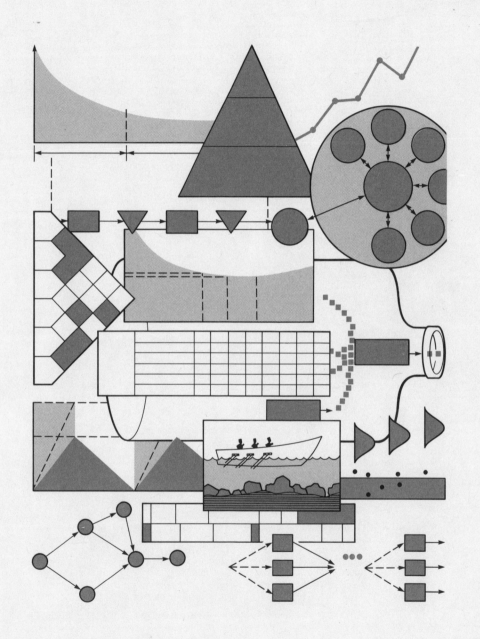

Production/Operations Management

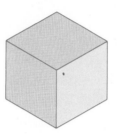

THE IRWIN SERIES IN QUANTITATIVE ANALYSIS FOR BUSINESS
CONSULTING EDITOR: ROBERT B. FETTER, YALE UNIVERSITY

PRODUCTION/OPERATIONS MANAGEMENT

WILLIAM J. STEVENSON
ROCHESTER INSTITUTE OF TECHNOLOGY

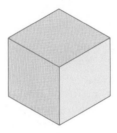

THIRD EDITION

HOMEWOOD, IL 60430
BOSTON, MA 02116

THIS BOOK IS DEDICATED TO YOU

© **RICHARD D. IRWIN, INC., 1982, 1986, and 1990**

SPONSORING EDITOR: Richard T. Hercher, Jr.
DEVELOPMENTAL EDITOR: Nancy Barbour
PROJECT EDITOR: Margaret Haywood
PRODUCTION MANAGER: Carma W. Fazio
DESIGNER: John Rokusek, Rokusek Design
COMPOSITOR: Better Graphics, Inc.
TYPEFACE: 10/12 Bembo
PRINTER: R. R. Donnelley & Sons Company

Library of Congress Cataloging-in-Publication Data

Stevenson, William J.
    Production/operations management/William J. Stevenson.—3rd ed.
        p.   cm.
     ISBN 0-256-08029-1—ISBN 0-256-09875-1 (International ed.)
     1. Production management.   I. Title.
   TS155.S7824 1990   89–19864
   658.5—dc20   CIP

Printed in the United States of America

3 4 5 6 7 8 9 0 D O 7 6 5 4 3 2 1

PREFACE

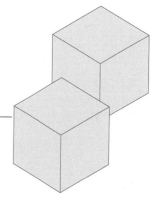

The material in this book is intended as an introduction to the field of production and operations management. It is suitable for both undergraduate and graduate students.

The subject matter is somewhat technical in parts. It represents a blend of concepts from industrial engineering, cost accounting, general management, quantitative methods, and statistics. Even so, readers should find the material interesting and informative. Production and operations activities, such as forecasting, choosing a location for an office or plant, allocating resources, designing products and services, scheduling activities, and assuring quality are core activities of most business organizations. Very often, the majority of employees and assets of an organization are controlled by the production/operations function. Some of you are—or will be—employed directly in a production/operations capacity, while others will have jobs that are indirectly related to this area. So whether this is your field of study or not, this field will probably have an impact on your work.

Historically, production and operations management (POM) techniques developed in manufacturing organizations. However, as time went on, it became more and more apparent that nonmanufacturing organizations have to contend with problems similar to those encountered in manufacturing settings. Consequently, the scope of POM has been expanded to cover both manufacturing and service organizations. Moreover, many of the techniques can be directly applied to both areas without modification.

This edition continues with many of the features of the second edition, such as:

1. Each chapter begins with an outline of topics covered and a set of learning objectives.
2. Concepts and techniques are presented in such a way that they are both interesting and fairly easy to grasp.

v

3. This book offers more examples, solved problems, and end-of-chapter problems than most other books. Students seem to benefit greatly from being able to review the solved problems.

4. The answers to many problems are given—but not solutions.

5. Materials and problems have been thoroughly class-tested and revised accordingly.

6. Many chapters have a short reading or a case suitable either for class discussion or for homework assignments.

7. There is a great deal of flexibility permitted in terms of depth and order of coverage of topics.

8. Manufacturing and service are integrated rather than separated.

9. Forecasting is covered early in the text (Chapter 3).

10. Productivity and quality assurance are emphasized.

Some of the key revisions and additions incorporated in this third edition are:

1. An entire chapter is devoted to just-in-time production systems.

2. The material on international competition has been expanded.

3. Operations strategy issues have been added to many chapters.

4. Line balancing procedures have been revised, and the linear programming supplement has been reworked.

5. Material has been added on maintenance, materials management, and capacity requirements planning.

6. The record keeping in MRP has been simplified.

7. The material on process selection has been expanded.

8. New readings have been added.

9. New problems have been added.

10. The quality assurance chapter has been revised and new materials and problems have been added.

11. Several new cases have been added.

The text contains more material than one could normally hope to cover in a one-semester course. Rather than relying on the author's personal bias, each instructor can choose those topics most suited to his or her own proclivities. Those who prefer quantitative emphasis, for example, will be quite comfortable with the abundance of student problems. Those who prefer a more qualitative approach will welcome the fact that some of the more quantitative material is placed in chapter supplements. Moreover, some of the chapter problems are less quantitative than others, and the cases and readings tend to be qualitative. Obviously, there are many possibilities between these two extremes.

I have gained a great deal in revising this book. I was fortunate again to have an excellent panel of reviewers who contributed significantly to the final product. I want to thank them for a job done well. They are: Professor Paul Bobrowski, University of Oregon; Professor Francis D. Booth, University of Montana; Professor Chandra Das, University of Northern Iowa; Professor Mustafa El Agizy, California Polytechnic University–Pomona; Professor Norbert L. Enrick, Kent State University; Professor P. K. Eswaran, Ohio University; Professor Joseph R. Munn, Baylor University; Professor Michael H. Peters, Louisiana State University; Professor David Ronen, University of Missouri–St. Louis; Professor Roberta Russell, Virginia Polytechnic Institute and State University; Professor M. Hossein Safizadeh, Wichita State University; Professor Britt M. Shirley, Columbus College; Professor R. Stansbury Stockton, Indiana University–Bloomington; Professor Richard Tellier, California State University, Fresno; Professor Paul Van Ness, Rochester Institute of Technology; and Professor Walter Warrick, Drake University.

Further thanks goes to Stan Stockton and his colleagues at Indiana University–Bloomington for all their suggestions and examples. In addition, several of my colleagues at Rochester Institute of Technology offered suggestions for improvement, and I want to thank them: George Johnson, Erhan Mergen, and the late Bob Wilferth.

I also want to thank Professor Robert Fetter, Irwin's consulting editor, for his comments and encouragement. Many students offered comments and suggestions, and many others are to be commended for suffering through revisions of problems and solutions and text material. The manuscript went through several stages of proofing and error-checking. Derek deSa of the University of Alabama, Buddhadev Roychoudhury of Indiana University–Bloomington, and Ronald Reimer of Indiana University, Southeast, tirelessly endeavored to ensure the accuracy of the final product and I owe them a great debt of thanks. All three did a terrific job.

Special thanks goes to Byron Finch and Rich Luebbe of Miami University of Ohio who developed the *Spreadsheet Applications* text (which may be used with this as well as other POM texts) and Vahid Lotfi and Carl Pegels who developed the *Decision Support System Production/Operations Management* software package. I would also like to acknowledge the following companies who kindly allowed us to use their photos for the text and segments for the video: Allen-Bradley; Apple Computer, Inc.; Bethlehem Steel Corporation; Chrysler Corporation; The Credo Company; Hewlett-Packard Company; International Business Machines Corporation; John Deere Horicon Works; Kawasaki Motors Manufacturing Corp.; The Lincoln Electric Company; Porsche Cars North America, Inc.; Sony Corporation of America; and Xerox Corporation.

Finally, I extend my thanks to all the people at Irwin for all of their effort and support. It was a pleasure to be able to work with such a competent and professional group of people. Special thanks go to Dick Hercher, Nancy Barbour, and Margaret Haywood.

William J. Stevenson

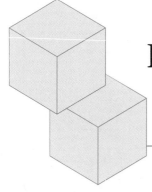

NOTE TO THE STUDENT

The material in this text is part of the core knowledge in your education. Consequently, you will derive considerable benefit from your study of operations management, *regardless of your major*. Practically speaking, production and operations is a course in *management*.

This book describes principles and concepts of production and operations management. You should be aware that many of these principles and concepts are applicable to other aspects of your professional and personal life. Consequently, you should expect the benefits of your study of production and operations management to serve you in these other areas.

After reading each chapter or supplement in the text, attending related classroom lectures, and completing assigned questions and problems, you should be able to do each of the following:

1. *Identify the key features* of that material.
2. *Define and use terminology.*
3. *Solve typical problems.*
4. *Recognize applications* of the concepts and techniques covered.
5. *Discuss the assumptions and limitations* which underlie each model or technique covered.

You will encounter a number of chapter supplements. Check with your instructor to determine whether or not to study them.

This book places an emphasis on problem solving. There are many examples throughout the text illustrating solutions. In addition, at the end of most chapters and supplements you will find a group of solved problems. The examples within the chapter itself serve to illustrate concepts and techniques. Too much detail at those points would be detrimental to learning. However, later on, when you begin to solve the end-of-chapter problems, you will find the *solved problems* quite helpful. Moreover, those solved problems usually illustrate more and different details than the problems within the chapter.

I suggest the following approach for studying and problem solving:

1. Look over the chapter outline and learning objectives.
2. Read the chapter summary.
3. Read the chapter and reread the summary.
4. Look over and try to answer the discussion and review questions.
5. Solve the problems, referring to the solved problems and chapter examples as needed.

Note that the answers to many problems are given at the end of the book. Try to solve each problem before turning to the answer. Remember—tests don't usually come with answers.

A study guide is also available. If your bookstore does not stock it, you can ask them to order it for you.

Good luck!

W. J. S.

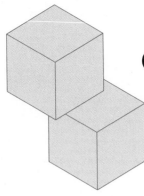

CONTENTS

INTRODUCTION

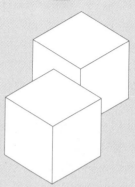

Chapter 1 outlines the nature and scope of operations management. In that chapter, you will learn that operations is one of the three main functions of most organizations, along with marketing and finance; what the function of operations involves; some of the different ways operations systems are classified; and what some of the current issues in operations management are. You will also read about a topic that is causing great concern throughout the world: *productivity*.

Chapter 2 focuses on decision making, with emphasis on operations decisions. The use of linear programming as a decision tool is described in the supplement to Chapter 2.

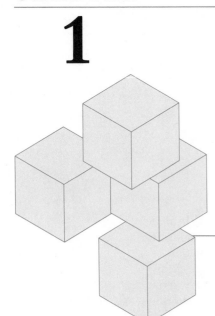

Production and Operations Management

LEARNING OBJECTIVES

After completing this chapter, you should be able to:

1. Define the term *operations management* and give examples.
2. Identify the three major functional areas of organizations and briefly describe how they interrelate.
3. Describe the operations function and the nature of the operations manager's job.
4. Differentiate between design and operation of production systems.
5. Discuss productivity in terms of what it is, why it is important, who is primarily responsible for it, and ways of increasing it.
6. Compare and contrast service and manufacturing.
7. Identify some of the current issues in operations management.
8. Describe the hierarchy of operations management decisions.
9. Explain the importance of including operations people in strategy formulation.
10. Describe the *Pareto phenomenon* and tell why it is important in problem solving.

CHAPTER OUTLINE

This book is about production and operations management (POM). The subject matter is fascinating and very timely: productivity, quality, foreign competition, and the use of robots in manufacturing are very much in the news. These are all a part of production and operations management. This first chapter presents an introduction and overview of POM. Among the issues it addresses are: What is operations management? Why is it important? What does an operations manager do? What is productivity, and why is it important? How does operations strategy relate to organization strategy and to the competitiveness of an organization's products and services?

The goal of the book is to present a broad conceptual framework for the management of the operations function in organizations. This chapter lays the groundwork for the book. It begins with a brief description of the various functions of business organizations and their relationships to each other. Then the operations function is described in more detail, including a description of methods of classifying production systems and a comparison of manufacturing and service systems. The chapter concludes with a discussion of the major issues that confront POM managers today, including productivity, competitiveness, and strategy.

INTRODUCTION

To many people, the term *production* conjures up images of factories, machines, and assembly lines. Interestingly enough, the field of production management in the past focused almost exclusively on manufacturing management. Heavy emphasis was placed on methods and techniques that dealt with operating a factory. In recent years, the scope of production management has broadened considerably. Currently, production concepts and techniques are being applied to a wide range of activities and situations *outside* of manufacturing (i.e., in *services*) as well as in manufacturing. Among the services are health care, food service, recreation, banking, hotel management, retail sales, education, transportation, and government. Because of this broadened scope, the field has taken on the name *operations management*, which more closely reflects the diverse nature of activities to which its concepts and techniques are applied.

Operations management is responsible for the management of productive systems, that is, systems that either *create goods* or *provide services* (or both). As an example of an operations management system, consider a luxury cruise ship. Most of the activities performed by the captain and crew during a cruise or in preparation for the cruise fall within the realm of operations management.

Among those activities are running the ship, managing food service, providing medical services, supervision and training of the crew, overseeing activities of passengers, and housekeeping. Navigation, maintenance, and general repairs are required to keep the ship on course and in good operating condition. Food and beverages must be ordered, meals must be prepared and served in an appetizing manner, and eating areas must be kept clean. Medical supplies must be on hand and personnel sufficiently prepared to handle a wide range of illnesses and emergencies. Motivation, training, productivity, job assignments, and personal appearance of crew members are important. Passengers must be assigned to cabins, activities must be scheduled, trips ashore at ports of call must be arranged, and other needs must be attended to in order to maintain satisfactory customer relations. Of course, there are other activities involved in operating a luxury ship, but this gives you some idea of the nature and scope of operations management in that regard.

Now consider managing a factory. Decisions have to be made on what raw materials to order, how much to order, and when to order; determination must be made as to what products to make and when and how much to make; work assignments have to be set; workers may have to be hired and trained; quality levels must be established and achieved; inventories of parts and supplies, raw materials, and finished goods must be maintained; worker grievances must be dealt with; workers must be motivated; production bottlenecks and equipment breakdowns must not be allowed to disrupt output; new equipment and production methods must be integrated with existing equipment and methods; and products must be periodically redesigned to incorporate new features and to meet the competition. Moreover, in some cases, locations for new facilities must be found, new factories must be designed and built, and decisions must be made on the layout (arrangement) of departments and equipment.

Although on the surface it may appear that the managing of a cruise ship and the managing of a manufacturing facility are quite different, in reality both involve many of the same elements: facilities, work force, inventories, scheduling, and quality assurance. Hence, as diverse as these two examples are, they both reflect activities that fall within the realm of production and operations management. The cruise ship involves *services,* the factory involves *goods*.

FUNCTIONS WITHIN BUSINESS ORGANIZATIONS

There are three primary functions in most business organizations: operations, finance, and marketing, as depicted in Figure 1–1. The three circles suggest that these three functions overlap: they do not exist or function independently of each other. Rather, they interact to achieve the goals and objectives of the organization; they are dependent on each other, and each has an important contribution to make. Often the success of an organization depends not only on how well each area performs but also on how well the areas *interface* with each other. For instance, in manufacturing, it is essential that production and marketing work together. Otherwise, marketing may attempt to promote goods that production cannot profitably produce, and production may turn out items for which there is no demand. Similarly, unless finance and production people work closely, funds for expansion or new equipment may not be available when needed.

Aside from these three primary functions, there are a number of supporting functions in many organizations, such as personnel, accounting, and engineering. Obviously, the presence of these functions and the emphasis placed on

FIGURE 1–1

*The three major
functions of business
organizations overlap*

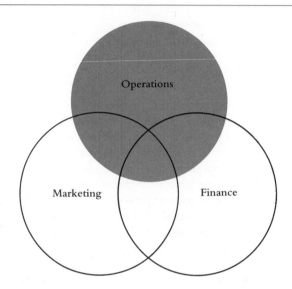

each one depend on the type of business a firm is engaged in. Thus, non-manufacturing firms would be less apt to have an engineering department than manufacturing firms.

Let's take a closer look at these functions, beginning with the three primary ones.

Operations

The operations function consists of all activities that are *directly* related to producing goods or providing services. The production function exists not only in manufacturing and assembly operations, which are *goods-oriented*, but also in such areas as health care, transportation, food handling, and retailing,

TABLE 1–1

*Examples of types
of operations*

Type of operation	Examples
Physical	Farming, mining, construction, manufacturing, power generation
Storage/transportation	Warehousing, trucking, mail service, moving, taxis, buses, hotels, airlines
Exchange	Retailing, wholesaling, banking, renting or leasing, library loans
Entertainment	Films, radio and television, plays, concerts, recording
Communication	Newspapers, radio and TV newscasts, telephone, satellites

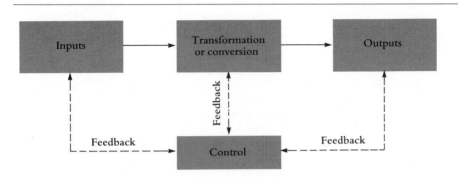

which are primarily *service-oriented*. Table 1–1 provides some examples that illustrate the diversity of operations management settings.

The operations function is the core of most business organizations; operations is responsible for the creation of an organization's products or services. Inputs of labor, materials, energy, and time are used to obtain finished goods or services using one or more *transformation processes* (e.g., storing, transporting, cutting), thereby *adding value*. To insure that the desired outputs are obtained, measurements are taken at various points in the transformation process (feedback) and then compared to previously established standards to determine if corrective action is needed (control). Figure 1–2 shows the conversion process.

Table 1–2 provides some examples of inputs, transformation processes, and outputs.

Finance

The finance function comprises activities related to securing monetary resources at favorable prices and allocating those resources throughout the organization. Finance and operations management personnel cooperate in exchange of information and expertise in such activities as:

1. *Budgeting*. Budgets must be periodically prepared in order to plan financial requirements. Budgets must sometimes be adjusted, and performance relative to budget must be evaluated.

2. *Economic analysis of investment proposals*. Evaluation of alternative investments in plant and equipment requires inputs from both operations and finance people.

3. *Provision of funds*. The necessary funding of operations and the amounts and timings of funding can be important and even critical when funds are tight. Careful planning can help avoid cash flow problems. Note that most for-profit firms obtain the majority of their funds through the revenues generated by sales of goods and services.

TABLE 1–2

Examples of inputs, transformation, and outputs

Inputs	Transformation	Outputs
Human	Processes	Goods
Physical	Cutting, drilling	Houses
Intellectual	Storing	Automobiles
Raw materials	Transporting	Textbooks
Energy	Extracting	Clothing
Water	Farming	Typewriters
Chemicals	Teaching	Machines
Metals	Assembling	Televisions
Lumber	Equipment	Food
Fibers	Machines	Energy
Other	Computers	Furniture
Technology	Typewriters	Services
Information	Trucks	Health care
Time	Buses	Entertainment
	Facilities	Car repair
	Factories	Car wash
	Schools	Transportation
	Hospitals	Delivery
	Service garages	Gift wrapping
	Offices	Banking
	Retail stores	Education
	Warehouses	

Marketing

The marketing function's main concern is with selling the organization's products or services. Primary marketing activities in addition to selling include advertising and promotion, generally developing and maintaining a market, and sales forecasting. Marketing is in a position to measure the needs and preferences of consumers, and marketing can be a valuable source of information relating to ideas for product or service improvement as well as for ideas for new products or services. One important piece of information marketing needs from operations is manufacturing or service *lead time* so that customers can be given realistic estimates of how long it will take to fill their orders.

Thus, marketing and operations need to interface on product and process design, forecasting, setting realistic schedules, quality and quantity decisions, and keeping each other informed on the other's strengths and weaknesses.

Other Functions

There are a host of other, supporting functions that interface with the main three. Among them are accounting and purchasing. In addition, depending on

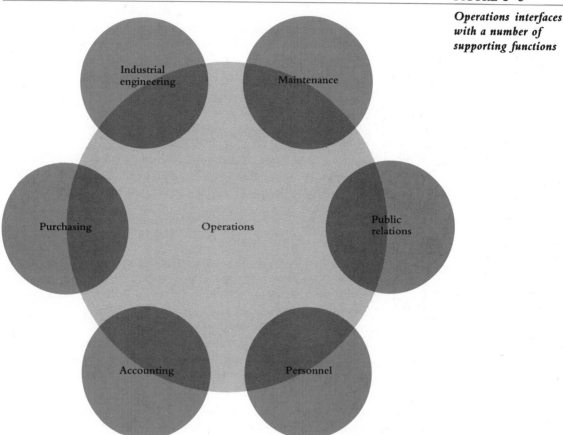

the nature of the organization, there may be personnel, product design and development, industrial engineering, and maintenance (see Figure 1–3).

Accounting has responsibility for preparing the financial statements, including the income statement and balance sheet. It also supplies cost data on labor, materials, and overhead and may provide reports on such items as scrap, downtime, and inventories. It must keep track of receivables, payables, and insurance costs and prepare tax statements for the firm.

Purchasing is charged with procurement of materials, supplies, and equipment. Close contact with operations is necessary to ensure correct quantities and timing of purchases. Also, the purchasing department is often called on to evaluate vendors for quality, reliability, service, price, and ability to adjust to changing demand. Purchasing also involves shipping, receiving, and inspecting the purchased goods.

The *personnel* department is concerned with recruitment and training of personnel, labor relations, contract negotiations, wage and salary administration, assisting in manpower projections, and ensuring the health and safety of employees.

Public relations has the responsibility for building and maintaining a positive public image of the organization. This might involve sponsoring a little league team, donating to cultural events, giving public tours of facilities, sponsoring community affairs (e.g., marathons, bike races), and so on. Donating the use of facilities and providing public service messages and information about the organization, its employees, its products, and its services all fall under the heading of public relations. There are many potential benefits of good public relations. An obvious one is in the marketplace. Other potential benefits include being regarded as a good place to work (labor supply), improving chances of getting zoning change requests approved, getting community acceptance of expansion plans, and generating a positive attitude among employees.

Industrial engineering is often concerned with scheduling, performance standards, work methods, quality control, and material handling. This function is typically found in manufacturing plants in medium and large firms.

Maintenance is responsible for general maintenance and repair of equipment, maintenance of buildings and grounds, heating and air conditioning, removing toxic wastes, parking, and perhaps security.

Many of these interfaces are elaborated on in later chapters.

The importance of production and operations management, both for organizations and for society, should be fairly obvious: The consumption of goods and services is an integral aspect of society as we know it. Production and operations management is responsible for creating those goods and services. Organizations exist primarily for the purpose of providing services or creating goods. Hence, production is the *core function* of an organization. Without this core, there would be no need for any of the other functions—the organization would have no purpose. Given the central nature of its function in our society, it is not surprising that more than half of all employed people in this country have jobs within the production/operations area. Furthermore, the operations function controls a major portion of the assets in most organizations.

THE OPERATIONS MANAGEMENT FUNCTION

We have already noted that the operations manager is responsible for the creation of goods and services. This encompasses acquisition of resources and the conversion of their inputs into outputs using one or more transformation processes. This involves planning, coordinating, and controlling the elements that make up the process, including workers, equipment, facilities, allocation of resources, and work methods. It also includes product and/or service design. This is a vital, ongoing process that most organizations must do. It is an activity that operations performs in conjunction with marketing. As previously noted, marketing people can be a source of ideas concerning new products and services as well as improvements to existing products and services. Operations people can also be a source of new ideas for improvements related to the production aspect of the organization. These can include ideas on new procedures for fabrication and assembly as well as improved designs, handling and storage procedures, and so on. From a practical standpoint, product and service design can be the lifeblood of a competitive organization.

The main function of the operations manager is to guide the system through decision making. Generally speaking, there is a major emphasis on productive use of resources.

There are various ways of classifying the decisions that an operations manager must make, such as qualitative versus quantitative, according to the management process (planning, staffing, etc.), and according to whether the decisions relate to system design or system operation. Each of these approaches has its merits. The approach used in this text—indeed, the framework of the entire book—is the last approach: the material is arranged according to topics that relate primarily to *design* and according to topics that relate primarily to system *operation*. The following section examines this approach in more detail.

Designing and Operating Production Systems

System design involves decisions that relate to system capacity, the geographic location of facilities, arrangement of departments and placement of equipment within physical structures, product and service planning, and acquisition of equipment. These are usually, but not always, decisions that require long-term commitments. **System operation** involves management of personnel, inventory planning and control, scheduling, project management, and quality assurance. In many instances, the operations manager is more involved in day-to-day operating decisions than with decisions relating to system design. In fact, much of systems design lies in the province of top management. However, the operations manager has a vital stake in system design because *system design essentially determines many of the parameters of system operation*. For example, costs, space, capacities, and quality are all directly affected by design decisions. Even though the operations manager is not responsible for making certain design decisions, he or she can provide a wide range of information to decision makers, which will have a bearing on those decisions.

A brief description of design and operating decisions is given in Table 1–3

These decisions are generally *hierarchical* in nature; plans and designs are usually sequential, and those at the lower levels are constrained to a certain extent by higher level plans and decisions. At the highest level are *strategic* decisions. These are broad in scope and involve choice of products and services, new facilities and locations, and general policies of the organization. For the most part, strategic decisions have long-term implications for the organization. At the next level are *tactical* decisions. These are narrower in

TABLE 1—3

Design and operating decisions

Decision area	Basic questions	Chapter
Forecasting	How much will be demanded? When, and what products and services?	3
Design		
Product and service selection	What products and services should the organization offer?	4, 6
Capacity (long range)	How much capacity will be needed? How can the organization best meet capacity requirements?	6
Location	What is a satisfactory location for a facility (factory, store, etc.)?	5
Layout	What is the best arrangement for departments, equipment, work flow, and storage in terms of cost, productivity?	7
Product and service design	How can products and services be improved?	4
Design of work systems	What is the best way to motivate employees? How can productivity be improved? How to measure work? How to improve work methods?	8
Operation		
Aggregate planning	How much capacity will be needed over the intermediate range? How can capacity needs best be met?	9
Inventory management	How much to order? When to reorder? Which items should get the most attention?	10
Materials requirements planning	What materials, parts, and subassemblies will be needed, and when?	11
Scheduling	How can jobs best be scheduled? Who will do which job? Which equipment to use?	13
Project management	Which activities are the most critical to the success of a project? What are the goals of a project? What resources will be needed, and when will they be needed?	14
Waiting lines	How can bottlenecks be reduced? What is effective capacity?	15
Quality assurance	How can quality be improved? Are processes performing adequately? What standards should be used? Are standards being met?	16

FIGURE 1—4

Hierarchy of operations management decisions

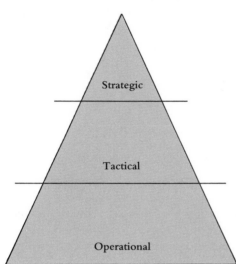

Broad scope

Examples include:
  Product selection
  New facility construction
  Choice of location
  Choice of technology

Moderate scope

Examples include:
  Employment levels
  Output levels
  Equipment selection
  Allocating financial resources

Narrow scope

Examples include:
  Scheduling personnel
  Adjusting output rates
  Controlling quality
  Inventory replenishment

scope than the strategic decisions. Tactical decisions often involve allocating financial resources, equipment selection and use, and planning work force levels, output rates, and inventory levels. Tactical decisions are made within the framework established by strategic decisions. At the lowest level are *operating* decisions. These involve such activities as scheduling of equipment and personnel, adjusting production rates, and handling equipment break-downs, absenteeism, shortages, inventory replenishment, and quality control. Operating decisions are made within the framework established by tactical decisions. The decision hierarchy is illustrated in Figure 1—4.

The Operations Manager and the Management Process

The operations manager is the key figure in the system: he or she has the ultimate responsibility for the creation of goods or services.

As you might imagine, the kinds of jobs that operations managers oversee vary tremendously from organization to organization, largely because of the differences in products or services different organizations are involved with. Thus, managing a banking operation obviously requires a different kind of expertise than managing a steel-making operation. However, in one very important respect, the jobs are the same: They are both essentially *managerial*. In fact, the same thing can be said for the job of any operations manager, regardless of the kinds of goods or services being created. In every case, the operations manager must coordinate the use of resources through the management process, which involves planning, organizing, staffing, directing, and controlling.

TABLE 1—4

Responsibilities of
operations managers

Planning	Organizing
Capacity	Degree of centralization
Location	Make or buy
Products and services	Subcontracting
Layout	Staffing
Projects	Use of overtime
Scheduling	Hiring/laying off
Controlling	Directing
Inventory control	Incentive plans
Quality control	Issuance of work orders
	Job assignments

Planning involves determining a future course of action. The planning process begins by deciding what is desired; then a way is designed for accomplishing that objective.

Organizing refers to the administrative structure of the organization. It involves putting the pieces of the system together in such a way that desired results can be achieved. It requires decisions regarding who, what, where, when, and how.

Staffing involves selection and training of the personnel who will operate the system.

Directing refers to the issuance of commands or orders, making suggestions, or otherwise motivating subordinates to perform their assigned duties in a timely and efficient manner.

Controlling involves measuring the results of operations, deciding if they are acceptable, and instituting corrective action if need be.

Examples of the responsibilities of operations managers according to these classifications are given in Table 1—4.

PRODUCTIVITY

One of the primary responsibilities of an operations manager is to achieve productive use of resources. **Productivity** measures the relationship between outputs (goods or services) and inputs (labor, capital, materials, or other resources) used to produce them. Productivity is usually expressed as the ratio of quantity of output to quantity of input:

$$\text{Productivity} = \frac{\text{Output}}{\text{Input}}$$

Two types of productivity measurements are generally employed: labor productivity and multifactor productivity. *Labor productivity* reflects output relative to labor hours worked, and *multifactor productivity* reflects a combination of some or all of the resources used to obtain a certain output.

Examples of labor productivity include:

$$\frac{\text{Yards of carpet installed}}{\text{Labor hours}} = \text{Yards per hour}$$

$$\frac{\text{Number of offices cleaned}}{\text{Number of shifts}} = \text{Offices per shift}$$

$$\frac{\text{Board feet of lumber cut}}{\text{Number of weeks}} = \text{Feet per week}$$

Similar examples can be listed for *machine productivity* (e.g., the number of pieces per hour turned out by a machine).

Calculations of multifactor productivity involve measuring inputs and outputs using a common unit of measurement, such as cost or value. For instance, the measure might use cost of inputs and price of the output:

$$\frac{\text{Quantity of production at standard price}}{\text{Labor cost + Materials cost + Overhead}}$$

In essence, productivity measurements serve as scorecards of the effective use of resources. Government leaders in every country are concerned with national productivity because there is a close relationship between productivity and the standard of living of a nation's people. High levels of productivity are largely responsible for the relatively high standards of living enjoyed by industrial nations. Moreover, wage and price increases that are not accompanied by productivity increases create inflationary pressures on the economy. Business leaders are also concerned with productivity as a key factor in *competitiveness*. If two competing firms each have the same level of output, but one of the firms is able to achieve this with a lower level of input, that firm will be at an advantage; it can charge the same price for its output and achieve a higher level of profit than its less productive competitor, or it can charge a lower price and thereby increase its sales at the expense of its less productive competitor.

U.S. productivity is the highest in the world. However, a significant portion of this relates to *agricultural* productivity; *manufacturing* productivity is closer to that of other industrial nations. Even so, there is serious concern on the part of the U.S. government and industrial leaders because U.S. productivity *increases* in many industries have lagged far behind those of other nations, particularly Japan and Korea. Figure 1–5 summarizes annual percentage changes in productivity ratios for 1981 to 1985 for selected countries.

The obvious question is: How are certain nations, industries, or companies able to achieve productivity gains while others are not? Actually, there are many reasons cited by theorists and researchers. Among the most prominent are:

1. A lower propensity to save and a higher propensity to consume in the United States and some other Western nations have slowed capital formation and attracted foreign goods.

FIGURE 1—5

Annual growth in gross domestic product per employee, 1981–1985

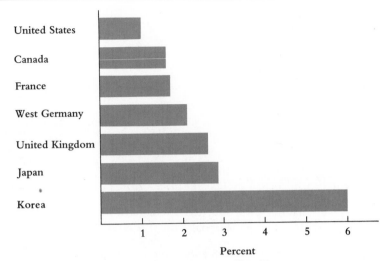

Percent

Source: American Productivity Center, *Productivity Perspectives,* 1987 edition.

2. Increasing government regulations have added to the administrative (and nonproductive) burden of many companies.

3. Increased legal staffs are needed to handle product liability claims.

4. There has been an increasing demand for services, which are generally less efficient than manufacturing operations.

5. There is often emphasis on *short-run* performance (e.g., annual profits and sales), and this reduces the incentive to develop long-term solutions to problems. In addition, in periods of inflation and increased costs of borrowed money, managers are, perhaps understandably, hesitant to commit funds for long periods of time because it reduces their flexibility to take advantage of other opportunities that might arise in the meantime.

Many authorities place much of the responsibility for lagging productivity improvements on management. They point out that foreign competitors have had to deal with similar (or worse) conditions than their U.S. counterparts and yet have come out ahead on productivity improvements. It should be noted that some argue that most foreign competitors started out with productivity so low that the improvements merely reflect catching up to U.S. manufacturers. To a certain extent, that is true. Moreover, foreign competitors were able to learn much about quality and productivity improvements by studying Western methods. However, many of those companies have achieved productivity levels that equal or surpass those of their U.S. counterparts. It seems that they are using the lessons learned to go beyond their teachers. Some cite the inability of U.S. managers to successfully integrate technological improvements into the production process; a common complaint is that U.S. managers seem to be "throwing technology at the problem" rather than wisely analyzing their processes to see if and how technology can be used to gain competitive advantage.

Factors that Affect Productivity

There are numerous factors that affect productivity. Among them are methods, capital, quality, technology, and management.

Consider the student who plans to type a lengthy term paper. The student is an average typist and can turn out about three pages per hour. How could the student increase productivity (i.e., turn out more pages per hour)? One way would be to enroll in a short course offered by the college to improve typing skills (method). Another possibility might be to replace a manual typewriter with a more expensive electric typewriter (capital) to gain the speed of automatic features. If quality (e.g., typing errors) is a problem, an even more expensive word processor (capital) that will allow errors to be corrected before they appear on the page could help. Still other productivity improvements might be achieved through improving organization and preparation for the actual typing (management). The incentive of receiving a good grade and the personal pride of doing a good job might also be important. The point is that all of these factors are potential sources of productivity, not only for typing papers but for any kind of work, and it is generally up to the manager to see to it that they are fully exploited.

A commonly held misconception is that workers are the main determinant of productivity. According to that theory, the route to productivity gains involves getting employees to work harder. However, the fact is that many productivity gains in the past have come from *technological* improvements. Familiar examples include:

Paint rollers	Long-distance direct dialing, pay-
Power lawn mowers	by-phone, cellular phones
Electronic typewriters	Computerized billing and
Copying machines	inventories
Microwave ovens	Automation
Automatic washers, dryers, dish-	Calculators
washers, electric blenders	Computers, personal computers

However, as noted in the previous section, technology alone won't produce productivity gains; it must be used wisely and thoughtfully. In fact, without careful planning, technology can actually *reduce* productivity, especially if it leads to inflexibility, high costs, or mismatched operations.

Improving Productivity

There are a number of key steps that a company or a department can take toward improving productivity:

1. Develop productivity measures for all operations; measurement is the first step in managing and controlling an operation.

FIGURE 1–6

Bottleneck operation

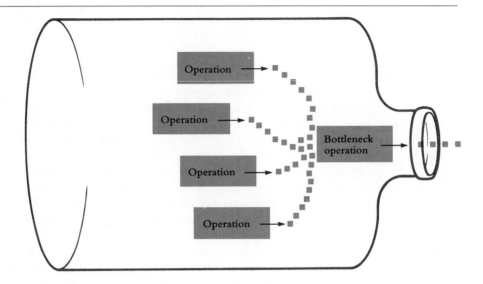

2.   Look at the system as a whole in deciding which operations to concentrate on; it is overall productivity that is important. This concept is illustrated in Figure 1–6, which shows several operations feeding their output into a *bottleneck* operation. The capacity of the bottleneck operation is less than the combined capacities of the operations that provide input, so units queue up waiting to be processed; hence the term bottleneck. Productivity improvements to any nonbottleneck operation will not affect the productivity of the system. Improvements in the bottleneck operation *will* lead to increased productivity, up to the point that the output rate of the bottleneck equals the output rate of the operations feeding it.

3.   Develop methods for achieving productivity improvements, such as soliciting ideas from workers (perhaps organizing teams of workers, engineers, and managers to work on this), studying how other firms have increased productivity, and reexamining the way work is done.

4.   Establish reasonable goals for improvement.

5.   Make it clear that management supports and encourages productivity improvement. Consider incentives to reward workers for contributions.

6.   Measure improvements, and publicize them.

CLASSIFYING PRODUCTION SYSTEMS

There are a number of ways to classify production systems. A brief discussion of some of these ways will help you to develop a better picture of the nature and scope of operations management. The three ways described here are:

degree of standardization, type of operation, and manufacturing versus service operations.

Degree of Standardization

Production systems produce output that ranges from highly standardized to highly customized. *Standardized* output means that there is a high degree of uniformity in goods or services. Examples of goods are radios, televisions, typewriters, newspapers, canned foods, automobile tires, pens, and pencils. Examples of services are automatic car washes, televised newscasts, taped lectures, and commercial airline service. *Customized* output means that the product or service is designed for a specific case or individual. Goods include eyeglasses, custom-fitted clothing, window glass (cut to order), and customized drapery. Examples of services are tailoring, taxi rides, and surgery.

Systems with standardized output can generally take advantage of standardized methods, materials, and mechanization, all of which contribute to higher volumes and lower unit costs. With specialized systems, on the other hand, each job is different enough that workers must be more skilled, the work moves slower, and the work is less susceptible to mechanization.

Type of Operation

The degree of standardization of a product or service and the volume of output influence the way that production is organized. On one end of the scale is a single, large-scale product or service such as the launching of a space shuttle (service) or the construction of a skyscraper (product). On the other end is a continuous process, such as oil refining. In between these extremes are small batches or individual units of output—such as custom-made furniture, lamps, special-purpose machines, and auto repair—all the way to mass production (high volume of output), such as automobiles, typewriters, and appliances.

Let's take a closer look at these different types of operations.

A *project* is a set of activities directed toward a unique goal. Usually, projects are relatively large scale. Examples of situations in which a project approach would be used are development of a new product, installation of a computerized production line, transfer of equipment to a new facility from a current one, and construction of a hospital. Sometimes the situations are of a more personal nature, such as planning for the visit of foreign dignitaries, planning an extended vacation that involves travel, and organizing a walk-for-water or other charitable activity. A key feature of all of these projects is their limited time frame. That is, they do not continue indefinitely; they have specific starting and ending points.

Unit or *batch* production is typically performed by a *job shop*. A job shop maintains the ability to render certain types of production but generally is not responsible for specific products. Instead, it performs to customer specifications; jobs tend to vary according to the needs of customers. Examples of job shops are organizations that do repair work (on appliances, televisions, stereos, automobiles), health care, printing, and so on. Some of these are highly customized; others offer a list of services or products of a more standardized nature from which customers can select.

On the other extreme of the scale of output volume is *mass production*. Organizations using this type of operation generally confine output to one or a relatively small number of similar products or services and function in such a way as to accomplish production as efficiently as possible. Both the work and the output tend to be highly standardized. Mass production systems are examples of *repetitive* production. This type of production lends itself to automation or other specialized equipment.

Continuous processing is employed when a homogeneous product or service is produced or rendered. Processing of chemicals, photographic film, newsprint, and oil products are all examples of this type of operation. Machines often provide continuous services, such as air conditioning, heating, continuous cleaning, and monitoring systems.

Manufacturing Operations versus Service Operations

Manufacturing implies production of a *tangible output,* such as an automobile, a clock radio, a golf ball, a refrigerator, or anything else that we can see or touch. Service, on the other hand, generally implies an *act*. A doctor's examination, TV and auto repair, lawn care, and showing a film are examples of services.

Manufacturing and service are often similar in terms of *what* is done but different in terms of *how* it is done. For example, both involve design and operating decisions. Manufacturers must decide how large a factory is needed, and service organizations (e.g., hospitals) must decide how large a building they need. Both must make location decisions, and both become involved in scheduling and controlling operations and allocating scarce resources.

Most of the differences between manufacturing and service organizations relate to manufacturing being product-oriented and service being act-oriented. The differences involve the following:

1. The nature and consumption of output.
2. Uniformity of input.
3. Labor content of jobs.
4. Uniformity of output.
5. Measurement of productivity.

Let us briefly consider each of these differences.

1. By its very nature, service involves a much higher degree of customer contact than manufacturing does. The performance of a service typically occurs at the point of consumption. That is, the two often occur simultaneously. For example, repairing a leaky roof must take place where the roof is, and surgery requires the presence of the surgeon and the patient. On the other hand, manufacturing allows a separation of production

and consumption, so that manufacturing often occurs in an isolated environment, away from the consumer. This permits a fair degree of latitude in selecting work methods, assigning jobs, scheduling work, and exercising control over operations. Service operations, because of their contact with customers, can sometimes be much more limited in their range of options in these areas. Moreover, customers are sometimes a part of the system (e.g., self-service operations such as gas stations, shopping), so tight control is not possible. Then, too, product-oriented operations can build up inventories of finished goods, which enables them to absorb some of the shocks caused by varying demand. However, service operations cannot build up inventories of *time,* so service capacity is much more sensitive to demand variability. Thus, banks and supermarkets alternate between lines of customers waiting for service and idle tellers or cashiers waiting for customers.

2. Service operations are subject to more variability of inputs than typical manufacturing operations are. Each patient, each lawn, and each TV presents a specific problem that often must be diagnosed before it can be remedied. There is often the ability in manufacturing to carefully control the amount of variability of inputs, so it is often possible to achieve low variability. Consequently, job requirements for manufacturing are generally more uniform than for services.

3. Because of the on-site consumption of services and because of the high degree of variation of inputs, services require a higher labor content, whereas manufacturing can be more capital-intensive (i.e., mechanized), although there are exceptions.

4. High mechanization generates products with low variability, so manufacturing tends to be smooth and efficient; service activities sometimes appear to be slow and awkward, and output is more variable.

5. Measurement of productivity is relatively straightforward in manufacturing due to the high degree of uniformity of most manufactured items. However, in many cases, variations in demand intensity, as well as variations in service requirements from job to job, make productivity measurement considerably more difficult. For example, the work load of two doctors might be compared. One may have had a large number of routine cases while the other did not, so their productivity would appear to differ unless a very careful analysis was made.

Table 1–5 gives an overview of manufacturing and service operation differences.

Although at times it may be convenient to think in terms of systems that are exclusively devoted to goods or services, most real systems are a blend of the two. For instance, maintenance and repair of equipment are two services performed by virtually every manufacturing firm. Similarly, most so-called service organizations typically sell goods that complement their services. Thus, a lawn care firm usually sells such goods as weed killers, fertilizers, and

TABLE 1–5

Differences between manufacturing and service

Characteristic	Manufacturing	Service
Output	Tangible	Intangible
Customer contact	Low	High
Labor content	Low	High
Uniformity of output	High	Low
Measurement of productivity	Easy	Difficult

grass seed. Hospitals dispense medical and surgical supplies along with health services. Restaurants sell food. Movie theaters sell popcorn, candy, and beverages.

Implications for Production Systems

These different ways of classifying production systems have important implications for designing and operating them. The degree of standardization of output, the type of operation, and whether the system involves mainly goods, mainly service, or some combination of goods and services have a bearing on capital requirements, choice of equipment, capacity planning, location planning, layout, inventory management, work force requirements, scheduling, and quality assurance.

Management of a project is quite different from management of an assembly line, and managing a job shop operation is different than managing a project or a high-volume operation. Forecasting requirements are different for the three types of systems. A high-volume operation requires a steady rate of output, and it can be costly as well as difficult to vary that rate. Hence, a good forecast is necessary to adequately design the system. Conversely, a job shop has a great deal more flexibility, so forecasting is less crucial at the design stage. Inventory requirements for a job shop are different from those for a system making standard products. Job shops typically make products to order. Thus, they would have little or no finished goods inventories. They may carry raw materials and supplies for frequently used operations. In repetitive manufacturing systems, an inventory of both raw materials and finished goods generally exists. However, purchasing is standardized, as are most of the activities associated with the operations. Projects tend to be unique, and their requirements vary considerably.

In terms of actual operation, repetitive systems exhibit the highest degree of certainty, job shops the next highest, and projects the lowest. Consequently, repetitive systems involve a more routine set of activities than do job shops, which involve a more routine set of activities than do projects. The differences among the systems and their implications for operations management will be elaborated on in the remainder of the book.

CONTEMPORARY ISSUES AND DEVELOPMENTS

A number of important issues and recent developments in the practice of operations management are currently influencing managerial decisions. This section presents a brief overview of the major ones, which are:

1. Productivity.
2. Government regulation.
3. The international scope of operations.
4. Foreign competition.
5. Cost and quality.
6. Technology.
7. The increasing importance of service operations.
8. Managerial attention to employee viewpoints.
9. Competitiveness.
10. Operations strategy.

A key issue in all organizations is *productivity*. In many cases, it has become a key measure of the effectiveness of management. Moreover, as noted earlier in the chapter, a major objective of operations management is to improve productivity. Management has always been concerned with productivity. However, U.S. productivity gains in recent years have lagged behind those of foreign competitors such as Japan and Korea.

Pollution control has also had a tremendous impact on some industries in terms of design and operation, and the government continues to strengthen standards on waste disposal and emission controls. When local or state government regulations differ from national standards, business organizations face the burden of designing for both. For instance, California emission control requirements are more stringent than most other states', and automotive firms have been forced to create special designs and pricing policies to compensate for them.

Increasing *consumer awareness*, particularly in the area of *product safety*, has emerged as a new force that must be reckoned with. Through pressures by the government and concerned consumers, major manufacturer recalls have been made on TVs, hairdryers, tires, bicycles, medicines, canned foods, coffee pots, and other items. Designers and quality inspectors have had to reconsider their activities.

Government regulations related to *worker safety* (OSHA) and *hiring practices* (EEO) have had an impact on the design of work systems.

The *international scope of operations* has increased opportunities to develop foreign markets, created additional sources for raw material and labor inputs, and forced numerous organizations to reassess their strategies. It has also brought an increase in multinational companies. It is becoming more and more common to encounter firms that obtain their raw materials in one country, fabricate parts in another, and assemble the final products in still another country. Managing such far-flung operations poses new challenges for managers as well as new opportunities.

Foreign competition has made serious inroads in areas traditionally dominated by U.S. firms. West Germany, Japan, Taiwan, and Korea are notable examples of major foreign competitors. Some U.S. firms have suffered substantial losses in market share to these competitors. This is a continuing problem that must be dealt with in order to avoid even more serious consequences. Beyond that, members of the European Common Market are expecting to form a closer trade alliance in 1992 called the European Economic Community. As part of that alliance, trade barriers among member nations will be removed, possibly making it more difficult for U.S. companies to compete in those markets.

Part of the reason for the success of foreign competitors has been their ability to provide high quality goods at reasonable cost. This has led U.S. firms to place greater importance on *quality* and *cost effectiveness* because they are discovering that consumers are placing more importance on product quality and that foreign competitors can often provide this quality at a relatively lower cost than many U.S. companies. The implication is that foreign producers are able to produce at lower costs; the costs of transforming inputs into outputs are lower. This emphasis on cost and quality has spread to service industries as well, to the point where it is now safe to say that there is a major emphasis on cost and quality that pervades thinking in production and operations management. Furthermore, quality, cost-effectiveness, and productivity are interrelated, making these topics among the most prominent in management today.

Technological changes are an increasingly important factor in operations management. New products and services are being developed as firms attempt to maintain competitiveness, and new production technologies are appearing that must be integrated into production systems. Robotics is an important example of this, particularly in the automotive industry (but also in other industries). Robots offer certain advantages in automation and have some of the benefits of flexibility not generally associated with automation. The increased use of computers has enlarged the decision-making capabilities of managers, enabling them to use more quantitative techniques in analyzing decisions, and its use has greatly enlarged information storage and handling capabilities.

As previously noted, *service systems* are becoming increasingly important in operations due to the growth in the number of such systems and because of the challenges that they present to the operations manager.

In an effort to improve quality and productivity, managers are encouraging *employee input* in the form of suggestions, quality circles, and other vehicles. Although this input is quite small, some feel that it will become more important in the years ahead.

The last two issues, competitiveness and strategy, are discussed in the following sections.

COMPETITIVENESS

Business organizations compete with one another in a variety of ways. Key among them are price, quality, product or service differentiation, flexibility, and delivery time.

1. **Price** is the amount a customer must pay for the product or service. Generally, the price a buyer is willing to pay relates to the other factors involved (quality, delivery time, etc.), as well as to the price and features of competitors. Organizations that compete on price may settle for lower profit margins, but most focus on lowering production *costs*.

2. **Quality** refers to materials and workmanship as well as design. Generally, it relates to the buyer's perceptions of how well the product or service will serve its intended purpose.

3. **Product differentiation** refers to any special features (design, cost, quality, ease of use, convenient location, warranty, etc.) that cause a product or service to be perceived by the buyer as more suitable than a competitor's product or service.

4. **Flexibility** refers to the ability to respond to changes. The better a company or department is able to respond to changes, the greater its competitive advantage over another company that is not as able to respond. The changes might relate to increases or decreases in volume demanded, changes in product mix, or to design changes in product or service features.

5. **Delivery time** refers to the length of time between placing an order and receiving the product or service ordered. Obviously, short delivery times are preferred over longer times. Occasionally, the ability to *schedule* delivery (e.g., of furniture, appliance, or other household item repairs) is an important consideration.

Although managers generally recognize some or all of these factors, they do not always use them for competitive advantage. One reason is that they are unsure of the mix of factors that matters most to buyers. This means that they must do a better job in carefully assessing buyer wants and needs. This is primarily the function of marketing research. Another reason is that they are unable to achieve desired levels of these factors. This is primarily the responsibility of production. Thus, if a firm is to compete effectively, it must understand its markets and be able to achieve suitable levels of quality, cost, delivery time, differentiation, and flexibility. It must also be aware of what its competitors are doing in these areas, and perhaps make some predictions about future behavior of competitors in order to have the necessary time to respond.

STRATEGY

In 1960, Japan accounted for only 1 percent of the free world's output of automobiles, while the United States accounted for 51 percent. By 1980, Japan's share of the output had climbed all the way to 24 percent, while the U.S. share had fallen to 22 percent. Over the next decade, these shares both slipped a few percentage points as other foreign producers gained a foothold in automobile production. Furthermore, markets that were once dominated by U.S. manufacturers, such as for TVs, VCRs, cassette players, minor appliances, and cameras, have rapidly lost market share to foreign competitors, with a large share of those markets going to Japanese companies. How did this happen? In retrospect, it appears that many foreign producers had strategies that were superior to strategies of U.S. producers.

Strategic decisions have a long-range impact on the general direction, and on the basic character, of a company. In large measure, strategic decisions determine the ability of an organization to compete. In fact, strategic decisions and their results weighed heavily in the relative success of Japanese manufacturers. Let's take a look at how this happened.

Japanese versus U.S. Strategy

As a nation, Japan is crowded and has little in the way of natural resources. After World War II, much of Japan's industrial base was in ruins. Japan sorely needed money from manufacturer exports to rebuild its economy. However, Japanese companies had a reputation as producers of shoddy goods. Japanese leaders agreed that a national priority was to overcome that reputation.

In an unprecedented move, managers at all levels of Japanese manufacturing companies were schooled in U.S. quality control concepts and procedures. Next, marketing departments were asked to identify products that corresponded to manufacturing capabilities. The strategy was to identify products that were in mature stages of development (i.e., for which there was a high-volume, stable market, with well-defined production technology and with competition based on price and quality). This strategy avoided the need to invest in product and market development; the markets already existed, and no major product innovations were needed. This permitted Japanese firms to invest money in robots and automatic production equipment and in programs to reduce cost and improve quality. In addition, efforts were made to develop long-term relationships with suppliers and shippers. And, because of crowded conditions and scarcity of natural resources, it was important to reduce waste and minimize inventories.

Efforts to improve quality had tremendous benefits. Not only did market share increase, but the resulting reduction in scrap and rework improved productivity and reduced costs. The use of robots and automatic processing equipment also added to quality improvements. Meanwhile, inventory reductions and the now-famous "just-in-time" production methods (which are described in Chapter 12) contributed to improving work flow, cost reduction, and productivity.

Now consider the U.S. experience. During World War II, the war effort was the overwhelming national priority. Production reigned supreme. Marketing and finance took a back seat to manufacturing. Quality control concepts and techniques were developed and applied to a wide range of products. Efficiency was important. When the war ended, U.S. industries were basically intact. Manufacturing shifted from the production of war goods to the production of consumer goods. Unlike their Japanese counterparts, U.S. manufacturers had to deal with excess capacity. Marketing became important as companies focused on creating demand for their goods and services. This spilled over into education, where many students became marketing majors because that was where the glamour jobs were. Manufacturing became less important in strategic planning than marketing.

Then, during the 1970s, finance and legal fields began to capture much of the attention as mergers and acquisitions became common. Often, mergers were made on a purely financial basis rather than for considerations based on similar or complementary *operations*. Many CEOs (chief executive officers) came from finance, law, or marketing, with little or no understanding of the operations side of their businesses. Operations was often not even represented on the board of directors. Marketing and/or finance became the basis of corporate strategy, with operations playing a reactive role: once it was decided *what* was to be done, it was left to operations to decide *how* to do it. But because operations people had little or no input at the strategic level, operations capabilities were sometimes not well suited to achieving the goals set by planners.

For example, in the auto industry, it became fashionable to offer car buyers a wide range of options. The reasoning was that this made a company competitive without adding much labor cost to a car. Although that was true, and although car buyers seemed to appreciate "designing their own cars," this created an immense burden for manufacturing: scheduling became increasingly difficult, inventories to support all of the different options became necessary, and equipment needed to accommodate the options (e.g., different tools, dies, fixtures) as well as the variety of methods used proliferated, greatly adding to the *indirect* cost and negatively impacting productivity. Similar effects were felt in other industries, primarily due to the lack of input from operations at the strategic stages of decision making.

Needless to say, there is currently a renewed interest in the United States in production and operations management as companies seek to maintain or regain their competitive edge in both foreign and domestic markets. An important element in these endeavors will be the strategic decisions that are made, and how well they serve the *mission* of the organization.

Mission

Every organization has a mission. The **mission** describes the purpose of the organization, the reason for its existence. Thus, different organizations will have different missions. A medical research organization might have as its mission to make a contribution to finding a cure for cancer; a consulting firm might have as its mission providing consulting services for new businesses; and a construction firm might have as its mission the remodeling of existing residences. Of course, part of the mission of for-profit firms is to make a profit for the owners. A statement of mission should answer the question: What business are we in?

The mission provides a general direction for an organization; it is the basis for organizational goals (e.g., increase market share at the rate of 5 percent a year for the next five years). Strategies must then be developed that will lead to the realization of the goals. **Strategies** are plans for accomplishing goals. By nature, they relate to the long term, providing *focus* for achieving the mission of the organization. Often, the success of an organization depends on how all the strategies match the organization's mission.

However, in some organizations, the mission is not clearly defined, making it difficult for decision makers (or even owners) to develop good strategies. Hence, it is extremely important for management to have a clear understanding of the mission of the organization in order to have a basis for formulating company, or *corporate*, strategy.

Corporate Strategy

Corporate strategy is the overall strategy of an organization. It provides the basis of the individual strategies of functional units (i.e., marketing, finance, and operations). Corporate strategy should take into account certain external and internal factors that might have an impact on the organization. Key external factors are:

1. *Economic conditions.* These include the general health and direction of the economy, inflation and deflation, interest rates, tax laws, and tariffs.
2. *Political conditions.* These include favorable or unfavorable attitudes toward business, political stability or instability, and wars.
3. *Legal environment.* This includes antitrust laws, government regulations, trade restrictions, minimum wage laws, product liability laws and recent court experience, labor laws, and patents.
4. *Technology.* This can include the rate at which product innovations are occurring, current and future process technology (equipment, materials handling), and design technology.
5. *Competition.* This includes the number and strength of competitors, the

basis of competition (e.g., price, quality, special features), and the ease of market entry.

6. *Markets*. This includes size, location, brand loyalties, ease of entry, potential for growth, long-term stability, and demographics.

Each of these external factors must be examined in light of the organization's mission and evaluated in terms of its potential for contributing to, or conflicting with, the mission. They must also be matched with certain internal factors. Possible internal factors relate to strengths and weaknesses of the organization and the potential for changing weaknesses and improving or retaining strengths. Among the key internal factors are:

1. *Human resources*. This includes the skills and abilities of managers, workers, and staff personnel; special talents (e.g., creativity, designing, problem solving); loyalty to the organization; expertise; dedication; and experience.

2. *Facilities and equipment*. Capacities, location, age, and cost to maintain or replace can have significant impact on operations.

3. *Financial resources*. Cash flow, access to additional funding, existing debt burden, and cost of capital are important considerations.

4. *Customers*. Loyalty, existing relationships, and understanding of wants and needs are important.

5. *Products and services*. This includes existing products and services as well as potential for new products and services.

6. *Technology*. This includes existing technology, the ability to integrate new technology, and the probable impact of technology on current and future operations.

7. *Suppliers*. Supplier relationships, dependability of suppliers, quality, flexibility, and service are typical considerations.

8. *Other*. Other factors include patents, labor relations, company or product image, distribution channels, relationships with distributors, maintenance of facilities and equipment, access to resources, and access to markets.

Figure 1–7 portrays the relationships between mission, corporate strategy, and functional strategies. The implication is that mission and the external and internal conditions combine to shape corporate strategy, which, in turn, shapes functional strategies. It is important to include inputs from functional areas in formulating corporate strategies; functional areas should be *proactive* rather then merely *reactive*. Otherwise, there is a significant risk that corporate strategies will not match functional capabilities and potential capabilities, thereby lessening the success of corporate strategies.

Table 1–6 contains a list of decision areas of corporate strategy.

FIGURE 1—7

Corporate strategy is based on mission and on external and internal conditions

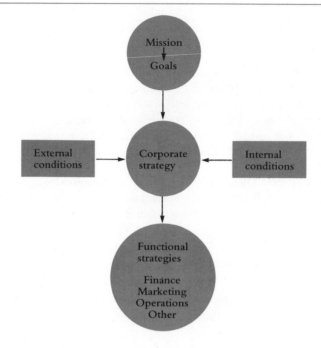

TABLE 1—6

Decision areas included in corporate strategy	Product and service selection
	Location of facilities
	Capacity
	Process selection
	Layout
	Human resource policies
	Bases of competition
	Technology
	Organization type

OPERATIONS STRATEGY

Operations strategy can be a key element in achieving strategic corporate objectives. As noted earlier, it is essential to have input from all of the functional areas, including operations, in formulating corporate strategy. This increases the likelihood that corporate strategies will be matched with functional capabilities.

Operations strategy should be formulated on the basis of corporate strategy. Strategic decisions in operations generally relate to *cost, quality/reliability, flexibility,* and *availability.* Cost reduction and the elimination of waste has been a successful strategy used by many Japanese competitors. And many Japanese companies have made quality a central part of their strategy. Reliability pertains both to the output and to equipment (e.g., breakdowns, ability to perform as required). High equipment reliability means fewer work disruptions. Flexibility can refer to the ability to respond to changing volume requirements, changing product or service requirements, or necessary changes in the mix of goods or services produced. Flexibility sometimes relates to the ability of an organization to make its products and services available on short notice. One way of ensuring availability is to maintain an inventory that can be drawn upon as needed.

The last two decision areas, availability and flexibility, pertain to **lead time,** which is the time needed to respond, say, to a change or to customer demand. In fact, recent literature on competition and operations strategy stresses *time management.* The implication is that operations managers could gain a different perspective on improving operations by focusing on reducing the time needed to accomplish each stage of the production process. Time management seems destined to become an important aspect of operations strategy as a competitive factor.

Operations areas that could stand improvement sometimes come to the manager's attention as problems; at other times, they are hidden and must be uncovered. It is a well-known axiom that relatively few factors account for a major share of the problems experienced and that improvements in a few key areas will have much more of an impact than improvements in many other areas. This is referred to as the **Pareto phenomenon.** It basically means that things are not all equal; some things (a few) will be very important in achieving an objective or solving a problem, and other things (many) will not. The implication is that a manager should examine the situation, searching for the few factors that will contribute the most to improvement, and then concentrate on those; little or nothing will be gained by focusing efforts on other, less important factors. This is one of the most important and pervasive concepts in operations management. In fact, as you read through this book, try to find a chapter or topic area where this concept does *not* apply. You may come to the conclusion that the concept can be applied at all levels of management and to every aspect of decision making, both professional and personal.

SUMMARY

The goal of this book is to present a broad conceptual framework for operations management. Operations, finance, and marketing are seen as the three primary functions of most business organizations. Although it has been traditionally regarded as primarily manufacturing-oriented, in recent years the scope of operations management has expanded greatly, and it is currently applied to both manufacturing and service activities. Operations management oversees all activities that are directly related to making a product or providing a service. Operations management is charged with transforming inputs of people, materials, energy, money, and information into useful goods and services. There are two main decision areas within operations: system design and system operation. System design is concerned with decisions related to capacity, location, layout, and product and process design. System operation is concerned with human resources, scheduling, project management, inventory management, and quality assurance.

One of the major responsibilities of the operations manager is productivity; much effort is typically devoted to maintaining and improving productivity.

Current issues in operations management include an increased emphasis on service systems, operating under increasing and changing government regulations, foreign competition, and integrating technological changes into production systems. Increasing emphasis is being placed on cost, quality, flexibility, and lead times. In addition, there is a greater awareness of the importance of integrating operations.

KEY TERMS

corporate strategy, 28
delivery time, 25
flexibility, 25
lead time, 31
mission, 28
operations management, 4
Pareto phenomenon, 31

price, 25
product differentiation, 25
productivity, 14
quality, 25
strategies, 28
system design, 11
system operation, 11

DISCUSSION AND REVIEW QUESTIONS

1. Briefly describe the three primary functions that exist within most business organizations.

2. What are the categories used to describe each of these: Inputs? Transformation? Outputs?

3. How does POM interface with marketing? How does it interface with finance?

4. Contrast system design and system operation. Give four examples of topics for each.

5. What are five important differences between manufacturing and service operations?

6. What is productivity, and why is it important? Who in the organization is primarily responsible for productivity?

7. What are some of the possible reasons offered in this chapter for the recent slump in productivity in some U.S. companies?

8. From time to time, various groups clamor for import restrictions on automobiles to help American manufacturers. In what ways might those restrictions be helpful? What disadvantages do you feel such restrictions might entail?

9. Much of the quality and productivity gain accomplished by the Japanese can be

traced to their use of industrial robots. Assuming this is true, why do you feel that U.S. companies have not made more extensive use of robots?

10. The United States has the highest productivity in agriculture of any country in the world and also ranks among the highest in textiles. What are some of the reasons for this high productivity?

11. Most experts agree that American workers are not primarily responsible for productivity problems. Nonetheless, workers sometimes contribute to the problem. Outline some of the ways this can happen.

12. Why study operations management?

13. Comment on the drawing on this page. What are its implications?

14. Describe the Pareto phenomenon and indicate why it is an important concept.

15. What strategies did Japanese manufacturers adopt after WWII that caused them to become successful competitors in U.S. markets?

16. List and briefly explain the five key ways business organizations compete with one another.

17. List the key external and internal factors that affect corporate strategy.

18. What are some competitive strategies? What are their advantages and disadvantages?

"If only people would work a little harder, we could increase productivity."

SELECTED BIBLIOGRAPHY

Buffa, E. S. *Meeting the Competitive Challenge: Manufacturing Strategies for U.S. Companies.* Homewood, Ill: Richard D. Irwin, 1984.

Chase, Richard, and Nicholas Aquilano. *Production and Operations Management.* 5th ed. Homewood, Ill.: Richard D. Irwin, 1989.

Hayes, Robert H., and Steven C. Wheelwright. *Restoring Our Competitive Edge: Competing through Manufacturing.* New York: John Wiley & Sons, 1984.

Hendrick, Thomas, and Franklin G. Moore, *Production/Operations Management.* 9th ed. Homewood, Ill.: Richard D. Irwin, 1985.

Hill, Terry. *Manufacturing Strategy.* Homewood, Ill.: Richard D. Irwin, 1989.

NBC White Paper: *"If Japan Can . . . Why Can't We?"* (Film available from Films, Inc.)

Porter, Michael E. *Competitive Advantage: Creating and Sustaining Superior Performance.* New York: The Free Press, 1984.

Peterson, Ronald S. "The Critical Issues for Manufacturing Management." *Operations Management Review* 2, no. 4, 1984, pp. 15–20.

Skinner, Wickham. "Manufacturing—Missing Link in Corporate Strategy." *Harvard Business Review,* May–June 1969, pp. 136–45.

Wheelwright, Steven C. "Japan—Where Operations Really Are Strategic." *Harvard Business Review,* July–August 1981, pp. 67–74.

READING

SPECIAL REPORT: PRODUCTIVITY

Karen Pennar

Someone else, or something else, was always to blame: The big spenders in Congress had let the budget deficit get too large. The Federal Reserve Board had cranked interest rates up too far. The dollar had soared too high. The Japanese were dumping products in the U.S. but shutting American companies out of their market. Whatever the excuse, though, the facts were the same: The U.S. was losing its competitive edge and had a ballooning trade deficit to prove it.

Then, as the dollar plunged and the deficits seemed intractable, the realization began to dawn: Was it possible that some of the blame lay right here? Maybe U.S. companies simply were not as productive, not as capable of turning out quality products at competitive prices as other industrial powers?

Management consultants and investment bankers sprang into action. Manufacturing executives took the bait. They restructured, downsized, merged, and streamlined in a desperate attempt to cut costs and survive. They poured money into the latest manufacturing technologies. Last year alone they added computers and new process-control equipment to the tune of $17 billion.

Receding Target

The results? Labor productivity in goods-producing industries leaped, pushing the annual growth rate to an average 3.5% for this decade, up from the paltry 1.4% of 1973 to 1979. Exports are climbing at double-digit rates. U.S. manufacturing is humming again. On the face of it, things are going swimmingly.

Look a little closer, though, and it's clear that a new paradox has emerged: The more Corporate America tries to boost productivity, the more elusive that goal becomes. In the first three years of the expansion, productivity growth topped 5% (see the chart), but since then it has slowed down to its current 3% level. That's decent enough, but experts worry that it's an unsustainable rate and in danger of falling further.

While a few companies have achieved astonishing results from carefully integrating automation into their operations, many that raced to spend on new technologies were burned. General Motors Corp. spent "more on automation than the gross national products of many countries," says Stephen G. Payne, chief executive of the PA Consulting group in Princeton, N.J., and had little to show for it. In April the No. 1 auto maker finally conceded that its market had shrunk, and it started downsizing. For GM and many other companies, the productivity payoff from automation is nowhere in sight.

Finally, the big catch is that despite the efficiency improvements, and despite cuts in unit labor costs, the U.S. still lags behind such nations as Japan, Britain, and France in productivity growth. And nations such as Korea and Taiwan are also logging big gains in productivity—enhancing their competitive position in world markets.

All the fuss is because rising productivity is the lever of economic development and growth: It provides what economists call "costless" growth. When labor and capital, the two key factors of production, are most productive, the economy is getting the biggest bang for its buck—the most output for a given level of input. Wages can rise, profits can climb, and investments can be made—all without prices escalating—because work has been reorganized or innovations introduced.

How to capture those benefits? How to build on earlier gains and boost U.S. competitiveness? How best to invest? Indeed, how do you even measure this thing called productivity?

Big Shift

The answers may come from a handful of companies that have developed a new math for productivity. They have tossed aside traditional cost accounting methods and made their capital investment decisions in novel ways. Instead of automating to cut costs, these executives invest to keep customers—and win new ones. Instead of buying a new machine to save on labor, they buy it to cut lead times, boost quality, reduce inventories, and add flexibility.

That approach marks a big shift from the early 1980s, when manufacturing executives on the defensive adopted slash-and-burn techniques to cut costs to the bone. Manufacturing employment plummeted from its peak of 21 million workers in 1979 to 18.4 million in 1983. Goods-producing industries added workers very slowly in the following years, then stepped up the pace when export demand picked up in 1986 and 1987. Yet even today, at 19.5 million, manufacturing employment stands well below the post-World War II peak.

At the same time as employers were cutting their work forces they were shuttering inefficient plants and drastically reducing capacity in the process. In the steel industry, capacity shrank by 25%, while capacity in the aluminum industry contracted 20%. The measures worked. From 1983 to 1985, while manufacturing output limped along, productivity shot up. But economists are skeptical that this marks any fundamental improvement. "If productivity goes up because industrial capacity was driven out, is that good?" asks Edward F. Denison, an economist at Brookings Institution.

What's more, once the fat has been trimmed—a worthy enough objective—that method of boosting productivity is exhausted. Closing plants and laying off workers are "one-time shots," says Lawrence Chimerine, chairman of the WEFA Group in Bala-Cynwyd, Pa. "These actions raise the level of productivity, but they don't improve its growth rate."

Unfulfilled Promise

It's obvious in the more recent productivity numbers that the benefits of slimming down and restructuring are running out. Now that manufacturing output has picked up, producers are beginning to bump up against capacity constraints, and their typical response has been to add more workers. A case in point: In the fourth quarter of 1987, manufacturing employment rose at a 6.7% annual rate while output rose 7.5%. The difference, 0.8%, was the meager gain in productivity. That's only one quarter's

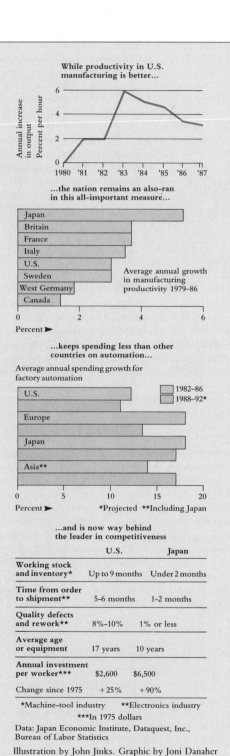

While productivity in U.S. manufacturing is better...

...the nation remains an also-ran in this all-important measure...

Average annual growth in manufacturing productivity 1979–86

...keeps spending less than other countries on automation...

Average annual spending growth for factory automation

1982–86
1988–92*

*Projected **Including Japan

...and is now way behind the leader in competitiveness

	U.S.	Japan
Working stock and inventory*	Up to 9 months	Under 2 months
Time from order to shipment**	5-6 months	1-2 months
Quality defects and rework**	8%–10%	1% or less
Average age or equipment	17 years	10 years
Annual investment per worker***	$2,600	$6,500
Change since 1975	+25%	+90%

*Machine-tool industry   **Electronics industry
***In 1975 dollars

Data: Japan Economic Institute, Dataquest, Inc., Bureau of Labor Statistics

Illustration by John Jinks. Graphic by Joni Danaher

number, of course, but it's a troubling example of the easy way to raise output—simply boost employment. "The trick is to get more output without a surge in employment," says Carl G. Thor, president of the American Productivity Center in Houston.

It's technology, of course, that should do the trick. So bring on automation, from office PCs to process-control devices. In theory, productivity should soar. In practice, the promise of technology hasn't been fulfilled. In the broadly defined service sector, from banks to health care clinics, capital spending on computers and office equipment has boomed over the last decade—and productivity has languished. This has dragged down the growth rate for productivity in the overall economy.

The goods-producing sector, meanwhile, has had mixed success with automation. Indeed, it's the computer industry itself that seems to have taken the greatest strides in improving productivity—its own capacity to produce computers, that is. Martin N. Baily, an economist at the Brookings Institution, calculates that in the years 1979 to 1985 productivity improvements in computers and related nonelectrical machinery account for a full percentage point of the "multifactor" productivity growth rate—a concept that weights the relative input of labor and capital in calculating productivity.

Variety

But the high-tech additions to capital don't seem to have had similar success in boosting output in other industries. One reason may be that changes in low tech must accompany the introduction of high tech. The way workers, supervisors, and managers interact may have to change at the same time as new manufacturing systems are adopted. Moreover, those new systems themselves aren't yet commonplace enough to make a difference in the overall productivity results. Says the American Productivity Center's Thor: "You need a decade's worth of that [kind of investment] to have an effect."

Eventually, though, they will have to. For now, the dollar is weak and demand strong—just the ticket for U.S. manufacturers. But if manufacturing executives want to ensure that they are competitive for the long haul, they should take this opportunity to invest more. Though capital spending is expected to jump 10% or so this year, many fear that it's still not enough and, worse yet, not of the right variety to boost productivity. While some executives worry that demand may lag in the future, those concerns shouldn't deter them from investing. "These investments have nothing to do with demand," says Thor. "In fact, if there's lower demand for your product, the investment might be your salvation."

That's advice that more manufacturers should heed, even if the numbers don't crunch right or the rates of return don't seem to justify the spending. Otherwise, they may wind up correctly calculating the wrong way to go—and lose more and more battles in the war to gain world markets.

READING

AN AMERICAN TRAGEDY: HOW A GOOD COMPANY DIED

Zachary Schiller

The Rust Belt is back. So say bullish observers as U.S. exports surge, long-moribund industries glow with newfound profits, and unemployment dips to lows not seen in a decade. But in the smokestack citadels, there's disquiet. Too many machine-tool and auto-parts factories are silent; too many U.S. industries still can't hold their own.

What went wrong since the heyday of the 1960s?

That's the issue Max Holland, a contributing editor of *The Nation,* takes up in his nutsy-boltsy but fascinating study *When the Machine Stopped.**

The focus of the story is Burgmaster Corp., a Los Angeles-area machine-tool maker founded in 1944 by Czechoslovakian immigrant Fred Burg. Holland's father worked there for 29 years, and the author interviewed 22 former employees. His shop-floor view of this small company is a refreshing change from academic treatises on why America can't compete.

The discussions of spindles and numerical control can be tough going. But Holland compensates by conveying the excitement and innovation of the company's early days and the disgust and cynicism accompanying its decline. Moreover, the fate of Burgmaster and its brethren is crucial to the U.S. industrial economy: Any manufactured item is either made by a machine tool or by a machine made by a machine tool.

Producing innovative turret drills used in a wide variety of metalworking tasks, Burgmaster was a thriving enterprise by 1965, when annual sales amounted to about $8 million. The company needed backing to expand, however, so it sold out to Buffalo-based conglomerate Houdaille Industries Inc. Houdaille was in turn purchased in a 1979 leveraged buyout led by Kohlberg Kravis Roberts & Co. By 1982, when debt, competition, and a sickly machine-tool market had battered Burgmaster badly, Houdaille went to Washington with a petition to withhold the investment tax credit for certain Japanese-made machine tools.

Thanks to deft lobbying, the Senate passed a resolution supporting Houdaille's position, but President Reagan refused to go along. Houdaille's subsequent attempt to link Burgmaster up with a Japanese rival also failed, and Burgmaster was closed.

Holland uses Burgmaster's demise to explore some key issues of economic and trade policy. Houdaille's charge that a cartel led by the Japanese government had injured U.S. toolmakers, for example, became a rallying point for those who would blame a fearsome Japan Inc. for the problems of U.S. industry.

Holland describes the Washington wrangling over Houdaille in painful detail. But he does show that such government decisions are often made without much knowledge of what's going on in industry. He shows, too, that Japanese producers succeeded less because of government help than because they made better, cheaper machines.

For those who see LBOs as a symptom of what ails the U.S. economy, Holland offers plenty of ammunition. He argues persuasively that the LBO crippled Burgmaster by creating enormous pressure to generate cash. As Burgmaster pushed its products out as fast as possible, he writes, it routinely shipped defective machines. It promised customers features that engineers hadn't yet designed. And although KKR disputes the claim, Holland concludes that the LBO choked off Burgmaster's investment funds just when foreign competition made them most necessary. As for Houdaille, it was recapitalized and sold to Britain's Tube Investments Group.

But Burgmaster's problems had started even before the LBO. Holland's history of the company under Houdaille is a veritable catalog of modern management techniques that flopped. One of the most disastrous was a system for computerizing production scheduling that was too crude for complex machine-tool manufacturing. Holland gives a dramatic depiction of supply snafus that resulted in delays and cost increases.

As an independent company, "Burgmaster thrived because the Burgs knew their business," Holland writes. Their departure under Houdaille was followed by an "endless and ultimately futile search for a better formula." But, he concludes: "No formula was a substitute for management involvement on the shop floor."

In the end, however, Holland puts most of the blame for the industry's decline on government policy. He targets tax laws and macroeconomic policies that encourage LBOs and speculation instead of productive investment. He also criticizes Pentagon procurement policies for favoring exotic, custom

* Max Holland, *When the Machine Stopped: A Cautionary Tale from Industrial America* (Boston, Mass.: Harvard Business School Press, 1988).

machines over standard, low-cost models. This adds up to an industrial policy, Holland writes—a bad one.

The point is well taken, but Holland gives it excessive weight. Like their brethren in Detroit and Pittsburgh, domestic tool-makers in the 1970s were too complacent when imports seized the lower end of the product line. The conservatism that had for years served them in their cyclical industry left them ill-prepared for change. Even now some of the largest U.S. tool-makers are struggling to restructure. Blame the government, yes. But blame the industry, too.

Questions

1. How important are machine tools to manufacturing? Why?
2. How did the leveraged buyout affect Burgmaster?
3. Other than the LBO, what factors contributed to the firm's failure?

2

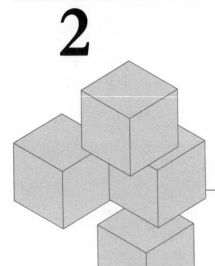

Decision Making

LEARNING OBJECTIVES

After completing this chapter, you should be able to:

1. Explain the importance of decision making.
2. Outline the steps in the decision-making process.
3. Discuss the characteristics of operations decisions.
4. Describe the different environments under which operations decisions are made.
5. Describe and use techniques that apply to decision making under uncertainty.
6. Describe and use the expected-value approach.
7. Construct a decision tree and use it to solve a problem.
8. Compute the expected value of perfect information.
9. Conduct sensitivity analysis on a simple decision problem.

Chapter Outline

The chief role of the operations manager is that of decision maker. In this capacity, the operations manager has considerable influence over the degree to which the goals and objectives of the organization are achieved.

Throughout this book you will be exposed to a broad range of decision areas that are encountered in operations management and to the tools necessary to handle those decisions. In this chapter the process of decision making is examined, as are typical reasons for poor decisions, the characteristics of operations decisions, and the classification of decision problems according to degree of certainty. The chapter concludes with a discussion of decision theory, which is a general approach to decision making that has applications in many areas of operations management.

THE DECISION PROCESS

Decision making is a fundamental process of management, and most of the efforts of managers are related to this process. Unfortunately, decisions do not always turn out as planned. Most successful decision making follows a process that consists of these steps:

1. Identify the problem.
2. Specify objectives and the decision criteria for choosing a solution.
3. Develop alternatives.
4. Analyze and compare alternatives.
5. Select the best alternative.
6. Implement the chosen alternative
7. Monitor the results to ensure that desired results are achieved.

Success or failure in decision making often depends on how well each of these steps is handled.

Identifying the problem is the focal point of the process. Unless it is done carefully, the remaining steps can be misdirected. One danger is that problem-solving efforts will be directed toward removing the *symptoms* of the problem rather than the actual problem itself, leaving the problem to resurface at a later time. For instance, athletic injuries are sometimes treated with pain-killing drugs that can effectively mask the symptoms. However, the drugs do not heal the actual injury. Even worse, the person may feel so much better that he or she returns to action and risks aggravating the injury. Or consider the young driver who became so annoyed at the strange noises coming from his car's engine that he was forced to turn up the volume on the car's radio to drown them out. *Solutions must address the basic problem, not the symptoms.*

The decision maker must *identify the criteria* by which proposed solutions will be judged. Common criteria often relate to costs, profits, return on investment, increased productivity, risk, company image, impact on demand, and similar variables.

The ability to satisfactorily handle problems often depends on the degree of success one has in *developing suitable alternatives.* In the search for alternatives, there is always the danger that one or more potentially superior alternatives will be overlooked. Consequently, the optimal alternative may turn out to be less than optimum. Obviously, there is a limit to the number of possible alternatives that can be identified. Much depends on the experience and creativity of the decision maker as well as on the nature of the situation. However, as a general rule, efforts expended in carefully identifying alternatives can yield substantial dividends in terms of the overall decision. One alternative that is frequently overlooked, possibly because it seems too simple, is to do nothing. The beauty of doing nothing lies not only in the fact that no time or effort is needed, but also in that it may cost nothing and requires no implementation.

Analyzing and comparing alternatives often benefits from the use of mathematical or statistical techniques. Many of these are described and demonstrated throughout this book.

Selection of the best alternative will depend on the objectives of the decision maker and the criteria that are being used to evaluate alternatives.

Implementing a solution simply means carrying out the actions indicated by the chosen alternative. Examples include buying the machine, refusing the loan application, beginning development of a new product, and authorizing the use of overtime. Of course, if the alternative selected is to do nothing, no action will be required to implement it. Note that many decision makers use this approach by default: By the time they get around to making a decision, it is too late!

Effective decision making requires that the results of the decision be *monitored* to make certain that the desired consequences have been achieved. If they have not, the decision maker may have to repeat the entire process; or perhaps a review of the situation may reveal an error in the actual implementation, an error in calculations, a wrong assumption, or some similar point that will allow the situation to be remedied rather quickly.

It should be noted that the decision process is not always completed in a sequential manner. Instead, there is usually a certain amount of backtracking and feedback involved, especially in terms of developing and analyzing alternatives. For example, if none of the alternatives analyzed can achieve the desired results, additional alternatives must be developed. Or perhaps the problem has not been clearly identified, and so additional work must be done there as well as on the other steps in the process.

Reasons for Poor Decisions

Occasionally, despite the best efforts of a manager, a decision turns out rather poorly due to unforeseeable circumstances. However, such occurrences are not all that common. More often, failures can be traced to some combination of the following reasons: mistakes made in the decision process, bounded rationality, or suboptimization.

In many cases, managers fail to appreciate the importance of each step in the decision process that was just outlined. They may skip a step or not devote enough effort to completing it before jumping to the next step. Sometimes this is due to a manager's style of making quick decisions or to failure to recognize the consequences of a poor decision. The manager's ego can be a factor. This sometimes happens after a period in which the manager has experienced a series of successes—important decisions that all turned out right. Under these circumstances, some managers begin to get the impression that they can do no wrong, and soon the trouble begins. This is enough to bring some managers back down to earth, but others seem oblivious to the negative results and continue the process they associate with their previous successes, not recognizing that some of that success was due more to luck than to any special abilities of their own. A part of the problem may be related to the manager's unwillingness to admit a mistake. Then, too, some managers demonstrate an inability to make a decision: they hem and haw, stalling long past the time when the decision should have been rendered.

Of course, all managers do not fall into these traps. In fact, it would seem safe to say that the majority do not. Even so, this does not necessarily mean that every decision works out as expected. Another factor with which managers must contend is **bounded rationality,** a term that refers to the limits imposed on decision making because of costs, human abilities, time, technology, and the availability of information. Because of these limitations, managers cannot always expect to reach decisions that are optimal in the sense of providing the best possible outcome (e.g., highest profit, least cost). Instead, they must often resort to achieving a *satisfactory* solution.

Still another source of poor decisions arises because organizations typically departmentalize decisions. Naturally, there is a great deal of justification for the use of departments in terms of overcoming span-of-control problems and human limitations. However, one problem that can arise is **suboptimization.** This occurs as a result of different departments each attempting to reach a solution that is optimum for that department. Unfortunately, what is optimum for a specific department may not be optimum for the organization as a whole. For example, the quality control department of a wire manufacturer may want to introduce a program that will guarantee that every nail produced is perfect. However, to cover costs, the price charged might be so ridiculously high that it would be unlikely that anyone would be willing to buy the product!

CHARACTERISTICS OF OPERATIONS DECISIONS

Operations decisions are often characterized by the use of models, by quantitative methods, by analysis of trade-offs, by sensitivity analysis, and by a systems approach. These characteristics are discussed in this section.

The Use of Models

A **model** is an abstraction of reality. That is, a model presents a simplified, incomplete version of something. For example, a child's toy car is a model of a real automobile: it has many of the same visual features (shape, relative proportions, wheels), which makes it quite suitable for its intended purpose in terms of the child's learning and playing. However, it does not have a real engine, it cannot transport people, and it does not weigh 2,000 pounds. Similarly, an instructor commonly uses chalk markings on a blackboard to represent just about anything under the sun. Again, these are models, for although they often communicate a point rather effectively, they are merely bits of chalk dust arranged on the blackboard.

Some common examples of models include wind tunnels, which are designed to model the effects of air turbulence on the outer surfaces of airplanes; formulas; graphs and charts; balance sheets and income statements; and financial ratios. Common statistical models include descriptive statistics such as the mean, median, mode, range, and standard deviation, as well as random sampling, the normal distribution, and regression equations.

Models are sometimes classified as physical, schematic, and mathematical:

Physical models look like their real-life counterparts. Examples include miniature cars, trucks, airplanes, toy animals and trains, and scale-model buildings. The advantage of these models is their visual correspondence with reality.

Schematic models are more abstract than their physical counterparts. That is, they have less resemblance to the physical reality. Examples include graphs and charts, blueprints, pictures, and drawings. The advantage of these models is that they are often relatively simple to construct and to change. Moreover, they have some degree of visual correspondence.

Mathematical models are the height of abstraction; they do not look at all like their real-life counterparts. Examples include numbers, formulas, and certain symbols. These models are usually the easiest to manipulate, and they are essential forms of inputs for computers and calculators.

The variety of models in use is enormous. Models range from the simple to the exotic; some are very crude, and others are extremely elegant. Nonetheless, they all have certain common features: They are all considered decision-making aids, and they are all abstractions (simplifications) of more complex real-life phenomena. The extensive use of models stems from the fact that real life involves an overwhelming amount of detail, much of which is irrelevant for any particular problem. Models strip away these unimportant details so that attention can be concentrated on the relatively few important aspects of the situation, thus increasing the opportunity for effective understanding of a problem and its solution.

The underlying goal in modeling is to develop a model that adequately portrays some real-life phenomenon. Once a model has been developed, a great deal can be learned about it by manipulating its variables and observing the results. If the model is a good one, a great deal can be learned about its real-life counterpart.

Since models play a significant role in operations management decision making, they are heavily integrated into the subject matter of this text. As you progress through the text, you will encounter a fair number of these models. For each model, try to learn (1) the purpose of the model, (2) how to use the model to generate results, (3) how results are interpreted and used, and (4) what assumptions and limitations apply.

The last point is particularly important because virtually every model has an associated set of requirements that indicate the conditions under which the model is valid. Failure to satisfy all of the assumptions (i.e., to try to use a model where it isn't meant to be used) will make the results suspect. Attempts to apply the results to a problem under such circumstances can lead to disastrous consequences. Hence, it is extremely important to be aware of the assumptions and limitations of each model.

Managers use models in a variety of ways and for a variety of reasons. Among them are the following:

1. They are generally easy to use and less expensive than dealing directly with the actual situation.
2. They require users to organize and sometimes quantify information and, in the process, often indicate areas where additional information is needed.
3. They provide a systematic approach to problem solving.
4. They increase understanding of the problem.
5. They enable managers to ask "what if . . . ?" questions.
6. They require users to be very specific about objectives.
7. They serve as a consistent tool for evaluation.
8. They enable users to bring the power of mathematics to bear on a problem.
9. They provide a standardized format for analyzing a problem.

This impressive list of benefits notwithstanding, there are certain limitations of models that you should also be aware of. Some of the more important limitations are:

1. Quantitative information may be emphasized at the expense of qualitative information.
2. Models may be incorrectly applied, and/or results can be misinterpreted. The widespread use of computerized models adds to this risk because highly sophisticated models may be placed in the hands of users who are not sufficiently grounded in mathematics to appreciate the subtleties of a particular model; they generally cannot fully comprehend the circumstances under which the model can be successfully employed.
3. Model building can become an end in itself.

Quantitative Approaches

Quantitative approaches to problem solving often embody an attempt to obtain mathematically optimum solutions to managerial problems. Although quantitative techniques have traditionally been associated with production and operations management, it was not until World War II that major efforts were made to develop these techniques. In order to handle complex logistics problems associated with military activity, interdisciplinary teams were assembled (e.g., psychologists, mathematicians, economists) that combined efforts in search of workable solutions. These efforts continued and expanded after the war, and many of the resulting techniques found applications in operations management. *Linear programming* and related mathematical techniques are widely used for optimum allocation of scarce resources. *Queuing techniques,* which originated around 1920 in telephone work but remained dormant until work was greatly expanded in the 1950s and 1960s, are useful for analyzing situations in which waiting lines form. *Inventory models,* also popular after some early work, went through a long period of low interest and are now widely used to control inventories. *Project models* such as PERT (program evaluation and review technique) and CPM (critical path method) are useful for planning, coordinating, and controlling large-scale projects. *Forecasting techniques* are increasingly being used as a basis for planning and scheduling. *Statistical models* are currently used in all areas of decision making where elements of risk are present.

In large measure, quantitative approaches to decision making in operations management (as well as in other areas of decision making) have been accepted because of the introduction of calculators and the availability of high-speed computers that are capable of handling the required calculations. Computers have had an enormous influence on the practice of operations management, particularly in the areas of scheduling and inventory control. Because of their capability for rapid, error-free computations and the ability to keep track of thousands of bits of information with instantaneous retrieval, computers have made significant inroads in handling some very difficult problem areas. Moreover, the growing availability of software packages covering virtually every quantitative technique in use has greatly enhanced management's use of the computer for problem solving. Many heretofore impractical techniques, such as multiple regression analysis and linear programming, can now be handled with virtual ease, thanks to computer packages and the widespread availability of computers.

Computers have proven invaluable in simulation studies, where analysts explore real-life problems that do not lend themselves to solution using formulas, by varying parameters in repeated computer trials and analyzing the results in order to better understand a problem and to generate alternative solutions.

Because of the emphasis on quantitative approaches in operations management decision making, it is important that you not lose sight of the fact that managers typically use a combination of qualitative and quantitative approaches, and many important decisions are based on *qualitative* approaches. The reason for the emphasis on quantitative methods lies in the fact that quantitative analysis is typically more difficult to understand without a fair amount of explanation and demonstration problems.

Analysis of Trade-Offs

The decisions encountered by operations managers can be described as *trade-off* decisions. For example, in deciding on the amount of inventory to stock, the manager's eventual decision must take into account the trade-off between the increased level of customer service that increasing the amount stocked would yield and the increase in costs required to stock that amount. Similarly, in choosing a level of quality inspection, a manager must evaluate the merits of fewer defectives slipping through by increasing inspection efforts versus the increase in costs that would be required. In allocating funds, the manager may have to weigh the potential for increased profits from a certain action against the higher risk of loss relative to what another proposal might entail. Use of overtime to increase output is another example. In that case, the manager must weigh the value of the increased output against the increased costs of overtime (e.g., lower productivity, higher labor costs, lower quality, and increased risk of accidents).

Throughout this book you will be presented with decision models that reflect these kinds of trade-offs. Managers often deal with decisions of this nature by listing the advantages and disadvantages of opposing courses of action in an effort to obtain a better understanding of the consequences of potential decisions.

Sensitivity Analysis

A key feature of many quantitive techniques is the ability of the user to perform **sensitivity analysis** on a solution, that is, the user's ability to test how sensitive a given solution is to a change in one or more of the parameters (i.e., the "numbers") taken as givens in a problem. For instance, suppose a manager has these two models:

$$\text{Profit A} = 2x + 4{,}000 \quad \text{and} \quad \text{Profit B} = 2x + 4$$

Suppose also that the variable x typically takes on a value of approximately 5.0. The manager may have estimated the coefficient of x (i.e., 2) in both models and now wants to know how sensitive the profit computed with the equation is to that value. Suppose that the manager feels the true value may be closer to 1 than to 2. For profit A, substituting 1 into the equation with $x = 5$ yields a profit of 4,005; substituting a 2 into the equation with $x = 5$ yields a profit of 4,010. There is little difference between the profits of A determined with these two different values of the coefficient.

Now let's see what happens in the case of profit B, again with $x = 5$. For a coefficient of 1, profit B is 9; for a coefficient of 2, profit B is 14. Comparing these two cases, we see that the model for profit B is quite sensitive to a possible estimation error of the magnitude given, whereas the model for profit A is rather insensitive.

The knowledge provided by sensitivity analysis can be useful in a variety of ways. One is that it allows a manager to learn whether additional effort is needed to pin down an estimate of a parameter. If the solution is not particularly sensitive to a change of a reasonable magnitude, the manager can use the solution with a certain degree of confidence. Conversely, if a solution is sensitive to such a change, the manager will probably want to devote more attention to obtaining a reasonably accurate estimate of the parameter.

Another use of sensitivity analysis is to enable managers to explore how certain changes might affect a solution. For instance, the limited availability of a resource (e.g., raw material) very often constrains a solution. A manager might have the opportunity to obtain an additional amount of the resource for a given cost. In order to decide whether or not to buy an additional amount of the resource, the manager will want to know how much improvement in profit the resource will generate and then compare that to the added cost.

The Systems Approach

A systems viewpoint is almost always beneficial in decision making. A **system** can be defined as a set of interrelated parts that must work together. In the case of a business organization, the organization is viewed as a system composed of subsystems (e.g., marketing subsystem, operations subsystem, finance subsystem), which in turn are composed of lower subsystems. The systems approach emphasizes interrelationships among subsystems, but its main theme is that *the whole is greater than the sum of its individual parts*. Hence, from a systems viewpoint, the output and objectives of the organization as a whole take precedence over those of any one subsystem and should be optimized even if this requires a less-than-optimum result in one or more subsystems. An alternative approach would be to concentrate on efficiency within subsystems and thereby achieve overall efficiency. That view tends to overlook the fact that organizations must operate in an environment of scarce resources and that subsystems are often in direct competition for those scarce resources, so that an orderly approach to the allocation of resources is called for.

One important implication relative to quantitative techniques is that many of the techniques tend to produce solutions that are optimal in a narrow sense but that may not be optimal in a broader sense (e.g., in terms of a department, plant, division, or overall organization). Consequently, managers must evaluate "optimal" solutions produced by quantitative techniques in terms of the larger framework and perhaps modify decisions accordingly.

An interesting problem that has system connotations involves world hunger. We read in the newspapers about how people in some parts of the world are starving, while in other parts of the world there is an overabundance of food—food that is rotting and being destroyed. The solution seems simple enough: Why not send the surplus food to those who need it? Unfortunately, that "solution" does not deal with the realities of the system. There are other key aspects of this problem that must be overcome. One is transporting the surplus food from current locations to those areas where it is needed. This is a fairly demanding task. The locations with surplus food have to be identified, the food has to be temporarily stored, and arrangements for shipping have to be made (schedules, timing, who will pay for shipping, finding available shipping capacity, and so on). An even more formidable task is distributing the food once it reaches the country in which it is needed. Not only must the political system of that country be dealt with, as well as possible graft and corruption, but also the transportation system of the region. More often than not, the region will have poor roads and very limited capacity for moving goods from ports to inland areas. Suitable landing fields are usually nonexistent in these areas. And even if all these problems could be overcome, the "solution" would only be a temporary one in that the broader problem that must be addressed is how to permanently solve the hunger problem in the region. Thus, taking a systems perspective enables us to achieve a truer picture of a problem and increases the chances that a meaningful resolution to the overall problem will be realized.

Priority Recognition

In virtually every situation a manager must deal with, certain aspects are more important than others. Recognizing this fact of life will enable the manager to direct his or her efforts to where they will do the most good and to avoid wasting time and energy on insignificant aspects of the situation.

Consider an automobile. It has many parts and systems that can malfunction. Some of these are critical to the operation of the automobile: it will not function without them or would be dangerous to operate without them. Critical items include the engine and drive train, steering, brakes, tires, electrical system, and cooling system. In terms of maintaining and repairing the car, these items should receive the highest priority if the goal is to have reliable transportation.

There are other items that are of much less importance, such as scratches in the paint, minor dents, a missing piece of chrome, and worn seatcovers. In terms of transportation, these should receive attention only after other, more important items have been attended to.

Between these two extremes lies a range of items of intermediate priority. These would be given attention corresponding to their importance to the overall goal. The list might include soft tires, weak battery, wheel alignment, noisy muffler, body rust, inoperative radio, and headlights that need adjustment.

It is fairly obvious that certain parts of an automobile are more critical to its operation than others. The same concept applies to management. By recognizing this and setting priorities, a manager will be in a position to more effectively deal with problems as they arise and to prevent many problems from arising at all.

Decision Environments

The environments in which operations management decisions are made can be classified according to the degree of certainty present. There are three basic categories: certainty, risk, and uncertainty.

Certainty implies that relevant parameters such as costs, capacity, and demand have known values.

Risk implies that certain parameters have probabilistic outcomes.

Uncertainty implies that it is impossible to assess the likelihood of various possible future events.

Consider these situations:

1. Profit per unit is $5. We have an order for 200 units. How much profit will we make? (This is an example of *certainty* since unit profits and total demand are known.)
2. Profit is $5 per unit. Based on previous experience, there is a 50 percent chance of an order for 100 units and a 50 percent chance of an order for 200 units. What is expected profit? (This is an example of *risk* since demand outcomes are probabilistic.)
3. Profit per unit is $5. The probabilities of potential demands are unknown. (This is an example of *uncertainty*.)

The importance of these three decision environments is that they require different techniques of analysis. Some techniques are better suited for one category than for others. You should make note of the environment for which each technique is appropriate.

DECISION THEORY

Decision theory represents a general approach to decision making. It is suitable for a wide range of operations management decisions. Among them are capacity planning, product and service design, equipment selection, and location planning. Decisions that lend themselves to a decision theory approach tend to be characterized by these elements:

1. A set of possible future conditions exists that will have a bearing on the results of the decision.
2. The manager has a list of alternatives to choose from.
3. There is a known payoff for each alternative under each possible future condition.

In order to use this approach, a decision maker would employ this process:

1. Identify the possible future conditions (e.g., demand will be low, medium, or high; the number of contracts awarded will be one, two, or three; the competitor will introduce a new product, or the competitor will not introduce a new product). These are called *states of nature*.

2. Develop a list of possible *alternatives,* one of which may be to do nothing.

3. Determine or estimate the *payoff* associated with each alternative for every possible future condition.

4. If possible, estimate the *likelihood* of each possible future condition.

5. Evaluate alternatives according to some *decision criterion* (e.g., maximize expected profit), and select the best alternative.

The information for a decision is often summarized in a **payoff table,** which shows the expected payoffs for each alternative under the various possible states of nature. These tables are helpful in choosing among alternatives because they facilitate comparison of alternatives. Consider the payoff table below, which illustrates a capacity planning problem.

	Possible future demand		
Alternatives	*Low*	*Moderate*	*High*
Small facility	$10*	$10	$10
Medium facility	7	12	12
Large facility	(4)	2	16

*Present value in $ millions.

The payoffs are shown in the body of the table. In this instance, the payoffs are in terms of present values, which represent equivalent current dollar values of expected future income minus costs. This is a convenient measure because it places all alternatives on a comparable basis. We see in the table that if a small facility is built, the payoff will be the same for all three possible states of nature. For a medium facility, low demand will have a present value of $7 million, whereas both moderate and high demand will have present values of $12 million. A large facility will have a loss of $4 million if demand is low, a present value of $2 million if demand is moderate, and a present value of $16 million if demand is high.

The problem for the decision maker is to select one of the alternatives, taking the present values into account.

Evaluation of the alternatives differs depending on the degree of certainty associated with the possibie future conditions. Again, there are three possibilities to consider: complete certainty, risk, and uncertainty.

Decision Making under Certainty

When it is known for certain which of the possible future conditions will actually happen, the decision is usually relatively straightforward: Simply choose the alternative that has the highest payoff under that state of nature. This is illustrated in Example 1.

EXAMPLE 1

Determine the best alternative in the preceding payoff table, if it is known with certainty that demand will be: *(a)* low, *(b)* moderate, *(c)* high.

Solution

Choose the alternative with the highest payoff. Thus, if we know demand will be low, we would elect to build the small facility and realize a payoff of $10 million. If we know demand will be moderate, a medium facility would yield the highest payoff ($12 million versus either $10 or $2 million). For high demand, a large facility will provide the highest payoff.

Although complete certainty is rare in such situations, exercises such as the preceding one do provide some perspective on the analysis. Moreover, in some instances, there may be an opportunity to consider allocation of funds to research efforts, which may reduce or remove some of the uncertainty surrounding the states of nature.

Decision Making under Uncertainty

At the opposite extreme is complete uncertainty: no information is available on how likely the various states of nature are. Under those conditions, four possible decision criteria are *maximin, maximax, Laplace,* and *minimax regret.* These approaches can be defined as follows.

Maximin—Determine the worst possible payoff for each alternative, and then choose the alternative that has the "best worst."

Maximax—Determine the best possible payoff, and choose the alternative with that payoff.

Laplace—Determine the average payoff for each alternative, and choose the alternative with the best average.

Minimax regret—Determine the worst regret for each alternative, and choose the alternative with the "best worst."

The next two examples illustrate these decision criteria.

EXAMPLE 2

Referring to the preceding payoff table, determine which alternative would be chosen under each of these strategies:

a. Maximin
b. Maximax
c. Laplace

Solution

a. The worst payoffs for the alternatives are:

Small facility:	$10 million
Medium facility:	$7 million
Large facility:	−$4 million

Hence, since $10 million is the best, choose to build the small facility using the maximin strategy.

b. The best overall payoff is the $16 million in the third row. Hence, the maximax criterion leads to building a large facility.

c. For the Laplace criterion, first find the row totals, and then divide each of those amounts by the number of states of nature (three in this case). Thus, we have:

	Row total	Row average
Small facility	30	10.00
Medium facility	31	10.33
Large facility	14	4.67

Since the medium facility has the highest average, it would be chosen under the Laplace criterion.

The maximin approach is essentially a pessimistic one in that it takes into account only the worst possible outcome for each alternative. The actual outcome may not be as bad as that, but this approach establishes a "guaranteed minimum."

The maximax approach is an optimistic, "go for it" strategy; it does not take into account any payoff other than the best.

The Laplace approach treats the states of nature as equally likely.

EXAMPLE 3

Determine which alternative would be chosen using a minimax regret approach to the capacity planning problem.

EXAMPLE 3 *(concluded)*

Solution

The first step in this approach is to prepare a table of **opportunity losses,** or **regrets.** To do this, subtract every payoff *in each column* from the largest positive payoff in that column. For instance, in the first column, the largest positive payoff is 10, so each of the three numbers in that column must be subtracted from 10. Going down the column, the regrets will be $10 - 10 = 0$, $10 - 7 = 3$, and $10 - (-4) = 14$. In the second column, the largest positive payoff is 12. Subtracting each payoff from 12 yields 2, 0, and 10. In the third column, 16 is the largest payoff. The regrets are 6, 4, and 0. These results are summarized in a regret table:

	Regrets			
Alternatives	*Low*	*Moderate*	*High*	*Worst*
Small facility	0	2	6	6
Medium facility	3	0	4	4
Large facility	14	10	0	14

The second step is to identify the worst regret for each alternative. For the first alternative, the worst is 6; for the second, the worst is 4; and for the third, the worst is 14.

The best of these "worsts" would be chosen using minimax regret. The lowest regret is 4, which is for a medium facility. Hence, that alternative would be chosen.

Solved Problem 6 at the end of the chapter illustrates decision making under uncertainty when the payoffs represent costs.

The main weakness of these approaches (except for Laplace) is that they do not take into account *all* of the payoffs. Instead, they focus on the worst or best, and so they lose some information. The weakness of Laplace is that it treats all states of nature as equally likely. Still, for a given set of circumstances, each has certain merits that can be helpful to a decision maker.

Decision Making under Risk

Between the two extremes of certainty and uncertainty lies the case of risk: the probability of occurrence for each state of nature can be estimated. (Note that because the states are mutually exclusive and collectively exhaustive, these probabilities must add to 1.00.) A widely used approach under such circumstances is the *expected monetary value criterion.* The expected value is computed for each alternative, and the one with the highest expected value is selected. The expected value is the sum of the payoffs for an alternative where each payoff is *weighted* by the probability for the relevant state of nature. Thus, the approach is:

Expected monetary value criterion (EMV)—Determine the expected payoff of each alternative, and choose the alternative that has the best expected payoff.

EXAMPLE 4

Using the expected monetary value criterion, identify the best alternative for the previous payoff table for these probabilities: low = .30, moderate = .50, and high = .20.

Solution

Find the expected value of each alternative by multiplying the probability of occurrence for each state of nature by the payoff for that state of nature and summing them:

$$EV_{small} = .30(\$10) + .50(\$10) + .20(\$10) = \$10$$
$$EV_{medium} = .30(\$7) + .50(\$12) + .20(\$12) = \$10.5$$
$$EV_{large} = .30(-\$4) + .50(\$2) + .20(\$16) = \$3$$

Hence, choose the medium-size facility because it has the highest expected value.

The expected monetary value approach is most appropriate when a decision maker is nether risk-averse nor risk-seeking, but instead is risk-neutral. Typically, well-established organizations with numerous decisions of this nature tend to use expected value since it provides an indication of the long-run, average payoff. That is, the expected-value amount (e.g., $10.5 million in the last example) is not an actual payoff but an expected or average amount that would be approximated if a large number of identical decisions were to be made. Hence, if a decision maker applies this criterion to a large number of similar decisions, the expected payoff for the total will equal the sum of the individual expected payoffs.

Decision Trees

A **decision tree** is a schematic representation of the alternatives available to a decision maker and their possible consequences. The term gets its name from the treelike appearance of the diagram (see Figure 2–1). Although tree diagrams can be used in place of a payoff table, they are particularly useful for analyzing situations that involve *sequential* decisions. For instance, a manager may initially decide to build a small facility only to discover that demand is much higher than anticipated. In this case, the manager may then be called upon to make a second decision on whether to expand or build an additional facility.

FIGURE 2–1

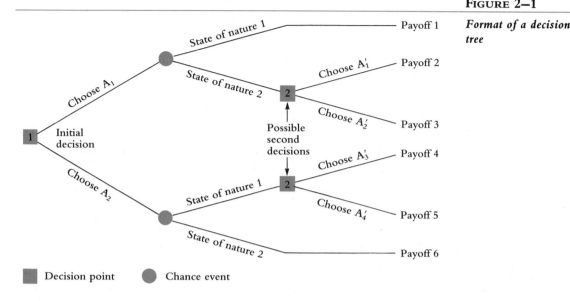

Format of a decision tree

Decision point ■   Chance event ●

A decision tree is composed of a number of *nodes* that have *branches* emanating from them (see Figure 2–1). Square nodes are used to denote decision points, and circular nodes are used to denote chance events. The tree is read from left to right. Branches leaving square nodes represent alternatives; branches leaving circular nodes represent chance events (i.e., the possible states of nature).

After the tree has been drawn, it is analyzed from *right to left* (i.e., starting with the last decision that might be made). For each decision, choose the alternative that will yield the greatest return. If chance events follow a decision, choose the alternative that has the highest expected monetary value (or lowest expected loss).

Expected Value of Perfect Information

In certain situations it is possible to ascertain which state of nature will actually occur in the future. For instance, the choice of location for a restaurant may weigh heavily on whether a new highway will be constructed or whether a zoning permit will be issued. A decision maker may have probabilities for these states of nature; however, it may be possible to delay a decision until it is clear which state of nature will exist. This might involve taking an option to buy the land. If the state of nature is favorable, the option can be exercised; if the state is unfavorable, the option can be allowed to expire. The question to consider is whether the cost of the option will be less than the expected gain due to delaying the decision (i.e., the expected payoff *above* the expected value). This is known as the *expected value of perfect information,* or EVPI.

EXAMPLE 5

Analyze the decision tree below and determine which initial alternative (build small or build large) should be chosen in order to maximize expected monetary value.

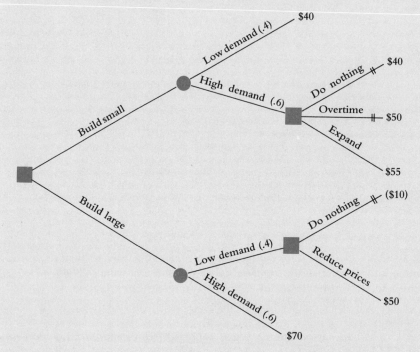

Solution

The dollar amounts at the branch ends indicate the estimated payoffs (usually in terms of present value) if the sequence of chance events and decisions that is traced back to the initial decision occurs. For example, if the initial decision is to build a small facility and it turns out that demand is low, the expected value will be $40 (thousand). Similarly, if a small facility is built, demand turns out high, and a later decision is made to expand, the expected value will be $55. The figures in parentheses on branches leaving the chance nodes indicate the probabilities of those states of nature. Hence, the probability of low demand is .4, and the probability of high demand is .6.

Analyze the decisions from right to left:

1. Determine which alternative would be selected for each possible second decision. For a small facility with high demand, there are three choices: *do nothing, work overtime,* and *expand.* Since *expand* has the highest payoff, it would be chosen. Indicate this by placing a double slash through each of the other alternatives. Similarly, for a large facility with low demand, there would be two choices: *do nothing* and *reduce prices. Reduce prices* would be

EXAMPLE 5 *(concluded)*

chosen because it has the higher expected value, so a double slash is placed on the other branch.

2. Determine the product of the chance probabilities and their respective payoffs for the remaining branches:

Build small
Low demand   .4($40) = $16
High demand   .6($55) = 33
Build large
Low demand   .4($50) = 20
High demand   .6($70) = 42

3. Determine the expected value of each initial alternative:

Build small: $16 + $33 = $49
Build large: $20 + $42 = $62

Hence, the choice should be to build the large facility because it has a larger expected value than the small facility.

Expected value of perfect information—the difference between the expected payoff under certainty and the expected payoff under conditions of risk.

Other possible ways of obtaining perfect information depend somewhat on the nature of the decision being made. For example, information about consumer preferences might come from market research; additional information about a product could come from product testing; legal experts might be called on; and so on.

There are two ways to determine the EVPI. One is to compute the expected payoff under certainty and subtract the expected payoff under risk. Thus,

$$\text{Expected value of perfect information} = \text{Expected payoff under certainty} - \text{Expected payoff under risk.} \quad (2\text{--}1)$$

EXAMPLE 6

Using the information from Example 4, determine the expected value of perfect information using Formula 2–1.

Solution

First, compute the expected payoff under certainty. To do this, identify the best payoff under each state of nature. Then combine these by weighting each payoff by the probability of that state of nature and adding the amounts. Thus, the best payoff under low demand is $10, the best under moderate demand is $12,

EXAMPLE 6 *(concluded)*

and the best under high demand is $16. The expected payoff under certainty is, then:

$$.30(\$10) + .50(\$12) + .20(\$16) = \$12.2$$

The expected payoff under risk, as computed in Example 4, is $10.5. The EVPI is the difference between these:

$$\text{EVPI} = \$12.2 - \$10.5 = \$1.7$$

This figure indicates the upper limit on the amount the decision maker should be willing to spend to obtain perfect information in this case. Thus, if the cost equals or exceeds this amount, the decision maker would be better off not spending additional money and simply going with the alternative that has the highest expected payoff.

A second approach is to use the regret table to compute the EVPI. To do this, find the expected regret for each alternative. The minimum expected regret is equal to the EVPI.

EXAMPLE 7

Determine the expected value of perfect information for the capacity-planning problem using the expected regret approach.

Solution

Using information from Examples 2, 3, and 4, we can compute the expected regret for each alternative. Thus:

Small facility	.30(0) + .50(2) + .20(6) = 2.2
Medium facility	.30(3) + .50(0) + .20(4) = 1.7[minimum]
Large facility	.30(14) + .50(10) + .20(0) = 9.2

The lowest expected regret is 1.7, which is associated with the second alternative. Hence, the EVPI is $1.7 million, which agrees with the previous example using the other approach.

Sensitivity Analysis

Generally speaking, in a decision problem such as the kind being discussed here, both the payoffs and the probabilities are estimated values. Consequently, it can be useful for the decision maker to have some indication of how sensitive the choice of an alternative is to changes in one or more of these values. Unfortunately, it is impossible to consider all possible combinations of every variable in a typical problem. Nevertheless, there are certain things a decision maker can do to judge the sensitivity.

One thing that can be done is to compare the expected values of the alternatives. If one or more of the expected values of other alternatives is close to the best one, it is reasonable to conclude that a modest change in a payoff or a probability could result in another alternative having the best expected value. Moreover, very often one or a few values are suspect: the decision maker usually has certain estimates that are less firm than others, and these are the ones he or she would focus on. Hence, an intuitive approach to the problem can be useful.

A more formal approach that can be useful when there are two states of nature involves constructing a graph and then using algebra to determine a range of probabilities for which a given solution is best. In effect, the graph provides a visual indication of the range of probability over which the various alternatives are optimal, and the algebra provides exact values of the endpoints of the ranges. The following example illustrates the procedure.

EXAMPLE 8

Given the following table, determine the range of probability for state of nature #2, that is, $P(2)$, for which each alternative is optimal under the expected-value approach.

	State of nature	
	#1	**#2**
A	4	12
Alternative B	16	2
C	12	8

Solution

First, plot each alternative relative to $P(2)$. To do this, plot the #1 value on the left side of the graph and the #2 value on the right side. For instance, for alternative A, plot 4 on the left side of the graph and 12 on the right side. Then connect these two points. The three alternatives are plotted on the graph as shown on the next page.

The graph shows the range of values of $P(2)$ over which each alternative is optimal. Thus, we see that for low values of $P(2)$ [and thus high values of $P(1)$, since $P(1) + P(2) = 1.0$], alternative B will have the highest expected value; for intermediate values of $P(2)$, alternative C is best; and for higher values of $P(2)$, alternative A is best.

For exact values of the ranges, we need to determine where the upper parts of the lines intersect. Note that at the intersections, the two alternatives represented by the lines would be equivalent in terms of expected value. Hence, the decision maker would be indifferent between the two at that point. To determine the intersections, we must obtain the equation of each line. This is relatively simple to do. Since these are straight lines, they have the form $y = a + bx$, where a is the y-intercept value at the left axis, b is the slope of the line, and x is $P(2)$. Slope

EXAMPLE 8 *(concluded)*

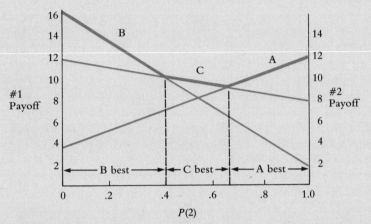

is defined as the change in y for a one-unit change in x. In this type of problem, the distance between the two vertical axes is 1.0. Consequently, the slope of each line is equal to the right-hand value minus the left-hand value. The slopes and equations are:

	#1	*#2*	*Slope*	*Equation*
A	4	12	12 − 4 = + 8	4 + 8P(2)
B	16	2	2 − 16 = −14	16 − 14P(2)
C	12	8	8 − 12 = − 4	12 − 4P(2)

From the graph, we can see that alternative B is best from $P(2) = 0$ to the point where that straight line intersects the straight line of alternative C, and that begins the region where C is better. To find that point, we can solve for the value of $P(2)$ at their intersection. This requires setting the two equations equal to each other and solving for $P(2)$. Thus,

$$16 - 14P(2) = 12 - 4P(2)$$

Rearranging terms gives us

$$4 = 10P(2)$$

Solving, we obtain $P(2) = .40$. Thus, alternative B is best from $P(2) = 0$ up to $P(2) = .40$. B and C are equivalent at $P(2) = .40$.

Alternative C is best from that point until its line intersects alternative A's line. To find that intersection, we set those two equations equal and solve for $P(2)$. Thus,

$$4 + 8P(2) = 12 - 4P(2)$$

Rearranging terms, we have

$$12P(2) = 8$$

Solving, we obtain $P(2) = .67$. Thus, alternative C is best from $P(2) > .40$ up to $P(2) = .67$, where A and C are equivalent. For values of $P(2)$ greater than .67 up to $P(2) = 1.0$, A is best.

Note: If a problem calls for ranges with respect to $P(1)$, find the $P(2)$ ranges as above, and then subtract each $P(2)$ from 1.00 (e.g., .40 becomes .60 and .67 becomes .33).

SUMMARY

Decision making is an integral part of operations management. Successful decision making comprises a number of steps, the first of which is to carefully define the problem.

Operations decision making frequently involves the use of quantitative models, a systems approach, and sensitivity analysis of solutions.

Decision theory is a general approach to decision making that is useful in many different aspects of operations management. Decision theory provides a framework for analysis of decisions. It includes a number of different techniques that can be classified according to the degree of uncertainty associated with a particular decision problem. Two visual tools useful for analyzing some decision problems are decision trees and graphical sensitivity analysis.

KEY TERMS

bounded rationality, 44
certainty, 51
decision tree, 56
expected monetary value
  (EMV), 56
expected value of perfect
  information (EVPI), 59
Laplace, 53
maximax, 53
maximin, 53
minimax regret, 53

model, 44
  mathematical, 45
  physical, 45
  schematic, 45
opportunity losses, 55
payoff table, 52
regrets, 55
risk, 51
sensitivity analysis, 48
suboptimization, 44
system, 49
uncertainty, 51

SOLVED PROBLEMS

The solved problems in this chapter refer to the following payoff table:

		New bridge built	*No new bridge*
Alternative locations	A	1	14
for new	B	2	10
warehouse	C	4	6

1. Assume the payoffs represent profits. Determine the alternative that would be chosen under each of these decision criteria:
   a. Maximin.
   b. Maximax.
   c. Laplace.

Solution

	New bridge	No new bridge	Maximin (worst)	Maximax (best)	Laplace (average)
A	1	14	1	14[best]	15 ÷ 2 = 7.5[best]
B	2	10	2	10	12 ÷ 2 = 6
C	4	6	4[best]	6	10 ÷ 2 = 5

Thus, the alternatives chosen would be C under maximin, A under maximax, and A under Laplace.

2. Using graphical sensitivity analysis, determine the range of probability for no new bridge for which each alternative would be optimal.

Solution

Plot a straight line for each alternative. Do this by plotting the payoff for new bridge on the left axis and the payoff for no new bridge on the right axis and then connecting the two points. Each line represents the ex-

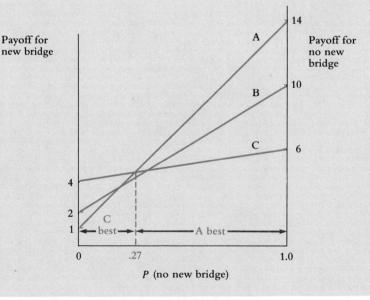

pected profit for an alternative for the entire range of probability of no new bridge. Because the lines represent expected profit, the line that is highest for a given value of *P*(no new bridge) is optimal. Thus, from the graph, we can see that for low values of this probability, alternative C is best, and for high values, alternative A is best (B is never the highest line, so it is never optimal).

The dividing line between the ranges where C is optimal and where A is optimal occurs where the two lines intersect. To find that probability, we must first formulate the equation for each line. To do this, let the intersection with the left axis be the *y*-intercept; the slope equals the right-side payoff minus the left-side payoff. Thus, for C we have $4 + (6-4)P$, which is $4 + 2P$. For A we have $1 + (14-1)P$, which is $1 + 13P$. Setting these two equal to each other, we can solve for P:

$$4 + 2P = 1 + 13P$$

Solving, $P = .27$. Therefore, the ranges for *P* (no new bridge) are:

$$\text{A:} \quad .27 \leq P \leq 1.00$$
$$\text{B:} \quad \text{never optimal}$$
$$\text{C:} \quad 0 \leq P \leq .27$$

3. Using the information in the payoff table, develop a table of regrets, and then:
   a. Determine the alternative that would be chosen under minimax regret.
   b. Determine the expected value of perfect information using the regret table, assuming that the probability of a new bridge being built is .60.

Solution

To obtain the regrets, subtract all payoffs in each column from the best payoff in the column. The regrets are:

	New bridge	No new bridge
A	3	0
B	2	4
C	0	8

   a. Minimax regret involves finding the worst regret for each alternative and then choosing the alternative that has the "best" worst. Thus, A would be chosen:

	Worst
A	3[best]
B	4
C	8

b. Once the regret table has been developed, the EVPI can be computed as the smallest expected regret. Since the probability of a new bridge is given as .60, we can deduce that the probability of no new bridge is $1.00 - .60 = .40$. The expected regrets are:

$$A: \quad .60(3) + .40(0) = 1.80$$
$$B: \quad .60(2) + .40(4) = 2.80$$
$$C: \quad .60(0) + .40(8) = 3.20$$

Hence, the EVPI is 1.80.

4. Using the probabilities of .60 for a new bridge and .40 for no new bridge, compute the expected value for each alternative in the payoff table, and identify the alternative that would be selected under the expected-value approach.

Solution

$$A: \quad .60(1) + .40(14) = 6.20[best]$$
$$B: \quad .60(2) + .40(10) = 5.20$$
$$C: \quad .60(4) + .40(6) \ = 4.80$$

5. Compute the EVPI using the information from the previous problem.

Solution

Using Formula 2–1, the EVPI is the expected payoff under certainty minus the maximum expected value. The expected payoff under certainty involves multiplying the best payoff in each column by the column probability and then summing those amounts. The best payoff in the first column is 4, and the best in the second is 14. Thus,

$$\text{Expected payoff under certainty} = .60(4) + .40(14) = 8.00$$

The expected value of perfect information is then

$$EVPI = 8.00 - 6.20 = 1.80$$

6. Suppose now that the values in the payoff table represent *costs* instead of profits.
   a. Determine the choice that would be made under each of these strategies: maximin, maximax, and Laplace.
   b. Develop the regret table, and identify the alternative that would

be chosen using minimax regret. Then find the EVPI if P(new bridge) = .60.

c. Using sensitivity analysis, determine the range of P(no new bridge) for which each alternative would be optimal.

d. If P(new bridge) = .60 and P(no new bridge) = .40, find the alternative that would be chosen to minimize expected cost.

Solution

a.

	New bridge	No new bridge	Maximin (worst)	Maximax (best)	Laplace (average)
A	1	14	14	1[best]	15 ÷ 2 = 7.5
B	2	10	10	2	12 ÷ 2 = 6
C	4	6	6 [best]	4	10 ÷ 2 = 5 [best]

b. Develop the regret table by subtracting the *lowest cost* in each column from each of the values in the column.

	New bridge	No new bridge	Worst
A	0	8	8
B	1	4	4
C	3	0	3 [best]

EVPI = .60(3) + 40(0) = 1.80

c. The graph is identical to that shown in Solved Problem 2. However, because the lines now represent expected *costs*, the

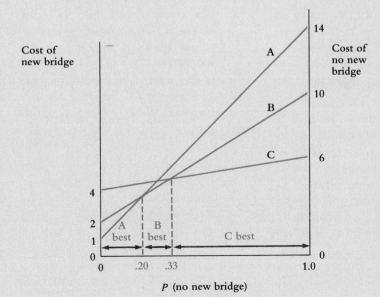

P (no new bridge)

best alternative for a given value of P(no new bridge) is the *lowest* line. Hence, for very low values of P(no new bridge), A is best; for intermediate values, B is best; and for high values, C is best. We can set the equations of A and B, and B and C, equal to each other in order to determine the values of P(no new bridge) at their intersections. Thus,

$$A\text{–}B: \quad 1 + 13P = 2 + 8P; \text{ solving, } P = .20$$
$$B\text{–}C: \quad 2 + 8P = 4 + 2P; \text{ solving, } P = .33$$

Hence, the ranges are:

$$\begin{aligned} A \text{ best:} & \quad 0 \le P < .20 \\ B \text{ best:} & \quad .20 < P < .33 \\ C \text{ best:} & \quad .33 < P \le 1.00 \end{aligned}$$

d. Expected-value computations are the same whether the values represent costs or profits. Hence, the expected payoffs for costs are the same as the expected payoffs for profits that were computed in Solved Problem 4. However, now we want the alternative that has the *lowest* expected payoff rather than the one with the highest payoff. Consequently, alternative C is the best because its expected payoff is the lowest of the three.

DISCUSSION AND REVIEW QUESTIONS

1. What is the chief role of the operations manager?

2. Outline the steps in the decision-making process.

3. What are the main characteristics of operations decisions?

4. What is a model? What are the primary advantages and limitations of models?

5. How would you respond to this criticism of models: "Because all models are incomplete—they leave out one or more variables—they are misleading"?

6. What are some of the reasons given in the chapter for poor decisions?

7. What is sensitivity analysis, and how can it be useful to a decision maker?

8. Contrast maximax and maximin decision strategies. Under what circumstances would one rather than the other be appropriate?

9. Under what circumstances is expected monetary value appropriate as a decision criterion? When isn't it appropriate?

10. What is a systems approach, and how can failure to use this approach lead to poor decisions?

11. Explain or define each of these terms:
    a. Laplace criterion.
    b. Minimax regret.
    c. Expected value.
    d. Expected value of perfect information.

12. What information does a decision maker need to do an expected-value analysis of a problem? What options are available to the decision maker if the probabilities of the states of nature are unknown? Can you think of a way sensitivity analysis might be useful in such a case?

13. Explain why a systems approach to productivity improvements would be beneficial and why, without that perspective, actual improvements might end up being less than anticipated.

PROBLEMS

1. A small building contractor has recently experienced two successive years in which work opportunities exceeded the firm's capacity. The contractor must now make a decision on capacity for next year. He has estimated profits under each of the two states of nature he believes might occur, as shown in the table below. Which alternative should be selected if the decision criterion is:

  a. Maximax?
  b. Maximin?
  c. Laplace?
  d. Minimax regret?

	Next year's demand	
Alternative	Low	High
Do nothing	$50*	$60
Expand	20	80
Subcontract	40	70

* Profit in $ thousands.

2. (Refer to the previous problem.) Suppose after a certain amount of discussion, it turns out that the contractor is able to subjectively assess the probabilities of low and high demand: $P(\text{low}) = .3$ and $P(\text{high}) = .7$.

  a. Determine the expected profit of each alternative. Which alternative is best? Why?
  b. Analyze the problem using a decision tree. Show the expected profit of each alternative on the tree.
  c. Compute the expected value of perfect information. How could the manager use this knowledge?

3. (Refer to the previous two problems.) Construct a graph that will enable you to perform sensitivity analysis on the problem. Over what range of $P(\text{high})$ would the alternative of doing nothing be best? Expand? Subcontract?

4. A firm that plans to expand its product line must decide whether to build a small or a large facility to produce the new products. If it builds a small facility and demand turns out to be low, the net present value after deducting for building costs will be $400,000. If demand turns out to be high, the firm can either maintain the small facility or expand it. Expansion would have a net present value of $300,000, and maintaining the small facility would have a net present value of $50,000.

If a large facility is built and demand is high, the estimated net present value is $800,000. If demand turns out to be low, the net present value will be −$10,000.

The probability that demand will be high is estimated to be .60, and the probability of low demand is estimated to be .40.

  a. Analyze using a tree diagram.
  b. Compute the EVPI. How could this information be used?

5. (Refer to the previous problem.) Determine the range over which each alternative would be best in terms of the value of P(demand low).

6. The lease of Theme Park, Inc. is about to expire, and management must decide whether to renew the lease for another 10 years or to relocate near the site of a proposed motel. The town planning board is currently debating the merits of granting approval to the motel. A consultant has estimated the net present values of Theme Park's two alternatives under each state of nature as shown below. What course of action would you recommend using:

 a. Maximax?
 b. Maximin?
 c. Laplace?
 d. Minimax regret?

Options	Motel approved	Motel rejected
Renew	$ 500,000	$4,000,000
Relocate	5,000,000	100,000

7. (Refer to the previous problem.) Suppose that, after some thought, the manager has decided that there is a .35 probability that the motel's application will be approved.
 a. If the manager uses maximum expected monetary value as the decision criterion, which alternative should be chosen?
 b. Represent this problem in the form of a decision tree.
 c. If the manager has been offered the option of a temporary lease while the town planning board considers the motel's application, would you advise the manager to sign the lease? The lease will cost $24,000.

8. Construct a graph that can be used for sensitivity analysis for the preceding problem.

 a. How sensitive is the solution to the problem in terms of the probability estimate of .35?
 b. Suppose that, after consulting with a member of the town planning board, management decides that an estimate of approval is approximately .45. How sensitive is the solution to this revised estimate? Explain.
 c. Suppose the manager is confident of all the estimated payoffs except the $4 million. If the probability of approval is .35, for what range of payoff for Renew/rejected will the alternative selected using maximum expected value remain the same?

9. A firm must decide whether to construct a small, medium, or large stamping plant. A consultant's report indicates a .20 probability that demand will be low and an .80 probability that demand will be high.

 If the firm builds a small facility and demand turns out to be low, the net present value will be $42 million. If demand turns out to be high, the firm can either subcontract and realize the net present value of $42 million or expand greatly for a net present value of $48 million.

 A medium-size facility could be built as a hedge: if demand turns out to be low, its net present value is estimated at $22 million; if demand turns out to be high, the firm could do nothing and realize a net present value of $46 million, or it could expand and realize a net present value of $50 million.

 If the firm builds the large facility and demand is low, the net present value will be $-\$20$ million, whereas high demand will result in a net present value of $72 million.
 a. Analyze this problem using a decision tree.
 b. What would the maximin alternative be?

c. Compute the EVPI and interpret it.

d. Perform sensitivity analysis on P(high).

10. A manager must decide how many machines of a certain type to buy. The machines will be used to fill demand for a new gear. The manager has narrowed the decision down to two alternatives: buy one machine or buy two. If only one machine is purchased and demand is more than it can handle, a second machine can be purchased at a later time. However, the cost per machine would be lower if the two machines were to be purchased at the same time.

The estimated probability of low demand is .30, and the estimated probability of high demand is .70.

The net present value associated with the purchase of two machines initially is $75,000 if demand is low and $130,000 if demand is high.

The net present value for one machine and low demand is $90,000. If demand is high, there are three options. One option would be to do nothing, and it would have a net present value of $90,000. A second option would be to subcontract; it would have a net present value of $110,000. The third option would be to purchase a second machine. This option would have a net present value of $100,000.

How many machines should the manager purchase initially? Use a decision tree to analyze this problem.

11. Determine the course of action that has the highest EMV for the accompanying tree diagram. (See diagram on page 72.)

12. Space engineers have three alternative designs from which to choose the configuration of a component for an unmanned space shot. The space vehicle is likely to encounter one of four different conditions, which have probabilities of occurrence as listed in the following payoff table along with the payoffs for each combination of design and state of nature. Additional data from previous flights are available but will require additional expenditures to analyze. However, the project director is quite confident that analysis of the data will clearly indicate which state of nature will be encountered. What amount would be justified for the data analysis?

	States of nature			
	A	**B**	**C**	**D**
Probability:	*.3*	*.4*	*.2*	*.1*
Design				
001	20*	10	10	0
002	15	10	0	40
003	10	20	30	30

*($100).

13. The director of social services of a certain county has just learned of additional information requirements mandated by the state. This will place an additional burden on the agency. The director has identified three acceptable alternatives to handle the increased work load. One is to reassign present staff members, another is to hire and train two new workers, and the third is to redesign current practice so that workers can readily collect the information with little additional effort. An unknown factor is the caseload for the coming year, during which time the new data will be collected on a trial basis. The estimated costs for various options and caseloads are shown in the table that follows:

	Caseload		
	Moderate	*High*	*Very high*
Reassign staff	$50*	60	85
New staff	60	60	60
Redesign collection	40	50	90

*Cost in thousands

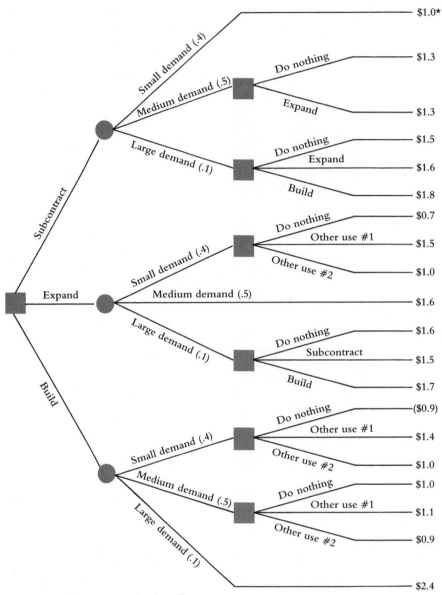

*Net present value in millions

Assuming that probabilities of various case-loads are unreliable, based on past experience, what decision would be appropriate using each of the following criteria?

a. Maximin.
b. Maximax.
c. Minimax regret.
d. Laplace.

14. After contemplating the caseload question, the director mentioned in the previous problem has decided that reasonable caseload probabilities are .10 for moderate, .30 for high, and .60 for very high.
   a. Which alternative will yield the minimum expected cost?
   b. Construct a decision tree for this problem. Indicate the expected costs for the three decision branches.
   c. Determine the expected value of perfect information using an opportunity loss table.

15. Suppose the director of social services will have the option of hiring an additional staff member if one staff member is hired initially and the caseload turns out to be high or very high. Under that plan, the first entry in row 2 of the cost table (see Problem 13) will be 40 instead of 60, the second entry will be 75, and the last entry will be 80. Assume the caseload probabilities are as noted in Problem 14. Construct a decision tree that shows the sequential nature of this decision, and determine which alternative will minimize expected cost.

16. A manager has compiled estimated profits for various alternative courses of action but is reluctant to assign probabilities to the states of nature. The payoff table is:

| | | State of nature | |
		#1	**#2**
	A	20	140
Alternative	B	120	80
	C	100	40

a. Plot the expected-value lines on a graph.
b. Is there any alternative that would never be appropriate in terms of maximizing expected profit? Explain on the basis of your graph.
c. For what range of $P(2)$ would alternative A be the best choice if the goal is to maximize expected profit?
d. For what range of $P(1)$ would alternative A be the best choice if the goal is to maximize expected profit?

17. Repeat all parts of the preceding question assuming the values in the payoff table are estimated *costs* and the goal is to minimize expected costs.

18. The research staff of a marketing agency has assembled the following payoff table of estimated profits:

		Receive contract	Not receive contract
	#1	10	−2
	#2	8	3
Proposal	#3	5	5
	#4	0	7

Relative to the probability of not receiving the contract, determine the range of probability for which each of the proposals would maximize expected profit.

19. Given this payoff table:

| | | State of nature | |
		#1	**#2**
	A	120	20
	B	60	40
Alternative	C	10	110
	D	90	90

a. Determine the range of $P(1)$ for which each alternative would be best, treating the payoffs as profits.
b. Answer part *a* treating the payoffs as costs.

SELECTED BIBLIOGRAPHY

Bierman, Harold; Charles P. Bonini; and Warren H. Hausman. *Quantitative Analysis for Business Decisions*. 6th ed. Homewood, Ill.: Richard D. Irwin, 1981.

Eppen, G. D.; F. J. Gould; and C. P. Schmidt. *Introductory Management Science*. 2nd ed. Englewood Cliffs, N.J.: Prentice-Hall, 1987.

Levin, Richard I.; Charles A. Kirkpatrick; and David S. Rubin. *Quantitative Approaches to Management*. 5th ed. New York: McGraw-Hill, 1982.

Stevenson, William J. *Introduction to Management Science*. Homewood, Ill.: Richard D. Irwin, 1989.

Taylor, Bernard W. *Introduction to Management Science*. 2nd ed. Dubuque, Iowa: Wm. C. Brown, 1986.

Ulvila, J. W., and R. V. Brown. "Decision Analysis Comes of Age." *Harvard Business Review*, September–October 1982, p. 130.

Linear Programming

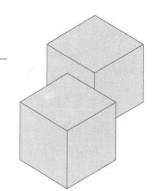

LEARNING OBJECTIVES

After completing this supplement, you should be able to:

1. Describe the type of problem that would lend itself to solution using linear programming.
2. Formulate a linear programming model from a description of a problem.
3. Solve a simple linear programming problem using the graphical method.
4. Use the simplex technique to solve linear programming problems.
5. Interpret computer solutions of linear programming problems.
6. Do sensitivity analysis on the solution of a linear programming problem.

SUPPLEMENT OUTLINE

INTRODUCTION

In 1947, George Danzig developed the use of linear algebra for determining optimal solutions to problems that involved restrictions, or *constraints*. For example, a problem might relate to determining the optimal quantities of several products to produce given each product's profit per unit, as well as such constraints as labor hours, machine time, and raw materials needed to make the products. The result was a class of techniques generally known as *linear programming,* and these techniques are now widely used to solve constrained optimization problems.

In essence, linear programming (LP) consists of a sequence of steps that will lead to an optimal solution to a class of problems, in cases where an optimum exists. There are a number of different linear programming techniques, some of which are special-purpose (i.e., used to find solutions for specific types of problems) and others that are more general in scope. This supplement describes the two general-purpose solution techniques: graphical linear programming and the simplex method. Graphical linear programming is presented because it provides a visual portrayal of many of the important concepts of linear programming. However, it is limited to problems that involve only two variables. Simplex is a mathematical approach, and thus lacks the visual features of the graphical approach, but it can handle more than two variables, making it much more useful for solving real problems, which often involve a large number of variables.

Linear programming models are used to help operations managers make decisions in many different areas. These include allocation of scarce resources, assignment problems (assigning workers to jobs, jobs to machines, and so on), transportation problems (determining distribution plans for shipping goods from multiple origins to multiple destinations, such as from 4 warehouses to 10 retail outlets), blending problems (petroleum products, diets), and other problems. As you can see, linear programming has a broad range of application. Moreover, in all applications, the use of linear programming guarantees an optimal solution to the mathematical model.

LINEAR PROGRAMMING MODELS

Linear programming models are mathematical representations of linear programming problems. These models have certain characteristics in common. Knowledge of these characteristics enables us to recognize problems that can be solved using linear programming. In addition, it also can help us formulate LP models. The characteristics can be grouped into two categories: components and assumptions. First, let's consider the components.

There are four components that provide the structure of a linear programming model:

1. Objective.
2. Decision variables.

3. Constraints.

4. Parameters.

Linear programming algorithms require that a single goal or **objective,** such as the maximization of profits, be specified. There are two general types of objectives: maximization and minimization. A maximization problem might involve profits, revenues, efficiency, or rate of return. Conversely, a minimization problem might involve cost, time, distance traveled, or scrap. The profit, cost, etc., per unit of output or input is summarized by an **objective function.**

Decision variables represent choices available to the decision maker in terms of amounts of either inputs or outputs. For example, some problems involve choosing a combination of inputs that will minimize total costs, while others involve selecting a combination of outputs that will maximize profits or revenues.

Constraints are limitations that restrict the alternatives available to decision makers. There are three types of constraints: less than or equal to ($\leq$), greater than or equal to ($\geq$), and simply equal to ($=$). A $\leq$ constraint implies an upper limit on the amount of some scarce resource (e.g., machine hours, labor hours, materials) available for use. A $\geq$ constraint specifies a lower bound that must be achieved in the final solution (e.g., must contain at least 10 percent real fruit juice, must get at least 30 MPG on the highway). The $=$ constraint is more restrictive in the sense that it specifies *exactly* what a decision variable should equal (e.g., make 200 units of product A). A linear programming model can consist of one or more constraints. In cases where there are multiple constraints, they may all be of the same type (e.g., all $\leq$ constraints), or they might be a mixture of types (e.g., three $\leq$ constraints and one $\geq$ constraint). Many possibilities exist. Taken as a whole, the constraints related to a given problem define the set of all feasible combinations of decision variables, which is referred to as the **feasible solution space.** Linear programming algorithms are designed to search the feasible solution space for the combination of decision variables that will yield an optimum in terms of the objective function.

An LP model consists of a mathematical statement of the objective and a mathematical statement of each constraint. These statements consist of symbols (e.g., x_1, x_2) that represent the decision variables and numerical values, called **parameters.** The parameters are fixed values; the model is solved *given* those values.

In order for linear programming models to be used effectively, certain *assumptions* must be satisfied. These are:

1. Linearity: the impact of decision variables is linear in constraints and the objective function.

2. Divisibility: noninteger values of decision variables are acceptable.

3. Certainty: values of parameters are known and constant.

4. Non-negativity: negative values of decision variables are unacceptable.

The following example illustrates the components of an LP model.

EXAMPLE S–1

Decision variables $\begin{cases} x_1 = \text{Quantity of product 1 to produce} \\ x_2 = \text{Quantity of product 2 to produce} \\ x_3 = \text{Quantity of product 3 to produce} \end{cases}$

Maximize	$5x_1 + 8x_2 + 4x_3$ (profit)	(Objective function)
subject to		
Labor	$2x_1 + 4x_2 + 3x_3 \leq 250$ hours	
Material	$7x_1 + 6x_2 + 5x_3 \leq 100$ pounds	(Constraints)
Product 1	$x_1 \qquad\qquad \geq 10$ units	
	$x_1, x_2, x_3 \geq 0$	(Non-negativity constraints)

First, the decision variables are listed and defined. These typically represent *quantities*. In this case, they are quantities of three different products that might be produced.

Next, the objective function is stated. It includes every decision variable in the model and the contribution (profit per unit) of each decision variable. Thus, product x_1 has a profit of \$5 per unit. The profit from product x_1 for a given solution will be 5 times the value of x_1 specified by the solution; the total profit from all products will be the sum of the individual product profits. Thus, if $x_1 = 10$, $x_2 = 0$, and $x_3 = 12$, the value of the objective function would be:

$$5(10) + 8(0) + 4(12) = 98$$

The objective function is followed by a list (in no particular order) of three constraints. Each constraint has a right-side numerical value (e.g., the labor constraint has a right-side value of 250) that indicates the amount of the constraint and an algebraic sign that indicates whether that amount is a maximum ($\leq$), a minimum ($\geq$), or an equality ($=$). The left side of each constraint consists of the variables that are subject to that particular constraint and a coefficient for each variable that indicates how much of the right-side quantity *one unit* of the decision variable represents. For instance, for the labor constraint, one unit of x_1 will require two hours of labor. The sum of the values on the left side of each constraint represents the amount of that constraint used by a solution. Thus, if $x_1 = 10$, $x_2 = 0$, and $x_3 = 12$, the amount of labor used would be:

$$2(10) + 4(0) + 3(12) = 56 \text{ hours}$$

Because this amount does not exceed the quantity on the right-hand side of the constraint, it is feasible.

Note that the third constraint refers to only a single variable; x_1 must be at least 10 units. Its coefficient is, in effect, 1, although it is not shown.

Finally, there are the non-negativity constraints. These are listed on a single line; they reflect the condition that no decision variable is allowed to have a negative value.

Model Formulation

An understanding of the components of linear programming models is necessary for model formulation. This helps provide organization to the process of assembling information about a problem into a model.

Naturally, it is important to obtain valid information on what constraints are appropriate, as well as on what values of the parameters are appropriate. If this is not done, the usefulness of the model will be questionable. Consequently, in some instances, considerable effort is expended to obtain that information.

Once all the information has been obtained, the next step is to assemble a model. There are a number of different procedures that might be employed. One approach is to identify the decision variables, then write out the objective function, and then formulate each of the constraints. This appproach follows a logical sequence from beginning to end. Another approach is to let the problem guide you in formulating a model. With this approach, pieces of the model are identified in the order in which they occur in the problem statement. For instance, if the first words of a problem are "A manager wants to maximize profits," this would lead to:

Maximize   (profits)

But if the first words are "A department has 2,000 pounds of raw material with which to prepare its products," this would lead to:

subject to
  Raw material $\leq$ 2,000 pounds

Or the first words may be "A supervisor would like to know how much of each of two products to make." This would lead to:

x_1 = Quantity of product 1
x_2 = Quantity of product 2

Following this approach will cause you to skip around the model according to the sequence of the problem statement; following the first approach will cause you to skip around the problem statement. Try both approaches, and decide what works best for you.

Once a model has been formulated, we can move on to solving the problem. In the following sections, three approaches to problem solution are described: graphical solutions, simplex solutions, and computer solutions.

GRAPHICAL LINEAR PROGRAMMING

Graphical linear programming is a method for finding optimal solutions to two-variable problems. This section describes that approach.

Outline of Graphical Procedure

The graphical method of linear programming involves plotting the constraints on a graph and identifying an area that satisfies all of the constraints. This is known as the *feasible solution space*. Next, the objective function is plotted and used to identify the optimal point in the feasible solution space. The coordinates of the point can sometimes be read directly from the graph, although generally an algebraic determination of the coordinates of the point is necessary.

The general procedure followed in the graphical approach is:

1. Set up the objective function and the constraints in mathematical format.
2. Plot the constraints.
3. Identify the feasible solution space.
4. Plot the objective function.
5. Determine the optimum solution.

The technique can best be illustrated through solution of a typical problem. Consider the following:

Two products, x_1 and x_2, can be produced on a certain machine. There are 12 hours of machine time available to produce these products. Product x_1 requires 1 hour per unit, and product x_2 requires 3 hours per unit. Both products require one raw material: product x_1 uses 4 pounds of raw material per unit, and product x_2 uses 3 pounds. There are 24 pounds of this raw material available for these two products. If the goal is to maximize the profit from these two products, and product x_1 contributes \$4 per unit to profit and product x_2 contributes \$5 per unit, what quantity of each should be produced?

To solve this problem, we must first set it up in mathematical format. This involves the following:

1. Identify the decision variables. In this case, they are product x_1 and product x_2.
2. Formulate the objective function. It is:

   Maximize $Z = 4x_1 + 5x_2$

3. Identify and formulate the constraints. There are two constraints: machine time and raw material. The constraints are:

   Machine time $x_1 + 3x_2 \leq 12$
   Raw material $4x_1 + 3x_2 \leq 24$

4. Add the non-negativity constraints. They are $x_1, x_2, \geq 0$.

Thus, the problem is:

Maximize $Z = 4x_1 + 5x_2$
subject to
  Machine time $x_1 + 3x_2 \leq 12$
  Raw material $4x_1 + 3x_2 \leq 24$
          $x_1, x_2 \geq 0$

The next step is to plot the constraints.

Plotting Constraints

The procedure for plotting constraints is quite simple:

1. Replace the inequality sign with an equal sign. This transforms the constraint into an equation of a *straight line*.
2. Determine where the line intersects each axis.
    a. To find where it crosses the x_2 axis, set x_1 equal to zero and solve the equation for the value of x_2.
    b. To find where it crosses the x_1 axis, set x_2 equal to zero and solve the equation for the value of x_1.
3. Mark these intersections on the axes, and connect them with a straight line.
4. Indicate by shading (or by arrows at the ends of the constraint line) whether the inequality is greater than or less than. (A general rule to determine which side of the line satisfies the inequality is to pick the point (0,0) and see whether it is greater than or less than the constraint amount.)
5. Repeat steps 1–4 for each constraint.

First, let's plot the machine hours constraint, which is $x_1 + 3x_2 \leq 12$.

1. Make it an equality: $x_1 + 3x_2 = 12$.
2. Set $x_1 = 0$ and solve for x_2: $(0) + 3x_2 = 12$, so $x_2 = 4$.
    Set $x_2 = 0$ and solve for x_1: $x_1 + 3(0) = 12$, so $x_1 = 12$.
3. Mark the points on the graph, and connect them with a straight line.
4. Shade the area that satisfies the constraint. (Inserting $x_1 = 0$, $x_2 = 0$ into the equation yields a value of 0, which is less than 12. Hence, all points on that side of the line are less than 12.) See Figure 2S–1. Note that only the area in the first quadrant is shaded due to the non-negativity constraints.

The second constraint can be plotted similarly.

1. Make it an equality: $4x_1 + 3x_2 = 24$.

FIGURE 2S–1

The machine constraint

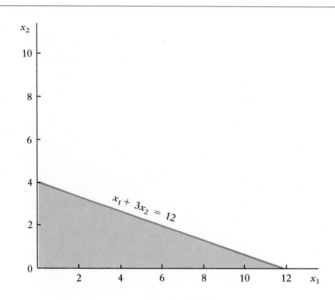

2. Set $x_1 = 0$ and solve for x_2: $4(0) + 3x_2 = 24$, so $x_2 = 8$.
   Set $x_2 = 0$ and solve for x_1: $4x_1 + 3(0) = 24$, so $x_1 = 6$.
3. Mark the points on the graph, and connect them with a straight line.
4. Shade in the area that satisfies this constraint (see Figure 2S–2). Note that some of the points satisfy only one of the constraints, and other points satisfy both.

FIGURE 2S–2

The raw material constraint is added to the graph

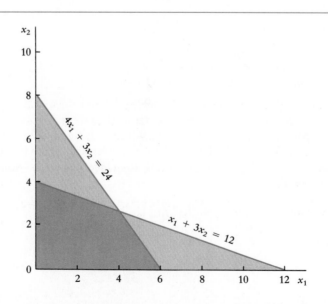

Identifying the Feasible Solution Space

The feasible solution space is the set of all points (i.e., the *area*) that satisfies all constraints. (Recall that the x_1 and x_2 axes form non-negativity constraints). The heavily shaded area shown in Figure 2S–2 is the feasible solution space for our problem.

Plotting the Objective Function Line

The objective function is actually a *family* of lines; the lines are parallel, but each represents a different amount. For example, one line could be $4x_1 + 5x_2 = 20$, another $4x_1 + 5x_2 = 40$, and another $4x_1 + 5x_2 = 60$. These lines are illustrated in Figure 2S–3. Note that the lines are *parallel* and that the farther away from the origin the line is, the greater the value of the objective function. In addition, each line is an *isoprofit* line: every combination of x_1 and x_2 on the line will yield the same profit (e.g., $40).

These are but a few of the many different lines that could be drawn. Some of these lines would cross the feasible solution space, and some would not. This is important since points that do not lie within the feasible solution space cannot possibly be feasible solutions. Given the three lines in Figure 2S–3, only the line $4x_1 + 5x_2 = 20$ has points within the feasible solution space. However, it is not difficult to see that other lines parallel to this, but farther from the origin, could be drawn. What we want is the last line that just touches the feasible solution space because it will yield the greatest *feasible* value for the objective function.

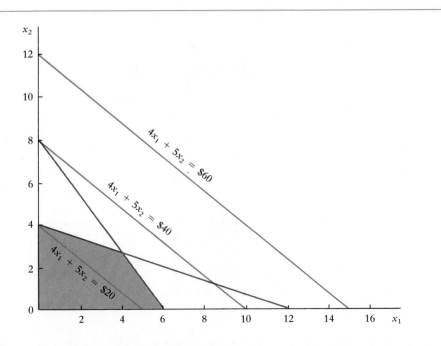

FIGURE 2S–4

The optimum point

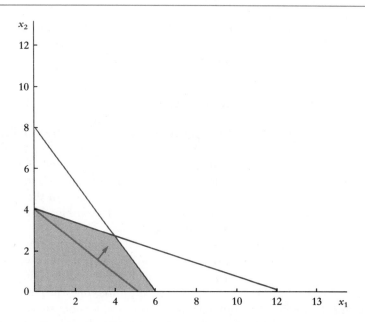

Instead of using trial and error, we can easily identify the line that will yield the maximum profit for an x_1, x_2 combination in the feasible solution space. All we need is an isoprofit line that crosses the feasible solution space.[1]

To plot the objective function, select a value to set it equal to. One easy-to-use value is the product of the x_1 and x_2 coefficients (in this case, 4 and 5: $4 \times 5 = 20$). This is one of the lines plotted in Figure 2S–3. Note that it does cross the feasible solution space. However, that will not always happen. When a line is outside of the feasible solution space, divide the selected value of the objective function (e.g., 60) by a constant so that it does cross the feasible solution space (e.g., $60/3 = 20$, and 20 crosses the space). Conversely, if the line crosses the feasible solution space but is too close to the origin to be useful, multiply the value by a constant—1.5, 2, 10, 100, or some other number—to obtain a more useful line.

Plot the line as you would a constraint line: set $x_1 = 0$ and solve for x_2, and then set $x_2 = 0$ and solve for x_1.

Since the profit increases as the line moves away from the origin, "slide" the line—parallel to its original position—away from the origin (imagine a series of parallel lines being drawn). The objective is to identify the farthest point in the feasible solution space touched by one of the parallel lines. The x_1 and x_2 coordinates of that point indicate the quantities of x_1 and x_2 that will maximize the objective function. (See Figure 2S–4.) In this example, the point is where

---

[1] Strictly speaking, the line need not cross the feasible solution space. However, it is convenient to work with such a line.

the two constraints intersect. Although we can read this directly from the graph in some cases, it is usually best to use algebra to determine the exact coordinates of the intersection. We can do this by solving the equations of the two lines simultaneously (i.e., find the one value of x_1 and one value of x_2 that will satisfy both equations). To do this, we make both constraints equalities:

$$x_1 + 3x_2 = 12$$
$$4x_1 + 3x_2 = 24$$

We have two equations and two unknowns. What we want is one equation with one unknown since this would enable us to readily determine the value of one of the two variables. Then by substituting that value into one of the two constraints, the value of the other variable can be determined.

When solving equations simultaneously, we usually have to modify one or both of the equations to obtain one set of coefficients that are equal. Following such modification, when we subtract one equation from the other, one of the terms will drop out, leaving us with the one variable in a single equation. In this instance, the x_2 coefficients are equal, so modifying is not necessary. (The first solved problem at the end of this section illustrates the more general case.) Hence, merely subtracting one from the other will produce the desired result:

$$
\begin{array}{rcl}
4x_1 + 3x_2 &=& 24 \\
-(\; x_1 + 3x_2 &=& 12) \\
\hline
3x_1 \quad\;\; &=& 12
\end{array}
$$

Solving, we find that $x_1 = 4$. Next, we substitute this value into one of the equations to find the value of x_2. Either equation will do. For example, the second equation yields:

$$4 + 3x_2 = 12$$

Solving, we find $x_2 = 8/3$, or 2.67.

Thus, the solution to the problem that will maximize profit is to produce 4 units of x_1 and 2.67 units of x_2. Substituting these values into the objective function will indicate the optimal profit:

$$4(4) + 5(2.67) = 29.35$$

Solutions and Corner Points

The feasible solution space in graphical linear programming is a polygon. Moreover, the solution to any problem will be at one of the corner points of the polygon. In rare instances, the objective function will be parallel to one of the constraint lines. In such a case, *every* combination of x_1 and x_2 on the segment of the constraint that touches the feasible solution space is optimal. Hence, there are multiple optimal solutions to the problem. Even in such a case, the solution will also be a corner point. In fact, the solution will be at *two* corner points: those at the ends of the segment that touches the feasible solution space. Figures 2S–5 and 2S–6 illustrate solutions at corner points and

FIGURE 2S–5

The solution is always at a corner point

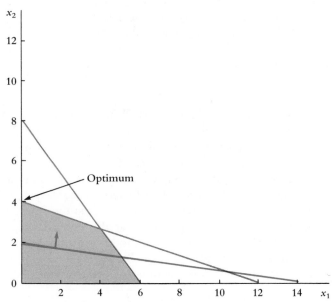

an objective function line that is parallel to a constraint line, respectively. Figure 2S–5 shows the same problem that was solved in this section with a different objective function: $Z = 2x_1 + 14x_2$.

FIGURE 2S–6

The objective function is parallel to one of the constraint lines

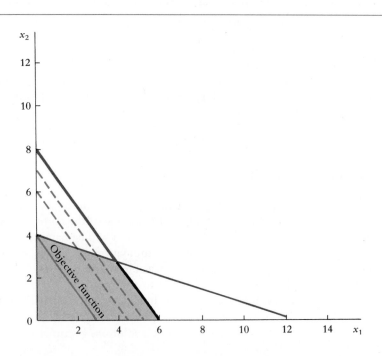

Minimization

Graphical minimization problems are quite similar to maximization problems. There are, however, two important differences. One is that the constraints are usually of the "greater than or equal to" type instead of "less than or equal to." This causes the feasible solution space to be outside of the polygon instead of inside. The other difference is that the objective is to *minimize* (e.g., minimize cost, distance, scrap). The optimum corner point is found by sliding the objective function (which is an *isocost* line) *toward* the origin instead of away from it.

EXAMPLE S–2

Solve the following problem using graphical linear programming.

Minimize $Z = 8x_1 + 12x_2$
subject to $5x_1 + 2x_2 \geq 20$
                        $4x_1 + 3x_2 \geq 24$
                                $x_2 \geq 2$

Solution

1. Plot the constraints (shown in Figure 2S–7).
   a. Change constraints to equalities.
   b. For each constraint, set $x_1 = 0$ and solve for x_2; then set $x_2 = 0$ and solve for x_1.

FIGURE 2S–7

The constraints define the feasible solution space

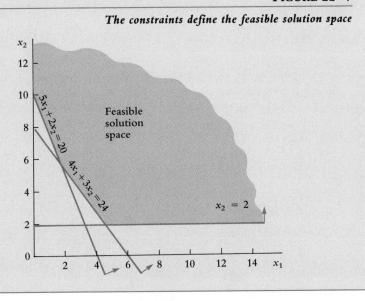

EXAMPLE S–2 *(concluded)*

    c. Graph each constraint. Note that $x_2 = 2$ is a horizontal line parallel to the x_1 axis and 2 units above it.

2. Shade the feasible solution space (see Figure 2S–7).

3. Plot the objective function.

    a. Select a value for the objective function that causes it to cross the feasible solution space. Try $8 \times 12 = 96$; $8x_1 + 12x_2 = 96$ (acceptable).

    b. Graph the line (see Figure 2S–8).

FIGURE 2S–8

The optimum is the last point the objective function touches as it is moved toward the origin

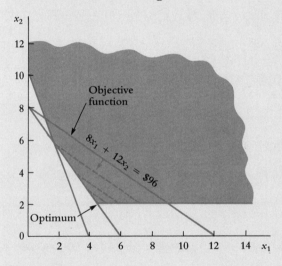

4. Slide the objective function toward the origin, being careful to keep it parallel to the original line.

5. The optimum (last feasible point) is shown in Figure 2S–8. The x_2 coordinate ($x_2 = 2$) can be determined by inspection of the graph. Note that the optimum point is at the intersecton of the line $x_2 = 2$ and the line $4x_1 + 3x_2 = 24$. Substituting the value of x_2 into the latter equation will yield the value of x_1 at the intersection:

$$4x_1 + 3(2) = 24 \qquad x_1 = 4.5$$

Thus, the optimum is $x_1 = 4.5$ units and $x_2 = 2$.

6. Compute the minimum cost:

$$8x_1 + 12x_2 = 8(4.5) + 12(2) = 60$$

SLACK AND SURPLUS

If a constraint forms the optimal corner point of the feasible solution space, it is called a **binding constraint.** In effect, it limits the value of the objective function; if the constraint could be relaxed (less restrictive), an improved solution would be possible. For constraints that are not binding, making them less restrictive will have no impact on the solution.

If the optimal values of the decision variables are substituted into the left side of a binding constraint, the resulting value will exactly equal the right-hand value of the constraint. However, for a nonbinding constraint, there will be a difference. If the left side is greater than the right side, we say that there is **surplus;** if the left side is less than the right side, we say that there is **slack.** Slack can only occur in a $\leq$ constraint; it is the amount by which the left side is less than the right side when the optimal values of the decision variables are substituted into the left side. And surplus can only occur in a $\geq$ constraint; it is the amount by which the left side exceeds the right side of the constraint when the optimal values of the decision variables are substituted into the left side.

For example, suppose the optimal values for a model are $x_1 = 10$ and $x_2 = 20$. If one of the constraints is

$$3x_1 + 2x_2 \leq 100$$

substituting the optimal values into the left side yields

$$3(10) + 2(20) = 70$$

Because the constraint is $\leq$, the difference between the values of 100 and 70 (i.e., 30) is slack. Suppose the optimal values had been $x_1 = 20$ and $x_2 = 20$. Substituting these values into the left side of the constraint would yield $3(20) + 2(20) = 100$. Because the left side equals the right side, this is a binding constraint; slack is equal to zero.

Now consider the constraint

$$4x_1 + x_2 \geq 50$$

If the optimal values are $x_1 = 10$ and $x_2 = 15$, substituting into the left side yields

$$4(10) + 15 = 55$$

Because this is a $\geq$ constraint, the difference between the left and right side values is *surplus.* If the optimal values had been $x_1 = 12$ and $x_2 = 2$, substitution would result in the left side being equal to 50. Hence, the constraint would be a binding constraint, and there would be no surplus (or surplus would be zero).

THE SIMPLEX METHOD

The **simplex** method is a general-purpose linear programming algorithm that is widely used to solve large-scale problems. Although it lacks the intuitive appeal of the graphical approach, its ability to handle problems with more than two decision variables makes it extremely valuable for solving problems often encountered in operations management.

The simplex technique involves a series of iterations; successive improvements are made until an optimal solution is achieved. The technique requires simple mathematical operations (addition, subtraction, multiplication, and division), but the computations are lengthy as well as tedious, and the slightest error can lead to a good deal of frustration. For these reasons, most users of the technique rely on computers to handle the computations while they concentrate on the solutions. Still, some familiarity with manual computations is helpful in understanding the simplex process. You will discover that it is better *not* to use your calculator in working through these problems because rounding can easily distort the results. Instead, it is best to work with numbers in fractional form.

Even though simplex can readily handle three or more decision variables, you will gain considerable insight on the technique if we use a two-variable problem to illustrate it because you will be able to compare what is happening in the simplex calculations with a graphical solution to the problem.

We will consider the simplex solution to the same problem that was used to illustrate a graphical solution. That problem is repeated here:

Maximize $Z = 4x_1 + 5x_2$
subject to $x_1 + 3x_2 \leq 12$
$4x_1 + 3x_2 \leq 24$
$x_1, x_2 \geq 0$

The solution is shown graphically in Figure 2S–9. Now let's see how the simplex technique can be used to obtain the solution.

The simplex technique involves generating a series of solutions in tabular form, called **tableaus**. By inspecting the bottom row of each tableau, one can

FIGURE 2S–9

Graphical solution

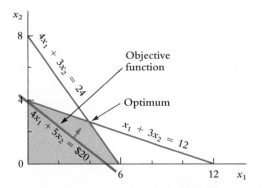

immediately tell if it represents the optimal solution. Each tableau corresponds to a corner point of the feasible solution space. The first tableau corresponds to the origin. Subsequent tableaus are developed by shifting to an adjacent corner point in the direction that yields the highest rate of profit. This process continues as long as a positive rate of profit exists. Thus, the process encompasses the following steps:

1. Set up the initial tableau.
2. Develop a revised tableau using the information contained in the first tableau.
3. Inspect to see if it is optimum.
4. Repeat steps 2 and 3 until no further improvement is possible.

Let's see how it works.

Setting Up the Initial Tableau

Obtaining the initial tableau is a two-step process. First, we must rewrite the constraints and objective function so that they are in the necessary form. Then we put this information into a table and supply a few computations that are needed to complete the table.

Rewriting the objective function and constraints involves the addition of *slack variables,* one for each constraint. These variables represent the amount of each resource that will not be used if the solution is implemented. In the initial solution, with each of the real variables equal to zero, the solution consists solely of slack. The constraints with slack added become equalities:

(1) $\quad x_1 + 3x_2 + 1s_1 \qquad\quad = 12$
(2) $\quad 4x_1 + 3x_2 \qquad + 1s_2 = 24$

It is useful in setting up the table to represent each slack variable in every equation. Hence, we can write these equations in an equivalent form:

(1) $\quad x_1 + 3x_2 + 1s_1 + 0s_2 = 12$
(2) $\quad 4x_1 + 3x_2 + 0s_2 + 1s_2 = 24$

The objective function can be written in similar form:

$$Z = 4x_1 + 5x_2 + 0s_1 + 0s_2$$

The slack variables are given coefficients of zero in the objective function because they do not produce any contributions to profits. Thus, the information above can be summarized as:

$$\text{Maximize} \quad Z = 4x_1 + 5x_2 + 0s_1 + 0s_2$$
$$\text{subject to}$$
$$(1) \quad x_1 + 3x_2 + 1s_1 + 0s_2 = 12$$
$$(2) \quad 4x_1 + 3x_2 + 0s_1 + 1s_2 = 24$$

TABLE 2S–1

Partial initial tableau	*Profit per unit for variables in solution*		*Decision variables*				
	C		*4*	*5*	*0*	*0*	*Objective row*
		Variables in solution	x_1	x_2	s_1	s_2	*Solution quantity*
	0	s_1	1	3	1	0	12
	0	s_2	4	3	0	1	24

This forms the basis of our initial tableau, which is shown in Table 2S–1.

To complete the first tableau, we will need two additional rows, a Z row and a $C - Z$ row. The Z row values indicate the reduction in profits that would occur if one unit of the variable in that column were added to the solution. The $C - Z$ row shows the potential for increasing profits if one unit of the variable in that column were to be added to the solution.

To compute the Z values, multiply the coefficients in each column by their respective row profit per unit amounts, and sum within columns. To begin with, all values are zero:

C	x_1	x_2	s_1	s_2	*Quantity*
0	(1)0	(3)0	(1)0	(0)0	(12)0
0	(4)0	(3)0	(0)0	(1)0	(24)0
Z	0	0	0	0	0

The last value in the Z row indicates the total profit associated with a given solution (tableau). Since the initial solution has $x_1 = 0$ and $x_2 = 0$, it is not surprising that profit is 0.

Values in the $C - Z$ row are computed by subtracting the Z value in each column from the value of the objective row for that column. Thus:

Variable row:	x_1	x_2	s_1	s_2
Objective row (C):	4	5	0	0
Z	0	0	0	0
C – Z	4	5	0	0

The completed tableau is shown in Table 2S–2.

C→		4	5	0	0	
↓	Variables in solution	x_1	x_2	s_1	s_2	Solution quantity
0	s_1	1	3	1	0	12
0	s_2	4	3	0	1	24
	Z	0	0	0	0	0
	C − Z	4	5	0	0	

The Test for Optimality

If all the values in the $C - Z$ row of any tableau are zero or negative, the optimal solution has been obtained. In this case, the $C - Z$ row contains two positive values, 4 and 5, indicating that improvement is possible.

Developing the Second Tableau

Values in the $C - Z$ row reflect the profit potential for each unit of the variable in a given column. For instance, the 4 indicates that each unit of variable x_1 added to the solution will increase profits by $4. Similarly, the 5 indicates that each unit of x_2 can contribute $5 to profits. Given a choice between $4 per unit and $5 per unit, we select the larger and focus on that column, which means that x_2 will come into the solution. Now we must determine which variable will leave the solution. (At each tableau, one variable will come into the solution, and one will go out of solution, keeping the number of variables in the solution constant. Note that the number of variables in the solution must always equal the number of constraints. Thus, since in this problem there are two constraints, all solutions will have two variables.)

To determine which variable will leave the solution, we use the numbers in the body of the table in the column of the entering variable (i.e., 3 and 3). These are called **row pivot values.** Divide each one into the corresponding solution quantity amount, as shown in Table 2S–3. The smaller of these two ratios indicates the variable that will leave the solution. Thus, variable s_1 will leave and be replaced with x_2. In graphical terms, we have moved up the x_2 axis to the next corner point. By determining the smallest ratio, we have found which constraint is the limiting factor. Turn back to Figure 2S–2. Note that the two constraints intersect the x_2 axis at 4 and 8, the two row ratios we have just computed. The second tableau will describe this corner point; it will indicate the profits and quantities associated with that corner point. It will also

TABLE 2S–3

*The leaving and
entering variables*

C		4	5	0	0	
	Variables in solution	x_1	x_2	s_1	s_2	Solution quantity
0	s_1	1	3	1	0	12/3 = 4 ← *Leaving variable*
0	s_2	4	3	0	1	24/3 = 8
	Z	0	0	0	0	0
	C − Z	4	5	0	0	

↑
*Entering
variable*

reveal if the corner point is an optimum, or if we must develop another tableau.

At this point we can begin to develop the second tableau. The row of the leaving variable will be transformed into the **new main row** of the second tableau. This will serve as a foundation on which to develop the other rows. To obtain this new main row, we simply divide each element in the s_1 row by the row pivot (intersection of the entering column and leaving row), which is 3. The resulting numbers are:

	x_1	x_2	s_1	s_2	Solution quantity
Main-row value	1/3	1	1/3	0	4

These numbers become the new x_2 row of the second tableau.

The main-row numbers are used to compute the values for the other constraint rows (in this instance, the only other constraint row is the s_2 row). The procedure is:

1. Find the value that is at the intersection of the constraint row (i.e., the s_2 row) and the entering variable column. It is 3.
2. Multiply each value in the new main row by this value.
3. Subtract the resulting values, column by column, from the current row values.

	x_1	x_2	s_1	s_2	Quantity
Current value:	4	3	0	1	24
−3 × (main row)	−3(1/3)	−3(1)	−3(1/3)	−3(0)	−3(4)
New row value	3	0	−1	1	12

C		4	5	0	0	
	Variables in solution	x_1	x_2	s_1	s_2	Solution quantity
5	x_2	1/3	1	1/3	0	4
0	s_2	3	0	−1	1	12

Partially completed second tableau

The two new rows are shown in Table 2S–4. The new Z row can now be computed. Multiply the row unit profits and the coefficients in each column for each row. Sum the results within each column. Thus:

Row	Profit	x_1	x_2	s_1	s_2	Quantity
x_2	5	5(1/3)	5(1)	5(1/3)	5(0)	5(4)
s_1	0	0(3)	0(0)	0(−1)	0(1)	0(12)
New Z row		5/3	5	5/3	0	20

Next, we compute the $C - Z$ row:

	x_1	x_2	s_1	s_2
C	4	5	0	0
Z	5/3	5	5/3	0
$C - Z$	7/3	0	−5/3	0

The completed second tableau is shown in Table 2S–5. It tells us that, at this point, 4 units of variable x_2 are the most we can make (see column *Solution quantity*, row x_2) and that the profit associated with $x_2 = 4$, $x_1 = 0$ is $20 (see row Z, column *Solution quantity*).

The fact that there is a positive value in the $C - Z$ row tells us that this is not the optimal solution. Consequently, we must develop another tableau.

C		4	5	0	0	
	Variables in solution	x_1	x_2	s_1	s_2	Solution quantity
5	x_2	1/3	1	1/3	0	4
0	s_2	3	0	−1	1	12
	Z	5/3	5	5/3	0	20
	$C - Z$	7/3	0	−5/3	0	

Completed second tableau

Developing the Third Tableau

The third tableau will be developed in the same manner as the previous one.

1. Determine the entering variable: Find the column with the largest positive value in the $C - Z$ row (7/3, in the x_1 column).
2. Determine the leaving variable: Divide the solution quantity in each row by the row pivot. Hence,

$$\frac{4}{1/3} = 12 \qquad 12/3 = 4$$

The smaller ratio indicates the leaving variable, s_2. See Table 2S–6.

3. Divide each value in the row of the leaving variable by the row pivot (3) to obtain the new main-row values:

	x_1	x_2	s_1	s_2	Quantity
Current value	3	0	-1	1	12
New main-row value	1	0/3	$-1/3$	1/3	12/3 = 4

4. Compute values for the x_2 row: Multiply each new main-row value by the x_2 row pivot value (i.e., 1/3) and subtract the product from corresponding current values. Thus,

TABLE 2S–6

The leaving and entering variables

C		*4*	*5*	*0*	*0*	
Variables in solution		x_1	x_2	s_1	s_2	Solution quantity
5	x_2	1/3	1	1/3	0	$\frac{4}{1/3} = 12$
0	s_2	3	0	-1	1	12/3 = 4 ← *variable is s_2*
	Z	5/3	5	5/3	0	20
	C − Z	7/3	0	$-5/3$	0	

↑
Entering variable is x_1

Leaving

	x_1	x_2	s_1	s_2	Quantity
Current value:	1/3	1	1/3	0	4
$-1/3 \times$ (main row)	$-1/3(1)$	$-1/3(0)$	$-1/3(-1/3)$	$-1/3(1/3)$	$-1/3(4)$
New row value	0	1	4/9	$-1/9$	8/3

5. Compute new Z row values. Note that now variable x_1 has been added to the solution mix; that row's unit profit is \$4.

Row	Profit	x_1	x_2	s_1	s_2	Quantity
x_2	\$5	5(0)	5(1)	5(4/9)	5($-1/9$)	5(8/3)
x_1	\$4	4(1)	4(0)	4($-1/3$)	4(1/3)	4(4)
New Z row		4	5	8/9	7/9	88/3

6. Compute the $C - Z$ row values:

	x_1	x_2	s_1	s_2
C	4	5	0	0
Z	4	5	8/9	7/9
$C - Z$	0	0	$-8/9$	$-7/9$

The resulting values of the third tableau are shown in Table 2S–7. Note that each of the $C - Z$ values is either 0 or negative, indicating that this is the final solution. The optimal values of x_1 and x_2 are indicated in the quantity column: $x_2 = 8/3$, or 2⅔, and $x_1 = 4$. (The x_2 quantity is in the x_2 row and the x_1 quantity in the x_1 row.) Total profit is 88/3, or 29.33 (quantity column, Z row).

TABLE 2S–7

The third tableau contains the optimal solution

C		4	5	0	0	
	Variables in solution	x_1	x_2	s_1	s_2	Solution quantity
5	x_2	0	1	4/9	$-1/9$	8/3
4	x_1	1	0	$-1/3$	1/3	4
	Z	4	5	8/9	7/9	88/3
	$C - Z$	0	0	$-8/9$	$-7/9$	

FIGURE 2S–10

Graphical analogies to
simplex tableaus

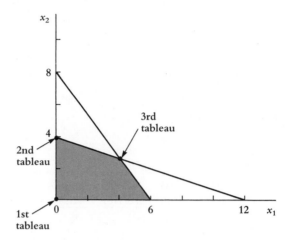

At this point, it will be useful to consider the tableaus in relation to a graph of the feasible solution space. This is shown in Figure 2S–10.

Handling ≥ and = Constraints

Up to this point, we have experienced ≤ constraints. Constraints that involve equalities and ≥ constraints are handled in a slightly different way.

When an equality constraint is present, use of the simplex method requires addition of an **artificial variable.** The purpose of such variables is merely to permit development of an initial solution. For example, the equalities

$$(1) \quad 7x_1 + 4x_2 = 65$$
$$(2) \quad 5x_1 + 3x_2 = 40$$

would be rewritten in the following manner using artificial variables a_1 and a_2:

$$(1) \quad 7x_1 + 3x_2 + 1a_1 + 0a_2 = 65$$
$$(2) \quad 5x_1 + 3x_2 + 0a_1 + 1a_2 = 40$$

Slack variables would not be added. The objective function, say, $Z = 2x_1 + 3x_2$, would be rewritten as:

$$Z = 2x_1 + 3x_2 + Ma_1 + Ma_2$$

where

$$M = \text{A large number (e.g., 999)}$$

Since the artificial variables are not desired in the final solution, selecting a large value of M (much larger than the other objective coefficients) will insure their deletion during the solution process.

For a $\geq$ constraint, surplus variables must be *subtracted* instead of added to each constraint. For example, the constraints

$$
\begin{align}
(1) \quad & 3x_1 + 2x_2 + 4x_3 \geq 80 \\
(2) \quad & 5x_1 + 4x_2 + x_3 \geq 70 \\
(3) \quad & 2x_1 + 8x_2 + 2x_3 \geq 68
\end{align}
$$

would be rewritten as equalities:

$$
\begin{align}
(1) \quad & 3x_1 + 2x_2 + 4x_3 - 1s_1 - 0s_2 - 0s_3 = 80 \\
(2) \quad & 5x_1 + 4x_2 + x_3 - 0s_1 - 1s_2 - 0s_3 = 70 \\
(3) \quad & 2x_1 + 8x_2 + 2x_3 - 0s_1 - 0s_2 - 1s_3 = 68
\end{align}
$$

As equalities, each constraint must then be adjusted by inclusion of an artificial variable. The final result looks like this:

$$
\begin{align}
(1) \quad & 3x_1 + 2x_2 + 4x_3 - 1s_1 - 0s_2 - 0s_3 + 1a_1 + 0a_2 + 0a_3 = 80 \\
(2) \quad & 5x_1 + 4x_2 + x_3 - 0s_1 - 1s_2 - 0s_3 + 0a_1 + 1a_2 + 0a_3 = 70 \\
(3) \quad & 2x_1 + 8x_2 + 2x_3 - 0s_1 - 0s_2 - 1s_3 + 0a_1 + 0a_2 + 1a_3 = 68
\end{align}
$$

If the objective function happened to be

$$5x_1 + 2x_2 + 7x_3$$

it would become

$$5x_1 + 2x_2 + 7x_3 + 0s_1 + 0s_2 + 0s_3 + Ma_1 + Ma_2 + Ma_3$$

Summary of Maximization Procedure

The main steps in solving a maximization problem with only $\leq$ constraints using the simplex algorithm are:

1. Set up the initial tableau.
    a. Rewrite the constraints so that they become equalities; add a slack variable to each constraint.
    b. Rewrite the objective function to include the slack variables. Give slack variables coefficients of 0.
    c. Put the objective coefficients and constraint coefficients into tableau form.
    d. Compute values for the Z row; Multiply the values in each constraint row by the row's C value. Add the results within each column.
    e. Compute values for the $C - Z$ row.
2. Set up subsequent tableaus.
    a. Determine the entering variable (the largest positive value in the $C - Z$ row). If a tie exists, choose one column arbitrarily.
    b. Determine the leaving variable: Divide each constraint row's solution quantity by the row's pivot value; the smallest positive ratio

indicates the leaving variable. If a tie occurs, divide the values in each row by the row pivot value, beginning with slack columns and then other columns, moving from left to right. The leaving variable is indicated by the lowest ratio in the first column with unequal ratios.

c. Form the new main row of the next tableau: Divide each number in the leaving row by the row's pivot value. Enter these values in the next tableau in the same row positions.

d. Compute new values for remaining constraint rows: For each row, multiply the values in the new main row by the constraint row's pivot value, and subtract the resulting values, column by column, from the original row values. Enter these in the new tableau in the same positions as the original row.

e. Compute values for Z and $C - Z$ rows.

f. Check to see if any values in the $C - Z$ row are positive; if they are, repeat 2a–2f. Otherwise, the optimal solution has been obtained.

Minimization Problems

The simplex method handles minimization problems in essentially the same way it handles maximization problems. However, there are a few differences. One is the need to adjust for $\geq$ constraints, which requires both artificial variables and surplus variables. This tends to make manual solution more involved. A second major difference is the test for the optimum: A solution is optimal if there are no *negative* values in the $C - Z$ row.

EXAMPLE S–3

Solve the following problem for the quantities of x_1 and x_2 that will minimize cost.

$$\text{Minimize} \quad Z = 12x_1 + 10x_2$$
$$\text{subject to} \quad x_1 + 4x_2 \geq 8$$
$$3x_1 + 2x_2 \geq 6$$

Solution

1. Rewrite the constraints so that they are in the proper form:

    $x_1 + 4x_2 \geq 8$ becomes $x_1 + 4x_2 - 1s_1 - 0s_2 + 1a_1 + 0a_2 = 8$
    $3x_1 + 2x_2 \geq 6$ becomes $3x_1 + 2x_2 - 0s_1 - 1s_2 + 0a_1 + 1a_2 = 6$

2. Rewrite the objective function (coefficients of C row):

    $$12x_1 + 10x_2 + 0s_1 + 0s_2 + 999a_1 + 999a_2$$

EXAMPLE S–3 *(continued)*

3. Compute values for rows Z and $C - Z$:

C	x_1	x_2	s_1	s_2	a_1	a_2	Quantity
999	1(999)	4(999)	−1(999)	0(999)	1(999)	0(999)	8(999)
999	3(999)	2(999)	0(999)	−1(999)	0(999)	1(999)	6(999)
Z	3,996	5,994	−999	−999	999	999	13,986
$C - Z$	−3,984	−5,984	999	999	0	0	

4. Set up the initial tableau:

C		12	10	0	0	999	999	
	Variables in solution	x_1	x_2	s_1	s_2	a_1	a_2	Solution quantity
999	a_1	1	4	−1	0	1		8
999	a_2	3	2	0	−1	0	1	6
	Z	3,996	5,994	−999	−999	999	999	13,986
	$C - Z$	−3,984	−5,984	999	999	0	0	

5. Find the entering variable (largest negative $C - Z$ value: x_2 column) and leaving variable (smaller of $8/4 = 2$ and $6/2 = 3$; hence, row a_1.

6. Divide each number in the leaving row by the pivot value (4, in this case) to obtain values for the new main row of the second tableau:

$$1/4 \quad 4/4 = 1 \quad -1/4 \quad 0/4 \quad 1/4 \quad 0/4 \quad 8/4 = 2$$

7. Compute values for other rows. a_2 is:

	x_1	x_2	s_1	s_2	a_1	a_2	Quantity
Current value	3	2	0	−1	0	1	6
−2 × (new main row)	−2/4	−2	2/4	−0/4	−2/4	−0/4	−4
New row	10/4	0	+2/4	−1	−2/4	1	2

8. Compute a new Z row:

Row	Cost	x_1	x_2	s_1	s_2	a_1	a_2	Quantity
x_2	10	10(1/4)	10(1)	10(−1/4)	10(0)	10(1/4)	10(0)	10(2)
a_2	999	999(10/4)	999(0)	999(2/4)	999(−1)	999(−2/4)	999(1)	999(2)
Z		2,500	10	497	−999	−497	999	2,018

9. Compute the $C - Z$ row:

	x_1	x_2	s_1	s_2	a_1	a_2
C	12	10	0	0	999	999
Z	2,500	10	497	−999	−497	999
$C - Z$	−2,488	0	−497	999	1,496	0

EXAMPLE S–3 *(continued)*

10. Set up the second tableau:

C		12	10	0	0	999	999	
	Variables in solution	x_1	x_2	s_1	s_2	a_1	a_2	Quantity
10	x_2	1/4	1	−1/4	0	1/4	0	2
999	a_2	10/4	0	2/4	−1	−2/4	1	2
	Z	2,500	10	497	−999	−497	999	2,018
	C − Z	−2,488	0	−497	999	1,496	0	

11. Repeat the process.
   a. Check for optimality: It is not optimum because of negatives in $C − Z$ row.
   b. Determine the entering variable: The largest negative is in column x_1.
   c. Determine the leaving variable: $2/(1/4) = 8, 2/(10/4) = 0.8$. Therefore, it is row a_2.
   d. Find new main-row value using the pivot value of 10/4:

$$1 \quad 0 \quad 0.2 \quad −0.4 \quad −0.2 \quad 0.4 \quad 0.8$$

   e. Determine values for new x_2 row:

$$0 \quad 1 \quad −0.3 \quad 0.1 \quad 0.3 \quad −0.1 \quad 1.8$$

   f. Determine new values for row Z:

Row	Cost	x_1	x_2	s_1	s_2	a_1	a_2	Quantity
x_2	10	10(0)	10(1)	10(−0.3)	10(0.1)	10(0.3)	10(−0.1)	10(1.8)
x_1	12	12(1)	12(0)	12(0.2)	12(−0.4)	12(−0.2)	12(0.4)	12(0.8)
Z		12	10	−0.6	−3.8	0.6	3.8	27.6

   g. Determine values for the $C − Z$ row:

	x_1	x_2	s_1	s_2	a_1	a_2
C	12	10	0	0	999	999
Z	12	10	−0.6	−3.8	0.6	3.8
C − Z	0	0	0.6	3.8	998.4	995.2

EXAMPLE S–3 *(concluded)*

h. Set up the next tableau. Since no $C - Z$ values are negative, the solution is optimal. Hence, $x_1 = 0.8$, $x_2 = 1.8$, and the minimum cost is 27.60.

C		12	10	0	0	999	999	
	Variables in solution	x_1	x_2	s_1	s_2	a_1	a_2	**Quantity**
10	x_2	0	1	−0.3	0.1	0.3	−0.1	1.8
12	x_1	1	0	0.2	−0.4	−0.2	0.4	0.8
	Z	12	10	−0.6	−3.8	0.6	3.8	27.6
	$C - Z$	0	0	0.6	3.8	998.4	995.2	

SENSITIVITY ANALYSIS

A decision maker is often interested in more than the immediate solution to a problem. The decision maker can benefit from sensitivity analysis of the solution in several ways. In preparing the problem for a linear programming solution, the decision maker may have used subjective estimates for certain parameters (e.g., the coefficients of the constraints, the coefficients of the objective function, and the right-hand-side values of the constraints). Understandably, the decision maker would want to know how sensitive the optimal solution is to changes in the value of one or more of those parameters. If the solution is relatively insensitive to reasonable changes, the decision maker can feel more confident in implementing the solution. Conversely, if the solution is sensitive to such changes, the decision maker will undoubtedly want to obtain more precise estimates of the suspect parameters.

A related issue involves a specific change in a parameter. For instance, there may be a price change that would alter a coefficient in the objective function. Similarly, a change in a production process could require a change in a coefficient of one of the constraints. Again, sensitivity analysis could provide the decision maker with the necessary insight.

A third possibility is the question of whether it might be beneficial to obtain larger amounts of certain resources. This question often arises when large amounts of some resources are unused by the optimal solution; by adding more of the other resources, it may be possible to realize a disproportionate increase in the value of the objective function.

Thus, we see that there are a number of reasons that a decision maker might want to pursue sensitivity analysis. We will explore two of these possibilities: a change in an objective function coefficient and a change in the right-hand-side value of a constraint. We will not consider a change in a coefficient of a constraint. Also, the following discussion pertains to *one* change, with all other parameters remaining unchanged. In a situation where more than one change is of interest, the problem must be reworked with the changed values.

Much of the information needed for sensitivity analysis is contained in the final simplex tableau. That plus the original problem statement will suffice to perform the analysis. Let's see how sensitivity analysis could be applied to the maximization problem that was solved using simplex earlier in this section. That problem and its final tableau are reproduced in Table 2S–8 for easy reference.

First, let us consider changes to one of the objective function coefficients. Sensitivity analysis will answer this question for a variable in the solution: For what range of values will the solution quantities of all the decision variables remain the same? This is known as the **range of optimality.** Of course, if one of the coefficients of the objective function is changed, the total profit (e.g., 88/3) will change even if the optimal quantities of x_1 and x_2 do not change.

The analysis involves computing a series of ratios using the $C - Z$ row of the final tableau and the row corresponding to the variable whose range of optimality is to be determined. The elements of the bottom row are divided by the corresponding elements of the variable's row. For instance, for variable x_1, the ratios are:

$$\frac{C - Z:}{x_1:} \quad \frac{0}{1} = 0 \quad \frac{0}{0} = \text{(undefined)} \quad \frac{-8/9}{-1/3} = 8/3 \quad \frac{-7/9}{1/3} = -7/3$$

The positive ratio closest to zero indicates the amount by which the original coefficient of x_1 in the objective function could be increased without changing the optimal solution quantities. Thus, the 4 could be increased by 8/3 = 2.67 (i.e., to 6.67) and not change the solution. Similarly, the 4 could be decreased by the negative amount closest to zero (i.e., $-7/3 = 2.33$) and not change the solution quantities. Hence, the range of optimality for the x_1 coefficient is:

$$4 - 2.33 \le c_1 \le 4 + 2.67$$

TABLE S2–8

Maximize $Z = 4x_1 + 5x_2$
subject to $x_1 + 3x_2 \le 12$
                       $4x_1 + 3x_2 \le 24$

C		4	5	0	0	
	Variables in solution	x_1	x_2	s_1	s_2	Solution quantity
5	x_2	0	1	4/9	−1/9	8/3
4	x_1	1	0	−1/3	1/3	4
	Z	4	5	8/9	7/9	88/3
	C − Z	0	0	−8/9	−7/9	

If c_1 remains at 4, the range of optimality for x_2 is determined as follows:

$$\frac{C - Z:}{x_2} \qquad \frac{0}{0} = \text{(undefined)} \qquad \frac{0}{1} = 0 \qquad \frac{-8/9}{4/9} = -2 \qquad \frac{-7/9}{-1/9} = 7$$

The smallest positive ratio is 7; hence, the original coefficient of 5 can be increased by 7, or up to $5 + 7 = 12$. The negative ratio closest to zero is -2. Hence, the original x_2 coefficient can be decreased by that amount. Therefore, its lower bound is $5 - 2 = 3$. Thus, the range of optimality for c_2 is 3 to 12.

In this example, there are two decision variables, and both are in the solution. In some cases one or more of the decision variables will not be in the solution. In those situations, we talk about the *range of insignificance*, which refers to the range over which that variable will remain out of the solution. In order for that variable to come into the solution, its objective function coefficient would have to increase by an amount greater than the value that appears in row $C - Z$ in this variable's column. For instance, if -4 appeared, the variable's objective function coefficient would have to increase by more than 4 for it to come into the solution. Its range of insignificance would be 0 to 4.

Now let's consider changes to the right-hand side of a constraint. Again, remember that only one constraint is assumed to change; all others remain fixed at their original amounts. First, it should be noted that some constraints are not candidates for change; nothing beneficial would be accomplished by increasing their amounts (assuming a $\leq$ constraint). This is the case for constraints that are slack in the final solution, since such constraints are not limiting factors on the problem. Hence, the **range of feasibility** for a slack constraint on the *down* side is equal to its value in the final solution. Thus, if $s_1 = 250$ in the final solution of a problem, the first constraint's right-side original amount can be decreased by that amount and not change the solution. On the *up* side, the right-side value can be increased by any amount and not change the solution; increasing it will merely increase the amount of slack. Note that a constraint that is slack will have a 0 in the $C - Z$ row for the column that corresponds to that slack variable.

If a constraint is a limiting factor, its slack variable will not appear in the final solution. (In some rare instances, a slack variable will appear but have a solution quantity equal to zero. In effect, there is no slack for that constraint even though it appears in the solution.) For slack variables not in the solution, there will be a negative value under its column in the $C - Z$ row. These negative amounts are known as **shadow prices.** They indicate how much a one-unit decrease in the original amount of a constraint would decrease the final value of the objective function. Thus, we can see in Table 2S–8 that a one-unit decrease in the first constraint of that problem would lead to a decrease in the final value of the objective function of $8/9 = 0.89$. Similarly, a decrease of one unit in the second constraint would lead to a decrease in the objective function of $7/9 = 0.78$. Conversely, a one-unit *increase* in one of these values would have the opposite effect: a one-unit increase in the first constraint would increase the optimal value of the objective function by 0.89, and a one-unit increase in the second constraint would lead to an increase of 0.78. The question that can be answered by sensitivity analysis is this: Over what range of right-side values of a constraint will these shadow prices remain valid?

To determine the range of feasibility for a constraint, first identify the values in the body of the final tableau under the column for that constraint's slack variable. For instance, for s_1 in Table 2S–8, the values are 4/9 and $-1/3$. Next, divide these values into the corresponding values in the quantity column. For s_1, the results are:

$$\frac{8/3}{4/9} = +6$$

$$\frac{4}{-1/3} = -12$$

The positive ratio closest to zero indicates the amount by which the original constraint can be *decreased,* and the negative ratio closest to zero indicates the amount by which the original value of the constraint can be *increased.* In this instance, the first constraint's original right-side value was 12. It could be decreased by as much as 6 units or increased by as much as 12 units and have an impact of 8/9 = 0.89 per unit on the optimal value of the objective function. Similarly, the ratios for s_2 are:

$$\frac{8/3}{-1/9} = -24$$

$$\frac{4}{1/3} = +12$$

Hence, if the first constraint remained unchanged, the second could be increased by as much as 24 units or decreased by as much as 12 units and have an impact of 7/9 = 0.78 per unit on the optimal value of the objective function.

COMPUTER SOLUTIONS

The simplex procedure provides an all-purpose method for solving linear programming problems. Unfortunately, for all but the smallest problems, the computational burden imposed by the simplex procedure is considerable. This is true even for problems that are moderate in size; for larger problems, manual computations would require a herculean effort for solution. Fortunately, standard computer packages for solving linear programming problems using simplex are widely available. In practice, they are used almost exclusively in lieu of manual computations. Therefore, computer solutions represent the most realistic avenue for handling LP problems.

One of the most widely used linear programming packages is **LINDO.** Developed by Linus Schrage of the University of Chicago, it is available in both mainframe and personal computer versions. Also, there are many other packages available for mainframes and personal computers. Although these packages have a high degree of similarity in terms of input and output, they do have minor differences. Therefore, rather than describe a particular package, the discussion here will present a generic overview of how computers are used to obtain solutions to linear programming models.

Consider this LP model:

Maximize $60x_1 + 50x_2$
subject to $4x_1 + 10x_2 \leq 100$
$\quad 2x_1 + x_2 \leq 22$
$\quad 3x_1 + 3x_2 \leq 39$
$\quad x_1, x_2 \geq 0$

The problem, as input into the computer, would look something like this:

```
MAX  60X1 + 50X2
 ST

      4X1 + 10X2 < = 100
      2X1 +  X2 < = 22
      3X1 + 3X2 < = 39
```

(Caps for letters may or may not be required. If not, the first constraint would look like this: 4x1 + 10x2 < = 100.) Note the key differences between this input and our basic model:

1. Two keystrokes are used for the $\leq$ constraints. (Some programs treat $<$ as the equivalent of $\leq$ and require only a single keystroke.)

2. The non–negative constraints are not needed; they are automatically assumed by the computer code (program).

3. Slack and surplus variables are not used; the computer uses them automatically, as needed.

4. Although this particular model does not involve any coefficients expressed as fractions (e.g., $\frac{1}{2}x_1$, $\frac{1}{4}x_2$), fractions are not allowed. Instead, all coefficients must be integers or decimals (e.g., $.5x_1$, $.25x_2$).

Often, users have the option of choosing the type of output they want. One option is to be given all of the tableaus; another is to be given only the final tableau; and still another is to be given only the final solution. Beyond that, most programs provide additional information on sensitivity analysis.

Table 2S–9 presents an example of how the computer output might appear for the preceding LP model. The output shows the optimal values of the variables and the optimal value of the objective function. The terms *reduced cost* and *dual price* will be explained later in this section.

However, the numbers are those that appear in the $C - Z$ row of the final tableau.

A slighty different version of computer output is shown in Table 2S–10. Aside from a slightly different format, the main difference between the two

TABLE 2S-9

Sample computer output

```
AFTER 2 ITERATIONS
THIS SOLUTION IS OPTIMAL:

     VARIABLE      QUANTITY
        S1            24
        X1             9
        X2             4

OPTIMAL Z   =     740

     VARIABLE    REDUCED  COST
        X1             0
        X2             0
                   DUAL PRICE
        S1             0
        S2           −10
        S3           −13.33
```

TABLE 2S-10

A second sample of computer output

```
        LP OPTIMUM FOUND AT STEP 3

          OBJECTIVE FUNCTION VALUE

     1)          740.000

VARIABLE           VALUE        REDUCED COST
      X1         9.00000          0.00000
      X2         4.00000          0.00000

ROW        SLACK OR SURPLUS   DUAL PRICES
   2)          24.00000          0.00000
   3)           0.00000         10.00000
   4)           0.00000         13.33334
```

sets of output is that one program reports the dual prices as negative amounts, and the other reports them as positives.

Computer packages generally have the capability of providing individual tableaus in addition to providing the optimal solution. For instance, a LINDO printout of the tableaus would appear as follows:

```
MAX      60 X1 +  50 X2
SUBJECT TO
   2)      4 X1 +  10 X2 <= 100
   3)      2 X1 +     X2 <=  22
   4)      3 X1 +   3 X2 <=  39
END
```

THE TABLEAU

```
ROW  (BASIS)           X1             X2 SLK    2  SLK     3  SLK     4
   1 ART             -60.000      -50.000     0.000      0.000     0.000      0.000
   2 SLK     2         4.000       10.000     1.000      0.000     0.000    100.000
   3 SLK     3         2.000        1.000     0.000      1.000     0.000     22.000
   4 SLK     4         3.000        3.000     0.000      0.000     1.000     39.000

         X1 ENTERS AT VALUE      11.000         IN ROW      3 OBJ. VALUE =   660.00
```

THE TABLEAU
```
ROW (BASIS)            X1             X2 SLK    2  SLK     3  SLK     4
   1 ART                0.000      -20.000     0.000     30.000     0.000    660.000
   2 SLK     2          0.000        8.000     1.000     -2.000     0.000     56.000
   3         X1         1.000        0.500     0.000      0.500     0.000     11.000
   4 SLK     4          0.000        1.500     0.000     -1.500     1.000      6.000

         X2 ENTERS AT VALUE      4.0000          IN ROW      4 OBJ. VALUE =   740.00
```

THE TABLEAU
```
ROW  (BASIS)           X1             X2 SLK    2  SLK     3  SLK     4
   1 ART                0.000        0.000     0.000     10.000    13.333    740.000
   2 SLK     2          0.000        0.000     1.000      6.000    -5.333     24.000
   3         X1         1.000        0.000     0.000      1.000    -0.333      9.000
   4         X2         0.000        1.000     0.000     -1.000     0.667      4.000

      LP OPTIMUM FOUND AT STEP          2
          OBJECTIVE FUNCTION VALUE
   1)          740.000000

   VARIABLE          VALUE          REDUCED COST
         X1         9.000000           0.000000
         X2         4.000000           0.000000

   ROW          SLACK OR SURPLUS     DUAL PRICES
      2)          24.000000            0.000000
      3)           0.000000           10.000000
      4)           0.000000           13.333333

   NO. ITERATIONS =    2
```

The output is somewhat self-explanatory, with the addition of a few comments. The top row of each tableau has the label ART. This stands for *artificial*, and the values in the row are the negative of what ordinarily appears in the bottom row of a tableau. Thus, in the last tableau 10.000 and 13.333 appear in the top row, and in Table 2S–9 these appear as negatives. Hence, the top row is $Z - C$ rather than $C - Z$. Note, too, that row Z does not appear at all. Finally, SLK refers to a slack variable. However, LINDO begins numbering with the top row, so s_1 is labeled SLK 2, s_2 is SLK 3, and so on. Also, the spacing along the top labels is such that the number of each slack variable appears directly over the appropriate column, but its label is shifted a bit to the left. Thus, the third column is SLK 2.

Computers handle linear programming problems with such ease, speed, and accuracy that you may wonder why you should even learn how to solve problems manually. Actually, there are several benefits of the manual approach. One is to gain insight into how solutions are generated. Without this knowledge, the computer becomes a black box that mysteriously comes up with solutions. People who use computers under those circumstances rarely fare as well as those who possess a basic understanding of the underlying process, either in formulating problems or in understanding the results. Therefore, solving a small number of manageable problems manually can provide valuable insight that is not readily obtainable another way. In addition, the opportunity to sharpen quantitative skills is important; the world is becoming increasingly quantitative, and those who have the ability to deal with quantitative information in a confident manner are less likely to be intimidated either by quantitative information or by computers. Still another benefit of manual solution is that other techniques for solving linear programming problems use procedures that are very simlar to some of those used in simplex. Consequently, learning and understanding those techniques is easier after exposure to the simplex procedure.

Manual calculations for sensitivity analysis problems yield a tremendous amount of insight into sensitivity analysis. Nonetheless, as a practical matter, the speed and accuracy delivered by a computer solution makes that the preferred approach for solving real problems. Moreover, most computer packages either automatically include sensitivity analysis or provide the option of obtaining that information in addition to the optimal solution. Needless to say, various software packages differ in how they present the results. However, these differences usually are minor; all packages present much the same general information.

With that in mind, let us consider a sample of computer output. Table 2S–11 repeats the final tableau of the preceding LP solution for reference, and Table 2S–12 illustrates a computer printout of sensitivity analysis of the microcomputer problem.

The printout begins with the original problem and the optimal values of the variables. The optimal values of the decision variables are given first, under the

TABLE 2S–11

Final tableau

C		60	50	0	0	0	
Variables in solution		x_1	x_2	s_1	s_2	s_3	*Solution quantity*
0	s_1	0	0	1	6	$-40/3$	24
60	x_1	1	0	0	1	$-1/3$	9
50	x_2	0	1	0	-1	$2/3$	4
	Z	60	50	0	10	$40/3$	740
	$C - Z$	0	0	0	-10	$-40/3$	

```
MAX  60X1 + 50X2

SUBJECT TO
  2)  4X1 + 10X2 ≤ 100
  3)  2X1 +   X2 ≤ 22
  4)  3X1 +  3X2 ≤ 39
END

      LP OPTIMUM FOUND AT STEP  3
         OBJECTIVE FUNCTION VALUE
              740.00
```

VARIABLE	VALUE	REDUCED COSTS
X1	9.00	0.00
X2	4.00	0.00

ROW		SLACK OR SURPLUS	DUAL PRICES
	2	24.00	0.00
	3	0.00	10.00
	4	0.00	13.33

```
         SENSITIVITY ANALYSIS
            OBJECTIVE COEFFICIENT RANGES
```

VARIABLE	CURRENT VALUE	ALLOWABLE INCREASE	ALLOWABLE DECREASE
X1	60.00	40.00	10.00
X2	50.00	10.00	20.00

```
            RIGHT-HAND SIDE RANGES
```

ROW	CURRENT VALUE	ALLOWABLE INCREASE	ALLOWABLE DECREASE
2	100.000	INFINITY	24.00
3	22.00	4.00	4.00
4	39.00	4.50	6.00

VARIABLE heading, followed by the optimal values of the slack variables, which are listed under the ROW heading. Just to the right of the optimal values of the decision variables are reduced costs, and to the right of the optimal slack values are dual prices. Here, row 2 refers to s_1, row 3 refers to s_2, and row 4 refers to s_3. The dual prices are equal to the values in row $C - Z$ of the final tableau (see Table 2S-11). Recall that for variables that are in the solution, the $C - Z$ values will be equal to zero. A nonzero reduced cost, then, would appear if a decision variable was not in the solution; that nonzero reduced cost would indicate the amount by which the variable's objective function coefficient could be increased without it coming into the solution. Thus, if a reduced cost was 2.00, that variable's objective function would have to be increased by more than 2.00 in order for it to be in the solution if the problem were to be reworked with that one change.

The dual prices are the shadow prices for the slack or surplus variables (slack variables in this case).

In the remaining portion of the printout, sensitivity analysis results are shown. First, the objective coefficient ranges (ranges of optimality) are shown, followed by the right-hand-side ranges (ranges of feasibility). For each decision variable, current value refers to its objective function coefficient; the next column indicates the amount of possible increase and the next column the amount of possible decrease that will result in the same optimal values of the variables that are in the solution. For the right-side ranges, the slack variables are listed (actually, row 2 refers here to s_1, row 3 to s_2, and row 4 to s_3). CURRENT VALUE refers to the original right-side values of the constraints. The next two columns show the amount by which the right side of a constraint can be changed and still be within the range of feasibility.

KEY TERMS

artificial variable, 98
binding constraint, 89
constraints, 77
decision variables, 77
feasible solution space, 77
graphical linear programming, 79
LINDO, 106
new main row, 94
objective, 77
objective function, 77

parameter, 77
range of feasibility, 105
range of optimality, 104
row pivot value, 93
simplex, 90
shadow price, 105
slack, 89
surplus, 89
tableau, 91

SOLVED PROBLEMS

1. A small construction firm specializes in building and selling single-family homes. The firm offers two basic types of houses, model A and model B. Model A houses require 4,000 labor hours, 2 tons of stone, and 2,000 board feet of lumber. Model B houses require 10,000 labor hours, 3 tons of stone and 2,000 board feet of lumber. Due to long lead times for ordering supplies and the scarcity of skilled and semiskilled workers in the area, the firm will be forced to rely on its present resources for the upcoming building season. It has 400,000 hours of labor, 150 tons of stone, and 200,000 board feet of lumber. What mix of model A and B houses should the firm construct if model As yield a profit of $1,000 per unit and model Bs yield $2,000 per unit? Assume that the firm will be able to sell all the units it builds.

Solution

   a. Formulate the objective function and constraints.[2]

       Maximize $Z = 1{,}000A + 2{,}000B$
       subject to

Labor	$4{,}000A + 10{,}000B \leq 400{,}000$	labor hours
Stone	$2A + 3B \leq 150$	tons
Lumber	$2{,}000A + 2{,}000B \leq 200{,}000$	board feet

   b. Graph the constraints and objective function, and identify the optimum corner point (see graph). Note that the lumber constraint is *redundant:* it does not form a boundary of the feasible solution space.

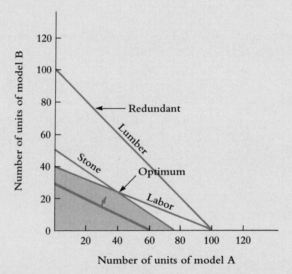

Number of units of model A

   c. Determine the optimal quantities of model A and B, and compute the resulting profit. Since the optimum point is at the intersection of the stone and labor constraints, we solve those two equations for their common point.

$$\begin{array}{rrr}
\text{Labor} \quad 4{,}000A + & 10{,}000B = & 400{,}000 \\
-2{,}000 \times (\text{Stone} \quad 2A + & 3B = & 150) \\
\hline
& 4{,}000B = & 100{,}000 \\
& B = & 25
\end{array}$$

[2] For the sake of consistency, we will assign to the horizontal axis the first decision variable mentioned in the problem. Hence, in this case, variable A will be represented on the horizontal axis and variable B on the vertical axis.

Substitute $B = 25$ in one of the equations, and solve for A:

$$2A + 3(25) = 150, \qquad A = 37.5$$

If we decide that it would be unreasonable to make 37.5 model A houses, we could simply round *down* and make 37 (check to see if 37 is a feasible solution). Profits would be $\$1{,}000(37) + \$2{,}000(25) = \$87{,}000$.

2. Solve the following problem using graphical linear programming:

Maximize $Z = 12x_1 + 6x_2$
subject to   (1) $2x_1 + 4x_2 \leq 16$
             (2) $5x_1 + 3x_2 \geq 15$
             (3) $\ x_1 \qquad\quad \leq 5$

Solution

a. Plot constraints, shade in the feasible solution space, and plot the objective function (see graph).

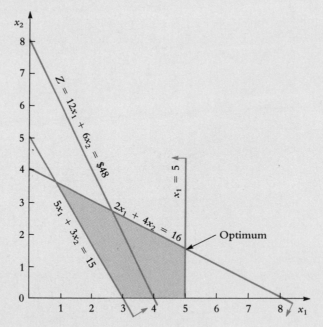

b. It is apparent from the graph that $x_1 = 5$ at the optimum. To determine the value of x_2, substitute $x_1 = 5$ in the equation $2x_1 + 4x_2 = 16$, and solve for x_2:

$$2(5) + 4x_2 = 16, \qquad x_2 = 1.5$$

c. Compute the value of the objective function at $x_1 = 5$, $x_2 = 1.5$.

$$Z_{max} = \$12(5) + \$6(1.5) = \$69$$

3. Solve the following problem for the quantities of x, y, and w that will maximize the objective function.

Maximize $Z = 20x + 16y + 10w$
subject to   (1) $4x + 2y + 3w \leq 120$
                     (2) $5x + 4y + 2w \leq 100$
                     (3) $2x + 3y + 3w \leq 90$

Solution

a. Start by rewriting the constraints as equalities using slack variables:

(1) $4x + 2y + 3w + 1s_1 + 0s_2 + 0s_3 = 120$
(2) $5x + 4y + 2w + 0s_1 + 1s_2 + 0s_3 = 100$
(3) $2x + 3y + 3w + 0s_1 + 0s_2 + 1s_3 = 90$

b. Next, develop the initial tableau:

TABLEAU 1

C		20	16	10	0	0	0	
	Variable	x	y	w	s_1	s_2	s_3	Quantity
0	s_1	4	2	3	1	0	0	120
0	s_2	5	4	2	0	1	0	100
0	s_3	2	3	3	0	0	1	90
	Z	0	0	0	0	0	0	0
	C − Z	20	16	10	0	0	0	

c. Identify the entering variable (column with the largest *positive* $C - Z$ value). Divide the numbers in that column (i.e., 4, 5, and 2) into their respective row quantities. The smallest resultant indicates the leaving variable. Hence, x is the entering variable, and s_2 is the leaving variable.

d. Divide all numbers in the s_2 row by the pivot number (i.e., 5) to obtain the main row of the next tableau. To compute new s_1 and s_3 rows, use the pivot number for each row (e.g., 4 for s_1 row) to multiply each main-row value, and subtract the resulting values from the corresponding values of the previous tableau.

e. Compute values for the Z and $C - Z$ rows.

f. If the $C - Z$ row values are all negative or zero, the optimal solution has been found. If any positive values appear, repeat steps c–e.

g. The second and third tableaus are as follows. The optimal quantities are: $x = 10.91$, $y = 0$, $w = 22.73$. The corresponding value of the objective function with those quantities is 445.46. In addition, note that constraints 2 and 3 have been fully used, but 8.18 of constraint 1 remains.

TABLEAU 2

C		20	16	10	0	0	0	
	Variable	x	y	w	s_1	s_2	s_3	Quantity
0	s_1	0.0	−1.2	1.4	1.0	−0.8	0.0	40.0
20	x	1.0	0.8	0.4	0.0	0.2	0.0	20.0
0	s_3	0.0	1.4	2.2	0.0	−0.4	1.0	50.0
	Z	20.0	16.0	8.0	0.0	4.0	0.0	400.0
	$C - Z$	0.0	0.0	2.0	0.0	−4.0	0.0	

TABLEAU 3

C		20	16	10	0	0	0	
	Variable	x	y	w	s_1	s_2	s_3	Quantity
0	s_1	0.0	−2.09	0.0	1.0	−0.55	−0.64	8.18
20	x	1.0	0.55	0.0	0.0	0.27	−0.18	10.91
10	w	0.0	0.64	1.0	0.0	−0.18	0.45	22.73
	Z	20.0	17.27	10.0	0.0	3.64	0.91	445.46
	$C - Z$	0.0	−1.27	0.0	0.0	−3.64	−0.91	

4. Given the third tableau of the preceding problem, perform sensitivity analysis. Specifically, do the following:

a. Determine the range of insignificance of variable y.

b. Determine the range of optimality for the coefficient of variable x.

c. Determine the range of feasibility for the third constraint.

d. If the third constraint can be increased at a cost of $.20 per unit and 200 units are available, how many should the firm purchase?

Solution

a. The value of -1.27 for the y column in row $C - Z$ indicates that the unit contribution of y in the objective function would have to increase by more than $1.27 in order for it to come into solution. Its range of insignificance is $0 to $17.27.

b. Dividing the values in row $C - Z$ by the values in row x produces these ratios:

x	y	w	s_1
$\dfrac{0.0}{1.0} = 0$	$\dfrac{-1.27}{0.55} = -2.31$	$\dfrac{0.0}{0.0} = \text{und.}$	$\dfrac{0.0}{0.0} = \text{und.}$

s_2	s_3
$\dfrac{-3.64}{0.27} = -13.5$	$\dfrac{-0.91}{-0.18} = +5.06$

The smallest positive ratio is 5.06, and the negative ratio closest to zero is -2.31. Hence, the coefficient of x of $20 can be decreased by as much as $2.31 and increased by as much as $5.06 and not affect the optimal solution quantities. Hence, its range of optimality is $17.69 to $25.06.

c. First, divide the values in the quantity column by the corresponding values in the s_3 column since we are interested in the third constraint. The ratios are:

$$\frac{8.18}{-0.64} = -12.78$$

$$\frac{10.91}{-0.18} = -60.61$$

$$\frac{22.73}{0.45} = 50.51$$

The smallest positive ratio indicates the amount by which the right-hand side can be decreased, and the negative ratio closest to zero (i.e., -12.78) indicates the maximum amount of increase. Hence, the range of feasibility for the third constraint is (using the original right-hand-side value of 90):

$$90 - 50.51 = 39.49 \quad \text{to} \quad 90 + 12.78 = 102.78$$

d. The shadow price of the third slack variable is -0.91, which means an increase of $.91 in the value of the objective function for each unit of increase in the third constraint's right-side value *up to the upper end of the range of feasibility.* Since the cost to acquire additional units is $.20 each, the net increase will be +$.71 per unit. Thus, acquire as many units as possible. In part *c* we found that an increase of 12.78 units was possible. Thus, acquire that amount. Note that beyond that point, the shadow price will change, so additional units of this constraint might just add to slack; another constraint would become binding (limiting) on the solution.

DISCUSSION AND REVIEW QUESTIONS

1. For which decision environment is linear programming most suited?
2. What is meant by the term *feasible solution space?* What determines this region?
3. In graphical linear programming problems, what is the upper limit on the number of:
   a. Variables in a problem?
   b. Constraints in a problem?
4. What is an isocost line? An isoprofit line?
5. What does sliding an objective function line toward the origin represent? Away?
6. In the simplex technique, how is the entering variable determined for a maximization problem? How is the leaving variable determined?
7. With what aspect of a graphical solution does a simplex tableau correspond? To what does the initial tableau correspond?
8. In what direction does the second solution move away from the initial solution in a two-variable problem?
9. After the optimal solution has been ob-

tained, it is possible to consider acquisition of additional scarce resources in a maximization problem. How does one determine:
   a. If it is worthwhile to add a given resource?
   b. The change in the value of the objective function for a change within the feasible range?
10. Explain what is meant by the terms *slack variable* and *artificial variable.*
11. What mix of surplus, slack, and artificial variables are used in each of the following constraints?
    a. ≤   b. =   c. ≥
12. Is there any theoretical limit to the number of decision variables that can be handled by the simplex method?
13. How are the numbers in the $C - Z$ row in slack columns interpreted?
14. At what point does it become apparent that a tableau contains the optimal solution in a maximization problem?

PROBLEMS

1. Solve for the optimal quantities using graphical linear programming:
   a. Maximize $Z = 10x_1 + 20x_2$ (profit)
      subject to
      Cutting $5x_1 + 2x_2 \le 40$ labor hours
      Sewing $4x_1 + 4x_2 \le 48$ labor hours

   b. Maximize $Z = 6A + 3B$ (revenue)
      subject to
      Material $20A + 5B \le 600$ lb.
      Machinery $25A + 20B \le 1{,}000$ hr.
      Labor $20A + 30B \le 1{,}200$ hr.
2. Use graphical linear programming to de-

termine the quantities that will minimize cost:

a. Minimize $Z = 1.80S + 2.20T$
   subject to

Potassium	$5S + 8T \geq 200$ gr.	
Carbohydrate	$15S + 6T \geq 240$ gr.	
Protein	$4S + 12T \geq 180$ gr.	
	$T \geq 10$ gr.	

b. Minimize $Z = 1.50C + 1.20D$
   subject to
     (1) $-8C + 4D \leq 104$
     (2) $30C + 5D \geq 210$
     (3) $7C + 7D \geq 133$

3. An appliance manufacturer produces two models of microwave ovens: H and W. Both models require fabrication and assembly work; each H uses four hours of fabrication and two hours of assembly, and each W uses two hours of fabrication and six hours of assembly. There are 600 fabrication hours available this week and 480 hours of assembly. Each H contributes $40 to profits, and each W contributes $30 to profits. What mix of H and W will maximize profits?

4. A small candy shop is preparing for the holiday season. The owner must decide how many bags of deluxe mix and how many bags of standard mix of Peanut/Raisin Delite to put up. The deluxe mix has ⅔ pound raisins and ⅓ pound peanuts, and the standard mix has ½ pound raisins and ½ pound peanuts per bag. The shop has 90 pounds of raisins and 60 pounds of peanuts to work with.

   Peanuts cost $.60 per pound and raisins cost $1.50 per pound. The deluxe mix will sell for $2.90 per pound, and the standard mix will sell for $2.55 per pound. The owner estimates that no more than 110 bags of one type can be sold.

   If the goal is to maximize *profits,* how many bags of each type should be prepared? What is the expected profit?

5. A firm produces cast-iron parts that require three basic operations: casting, grinding, and drilling. Available time for casting is 36,000 minutes; for grinding, 2,250 minutes; and for drilling, 3,600 minutes per week. Two products, x and y, require these operations. Product x requires 80 minutes for casting, 2.5 minutes for grinding, and 9 minutes for drilling per unit. Product y requires 60 minutes for casting, 4.5 minutes for grinding, and 4 minutes for drilling per unit. Each unit of x contributes $4 to profits, and each unit of y contributes $2. What combination of x and y will maximize profits on a weekly basis?

6. A retired couple supplement their income by making fruit pies, which they sell to a local grocery store. During the month of September they produce apple and grape pies. The apple pies are sold for $1.50 to the grocer, and the grape pies are sold for $1.20. The couple is able to sell all of the pies they produce due to the high quality they maintain. They follow a policy, for instance, of always using fresh ingredients. Flour and sugar are purchased once each month. For the month of September, they have 1,200 cups of sugar and 2,100 cups of flour. Each apple pie requires 1½ cups of sugar and 3 cups of flour, and each grape pie requires 2 cups of sugar and 3 cups of flour. Determine the number of grape and number of apple pies that will maximize revenues if the couple working together can make an apple pie in six minutes and a grape pie in three minutes. They plan to work no more than 60 hours. In addition, determine the amounts of sugar and/or flour that will be unused.

7. Solve Problem 1a using simplex.

8. Solve Problem 1b using simplex, and then determine the following:
   a. The range of feasibility for each constraint.
   b. The range of optimality or insignificance, whichever is appropriate, for the coefficients of the objective function.

9. Solve Problem 3 using simplex, and interpret your answer. Then:

a. Find the range of feasibility for each constraint, and interpret your answers.

b. Determine the range of insignificance or optimality, whichever is appropriate, for each coefficient of the objective function. Interpret your results.

10. Repeat the preceding procedure for Problem 5.

11. Given this information:

Maximize
$$Z = 10.50x + 11.75y + 10.80z$$
subject to
Cutting $5x + 12y + 8z \leq 1,400$ minutes
Stapling $7x + 9y + 9z \leq 1,250$ minutes
Wrapping $4x + 3y + 6z \leq 720$ minutes

a. Solve for the quantities of products x, y, and z that will maximize revenue.

b. Follow the instructions in parts a and b of Problem 9 for this problem.

12. A small firm makes three similar products, which all follow the same three-step process, consisting of milling, inspection, and drilling. Product a requires 12 minutes of milling, 5 minutes for inspection, and 10 minutes of drilling per unit; product b requires 10 minutes of milling, 4 minutes for inspection, and 8 minutes of drilling per unit; and product c requires 8 minutes of milling, 4 minutes for inspection, and 16 minutes of drilling. The department has 20 hours available during the next period for milling, 15 hours for inspection, and 24 hours for drilling. Product a contributes $2.40 per unit to profit, b contributes $2.50 per unit, and c contributes $3.00 per unit. Use the simplex method to determine the optimal mix of products in terms of maximizing contribution to profits for the period. Then, find the range of optimality or insignificance, whichever is appropriate, for the profit coefficient of each variable.

13. Use the simplex method to solve these problems:

a. Minimize $Z = 21x_1 + 18x_2$
subject to
(1) $5x_1 + 10x_2 \geq 100$
(2) $2x_1 + 1x_2 \geq 20$

b. Minimize $Z = 5x + 2y + 3z$
subject to
(1) $16x + 10y + 18z \geq 340$
(2) $11x + 12y + 13z \geq 300$
(3) $2x + 6y + 5z \geq 120$

14. Determine the combination of variables x_1, x_2, x_3, and x_4 that will maximize profits given this LP model:

Maximize
$$Z = 34x_1 + 18x_2 + 27x_3 + 40x_4$$

subject to
Labor $x_1 + x_2 + x_3 + x_4 \leq 4,000$
Product 4 $x_4 \geq 500$
Machine $2x_1 + x_2 + 3x_3 \leq 4,200$
Material A $4x_2 + 3x_4 \leq 2,000$
Material B $x_1 + x_2 + 2x_4 \leq 2,300$

15. Find the combination of A, B, C, D, and E that will maximize revenues given the following information:

Maximize $Z = 1.50A + 2.10B + 3.00C + 1.40D + 1.80E$
subject to
(1) $2A + 8B + D \leq 220$
(2) $A + 3C + E \leq 140$
(3) $4B + 3D + 2E \leq 150$
(4) $5A + 2B + C + 3E \leq 185$
(5) $A + B + C + D + E \leq 50$
(6) $C \leq 10$

16. A wood products firm uses leftover time at the end of each week to make goods for stock. Currently, there are two products on the list of items that are produced for stock: a chopping board and a knife holder. Both items require three operations: cutting, glu-

ing, and finishing. The manager of the firm has collected the followng data on these products:

Item	Profit/Unit	Time per unit (minutes)		
		Cutting	Gluing	Finishing
Chopping board	$2	1.4	5	12
Knife holder	$6	0.8	13	3

The manager has also determined that, during each week, 56 minutes are available for cutting, 650 minutes are available for gluing, and 360 minutes are available for finishing.

a. Determine the optimal quantities of the decision variables.

b. Which resources are not completely used by your solution? How much of each resource is unused?

17. A dietitian has been asked by the athletic director of a university to develop a snack that athletes can use in their training programs. The dietitian intends to mix two separate products together to make the snack. The following information has been obtained by the dietitian:

Nutrient	Minimum amount required (gr.)	Contribution per ounce (gr.)	
		Product A	Product B
Carbohydrates	20	2	5
Protein	12	6	1
Calories	450	90	50

Product A costs $.20 per ounce, and product B costs $.10 per ounce.

a. Determine the optimal quantities of the two products for cost minimization. What is the cost per snack?

b. Are any requirements exceeded? If so, which ones, and by how much?

18. The manager of the deli section of a grocery superstore has just learned that the department has 112 pounds of mayonnaise, of which 70 pounds is approaching its expiration date and must be used. In order to use up the mayonnaise, the manager has decided to prepare two items: a ham spread and a deli spread. Each pan of the ham spread will require 1.4 pounds of the mayonnaise, and each pan of the deli spread will require 1.0 pound. The manager has received an order for 10 pans of ham spread and 8 pans of the deli spread. In addition, the manager has decided to have at least 10 pans of each spread available for sale. Both spreads will cost $3 per pan to make, but ham spread sells for $5 per pan and deli spread sells for $7 per pan.

a. Determine the solution that will minimize cost.

b. Determine the solution that will maximize profit.

19. An advertising firm often uses linear programming to determine an optimal allocation of advertising budgets. Recently, a client asked for a plan that would allocate a $12,000 budget among radio, TV, and newspaper advertisements with the stipulation that no more than 40 percent of the budget be allocated to any one medium. The client wanted a plan that would maximize the effectiveness of advertisements.

The advertising firm did some research that yielded an effectiveness index for each medium and also determined the cost for an ad for each medium, as shown:

Medium	Effectiveness	Cost per ad
Radio	2.4	$200
TV	3.2	400
Newspaper	1.6	300

Determine the number of ads in each medium in order to maximize effectiveness.

20. The owner of a business that makes and sells wood products intends to expand the work schedule by one-half day each week and wants to optimize the use of that additional time. The firm makes five different items: a chair, a table, a desk, a bookcase, and a food serving cart. The respective profits per unit are $16, $30, $40, $42, and $32. The products require essentially the same basic operations: cutting, sanding and finishing, and assembly. The times for these operations differ for the various items. However, the times are fairly standard. They are shown in the following table:

		Time (minutes) per operation	
Item	*Cutting*	*Sanding and finishing*	*Assembly*
Chair	8	12	4
Table	6	10	3
Desk	9	15	5
Bookcase	9	12	4
Food cart	12	8	6

There are 320 minutes available for cutting, 400 for sanding and finishing, and 270 for assembling. What combination of products should be produced in the additional period each week in order to maximize profits? What will the total profit be?

21. A chocolate maker has contracted to operate a small candy counter in a fashionable store. To start with, the selection of offerings will be intentionally limited. The counter will offer a regular mix of candy made up of equal parts of cashews, raisins, caramels, and chocolates, and a deluxe mix that is one-half cashews and one-half chocolates. These will be sold in one-pound boxes. In addition, the candy counter will offer individual one-pound boxes of cashews, raisins, caramels, and chocolates.

A major attraction of the candy counter is that all candies are made fresh right at the counter. However, there is limited storage space for supplies and ingredients. Bins are available that can hold the amounts shown in the table:

Ingredient	*Capacity (pounds per day)*
Cashews	120
Raisins	200
Caramels	100
Chocolates	160

In order to present a good image and to encourage purchases, the counter will make at least 20 boxes of each type of product each day. Any leftover boxes at the end of the day will be removed and given to a nearby nursing home for goodwill.

The profit per box for the various items has been determined as follows:

Item	*Profit per box*
Regular	$.80
Deluxe	.90
Cashews	.70
Raisins	.60
Caramels	.50
Chocolates	.75

a. Formulate the LP model.

b. Solve for the optimal values of the decision variables and the maximum profit.

22. Given the following model:

x_1 = Quantity of regular blend
x_2 = Quantity of extra blend
x_3 = Quantity of Puppy Delite

Maximize $0.20x_1 + 0.18x_2 + 0.25x_3$
subject to

K9	$\frac{1}{3}x_1 + \frac{1}{2}x_2 \leq 1,500$ lbs.
K8	$\frac{1}{3}x_1 + \frac{1}{4}x_2 + \frac{1}{10}x_3 \leq 1,000$ lbs.
K1	$\frac{1}{3}x_1 + \frac{1}{4}x_2 + \frac{9}{10}x_3 \leq 1,000$ lbs.

$x_1, x_2, x_3 \geq 0$

FINAL TABLEAU

C		0.20	0.18	0.25	0	0	0	
	Variables	x_1	x_2	x_3	s_1	s_2	s_3	Quantity
0.18	x_2	0	1	−3.6	4	0	−4	2,000
0	s_2	0	0	−0.8	0	1	−1	0
0.20	x_1	1	0	5.4	−3	0	6	1,500
	Z	0.2	0.18	0.432	0.12	0	0.48	660
	C − Z	0	0	−0.182	−0.12	0	−0.48	

The final tableau is shown above.

a. What is the marginal value of a pound of K9? Over what range is the value valid?

b. By how much would profit decrease if there was one less pound of K1 available?

c. The manager believes it is possible to increase the profit per pound of puppy delite to $.40. Would that alter the optimal solution? Explain.

d. If the profit per unit of the extra blend dropped to $.16 a pound, would the optimal quantities of the variables in solution change? Would the optimal value of the objective function change? If so, what would its new value be?

23. A garden store prepares various grades of pine bark for mulch: nuggets (x_1), mini-nuggets (x_2), and chips (x_3). The process requires pine bark, machine time, labor time, and storage space. The following model has been developed:

Maximize $9x_1 + 9x_2 + 6x_3$ (profit)
subject to
Bark $5x_1 + 6x_2 + 3x_3 \le 600$ pounds
Machine $2x_1 + 4x_1 + 5x_2 \le 660$ minutes
Labor $2x_1 + 4x_2 + 3x_3 \le 480$ hours
Storage $1x_1 + 1x_2 + 1x_3 \le 150$ bags
$x_1, x_2, x_3 \le 0$

In addition, the optimal tableau shown below was obtained:

a. What is the marginal value of a pound of pine bark? Over what range is this price value appropriate?

b. What is the maximum price the store would be justified in paying for additional pine bark?

OPTIMAL TABLEAU

C		9	9	6	0	0	0	0	
	Variables	x_1	x_2	x_3	s_1	s_2	s_3	s_4	Quantity
9	x_1	1	1.5	0	0.5	0	0	1.5	75
0	s_2	0	3.5	0	1.5	1	0	−9.5	135
0	s_3	0	2.5	0	0.5	0	1	−4.5	105
6	x_3	0	−0.5	1	−0.5	0	0	2.5	75
	Z	9	10.5	6	1.5	0	0	1.5	1,125
	C − Z	0	−1.5	0	−1.5	0	0	−1.5	

c. What is the marginal value of labor? Over what range is this value in effect?

d. The manager obtained additional machine time through better scheduling. How much additional machine time can be effectively used for this operation? Why?

e. If the manager can obtain *either* additional pine bark *or* additional storage space, which one should be chosen, and how much should be obtained (assuming additional quantities cost the same as usual)?

f. If a change in the chip operation would increase the profit on chips from $6 per bag to $7 per bag, would the optimal quantities change? Would the value of the objective function change? If so, what would the new value(s) be?

SELECTED BIBLIOGRAPHY

Anderson, David R.; Dennis J. Sweeney; and Thomas A. Williams. *An Introduction to Management Science: Quantitative Approaches to Decision Making*. 5th ed. St. Paul, Minn.: West Publishing, 1988.

Bierman, Harold; Charles P. Bonini; and Warren H. Hausman. *Quantitative Analysis for Business Decisions*. 7th ed. Homewood, Ill.: Richard D. Irwin, 1986.

Cook, Thomas M., and Robert A. Russell. *Introduction to Management Science*. 3rd ed. Englewood Cliffs, N.J.: Prentice-Hall, 1985.

Eppen, G. D.; F. J. Gould; and C. P. Schmidt. *Introductory Management Science*. 2nd ed. Englewood Cliffs, N.J.: Prentice-Hall, 1987.

Levin, Richard; Charles A. Kirkpatrick; and David S. Rubin. *Quantitative Approaches to Management*. 5th ed. New York: McGraw-Hill, 1982.

Stevenson, W. J. *Introduction to Management Science*. Homewood, Ill.: Richard D. Irwin, 1989.

FORECASTING

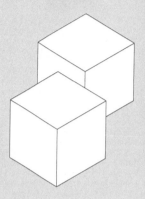

This part deals solely with forecasting (Chapter 3). It is presented early in the book because forecasts are the basis for a wide range of design and operating decisions. Consequently, this chapter serves as a basis for many of the remaining chapters. .

Although forecasts are frequently developed as part of the marketing function, operations people are often called upon to assist in forecast development. More important, though, is the fact that *operations makes major use of forecasts*. Hence, the subject of forecasting is exceedingly important for operations management.

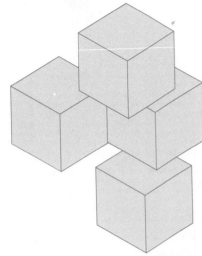

Forecasting

LEARNING OBJECTIVES

After completing this chapter, you should be able to:

1. Describe at least four qualitative forecasting techniques and the advantages and disadvantages of each.
2. Compare and contrast qualitative and quantitative approaches to forecasting.
3. Briefly describe averaging techniques, trend and seasonal techniques, and regression analysis, and solve typical problems.
4. Describe two measures of forecast accuracy.
5. Describe two ways of evaluating and controlling forecasts.
6. Identify the major factors to consider when choosing a forecasting technique.
7. List the elements of a good forecast.
8. Outline the steps in the forecasting process.

Chapter Outline

Planning is an integral part of a manager's job. If uncertainties cloud the planning horizon, it can be quite difficult for a manager to plan effectively. Forecasts can help managers by reducing some of the uncertainty, thereby enabling them to develop more meaningful plans than they might otherwise. A **forecast** is a statement about the future.

This chapter deals with business forecasting. Its purpose is to provide a survey of business forecasting. It covers basic forecasting techniques, how to monitor a forecast, the necessary steps in preparing a forecast, and elements that are common to forecasts.

INTRODUCTION

At one time or another, most of us have witnessed weather forecasts that were flops, even though most of the time the forecasters are close in predicting what the weather will be like. Forecasting demand is a lot like forecasting the weather. In both instances, there is no such thing as a sure bet: predictions usually turn out to be in the ballpark, but occasionally they miss the mark completely. Moreover, in both instances, the forecasts serve as a *basis for planning*. Weather forecasts influence travel and recreation plans, choice of clothing each day, and whether to walk or ride to work. Farmers rely on weather forecasts to determine when to plant and harvest and when to take precautionary steps (e.g., protect against frost). In business, forecasts are the basis for capacity planning, budgeting, sales planning, production and inventory planning, manpower planning, purchasing planning, and more. Forecasts play such an important role in the planning process because they enable managers to *anticipate the future* and to *plan* accordingly.

In a sense, there are two uses of forecasts. One is to help managers *plan the system,* and the other is to help them *plan the use of the system.* Planning the system generally involves making long-range plans concerning the types of products and services to offer, what facilities and equipment to have, where to locate, and so on. Planning the use of the system refers to short- and intermediate-range planning, which involve such tasks as planning inventory and work force levels, planning purchasing and production, budgeting, and scheduling.

It should be noted that business forecasting pertains to more than predicting demand. Forecasts are also used to predict profits, revenues, costs, productivity changes, prices and availability of energy and raw materials, interest rates, movements of key economic indicators (e.g., GNP, inflation, government borrowing), and prices of stocks and bonds, as well as other variables. However, for the sake of simplicity, the focus of the chapter will be on forecasting demand. Nevertheless, the concepts and techniques apply equally well to these other variables.

In spite of the use of computers and sophisticated mathematical models in forecasting, it is not an exact science. Instead, successful forecasting often requires a skillful blending of art and science. Experience, judgment, and technical expertise all play a role in developing useful forecasts. Even so, a certain amount of luck and a dash of humility can be helpful, since the worst forecasters occasionally produce a very good forecast, and even the best forecasters sometimes miss completely. Forecasting techniques currently in use range from the mundane to the exotic. Some work better than others, but no one technique works all of the time.

Generally speaking, the responsibility for preparing demand forecasts lies with marketing or sales rather than operations. Nonetheless, operations people are called on to make certain forecasts as well as to help others to prepare forecasts. In addition, since forecasts are major inputs for many operations decisions, it is essential for operations managers and staff to be knowledgeable about the kinds of forecasting techniques that are available, the assumptions that underlie their use, and their limitations. In other words, forecasting is an integral part of operations management.

FEATURES COMMON TO ALL FORECASTS

There is a wide variety of forecasting techniques in use. In many respects, they are quite different from each other, as you shall soon discover. Nonetheless, there are certain features that are common to all, and it is important to recognize them.

1. Forecasting techniques generally assume that the same underlying causal system that existed in the past will continue to exist in the future.

2. Forecasts are rarely perfect; actual results usually differ from predicted values. The inability to predict precisely how an often-large number of related factors will impinge upon the variable being forecast and the presence of randomness preclude a perfect forecast. Allowances should be made for inaccuracies.

3. Forecasts for groups of items tend to be more accurate than forecasts for individual items because forecasting errors among items in a group usually have a canceling effect. Opportunities for grouping may arise if parts or raw materials are used for multiple products or if a service is demanded by a number of independent sources.

4. Forecast accuracy decreases as the time period covered by the forecast (i.e., the time *horizon*) increases. Generally speaking, short-range forecasts must contend with fewer uncertainties than longer-range forecasts, so they tend to be more accurate.

STEPS IN THE FORECASTING PROCESS

There are five basic steps in the forecasting process:

1. *Determine the purpose* of the forecast and when it will be needed. This will provide an indication of the level of detail required in the forecast, the amount of resources (manpower, computer time, dollars) that can be justified, and the level of accuracy necessary.

2. *Establish a time horizon* that the forecast must cover, keeping in mind that accuracy decreases as the length of the forecast period increases.

3. *Select a forecasting technique.*

4. *Gather and analyze the appropriate data,* and then *prepare the forecast. Identify any assumptions* that are made in conjunction with preparing and using the forecast.

5. *Monitor the forecast* to see if it is performing in a satisfactory manner. If it is not, reexamine the method, assumptions, validity of data, and so on; modify as needed; and prepare a revised forecast.

APPROACHES TO FORECASTING

There are two general approaches to forecasting: qualitative and quantitative. Qualitative methods consist mainly of subjective inputs, which often defy precise numerical description. Quantitative methods involve either the extension of historical data or development of associative models that attempt to utilize *causal variables* to make a forecast.

Qualitative techniques permit inclusion of soft information (human factors, personal opinions, hunches) in the forecasting process. The factors are often omitted or downplayed when quantitative techniques are used because they are difficult or impossible to quantify. Quantitative techniques consist mainly of analyzing objective, or hard, data. They usually avoid personal biases that sometimes contaminate qualitative methods. In practice, either or both approaches might be used to develop a given forecast. Sometimes the two approaches can serve as a check on each other.

Forecasts Based on Judgment and Opinion

Judgmental forecasts rely on analysis of subjective inputs obtained from various sources, such as consumer surveys, the sales staff, managers and executives, and panels of experts. Quite frequently, these sources provide insights that are not otherwise available.

Forecasts Based on Historical Data

Some forecasting techniques depend on uncovering relationships between variables that can be used to predict future values of one of them; others simply attempt to project past experience into the future. The second of these approaches exemplifies forecasts that use historical, or time series, data. The theme of that approach is that the future will be like the past. Some of the models merely attempt to smooth out random variations in historical data, and others attempt to identify specific patterns in the data. In effect, approaches based on historical data treat the data as a mirror that reflects the combination of all forces influencing the variable of interest (e.g., demand), without trying to identify or measure those forces directly.

Associative Forecasts

Associative models involve identification of one or more variables that can be used to predict future demand. For example, demand for paint might be related to such variables as the price per gallon and the amount spent on advertising, as well as specific characteristics of the paint (e.g., drying time, ease of cleanup). The analysis in such cases yields a mathematical equation that enables the manager to predict volume of sales, for example, on the basis of given values of the "explaining" variable(s).

The discussion of forecasting techniques begins with techniques that are based on judgment and opinion.

FORECASTS BASED ON JUDGMENT AND OPINION

When a forecast must be prepared quickly, there is usually not enough time to gather and analyze quantitative data. At other times, especially when political and economic conditions are changing, available data may be obsolete, and more up-to-date information might not yet be available. Similarly, the introduction of new products, as well as the redesign of existing products or packaging, all suffer from the absence of historical data that would be useful in forecasting. In such instances, forecasts based on judgment and experience are commonly used. Among those techniques are forecasts that use executive opinions, consumer surveys, opinions of the sales staff, and opinions of experts.

Executive Opinions

A small group of upper-level managers (e.g., marketing, product, engineering, manufacturing, and financial managers) may meet and collectively develop a forecast. This approach is often used as a part of long-range planning and new product development. It has the advantage of bringing together the considerable knowledge and talents of these top management people. However, there is the risk that the view of one person will prevail, as well as the possibility that diffusing responsibility for the forecast over the entire group may result in less pressure to produce a good forecast.

Sales Force Composite

The sales staff is often a good source of information because of its direct contact with consumers. Thus, these people are often aware of any plans the customers may be considering for the future. There are, however, several drawbacks to this approach. One is that salespeople may be unable to distinguish between what customers would *like* to do and what they actually *will* do. Another is that salespeople are sometimes overly influenced by recent experiences. Thus, after several periods of low sales, their estimates may tend to become pessimistic, and after several periods of good sales, they may tend to be too optimistic. In addition, if forecasts are to be used to establish sales quotas, there will be a conflict of interest because it would be to the salesperson's advantage to provide low sales estimates.

Consumer Surveys

Since the consumer is the one who will ultimately determine demand, it seems natural to solicit input from consumers. In some instances, every customer or potential customer can be contacted. In most cases, however, there are either too many customers or there is no way to identify all potential customers. Because of these and similar factors, organizations that seek consumer input usually resort to the use of consumer surveys, which enable them to *sample* consumer opinions. The obvious advantage of such surveys is that they can tap information that might not be available elsewhere. On the other hand, surveys require a considerable amount of skill to handle correctly. A great deal of care is necessary to construct a survey, administer it, and correctly interpret the results in order to obtain valid information. In addition, even under the best of conditions, surveys involving the general public must contend with the possibility of irrational behavior patterns. For example, much thoughtful information gathering done by consumers before purchasing a new car is often undermined by the glitter of a new car showroom or a high-pressure sales pitch. Along the same lines, low response rates to a mail survey should (but often don't) make the results suspect.

   If these and similar pitfalls can be avoided, surveys can produce useful information both for forecasting and for product design and promotion.

Outside Opinion

Occasionally, outside opinions are needed to make a forecast. This may concern advice on political or economic conditions in the United States or in a foreign country or some other aspect of interest with which an organization lacks familiarity.

Opinions of Managers and Staff

A manager may use staff to generate a forecast or to provide several forecasting alternatives from which to choose. At other times, a manager may solicit opinions from a number of other managers and/or staff people. The **Delphi method** is sometimes useful in this regard. It involves circulating a series of questionnaires among those individuals who possess the knowledge and ability to contribute meaningfully. Responses are kept anonymous, which tends to encourage honest responses. Each new questionnaire is developed using any information extracted from the previous one, thus enlarging the scope of information on which participants can base their judgments. The goal is to achieve a consensus forecast.

The Delphi technique originated in the Rand Corporation in 1948, where it was used to assess the potential impact of an atomic bomb attack on the United States. Since that time, it has been applied to a variety of situations, not all of which involve forecasting. However, the discussion here will be limited to its use as a forecasting tool.

As a forecasting tool, the Delphi technique is useful for *technological* forecasting. That is, the technique is a method for assessing changes in technology and their impact on an organization. Often the goal is to predict *when* a certain event will occur. For instance, the goal of a Delphi forecast might be to predict when video telephones might be installed in at least 50 percent of residential homes or when a vaccine for a disease might be developed and ready for mass distribution. For the most part, these are long-term, single-time forecasts. In these situations, there is usually very little hard information to go by, or data are costly to obtain, so the problem does not lend itself to analytical techniques. Rather, judgments of experts or others who possess sufficient knowledge to make predictions are used.

The first step in the Delphi process is the establishment of a small group of individuals who will design the study. This group is the Delphi committee. They will first decide the channel of communication (e.g., mail, hand delivery, computer), the size of the group to be queried, and the participants. Next, the initial questionnaire must be developed. It must be constructed in such a way that it elicits opinions unambiguously. This is essential to achieve a true consensus from the group. The initial questionnaire must introduce the desired purpose and scope and focus on the desired points, factors, and opinions. Pretesting of the questionnaire to insure its validity is very important. Next, the questionnaire is distributed to the participants for their initial inputs and returned to the Delphi committee, which then compiles the results. Using this information, the committee develops and distributes a second questionnaire. This second questionnaire usually asks respondents to expand on key factors or place priorities on key items. This questionnaire receives cursory pretesting to eliminate ambiguities along with the results of the initial questionnaire. The reason for including the initial results is to exert pressure to conform; since it is human nature to conform, the feedback these results provide helps the process. The process is repeated with a third questionnaire. If there is to be a consensus, it will usually be achieved by this point. Hence, the process usually terminates after the third questionnaire. At that point, the forecast can be made, assuming consensus has been reached. Otherwise, the process may be started all over, perhaps with some new participants, a revised questionnaire, or a completely different approach to the problem (e.g., a face-to-face meeting of a few key experts).

There are a number of reasons for considering a Delphi approach. Among them are the following:

1. A group of experts can provide needed judgmental input.
2. More individuals may be needed than can effectively interact in a face-

to-face situation, and/or the individuals cannot be conveniently assembled in one place. Time and cost can also be factors.

3. It is important to avoid a "bandwagon effect."

4. It is desirable to preserve the anonymity of the participants.

5. There is controlled feedback between rounds and a statistical summary
    of group responses.

6. It is highly useful for situations that involve the creation of event sce-
    narios ("what if . . . ?").

There are also a number of weaknesses in the Delphi approach, some of
them fairly serious. Among them are the following:

1. The questions may contain ambiguous phrasing so that panel members
    reach a false consensus.

2. Panel membership may change, especially if the process requires a long
    time (some may take a year or more).

3. The "experts" may not be experts.

4. Studies have failed to prove that Delphi forecasts generally achieve a
    high degree of accuracy.

5. The process (questionnaire development, administration, and evalua-
    tion) in many instances does not meet the criteria of the American
    Psychological Association.[1]

6. Preserving anonymity removes accountability and responsibility.

7. Results are difficult or impossible to replicate.

FORECASTS THAT USE TIME SERIES DATA

A **time series** is a time-ordered sequence of observations taken at regular
intervals over a period of time (hourly, daily, weekly, monthly, quarterly,
annually, and so on). Common examples include measurements of demand,
earnings, profits, shipments, accidents, output, precipitation, productivity,
and the consumer price index. Forecasting techniques that are based on time
series data are predicated on the assumption that future values of the series can
be estimated from past values of the series. In spite of the fact that no attempt is
made to identify variables that influence the series, these methods are widely
used, often with very satisfactory results.

Analysis of time series data requires the analyst to identify the underlying
behavior of the series. This can often be accomplished by merely *plotting* the
data and visually examining the plot. One or more of the following behaviors
might appear: trend, seasonal variations, cycles, and variations around an
average. In addition, there can be random and irregular variations. These
behaviors can be described as follows:

---

[1] Harold Sackman, *Delphi Critique* (Lexington, Mass.: Lexington Books, 1975), p. 27.

1. **Trend** refers to a gradual, long-term movement in the data. Population shifts, changing incomes, and cultural changes often account for such movements.
2. **Seasonality** refers to short-term, fairly regular variations that are generally related to weather factors or to human-made factors such as holidays and vacations. Restaurants, supermarkets, and theaters experience weekly and even daily "seasonal" variations.
3. **Cycles** are wavelike variations of more than one year's duration. These are often related to a variety of economic and political factors and even agricultural conditions.
4. **Irregular variations** are due to unusual circumstances such as severe weather conditions, strikes, or a major change in a product or service. They do not reflect typical behavior, and inclusion in the series can distort the overall picture. Whenever possible, these should be identified and removed from the data.
5. **Random variations** are the residual variations that remain after all of the other behaviors have been accounted for. These behaviors are illustrated in Figure 3–1. The small "bumps" in the plots represent random variability.

In the remainder of this section, various approaches to the analysis of time series data are described. Before turning to those discussions, one point should be emphasized: A demand forecast should be based on a time series of past *demand* rather than sales. Sales would not truly reflect demand unless demand was less than the amount of a good or service available for sale. Similarly, shipments would not truly reflect demand if there are backlogs of orders; the timing of shipments would not correspond to the timing of demand.

Techniques for Averaging

Historical data typically contain a certain amount of random variation, or *noise,* that tends to obscure systematic movements in the data. This randomness arises from the combined influence of many—perhaps a great many—relatively unimportant factors, and it cannot be reliably predicted. Ideally, it would be desirable to completely remove any randomness from the data and leave only "real" variations, such as changes in the *level* of demand (e.g., a step or a ramp change). However, as a practical matter, it is usually impossible to distinguish these two kinds of variations, so the best one can hope for is to smooth out the randomness but leave the nonrandom variations intact. In effect, small variations are treated as random—they are smoothed out. Averaging techniques are often used for this purpose.

Averaging techniques smooth out some of the fluctuations in a time series because the individual highs and lows in the data offset each other when they are combined into an average. A forecast based on an average thus tends to exhibit less variability than the original data (see Figure 3–2). This can be

FIGURE 3–1

Trend, seasonal,
cyclical, random, and
irregular variations

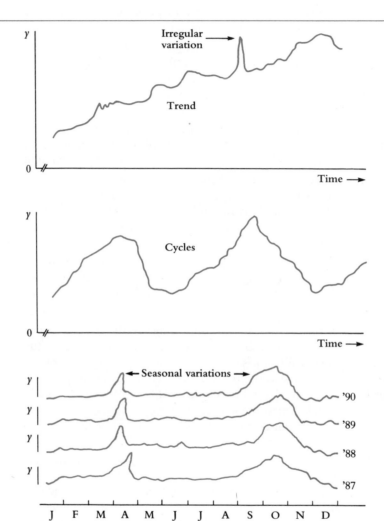

FIGURE 3–2

Averaging applied to
three possible patterns

Data

Forecast — — — —

Ideal   Step change   Gradual change

advantageous because many of these movements merely reflect random variability rather than a true change in level, or trend, in the series. Moreover, because response to changes in expected demand often can represent considerable cost (e.g., changes in production rate, changes in the size of a work force, inventory changes), it is desirable to avoid reacting to minor variations. In effect, minor variations are treated as random variations, whereas larger variations are viewed as more likely to reflect "real" changes, although these, too, are smoothed to a certain degree.

Averaging techniques generate a forecast that reflects recent values of a time series (e.g., the average value over the last several periods). These techniques work best when a series tends to vary around an average, although they can handle step changes or gradual changes in the level of the series. Three techniques for averaging are described in this section:

1. Naive forecasts.
2. Moving averages.
3. Exponential smoothing.

Naive Forecasts.   The simplest forecasting technique is the naive method. A **naive forecast** for any period equals the previous period's actual value. For example, if demand last week was 50 units, the naive forecast for the upcoming week is 50 units. Similarly, if demand in the upcoming week turns out to be 54 units, the forecast for the following week would be 54 units.

Although at first glance the naive approach may appear *too* simplistic, it is nonetheless a legitimate forecasting tool. Consider the advantages: It has vitually no cost, it is quick and easy to prepare a forecast because data analysis is nonexistent, and it is easy for users to understand. The main objection to this method is its inability to provide highly accurate forecasts. However, if resulting accuracy is acceptable, this approach deserves serious consideration. Moreover, even if other forecasting techniques offer better accuracy, they will almost always involve a greater cost. The accuracy of a naive forecast can serve as a standard of comparison against which to judge the cost and accuracy of other techniques. Hence, managers must answer the question: Is the increased accuracy of another method worth the additional resources required to achieve that accuracy?

The naive concept can also be applied to a series that exhibits seasonality or trend. For example, if monthly sales exhibit a seasonal pattern, demand for the current December can be based on demand for the preceding December, demand for January can be based on demand from the preceding January, and so on. Similarly, if trend is present, the increase (or decrease) from this period's actual demand to the next period's demand can be estimated as the same as the change observed between the last two periods. For instance, if June's demand is 90 units higher than May's demand, a naive forecast for July that allowed for trend would be June's actual demand plus an additional 90 units. Then, if July's demand was only 85 units greater than June's, August's forecast would be July's actual plus 85 units.

Moving Averages.   One weakness of the naive method is that it causes the forecast to *trace* the actual data, with a lag of one period; it does not smooth at all. But by expanding the amount of historical data a forecast is based on, this difficulty can be overcome. A **moving average** forecast uses a *number* of the most recent actual data values in generating a forecast. The moving average forecast can be computed using the following equation:

$$MA_n = \frac{\sum_{i=1}^{n} A_i}{n} \qquad (3\text{--}1)$$

where

$$i = \text{``Age'' of the data } (i = 1,2,3 \ldots)$$
$$n = \text{Number of periods in the moving average}$$
$$A_i = \text{Actual value with age } i$$

For example, MA_3 would imply a three-period moving average.

EXAMPLE 1

Compute a three-period moving average forecast given demand for shopping carts for the last five periods:

Period	Age	Demand
1	5	42
2	4	40
3	3	43
4	2	40
5	1	41

Solution

$$MA_3 = \frac{43 + 40 + 41}{3} = 41.33$$

If actual demand in period 6 turns out to be 39, the moving average forecast for period 7 would be:

$$MA_3 = \frac{40 + 41 + 39}{3} = 40.00$$

Note that in a moving average, as each new actual value becomes available, the forecast is updated by adding the newest value and dropping the oldest and then recomputing the average. Consequently, the forecast "moves" by reflecting only the most recent values.

In computing a moving average, the "age" column shown in the preceding example would not be included; it is shown merely to illustrate the concept.

FIGURE 3—3

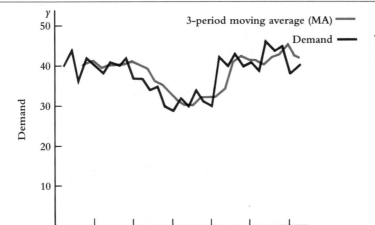

Instead, it would simplify computation to include a *moving total* column, which gives the sum of the *n* most current values from which the average will be computed. It is relatively simple to update the moving total: Subtract the oldest value from the newest value, and add that amount to the moving total for each update.

Figure 3–3 illustrates a three-period moving average forecast plotted against actual demand over 31 periods. Note how the moving average forecast lags the actual values and how smooth the forecasted values are compared to the actual values.

The moving average can incorporate as many data points as desired, beginning with the latest value and working backward. Hence, a 10-period moving average forecast would be the average of the latest 10 actual values. In selecting the number of periods to include in a moving average, the decision maker must take into account that the number of data points in the average determines its sensitivity to each new data point: The fewer the data points in an average, the more responsive the average tends to be, as depicted in Figure 3–4. Hence, if responsiveness is important, a moving average with relatively few data points should be used. This will permit quick adjustment to, say, a step change in the data, but it will also cause the forecast to be somewhat responsive even to random variations. Conversely, moving averages based on more data points will smooth more but be less responsive to "real" changes. Hence, the decision maker must weigh the cost of responding more slowly to changes in the data against the cost of responding to what might simply be random variations.

The advantages of a moving average forecast are that it is easy to compute and easy to understand. A disadvantage is that data storage requirements can be significant, especially if large numbers of moving average forecasts are being made. This is because individual values that make up the average must

FIGURE 3–4

The more periods in a moving average, the greater the forecast will lag changes in the data

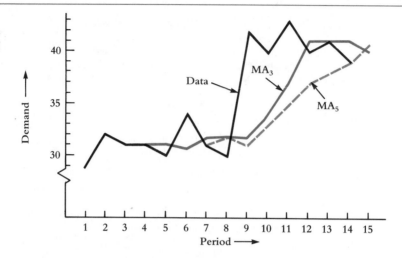

be separately identified so that with each new forecast, the oldest value can be discarded. A more serious consideration is that all values in the average are weighted equally. Hence, in a 10-period moving average, each value is given a weight of ⅟₁₀: the oldest value is given the *same weight* as the most recent value. Decreasing the number of values in the average will increase the weight of more recent values, but this will be at the expense of losing potential information from less recent values.

Exponential Smoothing. **Exponential smoothing** is an averaging technique that reduces these difficulties. Data storage requirements are minimal (only the most recent actual value must be stored), even though the forecast is based on many of the values in the series. In addition, the weights given to previous values are not equal; instead, they decrease with the age of the data, as illustrated in Figure 3–5.

FIGURE 3–5

Relative weights in exponential smoothing

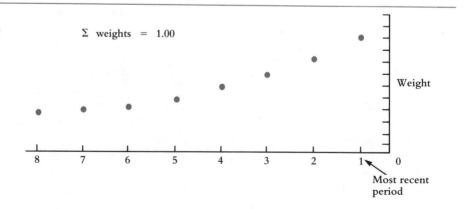

The method is relatively easy to use and understand. Each new forecast is based on the previous forecast plus a percentage of the difference between that forecast and the actual value of the series at that point. That is:

New forecast = Old forecast + α(Actual − Old forecast)

where α is a percentage and (Actual − Old forecast) represents the forecast error. More concisely,

$$F_t = F_{t-1} + \alpha(A_{t-1} - F_{t-1}) \tag{3–2}$$

where

$$
\begin{aligned}
F_t &= \text{Forecast for period } t \\
F_{t-1} &= \text{Forecast for period } t - 1 \\
\alpha &= \text{Smoothing constant} \\
A_{t-1} &= \text{Actual demand or sales for period } t - 1
\end{aligned}
$$

The smoothing constant, α, represents a percentage of the forecast error. Each new forecast is equal to the previous forecast plus a percentage of the previous error. For example, suppose the previous forecast was 42 units, actual demand was 40 units, and $\alpha = .10$. The new forecast would be computed as follows:

$$F_t = 42 + .10(40 - 42) = 41.8$$

Then, if the actual demand turns out to be 43, the next forecast would be:

$$F_t = 41.8 + .10(43 - 41.8) = 41.92$$

The sensitivity of forecast adjustment to error is determined by the smoothing constant, α. The closer its value is to zero, the slower the forecast will be to adjust to forecast errors (i.e., the greater the smoothing). Conversely, the closer the value of α is to 1.00, the greater the sensitivity and the less the smoothing. This is illustrated in the continuation of this series in Example 2.

Selecting a smoothing constant is basically a matter of judgment or trial and error. The goal is to select a smoothing constant that will balance the benefits of smoothing random variations with the benefits of responding to real` changes if and when they occur. Commonly used values range from .05 to .50.

Some computer packages include a feature that permits automatic modification of the smoothing constant if the forecast errors become unacceptably large.

EXAMPLE 2

Use exponential smoothing to develop a series of forecasts for the following data, and compute (Actual − Forecast) = Error for each period.

a.   Use a smoothing factor of .10.
b.   Use a smoothing factor of .40.

EXAMPLE 2 *(concluded)*

c. Plot the actual data and both sets of forecasts on a single graph.

t Period	Actual Demand
1	42
2	40
3	43
4	40
5	41
6	39
7	46
8	44
9	45
10	38
11	40
12	

Solution

t Period	Actual Demand	α = .10 Forecast	Error	α = .40 Forecast	Error
1	42	—	—	—	—
2	40	42	−2	42	−2
3	43	41.8	1.2	41.2	1.8
4	40	41.92	−1.92	41.92	−1.92
5	41	41.73	−0.73	41.15	−0.15
6	39	41.66	−2.66	41.09	−2.09
7	46	41.39	4.61	40.25	5.75
8	44	41.85	2.15	42.55	1.45
9	45	42.06	2.94	43.13	1.87
10	38	42.35	−4.35	43.88	−5.88
11	40	41.92	−1.91	41.53	−1.53
12		41.73		40.92	

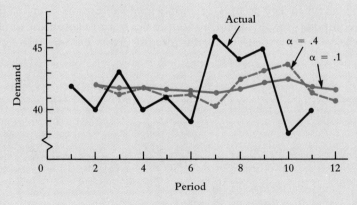

Exponential smoothing is one of the most widely used techniques in forecasting, partly because of its minimal data storage requirements and ease of calculation and partly because of the ease with which the weighting scheme can be altered (i.e., by simply changing the value of α).

A number of different approaches can be used to obtain a starting forecast (e.g., average the first several periods, use a subjective estimate, use the first actual as the forecast for the following period). One approach is to use an average of data over the *first n* periods, where *n* is computed as:

$$n = \frac{2}{\alpha} - 1 \qquad (3-3)$$

The resulting value should be rounded to the nearest integer. For example, suppose $\alpha = .10$. Then, $n = 2/.10 - 1 = 19$. One drawback of this approach is that small values of α produce large values of *n*, which requires considerable data that might not be available. An alternative would be to take an average of the *first four* values as a starting forecast.

The weighting pattern of exponential smoothing can be seen more readily by rewriting the equation

$$F_t = F_{t-1} + \alpha(A_{t-1} - F_{t-1})$$

by grouping the F_{t-1} terms:

$$F_t = \alpha A_{t-1} + (1 - \alpha)F_{t-1}$$

and then expanding:

$$F_t = \alpha A_{t-1} + (1 - \alpha)[\alpha A_{t-2} + (1 - \alpha)F_{t-2}]$$

We can continue to expand, to produce an equation of the form:

$$F_t = \alpha A_{t-1} + \alpha(1 - \alpha)A_{t-2} + \alpha(1 - \alpha)^2 A a_{t-3} + \alpha(1 - \alpha)^3 A_{t-4} + \cdots$$

For $\alpha = .2$, this becomes

$$F_t = .2A_{t-1} + .16A_{t-2} + .128A_{t-3} + .1024A_{t-4} + \cdots$$

and for $\alpha = .5$, this becomes:

$$F_t = .5A_{t-1} + .25A_{t-2} + .125A_{t-3} + .0625A_{t-4} + \cdots$$

Techniques for Trend

The trend component of a time series reflects the effects of any long-term factors on the series. Analysis of trend involves searching for an equation that will suitably describe trend (assuming that trend is, in fact, present in the data). The trend component may be linear, or it may not. Some commonly encountered nonlinear trend functions are illustrated in Figure 3–6. A simple plot of the data can often reveal the nature of the trend component. The discussion here will focus exclusively on linear trend because linear trends are fairly common and because they are the easiest to work with.

FIGURE 3–6

Graphs of some common nonlinear trends

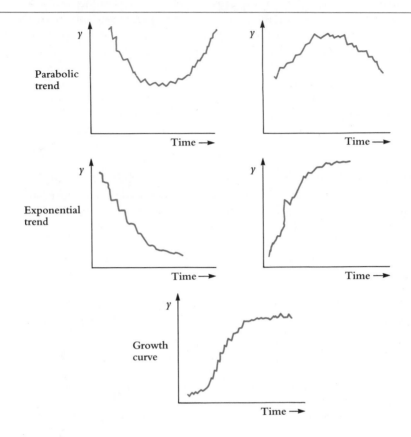

There are two important techniques that can be used to develop forecasts when trend is present. One involves use of a trend equation, and the other is an extension of exponential smoothing.

Trend equation. A **linear trend equation** has the form

$$y_t = a + bt \tag{3–4}$$

where

$$
\begin{aligned}
t &= \text{Specified number of time periods from } t = 0 \\
y_t &= \text{Forecast for period } t \\
a &= \text{Value of } y_t \text{ at } t = 0 \\
b &= \text{Slope of the line}
\end{aligned}
$$

For example, consider the trend equation $y_t = 45 + 5t$. The value of y_t when $t = 0$ is 45, and the slope of the line is 5, which means that, on the average, the value of y_t will increase by 5 units for each 1-unit increase in t. If $t = 10$, the forecast, y_t, is $45 + 5(10) = 95$ units. The equation can be plotted by finding two points on the line. One can be found by substituting some value of t into the equation (e.g., $t = 10$) and then solving for y_t. The other point is a (i.e., y_t at $t = 0$). Plotting those two points and drawing a line through them will yield a graph of the linear trend line.

The coefficients of the line, a and b, can be computed from historical data using these two equations:

$$b = \frac{n\Sigma ty - \Sigma t \Sigma y}{n\Sigma t^2 - (\Sigma t)^2} \tag{3-5}$$

$$a = \frac{\Sigma y - b\Sigma t}{n} \tag{3-6}$$

where

$$n = \text{Number of periods}$$
$$y = \text{Value of the time series}$$

These equations are identical to those used for computing a linear regression line, except that t replaces x in the equations. Manual computation of the coefficients of a trend line can be simplified by use of Table 3–1, which lists values of Σt and Σt^2 for up to 20 ($n = 20$) periods.

TABLE 3–1

Values of Σt and Σt^2

n	Σt	Σt^2
1	1	1
2	3	5
3	6	14
4	10	30
5	15	55
6	21	91
7	28	140
8	36	204
9	45	285
10	55	385
11	66	506
12	78	650
13	91	819
14	105	1,015
15	120	1,240
16	136	1,496
17	153	1,785
18	171	2,109
19	190	2,470
20	210	2,870

EXAMPLE 3

Calculator sales for a California-based firm over the last 10 weeks are shown in the following table. Plot the data, and visually check to see if a linear trend line would be appropriate. Then determine the equation of the trend line, and predict sales for weeks 11 and 12.

Week	Unit sales
1	700
2	724
3	720
4	728
5	740
6	742
7	758
8	750
9	770
10	775

Solution

a. A plot suggests that a linear trend would be appropriate:

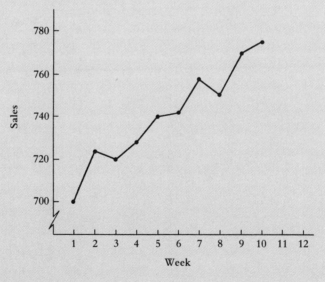

b.

Week (t)	y	ty
1	700	700
2	724	1,448
3	720	2,160
4	728	2,912

EXAMPLE 3 *(concluded)*

Week (t)	y	ty
5	740	3,700
6	742	4,452
7	758	5,306
8	750	6,000
9	770	6,930
10	775	7,750
	7,407	41,358

From Table 3–1, for $n = 10$, $\Sigma t = 55$ and $\Sigma t^2 = 385$. Using formulas 3–5 and 3–6, we can compute the coefficients of the trend line:

$$b = \frac{10(41,358) - 55(7,407)}{10(385) - 55(55)} = \frac{6,195}{825} = 7.51$$

$$a = \frac{7,407 - 7.51(55)}{10} = 699.40$$

Thus, the trend line is $y_t = 699.40 + 7.51t$, where $t = 0$ for period 0.

c. By substituting values of t into this equation, we can obtain forecasts for future periods. For the next two periods ($t = 11$ and $t = 12$), the forecasts are:

$$y_{11} = 699.40 + 7.51(11) = 782$$
$$y_{12} = 699.40 + 7.51(12) = 789.51$$

d. For purposes of illustration, the original data, the trend line, and the two projections (forecasts) are shown on the following graph:

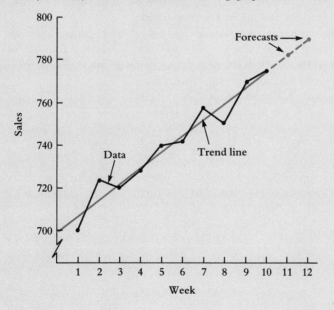

Trend–Adjusted Exponential Smoothing.   A variation of simple exponential smoothing can be used when a time series includes trend. It is called **trend-adjusted exponential smoothing** or, sometimes, *double smoothing,* to differentiate it from simple exponential smoothing, which is appropriate only when data vary around an average or have step or gradual changes. If a series exhibits trend, and simple smoothing is used on it, the forecasts will all *lag* the trend. For example, if the data are increasing, each forecast will be too low. Conversely, decreasing data will result in forecasts that are too high. Again, plotting the data can indicate when trend-adjusted smoothing would be preferable to simple smoothing.

The trend-adjusted forecast (TAF) is composed of two elements: a smoothed error and a trend factor:

$$TAF_{t+1} = S_t + T_t \qquad\qquad (3\text{–}7)$$

where

$$S_t = \text{Smoothed error}$$
$$T_t = \text{Current trend estimate}$$

and

$$S_t = TAF_t + \alpha_1(A_t - TAF_t)$$
$$T_t = T_{t-1} + \alpha_2(TAF_t - TAF_{t-1} - T_{t-1})$$

where α_1 and α_2 are smoothing constants. In order to use this method, one must select values of α_1 and α_2 (usually through trial and error) and make a starting forecast and an estimate of trend.

Suppose a manager estimates a trend of $+9.3$ units, based on the change from period 1 to 4 (see p. 150), and uses a starting forecast of 737.3 with $\alpha_1 = .4$ and $\alpha_2 = .3$. If the next actual value is 740, the TAF for the following period would be computed in this manner:

$$S_t = 737.3 + .4(740 - 737.3) = 738.38$$
$$T_t = 9.3 + .3(0) = 9.30$$
$$TAF_{t+1} = S_t + T_t = 738.38 + 9.30 = 747.68$$

Note that since this is the initial forecast, no previous error is available, so a value of zero is used for the $(TAF_t - TAF_{t-1} - T_{t-1})$ term. If the next actual value is 742, the next TAF would be:

$$S_{t+1} = 747.68 + .4(742 - 747.68) = 745.41$$
$$T_{t+1} = 9.30 + .3(747.68 - 737.30 - 9.30) = 9.62$$
$$TAF_{t+2} = 745.41 + 9.62 = 755.03$$

These are the first few calculations for the following example.

EXAMPLE 4

Using the calculator data from the previous example (where it was concluded that the data exhibited a linear trend), use trend-adjusted exponential smoothing to prepare forecasts for periods 5 through 11, with $\alpha_1 = .4$ and $\alpha_2 = .3$.

Solution

The initial estimate of trend is based on the net change of 28 for the *three* changes from period 1 to period 4, for an average of 9.30. The data and calculations are shown in Table 3–2.

A plot of the actual data and predicted values is shown below.

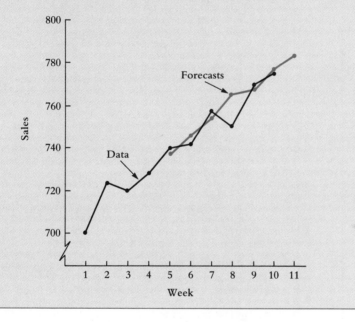

Although manual computations are somewhat more involved for trend-adjusted smoothing than for a linear trend line, trend-adjusted smoothing has the ability to adjust to *changes* in trend. Of course, trend projections are much simpler with a trend line than with trend-adjusted forecasts, so a manager must decide which benefits are most important in choosing between these two techniques for trend.

Techniques for Seasonality

Seasonal variations in time series data are regularly repeating upward or downward movements in series values that can be tied to recurring events. Familiar examples of seasonality relate to weather variations (e.g., sales of winter and summer sports equipment) and vacations or holidays (e.g., airline

TABLE 3–2

t (Period)	A_t (Actual)
1	700
2	724
3	720
4	728

Model development

Trend estimate $= \dfrac{728 - 700}{3} = \dfrac{28}{3} = 9.30$

Starting forecast $= 728 + 9.30 = 737.30$

$\mathrm{TAF}_t + \alpha_1(A_t - \mathrm{TAF}_t) = S_t$	$T_{t-1} + \alpha_2(\mathrm{TAF}_t - \mathrm{TAF}_{t-1} - T_{t-1}) = T_t$
$737.30 + .4(740 - 737.30) = 738.38$	$9.30 + .3(0) = 9.30$
$747.68 + .4(742 - 747.68) = 745.41$	$9.30 + .3(747.68 - 737.30 - 9.30) = 9.62$
$755.03 + .4(758 - 755.03) = 756.22$	$9.62 + .3(755.03 - 747.68 - 9.62) = 8.94$
$765.16 + .4(750 - 765.16) = 759.10$	$8.94 + .3(765.16 - 755.03 - 8.94) = 9.30$
$768.40 + .4(770 - 768.40) = 769.04$	$9.30 + .3(768.40 - 765.16 - 9.30) = 7.48$
$776.52 + .4(775 - 776.52) = 775.91$	$7.48 + .3(776.52 - 768.40 - 7.48) = 7.67$
$783.58 = 775.91 + 7.67$	

(Periods 5–10: Model test; Period 11: Forecast)

travel, greeting card sales, visitors at tourist and resort centers). Seasonality often is used to refer to regular annual variations. However, the term *seasonal variation* also is applied to daily, weekly, monthly, and other regularly recurring patterns in data. For example, rush hour traffic occurs twice a day: incoming in the morning and outgoing in the late afternoon. Theaters and restaurants often find weekly demand patterns, with demand higher later in the week than earlier. Banks may experience daily seasonal variations (heavier traffic during the noon hour and just before closing), weekly variations (heavier toward the end of the week), and monthly variations (heaviest around the end of the month because of social security checks, payrolls, and welfare checks being cashed or deposited). Mail volume; sales of toys, beer, automobiles, and turkeys; highway usage; hotel registrations; and gardening are common examples of seasonal variations.

Seasonality in data is expressed relative to the *average* value of a time series (i.e., to the value if seasonality were not present). Most often, seasonal variations are stated as *percentages* of the series average at a particular point in time. For example, the seasonal relative for November for toy sales may be 1.20, or 120 percent. This tells us that November toy sales are 20 percent *above* average. If the seasonal relative for March is .92, this means that March sales are 92 percent of average, or 8 percent *below* the average if seasonality were not present. Thus, a seasonal relative reflects the amount by which a value differs from the expected average for that time period.

Knowledge of seasonality variations is an important factor in planning and scheduling in many retail businesses. Moreover, seasonality can be an important factor in capacity planning for systems that must be designed to handle peak loads (e.g, public transportation, electric power plants, highways and bridges). Knowledge of the extent of seasonality in a time series can enable one to *remove* seasonality from the data (i.e., to "seasonally adjust" data) in order to discern other movement, or lack of movement, in the series. Thus, we frequently read or hear about "seasonally adjusted unemployment" and "seasonally adjusted personal income."

The simplest seasonal model is a variation of the naive technique described for averages. Instead of using the last *period's* actual demand as the forecast amount, the seasonal naive model uses last *season's* actual amount for the forecast. Hence, our forecast of theater attendance this Friday evening would equal last Friday's attendance using the seasonal naive model, and November toys sales in one year might be estimated based on toy sales in the preceding year. If trend and seasonal variations are present, the naive model might be the last seasonal's demand plus 10 percent, or whatever increase or decrease is appropriate. (See Figure 3–7.)

Again, the naive approach either can be used alone or can serve as a standard of comparison against which other, more refined techniques can be judged.

Centered Moving Average. A commonly used method for representing the trend portion of a time series involves a **centered moving average.** Computations are the same as for a moving average forecast, as are the

FIGURE 3—7

Naive approaches with seasonality

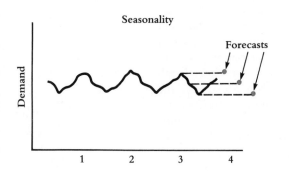
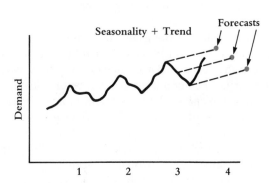

resulting values. However, the values are not projected as in a forecast; instead, they are *positioned in the middle* of the periods used to compute the moving average. The implication is that the average is most representative of that point in the series. For example, suppose we have the following time series data:

Period	Demand	Three-Period Centered Average	
1	40		
2	46	42.67	$\text{Average} = \dfrac{40 + 46 + 42}{3} = 42.67$
3	42		

The three-period average is 42.67. As a centered average, it would be positioned at period 2; the average is most representative of the series at that point. The ratio of demand at period 2 to this centered average at period 2 is an estimate of the seasonal relative at that point.

Because the ratio is $46/42.67 = 1.08$, the series is about 8 percent above average at this point. In order to achieve a reasonable estimate of seasonality for any season (e.g., Friday attendance at a theater), it is usually necessary to compute seasonal ratios for a number of seasons and then average these ratios. For instance, in the case of theater attendance, average the relatives of five or six Fridays for the Friday relative, average five or six Saturdays for the Saturday relative, and so on.

EXAMPLE 5

The manager of a parking lot has computed daily relatives for the number of cars per day in his lot. The computations are repeated here (about three weeks are shown for illustration). A seven-period centered moving average is used because there are seven days (seasons) per week.

Example 5 *(concluded)*

Day	Volume	Moving Total	Centered MA$_7$	Volume/MA
Tues	67			
Wed	75			
Thur	82			
Fri	98		71.86	98/71.86 = 1.36 (Friday)
Sat	90		70.86	90/70.86 = 1.27
Sun	36		70.57	36/70.57 = 0.51
Mon	55	503 ÷ 7 =	71.00	55/71.00 = 0.77
Tues	60	496 ÷ 7 =	71.14	60/71.14 = 0.84 (Tuesday)
Wed	73	494 etc.	70.57	73/70.57 = 1.03
Thur	85	497 .	71.14	85/71.14 = 1.19
Fri	99	498 .	70.71	99/70.71 = 1.40 (Friday)
Sat	86	494 .	71.29	86/71.29 = 1.21
Sun	40	498	71.71	40/71.71 = 0.56
Mon	52	495	72.00	52/72.00 = 0.72
Tues	64	499	71.57	64/71.57 = 0.89 (Tuesday)
Wed	76	502	71.86	76/71.86 = 1.06
Thur	87	504	72.43	87/72.43 = 1.20
Fri	96	501	72.14	96/72.14 = 1.33 (Friday)
Sat	88	503	73.00	88/73.00 = 1.21
Sun	44	507	73.57	44/73.57 = 0.60
Mon	50	505	72.71	50/72.71 = 0.69
Tues	70	511		
Wed	80	515		
Thurs	81	509		

   The estimated Friday relative is (1.36 + 1.40 + 1.33)/3 = 1.36. Relatives for other days can be computed in a similar manner. For example, the estimated Tuesday relative is: (0.84 + 0.89)/2 = 0.87.

   The number of periods needed in a centered moving average is equal to the number of data points within a season. Hence, with monthly data, a 12-period moving average would be needed. When the number of periods is even, one additional step is needed because the middle of an even set falls between two periods. The additional step involves taking a centered two-period moving average of the even-numbered centered moving average, which results in averages that "line up" with data points and, hence, permit determination of seasonal ratios. (See Solved Problem 4 at the end of this chapter for an example of this.)

   The reason a centered moving average is used to obtain representative values is that because it "looks forward" and "looks backward" by virtue of its centered position, it is able to closely follow data movements, regardless of whether they involve trends, cycles, or random variability alone. Figure 3–8 illustrates how a three-period centered moving average closely tracks the data originally shown in Figure 3–3.

   If both trend and seasonality appear in a series, each component can be determined separately, and they can then be combined to obtain a forecast.

FIGURE 3–8

A centered moving average closely tracks the data

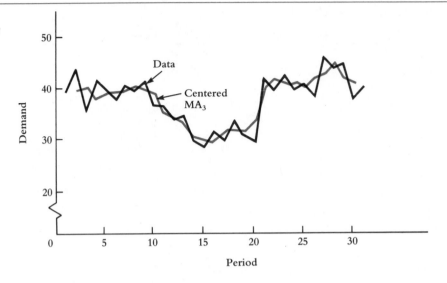

EXAMPLE 6

A furniture manufacturer wants to predict quarterly demand for a certain love-seat for periods 15 and 16, which happens to be the second and third quarters of a particular year. The series consists of both trend and seasonality. The trend portion of demand can be projected using the equation $y_t = 124 + 7.5t$. Quarter relatives are: $Q_1 = 1.20$, $Q_2 = 1.10$, $Q_3 = 0.75$, and $Q_4 = 0.95$. Use this information to predict demand for periods 15 and 16.

Solution

The trend values at $t = 15$ and $t = 16$ are:

$$y_{15} = 124 + 7.5(15) = 236.5$$
$$y_{16} = 124 + 7.5(16) = 244.0$$

Multiplying the trend value by the appropriate quarter relative will yield a forecast that includes both trend and seasonality. Since we are told that $t = 15$ is a second quarter and $t = 16$ is a third quarter, the forecasts are:

$$\text{Period 15} \quad 236.5(1.10) = 260.05$$
$$\text{Period 16} \quad 244.0(0.75) = 183.00$$

Techniques for Cycles

When cycles (up and down movement similar to seasonal variations, but of longer duration—say, two to six years between peaks) occur in time series data, they often are so irregular that it is difficult or impossible to project them from past data because turning points are difficult to identify. A short moving average or a naive approach may be of some value, although both will produce forecasts that lag cyclical movements by one or several periods.

The most commonly used approach is explanatory: Search for another variable that relates to, and *leads,* the variable of interest. For example, the number of housing starts (permits to build houses) in a given month often is an indicator of demand a few months later for products and services that are directly tied to construction of new homes (e.g., landscaping, sales of washers and dryers, sales of carpeting and furniture, new demands for shopping, transportation, schools, etc.). Thus, if an organization is able to establish a high correlation with such a *leading variable* (i.e., changes in the variable precede changes in the variable interest), an equation that describes the relationship can be developed, enabling forecasts to be made. It is important that there be a persistent relationship between the two variables. Moreover, the higher the correlation, the better the chances that the forecast will be on target.

Other Techniques for Time Series

A number of other techniques that can be used to analyze time series data are beyond the scope of this text. However, one of these, the *Box-Jenkins technique,* is worthy of note because of its increasing popularity and its ability to provide accurate forecasts.

The main advantage of the Box-Jenkins method is that it is better able to handle data that include complex patterns than are the techniques described previously. Also, the resulting forecasts often possess a high degree of accuracy compared to alternative methods. The main disadvantages of the technique relate to processing costs and complexity. The computations are fairly long and involved, and a computer program is essential. Furthermore, it is virtually impossible to communicate the assumptions that must be satisfied in order to obtain valid results to users who do not possess considerable mathematical sophistication.

If you are interested in learning more about this technique, consult the first reference at the end of this chapter.

ASSOCIATIVE FORECASTING TECHNIQUES

Associative techniques rely on identification of related variables that can be used to predict values of the variable of interest. For example, sales of beef may be related to the price per pound charged for beef as well as the prices of substitutes such as chicken, pork, and lamb; real estate prices are usually related to property location; and crop yields are related to soil conditions, as well as to amounts and timing of water and fertilizer applications.

The essence of associative techniques is the development of an equation that summarizes the effects of **predictor variables.** The primary method of analysis is known as **regression.** Although a detailed explanation of regression analysis is beyond the scope of this text, a brief overview of regression is given. This should suffice to place this approach into perspective relative to the other forecasting approaches described in the chapter.

Simple Linear Regression

The simplest and most widely used form of regression involves a linear relationship between two variables. A plot of the values might appear like that shown in Figure 3–9. The objective in linear regression is to obtain an equation of a straight line that minimizes the sum of squared vertical deviations of points around the line. This **least squares line** has the equation

$$y_c = a + bx \qquad (3\text{–}8)$$

where

y_c = Predicted (dependent) variable
x = Predictor (independent) variable
b = Slope of the line
a = Value of y_c when $x = 0$ (i.e, the height of the line at the y intercept)

(Note that it is conventional to represent values of the predicted variable on the y axis and values of the predictor variable on the x axis.) A graph of a linear regression line is illustrated in Figure 3–10.

The coefficients a and b of the line are computed using these two equations:

$$b = \frac{n(\Sigma xy) - (\Sigma x)(\Sigma y)}{n(\Sigma x^2) - (\Sigma x)^2} \qquad (3\text{–}9)$$

$$a = \frac{\Sigma y - b\Sigma x}{n} \text{ or } \bar{y} - b\bar{x} \qquad (3\text{–}10)$$

where

$$n = \text{Number of paired observations}$$

FIGURE 3–9

A straight line is fitted to a set of sample points

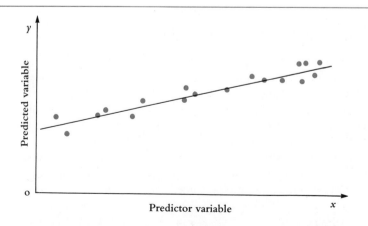

FIGURE 3–10

Equation of a straight line

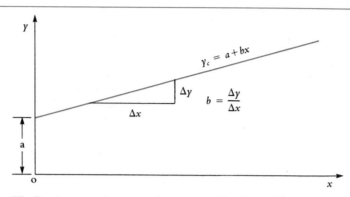

The line intersects the y axis where $y = a$. The slope of the line $= b$.

The accuracy of regression estimates depends on the extent to which sample data scatter around the line: the greater the scatter, the less accurate estimates will be. Scatter can be summarized using the standard error of estimate, s_e, where

$$s_e = \sqrt{\frac{\Sigma y^2 - a\Sigma y - b\Sigma xy}{n - 2}} \qquad (3\text{–}11)$$

EXAMPLE 7

Healthy Hamburgers has a chain of 12 stores in northern Illinois. Sales figures and profits for the stores are given in the following table. Obtain a regression line for the data, and predict profit for a store assuming sales of $10 million.

Sales, x (millions)	Profits, y (millions)
$ 7	$0.15
2	0.10
6	0.13
4	0.15
14	0.25
15	0.27
16	0.24
12	0.20
14	0.27
20	0.44
15	0.34
7	0.17

Solution

First, plot the data and decide if a linear model is reasonable (i.e., do the points seem to scatter around a straight line? Figure 3–11 suggests they do). Next,

EXAMPLE 7 *(continued)*

compute the quantities Σx, Σy, Σxy, and Σx^2. Calculations are shown for these quantities in Table 3–3. One additional calculation, Σy^2, is included for later reference.

Substituting into the equations, we find:

$$b = \frac{n(\Sigma xy) - (\Sigma x)(\Sigma y)}{n(\Sigma x^2) - (\Sigma x)^2} = \frac{12(35.29) - 132(2.71)}{12(1,796) - 132(132)} = 0.01593$$

$$a = \frac{\Sigma y - b(\Sigma x)}{n} = \frac{2.71 - 0.01593(132)}{12} = 0.0506$$

Thus, the regression equation is: $y_c = 0.0506 + 0.01593x$. For sales of $x = 10$ (i.e., $10 million), estimated profit is: $y_c = 0.0506 + 0.01593(10) = 0.2099$, or $209,900. (It may appear strange to you that substituting $x = 0$ into the equation produces a predicted profit of $50,600 because it seems to suggest that amount of profit will occur with no sales. However, the value of $x = 0$ is *outside of the range of observed values*. The regression line should only be used for the range of values it was developed from; the relationship may be nonlinear outside that range. The purpose of the a value is simply to establish the height of the line where it crosses the y axis.)

FIGURE 3–11

A linear model seems reasonable

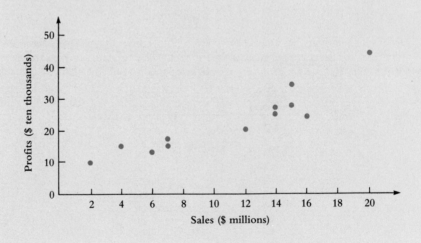

EXAMPLE 7 *(concluded)*

TABLE 3–3

Calculations for regression coefficients for healthy hamburgers

x	y	xy	x^2	y_2
7	0.15	1.05	49	0.0225
2	0.10	0.20	4	0.0100
6	0.13	0.78	36	0.0169
4	0.15	0.60	16	0.0225
14	0.25	3.50	196	0.0625
15	0.27	4.05	225	0.0729
16	0.24	3.84	256	0.0576
12	0.20	2.40	144	0.0400
14	0.27	3.78	196	0.0729
20	0.44	8.80	400	0.1936
15	0.84	5.10	225	0.1156
7	0.17	1.19	49	0.0289
132	2.71	35.29	1,796	0.7159

For the Healthy Hamburgers example, the standard error of estimate is

$$s_e = \sqrt{\frac{0.7159 - 0.0506(2.71) - 0.01593(35.29)}{12 - 2}} = 0.04074 \text{ or } \$40,740$$

A confidence interval for the predicted value of y (i.e., y_c) for a given value of x (i.e., x_g) can be obtained using the equation

$$\text{Confidence interval} = y_c \pm ts_{\text{reg}} \qquad (3\text{–}12)$$

where

$$s_{\text{reg}} = s_e \sqrt{1 + \frac{1}{n} + \frac{(x_g - \bar{x})^2}{\Sigma x^2 - [(\Sigma x)^2/n]}}$$

and

$\bar{x}$ = Mean of x values
x_g = Some given value of x
t = Standardized value obtained from a t table

For convenience, some selected values of t are listed in Table 3–4.
For the Healthy Hamburgers data, s_{reg} for $x_g = 10$ is

$$s_{\text{reg}} = 0.04074 \sqrt{1 + 1/12 + \frac{(10 - 11)^2}{1,796 - (132)^2/12}} = 0.04245$$

TABLE 3–4

	Degrees of freedom	t
Selected values of t for 95 percent confidence intervals	5 . . . . 2.57	
	6 . . . . 2.45	
	7 . . . . 2.37	
	8 . . . . 2.31	
	9 . . . . 2.25	
	10 . . . . 2.23	
	11 . . . . 2.20	
	12 . . . . 2.18	

Degrees of freedom = $n - 2$.

A 95 percent confidence interval for the predicted value of y is:

$$y_c \pm t(s_{reg}) = (0.506 + 0.01593(10)) \pm 2.23\,(0.04245)$$
$$= 0.2099 \pm 0.0947, \text{ or } 0.1152 \text{ to } 0.3046$$

That is, estimated profit on sales of $10 million is $209,900, and on the basis of the sample data we are 95 percent confident that actual profits will be in the range of $115,200 to $304,600.

It is interesting to note how wide the confidence interval is in this case, because after a certain point an interval can be so wide that it is meaningless. Although the interval here is somewhat wider than we would like, it does give an indication of the extent to which profits could vary on sales of $10 million.

Because the regression equation is developed from sample data that include random variability, there is always the risk that no real relationship exists between the variables. In that case, the average y would produce comparable predictions, so the added cost and effort of regression could be avoided. A simple test can be used to determine if a *significant* relationship exists (i.e., if the slope is nonzero):

$$t_{test} = b/s_b \tag{3–13}$$

where

$$b = \text{Slope of line}$$

$$s_b = s_e\sqrt{\frac{1}{\Sigma x^2 - [(\Sigma x)^2/n]}}$$

For Healthy Hamburgers, the standard error of the slope, s_b, is:

$$s_b = 0.04074\sqrt{\frac{1}{1,796 - (132)(132)/12}} = 0.0022$$

$$t_{test} = b/s_b = 0.01593/0.0022 = 7.24$$

This value must be compared to one found in a t table (see Table 3–4) using the appropriate degrees of freedom. Conclude the relationship is significant if $t_{test} > t$. (If $n > 30$, a z value obtained from the normal table can be used in place of t.) Since $t_{test} = 7.24$ and $t = 2.23$ from Table 3–4, we conclude that there is a relationship between the two variables.

One application of regression in forecasting relates to the use of indicators. These are uncontrollable variables that tend to lead or precede changes in a variable of interest. For example, changes in the federal reserve's discount rate may influence certain business activities. Similarly, an increase in housing starts during the spring and summer months may lead to increased demand for appliances, carpets, furniture, and similar items in the fall and winter months. Careful identification and analysis of indicators may yield insight into possible future demand in some situations. There are numerous published indexes from which to choose.[2] Among them are the following:

Net change in inventories on hand and on order
Interest rates for commercial loans
Industrial output
Consumer price index
The wholesale price index
Stock market prices

Other potential indicators are population shifts, local political climates, and activities of other firms (e.g., the opening of a shopping center may result in increased sales for nearby businesses).

In order for an indicator to be valid, three conditions are required:

1. There should be a logical explanation for the relationship between movements of an indicator and movements of the variable of interest.
2. Movements of the indicator must precede movements of the dependent variable by enough time so that the forecast isn't outdated before it can be acted upon.
3. There should be a fairly high correlation between the two variables.

Correlation measures the strength and direction of relationship between two variables. Correlation can range from -1.00 to $+1.00$. A correlation of $+1.00$ indicates that changes in one variable are always matched by changes in the other; a correlation of -1.00 indicates increases in one variable are matched by decreases in the other; and a correlation close to zero indicates little *linear* relationship between two variables. The correlation between two variables can be computed using the equation

$$r = \frac{n(\Sigma xy) - (\Sigma x)(\Sigma y)}{\sqrt{n(\Sigma x^2) - (\Sigma x)^2} \cdot \sqrt{n(\Sigma y^2) - (\Sigma y)^2}} \qquad (3\text{–}14)$$

---

[2] See for example, *The National Bureau of Economic Research, The Survey of Current Business, The Monthly Labor Review,* and *Business Conditions Digest.*

EXAMPLE 8

Sales of 19-inch color television sets and three-month lagged unemployment are shown in the following table. Determine if unemployment levels can be used to predict demand for 19-inch color TVs and, if so, derive a predictive equation.

Period	1	2	3	4	5	6	7	8	9	10	11
Units sold	20	41	17	35	25	31	38	50	15	19	14
Unemployment (three-month lag)	7.2	4.0	7.3	5.5	6.8	6.0	5.4	3.6	8.4	7.0	9.0

Solution

1. Plot the data to see if a linear model seems reasonable. In this case, a linear model seems appropriate *for the range of the data.*

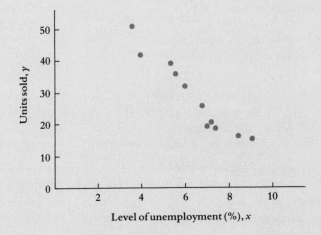

2. Compute the correlation coefficient to confirm that it is not close to zero.

x	y	xy	x^2	y^2
7.2	20	144.0	51.8	400
4.0	41	164.0	16.0	1,681
7.3	17	124.1	53.3	289
5.5	35	192.5	30.3	1,225
6.8	25	170.0	46.2	625
6.0	31	186.0	36.0	961
5.4	38	205.2	29.2	1,444
3.6	50	180.0	13.0	2,500
8.4	15	126.0	70.6	225
7.0	19	133.0	49.0	361
9.0	14	126.0	81.0	196
70.2	305	1,750.8	476.3	9,907

EXAMPLE 8 *(concluded)*

$$r = \frac{11(1,750.8) - 70.2(305)}{\sqrt{11(476.3) - (70.2)^2} \cdot \sqrt{11(9,907) - (305)^2}} = -.966$$

This is a fairly high correlation.

3. Compute the regression line:

$$b = \frac{11(1,750.8) - 70.2(305)}{11(476.3) - 70.2(70.2)} = -6.9145$$

$$a = \frac{305 - (-6.9145)(70.2)}{11} = 71.854$$

$$y = 71.85 - 6.91x$$

Note that the equation pertains only to unemployment levels that are in the range 3.6 to 9.0, since sample observations covered only that range. In addition, if you suspect that r is close to zero, test the slope, b, for significance; r is significant when b is.

Comments on the Use of Linear Regression Analysis

Use of simple regression analysis implies that certain assumptions have been satisfied. Basically, these are:

1. Variations around the line are random. If they are, no patterns such as cycles should be apparent when the line and data are plotted.
2. Deviations around the line should be normally distributed. A concentration of values close to the line with a small proportion of larger deviations supports the assumption of normality.
3. Predictions are being made only within the range of observed values.

If the assumptions are satisfied, regression analysis can be a powerful tool. Particularly useful are the confidence intervals for predicted values. To obtain the best results, observe the following:

1. Always plot the data to verify that a linear relationship is appropriate.
2. Always test the relationship (slope) for significance.
3. The data may be time-dependent. Check this by plotting the dependent variable versus time; if patterns appear, use analysis of time series instead of regression.
4. A small correlation may imply that other variables are important.

In addition, note these weaknesses of regression:

1. Simple linear regression applies only to linear relationships with *one* independent variable.

2. A considerable amount of data is needed to establish the relationship—in practice, say, 20 or more observations.

3. All observations are weighted equally.

4. The cost and complexity involved make this technique unattractive for situations that require forecasts for many individual items.

Curvilinear and Multiple Regression Analysis

Simple linear regression may prove inadequate to handle certain problems because a linear model is inappropriate or because more than one predictor variable is involved. When nonlinear relationships are present, curvilinear regression is called for; models that involve more than one predictor require the use of multiple regression analysis. Both of these techniques are beyond the scope of this text. However, you should be aware of the fact that such models are being used. For the most part, the computations lend themselves more to computers than to hand calculation. This usually adds to the cost of the forecast, as does the acquisition of additional data called for by the use of multiple predictor variables. In each case, it is necessary to weigh the additional cost and effort required against potential improvements in accuracy of predictions.

ACCURACY AND CONTROL OF FORECASTS

Accuracy and control of forecasts is a vital aspect of forecasting. To begin with, the complex nature of most real-world variables makes it almost impossible to correctly predict future values of those variables on a regular basis. Consequently, it is essential to include an indication of the extent to which the forecast might deviate from the value of the variable that actually occurs. This will provide the forecast user with a better perspective on how far off a forecast might be.

Moreover, because some techniques will provide more accuracy than others in a given situation, in choosing among different techniques, the decision maker needs a measure of accuracy that can be used as a basis for comparison.

Finally, some forecasting applications involve a series of forecasts (e.g., weekly revenues), whereas others involve a single forecast that will be used for a one-time decision (e.g., deciding on the size of a power plant). When periodic forecasts are made, it is important to monitor forecast errors to determine if the errors are within reasonable bounds. If they are not, it is necessary to take corrective action. This involves controlling the forecast.

Forecast **error** is the difference between the value that occurs and the value that was predicted for a given time period. Hence, Error = Actual − Forecast:

$$e_t = A_t - F_t \qquad\qquad (3\text{--}15)$$

Positive errors result when the forecast is too low, and negative errors result when the forecast is too high. For example, if actual demand for a week is 100 units and forecast demand was 90 units, the forecast was too low; the error is $100 - 90 = +10$.

There are two somewhat different ways in which forecast errors influence decisions. One is in making a choice between various forecasting alternatives, and the other is in evaluating the success or failure of a technique in use. We shall begin by examining two ways for summarizing forecast error over time and discovering how that information can be applied to a choice among forecasting alternatives. Then we shall consider several methods for controlling forecasts (i.e., evaluating the performance of a given forecasting method in use).

Measuring the Accuracy of Forecasts

There are two aspects of forecast accuracy that have potential significance in deciding among forecasting alternatives. One is the historical error performance of a forecast, and the other is the ability of a forecast to respond to changes.

Two commonly used measures for summarizing historical errors are the **mean absolute deviation (MAD)** and the **mean squared error (MSE).** MAD is the average absolute error, and MSE is the average of squared errors. The formulas used to compute MAD[3] and MSE are:

$$MAD = \frac{\Sigma|Actual - forecast|}{n} \qquad (3\text{--}16)$$

$$MSE = \frac{\Sigma(Actual - forecast)^2}{n - 1} \qquad (3\text{--}17)$$

The sample standard deviation, s, equals the square root of MSE.

The following example illustrates the computation of MAD and MSE.

EXAMPLE 9

Compute MAD and MSE for the following data.

Period	Actual	Forecast	(A–F) error	|Error|	Error^2
1	217	215	2	2	4
2	213	216	−3	3	9
3	216	215	1	1	1
4	210	214	−4	4	16
5	213	211	2	2	4
6	219	214	5	5	25
7	216	217	−1	1	1
8	212	216	−4	4	16
			−2	22	76

---

[3] The absolute value, represented by the two vertical lines in Formula 3–16, ignores minus signs: all data are treated as positive values. For example, −2 becomes +2.

EXAMPLE 9 *(concluded)*

Solution

Using the figures shown in the table,

$$MAD = \frac{\Sigma|e|}{n} = \frac{22}{8} = 2.75$$

$$MSE = \frac{\Sigma e^2}{n - 1} = \frac{76}{8 - 1} = 10.86$$

From a computational standpoint, the difference between these two measures is that one weights all errors evenly (MAD) and the other weights errors according to their *squared* values (MSE).

One use for these measures is to compare alternative forecasting methods. For instance, using either MAD or MSE, a manager could compare the results of exponential smoothing with values of .1, .2, and .3 and select the one that yielded the *lowest* MAD or MSE for a given set of data.

In some instances, historical error performance is secondary to the ability of a forecast to respond to changes in data patterns. Choice among alternative methods would then focus on the cost of not responding quickly to a change relative to the cost of responding to changes that are not really there (i.e., random fluctuations).

Overall, the operations manager must settle on the relative importance of historical performance versus responsiveness as well as on whether to use MAD or MSE to measure historical performance.

Controlling the Forecast

It is necessary to monitor forecast errors to insure that the forecast is performing adequately. This can be accomplished by comparing forecast errors to predetermined values, or *action limits,* as illustrated in Figure 3–12. Errors that fall within the limits would be judged acceptable, and errors outside of either limit would signal that corrective action is needed.

There are a variety of possible reasons for forecast errors. Among the primary sources of forecast errors are the following:

1. The model may be inadequate due to (a) the omission of an important variable, (b) a change or shift in the variable that the model cannot deal with (e.g., sudden appearance of a trend or cycle), or (c) the appearance of a new variable (e.g., new competitor).

2. Irregular variations due to severe weather or other natural phenomena, temporary shortages or breakdowns, catastrophes, or similar events may occur.

3. The forecasting technique may be used incorrectly, or the results may be misinterpreted.

FIGURE 3–12

Monitoring forecast errors

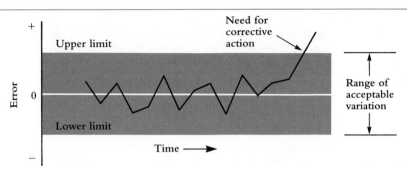

4. There are random variations in the data. Randomness is the inherent variation that remains in the data after all causes of variation have been accounted for.

A forecast is generally deemed to perform adequately when the errors exhibit only random variations. Hence, the key to judging when to reexamine the validity of a particular forecasting technique is whether forecast errors are random. If they are not random, an investigation must be made to determine which of the other sources is present and to correct the problem.

Forecasts can be monitored using either *tracking signals* or *control charts*. A **tracking signal** focuses on the ratio of *cumulative* forecast error to the corresponding value of MAD:

$$\text{Tracking signal} = \frac{\Sigma(\text{Actual} - \text{Forecast})}{\text{MAD}} \qquad (3\text{–}18)$$

The resulting values are compared to predetermined limits. These are based on judgment and experience and often range from ± 3 to ± 8. We shall use limits of ± 4 for the most part. These are roughly comparable to three standard deviation limits. Values within the limits suggest—but do not guarantee—that the forecast is performing adequately. After an initial value of MAD has been computed, MAD can be updated using exponential smoothing:

$$\text{MAD}_t = \text{MAD}_{t-1} + \alpha(|\text{Actual} - \text{Forecast}|_t - \text{MAD}_{t-1}) \qquad (3\text{–}19)$$

The **control chart** approach involves setting upper and lower limits for *individual* forecast errors (instead of cumulative errors, as is the case with a tracking signal). The limits are multiples of the square root of MSE. This method assumes the following:

1. Forecast errors are randomly distributed around a mean of zero.

2. The distribution of errors is normal.

In effect, the square root of MSE is an estimate of the standard deviation of the distribution of errors. That is,

$$s = \sqrt{\text{MSE}} \qquad (3\text{–}20)$$

Recall that for a normal distribution, approximately 95 percent of the values (errors in this case) can be expected to fall within limits of $0 \pm 2s$, and approximately 99 percent of the values can be expected to fall within $\pm$ 3s of zero. Hence, if the forecast is "in control," 99 percent or 95 percent of the errors should fall within the limits, depending on whether 3s or 2s limits are being used. Points that fall outside these limits should be regarded as evidence that corrective action is needed (i.e., that the forecast is not performing adequately). Figure 3–12 illustrates this concept.

In using a control chart, it can be very informative to plot the errors. A plot helps you to visualize the process and will enable you to check for possible patterns *within the limits* that suggest an improved forecast is possible.[4]

EXAMPLE 10

Monthly sales of leather jackets at the Lucky Leather Shoppe for the past 24 months are shown in the following table, as are the forecasts and errors for those months. Determine if the forecast is working using these approaches:

1. A tracking signal, beginning with month 10, updating MAD with exponential smoothing. Use limits of $\pm$ 4 and $\alpha = .2$.

2. A control chart with 2s limits. Use data from the first eight months to develop the control chart, then evaluate the remaining data with the control chart.

Month	A (sales)	F (forecast)	A − F (error)	|e|	Cumulative |e|
1	47	43	4	4	4
2	51	44	7	7	11
3	54	50	4	4	15
4	55	51	4	4	19
5	49	54	−5	5	24
6	46	48	−2	2	26
7	38	46	−8	8	34
8	32	44	−12	12	46
9	25	35	−10	10	56
10	24	26	−2	2	58
11	30	25	5	5	
12	35	32	3	3	
13	44	34	10	10	
14	57	50	7	7	
15	60	51	9	9	
16	55	54	1	1	
17	51	55	−4	4	

---

[4] The theory and application of control charts, as well as various methods for detecting patterns in the data, are covered in more detail in Chapter 16, on quality assurance.

EXAMPLE 10 (continued)

Month	A (sales)	F (forecast)	A − F (error)	|e|	Cumulative |e|
18	48	51	−3	3	
19	42	50	−8	8	
20	30	43	−13	13	
21	28	38	−10	10	
22	25	27	−2	2	
23	35	27	8	8	
24	38	32	6	6	
			−11		

Solution

a. The sum of absolute errors through the 10th month is 58. Hence, the initial MAD is $58/10 = 5.8$. The subsequent MADs are updated using the formula $MAD_{new} = MAD_{old} + .2(|e| - MAD_{old})$. The results are shown in the following table.

The tracking signal for any month is:

$$\frac{\text{Cumulative error at that month}}{\text{Updated MAD at that month}}$$

t (month)	|e|	$MAD_t = MAD_{t-1}$ $+ .2(|e| - MAD_{t-1})$	Cumulative error	Tracking signal = Cumulative error$_t$ ÷ MAD_t
10			−20	−20/5.800 = −3.45
11	5	5.640 = 5.8 + .2(5 − 5.8)	−15	−15/5.640 = −2.66
12	3	5.112 = 5.640 + .2(3 − 5.64)	−12	−12/5.112 = −2.35
13	10	6.090 = 5.112 + .2(10 − 5.112)	−2	−2/6.090 = −0.33
14	7	6.272 = 6.090 + .2(7 − 6.090)	5	5/6.272 = 0.79
15	9	6.818 = 6.272 + .2(9 − 6.272)	14	14/6.818 = 2.05
16	1	5.654 = 6.818 + .2(1 − 6.818)	15	15/5.654 = 2.65
17	4	5.323 = 5.654 + .2(4 − 5.654)	11	11/5.323 = 2.07
18	3	4.858 = 5.323 + .2(3 − 5.323)	8	8/4.858 = 1.65
19	8	5.486 = 4.858 + .2(8 − 4.858)	0	0/5.486 = 0.00
20	13	6.989 = 5.486 + .2(13 − 5.486)	−13	−13/6.989 = −1.86
21	10	7.591 = 6.989 + .2(10 − 6.989)	−23	−23/7.591 = −3.03
22	2	6.472 = 7.591 + .2(2 − 7.591)	−25	−25/6.472 = −3.86
23	8	6.778 = 6.472 + .2(8 − 6.472)	−17	−17/6.778 = −2.51
24	6	6.622 = 6.778 + .2(6 − 6.778)	−11	−11/6.622 = −1.66

Since the tracking signal is within ±4 of zero, there is no evidence of a problem.

b. (1) Check to make sure that the average error is approximately zero, since a large average would suggest a biased forecast.

$$\text{Average error} = \frac{\Sigma \text{ errors}}{n} = \frac{-11}{24} = -0.46 \quad [OK]$$

EXAMPLE 10 *(concluded)*

(2)   Compute the standard deviation:

$$s = \sqrt{\frac{\Sigma e^2}{n-1}}$$

$$= \sqrt{\frac{4^2 + 7^2 + 4^2 + 4^2 + (-5)^2 + (-2)^2 + (-8)^2 + (-12)^2}{24-1}} = 6.91$$

(3)   Determine $2s$ control limits:
$$0 \pm 2s = 0 \pm 2.(6.91) = -13.82 \text{ to } +13.82$$

(4)   (*a*) Check to see if all errors are within the limits. (They are.)
       (*b*) Plot the data (see the following graph), and check for nonrandom patterns. Note the strings of positive and negative errors. This suggests nonrandomness (and that an improved forecast is possible). The tracking signal did not reveal this.

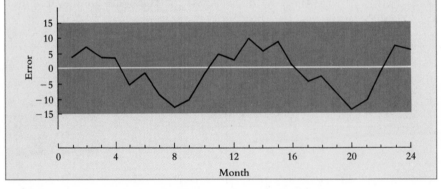

Like the tracking signal, a control chart focuses attention on deviations that lie outside predetermined limits. However, the control chart approach also involves checking for possible patterns in the errors, even if all errors are within the control limits. Some of the most common patterns are illustrated in Figure 3–13. Checking is usually done by visual inspection, although statistical tests are sometimes used. If a pattern is discovered, this means that errors are *predictable* and, thus, nonrandom. The implication is that the forecast can be improved. For example, trend in the errors means the errors are getting progressively worse. In time series data, adding or increasing a trend response may be needed. In an explanatory model, recomputing the slope or other adjustment may be called for.

Comment.   The control chart approach is generally superior to the tracking signal approach. A major weakness of the tracking signal approach is its use of cumulative errors: Individual errors can be obscured so that large

FIGURE 3–13

Examples of possible patterns

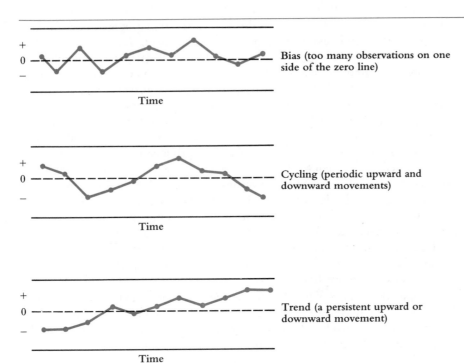

Bias (too many observations on one side of the zero line)

Cycling (periodic upward and downward movements)

Trend (a persistent upward or downward movement)

positive and negative values can cancel out each other. Conversely, with control charts, every error is judged individually. Hence, it can be misleading to rely on a tracking signal approach to monitor errors. In fact, the historical roots of the tracking signal approach relate to a time when using computers in business was just beginning. At that time, it was much more difficult to compute standard deviations than it was to compute average deviations; *for that reason,* the concept of a tracking signal was developed. Now, of course, modern computers and calculators can easily provide standard deviations. Nonetheless, the use of tracking signals has persisted, probably because users are unaware of its inferiority relative to the control chart approach.

CHOOSING A FORECASTING TECHNIQUE

There are many different kinds of forecasting techniques available, and no one technique works best in every situation. In selecting a technique for a given situation, the manager or analyst must take a number of factors into consideration.

Perhaps the two most important factors are *cost* and *accuracy*. How much money is budgeted for generating the forecast? What are the possible costs of error, and what are the possible benefits that might accrue from an accurate forecast? Generally speaking, the higher the accuracy, the higher the cost, so it is important to weigh cost-accuracy trade-offs carefully. The best forecast is not necessarily the most accurate or the least costly; rather, it is some combination of accuracy and cost deemed best by management.

Other factors include the availability of historical data; the availability of computers; the ability of decision makers to utilize certain techniques; the time needed to gather data, analyze them, and prepare the forecast; and any prior experience with a technique. The forecast horizon is important because some techniques are more suited to long-range forecasts and others work best for the short range. For example, moving averages and exponential smoothing are essentially short-range techniques, since they produce forecasts for the *next* period, whereas trend equations can be used to project over much longer time periods. Several of the qualitative techniques are well suited to long-range forecasts because they do not require historical data. The Delphi technique and executive opinion methods are often used for long-range planning. Since new products and services lack historical data, forecasts for these must be made on the basis of subjective estimates. In many cases, experience with similar items can be relevant. Table 3–5 provides some additional perspectives on forecasts in terms of the forecast horizon.

In some instances, a manager may decide to use more than one forecasting technique. The purpose would be to obtain independent forecasts. If the different methods produced approximately the same predictions, that would lend additional confidence to the results; disagreement among the forecasts would indicate that additional analysis may be needed.

The following section outlines some additional considerations that pertain both to choosing a forecasting methodology and to preparing a forecast.

TABLE 3–5

Forecast factors, by range of forecast	Factor	Short range	Intermediate range	Long range
	1. Frequency	Often	Occasional	Infrequent
	2. Level of aggregation	Item	Product family	Total output Type of product/ service
	3. Type of model	Smoothing Projection Regression	Projection Seasonal Regression	Managerial Judgment
	4. Degree of management involvement	Low	Moderate	High
	5. Cost per forecast	Low	Moderate	High

Elements of a Good Forecast

A properly prepared forecast must fulfill certain requirements:

1. The forecast should be *timely*. Usually, a certain amount of time is needed to respond to the information contained in a forecast. For example, capacity cannot be expanded overnight, nor can inventory levels be changed immediately. Hence, the forecasting horizon must cover the time necessary to implement possible changes.

2. The forecast should be *accurate,* and the degree of accuracy should be stated. This will enable users to plan for possible errors and will provide a basis for comparing alternative forecasts.

3. The forecast should be *reliable;* it should work. A technique that sometimes provides a good forecast and sometimes a poor one will leave users with the uneasy feeling that they are liable to get burned every time a new forecast is issued.

4. The forecast should be in *meaningful units*. Financial planners need to know how many *dollars* will be needed, production planners need to know how many *units* will be needed, and schedulers need to know what *machines* and *skills* will be required. Hence, choice of units will depend on user needs.

5. The forecast should be *in writing*. Although this will not guarantee that all concerned are using the same information, it will at least increase the likelihood of it. In addition, a written forecast will permit an objective basis for evaluating the forecast once actual results are in.

6. The forecasting technique should be *simple to understand and use*. Users often lack confidence in forecasts based on sophisticated techniques because they do not understand the circumstances in which the techniques are appropriate and the limitations of the techniques; misuse of techniques is an obvious consequence. Not surprisingly, fairly crude forecasting techniques enjoy widespread popularity because users are more comfortable using them.

USING FORECAST INFORMATION

A manager can take a *reactive* or a *proactive* approach to a forecast. A reactive approach views forecasts as probable descriptions of future demand, and a manager reacts to meet that demand (e.g., adjusts production rates, adjusts inventories, adjusts the work force). Conversely, a proactive approach seeks to actively influence demand (e.g., via advertising, pricing, or product/service changes).

Generally speaking, a proactive approach would require either an explanatory model (e.g., regression) or a subjective assessment of the influence on demand. It is possible, then, that a manager might use two forecasts: one to predict what will happen under the status quo and a second one based on a "what if . . ." approach, if the results of the status quo forecast are unacceptable.

OPERATIONS STRATEGY

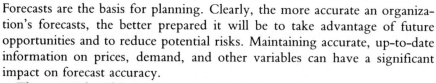

Forecasts are the basis for planning. Clearly, the more accurate an organization's forecasts, the better prepared it will be to take advantage of future opportunities and to reduce potential risks. Maintaining accurate, up-to-date information on prices, demand, and other variables can have a significant impact on forecast accuracy.

There are other things an organization can do to improve forecasts. These do not involve searching for improved techniques. Rather, they relate to the fact that accuracy tends to be inversely related to the forecast horizon; forecasts that cover shorter time frames tend to be more accurate than longer-term forecasts. Recognizing this, management might choose to devote efforts to shortening the time horizon that forecasts must cover. Essentially, this means shortening the *lead time* needed to respond to a forecast. This might involve building *flexibility* into operations to permit rapid response to changing demands for products and services, as well as changing volumes in quantities demanded. It might also mean shortening the lead time required to obtain supplies, equipment, and raw materials or the time needed to train or retrain employees. It can also mean shortening the time needed to *develop* new products and services.

SUMMARY

Forecasts are vital inputs for both the design and the operation of the productive systems because they help manages to anticipate the future.

Forecasting techniques can be classified as either qualitative or quantitative. Qualitative techniques rely on judgment, experience, and expertise to formulate forecasts, and quantitative techniques rely on the use of historical data or associations among variables to develop forecasts. Some of the techniques are quite simple, and others are quite complex. Some work better than others, but no technique works all the time. Moreover, all forecasts include a certain degree of inaccuracy, and some allowance should be made for this. All techniques assume that the same underlying causal system that existed in the past will continue to exist in the future.

The qualitative techniques described in this chapter include consumer surveys, sales force estimates, executive opinions, and manager and staff opinions. Two major quantitative approaches are described: analysis of time series data and associative techniques. The time series techniques rely strictly on the

TABLE 3-6

Approaches	Brief description

Qualitative:
  Judgmental methods:
    Consumer surveys . . . . Questioning consumers on future plans
    Sales force composites . . . . . Joint estimates obtained from salespeople
    Executive opinion . . . . Finance, marketing, and manufacturing managers join to prepare forecast
    Delphi technique . . . . Series of questionaires answered anonymously by managers and staff; successive questionnaires are based on information obtained from previous surveys
    Outside opinion . . . . Consultants or other outside experts prepare the forecast
Quantitative:
  Time series:
    Naive . . . . Next value in a series will equal the previous value
    Moving averages . . . . Forecast is based on an average of recent values
    Exponential smoothing . . . . Sophisticated form of averaging
  Associative models:
    Simple regression . . . . Values of one variable are used to predict values of another variable
    Multiple regression . . . . Two or more variables are used to predict values of another variable

examination of historical data; predictions are made by projecting past movements of a variable into the future without considering specific factors that might influence the variable. Associative techniques attempt to explicitly identify influencing factors and to incorporate that information into equations that can be used for predictive purposes.

Because all forecasts tend to be inaccurate, it is important to provide a measure of accuracy for each forecast. Several measures of forecast accuracy can be computed. These are often used to help managers evaluate the performance of a given technique as well as choose among alternative forecasting techniques. Control of forecasts involves deciding whether or not a forecast is performing adequately, using either a control chart or a tracking signal.

Selection of a forecasting technique involves choosing a technique that will serve the intended purpose at an acceptable level of cost and accuracy.

The various forecasting techniques are summarized in Table 3–6.

KEY TERMS

associative models, 131
centered moving average, 151
control chart, 167
correlation, 161
cycles, 135
Delphi method, 132
error, 164
exponential smoothing, 140
forecast, 128
irregular variation, 135
judgmental forecasts, 130
least squares line, 156
linear trend equation, 144

mean absolute deviation (MAD), 165
mean squared error (MSE), 165
moving average, 138
naive forecast, 137
predictor variable, 155
random variation, 135
regression, 155
seasonality, 135
seasonal variations, 149
time series, 134
tracking signal, 167
trend, 135
trend-adjusted exponential smoothing, 148

SOLVED PROBLEMS

1. *Exponential smoothing.* Using $\alpha = .5$, prepare a forecast for period 6 based on the information given in the following table.

Period	Number of complaints
1	60
2	65
3	55
4	58
5	64

Solution

$$n = \frac{2}{.5} - 1 = 3 \text{ periods}$$

Initial forecast (period 4): $\dfrac{60 + 65 + 55}{3} = 60$

$F_5 = F_4 + \alpha(A_4 - F_4) = 60 + .5(58 - 60) = 59$
$F_6 = F_5 + \alpha(A_5 - F_5) = 59 + .5(64 - 59) = 61.5$

2. *Time series analysis.* Apple's Citrus Fruit Farm ships boxed fruit anywhere in the continental United States. Using the following

information, forecast shipments for the first four months of next year.

Month	Seasonal relative
Jan.	1.2
Feb.	1.3
Mar.	1.3
Apr.	1.1
May	0.8
Jun.	0.7
Jul.	0.8
Aug.	0.6
Sep.	0.7
Oct.	1.0
Nov.	1.1
Dec.	1.4

Monthly forecast equation:

$$y_t = 402 + 3t$$

where

$$t_0 = \text{January of } last \text{ year}$$
$$y_t = \text{Number of shipments}$$

Solution

a. Determine trend amounts for the first four months of next year: January, $t = 24$; February, $t = 25$; etc. Thus,

$$Y_{\text{Jan}} = 402 + 3(24) = 474$$
$$Y_{\text{Feb}} = 402 + 3(25) = 477$$
$$Y_{\text{Mar}} = 402 + 3(26) = 480$$
$$Y_{\text{Apr}} = 402 + 3(27) = 483$$

b. Multiply each monthly trend by the corresponding seasonal relative for that month.

Month	Seasonal relative	Forecast
Jan.	1.2	474(1.2) = 568.8
Feb.	1.3	477(1.3) = 620.1
Mar.	1.3	480(1.3) = 624.0
Apr.	1.1	483(1.1) = 531.3

3. *Linear trend line.* Develop a linear trend line for the following data. Plot the line and the data on a graph, and visually verify that a linear trend line is appropriate. Then use the equation to predict the next two values of the series.

Period	Demand
1	44
2	52
3	50
4	54
5	55
6	55
7	60
8	56
9	62

Solution

Period, t	Demand, y	ty	
1	44	44	From Table 3–1, with $n = 9$,
2	52	104	
3	50	150	$\Sigma t = 45$ and $\Sigma t^2 = 285$
4	54	216	
5	55	275	
6	55	330	
7	60	420	
8	56	448	
9	62	558	
	488	2,545	

$$b = \frac{n\,\Sigma ty - \Sigma t\,\Sigma y}{n\Sigma t^2 - (\Sigma t)^2} = \frac{9(2,545) - 45(488)}{9(285) - 45(45)} = 1.75$$

$$a = \frac{\Sigma y - b\,\Sigma t}{n} = \frac{488 - 1.75(45)}{9} = 45.47$$

Thus, the trend equation is $y_t = 45.47 + 1.75t$. The next two forecasts are:

$$y_{10} = 45.47 + 1.75(10) = 62.97$$
$$y_{11} = 45.47 + 1.75(11) = 64.72$$

A plot of the data indicates that a linear trend line is appropriate:

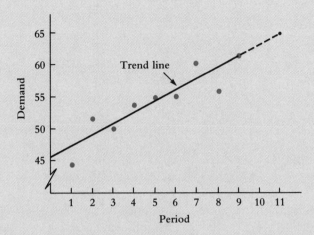

4. *Seasonal relatives.* Obtain estimates of quarter relatives for these data:

Year:		1				2				3			4
Quarter:	1	2	3	4	1	2	3	4	1	2	3	4	1
Demand:	14	18	35	46	28	36	60	71	45	54	84	88	58

(Note that each season has an *even* number of data points. See Example 5 in this chapter for an illustration of the procedure for an odd number of data points per season.)

Year	Quarter	Demand	MA_4	MA_2	Demand/MA_2
1	1	14			
	2	18			
	3	35	28.25	30.00	1.17
	4	46	31.75	34.00	1.35
2	1	28	36.25	39.38	0.71
	2	36	42.50	45.63	0.79
	3	60	48.75	50.88	1.18
	4	71	53.00	55.25	1.29
3	1	45	57.50	60.50	0.74
	2	54	63.50	65.63	0.82
	3	84	67.75	69.38	1.21
	4	88	71.00		
4	1	58			

		Quarter	
1	**2**	**3**	**4**
0.71	0.79	1.17	1.35
0.74	0.82	1.18	1.29
1.45	1.61	1.21	2.64
		3.56	
$\bar{x}$: 0.725	0.805	1.187	1.320

The sum of these relatives is 4.037. Multiplying each by 4.00/4.037 will make the total 4.00. The resulting relatives are: quarter 1, 0.718; quarter 2, 0.798; quarter 3, 1.176; quarter 4, 1.308.

5. *Regression analysis.* A large midwestern retailer has developed a linear relationship that summarizes the effect of advertising expenditures on sales volume, as shown in the following graph. Using the graph, determine an equation of the form $y = a + bx$ that describes this relationship.

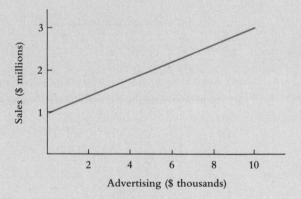

Solution

The linear equation has the form $y = a + bx$, where a is the value of y when $x = 0$ (i.e., where the line intersects the y axis) and b is the slope of the line (the amount by which y changes for a one-unit change in x).

Accordingly, $a = 1$ and $b = (3 - 1)/(10 - 0) = 0.2$, so $y = a + bx$ becomes $y = 1 + 0.2x$. [*Note:* (3 − 1) is the change in y.]

6. *Regression analysis.* The owner of a small hardware store has noted a sales pattern for window locks that seems to parallel the number of break-ins reported each week in the newspaper. The data are:

Sales:	46	18	20	22	27	34	14	37	30
Break-ins:	9	3	3	5	4	7	2	6	4

a. Plot the data to determine which type of equation, linear or nonlinear, is appropriate.
b. Obtain a regression equation for the data.
c. Test for significance.
d. Estimate sales if the number of break-ins is 5.
e. Place a 95 percent confidence interval around the estimate of sales for five break-ins.

Solution

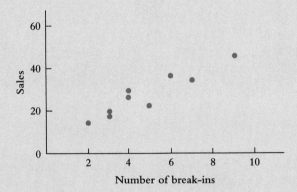

b. The computations for a straight line are:

x	y	xy	x²	y²
9	46	414	81	2,116
3	18	54	9	324
3	20	60	9	400
5	22	110	25	484
4	27	108	16	729
7	34	238	49	1,156
2	14	28	4	196
6	37	222	36	1,369
4	30	120	16	900
43	248	1,354	245	7,674

$$b = \frac{n(\Sigma xy) - (\Sigma x)(\Sigma y)}{n(\Sigma x^2) - (\Sigma x)^2} = \frac{9(1,354) - 43(248)}{9(245) - 43(43)} = 4.275$$

$$a = \frac{\Sigma y - b(\Sigma x)}{n} = \frac{248 - 4.275(43)}{9} = 7.129$$

Hence, the equation is: $y_c = 7.129 + 4.275x$.

c.   To test for significance, first compute s_e and then s_b:

$$s_e = \sqrt{\frac{\Sigma y^2 - a\Sigma y - b\Sigma xy}{n - 2}} = \sqrt{\frac{7,674 - 7.129(248) - 4.275(1,354)}{9 - 2}} = 4.092$$

$$s_b = s_e\sqrt{\frac{1}{\Sigma x^2 - [(\Sigma x)^2/n]}} = 4.092\sqrt{\frac{1}{245 - [(43)^2/9]}} = 0.651$$

Then compute:

$$t = b/s_b = 4.275/0.651 = 6.57$$

Since this greatly exceeds 2.0, conclude the slope is nonzero.

d.   For $x = 5$, $y_c = 7.129 + 4.275(5) = 28.50$.

e.   From Table 3–4 for $df = n - 2 = 7$, $t = 2.37$. The confidence interval for 95 percent is:

$$y_c \pm ts_{reg} = 28.50 \pm 2.73\left[4.092\sqrt{1 + \frac{1}{9} + \frac{(5 - 43/9)^2}{245 - (43)^2/9}}\right]$$
$$= 28.50 \pm 10.23, \text{ or } 18.27 \text{ to } 38.73$$

7.   *Accuracy and control of forecasts*. The marketing manager of a large manufacturer of industrial pumps must choose between two alternative forecasting techniques. Both techniques have been used to prepare forecasts for a six-month period. Using MAD as a criterion, which technique has the better performance record?

			Forecast	
Month		Demand	Technique 1	Technique 2
1		492	488	495
2		470	484	482
3		485	480	478
4		493	490	488
5		498	497	492
6		492	493	493

Solution

a.   Check to see that each forecast has an average error of approximately zero. (See computations that follow.)

b. Select the one with the smallest mean absolute error:

Month	Demand	Technique 1	e	$\lvert e \rvert$	Technique 2	e	$\lvert e \rvert$
1	492	488	4	4	495	−3	3
2	470	484	−14	14	482	−12	12
3	485	480	5	5	478	7	7
4	493	490	3	3	488	5	5
5	498	497	1	1	492	6	6
6	492	493	−1	1	493	−1	1
			−2	28		+2	34

$$\text{MAD}_1 = \frac{\Sigma \lvert e \rvert}{n} = \frac{28}{6} = 4.67$$

$$\text{MAD}_2 = \frac{\Sigma \lvert e \rvert}{n} = \frac{34}{6} = 5.67$$

Technique 1 is superior in this comparison, although six observations would generally be too few on which to base a realistic comparison.

8. Given the demand data that follow, prepare a naive forecast for periods 2 through 10. Then determine each forecast error, and use those values to obtain $2s$ control limits. If the next two periods' demands turn out to be 125 and 130, can you conclude that the forecasts are in control?

Period:	1	2	3	4	5	6	7	8	9	10
Demand:	118	117	120	119	126	122	117	123	121	124

Solution

For a naive forecast, each period's demand becomes the forecast for the next period. Hence, the forecasts and errors are:

Period	Demand	Forecast	Error	Error²
1	118	—	—	—
2	117	118	−1	1
3	120	117	3	9
4	119	120	−1	1
5	126	119	7	49
6	122	126	−4	16
7	117	122	−5	25
8	123	117	6	36
9	121	123	−2	4
10	124	121	3	9
			+6	150

$$s = \sqrt{\frac{\Sigma \ error^2}{n - 1}} \quad (n = \text{Number of errors})$$

$$= \sqrt{\frac{150}{9 - 1}} = 4.33$$

The control limits are 2(4.33) = ±8.66.

The forecast for period 11 was 124. Demand turned out to be 125, for an error of 125 − 124 = +1. This is within the limits of ±8.66. If the next demand is 130 and the naive forecast is 125 (based on the period 11 demand of 125), the error is +5. Again, this is within the limits, so we cannot conclude the forecast is not working properly. If we had more values, say, at least five or six, we could plot the errors to see if we could detect any patterns (which would suggest nonrandomness was present).

DISCUSSION AND REVIEW QUESTIONS

1. Which approach to forecasting, quantitative or qualitative, is superior?

2. What are the main advantages that quantitative techniques for forecasting have over qualitative techniques? What limitations do quantitative techniques have?

3. List the specific weaknesses of each of these approaches to developing a forecast:
   a. Consumer surveys.
   b. Sales force composite.
   c. Committee of managers or executives.

4. Briefly describe the Delphi technique. What are some of its main benefits and weaknesses?

5. What is the purpose of establishing control limits for forecasts?

6. What factors would you consider in deciding whether to use wide or narrow control limits for a forecast?

7. Contrast the use of MAD and MSE in evaluating forecasts.

8. What advantages does exponential smoothing have over moving averages as a forecasting tool?

9. How does the number of periods in a moving average affect the responsiveness of the forecast?

10. What factors enter into the choice of a value for the smoothing constant in exponential smoothing?

11. How accurate is your local five day weather forecast? Explain.

12. Explain how using a centered moving average with a length equal to length of a season eliminates seasonality from a time series.

13. Contrast the terms *sales* and *demand*.

14. Contrast the reactive and proactive approaches to forecasting. Give several examples of types of organizations or situations in which each type is used.

PROBLEMS

1. National Mixer, Inc. carries a line of electric blenders. Given the following monthly sales data:

a. Compute a three-month and a five-month moving average.

b. Plot the original data and the two moving averages on the same graph.

c. What effect does the number of periods in a moving average have on the extent of smoothing?

Month	Demand (000 units)	Month	Demand (000 units)
Jan.	20	Jul.	18
Feb.	24	Aug.	21
Mar.	18	Sept.	24
Apr.	14	Oct.	22
May	25	Nov. . . .	28
June	20	Dec.	32

2. National Mixer, Inc. also sells can openers. Monthly sales for a seven-month period were as follows:

Month	Sales (000 units)
Feb.	19
Mar.	18
Apr.	15
May	20
Jun.	18
Jul.	22
Aug.	20

a. Plot the monthly data on a sheet of graph paper.

b. Forecast September sales volume using each of the following:

(1) A linear trend equation.

(2) A five-month moving average.

(3) Exponential smoothing with a smoothing constant equal to .20, assuming a March forecast of 19.

(4) The naive approach.

c. Which method seems least appropriate? Why?

d. What does use of the term *sales* rather than *demand* presume?

3. Monthly sales of snowmobiles for a suburban Toronto dealer for the past year are:

Month	Units sold	Month	Units sold
Jan.	92	Jul.	4
Feb.	88	Aug.	3
Mar.	80	Sept.	6
Apr.	60	Oct.	12
May	10	Nov.	25
Jun.	1	Dec.	82

a. Smooth this data using a three-month *centered* moving average.

b. Plot the original sales data and the centered moving average on the same graph.

c. Would it make sense to use a three-month moving average to *predict* sales for the following January? Explain.

4. A dry cleaner uses exponential smoothing to forecast usage of equipment at its main plant. August usage was forecast to be 88 percent of capacity; actual usage was 89.6 percent of capacity. Forecasts use a smoothing constant of .1

a. Prepare a forecast for September.

b. Assuming actual September usage of 92 percent, prepare a forecast for October usage.

5. The owner of Wine Sales & Service is contemplating the use of exponential smoothing to forecast wine sales. Demand for the preceding eight years is shown in the following table.

a. Forecast demand for next year using $\alpha = .4$.

b. What would the naive forecast for the next year be?

Year	Demand (000 cases)
1	800
2	810
3	808
4	812
5	810
6	825
7	811
8	804

6. An electrical contractor's records during the last five weeks indicate the number of job requests:

Week:	1	2	3	4	5
Requests:	20	22	18	21	22

Predict the number of requests for week 6 using each of these methods:
a. Naive.
b. A four-period moving average.
c. Exponential smoothing with $\alpha = .30$.

7. Tread-On-Us Carpet & Tile Company sold 700,000 square feet of carpet last year, 800,000 square feet the year before, and 600,000 square feet the year before that. Using a three-year moving average, predict carpet sales for this year. Then, assuming actual sales for this year turn out to be 780,000 square feet, predict sales for next year.

8. A cosmetics manufacturer's marketing department has developed a linear trend equation that can be used to predict annual sales of its popular Hand & Foot Cream:

$$y_t = 80 + 15t$$

where

$$y_t = \text{Annual sales (000 bottles)}$$
$$t_0 = 1979$$

a. Are annual sales increasing or decreasing? By how much?
b. Predict annual sales for 1992 using the equation.

9. A management consultant, using historical sales data, has developed a predictive equation for sales of white pine trees for a tree farm:

$$y_t = 480 - 50t + 10t^2$$

where

$$y_t = \text{Number of trees sold in year } t$$
$$t = 0 \text{ at } 1988$$

a. Plot the equation for years 1983 to 1990.
b. Forecast sales of white pine trees for 1992.

10. From the following graph, determine the linear equation of the trend line using 1981 as the base year for Glib Sales, Inc.

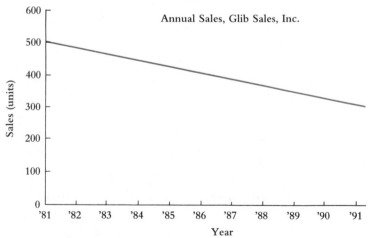

Annual Sales, Glib Sales, Inc.

11. Freight car loadings over a 12-year period at a busy port are:

Year	Number (00)	Year	Number (00)
1	220	7	350
2	245	8	360
3	280	9	400
4	275	10	380
5	300	11	420
6	310	12	450

a. Compute a linear trend line for freight car loadings.
b. Plot the trend line and the original data on a single sheet of graph paper.
c. Use the trend equation to predict loadings for year 15.

12. The following equation summarizes the trend portion of quarterly sales of automatic dishwashers over a long cycle. Sales also exhibit seasonal variations. Using the information given, prepare a forecast of sales for each quarter of 1992.

$$y_t = 40 - 6.5t + 2t^2$$

where

y_t = Unit sales
t = 0 at the fourth quarter of 1989

Quarter	Relative
1	1.1
2	1.0
3	.6
4	1.3

13. Develop a linear trend equation for the following data on bread deliveries, and use it to predict deliveries for periods 11 through 14.

Period	Dozen deliveries
1	200
2	214
3	211
4	228
5	235
6	222
7	248
8	241
9	253
10	267

14. Use trend-adjusted smoothing with $\alpha_1 = .3$ and $\alpha_2 = .2$ to smooth the bread delivery data in the preceding problem.

15. Refer to the freight car loading data in Problem 11. Because of the apparent trend in those data, the manager has decided to use trend-adjusted exponential smoothing to predict future loading demand.

a. Assume an initial forecast of 380 loadings. Use trend-adjusted smoothing with these constants: (1) $\alpha_1 = .2$, $\alpha_2 = .2$; (2) $\alpha_1 = .4$, $\alpha_2 = .2$; and (3) $\alpha_1 = .4$, $\alpha_2 = .40$. Use an initial trend estimate of 20. Start at period 9.
b. Which of the combinations in part a is the most accurate? Explain.
c. If there were more data, control charts could be constructed. How might those control charts be useful in comparing these forecasting alternatives?

16. Sales of waterbeds at a specialty store during the past seven weeks were:

Week:	1	2	3	4	5	6	7
Number sold:	26	24	29	33	32	37	36

a. Use two different appropriate methods to predict the number of units that will be sold during week 8. Explain why these methods are appropriate.
b. If actual sales during the next five weeks turn out to be 40, 45, 44, 50, and 53, which of the two methods would have provided a better forecast? Explain what probably occurred, based on a comparison of the new data with the original data.

17. A gift shop in a tourist center is open on weekends (Friday, Saturday, and Sunday).

The owner-manager hopes to improve scheduling of part-time employees by determining seasonal relatives for each of these days. Data on recent activity at the store (sales transactions per day) have been tabulated, and they are shown below. Develop seasonal relatives for the shop.

			Week			
	#1	#2	#3	#4	#5	#6
Friday	149	154	152	150	159	163
Saturday	250	255	260	268	273	276
Sunday	166	162	171	173	176	183

18. Use a naive trend approach to predict sales transactions for the gift shop in the previous problem for the following week.

19. An analyst must decide between two different forecasting techniques: a linear trend equation and the naive approach. The linear trend equation is $y_t = 124 + 2t$, and it was developed using data from periods 1 through 10. Based on data for periods 11 through 20 as shown, which of these two methods has the greater accuracy? (The data are for daily sales of trail bikes.)

t	Units Sold	t	Units Sold
11	147	16	152
12	148	17	155
13	151	18	157
14	145	19	160
15	155	20	165

20. The manager of a fashionable restaurant that is open Wednesday through Saturday has commented that the restaurant does about 30 percent of its business on Friday night, 35 percent on Saturday night, and 20 percent on Thursday night. What seasonal relatives would describe this situation?

21. Coal shipments from Mountain Coal Company's no. 4 mine for the past seven years are:

Year	Tons shipped (000)
1	405
2	410
3	420
4	415
5	412
6	420
7	424

a. Explain why simple exponential smoothing would not be an appropriate forecasting method.

b. Use an appropriate technique to develop a forecast for the next three years.

22. Obtain estimates of daily relatives for the number of customers at a restaurant for the evening meal, given the following data. (*Hint:* Use a seven-day moving average.)

Day	Number served
1	80
2	75
3	78
4	95
5	130
6	136
7	40
8	82
9	77
10	80
11	94
12	125
13	135
14	42
15	84
16	77
17	83
18	96
19	135
20	140
21	37
22	87
23	82
24	98

Day	Number served
25	103
26	144
27	144
28	48

23. A pharmacist has been monitoring sales of a certain over-the-counter pain reliever. Daily sales during the last 15 days were:

Day:	1	2	3	4	5	6	7	8	9
Number sold:	36	38	42	44	48	49	50	49	52
Day:	10	11	12	13	14	15			
Number sold:	48	52	55	54	56	57			

a. Without doing any calculations, which method would you suggest using to predict future sales—a linear trend equation or trend-adjusted exponential smoothing? Why?

b. If you now learn that on some of the days the store ran out of the pain reliever in question, would that knowledge cause you any concern? Explain.

c. Assume that the data refer to demand rather than sales. Using trend-adjusted smoothing with an initial forecast of 50 for week 8, an initial trend estimate of 2, and $\alpha_1 = \alpha_2 = .3$, develop forecasts for days 9 through 16. What is the MSE for the eight forecasts for which there are actual data?

24. Lawn mower sales for a dealer in Orange County, California, for the past year are shown in the following table, along with monthly (seasonal) relatives, which are supplied to the dealer by the regional distributor.

Month	Units sold	Index
Jan.	640	0.80
Feb.	648	0.80
Mar.	600	0.80
Apr.	761	0.94
May	735	0.89

Month	Units sold	Index
Jun.	850	1.00
Jul.	765	0.90
Aug.	1,000	1.17
Sept.	1,038	1.20
Oct.	1,026	1.14
Nov.	967	1.20
Dec.	1,107	1.23

a. Plot the data.

b. De-seasonalize lawn mower sales.

c. Plot the de-seasonalized data on the same graph as the original data. Comment on the two graphs.

25. A quality control analyst has kept a record of the defective rate of a process she has been working to improve during a period of about four weeks. The following data (percentages) were recorded:

	Week			
	1	2	3	4
Monday	10.2	9.4	8.4	7.8
Tuesday	8.2	7.3	7.0	6.5
Wednesday	7.2	6.8	6.3	5.0
Thursday	6.8	6.0	5.4	4.8
Friday	9.4	9.0	8.2	7.1

a. Determine daily relatives for the defective rate. Then use the relatives to remove seasonality from the data. (Hint: See Problem 24.)

b. Compute a linear trend equation for the de-seasonalized data.

c. Using the trend equation and seasonal relatives, predict the defective rate for each day of week 5.

26. A farming cooperative manager wants to estimate quarterly relatives for grain shipments, based on the data shown (quantities are in metric tons):

Year	Quarter			
	1	2	3	4
1	200	250	210	340
2	210	252	212	360
3	215	260	220	358
4	225	272	233	372
5	232	284	240	381

Determine quarter relatives. (*Hint:* Use a centered four-period moving average initially, and then use a centered two-period moving average of the four-period moving average.)

27. Long-Life Insurance has developed a linear model that it uses to determine the amount of straight life insurance a family of four should have, based on the current age of the head of the household. The equation is:

$$y = 32 - .1x$$

where

y = Insurance needed ($000)
x = Current age of head of household

a. Plot the relationship on a piece of graph paper.
b. Use the equation to determine the amount of straight life insurance to recommend for a family of four if the head of the household is 30 years old.

28. Timely Transport provides local delivery service for a number of downtown and suburban businesses. Delivery charges are based on distance and weight involved for each delivery: 10 cents per pound and 15 cents per mile. In addition, there is a $10 storage and handling fee per parcel.
a. Develop an expression that summarizes delivery charges.
b. Determine the delivery charge for transporting a 40-pound parcel 26 miles.

29. The following values represent summary information produced by a regression analysis of cash flow relative to sales.

$n = 14$, $\Sigma x = 50$, $\Sigma x^2 = 1,700$
$\Sigma xy = 1,540$, $\Sigma y = 200$, $\Sigma y^2 = 4,400$

a. Determine the least squares equation.
b. Compute the correlation coefficient.
c. Is the slope of the line significantly different from zero? Is the correlation significantly different from zero? Explain briefly.

30. The manager of a seafood restaurant was asked to establish a pricing policy on lobster dinners. Experimenting with prices produced the following data:

Average number sold per day, y	Price, x
200	$6.00
190	6.50
188	6.75
180	7.00
170	7.25
162	7.50
160	8.00

a. Plot the data and a regression line on the same graph.
b. Using the regression equation, obtain a 95 percent confidence interval for estimated demand for a price of $7.00.
c. Compute the correlation coefficient and interpret it.

31. The following data were collected during a study of consumer buying patterns.

Observation	x	y
1	15	74
2	25	80
3	40	84
4	32	81
5	51	96
6	47	95
7	30	83
8	18	78
9	14	70
10	15	72
11	22	85
12	24	88
13	33	90

a. Plot the data.

b. Fit a linear regression line to the data using the least squares method.

c. Is the slope of the line significantly different from zero?

d. Use the equation determined in part b to predict the value of y for $x = 41$.

e. Determine a 95 percent confidence interval for the predicted value of y for $x = 41$.

32. Lovely Lawns, Inc. intends to use sales of lawn fertilizer to predict lawn mower sales. The store manager feels that there is probably a six-week lag between fertilizer sales and mower sales. The pertinent data are:

Period	Fertilizer sales (tons)	Number of mowers sold (six-week lag)
1	1.6	10
2	1.3	8
3	1.8	11
4	2.0	12
5	2.2	12
6	1.6	9
7	1.5	8

a. Compute the correlation between the two variables. Does it appear that there is a relationship between these variables that will yield good predictions?

b. Use the least squares method to obtain a linear regression line for the data.

c. Predict lawn mower sales for the first week in August, given fertilizer sales six weeks earlier of 2 tons.

33. A financial planner wants to develop a linear regression model that he can use to evaluate clients' portfolios. He has collected relevant data on 20 clients, and he has used his microcomputer to analyze the data. The computer output included the following information:

$$y = 470.4 + 25.1x$$

where

$x = $ Beginning portfolio value

$y = $ Portfolio value two years later

$$s_e = 4.30$$
$$s_b = 6.21$$
$$r = +.924$$

a. Is the relationship significant? Explain.

b. How well does the regression equation fit the data? Explain.

c. If the planner determines that s_{reg} for a certain new client's portfolio of 98 is 3.70, develop a 95 percent confidence interval for the dependent variable, and interpret your answer.

34. The manager of a travel agency has been using a seasonally adjusted forecast to predict demand for packaged tours. The actual and predicted values are:

Period	Demand	Predicted
1	129	124
2	194	200
3	156	150
4	91	94
5	85	80
6	132	140
7	126	128
8	126	124
9	95	100
10	149	150
11	98	94
12	85	80
13	137	140
14	134	128

a. Compute MAD for the fifth period, then update it period by period using exponential smoothing with $\alpha = .3$.

b. Compute a tracking signal for periods 5 through 14 using the initial and updated MADs. If limits of ± 3 are used, what can you conclude?

35. Two independent methods of forecasting based on judgment and experience have been prepared each month for the past 10 months. The forecasts and actual sales are as follows.

Month	Sales	Forecast 1	Forecast 2
1 770	770	771	769
2 789	789	785	787
3 794	794	790	792
4 780	780	784	798
5 768	768	770	774
6 772	772	768	770
7 760	760	761	759
8 775	775	771	775
9 786	786	784	788
10 790	790	788	788

a. Compute the MSE and MAD for each forecast. Does either method seem superior? Explain.

b. Compute a tracking signal for the 10th month for each forecast. What does it show? (Use action limits of ± 4.)

c. Compute $2s$ control limits for each forecast.

d. Prepare a naive forecast for periods 2–11 using the given sales data. Compute each of the following: (1) MSE, (2) MAD, (3) tracking signal at month 10, and (4) $2s$ control limits. How do the naive results compare with the other two forecasts?

36. The classified department of a monthly magazine has used a combination of quantitative and qualitative methods to forecast sales of advertising space. Results over a 20-month period are as follows:

Month	Error
1	−8
2	−2
3	4
4	7
5	9
6	5
7	0
8	−3
9	−9
10	−4
11	1
12	6
13	8

Month	Error
14	4
15	1
16	−2
17	−4
18	−8
19	−5
20	−1

a. Compute a tracking signal for months 11 through 20. Compute an initial value of MAD for month 11, and then update it for each month using exponential smoothing with $\alpha = .1$. What can you conclude? Assume limits of ± 4.

b. Using the first half of the data, construct a control chart with $2s$ limits. What can you conclude?

c. Plot the last 10 errors on the control chart. Are the errors random? What is the implication of this?

37. A textbook publishing company has compiled data on total annual sales of its business texts for the preceding nine years:

Year:	1	2	3	4	5
Sales (000):	40.2	44.5	48.0	52.3	55.8
Year:	6	7	8	9	
Sales (000):	57.1	62.4	69.0	73.7	

a. Using an appropriate model, forecast textbook sales for each of the next five years.

b. Prepare a control chart for the forecast using the original data.

c. Suppose actual sales for the next five years turn out as follows:

Year:	10	11	12	13	14
Sales (000):	77.2	82.1	87.8	90.6	98.9

Is the forecast performing adequately? Explain.

38. The owner of a catering company wants to use exponential smoothing to forecast demand for the catering service. These historical values reflect recent experience:

Week: 1 2 3 4 5 6 7 8 9
Demand: 8 10 10 12 9 7 8 7 9
Week: 10 11 12 13 14
Demand: 10 13 12 11 10

a. Use the first half of the data to develop a model. Choose between a smoothing constant of .10 and one of .30.

b. Test your choice of a smoothing constant on the remainder of the data,

using a control chart with two standard deviation limits.

c. Forecast the expected demand for week 15.

d. If actual demand turns out to be 8, is the forecast in control? Forecast the demand for the following week. If actual demand turns out to be 13, is the forecast in control? Explain.

SELECTED BIBLIOGRAPHY

Box, G. E. P., and G. Jenkins. *Time Series Analysis: Forecasting and Control.* San Francisco: Holden-Day, 1970.

Chambers, John C.; S. K. Mullick; and Donald D. Smith. "How to Choose the Right Forecasting Technique." *Harvard Business Review,* July–August 1971, pp. 45–74.

Hanke, John E., and Arthur G. Reitsch. *Business Forecasting.* Boston: Allyn & Bacon, 1981.

Levenbach, Hans, and James P. Cleary. *The Modern Forecaster: The Forecasting Process through Data Analysis.* Belmont, Calif.: Lifetime Learning Publications, 1984.

Riggs, James L. *Production Systems: Planning, Analysis, and Control.* 3rd ed. New York: John Wiley & Sons, 1981.

Stevenson, William J. *Business Statistics: Concepts and Applications.* 2nd ed. New York: Harper & Row, 1985.

Tersine, R. J., and W. Riggs. "The Delphi Technique: A Long-Range Planning Tool." *Business Horizons* 19, no. 2, 1976.

Wheelwright, Steven C.; Spyros Madridakis; and Victor McGee. *Forecasting Methods and Applications.* 2nd. ed. New York: John Wiley & Sons, 1983.

CASE

WATCH OUR FORECASTS GROW

The annual budget meeting of a large commerical bank had just ended, and from the looks on their faces, it was obvious that Bud Thompson and Brad Smith were quite disappointed with the outcome. Brad was in charge of the commerical bank loan department, and Bud was director of personnel for the bank. Brad remarked, somewhat dryly, "What do they think we are, miracle workers?"

"I know what you mean," Bud responded. "Even if demand turns out to be lower than my forecast, I am still going to need those funds."

When they met for coffee the next morning, Bud offered a suggestion: "You know my brother, Bob, the salesman? I mentioned our little problem to him, and he said that most of the salesmen he knows tack on an additional 10 to 20 percent to their forecasts. Maybe we should do the same.

That way, even if they cut us back a bit, we would still get more than we do now. And who knows, demand might be higher than normal. And even if it isn't, I'm sure we will be able to come up with a reasonable explanation."

"I don't know if that would be wise," countered Brad. "You know how the old man pores over those figures before our meetings. I wouldn't want to have him come down on me in a meeting. But I'll tell you one thing," he continued. "If there is a substantial increase in demand, we could be in a real bind. By the time we can gear up, National will have grabbed a huge chunk of our accounts."

"It's a tricky business," Bud commented. "You're damned if you do and damned if you don't!"

Questions

1. Do you feel that inflated forecasts would be an appropriate alternative in this situation? Explain. Would inflated forecasts ever be appropriate? Why or why not?

2. What action could Bud and Brad take to try to improve the situation? Support your answer.

3. In what ways are banks similar to other organizations in terms of developing and using forecasts?

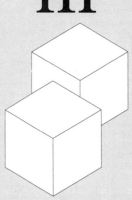

DESIGN OF PRODUCTION SYSTEMS

Production system design encompasses decisions involving:

1. Product and service design (Chapter 4).
2. Location planning (Chapter 5).
3. Process selection and capacity planning (Chapter 6).
4. Facilities layout (Chapter 7).
5. Design of work systems (Chapter 8).

Design decisions do not occur only when an organization is initially formed. Rather, they continue to be made periodically throughout the life of the organization. The importance of these decisions is related to the costs they often entail, the long-term commitments they often require, the constraints they place on the ongoing operations of the organization, and the difficulty of reversing them once they have been executed.

These areas are not always under the direct control of the operations manager. Nonetheless, the operations manager usually has some say in these matters, especially since they play a major role in setting the stage on which the operations manager must perform.

Product and service design often is the focal point of system design since it represents the purpose of the system. Capacity decisions create limits on the ability of the system to provide goods and services. Capacity and location decisions both influence operating costs, and location decisions also have an effect on transportation costs, labor supply and cost, material costs, and access to markets. Layout decisions affect the flow of work through the system. Work design focuses on the human component of production systems and how that component interfaces with other aspects of the system. It also involves a focus on productivity improvements.

Design decisions are primarily strategic in nature. They have a major impact on production systems.

4

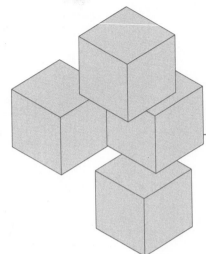

Product and Service Design

LEARNING OBJECTIVES

After completing this chapter, you should be able to:

1. Identify some of the reasons organizations become involved with product and service design.
2. Describe the contributions of R&D to product and service design.
3. Explain the concept of standardization and discuss the advantages and disadvantages of standardization.
4. Discuss the concept of modular design, including its advantages and disadvantages.
5. Define reliability, perform simple reliability computations, and suggest possible ways of improving reliability.

CHAPTER OUTLINE

The essence of any organization is the products or services it offers. Moreover, there is a close link between the design of these products or services and the realization of the goals of the organization. Because of this, organizations have a vital stake in product and service design. Two primary concerns are *function* and *cost*.

In this chapter, we shall consider the need for product and service design, the importance of research and development, the concept of standardization, and the concept of reliability.

THE NEED FOR PRODUCT/SERVICE DESIGN

It might seem that the matter of product or service design is a one-time necessity for new items, that once it is done, no further attention is needed. Practically speaking, this is not usually the case. The business environment in which most organizations must operate is fairly dynamic, so that questions related to product and service design can arise at any time. Pressures for design changes can come from customers, competitors, legal sources, and from within the organization.

Customers may indicate their dissatisfaction with a particular design either through direct complaints to the organization or some regulatory body, or indirectly through decreased purchases of the item. Thus, organizations often become involved in redesign to improve sales or to respond to complaints.

In competitive situations, organizations often strive to increase profits and market share by building "a better mousetrap," which then forces competitors to reevaluate their own designs in a never-ending battle. As soon as one bank comes up with a promotional gimmick, such as free checking or bank-by-mail, its competitors are sure to follow. Likewise, if one supermarket offers double-couponing, competitors may follow suit for fear of losing their market shares.

Organizations are faced with an increasing array of government agencies established to regulate their activities. Among the more familiar ones are the Food and Drug Administration, the Environmental Protection Agency, the National Highway Safety Commission, and the Consumer Products Safety Commission. Bans on cyclamates, red food dye, phosphates, and asbestos in recent years have sent designers scurrying back to their drawing boards to find alternative designs that will prove acceptable to both the government regulators and their customers. Similarly, pollution standards for automobiles and safety features such as seat belts, safety glass, and energy-absorbing bumpers and frames have had a substantial impact on automotive design. Much attention has been directed toward the design of toys with the idea of removing sharp edges, small pieces that can cause choking, and toxic materials. In the construction field, government regulations often require the use of lead-free paint, safety glass in entranceways, access to public buildings for handicapped persons, and standards for insulation, electrical wiring, plumbing, and so on.

In some cases, the cost or shortage of raw materials can necessitate design changes. For instance, gasoline shortages and price increases spurred efforts to develop fuel-efficient cars as well as the development of alternative sources of energy.

Product liability can be a strong incentive for design improvement. **Product liability** means that a manufacturer is liable for any injuries or damages caused by a faulty product, because of either poor workmanship or poor design. In recent years, many business firms have become involved in lawsuits related to their products, including the Firestone Tire & Rubber Co. (which underwent a major recall of its tires), the Ford Motor Co. (concerning, among other problems, the gas tank of its Pinto), General Motors Corp. (steering problems with its Corvair), manufacturers of hairdryers (asbestos particles), toy manufacturers, and countless others. Also, manufacturers are faced with the implied warranties created by state laws under the **Uniform Commercial Code**, which says, in effect, that products carry an implication of *merchantability* and *fitness* (i.e., a product must be usable for its intended purposes).

The suits and potential suits have resulted in increases in legal and insurance costs, expensive settlements with injured parties, and costly recalls. Moreover, increasing consumer awareness of product safety can adversely affect product image and subsequent demand for a product.

Because of these factors, it is extremely important to design products that are reasonably free of hazards. When hazards do exist, it is necessary to install safety guards or other devices for reducing accident potential. Adequate warning notices of risks must also be provided. Consumer groups, business firms, and various government agencies often work together to develop industry-wide standards that will help avoid some of the hazards. Major advances have been made in the area of toy manufacturing in terms of safety standards.

It is interesting to reflect on the role of operations management people in product and service design since operations will have the ultimate responsibility for *converting* the design into reality. During the conversion process, design errors and deficiencies are frequently detected, and ideas for improvements are generated. Many of the mistakes can be avoided by involving operations personnel in the design stages. In fact, it often happens that when operations people are not consulted during product or service design, they become involved by initiating redesign efforts.

Finally, a humorous look at some of the different ways that various individuals and departments in the design process can interpret the "design" is illustrated in Figure 4–1. The obvious point is that there must be sufficient information to determine what the customer wants as well as communication and agreement among those responsible for designing, producing, and marketing the product or service.

Product Life Cycles

Many new products go through a **product life cycle** in terms of demand. When an item is first introduced, it may be treated as a curiosity. Demand is generally low at this point because potential buyers have not had much time to

FIGURE 4—1

Differing views of design created through lack of information

Source: *Educational Center Newsletter*, Minneapolis, Minnesota.

As proposed by the marketing department.

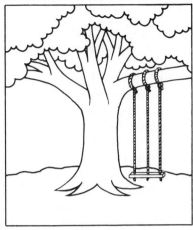

As specified in the product request.

As designed by the senior designer.

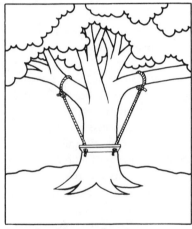

As produced by manufacturing.

As used by the customer.

What the customer wanted.

familiarize themselves with the item. Many potential buyers recognize that all of the bugs have probably not been ironed out and that the price may drop after the introductory period. With the passage of time, production and design improvements usually create a more reliable and less costly product. Demand then grows for these reasons and because of the increasing awareness of the product or service. At the next stage in the life cycle, the product reaches maturity: there are few, if any, design changes, and demand levels off. Eventually, the market becomes saturated, which leads to a decline in demand. These stages in the cycle are illustrated in Figure 4–2.

In the last stage of a life cycle, some firms adopt a defensive research posture whereby they attempt to prolong the useful life of a product or service by one or more of the following: improving the reliability of the product, reducing costs of producing the item (and, hence, the price), redesigning the item, or changing the packaging.

Some products do not seem to go through such a life cycle. For example, wooden pencils, paper clips, nails, knives, forks and spoons, drinking glasses, and similar items don't seem to exhibit life cycles, but most new products seem to. Current examples of items in various stages of life cycles include slide rules, black-and-white televisions, textbook editions, computers, calculator models, kitchen floor coverings, and TV series.

It is important to recognize that wide variations exist in the amount of time a particular product takes to pass through a given phase of its life cycle; some products pass through various stages in a relatively short period of time; others take considerably longer. Often it is a matter of the basic *need* for the item and the *rate of technological change*. For instance, some toys, novelty items, and style items have a life cycle of less than one year, whereas other, more crucial items, such as slide rules, may last for 50 years or more before yielding to technological change.

FIGURE 4–2

Products or services may exhibit life cycles over time

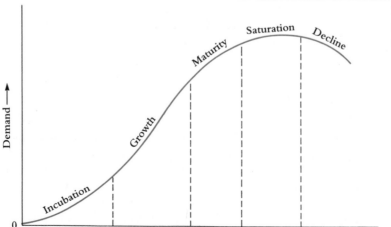

RESEARCH AND DEVELOPMENT

Most of the recent developments in semiconductors, medical technology, communications, and space technology can be traced to **research and development (R&D)**. The costs of much of these efforts were so great that only the largest companies and the government could afford to underwrite their expense. The research projects from which these and countless other scientific advancements have sprung are typically conducted by colleges and universities, research foundations, and large corporations. Some have come from basic research, and others, perhaps the majority, have come about through applied research and development. *Basic research* is intended to advance scientific knowledge (i.e., advance the state of the art), and it generally does not have any specific commercial purposes. *Applied research* is designed to produce commercial benefits. *Development* involves converting the results of applied research into useful commercial applications.

Because basic research does not yield results that can be considered immediately useful, only the largest companies, foundations, and the government can afford to underwrite such efforts. Applied research and development, because of its commercial possibilities, appeals more to smaller organizations. Even then, costs can be prohibitive, leading some to adopt a design-by-imitation approach. This is readily evident, for example, in the field of electronics.

The benefits of successful R&D can be tremendous. Some research leads to patents, with the potential for licensing and royalties. However, many discoveries are not patentable, or companies don't wish to divulge details of their ideas and so do not follow the patent route. Even so, the first organization to bring a new product or service to the market generally stands to profit from it before the others can catch up. (Recall the earlier discussion of life cycles; early products may be priced higher because a temporary monopoly exists until competitors bring their versions out.)

There are also a number of substantial risks involved in R&D. For example, an oil company may spend $5 million to drill a well even though the probability of success might be less than 10 percent. The fact is that most projects that have high potential gains also have high potential losses. Moreover, many projects must be terminated when it appears that they are not likely to yield enough to make them attractive.

STANDARDIZATION

A major contributing factor to the high rate of productivity achieved by industrialized nations is the standardization of parts. **Standardization** means that parts are made to conform to a specified standard, and regardless of when or where such a part was made, it can be interchanged with another part of the same type and serve just as well. Because of this, parts do not have to be custom-produced for a product, which would be a slow and expensive procedure. Instead, large volumes of standardized parts can be produced and used for subsequent assembly operations and for replacements in the field, thus permitting many economies in designing, fabricating, storing, inspecting, assembling, and repairing parts.

One of the main disadvantages of standardization is that it reduces the potential variety of products, reducing the range of customers to whom it may appeal. Generally, consumers must accept the standardized version or nothing at all. Another disadvantage is that a design may be frozen before it has been adequately improved. Once an item is standardized, there are compelling arguments for avoiding design modifications. A familiar example of this is the keyboard arrangement of a typewriter. Research has demonstrated that much more efficient arrangements are possible, but the cost of replacing or changing those already in service plus the need to retrain typists would entail a tremendous burden. Similarly, U.S.-made color TVs have a standard scanning rate (lines per inch) that is lower than that of foreign-made televisions, resulting in poorer resolution. Again, early freezing of the design is partly to blame.

The main advantages and disadvantages of standardization are outlined in Table 4–1.

Modular Design

Modular design is essentially standardization in chunks. Modules represent groupings of component parts into subassemblies, usually to the point where the individual parts lose their separate identity. One familiar example of modular design is a television set with easily removed control panels. Computers, too, have modular parts that can be replaced if they become defective. By arranging modules in different configurations, different computer capabilities can be obtained. Modular design is also found in the construction industry. One firm in Rochester, New York, makes prefabricated motel rooms complete with wiring, plumbing, and even room decorations in its factory and then moves the complete rooms via rail to the construction site, where they are integrated into the structure.

TABLE 4–1

Advantages and disadvantages of standardization

Advantages

1. Fewer parts to deal with in inventory and in manufacturing.
2. Reduces training costs and time.
3. Purchasing, handling, and inspection procedures become more routine.
4. Orders can be filled from inventory.
5. Provides opportunities for long production runs and automation.
6. Need for fewer parts justifies increased expenditures on perfecting designs and improving quality control procedures.

Disadvantages

1. Designs may be frozen with too many imperfections remaining.
2. High cost of design changes increases resistance to improvements.
3. Decreased variety results in less consumer appeal.

One advantage of modular design of equipment is that failures are often easier to diagnose and remedy because there are fewer pieces to investigate compared to a nonmodular design. Similar advantages are found in ease of repair and replacement; the faulty module is conveniently removed and replaced with a good one. The manufacture and assembly of modules generally involves simplifications: fewer parts are involved, so purchasing and inventory control become more routine, fabrication and assembly operations become more standardized, and training costs often are less.

The main disadvantages of modular design stem from the decrease in variety: the number of possible configurations of modules is much less than the number of possible configurations based on individual components. Another disadvantage that is sometimes encountered is the inability to disassemble a module in order to replace a faulty part; the entire module must be scrapped—usually a more costly procedure.

Metric Conversion

In 1975 Congress enacted legislation calling for voluntary conversion to the metric system of measurement from the present English system. At the time, this was regarded as a move to achieve standardization among industrial nations; most other countries use the metric system.

Since that time there has been some change, although it has perhaps not been as swift as most thought it would be, because of the costs associated with converting tools and equipment and because of public resistance. Some of the difficulty relates to controversy over whether to completely convert to a metric system, discarding present sizes and quantities, or to partially convert by relabeling current sizes and quantities. For instance, should milk and soft drinks be bottled and sold in liter-size containers, as some soft drink manufacturers are now doing, or would it be sufficient to relabel current sizes to reflect metric values (e.g., a quart would become 0.95 liters)? A complete conversion would be more in line with the original intention and would result in fewer sizes than now exist. Relabeling would involve considerably less tooling and equipment changes, making it less costly and much easier to convert.

Other resistance to metric conversion comes from adults, who will have to learn a whole new system of weights and measures, and even from businesses, because of the training requirements such a move would involve.

Furthermore, during the changeover period, it is highly likely that some firms will make the conversion more rapidly than others. This may create a situation in which firms, especially suppliers, will have to provide some customers with metric sizes and others with English sizes. In addition, dual dimensioning on blueprints and machinery will be necessary during the conversion.

Thus, although it appears that metric conversion has certain advantages for American industry, the cost burden and problems in actually making the conversion create a sizable degree of inertia that must be reckoned with by both government and business.

COMPUTER-AIDED DESIGN (CAD)

Computers are being increasingly used for product design, particularly for manufacturing. **Computer-aided design (CAD)** uses computer graphics for product design. The designer can modify an existing design or create a new one on a CRT by means of a light pen, a keyboard, a joystick, or a similar device. Once the design is entered into the computer, the designer can maneuver it on the screen: it can be rotated to provide the designer with different perspectives, it can be split apart to give the designer a view of the inside, and a portion of it can be enlarged for closer examination. When the design has been completed, the designer can obtain a printed version of the design. In addition, the design can be filed electronically, making it accessible to manufacturing personnel and others in the firm who have need for this information (e.g., marketing).

An increasing number of products are being designed in this way. Some of the products include transformers, automobile parts, aircraft parts, integrated circuits, and electric motors.

A major benefit of CAD is the increased productivity of designers. No longer is it necessary to laboriously prepare mechanical drawings of products or parts and revise them repeatedly to correct errors or incorporate revisions. A rough estimate is that CAD increases the productivity of designers from 3 to 10 times. A second major benefit of CAD is the creation of a data base for manufacturing that can supply needed information on product geometry and dimensions, tolerances, material specifications, and so on. It should be noted, however, that such a data base is necessary for CAD to function and that this entails a considerable amount of effort.

Some CAD systems allow the designer to perform engineering and cost analyses on proposed designs. For instance, the computer can determine the weight and volume of a part and do stress analysis as well. When there are a number of alternative designs, the computer can quickly go through the possibilities and identify the best one, given the designer's criteria.

The following reprint gives some indication of the breadth of use of computer-aided design. This article refers to CAD–CAM (CAM stands for computer-aided manufacturing).

COMPUTERS SPEED THE DESIGN OF MORE WORKADAY PRODUCTS

The same computer technology used to design cars and missiles now is being used to design sneakers and spoons. The reason: Computer-aided design and manufacturing systems have become cheaper and easier to use, encouraging even decidedly low-tech companies to trade their drafting tables for computer terminals.

"CAD–CAM companies have been beating down our doors for years," says Alfred Zeien, vice chairman of Gillette Co., whose Braun subsidiary in West Germany uses computers to design hair dryers and electric shavers. "We were finally convinced they could deliver."

Other makers of workaday products also have been convinced. Hasbro Bradley Inc. uses computers to design parts for GI Joe aircraft carriers; Craft Patterns does the same for dog houses. ITT Corp.'s computers draw fire hydrants; Oneida Ltd.'s make spoons and forks.

Computers take the drudgery out of design. Instead of laboriously drawing and redrawing blueprints, engineers create designs electronically and alter them at the push of a few buttons. Some computer programs also analyze the designs to see how well they handle stress or changes in temperature. Manufacturers say that encourages experimentation, yields better-quality goods, and helps them introduce products more quickly.

"It allows us to try blue-sky projects," says W. David Lee, who heads a product development group at the Arthur D. Little Inc. consulting firm. Using computerized design techniques, Mr. Lee's group produced a U.S. Army canteen that keeps coffee warm for eight hours in arctic temperatures and a gas stove that needs less insulation for Maytag Co.'s Hardwick Stove division.

Walter Stewart, a senior vice president at Oneida, says that adding CAD–CAM is "a matter of survival." Oneida estimates that it takes 70 weeks to design and produce a flatware set using conventional methods—nearly twice the time of Asian competitors who work longer hours and, Oneida contends, produce lower-quality goods. To compete better, Oneida began in 1983 to use computers to design flatware and to make dies that punch out stainless steel forks and knives.

As a result, Oneida says it now can match the turnaround time of its Asian competitors on some items. It also can bid on rush jobs that it might otherwise lost. Last summer, for instance, it produced spoon designs using the hot-selling Care Bear characters for General Mills Inc. in only two days. Oneida also says that more precise tooling reduces the number of imperfections in the flatware which must be laboriously ground or polished out.

Manufacturers also use CAD–CAM to customize products. The Kennedy Valve unit of ITT designs fire hydrants by piecing together computer drawings of different size nozzles and pipes. "It's like working with building blocks," says Bruce Platusich, manager of product engineering.

In a more sophisticated application, privately owned Techmedica Inc., Camarillo, Calif., produces artificial bones by computer. Techmedica uses cross-sections of a patient's bone produced by a CT scan, or computer tomography, as a basis for the bone design. The computer then directs a machine that cuts the replacement bone out of a block of titanium alloy.

Anthony Hedley, director of surgical research at the Huntington Arthritis Center in Phoenix, says Techmedica can deliver an artificial bone in two weeks—a fraction of the time of suppliers that aren't computerized. As a result of the speeded up delivery and precision design, he says, some bone cancer patients are spared amputations.

Manufacturers also say CAD–CAM fattens their profit margins. By reducing product development time with computers, Gillette says it can quickly "abort" a project that doesn't meet cost goals. Hasbro Bradley says it can gear up faster for mass production by using computers to design molds.

"With some toys you can sell all you can make by Thanksgiving," says Hugh Maxwell, Hasbro Bradley's senior vice president for operations. If the company can produce a mold just one week faster, he estimates, it can sell another $300,000 worth of some toys.

But CAD–CAM has some shortcomings. Longtime employees sometimes resist learning the technology. And because the systems are so complex, they can be out of commission as much as 30 percent of the time, says Harley Shaiken, a Massachusetts Institute of Technology researcher. Among reasons for the downtime, he says, are computer breakdowns, inexperienced workers, and management failure to devise schedules that take advantage of the technology. (Confirms Henry Eichfeld, an official at Computervision Corp., a large CAD–CAM maker: "Thirty percent downtime isn't atypical for the world of data processing.")

What's more, whatever cost savings result from the use of CAD–CAM don't necessarily translate into lower prices for consumers. Converse Inc., for instance, uses computers to design sneakers. But John O'Neil, president, says the company's large investment in CAD–CAM "means the cost of speeding up the process won't be reflected in the cost of the shoe."

Brian Smith, president of privately owned Craft Patterns, St. Charles, Illinois, has another problem with CAD–CAM. He says that he can only use his company's $165,000 design system at night because it saps too much power from the main computer. But he isn't complaining. He says the alternative—using pen and ink to design woodworking patterns for dog houses, high chairs, and other furniture—"is a total mess."

RELIABILITY

Reliability is a measure of the ability of a product, part, or system to perform its intended function under a prescribed set of conditions. The importance of reliability is underscored by the fact that prospective buyers use it when comparing alternatives and sellers use it as one determinant of price. Also, it can have an impact on repeat sales, it can reflect on the producer's image, and there may be legal implications if it is too low.

There are three important dimensions of reliability:

1. Reliability as a probability.
2. Definition of failure.
3. Prescribed operating conditions.

If an item has a reliability of, say, .90, this means that the probability it will function as intended is 90 percent and that the probability it will fail is $1 - .90 = 10$ percent. Hence, it is expected that, on the average, 1 of every 10 such items will fail or, equivalently, that the item will fail, on the average, once in every 10 trials. Similarly, a reliability of .985 implies 15 failures per 1,000 parts or trials.

The term **failure** is used to describe a situation in which an item does not perform as intended. This includes not only those instances in which the item does not function at all, but also instances in which performance is substandard and instances in which the item functions in a way not intended. For example, a smoke alarm might fail to respond to the presence of smoke (not operate at all), or it might sound an alarm that is too faint to provide an adequate warning (substandard performance), or it might sound an alarm even though no smoke is present (an unintended response).

Reliabilities are always specified with respect to some set of conditions, called **normal operating conditions**. These can include load, temperature, and humidity ranges, as well as operating procedures and maintenance schedules. Failure of users to heed such conditions often results in premature failure of parts or complete systems. For example, using a passenger car to tow heavy loads causes excess wear and tear on the drive train; driving over potholes or curbs often results in untimely tire failure; and using a calculator to drive nails usually has a marked impact on its usefulness for performing mathematical operations.

Measuring Reliability

Engineers and designers have a number of techniques at their disposal for assessing the reliability of parts, products, and systems. However, a discussion of those techniques is not within the scope of this text. Instead, let us turn our attention to the issue of measuring overall product or system reliability.

Two types of probability are important for assessing reliability:

1. The probability that the product or system will function on any given trial.
2. The probability that the product or system will function for a given length of time.

The first of these focuses on *one point in time* and is often used when a system must operate for one time or a relatively few number of times. The second of these focuses on the *length of service*. The distinction will become more evident as we examine each of these approaches in more detail.

The probability that a product or system will perform on a given trial is a function of the reliabilities of its component parts and how they are interrelated. Suppose a system is composed of two components and that both must operate in order for the system to function. The system reliability is the *product* of the reliabilities of the components. Thus, if $P(A) = .9$ and $P(B) = .8$, the system has a probability of .72.

Similarly, if three components with reliabilities of .9, .8, and .9 must all work, the system reliability is .648:

It is interesting to note that even though the individual components of a system might have high reliabilities, the system as a whole can have considerably less reliability because all components that are in series (as the ones in the preceding examples are) must function. Furthermore, as the number of series components increases, the system reliability decreases. For example, a system comprising eight components in series, each with a reliability of .99, has a reliability of only $.99^8 = .923$.

Obviously, many products and systems have a large number of component parts that must all operate, and some way to increase overall reliability is needed. One approach is to use **redundancy** in the design. This involves providing backup parts for some items. Consider the case of a component with a reliability of .9 and a backup with a reliability of .8 that automatically switches on if the original fails. The probability that the original part functions is .9. Of the 10 percent of the parts that fail (i.e., $1 - .9$), 80 percent will be "saved" by the backup. Hence, the resulting probability for this pair is $.9 + .8(.1) = .98$.

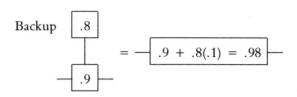

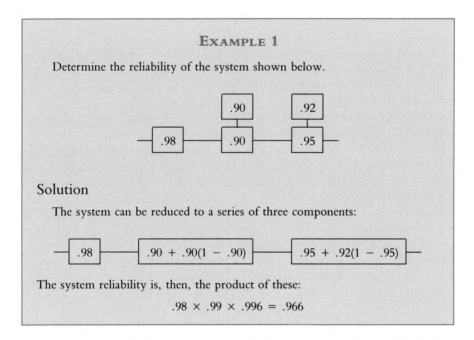

EXAMPLE 1

Determine the reliability of the system shown below.

Solution

The system can be reduced to a series of three components:

The system reliability is, then, the product of these:

$$.98 \times .99 \times .996 = .966$$

The second way of looking at reliability involves the incorporation of a time dimension: probabilities are determined relative to a specified length of time. This approach is commonly used in product warranties, which pertain to a given period of time after purchase of a product.

A typical profile of product failure rate over time is illustrated in Figure 4–3. Because of its shape, it is sometimes referred to as a "bathtub curve." It often happens that a number of items fail shortly after they are put into service, not because they wear out, but simply because they are defective to begin with. The rate of such failures decreases rapidly once the truly defective items are weeded out. During the second phase, there are few failures because most of the defective items have been eliminated, and it is too soon to encounter items that fail because they have worn out. In some cases, this phase can cover

FIGURE 4–3

*Failure rate is a
function of time*

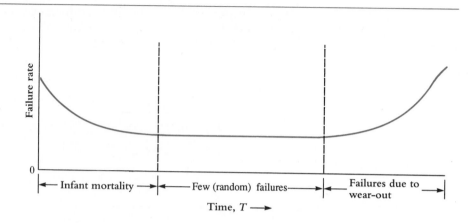

a relatively long period of time. In the third and final phase, failures due to wear-out occur, and the failure rate increases.

Information on the distribution and length of each phase requires the collection of historical data and analysis of those data. It often turns out that the **mean time between failures (MTBF)** can be modeled by a negative exponential distribution, such as that depicted in Figure 4–4. Equipment failures as well as product failures may occur in this pattern. In such cases, the exponential distribution can be used to determine various probabilities of interest. The probability that equipment or a product put into service at time 0 will fail *before* some specified time, T, is equal to the area under the curve between 0 and T. Reliability is concerned with the probability that a product will last *at least until* time T; reliability is equal to the area under the curve *beyond* T. (Note that the total area under the curve in each phase is treated as 100 percent for computational purposes.) Observe that as the specified length of service increases, the area under the curve to the right of that point (i.e., the reliability) decreases.

FIGURE 4–4

*An exponential
distribution*

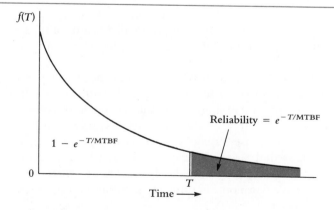

Determining values for the area under a curve to the right of a given point, T, is a relatively simple matter using a table of exponential values. An exponential distribution is completely described using a single parameter, the distribution mean, which reliability engineers often refer to as the mean time between failures. Using the symbol T to represent length of service, we can easily determine the probability that failure will not occur before time T (i.e., the area in the right tail):

$$P(\text{no failure before } T) = e^{-T/\text{MTBF}}$$

where

$$e = \text{Natural logarithm, } 2.7183. . .$$
$$T = \text{Length of service before failure}$$
$$\text{MTBF} = \text{Mean time between failures}$$

The probability that failure will occur before time T is 1.00 minus that amount:

$$P(\text{failure before } T) = 1 - e^{-T/\text{MTBF}}$$

Selected values of $e^{-T/\text{MTBF}}$ are listed in Table 4–2.

EXAMPLE 2

By means of extensive testing, a manufacturer has determined that its Super Sucker Vacuum Cleaner models have an expected life that is exponential with a mean of four years. Find the probability that one of these cleaners will have a life that ends:

a. After the initial four years of service.
b. Before four years of service are completed.
c. Not before six years of service.

Solution

$$\text{MTBF} = 4 \text{ years}$$

a. $T = 4$ years:

$$T/\text{MTBF} = \frac{4 \text{ years}}{4 \text{ years}} = 1.0$$

From Table 4–2, $e^{-1.0} = .3679$.

b. The probability of failure before $T = 4$ years is $1 - e^{-1}$, or $1 - .3679 = .6321$.

c. $T = 6$ years:

$$T/\text{MTBF} = \frac{6 \text{ years}}{4 \text{ years}} = 1.50$$

From Table 4–2, $e^{-1.5} = .2231$.

TABLE 4–2

Values of $e^{-T/MTBF}$

T/MTBF	$e^{-T/MTBF}$	T/MTBF	$e^{-T/MTBF}$
0.10	.9048	3.60	.0273
0.20	.8187	3.70	.0247
0.30	.7408	3.80	.0224
0.40	.6703	3.90	.0202
0.50	.6065	4.00	.0183
0.60	.5488	4.10	.0166
0.70	.4966	4.20	.0150
0.80	.4493	4.30	.0136
0.90	.4066	4.40	.0123
1.00	.3679	4.50	.0111
1.10	.3329	4.60	.0101
1.20	.3012	4.70	.0091
1.30	.2725	4.80	.0082
1.40	.2466	4.90	.0074
1.50	.2231	5.00	.0067
1.60	.2019	5.10	.0061
1.70	.1827	5.20	.0055
1.80	.1653	5.30	.0050
1.90	.1496	5.40	.0045
2.00	.1353	5.50	.0041
2.10	.1255	5.60	.0037
2.20	.1108	5.70	.0033
2.30	.1003	5.80	.0030
2.40	.0907	5.90	.0027
2.50	.0821	6.00	.0025
2.60	.0743	6.10	.0022
2.70	.0672	6.20	.0020
2.80	.0608	6.30	.0018
2.90	.0550	6.40	.0017
3.00	.0498	6.50	.0015
3.10	.0450	6.60	.0014
3.20	.0408	6.70	.0012
3.30	.0369	6.80	.0011
3.40	.0334	6.90	.0010
3.50	.0302	7.00	.0009

Product life can sometimes be modeled by a normal distribution. Obtaining probabilities involves the use of a table (refer to Table B in Appendix B). The table provides areas under a normal curve from (essentially) the left end of the curve to a specified point, z, where z is a *standardized* value computed using the formula:

$$z = \frac{T - \text{Mean wear-out time}}{\text{Standard deviation of wear-out time}}$$

FIGURE 4–5

A normal curve

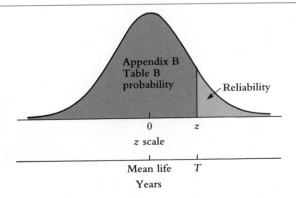

Thus, in order to work with the normal distribution, it is necessary to know the mean of the distribution and its standard deviation. A normal distribution is illustrated in Figure 4–5. Table 3 in Appendix B yields normal probabilities (i.e., the area that lies to the left of z). To obtain a probability that service life will not exceed some value, T, compute z and refer to the table. To find the reliability for time T, compute z, obtain the probability from Table B for the area to the left of z, and subtract this probability from 100 percent. To obtain the value of T that will provide a given probability, locate the nearest probability under the curve *to the left* in Table B. Then use the corresponding z in the preceding formula and solve for T.

EXAMPLE 3

The mean life of a certain ball bearing can be modeled using a normal distribution with a mean of six years and a standard deviation of one year. Determine each of the following:

a. The probability that a ball bearing will wear out *before* seven years of service.

b. The probability that a ball bearing will wear out *after* seven years of service (i.e., find its reliability).

c. The service life that will provide a wear-out probability of 10 percent.

Solution

Wear-out mean = 6 years

Wear-out standard deviation = 1 year

Wear-out life is normally distributed

a. Compute *z* and use it to obtain the probability directly from Table B (see diagram).

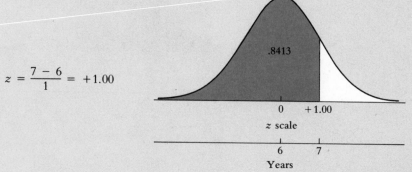

$$z = \frac{7 - 6}{1} = +1.00$$

Thus, $P(T < 7) = .8413$.

b. Subtract the probability determined in part *a* from 100 percent (see diagram).

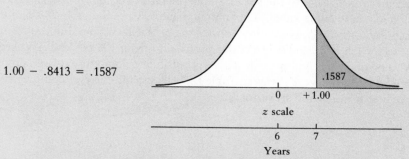

$$1.00 - .8413 = .1587$$

c. Turn to the normal table (Appendix B, Table B), and find the value of *z* that corresponds to an area under the curve of 10% (see diagram).

$$z = -1.28 = \frac{T - 6}{1}$$

90%

10%

$z = -1.28$ 0

z scale

4.72   6

Years

Solving for *T*, we find $T = 4.72$ years.

TABLE 4–3

1.	Improve component design.
2.	Improve production and/or assembly techniques.
3.	Improve testing.
4.	Use redundancy.
5.	Improve preventive maintenance procedures.
6.	Improve user education.
7.	Improve system design.

Potential ways to improve reliability

Improving Reliability

Reliability can be improved in a number of ways, some of which are listed in Table 4–3.

Because overall system reliability is a function of the reliability of individual components, improvements in their reliability can increase system reliability. Unfortunately, inadequate production or assembly procedures can negate even the best of designs, and this is often a source of failures. Part of the burden of reducing product failures lies with the quality control system, which must inspect output and indicate if changes are needed. As we have just seen, system reliability can be increased by the use of backup components. Failures in actual use can often be reduced by upgrading user education and refining maintenance recommendations or procedures. Finally, it may be possible to increase the overall reliability of the system by simplifying the system (and thereby reducing the number of components that could cause the system to fail) or altering component relationships (e.g., increasing the reliability of interfaces).

Perhaps the fundamental issue in improving reliability is: How much reliability is needed? The answer depends on the potential benefits of improvements and on the cost of those improvements. Generally speaking, reliability improvements become increasingly costly. Thus, although initially benefits may increase at a much faster rate than costs, eventually the opposite becomes true. The optimal level of reliability is the point where the incremental benefit received equals the incremental cost of obtaining it.

OPERATIONS STRATEGY

There are four major recommendations on operations strategy in the area of product and service design that can improve competitiveness:

1. Invest more in R&D.
2. Shift some emphasis away from short-term performance to long-term performance.
3. Work toward continual (albeit gradual) improvements instead of using a "big bang" attitude.
4. Work to shorten the product development cycle.

Dollars invested in research and development can have a tremendous impact on a company's *future* competitiveness, affecting quality and reliability, technological innovation, and product improvement. The average Japanese company invests a far greater share of its profits in R&D than the typical Western company. Western managers must be willing to initially sacrifice some short-term performance in favor of R&D that will eventually lead to *both* long-term and (later) short-term performance. However, accomplishing this will require a different attitude from the one that now prevails in many companies.

One of the hallmarks of Japanese success is the emphasis on *continual* improvement in products and processes. In contrast, many Western managers appear bent on making a big splash (the tortoise and the hare?). "Little" things such as product reliability improvements can have long-lasting effects on consumer attitudes and buying patterns.

Getting new products to the market before competitors do usually results in substantial profits. Over the last decade, Japanese producers of automobiles and major appliances have introduced new products and product innovations an average of one year earlier than their Western counterparts. The implication is clear: Western managers must devote efforts to shortening their product development cycles to be competitive.

Summary

Product and service design plays a central role in system design because the other aspects of the system must be designed with respect to the general products and services involved. Due to the ever-changing nature of the environment in which organizations must function, product and service design is subject to continual pressures for design improvements.

Research and development activities are one approach to developing new products. Because of the inherent costs involved, the number of firms that can afford R&D is limited. Another approach involves design by imitation. Regardless of whether firms undertake research themselves or use the services of other organizations, the value of removing uncertainty from a risk situation can be determined.

Two key aspects of product design relate to standardization and reliability. Standardization yields economies based on uniformity of output and related activities but results in a decrease in the amount of variety possible. Modular design is one form of standardization. Measuring and improving reliability are important aspects of successful systems design.

The primary concerns in product design are function and cost (manufacturability).

Key Terms

computer-aided design (CAD), 205
failure, 207

mean time between failures
(MTBF), 210

SOLVED PROBLEMS

1. A product design engineer must decide if a redundant component is cost-justified in a certain system. The system in question has a critical component that has a probability of .98 of operating. System failure would involve a cost of $20,000. A switch could be added that would automatically transfer the system to the backup component in the event of a failure, for a cost of $100. Should the backup be added if the backup probability is also .98?

Solution

Since no probability is given for the switch, we must assume its probability of operating when needed is 100 percent. The expected cost of failure (i.e., without the backup) is $20,000(1 − .98) = $400.

With the backup, the probability of *not* failing would be:

$$.98 + .02(.98) = .9996$$

Hence, the probability of failure would be 1 − .9996 = .0004. The expected cost of failure with the backup would be the added cost of the backup plus the failure cost:

$$\$100 + \$20,000(.0004) = \$108$$

Since this is less than the cost without the backup, it appears that adding the backup is definitely cost-justifiable.

2. Due to the extreme cost of interrupting production, a firm has two standby machines available in case a particular machine suffers a breakdown. The machine in use has a reliability of .94, and the backups have reliabilities of .90 and .80. In the event of a failure, either backup can be pressed into service, and if it fails, the other backup can be used. Compute the system reliability.

Solution

$$R_1 = .94, \ R_2 = .90, \text{ and } R_3 = .80$$

The system can be depicted in the manner shown:

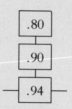

$$R_{\text{system}} = R_1 + R_2(1 - R_1) + R_3(1 - R_2)(1 - R_1)$$
$$= .94 + .90(1 - .94) + .80(1 - .90)(1 - .94) = .9988$$

3. A hospital has three *independent* fire alarm systems, with reliabilities of .95, .97, and .99. In the event of a fire, what is the probability that a warning would be given?

Solution

A warning would *not* be given if all three alarms failed. The probability that at least one alarm would operate is $1 - P(\text{none operate})$:

$$P(\text{none operate}) = (1 - .95)(1 - .97)(1 - .99) = .000015$$
$$P(\text{warning}) = 1 - .000015 = .999985$$

4. A weather satellite has an expected life of 10 years from the time it is placed into earth orbit. Determine its probability of no wear-out before each of the following lengths of service. (Assume the exponential distribution is appropriate.)

   a. 5 years.   *b.* 12 years.   *c.* 20 years   *d.* 30 years.

Solution

$$\text{MTBF} = 10 \text{ years}$$

Compute the ratio T/MTBF for $T = 5, 12, 20,$ and 30, and obtain the values of $e^{-T/\text{MTBF}}$ from Table 4–2. The solution is summarized in the following table.

	T	MTBF	T/MTBF	$e^{-T/\text{MTBF}}$
a.	5.	10	0.50	.6065
b.	12.	10	1.20	.3012
c.	20.	10	2.00	.1353
d.	30.	10	3.00	.0498

5. What is the probability that the satellite described in Solved Problem 4 will fail between 5 and 12 years after being placed into earth orbit?

Solution

$$P(5 \text{ years} < \text{Failure} < 12 \text{ years}) = P \text{ (failure after 5 years)}$$
$$- P(\text{failure after 12 years})$$

Using the probabilities shown in the previous solution, we find:

$$P(\text{failure after 5 years}) = .6065$$
$$- P(\text{failure after 12 years}) = \underline{.3012}$$
$$.3053$$

The corresponding area under the curve is illustrated as follows:

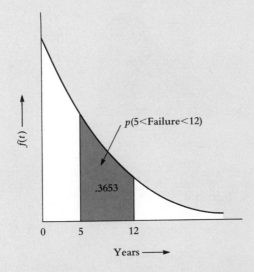

6. One line of radial tires produced by a large company has a wear-out
    life that can be modeled using a normal distribution with a mean of
    25,000 miles and a standard deviation of 2,000 miles. Determine each
    of the following:
    a. The percentage of tires that can be expected to wear out within
        ±2,000 miles of the average (i.e., between 23,000 miles and
        27,000 miles).
    b. The percentage of tires that can be expected to fail between
        26,000 miles and 29,000 miles.

Solution

Notes: (1) Miles are analogous to time and are handled in exactly the same
way time is; (2) the term *percentage* refers to a *probability*.
    a. The phrase "within ±2,000 miles of the average" translates to
        "within one standard deviation of the mean" since the standard

deviation equals 2,000 miles. Therefore, the range of z is $z = -1.00$ to $z = +1.00$, and the area under the curve between those points is found as the difference between $P(z < +1.00)$ and $P(z < -1.00)$, using values obtained from Appendix B, Table B:

$$\begin{array}{r} P(z < +1.00) = .8413 \\ -P(z < -1.00) = .1587 \\ \hline P(-1.00 < z < +1.00) = .6826 \end{array}$$

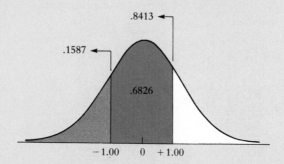

b.   Wear-out mean = 25,000 miles
     Wear-out standard deviation = 2,000 miles

$$P(26,000 < \text{Wear-out} < 29,000) = P(z < z_{29,000}) - P(z < z_{26,000})$$

$$z_{29,000} = \frac{29,000 - 25,000}{2,000} = +2.00 \rightarrow .9772$$

$$z_{26,000} = \frac{26,000 - 25,000}{2,000} = +0.50 \rightarrow .6915$$

The difference is $.9772 - .6915 = .2857$, which is the expected percentage of tires that will wear out between 26,000 miles and 29,000 miles.

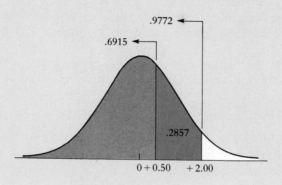

DISCUSSION AND REVIEW QUESTIONS

1. What are some of the factors that cause organizations to redesign their products and services?

2. Contrast applied research and basic research.

3. What is CAD? Describe some of the ways it can be used by a product designer.

4. What are some of the main advantages and disadvantages of standardization?

5. What is modular design, and what are its main advantages and disadvantages?

6. Define the term *reliability*.

7. Explain why a product or system might have an overall reliability that is low even though it is made up of components that have fairly high reliabilities.

8. What are some of the ways that reliability can be improved?

9. What is meant by the term *product life cycle*? Why would this be a consideration in product design?

10. Why is R&D a key factor in productivity improvement? What are some of the ways R&D contributes to productivity improvements?

11. What is redundancy and how can it improve product design?

PROBLEMS

1. Consider the following system:

Determine the probability that the system will operate under each of these conditions:
   a. The system as shown.
   b. Each system component has a backup with a probability of .90 and a switch that is 100 percent reliable.
   c. Backups with .90 probability and a switch that is 99 percent reliable.

2. A product is composed of four parts. In order for the product to function properly in a given situation, each of the parts must function. Two of the parts each have a probability of .96 of functioning, and two have a probability of .99 What is the overall probability that the product will function properly?

3. A system consists of three identical components. In order for the system to perform as intended, all of the components must perform. Each has the same probability of performance. If the system is to have a .92 probability of performing, what is the minimum probability of performing needed by each of the individual components?

4. A product engineer has developed the following equation for the cost of a system component: $C = (10P)^2$, where C is the cost in dollars and P is the probability that the component will operate as expected. The system is composed of two identical components, which must both operate in order for the system to operate. The engineer can spend \$173 for the two components. To the nearest two decimal places, what is the largest component probability that can be achieved?

5. The guidance system of a ship is controlled by a computer that has three major modules. In order for the computer to function properly, all three modules must function. Two of the modules have reliabilities of .97, and the other has a reliability of .99.
   a. What is the reliability of the computer?
   b. A backup computer identical to the one being used will be installed to improve

overall reliability. Assuming the new computer automatically functions if the main one fails, determine the resulting reliability.

c. If the backup computer must be activated by a switch in the event that the first computer fails, and the switch has a reliability of .98, what is the overall reliability of the system? (*Both* the switch and the backup computer must function in order for the backup to take over.)

6. One of the industrial robots designed by a leading producer of servomechanisms has four major components. Component reliabilities are .98, .95, .94, and .90. All of the components must function in order for the robot to operate effectively.

a. Compute the reliability of the robot.

b. Designers want to improve the reliability by adding a backup component. Due to space limitations, only one backup can be added. The backup for any component will have the same reliability as the unit it is a backup for. Which component should get the backup in order to achieve the highest reliability?

c. If one backup that has a reliability of .92 can be added to any one of the main components, which one should get it to obtain the highest overall reliability?

7. A production line comprises three machines, A, B, and C, with reliabilities of .99, .96, and .93, respectively. The machines are arranged in such a way that if one breaks down, the others must also shut down. Engineers are weighing two alternative designs for increasing the line's reliability. Plan 1 involves adding an identical backup *line*, and plan 2 involves providing a backup for each *machine*. In either case, three machines (A, B, and C) would be used with reliabilities equal to the original three.

a. Which plan will provide the higher reliability?

b. Explain why the two reliabilities are not the same.

c. What other factors might enter into the decision of which plan to adopt?

8. A water treatment plant has five major components that must all function in order for the plant to operate as intended. Assuming that each component of the system has the same reliability, what is the minimum reliability each one must have in order for the overall system to have a reliability of .98?

9. Repeat the previous problem under the condition that one of the components will have a backup with a reliability equal to that of any one of the other components.

10. Hoping to increase the chances of reaching a performance goal, the director of a research project has assigned three separate research teams the same task. The director estimates that the team reliabilities are .9, .8, and .7 for successfully completing the task in the allotted time. Assuming that the teams work independently, what is the probability that the task will not be completed in time?

11. An electronic chess game has a useful life that is exponential with a mean of 30 months. Determine each of the following:

a. The probability that any given unit will operate for at least: (1) 39 months, (2) 48 months, (3) 60 months.

b. The probability that any given unit will fail sooner than: (1) 33 months, (2) 15 months, (3) one–half year.

c. The length of service after which the percentage of units that have failed will approximately equal: (1) 50 percent, (2) 85 percent, (3) 95 percent, (4) 99 percent.

12. A manufacturer of programmable calculators is attempting to determine a reasonable free-service period for a model it will introduce shortly. The manager of product testing has indicated that the calculators have an expected life of 30 months. Assume product life can be described by an exponential distribution.

a. If service contracts are offered for the expected life of the calculator, what percentage of those sold would be expected to fail during the service period?

b. What service period would result in a failure rate of approximately 10 percent?

13. Lucky Lumen light bulbs have an expected life that is exponentially distributed with a mean of 5,000 hours. Determine the probability that one of these light bulbs will last:

a. At least 6,000 hours.

b. No longer than 1,000 hours

c. Between 1,000 hours and 6,000 hours.

14. Planetary Communications, Inc. intends to launch a satellite that will enhance reception of television programs in Alaska. According to its designers, the satellite will have an expected life of six years. Assume the exponential distribution applies. Determine the probability that it will function for each of these time periods:

a. More than 9 years.

b. Less than 12 years.

c. More than 9 years but less than 12 years.

d. At least 21 years.

15. An office manager has received a report from a consultant that includes a section on equipment replacement. The report indicates that typewriters have a service life that is normally distributed with a mean of 41 months and a standard deviation of 4 months. On the basis of this information, determine the percentage of typewriters that can be expected to fail in these time periods:

a. Before 38 months of service.

b. Between 40 and 45 months of service.

c. Within ±2 months of the mean life.

16. According to a study underwritten by a major television manufacturer, its 19-inch color TV picture tubes have a mean service life that can be modeled by a normal distribution that has a mean of six years and a standard deviation of one-half year.

a. What probability can you assign to these service lives: (1) Five years? (2) Six years? (3) Seven and one-half years?

b. If the manufacturer offers service contracts of four years on these picture tubes, what percentage can be expected to fail from wear-out during the service period?

17. In the previous problem, what service period would achieve an expected wear-out rate of:

a. 2 percent?

b. 5 percent?

SELECTED BIBLIOGRAPHY

Bierman, Harold, Jr.; Charles P. Bonini; and Warren H. Hausman. *Quantitative Analysis for Business Decisions.* 6th ed. Homewood, Ill.: Richard D. Irwin, 1981.

Groover, Mikell P. *Automation, Production Systems, and Computer-Aided Manufacturing.* Englewood Cliffs, N.J.: Prentice-Hall, 1980.

————, and E. W. Zimmers, Jr. *CAD/CAM: Computer-Aided Design and Manufacturing.* Englewood Cliffs, N.J.: Prentice-Hall, 1984.

Hare, Van Court, Jr. *Systems Analysis: A Diagnostic Approach.* New York: Harcourt Brace Jovanovich, 1967.

Hopeman, Richard J. *Production and Operations Management.* 4th ed. Columbus, Ohio: Charles E. Merrill Publishing, 1980.

Kushner, Lawrence M. "Product Safety Standards and Product Innovation, Too," *Harvard Business Review,* July–August 1980, p. 36.

Malott, Robert H. "Let's Restore Balance to Product Liability Law." *Harvard Business Review*, May–June 1983, p. 66.

Moore, Franklin G., and Thomas E. Hendrick. *Production/Operations Management.* 9th ed. Homewood, Ill.: Richard D. Irwin, 1984.

READING

TOYING WITH HIGH TECH

Andrew Pollack

What do you do with an exotic metal alloy that has the ability to "remember" its original shape and return to that shape when heated?

In the United States, the answer is: Use it to make pipe joints in fighter planes and think about using it for satellites that could be launched in compact form and would unfold automatically in space.

But in Japan, the answer is: Use the alloy to make eyeglass frames, air-conditioner louvers, and a toy in which a boy's head and a girl's head are separated by a wire made of the alloy. When the toy is dunked in hot water, the wire returns to a ring shape, bringing the heads together in a kiss.

The example illustrates a major difference between the two nations, which are now vying for world supremacy in high technology.

In the United States, technological emphasis is often on a big military or space project, with little regard for immediate commercial applications.

In Japan, which has no big military or space programs, the emphasis is overwhelming on commercial uses, particularly for consumers. Technology advances bit by bit, tested at each step in a variety of applications, some of them exceedingly trivial. Indeed, the Japanese have a penchant for finding low-tech applications for high-tech products.

"We are now in the age of popularization of advanced technology," said Masanori Moritani, senior researcher at the Nomura Research Institute, a division of the Nomura Securities Co. "Especially in Japan, companies are very eager to apply advanced technology."

James C. Abegglen, a Japan watcher associated with the Boston Consulting Group, agreed: "The Americans go for the home run. The Japanese get singles and steal bases."

Other examples of the difference in approach abound:

In the United States, one of the first feasible uses of solar electricity generation was to provide power to satellites. Japan came up with a more down-to-earth application—the solar-powered calculator. Now companies here are coming out with the solar-powered radio, the solar-powered watch, and the solar-powered rechargeable battery recharger.

In the United States, more than half the market for graphite composite materials—lightweight but strong materials being used as substitutes for metal—is for aerospace and aircraft uses. In Japan, 80 percent of the market is for tennis racquets, golf clubs, and other sports equipment, which account for but a small part of its American use.

In the United States, laser development has facilitated everything from surgery to fusion energy, and now lasers may be used for weapons to destroy enemy missiles. Japan produces the only existing consumer products using lasers—the laser videodisk system and the digital audiodisk system.

In new ceramics, the United States has emphasized military uses and the space shuttle heat shield. Japanese companies have come up with ceramic scissors, ballpoint pen tips, and sake warmers.

Which approach, the home run or the barrage of singles, will win the game is hotly debated, with each nation wishing it had some of the attributes of the other.

Some American electronics executives question the value of devoting so much technological research to military and space efforts with little commercial value. Many Japanese executives, however, are envious of the American system's ability to make great advances and are worried that their consumer-based technology is too limited.

Aside from Japan's lack of big military or space programs, another reason for the emphasis on consumer applications is that technology development programs run by the Ministry of International Trade and Industry do not always provide much money, despite the publicity they receive. So companies must find other ways to pay for technology development quickly.

"Whether we like it or not, our research efforts must be directed at smaller versions, to find a way to earn some profit," said Kazuo Iga, director of the corporate products development division of the Matsushita Electric Industrial Co. His company uses the shape memory alloy to make air-conditioner louvers that change direction depending on the temperature, directing hot air down to warm a room and cool air up to cool it.

Moreover, the intensely competitive nature of the Japanese consumer electronics industry leads each company to employ new technologies, no matter how frivolously, to make its product stand out. This practice is abetted by the Japanese love of novelty. One product, for example, is a voice-activated cradle, which starts rocking when the baby cries.

Such experimentation often produces benefits in allowing companies to hone their technology and reduce costs by mass production. "You can develop a high-technology base by developing low-technology products with high volume," said Bruce F. Rubinger, director of studies for the Global Competitiveness Council, a research organization in Boston.

Solar energy is an example. The Sanyo Electric Co. is producing four million solar batteries for calculators each month. Now it thinks it has forced the cost down enough to introduce a solar roof tile to provide electricity for homes.

In ceramics, as well, some experts think small consumer applications can help develop more serious ones.

The Japanese are even starting to apply their civilian technology to military systems, spurred in part by an agreement last year with the United States calling for more cooperation in defense technology.

Devices used to record images in video cameras have potential uses for missile guidance systems. Mitsubishi Heavy Industries has been approached by General Motors for help in designing tank transmissions.

Questions

1. What is the author's main point?
2. Can you think of any other examples that support the author's contention? Can you think of any that contradict it?

Source: "High Tech: Japan's Approach," *New York Times*, June 12, 1984. Copyright © 1984 by The New York Times Company. Reprinted by permission.

READING

MANAGING COMPLEXITY AND THE FLOW OF DOLLARS

By John Hagel III

Product complexity is not necessarily undesirable. It is often a concomitant of innovation and can play an important role in building, or maintaining, advantages over competing products. Managing complexity is, therefore, a matter of business judgment—of weighing its costs against its value to customers and, from that, its potential returns.

Why Design Matters

Intricacy of product design usually does not get the attention it deserves as a driver of product development expense. Although managers understand that such complexity boosts development expense to some degree, few realize how extraordinarily sensitive that expense can be to variations in complexity. In fact, intricacy of product design often has a far greater impact on expense than how product development is organized or managed—even though efforts to trim development spending have usually focused more on these latter choices than on complexity.

The pioneering research of software development expert Lawrence Putnam, on the relationship between complexity in product design and development expense, suggest that this relationship is not linear, but exponential. He found that increasing the number of lines of code in a software product would not just double the development expense—it would raise it by a power of three, holding other variables constant.

McKinsey's work on product development has turned up similar results. For example, we conducted a detailed comparison of the development projects of two companies that were introducing similar data networking products. Our analysis showed that one company had spent 13 times as much as the other. When we explored what factors were responsible for this enormous discrepancy, we discovered that product complexity accounted for about 74% of the differential.

The effect of design complexity on development expense does not end when a product is introduced; it creates a permanent burden that lives on in subsequent generations of the same product. In the case of the data networking products discussed above, we found that 25% of the ongoing development budget for product enhancement at the high-cost company could be traced directly to the choices it had made regarding product complexity when the product was first introduced.

This 25% complexity burden was not a result of efforts to make the product still more complex. It represented the incremental expense of implementing enhancements in a product that was already highly complex. To put the point another way, the high-cost company spent one-third more on continuing development activities than it would have if it had chosen to introduce the less complex product offered by its competitor. It had unintentionally built into its development budget a cost weight it would carry into the future.

If customers had valued the additional complexity highly enough—if it had led enough of them to buy the high-cost company's product instead of its competitor's—the firm's choice, of more complexity and more cost, might have made good business sense. As it turned out, they did not.

Cross-Functional Implications

Although the complexity of product design tends to have its most significant cost impact on development expense, it has other less direct effects as well. For example, manufacturing expense may increase with the complexity of product design. In some cases, complexity will increase the number of components used in a product, leading both to higher manufacturing costs and higher inventory investment. More complex designs may also require a tightening of performance standards for the manufacturing process and an expansion of quality testing procedures. These outcomes, in turn, lead to higher first-pass expense and raise reject rates.

Customer service expense can also rise with increases in the complexity of product design. Some product categories are typically accompanied by customer training programs. For example, factory equipment or advanced medical diagnostic instrumentation may undergo jumps in training program expense as customers require more handholding to learn how to use more complex products. Training expense may increase, at the same time and for the same reason, for the technical service organization. Field service expense may rise as well if more complex product designs increase either the need for preventive maintenance or the likelihood of product failure.

Even marketing and sales can be affected by the complexity of product design—as, for instance, when a company seeks to market a high-cost product to a customer segment that does not attach a high value to the complexity embedded in the product.

Why are so few companies aware of the full impact of product complexity? The main reason seems to be that managers' radar screens—the systems that define and shape the reality perceived by mangers—are rarely designed to track and highlight complexity. Complexity tends to remain in the shadows, hidden.

Complexity is so hard to see, in part, because the relevant dimensions of complexity vary so much from product to product. For each type of product, some dimensions of complexity will have disproportionate effects on development expense. In software products, for example, the key dimension of complexity is the number of lines of code; in printed circuit boards, it is the number of components and the density with which they are packed on the board.

Identifying the primary dimensions of product complexity and quantifying their impact on development spending can be a substantial, and difficult, undertaking. Existing financial or operations reports offer little help—not least because development programs are rarely organized in a way that directly corresponds to the primary dimensions of complexity.

Not surprisingly, it is rarely possible to quantify with confidence the impact of design complexity by comparing the numbers for actual projects. It is usually more productive to generate a series of detailed "what if" scenarios around a single development effort and, in this way, to explore the resource implications of stepping down the complexity of a product, feature by feature.

Although there are substantial difficulties in quantifying the impact of complexity on development expense, management can use some relatively quick tests to determine if complexity is likely to be an issue. First, a detailed feature/performance comparison between a company's products and those of its competitors may uncover a feature/performance

surplus. This surplus could represent unnecessary increments of complexity—or, if a customer values additional features highly enough, a source of competitive advantage.

Second, a comparison of development expense/revenue ratios could reveal that the yield from a firm's development spending is below that of its competition. Alternatively, management could analyze relative margin yields—how many dollars of gross margin a product line generates as compared with the percentage of the dollars spent on development.

To ascertain whether and to what extent potential customers value additional features, firms can employ conjoint analysis—in which respondents are presented with a series of choices between two packages of attributes. This methodology, which has been used for years to test options for consumer packaged goods, can help electronics companies pinpoint which increments of complexity are worth their costs.

Costs of complexity

Product complexity
can affect a
wide range of costs:

1. Prototype development
2. Manufacturing
3. Inventory
4. Quality testing
5. First-pass manufacturing
6. Eliminating rejects
7. Customer training
8. Field service

Source: *Electronic Business*, January 9, 1989, pp. 38–40.

5

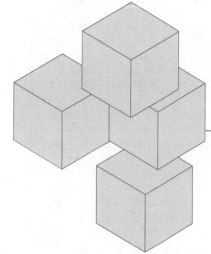

Location Planning

LEARNING OBJECTIVES

After completing this chapter, you should be able to:

1. List some of the main reasons organizations become involved in location decisions.
2. Explain why location decisions are important.
3. Discuss the options that are generally available in location decisions.
4. Describe some of the major factors that affect location decisions.
5. Outline the decision process that is generally followed in these kinds of decisions.
6. Use the techniques presented to solve typical problems.

CHAPTER OUTLINE

When a well-known real estate broker was asked what the three most important determinants of value of a property are, he said, "That's easy. Location, location, and location."

Evidently, in the residental market, location is a rather important factor. Although factors such as style of house, number of bedrooms and bathrooms, how well it has been maintained, and how modern the kitchen is undoubtedly enter into the picture, obviously some locations will be more desirable than others.

In many respects, the choice of location for a business organization is every bit as important as it is for a house, although for different reasons.

Location decisions represent an integral part of the strategic planning process of virtually every organization. Although it might appear that location decisions are mostly one-time problems pertaining to new organizations, the fact is that existing organizations often have a bigger stake in these kinds of decisions than new organizations have.

This chapter explores the issue of location analysis. It begins with a brief overview of the reasons firms become involved in location decisions, the nature of these decisions, and a general procedure for developing and evaluating location alternatives.

THE NEED FOR LOCATION DECISIONS

Existing organizations become involved in location decisions for a variety of reasons. Firms such as banks, fast-food chains, supermarkets, and retail stores view locations as a marketing strategy, and they look for locations that will help them to expand their markets. Basically, the location decisions in those cases reflect *addition* of new locations to an existing system.

A similar situation occurs when an organization experiences a growth in demand for its products or services that cannot be satisfied by expansion at an existing location. The addition of a new location to complement an existing system is often a realistic alternative.

Some firms become involved in location decisions through depletion of basic inputs. For example, fishing and logging operations are often forced to relocate due to the temporary exhaustion of fish or forests at a given location. Mining operations and petroleum operations face the same sort of situation, although usually over a longer horizon.

For other firms, a shift in their markets causes them to consider relocation, or the costs of doing business at a particular location reach a point where other locations begin to look more attractive.

THE NATURE OF LOCATION DECISIONS

Location decisions for many types of businesses are made rather infrequently, but they tend to have a significant impact on the organization. In this section we shall look at the importance of location decisions, the usual objectives managers have when making location choices, and some of the options that are open to them.

Importance of Location Decisions

There are two primary reasons that location decisions are a highly important part of production systems design. One is that they entail a long-term commitment, which makes mistakes difficult to overcome. The other is that location decisions often have an impact on operating costs (both fixed and variable) and revenues as well as on operations. For instance, a poor choice of location might result in excessive transportation costs, a shortage of qualified labor, loss of competitive advantage, inadequate supplies of raw materials, or some similar condition that would be detrimental to operations.

Objectives of Location Decisions

As a general rule, profit-oriented organizations base their decisions on profit potential, whereas nonprofit organizations strive to achieve a balance between cost and the level of customer service they provide. It might seem to follow, then, that these organizations would attempt to identify the "best" location available. However, this is not necessarily the case.

In many instances, there may be no one location that is significantly better than the others. There may be numerous acceptable locations from which to choose, as evidenced by the fact that successful organizations can be found in a wide variety of locations. Furthermore, the number of possible locations that would have to be examined in order to find the best location may be too large to make an exhaustive search practical. Consequently, most organizations do not set out with the intention of identifying the *one best* location; rather, they hope to find a number of *acceptable* locations from which to choose—and to avoid choosing a location that will create future problems.

Location Options

There are essentially four options that managers can consider in location planning. One is to expand an existing facility. This option can be attactive if there is adequate room for expansion, especially if the location has desirable features that are not readily available elsewhere. Furthermore, expansion costs are often less than those of other alternatives.

Another option is to add new locations while retaining existing ones, as is done in many retail operations. In such cases, it is essential to take into account what the impact will be on the total system. For instance, opening a new store in a shopping mall may simply draw customers who already patronize an existing store in the same chain rather than expand the market. On the other hand, adding locations can be a defensive strategy designed to maintain a market share or to prevent competitors from entering a market.

A third option is to shut down at one location and move to another. An organization must weigh the costs of a move and the resulting benefits against the costs and benefits of remaining in an existing location. As previously mentioned, a shift in markets, exhaustion of raw materials, and the cost of operations often cause firms to seriously consider this option.

Finally, organizations have the option of doing nothing. If a detailed analysis of potential locations fails to uncover benefits that make one of the previous three alternatives attractive, a firm may decide to maintain the status quo, at least in the short run.

GENERAL PROCEDURE FOR MAKING LOCATION DECISIONS

The way in which organizations approach location decisions often depends on the size of the organization and the nature or scope of its operations. New or small organizations tend to adopt a rather informal approach to location decisions. New firms typically locate in a certain area simply because that is where the owner lives. Similarly, managers of small firms often want to keep operations in their own backyard, so they tend to focus almost exclusively on local alternatives. Large established companies, particularly ones that already operate in more than one location, tend to take a more formal approach. Moreover, they generally consider a wider range of geographic locations. The discussion here pertains mainly to a formal approach to location decisions.

The general procedure for making location decisions usually consists of the following steps:

1. Determine the criteria that will be used to evaluate location alternatives, such as increased revenues or community service.
2. Identify factors that are important, such as location of markets or raw materials.
3. Develop location alternatives:
    a. Identify the general region for a location.
    b. Identify a small number of community-site alternatives.
4. Evaluate the alternatives and make a selection.

Step 1 is simply a matter of managerial preference. Steps 2 through 4 may need some elaboration.

FACTORS THAT AFFECT LOCATION DECISIONS

Many factors can influence location decisions. However, it often happens that one or a few factors are so important that they tend to dominate the location decision. For example, in manufacturing, the potentially dominating factors usually include availability of an abundant energy and water supply and nearness to raw materials. Thus, nuclear reactors require large amounts of water for cooling, heavy industries such as steel and aluminum production need large amounts of electricity, and so on. Transportation costs can also be a major factor in location decisions. In nonmanufacturing organizations, possible dominating factors are market-related and include traffic patterns, convenience, and competitors' locations, as well as nearness to the market. For example, car rental agencies locate near airports and midcity, since that is where their business comes from.

Once the most important factors have been determined, organizations typically try to narrow the search for suitable alternatives to one geographic region. Then a small number of community-site alternatives are identified and subjected to detailed analysis. Community and site factors are often so intertwined that it makes more sense to consider them jointly than to attempt to first decide on a community and then try to find an acceptable site.

Regional Factors

The primary regional factors involve raw materials, markets, and labor considerations.

1. *Location of raw materials.* There are three primary reasons firms locate near or at the source of raw materials: necessity, perishability, and transportation costs. In the *necessity* category are mining operations, farming, forestry, and fishing. Obviously, such operations must locate where the raw materials are. In the *perishability* category are firms involved in canning or freezing of fresh fruit and vegetables, processing of dairy products, baking, and so on. *Transportation costs* are important in industries where processing eliminates much of the bulk connected with a raw material, making it much less expensive to transport the product or material after processing. Examples include aluminum reduction, cheese making, and paper production. In situations where inputs come from different locations, some firms choose to locate near the geographic center of the sources. For instance, steel producers use large quantities of both coal and iron ore, and many are located somewhere between the Appalachian coal fields and places where the iron ore is mined. Transportation costs are often the reason that vendors locate near their major customers. Moreover, regional warehouses are used by supermarkets and other retail operations to supply multiple outlets. Often the choice of new locations and additional warehouses reflect the locations of existing warehouses or retail outlets.

2. *Location of markets.* Profit-oriented firms often locate near the markets they intend to serve as part of their competitive strategy, whereas nonprofit organizations choose locations relative to the needs of the users of their services. Other factors include distribution costs or the perishability of a finished product.

Retail sales and services are usually found near the center of the markets they serve. Examples include fast-food restaurants, service stations, dry cleaners, and supermarkets. Quite often their products and those of their competitors are so similar that they rely on convenience to attract customers. Hence, these businesses seek locations with high population densities or high traffic. The competition/convenience factor is also important in locating banks, hotels and motels, auto repair shops, drugstores, newspaper boxes, and shopping centers. Similarly, doctors, dentists, and lawyers typically serve clients who reside within a limited area, as do barbers and beauticians.

Competitive pressures for retail operations can be extremely important factors. In some situations, a market served by a particular location may be too small to justify two or more competitors (e.g., one hamburger stand per block), so that a search for potential locations would tend to concentrate on locations without competitors. In other cases, the opposite might be true: it could be desirable to locate near competitors. Large department stores often locate near each other, and small stores like to locate in shopping centers with large "anchor" stores. The large stores are able to attract large numbers of shoppers who become potential purchasers in the smaller stores or in the other large stores.

Some firms must locate close to their markets because of the perishability of their products. Examples include bakeries, flower shops, and stores that sell fresh seafood. For other types of firms, distribution costs are the main factor in closeness to market. For example, sand and gravel dealers usually serve a limited area because of the high distribution costs associated with their products. Still other firms require close customer contact, so they too tend to locate within the area they expect to serve. Typical examples are tailor shops, home remodelers, home repair services, cabinet makers, rug cleaners, and lawn and garden services.

Locations of many government services are near the markets they are designed to serve. Hence, post offices are typically scattered throughout large metropolitan areas. Police, fire, and emergency health care locations are frequently selected on the basis of client needs. For instance, fire stations would tend to locate in areas of high hazards, police patrols often concentrate on high crime areas, and emergency health care facilities are usually found in central locations because they provide ready access from all directions.

3. *Labor factors.* The primary labor considerations relate to the cost and availability of labor, wage rates in an area, labor productivity and attitudes toward work, and whether there is a serious potential for problems with unions.

Labor costs can be very important for organizations that are labor-intensive. The shift of the textile industry from the New England states to southern states was partly due to labor costs.

Skills of potential employees may be a factor, although some companies prefer to train their new employees rather than rely on previous experience alone. Increasing specialization in many industries makes this possibility even more likely than in the past. Although most companies concentrate on the supply of blue-collar workers, some firms are more interested in scientific and technical people as potential employees, and they look for areas with high concentrations of those types of workers.

Worker attitudes toward turnover, absenteeism, and similar factors may differ among potential locations. For example, workers in large urban centers may exhibit different attitudes than workers who reside in small towns or in rural areas. Furthermore, attitudes in different parts of the country, or in different countries, may be markedly different in this respect.

Some companies offer their current employees jobs when they move to a new location. However, in many instances, employees are reluctant to move, especially if it means leaving families and friends. Furthermore, in families with two wage earners, relocation would require that one wage earner give up a job and then attempt to find another job in the new location.

4. *Other factors.* Climate and taxes sometimes play a role in location decisions. For example, a string of unusually severe winters may cause some firms to seriously consider moving to a milder climate, especially if delayed deliveries and work disruptions caused by inability of employees to get to work have been frequent occurrences. Similarly, the business and personal income taxes in some northern states reduce their attractiveness to companies seeking new locations. Many companies have been attracted to the Sun Belt states by ample supplies of low-cost energy or labor, by the climate, and by tax considerations.

The growth in multinational operations over the past several decades is evidence of the importance of foreign locations. Some firms are attracted to foreign locations because those countries have important deposits of aluminum, copper, timber, oil, or other natural resources. Other firms view foreign locations as a way to expand their markets, and still others are attracted by ample supplies of labor. Some countries may offer financial incentives to companies in order to create jobs for their people. Developing countries may establish tariffs to protect their young industries from outside competition, which may also reduce the amount of "foreign" competition a firm must face if it located in such a country. (However, the Fisher-Price Toy Company factory in Atamoros, Mexico, is not allowed to sell the Muppet toys it makes in Mexico. In fact, under a trade agreement between the United States and Mexico, U.S. companies are encouraged to locate factories in Mexico and are allowed to import raw materials duty-free, but they are required to export all of their output.)

Many developing countries offer an abundant supply of cheap labor. For example, most of the clothes sold in the United States carry labels indicating that they were made in Korea, Hong Kong, or Taiwan. In some instances, it can be less expensive to ship raw materials or semifinished goods to foreign countries for fabrication and assembly and then ship them to their final destinations than it is to produce them in the United States. However, it is essential to recognize that the final cost per unit is the most important factor. In many cases, the low cost of labor in a foreign country can be negated by low productivity.

A firm contemplating a foreign location must carefully weigh the potential benefits against the potential problems it might encounter. One of the major factors is the ability of a country's government and its attitude toward American firms. Import restrictions can pose problems in terms of bringing in equipment and spare parts.

Some potential problems with a foreign location relate to language and cultural differences between the United States and the host country. American firms often find it necessary to use American technical personnel but find it sometimes difficult to convince workers to move to a foreign country; workers may have to leave their families behind or else subject them to substandard housing or educational systems. Companies usually exert additional efforts to reduce these obstacles. They are also improving their efforts to see to it that the people they send abroad are familiar with local customs and have a reasonable facility with the language of the host country.

Community Considerations

Many communities actively try to attract new businesses because they are viewed as potential sources of future taxes and as sources of new job opportunities. However, communities do not, as a rule, want firms that are going to create pollution problems or otherwise lessen the quality of life in the community. Local groups may actively seek to exclude certain companies on such grounds, and a considerable amount of effort may be required on the part of the company to convince local officials that the company will be a "responsible citizen." Furthermore, some organizations discover that even though overall community attitude is favorable, there may still be considerable opposition to specific sites from nearby residents who object to possible increases in levels of noise, traffic, or pollution. Examples of this include resistance to airport expansion, changes in zoning, construction of nuclear facilities, and highway construction.

From a company standpoint, there are a number of factors that determine the desirability of a community as a place for its workers and managers to live. They include facilities for education; shopping; recreation; transportation; religious worship; entertainment; the quality of police, fire, and medical services; local attitudes toward the company; and the size of the community. Community size can be particularly important if a firm will be a major employer in the community, because a future decision to terminate or reduce operations in that location could have a serious impact on the local economy.

Other community-related factors involve the cost and availability of utilities, environmental regulations, taxes (state and local, direct and indirect), and existence of development support (bond issues, tax abatement, low-cost loans, and grants).

Site-Related Factors

The primary considerations related to sites involve land, transportation, and zoning or other restrictions.

Evaluation of potential sites may require consulting with engineers or architects, especially in the case of heavy manufacturing or when large buildings or facilities with special requirements are to be erected. Soil conditions, load factors, and drainage rates can be critical and often necessitate certain kinds of expertise in evaluation.

Because of the long-term commitment usually required, land costs may be secondary to other site-related factors, such as room for future expansion, current utility and sewer capacities and any limitations on these that could hinder future growth, and sufficient parking space for employees and customers. In addition, many firms find access roads for trucks or rail spurs important.

Industrial parks may be worthwhile alternatives for firms involved in light manufacturing or assembly work, as well as for warehouse operations and customer service facilities. Typically, the land is already developed; power, water, and sewer hookups have been attended to; and zoning restrictions do not require special attention. On the negative side, industrial parks may place restrictions on the kinds of activities that can be concluded there, and that can limit options for future development of a firm's products and services as well as the processes it can consider. In addition, in some cases there can be rather stringent regulations governing the size, shape, and architectural features of buildings, which limits managerial choice in these matters; also, there may not be an adequate allowance for possible future expansion.

For firms with executives who travel frequently, the size and nearness of the airport or train station as well as travel connections can be important, although schedules and connections are subject to change.

A summary of the factors that affect location decisions is provided in Table 5–1, which is on the following page.

TRENDS IN LOCATION AND POSSIBLE FUTURE STRATEGIES

Recent trends in locating facilities, particularly manufacturing facilities, reflect a combination of competitive factors and technological factors. One such trend is for foreign producers, especially Japanese automotive firms, to locate plants in the United States. One reason for this is the fact that the United States represents a tremendous market for Japanese cars, trucks, and recreational vehicles. By locating in the United States, these firms can shorten delivery times and reduce delivery costs. Furthermore, they can avoid any future tariffs or quotas that might be applied to imports.

Another factor is just-in-time manufacturing techniques (see Chapter 12 for details), which encourage suppliers and customers to locate near each other in order to reduce supplier lead times. For this reason, some U.S. firms are reconsidering decisions to locate offshore. Moreover, in light manufacturing (e.g., electronics), low-cost labor is becoming less important than nearness to markets; users of electronics components want suppliers that are close to their manufacturing facilities. One offshoot of this is the possibility that the future will see a trend toward smaller factories located close to markets. In some

TABLE 5–1

	Level	Factors	Considerations
Factors that affect location decisions	Region/country	Location of raw materials or supplies	Proximity, modes and costs of transportation, quantity available
		Location of markets	Proximity, distribution costs, target market, trade practices/restrictions
		Labor	Availability (general and for specific skills), age distribution of work force, attitudes toward work, union or non-union, productivity, wage scales, unemployment compensation laws
	Community	Facilities	Schools, churches, shopping, housing, transportation, entertainment, etc.
		Services	Medical, fire, and police
		Attitudes	Pro/con
		Taxes	State/local, direct and indirect
		Environmental regulations	State/local
		Utilities	Cost and availability
		Development support	Bond issues, tax abatement, low-cost loans, grants
	Site	Land	Cost, degree of development required, soil characteristics, room for expansion, drainage, parking
		Transportation	Type (access roads, rail spurs, air freight)
		Environmental/legal	Zoning restrictions

industries, small, automated **microfactories** with a narrow product focus will be located near major markets to reduce response time.

Advances in information technology will enhance the ability of manufacturing firms to gather, track, and distribute information that links purchasing, marketing, and distribution with design, engineering, and manufacturing. This will reduce the need for these functions to be located close together, thereby permitting a strategy of locating production facilities near major markets.

EVALUATING LOCATION ALTERNATIVES

This section contains descriptions of two techniques that can be used to help managers evaluate location alternatives. The first technique is an extension of cost-volume analysis and relates to evaluation on economic terms. The second approach is more general in that it offers managers a way to combine both qualitative and quantitative inputs in the decision framework.

Locational Cost-Analysis Volume

The economic comparison of location alternatives is facilitated by the use of cost-volume-profit analysis. The analysis can be done numerically or graphically. The graphical approach will be demonstrated here because it enhances understanding of the concept and because it provides an indication of the ranges over which one of the alternatives is superior to the others.

The procedure for **locational cost–volume analysis** involves these steps:

1. Determine the fixed costs and the variable costs associated with each location alternative.
2. Plot the total-cost lines for all location alternatives on the same graph.
3. Determine which location has the lowest total cost for the expected level of output.

This method assumes the following:

1. Fixed costs are constant for the range of probable output.
2. Variable costs are linear for the range of probable output.
3. The required level of output can be closely estimated.
4. Only one product is involved.

EXAMPLE 1

Fixed and variable costs for four potential plant locations are shown below:

Location	Fixed cost per year	Variable cost per unit
A	$250,000	$11
B	110,000	30
C	150,000	20
D	200,000	35

a. Plot the total-cost lines for these locations on a single graph.
b. Identify the range of output for which each alternative is superior (i.e., has the lowest total cost).
c. If expected output at the selected location is to be 8,000 units per year, which location would provide the lowest total cost?

Solution

a. To plot the total-cost lines, select an output that is approximately equal to the expected output level (e.g., 10,000 units per year). Compute the total cost for each location at that level:

Example 1 (concluded)

	Fixed cost	+	Variable cost	=	Total cost
A	$250,000	+	$11(10,000)	=	$360,000
B	100,000	+	30(10,000)	=	400,000
C	150,000	+	20(10,000)	=	350,000
D	200,000	+	35(10,000)	=	550,000

Plot each location's fixed cost (at Output = 0) and the total cost at $10,000 units and connect the two points with a straight line. (See the accompanying graph.)

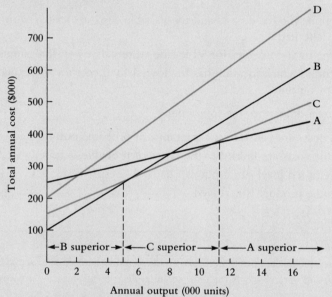

b. The *approximate* ranges for which the various alternatives will yield the lowest costs are shown on the graph. Note that location D is never superior. The *exact* ranges can be determined by finding the output level at which lines B and C and lines C and A cross. To do this, set their total cost equations equal and solve for Q, the break-even output level. Thus, for B and C we have:

$$\begin{array}{cc} (B) & (C) \\ \$100,000 + \$30Q = \$150,000 + \$20Q \end{array}$$

Solving, we find Q = 5,000 units per year.
    For C and A we have:

$$\begin{array}{cc} (C) & (A) \\ \$150,000 + \$20Q = \$250,000 + \$11Q \end{array}$$

We find Q = 11,111 units per year.

c. From the graph we can see that for 8,000 units per year, location C would provide the lowest total cost.

In a situation where the expected level of output is close to the middle of the range over which one alternative is superior, the choice is readily apparent. If the expected level of output is very close to the edge of a range, it simply means that the two alternatives will yield comparable annual costs, so management would be indifferent in choosing between the two *in terms of total cost*. However, it is important to recognize that in most situations, other factors besides costs must also be considered. A general scheme for including a broad range of factors is presented later in this section. Before turning to that, let's consider another kind of cost that is often considered in location decisions: transportation costs.

The Transportation Model

Transportation costs sometimes play an important role in location decisions. These can stem from either the movement of raw materials or the movement of finished goods. If the facility will be the sole source or destination of the shipments, then the transportation costs can be included in a locational cost-volume analysis by incorporating the transportation cost per unit being shipped into the variable cost per unit. (If raw materials are involved, the transportation cost must be converted into cost per unit of *output* in order to correspond to other variable costs.)

When a problem involves shipments of goods from multiple sending points to multiple receiving points, and a new location (sending or receiving point) is to be added to the system, a separate analysis of transportation should be undertaken. In such instances the *transportation model* of linear programming can be very helpful. It is a special-purpose algorithm that can be used to determine the minimum transportation cost that would result if a potential new location were to be added to an existing system. It can also be used if a *number* of new facilities are to be added or if an entire new system is being developed. The model is used to analyze each of the configurations being considered, and it reveals the minimum costs that each would entail. This information can then be included in the evaluation of location alternatives.

A description of the procedure for the transportation model and examples of its use in location decisions are the subject of the supplement to this chapter. A solved problem at the end of this chapter illustrates how results of a transportation analysis can be combined with the results of a locational cost-volume analysis.

Factor Rating

A typical location decision involves both qualitative and quantitative inputs, and these tend to vary from situation to situation depending on the needs of each particular organization. **Factor rating** is a general approach that is useful both for evaluating a given alternative and for comparing alternatives. The value of factor rating is that it provides a rational basis for evaluation and it facilitates comparison among alternatives by establishing a *composite* value for each alternative that summarizes all related factors. Factor rating enables decision makers to incorporate their personal opinions as well as quantitative information into the decision process.

The following procedure is used to develop a factor rating:

1. Determine the factors that are relevant (e.g., location of market, water supply, parking facilities, revenue potential).
2. Assign a weight to each factor that indicates its relative importance compared to all other factors. Typically, weights sum to 1.00.
3. Decide on a common scale for all factors (e.g., 0 to 100).
4. Score each location alternative.
5. Multiply the factor weight by the score for each factor, and sum the results for each location alternative.
6. Choose the alternative with the highest composite score. This procedure is illustrated in the next example.

EXAMPLE 2

A small manufacturing firm has recently decided to expand its operations to include several new lines, which it hopes to produce in a separate location because of space limitations in its existing plant. The following rating sheet illustrates relevant factors, factor weightings, and actual ratings for two alternative locations, along with the necessary computations to obtain composite scores for each alternative.

Factor	Weight	Scores (out of 100) Alt. 1	Alt. 2	Weighted scores Alternative 1	Alternative 2
Nearness to raw material	.10	100	60	.10(100) = 10.0	.10(60) = 6.0
Labor costs	.05	80	80	.05(80) = 4.0	.05(80) = 4.0
Water supply	.40	70	90	.40(70) = 28.0	.40(90) = 36.0
Transportation costs	.10	86	92	.10(86) = 8.6	.10(92) = 9.2
Climate	.20	40	70	.20(40) = 8.0	.20(70) = 14.0
Taxes	.15	80	90	.15(80) = 12.0	.15(90) = 13.5
	1.00			70.6	82.7

Thus, alternative 2 is better because it has the higher composite score.

In some cases, managers may prefer to establish minimum *thresholds* for composite scores. If an alternative fails to meet that minimum, it can be rejected without further consideration. If none of the alternatives meets the minimum, this means that either additional alternatives must be identified and evaluated or the minimum threshold must be reevaluated.

SUMMARY

Location decisions confront both new and existing organizations. Factors such as growth, market shifts, depletion of raw materials, and the introduction of new products and services are some of the reasons organizations become involved with location decisions. The importance of these decisions is underscored by the long-term commitment they typically involve and by their potential impact on the operating system.

The primary options available to existing organizations in terms of location are to expand an existing location, move to a new location, or maintain existing facilities while adding another facility in a new location.

Among the major factors that influence location decisions in practice are location of raw materials and sources of supply, labor supply, market considerations, community-related factors, site-related factors, and climate. Foreign locations may be attractive in terms of labor costs, abundance of raw materials, or as potential markets for a firm's products or services. Problems that are sometimes encountered in foreign countries involve language differences, cultural differences, anti-American sentiments, and political instability.

A common approach to narrowing the range of location alternatives is to first identify a country or region that seems to satisfy overall needs and then identify a number of community-site alternatives for more in-depth analysis. There are a variety of methods used to evaluate location alternatives. The ones described in the chapter include locational cost-volume analysis and factor rating. The transportation model is briefly mentioned; a more complete description of that subject is contained in the chapter supplement.

KEY TERMS

factor rating, 241   microfactories, 238
locational cost-volume analysis, 239

SOLVED PROBLEMS

1. A farm implements dealer is seeking a fourth warehouse location to complement three existing warehouses. There are three potential locations: Charlotte, Atlanta, and Columbia, S.C. Charlotte would involve a fixed cost of $4,000 per month and a variable cost of $4 per unit; Atlanta would involve fixed costs of $3,500 per month and a variable cost of $5 per unit; and Columbia would involve a fixed cost of $5,000 per month and a variable cost of $6 per unit. Use of the Charlotte location would increase system transportation costs by $19,000 per month, Atlanta would add $22,000 per month, and Columbia would add $18,000 per month to transportation costs.

Which location would result in the lowest total cost to handle 800 units per month?

Solution

Given: Volume = 800 units per month

	FC per month	VC per unit	Transportation cost per month
Charlotte	$4,000	$4	$19,000
Atlanta	3,500	5	22,000
Columbia	5,000	6	18,000

Monthly total cost = FC + VC + Transportation cost

Charlotte:	$4,000 + $4 per unit × 800 units + $19,000 = $26,200
Atlanta:	3,500 + 5 per unit × 800 units + 22,000 = 29,500
Columbia:	5,000 + 6 per unit × 800 units + 18,000 = 27,800

Hence, Charlotte would result in the lowest total cost for this monthly volume.

2. A small printing firm is about to lose its lease, so it must move to another location. Two sites are currently under consideration. Site A would have fixed costs of $8,000 per month, and site B would have fixed costs of $9,400 per month. Variable costs are expected to be $5 per unit at site A and $4 per unit at site B. Monthly demand has been steady at 8,800 units for the last several years and is not expected to deviate from that amount in the foreseeable future. Assume units sell for $6 per unit. Determine which location would yield the higher profit under these conditions.

Solution

Profit = (Revenue per unit) × Q − [FC + (VC per unit) × Q]

Site	Revenue	FC	VC	Monthly profit
A	$52,800	$8,000	$44,000	$ 800
B	$52,800	$9,400	$35,200	$8,200

Hence, site B is expected to yield the higher monthly profit.

DISCUSSION AND REVIEW QUESTIONS

1. In what ways can the location decision have an impact on the production system?

2. How would you respond to this statement: "The importance of the location decision is

often vastly overrated; the fact that virtually every type of business is located in every section of the country means there should be no problem in finding a suitable location"?

3. What are the community factors that influence location decisions?

4. In what ways are manufacturing and non-manufacturing location decisions similar? Different?

5. What are some of the potential benefits of locating in foreign countries? What are some of the possible drawbacks?

6. What is location rating, and how does it work?

7. Outline the general approach for developing location alternatives.

8. What are the basic assumptions in locational cost-volume analysis?

9. Discuss recent trends in location and possible future strategies.

PROBLEMS

1. A newly formed firm must decide on a plant location. There are two alternatives under consideration: locate near the major raw materials or locate near the major customers. Locating near the raw materials will result in lower fixed and variable costs than locating near the market, but the owners feel there would be a loss in sales volume because of the tendency of customers to favor local suppliers. Revenue per unit will be $185 in either case. Using the following information, determine which location would produce the greater profit.

	Omaha	Kansas City
Annual fixed costs ($ millions)	$1.2	$1.4
Variable cost per unit	$36	$47
Expected annual demand (units)	8,000	12,000

2. The owner of Genuine Subs, Inc. hopes to expand her present operation by adding one new outlet. Three locations have been studied. Each would have the same labor and materials costs (food, serving containers, napkins, etc.) of $0.76 cents per sandwich. Sandwiches sell for $1.65 each in all locations. Rent and equipment costs would be $5,000 per month for location A, $5,500 per month for location B, and $5,800 per month for location C.

   a. Determine the volume necessary at each location to realize a monthly profit of $10,000.

   b. If expected sales at A, B, and C are 21,000 per month, 22,000 per month, and 23,000 per month, respectively, which location would yield the greatest profits?

3. A small producer of machine tools wants to move a larger building. Two alternatives have been identified. Location A would have fixed costs of $800,000 per year and variable costs of $14,000 per unit; location B would have annual fixed costs of $920,000 and variable costs of $13,000 per unit. The finished items sell for $17,000 each.

   a. At what volume of output would the two locations have the same total cost?

   b. For what range of output would location A be superior? For what range would B be superior?

4. A company that produces pleasure boats has recently decided to expand one of its lines. Current facilities are insufficient to handle the increased workload, so the com-

pany is considering three alternatives, A (new location), B (subcontract), and C (expand existing facilities).

Alternative A would involve substantial fixed costs but relatively low variable costs: fixed costs would be $250,000 per year, and variable costs would be $500 per boat. Subcontracting would involve a cost per boat of $2,500, and expansion would require an annual fixed cost of $50,000 and a variable cost of $1,000 per boat.

a. For what range of output would each alternative yield the lowest total cost?

b. Which alternative would yield the lowest total cost for an expected annual volume of 150 boats?

c. What other factors might be considered in choosing between expansion and subcontracting?

5. Rework part *b* of the previous problem using this additional information: Expansion would result in an increase of $70,000 per year in transportation costs, subcontracting would result in an increase of $25,000 per year, and adding a new location would result in an increase of $4,000 per year.

6. A firm that has recently experienced an enormous growth rate is seeking to lease a small plant in either Memphis, Biloxi, or Birmingham. Prepare an economic analysis of the three locations given the following information: Annual costs for building, equipment, and administration would be $40,000 for Memphis, $60,000 for Biloxi, and $100,000 for Birmingham. Labor and materials are expected to be $8 per unit in Memphis, $4 per unit in Biloxi, and $5 per unit in Birmingham. The Memphis location would increase system transportation costs by $50,000 per year, the Biloxi location would increase them by $60,000 per year, and the Birmingham location would increase those costs by $25,000 per year. Expected annual volume is 10,000 units.

7. A retired auto mechanic hopes to open his own rustproofing shop. Customers would be area new-car dealers. Two locations are being considered, one in the center of the city and one on the outskirts of the city. The in-city location would involved fixed monthly costs of $7,000 and labor, materials, and transportation costs of $30 per car. The outside location would have fixed monthly costs of $4,700 and labor, materials, and transportation costs of $40 per car. Dealer price at either location will be $90 per car.

a. Which location will yield the greatest profit if monthly demand is (1) 200 cars? (2) 300 cars?

b. At what volume of output will the two sites yield the same monthly profit?

8. For each of the four types of organizations shown, rate the importance of each of the factors listed, using L = Low importance, M = Moderate importance, and H = High importance, in terms of making location decisions.

Factor	Local bank	Steel mill	Food ware-house	Public school
Convenience for customers	____	____	____	____
Attractiveness of building	____	____	____	____
Nearness to raw materials	____	____	____	____
Large amounts of power	____	____	____	____
Pollution controls	____	____	____	____
Labor cost and availability	____	____	____	____
Transportation costs	____	____	____	____
Construction costs	____	____	____	____

9. Using the following factor ratings, determine which location alternative should be

chosen on the basis of maximum composite score, A, B, or C.

Factor (100 points each)	Weight	Location A	B	C
Convenient	.15	80	70	60
Parking facilities	.20	72	76	92
Display area	.18	88	90	90
Shopper traffic	.27	94	86	80
Operating costs	.10	98	90	82
Neighborhood	.10	96	85	75
	1.00			

10. A manager has received an analysis of several cities being considered for a new office complex. The data (10 points maximum) are:

Factor	Location A	B	C
Business services	9	5	5
Community services	7	6	7
Real estate cost	3	8	7
Construction costs	5	6	5
Cost of Living	4	7	8
Taxes	5	5	4
Transportation	6	7	8

a. If the manager weights the factors equally, how would the locations stack up?

b. If business services and construction costs are given weights that are double the weights of the other factors, how would the locations stack up?

SELECTED BIBLIOGRAPHY

Adam, Everette E., Jr., and Ronald J. Ebert. *Production and Operations Management: Concepts, Models and Behavior.* 4th ed. Englewood Cliffs, N.J.: Prentice-Hall, 1989.

Buffa, E. S. *Operations Management: Problems and Models,* 3d ed. New York: John Wiley & Sons, 1972.

Hayes, Robert H., and Stephen Wheelright. *Restoring Our Competitive Edge: Competing through Manufacturing.* New York: Wiley, 1984.

Reed, R., Jr. *Plant Location, Layout, and Maintenance.* Homewood, Ill.: Richard D. Irwin, 1967.

Schmenner, R. W. "Look Beyond the Obvious in Plant Location." *Harvard Business Review,* January–February 1979, pp. 126–32.

Schollhammer, H. *Locational Strategies of Multinational Firms.* Los Angeles: Center for International Business, Los Angeles World Trade Center, 1974.

Toward a New Era in U.S. Manufacturing: The Need for a National Vision. Washington: National Academy Press, 1986.

"What Management Needs to Know before Picking a Plant Site." *Dun's Review,* October 1979, p. 14ff.

READING

U.S. SEMICONDUCTOR MAKERS AUTOMATE, CUT CHIP PRODUCTION IN SOUTHEAST ASIA

Steven P. Galante

PORTLAND, Maine—This New England city has lost jobs to Southeast Asia time and again over the past 15 years, in industries ranging from shoemaking to shipbuilding. Now Portland is striking back.

In a one-story factory owned by Schlumberger Ltd.'s Fairchild Camera & Instrument Corp. subsidiary, automated machines are doing the work once performed almost exclusively by hand in Southeast Asia. The machines are welding semiconductor chips, each smaller than an infant's fingernail, onto matchbook-sized metal frames.

"We think we can make more money doing it here than we can 10,000 miles away," says Kirk P. Pond, general manager of Fairchild's digital products division, explaining the decision to bring the assembly operation back to the U.S. from Singapore and Indonesia.

Such thinking would have been scoffed at just a few years ago. For more than a decade, American semiconductor makers have divided their production into onshore and offshore operations. Domestic plants have done the highly skilled tasks, and overseas facilities, where wages are low, have done the final work that requires a lot of labor but less skill.

Boon of Automation

Automation is changing that. Machines can now mount circuits onto their metal frames, wire the circuits in place and test the finished product for flaws—all far more rapidly than humans.

A Southeast Asia worker using manual equipment can wire as many as 120 integrated circuits to their frames in an hour. But the 34 automated machines here in Portland each can wire 640 circuits in an hour. And since one person can monitor eight machines at a time, the output per person is a stunning 5,120 circuits an hour.

Labor, obviously, becomes a smaller portion of the overall manufacturing cost. When transportation and inventory costs are considered, it becomes more economical to assemble chips at a U.S. plant than at an Asian plant—even if the Asian plant is equally automated, according to some analysts.

"The rise in the use of automated equipment is rapidly dispelling the advantages that used to exist for assembly in Asia," says Robert M. Clary, an electronics consultant at Rose Associates in Los Altos, Calif.

And that has major implications for countries such as Malaysia, the Philippines and Singapore, which have relied heavily on electronics for jobs and exports. A drift of assembly operations back to the U.S. could slow the industry's growth in Asia, and make it more difficult for Asian countries to acquire technological skills.

Plans Dropped

Advanced Micro Devices Inc., Sunnyvale, Calif., has dropped plans to enlarge its Singapore assembly plant and is slowing work on a facility in Bangkok. And Motorola Inc. of Schaumburg, Ill., has put plans to expand in Malaysia and Thailand on hold.

U.S. manufacturers aren't likely to scrap their existing Asian facilities just to replace them with automated U.S. plants, according to G. Dan Hutcheson, a vice president at VLSI Research Corp. in San Jose, Calif. "But as companies build new lines in the future," he says, "they're going to build them onshore."

Automation isn't the only factor prompting the chip makers to bring assembly back home. Economic changes sweeping through the marketplace are making it more important for producers to have assembly operations close to customers. Automation, however, is making that economically possible.

The "most profound thing" taking place in the industry is a move toward closer cooperation between chip makers and their customers, says Mr. Pond, the head of Fairchild's Portland plant.

Staying on Target

"I've got many, many customers to whom I can ship zero days late and no more than one day early," he says. Without onshore assembly, such timely deliveries would be difficult, unless Fairchild itself stocked a large and expensive inventory.

Southeast Asian governments are watching the trend towards onshore manufacturing with dismay. Singapore is considering more generous tax incentives and possibly even low-interest loans to lure U.S. semiconductor makers, says a spokesman for that country's Economic Development Board. Malaysian officials say they are reviewing their investment incentives, too.

Questions

1. How is the semiconductor industry changing? What impact is this having on location decisions? Why?

2. Why aren't U.S. manufacturers likely to scrap their existing Asian facilities?

3. Why are timely deliveries difficult without onshore assembly?

READING

RADIO SHACK INTERNATIONAL

In 1973, Radio Shack opened its first European store in Belgium. In 1977, the organization had 459 overseas outlets but had not added a new store in 18 months. In addition, it had lost $21 million from its European operations in the previous three years.

Charles D. Tandy had spent 13 years building Radio Shack into the leading merchandiser of amateur electronic gear in the United States. He bought Radio Shack Corporation in 1963 when it was in trouble. In the first nine months of fiscal 1977, the 6,000-store chain had earnings of $56.2 million on revenues of $732.6 million—respective increases of 14 percent and 32 percent. Retail stores accounted for 95 percent of the company's earnings and revenues.

Radio Shack's success in the United States appears to be a combination of well-located stores, discount prices, a wide product mix, and heavy advertising. Charles Tandy believes that this approach will work in Europe and that the four years of heavy losses are only temporary. Basically, he says, "I see nothing different about the people in Europe from the people in the United States." As a result, he plans to continue with the same strategies.

Others suggest that the problem is more fundamental—that discounting methods that work in the United States will not attract Europeans, who are highly brand and quality conscious. In a blitz operation, the European market was blanketed with hundreds of stores, many in poor locations.

In many cases, local laws and customs were overlooked or disregarded. When the first store was opened in Belgium, for example, Tandy overlooked a law that requires a government tax stamp on window signs. In Holland, the first Christmas promotion was geared to December 25. The company was not aware that the Dutch exchange holiday gifts on St. Nicholas Day, usually celebrated on December 6. In Germany, one of the biggest losses occurred when Radio Shack gave away flashlights to promote its stores—and was served with an injunction for violating German sales laws.

In the United States, citizens band radios are Radio Shack's best-selling item, accounting for 22 percent of sales. Belgium, Britain, and Holland bar citizens band radios; and various laws have curbed the sale of other items as well.

European competitors suggest that Europeans are willing to pay premium prices for top quality items and that Radio Shack's image as a discount house keeps customers away. The quality image is especially strong in France, where Radio Shack has only eight stores (none of which is in Paris).

Despite the losses, sales are slowly increasing; and Tandy is optimistic that his basic strategy will work. In fact, he predicts that the foreign operation will be profitable in two years.

Questions

1. How might planning be different in Europe than in the United States?

2. What recommendations would you have for Tandy after reading this chapter? Is he being optimistic or realistic in his planning?

3. What steps would you take to increase sales and profitability? What would you want to know about the different European countries?

4. What implications does this reading have for other international retail operations?

SUPPLEMENT TO CHAPTER 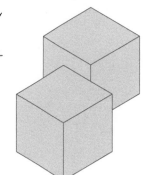 5

THE TRANSPORTATION MODEL

LEARNING OBJECTIVES

After completing this supplement, you should be able to:

1. Describe the nature of a transportation problem.
2. Solve transportation problems manually and interpret the results.
3. Set up transportation problems in the general linear programming format.
4. Interpret computer solutions.

SUPPLEMENT OUTLINE

INTRODUCTION

The transportation problem involves finding the lowest-cost plan for distributing stocks of goods or *supplies* from multiple origins to multiple destinations that *demand* the goods. For instance, a firm might have three factories that are all capable of producing identical units of the same product and four warehouses that stock or demand those products, as depicted in Figure 5S–1. The *transportation model* can be used to determine how to allocate the supplies available from the various factories to the warehouses that stock or demand those goods in such a way that total shipping cost (time, distance, etc.) is minimized. Usually, analysis of the problem will produce a shipping plan that pertains to a certain period of time (day, week), although once the plan is established, it will generally not change unless one or more of the parameters of the problem (supply, demand, unit shipping cost) changes.

Although the diagram in Figure 5S–1 illustrates the nature of the problem, in many real-life cases managers must deal with allocation problems that are considerably larger in scope. For instance, consider the case of a beer maker with four or five breweries and hundreds or even thousands of distributors, or the case of an automobile manufacturer with eight assembly plants scattered throughout the United States and Canada and the thousands of dealers that must be supplied with those cars. In such cases, the ability to identify the optimal solution makes the transportation model quite important.

FIGURE 5S–1

The transportation problem involves determining a minimum cost plan for shipping from multiple sources to multiple destinations

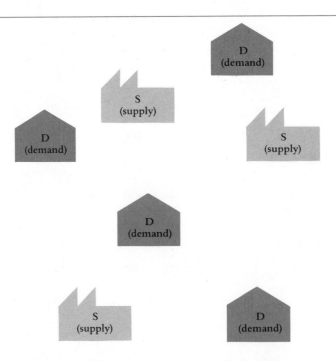

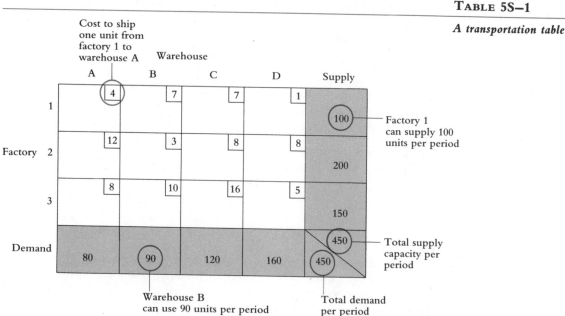

The shipping (supply) points can be factories, warehouses, departments, or any other place from which goods are sent. Destinations can be factories, warehouses, departments, or other points that receive goods. The information needed to use the model consists of the following:

1. A list of the origins and each one's capacity or supply quantity per period.
2. A list of the destinations and each one's demand per period.
3. The unit cost of shipping items from each origin to each destination.

This information is arranged into a *transportation table* such as the one shown in Table 5S–1.

The transportation model is one of a class of linear programming models, so named because of the linear relationships among problem variables. In the transportation model, transportation costs are treated as a direct linear function of the number of units shipped. For instance, if the unit cost to ship is $7 and 10 units are shipped, the cost would be 10($7) = $70. If 20 units are shipped, the cost would be 20($7) = $140. Hence, transportation cost is a linear function of the amount shipped.

Use of the transportation model implies that certain assumptions are satisfied. The major ones are:

1. The items to be shipped are homogeneous (i.e., they are the same regardless of their source or destination).

2. Shipping cost per unit is the same regardless of the number of units shipped.

3. There is only one route or mode of transportation being used between each source and each destination.

The transportation method is an iterative process. It starts with the development of a feasible solution, which is then sequentially tested and improved until an optimal solution is obtained. The description of the technique on the following pages focuses on each of the major steps in the process in this order:

1. Obtaining an initial solution.
2. Testing the solution for optimality.
3. Improving suboptimal solutions.

OBTAINING AN INITIAL SOLUTION

In order to begin the process, it is necessary to develop a feasible distribution plan. There are a number of different methods for obtaining such a plan. The discussion here will focus on two widely used approaches: the **northwest-corner method** and the **intuitive approach.** The latter is a heuristic approach that yields an initial solution that is often optimal or near optimal. The northwest-corner method is much less efficient; it merely provides a convenient starting point. Even so, it is an easy-to-understand approach that merits consideration. Each method will be demonstrated using the matrix illustrated in Table 5S–1.

These methods require that total supply equal total demand. If you refer to Table 5S–1, you will see that they are equal. Later you will learn what to do if they are not equal.

The Northwest-Corner Method

1. The northwest-corner method begins with the cell that is in the upper left-hand (northwest) corner of the matrix, allocating (assigning) as many units as possible to that cell. Factory 1 can supply 100 units, but warehouse A needs only 80 units. Hence, assign 80 units to cell 1–A, completely exhausting A's demand and leaving factory 1 with a supply of 20 units (see Table 5S–2).

2. Staying in row 1 and moving to column B, we see that warehouse B has a demand for 90 units, 20 of which can be supplied by factory 1. Assigning 20 units to cell 1–B exhausts factory 1's supply and leaves warehouse B with a demand for 70 additional units.

3. Staying in column B and dropping down to row 2, we observe that factory 2 has a supply of 200 units. Assigning 70 units to cell 2–B satisfies B's demand and leaves factory 2 with 130 units.

Warehouse

	A	B	C	D	Supply
1	① 4 80	② 7 20	7	1	100
Factory 2	12	③ 3 70	④ 8 120	⑤ 8 10	200
3	8	10	16	⑥ 5 150	150
Demand	80	90	120	160 450	450

4. Staying in row 2 and moving to column C, we observe that warehouse C has a demand for 120 units, which can be filled by factory 2. Assigning 120 units to cell 2–C satisfies C's demand and still leaves factory 2 with 10 units.

5. Staying in row 2 and moving to column D, we find that warehouse D has a demand of 160 units. Assigning 10 units to cell 2–D exhausts factory 2's supply and leaves D with a need for an additional 150 units.

6. The remaining demand of warehouse D for 150 units can be just satisfied by factory 3's supply. This is a consequence of starting with equal supply and demand. Hence, assign 150 units to be shipped from factory 3 to warehouse D.

Is this distribution plan optimal (i.e., does it minimize transportation costs)? In a moment, we shall see how to test it to determine if further improvements are possible. In the meantime, it will be instructive to compute the transportation costs associated with this initial solution. The cost for each cell is the product of units assigned to that cell and the unit transportation cost for the cell. (Empty cells have no cost.) Thus:

			Total cost
1–A	. . . . .	80($4) =	$ 320
1–B	. . . . .	20($7) =	140
2–B	. . . . .	70($3) =	210
2–C	. . . . .	120($8) =	960
2–D	. . . . .	10($8) =	80
3–D	. . . . .	150($5) =	750
			$2,460

As previously mentioned, the northwest-corner method is merely a convenient way to obtain a feasible solution. Because it does not take costs into account, it frequently does not yield the optimal solution. Note that with the given supplies and demands, the same solution would be generated even if the costs were quite different. It will be interesting, then, to see how well the intuitive method does, since it explicitly takes costs into account in obtaining an initial solution.

The Intuitive Approach

With the intuitive approach, cell allocations are made according to cell cost, beginning with the lowest cost. The procedure involves these steps:

1. Identify the cell with the lowest cost.
2. Allocate as many units as possible to that cell, and cross out the row or column (or both) that is exhausted by this.
3. Find the cells with the next lowest cost from among the *feasible* cells.
4. Repeat steps 2 and 3 until all units have been allocated.

Cell 1–D has the lowest cost ($1) (see Table 5S–3). The factory 1 supply is 100, and the warehouse D demand is 160. Therefore, the most we can allocate to this cell is 100 units. Since the supply of 100 is exhausted, we cross out the costs in the first row as well as the supply of 100. In addition, we must adjust the column total to reflect the allocation, which leaves 60 units of unallocated demand in column D.

The next lowest cost is $3 in cell 2–B. Allocating 90 units to this cell exhausts the column total and leaves 110 units for the supply of factory 2 (see Table 5S–4). Next, we cross out the costs for column B.

TABLE 5S–3

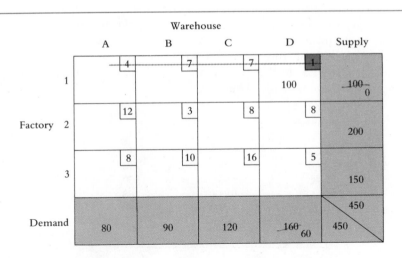

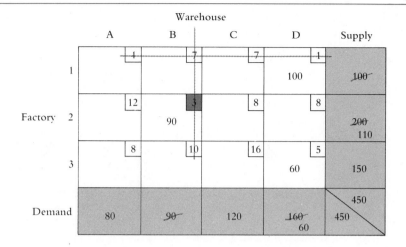

The next lowest cost (that is not crossed out) is the $5 in cell 3–D. Allocating 60 units to this cell exhausts the column total and leaves 90 units for row 3. We now cross out the costs in column D (see Table 5S–5).

At this point, there is a *tie* for the next lowest cell cost: cell 3–A and cell 2–C each have a cost of $8. Break such a tie arbitrarily. Suppose we choose cell 3–A. There is a demand of 80 units, and there is a remaining supply of 90 units in the row. The smaller of these is 80, so that amount is placed in cell 3–A (see Table 5S–6). This exhausts the column, so we cross out the cell costs in column A. Also, the remaining supply in factory 3 is now 10.

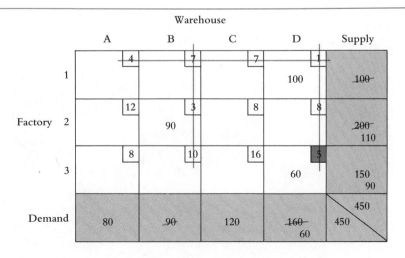

TABLE 5S–6

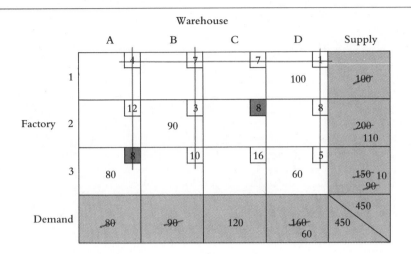

The other cell in the tie, cell 2–C, still remains. There is a supply of 110 remaining in the row and a demand of 120 in the column. The smaller of these two amounts, 110, is assigned to the cell, and the row costs are crossed out. The row total is changed to zero, and the column total is changed to 10 units. The only remaining cell with a cost that has not been crossed out is cell 3–C. Both supply and demand are 10 units, so 10 units are assigned to the cell. This completes the initial allocation. (See Table 5S–7.)

Now let's determine if this initial solution obtained using the intuitive method is optimum.

TABLE 5S–7

Initial allocation using intuitive approach

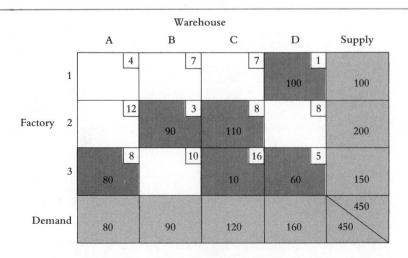

TESTING FOR OPTIMALITY

Testing for optimality and revising suboptimal solutions are the same regardless of how the initial solution was developed (e.g., northwest–corner method or intuitive). The process involves analysis of each unused or empty cell to determine if there is a potential for reducing the total cost of the solution. This is accomplished by transferring one unit into an empty cell and noting the impact this has on costs. If costs are increased, then this implies that using the cell would increase total costs. If costs remain the same, this would imply that an alternative option with the same total cost as the current plan exists. However, if analysis reveals a cost decrease, this implies that an improved solution is possible. The test for optimality requires that *every* unused cell be evaluated for potential improvement. Either of two methods can be used: stepping-stone or MODI.

Evaluating Empty Cells: The Stepping-Stone Method

In the **stepping-stone method,** cell evaluation proceeds by borrowing one unit from a full cell and using it to assess the impact that shifting units into the empty cell would produce. For instance, if a shift of one unit causes an increase of $5, then it can be assumed that total costs would be increased by $5 times the number of units shifted into the cell. Obviously, such a move would be unwise since the objective is to decrease costs.

The name *stepping-stone* derives from early descriptions of the method that likened the procedures to crossing a shallow pond by stepping from stone to stone. Here, the occupied cells are the "stones"; shifting units into empty cells requires borrowing units from occupied cells. In order to maintain the balance of supply and demand for every row and column, a shift of one unit into an empty cell requires a series of shifts from other occupied cells.

The best way to understand the evaluation process is to consider a simple example. Suppose we want to evaluate cell 1–A (see Table 5S–8). We must shift one unit into that cell, which would imply that one unit will be shipped from factory 1 to warehouse A. However, factory 1 has only 100 units it can ship, and all are allocated to warehouse D. Therefore, in order to ship one unit to A, we borrow a unit from cell 1–D. This creates two problems: Column A now has one extra unit, and column D is short one unit (i.e., A has 1 + 80 = 81 units but needs only 80 units, and D has 99 + 60 = 159 but needs 160 units). We can remedy these problems by subtracting one unit from cell 3–A and adding it to cell 3–D; this gives column A a total of 1 + 79 = 80 and column D a total of 99 + 61 = 160. (Note that instead of actually making each addition or subtraction of the single unit, a + or − sign is simply inserted in the appropriate cell to signify the operation.)

Let's see what effect such a shift would have on costs. For each cell to which a unit is added, the cost will increase by the transportation cost for that cell; for cells that gave up a unit, costs will decrease by the cell's transportation cost. We can summarize this with a *T account* as follows.

TABLE 5S–8

Evaluation path for cell 1–A

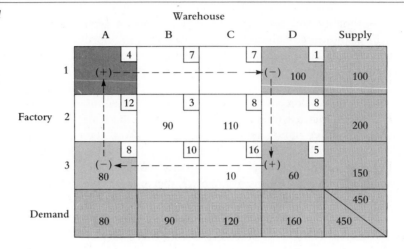

Cell 1–A

+		−	
(1–A)	+4	(1–D)	−1
(3–D)	+5	(3–A)	−8
	+9		−9
		0	

Thus, shifting units around this path would have no impact whatsoever on transportation costs: use of cell 1–A would be an equivalent-cost alternative. Management may prefer to use it for other reasons, or management may prefer to stay with the original solution. In any case, knowledge of such alternatives gives a certain degree of added flexibility in decision making.

So far, we have not discovered any improvement potential. But there are still five unused cells that must be analyzed. However, before we evaluate the remaining empty cells, it is important to mention that constructing paths using the stepping-stone method requires a minimum number of occupied cells and unless that number exists, it will be impossible to evaluate all the empty cells in this manner. The number of occupied cells must equal the sum of the number of rows and columns minus 1: $R + C - 1$, where R = Number of rows and C = Number of columns. In this example, $R = 3$ and $C = 4$, so we must have $3 + 4 - 1 = 6$ used or completed cells (which we do have). If there are too few occupied cells, the matrix is said to be *degenerate*. A method for overcoming this problem is explained later in this supplement.

For now, let's continue evaluating the unused cells. Suppose we now consider cell 2–A. Begin by adding a unit to the empty cell. Moving to the right in row 2, we have what seems to be a choice: borrow a unit from 90 or from 110. However, borrowing from 90 will leave column B one unit short, and since adding and borrowing must involve occupied cells and there are no others in the B column, the 90 cannot be used. Instead, we must borrow from the 110 and add one unit to the 10 in cell 3–C. We can complete our path back to the original cell by subtracting a unit from the 80 units in cell 3–A. The +/− path is shown in Table 5S–9. The impact on total cost for the path associated with cell 2–A would be:

Cell 2–A

+			−	
(2–A)	+12	(2–C)	−8
(3–C)	+16	(3–A)	−8
	+28		−16

+12

This means that for every unit shifted into cell 2–A, the total cost would *increase* by $12. Hence, we should avoid shipping units from factory 2 to warehouse A.

At this point, let's pause for a moment and consider some helpful rules for obtaining evaluation paths, since you may still be a little unsure of how to actually do it.

1. Start by placing a + sign in the cell you wish to evaluate.
2. Move horizontally (or vertically) to a completed cell. Choose a cell that will permit your next move to another completed cell. Assign a − sign to the cell.
3. Change direction and move to another completed cell. Again, choose one that will permit your next move. Assign a + sign to the cell.

TABLE 5S–9

Evaluation path for cell 2–A

TABLE 5S–10

Evaluation path for cell 3–B

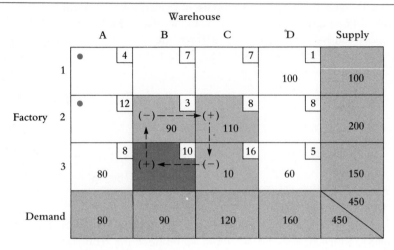

• Previously evaluated

4. Continue this process of moving to completed cells and alternating + and − signs until you can complete a closed path back to the original cell. Make only horizontal and vertical moves.

5. You may find it helpful to place a small dot or checkmark in cells that have been evaluated to help keep track of them.

Let's try another one, say, 3–B. Start by placing a + sign in cell 3–B. Move to the 90 in cell 2–B, and place a − sign there. Move to the 110 in cell 2–C, and place a + sign there. Move to cell 3–C, and give it a − sign. The path is shown in Table 5S–10. This one was fairly easy. Let's see what the impact on cost would be:

Cell 3–B

+		−	
(3–B)	+10	(2–B)	−3
(2–C)	+8	(3–C)	−16
	+18		−19

$$\boxed{-1}$$

The −1 indicates that for each unit we can shift into cell 3–B, our cost will decrease by $1. Hence, if we could shift 100 units, we could save $100 over the present solution. However, at this point we are not ready to make any changes since there may be some other empty cell that would yield even greater savings, and we can only make one shift at a time.

Evaluation of cell 2–D is quite similar to the evaluation of cell 3–B. The evaluation path is shown in Table 5S–11. The cost impact would be:

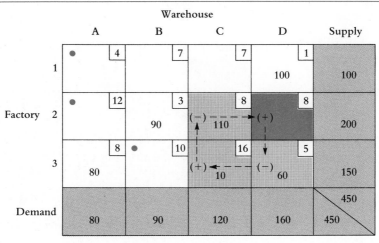

• Previously evaluated

Cell 2–D

+		−	
(2–D)	+8	(3–D)	−5
(3–C)	+16	(2–C)	−8
	+24		−13

+11

Thus, no improvement is possible.

There are two cells remaining to be evaluated: 1–B and 1–C. Let's consider 1–B first. It is a little more involved than the previous paths. Begin by placing a + in cell 1–B. Move to cell 1–D (100 units) and give it a −. Move vertically to 3–D (60 units) and give it a +. Move to the left and put a − in cell 3–C (10 units). Move up to 110 and put a + in that cell. Move to the left to 90 units (cell 2–B) and give it a − sign, completing the path. The path is shown in Table 5S–12. The cost impact of the path would be:

Cell 1–B

+		−	
(1–B)	+7	(1–D)	−1
(3–D)	+5	(3–C)	−16
(2–C)	+8	(2–B)	−3
	+20		−20

0

Again, no improvement is possible using this cell path.

TABLE 5S–12

Evaluation path for cell 1–B

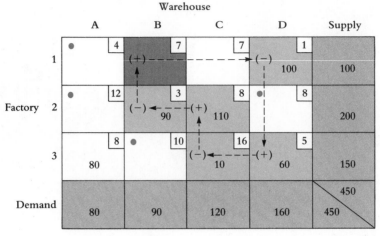

● Previously evaluated

The last empty cell 1–C. Its evaluation path is shown in Table 5S–13. Begin with 1–C as +, 1–D as −, 3–D as +, and 3–C as −. The cost impact would be:

Cell 1–C

+		−	
(1–C)	+7	(3–D)	−1
(3–D)	+5	(3–C)	−16
	+12		−17

$$\left(-5\right)$$

Hence, for each unit we can transfer into this empty cell, we improve the cost by $5.

At this point, each of the unused cells has been evaluated. The resulting costs are summarized below.

Cell	1–A	2–A	3–B	2–D	1–B	1–C
Cost	0	+12	(−1)	+11	0	(−5)

Cells with a positive total do not present opportunities for improvement. The fact that 1–A and 1–B are both zero indicates that at least one other equivalent alternative exists. The interesting fact here is that two cells have negative evaluations, indicating that the present solution is not an optimum. In a later section, you will learn how to develop an improved solution.

• Previously evaluated

Evaluating Empty Cells: The MODI Method

Another method for evaluating empty cells is the **modified distribution method (MODI).** It involves computing row and column index numbers that can be used for cell evaluation. In many respects, it is simpler than the stepping-stone method because it avoids having to trace cell evaluation paths. However, the cell evaluations it produces are identical to those obtained using the stepping-stone method. Note, though, that if a solution is not optimal, *one* stepping-stone path must be traced to obtain an improved solution. This is explained in detail in the next section.

The MODI procedure consists of these steps:

1. Make an initial allocation using the northwest-corner or intuitive method. Check for degeneracy, and adjust if necessary.
2. Obtain an index number for each row and column. Do this using only *completed* cells. Note that there will always be at least one completed cell in each row and in each column.
   a. Begin by assigning a zero to the first row.
   b. Determine the column index for any completed cells in row 1 using the relationship: Column index = Cell cost − Row index. For example, if a cell cost is $8 per unit, the column index will be 8 − 0 = 8.
   c. Each new column value will permit the calculation of *at least* one new row value, and vice versa. Continue until all rows and columns have index numbers, using only completed cells.

3. Obtain cell evaluations for *empty* cells using the relationship:

$$\text{Cell evaluation} = \text{Cell cost} - \text{Row index} - \text{Column index}$$

Obtain these in any order.

Comments:

1. Row or column values may be positive, negative, or zero.
2. A reallocation requires that new row and column cost values be calculated.

Let's see how the MODI method can be used for cell evaluations.

We begin by assigning a zero to row 1 (see Table 5S–14). Since we can only work with occupied cells and since cell 1–D is the only such cell in row 1, we focus on it. Since the sum of the row and column index numbers must add to the cell cost (which is 1), we can see that the index number for column D must be 1. There are no other occupied cells in row 1, so we shift to column D, cell 3–D. Again, the sum of the row and column index numbers must add to the cell cost (which is 5). Since the column index for D is 1, the index number for row 3 must be 4: 4 + 1 = 5.

We can use this row 3 index number and the other two occupied cells in row 3 to obtain index numbers for columns A and C. For column A, the A index number plus 4 must equal the 3–A cell cost of 8. Hence, the index for A is 4: 4 + 4 = 8. For C, the index plus 4 must equal 16; hence, the index number is 12.

Next, for row 2, using cell 2–C and a C index of 12, the row index is −4. Then, using cell 2–B, the column index is 7: 7 + (−4) = 3. This completes the row and column index numbers.

TABLE 5S–14

MODI index numbers

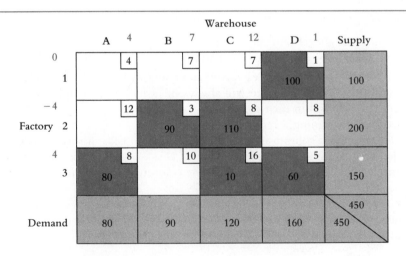

Cell	Evaluation
1–A	$4 - [0 + 4] = 0$
1–B	$7 - [0 + 7] = 0$
1–C	$7 - [0 + 12] = -5$
2–A	$12 - [-4 + 4] = 12$
2–D	$8 - [-4 + 1] = 11$
3–B	$10 - [4 + 7] = -1$

MODI cell evaluation

The cell evaluation for each empty cell is determined by subtracting from the cost of the empty cell the sum of the row and column index numbers:

Cell evaluation = Cell cost − (Row index + Column index)

This is shown in Table 5S–15. Note that these agree with the evaluations obtained using the stepping-stone method. Again, because some evaluations are negative, the solution is not optimal.

OBTAINING AN IMPROVED SOLUTION

The presence of negative cell evaluations is evidence that an improved solution is possible. By the same token, if no negatives appear, an optimum has been achieved.

In this case, there are two cells with negative evaluations: 3–B, with a value of −1, and 1–C, with a value of −5. Select the value that implies more improvement (i.e., −5), and ignore the other.

The implication of the −5 is that a savings of $5 per unit will be realized for every unit that can be shifted into cell 1–C. Recall the path used to evaluate the cell; it is reproduced in Figure 5S–16A. In the course of the evaluation, a single unit was added or subtracted to certain cells, as denoted by the + and − signs. We want to repeat that procedure, but instead of shifting *one* unit, we want to shift *as many as possible*. The *quantities* in the cells that have − signs (i.e., 10 in cell 3–C and 100 in cell 1–D) are potential candidates for shifting, since the − implies units are subtracted from those cells. It is the *smaller* of these quantities that is the limiting factor. That is, we can subtract 10 from both numbers (10 and 100), but if we try to subtract 100 from both, we end up with 0 and −90. The negative value would imply shipping from the warehouse back to the factory! Hence, 10 units can be shifted. In general, shift the minimum quantity that occupies a negative position in the ± path.

To accomplish the shift, add 10 units to each cell that has a + sign and subtract 10 units from each cell with a − sign. (Because the signs alternate, the row and column totals will still be satisfied.) This is shown in Table 5S–16.

Table 5S–16

Evaluation path for cell 1–C (see A) and reallocation of 10 units around the path (see B)

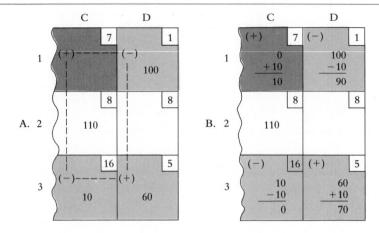

The improved solution is shown in Table 5S–17. The total costs are:

				Total cost
1–C	. . . . .	10($7)	=	$ 70
1–D	. . . . .	90($1)	=	90
2–B	. . . . .	90($3)	=	270
2–C	. . . . .	110($8)	=	880
3–A	. . . . .	80($8)	=	640
3–D	. . . . .	70($5)	=	350
				$2,300

Table 5S–17

Revised solution

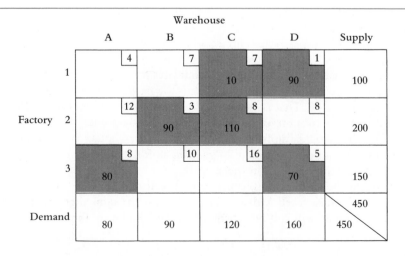

Note that the revised solution has a total cost that is $50 less than the previous solution ($2,300 versus $2,350), which is exactly equal to the cell evaluation value times the number of units shifted: -5×10 units $= -\$50$.

Is this the optimum? Once again, we must evaluate each empty cell to determine if further improvements are possible. Recall that it is necessary to check to see that there are enough completed cells to allow all empty cells to have evaluation paths. Thus,

$$R + C - 1 = 3 + 4 - 1 = 6$$

Since there are six completed cells, the second round of cell evaluations can proceed. The cell paths and their values are shown in Tables 5S–18 to 5S–23. Since all are either zero or positive, this solution is the optimum. (*Note:* MODI could have been used instead of stepping-stone.)

SPECIAL PROBLEMS

Not all transportation problems are as straightforward to deal with as the one just presented. Various irregularities often crop up, which require certain adjustments before a solution can be obtained. Two of the most common irregularities are unequal supply and demand and degeneracy, a term that refers to an insufficient number of completed cells to allow evaluation of every empty cell.

TABLE 5S–18

Evaluation of cell 1–A

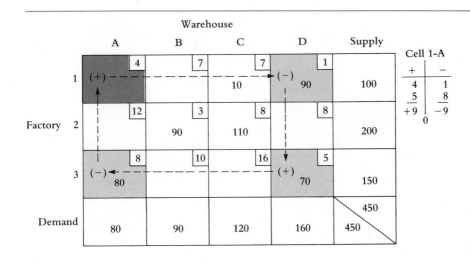

TABLE 5S–19

Evaluation of cell 1–B

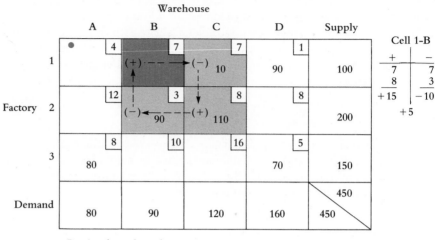

● Previously evaluated

TABLE 5S–20

Evaluation of cell 2–A

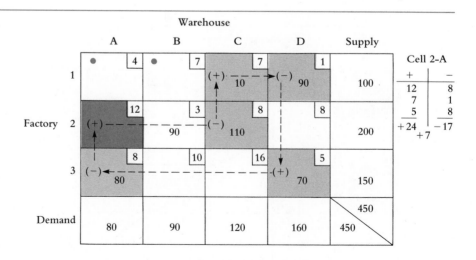

TABLE 5S–21

Evaluation of cell 2–D

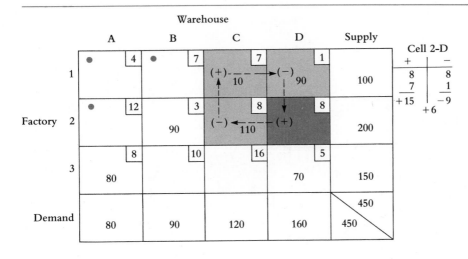

TABLE 5S–22

Evaluation of cell 3–B

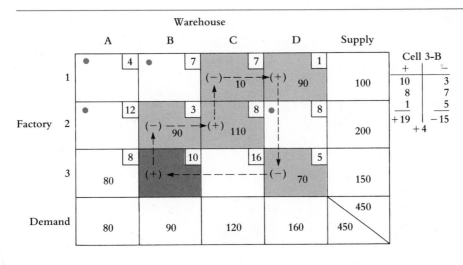

TABLE 5S–23

Evaluation of cell 3–C

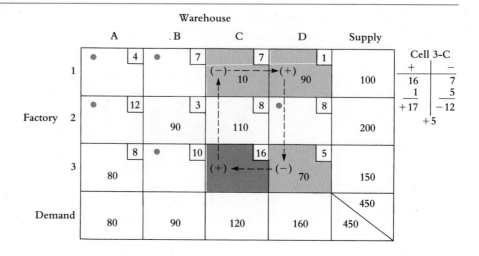

Unequal Supply and Demand

A frequently encountered situation is one in which supply and demand are not equal. Table 5S–24 illustrates such a case. Total supply (capacity) of the two sources is 200 units, but total demand of the destinations is only 170. Hence, there is a deficiency in demand of 30 units. This condition can be remedied by adding a **dummy** destination with a demand equal to the difference between supply and demand. Since there is no such destination, no units will actually be shipped, and unit shipping costs for each dummy cell are $0. This is illustrated in Table 5S–25.

Once the dummy has been added, the transportation method can then be applied in the usual manner. The final solution will have a total number of

TABLE 5S–24

Supply exceeds demand by 30 units

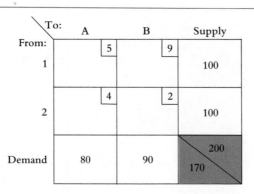

TABLE 5S–25

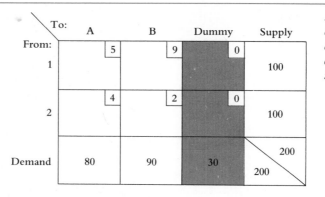

TABLE 5S–25

A dummy column with a demand of 30 units is added to the matrix; dummy cell costs are zero

units assigned to the dummy that equals the original difference between supply and demand (see Table 5S–26). These numbers indicate which source(s) (e.g., factories) will hold the extra units or will have excess capacity. In the example shown, factory 1 will ship only 70 units even though it has the capacity to ship 100 units.

A similar situation exists when demand exceeds supply (see Tables 5S–27). In those cases a dummy *row* (e.g., factory) with a supply equal to the difference between supply and demand must be added (see Table 5S–28). Again, units will not actually be shipped, so transportation costs are $0 for each cell in the dummy row. Units in the dummy row in the final solution indicate the destinations that will not receive all the units they desire and the amount of the shortage for each. For example, Table 5S–29 indicates that destination A will be 20 units short and destination B 30 units short.

TABLE 5S–26

Units in the dummy column are not shipped; factory 1 will ship only 70 units

To:	A	B	Dummy	Supply
From: 1	70 (5)	(9)	30 (0)	100
2	10 (4)	90 (2)	(0)	100
Demand	80	90	30	200 / 200

TABLE 5S–27

Demand exceeds supply by 50 units

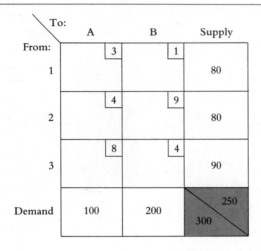

TABLE 5S–28

A dummy row with a supply of 50 units is added to the matrix so supply will equal demand

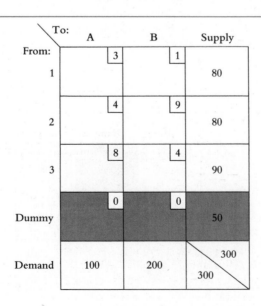

To:	A	B	Supply
From:			
1	3	1 80	80
2	4 80	9	80
3	8	4 90	90
Dummy	0 20	0 30	50
Demand	100	200	300 / 300

Units in the dummy row will not be shipped; destination A will receive 100 − 20 = 80 units and B will receive 200 − 30 = 170 units

The total transportation cost for this distribution plan is:

			Total cost
1–B	. . . . . . 80($1)	=	$ 80
2–A	. . . . . . 80($4)	=	320
3–B	. . . . . . 90($4)	=	360
Dummy–A	. . . . . . 20($0)	=	0
Dummy–B	. . . . . . 30($0)	=	0
			$760

Degeneracy

We have seen that the transportation method involves evaluation of empty cells using completed cells as "stepping stones." **Degeneracy** exists if there are too few completed cells to allow all necessary paths to be constructed. The condition occurs if an allocation (other than the final one) exhausts *both* the row (supply) and the column (demand) quantities. It can occur in an initial solution or in subsequent solutions, so it is necessary to test for degeneracy after each iteration using $R + C - 1$.

An example of a matrix with too few completed cells is shown in Table 5S–30. Note that there are only four completed cells, although the necessary number is five: $3 + 3 - 1 = 5$. Because of this, it is impossible to develop an evaluation path for cells 1–B, 1–C, 2–A, or 3–A. The situation can be

TABLE 5S–30

There are too few completed cells; some empty cells cannot be evaluated

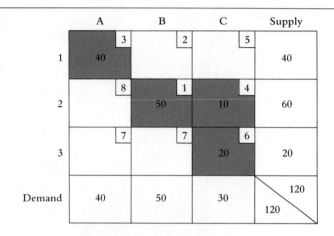

	A	B	C	Supply
1	3 / 40	2	5	40
2	8	1 / 50	4 / 10	60
3	7	7	6 / 20	20
Demand	40	50	30	120 / 120

remedied by placing a very small quantity, represented by the symbol ε, into one of the empty cells and then treating it as a completed cell. The quantity is so small that it is negligible; it will be ignored in the final solution.

The idea is to select a position for ε that will permit evaluation of all remaining empty cells. For example, putting it in cell 3–A will permit evaluation of all empty cells (see Table 5S–31). Some experimentation may be needed to find the best spot for ε, since not every cell will enable construction of evaluation paths for the remaining cells. Moreover, avoid placing ε in a minus position of a cell path that turns out to be negative because reallocation requires shifting the smallest quantity in a minus position. Since the smallest quantity is ε, which is essentially zero, no reallocation will be possible.

The cell evaluations (not shown) are all positive, so this solution is optimal.

TABLE 5S–31

Cell 3–A becomes a completed cell with the addition of a very small quantity, represented by the symbol ε

	A	B	C	Supply
1	3 / 40	2	5	40
2	8	1 / 50	4 / 10	60
3	7 / ε	7	6 / 20	20
Demand	40	50	30	120 / 120

(Note that cell 3–A is considered to be a completed cell and is therefore *not* evaluated.)

SUMMARY OF PROCEDURE

1. Make certain tha supply and demand are equal. If they are not, determine the difference between the two amounts. Create a dummy source or destination with a supply (or demand) equal to the difference so that demand and supply are equal.
2. Develop an initial solution using either the northwest-corner method or the intuitive approach.
3. Check to see that the number of completed cells is equal to $R + C - 1$. If it isn't, the solution is degenerate and will require insertion of a minute quantity, ϵ, in one of the empty cells.
4. Evaluate each of the empty cells. If any evaluations turn out to be negative, an improved solution is possible. Identify the cell that has the largest negative evaluation. Reallocate units around its evaluation path.
5. Repeat steps 3 and 4 until all cells have zero or positive values. When that occurs, the optimal solution has been achieved.

LOCATION DECISIONS

The transportation model can be used to compare location alternatives in terms of their impact on the total distribution costs for a system. The procedure involves working through a separate problem for each location being considered and then comparing the resulting total costs. Let's consider a simple example of this.

A previous example dealt with unequal supply and demand. The original matrix is reproduced in Table 5S–32. Suppose the firm has recently decided to open a third distribution center that will have an expected demand of 30 units,

TABLE 5S–32

Supply exceeds demand by 30 units

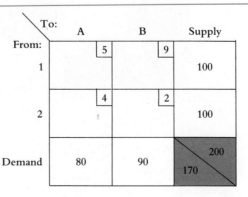

TABLE 5S-33

Transportation costs for Boston and Albany	Cost per unit to Boston	Cost per unit to Albany
	From:	From:
	1 . . . . $3	1 . . . . $4
	2 . . . . $6	2 . . . . $1

which will result in equality of supply and demand. The question is whether to locate in a suburb of Boston or in Albany, New York. The transportation costs for each location are shown in Table 5S–33. In order to determine which will yield the lower transportation costs for the system, we must work the problem twice—once using the Boston costs and once using the Albany costs. The resulting optimal solution for each location and its total cost are shown in Tables 5S–34 and 5S–35. The total cost with the Boston location is $10 less than with the Albany location, making Boston the better location *on the basis of transportation cost*. Of course, we have already seen that there are many aspects of location decisions, and transportation cost is only one of them. There may be other, more important factors that favor one location over the other.

You may also be wondering how important a difference of $10 is. Remember that this is simply an example designed to demonstrate use of the method in location decisions. Of course, if an actual situation produced such a small difference, for practical purposes the locations would undoubtedly be rated even in terms of transportation costs. However, suppose the units of supply and demand are in hundreds. Then the cost difference would be 100 ($10) = $1,000. In addition, the supply and demand quantities are generally for a short period of time (e.g., week, month, or quarter). Consequently, the difference on an annual basis would be much larger. For instance, if the

TABLE 5S-34

Optimal plan using Boston warehouse

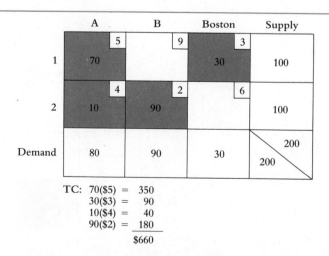

TC: 70($5) = 350
     30($3) = 90
     10($4) = 40
     90($2) = 180
             _____
             $660

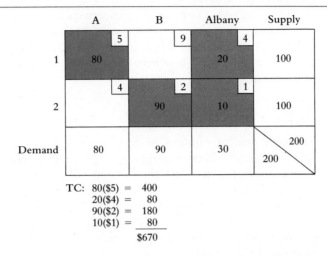

TC: 80($5) = 400
20($4) = 80
90($2) = 180
10($1) = 80
————
$670

amounts are in hundreds of units per week, the annual difference would be $1,000(52) = $52,000, which would undoubtedly be regarded as significant.

If there are other costs that differ among locations, such as production costs, these can easily be included in the analysis, provided they can be determined on a per-unit basis. In this regard, it should be noted that merely adding or subtracting a constant to all cost values in any row or column will not affect the optimum solution, so any additional costs should only be included if they have a varying effect within a row or column.

OTHER APPLICATIONS

We have seen how the transportation model can be used to minimize the costs associated with distributing goods, and we have seen how the model can be used for comparing location alternatives. You should be aware of the fact that the model is also used in a number of other ways. For example, in a slight variation of the model, profits can be used in place of costs. In such cases, each of the cell profits can be subtracted from the largest profit, and the remaining values (opportunity costs) can be treated in the same manner as shipping costs.

Some of the other uses of the model include production planning and scheduling (see Chapter 9), problems involving assignment of personnel or jobs to certain departments or machines (see Chapter 13), capacity planning, and transshipment problems.[1]

The use of the transportation model for capacity planning parallels its use for location decisions. Proposed capacity alternatives can be subjected to

---

[1] Transshipment relates to problems with major distribution centers that in turn redistribute to smaller market destinations. See, for example, W. J. Stevenson, *Introduction to Management Science* (Homewood, Ill.: Richard D. Irwin, 1989).

transportation analysis to determine which one would generate the lowest total shipping cost. For example, it is perhaps intuitively obvious that a factory or warehouse that is close to its market—or has low transportation costs for some other reason—should probably have a larger capacity than other locations. Of course, many problems are not so simple, and they require actual use of the model.

COMPUTER SOLUTIONS

Although manual solution of transportation problems is fairly straightforward, computer solutions are generally preferred, particularly for moderate or large problems. Many software packages call for data input in the same tabular form used throughout this chapter. A more general approach is to format the problem as a standard linear programming model (i.e., specify the objective function and a set of constraints). That approach enables one to use the more general version of an LP package (such as LINDO) to solve a transportation problem. Let's consider this general approach.

Table 5S–36 repeats the transportation model presented earlier in this supplement. The decision variables for a transportation model are the quantities to be shipped. Because each cell represents a potential transportation route, each must have a decision variable. We can use the symbol x_{1A} to represent the decision variable for cell 1–A, x_{1B} for cell 1–B, and so on. The objective function consists of the cell costs and these cell symbols:

Minimize $4x_{1A} + 7x_{1B} + 7x_{1C} + 1x_{1D} + 12x_{2A} + 3x_{2B} + 8x_{2C}$
$+ 8x_{2D} + 8x_{3A} + 10x_{3B} + 16x_{3C} + 5x_{3D}$

Because the amounts allocated in any row or column must add to the row or column total, each row and column must have a constraint. Thus, we have

TABLE 5S–36

		Warehouse				
		A	B	C	D	Supply
Factory	1	4	7	7	1	100
	2	12	3	8	8	200
	3	8	10	16	5	150
						450
Demand		80	90	120	160	450

$$
\begin{aligned}
\text{Supply (row)} \quad & x_{1A} + x_{1B} + x_{1C} + x_{1D} = 100 \\
& x_{2A} + x_{2B} + x_{2C} + x_{2D} = 200 \\
& x_{3A} + x_{3B} + x_{3C} + x_{3D} = 150
\end{aligned}
$$

$$
\begin{aligned}
\text{Demand (column)} \quad & x_{1A} + x_{2A} + x_{3A} = 80 \\
& x_{1B} + x_{2B} + x_{3B} = 90 \\
& x_{1C} + x_{2C} + x_{3C} = 120 \\
& x_{1D} + x_{2D} + x_{3D} = 160
\end{aligned}
$$

We do not need a constraint for the total; the row and column constraints take care of this.

If supply and demand are not equal, add the appropriate dummy row or column to the table before writing the constraints.

KEY TERMS

degeneracy, 275
dummy, 272
intuitive approach, 254

modified distribution method
(MODI), 265
northwest-corner method, 254
stepping-stone method, 259

SOLVED PROBLEMS

1. Use the intuitive technique to develop an initial solution to the following problem, and then determine if the solution is optimal. If it is not, develop the optimal solution.

To: From:	A	B	Supply
1	9	6	75
2	5	3	75
Demand	80	90	

Solution

a. First check to see if supply and demand are equal. Total demand = 170 and total supply = 150; therefore, it will be necessary to create a dummy origin (supply) with zero transportation costs in each of its cells (see following table).

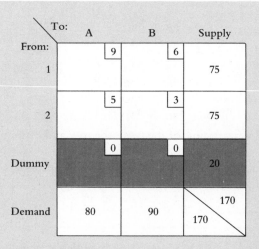

b. Find the cell that has the lowest unit transportation cost. When a dummy is present and the intuitive method is being used, leave the dummy allocation until last. Thus, aside from the $0 costs in the dummy row, the lowest cost is $3 for cell 2–B. Assign as many units as possible to this cell. The column total is 90, and the row total is 75. Because 75 is the smaller of the two, assign 75 to cell 2–B. This exhausts the row total, so cross out the 75, and cross out the cell costs for the second row. Revise the column total to 15.

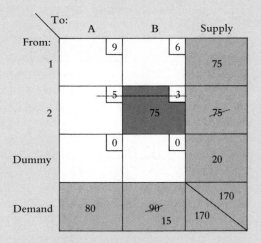

The next smallest cell cost is $6 in cell 1–B. We want to assign as many units as possible to this route (cell). The remaining demand for column B is 15, and the row total is 75. We assign the smaller of these, 15, to cell 1–B, thereby exhausting the column and reducing the row supply to 60. Next we draw a line through the cell costs of column B.

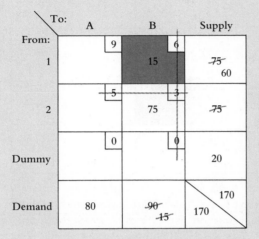

Still ignoring the dummy row, the next lowest cell cost is $9 in 1–A, where a supply of 60 and a demand of 80 exists. We assign the smaller of these, 60 units, to cell 1–A, so row 1 costs must be crossed out. Also, the revised column A total becomes 20.

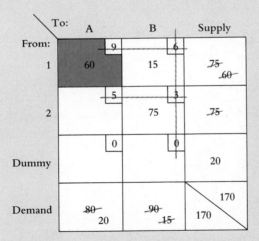

At this point, only the dummy row remains. Cell dummy–A has a supply and a demand of 20; assigning this amount to the cell exhausts both the supply and the demand, finishing the initial allocation.

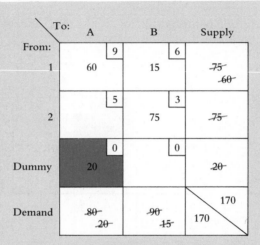

c. The next step is to evaluate this solution to determine if it is the
optimal solution. First we must check for degeneracy: $R + C -
1 = 3$ (rows) $+ 2$ (columns) $- 1 = 4$, the required number of
filled or completed cells. Because there are four completed cells,
the solution is not degenerate.

The evaluation can use either the stepping-stone method or
MODI. Suppose we use MODI. We always begin by placing a
zero at the left edge of row 1. This is the row 1 index number.
We can use it to find the column index number for any cell in
row 1 that is a completed cell. Because both cell 1–A and cell
1–B are completed, we can obtain both of their column index
numbers. For completed cells, the sum of the row and the
column index numbers must equal the cell cost. For cell 1–A,

To:	A 9	B 6	Supply
From: 0 / 1	[9] 60	[6] 15	75
−3 / 2	[5]	[3] 75	75
−9 / Dummy	[0] 20	[0]	20
Demand	80	90	170 / 170

0 + Column index = 9, so the column A index must be 9. Similarly, for cell 1–B, 0 + Column index = 6, so the column index must be 6. Next, these index numbers are used to find values of row index numbers for completed cells in their respective columns. Thus, for cell 2–B, 6 + Row index = 3, so the row index must be −3. For dummy–A, 9 + Row index = 0, so the row index must be −9.

Next, we use these index numbers to evaluate the empty cells. A cell evaluation is determined by subtracting from the cell cost the sum of its row and column index numbers. Thus, for cell 2–A, we have 5 − (−3 + 9) = −1, and for cell dummy–B, we have 0 − (−9 + 6) = 3.

The appearance of a negative cell evaluation tells us that this solution can be improved on. When negatives appear, we select the cell with the largest negative as the focal point of our effort to improve the solution. Because there is only one such cell, it is the one we select.

d. The −1 in cell 2–A tells us that for every unit we can move into this cell, we can reduce the total cost of the solution by $1. Obviously, we would like to put as many units as possible into this cell. Naturally, we are limited by the row and column totals (row 2 and column A), but we are also constrained by the need for all row and column totals to be maintained. In order to put units into cell 2–A, we must take them from some other cell, which will be in another row or column. Fortunately, this matter is simple to resolve: Determine the stepping-stone path for cell 2–A, and use it to guide the reallocation. That path is illustrated in the following table:

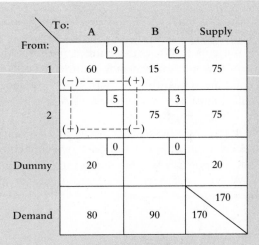

The amount that can be shifted into cell 2–A is the *smallest* quantity that appears in a *negative position* of the path. Note that there are two such quantities, 60 and 75. Because 60 is the smaller of these, it is shifted around the entire path (i.e., added where there is a + sign and subtracted where there is a − sign). The result is our revised solution:

e. This improved solution may be optimal, or it may need further revision. To find out, we must evaluate it.

First, we check for degeneracy: $R + C - 1 = 3 + 2 - 1 = 4$. Because there are four completed cells, the solution is not degenerate.

Next, we develop MODI index numbers using the completed cells. We always begin by assigning an index of 0 to the first row. Then, for any completed cell in the first row, the column index number is the same as the cell cost. Thus, because cell 1–B has a cell cost of 6, the column B index number is 6. Using this value and the cell cost for completed cell 2–B enables us to find the index number for row 2: Cell cost − Column index = Row index. Thus, $3 - 6 = -3$. This row 2 index number can be used with the cell cost of completed cell 2–A to find the column A index number, $5 - (-3) = 8$, and the index of 8 can be used with the cell cost of dummy–A to find the dummy index number: $0 - 8 = -8$. These index numbers are shown in the following table.

To: From:	A 8	B 6	Supply
0 1	9	6 75	75
−3 2	5 60	3 15	75
−8 Dummy	0 20	0	20
Demand	80	90	170 170

Evaluations for the empty cells can now be determined.

Cell 1–A: $9 - (0 + 8) = 1$
Cell dummy–B: $0 - (-8 + 6) = 2$

Because there are no negative evalutions, the current solution is optimal: Ship 75 units from 1 to B, 60 units from 2 to A, and 15 units from 2 to B. The 20 units in dummy–A means that destination A will be 20 units short of satisfying its demand of 80 units.

The total cost of the optimal solution is $795:

$$
\begin{array}{rcl}
75(6) &=& 450 \\
60(5) &=& 300 \\
15(3) &=& 45 \\
20(0) &=& \underline{0} \\
&& 795
\end{array}
$$

2. A firm that specializes in nonferrous casting must decide between locating a new foundry in Chicago or Detroit. Transportation costs from each proposed location to existing warehouses are shown in the following table, along with transportation costs for existing locations for a certain type of casting. Each will be able to supply 2,500 units per month. Explain how to determine which location should be chosen on a transportation cost basis.

From Detroit to:	Cost per unit	From Chicago to:	Cost per unit
A	$10	A	$12
B	8	B	13
C	15	C	5

To: From:	Warehouse A	Warehouse B	Warehouse C	Supply (hundreds of units/month)
Foundry 1	17	10	6	30
Foundry 2	7	12	14	20
Demand (hundreds of units/month)	25	10	40	

Solution

This decision requires solving two transportation problems, one using Detroit costs and the other using Chicago costs.

a. Set up the two transportation matrices.

	Warehouse A	Warehouse B	Warehouse C	Supply
1	17	10	6	30
2	7	12	14	20
Detroit	10	8	15	25
Demand	25	10	40	

| | Warehouse | | | |
	A	B	C	Supply
1	17	10	6	30
2	7	12	14	20
Chicago	12	13	5	25
Demand	25	10	40	

b. Solve each problem.

c. The problem that yields the lowest total cost will indicate the preferred location.

DISCUSSION AND REVIEW QUESTIONS

1. What information is needed to use the transportation model?

2. What check must you make before proceeding to develop an initial solution? What corrective action might need to be taken?

3. Would it ever make sense to have a situation that required both a dummy row and a dummy column? Explain briefly.

4. What is *linear* in a transportation problem?

5. Why do the + and − signs alternate in cell evaluation paths?

6. How do you know if a solution is optimal?

7. What does a zero value for an evaluation path indicate?

8. If a solution is not optimal:
   a. How do you decide which empty cell to shift units into?

   b. How do you know which cells to include in the shifting operation?

   c. How do you decide how many units to shift?

9. What is meant by the term *degeneracy?* How is it overcome?

10. How is the transportation model useful in location decisions? How does use of the transportation model in location decisions differ from its use as a tool to develop an optimal distribution plan for a given set of sources and destinations?

11. How are total costs determined for a given distribution plan?

12. What interpretation is given to quantities allocated to dummy destinations? Dummy sources?

13. What is the MODI method? How does it differ from the stepping-stone method?

PROBLEMS

1. Obtain the optimal distribution plan for the following transportation problem. Develop the initial solution using:

a. The northwest-corner method.

b. The intuitive approach.

Use the stepping-stone method for cell evaluations.

To: From:	A	B	C	Supply
1	3	4	2	40
2	5	1	7	60
3	8	7	4	50
Demand	30	45	75	150 / 150

2. A given shipping combination may be undesirable for a reason other than shipping cost. Use of that combination can be avoided by replacing that cell's unit cost with a larger cost. Assume cell 3–C in the previous problem represents such a case. Assign a unit cost of $100 to that cell, and find the minimum cost solution using the intuitive method for the initial allocation.

3. Given the following transportation problem, do each of the following:

a. Develop an initial feasible solution using each of the two methods described in this supplement.

b. Use the stepping-stone method to evaluate the northwest-corner solution.

c. Repeat part *b* using MODI.

d. Find the optimal solution.

To: From	A	B	C	D	Supply
1	18	12	14	16	40
2	23	24	27	33	80
3	42	34	31	26	130
Demand	90	80	30	50	

4. Using the intuitive method to generate an initial solution, determine the optimal distribution plan for the following problem, and compute the total cost for that plan. Use the MODI method for cell evaluation.

To: From:	A	B	C	D	Supply
1	14	24	18	28	48
2	17	18	25	16	56
3	30	16	22	30	32
Demand	41	34	35	20	

5. Refer to problem 3. Due to a temporary condition, origin 3 has experienced a capacity reduction of 20 units per period. Using the intuitive method to develop an initial solution, determine a temporary distribution plan that will minimize transportation costs.

6. Refer to problem 4. The market supplied by destination D is experiencing a period of rapid growth. Projected demand is for 60 units per period. A new factory with a capacity of 50 units is planned for one of two locations, Baltimore or Philadelphia. Transportation costs are as follows. Which location would result in the lower total cost? Use the MODI method for cell evaluation.

From Baltimore to:	Cost per unit	From Philadelphia to:	Cost per unit
A	$18	A	$31
B	16	B	25
C	22	C	19
D	27	D	20

7. Determine the optimal shipping plan for the following transportation matrix. Use the initiative method to develop the initial solution. What is the total cost for your plan?

To: From:	Dallas	Buffalo	Miami	Supply
Chicago	4	9	6	25
Milwaukee	12	10	7	55
Cleveland	11	5	8	40
Demand	35	40	45	

8. A toy manufacturer wants to open a third warehouse that will be used to supply three retail outlets. The new warehouse will have a capacity to supply 500 units of backyard playsets per week. Two locations are being studied, N1 and N2. Transportation costs for location N1 to stores A, B, and C would be $6, $8, and $7, respectively; for location N2, the costs would be $10, $6, and $4, respectively. The existing system is shown in the following table. Use the intuitive method to develop an initial solution. Which location would result in the lower transportation costs for the system?

To: From:	Store A	B	C	Capacity (units/week)
Warehouse 1	8	3	7	500
Warehouse 2	5	10	9	400
Demand (units/week)	400	600	350	

9. A large firm is contemplating construction of a new manufacturing facility. The two leading locations are Toledo and Cincinnati. The new factory would have a supply capacity of 160 units per week. Transportation costs from each potential location are shown in the following table. Also shown are transportation costs for existing locations. Using the intuitive method to develop an initial solution, determine which location would provide the lower transportation costs.

From Toledo to:	Cost per unit	From Cincinnati to:	Cost per unit
A	$18	A	$ 7
B	8	B	17
C	13	C	13

	A	B	C	Supply (Units/week)
1	10	14	10	210
2	12	17	20	140
3	11	11	12	150
Demand (Units/week)	220	220	220	

10. A large retailer is planning to open a new store. Three locations are currently under consideration: South Coast Plaza, Fashion Island, and Laguna Hills. Transportation costs for the locations are shown below. Also shown are costs, demands, and supplies for existing locations and warehouses (origins). Each of the locations has a demand potential of 300 units per week. Use the intuitive method to develop the initial solution. Which location would yield the lowest transportation costs for the system?

From warehouse:	To: SCP	FI	LH
1	$ 4	$7	$5
2	11	6	5
3	5	5	6

	A	B	Supply (Units/week)
1	15	9	660
2	10	7	340
3	14	18	200
Demand (Units/week)	400	500	

11. Set up problem 1 in a general linear programming format using an objective function and a set of constraints.
12. Set up problem 3 in a general linear programming format using an objective function and a set of constraints.
13. A soft drink manufacturer has recently begun negotiations with brokers in areas where it intends to distribute new products. Before finalizing agreements, however, the firm wants to determine shipping routes and costs. The firm has three plants with capacities as follows:

Plant	Capacity (cases per week)
Metro	40,000
Ridge	30,000
Colby	25,000

Estimated demands in each of the warehouse localities are:

Warehouse	Demand (cases per week)
SR1	24,000
SR2	22,000
SR3	23,000
SR4	16,000
SR5	10,000

The estimated shipping costs per case for the various routes are:

From:	To: RS1	RS2	RS3	RS4	RS5
Metro	.80	.75	.60	.70	.90
Ridge	.75	.80	.85	.70	.85
Colby	.70	.75	.70	.80	.80

Determine the optimal shipping plan that will minimize total shipping cost under these conditions:
a. Route Ridge-RS4 is unacceptable
b. All routes are acceptable.
c. What is the additional cost of the Ridge-RS4 route not being acceptable?

14. Solve this LP problem using the transportation method. Find the optimal transportation plan and the minimum cost. Also, decide if there is an alternate solution. If there is one, identify it.

minimize $8x_{11} + 2x_{12} + 5x_{13} + 2x_{21} + x_{22} + 3x_{23} + 7x_{31} + 2x_{32} + 6x_{33}$

subject to

$$x_{11} + x_{12} + x_{13} = 90$$
$$x_{21} + x_{22} + x_{23} = 105$$
$$x_{31} + x_{32} + x_{33} = 105$$
$$x_{11} + x_{21} + x_{31} = 150$$
$$x_{12} + x_{22} + x_{32} = 75$$
$$x_{13} + x_{23} + x_{33} = 75$$

All variables ≥ 0

SELECTED BIBLIOGRAPHY

Bierman, Harold; Charles P. Bonini; and Warren H. Hausman. *Quantitative Analysis for Business Decisions.* 7th ed. Homewood, Ill.: Richard D. Irwin, 1985.

Eppen, G. D.; F. J. Gould; and C. P. Schmidt. *Introductory Management Science,* 2nd ed. Englewood Cliffs, N.J.: Prentice-Hall, 1987.

Levin, Richard I.; Charles A. Kirkpatrick; and David Rubin. *Quantitative Approaches to Management.* 5th ed. New York: McGraw-Hill, 1982.

Stevenson, William J. *Introduction to Management Science.* Homewood, Ill.: Richard D. Irwin, 1989.

6

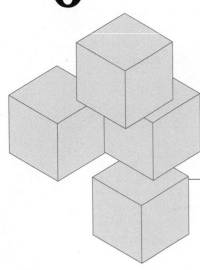

Process Selection and Capacity Planning

After completing this chapter, you should be able to:

1. Explain the importance of process selection and how process selection relates to product and service design and capacity planning.
2. Describe the different types of processing.
3. Describe automated approaches to processing.
4. Indicate the need for management of technology.
5. Explain the importance of capacity planning.
6. Discuss ways of defining and measuring capacity.
7. Describe some of the factors that determine effective capacity.
8. Discuss the major considerations related to developing capacity alternatives.
9. Briefly describe approaches that are useful for evaluating process selection and capacity alternatives.

CHAPTER OUTLINE

Product and service choices, process selection, capacity planning, location, and layout are among the most basic decisions managers must make, for those decisions have long-term consequences for the organization.

In this chapter, process selection and capacity planning are examined. Process selection is both exciting and challenging; technological advances in processing provide many new options for competitive advantage, but they also pose numerous risks for the unwary decision maker. The first half of the chapter is devoted to process planning. The remainder of the chapter explores issues related to capacity planning.

PROCESS SELECTION

Process selection refers to the way an organization chooses to produce or provide its goods or services. Essentially it involves choice of technology and related issues, and it has major implications for capacity planning, layout of facilities, equipment, and design of work systems. Figure 6–1 provides an overview of where process selection fits into system design.

Process selection occurs naturally when new products or services are being planned. However, it also occurs periodically due to technological changes in equipment as well as changes of products or services.

Make or Buy

The very first step in process planning is the issue of whether to make or buy some or all of the product or to subcontract some or all of a service. A manufacturer might decide to purchase certain parts rather than make them; in many instances, the majority of parts are purchased, with the manufacturer simply doing assembly operations. Many firms contract out janitorial service, and some contract for repair services. If a decision is made to buy or contract, this lessens or removes the need for process selection.

FIGURE 6–1

Process selection and system design.

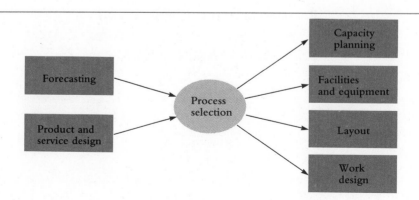

In make or buy decisions, a number of factors are commonly considered, such as:

1. *Available capacity*. If an organization has available capacity, it often makes sense for the organization to produce an item or perform a service itself. The additional costs involved would be relatively small compared to those required to buy items or subcontract services.
2. *Expertise*. If a firm lacks the expertise to do a satisfactory job, buying might be a more reasonable alternative.
3. *Quality considerations*. Firms that specialize can usually offer higher quality than an organization can obtain itself. Conversely, special quality requirements or the ability to closely monitor quality may cause a firm to perform the work itself.
4. *The nature of demand*. When demand for an item is high and steady, the organization is usually better off doing the work itself. However, wide fluctuations in demand or small orders are usually better handled by others who are able to combine orders from multiple sources, which results in higher volume and tends to offset individual buyer fluctuations.
5. *Cost*. Any cost savings achieved from buying or making must be weighed against the preceding factors. Cost savings might come from the item itself or from transportation cost savings realized by making the item rather than buying it.

In some cases, a firm might choose to perform part of the work itself and let others handle the rest in order to maintain flexibility and to hedge against loss of a subcontractor. Moreover, this gives the organization a bargaining tool in negotiations with contractors and a head start if it decides later to take over the operation entirely.

If the decision is made to have the organization provide some or all of the processing, then the issue involves the type of processing to employ.

Types of Processing

There are basically three types of processing systems: continuous systems, intermittent systems, and projects. Continuous systems are highly specialized systems designed to provide high volumes of output of one or a few standardized items. Intermittent systems are more generalized, making them more suited to handle lower volumes of items that present a variety of processing requirements. Projects have limited life spans and are best suited to complex, special-purpose jobs. Each of these systems is briefly described in the following sections.

Continuous Processing. **Continuous processing** systems are sometimes referred to as *flow systems* because of the rapid rate at which items move through the system. This form of processing is used when highly standardized products are involved. Typical examples of goods produced by these systems are typewriters, automobiles, calculators, televisions, and tape players. All of these items involve discrete, or countable, goods. In some instances, though, the output is not discrete, but continuous. For example, petroleum refining, water treatment, and much food manufacturing are measured rather than counted. And, in some cases, goods begin in continuous form but end up as discrete units. Spaghetti is one example of this; plastic pipe is another. The highly repetitive nature of operations lends itself to specialization of both labor and equipment. Because of the division of labor, there are usually low-skill labor requirements. Specialized equipment, on the other hand, although expensive, can usually be justified by the high volumes characteristic of such systems, which makes the cost per unit relatively low. As a general rule, such products are made for inventory rather than for customer order. Examples in the service area include programs for mass inoculations, automatic car washes, mechanical harvesters, mail service, and fast-food operations. Applications in services are less plentiful because services tend to be more customized on a per unit basis.

Intermittent Processing.   **Intermittent processing** is used when systems handle a variety of processing requirements. Processing is done in batches, and volume is much lower than in flow systems. In addition to relatively low volumes of output, these systems are characterized by general-purpose equipment that can satisfy a variety of processing requirements, semiskilled or skilled workers who operate the equipment, and a narrower span of supervision than for most continuous systems. Differences in job processing requirements present routing and scheduling challenges, as well as a frequent need to adjust equipment settings or make other alterations for successive jobs. In manufacturing systems, items are often processed in *batches* or *lots;* in nonmanufacturing applications, processing occurs both by lots and on an individual basis. Processing cost per unit is generally higher than it would be under continuous processing. Typical examples of intermittent processing are textbook publication, bakeries, health care systems, and educational systems. In some cases, the outputs are made for inventory (clothing, automobile tires), and in others, they are designed to meet customer needs (health care) or specifications (special tools, parts, or equipment). Marketing efforts in such systems are often directed toward promoting system capabilities or customized services.

Projects.   **Projects** are set up to handle complex jobs that involve unique sets of activities. Projects include large or unusual construction projects, new product development or promotion, planning and coordinating space missions, and organizing and handling the logistics of disaster relief efforts. Because of their limited life spans and the nonrepetitive nature of activities, these systems differ considerably from continuous and intermittent processing systems. Projects are discussed at length in Chapter 14.

Automation

Automation is the substitution of machinery for human labor. The machinery includes sensing and control devices that enable it to operate automatically. A key question in process planning is whether to automate or not. And if the decision is made to automate, the question becomes how much to automate. Automation can range from factories that are completely automated to a single automated operation.

Automation offers a number of advantages over human labor. One is that human labor is inherently variable: it is difficult for a human to perform a task in exactly the same way, and in the same amount of time, on a repetitive basis. Variability is detrimental to quality and to meeting schedules. Moreover, machines do not get bored or distracted, nor do they go out on strike, ask for higher wages, or file labor grievances.

Automation is frequently touted as a necessary strategy for being competitive. However, automation also has certain disadvantages and limitations compared to human labor. To begin with, automation can be costly; technology can be expensive. Automation is much less flexible than humans; once a process has been automated, there is substantial reason for not changing it. Moreover, automation often becomes an emotional issue with workers because of the fear of job loss.

The implication of this for process selection is that automation has potential advantages as well as disadvantages, so the issue of whether to automate or the degree to which automation should be used must be carefully examined so that all the ramifications are clearly understood by decision makers.

Computer-Aided Manufacturing (CAM)

Computer-aided manufacturing (CAM) refers to the use of computers in process control, ranging from numerically controlled machines to robots to automated assembly systems. These systems replace human functions with machine functions. They have the advantage of reducing labor; handling dangerous, dirty, or boring tasks; and yielding high, consistent quality. As you might suppose, such equipment can be very expensive.

Numerically controlled (N/C) machines are programmed to follow a set of processing instructions based on mathematical relationships that tell the machine the details of the operations to be performed. The instructions are stored on a device such as a floppy disk, magnetic tape, or a microprocessor. Although N/C machines have been used for many years, they are an important part of new approaches to manufacturing. Individual machines may have their own computer; this is referred to as *computerized numerical control (CNC)*.

FIGURE 6–2

Examples of robot "hands"

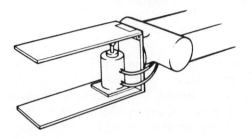

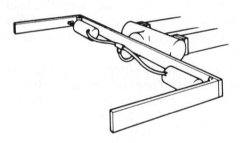

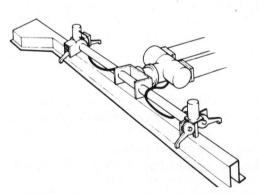

Special hand with one movable jaw

A hand with single-acting jaw should be considered when there is any access underneath a part, as when it is on a rack. Where this hand can be applied, it will scoop up a part quite quickly. Simplicity of the design makes this one of the most economical hands.

Special hand for cartons

The dual-jaw hand will open wide to grasp inexactly located objects of light weight. Lifting and placement of carboard cartons is an application. Actuators and jaws can be remounted in any of several positions on the fixed back plate, making it practical for the same dual-jaw hand to move large cartons on one day and smaller cartons the next.

Special hand with modular gripper

This special hand, with pair of pneumatic actuators, is one of the many special hand designs for industrial robots. It would be suitable for parts of light weight. Lifting capacity is dependent upon friction developed by the fingers, but heavier parts could be handled if the fingers could secure a more positive purchase—as under a flange or lip.

Or one computer may control a number of N/C machines, which is referred to as *direct numerical control (DNC)*.

The use of **robots** in manufacturing is increasing. A robot consists of three parts: a mechanical arm, a power supply, and a controller. Unlike film versions of robots, which vaguely resemble human beings, industrial robots are much less glamorous in appearance and much less mobile: most robots are stationary except for their movable "arms."

Robots are used to handle a wide variety of tasks, including welding, assembly, loading and unloading machines, painting, and testing. They relieve humans from heavy or dirty work; robots are typically used to eliminate drudgery tasks.

Some uses of robots are fairly simple, whereas others are much more complex. At the lowest level are robots that follow a fixed set of instructions. Next are programmable robots, which can repeat a set of movements after being led through the sequence. In effect, these robots "play back" a mechanical sequence much as a video recorder plays back a visual sequence. At the next level up are robots that follow instructions from a computer. At the top end are robots that can recognize objects and make certain decisions.

Robots move in one of two ways. Point-to-point robots move to predetermined points and perform a specified operation; they then move on to the next point and perform another operation; and so on. Continuous-path robots follow a continuous (moving) path while performing an operation.

Robots can be powered in one of three ways: pneumatically (air-driven), hydraulically (fluids under pressure), or electronically.

Figures 6–2 through 6–5 illustrate robots. Table 6–1 describes in more detail some of the various kinds of robots currently being used.

FIGURE 6–3

Work comes to robot

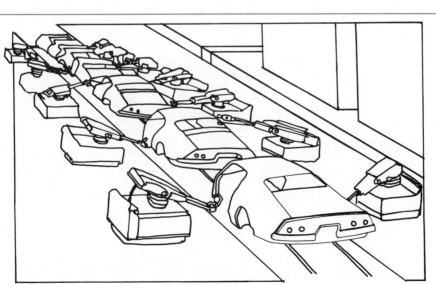

FIGURE 6–4

*Robots on an assembly
line*

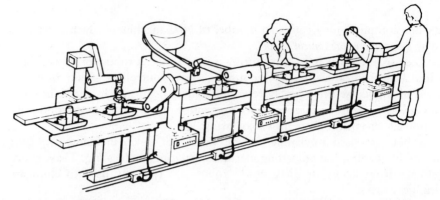

FIGURE 6–5

***Typical articulations of
a playback robot with
point-to-point control***

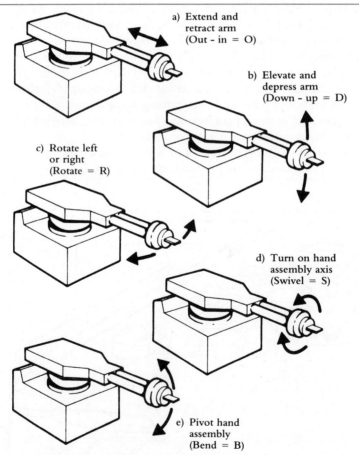

a) Extend and
retract arm
(Out - in = O)

b) Elevate and
depress arm
(Down - up = D)

c) Rotate left
or right
(Rotate = R)

d) Turn on hand
assembly axis
(Swivel = S)

e) Pivot hand
assembly
(Bend = B)

TABLE 6—1

Industrial robots

Industrial robots all have armlike projections and grippers that perform factory work customarily done by humans. The term is usually reserved for machines with some form of built-in control system and capable of stand-alone operation. But in Japan, it also includes manipulators operated by humans, either directly or remotely.

A *pick-and-place robot* is the simplest version, accounting for about one third of all U.S. installations. The name comes from its usual application in materials handling: picking something from one spot and placing it at another. Freedom of movement is usually limited to two or three directions—in and out, left and right, and up and down. The control system is electromechanical. Prices range from $5,000 to $30,000.

A *servo robot* is the most common industrial robot because it can include all robots described below. The name stems from one or more servomechanisms that enable the arm and gripper to alter direction in midair, without having to trip a mechanical switch. Five to seven directional movements are common, depending on the number of "joints," or articulations, in the robot's arm.

A *programmable robot* is a servo robot directed by a programmable controller that memorizes a sequence of arm-and-gripper movements; this routine can be repeated perpetually. The robot is reprogrammable by leading its gripper through the new task. The price range is $25,000 to $90,000.

A *computerized robot* is a servo model run by a computer. The computer controller does not have to be taught by leading the arm and gripper through a routine; new instructions can be transmitted electronically. The programming for such "smart" robots may include the ability to optimize work routine instructions. Prices start at about $35,000.

A *sensory robot* is a computerized robot with one or more artificial senses, usually sight or touch. Prices for early models start at about $75,000.

An *assembly robot* is a computerized robot, probably a sensory model, designed specifically for assembly line jobs. For light, batch-manufacturing applications, the arm's design may be fairly anthropomorphic.

A **flexible manufacturing system (FMS)** is a group of machines including supervisory computer control, automatic material handling, and possibly robots or other automated processing equipment. Reprogrammable controllers enable these systems to produce a variety of *similar* products. Systems may range from three to four machines to more than a dozen. They are designed to handle intermittent processing requirements with some of the benefits of automation and with some of the flexibility of individual, or stand-alone, machines (e.g., N/C machines). Flexible manufacturing systems offer reduced labor costs compared with more traditional manufacturing methods, lower capital investment and higher flexibility than "hard" automation, relatively quick changeover time, and more consistent quality than traditional manufacturing methods.

Although these are important benefits, there are also certain limitations to FMS. One is that these systems can handle a relatively narrow range of part variety, so they must be used for a family of similar parts that all require similar machining. Also, FMS involves longer planning and development times than more conventional processing equipment because of the increased complexity and cost. Furthermore, companies sometimes prefer a gradual approach to automation, and FMS represents a sizable chunk of technology.

Computer-integrated manufacturing (CIM) is a system for linking a broad range of manufacturing activities through an integrating computer system, including engineering design, flexible manufacturing systems, and production planning and control, although not all elements are absolutely necessary. For instance, CIM might be as simple as linking two or more FMSs by a host computer. More encompassing systems can link scheduling, purchasing, inventory control, shop control, and distribution. In effect a CIM system integrates information from other areas of an organization with manufacturing.

The overall goal of using CIM is to link various areas of an organization to achieve rapid response to customer orders and/or product changes, to allow rapid production, and to reduce *indirect* labor costs.

OPERATIONS STRATEGY

Process selection often requires engineering expertise. Many U.S. managers in this position have little technical knowledge; their education and experience lie in the fields of marketing, finance, and the like. In contrast, many Japanese managers faced with the same decisions do have engineering backgrounds. Consequently, there seems to be a tendency in Western firms to delegate technical decisions to engineers. Engineering white elephants are not uncommon, and neither are systems based on narrow viewpoints of problems and solutions. In the long run, greater emphasis should be placed on hiring and promoting managers who have both managerial and technical skills and expertise. In the short run, managers must work with technical experts, asking questions and increasing their understanding of the benefits and limitations of sophisticated processing equipment and technology, and ultimately making decisions themselves. Thus, there is a real need for *management of technology*.

Throughout this book, the importance of *flexibility* as a competitive strategy is stressed. However, flexibility does not always offer the best choice in processing decisions. Flexible systems or equipment are often more expensive and less efficient than less flexible alternatives. And, in certain instances, flexibility is not needed because products are in mature stages, requiring few design changes, and there is a high volume of output. Ordinarily, this type of situation calls for specialized processing equipment, with no need for flexibility. The implication is clear: Flexibility should be adopted with great care; applications should be matched with situations in which a *need* for flexibility clearly exists.

CAPACITY PLANNING

In this section, we examine the importance of capacity decisions, the measurement of capacity, how capacity requirements are determined, and the development and evaluation of capacity alternatives.

The term **capacity** refers to an upper limit or ceiling on the load that an operating unit can handle. The operating unit might be a plant, a department, a machine, a store, or a worker. The load can be specified in terms of either inputs or outputs. For instance, a machine may be able to process 45 pounds of raw material per hour. Hence, its input capacity is 45 pounds per hour. Another machine might produce 18 castings per hour; its capacity in terms of the castings output is 18 pieces per hour. Whether to use input or output capacity is sometimes a matter of choice, and sometimes it is dictated by the situation, as we shall see.

The capacity of an operating unit is an important piece of information for planning purposes: It enables managers to quantify production capability, in terms of either inputs or outputs, and thereby make other decisions or plans related to those quantities. The basic questions in capacity planning of any sort are the following:

1. What kind of capacity is needed?
2. How much is needed?
3. When is it needed?

The question of what kind of capacity is needed relates to the products and services that management intends to produce or provide. Hence, in a very real sense, capacity planning is governed by those choices.

The most fundamental decisions in any organization relate to the products and/or services it will offer. Virtually all other decisions relative to capacity, facilities, location, and the like are governed by product and service choices. Thus, a decision to produce high-quality steel will necessitate certain types of processing equipment and certain kinds of labor skills, and it will suggest certain types of arrangement of facilities. It will influence the size and type of building as well as the plant location. Notice how different each of these factors would be if the choice were to operate a family restaurant, and how still different each of these factors would be in another situation, in which the choice is to operate a hospital.

In some instances, capacity choices are made very infrequently, and in others, they are made much more regularly, as part of an ongoing process. Generally speaking, the factors that influence this frequency are the stability of demand, the rate of technological change in both equipment and product design, and competitive factors. Other factors relate to the type of product or service and whether style changes are important, as for automobiles and clothing. In any case, it is important for management to periodically review product and service choices in order to insure that changes will be made when they are needed for cost, competitive effectiveness, or other reasons.

Importance of Capacity Decisions

Capacity decisions are among the most fundamental of all the design decisions managers are called on to make. One reason for the importance of capacity decisions relates to their potential impact on the ability of the organization to meet future demands for products and services; capacity essentially limits the rate of output possible. A second reason for the importance of capacity stems from the relationship between capacity and operating costs. Ideally, capacity and demand requirements will be matched, which will tend to minimize operating costs. In practice, this is not always achieved, either because actual demand differs from expected demand or because demand tends to vary (e.g., cyclically). In such cases, a decision might be made to attempt to balance the costs of over- and undercapacity. A third reason for the importance of capacity decisions is the initial cost involved, of which capacity is usually a major determinant. Typically, the greater the capacity of a productive unit, the greater its cost. This does not necessarily imply a one-for-one relationship; larger units tend to cost *proportionately* less than smaller units. A fourth reason for the importance of capacity decisions stems from the long-term commitment of resources that is often required and the fact that, once they are implemented, it may be difficult or impossible to modify those decisions without incurring major costs.

Defining and Measuring Capacity

Capacity often refers to an upper limit on the *rate* of output. Even though this seems simple enough, there are subtle difficulties in actually measuring capacity in certain cases. These difficulties arise because of different interpretations of the term *capacity* and problems with identifying suitable measures for a specific situation.

In selecting a measure of capacity, it is important to choose one that does not require revision. For example, dollar amounts are often a poor measure of capacity (e.g., capacity of $30 million a year) because price changes necessitate continual updating of that measure.

In situations where only one product or service is involved, the capacity of the productive unit may be expressed in terms of that item. However, when multiple products or services are involved, as is often the case, using a single measure of capacity based on units of output can be misleading. For example, an appliance manufacturer may produce both refrigerators and freezers. If the output rates for these two products are different, it would not make sense to simply state capacity in units without reference to either refrigerators or freezers. The problem is compounded if the firm in question has other products. One possible solution is to state capacities in terms of each product. Thus, the firm may be able to produce 100 refrigerators per day *or* 80 freezers per day. In some cases, this approach is helpful, but in others it is not. For instance, in a situation where an organization has many different products or services, it may not be practical to list all of the relevant capacities. This is especially true if there are frequent changes in the mix of output, because this would necessitate a continually changing composite index of capacity. The preferred alternative in such cases is to use a measure of capacity that refers to *availability of resources.* Thus, a hospital has a certain number of beds, a factory has a certain number of machine hours available, and a bus has a certain number of seats and a certain amount of standing room.

No single measure of capacity will be appropriate in every situation. Rather, the measure of capacity must be somewhat tailored to the situation at hand. Table 6–2 provides some examples of commonly used measures of capacity.

Up to this point, we have been using a working definition of capacity. Although it is functional, it could stand some refinement. There are, in fact, three different definitions of capacity that are useful:

1. *Design capacity:* the maximum output that can possibly be attained.
2. *Effective capacity:* the maximum possible output given a product mix, scheduling difficulties, machine maintenance, quality factors, and so on.
3. *Actual output:* the rate of output actually achieved. It cannot exceed effective capacity and is often less than effective capacity due to breakdowns, defective output, shortages of materials, and similar factors.

Design capacity is the maximum rate of output achieved under ideal conditions. Effective capacity is usually less than design capacity (it cannot exceed design capacity) owing to realities of changing product mix, the need for periodic maintenance of equipment, lunch breaks, coffee breaks, problems in scheduling and balancing operations, and similar circumstances. Actual output

	Measure of capacity		**TABLE 6–2**
Type of business	**Resources available**	**Output**	*Examples of commonly used measures of capacity*
Automobile manufacturing	Labor hours, machine hours	Number of cars or trucks per shift	
Steel mill	Size of furnace	Tons of steel per week	
Oil refinery	Size of refinery	Gallons of fuel oil per day	
Farm	Number of acres, cows	Tons of grain per year, gallons of milk per week	
Restaurant	Number of tables	Number of meals served per day	
Theater	Number of seats	Number of performances per week	
Retail sales	Size of display area, number of cashiers	Units sold per day	

cannot exceed effective capacity and is often less than effective capacity because of machine breakdowns, absenteeism, and other problems outside the control of the operations managers.

These different measures of capacity are useful in defining two measures of system effectiveness: efficiency and utilization. *Efficiency* is the ratio of actual output to effective capacity. *Utilization* is the ratio of actual output to design capacity.

$$\text{Efficiency} = \frac{\text{Actual output}}{\text{Effective capacity}} \qquad (6-1)$$

$$\text{Utilization} = \frac{\text{Actual output}}{\text{Design capacity}} \qquad (6-2)$$

It is quite common for managers to focus exclusively on efficiency, but in many instances, such emphasis can be misleading. This happens when effective capacity is low compared to design capacity. In those cases, high efficiency would seem to indicate effective use of resources when that is not the case. The following example illustrates this point.

EXAMPLE 1

Given the information below, compute the efficiency and the utilization of the vehicle repair department:

Design capacity = 80 trucks per day
Effective capacity = 40 trucks per day
Actual output = 36 units per day

Solution

$$\text{Efficiency} = \frac{\text{Actual output}}{\text{Effective capacity}} = \frac{36 \text{ units per day}}{40 \text{ units per day}} = 90\%$$

$$\text{Utilization} = \frac{\text{Actual output}}{\text{Design capacity}} = \frac{36 \text{ units per day}}{80 \text{ units per day}} = 45\%$$

Thus, compared to the effective capacity of 40 units per day, 36 units per day looks pretty good. However, compared to the design capacity of 80 units per day, 36 units per day is much less impressive although probably more meaningful.

Because effective capacity acts as a lid on actual output, the real key to improving capacity utilization is to increase effective capacity. Consider the following example. George H. wants to travel from his home in Washington, D.C., to his sister's home in Baltimore, which is 60 miles away. He could borrow his son's bike or borrow his son's car. Instead of using the bike and concerning himself with pedaling as *efficiently* as possible, he could make the trip in less time (same output in a shorter time) by using the car.

Hence, increasing utilization depends on being able to increase effective capacity, and this requires a knowledge of what is constraining effective capacity. The following section explores some of the main determinants of effective capacity.

Determinants of Effective Capacity

Many decisions made with respect to system design have an impact on capacity. The same is true for many operating decisions. Some of these factors are briefly described in this section and then elaborated on at other points in the book. The main factors relate to the following:

1. Facilities.
2. Products or services.
3. Processes.
4. Human considerations.
5. Operations.
6. External forces.

Facilities factors. The design of facilities, including size and provision for expansion, is very important. Locational factors, such as transportation costs, distance to market, labor supply, energy sources, and room for expansion, are also important. Likewise, layout of the work area often determines how smoothly work can be performed, and environmental factors such as heating, lighting, and ventilation also play an important role in determining whether personnel can perform effectively or whether they must struggle to overcome poor design characteristics.

Product/service factors. Product or service design can have a tremendous influence on capacity. For example, when items are highly similar, the ability of the system to produce those items is generally much greater than when successive items tend to differ. For example, a restaurant that offers a limited menu can usually prepare and serve meals at a faster rate than a restaurant with a very extensive menu. Generally speaking, the more uniform the output, the more opportunities there are for standardization of methods and materials, which leads to greater capacity. The particular mix of products or services rendered must also be considered since different items will have different rates of output.

Process factors. The quantity capability of a process is an obvious determinant of capacity. A more subtle determinant is the influence of output *quality*. For instance, if quality of output does not meet standards, the rate of output will be slowed by the need for inspection and rework activities.

Human factors.   The tasks that make up a job, the variety of activities involved, and the training, skill, and experience required to perform a job all have an impact on the potential and actual output. In addition, employee motivation has a very basic relationship to capacity, as do absenteeism and labor turnover.

Operation factors.   If there are any differences in equipment capabilities for alternative pieces of equipment and/or for differences in job requirements, there can be scheduling problems. Inventory stocking decisions, late deliveries, and acceptability of purchased materials and parts can all influence effective capacity. Quality inspection and control procedures also have an impact on effective capacity.

An example of inventory problems having a negative impact on capacity occurred when General Motors first introduced its front-wheel-drive cars.

TABLE 6–3

Factors that determine effective capacity

A. Facilities
    1. Design
    2. Location
    3. Layout
    4. Environment
B. Product/service
    1. Design
    2. Product or service mix
C. Process
    1. Quantity capabilities
    2. Quality capabilities
D. Human factors
    1. Job content
    2. Job design
    3. Training and experience
    4. Motivation
    5. Compensation
    6. Learning rates
    7. Absenteeism and labor turnover
E. Operational
    1. Scheduling
    2. Materials management
    3. Quality assurance
    4. Maintenance policies
    5. Equipment breakdowns
F. External factors
    1. Product standards
    2. Safety regulations
    3. Unions
    4. Pollution control standards

Unexpected high demand created by shortages and rapid price increases of gasoline exceeded the supply of cars. Company officials lamented the fact that they could not take advantage of the opportunity to increase sales because of a shortage of component parts, which the company could not quickly overcome. Thus, insufficient capacity in one area affected overall capacity.

External factors. Product standards, especially minimum quality and performance standards, can restrict management's options in increasing and using capacity. Thus, pollution standards on either products or equipment often reduce effective capacity. So, too, does paperwork required by government regulatory agencies by engaging employees in nonproductive activities. A similar effect occurs when a union contract limits the number of hours and type of work an employee may do.

A summary of these factors is presented in Table 6–3.

Determining Capacity Requirements

Capacity planning decisions involve both long-term and short-term considerations. Long-term considerations relate to overall *level* of capacity, such as facility size; short-term considerations relate to probable *variations* in capacity requirements created by such things as seasonal, random, and irregular fluctuations in demand. Because the time intervals covered by each of these categories can vary significantly from industry to industry, it would be misleading to attempt a precise definition for these terms. Nevertheless, the distinction will serve as a framework within which to discuss capacity planning.

Long-term capacity needs are determined by forecasting demand over a time horizon and then converting those forecasts into capacity requirements. Some of the basic demand patterns that might be identified by a forecast are illustrated in Figure 6–6. In addition to these basic patterns are more complex patterns, such as a combination of cycles and trends.

When trends are identified, the fundamental issues are (1) how long the trend might persist, since few things last forever, and (2) the slope of the trend. If cycles are identified, interest focuses on (1) the approximate length of the cycles, since cycles are rarely uniform in duration, and (2) the amplitude of the cycles (i.e., deviation from average).

Short-term capacity needs are less concerned with cycles or trends than with seasonal variations and other variations from average. These deviations are particularly important because they can place a severe strain on a system's ability to satisfy demand at some times and yet result in idle capacity at other times.

Seasonal patterns can be identified using standard forecasting techniques. Although commonly thought of as annual fluctuations, seasonal variations are often reflected in monthly, weekly, and even daily capacity requirements. Table 6–4 provides some examples of items that tend to exhibit seasonal demand patterns.

FIGURE 6–6

Some possible demand patterns

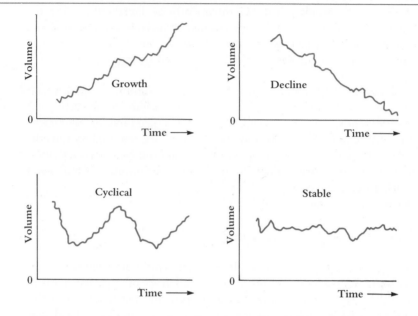

When time intervals that are too short to have seasonal variations are analyzed, variations in demand may often be described by probability distributions such as the normal, uniform, or Poisson distribution. For example, the amount of coffee served during the midday meal at a luncheonette may be described by a normal distribution with a certain mean and standard deviation. The number of customers that enter a branch of a bank on Monday mornings may be described by a Poisson distribution with a certain mean. It does not follow, however, that *every* instance of random variability will lend itself to description by a standard statistical distribution. Service systems in particular may experience a considerable amount of variability in capacity requirements unless requests for service can be scheduled. Production systems, because of their typical isolation from customers and the more uniform nature of produc-

TABLE 6–4

Examples of seasonal demand patterns

Period	Items
Year	Beer sales, toy sales, airline traffic, clothing, vacations, tourism, power usage, gasoline consumption, sports and recreation, education
Month	Welfare and social security checks, bank transactions
Week	Retail sales, restaurant meals, automobile traffic, automotive rentals, hotel registrations
Day	Telephone calls, power usage, automobile traffic, public transportation, classroom utilization, retail sales, restaurant meals

tion, are less likely to experience them. Queuing models are sometimes useful in analyzing service systems.

Perhaps the most troublesome variations are the irregular ones because they are virtually impossible to predict. They are created by such diverse forces as freak storms that disrupt normal routines, foreign political turmoil that causes oil shortages, major equipment breakdowns, discovery of health hazards (nuclear accidents, unsafe chemical dumping grounds, carcinogens in food and drink), and so on.

Developing Capacity Alternatives

Aside from the general considerations outlined in Chapter 2 regarding the development of alternatives (i.e., conduct a reasonable search for possible alternatives, consider doing nothing, take care not to overlook nonquantitative factors), there are some specific considerations revelant to developing capacity alternatives. Among the considerations to be discussed in this section, are the following:

1. Design flexibility into systems.
2. Take a "big picture" approach to capacity changes.
3. Prepare to deal with capacity "chunks."
4. Attempt to smooth out capacity requirements.
5. Identify the optimal operating level.

The long-term nature of many capacity decisions and the risks inherent in long-term forecasts suggest potential benefits from designing flexible systems. For example, in many instances, provision for future expansion in the original design of a structure can be obtained at a small price compared to what it would cost to remodel an existing structure that did not have such a provision. Hence, if future expansion of a restaurant seems likely, water lines, power hookups, and waste disposal lines can be put in place initially so that if expansion becomes a reality, modification to the existing structure can be minimized. Similarly, a new golf course may start as a 9-hole operation, but unless provision is made for future expansion by obtaining options on adjacent land, it may never progress to a larger (18-hole) course. Other considerations in flexible design involve layout of equipment, location, equipment selection, production planning, scheduling, and inventory policies. These are discussed in later chapters.

In developing capacity alternatives, it is important to consider how parts of the system interrelate. For example, a decision to increase the number of rooms that a motel has should also take into account probable increased demands for parking, entertainment and food, and housekeeping. This is a "big picture" approach.

Capacity increases are often acquired in fairly large chunks rather than smooth increments, making it difficult to achieve a match between desired capacity and feasible capacity. For instance, the desired capacity of a certain operation may be 55 units per hour, but suppose that machines used for this operation are able to produce 40 units per hour each. One machine by itself would cause capacity to be 15 units per hour short of what is needed, but two machines would result in an excess capacity of 25 units per hour. The illustration becomes even more extreme if the topic shifts, say, to open-hearth furnaces or to the number of airplanes needed to provide a desired level of capacity.

Unevenness in capacity requirements can create certain problems. For instance, during periods of inclement weather, public transportation ridership tends to increase substantially relative to periods of pleasant weather. Consequently, the system tends to alternate between underutilization and overutilization. Increasing the number of buses or subway cars will reduce the burden during periods of heavy demand, but this will aggravate the problem of overcapacity at other times and most certainly add to the cost of operating the system. Unfortunately, there do not seem to be any simple solutions to such problems.

The unevenness in demand for products and services can be traced to a variety of sources. The bus ridership problem is weather-related to a certain extent, but demand could be considered to be partly random (i.e., varying because of chance factors). Still another source of varying demand is seasonality. However, seasonal variations are generally easier to cope with than random variations because they are *predictable*. Consequently, allowances can be made in planning and scheduling activities and inventories. However, seasonal variations can still pose problems because of their uneven demands on the system: at certain times the system will tend to be overloaded, and at certain other times it will tend to be underloaded. One possible approach to this problem is to try to identify products or services that have complementing demand patterns (i.e., patterns that tend to offset each other). For instance, demand for snow skis and demand for water skis might complement each other: demand for water skis is greater in the spring and summer months, and demand for snow skis is greater in the fall and winter months. The same might apply to heating and air conditioning equipment. The ideal case is one in which products or services with complementing demand patterns involve the use of the same resources but at different times, so that overall capacity requirements remain fairly stable. Figure 6–7 illustrates complementing demand patterns.

Possible strategies for handling variations in a narrower time frame include subcontracting, working overtime, and using inventories to absorb demand fluctuations. These and other strategies are discussed in more detail in later chapters.

Production units typically have an ideal or optimal level of operation in terms of unit cost of output. At the ideal level, cost per unit is the lowest for that production unit; larger or smaller rates of output will result in a higher unit cost. This concept is illustrated in Figure 6–8. Notice how unit costs rise as the rate of output varies from the optimal level.

FIGURE 6–7

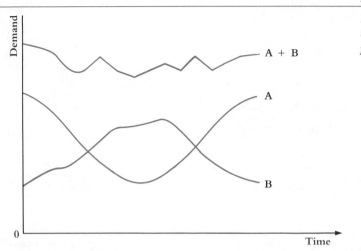

The explanation for the shape of the cost curve follows: At low levels of output, the costs of facilities and equipment must be absorbed (paid for) by very few units. Hence, the cost per unit is high. As output is increased, there are more units to absorb the "fixed" cost of facilities and equipment, so unit costs decrease. However, beyond a certain point, unit costs will start to rise. To be sure, the fixed costs are being spread over even more units, so that does not account for the increase. Other factors then become important, such as worker fatigue; equipment breakdowns; the loss of flexibility, which leaves

FIGURE 6–8

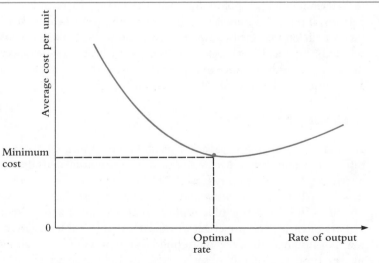

Production units have an optimal rate of output for minimum cost

FIGURE 6-9

Minimum cost and optimal operating rate are functions of size of a production unit

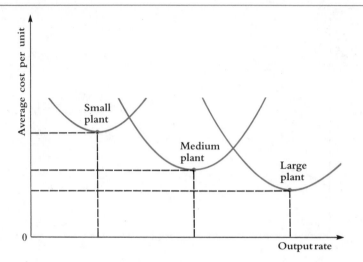

less of a margin for error; and, generally, more difficulty in coordinating operations.

The optimal operating rate and the amount of the minimum cost both tend to be a function of the general capacity of the operating unit. As the general capacity, say, of a plant increases, the optimal output rate increases, and the minimum cost for the optimal rate decreases. Thus, larger plants tend to have higher optimal output rates and smaller minimum costs than smaller plants. These points are illustrated in Figure 6-9.

In choosing the capacity of an operating unit, management must take these relationships into account along with the availability of financial and other resources and forecasts of expected demand. In order to do this, it is necessary to determine enough points for each size facility to be able to make a comparison among different sizes. In some instances, facility sizes are givens, whereas in others, facility size is a continuous variable (i.e., any size can be selected). In the latter case, an ideal facility size can be selected. In most instances, though, a choice must be made from given sizes, and none may have a minimum at the desired rate of output.

Evaluating Alternatives

Alternatives for future capacity need to be examined from a number of different perspectives. Most obvious are economic considerations: Will an alternative be economically feasible? How much will it cost? How soon can we have it? What will operating and maintenance costs be? What will the useful life be? Will it be compatible with present personnel and present operations?

Less obvious, but nonetheless important, is possible negative public opinion. For instance, the decision to build a new power plant is almost sure to stir up reaction, whether it is to be coal-fired, hydroelectric, or nuclear. Any option that has the possibility of disrupting lives and property is bound to generate hostile reactions. Construction of new facilities may necessitate moving personnel to a new location. Embracing a new technology may mean retraining certain people and even terminating some. Relocation can cause unfavorable reactions, particularly if a town is about to lose a major employer. Conversely, community pressure in a new location may arise if the presence of the company is viewed unfavorably (noise, traffic, pollution).

There are a number of techniques that are useful in evaluating capacity alternatives from an economic standpoint. Some of the more common ones are cost-volume analysis, financial analysis, decision theory, and queuing analysis. Cost-volume analysis is described in this chapter. Financial analysis is mentioned briefly and described in more detail in the chapter supplement, and decision theory and queuing theory are described in other chapters.

Cost-Volume Analysis. Cost-volume analysis, or **break-even analysis,** as it is commonly referred to, focuses on relationships between cost, revenue, and volume of output. The purpose of cost-volume analysis is to estimate the income of an organization that will occur under different operating conditions. It can be particularly useful as a tool for comparing capacity alternatives.

Use of the technique requires identification of all costs related to the production of a given product. These costs are then assigned to one of two categories: fixed costs or variable costs. *Fixed costs* are those that tend to remain constant regardless of volume of output. Examples include rental costs, property taxes, equipment costs, heating and cooling expenses, and certain administrative costs. *Variable costs* vary directly with volume of output. The major components of variable costs are generally materials and labor costs. It is assumed that variable cost per unit remains the same regardless of volume of output.

The total cost associated with a given volume of output is equal to the sum of the fixed cost and the variable cost per unit times volume:

$$\text{Total cost} = \text{Fixed cost} + \text{Variable cost per unit} \times Q \text{ units} \quad (6-3)$$

Figure 6–10A shows the relationship between volume of output and fixed costs, total variable costs, and total (fixed plus variable) costs.

Revenue per unit, like variable cost per unit, is assumed to be the same regardless of quantity of output. Thus, it too will have a linear relationship to output, as illustrated in Figure 6–10B. It is assumed that all of the output can be sold. The total revenue associated with a given quantity of output, Q, is:

$$\text{Total revenue} = \text{Revenue per unit} \times Q \quad (6-4)$$

Figure 6–10C describes the relationship between profit—which is the difference between total revenue and total (i.e., fixed plus variable) cost—and volume of output. The volume at which total costs and total revenue are equal is referred to as the **break-even point (BEP).** When volume is less than the break-even point, there is a loss rather than a profit; for volume greater than

FIGURE 6–10

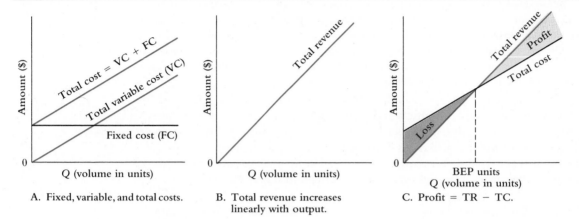

A. Fixed, variable, and total costs.

B. Total revenue increases linearly with output.

C. Profit = TR − TC.

the break-even point, there is a profit. The greater the deviation from this point, the greater the profit or loss. Total profit can be computed using the formula:

$$\begin{aligned} \text{Profit} &= \text{Total revenue} - \text{Total cost} \\ &= \text{Revenue per unit} \times Q - (\text{fixed cost} \\ &\quad + \text{Variable cost per unit} \times Q) \end{aligned} \qquad (6\text{--}5)$$

The required volume needed to generate a specified profit is:

$$\text{Volume} = \frac{\text{Specified profit} + \text{Fixed cost}}{\text{Revenue per unit} - \text{Variable cost per unit}} \qquad (6\text{--}6)$$

A special case of this is the volume of output needed for total revenue to equal total cost. This is the break-even point, and it can be computed using the formula:

$$Q_{\text{BEP}} = \frac{\text{Fixed cost}}{\text{Revenue per unit} - \text{Variable cost per unit}} \qquad (6\text{--}7)$$

The break-even symbols and formulas are summarized in Table 6–5. The use of these formulas is illustrated in the following example.

EXAMPLE 2

Old-Fashioned Berry Pies, Ltd. currently operates a single bakery but is now considering a second location in a new shopping mall. The owner, S. Simon, estimates that fixed costs would be $3,000 per week and that labor and materials to produce pies at that location will be 60 cents per pie. Pies will be sold for $1.60 each.

EXAMPLE 2 *(concluded)*

1. What number of pies must be sold in order to break even?
2. What profit (or loss) would there be on sales of 10,000 pies in one week?
3. What volume would be required in order to realize a profit of $12,000?

Solution

1. FC = $3,000, VC = $0.60 per unit, Rev = $1.60 per unit

$$Q_{BEP} = \frac{FC}{Rev - VC} = \frac{\$3,000}{\$1.60 - \$0.60} = 3,000 \text{ pies per week}$$

2. $P = Rev \times Q - (FC + VC \times Q)$
   $= \$1.60(10,000) - (\$3,000 + \$0.60) \times (10,000)$
   $= \$7,000$

3. $\text{Volume} = \dfrac{SP + FC}{Rev - VC} = \dfrac{\$12,000 + \$3,000}{\$1.60 - \$0.60}$

   $= 15,000 \text{ pies}$

Before the break-even model is used, it is necessary to make certain that the assumptions of the model are reasonably satisfied. The assumptions are:

1. One product is involved.
2. Everything that is produced can be sold.
3. The variable cost per unit is the same regardless of the volume.

TABLE 6–5

Summary of break-even formulas

FC = Fixed costs	Q_{BEP} = Break-even quantity
VC = Variable cost per unit	TR = Total revenue
TC = Total cost	P = Profit
Rev = Revenue per unit	SP = Specified profit
Q = Quantity of output	

1. $TC = FC + VC \times Q$
2. $TR = Rev \times Q$
3. $P = TR - TC = Rev \times Q - (FC + VC \times Q) = Q(Rev - VC) - FC$

4. $Q_{BEP} = \dfrac{FC}{Rev - VC}$

5. Volume needed to generate a specified profit:

$$Q = \frac{SP + FC}{Rev - VC}$$

4.   Fixed costs do not change with volume changes.

5.   The revenue per unit is the same regardless of volume.

Cost-volume analysis can be a valuable tool for comparing location decisions. As is the case with any quantitative tool, it is important to verify that the assumptions on which the technique is based are reasonably satisfied for a particular situation. For example, revenue per unit or variable cost per unit are not always constant. In addition, fixed costs may not be constant over the range of possible output. If demand is subject to random variations, it will be necessary to take that into account in the analysis. Cost-volume analysis requires that fixed and variable costs can be separated, and this is sometimes exceedingly difficult to accomplish.

Cost-volume analysis works best when one product or a few products that have the same cost characteristics are involved. Otherwise, the analysis can become fairly complex, although it is not impossible to deal with such cases.

In any case, an important benefit of cost-volume considerations is the conceptual framework it provides for integrating cost, revenue, and profit estimates into capacity decisions.

Financial Analysis.   A problem that is universally encountered by managers is how to allocate scarce funds. A common approach is to use *financial analysis* to rank investment proposals. At this point, it is unnecessary to go into much detail about these methods. However, for those so inclined, the chapter supplement describes some of the techniques commonly used for financial analysis and provides examples of each.

The purpose of this section is to define some of the terms that are used elsewhere in the reading material and to provide some perspective on where financial analysis methods fit into the spectrum of evaluation techniques available to managers.

Two important terms in financial analysis are *cash flow* and *present value*.

Cash flow refers to the difference between the cash received from sales (of goods or services) and other sources (e.g., sale of old equipment) and the cash outflow for labor, materials, overhead and taxes.

Present value expresses in current value the sum of all future cash flows of an investment proposal.

The three most commonly used methods of financial analysis are payback, present value, and internal rate of return.

Payback is a crude but widely used method that focuses on the length of time it will take for an investment to return its original cost. For example, an investment with an original cost of $6,000 and a monthly net cash flow of $1,000 has a payback period of six months. Payback ignores the *time value of money*. Its use is easier to rationalize for short-term projects than for long-term ones. However, some now feel that use of this method is one of the contributing factors in the failure of U.S. firms to match productivity increases achieved by other nations.

The *present value (PV)* method summarizes the initial cost of an investment, its estimated annual cash flows, and any expected salvage value in a single value called the *equivalent current value,* taking into account the time value of money (i.e., interest rates).

The *internal rate of return (IRR)* summarizes the initial cost, expected annual cash flows, and estimated future salvage value of an investment proposal in an *equivalent interest rate.* In other words, this method identifies the rate of return that equates the estimated future returns and the initial cost.

These techniques are appropriate when there is a high degree of *certainty* associated with estimates of future cash flows. In many instances, operations managers and other managers must deal with situations that can be better described by risk or uncertainty. The certainty methods are described in the chapter supplement; methods for dealing with financial analysis under conditions of risk or uncertainty are often handled using decision theory.

Decision Theory.   Decision theory is a helpful tool for financial comparison of alternatives under conditions of either risk or uncertainty. It is suited to capacity decisions as well as to a wide range of other decisions managers are called on to make. Decision theory was described in Chapter 2, but the same approaches can be applied to capacity decisions. Some of the problems at the end of this chapter require the use of decision theory. There would be little benefit in repeating the discussion that appears in Chapter 2. Suffice it to say that decision theory is an important managerial tool for capacity decisions.

Queuing Theory.   Queuing theory is often useful for designing service systems. Waiting lines have a tendency to form in a wide variety of service systems (e.g., airport ticket counters, telephone calls to a cable television company, and hospital emergency rooms). The lines are symptoms of bottleneck operations. Queuing theory is useful in helping managers choose a capacity level that will be cost-effective through balancing the cost of having customers wait with the cost of providing additional capacity. Queuing theory can aid in the determination of expected costs for various levels of service capacity.

This topic is described in detail in Chapter 15.

SUMMARY

Process selection is an important aspect of the design of a production system, and it can have major implications on productivity, cost, competitiveness, and flexibility. New products and services, changes in products or services, and technological changes are some of the reasons organizations become involved in process selection.

Basic issues in process selection relate to the type of processing in use (e.g., steady, high-volume; intermittent, lower-volume; or one-of-a-kind, large-scale projects), the level of automation or computer-assisted processing to use, the amount of flexibility to build in, and costs of processing.

Capacity refers to a system's potential for producing goods or delivering services over a specified time interval. Capacity decisions are doubly important: Capacity limitations act as a ceiling on output, and capacity is a major determinant of operating costs.

As a general rule, a variety of factors interfere with capacity utilization, so that effective capacity is somewhat less than design capacity. These factors involve such things as facilities design and layout, human factors, product/service design, equipment failures, scheduling problems, and quality considerations.

Capacity planning involves long-term and short-term considerations. Long-term concern relates to the overall level of capacity, and short-term concern relates to variations in capacity requirements due to seasonal, random, and irregular fluctuations in demand. Ideally, capacity will match demand, since it is typically most efficient to operate at or close to full capacity. For this reason, there is a close link between forecasting and capacity planning, particularly in the long term. In the short term, emphasis shifts to describing and coping with variations in demand.

Development of capacity alternatives is enhanced by taking a systems approach to planning, by recognizing that capacity increments are often acquired in chunks, by designing flexible systems, and by considering product/service complements as a way of dealing with various patterns of demand.

Evaluating capacity alternatives contains both quantitative and qualitative aspects. Quantitative analysis usually reflects economic factors, and qualitative considerations include such intangibles as public opinion and personal preferences of managers. Cost-volume analysis, financial analysis, decision theory, and queuing theory are possible tools for analyzing alternatives.

KEY TERMS

automation, 299
break-even analysis, 317
break-even point (BEP), 317
capacity, 305
cash flow, 320
computer-aided manufacturing (CAM), 299
computer-integrated manufacturing (CIM), 304

continuous processing, 297
flexible manufacturing systems (FMS), 303
intermittent processing, 298
numerically controlled (N/C) machines, 299
present value, 320
projects, 298
robots, 301

SOLVED PROBLEMS

1. *Make or buy.* A firm's manager must decide whether to make or buy a certain item used in the production of vending machines. Cost and volume estimates are as follows:

	Make	Buy
Annual fixed cost	$150,000	None
Variable cost/unit	$60	$80
Annual volume (units)	12,000	12,000

a. Given these figures, should the firm buy or make this item?

b. There is a possibility that volume could change in the future. At what volume would the manager be indifferent between making and buying?

Solution

a. Determine the annual cost of each alternative:

$$TC = \text{Fixed cost} + \text{Volume} \times \text{Variable cost}$$

Make: $150,000 + 12,000(\$60) = \$870,000$
Buy: $0 + 12,000(\$80) = \$960,000$

Because the annual cost of making is less than the annual cost of buying, it would seem reasonable for the manager to choose to make the item.

b. To determine the volume at which the two choices would be equivalent, set the two total costs equal to each other, and solve for volume: $TC_{make} = TC_{buy}$. Thus, $\$150,000 + Q(\$60) = 0 + Q(\$80)$. Solving $Q = 7,500$ units. Therefore, at a volume of 7,500 units a year, the manager would be indifferent between making and buying. For lower volumes, the choice would be to buy, and for higher volumes, the choice would be to make.

2. A small firm produces and sells novelty items in a five-state area. The firm expects to consolidate assembly of its electric turtle line at a single location instead of the current situation, which consists of three widely scattered operations. The leading candidate for location will have a monthly fixed cost of $42,000 and variable costs of $3 per turtle. Turtles sell for $7 each. Prepare a table that shows total profits, fixed costs, variable costs, and revenues for monthly volumes of 10,000, 12,000, and 15,000 units.

Solution

$$\text{Revenue} = \$7 \text{ per unit}$$
$$\text{Variable cost} = \$3 \text{ per unit}$$
$$\text{Fixed cost} = \$42,000 \text{ per month}$$

$$\text{Profit} = \text{Revenue} \times \text{Volume} - (FC + VC \times \text{Volume})$$
$$\text{Total cost} = FC + VC$$

Volume	Total revenue	Total VC	Fixed cost	Total cost	Total profit
10,000	$ 70,000	$30,000	$42,000	$72,000	$ (2,000)
12,000	84,000	36,000	42,000	78,000	6,000
15,000	105,000	45,000	42,000	87,000	18,000

3. (Refer to the previous problem.) Develop an equation that can be used to compute profit for any volume using the information in the previous problem, and use that equation to determine profit for the case where volume equals 22,000 units.

Solution

$$\text{Profit} = \$7/\text{unit} \times Q - (\$42,000 + \$3/\text{unit} \times Q)$$

where Q = volume. For Q = 22,000, profit is

$$\$7(22,000) - (\$42,000 + \$3 \times 22,000) = \$46,000$$

DISCUSSION AND REVIEW QUESTIONS

1. Explain the importance of process selection in system design.

2. Briefly describe continuous processing, intermittent processing, and projects, and indicate the kinds of situations in which each would be used.

3. Briefly discuss the advantages and disadvantages of automation.

4. Briefly describe computer-assisted approaches to production.

5. What is a flexible manufacturing system, and why is it important?

6. Why is *management of technology* important?

7. Why might the choice of equipment that provides flexibility sometimes be viewed as a management cop-out?

8. Contrast *design* and *effective* capacity.

9. List and briefly explain three factors that may inhibit capacity utilization.

10. How do long-term and short-term capacity considerations differ?

11. Give two examples of items that exhibit these seasonal demand patterns:
    a. Annual.
    b. Monthly.
    c. Weekly.
    d. Daily.

12. Give some examples of ways that flexibility can be built into system design.

13. Why is it important to adopt a "big picture" approach to capacity planning?

14. What is meant by "capacity in chunks," and why is that a factor in capacity planning?

15. What kinds of capacity problems are currently being experienced by many elementary and secondary schools? What are some of the alternatives being used to deal with those problems?

16. How can a systems approach to capacity planning be useful?

17. How do capacity decisions influence productivity?

PROBLEMS

1. A producer of pottery is considering the addition of a new plant to absorb the backlog of demand that now exists. The primary location being considered will have fixed costs of $9,200 per month and variable costs of 70 cents per unit produced. Each item is sold to retailers at a price that averages 90 cents.
   a. What volume per month is required in order to break even?
   b. What profit would be realized on a monthly volume of (1) 61,000 units? (2) 87,000 units?
   c. What volume would be needed to obtain a profit of $16,000 per month?
   d. What volume is required to provide a revenue of $23,000 per month?
   e. Plot the total cost and total revenue lines.

2. A small firm intends to increase the capacity of a bottleneck operation by adding a new machine. Two alternatives, A and B, have been identified, and the associated costs and revenues have been estimated: Annual fixed costs would be $40,000 for A and $30,000 for B; variable costs per unit would be $10 for A and $12 for B; and revenue per unit would be $15 for A and $16 for B.
   a. Determine each alternative's break-even point in units.
   b. At what volume of output would the two alternatives yield the same profit?
   c. If expected annual demand is 12,000 units, which alternative would yield the higher profit?

3. A producer of felt-tip pens has received a forecast of a demand of 30,000 pens for the coming month from its marketing department. Fixed costs of $25,000 per month are allocated to the felt-tip operation, and variable costs are 37 cents per pen.
   a. Find the break-even quantity if pens sell for $1 each.

   b. What price must pens be sold for to obtain a monthly profit of $15,000, assuming that estimated demand materializes?

4. A real estate agent is considering installing a cellular telephone in her car. There are three billing plans to choose from, all of which involve a weekly charge of $20. Plan A has a cost of $.45 a minute for daytime calls and $.20 a minute for evening calls. Plan B has a charge of $.55 a minute for daytime calls and a charge of $.15 a minute for evening calls. Plan C has a flat rate of $80 with 200 minutes of calls allowed per week and a cost of $.40 per minute beyond that, day or evening.
   a. Determine the total charge under each plan for this case: 120 minutes of day calls and 40 minutes of evening calls in a week.
   b. Prepare a graph that shows total weekly cost for each plan versus daytime call minutes.
   c. If the agent will use the service mainly for daytime calls, over what range of call minutes will each plan be optimal?

5. (Refer to the previous question.) Suppose that the agent expects both day and evening calls. At what point (i.e., proportion of call minutes for daytime calls) would she be indifferent between plans A and B?

6. Good Labels, Inc. supplies labels for wine bottles to regional vineyards. Increased demand for wine is expected to exceed label capacity in the near future. Consequently, Good Labels is exploring several options for increasing its capacity relative to doing nothing. Net present values (in $ millions) for the various options are shown in the following table. Which option would be indicated under each of these conditions?
   a. The firm uses maximax.
   b. The firm uses maximin.
   c. The firm uses maximum expected

value, and probabilities of the demands listed are equally likely.

d. The firm uses maximum expected value, and $P(40) = .2$, $P(45) = .4$, $P(50) = .3$, and $P(55) = .1$.

	Demand (boxes per day)			
Options	40	45	50	55
Do nothing	0	5	5	5
Expand	−5	0	5	10
Additional plant	−20	−5	10	25

7. A regional airline has recently added a "long-hop" commuter route and is now considering the purchase of a jet to use on that route. Information concerning the estimated payoffs under various levels of customer demand are shown for the alternatives being considered. The figures have been adjusted for purchase cost of the planes. What alternative would be appropriate for each of the following decision criteria?

a. Maximax.

b. Maximin.

c. Minimax regret.

d. Maximum expected value if probabilities for low, moderate, and high demand, respectively, are: (1) .1, .4, and .5; (2) .2, .3, and .5.

	Demand		
	Low	Moderate	High
Do nothing	2*	3	3
Buy 80 passenger	0	4	6
Buy 120 passenger . . .	(5)	0	7
Buy 200 passenger . . .	(10)	1	10

* Net present value in $ millions.

8. A motel has received numerous complaints from potential guests whose reservations could not be honored due to overbooking. Discussions with the assistant manager of the motel have revealed that each overbooking results in a loss of profit and goodwill that has a value of $30. Thus, if two rooms are overbooked, the loss will be $60. On the other hand, the assistant manager estimates that "no-shows" reflect a profit loss of $12 each.

a. Construct a payoff matrix for overbooking strategies of 0, 1, 2, 3, and 4 for 0 through 5 no-shows.

b. What decision should be made if the criterion is (1) maximax? (2) maximin?

c. If no-show probabilities for 0, 1, 2, 3, 4, and 5 are .2, .3, .2, .1, .1, and .1, respectively, which strategy would be selected in order to minimize expected loss?

9. A firm plans to begin production of a new small appliance soon. The manager must decide whether to purchase the motors for the appliance from a vendor at $7 each or to produce them in-house. Either of two processes could be used for in-house production; one would have an annual fixed cost of $160,000 and a variable cost of $5 per unit, and the other would have an annual fixed cost of $190,000 and a variable cost of $4 per unit. Determine the range of annual volume for which each of the alternatives would be best.

10. A manager is trying to decide whether to purchase a certain part or to have it produced internally. Internal production could use either of two processes. One would entail a variable cost of $17 per unit and an annual fixed cost of $200,000; the other would entail a variable cost of $14 per unit and an annual fixed cost of $240,000. Three vendors are willing to provide the part. Vendor A has a price of $20 per unit for any volume up to 30,000 units. Vendor B has a price of $22 per unit for demand of 1,000 units or less, and $18 per unit for larger quantities. Vendor C offers a price of $21 per unit for the first 1,000 units, and $19 per unit for additional units.

a. If the manager anticipates an annual volume of 10,000 units, which alternative would be best from a cost standpoint? For 20,000 units, which alternative would be best?

b. Determine the range for which each alternative is best. Are there any alternatives that are never best? Which?

11. A company manufactures a product using three-machine cells. Each cell has a design capacity of 250 units per day and an effective capacity of 230 units per day. At present, actual output averages 200 units per cell, but the manager estimates that productivity improvements soon will increase that to 225 units per day. Annual demand is currently 50,000 units. It is forecasted that within two years, annual demand will triple. The company could produce at the rate of 400 per day using available capacity. How many cells should the company plan for in order to satisfy predicted demand under these conditions? Assume 240 workdays per year.

SELECTED BIBLIOGRAPHY

Abramowitz, Irving. *Production Management: Concepts and Analysis for Operation and Control.* New York: Ronald Press, 1967.

Adam, Everette E., Jr., and Ronald J. Ebert. *Production and Operations Management: Concepts, Models and Behavior.* 4th ed. Englewood, Cliffs, N.J.: Prentice-Hall, 1989.

Buffa, Elwood, and James S. Dyer. *Essentials of Management/Operations Research.* New York: John Wiley & Sons, 1978.

Hill, Terry. *Manufacturing Strategy.* Homewood, Ill.: Richard D. Irwin, 1989.

Monks, Joseph G. *Operations Management: Theory and Problems.* New York: McGraw-Hill, 1982.

Moore, Franklin, and Thomas E. Hendrick. *Production/Operations Management.* 9th ed. Homewood, Ill.: Richard D. Irwin, 1985.

Toward a New Era in U.S. Manufacturing: The Need for a National Vision. Washington, D.C.: National Academy Press, 1986.

READING

MATCH THE PROCESS AND THE PRODUCT

The difference between success and failure in production can sometimes be traced to choice of process. Products range from highly customized to highly standardized. Generally, volume requirements tend to increase as standardization increases; customized products tend to be low volume, and standardized products tend to be high volume. These factors should be considered in determining the process to be used.

Certain processes are more amenable to low-volume, customized products, while others are more suited to moderate-variety products, and still others to higher volume, highly standardized products. By matching product requirements with process choices, producers can achieve the greatest degree of efficiency in their operations. The following table illustrates this important concept. Examples of products are placed in their ideal positions.

Notice that the examples all line up along the diagonal of the table. This is the most efficient position. If a producer should choose some other combination (e.g., assembly line for a customized product or service), he would find that the highly customized requirements of the various products were in direct conflict with the more uniform requirements needed to effectively operate in the assembly-line mode. Similarly, a job shop arrangement (machines and personnel are capable of handling a wide variety of processing requirements) would be wasted on a highly standardized product; equipment and personnel need to be highly specialized.

The table can provide insights to those making process selections as well as to those managing existing operations. For process choice, decision makers should make every attempt to achieve the aforemen-

	Product			
	Customized (low volume)	*High variety (low–moderate)*	*Moderate variety (moderate)*	*Standardized (high volume)*
Job shop	Advertising Dental work Equipment repair			
Batch		Magazines Pastry shop		
Assembly line			Autos TVs	
Continuous flow				Sugar Flour

Sources: Adapted from Robert H. Hayes and Stephen C. Wheelwright, "Link Manufacturing Product and Process Life Cycles," *Harvard Business Review*, Jan-Feb 1979, pp. 133–40; and Irwin Business Insights video tape series, 1988.

tioned matching of product and process requirements. For an ongoing operation, a manager should examine existing processes in light of the table in order to see how well processes and products are matched. Poor matches would suggest the potential for improvement, perhaps with a substantial increase in efficiency and lowering of cost.

A second important concept is that products and services often go through *life cycles* that begin with low volume that increases as products or services become more well known. When that happens, a manager must know when to shift from one type of process (e.g., job shop) to the next (e.g., batch), and perhaps to the next (e.g., assembly line). Of course, some operations remain at a certain level (e.g., magazine publishing), while others increase (or decrease

as markets become saturated) over time. Again, it is important for a manager to assess his or her products and services and make a judgment on whether to plan for changes in processing over time.

Questions

1. Describe the product-process matrix, and give additional examples of products and services in each category.

2. Why is it important to achieve a position along the diagonal of the matrix?

3. How could the above table be used to audit existing processes? What benefits might this lead to?

FINANCIAL ANALYSIS

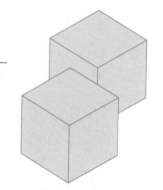

LEARNING OBJECTIVES

After completing this supplement, you should be able to:

1. Define or explain these terms:
   a. Economic life.
   b. Cash flow.
   c. Salvage value.
   d. Depreciation.
   e. Time value of money.
2. Give examples of decisions that require the operations manager to use financial analysis.
3. Describe and use each of these methods of evaluation:
   a. Payback.
   b. Net present value.
   c. Internal rate of return.

SUPPLEMENT OUTLINE

In both the public and private sectors, operations managers must continually make decisions concerning the allocation of funds among investment alternatives. In private firms, the objective is to obtain a reasonable return on owners' capital; in public organizations, the objective is usually to provide a given level of service at the lowest cost or to obtain the highest possible level of service for a given cost.

Typical investment decisions usually involve the following:

1. Acquisition of facilities.
2. Acquisition of equipment.
3. Revision or expansion of existing facility layout.
4. Research and development.
5. Make or buy.
6. New products.
7. Repair and maintenance of equipment and facilities.

In comparing investment alternatives, operations managers generally take into account the economic life of an investment, its initial cost, the expected cash flows, depreciation and taxes, salvage values, and the time value of money. Before discussing these methods, it will be helpful to briefly review some of the terms commonly used in financial analysis.

TERMINOLOGY

Among the key terms in financial analysis are the following:

Economic Life

The **economic life** of an asset or other investment alternative is the period of time that it will perform a useful service to the organization. It can differ from the *accounting life* of an asset (period of time over which the asset is depreciated) as well as from the *productive life* of an asset (period of time over which the asset could perform). The productive life of equipment often exceeds its useful (economic) life to the organization because technological changes make the original equipment obsolete or because the needs of the organization change. The accounting life of an asset is often a matter of tax laws and tax strategies.

Net Cash Flow

Net cash flow is the annual difference between revenues and expenses related to an investment proposal. Although cash flows might occur throughout the year, for purposes of financial analysis they are treated as occurring at the end of the year.

Salvage Value

The **salvage value** is generally the estimated income that will be received from the sale of an asset. Sometimes this will be a negative amount (e.g., the organization must incur a cost in disposing of the asset).

Depreciation

Depreciation is an accounting term that relates to an annual reduction in the value of an asset on the books of a firm. A detailed discussion of depreciation is beyond the scope of this text. However, the importance of depreciation in terms of financial analysis should be noted: Depreciation has an effect on income taxes, which in turn affect the actual cash flow, even though depreciation itself is *not* a cash flow.

Time Value of Money

The timing of cash flows from an asset has a lot to do with the desirability of the investment. Investment alternatives that produce the same total returns, but with differing times, are not usually equally attractive, due to the time value of money. The **time value of money** refers to the fact that money can be invested (e.g., in new investments, deposited in a bank account) to produce a return. The timing of cash flows of an investment proposal is important because the sooner the money becomes available, the sooner it can be used for other worthwhile purposes.

Consider this example. You are given a choice of receiving $100 now, or $100 in two years. Suppose that you will not need this money for another two years, so if you receive it now you will put it into a bank account that yields 6 percent a year. If you decide to take the money now and deposit it in the bank, the future value, F, after *one* year will equal the present value P ($100), plus a dividend equal to the amount deposited times the interest rate, i. Thus,

$$F_1 = \$100 + \$100(.06) = \$106$$

Assuming the total amount remained in the account for the second year, the interest would be paid on $106 for the second year, and the account balance at the end of that year would be:

$$F_2 = \$106 + \$106(.06) = \$112.36$$

Hence, by receiving the money at the present time and investing it, you would have $12.36 *more* than if you chose to take the $100 at the end of the second year. This difference reflects the time value of money.

In general, the future value after one year can be determined using the formula:

$$F_1 = P + Pi$$
$$= P(1 + i)$$ (6S–1)

where

$F_1 = $ Future value at the end of period 1
$P = $ Present value
$i = $ Interest rate

For year 2, the formula becomes:

$$F_2 = P(1 + i) + P(1 + i)i$$
$$= P(1 + i)(1 + i)$$
$$= P(1 + i)^2$$

In a similar fashion, the total value after n years would be:

$$F_n = P(1 + i)^n$$ (6S–2)

An interesting question is what the present value of the other alternative is (i.e., receive \$100 at the end of two years). In other words, what sum of money, invested for two years at 6 percent interest, would produce \$100?

FIGURE 6S–1

Cash values in given years can be restated relative to the present time or to some point in the future

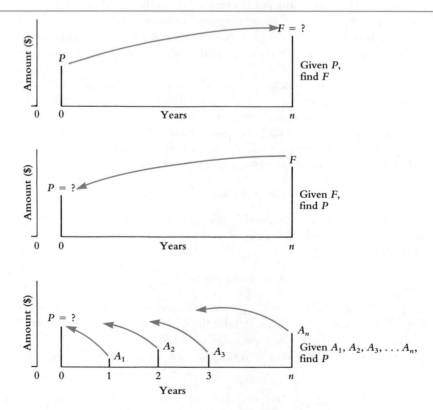

A general formula for P, given F, n, and i, can be derived by solving the general formula for F in terms of P. Solving for P yields:

$$P = \frac{F_n}{(1 + i)^n} \qquad (6S\text{--}3)$$

Hence, the required sum needed now to produce a future value of $100 in two years is:

$$P = \frac{\$100}{(1 + .06)^2} = \$89$$

An extension of this concept involves determining either the present or the future value of a series of annual amounts, A_1, A_2, . . . , A_n, which may or may not be equal. You will see in the next section how to do this. For now, it will be instructive to compare these three concepts: given F, find P; given P, find F; and given A, find P. These are illustrated in Figure 6S–1.

TAX CONSIDERATIONS

Federal income taxes can have important implications in financial decision making. Tax rates and provisions for applying them change from time to time, so precise statements about tax laws are difficult to make. Nonetheless, certain observations concerning taxes can be made.

Taxes and depreciation on plant and equipment are closely linked. Depreciation allows companies to write off a portion of an investment against current income. This reduces the amount of taxable income and thereby frees funds for other uses (e.g., invest in additional equipment). Generally speaking, analysis of investment alternatives on a before-tax basis leads to the same ranking as an after-tax basis, although differences may occur in cases where lease versus buy is involved. Consequently, because it is less complicated to use before-tax analysis, or to assume taxes have already been handled, we can avoid a detailed discussion of income taxes. However, a consideration of taxes is important in choosing a method of depreciation, since different methods will generally result in different tax consequences in certain years. In other words, choice of depreciation methods can result in shifting the tax burden to different years, and this can have important benefits in terms of cash flow by preserving funds that would otherwise have to be paid out in the form of income taxes.

Also, in certain years, businesses have been allowed to take an *investment tax credit,* which is a direct reduction in taxes. Again, the underlying philosophy is to encourage business investment.

METHODS OF EVALUATION

We shall examine three commonly used methods for evaluating alternatives: payback period, present value, and internal rate of return.

Payback Period

The **payback period** is a crude but widely used method for evaluating the desirability of a financial investment. As its name implies, it focuses on the length of time it will take to recoup the original investment.

EXAMPLE S–1

Determine the payback period for each of the following investment proposals, given their estimated cash flows. Assume each requires an initial investment of $40,000.

Year	A	B	C
1	$10,000	$20,000	$ 1,000
2	10,000	20,000	5,000
3	10,000	2,000	10,000
4	10,000	1,000	20,000
5	10,000	100	40,000
6	10,000	0	80,000

Solution

Calculate the cumulative cash flows for each alternative, and note when the cumulative amount equals the original investment. Hence,

Year	A	B	C
1	$10,000	$20,000	$ 1,000
2	20,000	40,000	6,000
3	30,000	42,000	16,000
4	40,000		36,000
5			76,000

Thus, A's payback period is exactly four years, B's is exactly two years, and C's is between four and five years. From a payback standpoint, the most attractive alternative is B. C is the least attractive.

One obvious disadvantage of the payback method is that it does not consider cash flows beyond the payback period. Nor does it take salvage value into account. In the preceding example, note that B's cash flows are quite small beyond the payback period, in contrast to C's, which get larger and larger. Another disadvantage is that no allowance is made for the time value of money, at least not directly. Indirectly, the rationale of the payback approach is to recoup the initial investment as quickly as possible to have the funds available for future opportunities. In fact, this method is especially appealing to firms that have a cash shortage. Other firms like its simplicity, and many firms like to use it in situations where the payback period is fairly short (e.g., six months to a year).

Net Present Value

The present value method involves finding the present value of each of the future cash flows (including salvage value) and summing the results. The **net present value** of an alternative is equal to this sum minus the initial cost of the proposed investment:

$$\text{Net present value} = \frac{\text{Present value of}}{\text{future cash flows}} - \text{Initial cost} \qquad \text{(6S–4)}$$

There are essentially two kinds of situations that arise in terms of annual cash flows:

1. Annual cash flows are all the same amount.
2. Annual cash flows are not all the same.

In the first situation, a single computation is required; in the second, a separate computation is usually required for each cash flow (i.e., the present value of

TABLE 6S–1

Present value of an annuity of $1: Given equal As, find P

Year	5%	6%	7%	8%	9%	10%	12%	14%	16%	18%	20%	24%	28%
1	0.952	0.943	0.935	0.926	0.917	0.909	0.893	0.877	0.862	0.847	0.833	0.806	0.781
2	1.859	1.833	1.808	1.783	1.759	1.736	1.690	1.647	1.605	1.566	1.528	1.457	1.392
3	2.723	2.673	2.624	2.577	2.531	2.487	2.402	2.322	2.246	2.174	2.106	1.981	1.868
4	3.546	3.465	3.387	3.312	3.240	3.170	3.037	2.914	2.798	2.690	2.589	2.404	2.241
5	4.329	4.212	4.100	3.993	3.890	3.791	3.605	3.433	3.274	3.127	2.991	2.745	2.532
6	5.076	4.917	4.766	4.623	4.486	4.355	4.111	3.889	3.685	3.498	3.326	3.020	2.759
7	5.786	5.582	5.389	5.206	5.033	4.868	4.564	4.288	4.039	3.812	3.605	3.242	2.937
8	6.463	6.210	5.971	5.747	5.535	5.335	4.968	4.639	4.344	4.078	3.837	3.421	3.076
9	7.108	6.802	6.515	6.247	5.985	5.759	5.328	4.946	4.607	4.303	4.031	3.566	3.184
10	7.722	7.360	7.024	6.710	6.418	6.145	5.650	5.216	4.833	4.494	4.193	3.682	3.269
11	8.306	7.887	7.499	7.139	6.805	6.495	5.988	5.453	5.029	4.656	4.327	3.776	3.335
12	8.863	8.384	7.943	7.536	7.161	6.814	6.194	5.660	5.197	4.793	4.439	3.851	3.387
13	9.394	8.853	8.358	7.904	7.487	7.103	6.424	5.842	5.342	4.910	4.533	3.912	3.427
14	9.899	9.295	8.745	8.244	7.786	7.367	6.628	6.002	5.468	5.008	4.611	3.962	3.459
15	10.380	9.712	9.108	8.559	8.060	7.606	6.811	6.142	5.575	5.092	4.675	4.001	3.483
16	10.838	10.106	9.447	8.851	8.312	7.824	6.974	6.265	5.669	5.162	4.730	4.033	3.503
17	11.274	10.477	9.763	9.122	8.544	8.022	7.120	6.373	5.749	5.222	4.775	4.059	3.518
18	11.690	10.828	10.059	9.372	8.756	8.201	7.250	6.467	5.818	5.273	4.812	4.080	3.529
19	12.085	11.158	10.336	9.604	8.950	8.365	7.366	6.550	5.877	5.316	4.844	4.097	3.539
20	12.462	11.470	10.594	9.818	9.128	8.514	7.469	6.623	5.929	5.353	4.870	4.110	3.546
25	14.094	12.783	11.654	10.675	9.823	9.077	7.843	6.873	6.097	5.467	4.948	4.147	3.564
30	15.373	13.765	12.409	11.258	10.274	9.427	8.055	7.003	6.177	5.517	4.979	4.160	3.569

each cash flow must be determined). In both cases, the actual determination of the present values is greatly simplified by the use of tables. In order to use the tables, decide which of these two situations describes the problem. In the first stituation, use Table 6S–1. Find the factor in the table for the number of years and the cost of capital (e.g., for $n = 2$ and $i = 5$ percent, the factor is 1.859). Multiply this factor by the annual cash flow to determine the present value.

EXAMPLE S–2

Determine the net present value of a proposal that has an economic life of nine years, an initial cost of $30,000, and an annual cash flow of $10,000. The firm's cost of capital is 12 percent.

Solution

$$n = 9, \ A = \$10,000, \ \text{Initial cost} = \$30,000, \ \text{and} \ i = 12\%$$

1. Find the annuity factor from Table 6S–1: 5.328.
2. Find the present value of cash flows: $10,000(5.328) = $53,280.
3. Determine the net present value: $53,280 − $30,000 = $23,280.

In the second case, a separate computation must be made for each cash flow.

EXAMPLE S–3

A newspaper is considering two investment proposals for a new piece of equipment. Proposal A has an initial cost of $2,000, and proposal B has an initial cost of $1,000. Given the following cash flow information and the firm's cost of capital of 10 percent, determine which proposal has the higher present value.

	Cash flows	
Year	Proposal A	Proposal B
1	$1,000	$2,000
2	2,000	1,000
3	3,000	800
4		100

Solution

Using Table 6S–2, find the *present value factor (PVF)* for each year in the 10 percent column. Multiply that amount by the year's cash flow and sum the results. Subtract the initial cost from the sum to obtain the net present value:

Example S–3 *(concluded)*

1. Find the present value of cash flows.

Year	Proposal A			Proposal B		
	Cash flow × PVF =		PV	Cash flow × PVF =		PV
1	$1,000	.909	$ 909	$2,000	.909	$1,818
2	2,000	.826	1,652	1,000	.826	826
3	3,000	.751	2,253	800	.751	601
4				100	.683	68
			$4,814			$3,313

2. Subtract the initial investments to find the present value of each investment:

   Proposal A: $4,814 − $2,000 = $2,814
   Proposal B: $3,313 − $1,000 = $2,313

   Hence, proposal A has a higher present value.

TABLE 6S–2

Present value of $1: Given F, find P

Year	5%	6%	7%	8%	9%	10%	12%	14%	15%	16%	18%	20%	24%	28%
1	0.952	0.943	0.935	0.926	0.917	0.909	0.893	0.877	0.870	0.862	0.847	0.833	0.806	0.781
2	0.907	0.890	0.873	0.857	0.842	0.826	0.797	0.769	0.756	0.743	0.718	0.694	0.650	0.610
3	0.864	0.840	0.816	0.794	0.772	0.751	0.712	0.675	0.658	0.641	0.609	0.579	0.524	0.477
4	0.823	0.792	0.763	0.735	0.708	0.683	0.636	0.592	0.572	0.552	0.516	0.482	0.423	0.373
5	0.784	0.747	0.713	0.681	0.650	0.621	0.567	0.519	0.497	0.476	0.437	0.402	0.341	0.291
6	0.746	0.705	0.666	0.630	0.596	0.564	0.507	0.456	0.432	0.410	0.370	0.335	0.275	0.227
7	0.711	0.665	0.623	0.583	0.547	0.513	0.452	0.400	0.376	0.354	0.314	0.279	0.222	0.178
8	0.677	0.627	0.582	0.540	0.502	0.467	0.404	0.351	0.327	0.305	0.266	0.233	0.179	0.139
9	0.645	0.592	0.544	0.500	0.460	0.424	0.361	0.308	0.284	0.263	0.226	0.194	0.144	0.108
10	0.614	0.558	0.508	0.463	0.422	0.386	0.322	0.270	0.247	0.227	0.191	0.162	0.116	0.085
11	0.585	0.527	0.475	0.429	0.388	0.350	0.287	0.237	0.215	0.195	0.162	0.135	0.094	0.066
12	0.557	0.497	0.444	0.397	0.356	0.319	0.257	0.208	0.187	0.168	0.137	0.112	0.076	0.052
13	0.530	0.469	0.415	0.368	0.326	0.290	0.229	0.182	0.163	0.145	0.116	0.093	0.061	0.040
14	0.505	0.442	0.388	0.340	0.299	0.263	0.205	0.160	0.141	0.125	0.099	0.078	0.049	0.032
15	0.481	0.417	0.362	0.315	0.275	0.239	0.183	0.140	0.123	0.108	0.084	0.065	0.040	0.025
16	0.458	0.394	0.339	0.292	0.252	0.218	0.163	0.123	0.107	0.093	0.071	0.054	0.032	0.019
17	0.436	0.371	0.317	0.270	0.231	0.198	0.146	0.108	0.093	0.080	0.060	0.045	0.026	0.015
18	0.416	0.350	0.296	0.250	0.212	0.180	0.130	0.095	0.081	0.069	0.051	0.038	0.021	0.012
19	0.386	0.331	0.276	0.232	0.194	0.164	0.116	0.083	0.070	0.060	0.043	0.031	0.017	0.009
20	0.377	0.319	0.258	0.215	0.178	0.149	0.104	0.073	0.061	0.051	0.037	0.026	0.014	0.007
25	0.295	0.233	0.184	0.146	0.116	0.092	0.059	0.038	0.030	0.024	0.016	0.010	0.005	0.002
30	0.231	0.174	0.131	0.099	0.075	0.057	0.033	0.020	0.015	0.012	0.007	0.004	0.002	0.001

If it happens that an investment is expected to have a uniform cash flow but a different salvage value, handle the uniform flows using Table 6S–1 and the salvage value using Table 6S–2. Then add the results.

EXAMPLE S–4

$$\text{Annual cash flow} = \$5,000 \qquad i = 14\%$$
$$\text{Initial cost} = \$12,000 \qquad n = 10$$
$$\text{Salvage value} = \$2,000 \text{ in year } 10$$

Find the net present value.

Solution

1. Find the present value of the equal cash flows using Table 6S–1:

$$P = \$5,000(5.216) = \$26,080$$

2. Find the present value of the salvage using Table 6S–2:

$$P = \$2,000(.270) = \$540$$

3. Determine the net present value:

$$\text{Net present value} = (\$26,080 + \$540) - \$12,000 = \$14,620$$

Among the disadvantages of the present value approach are the assumption that the funds can be reinvested as they are received at the cost of capital and the fact that it does not consider the length of time needed to recoup the original cost. Its advantages are that it incorporates a time value dimension, it facilitates total value comparisons among alternatives, and it can handle uneven cash flows.

Internal Rate of Return

Another popular method used to evaluate investment alternatives involves finding the interest rate that will equate the present value of future cash flows with the initial investment. The resulting interest rate is called the **internal rate of return (IRR).**

When annual expected cash flows are equal and there is no expected salvage value, computations are straightforward. Simply compute the ratio of the initial cost to the annual cash flow, and refer to Table 6S–1 to determine the approximate interest rate for the specified life of the investment. That is:

$$PVA_n = \frac{\text{Initial investment}}{\text{Annual cash flow}} = \frac{I}{A} \qquad (6S–5)$$

where

PVA_n = Present value factor for n years (found in Table 6S–1)

EXAMPLE S–5

An automatic bottlecapping machine requires an initial investment of $9,000. During its estimated useful life of 11 years, it will provide an annual cash flow of $1,800. At the end of 11 years, the machine will have no salvage value. Determine the internal rate of return.

Solution

$$I = \$9,000$$
$$A = \$1,800$$
$$n = 11 \text{ years}$$
$$\frac{I}{A} = \frac{\$9,000}{1,800} = 5.00$$

Referring to Table 6S–1 for $n = 11$, we find PVA = 5.029 for $i = 16$ percent and PVA = 4.656 for $i = 18$ percent. Since the computed value is approximately 5.029, we conclude the IRR is approximately 16 percent.

When cash flows are nonuniform and/or when salvage value is nonzero, determination of the IRR is a good deal more complex and involves a trial-and-error search for the approximate interest rate. A present value computation of each cash flow must be done for a number of i's until the approximate value of i can be narrowed down, using Table 6S–2.

EXAMPLE S–6

An investment proposal will have cash flows of $2,000 in the first year, $5,000 in the second, $4,000 in the third, and a salvage value of $1,000 in the fourth. Initial cost is $10,000. Determine the approximate internal rate of return.

Solution

Try several i's (perhaps including 6 percent and 10 percent):

Year	Cash flow	6 percent	10 percent
1	$2,000	.943 = 1,886	.909 = 1,818
2	5,000	.890 = 4,450	.826 = 4,130
3	4,000	.840 = 3,360	.751 = 3,004
4	1,000	.792 = 792	.683 = 683
		10,488	9,635

A rate of 6 percent results in a value that is slightly greater than the initial cost, and the 10 percent rate results in a value that is slightly less than the initial cost. Thus, a rate between these two would be appropriate. A rate of 8 percent resulted in $10,048 (calculations not shown), so we can conclude the internal rate of return is approximately 8 percent.

Several points related to the IRR are worth noting:

1. The internal rate of return and present value methods often yield the same choice in an evaluation of alternatives.
2. Some organizations have a threshold for the IRR below which investments are not considered.
3. Financial calculators and computer programs greatly simplify determination of the internal rate of return.

The disadvantages of the IRR method are that it does not consider the *amount* involved, nor does it indicate the payback period. Its advantages are that it permits comparisons among alternatives, it adjusts for the time value of money, and it can be compared to the firm's cost of capital (which can serve as a lower threshold for acceptable investments).

SUMMARY

Operations managers rely on financial analysis to help them in ranking investment proposals in order to allocate limited funds. The underlying theme of financial anaylsis is that money has a time value: a dollar today is worth more than a dollar five years from today because today's dollar can be *invested* (i.e., it has the potential to produce additional gains). Using financial techniques, managers can compare alternative investment proposals, which often differ in terms of useful life, amount of initial investment required, amounts and distributions of annual cash flows, salvage value, and interest rates. Three widely used methods of evaluation are described in this supplement: payback, present value, and internal rate of return.

KEY TERMS

depreciation, 331
economic life, 330
internal rate of return (IRR), 338
net cash flow, 330

net present value, 335
payback period, 334
salvage value, 331
time value of money, 331

SOLVED PROBLEMS

1. Recreation-Can-Be-Fun, Inc. has developed a proposal to erect a temporary indoor tennis court. Profit projections are $5,000 for the first year of operation and $2,000 for years 2 through 5. The structure will be dismantled at the end of the fifth year at a contracted cost of $3,000. Initial cost is $7,500.

a.   What is the present value of this proposal for a cost of capital of
16 percent?

b.   What rate of return would equate the cash flows to the original
cost?

Solution

The cash flows are:

Year	Cash flow
1	$5,000
2	2,000
3	2,000
4	2,000
5	−1,000

For fifth year, $2,000 − $3,000 = $−1,000.
$I = $7,500, n = 5.$

a. $i = 16$ percent.

Year	Cash flow	PVF (Table 6S–2)	PV = Cash flow × PVF
1	$5,000	.862	$4,310
2	2,000	.743	1,486
3	2,000	.641	1,282
4	2,000	.552	1,104
5	−1,000	.476	− 476
			$7,706
			−7,500
			$ 206

b.   Noting that the present value is close to zero at $i = 16$ percent
and observing that increasing the interest rate causes a decrease
in present value, we can try $i = 18$ percent:

Year	Cash flow	PVF (Table 6S–2)	PV
1	$5,000	.847	$4,235
2	2,000	.718	1,436
3	2,000	.609	1,218
4	2,000	.516	1,032
5	−1,000	.437	− 437
			$7,484
			−7,500
			$ − 16

Hence, the IRR is approximately 18 percent.

2. Determine the present value of an investment that has an initial cost of $9,300, zero salvage value, and cash flows of $4,000 per year for the first two years of the investment, then $1,000 for the next five years, and nothing after that point, if the cost of capital is 14 percent.

Solution

The problem can be simplified by viewing the cash flows as two annuities: one of $3,000 per year and the other of $1,000 per year:

Year	Cash flow $\longrightarrow$ Annuity 1		Annuity 2
1	$4,000	$3,000	$1,000
2	4,000	3,000	1,000
3	1,000		1,000
4	1,000		1,000
5	1,000		1,000
6	1,000		1,000
7	1,000		1,000

Then:

$$PV = \$3000 \times (PVA: n = 2, i = 14\%) + \$1,000 \times (PVA: n = 7, i = 14\%) - \$9,300$$

From Table 6S–1, for $n = 2$ and $i = 14$ percent, PVA = 1.647. For $n = 7$ and $i = 14$ percent, PVA = 4.288. Thus,

$$PV = \$3,000 \times 1.647 + \$1,000 \times 4.288 - \$9,300 = \$-71$$

DISCUSSION AND REVIEW QUESTIONS

1. Briefly define or explain each of these terms:
   a. Cash flow.
   b. Salvage value.
   c. Economic life.
   d. Depreciation.
   e. Time value of money.

2. What are the advantages and disadvantages of each of these methods of evaluation?
   a. Payback.
   b. Present value.
   c. Internal rate of return.

PROBLEMS

1. A dairy cooperative is considering construction of a processing plant, which will require an outlay of $2.1 million initially. Annual income from the plant is expected to be $300,000. Plant life will be 15 years. Determine the internal rate of return on this investment for each of these cases:
   a. The plant is expected to have no salvage value.

b. A salvage value of $250,000 is anticipated.

2. Referring to the previous problem:
   a. Determine the payback period.
   b. Determine the present value, assuming a cost of capital of 10 percent for each salvage value.

3. A photo finisher must decide whether to lease or buy a delivery van that will have an expected useful life of four years. Purchase cost would be $8,000, and salvage value is estimated at $1,500. Two lease options are available: Option A requires a downpayment of $4,000 initially and an annual payment of $1,000; B requires an initial payment of $5,000 and an annual payment of $600. The firm's cost of capital is 14 percent. Which alternative is better?

4. City Hospital is currently involved in a campaign to update its X-ray diagnostic equipment. Two machines are being considered. Machine A would require an initial investment of $24,000 and would return $5,000 yearly for 10 years. Machine B would return $6,000 per year for 12 years with an initial investment of $30,000. Assume the cost of capital is 12 percent. Determine the present value of each machine for these cases:
   a. Neither machine has any salvage value.
   b. A will have a salvage value of $4,000, and B will have a salvage value of $3,000.

5. Determine the payback periods for machines A and B in the preceding problem.

6. Determine the internal rate of return for each of the investment proposals shown below.

	Proposal		
	A	**B**	**C**
Initial amount . . .	$60,000	$60,000	$50,000
Cash flow			
(per year)			
1	20,000	20,000	20,000
2	30,000	40,000	20,000
3	30,000	30,000	20,000
4	10,000	−10,000	20,000

7. Compute the present value for each proposal in the previous problem using a cost of capital of 18 percent.

8. Commercial Utilities is considering a proposed $6.4 million coal-fired power plant, which will have an expected operating life of 30 years. Estimated annual returns after taxes and depreciation are $0.8 million for the first 10 years, $1.0 million for the next 5 years, and $0.7 million for the remaining years. A salvage value of $2.0 million is projected.
   a. Determine the present value of the proposal for interest rates of (1) 12 percent and (2) 16 percent.
   b. What is the approximate internal rate of return for the power plant?
   c. Determine the payback period for this investment.

9. A bank manager of a suburban branch of a large savings bank is considering two proposals for meeting increased demand for bank services. Proposal 1 would involve remodeling the bank; proposal 2 would involve installation of automatic equipment and different processing routines than are now being used. Substantial retraining costs would be associated with the second proposal. The manager foresees three possible future states of nature—A, B, and C—with estimated likelihoods of .20 for A, .30 for B, and .50 for C. If the manager's decision criterion is maximum expected present value, which proposal should be selected? Why? Assume a cost of capital of 16 percent. Net cash flows under each state of nature for each proposal's life are as follows:

Remodel: Initial cost = $80,000

Year	A	B	C
1	40*	60	50
2	40	60	50
3	40	40	50
4	40	30	50
5	40	20	−10

* Net cash flows in $000s.

Automate: Initial cost = \$120,000

Year	A	B	C
1	50*	40	40
2	50	45	40
3	50	50	50
4	50	55	60
5	50	60	60

* Net cash flows in \$000s.

SELECTED BIBLIOGRAPHY

Anthony, Robert N., and James S. Reece. *Management Accounting Principles*. 3rd ed. Homewood, Ill.: Richard D. Irwin, 1975.

Bierman, H., and S. Smidt. *The Capital Bugeting Decision*. 6th ed. New York: Macmillan, 1984.

Chase, Richard B., and Nicholas J. Aquilano. *Production and Operations Management*. 4th ed. Homewood, Ill.: Richard D. Irwin, 1985.

Grant, Eugene L.; W. Grant Ireson; and Richard R. Leavenworth. *Principles of Engineering Economy*. 6th ed. New York: Ronald Press, 1976.

Horngren, Charles T. *Cost Accounting: A Managerial Emphasis*. 4th ed. Englewood Cliffs, N.J.: Prentice-Hall, 1977.

Weston, J. Fred, and Eugene F. Brigham. *Essentials of Managerial Finance*. 4th ed. Hinsdale, Ill.: Dryden Press, 1979.

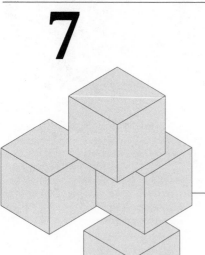

Facilities Layout

After completing this chapter, you should be able to:

1. List some of the different reasons for redesign of layouts.
2. List the primary advantages and limitations of both product and process layouts.
3. Solve simple line balancing problems.
4. Develop simple process layouts.
5. Describe new approaches to production.

Chapter Outline

This is the fourth of a series of chapters on design of operating systems. The previous chapters dealt with location, products, and process and capacity planning; this chapter examines layout design. Layout concerns the configuration of departments, work centers, and equipment, with particular emphasis on movement of work (customers or materials) through the system. Decisions in any one of these four design areas usually have impacts on the others. Thus, both layout and location decisions affect capacity. Conversely, efforts to increase capacity may involve modifications in layout and changes in location. Moreover, any time a new location is established, or products or services are introduced or changed, there are layout implications.

This chapter describes the main types of layout designs along with models used to evaluate design alternatives.

INTRODUCTION

As in other areas of system design, layout decisions are important for three basic reasons: (1) they require substantial investments of both money and effort, (2) they involve long-term commitments, which make mistakes difficult to overcome, and (3) they have a significant impact on the cost and efficiency of short-term operations. In addition, personnel may resist changes to an existing layout because such changes often require them to alter daily routines or to undergo retraining.

The Need for Layout Decisions

The need for layout planning can arise as part of the process of design of new facilities as well as in the redesign of existing facilities. In the latter instance, the most common reasons for redesign of layouts include the following:

1. Inefficient operations (e.g., high cost, bottlenecks).
2. Accidents or safety hazards.
3. Changes in the design of products or services.
4. The introduction of new products or services.
5. Changes in the volume of output or mix of outputs.
6. Changes in methods or equipment.
7. Changes in environmental or other legal requirements.
8. Morale problems (e.g., lack of face-to-face contact).

Naturally, the reasons for layout redesign influence the objectives being sought. For instance, if morale or safety problems exist, the objectives of a new layout plan would include remedying those problems. Even so, the main objectives in the majority of layout analyses relate to minimizing either the cost of materials handling or the movement of customers within a system, along with concerns for productivity and other operating characteristics of the system.

BASIC LAYOUT TYPES

There are three basic types of layouts, and these correspond roughly to the three types of processing systems. *Product layouts* are most conducive to repetitive processing, *process layouts* are used for intermittent processing, and *fixed-position layouts* are used when projects require layouts, although not all projects do. In addition, fixed-position layouts find applications in other situations, as you will soon discover. The characteristics of each layout type will be described in this section, along with the advantages and disadvantages associated with each. Hybrid layouts, which are combinations of these pure types, are also briefly described.

Product Layouts

Product layouts are used to achieve a smooth and rapid flow of large volumes of products or customers through a system. This is made possible by highly standardized products or services that require highly standardized (repetitive) processing operations. A job is divided into a series of standardized tasks, permitting specialization of both labor and equipment. The large volumes handled by these systems usually make it economical to invest substantial sums of money in equipment and in job design. Because only one or a few very similar items are involved, it is feasible to arrange an entire layout to correspond to the technological processing requirements of the product or service involved. For instance, if a portion of a manufacturing operation required the sequence mill–drill–deburr, the appropriate pieces of equipment would be arranged in that same sequence. Moreover, because each item follows the same sequence of operations, it is often possible to utilize fixed-path material-handling equipment such as conveyors to transport items between operations. The resulting arrangement forms a line like the one depicted in Figure 7–1. In manufacturing environments, the lines are referred to as **production lines** or **assembly lines,** depending on the type of activity involved. In nonmanufacturing processes, the term *line* may or may not be

---

FIGURE 7–1

A flow line for production or service

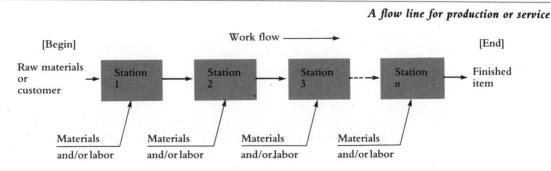

FIGURE 7–2

Cafeteria line

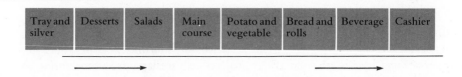

used. For instance, it is common to refer to a cafeteria line as such but not a car wash, although, from a conceptual standpoint, the two are nearly identical. Figure 7–2 illustrates a typical cafeteria serving-line layout. Examples of this type of layout are less plentiful in nonmanufacturing environments because processing requirements usually exhibit too much variability to make standardization feasible. Without high standardization, many of the benefits of continuous processing are lost. When lines are used, certain compromises may be made. For instance, an automatic car wash provides equal treatment to all cars—the same amount of soap, water, and scrubbing—even though cars may differ considerably in cleaning needs. As a result, some very dirty cars do not come out completely clean, and relatively clean cars that go through the system mean some waste of soap, water, and energy.

Product layouts achieve a high degree of both labor and equipment utilization, and that tends to offset the high equipment costs usually associated with this type of layout. Because items move quickly from operation to operation, investment in work-in-process is often minimal. However, operations are so closely tied to each other that the entire system has a high vulnerability to being shut down due to either mechanical failure or high absenteeism. Maintenance procedures are geared to this. Preventive maintenance—periodic inspection and replacement of worn parts or those with high failure rates—is used to reduce the probability of breakdowns during operations. Of course, no amount of preventive activity can completely eliminate failures, so measures designed to provide quick repair must also be taken, which include maintaining an inventory of spare parts and having repair personnel available to quickly restore equipment to normal operation. These procedures are fairly expensive; because of the specialized nature of equipment, problems become more difficult to diagnose and resolve, and spare part inventories can be extensive.

The main advantages of product layouts are:

1. There is a high rate of output.
2. Units costs are low due to high volume; the high cost of specialized equipment is spread over many units.
3. Labor specialization reduces training costs and time and results in a wide span of supervision.
4. Material-handling costs are low per unit, and material handling is simplified because units follow the same sequence of operations.
5. There is a high utilization of labor and equipment.

6. Routing and scheduling are encompassed in the initial design of the system and do not require much attention once the system is in operation.

7. Accounting, purchasing, and inventory control are fairly routine.

The primary disadvantages of product layouts include:

1. The intensive division of labor usually creates dull, repetitive jobs, which do not provide much opportunity for advancement and may lead to morale problems.

2. Poorly skilled workers may exhibit little interest in maintaining equipment or in quality of output.

3. The system is fairly inflexible in response to either changes in the volume of output or changes in product or process design.

4. The system is highly susceptible to shutdowns caused by equipment breakdowns or excessive absenteeism.

5. Preventive maintenance, the capacity for quick repairs, and spare parts inventories are necessary expenses.

6. Incentive plans tied to individual output are impractical since they would tend to cause variations among outputs of individual workers that would adversely affect high utilization of labor and equipment.

Process Layouts

Process layouts are designed to facilitate processing items or providing services that present variations in their processing requirements. The layouts feature departments or other functional groupings in which similar kinds of activities are performed. For example, machine shops usually have separate departments for milling, grinding, drilling, and so on. Items that require those operations are frequently moved in batches to the departments in a sequence dictated by technical considerations. Different products may present quite different processing requirements and sequences of operations. Consequently, variable-path material-handling equipment (forklift trucks, jeeps, tote boxes) is needed to handle the variety of routes and items. The use of general-purpose machines provides the flexibility necessary to handle a wide range of processing requirements. Workers who operate the equipment are usually skilled or semiskilled. Figure 7–3 illustrates the departmental arrangement typical of process layouts.

Process layouts are also common in nonmanufacturing environments. Examples include hospitals, colleges and universities, banks, auto repair shops, airlines, and public libraries. For instance, hospitals have departments or other units that specifically handle surgery, maternity, pediatrics, psychiatric, emergency, and geriatric care. Similarly, universities have separate schools or departments that concentrate on such areas of study as business, engineering, science, and math. Most business organizations have administrative departments such as accounting and payroll.

FIGURE 7–3

A process layout is typified by departmental work centers

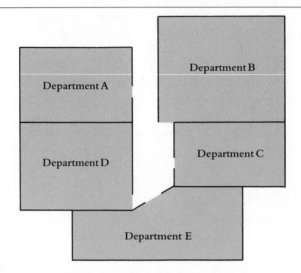

Because process layouts arrange equipment by type rather than according to processing sequence, the system is much less vulnerable to shutdown caused by either mechanical failure or absenteeism. In manufacturing systems especially, idle equipment is usually available to replace machines that are temporarily out of service. Moreover, since items are often processed in lots, there is considerably less interdependence between successive operations than with a product layout. Maintenance costs tend to be lower because the equipment is less specialized than with product layouts, and grouping of machinery permits repair personnel to become somewhat specialized in handling repairs. And machine similarity reduces the necessary investment in spare parts. On the negative side, routing and scheduling must be done on a continual basis in order to accommodate the variety of processing demands typically imposed on these systems. Material handling is inefficient, and unit handling costs are generally much higher than in product layouts. In-process inventories can be substantial due to batch processing. Furthermore, it is not uncommon for such systems to have equipment utilization rates under 50 percent because of routing and scheduling complexities related to the variety of processing demands being handled.

In sum, the advantages of process layouts include:

1. Systems can handle a variety of processing requirements.
2. The system is not particularly vulnerable to equipment failures.
3. General-purpose equipment is often less costly than the specialized equipment used in product layouts and is easier and less costly to maintain.
4. It is possible to use individual incentive systems.

Disadvantages of process layouts include:

1. In-process inventory costs can be high if batch processing is used in manufacturing systems.
2. Routing and scheduling pose continual challenges.
3. Equipment utilization rates are low.
4. Material handling is slow and inefficient and more costly per unit than under product layouts.
5. Job complexities often reduce the span of supervision and result in higher supervisory costs than product layouts do.
6. Special attention for each product or customer (routing, scheduling, machine setups, and so on) and low volumes result in higher unit costs than with product layouts.
7. Accounting, inventory control, and purchasing are much more involved than under product layouts.

Fixed-Position Layouts

In **fixed-position layouts,** the item being worked on remains stationary, and workers, materials, and equipment are moved about as needed. This is in marked contrast to product and process layouts. Almost always, the nature of the product dictates this kind of arrangement: weight, size, bulk, or some other factor makes it undesirable or extremely difficult to attempt to move the product. Fixed-position layouts are used in large construction projects (buildings, power plants, dams), shipbuilding, and production of large aircraft and the rockets used to launch space missions. In those instances, attention is focused on timing of material and equipment deliveries so as not to clog up the work site and to avoid having to relocate materials and equipment around the work site. Lack of storage space can present significant problems, for example, at construction sites in crowded urban locations. Because of the many diverse activities being carried out on large projects and because of the wide range of skills required, special efforts are needed to coordinate the activities, and the span of control can be quite narrow. For these reasons, the administrative burden is often much higher than it would be under either of the other layout types. Material handling may or may not be a factor: in many cases, there is no tangible product involved (e.g., designing a computerized inventory system). When goods and materials are involved, material handling often resembles process-type, variable-path, general-purpose equipment, even though the actual equipment used might differ somewhat depending on the nature of the work. Projects might require use of earth-moving equipment and trucks to haul materials to, from, and around the work site, for example.

Fixed-position layouts are widely used for farming, firefighting, road building, home building, remodeling and repair, and drilling for oil. In each case, there are compelling reasons for bringing workers, materials, and equipment to the "product's" location instead of the other way around.

Combination Layouts

The three basic layout types are ideal models that may be altered to satisfy the needs of a particular situation. In fact, it is not unusual to discover layouts that represent some combination of these pure types. For instance, supermarket layouts are essentially of a process nature, and yet we find most use fixed-path material-handling devices such as roller-type conveyors both in the stockroom and at checkouts and belt-type conveyors at the cash registers. Hospitals also use the basic process arrangement, although frequently patient care involves more of a fixed-position approach, in which nurses, doctors, medicines, and special equipment are brought to the patient. By the same token, faulty parts made in a product layout may require off-line reworking, which involves customized processing. And one frequently observes use of conveyors in both farming and construction activities.

Process layouts and product layouts represent two ends of a continuum from small batches to continuous production. Process layouts are conducive to the production of a wider range of products or services than product layouts, which is desirable from a customer standpoint where customized products are often in demand. However, process layouts tend to be less efficient than product layouts, and they involve higher unit production costs than product layouts and sometimes lower quality. Some manufacturers are attempting to move away from process layouts in an effort to capture some of the benefits of product layouts. Ideally, a system would be flexible and yet be efficient with low unit production costs. Cellular manufacturing, group technology, and flexible manufacturing systems represent efforts to move toward this ideal.

CELLULAR LAYOUTS

Cellular Manufacturing

Cellular manufacturing is a type of layout in which machines are grouped into what is referred to as a *cell*. Groupings are determined by the operations needed to perform work for a set of similar items, or *part families,* that require similar processing. In effect, the cells become miniature versions of product layouts. The cells can consist of one machine, a group of machines with no conveyorized movement of parts between machines (automatic transfer), or a flow line connected by a conveyor. A comparison of a typical functional (process) layout and a cellular manufacturing layout is given in Figure 7–4. Observe that in the cellular layout, machines are arranged to handle all of the operations necessary for a group (family) of similar parts. Thus, all of the parts

FIGURE 7—4

*Comparison of
functional and cellular
manufacturing layouts*

Part
families $\left\{ \begin{array}{l} 1111111111 \\ 2222222222 \\ 3333333333 \\ 4444444444 \end{array} \right.$

Functional layout

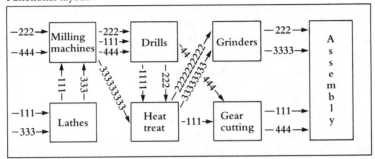

Cellular manufacturing layout

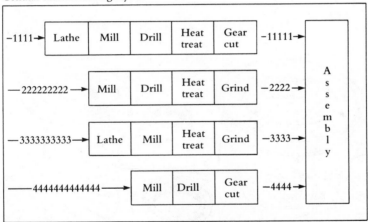

Source: Adapted from D. Fogarty and T. Hoffman, *Production and Inventory Management* (Cincinnati: South-Western Publishing, 1983), p. 472.

follow the same route, although minor variations (e.g., skip an operation) are possible. In contrast, the functional layout involves multiple paths for parts. Moreover, there is little effort or need to identify part families; the distinction in the figure is merely for purposes of comparison.

There are numerous benefits of cellular manufacturing. These relate to the grouping of equipment. They include faster throughput time, less material handling, less work-in-process inventory, and reduced setup time.

Group Technology

For cellular manufacturing to be effective, there must be groups of items that have similar processing characteristics. Moreover, these items must be identified. The grouping process is known as **group technology** and involves identifying items that have similarities in either *design characteristics* or *manufacturing characteristics* and grouping them into part families. Design characteristics include size, shape, and function; manufacturing or processing characteristics involve the type and sequence of operations required. In many cases, design and processing characteristics are correlated, although this is not always the case. Thus, design families may be different from processing families. Figure 7–5 illustrates a group of parts that have similar processing characteristics but different design characteristics.

Once similar items have been identified, items can be classed according to their families, and a coding system can be developed. The coding system facilitates retrieval from a data base for purposes of design and manufacturing. For instance, a designer can readily determine if there is an existing part that is

FIGURE 7–5

A group of parts with similar manufacturing process requirements but different design attributes

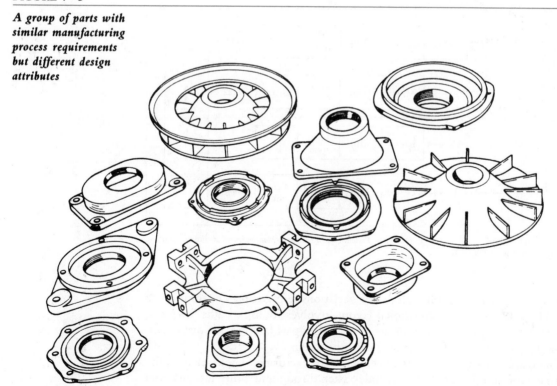

Source: Mikell P. Groover, *Automation, Production Systems, and Computer-Aided Manufacturing* © 1980, p. 540. Reprinted by permission of Prentice-Hall, Inc., Englewood Cliffs, New Jersey.

similar or identical to one that needs to be designed. It may happen that an existing part, with some modification, would be satisfactory. This greatly enhances the productivity of design. Similarly, planning manufacturing for a new part would involve matching it with one of the part families in existence, thereby alleviating much of the burden of specifying processing details.

The conversion to group technology and cellular manufacturing involves a systematic analysis of parts to identify the part families. This often represents a major undertaking; it is a time-consuming job that involves the analysis of a considerable amount of data. Three primary methods for accomplishing this are visual inspection, examination of design and production data, and production flow analysis.

Visual inspection is the least accurate of the three but also the least costly and the simplest to perform. Examining design and production data is more accurate but much more time-consuming; it is perhaps the most commonly used method of analysis. Production flow analysis involves examination of operations sequences and machine routings to uncover similarities. Hence, the analysis has a manufacturing perspective and not a design perspective. Moreover, the operation sequences and routings are taken as givens; in reality the existing procedures may be far from optimal.

Conversion to cellular manufacturing can involve costly realignment of equipment. Consequently, a manager must weigh the benefits of a switch from a process layout to a cellular one against the costs of moving equipment as well as the cost and time needed for grouping parts.

Flexible Manufacturing Systems

As discussed in Chapter 6, flexible manufacturing systems (FMSs) are more fully automated versions of cellular manufacturing: A computer controls the transfer of parts from machine to machine as well as the start of work at each machine. As you might suspect, these systems are quite expensive. However, they enable manufacturers to achieve some of the benefits of product layouts with small batch sizes and much greater flexibility with a system that is capable of operating with little or no human intervention.

LINE BALANCING

Many of the benefits of a product layout relate to the ability to divide required work into a series of elemental tasks (e.g., "assemble parts *C* and *D*") that can be performed quickly and routinely by low-skill workers or by specialized equipment. The durations of these elemental tasks typically range from as little as a few seconds to 15 minutes or more. Most of the times are so brief that it would be impractical to assign only one task to each worker. For one thing, most workers would quickly become bored by the limited job requirements. For another, the number of workers required to complete even a simple product or service would be enormous. Instead, tasks are usually grouped into manageable bundles that are assigned to workstations manned by one or two operators.

The process of deciding how to assign tasks to workstations is referred to as **line balancing.** The goal of line balancing is to obtain task groupings that represent approximately equal time requirements. This minimizes the idle time along the line and results in a high utilization of labor and equipment. Idle time occurs if task times are not equal among workstations because some stations will have the capability to produce at higher rates than others. These "fast" stations will experience periodic waits for the output from slower stations or else be forced into idleness to avoid buildups of work between stations. Unbalanced lines are undesirable both in terms of inefficient utilization of labor and equipment and because they may create morale problems for workers at the slower stations who must work continuously.

Lines that are perfectly balanced will have a smooth flow of work because activities along the line are synchronized to achieve maximum utilization of labor and equipment. The major obstacle in attaining a perfectly balanced line is the inability to obtain task bundles that have the same durations. One reason for this is the fact that it may not be feasible to combine certain activities into the same bundle either because of differences in equipment requirements or because the activities are not compatible (e.g., risk of contamination of painting from sanding). Another reason is that differences among elemental task lengths can not always be overcome by grouping tasks. A third reason for the inability to perfectly balance a line is that a required technological sequence may prohibit otherwise desirable task combinations. For instance, consider a series of three operations that have durations of two minutes, four minutes, and two minutes, as shown in the following diagram. Ideally, the first and third operations could be combined at one workstation and have a total time equal to that of the second operation. However, it may not be possible to combine the first and third operations. For instance, in the case of an automatic car wash, scrubbing and drying operations could not be realistically combined at the same workstation due to the need to rinse cars between these two operations:

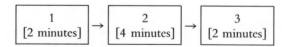

A key aspect of an assembly line is its **cycle time.** This is the amount of time each workstation has to complete its set of tasks before the product moves to the next station. The cycle time also determines the rate of output for the line. For instance, if a line has a cycle time of five minutes, completed units will reach the end of the line at the rate of one every five minutes, or 12 per hour.

We can gain some insight into task groupings and cycle time by considering a simple example.

Suppose that the work required to fabricate a certain product can be divided up into five elemental tasks, with the task times and precedence relationships as shown below.

$$\rightarrow \boxed{0.1 \text{ min.}} \rightarrow \boxed{0.7 \text{ min.}} \rightarrow \boxed{1.0 \text{ min.}} \rightarrow \boxed{0.5 \text{ min.}} \rightarrow \boxed{0.2 \text{ min.}} \rightarrow$$

Two important pieces of information in any listing of elemental task times are the sum of the task times and the length of the longest elemental task. The longest task (one minute in this case) indicates the *minimum* possible cycle time (the time interval between units coming off the line), and the sum of the times (2.5 minutes) indicates the *maximum* cycle time that would make sense. Thus, combining the tasks at a single workstation would require a cycle time of two and one-half minutes. At the other extreme, even by assigning each task to a different workstation, the cycle time could not be less than one minute, since the third task requires that length of time. The maximum and minimum cycle times are important because they can be used to determine upper and lower bounds on a line's output potential. Once the cycle time has been decided on, daily capacity of the line can be found by dividing operating time per day by a line's cycle time:

$$\text{Output capacity} = \frac{OT}{CT} \qquad (7–1)$$

where

OT = Operating time per day
CT = Cycle time

For instance, assume that the line will operate for eight hours per day (480 minutes). With a cycle time of 1.0 minute, output would be:

$$\frac{480 \text{ minutes per day}}{1.0 \text{ minute per unit}} = 480 \text{ units per day}$$

With a cycle time of 2.5 minutes, the output would be:

$$\frac{480 \text{ minutes per day}}{2.5 \text{ minutes per unit}} = 192 \text{ units per day}$$

Assuming that no parallel activities are to be employed (e.g., two lines), the output selected for the line must fall in the range of 192 units per day to 480 units per day.

As a general rule, the cycle time is determined by the desired output. That is, a desired output level is selected, and the cycle time is computed. If the cycle time does not fall between the maximum and minimum bounds, the desired output rate must be revised. The cycle time can be computed using this formula:

$$CT = \frac{OT}{D} \tag{7-2}$$

where D = Desired output rate

For example, suppose that the desired output rate is 480 units. Using Formula 7–2, we can compute the necessary cycle time:

$$\frac{480 \text{ minutes per day}}{480 \text{ units per day}} = 1.0 \text{ minute per unit}$$

The number of workstations that will be needed is a function of both the desired output rate and our ability to combine elemental tasks into workstations. The *theoretical minimum* number of stations necessary to provide a specifed rate of output can be determined as follows:

$$N_{\text{min}} = \frac{D \times \Sigma t}{OT} \tag{7-3}$$

where

N_{min} = Theoretical minimum number of stations
D = Desired output rate
Σt = Sum of task times
OT = Operating time

Suppose the desired rate of output is the maximum of 480 units per day.[1] (This will require a cycle time of 1.0 minute.) The minimum number of stations required to achieve this goal is:

$$N_{\text{min}} = \frac{480 \text{ units per day} \times 2.5 \text{ minutes per unit}}{480 \text{ minutes per day per station}} = 2.5 \text{ stations}$$

Because 2.5 stations is not feasible, it is necessary to *round up* (because 2.5 is the minimum) to three stations. Thus, the actual number of stations used will equal or exceed three, depending on how successfully the tasks can be grouped into work bundles.

---

[1] At first glance, it might seem that the desired output would logically be the maximum possible output. However, you will soon learn why that is not always the best arrangement.

EXAMPLE 1

Combine the five elemental tasks described in the preceding illustration into three workstations. Assign tasks to workstations according to precedence, beginning with the first task. Use a cycle time of 1.0 minute.

Solution

The cycle time of 1.0 minute represents an upper constraint on the sum of task times assigned to any workstation. With this in mind, we assign the first two tasks to the first workstation since their times sum to 0.8 minute. Obviously, the next task must be assigned to a separate workstation because its length equals the cycle time. The remaining two tasks can be assigned to the third workstation, for a station time of 0.7 minute. The resulting assignments are illustrated below.

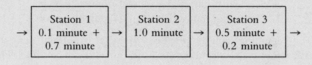

Because the goal of line balancing is to minimize idle time, the percentage of idle time associated with a given assignment of tasks to workstations is of particular interest. The idle time per cycle for each station is:

$$\text{Idle time per station} = \text{Cycle time} - \text{Station time}$$

The idle times for the above assignments and a cycle time of 1.0 minute are shown in the table below:

Station	Station time	Station idle time
1	0.8	0.2
2	1.0	0.0
3	0.7	0.3
		0.5

The percentage of idle time is the ratio of idle time per cycle to total time available per cycle:

$$\text{Percentage of idle time} = \frac{\text{Idle time per cycle}}{N \times CT} = \frac{0.5}{3(1.0)} = .167 \text{ or } 16.7\%$$

Efficiency can also be computed. It equals $1 -$ percentage of idle time. Note that an idle time percentage of zero means the line is perfectly balanced.

The extent to which workstations can be *packed* influences both the number of stations needed and the percentage of idle time.

EXAMPLE 2

Assign the given tasks to workstations in a way that minimizes idle time, and compute the resulting percentage of idle time and the efficiency. (Note that the total task times and the longest task time are the same as in the preceding example.) Assume $D = 480$ units per day.

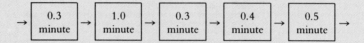

Solution

An output of 480 units per day will require a cycle time of 1.0 minute:

$$CT = \frac{\text{Operating time per day}}{\text{Desired output rate}} = \frac{480 \text{ minutes per day}}{480 \text{ units per day}} = 1.0$$

Assign tasks, beginning with the first task. The first station will consist solely of the first task because the second task's time equals the cycle time. The second station will consist of the second task; the third station will consist of the third and fourth tasks; and a fourth station will be required to handle the last task. These assignments are shown below.

	Station 1		Station 2		Station 3		Station 4	
→	0.3 minute	→	1.0 minute	→	0.3 minute + 0.4 minute	→	0.5 minute	→

The resulting idle times for this assignment are:

Station	Station time	Station idle time
1	0.3	0.7
2	1.0	—
3	0.7	0.3
4	0.5	0.5
		1.5

The percentage of idle time is:

$$\text{Percentage of idle time} = \frac{\text{Idle time per cycle}}{N \times CT} = \frac{1.5}{4(1.0)} = 37.5 \text{ percent}$$

Efficiency is $1 - .375 = .625$, or 62.5%.

Note that the overall efficiency is lower in Example 2 than it was in Example 1 (the percentage of idle time is greater), even though the sum of the task times and the cycle time are identical. The reason for the decrease in efficiency can be attributed to the use of a fourth workstation in the second example. Of course, that station was unavoidable because of the inability to obtain as high a degree of packing of the first three stations as was possible in Example 1.

This brings us back to the question of whether the selected level of output should equal the maximum output possible. The minimum number of workstations needed is a function of the desired output rate:

$$N = \frac{D \times \Sigma t}{OT}$$

Therefore, a lower rate of output may produce a need for fewer stations. Hence, the manager must consider whether the potential savings that could be realized by having fewer workstations would be greater than the decrease in contribution resulting from producing fewer units.

The preceding examples serve to illustrate some of the fundamental concepts of line balancing. Nonetheless, compared to most real-life situations, they are rather simple; the number of branches and tasks involved are often much greater than in these examples. Consequently, the job of line balancing can be a good deal more complex than you might suspect. In fact, in many instances, the number of alternatives for grouping tasks is so great that it would be virtually impossible to conduct an exhaustive review of all possibilities. For this reason, many real-life problems of any magnitude are solved using *heuristic* approaches. The purpose of the heuristic approaches is to reduce the number of alternatives that must be considered, but they do not guarantee an optimal solution.

Some of the heuristic rules used in practice are:

1. Assign tasks to workstations, longest tasks first, and continue until all tasks have been assigned.
2. Assign tasks in order of most number of following tasks.
3. Assign tasks in order of most number of preceding tasks.
4. Assign tasks according to *positional weight,* which is the sum of a task's time and the times of all following tasks.

Unfortunately, none of these rules works all the time, so it is usually necessary to try several rules in the hopes of discovering a good solution to a problem. Although heuristic rules do not guarantee an optimal solution to line balancing problems, they often provide reasonably good solutions with a limited amount of effort. Moreover, they are intuitively appealing: The rules offer rational, step-by-step handling of fairly complex problems.

Computerized approaches to the line balancing problem may incorporate heuristic rules such as those listed above, or they may use dynamic programming.[2]

All tasks have precedence relationships, which govern the sequence in which they must be performed (i.e., certain tasks must be completed before

---

[2] See, for example, M. Held, R.M. Karp, and R. Sharesian, "Assembly-Line Balancing: Dynamic Programming with Precedence Constraints," *Operations Research* 11, no. 3 (May–June 1963).

others can begin). Some clarifying notes on line balancing follow, courtesy of the Operations and Systems Management Department at Indiana University:

LINE BALANCING

In balancing an assembly line, tasks are assigned *one at a time* to the line, starting at the first workstation. At each step, the unassigned tasks are checked to determine which of them are eligible for assignment. Next, the eligible tasks are checked to see which of them will fit in the workstation being loaded. Then a heuristic is used to select one of the tasks that will fit, and the task is assigned. This process is repeated until there are no eligible tasks that will fit. Then we start loading the next workstation. This continues until all tasks are assigned. The objective is to minimize the idle time for the line subject to technological and output constraints.

Technological constraints tell us which elemental tasks are *eligible* to be assigned at a particular position on the line. Technological constraints can result from the precedence or ordering relationships among the tasks. The precedence relationships require that certain tasks must be performed before others (and so, must be assigned to workstations before others). Thus, in a car wash, the rinsing operation must be performed before the drying operation. The drying operation, then, is not eligible for assignment until the rinsing operation is assigned. Technological constraints may also result from two tasks being "in-compatible" (e.g., because of space restrictions or the nature of the operations, they cannot be placed in the same work center). For example, sanding and painting operations would not be assigned to the same work center because of the dust from the sanding operation.

Output constraints, on the other hand, determine the maximum amount of work that can be assigned to each workstation, and this determines whether an eligible task *will fit* at a workstation. The desired output rate determines the cycle time, and the sum of the task times assigned to any workstation must not exceed the cycle time. If a task can be assigned to a workstation without exceeding the cycle time, then the task will fit.

Once we know which tasks are *eligible* and *will fit*, we still need to select the task to be assigned (if there is more than one to choose from). This is where the heuristic rules come in. They help us decide which task to assign from among those that are eligible and will fit.

Just to clarify the terminology a bit, *following tasks* are all tasks that you would encounter by following all paths from the task in question through the precedence diagram. Similarly, *preceding tasks* are all tasks

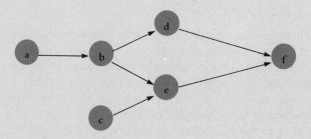

you would encounter by tracing all paths *backward* from the task in question. In the precedence diagram below, tasks B, D, E, and F are followers of task A. Tasks A, B, and C are preceding tasks for E.

The *positional weight* for a task is the sum of the task times for itself and all its following tasks.

None of the heuristics described above *guarantees* the *best* solution, or even a good solution to the line-balancing problem, but they do provide guidelines for developing a solution. It may be useful to apply several different heuristics to the same problem and pick the best (least idle time) solution out of those developed.

It can be helpful in line balancing to work with a **precedence diagram,** which shows the sequence of operations. This diagram can easily be constructed from a list of sequential activities. Example 3 illustrates the use of such a diagram and the use of the heuristic rules for task assignments.

EXAMPLE 3

Using the information contained in the table shown, do each of the following:

1. Draw a precedence diagram.
2. Assuming an eight-hour workday, compute the cycle time needed to obtain an output of 400 units per day.
3. Determine the minimum number of workstations required.
4. Assign tasks to workstations using this rule: Assign tasks according to greatest number of following tasks. In case of a tie, use the tiebreaker of assigning the task with the longest processing time first.

Task	Immediate predecessor	Task time
a	—	0.2
b	a	0.2
c	—	0.8
d	c	0.6
e	b	0.3
f	d,e	1.0
g	f	0.4
h	g	0.3
	$\Sigma t =$	3.8

Solution

1. Drawing a precedence diagram is a relatively straightforward task. Begin with activities with no predecessors. We see from the list that a and c have no immediate predecessors. We build from here.

EXAMPLE 3 *(continued)*

Task b follows a, and
d follows c.

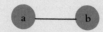

Task e follows b.

Task f follows e and d.

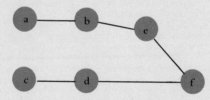

Task g follows f, and h
follows g.

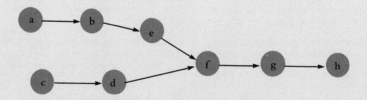

2. $CT = \dfrac{OT}{D} = \dfrac{480 \text{ minutes per day}}{400 \text{ units per day}} = 1.2 \text{ minutes per cycle}$

3. $N = \dfrac{D \times \Sigma t}{OT} = \dfrac{400 \text{ units per day} \times 3.8 \text{ minutes per unit}}{480 \text{ minutes per day per station}}$

   $= 3.17 \text{ stations (round to 4)}$

EXAMPLE 3 *(concluded)*

4. Beginning with station 1, make assignments following this procedure: Determine from the precedence diagram which tasks are eligible for assignment. Then determine which of the eligible tasks will fit the time remaining for the station. Use the tiebreaker if necessary. Once a task has been assigned, remove it from consideration. When a station cannot take any more assignments, go on to the next station. Continue until all tasks have been assigned.

Station	Time remaining	Eligible	Will fit	Assign (task time)	Idle
1	1.2 min.	a,c*	a,c*	a (0.2)	
	1.0	c,b**	c,b**	c (0.8)	
	0.2	b,d	b	b (0.2)	
	0	e,d	None	—	0
2	1.2	e,d	e,d	d (0.6)	
	0.6	e	e	e (0.3)	
	0.3***	f	None	—	0.3
3	1.2	f	f	f (1.0)	
	0.2	g	None	—	0.2
4	1.2	g	g	g (0.4)	
	0.8	h	h	h (0.3)	
	0.5	—	—	—	0.5
					1.0 min.

* Neither a nor c have any predecessors, so both are eligible. Task a was assigned since it has more followers.

** Once a is assigned, b and c are now eligible. Both will fit in the time remaining of 1.0 minute. The tie cannot be broken by the "most followers" rule, so the longer task is assigned.

*** Although f is eligible, this task will not fit, so station 2 is left with 0.3 minute of idle time per 1.2-minute cycle.

These assignments are shown in the following diagram. If you look carefully at this solution, you may discover that it can be improved upon. Thus, this solution is not necessarily optimal. The point is that one should not expect that heuristic solutions will produce optimal solutions; they merely provide a practical way to deal with what can be a highly complex problem that does not lend itself to optimizing techniques.

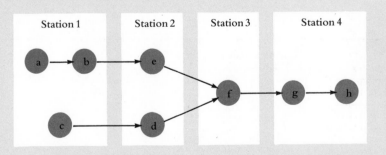

Other Factors

The preceding discussion on line balancing presents a relatively straightforward approach to approximating a balanced line. In practice, the ability to do this usually involves additional considerations, some of which are technical and some of which are not.

Technical considerations include skill requirements of different tasks. If skill requirements of tasks are quite different, it may not be feasible to place the tasks in the same workstation. Similarly, if the tasks themselves are in conflict, such as sanding and painting or use of fire and use of volatile liquids, it may not be feasible to place them in the same workstation, or even in stations that are near to each other.

Although it can be convenient to treat assembly operations as if they occur at the same rate time after time, it is more realistic to assume that whenever humans are involved, variability in task completion times will occur. The reasons for the variations are numerous, including fatigue, boredom, and non-work-related thoughts. Hence, even in a "perfectly balanced line," the actual performance may not reflect a perfect balance. Likewise, absenteeism can affect line balance.

Thus, developing a workable plan for balancing a line requires consideration of other factors besides precedence relationships, such as human factors, equipment and space limitations, and incompatible operations.

DESIGNING PROCESS LAYOUTS

The main issue in design of process layouts concerns the relative positioning of the departments involved. As illustrated in Figure 7–6, a list of departments must be assigned to a list of locations. The problem is to develop a reasonably good layout; some combinations will be more desirable than others. For example, some departments may benefit from adjacent locations, and others should be separated. Painting and sanding departments that are too close to each other could cause painting to be contaminated by particles from the sanding operations. Conversely, two departments that share some of the same equipment would benefit from being close together.

FIGURE 7–6

Work centers must be assigned to locations

Locations		
A	B	C
D	E	F

Work centers to be assigned

1
2
3
4
5
6

Layouts can also be influenced by such external factors as the locations of entrances, loading docks, elevators, windows, and areas of reinforced flooring.

In a few instances, such as in the layouts of supermarkets, gas stations, and fast-food chains, there are sufficient numbers of installations with similar characteristics to justify development of standardized layouts. A good example of standardized layouts is provided by McDonald's hamburger outlets. The use of the same basic pattern in all outlets facilitates construction of new structures and employee training. Food preparation, order taking, and customer service follow the same pattern throughout the chain. Moreover, installation and service of equipment are also standardized. Supermarkets also benefit from standardized layouts, although in a different respect. Customers acquainted with the layout of any store in the chain can readily locate desired items in other stores in the chain. In addition, most supermarkets locate departments such as meat, produce, and bakery around the perimeter of the store and provide wide aisles to permit customers to ponder choices and to achieve customer circulation throughout the store. Bread and milk are often placed away from the entrance in order to expose customers who stop in just to pick up those items to additional merchandise.

The majority of layout problems involve single locations rather than multiple locations, and they present unique combinations of factors that do not lend themselves to a standardized approach. Consequently, these layouts require customized designs.

The major obstacle in finding the most efficient layout of departments is the large number of assignments that are possible. For example, there are over 50,000 different ways that nine departments can be assigned to nine locations if the locations form a single line. Different location configurations (e.g., nine departments in a 3×3 grid) often reduce the number of possibilities, as do any special requirements (e.g., the stamping department may have to be assigned to a location with reinforced flooring). Still, the remaining number of layout possibilities usually is too large to allow each one to be examined, even with computer assistance. Unfortunately, no algorithms exist that can identify the best layout arrangement under all circumstances. Often planners must rely on heuristic rules to guide trial-and-error efforts to obtain a satisfactory solution to each problem.

Measures of Effectiveness

One advantage of process layouts is their ability to satisfy a variety of processing requirements. Customers or materials in these systems require different operations and different sequences of operations, which causes them to follow different paths through the system. Material-oriented systems necessitate the use of variable-path material-handling equipment to move materials from work center to work center, and in customer-oriented systems, people must travel or be transported from work center to work center. In both cases, transportation costs or time can be significant. Because of this factor, one of the major objectives in process layout is to minimize transportation cost, distance, or time. This is usually accomplished by locating departments with relatively high interdepartmental work flows as close together as possible.

Other measures that may be used in choosing among alternative layouts include initial costs in setting up the layout, expected operating costs, the amount of effective capacity created, and the ease with which the system could be modified if the need arose.

In situations that involve efforts to improve an existing layout, costs of relocating any work center must be weighed against the potential benefits of such a move.

Information Requirements

The design of process layouts requires the following information:

1. A list of departments or work centers to be arranged, their approximate dimensions, and the dimensions of the building or buildings that will house the departments.
2. A projection of future work flows between the various work centers.
3. The distance between locations and the cost per unit of distance to move loads between various locations.
4. The amount of money to be invested in the layout.
5. A list of any special considerations (e.g., heavy equipment will require reinforced flooring, and sanding and painting operations should be separated to avoid contamination).

An ideal situation would be to first develop a layout and then design the physical structure around that layout, which would permit maximum flexibility in design. In fact, this procedure is commonly followed when new facilities are being constructed. Nonetheless, many layouts must be developed in situations where there is an existing structure. In those instances, floor space, the

FIGURE 7–7

Buildings can have a variety of shapes

How They Do It...

Kawasaki

Motorcycle assembly line at the
Kawasaki plant in
Lincoln, Nebraska.

*Photos courtesy of Kawasaki Motors
Manufacturing Corp., U.S.A.*

Wheels are manufactured
at the same plant.

A similar assembly line at the plant
is set up for all-terrain vehicles.

CHRYSLER

The tilt line at Chrysler's Newark plant permits more comfortable worker access.

Material-handling robot. One of 219 robots in service, it moves a 2,000-pound car frame easily.

Photos courtesy of Chrysler Corporation

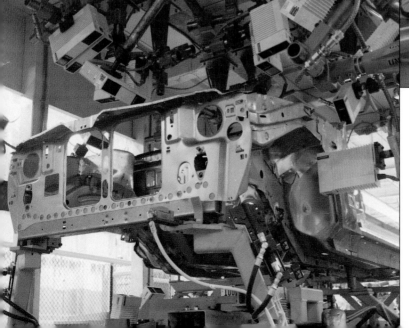

Chrysler also employs an optical gauging system using lasers to check quality.

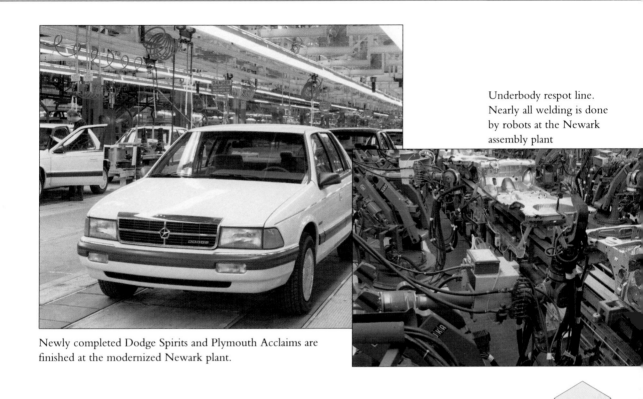

Underbody respot line. Nearly all welding is done by robots at the Newark assembly plant

Newly completed Dodge Spirits and Plymouth Acclaims are finished at the modernized Newark plant.

PORSCHE

Each Porsche is assembled only after being ordered, providing "customized" production.
Courtesy of Porsche Cars North America, Inc.

HEWLETT-PACKARD

Employees assemble computers using just-in-time (JIT) procedures to reduce costs and increase productivity.
Photos courtesy of Hewlett-Packard Company

H-P personal computers provide many test instrumentation functions to monitor production processes such as wave soldering

H-P Industrial Touch display terminal has tiltable mounting base for operator efficiency and comfort.

Quality control of H-P manufacturing requires careful loading and inspection of its printed circuit boards.

Terminals in an "aging area" are placed in a self-test mode to reach operating temperatures prior to final display adjustments to weed out any infant failures.

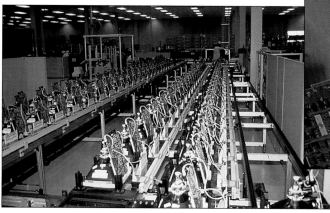

XEROX

Human / robot cooperation in assembling the 10-90 parts.

Photos courtesy of Xerox Corporation

An automated storage-handling shuttle car at the Xerox facility in Webster, New York.

ALLEN – BRADLEY
CIM AT ALLEN – BRADLEY

In the control room at the Allen-Bradley Milwaukee plant, production can be monitored with color graphics computers.

Photos courtesy of Allen-Bradley

The "world contactor"
assembly line at
Allen-Bradley

BETHELEHEM STEEL

At Bethelehem Steel,
continuous casting can
produce 2.9 million tons of
steel slabs a year.
*Courtesy of Bethelehem Steel
Corporation*

Painted mower decks with "kits" of yellow parts at the John Deere Horicon Works in Wisconsin.

Photos courtesy of John Deere Horicon Works

Homogenized mower deck subassembly line at the Horicon Works.

Hardware delivery cart with dedicated, "triggered" tote pans.

Engines are unpacked, subassembled, and loaded directly onto the assembly vehicle.

From subassembly line, the mower deck is loaded directly onto the assembly vehicle.

APPLE

The Macintosh assembly line in Fremont, California
Photos courtesy of Apple Computer, Inc.

Completed Macintosh computers ready for distribution

LINCOLN ELECTRIC

A multiple-head machining center at the Lincoln Electric manufacturing facility.
Photos courtesy of The Lincoln Electric Company

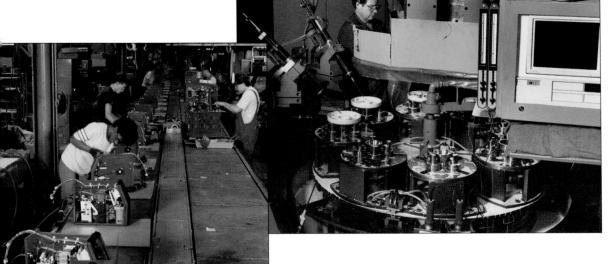

An assembly line at the Lincoln Electric facility in Cleveland, Ohio.

CREDO

The automated warehouse at Credo Company in Woodburn, Oregon.
Courtesy of The Credo Company

SONY

Quality control inspection at Sony.

Assembling televisions at the Sony San Diego plant.
Photos courtesy of Sony Corporation of America

A quality check of a new Sony color television monitor.

ROBOTICS

Robots welding, painting, and assembling at the General Motors Canadian group plant.

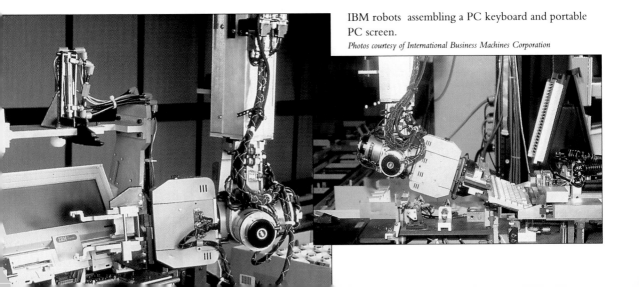

IBM robots assembling a PC keyboard and portable PC screen.

Photos courtesy of International Business Machines Corporation

dimensions of the building, location of entrances and elevators, and other similar factors must be carefully weighed in designing the layout. Some of the building shapes resulting from layout development are illustrated in Figure 7–7. Muliple-level structures pose special problems for layout planners.

Minimizing Transportation Costs or Distances

The most common goals in designing process layouts relate to minimization of transportation costs or distances traveled. In such cases, it can be very helpful to summarize the necessary data in *from-to charts* like those illustrated in Tables 7–1 and 7–2. Table 7–1 indicates the distance between each of the locations, and Table 7–2 indicates actual or projected work flows between each pair. For instance, the distance chart reveals that a trip from location A to location B will involve a distance of 20 meters. (Distances are often measured between department centers.) Oddly enough, the length of a trip between location A and B may differ depending on the *direction* of the trip, due to one-way routes, escalators, or other factors. To simplify the discussion, we shall assume a constant distance between any two locations regardless of direction. However, it would not be realistic to assume that interdepartmental work flows are equal; there is no reason to suspect that department 1 will send as much work to department 2 as department 2 sends to 1. For example, several departments may send goods to packaging, but packaging may send only to the shipping department.

TABLE 7–1

Distance between locations (meters)

From \ To		Location A	B	C
A		—	20	40
B		20	—	30
C		40	30	—

TABLE 7–2

Interdepartmental work flow (loads per day)

From \ To		Department 1	2	3
1		—	10	80
2		20	—	30
3		90	70	—

Transportation costs can also be summarized in from-to charts, but to avoid the added complexity that would entail, we shall assume that costs are a direct, linear function of distance.

Example 4

Assign the three departments shown in Table 7–2 to locations A, B, and C, which are separated by the distances shown in Table 7–1, in such a way that transportation cost is minimized. Use this heuristic: Assign departments with the greatest interdepartmental work flows first.

Solution

Ranking departments according to highest work flows and locations according to highest interlocation distances helps in making assignments. If interlocation distances are independent of direction of flow, work flows between departments can be summed to achieve a clearer picture of the need for closeness. Thus:

Trip	Distance (meters)	Department pair	Work flow	
A–B	20	3–1	90	} 170
B–A	20	1–3	80	
B–C	30	3–2	70	} 100
C–B	30	2–3	30	
A–C	40	2–1	20	} 30
C–A	40	1–2	10	

From these listings, we can see that departments 1 and 3 have the highest interdepartmental work flows and that locations A and B are the closest. Thus, it would seem reasonable to consider assigning 1 and 3 to locations A and B, although it is not yet obvious which department should be assigned to which location. Further inspection of the work flow list reveals that 2 and 3 have higher work flows than 1 and 2, so 2 and 3 should probably be located more closely than 1 and 2. Hence, it would seem reasonable to place 3 between 1 and 2, or at least centralize that department with respect to the other two. The resulting assignments might appear as illustrated in Figure 7–8.

Figure 7–8

Interdepartmental work flows for assigned departments

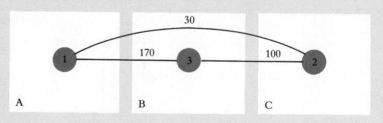

EXAMPLE 4 *(concluded)*

Note that work flows between departments in the diagram are the sum of the flow each way (e.g., the 170 between 1 and 3 is the combined flow of 90 loads from 3 to 1 and 80 loads from 1 to 3).

If we assume that the cost per meter to move any load is $1, we can compute the total daily transportation cost for this assignment by multiplying each department's number of loads by the trip distance and summing those quantities:

Department	Number of loads to:	Location	Distance to:	Loads × Distance
1	2: 10	A	C: 40	10 × 40 = 400
	3: 80		B: 20	80 × 20 = 1,600
2	1: 20	C	A: 40	20 × 40 = 800
	3: 30		B: 30	30 × 30 = 900
3	1: 90	B	A: 20	90 × 20 = 1,800
	2: 70		C: 30	70 × 30 = 2,100
				7,600

At $1 per load-meter, the cost for this plan would be $7,600 per day. Even though it might appear that this arrangement yields the lowest transportation cost, we cannot be absolutely positive of that without actually computing the total cost for every alternative and comparing it to this one. Although we could do so in this case, where the number of alternatives is quite small (i.e., there are 3! = 6 possible arrangements), in problems with more departments, the number is likely to be too large to even consider examining every alternative. Instead, we must rely on the choice of reasonable heuristic rules such as those demonstrated above to guide us to a solution that will be satisfactory, if not optimal.

Closeness Ratings

Even though the preceding approach is widely used, it suffers from the limitation of being able to focus on only one objective, and many situations involve multiple criteria. Richard Muther developed a more general approach to the problem, which allows for subjective input from analysts or managers to indicate the relative importance of each combination of department pairs.[3] That information is then summarized in a grid like the one shown in Figure 7–9. The grid is read in the same way as the mileage chart on a road map, except that letters rather than distances appear at the intersections. The letters represent the importance of closeness for each department pair, with A being the most important and X being an undesirable pairing. Thus, in the grid we can see that it is "absolutely necessary" to locate 1 and 2 close to each other because there is an A at the intersection of those departments on the grid. On the other hand, we also can see that 1 and 4 should not be close together

---

[3] R. Muther, *Systematic Layout Planning* (Boston: Industrial Education Institute, 1961).

FIGURE 7—9

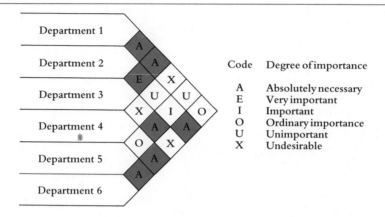

Code	Degree of importance
A	Absolutely necessary
E	Very important
I	Important
O	Ordinary importance
U	Unimportant
X	Undesirable

because their intersection has an X. In practice, the letters on the grid are often accompanied by numbers that indicate the reason for each assignment; they are omitted here to simplify the illustration. Muther suggests the following list:

1. Use same equipment or facilities.
2. Share the same personnel or records.
3. Sequence of work flow.
4. Ease of communication.
5. Unsafe or unpleasant conditions.
6. Similar work performed.

As with the previous examples, no optimizing algorithm exists, so trial-and-error alternatives must be developed and compared using heuristic rules.

EXAMPLE 5

Assign the six departments in Figure 7–9 to a 2 × 3 set of locations using the heuristic rule: Assign critical departments first.

Solution

Critical pairs of departments are those with A or X ratings. We can prepare a list of those by referring to the grid:

As	*Xs*
1–2	1–4
1–3	3–6
2–6	3–4
3–5	
4–6	
5–6	

EXAMPLE 5 *(concluded)*

Next, form a cluster of A links, beginning with the department that appears most frequently in the A list (in this case, 6). For instance:

Take the remaining As in order, and add them on to this main cluster where possible, rearranging the cluster as necessary. Form separate clusters for departments that do not link with the main cluster. In this case, they all link with the main cluster:

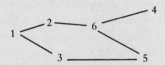

Next, graphically portray the Xs:

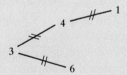

Observe that, as it stands, the cluster of As also satisfies the X separations, and it is a fairly simple exercise to fit the cluster into a 2 × 3 arrangement:

1	2	6
3	5	4

It is interesting to note that the lower-level ratings have also been satisfied with this arrangement, even though no attempt was made to explicitly consider these E and I ratings. Naturally, not every problem will yield the same results, so it may be necessary to do some additional juggling to see if improvements can be made, keeping in mind that the A and X assignments deserve the greatest consideration.

Note that departments are considered close not only when they touch side to side, but also if they touch corner to corner.

The value of this rating approach lies in the fact that it permits the use of multiple objectives and subjective inputs. Its limitations relate to the use of subjective inputs in general: they are imprecise and unreliable.

Computer Analysis

The size and complexity of process layout problems led to the development of a number of computerized packages. Three of the most well-known packages are ALDEP, CORELAP, and CRAFT.

ALDEP (automated layout design program) and CORELAP (computerized relationship layout planning) both use preferences ratings (A-E-I-O-U-X format) and either building or space requirements. ALDEP processing involves an initial random selection of a department and location and then a search of remaining departments' closeness ratings with the chosen department to assign locations. That procedure is continued until all departments have been assigned. The completed layout is evaluated and scored according to how well the preferences have been satisfied. The program is rerun a number of times, and the best layout is identified. CORELAP processes location assignments using the preference ratings to order choice of departments. Hence, the program begins with a department pair that has an A rating, then another A pair, and so on until all A relationships have been assigned. Next, the E relationship pairs are assigned, and so on down the line until all departments have been assigned to locations.

CRAFT (computerized relative allocation of facilities technique) seeks to minimize material flow cost. The program requires information on material flow rates between departments, unit-distance transportation costs, and an initial layout. The program exchanges department pairs until no further improvement can be achieved. The output is a printout of a rectangular layout that may or may not be optimal.

The obvious advantage of computerized analyses of layout problems is the ability to handle large problems and to consider many different layout alternatives. Even so, in most instances, the results of computer analysis require additional manual adjustments before they can be used. In some cases, this is due to irregularly shaped layouts produced by the program, and in others there is the need to check the logic of certain assignments. In the case of the CRAFT program, where the analyst must submit an initial feasible layout, different initial layouts will sometimes lead to different final solutions, so the experience and judgment of the analyst in preparing the initial layout can be an important factor.

Other computer programs exist to handle layout assignments, and it is highly likely that additional packages will be developed in the future. Although current programs cannot guarantee optimal solutions to problems, it is impossible to predict what course new program developments will take. For the present, it appears that knowledge and experience are valuable resources for dealing with process layout problems.

SUMMARY

Layout decisions are an important aspect of the design of productive systems, affecting operating costs and efficiency. Layout decisions are related to decisions involving location, products or services, and capacity.

A major determinant of layout design is the type of processing required of a system. The three basic types are continuous, intermittent, and project. Continuous processing is characterized by a high volume of one or a few similar products or services. Intermittent processing provides the processing capability needed to deal with a broader range of products or services than continuous processing allows. Projects are used to plan and coordinate complex jobs with relatively brief life spans. Product layouts are typically used for continuous processing, process layouts for intermittent processing, and fixed-position layouts for projects, although some projects do not require layouts. Product layouts are geared to high-volume output of standardized items. Workers and equipment are arranged according to the technological sequence required by the product or service involved. Emphasis in design is on work flow through the system. Very often, specialized processing and handling equipment is used. Although costly, such equipment contributes to rapid processing, and the resulting high volume of output means cost per unit is relatively low. Product layouts are highly vulnerable to breakdowns, and preventive maintenance is often used to reduce the occurrence of breakdowns.

Process layouts involve grouping like activities into departments or other work centers. Such systems can handle a wide range of processing requirements and are less susceptible to breakdowns. However, the variety of processing requirements necessitates continual routing and scheduling and the use of variable-path material-handling equipment. Also, the rate of output of such systems is generally much lower than that of product layouts. Fixed-position layouts are used when size, fragility, cost, or other factors makes it undesirable or impractical to move a product through a system. Instead, workers, equipment, and materials are brought to the product.

The main design efforts in product layout development focus on dividing up the work required to produce a product or service into a series of tasks that are as nearly equal as possible, in an effort to achieve a high degree of utilization of labor and equipment. In process layout, design efforts often focus on the relative positioning of department to minimize transportation costs or to meet other requirements concerning nearness of certain department pairs.

Many layout problems possess such a large number of possible alternatives that it is virtually impossible to examine each one. Instead, heuristic rules are used to guide discovery of alternatives. The solutions thus obtained are usually satisfactory although not necessarily optimal. Computer packages are available to reduce the effort required to obtain solutions to layout problems. For the most part, these too rely on heuristic methods.

KEY TERMS

assembly lines, 349
cellular manufacturing, 354
cycle time, 358
fixed-position layouts, 353
group technology, 356

line balancing, 358
precedence diagrams, 365
process layouts, 351
product layouts, 349
production lines, 349

SOLVED PROBLEMS

1. The tasks shown in the following precedence diagram are to be assigned to workstations with the intent of minimizing idle time. Management has designed an output rate of 275 units per day. Assume 440 minutes are available per day.
   a. Determine the appropriate cycle time.
   b. What is the minimum number of stations possible?
   c. Assign tasks using the "positional weight" rule: Assign tasks with highest following times (including a task's own time) first. Break ties using greatest number of following tasks.

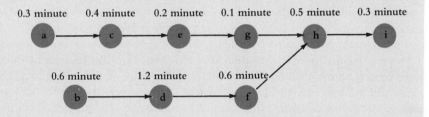

Solution

a. $CT = \dfrac{\text{Operating time}}{\text{Desired output}} = \dfrac{440 \text{ minutes per day}}{275 \text{ units per day}} = 1.6 \text{ minutes}$

b. $N = \dfrac{\text{Desired output} \times \Sigma t}{\text{Operating time}} = \dfrac{275 \text{ per day} \times 4.2}{440 \text{ minutes per day}} = 2.6 \text{ (round to 3)}$

c.

Station	Assigned Task	Time remaining	Time	Station Time Remaining	Feasible next task
1	b	3.2	0.6	1.0	a
	a	1.8	0.3	0.7	c
	c	1.5	0.4	0.3	None
2	d	2.6	1.2	0.4	e
	e	1.1	0.2	0.1	g
	g	0.9	0.1	0.0	None
3	f	1.4	0.6	1.0	h
	h	0.8	0.5	0.5	i
	i	0.3	0.3	0.2	None

The resulting assignments are shown below.

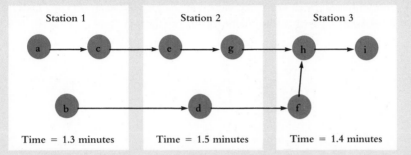

(Note that the time needed to produce 275 units will be 275 × 1.5 minutes = 412.5 minutes. With 440 minutes per day available, this leaves 27.5 minutes of "slack."

2. Assign nine departments to locations in 3 × 3 grid so that the closeness ratings in the following matrix are satisfied. (The unimportant and ordinary-importance pair ratings have been omitted to simplify the example.) The location of department 4 must be in the upper right-hand corner of the grid to satisfy a town ordinance.

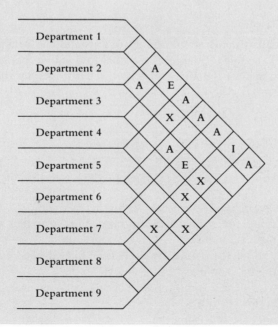

Solution

Note that department 1 has many A ratings, making it a strong candidate for the center position in the grid. We can form a cluster of departments that should be close together:

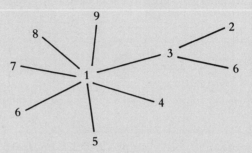

Next, we can identify departmental pairings that should be avoided:

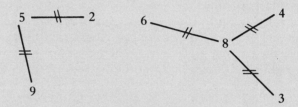

These departments should be spaced around the perimeter of the grid. After a bit of juggling, the final grid shown below emerged. Check it against the rating matrix to see if it satisfies the ratings.

2	3	4
9	1	6
8	7	5

3. For the set of tasks given below, do the following:
   a. Develop the precedence diagram. This describes the technological constraints.
   b. Determine the maximum cycle time for a desired output of 500 units in a 7-hour day.
   c. Determine the minimum number of work stations for output of 500 units per day.
   d. Balance the line using the *largest positional weight* heuristic. Break ties with the *most following tasks* heuristic.

e. Calculate the percentage idle time for the line.

Task	Task time	Immediate predecessors
A	45 sec.	—
B	11	A
C	9	B
D	50	—
E	26	D
F	11	E
G	12	C
H	10	C
I	9	F, G, H
J	10	I
	193 sec.	

Solution

a.

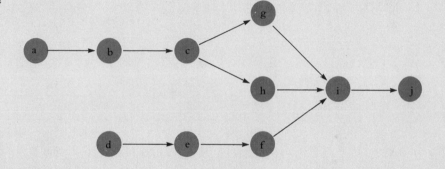

b. $\quad CT = \dfrac{OT}{D} = \dfrac{7(60)}{500} = .84$ minutes $= 50.4$ seconds

c. $\quad N = \dfrac{(D)(\Sigma t)}{OT} = \dfrac{(500)(193)}{(420)(60)} = 3.83$ or 4 stations

d.

Task	Followers	Positional Weight
A	B, C, G, H, I, J	106
B	C, G, H, I, J	61
C	G, H, I, J	50
D	E, F, I, J	106
E	F, I, J	56
F	I, J	30
G	I, J	31
H	I, J	29
I	J	19
J	—	10

Worksheet

Station	Time remaining	Eligible	Will fit	Assign	Idle
I	50.4	A, D	A, D	A (tie)	
	5.4	B, D	—	—	5.4
II	50.4	B, D	B, D	D	
	.4	B, E	—	—	.4
III	50.4	B, E	B, E	B	
	39.4	C, E	C, E	E	
	13.4	C, F	C, F	C	
	4.4	F, G, H	—	—	4.4
IV	50.4	F, G, H	F, G, H	G	
	38.4	F, H	F, H	F	
	27.4	H	H	H	
	17.4	I	I	I	
	8.4	J	—	—	8.4
V	50.4	J	J	J	
	40.4	—	—	—	40.4
					59.0

I	II	III	IV	V
A	D	B, E, C	G, F, H, I	J

e. $\dfrac{\text{Percentage of}}{\text{idle time}} = \dfrac{\text{Total idle time}}{(\text{Number of stations})(\text{CT})} = \dfrac{59.0}{5(50.4)} = .236 \text{ or } 23.6\%$

DISCUSSION AND REVIEW QUESTIONS

1. List some common reasons for redesign of layouts.

2. Briefly describe each of the three basic layout types.

3. What are the main advantages of a product layout? The main disadvantages?

4. What are the main advantages of a process layout? The main disadvantages?

5. What is the goal of line balancing? What happens if a line is unbalanced?

6. Why are routing and scheduling continual problems in a process layout?

7. Compare equipment maintenance strategies in produce and process layouts.

8. Briefly outline the impact that job sequence has on each of the layout types.

9. The City Transportation Planning Committee must make a decision on whether to begin a long-term project to build a subway system or to upgrade bus service.

Since you are an expert in fixed-path and variable-path material-handling equipment, your counsel has been sought on this matter. How would you compare the advantages and limitations of subway versus bus?

10. Identify the fixed-path and variable-path material-handling equipment commonly found in supermarkets.

11. What are heuristic approaches, and why are they used in designing layouts?

12. Why are product layouts atypical in non-manufacturing environments?

13. According to a recent study by the Alliance of American Insurers, it would cost more than three times the original purchase price in parts and labor to replace a totally wrecked Chevrolet. Explain some of the reasons for this large discrepancy in terms of the processes used to assemble the original car versus those required to reconstruct the wrecked car.

14. What are some of the ways that layout can help or hinder productivity?

15. What is cellular manufacturing? What are its main benefits and limitations?

16. What is group technology?

17. What is a flexible manufacturing system?

PROBLEMS

1. An assembly line with 17 tasks is to be balanced. The longest task is 2.4 minutes, and the sum of task times is 18 minutes. The line will operate for 450 minutes per day.
   a. Determine the minimum and maximum cycle times.
   b. What range of output is theorectically possible for the line?
   c. What is the minimum number of stations needed if the maximum output rate is to be sought?
   d. What cycle time will provide an output rate of 125 units per day?
   e. What output potential will result if the cycle time is (1) 9 minutes? (2) 15 minutes?

2. A large manufacturer of plastic saddles is planning to add a new line of multicolored saddles, and you have been asked to balance the process, given the following task times and precedence relationships. Assume that cycle time is to be the minimum length possible.

Task	Length (minutes)	Immediate predecessor
a	0.2	—
b	0.4	a
c	0.3	—
d	1.3	b,c
e	0.1	—
f	0.8	e
g	0.3	d,f
h	1.2	g

Do each of the following:
   a. Draw the precedence diagram.
   b. Assign tasks to stations in order of greatest number of following tasks.
   c. Determine the percentage of idle time.
   d. Compute the rate of output that could be expected for this line assuming a 420-minute working day.

3. In the previous problem:
   a. What is the shortest cycle time that will permit use of only two workstations? Is this cycle time feasible? Identify the tasks you would assign to each station.

b. Determine the percentage of idle time that would result if two stations were to be used.

c. What would the daily output be under this arrangement?

d. Determine the output rate that would be associated with the maximum cycle time.

4. As part of a major plant renovation project, the industrial engineering department has been asked to balance a revised assembly operation to achieve an output of 480 units per eight-hour day. Task times and precedence relationships are as follows:

Task	Duration (minutes)	Follows task
a	0.1	—
b	0.2	a
c	0.1	b
d	0.2	—
e	0.6	d
f	0.6	c
g	0.5	e,f

Do each of the following:

a. Draw the precedence diagram.

b. Determine the maximum cycle time.

c. Determine the minimum number of stations needed.

d. Assign tasks to stations on the basis of greatest number of following tasks; use longest processing time as a tiebreaker. If ties still exist, assume indifference in choice.

e. Compute the percentage of idle time for the assignment in part *d.*

f. Assign tasks to workstations in order of greatest number of preceding tasks, using the same tiebreaker as in *d.*

g. Compute the percentage of idle time for the assignment in part *f.*

5. Twelve tasks, with times and precedence requirements as shown in the following table, are to be assigned to workstations using a cycle time of 1.5 minutes. Three heuristic rules will be tried: (1) greatest positional weight, (2) greatest number of following tasks, and (3) longest task first.

In each case, the tiebreaker will be shortest task time.

Task	Length (minutes)	Follows
a	0.1	—
b	0.2	a
c	0.9	b
d	0.6	c
e	0.1	—
f	0.2	d,e
g	0.4	f
h	0.1	g
i	0.2	h
j	0.7	i
k	0.3	j
l	0.2	k

a. Draw the precedence diagram for this line.

b. Assign tasks to stations under each of the three rules.

c. Compute the percentage of idle time for each rule.

6. Arrange six departments into a 2 × 3 grid so that these conditions are satisfied: 1 close to 2, 5 close to 6, 2 close to 5, and 3 not close to 1.

7. Using the information given in the preceding problem, develop a Muther-type grid using the letters A, O, and X. Assume any pair combinations not mentioned have an O rating.

8. Using the information in the following grid, determine if the department locations shown are appropriate. If they are not, modify the assignments so that the conditions are satisfied.

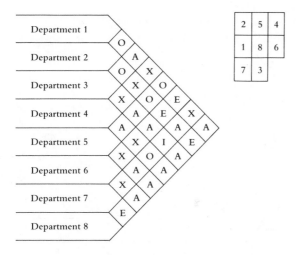

9. Arrange the eight deparments shown in the accompanying Muther grid into a 2 × 4 format. Note: Department 1 must be in the location shown.

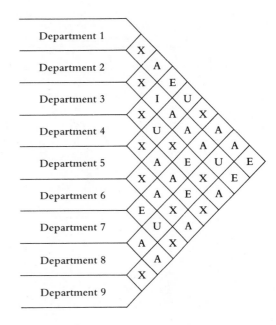

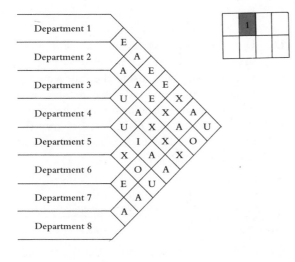

10. Arrange the departments so they satisfy the conditions shown in the following rating grid into a 3 × 3 format. Place department 5 in the lower left corner of the 3 × 3 grid.

11. Assign six work centers to locations A–F, given the following information, so that the total distance traveled is minimized. Assume work center 6 must be in location A. Compute the total cost of your plan if the transportation cost is $2 per load per foot. Assume the reverse distances are equal (e.g., B to A = 50 feet = A to B).

From	To	A	B	C	D	E	F
			Distance between locations (feet)				
A		—	50	100	50	80	130
B			—	50	90	40	70
C				—	140	60	50
D					—	50	120
E						—	50
F							—

Number of trips per day between centers

From \ To	1	2	3	4	5	6
1	—	90	25	23	11	18
2	35	—	8	5	10	16
3	37	2	—	1	0	7
4	41	12	1	—	4	0
5	14	16	0	9	—	3
6	32	38	13	2	2	—

Distances (meters)

From \ To	A	B	C	D	E	F	G	H
A	—	40	40	60	120	80	100	110
B		—	60	40	60	140	120	130
C			—	45	85	40	70	90
D				—	40	50	40	45
E					—	90	50	40
F						—	40	60
G							—	40
H								—

A	B	C
D	E	F

Loads per day

From \ To	1	2	3	4	5	6	7	8
1	—	10	5	90	365	135	125	0
2	0	—	140	10	0	35	0	120
3	0	220	—	110	10	0	0	200
4	0	110	240	—	10	0	0	170
5	5	40	100	180	—	10	40	10
6	0	80	40	70	0	—	10	20
7	0	45	20	50	0	40	—	20
8	0	0	0	20	0	0	0	—

12. Eight work centers must be arranged in an L-shaped building. The locations of centers 1 and 3 are designated as shown in the accompanying diagram. Assuming transportation costs are $1 per load per meter, develop a suitable layout that minimizes transportation costs using the given information. Compute the total cost. (Assume the reverse distances are the same.)

A 1	B	
C	D	E 3
F	G	H

13. Develop a process layout that will minimize the total distance traveled by patients at a medical clinic, using the following information on projected departmental visits by patients and distance between locations. Assume a distance of 35 feet between the reception area and each potential location. Use the format shown.

Distance between locations (feet)

From \ To	A	B	C	D	E	F
A	—	40	80	100	120	160
B		—	40	60	80	120
C			—	20	40	80
D				—	20	40
E					—	40
F						—

Trips between departments (per day)							
From \ To	1	2	3	4	5	6	Reception
Reception	10	10	200	20	0	100	—
1	—	0	0	80	20	40	10
2	0	—	0	0	0	20	40
3	40	0	—	10	190	10	10
4	30	50	0	—	10	70	0
5	60	40	60	30	—	20	10
6	10	100	0	20	0	—	30

Number of trips per day between departments										
From \ To	1	2	3	4	5	6	7	8	9	10
1	—	40	1	20	20	4	0	2	6	5
2	0	—	2	15	25	10	2	12	13	6
3	50	35	—	10	13	4	0	4	7	1
4	6	1	8	—	0	14	10	20	22	11
5	3	2	7	35	—	22	5	9	19	10
6	5	5	10	0	2	—	15	0	1	20
7	20	16	50	4	9	2	—	1	3	0
8	10	6	14	2	4	44	13	—	1	25
9	5	5	18	1	2	40	30	42	—	32
10	30	30	35	20	15	5	40	10	15	—

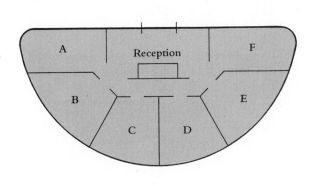

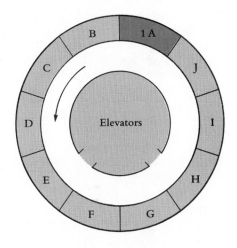

14. Ten labs will be assigned to the circular layout shown. Recalling a similar layout's congestion in the halls, the new lab manager has requested an assignment that will minimize traffic between offices. In addition, movement in the halls is restricted to a counterclockwise route. Develop a suitable layout using the following information.

15. Rebalance the assembly line in Solved Problem 3. This time, use the *longest operation time* heuristic. Break ties with the *most following tasks* heuristic. What is the percent idle time for your line?

16. Repeat Problem 15, but with this additional constraint: Task B and Task F may not be performed at the same workstation. How does this affect the mix of tasks at each station? The idle time percentage for the line?

SELECTED BIBLIOGRAPHY

Fogarty, Donald W., and Thomas R. Hoffman. *Production and Inventory Management*. Cincinnati: South-Western Publishing, 1983.

Foulkes, Fred K., and J. L. Hirsch. "People Make Robots Work." *Harvard Business Review*, January–February 1984, p. 94.

Francis, R. L., and J. A. White. *Facility Layout and Location: An Analytical Approach*. Englewood Cliffs, N.J.: Prentice-Hall, 1974.

Freeman, D. R., and J. V. Jucker. "The Line Balancing Problem." *Journal of Industrial Engineering* 18 (1967), p. 361.

Gerwin, D. "Do's and Don'ts of Computerized Manufacturing." *Harvard Business Review*, March–April 1982, pp. 107–16.

Gold, B. "CAM Sets New Rules for Production." *Harvard Business Review*, November–December 1982, pp. 88–94.

Groover, Mikell P. *Automation, Production Systems, and Computer-Aided Manufacturing*. Englewood Cliffs, N.J.: Prentice-Hall, 1980.

Helgeson, W. B., and D. P. Bernie. "Assembly Line Balancing Using the Ranked Positional Weight Technique." *Journal of Industrial Engineering* 12, no. 6 (November–December 1961).

Hendrick, T. E., and F. G. Moore. *Production/Operations Management*. 9th ed. Homewood, Ill.: Richard D. Irwin, 1985.

Hicks, P. E., and T. E. Cowan. "CRAFT-M for Layout Rearrangement." *Industrial Engineering* 8(May 1976), pp. 30–35.

Ignall, E. J. "A Review of Assembly Line Balancing." *Journal of Industrial Engineering* 16 (1965).

Kilbridge, M. D., and L. Wester. "A Heuristic Method of Assembly Line Balancing." *Journal of Industrial Engineering* 12 (July–August 1961).

Lee, R. C., and J. M. Moore. "CORELAP-Computerized Relationship Layout Planning." *Journal of Industrial Engineering* 18 (March 1967), pp. 195–200.

Mastor, A. A. "An Experimental Investigation and Comparative Evaluation of Production Line Balancing Techniques." *Management Science* 16, no. 11 (July 1970), pp. 728–46.

Moore, J. M. *Plant Layout and Design*. New York: Macmillan, 1962.

Muther, R., and K. McPherson. "Four Approaches to Computerized Layout Planning." *Industrial Engineering* 2 (1970), pp. 39–42.

Reed, R. *Plant Location, Layout and Maintenance*. Homewood, Ill.: Richard D. Irwin, 1967.

READING

THE TECHNOCRATIC HAMBURGER

Nowhere in the entire service sector are the possibilities of the manufacturing mode of thinking better illustrated than in fast-food franchising. Nowhere have manufacturing methods been employed more effectively to control the operation of distant and independent agents. Nowhere is "service" better.

Few of today's successful new commercial ventures have antecedents that are more humble and less glamorous than the hamburger. Yet the thriving nationwide chain of hamburger stands called "McDonald's" is a supreme example of the application of manufacturing and technological brilliance to problems that must ultimately be viewed as marketing problems. From 1961 to 1970 McDonald's sales rose from approximately $54 million to $587 million. During this remarkable ascent, the White Tower chain, whose name had theretofore been practically synonymous throughout the land with low-priced, quick-service hamburgers, practically vanished.

The explanation of McDonald's thundering success is not a purely fiscal one—i.e., the argument that it is financed by independent local entrepreneurs who bring to their operations a quality of commitment and energy not commonly found among hired workers. Nor is it purely geographical one—i.e., the argument that each outlet draws its patronage from a relatively small geographic ring of customers, thus enabling the number of outlets easily and quickly to multiply. The relevant explanation must deal with the central question of why each separate McDonald's outlet is so predictably successful, why each is so certain to attract many repeat customers.

Entrepreneurial financing and careful site selection do help. But most important is the carefully controlled execution of each outlet's central function—the rapid delivery of a uniform, high-quality mix of prepared foods in an environment of obvious cleanliness, order and cheerful courtesy. The systematic substitution of equipment for people, combined with the carefully planned use and positioning of technology, enables McDonald's to attract and hold patronage in proportions no predecessor or imitator has managed to duplicate. Consider the remarkable ingenuity of the system, which is worth examining in some detail:

To start with the obvious, raw hamburger patties are carefully prepacked and premeasured, which leaves neither the franchisee nor his employees any discretion as to size, quality, or raw-material consistency. This kind of attention is given to all McDonald's products. Storage and preparation space and related facilities are expressly designed for, and limited to, the predetermined mix of products. There is no space for any foods, beverages, or services that were not designed into the system at the outset. There is not even a sandwich knife or in fact, a decent place to keep one. Thus the owner has no discretion regarding what he can sell—not because of any contractual limitations, but because of facilities limitations. And the employees have virtually no discretion regarding how to prepare and serve things. Discretion is the enemy of order, standardization, and quality. On an automobile assembly line, for example, a worker who has discretion and latitude might possibly produce a more personalized car, but one that is highly unpredictable. The elaborate care with which an automobile is designed and an assembly line is structured and controlled is what produced quality cars at low prices, and with surprising reliability considering the sheer volume of the output. The same is true at McDonald's, which produces food under highly automated and controlled conditions.

French-fried automation

While in Detroit the significance of the technological process lies in production, at McDonald's it lies in marketing. A carefully planned design is built into the elaborate technology of the food-service system in such a fashion as to make it a significant marketing device. This fact is impressively illustrated by McDonald's handling of that uniquely plebeian American delicacy, french-fried potatoes.

French fries become quickly soggy and unappetizing; to be good, they must be freshly made just before serving. Like other fast-food establishments, McDonald's provides its outlets with precut, partially cooked, frozen potatoes that can be quickly finished in an onpremises, deep-fry facility. The McDonald's fryer is neither so large that it produces too many fresh fries at one time (thus allowing them to become soggy) nor so small that it requires frequent and costly frying.

The fryer is emptied onto a wide, flat tray adjacent to the service counter. This location is crucial. Since the McDonald's practice is to create an impression of abundance and generosity by slightly overfilling each bag of french fries, the tray's location next to the service counter prevents the spillage from an overfilled bag from reaching the floor. Spillage creates not only danger underfoot but also an unattractive appearance that causes the employees to become accustomed to an unclean environment. Once a store is unclean in one particular, standards fall very rapidly and the store becomes unclean and the food unappetizing in general.

While McDonald's aims for an impression of abundance, excessive overfilling can be very costly for a company that annually buys potatoes almost by the trainload. A systematic bias that puts into each bag of french fries a half ounce more than is intended can have visible effects on the company's annual earnings. Further, excessive time spent at the tray by each employee can create a cumulative service bottleneck at the counter.

McDonald's has therefore developed a special wide-mouthed scoop with a narrow funnel in its handle. The counter employee picks up the scoop and inserts the handle end into a wall clip containing the bags. One bag adheres to the handle. In a continuous movement the scoop descends into the potatoes, fills the bag to the exact proportions its designers intended, and is lifted, scoop facing the ceiling, so that the potatoes funnel through the handle into the attached bag, which is automatically disengaged from the handle by the weight of the contents. The bag comes to a steady, nonwobbling rest on its flat bottom.

Nothing can go wrong—the employee never soils his hands, the floor remains clean, dry, and safe, and the quantity is controlled. Best of all, the customer gets a visibly generous portion with great speed, the employee remains efficient and cheerful, and the general impression is one of extravagantly good service.

Mechanized marketing

Consider the other aspects of McDonald's technological approach to marketing. The tissue paper used to wrap each hamburger is color-coded to denote the mix of the condiments. Heated reservoirs hold pre-prepared hamburgers for rush demand. Frying surfaces have spatter guards to prevent soiling of the cook's uniform. Nothing is left to chance or the employees' discretion.

The entire system is engineered and executed according to a tight technological discipline that ensures fast, clean, reliable service in an atmosphere that gives the modestly paid employees a sense of pride and dignity. In spite of the crunch of eager customers, no employee looks or acts harassed, and therefore no harassment is communicated to the customers.

But McDonald's goes even further. Customers may be discouraged from entering if the building looks unappealing from the outside; hence considerable care goes into the design and appearance of the structure itself.

Some things, however, the architect cannot control, especially at an establishment where people generally eat in their parked cars and are likely to drop hamburger wrappings and empty beverage cartons on the ground. McDonald's has anticipated the requirement: its blacktop parking facilities are dotted like a checkerboard with numerous large, highly visible trash cans. It is impossible to ignore their purpose. Even the most indifferent customer would be struck with guilt if he simply dropped his refuse on the ground. But, just in case he drops it anyway, the larger McDonald's outlets have motorized sweepers for quick and easy cleanup.

What is important to understand about this remarkably successful organization is not only that it has created a highly sophisticated piece of technology, but also that it has done this by applying a manufacturing style of thinking to a people-intensive service situation. If machinery is to be viewed as a piece of equipment with the capability of producing a predictably standardized, customer-satisfying output while minimizing the operating discretion of its attendant, that is what a McDonald's retail outlet is. It is a machine that produces, with the help of totally unskilled machine tenders, a highly polished product. Through painstaking attention to total design and facilities planning, everything is built integrally into the machine itself, into the technology of the system. The only choice available to the attendant is to operate it exactly as the designers intended.

Questions

1. Describe McDonald's production-line approach to fast-food service.

2. What are the advantages of this approach?

3. Which operation—a takeout shop specializing in pizza, or a famous expensive restaurant with a large menu—would be most amenable to the production-line approach? Why?

4. Can you think of any other nonmanufacturing examples that parallel the McDonald's approach?

Source: Reprinted by permission. Excerpted from Theodore Levitt, "Production-Line Approach to Service," *Harvard Business Review* (September–October 1972), pp. 41–52. Copyright © 1972 by the President and Fellows of Harvard College; all rights reserved.

8

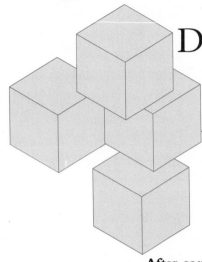

Design of Work Systems

LEARNING OBJECTIVES

After completing this chapter, you should be able to:

1. Briefly describe the two basic approaches to job design.
2. Discuss the advantages and disadvantages of specialization and automation.
3. Explain the term *sociotechnical system*.
4. Explain the purpose of methods analysis and describe how methods studies are done.
5. Describe four commonly used techniques for motion study.
6. Discuss the impact of working conditions on job design.
7. Define a standard time.
8. Discuss and compare time study methods.
9. Describe work sampling and perform calculations.
10. Compare stopwatch time study and work sampling.
11. Contrast time and output pay systems.

Chapter Outline

This chapter concludes our discussion of the design of operations systems. Previous chapters in this part have dealt with process and capacity planning, location, product/service design, and layout. In this chapter, we turn our attention to the design of the work system. Work design involves job design, establishment of time standards, and worker compensation.

As you read this chapter, note how decisions in the other design areas have an impact on work systems, and how decisions on work design have an impact on the other areas. For example, product or service design decisions (e.g., operate a coal mine, offer computer dating service, sell sports equipment) in large measure determine the kinds of activities workers will be involved with. Similarly, layout decisions often influence work design. Process layouts tend to necessitate broader job content than product layouts. The implication of these interrelationships is that it is essential to adopt a systems approach to design; decisions in one area must be related to the overall system.

The importance of work system design is underscored by the fact that the organization depends on human efforts (i.e., work) to accomplish its goals. Work design is one of the oldest areas of operations management. In the past, it has often been deemphasized in operations management courses in favor of other topics. In recent years, however, there has been renewed interest in this area, which has come from somewhat different directions. Some of the interest has come about from studies that suggest a general dissatisfaction on the part of many workers with their jobs. Interest has also been sparked by increasing concerns over productivity. Paradoxically, the very jobs that yield the highest productivity levels are also the ones that appear to generate the greatest amount of worker dissatisfaction, posing somewhat of a dilemma for job designers.

JOB DESIGN

Job design is concerned with specifying the contents and methods of jobs. In general, the goal of job design is to create a work system that is productive and efficient, taking into consideration costs and benefits of various alternatives. Practically speaking, job designers are concerned with *who* will do a job, *how* the job will be done, and *where* the job will be done.

In order for job design to be successful, it must be:

1. Carried out by experienced personnel who have the necessary training and background.
2. Consistent with the goals of the organization.
3. In written form.
4. Understood and agreed to by both management and employees.

The factors that affect job design and the implications of various alternatives are often so complex that a person without a good background in job design is likely to overlook important aspects of it. Workers and managers alike should be consulted in order to take advantage of their knowledge as well as to keep them informed. Because they are intimately involved with the work, employees are frequent sources of valuable suggestions relative to job improvements. Managerial support depends on the commitment and involvement of managers in job design. It is usually easier to sell a design to these two groups if they have been included in the process. Finally, establishing a written record of the job design can serve as a basis for referral if questions arise about it.

Current practice in job design contains elements of two basic schools of thought. One might be called the *efficiency* school because it emphasizes a systematic, logical approach to job design; the other is called the *behavioral* school because it emphasizes satisfaction of wants and needs.

The efficiency approach is a refinement of Frederick Winslow Taylor's scientific management concepts and has received considerable emphasis in the past. The behavioral approach emerged during the 1950s and has continued to make inroads into many aspects of job design. One of the main contributions of the behavioral approach is that it has awakened managers to the fact that humans are complex beings, and the efficiency approach may not be appropriate in every instance.

The behavioral view received a shot in the arm in 1973, when the report *Work in America* was released, detailing some of the problems that currently exist in our work systems.[1] The report revealed an apparently widespread dissatisfaction on the part of workers across the spectrum of jobs. Two points were of special interest to job designers. One was that many workers felt that their jobs were not interesting; the other was that workers wanted more control over their jobs. The central issue seemed to be the degree of specialization associated with their jobs; high specialization appeared to generate the most dissatisfaction. It is noteworthy that specialization is a primary source of disagreement between the efficiency and behavioral approaches.

Specialization

Specialization is a term used to describe jobs that have a very narrow scope. Examples range from assembly lines to medical specialties. College professors often specialize in teaching certain courses, some auto mechanics specialize in transmission repair, and some bakeries specialize in wedding cakes. The main rationale for specialization is the ability to concentrate one's efforts and thereby become proficient in some aspect of a product or service. Sometimes the amount of knowledge or training required of a specialist and the complexity of the work suggest that individuals who choose such work are not unhappy with their jobs. This seems to be especially true in the professions (doctors, lawyers, professors, etc.). However, at the other end of the scale are assembly line workers, who are also specialists, although with a lot less

---

[1] Upjohn Institute for Employment Research, *Work in America* (Cambridge, Mass.: MIT Press, 1973).

glamour. The rationale for these highly specialized jobs is that they yield high productivity and low unit costs. In fact, such specialization is largely responsible for the high standard of living that exists today in industrial nations.

Unfortunately, many of these jobs can be described as monotonous or downright boring, and they are apparently the source of much of the dissatisfaction that exists in industry today. Even so, it would be wrong to conclude that all workers oppose this type of work. Some workers undoubtedly prefer a job with limited requirements and responsibility for making decisions. Others are not capable of handling jobs with larger scopes. Nonetheless, many workers are frustrated in such jobs, and this manifests itself in a number of ways. Turnover and absenteeism are often high in these jobs. For example, in the automotive industry, absenteeism runs as high as 20 percent, although not every absentee is a frustrated worker on an assembly line. Workers may also take out their frustrations through disruptive tactics, deliberate slowdowns, or poor attention to product quality.

The seriousness of these problems has caused job designers and others to seek ways of alleviating them. Some of those approaches are discussed in the following sections. Before we turn to them, it will be helpful to reflect on the advantages and disadvantages of specialization, which are summarized in Table 8–1.

Behavioral Approaches to Job Design

In an effort to make jobs more interesting and meaningful, job designers frequently consider job enlargement, job rotation, job enrichment, and increased use of mechanization.

Job enlargement involves giving a worker a larger portion of the total task. This constitutes horizontal loading in the sense that the additional work is

---

TABLE 8–1

Major advantages and disadvantages of specialization in business		
	Advantages	
	For management:	For labor:
	1. Simplifies training	1. Low education and skill requirements
	2. High productivity	2. Minimum responsibilities
	3. Low wage costs	3. Little mental effort needed
	Disadvantages	
	For management:	For labor:
	1. Difficult to motivate quality	1. Monotonous boring work
	2. Worker dissatisfaction, possibly resulting in absenteeism, turnover, etc.	2. Limited opportunities for advancement
		3. Little control over work
		4. Little opportunity for self-fulfillment

on the same level of skill and responsibility as the original job. Schematically, this can be depicted as:

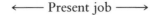

The goal is to make the job more interesting by increasing the variety of skills required and by providing the worker with a more recognizable contribution to the overall output. For example, in a supermarket setting, instead of having employees work exclusively in the produce or meat department, they might be given assignments that involve work in two or more of these departments. Similarly, a production worker's job might be expanded so that he or she is responsible for a *sequence* of activities instead of only one activity.

Job rotation involves periodically having workers exchange jobs. This approach can be used to avoid having one or a few employees stuck in boring or monotonous jobs. It works best when workers can be transferred to more interesting jobs; there is little advantage in merely having workers exchange one boring job for another. Job rotation allows workers to broaden their learning experience and enables workers to fill in for others in the event of sickness or absenteeism.

Job enrichment involves an increase in the level of responsibility for planning and coordination tasks. In effect, it represents a vertical loading:

Present job

An example of this is to permit stock clerks in supermarkets to handle reordering of goods, thus increasing their responsibilities. Job enrichment approaches focus on the motivating potential of jobs via worker satisfaction. Among the proponents of this approach is Frederick Herzberg, who published a study indicating that factors such as achievement, recognition, and responsibility have the potential for generating satisfaction but not dissatisfaction, while factors such as supervision, pay, and working conditions have the opposite potential of leading to dissatisfaction but not satisfaction.[2] According to this view, job enrichment could be a source of satisfaction by adding more of the factors that have satisfying potential.

In a later study, Richard Hackman and G.R. Oldham proposed that job enrichment can lead to improved worker performance if the worker perceives that the work is meaningful, accepts responsibility for the outcome, and receives knowledge of the results.[3] However, they point out that job enrichment should not be used without a careful investigation of the need for changes and of what changes are most apt to succeed. In effect, they warn that

[2] F. Herzberg, B. Mausner, and B. Snyderman, *The Motivation to Work* (New York: John Wiley & Sons, 1959).

[3] J. Richard Hackman, G. R. Oldham, Jane L. Pearce, and Jane Caminis, "A New Strategy for Job Enrichment," *California Management Review*, Summer 1975, pp. 57–77.

not all jobs or workers are amenable to job enrichment, nor would they necessarily benefit from enrichment. Toward that end, they have developed a questionnaire that can be used to diagnose the motivating potential of job enrichment.[4] The diagnosis focuses on four dimensions:

1. Is there a problem with motivation and job satisfaction?
2. What is the motivating potential of the job?
3. What aspects of the job are causing difficulty?
4. Will employees accept the necessary changes?

Increased use of mechanization often enables designers to free workers from repetitive work, which tends to be monotonous and boring. Increased mechanization may take the form of automation, which is discussed more fully in the following section.

The essence of these approaches to job design is that they attempt to increase the motivational aspect of jobs by increasing worker satisfaction through improvement in the *quality of work life*. Many firms are currently involved in or seriously considering programs related to quality of work life. In addition to the aforementioned approaches, organizations are also experimenting with choice of locations (e.g., medium-sized cities or campus-like settings, when feasible), flexible work hours, and quality circles, which are described in the chapter on quality assurance.

Automation

The use of mechanical and/or electronic devices in place of human effort is referred to as **automation.** Under this heading come automatic processing equipment, computers, industrial robots, and similar devices. A key feature of these devices is their ability to exert control over a process without human intervention. There are numerous benefits, as well as potential drawbacks, associated with automation.

Among the benefits of automation are the following:

1. The jobs that are most susceptible to automation are those that are repetitive, boring, and monotonous. Hence, the jobs that are least desirable from a human standpoint often lend themselves to automation.
2. Automation yields a highly uniform output and generally results in higher quality compared to human-generated output.
3. The rate of output generally exceeds human capabilities.
4. Human conflicts are avoided.

---

[4] J. Richard Hackman and G. R. Oldham, "Development of the Job Diagnostic Survey," *Journal of Applied Psychology* 60 (1975), pp. 159–70.

Among the potential drawbacks of automation are the following:

1. The traditional argument against automation is that it displaces humans. Although it has been shown that automation results in more jobs rather than fewer, and the jobs created are more interesting than those lost, the fact remains that workers must be retrained, which adds to the cost. Moreover, workers often tend to resist any sort of change.

2. Automated systems often involve substantial costs, and this usually means that a fairly high volume of output is needed to make the system economical.

3. Automated systems can be inflexible because they are often restricted by design to a narrow range of tasks.

Compared to American firms, the Japanese are much greater users of automated processing in the automotive and steel industries, but they are considerably less automated in agriculture. The successes that the Japanese have had in the areas of quality and productivity in industrial applications of automation, and the U.S. successes in agriculture, have caused managers in many U.S. firms to give more attention to the possible benefits of automation. There has not yet been a wholesale rush toward it. One possible reason is the resistance of labor unions. Another is the enormous cost involved, coupled with a long period of time before payoffs can be realized. Still another possible reason involves the costs and difficulties of retraining employees and the problems associated with integrating automated systems into current operations.

Sociotechnical Systems

The **sociotechnical systems** approach is concerned with the human-technology interface. Specifically, it recognizes that choice of technology can and often does have an impact on the social structure within an organization and that technological changes (redesign of layout, automation, introduction of new techniques) can and often do have detrimental effects on worker performance. Furthermore, proponents of this approach argue that there are often technological alternatives that would produce desired results and still be consistent with sociological considerations. Hence, the focus is on finding a design that is consistent with both technological efficiency and the existing sociological system. In many respects, this approach is very similar to job enrichment in that it seeks task variety, skill variety, task autonomy, and feedback. It goes beyond that approach in terms of giving the workers more say in how the work is actually done and in allowing workers to self-organize. Because of this, there is a certain amount of controversy surrounding the sociotechnical approach, and there has not been widespread acceptance of this approach, although some foreign firms are using it. It may be that such an approach would be more suited to Japan's work environment, where staff personnel such as industrial engineers and quality control experts are viewed as consultants, available to assist workers but not to specify work procedures. One of the major obstacles to greater use of the sociotechnical approach appears to be the reluctance of managers to entrust more of their authority to their workers. Although in some cases such fears are somewhat unfounded, in other cases they are not. Consequently, much additional work remains to be done before it will be possible to say how, and to what extent, sociotechnical systems can be used in job design.

Methods Analysis

Job design often begins with a methods analysis of an overall operation. You might call it a macro view of the job. It then moves from the general to specific details of the job, concentrating on arrangement of the workplace and movements of the worker.

The need for methods analysis can come from a number of different sources, such as:

1. Changes in tools and equipment.
2. Changes in product design.
3. New products.
4. Changes in materials or procedures.
5. Government regulations or contractual agreements.

Methods analysis is done both for existing jobs and for jobs that have not yet been performed. At first glance, it might seem strange to analyze methods of a nonexisting job. However, someone has to establish a method for a new job, and it is usually wise to have a person who is trained to handle this do it at the start rather than allow the job to begin and then try to improve it later.

When an existing job is involved, the procedure is generally to have the analyst first observe the job as it is currently being done and then devise ways to improve the job. For a brand new job, the analyst must rely on a description of the job and an ability to visualize the operation in advance. Methods analysis can be a good source of productivity improvements.

The basic procedure in methods analysis is:

1. Identify the operation to be studied, and gather all pertinent facts regarding tools, equipment, materials, and so on.
2. If the job is currently being done, discuss the job with the operator and supervisor to get their inputs.
3. Study and document the present method of an existing job using process charts. For new jobs, develop charts based on information about the activities involved.
4. Analyze the job.

5. Propose new methods.
6. Install the new methods.
7. Follow up installation to assure that improvements have been achieved.

Selecting the operation to study. Sometimes a foreman or supervisor will request that a certain operation be studied. At other times, methods analysis will be part of an overall program to increase productivity and reduce costs. Some general guidelines for selecting a job to study are to seek jobs that:

1. Have a high labor content.
2. Are done frequently.
3. Are unsafe, tiring, unpleasant, and/or noisy.
4. Are designated as problems (e.g., quality problems, scheduling bottlenecks).

Documenting the present method. Use charts, graphs, and verbal descriptions of the way the job is now being done. This will provide a better understanding of the job and serve as a basis of comparison against which revisions can be judged.

Analyzing the job and proposing new methods. Analyzing the job requires that the analyst carefully consider the what, why, when, where, and who of the job. Often, simply going through these questions will clarify the review process by encouraging the analyst to take a "devil's advocate" attitude toward both the present and the proposed methods.

Analyzing and improving methods is facilitated by the use of various charts such as *flow process charts* and *worker-machine charts*. Another chart that is sometimes useful is *a gang process chart*.

Flow process charts are used to review and critically examine the overall sequence of an operation by focusing on either the movements of the operator or the flow of materials. These charts can be very helpful in identifying nonproductive parts of the process (e.g., delays, temporary storages, distances traveled).

Figure 8–1 describes the symbols used in constructing a flow process chart, and Figure 8–2 illustrates a flow process chart.

Some of the uses of flow process charts include studying the flow of material through a department, studying the sequence that documents or forms take, analyzing movement and care of surgical patients, layout of department and grocery stores, and mail handling.

Experienced analysts usually develop a checklist of questions they ask themselves to generate ideas for improvements. Some representative questions are:

1. Why is there a delay or storage at this point?
2. How can travel distances be shortened or avoided?

FIGURE 8–1

Process chart symbols

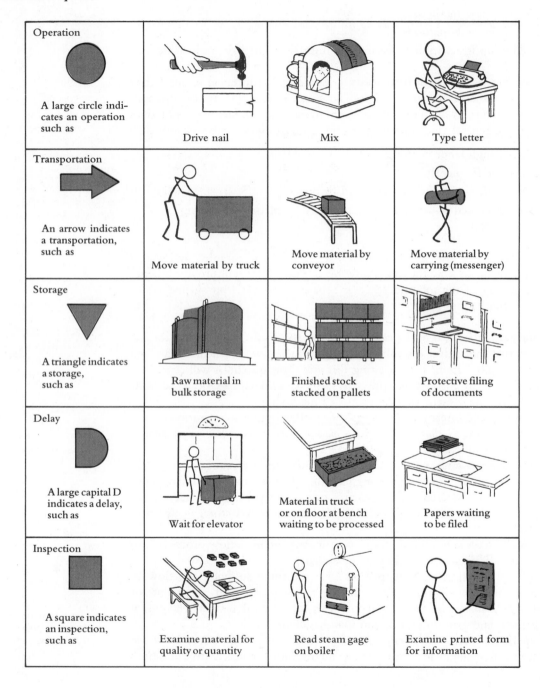

Operation	Drive nail	Mix	Type letter
A large circle indicates an operation such as			
Transportation	Move material by truck	Move material by conveyor	Move material by carrying (messenger)
An arrow indicates a transportation, such as			
Storage	Raw material in bulk storage	Finished stock stacked on pallets	Protective filing of documents
A triangle indicates a storage, such as			
Delay	Wait for elevator	Material in truck or on floor at bench waiting to be processed	Papers waiting to be filed
A large capital D indicates a delay, such as			
Inspection	Examine material for quality or quantity	Read steam gage on boiler	Examine printed form for information
A square indicates an inspection, such as			

Source: Benjamin W. Niebel, *Motion and Time Study*, 6th ed. (Homewood, Ill.: Richard D. Irwin, 1976), p. 28. © 1976 by Richard D. Irwin, Inc. Reprinted by permission.

FIGURE 8—2

Format of a flow process chart

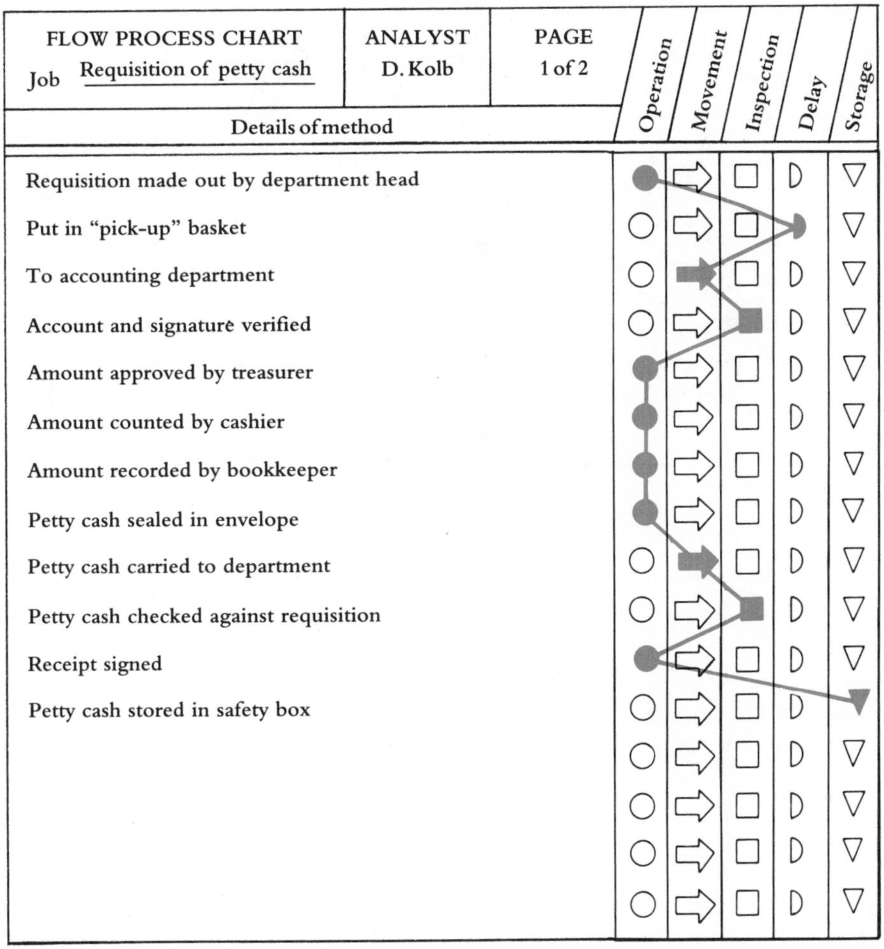

FLOW PROCESS CHART	ANALYST	PAGE	Operation	Movement	Inspection	Delay	Storage
Job Requisition of petty cash	D. Kolb	1 of 2					
Details of method							
Requisition made out by department head			●	⇨	☐	D	▽
Put in "pick-up" basket			○	⇨	☐	●	▽
To accounting department			○	⇨	☐	D	▽
Account and signature verified			○	⇨	☐	D	▽
Amount approved by treasurer			●	⇨	☐	D	▽
Amount counted by cashier			●	⇨	☐	D	▽
Amount recorded by bookkeeper			●	⇨	☐	D	▽
Petty cash sealed in envelope			●	⇨	☐	D	▽
Petty cash carried to department			○	⇨	☐	D	▽
Petty cash checked against requisition			○	⇨	☐	D	▽
Receipt signed			●	⇨	☐	D	▽
Petty cash stored in safety box			○	⇨	☐	D	▼
			○	⇨	☐	D	▽
			○	⇨	☐	D	▽
			○	⇨	☐	D	▽
			○	⇨	☐	D	▽

Source: Elias M. Awad, *Systems Analysis and Design* (Homewood, Ill.: Richard D. Irwin, 1979), p. 113.
© 1979 by Richard D. Irwin, Inc. Reprinted by permission.

3. Can materials handling be reduced?
4. Would a rearrangement of the workplace result in greater efficiency?
5. Can similar activities be grouped?
6. Would the use of additional or improved equipment be helpful?
7. Does the worker have any ideas for improvements?

A **worker-machine chart** is helpful for visualizing the portions of a work cycle during which an operator and equipment are busy or idle. The analyst can easily see when the operator and machine are working independently as

FIGURE 8–3

Worker-machine chart

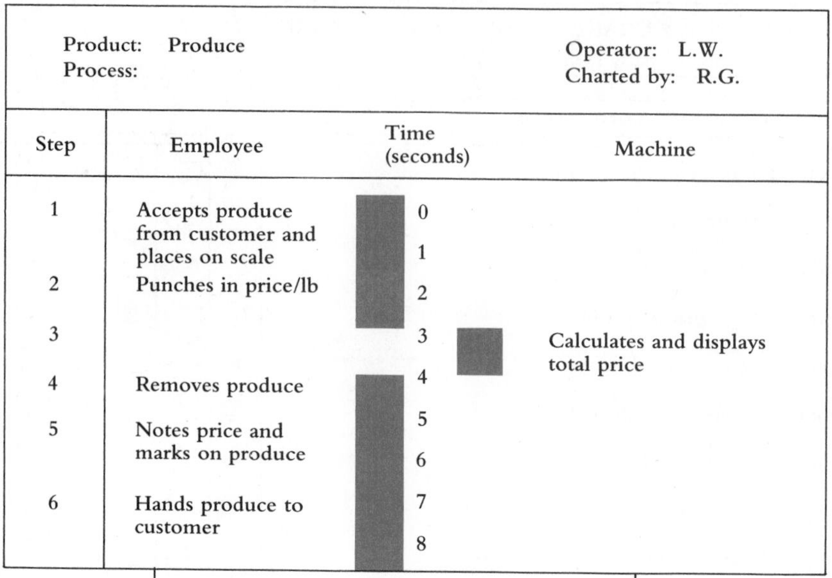

Product: Produce			Operator: L.W.
Process:			Charted by: R.G.

Step	Employee	Time (seconds)	Machine
1	Accepts produce from customer and places on scale	0 1	
2	Punches in price/lb	2	
3		3	Calculates and displays total price
4	Removes produce	4	
5	Notes price and marks on produce	5 6	
6	Hands produce to customer	7 8	

Summary

	Employee		Machine	
	Time (seconds)	%	Time (seconds)	%
Work	7	87.5	1	12.5
Idle	1	12.5	7	87.5

well as when their work overlaps or is interdependent. One use of this type of chart is to determine how many machines or how much equipment the operator can manage.

An example of a worker-machine chart is presented in Figure 8–3. Among other things, the chart highlights worker and machine utilization.

Another multiactivity chart is the **gang process chart.** It is useful in coordinating and analyzing a *team* of workers because it provides a cross-sectional view of the work at any point. The chart also reveals individual utilizations. An example of this kind of chart is shown in Figure 8–4.

Installing the improved method.   Successful implementation of proposed method changes requires convincing management of the desirability of the new method and obtaining the cooperation of the worker. If the worker has been consulted throughout the process and has made suggestions that are incorporated in the proposed changes, this part of the task will be considerably easier than if the analyst has assumed sole responsibility for the development of the proposal.

FIGURE 8—4

Multiactivity chart (gang process): Hydraulic extrusion process, proposed method

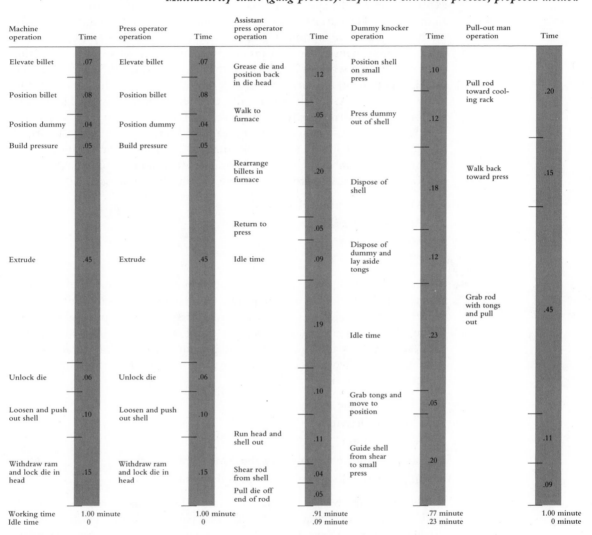

Machine operation	Time	Press operator operation	Time	Assistant press operator operation	Time	Dummy knocker operation	Time	Pull-out man operation	Time
Elevate billet	.07	Elevate billet	.07	Grease die and position back in die head	.12	Position shell on small press	.10	Pull rod toward cooling rack	.20
Position billet	.08	Position billet	.08	Walk to furnace	.05	Press dummy out of shell	.12		
Position dummy	.04	Position dummy	.04						
Build pressure	.05	Build pressure	.05	Rearrange billets in furnace	.20	Dispose of shell	.18	Walk back toward press	.15
				Return to press	.05	Dispose of dummy and lay aside tongs	.12		
Extrude	.45	Extrude	.45	Idle time	.09				
					.19	Idle time	.23	Grab rod with tongs and pull out	.45
Unlock die	.06	Unlock die	.06		.10	Grab tongs and move to position	.05		
Loosen and push out shell	.10	Loosen and push out shell	.10	Run head and shell out	.11	Guide shell from shear to small press	.20		.11
Withdraw ram and lock die in head	.15	Withdraw ram and lock die in head	.15	Shear rod from shell	.04				.09
				Pull die off end of rod	.05				
Working time	1.00 minute		1.00 minute		.91 minute		.77 minute		1.00 minute
Idle time	0		0		.09 minute		.23 minute		0 minute

Source: Benjamin W. Niebel, *Motion and Time Study*, 6th ed. (Homewood, Ill.: Richard D. Irwin, 1976), p. 132. © 1976 by Richard D. Irwin, Inc. Reprinted by permission.

If the proposed method constitutes a major change from the way the job has been performed in the past, workers may have to undergo a certain amount of training, and full implementation may take some time to achieve.

The follow-up.   In order to insure that changes have been made and that the proposed method is functioning as expected, the analyst should review the operation after a reasonable period and consult again with the operator.

Motion Study

Motion study is the systematic study of the human motions used to perform an operation. The purpose is to eliminate unnecessary motions and to identify the best sequence of motions for maximum efficiency. Hence, motion study can be an important avenue for productivity improvements. Present practice evolved from the work of Frank Gilbreth, who originated the concepts in the bricklaying trade in the early part of this century. Through the use of motion study techniques, Gilbreth is generally credited with increasing the average number of bricks laid per hour by a factor of 3, even though he was not a bricklayer by trade. When you stop to realize that bricklaying had been carried on for centuries, Gilbreth's accomplishment is even more remarkable.

There are a number of different techniques that motion study analysts can use to develop efficient procedures. The most used techniques are:

1. Motion study principles.
2. Analysis of therbligs.
3. Micromotion study.
4. Charts.

The work of Gilbreth laid the foundation for development of **motion study principles,** which are guidelines for designing motion-efficient work procedures. The guidelines are divided into three categories: principles for use of the body, principles for arrangement of the workplace, and principles for the design of tools and equipment. The principles are listed in Table 8–2.

In developing work methods that are motion-efficient, some of the things the analyst tries to do are:

1. Eliminate unnecessary motions.
2. Combine activities.
3. Reduce fatigue.
4. Improve the arrangement of the workplace.
5. Improve the design of tools and equipment.

Therbligs are basic elemental motions. The name *therblig* is Gilbreth spelled backwards (except for the *th*). The idea behind the development of therbligs is to break jobs down into minute elements and base improvements on analysis of these basic elements by eliminating, combining, or rearranging them.

Although a complete description of therbligs is outside the scope of this text, a list of some common ones will give you some idea of the nature of these basic elemental motions:

Search implies hunting for an item with hands and/or the eyes.
Select means to choose from a group of objects.
Grasp means to take hold of an object.
Hold refers to retention of an object after it has been grasped.

TABLE 8—2

Motion study principles

Human body

1. Begin and end motions of both hands at the same time.
2. Do not allow both hands to be idle at the same time except during rest periods.
3. Make sure that motions of arms are in opposite and symmetrical directions and at the same time.
4. Confine hand and body motions to the simplest movements that will do the work.
5. Use momentum to assist where helpful, but reduce it if it must be overcome by muscular effort.
6. Use smooth, continuous curved motions in preference to straight-line motions that involve sudden changes in direction.
7. Remember that ballistic motions are faster, easier, and more accurate than controlled movements.
8. Arrange work to permit use of natural rhythm wherever possible.
9. Keep eye fixations as few and as close together as possible.

Workplace

10. Keep all tools and materials in a definite and fixed place.
11. Keep tools, materials, and controls close to the point of use.
12. Use gravity feed bins and containers to deliver material close to the point of use.
13. Use drop deliveries wherever possible.
14. Locate materials and tools to permit the best sequence of motions.
15. Provide proper illumination, heating, and ventilation.
16. Arrange the height of the workplace and the chair so that alternate sitting and standing is easily possible.
17. Provide a chair that permits good posture for every worker.

Tools and equipment

18. Relieve the hands of all work that can be done by jigs, fixtures, and foot-operated devices.
19. Combine two or more tools wherever possible.
20. Pre-position tools and materials to reduce motions of searching, finding, and selecting as much as possible.
21. Distribute the load on each finger in accordance with the inherent capabilities of the fingers.
22. Locate levers, crossbars, and handwheels so that the operator can manipulate them with the least change in body position and with the greatest mechanical advantage.

Source: Ralph M. Barnes, *Motion and Time Study: Design and Measurement of Work,* 6th ed. (New York: John Wiley & Sons, 1968), p. 220. Reprinted by permission of the publisher.

Transport loaded means movement of an object after hold.

Release load means to deposit the object.

Some other therbligs are *inspect, position, plan, rest,* and *delay.*

Description of a job using therbligs often involves a substantial amount of work. However, for short, repetitive jobs, therbligs analysis may be justified.

Frank Gilbreth and his scientist wife, Lillian, were also responsible for introducing motion pictures for studying motions, called **micromotion study.** This approach is used not only in industry but in many other areas of human endeavor, such as sports and health care. Use of the camera and slow-motion replays enables analysts to study motions that would otherwise be too rapid to see. In addition, the resulting films provide a permanent record that can be referred to for training workers and analysts as well as for settling job disputes involving work methods.

The cost of micromotion study limits its use to repetitive activities, where even minor improvements can yield substantial savings owing to the number of times an operation is repeated, or where other considerations justify its use (e.g., surgical procedures).

Motion study analysts often use charts as a tool for analyzing and recording motion studies. Activity charts and process charts such as those described earlier can be quite helpful. In addition, a *simo chart* like the one shown in Figure 8–5 can be used to study simultaneous motions of the hands. These charts are invaluable in studying operations such as typing, sewing, surgical and dental procedures, and certain assembly operations.

Working Conditions

Working conditions are an important aspect of job design. Physical factors such as temperature, humidity, ventilation, illumination, color, and noise can have a significant impact on worker performance in terms of productivity, quality of output, and accidents.

1. *Temperature and humidity.* Although human beings can function under a fairly wide range of temperatures, work performance tends to be adversely affected if temperatures are outside a very narrow *comfort band.* Although individuals tend to differ in terms of what they consider comfortable ranges, it is generally agreed that office workers and others who exert little physical effort on the job function best when temperatures are between 65° F and 72° F. For moderately strenuous activities, temperatures in the range of 60° F to 70° F are preferable, and for very strenuous activities, temperatures in the range of 55° F to 65° F are best.

Heating and cooling are less of a problem in offices than in factories and other work environments where high ceilings allow heat to rise and where there is often a constant flow of trucks and other moving and handling equipment through large doors. This makes it difficult to maintain a constant temperature. Solutions range from selection of suitable clothing to space heaters and other localized heating or cooling devices.

FIGURE 8—5

*A simultaneous
motion chart*

SIMO CHART

OPERATOR: Ken Reisch
DATE: May 21,
OPERATION: Assembly
PART: Lace Finger
METHOD: Proposed
CHART BY: Joseph Riley

TIME SCALE (winks)	ELEMENT TIME	LEFT-HAND DESCRIPTION	SYMBOL	MOTION CLASS	SYMBOL	RIGHT-HAND DESCRIPTION	ELEMENT TIME	TIME SCALE (winks)
4548	12	Reach for finger	RE		RE	Reach for finger	12	4548
4560	19	Grasp finger	G		G	Grasp finger	19	4560
4579	31	Move finger	M		M	Move finger	31	4579
4610	75	Position and release finger	P RL		P RL	Position and release finger	75	4610
4685	15	Reach for clamp	RE		RE	Reach for clamp	15	4685
4700	15	Grasp clamp	G		G	Grasp clamp	15	4700
4715								4715
7541	12	Grasp assembly	G		G	Grasp assembly	12	7541
7559	18	Move and release assembly	M RL		M RL	Move and release assembly	18	7559

SUMMARY

%	TIME	LEFT HAND SUMMARY	SYM.	RIGHT HAND SUMMARY	TIME	%
8.56	249	Reach	RE	Reach	245	8.4
7.49	218	Grasp	G	Grasp	221	7.5
12.16	354	Move	M	Move	413	14.2
30.45	887	Position	P	Position	1124	38.7
39.3	1145	Use	U	Use	876	30.1
1.03	30	Idle	I	Idle	0	0.0
.96	28	Release	RL	Release	32	1.1
100.0	3011	TOTALS			3011	100.0

Source: Benjamin W. Niebel, *Motion and Time Study,* 6th ed. (Homewood, Ill.: Richard D. Irwin, 1976), p. 204. © 1976 by Richard D. Irwin, Inc. Reprinted by permission.

Humidity is generally an important variable in maintaining a comfortable working environment. Humidities in the range of 30 percent to 50 percent are most conducive to comfort, although, as a general rule, choice of temperature levels depends on humidity levels because humans tend to be more sensitive to variations in temperature at high humidities. Therefore, high humidity will require more cooling on a warm day, and more heating on a cold day, than low humidity.

2. *Ventilation.* Unpleasant and noxious odors can be distracting as well as dangerous to workers. Moreover, unless smoke and dust are periodically removed, the air can quickly become stale and unpleasant. Large fans and air conditioning equipment are commonly used to exchange and recondition the air.

3. *Illumination.* The amount of illumination required depends largely on the type of work being performed. The more detailed the work, the higher the level of illumination needed for adequate performance. Other important considerations are the amount of glare and contrast. From a safety standpoint, good lighting in halls, stairways, and other dangerous points is important. However, because illumination is expensive, high illumination in all areas is not generally desirable.

Sometimes natural daylight can be used as a source of illumination. Not only is it free, but it also provides some psychological benefits. Workers in windowless rooms may feel "cut off" from the outside world and experience various psychological problems. However, the inability to control natural light (e.g., cloudy days) can result in dramatic changes in light intensity.

4. *Color.* There are two features of color that are important in job design. One is the ability of colors to affect moods and feelings, and the other is the visual discriminations it permits.

Color produces emotional and psychological effects in many situations. Some of the effects of various colors are:

Red conveys warmth, action, and stimulation. It is a high-visibility color.
Yellow is also a high-visibility color. It can give the impression of cheerfulness and freshness.
Blue is a low-visibility color. It may convey coolness and may promote thoughtfulness or depression.
Green is another low-visibility color. It is often associated with calm and restfulness.
Brown is a natural color. Earth tones impart a natural, peaceful feeling. It is a low-visibility color.
Orange is a high-visibility color that attracts attention more than any other color. It imparts feelings of warmth and stimulation.

The implications for job designers relate to the type of atmosphere and emotions that are best suited for the job. Red is generally taboo in hospitals, whereas green is widely used. Bright colors lend themselves to coloring the surroundings in jobs that involve a high degree of creativity; browns are used to convey peaceful surroundings, and blues are more appropriate where quiet deliberations are involved. Of course, these are broad generalizations, but the point is that colors should be a part of job design.

Colors are also used to designate safe or hazardous areas or conditions. Some common uses are:

Red is frequently used for fire protection equipment, gasoline storage containers, danger signs, emergency warning lights, and hot pipes.

Yellow indicates caution. It is frequently used to designate walkways, edges of stairs, corners, and ends of loading docks. Heavy equipment, school buses, and forklifts are usually yellow because of its high visibility.

Blue is sometimes used to mark control devices, water pipes, and valves.

Green is used to designate safety areas or equipment.

Purple is used for radiation hazards.

Orange is frequently used to indicate dangerous parts of equipment and safety starting buttons and switches.

Color coding is also used as a means of identifying electrical wiring, especially where a number of different wires might need to be traced through partitions or equipment.

5. *Noise and vibration.* Noise is unwanted sound. It is caused by vibrations of machines or equipment as well as by humans. Noise can be annoying or distracting, leading to errors and accidents. It can also damage or impair hearing if it is loud enough. Figure 8–6 illustrates loudness levels of some typical sounds.

Successful sound control begins with measurement of the offending sounds. In a new operation, selection and placement of equipment can eliminate or reduce many potential problems. In the case of existing equipment, it may be possible to redesign the equipment or substitute other equipment. In some instances, the source of noise can be isolated from other work areas. If that isn't feasible, acoustical walls and ceilings or baffles that deflect sound waves may prove useful. Sometimes the only alternative is to provide protective devices for those in the immediate vicinity (e.g., personnel who guide jet aircraft into landing gates wear protective devices over their ears).

Vibrations can be a factor in job design even without a noise component, so merely eliminating sound may not be sufficient in every case. Vibrations can come from tools, machines, vehicles, human activity, air conditioning systems, pumps, and other sources. Corrective measures include padding, stabilizers, shock absorbers, cushioning, and rubber mountings.

6. *Work breaks.* The frequency, length, and timing of work breaks can have a significant impact on both productivity and quality of output. One indication of the relationship between worker efficiency and work breaks is

FIGURE 8—6

Decibel values of typical sounds (db)

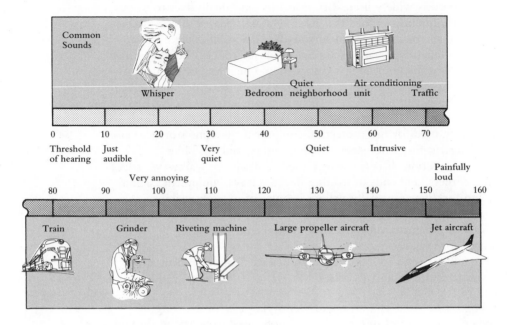

Source: Benjamin W. Niebel, *Motion and Time Study,* 6th ed. (Homewood, Ill.: Richard D. Irwin, 1976), p. 221. © 1976 by Richard D. Irwin, Inc. Reprinted by permission.

FIGURE 8—7

A typical relationship between worker efficiency and the time of day

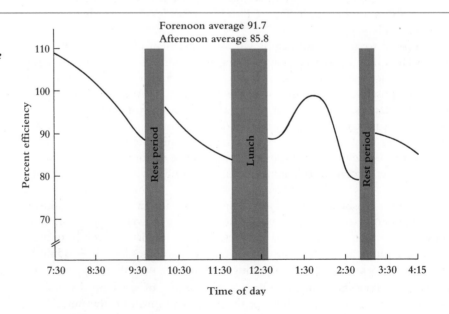

Source: Benjamin W. Niebel, *Motion and Time Study,* 6th ed. (Homewood, Ill.: Richard D. Irwin, 1976), p. 243. © 1976 by Richard D. Irwin, Inc. Reprinted by permission.

illustrated in Figure 8–7. It reveals that efficiency generally declines as the day wears on, but it also shows how breaks for lunch and rest can cause an upward shift in efficiency.

An important variable in the rate of decline of efficiency and potential effects of work breaks is the amount of physical and/or mental requirements of the job. Steelworkers, for instance, may need rest breaks of 15 minutes per hour due to the strenuous nature of their jobs. Physical effort is not the only condition that indicates the need for work breaks. People working at CRTs also need periodic breaks. Moreover, you have undoubtedly experienced the benefits of study breaks.

7. *Safety.* Worker safety is one of the most basic issues in job design. This is an area that needs constant attention from management, employees, and designers. Workers cannot be effectively motivated if they feel they are in physical danger.

From an employer standpoint, accidents are undesirable because they are expensive (insurance and compensation); they usually involve damage to equipment and/or products; they require hiring, training, and makeup work; and they generally interrupt work. From a worker standpoint, accidents mean physical suffering, mental anguish, potential loss of earnings, and disruption of the work routine.

It is generally agreed that the two basic causes of accidents are worker *carelessness* and accident *hazards*. Under the heading of carelessness come unsafe acts. Examples include driving at high speeds, drinking and driving, failure to use protective equipment, overriding safety controls (e.g., taping control buttons down), disregarding safety procedures (e.g., running, throwing objects, cutting through, failing to observe one-way signs), improper use of tools and equipment, and failure to use reasonable caution in danger zones. Unsafe conditions include unprotected pulleys, chains, material-handling equipment, machinery, and so on. Also, poorly lit walkways, stairs, and loading docks constitute hazards. Toxic wastes, gases and vapors, and radiation hazards must be contained. In many instances, these cannot be detected without special equipment, so they would not be obvious to workers or emergency personnel. Protection against hazards involves use of proper lighting, clearly marking danger zones, use of protective equipment (e.g., hardhats, goggles, earmuffs, gloves, heavy shoes and clothing), safety devices (e.g., machine guards, dual control switches that require an operator to use both hands), emergency equipment (e.g., emergency showers, fire extinguishers, fire escapes) and thorough instruction in safety procedures and use of regular and emergency equipment. Housekeeping (clean floors, open aisles, waster removal, etc.) is another important safety factor.

An effective program of safety and accident control requires the cooperation of both workers and management. Workers must be trained in proper procedures and attitudes, and they can contribute to a reduction in hazards by pointing out hazards to management. Management must enforce safety procedures and use of safety equipment. If supervisors allow workers to ignore safety procedures or look the other way when they see violations, workers will be less likely to take proper precautions. Some firms use contests that compare departmental safety records. However, accidents cannot be completely eliminated, and a freak accident may seriously affect worker morale and might even contribute to additional accidents. Posters can be very effective, particularly if they communicate in specific terms *how* to avoid accidents. For example, the admonition to "be careful" is not nearly as effective as "wear hardhats," "walk, don't run," "hold on to rail," and so on.

Effective accident control begins with measurement of accident experience. Commonly used measures include frequency of accidents, severity, and average seriousness. Accidents that cause serious injury and loss of work time beyond the day of the injury are called **lost-time accidents,** and these cases are the ones generally used to quantify experience, although minor accidents can serve as a warning of impending major accidents. Frequency, severity, and seriousness are defined as follows:

$$\text{Frequency} = \text{Number of lost-time accidents per million labor hours worked}$$
$$\text{Severity} = \text{Number of days lost per million labor hours worked}$$
$$\text{Average seriousness} = \text{Severity} \div \text{Frequency}$$

Use of hours worked is standard practice because it allows for meaningful comparisons based on *exposure*. However, the last measure, average seriousness, avoids the need to determine the number of hours worked. The frequency of accidents is useful as a measure of how often accidents are occurring; severity can be high because of numerous accidents with little time lost per accident or because of one or two very serious accidents. The lost-time figure is based on the number of days a worker is actually absent from his regular job plus possible standard changes based on the nature of the injury. For instance, loss of a portion of a finger or toe results in a specified charge of lost-time in addition to time actually lost.

Accident measures are necessary to assess a department's or company's experience over time, as well as to judge the experience of a company against that of the industry as a whole. In other words, frequency and severity of accidents vary by type of work; the nature and seriousness of accident hazards in electrical work, office work, logging, steel work, and so on are quite different. In order to get a clear picture of any firm's accident experience, it is necessary to compare its record with other firms engaged in the same type of business, since jobs in these firms will have the same hazards. In addition, accident records can be used to help management pinpoint areas where corrective action is needed, although it is infinitely better to *prevent* accidents rather than emphasize corrective action. Still, hazards are not always obvious, and corrective action can prevent *future* accidents.

The importance of safety considerations in systems design was heightened by the enactment of the Occupational Safety and Health Act (**OSHA**) in 1970.

The law was intended to ensure that workers in all organizations have healthy and safe working conditions. It provides specific safety regulations as well as inspectors to see that they are adhered to. Inspections are carried out randomly and to investigate complaints of unsafe conditions. OSHA officials are empowered to issue warnings, to impose fines, and even to invoke court-ordered shutdowns for unsafe conditions.

Early experience with OSHA was mixed. Although OSHA caused a general improvement in working conditions and safety records, sometimes overzealous inspectors demanded strict compliance with regulations. Moreover, many employers felt that certain regulations were too detailed and unrealistic in terms of costs and benefits. Congress subsequently ordered OSHA to eliminate nuisance regulations and to try to be more realistic in administering federal regulations.

OSHA must be regarded as a major influence on operations management decisions in all areas relating to worker safety. OSHA has promoted the welfare and safety of workers in its role as a catalyst, spurring companies to make changes that they knew were needed but "hadn't gotten around to making yet."

WORK MEASUREMENT

Job design and methods analysis concentrate on *how* a job is done. Work measurement is concerned with determining the *length of time* it should take to complete the job. Job times are vital inputs for manpower planning, estimating labor costs, scheduling, budgeting, and designing incentive systems. Moreover, from the workers' standpoint, time standards provide an indication of expected output. Time standards reflect the amount of time it should take an average worker to do a given job working under typical conditions. The standards include expected activity time plus allowances for probable delays.

More formally, a **standard time** is the amount of time it should take a qualified worker to complete a specified task, working at a sustainable rate, using given methods, tools and equipment, raw material inputs, and workplace arrangement. Whenever a time standard is developed for a job, it is essential to provide a complete description of the parameters of the job because the actual time to do the job is sensitive to all of these factors; changes in any one of the factors can materially affect time requirements. For instance, changes in product design or changes in the way a job is performed brought about by a methods study should trigger a new time study to update the standard time. As a practical matter, though, minor changes are occasionally made that do not justify the expense of restudying the job. Consequently, the standards for many jobs may be slightly inaccurate. Periodic time studies may be used to update the standards.

There are a number of different ways organizations develop time standards. Although some small manufacturers and service organizations rely on subjective estimates of job times, the most commonly used methods of work measurement are:

1. Stopwatch time study.
2. Historical times.
3. Predetermined data.
4. Work sampling.

Each of these techniques is described in some detail on the following pages.

Stopwatch Time Study

Stopwatch time study was formally introduced by Frederick Winslow Taylor late in the last century. Today it is the most widely used method of work measurement. It is especially appropriate for short, repetitive tasks.

Stopwatch time study involves developing a time standard based on observations of one worker taken over a number of cycles. Once established, it is then applied to the work of all others in the organization who perform the same task. The basic steps in a time study are:

1. Define the task to be studied, and inform the worker who will be studied.
2. Determine the number of cycles to observe.
3. Time the job, and rate the worker's performance.
4. Compute the standard time.

The analyst who will study the job should be thoroughly familiar with it since it is not unusual for workers to attempt to include extra motions during the study in hope of gaining a standard that allows more time per piece (i.e., the worker will be able to work at a slower pace and still meet the standard). Furthermore, the analyst will want to check to see if the job is being performed efficiently before setting the time standard.

In most instances, an analyst will want to break all but very short jobs down into basic elemental motions (e.g., reach, grasp) and obtain times for each element. There are several reasons for this. One is that some elements are not done in every cycle, and the breakdown enables the analyst to get a better perspective on them. Another is that the worker's proficiency may not be the same for all elements of the job, so an elemental breakdown become necessary. A third reason for an elemental breakdown is to build a file of elemental times that can be used to set times for other jobs. This use will be described a bit later.

It is important to inform the worker who will be observed about the study in order to avoid suspicion or misunderstandings. Workers sometimes feel uneasy about being studied, and they may fear changes that might result. The analyst should make an attempt to discuss these things with the worker prior to studying the operations to allay such fears and to enlist the cooperation of the worker.

The number of cycles that must be timed is a function of three things: (1) the variability of observed times, (2) the desired accuracy, and (3) the desired level of confidence for the estimated job time. Very often the desired accuracy is expressed as a percentage of the mean of the observed times. For example, the goal of a time study may be to achieve an estimate that is within 10 percent of the actual mean. The sample size that will be needed to achieve that goal can be determined using this formula:

$$n = \left(\frac{zs}{a\overline{x}}\right)^2 \qquad (8\text{--}1)$$

where

z = Number of normal standard deviations needed for desired confidence
s = Sample standard deviation
a = Desired accuracy percentage
$\overline{x}$ = Sample mean

Typical values of z used in this computation are:[5]

Desired confidence percent	z value
90	1.65
95	1.96
95.5	2.00
98	2.33
99	2.58

Of course, the value of z for any desired confidence can be obtained from the normal table in Appendix B, (Table A or Table B).

An alternate formula that is used when the desired accuracy is stated as an *amount* (e.g., within one minute of the true mean) instead of a percentage is:

$$n = \left(\frac{zs}{e}\right)^2 \qquad (8\text{--}2)$$

where

e = Accuracy or maximum error desired

To make a preliminary estimate of sample size, it is typical to take a small number of observations (say, 10 to 20) and then compute values of $\overline{x}$ and s to use in the formula for n. Toward the end of the study, the analyst may want to recompute n using revised estimates of $\overline{x}$ and s based on the increased data available.

---

[5] Theoretically, a t value rather than a z should be used because the population standard deviation in unknown. However, the use of z is simpler and provides reasonable results when the number of observations is 30 or more as it generally is. In practice, z is used almost exclusively.

EXAMPLE 1

A time study analyst wants to estimate the time required to perform a certain job. A preliminary study yielded a mean of 6.4 minutes and a standard deviation of 2.1 minutes. The desired confidence is 95 percent. How many observations will be needed (including those already taken) if the desired maximum error is:
a. ± 10 percent of the sample mean?
b.   One-half minute?

Solution

a. $s = 2.1$ minutes $z = 1.96$
     $\overline{x} = 6.4$ minutes $a = 10\%$

$$n = \left(\frac{zs}{a\overline{x}}\right)^2 = \left(\frac{1.96(2.1)}{.10(6.4)}\right)^2 = 41.36 \text{ (round up to 42)}$$

b. $e = .5$ $n = \left(\frac{zs}{e}\right)^2 = \left(\frac{1.96(2.1)}{.5}\right)^2 = 67.77 \text{ (round up to 68)}$

In an actual situation, the analyst would not be "given" the value of s but would be expected to compute it from sample data. This can be done using either of two formulas:

$$s = \sqrt{\frac{\Sigma(x_i - \overline{x})^2}{n - 1}} \quad \text{or} \quad s = \sqrt{\frac{\Sigma x_i^2 - (\Sigma x_i)^2/n}{n - 1}} \qquad (8\text{--}3)$$

An example of this computation is provided as a solved problem at the end of this chapter.

Development of a time standard involves computation of three times: the *observed time* (OT), the *normal time* (NT), and the *standard time* (ST).

Observed time.   The observed time is simply the average of the observed times. Thus,

$$OT = \frac{\Sigma x_i}{n} \qquad (8\text{--}4)$$

where

$$OT = \text{Observed time}$$
$$\Sigma x_i = \text{Sum of observed times}$$
$$n = \text{Number of observations}$$

Normal time.   The normal time is the observed time adjusted for worker performance. It is computed by multiplying the observed time by a *performance rating*. That is,

$$NT = OT \times PR \qquad (8\text{--}5)$$

where

$$NT = \text{Normal time}$$
$$PR = \text{Performance rating}$$

This assumes that a single performance rating has been made for the entire job. If ratings are made on an element-by-element basis, the normal time is obtained by multiplying each element's average time by its performance rating and summing those values:

$$NT = \Sigma(\overline{x}_j \cdot PR_j) \qquad (8-6)$$

where

$$\overline{x}_j = \text{Average time for element } j$$
$$PR_j = \text{Performance rating for element } j$$

The reason for including this adjustment factor is that the worker being observed may be working at a rate that is different from a "normal" rate, either because of an attempt to deliberately slow the pace or because the worker's natural abilities differ from the norm. For this reason, an efficiency factor, or performance rating, is made by the observer to adjust the observed times to an "average" pace. For instance, a performance rating of 0.9 indicates a pace that is 90 percent of normal, whereas a rating of 1.05 indicates a pace that is slightly faster than normal. For long jobs, each element may be rated; for short jobs, a single rating may be made for an entire cycle.

In assessing performance, the analyst must compare the observed performance to his or her concept of normal. Obviously, there is room for debate about what constitutes normal performance, and performance ratings are sometimes the source of considerable conflict between labor and management. Although no one has been able to suggest a way around these subjective evaluations, sufficient training and periodic *recalibration* of analysts using training films can provide a high degree of consistency in the ratings of different analysts.

Standard time. Normal time is the length of time a worker should take to perform a job if there are no delays or interruptions. It does not take into account such factors as personal delays (getting a drink of water or going to the restroom), unavoidable delays (machine adjustments and repairs, talking to a supervisor, waiting for materials), or rest breaks. The standard time for a job is the normal time adjusted for these delays using an allowance factor:

$$ST = NT \times AF \qquad (8-7)$$

where

$$ST = \text{Standard time}$$
$$AF = \text{Allowance factor}$$

The allowance factor can be computed in one of two ways, depending on how allowances are specified. If allowances are based on the *job time,* the allowance factor must be computed using the formula:

$$AF_{job} = 1 + A \qquad (8-8)$$

where

$$A = \text{Allowance percentage based on job time}$$

If allowances are based on a percentage of the time worked (i.e., the *workday*), the appropriate formula is:

$$AF_{day} = \frac{1}{1 - A} \qquad (8-9)$$

where

$$A = \text{Allowance percentage based on workday.}$$

Some typical allowance percentages (A) are listed in Table 8–3.

EXAMPLE 2

Compute the allowance factor for these two cases:

a.   The allowance is 20 percent of *job* time.
b.   The allowance is 20 percent of *work* time.

Solution

$$A = .20$$

a. $AF = 1 + A = 1.20$, or 120%.

b. $AF = \dfrac{1}{1 - A} = \dfrac{1}{1 - .20} = 1.25$, or 125%.

TABLE 8–3

Typical allowance percentages for working conditions

	Percent
A. Constant allowances:	
1. Personal allowance	5
2. Basic fatigue allowances	4
B. Variable allowances:	
1. Standing allowance	2
2. Abnormal position allowance:	
a. Slightly awkward	0
b. Awkward (bending)	2
c. Very awkward (lying, stretching)	7

TABLE 8–3

	Percent	*(concluded)*

3. Use of force or muscular energy (lifting, pulling, or pushing):
   Weight lifted, pounds:

5	0
10	1
15	2
20	3
25	4
30	5
35	7
40	9
45	11
50	13
60	17
70	22

4. Bad light:
   a. Slightly below recommended   0
   b. Well below   2
   c. Quite inadequate   5
5. Atmospheric conditions (heat and humidity)—variable   0–10
6. Close attention:
   a. Fairly fine work   0
   b. Fine or exacting   2
   c. Very fine or very exacting   5
7. Noise level:
   a. Continuous   0
   b. Intermittent—loud   2
   c. Intermittent—very loud   5
   d. High-pitched—loud   5
8. Mental strain:
   a. Fairly complex process   1
   b. Complex or wide span of attention   4
   c. Very complex   8
9. Monotony:
   a. Low   0
   b. Medium   1
   c. High   4
10. Tediousness:
   a. Rather tedious   0
   b. Tedious   2
   c. Very tedious   5

EXAMPLE 3

A time study of an assembly operation yielded the following observed times, for which the analyst gave a performance rating of 1.10. Using an allowance of 15 percent of *job* time, determine the appropriate standard time for this operation.

Observation	Time (minutes)	Observation	Time (minutes)
1	4.20	6	4.18
2	4.15	7	4.14
3	4.08	8	4.14
4	4.12	9	4.19
5	4.15		37.35

Solution

$$n = 9, \ PR = 1.10, \text{ and } A = .15$$

a. $OT = \dfrac{\Sigma x_i}{n} = \dfrac{37.35}{9} = 4.15 \text{ minutes.}$

b. $NT = OT \times PR = 4.15(1.10) = 4.565 \text{ minutes.}$

c. $ST = NT \times (1 + A) = 4.565(1.15) = 5.25 \text{ minutes.}$

The formulas and symbols used for time study computations are summarized in Table 8–4.

In spite of the obvious benefits that can be derived from work measurement using time study, there are also some limitations that must be mentioned. One limitation relates to the subjective nature of performance rating. This has created innumerable conflicts between labor and management and in some companies is a continual sore spot. Another limitation is the fact that only those jobs that can be observed can be studied. This eliminates most managerial and creative jobs, which involve mental as well as physical aspects. In addition, the cost of making the study rules out its use for irregular operations and infrequently occurring jobs. Finally, it disrupts the normal work routine, and workers resent it in many cases.

Standard Elemental Times

Standard elemental times are derived from a firm's own historical time study data. Over the years, a time study department can accumulate a file of elemental times that are common to many jobs. After a certain point, many such times can be taken from the file, instead of the analysts having to go through a complete time study to get them, although others may require actual timing.

TABLE 8—4

Summary of time study computations

A. Sample size

$$n = \left(\frac{zs}{a\overline{x}}\right)^2 \qquad (8\text{--}1)$$

$$n = \left(\frac{zs}{e}\right)^2 \qquad (8\text{--}2)$$

B. Observed time

$$\text{OT} = \frac{\Sigma x_i}{n} \qquad (8\text{--}4)$$

C. Normal time

$$\text{NT} = \text{OT} \cdot \text{PR} \qquad (8\text{--}5)$$

D. Standard time

$$\text{ST} = \text{NT} \cdot \text{AF} \qquad (8\text{--}7)$$

where

$$\text{AF}_{job} = 1 + A \qquad (8\text{--}8)$$

$$\text{AF}_{day} = \frac{1}{1 - A} \qquad (8\text{--}9)$$

Symbols:

a = Allowable error as a percentage of average time
A = Allowance percentage
AF = Allowance factor
AF_{job} = Allowance expressd as a percentage of job time
AF_{day} = Allowance expressed as a percentage of working day
n = Number of observations needed
NT = Normal time
OT = Observed, or average, time
s = Standard deviation of observed times
x_i = Time for ith observation (i = 1,2,3, . . . ,n)
ST = Standard time

The procedure for using standard elemental times consists of the following steps:

1. Analyze the job to identify the standard elements.
2. Check the file to see which elements have historical times, and record them. Use time study to obtain others, if necessary.
3. Modify the file times if necessary (explained below).
4. Sum the elemental times to obtain the normal time, and factor in allowances to obtain the standard time.

In some cases, the file times may not pertain exactly to a specific task. For instance, standard elemental times might be on file for "move the tool 3 centimeters'' and ''move the tool 9 centimeters,'' when the task in question involves a move of 6 centimeters. However, it is often possible to interpolate between values on file to obtain the desired time estimate.

One obvious advantage of this approach is the potential savings in cost and effort created by not having to conduct a complete time study for each job. A second advantage is that there is less disruption of work, again because the analyst does not have to time the worker. A third advantage is that performance ratings do not have to be done; they are generally *averaged* in the file times. The main disadvantage of this approach are that times may not exist for enough standard elements to make it worthwhile, and the file times may be biased or inaccurate.

The method described in the following section is a variation of this that helps avoid some of these problems.

Predetermined Time Standards

Predetermined time standards involve the use of published data on standard elemental times. A commonly used system is *MTM* (methods time measurement), which was developed in the late 1940s by the Methods Engineering Council. The MTM tables are based on extensive research on basic elemental motions and times. In order to use this approach, the analyst is required to divide the job into its basic elements (reach, move, turn, disengage), measure the distances involved (if applicable), rate the difficulty of the element, and then refer to the appropriate table of data to obtain the time for that element. The standard time for the job is obtained by adding the times for all of the basic elements. Times of the basic elements are measured in time measurement units (TMUs); one TMU equals 0.0006 minutes. One minute of work may involve 100 or more basic elements, and a typical job may involve several hundred or more of these basic elements. This requires a considerable amount of skill on the part of the analyst to adequately describe the operation and develop realistic time estimates. A few of the MTM tables are presented in Table 8–5 to give you an idea of the kind of information they provide.

A great deal of skill is required to generate a predetermined time standard. Analysts generally take training or certification courses to develop the necessary skills to do this kind of work.

Among the advantages of predetermined time standards are the following:

1. They are based on large numbers of workers under controlled conditions.
2. The analyst is not required to rate performance in developing the standard.
3. There is no disruption of the operation.
4. Standards can be established even before a job is done.

Although proponents of predetermined standards claim that the approach provides much better accuracy than stopwatch studies, not everyone agrees

TABLE 8–5

A portion of the MTM tables

Table II—Move—M

Distance moved (inches)	Time (TMU)				Weight Allowance			Case and description
	A	B	C	Hand in motion B	Weight (pounds) up to:	Dy-namic factor	Static con-stant TMU	
¾ or less	2.0	2.0	2.0	1.7				
1	2.5	2.9	3.4	2.3	2.5	1.00	0	A. Move object to other hand or against stop.
2	3.6	4.6	5.2	2.9				
3	4.9	5.7	6.7	3.6	7.5	1.06	2.2	
4	6.1	6.9	8.0	4.3				
5	7.3	8.0	9.2	5.0	12.5	1.11	3.9	
6	8.1	8.9	10.3	5.7				
7	8.9	9.7	11.1	6.5	17.5	1.17	5.6	
8	9.7	10.6	11.8	7.2				
9	10.5	11.5	12.7	7.9	22.5	1.22	7.4	B. Move object to approxi-mate or indefinite location.
10	11.3	12.2	13.5	8.6				
12	12.9	13.4	15.2	10.0	27.5	1.28	9.1	
14	14.4	14.6	16.9	11.4				
16	16.0	15.8	18.7	12.8	32.5	1.33	10.8	
18	17.6	17.0	20.4	14.2				
20	19.2	18.2	22.1	15.6	37.5	1.39	12.5	
22	20.8	19.4	23.8	17.0				C. Move object to exact location.
24	22.4	20.6	25.5	18.4	42.5	1.44	14.3	
26	24.0	21.8	27.3	19.8				
28	25.5	23.1	29.0	21.2	47.5	1.50	16.0	
30	27.1	24.3	30.7	22.7				
Additional	0.8	0.6	0.85		TMU per inch over 30 inches			

Table III A—Turn—T

Weight	Time (TMU) for degrees turned										
	30°	45°	60°	75°	90°	105°	120°	135°	150°	165°	180°
Small—0 to 2 pounds	2.8	3.5	4.1	4.8	5.4	6.1	6.8	7.4	8.1	8.7	9.4
Medium—2.1 to 10 pounds	4.4	5.5	6.5	7.5	8.5	9.6	10.6	11.6	12.7	13.7	14.8
Large—10.1 to 35 pounds	8.4	10.5	12.3	14.4	16.2	18.3	20.4	22.2	24.3	26.1	28.2

with that claim. Some argue that many activity times are too specific to a given operation for them to be generalized from published data. Others aruge that different analysts perceive elemental activity breakdowns in different ways, and that this adversely affects the development of times and produces varying time estimates among analysts. A third argument is that analysts can differ on the degree of difficulty they assign a given task and thereby obtain different time standards.

Work Sampling

Work sampling is a technique for estimating the proportion of time that a worker or machine spends on various activities. Introduced by L. H. C. Tippett in 1934 in the textile industry, it is now widely used to study work activities.

Unlike time study, work sampling does not require timing an activity. In fact, it does not even involve continuous observation of the activity. Instead, an observer is required to make brief observations of a worker or machine at random intervals over a period of time and simply note the nature of the activity. For example, a machine may be busy or idle; a secretary may be typing, filing, talking on the telephone, and so on; and a carpenter may be carrying supplies, taking measurements, cutting wood, and so on. The resulting data are *counts* of the number of times each category of activity or nonactivity was observed.

Although work sampling is occasionally used to set time standards, its two primary uses are in (1) ratio-delay studies, which concern the percentage of a worker's time that involves unavoidable delays or the proportion of time a machine is idle, and (2) analysis of nonrepetitive jobs. In a ratio-delay study, a hospital administrator, for example, might want to estimate the percentage of time that a certain piece of X-ray equipment is not in use. In a nonrepetitive job, such as secretarial work or maintenance, it can be important to establish the percentage of time an employee spends doing various tasks.

Nonrepetitive jobs typically involve a broader range of skills than repetitive jobs, and workers in these jobs are often paid on the basis of the highest skill involved. Therefore, it is important to determine the proportion of time spent on the high-skill level. For example, a secretary may take dictation, type, file, answer the telephone, schedule appointments, and do other routine office work. If the secretary spends a high percentage of time filing instead of typing or taking shorthand, the compensation should be lower than for a secretary who spends a high percentage of time typing and taking shorthand. Work sampling can be used to verify those percentages and can therefore be an important tool in developing the job description. In addition, work sampling can be part of a program for validation of job content that is needed for "bona fide occupational qualifications" (i.e., advertised jobs must require the skills that are specified).

Work sampling estimates include some degree of error; the same number of observations taken at different times during the week will probably produce slightly different estimates, and all estimates will usually differ from the actual (but unknown) values. Hence, it is important to treat work sampling estimates as *approximations* of the actual proportion of time devoted to a given activity. The goal of work sampling is to obtain an estimate that provides a specified confidence of not differing from the true value by more than a specified error. For example, a hospital administrator might request an estimate of X-ray idle time that will provide a 95 percent confidence of being within 4 percent of the actual percentage. Hence, work sampling is designed to produce a value, $\hat{p}$, which estimates the true proportion, p, within some allowable error, e: $\hat{p} \pm e$. The variability associated with sample estimates of p tends to be approximately normal for large sample sizes. Consequently, the normal distribution can be used to construct a confidence interval and to determine required sample sizes. One (nonclassical) way to view the sampling distribution is to imagine all of the *possible* true proportions that could produce a given sample value of $\hat{p}$. The result is a distribution of possible true proportions that is (1) normal and (2) centered around the sample proportion. The most likely values of the actual proportion are quite close to the sample proportion; a true value close to the center of the distribution is much more likely than a value in one of the tails. This concept is illustrated in Figure 8–8. The degree to which this distribution is narrow or spread out is a function of the sample size and p. The amount of maximum probable error is a function of both the sample size and the desired level of confidence.

For large samples, the maximum error, e, can be computed using the formula:

$$e = z \sqrt{\frac{\hat{p}(1 - \hat{p})}{n}} \qquad (8\text{–}10)$$

where

z = Number of standard deviations needed to achieve desired confidence
$\hat{p}$ = Sample proportion
n = Sample size

FIGURE 8–8

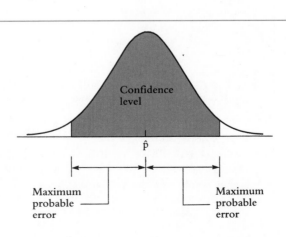

A confidence interval for the estimate of the true proportion is based on a normal distribution

Confidence level

$\hat{p}$

Maximum probable error

Maximum probable error

In most instances, management will be required to specify the desired confidence level and the amount of allowable error, and the analyst will be required to determine a sample size that will be sufficient to obtain those results. The appropriate value for n can be determined by solving Formula 8–10 for n, which yields:

$$n = \left(\frac{z}{e}\right)^2 \hat{p}(1 - \hat{p}) \qquad (8–11)$$

Note: If the resulting value of n is noninteger, round *up*.

EXAMPLE 4

The manager of a small supermarket chain wants to estimate the proportion of time stock clerks spend making price changes to previously marked merchandise. The manager wants a 98 percent confidence that the resulting estimate will be within 5 percent of the true value. What sample size should be used?

Solution

$$e = .05, \qquad z = 2.33 \text{ (see p. 417)}$$
$$\hat{p} = \text{Unkown}$$

When no sample estimate of p is available, a preliminary estimate of sample size can be obtained using $\hat{p} = .50$. Then, after 20 or so observations, a new estimate of $\hat{p}$ can be obtained from those observations and a revised value of n computed using the new $\hat{p}$. In fact, it would be prudent to recompute the value of n at two or three points during the study to obtain a better indication of the necessary sample size. Thus, the initial estimate of n is:

$$n = \left(\frac{2.33}{.05}\right)^2 .50(1 - .5) = 542.89, \text{ or } 543 \text{ observations}$$

Suppose that, in the first 20 observations, stock clerks were found to be changing prices twice, making $p = 2/20 = .10$. The revised estimate of n at that point would be:

$$n = \left(\frac{2.33}{.05}\right)^2 .1(1 - .1) = 195.44, \text{ or } 196$$

Suppose a second check is made after a total of 100 observations, and assume $\hat{p} = .11$ at this point (including the initial 20 observations). Recomputing n yields:

$$n = \left(\frac{2.33}{.05}\right)^2 .11(.89) = 212.60, \text{ or } 213$$

Perhaps one more check might be made to settle on a final value for n. If the computed value of n is less than the number of observations already taken, sampling would be terminated at that point.

Determining the sample size is only one part of work sampling. The overall procedure consists of the following steps:

1. Clearly identify the worker(s) or machine(s) to be studied.
2. Notify the workers and supervisors of the purpose of the study to avoid arousing suspicions.
3. Compute an initial estimate of sample size using a preliminary estimate of p, if available (say, from analyst experience or past data.) Otherwise, use $\hat{p} = .50$.
4. Develop a random observation schedule.
5. Begin taking observations. Recompute the required sample size several times during the study.
6. Determine the estimated proportion of time spent on the specified activity.

As always, careful problem definition can prevent mistakes such as studying the wrong worker or wrong activity. Similarly, it is important to inform related parties of the purpose and scope of the study in order to reduce unnecessary fears that might be generated by unannounced data collection. It is also important to obtain random observations in order to achieve valid results.

Observations must be spread out over a period of time so that a true indication of variability is obtained. If observations are bunched too closely in time, there is some risk that the behaviors observed during that time will not genuinely reflect typical performance. The degree to which observations should be spread out will depend in part on the nature of the activity being studied, and a decision on this is usually best left to the analyst. Determination of a random observation schedule involves the use of a **random number table** (see Table 8–6), which consists of *unordered sequences* of numbers (i.e.,

TABLE 8–6

Portion of a random number table

	1	2	3	4	5	6
1	6912	7264	2801	8901	4627	8387
2	3491	1192	0575	7547	2093	4617
3	4715	2486	2776	2664	3856	0064
4	1632	1546	1950	1844	1123	1908
5	8510	7209	0938	2376	0120	4237
6	3950	1328	7343	6083	2108	2044
7	7871	7752	0521	8511	3956	3957
8	2716	1396	7354	0249	7728	8818
9	2935	8259	9912	3761	4028	9207
10	8533	9957	9585	1039	2159	2438
11	0508	1640	2768	4666	9530	3352
12	2951	0131	4359	3095	4421	3018

random). Use of such tables enables the analyst to incorporate randomness into the observation schedule. Numbers obtained from the table can be used to identify observation times for a study. Any size number (i.e., any number of digits read as one number) can be obtained from the table. The digits are in groups of four for convenience only. The basic idea is to obtain numbers from the table and to convert each one so that it corresponds to an observation time. There are a number of different ways to accomplish this. The approach we will use is as follows. We will obtain three sets of numbers from the table for each observation: the first set will correspond to the *day,* the second to the *hour,* and the third to the *minute* when the observation is to be made. The number of digits necessary for any set will equal the number of days in the study, the number of hours per day, and minutes per hour. For instance, if the study will cover 47 days, a two-digit number will be needed; and if the activity is performed for eight hours per day, a one-digit number will be needed for hours. Of course, since each hour has 60 minutes, a two-digit number will be needed for minutes. Thus, we would need a two-digit number for the day, a one-digit number for the hour, and a two-digit number for minutes. For a study that requires observations over a seven-day period in an office that works nine hours per day, one-digit numbers would be needed for days, one-digit numbers for hours, and two-digit numbers for minutes.

Suppose we want three observations in this last case (i.e., 7 days, 9 hours, 60 minutes). We might begin by determining the days on which observations will be made, then the hours, and finally the minutes. Let's begin at the upper left-hand corner of Table 8–6 and read across: The first number is 6, which indicates day 6. The second number is 9. Since it exceeds the number of days in the study, it is simply ignored. The third number is 1, indicating day 1, and the next is 2, indicating day 2. Hence, observations will be made on days 6, 1, and 2. Next we determine the hours. Suppose we read the second row of column 1, again obtaining one-digit numbers. We find:

$$3 (= \text{3rd hour}), 4 (= \text{4th hour}), 9 (= \text{9th hour})$$

Moving to the next row and reading two-digit numbers, we find:

$$47 (= \text{47th minute}), 15 (= \text{15th minute}), 24 (= \text{24th minute})$$

Combining these results yields:

Day	Hour	Minute
6 3		47
1 4		15
2 9		24

This means that on day 6 of the study, an observation is to be made during the 47th minute of the 3rd hour; on day 1, during the 15th minute of the 4th hour; and on day 2, during the 24th minute of the 9th hour. For simplicity, these times can be put in chronological order by day. Thus,

Day	Hour	Minute
1 4		15
2 9		24
6 3		47

A complete schedule of observations might appear as follows, after all numbers have been arranged in chronological order.

Day 1					Day 2			
Observa-tion	Time	Busy (✔)	Idle (✔)		Observa-tion	Time	Busy (✔)	Idle (✔)
1	4:15				24	8:04		
2	8:42				25	9:15		
3	9:02				26	9:24		
4	9:31				27	9:35		
5	9:48				28	10:12		
6	9:57				29	10:27		
7	10:20				30	10:38		
8	11:02				31	10:58		
9	11:13				32	11:50		
10	11:55				33	1:14		
11	1:29				34	1:43		
12	1:41				35	1:57		
13	2:00				36	3:10		
14	2:33							

The general procedure for using a random number table is to read the numbers in some sequence (across rows, down or up columns), discarding any that lack correspondence. It is important to vary the starting point from one study to the next in order to avoid taking observations at the same times, since the times would quickly become known to workers and the random element would be lost. There are various ways to choose a starting point. One is to use the serial number on a dollar bill to select a starting point. However, so that everyone ends up with the same results, you will be instructed in each problem as to the starting point and as to the direction to read in.

In sum, the procedure for identifying random times at which to make work sampling observations involves the following steps:

1. Determine the number of days in the study and the number of hours per day. This will indicate the required number of digits for days and hours.

TABLE 8–7

Advantages and disadvantages of work sampling compared to stopwatch time study

Advantages

1. Observations are spread out over a period of time, making results less susceptible to short-term fluctuations.
2. There is little or no disruption of work.
3. Workers are less resentful.
4. Studies are less costly and less time-consuming, and the skill requirements of the analyst are much less.
5. The study can be interrupted without affecting the results.
6. Many different studies can be conducted simultaneously.
7. No timing device is required.
8. Lends itself to nonrepetitive tasks.

Disadvantages

1. There is much less detail on the elements of a job.
2. Workers may alter their work patterns when they spot the observer, thereby invalidating the results.
3. In many cases, there is no record of the method used by the worker.
4. Observers may fail to adhere to a random schedule of observations.
5. It is not well suited for short, repetitive tasks.
6. Much time may be required to move from one workplace to another and back to satisfy the randomness requirement.

---

2. Obtain the necessary number of sets for *days,* ignoring any sets that exceed the number of days.

3. Repeat step 2 for *hours.*

4. Repeat step 2 for *minutes.*

5. Link the days, hours, and minutes in the order that they were obtained.

6. Place the observation times in chronological order.

A comparison of work sampling and time study is presented in Table 8–7. It suggests that work sampling is a less formal, less detailed approach to determining job times that is best suited to nonrepetitive jobs.

COMPENSATION

A significant issue that relates to the design of work systems is worker compensation. It is important for organizations to develop suitable compensation plans for their employees, especially since the success or failure of a firm depends in large measure on the efforts of its employees. If wages are set too low, organizations may find it difficult to attract and hold competent workers and managers. Conversely, if wages are set too high, the increased costs may result in lower profits or force the organization to increase its prices, which might adversely affect demand for the organization's products or services.

Organizations use two basic systems for compensating employees: *time-based systems* and *output-based systems*. **Time-based systems,** also known as *hourly* and *measured daywork* systems, compensate employees for the time the employee has worked during a pay period. Salaried workers also represent a form of time-based compensation. **Output-based (incentive) systems** compensate employees according to the amount of output they produce during a pay period, thereby tying pay directly to performance.

Time-based systems are more widely used than incentive systems, particularly for office, administrative, and managerial employees, but also for blue-collar workers. One of the reasons for this is that computation of wages is straightforward and managers can readily estimate labor costs for a given manpower level. Employees often prefer time-based systems because the pay is steady and they know how much they will receive for each pay period. In addition, employees may resent the pressures associated with an output-based system.

Another reason for using time-based systems is that many jobs do not lend themselves to the use of incentives. In some cases it may be difficult or impossible to measure output. For example, jobs that require creative or mental work cannot be easily measured on an output basis. Other jobs may include irregular activities or have so many different forms of output that measuring output and determining pay is fairly complex. Also, in the case of assembly lines, the use of *individual* incentives would disrupt the even flow of work. However, *group* incentives are sometimes used successfully in such cases. Finally, *quality* considerations may be more important than *quantity*. For example, in health care, greater emphasis is generally placed on the quality of patient care than on the number of patients processed.

On the other hand, there are situations in which the use of incentives is desirable. Incentives reward workers for their output, which presumably causes some workers to produce more than they might under a time-based system. The advantage is that certain (fixed) costs do not vary with increases in output, so the overall cost per unit decreases if output increases. Workers may prefer incentive systems because they see a relationship between their efforts and their pay and because it presents the opportunity for them to earn more than they might under a time-based system.

On the negative side, incentive systems involve a considerable amount of paperwork, computation of wages is more difficult than under time-based systems, output has to be measured and standards have to be set, cost-of-living increases are difficult to integrate into incentive plans, and contingency arrangements for unavoidable delays have to be developed.

The main advantages and disadvantages of time-based and output-based plans are outlined in Table 8–8.

In order to obtain the maximum benefit from an incentive plan, the plan should be:

1. Accurate.
2. Easy to apply.

TABLE 8–8

Comparison of time-based and output-based pay systems

	Management	Worker
Time-based		
Advantages	1. Stable labor costs 2. Easy to administer 3. Simple to compute pay 4. Stable output	1. Stable pay 2. Less pressure to produce than under output system
Disadvantages	1. No incentive for workers to increase output	1. Extra efforts not rewarded
Output-based		
Advantages	1. Lower cost per unit 2. Greater output	1. Pay related to efforts 2. Opportunity to earn more
Disadvantages	1. Wage computation more difficult 2. Need to measure output 3. Quality may suffer 4. Difficult to incorporate wage increases 5. Increased problems with scheduling	1. Pay fluctuates 2. Worker may be penalized because of factors beyond their control (e.g., machine breakdowns)

3. Consistent.
4. Easy to understand.
5. Fair.

In addition, there should be an obvious relationship between effort and reward, and there should not be a limit on earnings.

Incentive systems may focus on the output of each individual or on the output of a group. Each of these approaches is briefly described below.

Individual Incentive Plans

Individual incentive plans take a variety of forms. The simplest plan is *straight piecework*. Under this plan, a worker's pay is a direct linear function of his or her output. In the past, piecework plans were fairly popular. Now minimum wage legislation makes them somewhat impractical. Even so, many of the plans currently in use represent variations of the straight piecework plan. They typically incorporate a base rate that serves as a floor: workers are guaranteed that amount as a minimum, regardless of output. The base rate is tied to an output standard: if the worker produces less than the standard, that worker will be paid at the base rate. This protects workers from pay loss due to delays, breakdowns, and similar problems. In most cases, incentives are paid for output above standard, and the pay is referred to as a *bonus*.

Group Incentive Plans

Group incentive plans stress sharing of productivity gains with employees. There are a variety of plans in use. Some focus exclusively on output, and others reward employees for output and for reductions in material and other costs. The following four well-known plans reflect the main features of most of the plans currently in operation.

The *Scanlon plan* was developed by the late Joseph Scanlon during the 1930s in cooperation with the management of a machine tool company that was on the brink of bankruptcy. The main feature of the plan was to encourage reductions in labor costs by allowing workers to share in any reductions achieved. The plan involved formation of worker committees to actively seek out areas for improvement.

The *Kaiser plan* was introduced during the 1960s. Like the Scanlon plan, it involved the use of committees to suggest ways of reducing costs, with savings shared by employees. However, in addition to reductions in labor costs, it also provided for workers to share in reductions in material and supply costs.

The *Lincoln plan* was developed over a period of about 20 years (1914 to 1934) at the Lincoln Electric Company in Cleveland, Ohio. It includes profit sharing, job enlargement, and participative management. Like the other plans, it involves the use of evaluation committees to generate suggestions. The three main components of the plan are a piecework system, an annual bonus, and a stock purchase provision. Lincoln officials credit the plan with enabling the company to increase its market share and profitability and with reducing the unit cost of its basic product while competitors have experienced substantial increases in their costs.

The *Kodak plan* uses a combination of premium wage levels and an annual bonus related to company profits instead of more traditional incentives. Workers are encouraged to help set goals and to decide on reasonable performance levels with the idea that because of their involvement, they will be more apt to produce at a premium rate.

OPERATIONS STRATEGY

It is important for management to make design of work systems a key element of its operations strategy. In spite of the major advances in computers and manufacturing technology, people are still the heart of a business; they can make or break it, regardless of the technology being used. That is not to say that technology is unimportant, but that technology alone is not enough.

Methods analysis, motion study, work standards, and incentives all have an impact on productivity. Methods analysis and motion study get at the nitty-gritty aspects of productivity. They lack the glamour of high tech; they are closer to the back-to-the-basics fundamentals of industrial engineering.

Workers can be a valuable source of insight and creativity since they are closest to the jobs and to the problems that arise. All too often, managers have overlooked contributions and potential contributions of employees, sometimes because of ignorance and sometimes because of a false sense of pride. Union-management differences also contribute to this. More and more, though, companies are attempting to develop a spirit of cooperation between employees and managers, based in part on successes of Japanese companies.

In the same vein, more and more companies are focusing some of their attention on improving the quality of work life and on instilling pride and respect among workers.

Summary

The design of work systems involves job design, work measurement, and compensation.

Job design is concerned with the content of jobs and work methods. In the past, job design has tended to focus on efficiency. However, there now seems to be an increasing awareness of and an attempt to consider the behavioral aspects of work and worker satisfaction. Current concern about productivity has thrust job design into the limelight. However, the jobs usually associated with high productivity are often the same jobs that are the greatest source of worker dissatisfaction, creating somewhat of a paradox for job designers.

Methods analysis and motion study techniques are often used to develop the "efficiency" aspects of jobs but do not directly address their behavioral aspects. Nonetheless, they are an important part of job design. Working conditions are also an important aspect of job design, not only because of the behavioral and efficiency factors, but also because of concern for the health and safety of workers.

Work measurement is concerned with specifying the length of time needed to complete a job. Such information is vital for personnel planning, cost estimating, budgeting, scheduling, and worker compensation. Commonly used approaches include stopwatch time study and predetermined times. A related technique is work sampling, which can also be used to obtain data on activity times. More commonly, work sampling is used to estimate the proportion of time a worker spends on a certain aspect of the job.

Organizations can choose from a variety of compensation plans. It is important to do so carefully, for compensation is important to both the worker and the organization, and, once adopted, it is usually difficult to substantially change a compensation plan.

KEY TERMS

automation, 398
flow process chart, 401
gang process chart, 404
job design, 394
job enlargement, 396
job enrichment, 397
job rotation, 397
lost-time accident, 414
micromotion study, 408
motion study, 406
motion study principles, 406
OSHA, 414

output-based system, 433
predetermined time standards, 424
random number table, 429
sociotechnical systems, 399
specialization, 395
standard elemental times, 422
standard time, 415
stopwatch time study, 416
therblig, 406
time-based system, 433
work sampling, 426
worker-machine chart, 403

SOLVED PROBLEMS

1. Compute the mean and standard deviation of these observed times:

Observation	Time (minutes)
1	3.6
2	4.1
3	4.4
4	3.7
5	4.2

Solution

$$\bar{x} = \text{Average time} = \frac{3.6 + 4.1 + 4.4 + 3.7 + 4.2}{5} = \frac{20.0}{5} = 4.0$$

Using $s = \sqrt{\dfrac{\Sigma(x_i - \bar{x})^2}{n - 1}}$:

x_i	$\bar{x}$	$(x_i - \bar{x})$	$(x_i - \bar{x})^2$
3.6	4.0	-0.4	0.16
4.1	4.0	0.1	0.01
4.4	4.0	0.4	0.16
3.7	4.0	-0.3	0.09
4.2	4.0	0.2	0.04
		0.0	0.46

$$s = \sqrt{\frac{0.46}{5 - 1}} = 0.34 \text{ minutes}$$

Using $s = \sqrt{\frac{\Sigma x_i^2 - (\Sigma x_i)^2/n}{n - 1}}$:

x_i	x_i^2
3.6	12.96
4.1	16.81
4.4	19.36
3.7	13.69
4.2	17.64
20.0	80.46

$$s = \sqrt{\frac{80.46 - 20^2/5}{5 - 1}}$$

$$= 0.34 \text{ minutes}$$

2. *Work sampling.* An analyst has been asked to prepare an estimate of the proportion of time that a turret lathe operator spends adjusting the machine, with a 90 percent confidence level. Based on previous experience, the analyst believes the proportion will be approximately 30 percent.

   a. If the analyst uses a sample size of 400 observations, what is the maximum possible error that will be associated with the estimate?

   b. What sample size would the analyst need in order to have the maximum error be no more than ± 5 percent?

Solution

$$\hat{p} = .30, \ z = 1.65 \text{ (for 90 percent confidence)}$$

a. $e = z \sqrt{\dfrac{\hat{p}(1 - \hat{p})}{n}} = 1.65 \sqrt{\dfrac{.3(.7)}{400}} = .038$

b. $n = \left(\dfrac{z}{e}\right)^2 \hat{p}(1 - \hat{p}) = \left(\dfrac{1.65}{.05}\right)^2 (.3)(.7) = 228.69, \text{ or } 229$

3. *Work sampling.* The owner of a large gift shop wants to estimate the proportion of time shoppers spend in a certain part of the store. The shop is open nine hours a day, six days a week. Twelve observations will be taken over a 30-day period. Determine the random observation times using Table 8–6 and these instructions:

   a. For days, read the first two digits of column 2, going down, and then the first two digits of column 3, going down.

   b. For hours, read one-digit numbers in row 4 from left to right.

   c. For minutes, read one-digit numbers using the first two digits in column 1, going down, and then the second two digits in column 1, going down.

Solution

a. Days:	*b.* Hours:	*c.* Minutes:
Random number	*Random number*	*Random number*
72*	1	69†
11	6	34
24	3	47
15	2	16
72*	1	85†
13	5	39
77*	4	78†
13	6	27
82*	1	29
99*	9	85†
16	5	05
01	0‡	29
28	1	12
05		91†
27		15
19		32
09		10

*Since there will be 30 days in the study, random numbers larger than 30 are not relevant.

†There are 60 minutes per hour. Larger number do not correspond, so they are discarded.

‡The store is open nine hours per day. The numbers 1–9 correspond to the hours 1–9; 0 is not applicable.

Combining these results, in the order they appeared, produces the following results:

Day	Hour	Minute
11 1		34
24 6		47
15 3		16
13 2		39
13 1		27
16 5		29
01 4		05
28 6		29
05 1		12
27 9		15
19 5		32
09 1		10

Arranging the results chronologically by day, hour, and minute (but maintaining the same *combinations*) produces this list of observation times:

Observations	Day	Hour	Minute
1 01		4	05
2 05		1	12
3 09		1	10
4 11		1	34
5 13		1	27
6 13		2	39
7 15		3	16
8 16		5	29
9 19		5	32
10 24		6	47
11 27		9	15
12 28		6	29

DISCUSSION AND REVIEW QUESTIONS

1. What is job design, and why is it important?

2. What are some of the main advantages and disadvantages of specialization from a management perspective? From a worker's perspective?

3. Contrast the meanings of the terms *job enlargement* and *job enrichment*.

4. What is the purpose of job enlargement and job enrichment?

5. Explain what is meant by the term *sociotechnical approach*.

6. What are some of the ways in which automation can improve production operations? What are some of the potential problems that a manager should be aware of when considering automation?

7. Some Japanese firms have a policy of rotating their managers among the different managerial jobs. In contrast, American managers are more likely to specialize in a certain area (e.g., finance or operations). Discuss the advantages and disadvantages of each of these approaches. Which do you prefer? Why?

8. What are motion study principles? How are they classified?

9. What are some of the reasons that methods analyses are needed? How is methods analysis linked to productivity improvements?

10. How are devices such as flow process charts and worker-machine charts useful?

11. What is a time standard? What factors must be taken into account when developing standards?

12. What are some of the main uses of time study information?

13. Could performance rating be avoided by studying a group of workers and averaging their times? Explain briefly.

14. If an average worker could be identified, what advantage would there be in using that person for a time study? What are some of the reasons that an average worker might not be studied?

15. What are some of the main limitations of time study?

16. Comment on the following: "At any given instant, the standard times for many jobs will not be strictly correct."
    a. Why is this so?
    b. Does this mean that those standards are useless? Explain.

17. Why do workers sometimes resent time studies?

18. List advantages and disadvantages of:
    a. Time-based pay plans?
    b. Incentive plans?

PROBLEMS

1. An analyst has timed a metal-cutting operation for 50 cycles. The average time per cycle was 10.40 minutes, and the standard deviation was 1.20 minutes for a worker with a performance rating of 125 percent. Assume an allowance of 16 percent of job time. Find the standard time for this operation.

2. A job was timed for 60 cycles and had an average of 1.2 minutes per piece. The performance rating was 95 percent, and allowances are 10 percent, based on an eight-hour day. Determine each of the following:
   a. Observed time.
   b. Normal time.
   c. Standard time.

3. A time study was conducted on a job that contains four elements. The observed times and performance ratings for six cycles are shown in the following table.

Element	Performance rating	Observations (minutes per cycle)					
		1	2	3	4	5	6
1	90%	0.44	0.50	0.43	0.45	0.48	0.46
2	85	1.50	1.54	1.47	1.51	1.49	1.52
3	110	0.84	0.89	0.77	0.83	0.85	0.80
4	100	1.10	1.14	1.08	1.20	1.16	1.26

a. Determine the average cycle time for each element.
b. Find the normal time for each element.
c. Assuming an allowance factor of 15 percent of job time, compute the standard time for this job.

4. A worker-machine operation was found to involve 3.3 minutes of machine time per cycle in the course of 40 cycles of stopwatch study. The worker's time averaged 1.9 minutes per cycle, and she was given a rating of 120 percent (machine rating is 100 percent). Midway through the study, the worker took a 10-minute rest break. Assuming an allowance factor of 12 percent of labor time, determine the standard time for this job.

5. A recently negotiated union contract allows workers in a grinding department 48 minutes for rest, 20 minutes for personal time, and 28 minutes for delays for an eight-hour shift. A time study analyst observed a job that is performed continuously and found an average time of 6.0 minutes per cycle for a worker he rated at 95 percent. What standard time is applicable for that operation?

6. The data in the table at the bottom of the page represent time study observations for a woodworking operation.
a. Based on the observations, determine the standard time for the operation, assuming an allowance of 15 percent based on job time.
b. How many observations would be needed to estimate the mean time for

element 2 within 1 percent of its true value with a 95.5 percent confidence?
c. How many observations would be needed to estimate the mean time for element 2 to within .01 minute of its true value with a 95.5 percent confidence?

7. How many observations should a time study analyst plan for in the case of an operation that has a standard deviation of 1.5 minutes per piece if the goal is to estimate the mean time per piece to within 0.4 minutes and obtain a confidence of 95.5 percent?

8. About how many work cycles should be timed in order to estimate the average cycle time to within 2 percent of the sample mean with a confidence of 99 percent if a pilot study yielded these times (minutes): 5.2, 5.5, 5.6, 5.3, 5.5, and 5.3?

9. In an initial survey designed to estimate the percentage of time air-express cargo loaders are idle, an analyst found that loaders were idle in 6 of the 50 observations.
a. Estimate the percentage of idle time.
b. Based on the intial results, approximately how many observations would you require in order to estimate the actual percentage of idle time to within 5 percent with a confidence of 95 percent?

10. A certain job in an insurance office involves telephone conversations with policyholders. The office manager estimates that about half of this person's time is spent

Element	Performance rating	Observation (minutes per cycle)					
		1	2	3	4	5	6
1	110%	1.20	1.17	1.16	1.22	1.24	1.15
2	115	0.83	0.87	0.78	0.82	0.85	1.32*
3	105	0.58	0.53	0.52	0.59	0.60	0.54

*Unusual delay; disregard time.

on the telephone. How many observations would be needed in a work sampling study to estimate that time percentage to within 6 percent and have a confidence of 98 percent?

11. Design a schedule of work sampling observations in which there are eight observations made during one eight-hour day. Using Table 8–6, read the *last digit* going down column 4 for hour (e.g., 1 7 4 4 6 . . .), and then read across row 3 from left to right in sets of two for minutes (e.g., 47 15 24 86 . . .). Arrange the times chronologically.

12. The manager of a large office intends to conduct a work sampling of the time the staff spends on the telephone. The observations will be taken over a period of 50 workdays. The office is open five days a week for eight hours a day. Although the study will consist of 200 random observations, in this problem you will be asked to determine times for 11 observations. Use random numbers from Table 8–6.
    a. Determine times for 11 observations. For days, read sets of two-digit numbers going across row 4 from left to right (e.g., 16 32 15 46 . . .), and do the same in row 5.
    b. For hours, read one-digit numbers going *down,* using the first digit of column 1 (e.g., 6 4 3 1 . . .).
    c. For minutes, read two-digit numbers going *up* column 4 using the first two

digits (e.g., 30 46 10 . . .), and then repeat for the second two digits going *up* column 4 (e.g., 95 66 39 . . .).
    d. Arrange the combinations chronologically by day, hour, and minute.
    e. Assume March 1 is a Monday and that there are no holidays in March, April, or May. Convert your observation days to dates in March, April, and May.

13. A work sampling study is to be conducted on rush-hour traffic (4 to 7 P.M) 5 days per week. The study will encompass 40 days. Determine the day, hour, and minute for 10 observations using the following procedure:
    a. Read two-digit numbers going *down* the first two digits of column 5 (e.g., 46 20 38 . . .), and then down the second two digits of that column (e.g., 27 93 56 . . .) for days.
    b. For hours, read one-digit numbers going from left to right across row 1 and then across row 2. (Read only 4s, 5s, and 6s.)
    c. For minutes, read two-digit numbers going *down* column 6, first using the *last* two digits (e.g., 87 17 64 . . .), and then, after exhausting those numbers, repeat using the first two digits of that column (e.g., 83 46 00 19 . . .).
    Arrange your times chronologically by day, then hour, and then minute.

SELECTED BIBLIOGRAPHY

Barnes, Ralph M. *Motion and Time Study: Design and Measurement of Work.* 8th ed. New York: John Wiley & Sons, 1980.

Buffa, Elwood Spencer. *Operations Management: The Management of Productive Systems.* 2d ed. New York: John Wiley & Sons, 1980.

Chase, Richard B., and Nicholas J. Aquilano. *Production and Operations Management.* 4th ed. Homewood, Ill.: Richard D. Irwin, 1985.

Davis, L. E. "Job Satisfaction Research: The Post-Industrial View." *Industrial Relations* 10 (1971), pp. 176–93.

————, and A. B. Cherns, eds. *Quality of Working Life; Cases.* Vol. 2. New York: Free Press, 1975.

————, and J. C. Taylor, eds. *Design of Jobs.* Middlesex, England: Penguin Books, 1972.

Dickson, Paul. *The Future of the Workplace.* New York: Weybright and Talley, 1975.

Fory, N., and H. Gordon. "Worker Participation: Contrasts in Three Countries." *Harvard Business Review* 54, no. 3 (May–June 1976), pp. 71–83.

Herbst, P. G. *Socio-technical Design: Strategies in Multidisciplinary Research.* London: Tavistock, 1974.

Herzberg, Frederick. "One More Time: How Do You Motivate Employees?" *Harvard Business Review,* January–February 1968.

Hopeman, Richard J. *Production and Operations Management.* 4th ed. (Columbus, Ohio: Charles E. Merrill Publishing, 1980).

Huchinson, R. D. *New Horizons for Human Factors in Job Design.* New York: McGraw-Hill, 1981.

Konz, S. *Work Design: Industrial Ergonomics.* 2nd ed. New York: John Wiley & Sons, 1981.

Monks, Joseph G. *Operations Management: Theory and Problems.* New York: McGraw-Hill, 1977.

Moore, Franklin and Thomas Hendrick. *Production/Operations Management.* 8th ed. Homewood, Ill.: Richard D. Irwin, 1980.

Mundel, Marvin E. *Motion and Time Study.* 5th ed. Englewood Cliffs, N.J.: Prentice-Hall, 1978.

Nadler, G. *Work Design.* Rev. ed. Homewood, Ill.: Richard D. Irwin, 1970.

Niebel, Benjamin W. *Motion and Time Study.* 6th ed. Homewood, Ill.: Richard D. Irwin, 1976.

Smith, George L., Jr. *Work Measurement: A Systems Approach.* Columbus, Ohio: Grid Publishing, 1978.

Van Der Zwaan, A. H. "The Sociotechnical Systems Approach: A Critical Evaluation." *International Journal of Production Research* 13, no. 2 (1975), pp. 149–63.

READING

MAKING HOTPLATES

A group of 10 workers were responsible for assembling hotplates (instruments for heating solutions to a given temperature) for hospital and medical laboratory use. A number of different models of hotplates were being manufactured. Some had a vibrating device so that the solution could be mixed while being heated. Others heated only test tubes. Still others could heat solutions in a variety of different containers.

With the appropriate small tools, each worker assembled part of a hotplate. The partially completed hotplate was placed on a moving belt, to be carried from one assembly stage to the next. When the hotplate was completed, an inspector would check it over to insure that it was working properly. Then the last worker would place it in a specially prepared cardboard box for shipping.

The assembly line had been carefully "balanced" by industrial engineers, who had used a time and motion study to break the job down into subassembly tasks, each requiring about three minutes to accomplish. The amount of time calculated for each subassembly had also been "balanced" so that the task performed by each worker was supposed to take almost exactly the same amount of time. The workers were paid a straight hourly rate.

However, there were some problems. Morale seemed to be low, and the inspector was finding a relatively high percentage of badly assembled hotplates. Controllable rejects—those "caused" by the operator rather than by faulty materials—were running about 23 percent.

After discussing the situation, management decided to try something new. The workers were called together and asked if they would like to build the hotplates individually. The workers decided they would like to try this approach, provided they could go back to the old program if the new one did not work well. After several days of training, each worker began to assemble the entire hotplate.

The change was made at about the middle of the year. Productivity climbed quickly. By the end of the year, it had leveled off at about 84 percent higher than during the first half of the year, although no other changes had been made in the department or its personnel. Controllable rejects had dropped from 23 percent to 1 percent during the same period. Absenteeism had dropped from 8 percent to less than 1 percent. The workers had responded positively to the change, and their morale was higher. As one person put it, "Now, it is *my* hotplate." Eventually, the reject rate dropped so low that all routine final

inspection was done by the assembly workers themselves. The full-time inspector was transferred to another job in the organization.

Questions

1. What changes in the work situation might account for the increase in productivity and the decrease in controllable rejects?

2. What might account for the drop in absenteeism and the increase in morale?

3. What were the major changes in the situation? Which changes were under the control of the manager? Which were controlled by the workers?

4. What might happen if the workers were to go back to the old assembly line method?

CASE

ALLSTATE AUTOMOTIVE ANALYZERS, INC.

Allstate Automotive Analyzers manufactures a complete line of automobile testing equipment, ranging from basic timing lights and tachometers for the do-it-yourself owner-mechanic to superior quality console testers for the professional. Basic DC-powered timing lights are used to check timing, distributor action, centrifugal and vacuum advance; tachometers measure RPM, point resistance, and dwell angle. Allstate's professional quality analyzer checks the electrical output of alternators, generators, and voltage regulators and measures RPM, air-fuel ratios, and carbon monoxide levels of automobiles. When coupled with an oscilloscope, the tune-up analyzer diagnoses coil output, spark plug

voltage, polarity, point bounce, and other aspects of a secondary ignition circuit.

Allstate's products are advertised and sold nationally. Prior to the surge in prices of new cars in the early 1970s, the company was only moderately successful; following several years of significant price increases, Allstate has enjoyed strong demand for its equipment and resultant high profits. (The demand for the firm's analyzers is attributed to car owners keeping their automobiles longer and a tendency for the owner to save on expensive tune-ups.) Unit price on the firm's testers varies from $25 for the most basic timing lights to nearly $1,000 for the firm's most sophisticated console analyzer.

For several years, management of Allstate has had a number of its manufacturing operations on individual incentives. Before an operation is placed on an incentive wage plan, however, the firm's Industrial Engineering Department thoroughly analyzes the job, establishes standardized methods of performance, and sets production standards based on accepted work measurement techniques. The firm uses motion and time study as a basis for setting productivity expectations, and it has adopted the standard hour wage incentive plan for all operations that lend themselves to incentive pay.[1]

Eligible employees of Allstate are represented by a large national labor union which has gained a reputation for hard-nosed bargaining with employers on wages, hours, and conditions of employment. As a result of the union's effective bargaining, the base rates of pay for employees of Allstate are above average for the geographic region and type of work performed. One of the key factors which the union uses in negotiating for higher base rates of pay is the "tight" production standards set by management. Such tight standards, according to the union, restrict employees from earning "bonus" pay.

Basically, the wage incentive program has been a success for the company. With the exception of one department, very few grievances are filed with the union stewards. Whenever a grievance charging unfair standards is voiced, the steward (who has been trained in basic motion and time study) has the right to time the operation himself. Based on his analysis, the steward either processes the grievance or screens it out as being without merit or justification. A majority of the formal grievances and informal complaints over standards originate in the assembly department, where one of the union stewards works. (All stewards are regular employees of the company; each is given six hours each week for the purpose of

handling union business. While conducting union business, stewards earn the base rate of pay established for their particular jobs.) This steward recently transferred to the assembly department from another operation which is not on incentive pay because it is machine-controlled.

Management of Allstate contends that the existing production standards in all departments, as set by the Industrial Engineering Department, are fair. Moreover, they feel that the steward is bitter because of his inability to earn higher wages than he earned in his former job. (He cannot bump back into his old job because all other workers in the department have more seniority.) As a result of his situation, management argues, the steward continually stirs up trouble and acts as an agitator. To support its contention, management points out that most of the grievances over unjust standards never get to the second stage of the grievance procedure and, hence, are not put in writing as dictated by the union contract. Even so, the steward remains quite popular with many of his co-workers, who feel that he gives them better representation than the other stewards, who "bend over backward to get along with management."

Generally, the grievances filed by employees of the assembly department are based on standards which they consider "too tight," excessive downtime resulting from mechanical failures, and the introduction of new electric power drills and other assembly tools with which they must become familiar. In addition, they complain that the motion-and-time-study engineers use their positions to intimidate and harass by continually conducting time studies (with the implied threat of reducing time and increasing productivity requirements.)

On two occasions (once in the assembly department and once in a punch press operation), formal grievances led to retiming of operations and a reduction in standards. Following the change in standards, productivity increased by an average of 20 percent, thereby making the operations more costly for the company. Restriction of output, on the other hand,

[1] The standard hour plan expresses the work standard in terms of time. It incorporates a base rate of pay which workers earn if they fail to meet standards. For all productivity over standards, earnings are directly proportional to the output. For example, assume the base rate of pay for a job is $5 per hour and the time standard is one-half hour per unit. If a worker produces 20 units in one day, he or she earns 10 standard hours of pay, or $50. Productivity is 125 percent of standards; hence, earnings are 125 percent of base wages.

which results from standards that are too tight, makes it difficult for the firm to meet its production schedules. Consequently, management is baffled by the seemingly paradoxical situation.

Questions

1. Elvaluate the strengths and weaknesses of the standard hour plan used by Allstate Automotive Analyzers, Inc.

2. On what basis should production standards be set? Changed?

3. Discuss the handling of grievances which arise because of "tight" standards, new assembly tools, downtime, etc.

Source: This case was written by Jerry Kinard, Dean of the School of Business at Francis Marion College. All rights reserved. Reprinted by permission.

LEARNING CURVES

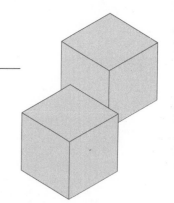

LEARNING OBJECTIVES

After completing this supplement, you should be able to:

1. Explain the concept of a learning curve.
2. Use the learning curve table to make activity time projections.
3. List and briefly describe some of the main applications of learning curves.
4. Outline some of the cautions and criticisms of learning curves.

SUPPLEMENT OUTLINE

A basic consideration in the design of work systems relates to the fact that learning is usually present when humans are involved. Consequently, it can be highly desirable to be able to predict how learning will affect task times and costs. This section addresses those issues.

THE CONCEPT OF LEARNING CURVES

Human activities typically show improvement when they are done on a repetitive basis: the time required to perform a task decreases with increasing repetitions. The degree of improvement and the number of tasks needed to realize the major portion of the improvement is a function of the task being done. If the task is short and somewhat routine, only a modest amount of improvement is apt to occur, and it generally occurs during the first few repetitions. On the other hand, if the task is fairly complex and has a longer duration, improvements will occur over a longer interval (i.e., a larger number of repetitions). Because of this, learning factors have little relevance for planning or scheduling routine activities, but they do have relevance for complex repetitive activities.

Figure 8S–1 illustrates the basic relationship between increasing repetitions and a decreasing time per repetition. It should be noted that the curve will never touch the x axis; that is, the time per unit will never be zero.

T. P. Wright drew attention to learning curves in a 1936 article in which he described how the direct labor cost of producing a certain airframe decreased with experience.[1] Since that time, a number of other studies have confirmed the general relationship that Wright described. Alternately referred to as a progress function or improvement function, it is now widely agreed that the

FIGURE 8S–1

The learning effect: Time per repetition decreases as the number of repetitions increases

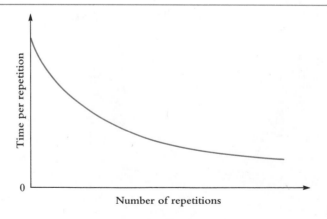

---

[1] T. P. Wright, "Factors Affecting the Cost of Airplanes," *Journal of the Aeronautical Sciences* 3 (February 1936).

learning effect is the result of factors in addition to actual worker learning. Some of the improvements can be traced to preproduction factors, such as selection of tooling and equipment, product design, methods analysis, and, in general, the amount of effort expended prior to the start of the work. Other contributing factors may involve changes once production has begun, such as changes in methods, tooling, and design. In addition, management can be an important factor through improvements in planning, scheduling, motivation, and control.

It is interesting to note that changes made once production is underway can cause a temporary *decrease* in output rate until workers adjust to the change, even though they eventually lead to an increased output rate. If a number of changes are made during production, the learning curve would be more realistically described by a series of scallops instead of a smooth curve, as illustrated in Figure 8S–2. Nonetheless, it is convenient to work with a smooth curve, which can be interpreted as the *average* effect.

From an organizational standpoint, the thing that makes the learning effect more than an interesting curiosity is its *predictability,* which becomes readily apparent if the relationship is plotted on a log-log scale (see Figure 8S–3). The straight line that results reflects a constant learning percentage, which is the basis of learning curve estimates: every *doubling* of repetitions results in a *constant percentage* decrease in the time per repetition. This applies both to the *average* time and to the *unit* time, as shown in Figure 8S–4. Typical decreases range from 10 percent to 20 percent. By convention, learning curves are referred to in terms of the *complements* of their improvement rates. For example, an 80 percent learning curve denotes a 20 percent decrease in unit (or average) time with each doubling of repetitions, and a 90 percent curve denotes a 10 percent improvement rate. Thus, a 100 percent curve would imply no improvement at all.

FIGURE 8S—2

Improvements may create a "scallop" effect in the curve

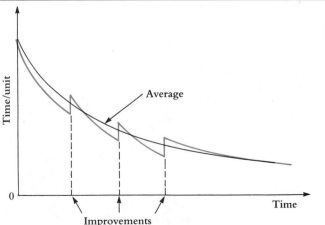

On a log-log graph, learning curves are straight lines

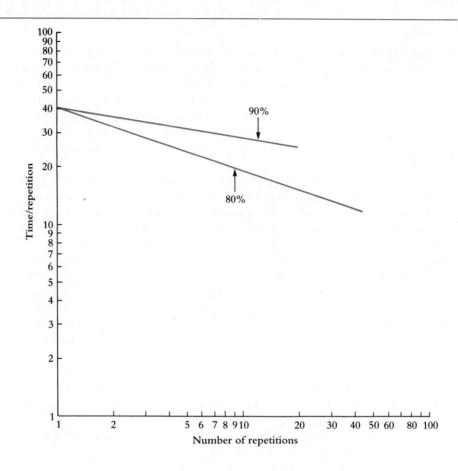

After the first unit, the unit and average curves are parallel

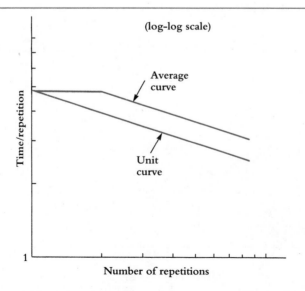

EXAMPLE S–1

An activity is known to have an 80 percent learning curve. It has just taken a worker 10 hours to produce the first unit. Determine expected completion times for these units: the 2nd, 4th, 8th, and 16th (note successive doubling of units).

Solution

Each time the cumulative output doubles, the time per unit for that amount should be approximately equal to the previous time multiplied by the learning percentage (80 percent in this case). Thus:

Unit	Unit time (hours)
1	10
2 . . . . 0.8(10)	= 8
4 . . . . 0.8(8)	= 6.4
8 . . . . 0.8(6.4)	= 5.12
16 . . . . 0.8(5.12)	= 4.096

This example illustrates an important point, and it also raises an interesting question. The point it makes is that the time reduction *per unit* becomes less and less as the number of repetitions increase. For example, the second unit required two hours less time than the first, and the improvement from the 8th to the 16th unit was only a bit more than one hour. The question the example raises is: How are times for values such as three, five, six, seven, and other units that don't fall into this pattern computed?

The unit time (i.e., the number of direct labor hours required) for the nth unit can be computed using the relationship:

$$T_n = T_1 \times n^b \qquad (8S–1)$$

where

$$T_n = \text{Time for } n\text{th unit}$$
$$T_1 = \text{Time for first unit}$$
$$b = \ln(\text{learning percent})/\ln 2$$

For example, for an 80 percent curve with $T_1 = 10$ hours, the time for the third unit would be computed as:

$$T_3 = 10(3^{\ln .8/\ln 2}) = 7.02$$

Generally, it is not necessary to use the formula; values can be determined using Table 8S–1.

The table shows two things for some selected learning percentages. One is a unit value for each of the outputs listed. It enables us to easily determine how long any unit will take to produce. The second is a cumulative value, which enables us to compute the total number of hours that will be needed to complete any given number of repetitions. The computation is a relatively

TABLE 8S–1

Learning curve coefficients

Unit number	70% Unit time	70% Total time	75% Unit time	75% Total time	80% Unit time	80% Total time	85% Unit time	85% Total time	90% Unit time	90% Total time
1	1.000	1.000	1.000	1.000	1.000	1.000	1.000	1.000	1.000	1.000
2	.700	1.700	.750	1.750	.800	1.800	.850	1.850	.900	1.900
3	.568	2.268	.634	2.384	.702	2.502	.773	2.623	.846	2.746
4	.490	2.758	.562	2.946	.640	3.142	.723	3.345	.810	3.556
5	.437	3.195	.513	3.459	.596	3.738	.686	4.031	.783	4.339
6	.398	3.593	.475	3.934	.562	4.299	.657	4.688	.762	5.101
7	.367	3.960	.446	4.380	.534	4.834	.634	5.322	.744	5.845
8	.343	4.303	.422	4.802	.512	5.346	.614	5.936	.729	6.574
9	.323	4.626	.402	5.204	.493	5.839	.597	6.533	.716	7.290
10	.306	4.932	.385	5.589	.477	6.315	.583	7.116	.705	7.994
11	.291	5.223	.370	5.958	.462	6.777	.570	7.686	.695	8.689
12	.278	5.501	.357	6.315	.449	7.227	.558	8.244	.685	9.374
13	.267	5.769	.345	6.660	.438	7.665	.548	8.792	.677	10.052
14	.257	6.026	.334	6.994	.428	8.092	.539	9.331	.670	10.721
15	.248	6.274	.325	7.319	.418	8.511	.530	9.861	.663	11.384
16	.240	6.514	.316	7.635	.410	8.920	.522	10.383	.656	12.040
17	.233	6.747	.309	7.944	.402	9.322	.515	10.898	.650	12.690
18	.226	6.973	.301	8.245	.394	9.716	.508	11.405	.644	13.334
19	.220	7.192	.295	8.540	.388	10.104	.501	11.907	.639	13.974
20	.214	7.407	.288	8.828	.381	10.485	.495	12.402	.634	14.608
21	.209	7.615	.283	9.111	.375	10.860	.490	12.892	.630	15.237
22	.204	7.819	.277	9.388	.370	11.230	.484	13.376	.625	15.862
23	.199	8.018	.272	9.660	.364	11.594	.479	13.856	.621	16.483
24	.195	8.213	.267	9.928	.359	11.954	.475	14.331	.617	17.100
25	.191	8.404	.263	10.191	.355	12.309	.470	14.801	.613	17.713
26	.187	8.591	.259	10.449	.350	12.659	.466	15.267	.609	18.323
27	.183	8.774	.255	10.704	.346	13.005	.462	15.728	.606	18.929
28	.180	8.954	.251	10.955	.342	13.347	.458	16.186	.603	19.531
29	.177	9.131	.247	11.202	.338	13.685	.454	16.640	.599	20.131
30	.174	9.305	.244	11.446	.335	14.020	.450	17.091	.596	20.727
31	.171	9.476	.240	11.686	.331	14.351	.447	17.538	.593	21.320
32	.168	9.644	.237	11.924	.328	14.679	.444	17.981	.590	21.911
33	.165	9.809	.234	12.158	.324	15.003	.441	18.422	.588	22.498
34	.163	9.972	.231	12.389	.321	15.324	.437	18.859	.585	23.084
35	.160	10.133	.229	12.618	.318	15.643	.434	19.294	.583	23.666
36	.158	10.291	.226	12.844	.315	15.958	.432	19.725	.580	24.246
37	.156	10.447	.223	13.067	.313	16.271	.429	20.154	.578	24.824
38	.154	10.601	.221	13.288	.310	16.581	.426	20.580	.575	25.399
39	.152	10.753	.219	13.507	.307	16.888	.424	21.004	.573	25.972
40	.150	10.902	.216	13.723	.305	17.193	.421	21.425	.571	26.543

TABLE 8S–1 *(concluded)*

Learning curve coefficients

Unit number	70% Unit time	70% Total time	75% Unit time	75% Total time	80% Unit time	80% Total time	85% Unit time	85% Total time	90% Unit time	90% Total time
41	.148	11.050	.214	13.937	.303	17.496	.419	21.844	.569	27.111
42	.146	11.196	.212	14.149	.300	17.796	.416	22.260	.567	27.678
43	.144	11.341	.210	14.359	.298	18.094	.414	22.674	.565	28.243
44	.143	11.484	.208	14.567	.296	18.390	.412	23.086	.563	28.805
45	.141	11.625	.206	14.773	.294	18.684	.410	23.496	.561	29.366
46	.139	11.764	.204	14.977	.292	18.975	.408	23.903	.559	29.925
47	.138	11.902	.202	15.180	.290	19.265	.405	24.309	.557	30.482
48	.136	12.038	.201	15.380	.288	19.552	.403	24.712	.555	31.037
49	.135	12.173	.199	15.579	.286	19.838	.402	25.113	.553	31.590
50	.134	12.307	.197	15.776	.284	20.122	.400	25.513	.552	32.142
51	.132	12.439	.196	15.972	.282	20.404	.398	25.911	.550	32.692
52	.131	12.570	.194	16.166	.280	20.684	.396	26.307	.548	33.241
53	.130	12.700	.192	16.358	.279	20.963	.394	26.701	.547	33.787
54	.128	12.828	.191	16.549	.277	21.239	.392	27.094	.545	34.333
55	.127	12.955	.190	16.739	.275	21.515	.391	27.484	.544	34.877
56	.126	13.081	.188	16.927	.274	21.788	.389	27.873	.542	35.419
57	.125	13.206	.187	17.144	.272	22.060	.388	28.261	.541	35.960
58	.124	13.330	.185	17.299	.271	22.331	.386	28.647	.539	36.499
59	.123	13.453	.184	17.483	.269	22.600	.384	29.031	.538	37.037
60	.122	13.574	.183	17.666	.268	22.868	.383	29.414	.537	37.574

simple operation: Multiply the table value by the time required for the first unit.

EXAMPLE S–2

Production Airlines is negotiating a contract involving production of 20 small jets. The initial jet required 400 labor days of direct labor. Estimate the expected number of labor days of direct labor for:

a. The 20th jet.
b. All 20 jets.

Assume an 80 percent learning curve is appropriate.

Solution

Using Table 8S–1 with $n = 20$ and an 80 percent learning percentage, we find these factors: Unit = .381, Cumulative = 10.485.

a. Expected time for 20th jet: 400(.381) = 152.4 labor days.
b. Expected total time for all 20: 400(10.485) = 4,194 labor days.

Use of the table requires a time for the first unit. If it happens that, for some reason, the completion time of the first unit is not available, or if the manager believes the completion time for some later unit is more reliable, it can be used to obtain a revised estimate of the initial time, and that value can be used in conjunction with the table.

EXAMPLE S–3

The manager in the previous problem feels there were some unusual problems encountered in producing the first jet and would like to revise that estimate based on a completion time of 276 labor days for the third jet.

Solution

The unit value for $n = 3$ and an 80 percent curve is .702 (Table 8S–1).
Divide the actual time for unit 3 by the table value to obtain the revised estimate for unit 1's time: 276 labor days ÷ .702 = 393.2 labor days.

APPLICATIONS OF LEARNING CURVES

Learning curve theory has found useful applications in a number of areas, including:

1. Manpower planning and scheduling.
2. Negotiated purchasing.
3. Pricing new products.
4. Budgeting, purchasing, and inventory planning.

Knowledge of output projections in learning situations can help managers make better decisions on how many workers they will need than they could from basing decisions on initial output rates. Of course, managers obviously recognize that improvement will occur; what the learning curve contributes is a method for quantifying expected future improvements.

Negotiated purchasing often involves contracting to supply specialized items that may have a high degree of complexity. Examples include aircraft, computers, and special-purpose equipment. The direct labor cost per unit of such items can be expected to decrease as the size of the order increases. Hence, negotiators first settle on the number of units and then negotiate price on that basis. The government requires learning curve data on contracts that involve large, complex items. For contracts that are terminated before delivery of all units, suppliers can use learning curve data to argue for an increase in the unit price for the smaller number of units. Conversely, the government can use that information to negotiate a lower price per unit on follow-on orders on the basis of projected additional learning gains.

Worker learning curves can help guide personnel job placement

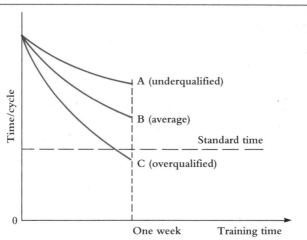

Organizations must establish prices for their products and services, often well in advance of producing a new product on a sufficiently large scale to make a firm determination of costs. Generalizing from the cost of the first few units will result in a much higher price than can be expected after a number of units have been produced. However, the manager needs to use the learning curve to avoid underpricing as well as overpricing. The manager may project initial costs, using the learning progression known to represent an organization's past experience, or else do a regression analysis of the initial results.

The learning curve projections help managers to plan costs and labor, purchasing, and inventory needs. For example, initial cost per unit will be high, and output will be fairly low, so purchasing and inventory decisions can reflect this. As productivity increases, purchasing and/or inventory actions must allow for increased usage of raw materials and purchased parts to keep pace with output. Because of learning effects, the usage rate will increase over time. Hence, failure to refer to a learning curve would lead to substantial *overestimates* of labor needs and *underestimates* of the rate of material usage.

These learning principles can sometimes be useful in evaluating new workers during training periods. This can be done by measuring each worker's performance, graphing the results, and then comparing them to an expected rate of learning. This can reveal which workers are underqualified, average, and overqualified for a given type of work (see Figure 8S–5). Moreover, measuring a worker's progress can help predict whether the worker will make a quota within a required period of time.

CAUTIONS AND CRITICISMS

Managers who use the learning curves should be aware of its limitations and pitfalls. This section briefly outlines some of the major cautions and criticisms of learning curves.

FIGURE 8S–6

Learning curves are useful for production start-up, but not usually for mass production

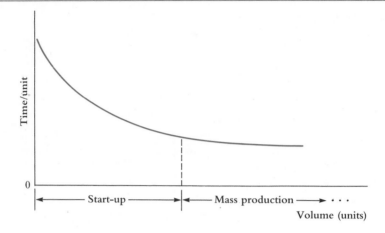

1. Learning rates may differ from organization to organization and by type of work. Therefore, it is best to base learning rates on empirical studies rather than on assumed rates.

2. Projections based on learning curves should be regarded as *approximations* of actual times and treated accordingly.

3. Because time estimates are based on the time for the first unit, considerable care should be taken to insure that the time is valid. It may be desirable to revise the base time as later times become available. Since it is often necessary to estimate the time for the first unit prior to production, this caution is quite important.

4. It is entirely possible that at some point the curve might level off or even tip upward, especially near the end of a job. The potential for savings at that point is so slight that most jobs do not command the attention or interest to sustain improvements. Then, too, some of the better workers may be shifted into new jobs that are starting up.

5. Some of the improvements may be more apparent than real: improvements in times may be caused in part by *increases* in *indirect* labor costs.

6. In situations that involve mass production, learning curves may be of use in predicting how long it will take before the process stabilizes. However, for the most part, the concept does not apply to mass production because the decrease in time per unit is imperceptible for all practical purposes (see Figure 8S–6).

7. Users of learning curves sometimes fail to include carryover effects; previous experience with similar activities can reduce initial activity times, although it should be noted that the *learning rate* remains the same.

SOLVED PROBLEMS

1. An assembly operation has a 90 percent learning curve. The line has just begun work on a new item, and the initial unit required 28 hours. Estimate the time that will be needed to complete:
   a. The first five units.
   b. Units 20 through 25.

Solution

(Use the cumulative portion of the 90 percent column of Table 8S–1.)
a. Table value: 4.339.
   Estimated time for five units: 28(4.339) = 121.49 hours.
b. The total time for units 20 through 25 can be determined by subtraction:

		Hours
Total time for 25 units:	28(17.713) =	495.96
−Total time for 19 units:	28(13.974) =	391.27
Total time for 20 through 25:		104.69

2. A manager wants to determine an appropriate learning rate for a new type of work his firm will undertake. He has obtained completion times for the initial six repetitions of a job of this type. What learning rate is appropriate?

Unit	Completion time (hours)
1	15.9
2	12.0
3	10.1
4	9.1
5	8.4
6	7.5

Solution

According to theory, the time per unit decreases at a constant rate each time the output *doubles* (e.g., unit 1 to 2, 2 to 4, and 3 to 6). The ratios of these observed times will give us an approximate rate. Thus,

$$\frac{\text{Unit 2}}{\text{Unit 1}} = \frac{12.0}{15.9} = .755 \quad \frac{\text{Unit 4}}{\text{Unit 2}} = \frac{9.1}{12.0} = .785 \quad \frac{\text{Unit 6}}{\text{Unit 3}} = \frac{7.5}{10.1} = .743$$

Not surprisingly, there is some variability; the rate is usually a smoothed approximation. Even so, the ratios are fairly close; a rate of 75 percent seems reasonable in this case.

DISCUSSION AND REVIEW QUESTIONS

1. If the learning phenomenon applies to all human activity, why isn't the effect noticeable in mass production or high-volume assembly work?

2. Under what circumstances might a manager prefer a learning rate of approximately 100 percent?

3. What would a learning percentage of 120 percent imply?

4. Explain how an increase in indirect labor cost can contribute to a decrease in direct labor cost per unit.

5. List the kinds of factors that create the learning effect.

6. Explain how changes in a process, once it is underway, can cause scallops in a learning curve.

7. What are some of the areas in which learning curves are useful?

8. What factors might cause a learning curve to "tip up" toward the end of a job?

9. What is the implication of item 7 in the list of cautions and criticisms in this supplement?

PROBLEMS

1. An aircraft company has an order to refurbish the interiors of 18 jet aircraft. The work has a learning curve percentage of 80. On the basis of previous experience with similar jobs, the industrial engineering department estimates that the first plane will require 300 hours to refurbish. Estimate the amount of time that will be needed to complete:
   a. The 5th plane.
   b. The first 5 planes.
   c. All 18 planes.

2. Estimate the time it will take to complete the 4th unit of a 12-unit job involving a large assembly if the initial unit required approximately 80 hours for each of these learning percentages:
   a. 72 percent.
   b. 87 percent.
   c. 95 percent.

3. A small contractor intends to bid on a job that will involve installation of 30 inground swimming pools. Because this will be a new line of work for the contractor, he believes there will be a learning effect for the job. After reviewing time records from a similar type of activity with his daughter, who is majoring in operations management at a nearby university, the contractor is convinced that an 85 percent curve is appropriate. He estimates that the first pool will take his crew eight days to install. How many days should the contractor budget for:
   a. The first 10 pools?
   b. The second 10 pools?
   c. The final 10 pools?

4. A manager wants to determine an appropriate learning percentage for a certain activity. Toward that end, times have been recorded for completion of each of the first six repetitions. They are:

Repetition	Time (minutes)
1	46
2	39
3	35
4	33
5	32
6	30

a. Determine the approximate learning percentage.

b. Using your answer from part a, estimate the average completion time per repetition assuming a total of 50 repetitions are planned.

5. Students in an operations management class have been assigned four transportation problems by their instructor. One student noted that it took her 50 minutes to complete the first problem. Assume that the four problems are quite similar and that a 70 percent learning curve is appropriate. How much time can this student plan to spend solving the remaining problems?

6. A subcontractor is responsible for outfitting six satellites that will be used for solar research. Four of the six have been completed in a total of 600 hours. If the crew has a 75 percent learning curve, how long should it take them to finish the last two units?

7. The 5th unit of a 40-unit job took 14.5 hours to complete. Answer the following questions, assuming a 90 percent learning curve is appropriate:

a. About how long should the last unit take to complete?

b. How much time should it take to complete the 10th unit?

c. Estimate the average time per unit for the 40 units.

8. The labor cost to produce a certain item is $8.50 per hour. Job setup costs $50, and material costs are $20 per unit. Overhead is charged at a rate of 50 percent of labor, materials, and setup costs.

The job has a 90 percent learning rate, and the foreman estimates that the initial unit will require five hours. The item can be purchased for $88.50 per unit.

a. Determine the unit cost for 20 units.

b. What is the minimum production quantity that would make production cost less than purchase cost?

9. The government agency for which a contractor has been working has notified the contractor of a desire to extend the original contract to include three additional units. The initial contract called for four units to be built and delivered. The contractor must now estimate the total time required to complete the next three units.

Upon reviewing records for the original contract, it was discovered that data for the second unit are inaccurate and cannot be used. It is known that the first unit required 16 days, the third 12.5 days, and the fourth 11.5 days.

Determine an estimated time for the next three units.

10. A firm has a training program for a certain operation. The progress of trainees is carefully monitored. A standard has been established that requires a trainee to be able to complete the sixth repetition of the operation in six hours or less. Those who are unable to do this are assigned to other jobs.

Currently, three trainees have each completed two repetitions. Trainee A had times of 9 hours for the first and 8 hours for the second repetition; trainee B had times of 10 hours and 8 hours for the first and second repetitions; and trainee C had times of 12 and 9 hours.

Which trainee(s) do you think will make the standard? Explain your reasoning.

SELECTED BIBLIOGRAPHY

Abernathy, W. J. "The Limits of the Learning Curve." *Harvard Business Review*, September–October 1974, pp. 109–19.

Andress, Frank J. "The Learning Curve as a Production Tool." *Harvard Business Review*, January–February 1954, pp. 87–95.

Fabrycky, W. J; P. M. Ghare; and P. E. Torgersen. *Industrial Operations Research*. Englewood Cliffs, N.J.: Prentice-Hall, 1972.

Holdham, J. H. "Learning Curves—Their Applications in Industry." *Production and Inventory Management* (fourth quarter 1970), pp. 40–55.

Yelle, Y. E. "The Learning Curve: Historical Review and Comprehensive Survey." *Decision Sciences* 10 (1979), pp. 302–28.

CASE

PRODUCT RECALL

An automobile manufacturer is conducting a product recall after it was discovered that a possible defect in the steering mechanism could cause loss of control in certain cars. The recall covers a span of three model years. The company has sent out letters to car owners promising to repair the defect at no cost at any dealership.

The company's policy is to pay the dealer a fixed amount for each repair. The repair is somewhat complicated, and the company expected learning to be a factor. In order to set a reasonable rate for repairs, company engineers conducted a number of repairs themselves. It was then decided that a rate of $88 per repair would be appropriate, based on a flat hourly rate of $22 per hour and a 90 percent learning rate.

Shortly after dealers began making repairs, the company received word that several dealers were encountering resistance from workers who felt the flat rate was much too low and who were threatening to refuse to work on those jobs. One of the dealers has collected data on job times and has sent that information to the company: Three mechanics each completed two repairs. Average time for the first unit was 9.6 hours, and average time for the second unit was 7.2 hours. The dealer has suggested a rate of $110 per repair.

You have been asked to investigate the situation and to prepare a report.

Questions

1. Prepare a list of questions that you will need to have answered in order to analyze this situation.

2. Prepare a list of observations regarding the information provided in the case.

3. What preliminary thoughts do you have on solutions/partial solutions to points you have raised?

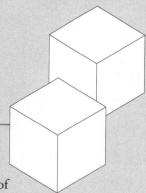

OPERATING AND CONTROLLING THE SYSTEM

The topics in this part relate to operating and controlling the production of goods and services.

The chapters in this section cover the following general topics:

1. Aggregate planning (Chapter 9).
2. Inventory management (Chapter 10).
3. Material requirements planning (Chapter 11).
4. Just-in-time systems (Chapter 12).
5. Scheduling (Chapter 13).
6. Project management (Chapter 14).
7. Waiting lines (Chapter 15).
8. Quality assurance (Chapter 16).

Chapter 9 serves as a link between the design decisions discussed in the Part III, and the operating decisions described in the remaining chapters. It deals with intermediate-range decisions.

Chapters 10 and 11 deal with various aspects of inventories. The first of these two chapters deals with general inventory management decisions, particularly as they relate to finished goods inventories. Chapter 11 deals with inventories in a manufacturing/assembly mode.

Chapter 12 describes just-in-time production systems.

Chapter 13 deals with scheduling decisions involving fairly routine types of activities. Chapter 14 deals with planning and scheduling projects, which generally include many nonroutine activities.

Chapter 15 is concerned with the analysis of waiting lines, which are commonly found in service systems when arrivals are random.

Chapter 16 discusses quality assurance, an increasingly important topic for many organizations.

9

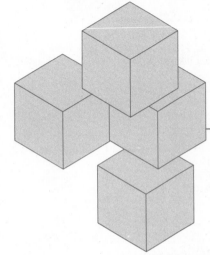

Aggregate Planning

LEARNING OBJECTIVES

After completing this chapter, you should be able to:

1. Explain what aggregate planning is and how it can be useful.
2. Identify the variables that decision makers have to work with in aggregate planning and some of the possible strategies they can use.
3. Describe some of the graphical and quantitative techniques planners use.
4. Prepare aggregate plans and compute their costs.

Chapter Outline

INTRODUCTION

Aggregate planning is medium-range capacity planning that typically covers a time horizon of anywhere from 2 to 18 months. The goal of aggregate planning is to achieve a production plan that will effectively utilize the organization's resources to satisfy expected demand. Planners must make decisions on output rates, employment levels and changes, inventory levels and changes, back orders, and subcontracting.

The purpose of this chapter is to introduce the concept of aggregate planning, discuss the pertinent costs and possible strategies, and illustrate some of the different approaches used in aggregate planning.

The Concept of Aggregation

Aggregate planning is essentially a "big picture" approach to planning. Planners generally try to avoid focusing on individual products or services unless, of course, the organization has only one major product or service. Instead, they focus on overall, or aggregate, capacity.

For purposes of aggregate planning, it is often convenient to think of capacity in terms of labor hours or machine hours per month, or output rates (barrels per month, units per month), without worrying about how much of this item or how much of that item will actually be involved. The reason for this approach is that it frees planners to make decisions about the use of resources in a general way without having to get into the complexities of individual product or service requirements. Often aggregation is done by product groupings, where products (or services) with similar requirements are lumped together for planning purposes. This makes the problem of obtaining an acceptable unit of aggregation easier since different product groupings may lend themselves to different aggregate measures.

It can be convenient to think of aggregate planning as a *macro approach* to developing a production plan. For instance, consider the task of planning a vegetable garden. Aggregate planning would consist of deciding on the overall size (capacity) of the garden; taking into account how much time and effort the gardener is willing to commit to the garden for preparing the soil, planting, weeding, watering, and fertilizing; as well as calculating the amount of funds available for plants, seeds, and supplies. In addition, the gardener must consider how much output is desired (e.g., enough to feed a family of four). This can be done without getting into the details of precisely how many tomato plants or cucumber plants there will be. Decisions of that nature are best left until the broad plans have been worked out.

Now consider how aggregate planning might work in a manufacturing setting. Think of an automobile manufacturer that makes a variety of cars and trucks. For purposes of aggregate planning, a decision on the number of cars and number of trucks to be produced will be made without specifying the breakdown of two-door versus four-door cars, options, etc. Similarly, a decision on four-cylinder and six-cylinder engines will be made without concern for which engines will go with which cars or trucks. Planners will generally take into account the expected demand for cars, trucks, and engine blocks and the available capacity for making those items. If expected demand and capacity are approximately equal, planners will devote their efforts to meeting demand as efficiently as possible. If capacity exceeds demand, advertising and promotion might be realistic options. If capacity is less than demand, contracting some of the work to outside firms may be an option. In any event, planners will be looking at aggregate measures of capacity in making their decisions.

Finally, consider how aggregate planning might work in a large department store. Space allocation is often an aggregate decision. That is, a manager might decide to allocate 20 percent of the available space in the clothing section to women's sportswear, 30 percent to juniors, and so on, without regard to what brand names will be offered, how much of juniors will be slacks, and so on. The aggregate measure might be square feet of space or racks of clothing.

In each of these examples, we see that an aggregate approach permits planners to make general decisions about intermediate-range capacity without having to deal with highly specific details. They can instead concern themselves with overall decisions on levels of output, employment, and inventories. They do this by lumping demand for all products into one or a few categories and planning on that level.

AGGREGATE PLANNING IN PERSPECTIVE

Organizations become involved with capacity decisions on three levels: long term, intermediate term, and short term. Long-term decisions relate to product and sevice selection (i.e., determining which products or services to offer), facility size and location, equipment decisions, and layout of facilities. These long-term decisions essentially define the capacity constraints within which intermediate, or aggregate, planning must function. Intermediate decisions, as we have said, relate to general levels of employment, output, and inventories. These, in turn, define the boundaries within which short-range capacity decisions must be made. Thus, short-term decisions essentially relate to deciding on the best way to achieve desired results within the constraints resulting from long-term and intermediate-term decisions. These involve scheduling jobs, machine loading, job sequencing, and the like. The three levels of capacity decisions are highlighted in Table 9-1.

Long-term capacity decisions were covered in preceding chapters, and scheduling and related matters are covered in a later chapter. This chapter covers the intermediate capacity decisions.

TABLE 9–1

Overview of planning levels

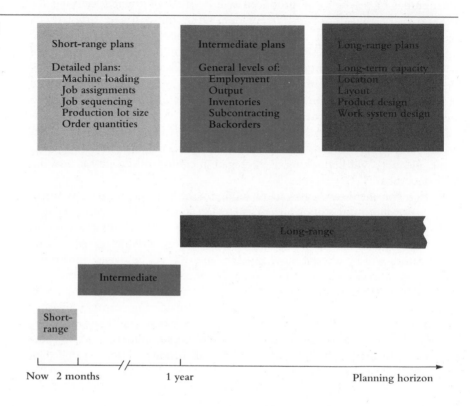

Short-range plans	Intermediate plans	Long-range plans
Detailed plans:	General levels of:	Long-term capacity
Machine loading	Employment	Location
Job assignments	Output	Layout
Job sequencing	Inventories	Product design
Production lot size	Subcontracting	Work system design
Order quantities	Backorders	

Now   2 months   1 year   Planning horizon

AN OVERVIEW OF AGGREGATE PLANNING

Aggregate planning begins with a forecast of expected demand for the intermediate range. This is followed by a general plan to meet demand requirements by setting output, employment, and inventory levels. A series of plans might be considered. Each plan must be examined in light of feasibility and cost. If a plan is reasonably good but has minor difficulties, it may be reworked. Conversely, a poor plan should be discarded and alternative plans considered until an acceptable one is uncovered. This process is illustrated in Figure 9-1. The production plan is essentially the output of aggregate planning. The process of evaluating various proposed plans in attempting to balance capacity (supply) and demand is known as **rough-cut capacity planning.** That is, the aggregate treatment of capacity prohibits something more than a rough, or approximate, balance of capacity and demand.

FIGURE 9–1

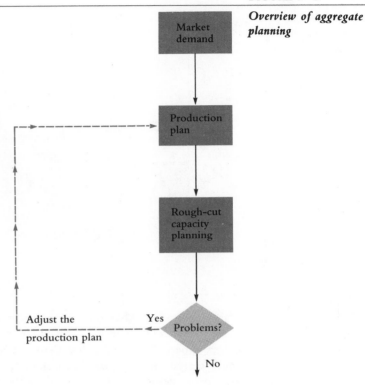

Overview of aggregate planning

THE PURPOSE AND SCOPE OF AGGREGATE PLANNING

In this section, we examine the basic problem that aggregate planning addresses—namely, the balancing of supply and demand—along with the purpose of aggregate planning, and the primary decision variable available to planners, and associated costs.

Demand and Capacity

Aggregate planners are concerned with the *quantity* and the *timing* of expected demand. If total expected demand for the planning period is much different from available capacity over that same period, the major approach of planners will be either to increase demand (if demand is less than capacity) or increase capacity (if demand exceeds capacity). On the other hand, even if capacity and demand are approximately equal for the planning period as a whole, planners may still be faced with the problem of dealing with *uneven* demand within the

FIGURE 9–2

Projected demand for a
12-period planning
horizon

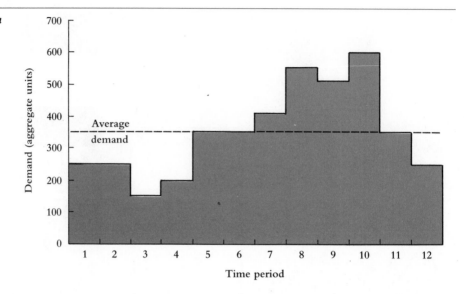

planning interval. The problem of uneven demand is illustrated in Figure 9-2. Note that in some periods, expected demand exceeds projected capacity, in others expected demand is less than projected capacity, and in some periods the two are roughly equal. The task of aggregate planners is to achieve rough equality of demand and capacity over the entire planning horizon.

The Purpose of Aggregate Planning

The purpose of aggregate planning is to develop a feasible production plan on an aggregate level that achieves a balance of expected demand and supply. Moreover, planners are usually concerned with minimizing the cost of the production plan, although cost is not the only consideration.

TABLE 9–2

Aggregate planning
inputs

Resources	Costs
Work force/production rates	Inventory carrying
Facilities and equipment	cost
Demand forecast	Back orders
	Hiring/firing
Policy statements on work force changes	Overtime
Subcontracting	Inventory changes
Overtime	Subcontracting
Inventory levels/changes	
Back orders	

Inputs to Aggregate Planning

There are a number of important informational needs for effective aggregate planning. First, the available resources over the planning period must be known, including facilities. Also, a forecast of expected demand must be available. Finally, planners must take into account any policies regarding changes in employment levels (e.g., some organizations view layoffs as very undesirable, so they would exclude that option from consideration or perhaps use it only as a last resort).

Table 9-2 lists the major inputs to aggregate planning.

Decision Variables and Costs

Management has a wide range of decision options at its disposal for purposes of aggregate planning. These include pricing, promotion, backlogging orders, using overtime, using part-time workers, subcontracting, adding or deleting extra shifts, and stockpiling inventories. Some of these, such as pricing and promotion, represent options that are intended to alter the pattern of demand. Others, such as using part-time workers, overtime, and subcontracting, represent decision options that are intended to alter capacity, or supply. Suppose we examine options in more detail.

The basic demand options are the following:

1. *Pricing.* Pricing differentials are commonly used to shift demand from peak periods to off-peak periods. Some airlines, for example, offer lower fares for midweek travel and charge higher fares other times. Many airlines also offer lower fares for night travel. Similarly, movie theaters may offer reduced rates for matinees, and some restaurants offer "early bird specials" in an attempt to shift some of the heavier dinner demand to an earlier time that traditionally has less traffic. Some restaurants may also offer smaller portions at reduced rates, and most have smaller portions and prices for children. The smaller portions act to decrease demand. To the extent that pricing is effective, demand will be shifted so that it more closely corresponds to capacity, albeit for an opportunity cost that represents the lost profit stemming from capacity insufficient to meet demand during certain periods.

An important factor to consider is the degree of price elasticity for the product or service; the more the elasticity, the more effective pricing will be in influencing demand patterns.

2. *Promotion.* Advertising and other forms of promotion, such as displays and direct marketing, can sometimes be very effective in shifting demand so that it conforms more closely to capacity. Obviously, timing these efforts and knowledge of response rates and response patterns will be needed to achieve the desired results. Unlike pricing policy, there is much less control over the timing of demand; there is always the risk that promotion can worsen the condition it was intended to improve.

3. *Back orders*. An organization can shift demand to other periods by allowing back orders. Hence, orders are taken in one period and deliveries promised for a later period. The success of this approach depends on how willing customers are to wait for delivery. Moreover, the cost associated with back orders can be difficult to pin down since it would include lost sales, annoyed or disappointed customers, and perhaps additional paperwork.

4. *New demand*. Many organizations are faced with the problem of having to provide products or services for peak demand in situations where demand is very uneven. For instance, demand for public transportation tends to be very intense during the morning and late afternoon rush hours but much lighter at other times. Creating new demand for the buses at other times (e.g., trips by schools, clubs, and senior citizen groups) would make use of the excess capacity during those slack times. Similarly, many fast-food restaurants are open for breakfast in order to use their capacities more fully, and some landscaping firms in northern climates use their equipment during the winter months for snow plowing. Manufacturing firms that experience seasonal demands for certain products (e.g., snowblowers) are sometimes able to develop a demand for a complementary product (e.g., lawn mowers, garden equipment) that makes use of the same production processes. They thereby achieve a more consistent use of labor, equipment, and facilities.

The basic options for altering the availability of capacity are the following:

1. *Hire and fire workers*. The extent to which operations are labor intensive determines the impact that changes in the level of a work force will have on capacity. The resource requirements of each worker can also be a factor. For instance, if a supermarket with 14 checkout lines generally has 10 operating, an additional four checkout workers could be added. Hence, the ability to add workers is constrained at some point by other resources needed to support the workers. Conversely, there may be a lower limit on the number of workers needed to maintain a viable operation (e.g., a skeleton crew).

Union contracts may restrict the amount of hiring and firing a company can do. Moreover, because firing and laying off can present serious problems for workers, many firms have policies that either prohibit or limit downward adjustments to a work force. On the other hand, hiring presumes an available supply of workers, This may change from time to time and, at certain times of low supply, have an impact on the ability of an organization to pursue this approach.

Use of hiring and firing entails certain costs. Hiring costs include recruitment, screening, and training to bring new workers "up to speed." Some savings may occur if workers who have recently been laid off are rehired. Firing costs include severance pay, the cost of realigning the remaining work force, and potential bad feelings toward the firm on the part of fired workers, as well as some loss of morale for workers who are retained (i.e., in spite of company assurances, some workers will nevertheless believe that they may also be laid off in time).

2. *Overtime/slack time.* Use of overtime or slack time is a less severe method for changing capacity than hiring and firing workers, and it can be used across the board or selectively as needed. It can also be implemented more quickly than hiring and firing and allows the firm to maintain a steady base of employees. The use of overtime can be especially attractive in dealing with seasonal demand peaks by reducing the need to hire and train people who will have to be laid off during the "off" season. It also maintains a skilled work force and allows employees a chance to increase earnings. Moreover, in situations that involve crews, it is often necessary to use a full crew rather than to hire one or two additional people. Thus, having the entire crew work overtime would be preferable to hiring some extra people.

On the negative side, some union contracts allow workers to refuse overtime. In those cases, it may be difficult to muster a full crew to work overtime or to get an entire production line into operation after regular hours. And although workers often like the additional income overtime can generate, they may not appreciate having to work on short notice or the fluctuations in income that result. Still other considerations relate to the fact that overtime often results in lower productivity, poorer quality, more accidents, and increased payroll costs, whereas idle time results in less efficient use of machines and other fixed assets.

3. *Part-time workers.* In certain instances, the use of part-time workers is a viable option. Much depends on the nature of the work, training and skills needed, and union agreements. Seasonal work requiring low-to-moderate job skills lends itself to part-time workers, who generally cost less than regular workers in both hourly wages and fringe benefits. However, unions may regard such workers unfavorably because they typically do not pay union dues and may lessen the power of unions. Department stores, restaurants, and supermarkets make use of part-time workers. So do parks and recreation departments, resorts, travel agencies, hotels, and other service organizations with seasonal demands. In order to be successful, these organizations must be able to hire part-time employees when they are needed.

4. *Inventories.* The use of inventories allows firms to produce goods in one period and sell or ship them in another period, albeit at a cost of holding or carrying those goods as inventory until they are needed. The cost includes not only storage costs and the cost of money tied up that could be invested elsewhere, but also the cost of insurance, obsolescence, deterioration, spoilage, breakage, and so on. In essence, inventories can be built up during periods when production capacity exceeds demand and drawn down in periods when demand exceeds production capacity. This method is more amenable to manufacturing than services since manufactured goods can be stored whereas services generally cannot. However, an analogous approach used by services is to make efforts to streamline services (e.g., standard forms) or otherwise do a portion of the service during slack periods (e.g., organize the workplace). In spite of these possibilities, services tend to be unable to make much use of inventories to alter capacity requirements.

5. *Subcontracting.* Subcontracting enables planners to acquire temporary capacity, although it affords less control over the output and may lead to higher costs as well as quality problems. The question of whether to make or buy (in a case that involves manufacturing) or whether to perform a service or hire someone else to do the work generally depends on such factors as available capacity, relative expertise, quality considerations, cost, and the amount and stability of demand.

In some cases, a firm might choose to perform part of the work itself and let others handle the rest in order to maintain flexibility and as a hedge against loss of a subcontractor. Moreover, this gives the organization a bargaining tool in negotiations with contractors and a head start if it decides at a later date to take over the operation entirely.

Basic Strategies for Meeting Uneven Demand

Managers have a wide range of decision options they can consider for achieving a balance of demand and capacity in aggregate planning. Since the options that are most suited to influencing demand generally fall more in the realm of marketing than in operations (with the exception of backlogging), we shall concentrate on the capacity options, which are in the realm of operations but include the use of back orders.

There are a number of strategies aggregate planners might adopt. Some of the more prominent ones are:

1. Maintain a level work force.
2. Maintain a steady output rate.
3. Match demand period by period.
4. Use a combination of decision variables.

There are other possible strategies that we might consider, but these will suffice to give you a sense of how aggregate planning operates in a vast number of organizations. The first three strategies are "pure" strategies in that each has a single focal point; the last strategy is "mixed" in that it lacks the single focus. Under the level work force strategy, variations in demand are met by using some combination of inventories, overtime, part-time workers, subcontracting, and back ordering. The essence is to maintain a steady rate of *regular-time* output, although *total* output could vary. Maintaining a steady rate of output implies absorbing demand variations with inventories, subcontracting, or backlogging. Matching capacity to demand implies a **chase strategy;** the planned output for any period would be the expected demand for that period.

Many organizations find a level work force strategy very appealing. Since work force changes through hiring and firing can have a major impact on the lives and morale of employees and can be disruptive for managers, organizations often prefer to handle uneven demand in other ways. Moreover, changes in work force size can be very costly, and there is always the risk that there will not be a sufficient pool of workers with the appropriate skills when needed. Aside from these considerations, such changes can involve a significant amount of paperwork. Unions tend to favor a level work force since the freedom to hire and fire workers diminishes union strengths.

In order to maintain a constant level of output and still meet demand requirements, an organization must resort to some combination of subcontracting, backlogging, and use of inventories to absorb fluctuations. Subcontracting requires an investment in evaluating sources of supply as well as possible increased costs, less control over output, and perhaps quality considerations. Backlogs can lead to lost sales, increased record keeping, and lower levels of customer service. Allowing inventories to absorb fluctuations can entail substantial costs by having money tied up in inventories, having to maintain relatively large storage facilities, and incurring other costs related to inventories. Furthermore, inventories are not usually an alternative for service-oriented organizations. However, there are certain advantages, such as minimum costs of recruitment and training, minimum overtime and idle-time costs, fewer morale problems, and stable use of equipment and facilities.

A chase strategy presupposes a great deal of ability and willingness on the part of managers to be flexible in adjusting to demand. A major advantage of this approach is that inventories can be kept relatively low, which can yield substantial savings for an organization. A major disadvantage is the lack of stability in operations; the atmosphere is one of dancing to demand's tune. When forecast and reality differ, morale can suffer since it quickly becomes obvious to all that efforts have been wasted.

Organizations may opt for a strategy that involves some combination of decision variables without a single guiding focus. This allows managers greater flexibility in dealing with uneven demand and perhaps in experimenting with a wide variety of approaches. However, the absence of a clear focus may lead to an erratic approach and confusion on the part of employees.

Choosing a Strategy

Whatever strategy an organization is considering, two important factors are *company policy* and *costs*. Company policy may set constraints on the available options or the extent to which they can be used. For instance, company policy may discourage firing and layoffs except under extreme conditions. Similarly, subcontracting may not be a viable alternative due to the desire to maintain secrecy about some aspect of the manufacturing of a product (e.g., a secret formula or blending process). Often, union agreements impose restrictions. For example, a union contract may specify both minimum and maximum numbers of hours part-time workers can be used.

As a general rule, aggregate planners seek to match supply and demand within the constraints imposed on them by policies or agreements and at minimum cost. In fact, alternatives are usually evaluated in terms of their overall costs. In the next section, a number of different techniques for aggregate planning are described along with some examples of cost evaluation of alternative plans.

TECHNIQUES FOR AGGREGATE PLANNING

There are numerous techniques that can be used to help decision makers with the task of aggregate planning. Generally, they fall into one of two categories: informal, trial-and-error techniques and mathematical techniques. In practice, the informal techniques are more commonly used. However, a considerable amount of research has been devoted to mathematical techniques, and even though they are not widely used, they often serve as a basis for comparing the effectiveness of alternative techniques for aggregate planning. Thus, it will be instructive to briefly examine them as well as the informal techniques.

A general procedure for aggregate planning consists of the following steps:

1. Determine demand for each period.
2. Determine capacities (regular time, overtime, subcontracting) for each period.
3. Determine company or departmental policies that are pertinent (e.g., maintain a safety stock of 5 percent of demand, maintain a reasonably stable work force).
4. Determine unit costs for regular time, overtime, subcontracting, holding inventories, back orders, and other relevant costs.
5. Develop alternative plans and compute the cost for each.
6. If satisfactory plans emerge, select the one that best satisfies objectives. Otherwise, return to step 5.

It can be helpful to use a worksheet that summarizes demand, capacity, and cost for each plan, such as the one illustrated in Table 9–3. In addition, graphs can be used to guide development of alternatives.

Informal Techniques

Informal approaches consist of developing simple tables or graphs that enable planners to visually compare projected demand requirements with existing capacity, and this provides them with a basis for developing alternative plans for achieving intermediate-range goals. Alternatives are usually evaluated in terms of their overall costs. The chief disadvantage of such techniques is that they do not necessarily result in the optimal aggregate plan.

Very often, graphs can be used to guide the development of alternatives. Some planners prefer cumulative graphs, and others prefer to see a period-by-

TABLE 9–3

Worksheet

Period	1	2	3	4	5			Total
Forecast								
Output								
Regular								
Overtime								
Subcontract								
Output—Forecast								
Inventory								
Beginning								
Ending								
Average								
Backlog								
Costs:								
Output								
Regular								
Overtime								
Subcontract								
Inventory								
Back orders								
Total								

period breakdown of a plan. For instance, Figure 9–3 shows a cumulative graph for a plan with steady output and inventory absorption of demand variations. Figure 9–4 shows a period-by-period breakdown of the same plan. The obvious advantage of a graph is that it provides a visual portrayal of a plan. The choice between these two types of graphs depends on the preference of the planner.

Two examples will be used to illustrate the development and comparison of aggregate plans. In the first example, regular output is held steady, with inventory absorbing demand variations. This plan is portrayed in Figures 9–3 and 9–4. In the second example, a lower rate of regular output is used, supplemented by use of overtime. In both examples, some backlogs are allowed to build up.

FIGURE 9–3

A cumulative graph and inventory profile

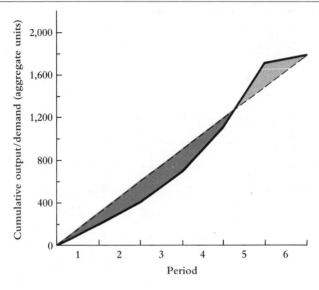

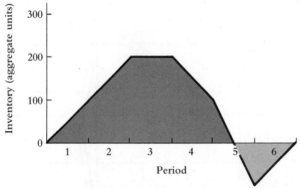

These examples and the other examples and problems in this chapter are based on the following assumptions:

1. The regular output capacity is the same in all periods. No allowance is made for holidays, different numbers of workdays in different months, and so on. This has been done for simplicity and ease of computation.
2. Cost (backlog, inventory, subcontracting, etc.) is a linear function composed of unit cost and number of units. This is often a reasonable approximation to reality, although there may be narrow ranges over which this is true. Cost is sometimes more of a step function.
3. Plans are feasible. That is, sufficient inventory capacity exists to accommodate a plan, subcontractors with appropriate quality and capacity are standing by, and changes in output can be made as needed.
4. All costs associated with a decision option can be represented by a lump

FIGURE 9—4

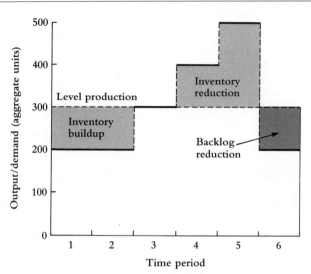

*Level production and
fluctuations in demand
absorbed by inventory*

sum or by unit costs that are independent of the quantity involved. Again, a step function may be more realistic; for purposes of illustration as well as simplicity, this assumption is appropriate.

5. Cost figures can be reasonably estimated and are constant for the planning horizon.

6. Inventories are built up and drawn down at a uniform rate throughout each period, and output occurs at a uniform rate throughout each period. However, backlogs are treated as if they exist for an entire period, even though in periods where they initially appear, they would tend to build up toward the end of the period. Hence, this assumption is a bit unrealistic for some periods, but it simplifies computations.

EXAMPLE 1

Planners are about to prepare the aggregate plan for a company that will cover six periods. They have assembled the following information:

Period	1	2	3	4	5	6	Total
Forecast	200	200	300	400	500	200	1,800

Costs:
  Output
    Regular time = $2 per unit
    Overtime   = $3 per unit
    Subcontract = $6 per unit
  Inventory   = $1 per unit per period on average inventory
  Back orders = $5 per unit per period

EXAMPLE 1 *(concluded)*

They now want to evaluate a plan that calls for a steady rate of regular-time output, mainly using inventory to absorb the uneven demand but allowing some backlog. They intend to start with zero inventory on hand in the first period. Prepare an aggregate plan and determine its cost using the preceding information. Assume a level output rate of 300 units per period with regular time (i.e., 1,800/6 = 300). Note that the planned ending inventory is zero.

Solution

Period	1	2	3	4	5	6	Total
Forecast	200	200	300	400	500	200	1,800
Output							
Regular	300	300	300	300	300	300	1,800
Overtime	—	—	—	—	—	—	
Subcontract	—	—	—	—	—	—	
Output − Forecast	100	100	0	(100)	(200)	100	0
Inventory							
Beginning	0	100	200	200	100	0	
Ending	100	200	200	100	0	0	
Average	50	150	200	150	50	0	600
Backlog	0	0	0	0	100	0	100
Costs:							
Output							
Regular	$600	600	600	600	600	600	$3,600
Overtime	—	—	—	—	—	—	—
Subcontract	—	—	—	—	—	—	—
Inventory	$ 50	150	200	150	50	0	$ 600
Back orders	$ 0	0	0	0	500	0	$ 500
Total	$600	750	800	750	1,150	600	$4,700

Note that the total regular-time output of 1,800 units equals the total expected demand. Ending inventory equals beginning inventory plus or minus the quantity Output − Forecast. Average inventory equals one half the sum of beginning and ending inventories. If Output − Forecast is negative, inventory is decreased in that period by that amount. If insufficient inventory exists, a backlog equal to the shortage amount appears, as in period 5. This is taken care of using the excess output in period 6.

The costs were computed as follows. Regular cost in each period equals 300 units × $2 per unit or $600. Inventory cost equals average inventory × $1 per unit. Back order cost is $5 per unit. The total cost for this plan is $4,700.

Note that the first two quantities in each column are givens. The remaining quantities in the upper portion of the table were determined working down each column, beginning with the first column. The costs were then computed based on the quantities in the upper part of the table.

EXAMPLE 2

After reviewing the plan developed in the preceding example, planners have decided to develop an alternative plan. They have learned that one person is about to retire from the company. Rather than replace him, they would like to stay with the smaller work force and use overtime to make up for the lost output. The reduced regular-time output is 280 units per period. The maximum amount of overtime output per period is 40 units. Develop a plan and compare it to the previous one.

Solution

Period	1	2	3	4	5	6	Total
Forecast	200	200	300	400	500	200	1,800
Output							
Regular	280	280	280	280	280	280	1,680
Overtime	0	0	40	40	40	0	120
Subcontract	—	—	—	—	—	—	—
Output − Forecast	80	80	20	(80)	(180)	80	0
Inventory							
Beginning	0	80	160	180	100	0	
Ending	80	160	180	100	0	0	
Average	40	120	170	140	50	0	520
Backlog	0	0	0	0	80	0	80
Costs:							
Output							
Regular	$560	560	560	560	560	560	$3,360
Overtime	0	0	120	120	120	0	$ 360
Subcontract	—	—	—	—	—	—	
Inventory	$ 40	120	170	140	50	0	$ 520
Back orders	$ 0	0	0	0	400	0	$ 400
Total	$600	680	850	820	1,130	560	$4,640

The amount of overtime that must be scheduled has to make up for lost output of 20 units per period for six periods, which is 120. This is scheduled toward the center of the planning horizon since that is where the bulk of demand occurs. Scheduling it earlier would increase inventory carrying costs; scheduling it later would increase the backlog.

Overall, the total cost for this plan is $4,640, which is $60 less than for the previous plan. Regular-time production cost is down, and inventory cost and overtime cost are up. However, this plan achieves savings in back order cost, making it somewhat less costly overall than the other plan.

These are only two of many possible options that could be tried. Perhaps some of the others would result in a lower cost. With trial and error, you can never be completely sure you have identified the lowest-cost alternative unless every possible alternative is evaluated. Of course, the purpose of these examples is to illustrate the process of developing and evaluating an aggregate plan, rather than to find the lowest-cost plan. However, some of the problems at the end of the chapter involve different alternatives for this situation.

In practice, successful achievement of a good plan depends on the resourcefulness and the persistence of the planner.

Mathematical Techniques

A number of mathematical techniques have been proposed over the last two decades to handle aggregate planning. They range from mathematical programming models to heuristic and computer search models. This section briefly describes some of the better-known techniques.

Linear Programming. Linear programming models are methods for obtaining optimal solutions to problems involving the allocation of scarce resources in terms of cost minimization or profit maximization. In terms of aggregate planning, the goal is usually to minimize the sum of costs related to regular labor time, overtime, subcontracting, inventory holding costs, and costs associated with changing the size of the work force. Constraints involve capacities of work force, inventories, and subcontracting.

E. H. Bowman proposed formulating the problem in terms of a transportation-type programming model (described in detail in the supplement to Chapter 5) as a way to obtain aggregate plans that would match capacities with demand requirements and minimize costs.[1] In order to use this approach, planners must identify capacity (supply) of regular time, overtime, subcontracting, and inventory on a period-by-period basis, as well as related costs of each variable.

The notation and setup of a transportation table is shown in Table 9–4. Note the systematic way that costs change as you move across a row from left to right. Note that regular cost, overtime cost, and subcontracting cost are at their lowest when the output is consumed (delivered, etc.) in the same period it is produced (at the intersection of period 1 row and column for regular cost, at the intersection of period 2 row and column for regular cost, and so on). If goods are made available in one period but carried over to later periods (i.e., moving across a row), holding costs are incurred at the rate of h per period. Thus, holding goods for two periods results in a unit cost of $2h$, irrespective of whether the goods came from regular production, overtime, or subcontracting. Conversely, in the case of back orders, the unit cost increases as you move

---

[1] E. H. Bowman, "Production Planning by the Transportation Method of Linear Programming," *Journal of Operations Research Society* 4 (February 1956), pp. 100–103.

TABLE 9–4

*Transportation notation
for aggregate planning*

r = Regular production cost per unit
t = Overtime cost per unit
s = Subcontracting cost per unit
h = Holding cost per unit per period
b = Back order cost per unit per period
n = Number of periods in planning horizon

Period		Period 1	Period 2	Period 3	$\cdots$	Ending inventory period n	Unused capacity	Capacity
	Beginning inventory	0	h	$2h$	$\cdots$	nh	0	I_0
1	Regular time	r	$r+h$	$r+2h$	$\cdots$	$r+nh$	0	R_1
	Overtime	t	$t+h$	$t+2h$	$\cdots$	$t+nh$	0	O_1
	Subcontract	s	$s+h$	$s+2h$	$\cdots$	$s+nh$	0	S_1
2	Regular time	$r+b$	r	$r+h$	$\cdots$	$r+(n-1)h$	0	R_2
	Overtime	$t+b$	t	$t+h$	$\cdots$	$t+(n-1)h$	0	O_2
	Subcontract	$s+b$	s	$s+h$	$\cdots$	$s+(n-1)h$	0	S_2
3	Regular time	$r+2b$	$r+b$	r	$\cdots$	$r+(n-2)h$	0	R_3
	Overtime	$t+2b$	$t+b$	t	$\cdots$	$t+(n-2)h$	0	O_3
	Subcontract	$s+2b$	$s+b$	s	$\cdots$	$s+(n-2)h$	0	S_3
	Demand				$\cdots$			Total

across a row from right to left, beginning at the intersection of a row and column for the same period (e.g., period 3). For instance, if some goods are produced in period 3 to satisfy back orders from period 2, a unit back order cost of b is incurred. And if goods in period 3 are used to satisfy back orders two periods back (e.g., from period 1), a unit cost of $2b$ is incurred. Unused capacity is generally given a unit cost of 0, although it is certainly possible to insert an actual cost if that seems relevant. Finally, beginning inventory is given a unit cost of 0 if it is used to satisfy demand in period 1. However, if it is held over for use in later periods, a holding cost of h per unit is added for each period. If the inventory is to be held for the entire planning horizon, a total unit cost of h times the number of periods, n, will be incurred.

Example 3 illustrates the setup and final solution of a transportation model of an aggregate planning problem.

In a case where backlogs are not permitted, the cell costs for the backlog positions can be made prohibitively high so that no backlogs will appear in the solution.

The main limitations of LP models are the assumptions of linear relationships among variables, the inability to continuously adjust output rates, and the need to specify a single objective (e.g., minimize costs) instead of using multiple objectives (e.g., minimize cost while stabilizing the work force.)

EXAMPLE 3

Given the following information, set up the problem in a transportation format and solve for the minimum-cost plan:

	Period		
	1	*2*	*3*
Demand	550	700	750
Capacity			
Regular	500	500	500
Overtime	50	50	50
Subcontract	120	120	100
Beginning			
inventory	100		
Costs			
Regular time	$60 per unit		
Overtime	80 per unit		
Subcontract	90 per unit		
Inventory			
carrying cost	$1 per unit per month		
Back order cost	$3 per unit per month		

Solution

The transportation solution (see the supplement to Chapter 5) is shown in Table 9–5. Some of the entries require additional explanation:

a.   In this example, inventory carrying costs are $1 per unit per period (costs are shown in the upper right-hand corner of each cell in the table). Hence, units produced in one period and carried over to a later period will incur a holding cost that is a linear function of the length of time held.

EXAMPLE 3 *(concluded)*

TABLE 9–5

Transportation solution

Period	Supply from	Demand for — Period 1	Period 2	Period 3	Unused capacity (dummy)	Total capacity available (supply)
Period	Beginning inventory	0 — 100	1	2	0	100
1	Regular time	60 — 450	61 — 50	62	0	500
1	Overtime	80	81 — 50	82	0	50
1	Subcontract	90	91 — 30	92	0 — 90	120
2	Regular time	63	60 — 500	61	0	500
2	Overtime	83	80 — 50	81	0	50
2	Subcontract	93	90 — 20	91 — 100	0	120
3	Regular time	66	63	60 — 500	0	500
3	Overtime	86	83	80 — 50	0	50
3	Subcontract	96	93	90 — 100	0	100
	Demand	550	700	750	90	2,090

b. Linear programming models of this type require that supply (capacity) and demand be equal. A "dummy" column has been added (unused capacity) to satisfy that requirement. Since it does not "cost" anything extra to not use capacity in this case, cell costs of $0 have been assigned.

c. No backlogs were needed in this example.

d. The quantities (e.g., 100 and 450 in column 1) are the amounts of output or inventory that will be used to meet demand requirements. Thus, the demand of 550 units in period 1 will be met using 100 units from inventory and 450 obtained from regular-time output.

Goal Programming. **Goal programming** is a variation of linear programming that permits the user to specify multiple goals in a priority-based way. The solution represents an attempt to optimize the goals according to priorities. Several applications of goal programming to aggregate planning have been reported in the literature.[2]

Linear Decision Rule. Another optimizing technique, the **linear decision rule,** was developed during the 1950s, by Charles Holt, Franco Modigliani, John Muth, and Herbert Simon.[3] It seeks to minimize the combined costs of regular payroll, hiring and layoffs, overtime, and inventory using a set of cost-approximating functions, three of which are *quadratic* (contain squared terms), to obtain a single quadratic equation. Using calculus, two linear equations (hence the name *linear decision rule*) can be derived from the quadratic equation. One of the equations can be used to plan the output for each period in the planning horizon, and the other can be used to plan the work force size for each period.

Although the model has found some applications, its chief function seems to be as a benchmark against which proposed techniques can be evaluated. In practice, the model suffers from three limitations: (1) a specific type of cost function is assumed, (2) considerable effort must usually be expended in obtaining relevant cost data and developing cost functions for each organization, and (3) the method can produce solutions that are not feasible or are impractical.

Management Coefficients. A heuristic model proposed by E. H. Bowman, **management coefficients,** attempts to incorporate previous managerial planning performance into a decision model.[4] The rationale for the model is based on improving performance rather than on trying to develop a "new" optimizing method. The procedure involves the use of multiple regression analysis to build a decision model.

Parametric Production Planning. A heuristic technique known as **parametric production planning** was proposed by C. H. Jones in the late 1960s.[5] The model uses a search routine to develop two decision rules for output and work force size. In some respects, it is similar to the linear decision rule: It uses quadratic cost-approximating functions and provides two decision

---

[2] See, for example, D. A. Goodman, "A New Approach to Scheduling Aggregate Production and Work Force," *AIIE Transactions* 5 (June 1973), pp. 153–41; and S. M. Lee and L. J. Moore, "A Practical Approach to Production Scheduling," *Production and Inventory Management* (1st quarter 1974), pp. 79–92.

[3] Charles C. Holt, Franco Modigliani, John F. Muth, and Herbert A. Simon, *Planning Production, Inventories and Work Force* (Englewood Cliffs, N.J.: Prentice-Hall, 1960).

[4] E. H. Bowman, "Consistence and Optimality in Managerial Decision Making," *Management Science* 4 (January 1963), pp. 100–103.

[5] C. H. Jones, "Parametric Production Planning," *Management Science* 13, no. 11 (July 1967), pp. 843–66.

rules. Unlike the linear decision model, it can be used with essentially any cost function.

Simulation Models.   A number of **simulation models** have also been developed for aggregate planning. (Simulation is described in detail in the supplement to Chapter 15.) The essence of the models is the development of computerized models that can be tested under a variety of conditions in an attempt to identify reasonably acceptable (although not always optimal) solutions to problems.

These models are summarized in Table 9–6.

Aggregate planning techniques other than trial and error do not appear to be widely used. Instead, in the majority of organizations, aggregate planning seems to be done more on the basis of experience, along with trial-and-error methods. It is difficult to say exactly why some of the mathematical techniques mentioned are not used to any great extent. We can only speculate. Perhaps the level of mathematical sophistication discourages greater use; or the assump-

TABLE 9–6

Technique	Solution approach	Characteristics	
Graphical/ charting	Trial and error	Intuitively appealing, easy to understand; solution not necessarily optimal	*Summary of planning techniques*
Linear programming	Optimizing	Computerized; linear assumptions not always valid	
Goal programming	Optimizing	Allows use of multiple goals	
Linear decision rule	Optimizing	Complex, requires considerable effort to obtain pertinent cost information and to construct model; cost assumptions not always valid	
Management coefficients	Heuristic	Uses multiple regression to incorporate past managerial performance into a model; attempts to use that as a base to improve performance	
Parametric planning	Heurisitic	Uses a search routine to develop two decision rules	
Simulation	Trial and error	Computerized models allow managers to examine models under a variety of conditions	

tions required in certain models may appear unrealistic; or the models may be too narrow in scope. But whatever the reasons, none of the techniques to date have captured the attention of aggregate planners on a broad scale. Goal programming and simulation are two techniques that seem to be gaining in favor. Suffice it to say that research on improved approaches to aggregate planning is continuing.

DISAGGREGATING THE AGGREGATE PLAN

For the production plan to be translated into meaningful terms for production, it is necessary to *disaggregate* the aggregate plan. This involves breaking down the aggregate plan into specific product requirements in order to determine labor requirements (skills, size of work force), materials, and inventory requirements. This process is discussed in some depth in Chapter 11, Material Requirements Planning. At this stage, however, it can be useful for you to be aware of the need for disaggregation, as well as to have some understanding of what the term implies.

Working with aggregate units facilitates intermediate planning. However, for the production plan to be operationalized, those aggregate units have to be converted, or decomposed, into units of actual products or services that are to be produced or offered. For example, a lawn mower manufacturer may have an aggregate plan that calls for 200 lawn mowers in January, 300 in February,

FIGURE 9–5

Disaggregating the aggregate plan

Aggregate plan	Month					
		Jan.	Feb.	Mar.	Apr.	May
	Planned output*	200	300	400	400	350

*Aggregate units

Master schedule	Month	Jan.	Feb.	Mar.
	Planned output*			
	Push	100	100	100
	Self-propelling	75	150	200
	Riding	25	50	100
	Total	200	300	400

*Actual units

and 400 in March. That company may produce push mowers, self-propelled mowers, and riding mowers. Although the mowers probably contain some of the same parts and involve some similiar or identical operations for fabrication and assembly, we expect certain basic differences in the materials, parts, and operations that each type requires. Hence, the 200, 300, and 400 aggregate lawn mowers that are to be produced during those three months must be translated into specific numbers of mowers of each type prior to actually purchasing the appropriate materials and parts, scheduling operations, and planning inventory requirements.

The result of disaggregating the aggregate plan is a **master schedule,** which simply shows the quantity and timing of *specific* goods or services for a schedule horizon. The master schedule then serves as the basis for *short-range* planning. It should be noted that whereas the aggregate plan covers an interval, say, of 12 months, the master schedule covers only a portion of this. In other words, the aggregate plan is disaggregated in stages, or phases, that may cover a few weeks to two or three months. Moreover, the master schedule may be updated monthly, even though it covers two or three months. For instance, the lawn mower master schedule would probably be updated at the end of January to include any revisions in planned output for February and March as well as new information on planned output for April.

The concept of disaggregating the aggregate plan is illustrated in Figure 9–5. The illustration makes a simple assumption in order to clearly show the concept of disaggregation: The totals of the aggregate and the disaggregated units are equal. However, that is not always true. As a consequence, it can require considerable effort to disaggregate the aggregate plan.

SUMMARY

Aggregate planning establishes general levels of employment, output, and inventories for periods of two months to one year. In the spectrum of planning, it falls between the broad design decisions of long-range planning and the very specific and detailed short-range planning decisions. It begins with an overall forecast for the planning horizon and ends with preparations for applying the plans to specific products and services.

The essence of aggregate planning is the aggregation of products or services into one "product" or "service." This permits planners to consider overall levels of employment and inventories without having to become involved with specific details that are better left to short-range planning. Planners often use informal graphical and charting techniques to develop plans, although various mathematical techniques have been suggested. It appears that the complexity and the restrictive assumptions of these techniques limit their widespread acceptance in practice.

KEY TERMS

aggregate planning, 466

chase strategy, 474

goal programming, 486

linear decision rule, 486

management coefficients, 486

master schedule, 489

parametric production planning, 486

rough–cut capacity planning, 468

simulation models, 487

SOLVED PROBLEM

A manager is attempting to put together an aggregate plan for the coming year. She has obtained a forecast of expected demand for the planning horizon. Basically, the plan must deal with demand that is highly seasonal; demand is relatively high in periods 3 and 4 and again in periods 10 and 11, as can be seen from the following forecasts:

Period	1	2	3	4	5	6	7	8	9	10	11	12	Total
Forecast	190	230	260	280	210	170	160	160	220	250	260	180	2,570

The department now has 20 full-time people, each of whom can produce 10 units of output per period at a cost of $6 per unit. Inventory carrying cost is $5 per unit per period, and backlog cost is $10 per unit per period. The manager is considering a plan that would involve hiring two people to start working in period 1, one on a temporary basis who would work only through period 5. This would cost $500 in addition to unit production costs.

a. What is the rationale for this plan?

b. Determine the total cost of the plan, including production, inventory and back order costs.

Solution

a. With the current work force of 20 people each producing 10 units per period, regular capacity is 2,400 units. That is 170 units less than expected demand. Adding one worker would increase regular capacity to 2,400 + 120 = 2,520 units. That would still be 50 units short, or just the amount one temporary worker could produce in five periods. Since one of the two seasonal peaks is quite early, it would make sense to start the temporary worker right away to avoid some of the back order cost.

b. The production plan for this strategy is as follows:

Period	1	2	3	4	5	6	7	8	9	10	11	12	Total
Forecast	190	230	260	280	210	170	160	160	220	250	260	180	2,570
Output													
Regular	220	220	220	220	220	210	210	210	210	210	210	210	2,570
Overtime	—	—	—	—	—	—	—	—	—	—	—	—	—
Subcontract	—	—	—	—	—	—	—	—	—	—	—	—	—
Output − Forecast	30	(10)	(40)	(60)	10	40	50	50	(10)	(40)	(50)	30	0
Inventory													
Beginning	0	30	20	0	0	0	0	20	70	60	20	0	
Ending	30	20	0	0	0	0	20	70	60	20	0	0	
Average	15	25	10	0	0	0	10	45	65	40	10	0	220
Backlog	0	0	20	80	70	30	0	0	0	0	30	0	230

Costs:													
Output													
Regular @ $6	$1,320	1,320	1,320	1,320	1,320	1,260	1,260	1,260	1,260	1,260	1,260	1,260	$15,420
Overtime													
Subcontract													
Inventory @ $5	$ 75	125	50	0	0	0	50	225	325	200	50	0	$ 1,100
Back order @ $10	0	0	200	800	700	300	0	0	0	0	300	0	$ 2,300
Total	$1,395	1,445	1,570	2,120	2,020	1,560	1,310	1,485	1,585	1,460	1,610	1,260	$18,820

The total cost for this plan is $18,820, plus the $500 cost for hiring and for the layoff, giving a total of $19,320. This plan may or may not be good. We would need information on other costs and options before settling on one plan.

Although the calculations are relatively straightforward, the backlogs can sometimes seem difficult to obtain. Consider these rules for computing the backlog:

1. Start with the Output − Forecast value. If it is positive and there was a backlog in the preceding period, reduce the backlog by this amount. If the amount exceeds the backlog, the difference becomes the ending inventory for the period. If they are exactly equal, the backlog and the ending inventory will both be equal to zero.

2. If Output − Forecast is negative, subtract it from the beginning inventory. If this produces a negative value, that value becomes the backlog for that period.

DISCUSSION AND REVIEW QUESTIONS

1. What three levels of planning involve operations managers? What kinds of decisions
   are made at the various levels?
2. What are the three phases of intermediate
   planning?
3. What is aggregate planning? What is its
   purpose?
4. Why is there a need for aggregate
   planning?
5. What are the most common decision variables for aggregate planning in a
   manufacturing setting? In a service setting?
6. What difficulty may an organization that
   offers a variety of products and/or services
   have to deal with in aggregate planning
   that an organization with one or a few
   similar products or services would not?
7. Briefly discuss the advantages and disadvantages of each of these planning
   strategies:

    a. Maintain a level rate of output, and let
   inventories absorb fluctuations in
   demand.
    b. Vary the size of the work force to
   correspond with predicted changes in
   demand requirements.
    c. Maintain a constant work force size,
   but vary hours worked to correspond
   to predicted demand requirements.
8. What are the primary advantages and limitations of informal graphical and charting
   techniques for aggregate planning?
9. Briefly describe the planning techniques
   listed below, and give an advantage and
   disadvantage for each one:
    a. Linear programming.
    b. Linear decision rule.
    c. Management coefficients.
    d. Simulation.

PROBLEMS

1. The solved problem illustrated an aggregate plan that involved use of hiring and a
   layoff as well as inventory absorption of
   demand variations and some buildup of
   backlogs. As noted, for the merits of that
   plan to be assessed, certain other information would be needed. If you were the manager, what information would you want?
   Be specific.
2. Prepare two graphs like those in Figure 9–3
   for the solved problem at the end of this
   chapter. Also, prepare a graph like the one
   in Figure 9–4.
3. (Refer to the solved problem.) Prepare two
   additional aggregate plans. Call the one in
   the solved problem plan A. For plan B, hire
   one more worker at a cost of $200 in that
   period. Make up any shortfall using subcontracting at $8 per unit, with a maximum

   of 20 units per period (i.e., use subcontracting to reduce back orders when the forecast
   exceeds regular output). Note that the ending inventory in period 12 should be zero.
   Therefore, Total forecast = Total output
   + Quantity subcontracted. An additional
   constraint is that back orders cannot exceed
   70 units in any period. For plan C, assume
   no workers are hired (so regular output is
   200 units per period instead of 210 as in plan
   B). Use subcontracting as needed, and try
   to minimize back orders. The constraints of
   20 units of subcontracting per period and 70
   units of back orders still apply. Compute
   the total cost of each plan. Which plan has
   the lowest cost?
4. (Refer to the solved problem.) Suppose another option is to use part-time workers to
   assist during seasonal peaks. The cost per

unit, including hiring and training, is $11. The output rate is 10 units per worker per period for all workers. A maximum of 10 workers can be used, and the same number of part-time workers must be used in all periods that have part-time workers. The ending inventory in period 12 should be 30 units. The limit on backlogs is 20 units per period. Try to make up backlogs as soon as possible. Compute the total cost for this plan, and compare it to the cost of the plan used in the solved problem.

5. (Refer to solved problem.) Prepare an aggregate plan that uses overtime ($9 per unit, maximum output 25 units per period) and inventory variation. Try to minimize backlogs. The ending inventory in period 12 should be zero, and the limit on backlogs is 60 units per period. Note that Total forecast = Total regular output + Quantity subcontracted. Compute the total cost of your plan, and compare it to the total cost of the plan used in the solved problem.

6. (Refer to the solved problem.) Prepare an aggregate plan that uses some combination of hiring ($200 per worker), layoff ($100 per worker), subcontracting ($8 per unit, maximum of 20 units per period, must use for a minimum of three consecutive periods), and overtime ($9 per unit, maximum of 25 per period, maximum of 100 for the planning horizon). Compute the total cost, and compare it to any of the other plans you have developed. Which plan has the lowest total cost?

7. (Refer to Example 1.) The president of the firm has decided to shut down the plant for vacation and installation of new equipment in period 4. After installation, the cost per unit will remain the same, but the output rate for regular time will be 450.

   a. Prepare graphs like those in Figures 9–3 and 9–4 for this revised case.

   b. Regular output is the same as in Example 1 for periods 1, 2, and 3; 0 for period 4; and 450 for each of the remaining periods. Note, though, that the forecast of 200 units in period 4 must be dealt with. Prepare the aggregate plan, and compute its total cost.

8. (Refer to Example 1.) Suppose that the regular output rate will drop to 290 units per period due to an expected change in production requirements. Costs will not change. Prepare an aggregate plan and compute its total cost for each of these alternatives:

   a. Use overtime at a fixed rate of 20 units per period as needed. Plan for an ending inventory of zero for period 6. Backlogs cannot exceed 90 units per period.

   b. Use subcontracting at a *maximum* rate of 50 units per period; the usage need not be the same in every period. Have an ending inventory of zero in the last period. Again, backlogs cannot exceed 90 units in any period. Compare these two plans.

9. (Refer to Example 2.) Do each of the following:

   a. Prepare graphs like those in Figures 9–3 and 9–4 for the data given in Example 2. Combine regular time and overtime, and use those amounts for output in the graphs.

   b. Suppose you can use a combination of overtime and subcontracting, but you cannot use subcontracting in more than two periods. Up to 50 units of subcontracting and either 0 or 40 units of overtime are allowed per period. Subcontracting is $6 per unit, and overtime is $3 per unit. (*Hint:* Use subcontracting only when overtime units are not sufficient to decrease backlogs to 80 units or fewer.) Plan for an ending inventory balance of 0 for period 6. Prepare a plan that will minimize total cost.

10. (Refer to Example 2.) Determine if a plan to use subcontracting at a maximum rate of 50 units per period as needed with no overtime would achieve a lower total cost than the plan shown in Example 2. Again, plan for a zero inventory balance at the end of period 6.

11. Verify the transportation solution shown in Example 3.

12. (Refer to Example 3.) Suppose that, due to an increase in warehousing costs and other costs, inventory carrying costs are now $2 per unit per month. All other costs and quantities remain the same. Determine a revised solution to this transportation problem.

13. (Refer to Example 3.) Suppose that regular-time capacity will be reduced to 440 units in Period 3 to accommodate a companywide safety inspection of equipment. What will the additional cost of the optimal plan be as compared to the one shown in Example 3? Assume all costs and quantities are the same as given in Example 3 except for period 3's regular-time output.

14. Solve the preceding problem using an inventory carrying cost of $2 per unit per period.

15. Dundas Bike Components Inc. of Wheelville, Illinois, manufactures bicycle wheels in two different sizes for the Big Bike Co. assembly plant located across town. David Dundas, the firm's owner-manager, has just received Big Bike's order for the next six months.

	20-inch wheels	24-inch wheels
Nov.	1,000 units	500 units
Dec.	900	500
Jan.	500	300
Feb.	700	500
Mar.	1,100	400
Apr.	1,100	600

a. Under what circumstances will it be possible for David to develop just one aggregate plan rather than two (one for each size wheel)? Explain in two to three sentences—no calculations.

b. Currently David employs 30 full-time, highly skilled employees, each of whom can produce 50 wheels per month. Because skilled labor is in short supply in the Wheelville area, David would like to develop a pure level output plan. There is no inventory of finished wheels on hand at present, but David would like to have 300 on hand at the end of April. Big Bike will tolerate back orders of up to 200 units per month. Show your level plan in tabular form.

c. Calculate the total annual cost of your plan using these costs:

Regular	$5.00	Hiring	$300
Overtime	$7.50	Layoff	$400
Part-time	NA	Inventory	$1.00
Subcontract	NA	Back order	$6.00

SELECTED BIBLIOGRAPHY

Buffa, Elwood S., and Jeffery G. Miller. *Production-Inventory Systems: Planning and Control.* 3rd ed. Homewood, Ill.: Richard D. Irwin, 1974.

Fogarty, Donald W., and Thomas R. Hoffmann. *Production and Inventory Management.* Cincinnati: South-Western Publishing, 1983.

Krajewski, L., and L. Ritzman. "Disaggregation in Manufacturing and Service Organizations." *Decision Sciences* 8, no. 1 (1977), pp. 1–18.

Leone, Robert A., and John R. Meyer. "Capacity Strategies for the 1980s." *Harvard Business Review,* November–December 1980, p. 133.

McLain, J. O., and L. J. Thomas. "Horizon Effects in Aggregate Production Planning with Seasonal Demand." *Management Science* 23, no. 7 (March 1977), pp. 728–36.

Posner, M. E., and W. Szwarc. "A Transportation Type Aggregate Production Model with Backor-dering." *Management Science* 29, no. 2 (February 1983), pp. 188–99.

Vollmann, Thomas E.; William L. Berry; and D. Clay Whybark. *Manufacturing Planning and Control Systems.* Homewood, Ill.: Richard D. Irwin, 1984.

10

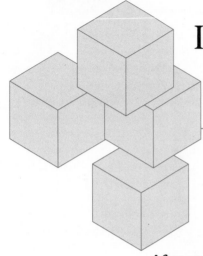

Inventory Management

LEARNING OBJECTIVES

After completing this chapter, you should be able to:

1. Define the term *inventory*.
2. Contrast independent and dependent demand.
3. List the major reasons for holding inventories.
4. List the main requirements for effective inventory management.
5. Discuss periodic and perpetual review systems.
6. Describe the A-B-C approach and explain how it is useful.
7. Discuss the objectives of inventory management.
8. Describe the basic EOQ model and its assumptions and solve typical problems.
9. Describe the economic run size model and solve typical problems.
10. Describe the quantity discount model and solve typical problems.
11. Describe reorder point models and solve typical problems.
12. Describe the single-period model and solve typical problems.

Chapter Outline

We proceed as follows. First look for a five-by-five-by-three-foot bin of gears or parts that looks like it has been there awhile. Pick up a gear and ask, casually, "How much is this worth?" You then ask, "How many of these are in the bin?" followed by, "How long has this bin been here?" and, "What's your cost of money for this company?" I recall one case in a nameless South American country where the unit cost times the number of parts times the time it had been there times the interest rate resulted in a cost-per-day figure that would insure comfortable retirement for the plant manager on the bank of the Rio de la Plata at one of the better resorts to be found there. The plant manager suddenly realized that what he was holding was not just a chunk of high-test steel, but was *real money*. He then pointed out that *he* now understood the value of the inventory but could I suggest a way to drive the point home to upper management? I suggested that he go to the accounting department and borrow enough money to be equal to the bin's value for as long as it had been sitting there, and pile it on the top of the bin. I further suggested that he do that for every bin on the production line. We rapidly figured out that by the time we had the money piled up on the bin, you would not even be able to *see* the bin. My opinion was that if the upper managers were given a tour of the line with the money piled up, they would *never forget it*.

Gene Woolsey, "On Doing Good Things and Dumb Things in Production and Inventory Control," *Interfaces* 5, no. 3 (May 1975). Copyright 1975, The Institute of Management Science. Reprinted by permission.

Good inventory management is essential to the successful operation of most organizations. There are a number of reasons for this. One is the amount of money inventory represents; another is the impact that inventories have on the daily operations of an organization. Some organizations have excellent inventory management, and many have satisfactory inventory management. But too many have unsatisfactory inventory management. In some instances, that is a sign that management does not recognize the importance of inventories. More often than not, though, the recognition is there. What is lacking is an understanding of what needs to be done and how to do it. In this chapter, the concepts that underlie good inventory management are explored.

The preceding chapter described *aggregate* inventory planning. This chapter and the next one narrow the focus to *individual items*. The next chapter deals with inventory methods that are best suited for managing inventories of component parts and subassemblies, while this chapter describes methods that are best suited for finished goods, raw materials, purchased parts, and retail items.

The chapter discusses the different functions of inventories, the requirements for effective inventory management, the objectives of inventory control, and techniques for determining *how much* to order and *when* to order.

INTRODUCTION

An **inventory** is a stock or store of goods. Many firms stock hundreds or even thousands of items, ranging from small things such as pencils, paper clips, screws, nuts, and bolts to large items such as machines, trucks, construction equipment, and airplanes. Naturally, many of the items a firm carries in inventory relate to the kind of business it engages in. Thus, manufacturing firms carry supplies of raw materials, purchased parts, partially completed items, and finished goods, as well as spare parts for machines, tools, and other supplies. Department stores carry clothing, furniture, carpeting, stationery, appliances, gifts, cards, and toys. Some also stock sporting goods, paints, and tools. Hospitals stock drugs, surgical supplies, life-monitoring equipment, sheets and pillow cases, and more. Supermarkets stock fresh and canned foods, packaged and frozen foods, household supplies, magazines, baked goods, dairy products, and miscellaneous items.

Independent and Dependent Demand

A major distinction in the way inventory planning and control is managed is whether demand for items in inventory is *independent* or *dependent*. **Dependent demand** items are typically subassemblies or component parts that will be used in the production of a final or finished product. In such cases, demand (i.e., usage) of subassemblies and component parts essentially *depends* on the number of finished units that will be produced. A classic example of this is demand for wheels for new cars. If each car is to have five wheels, then the total number of wheels required for a production run is simply a function of the number of cars that are to be produced in that run. For example, 200 cars would require $200 \times 5 = 1,000$ wheels. **Independent demand** items, on the other hand, are the finished goods or other end items. Generally speaking, these items are sold, or at least shipped out, rather than used in making another product. In such cases, there is usually no way to precisely determine how many of these items will be demanded during any given time period because demand typically includes elements of randomness. Therefore, forecasting plays an important role in stocking decisions, whereas for dependent demand items, stock requirements are determined by reference to the production plan. This chapter focuses on management of independent demand items, and the next chapter focuses on dependent demand.

Types of Inventories

An inventory of a typical firm can be classified as one of the following:

Raw materials and purchased parts.
Partially completed goods (work in process) or goods in transit.
Finished goods inventories (manufacturing firms) or merchandise (retail stores).
Replacement parts, tools, and supplies.

Functions of Inventory

Inventories serve a number of important functions. Among the most salient reasons for holding inventories are the following:

1. To meet anticipated demand.
2. To smooth production requirements.
3. To decouple components of the production-distribution system.
4. To protect against stock-outs.
5. To take advantage of order cycles.
6. To hedge against price increases.
7. To permit operations.

Let's take a look at each of these.

1. *To meet anticipated customer demand.* A customer can be a person who walks in off the street to buy a new stereo system, a mechanic who requests a tool at a tool crib, or a manufacturing operation. These inventories are referred to as *anticipation stocks* because they are held to satisfy planned or expected demand.

2. *To smooth production requirements.* Firms that experience seasonal patterns in demand often build up inventories during off-season periods in order to meet overly high requirements that exist during certain seasonal periods. These inventories are aptly named *seasonal inventories.*

3. *To decouple operations.* Unless successive steps in a production or distribution system have a buffer of inventories between them, they will be so interdependent that an interruption at one point will quickly cause the entire system to grind to a halt, as individual steps in the operations have to cease and operations shut down one after the other in domino fashion. Thus, an inventory of raw materials offers a manufacturer some protection from disruption in deliveries caused by the weather or problems with a supplier. Similarly, inventories between successive manufacturing steps act as a buffer that allows other operations to continue temporarily if some operations suffer breakdowns or other problems. Also, finished goods inventories separate manufacturing and selling operations, enabling income to be generated when a disruption in manufacturing occurs.

4. *To protect against stock-outs.* Delayed deliveries and unexpected increases in demand increase the risk of shortages. Delays can be due to weather conditions, supplier stock-outs, deliveries of wrong materials, quality problems, and so on. The risk of shortages can be reduced by holding *safety stocks,* which are stocks in excess of anticipated demand.

5. *To take advantage of order cycles.* To minimize purchasing and inventory costs, it is often necessary to buy quantities that exceed immediate usage requirements. This necessitates storing some or all of the purchased amount for later use. Similarly, it is usually economical to produce in large rather than small quantities. Again, the excess output must be stored for later use. Hence, inventory storage enables a firm to buy and produce in *economic lot sizes* without having to try to match purchases or production with demand requirements in the short run. This results in *periodic* orders, or order *cycles*. The resulting stock is known as *cycle stock*. Order cycles are not always due to economic order sizes. In some instances, it is practical or economical to group orders or to order at fixed intervals.

6. *To hedge against price increases.* Occasionally a firm will suspect that a substantial price increase is about to be made and purchase larger-than-normal amounts to achieve some savings.

7. *To permit operations.* The fact that production operations take a certain amount of time (i.e., they are not instantaneous) means that there will generally be some *work-in-process* inventory. In addition, intermediate stocking of goods—including raw materials, semifinished items, and finished goods at production sites, as well as goods stored in warehouses—leads to *pipeline* inventories throughout a production-distribution system.

Objectives of Inventory Control

Inadequate control of inventories can result in both understocking and overstocking of items. Understocking results in missed deliveries, lost sales, dissatisfied customers, and production bottlenecks; overstocking unnecessarily ties up funds that might be more productive elsewhere. Although overstocking may appear to be the lesser of the two evils, the price tag for excessive overstocking can be staggering when inventory holding costs are high, as illustrated by the little story about the bin of gears at the beginning of the chapter. Moreover, matters can easily get out of hand. For example, it is not unheard of for a manager to discover that his or her firm has more than a 100-year supply of some item. (No doubt the firm got a good buy on it!)

There are two main objectives of inventory control. One is to *maximize the level of customer service* (i.e., have the right goods, in sufficient quantities, in the right place, and at the right time.) The other is to *minimize the cost* of providing a certain level of customer service.

These two objectives are generally in opposition: high levels of customer service lead to high costs, and low costs usually are accompanied by low levels of customer service. Consequently, most inventory decisions are trade-offs involving a compromise between cost and customer service level. In practice, management may select a desired level of customer service, in which case the goal of inventory contol is to attain that level at the lowest possible cost. Conversely, management may set cost levels, in which case the goal is usually to attain the highest possible level of customer service under those conditions.

Toward this end, the decision maker's problem is to achieve a balance in stocking, avoiding both overstocking and understocking. The two fundamental decisions that must be made relate to the *timing* and *size* of orders (i.e., when to order and how much to order). The majority of material in this chapter is devoted to models that can be applied to assist in making those decisions.

REQUIREMENTS FOR EFFECTIVE INVENTORY MANAGEMENT

Management has two basic functions with respect to inventory. One is to establish a system of accounting for items in inventory, and the other is to make decisions regarding how much to order and when to order. To be effective, management must have the following:

1. A system to *keep track of the inventory* on hand and on order.
2. A reliable *forecast of demand* that includes an indication of possible *forecast error*.
3. Knowledge of *lead times* and *lead time variability*.
4. Reasonable estimates of inventory *holding costs, ordering costs,* and *shortage costs*.
5. A *classification system* for inventory items.

Let's take a closer look at each of these requirements.

Inventory Accounting Systems

Inventory accounting systems can be periodic or continuous. Under a **periodic system,** a physical count of items in inventory is made at periodic intervals (weekly, monthly) in order to decide how much to order of each item. Many small grocers use this approach; a manager periodically checks the shelves and stockroom to determine the quantity on hand. Then the manager estimates how much will be demanded prior to the next period's delivery and bases the order quantity on that information. An advantage of this type of system is that orders for many items occur at the same time, and there can be economies in processing and shipping orders. There are also several disadvantages of periodic reviews. One is that there is lack of control between reviews. Another is the need to protect against shortages between review periods by carrying extra stock. A third disadvantage is the need to make a decision on order quantities at each review.

A **continuous inventory system** (also known as a *perpetual* system) keeps track of removals from inventory on a continuous basis, so the system can provide information on the current level of inventory for each item. When the amount on hand reaches a predetermined minimum, a fixed quantity, Q, is ordered. An obvious advantage of this system is the control provided by the continuous monitoring of inventory withdrawals. Another advantage is the fixed-order quantity; management can identify an *economic order size* (this concept is discussed in detail later in the chapter). One disadvantage of this approach is the added costs of record keeping. Moreover, a physical count of inventories must still be performed periodically (e.g., annually) to verify records because of errors, pilferage, spoilage, and other factors than can reduce the effective amount of inventory. Bank transactions such as customer deposits and withdrawals are examples of continuous recording of inventory changes.

Continuous systems range from very simple to very sophisticated. A **two-bin** arrangement is an example of a very elementary system. It involves the use of two containers for inventory. Items are withdrawn from the first bin. When its contents are exhausted, it is time to reorder. Sometimes an order card is placed at the bottom of the first bin. The second bin contains enough stock to satisfy expected demand until the order is filled, plus an extra cushion of stock that will reduce the chance of a stock-out if the order is late or if usage is greater than expected. The advantage of this system is that there is no need to record each withdrawal from inventory; the disadvantage is that the reorder card may not be turned in for a variety of reasons (it is misplaced, the person who is supposed to turn it in forgets to, etc.).

Continuous systems can be either *batch* or *on-line*. In batch systems, inventory records are collected periodically and entered into the system. In on-line systems, the transactions are recorded instantaneously. The advantage of on-line systems is that the system is always up-to-date; with a batch system, a sudden surge in demand could result in reducing the amount of inventory below the reorder point between the periodic read-ins, although frequent batch collections can minimize that problem.

Supermarkets, discount stores, and department stores have always been major users of periodic accounting systems. However, in the last few years many have switched to computerized checkout systems using a laser scanning device that reads a **universal product code** (UPC), or bar code, printed on an item tag or on product packaging. A typical grocery product code is illustrated below.

The zero on the left identifies this as a grocery item, the first five numbers (14800) indicate the manufacturer (Mott's), and the last five numbers (23208) indicate the specific item (natural style applesauce). Items in small packages, such as candy and gum, use a six-digit number.

UPC scanners represent a major change in the inventory systems of stores that use them. In addition to the increase in speed and accuracy these systems provide, they give managers continuous information on inventories, they reduce the need for periodic inventories and order-size determinations, and they improve the level of customer service by indicating the price and quantity of each item on the customer's receipt, as illustrated below.

```
                  BRAVO CAPELLINI           .79
                  BUB YUM DBL LIME          .30 T
                  2/ LO FAT MILK H G       1.03
                  LACTAID MILK              .91
                  WEGMAN 2/ MILK QT         .55
                  NEWSPAPER                 .35
                  KR CAS BRICK CHEES       1.59
                  GRAPES-GREEN
         .91 LB @ .89 PER LB                .81

                  TAX DUE                   .02
                  TOTAL                    6.35

                  CASH                    20.00 *
                  CHANGE                  13.65

     10/07/90 18:01 21     16    23100   2570
```

Bar coding represents an important development for other sectors besides retailing. Manufacturing and service industries also benefit from the simplified production and inventory control it provides. In manufacturing, bar codes attached to parts, subassemblies, and finished goods greatly facilitate counting and monitoring activities. Automatic routing and scheduling is also a possibility with bar codes, as are automatic sorting and packaging. Outside of retailing, a system known as Code 39 is used rather than UPC for bar coding.

Demand Forecasts and Lead Time Information

Since inventories will be used to satisfy demand requirements, it is essential to have reliable estimates of the amount and timing of demand. Similarly, it is essential to know how long it will take for orders to be delivered. In addition, it is necessary to know the extent to which demand and lead times might vary; the more potential variability, the greater the need for additional stock to insure against a shortage between deliveries. Thus, there is a crucial link between forecasting and inventory management.

Cost Information

Three basic costs are associated with inventories: holding, transaction (ordering), and shortage costs.

Holding or **carrying costs** relate to physically holding items in storage. They include interest, insurance, taxes,[1] depreciation, obsolescence, deterioration, spoilage, pilferage, breakage, and warehousing costs (heat, light, rent,

---

[1] In some states.

security). Holding costs also include opportunity costs associated with having funds tied up in inventory that could be used elsewhere.

The significance of the various components of holding cost depends on the type of item involved, although taxes, interest, and insurance are generally based on the dollar value of an inventory. Items that are easily concealed (such as pocket cameras, transistor radios, and calculators) or fairly expensive (cars, TVs) are prone to theft. Fresh seafood, meats and poultry, produce, and baked goods are subject to rapid deterioration and spoilage. Other items, such as dairy products, salad dressings, medicines, batteries, and film, also have limited shelf lives.

Holding costs are stated in either of two ways. One way is to specify cost as a percentage of unit price, and the other is to specify a dollar amount per unit. In any case, typical annual holding costs range from 20 percent to 40 percent of the value of an item. Thus, to hold a $1 item for one year could cost from 20 cents to 40 cents.

Ordering costs are the costs associated with ordering and receiving inventory. These costs include determining how much is needed, typing up invoices, inspecting goods upon arrival for quality and quantity, and moving the goods to temporary storage. Ordering costs are generally expressed as a fixed dollar amount per order, regardless of order size.

When a firm produces its own inventory instead of ordering it from a supplier, the costs of machine setup (preparing equipment for the job by adjusting the machine, changing cutting tools, and so on) are analogous to ordering costs (i.e., they are expressed as a fixed charge per run, regardless of the size of the run).

Shortage costs result when demand exceeds the supply of inventory on hand. The costs can include the opportunity cost of not making a sale, loss of customer goodwill, lateness charges, and similar costs. Furthermore, if the shortage occurs in an item carried for internal use (e.g., to supply an assembly line), the cost of lost production or downtime is considered a shortage cost. Such costs can easily run into hundreds of dollars a minute or more.

Shortage costs are usually difficult to measure, and they are often subjectively estimated. Later in the chapter you will see how to evaluate the sensitivity of decisions to these estimates.

Classification System

An important aspect of inventory management concerns the fact that items kept in inventory are not of equal importance in terms of dollars invested, profit potential, sales or usage volume, and stock-out penalties. For instance, a producer of electrical equipment might have electric generators, coils of wire, and miscellaneous nuts and bolts among the items carried in inventory. It would be unrealistic to devote equal attention to each of these items. Instead, a more reasonable approach would be to allocate control efforts according to the relative importance of various items in inventory.

The **A-B-C approach** involves classifying inventory items according to some measure of importance—usually annual dollar usage (i.e., dollar value per unit multiplied by annual usage rate)—and then allocating control efforts accordingly. Typically, three classes of items are used: A (very important), B (moderately important), and C (least important). However, the actual number of categories may vary from organization to organization, depending on the extent to which a firm wants to differentiate control efforts. Generally speaking, with three classes of items, A items often account for about 5 percent to 10 percent of the *number* of items in inventory but about 60 percent to 70 percent of the *dollar usage*. At the other end of the scale, C items might account for about 60 percent of the number of items but only about 15 percent of the dollar usage of an inventory. These percentages vary from firm to firm, but the point is that, in most instances, a relatively small number of items will account for a large share of the value or cost associated with an inventory, and these items should receive a relatively greater share of control efforts. For instance, A items should receive close attention to make sure the customer service levels are attained, through frequent reviews of amounts on hand and control over withdrawals, where possible. The C items should receive only loose control (two-bin system, bulk orders), and the B items should have a control effort that lies between these two extremes.

The A-B-C concept is illustrated in Figure 10–1.

FIGURE 10–1

A typical A-B-C breakdown in percentage of dollar value and percentage of items by category

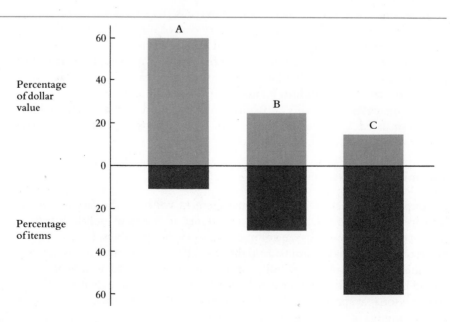

EXAMPLE 1

Classify the inventory items as A, B, or C based on annual dollar value, given the following information:

Item	Annual demand	Unit cost	Annual dollar value
1	1,000	$4,300	$4,300,000
2	5,000	720	3,600,000
3	1,900	500	950,000
4	1,000	710	710,000
5	2,500	250	625,000
6	2,500	192	480,000
7	400	200	80,000
8	500	100	50,000
9	200	210	42,000
10	1,000	35	35,000
11	3,000	10	30,000
12	9,000	3	27,000

Solution

Simply on an intuitive basis, you can see that the first two items have a relatively high annual dollar value. Hence, it would seem reasonable to classify them as A items. The next four items appear to have moderate annual dollar values and should be B items. The remainder should be C items, based on their relatively low dollar values.

HOW MUCH TO ORDER: ECONOMIC ORDER QUANTITY MODELS

The question of how much to order is frequently determined by using an **economic order quantity (EOQ)** model. EOQ models identify the optimal order quantity in terms of minimizing the sum of certain annual costs, which vary with order size.

Three order size models are described in the following sections:

1. The economic order quantity model.
2. The economic order quantity model with noninstantaneous delivery.
3. The quantity discount model.

Basic Economic Order Quantity (EOQ) Model

The basic EOQ model is the simplest of the three models. It is used to identify the order size that will minimize the sum of the annual costs of holding

TABLE 10–1

Assumptions of the basic EOQ model	1. There is only one product involved.
	2. Annual usage (demand) requirements are known.
	3. Usage is spread evenly throughout the year so that the usage rate is reasonably constant.
	4. Lead time does not vary.
	5. Each order is received in a single delivery.
	6. There are no quantity discounts.

inventory and the annual costs of ordering inventory. The unit purchase price of items in inventory is not generally included in the total cost because the unit cost is unaffected by the order size unless quantity discounts are a factor. (The quantity discount version of the basic model will be taken up shortly.) If holding costs are specified as a percentage of unit cost, then unit cost is indirectly included in the total cost as a part of holding costs.

The basic model involves a number of assumptions, some of which may appear to be idealistic. They are listed in Table 10–1. The implications of some of the assumptions can be seen in the diagram of an inventory cycle in Figure 10–2.

The cycle begins with receipt of an order of Q units. These are withdrawn at a constant rate over time. When the quantity on hand is just sufficient to satisfy demand during lead time (the time between submitting an order and receiving that order), an order for Q units is submitted to the supplier. Because it is assumed that both the usage rate and the lead time do not vary, the order

FIGURE 10–2

The inventory cycle: Profile of inventory level over time

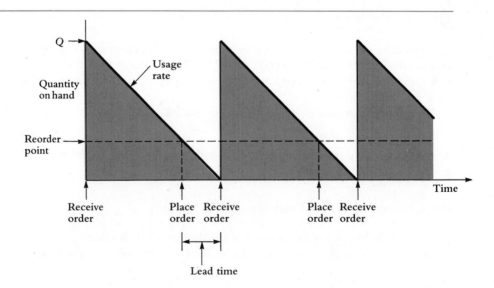

will be received at the precise instant that the inventory on hand falls to zero. Thus, orders are timed to avoid having excess stock on hand and to avoid stock-outs.

The optimal order quantity reflects a trade-off between carrying costs and ordering costs: as order size is varied, one type of cost will increase while the other one decreases. For example, if the order size is relatively small, the average inventory will be low, which will result in low carrying costs. However, a small order size will necessitate frequent orders, and that will drive up annual ordering costs. Conversely, annual ordering costs can be held down by ordering large quantities at infrequent intervals, but that would result in higher average inventory levels and therefore increased carrying costs. These two extremes are illustrated in Figure 10–3.

Thus, the ideal solution will typically be an order size that causes neither a few very large orders nor many small orders, but one that lies somewhere between those two extremes. The exact amount to order will depend on the relative magnitudes of carrying and ordering costs.

Annual carrying cost is computed by multiplying the average amount of inventory on hand by the cost to carry one unit for a year, even though any

FIGURE 10–3

Average inventory level and number of orders per year are inversely related: As one increases, the other decreases

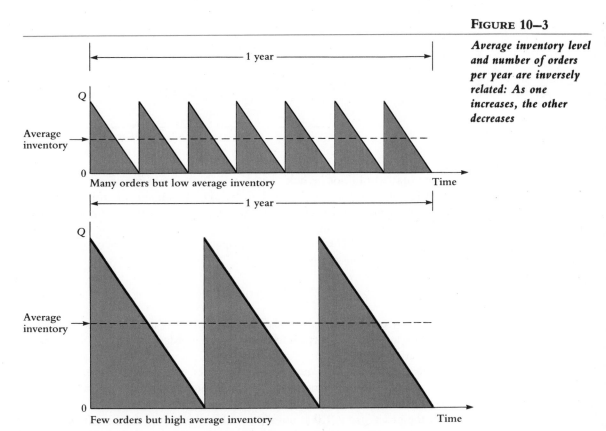

FIGURE 10–4

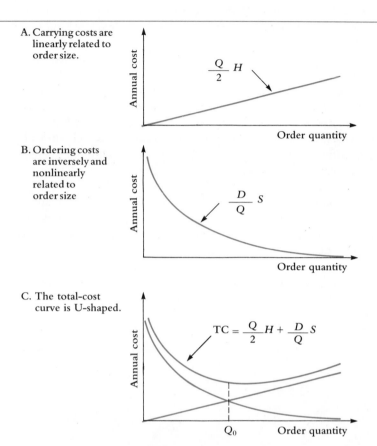

A. Carrying costs are linearly related to order size.

$$\frac{Q}{2}H$$

Annual cost

Order quantity

B. Ordering costs are inversely and nonlinearly related to order size

$$\frac{D}{Q}S$$

Annual cost

Order quantity

C. The total-cost curve is U-shaped.

$$TC = \frac{Q}{2}H + \frac{D}{Q}S$$

Annual cost

Q_0 Order quantity

given unit would not be held for a year. (Note, however, that 12 units each held for one month is equivalent to holding 1 unit for an entire year.) The average inventory is simply one half of the order quantity: the amount on hand decreases steadily from Q units to 0, for an average of $(Q + 0)/2$, or $Q/2$. Using the symbol H to represent the average annual carrying cost per unit, the *total annual carrying cost* is

$$\text{Annual carrying cost} = \frac{Q}{2}H$$

Carrying costs are thus a linear function of Q: carrying costs increase or decrease in direct proportion to changes in the order quantity Q, as illustrated in Figure 10–4A.

On the other hand, annual ordering costs will decrease as order size increases, since for a given annual demand, the larger the order size, the fewer the number of orders needed. For instance, if annual demand is 12,000 units and the order size is 1,000 units per order, there must be 12 orders over the year. But if $Q = 2,000$ units, only 6 orders will be needed; and if $Q = 3,000$

units, only 4 orders will be needed. In general, the number of orders per year will be D/Q, where D = Annual demand and Q = Order size. Unlike carrying costs, ordering costs are relatively insensitive to order size; regardless of the amount of an order, there are certain activities that must be done, such as determine how much is needed, periodically evaluate sources of supply, and prepare the invoice. Even inspection of the shipment to verify quality and quantity characteristics is not strongly influenced by order size since large shipments are sampled rather than completely inspected. Hence, there is a fixed ordering cost. *Annual ordering cost* is a function of the number of orders per year and the ordering cost per order:

$$\text{Annual ordering cost} = \frac{D}{Q}\,S$$

where S = Ordering cost.

Because the number of orders per year, D/Q, decreases as Q increases, annual ordering cost is inversely related to order size, as illustrated in Figure 10–4B.

The total annual cost associated with carrying and ordering inventory when Q units are ordered each time is:

$$
\begin{array}{rl}
& \text{Annual} \quad \text{Annual} \\
\text{TC} = & \text{carrying} + \text{ordering} \\
& \text{cost} \qquad \text{cost} \\
= & \dfrac{Q}{2}\,H + \dfrac{D}{Q}\,S
\end{array}
\qquad (10\text{--}1)
$$

where

$$
\begin{aligned}
D &= \text{Demand, in units per year} \\
Q &= \text{Order quantity, in units} \\
S &= \text{Ordering cost, in dollars} \\
H &= \text{Carrying cost, in dollars per unit per year}
\end{aligned}
$$

(Note that D and H must be in the same units, e.g., years.) Figure 10–4C reveals that the total-cost curve is U-shaped and that *it reaches its minimum at the quantity where carrying and ordering costs are equal*. An expression for the optimal order quantity, Q_0, can be obtained using calculus.[2] The result is the formula

$$Q_0 = \sqrt{\frac{2DS}{H}} \qquad (10\text{--}2)$$

---

[2] The minimum point of the total-cost curve can be found by differentiating TC with respect to Q, setting the result equal to zero, and solving for Q. Thus,

1. $\dfrac{d\text{TC}}{dQ} = \dfrac{dQ}{2}H + d(D/Q)S = H/2 - DS/Q^2$

2. $0 = H/2 - DS/Q^2$, so $Q^2 = \dfrac{2DS}{H}$ or $Q_0 = \sqrt{\dfrac{2DS}{H}}$.

Note, too, that the second derivative is positive, which indicates a minimum has been obtained.

Thus, given annual demand, the ordering cost per order, and the annual carrying cost per unit, the optimal (economic) order quantity can be computed.

The minimum total cost is:

$$TC_{min} = \frac{Q_0}{2} H + \frac{D}{Q_0} S \qquad\qquad (10\text{–}3)$$

EXAMPLE 2

A local distributor for a national tire company expects to sell approximately 9,600 steel-belted radial tires of a certain size and tread design next year. Annual carrying costs are $16 per tire, and ordering costs are $75. The distributor operates 288 days a year.
a. Determine the EOQ.
b. How many times per year does the store reorder?
c. Determine the length of an order cycle.

Solution

$$D = 9{,}600 \text{ tires per year}$$
$$H = \$16 \text{ per unit per year}$$
$$S = \$75$$

a. $Q_0 = \sqrt{\dfrac{2DS}{H}} = \sqrt{\dfrac{2(9{,}600)75}{16}} = 300 \text{ tires.}$

b. Number of orders per year: $D/Q_0 = \dfrac{9{,}600 \text{ tires}}{300 \text{ tires}} = 32.$

c. Length of order cycle: $Q_0/D = \dfrac{300 \text{ tires}}{9{,}600 \text{ tires}} = \frac{1}{32}$ of a year, which is $\frac{1}{32} \times (288)$, or nine workdays.

Carrying costs are sometimes stated as a percentage of the purchase price of an item rather than as a dollar amount per unit. However, as long as the percentage is converted into a dollar amount, the EOQ formula is still appropriate.

EXAMPLE 3

Piddling Manufacturing assembles television sets. It purchases 3,600 black-and-white picture tubes a year at $65 each. Ordering costs are $31, and annual carrying costs are 20 percent of the purchase price. Compute the optimal quantity and the total annual cost of ordering and carrying the inventory.

EXAMPLE 3 *(concluded)*

Solution

$$D = 3{,}600 \text{ picture tubes per year}$$
$$S = \$31$$
$$H = .20(\$65) = \$13$$

$$Q_0 = \sqrt{\frac{2DS}{H}} = \sqrt{\frac{2(3{,}600)(31)}{13}} = 131 \text{ picture tubes}$$

$$
\begin{aligned}
TC &= \text{Carrying costs} + \text{Ordering costs} \\
&= (Q_0/2)H + (D/Q_0)S \\
&= (131/2)13 + (3{,}600/131)31 \\
&= \$852 + \$852 = \$1{,}704
\end{aligned}
$$

Note that the ordering and carrying costs are equal at the EOQ, as illustrated in Figure 10–4C.

Comment. Holding and ordering costs are typically estimated values rather than values that can be precisely determined, say, from accounting records. In fact, holding costs are sometimes *designated* by managers instead of computed. Consequently, the EOQ should be regarded as an approximate quantity rather than an exact quantity. Thus, rounding the calculated value is perfectly acceptable; stating a value to several decimal places would tend to give an unrealistic impression of the precision involved. An obvious question, then, is this: How good is this "approximate" EOQ in terms of minimizing cost? The answer is that the EOQ is fairly robust; even if it is off by a large margin, the total cost suffers relatively little. For instance, an EOQ that varies by less than -20 percent to $+30$ percent from the true value will yield a total cost that is within ± 5 percent of the minimum. This is due to the way the EOQ is calculated: Errors may cancel each other out, and taking the square root reduces the effect of errors. Hence, there is actually a range or "zone" of workable values for the EOQ, as depicted in Figure 10–5.

EOQ with Noninstantaneous Replenishment

In the basic EOQ model, it is assumed that orders are delivered as whole units at a single point in time (instantaneous replenishment). However, in some instances such as when a firm is both a producer and user, or when deliveries are spread over time, inventories tend to build up gradually instead of instantaneously.

If usage and production (or delivery) rates are equal, there will not be an inventory buildup since all output will be used immediately, and the question

FIGURE 10–5

The total-cost curve is relatively flat near the EOQ

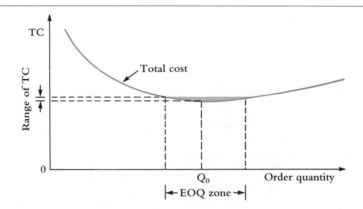

of lot size doesn't come up. In the more typical case, the production or delivery rate *exceeds* the usage rate, creating the situation depicted in Figure 10–6. In the production case, because the production rate is greater than the usage rate, production occurs over only a portion of each cycle, and usage occurs over the entire cycle. During the production phase of the cycle, inventory builds up at a rate equal to the difference between production and usage rates. For example, if the daily production rate is 20 units and the daily usage rate is 5 units, inventory will build up at the rate of $20 - 5 = 15$ units per day. As long as production occurs, the inventory level will continue to build; when production ceases, the inventory level will begin to decrease. Hence, the inventory level will be maximum at the point where production ceases. When the amount of inventory on hand is exhausted, production is resumed, and the cycle repeats itself.

FIGURE 10–6

EOQ with noninstantaneous replenishment

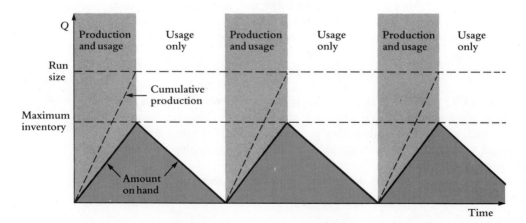

Since the firm makes the product itself, there are no ordering costs as such. Nonetheless, with every run there are setup costs, which are analogous to ordering costs. Like ordering costs, setup costs are also independent of the lot (run) size, and they are treated in the formula in exactly the same way as ordering costs. Hence, the larger the run size, the fewer the number of runs needed and, hence, the lower the annual setup cost. The number of runs is D/Q, and the annual setup cost is equal to the number of runs per year times the setup cost per run: $(D/Q)S$.

Total cost is:

$$TC_{min} = \text{Carrying cost} + \text{Setup cost} \quad\quad (10\text{--}4)$$

$$= \left(\frac{I_{max}}{2}\right)H + (D/Q_0)S$$

where I_{max} = Maximum inventory.

The economic run quantity is:

$$Q_0 = \sqrt{\frac{2DS}{H}}\sqrt{\frac{p}{p-u}} \quad\quad (10\text{--}5)$$

where

$$p = \text{Production or delivery rate}$$
$$u = \text{Usage or demand rate}$$

The maximum and average inventory levels are:

$$I_{max} = \frac{Q_0}{p}(p-u) \quad \text{and} \quad I_{average} = \frac{I_{max}}{2} \quad\quad (10\text{--}6)$$

The cycle time for the economic run size is a function of the run size and usage (demand) rate:

$$\text{Cycle time} = \frac{Q_0}{u} \quad\quad (10\text{--}7)$$

Similarly, the run time is a function of the run size and the production rate:

$$\text{Run time} = \frac{Q_0}{p} \qu\quad (10\text{--}8)$$

EXAMPLE 4

A toy manufacturer uses 48,000 rubber wheels per year for its popular dump truck series. The firm makes its own wheels, which it can produce at a rate of 800 per day. The toy trucks are assembled uniformly over the entire year. Carrying cost is $1 per wheel a year. Setup cost for a production run of wheels is $45. The firm operates 240 days per year. Determine each of the following:

EXAMPLE 4 *(concluded)*

a. The optimal run size.
b. The minimum total annual cost for carrying and setup.
c. The cycle time for the optimal run size.
d. The run time.

Solution

$$D = 48,000 \text{ wheels per year}$$
$$S = \$45$$
$$H = \$1 \text{ per wheel per year}$$
$$p = 800 \text{ wheels per day}$$
$$u = 48,000 \text{ wheels per 240 days, or 200 wheels per day}$$

a. $$Q_0 = \sqrt{\frac{2DS}{H}} \sqrt{\frac{p}{p - u}}$$

$$= \sqrt{\frac{2(48,000)45}{1}} \sqrt{\frac{800}{800 - 200}}$$

$$= 2,400 \text{ wheels}$$

b. $$TC_{min} = \text{Carrying cost} + \text{Setup cost}$$

$$= \left(\frac{I_{max}}{2}\right)H + (D/Q_0)S$$

Thus, we must first compute I_{max}:

$$I_{max} = \frac{Q_0}{p}(p - u) = \frac{2,400}{800}(800 - 200) = 1,800 \text{ wheels}$$

b. $$TC = \frac{1,800}{2} \times \$1 + \frac{48,000}{2,400} \times \$45$$

$$= 900 + 900 = \$1,800$$

Note again the equality of cost (in this instance, setup and carrying costs) at the EOQ.

c. Cycle time $$= \frac{Q_0}{u} = \frac{2,400 \text{ wheels}}{200 \text{ wheels per day}} = 12 \text{ days}$$

d. Run time $$= \frac{Q_0}{p} = \frac{2,400 \text{ wheels}}{800 \text{ wheels per day}} = 3 \text{ days}$$

Quantity Discounts

Quantity discounts are price reductions for large orders offered to customers to induce them to buy in large quantities. For example, a Chicago surgical supply company publishes the price list shown in Table 10–2 for boxes of gauze strips. Note that the price per box decreases as order quantity increases.

If quantity discounts are offered, the customer must weigh the potential

TABLE 10–2

Price list for extra-wide gauze strips

Order quantity	Price per box
1 to 44	$2.00
45 to 69	1.70
70 or more	1.40

benefits of reduced purchase price and fewer orders that will result from buying in large quantities against the increase in carrying costs caused by higher average inventories. Hence, the buyer's goal in the case of quantity discounts is to select the order quantity that will minimize total cost, where total cost is the sum of carrying cost, ordering cost, *and* purchasing cost:

$$\text{TC} = \text{Carrying cost} + \text{Ordering cost} + \text{Purchasing cost}$$

$$= \left(\frac{Q}{2}\right)H + \left(\frac{D}{Q}\right)S + PD \qquad (10\text{–}9)$$

where P = Unit price.

Recall that in the basic EOQ model, determination of order size does not involve the purchasing cost. The rationale for not including unit price is that under the assumption of no quantity discounts, price per unit is the same for all order sizes. Inclusion of unit price in the total-cost computation in that case

FIGURE 10–7

Adding PD doesn't change the EOQ

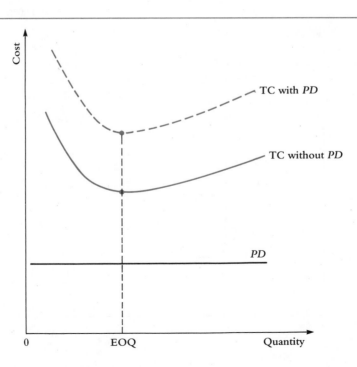

would merely increase the total cost by the amount P times D. A graph of total annual purchase cost versus quantity would be a horizontal line. Hence, including purchasing costs would merely raise the total-cost curve by the same amount (PD) at every point. That would not change the EOQ, however. This is illustrated in Figure 10–7.

When quantity discounts are present, there is a separate U-shaped total-cost curve for each unit price. Again, including unit prices merely raises each curve by a constant amount. However, because the unit prices are all different, each curve is raised by a different amount: smaller unit prices will raise a total-cost curve less than larger unit prices. In addition, no one curve applies to the entire range of quantities; each curve applies to only a *portion* of the range. This is illustrated in Figure 10–8. Hence, the applicable or *feasible* total cost is initially on the curve with the highest unit price and then drops down, curve by curve, at the *price breaks,* which are the minimum quantities needed to obtain the discounts. Thus, in Table 10–2, the price breaks for gauze strips are at 45 and 70 boxes. The result is a total-cost curve with *steps* at the price breaks.

Note that even though each curve has a minimum, those points are not necessarily feasible. For example, the minimum point for the $1.40 curve in Figure 10–8 appears to be about 65 units. However, the price list shown in

FIGURE 10–8

The total-cost curve with quantity discounts is composed of a portion of the total-cost curve for each price

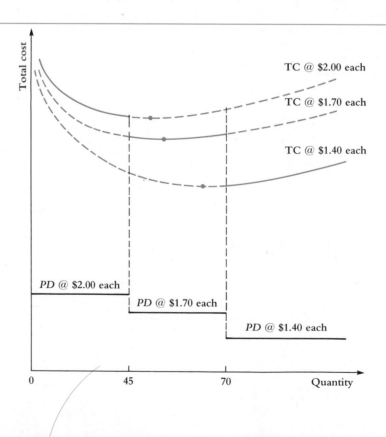

FIGURE 10–9

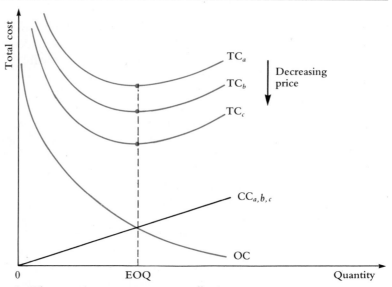

A. When carrying costs are constant, all curves
   have the same EOQ.

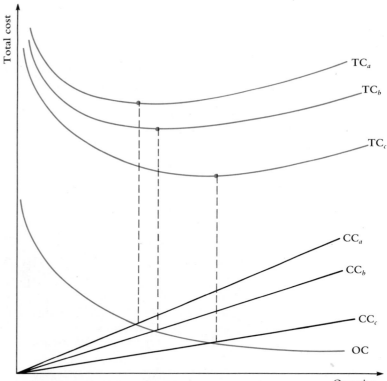

B. When carrying costs are given as a percentage of unit
   price, price decreases decrease carrying costs and
   that causes an increase in the EOQ.

Table 10–2 indicates that an order size of 65 boxes will involve a unit price of $1.70. The actual total-cost curve is denoted by the solid lines; only those price-quantity combinations are feasible. The objective of the quantity discount model is to identify an order quantity that will represent the lowest total cost for the entire set of curves.

There are two general cases of the model: in one carrying costs are constant (e.g., $2 per unit), and in the other carrying costs are stated as a percentage of purchase price (e.g., 20 percent of unit price). When carrying costs are constant, there will be a single EOQ that is the same for all of the cost curves. Consequently, the total-cost curves line up vertically, with the only differing feature among the curves being that lower unit prices are reflected by lower total-cost curves. This is illustrated in Figure 10–9A. For purposes of illustration, the horizontal purchasing cost lines have been omitted.

When carrying costs are specified as a percentage of unit price, each curve will have a different EOQ. Since carrying costs are a percentage of price, lower prices will mean lower carrying costs and larger EOQs. Thus, as price decreases, each curve's EOQ will be to the right of the next higher curve's EOQ, as illustrated in Figure 10–9B.

The procedure for determining the overall EOQ differs slightly, depending on which of these two cases is relevant. For carrying costs that are constant, the procedure is:

1. Compute the common EOQ.
2. Only one of the curves will have the EOQ in its feasible range since the ranges do not overlap. Identify that curve.
   a. If the feasible EOQ is on the lowest price curve, that is the optimal order quantity.
   b. If the feasible EOQ is on any other curve, compute the total cost for the EOQ and for the price breaks of all *lower* cost curves. Compare the total costs; the quantity (EOQ or price break) that yields the lowest total cost is the optimal order quantity.

EXAMPLE 5

The maintenance department of a large hospital uses 816 cases of liquid cleanser annually. Ordering costs are $12, carrying costs are $4 per case a year, and the new price schedule indicates that orders of less than 50 cases will cost $20 per case, 50 to 79 cases will cost $18 per case, 80 to 99 cases will cost $17 per case, and larger orders will cost $16 per case. Determine the optimal order quantity and the total cost.

Solution

See Figure 10–10.

EXAMPLE 5 *(continued)*

FIGURE 10–10

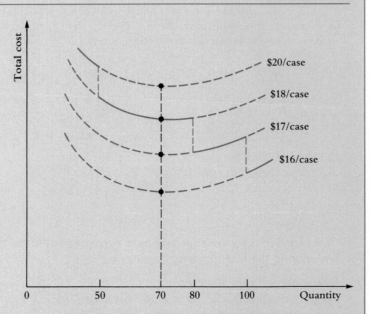

$$D = 816 \text{ cases per year}$$
$$S = \$12$$
$$H = \$4 \text{ per case per year}$$

Range	Price
1 to 49	$20
50 to 79	18
80 to 99	17
100 or more	16

1. Compute the common EOQ: $Q_0 = \sqrt{\dfrac{2DS}{H}} = \sqrt{\dfrac{2(816)12}{4}} = 70 \text{ cases}$

2. The 70 cases can be bought at $18 per case since 70 falls in the range of 50 to 79 cases. The total cost to purchase 816 cases a year, at the rate of 70 cases per order, will be:

$$
\begin{aligned}
TC_{70} &= \text{Carrying cost} + \text{Order cost} + \text{Purchase cost} \\
&= (Q/2)H + (D/Q_0)S + PD \\
&= (70/2)4 + (816/70)12 + 18(816) = \$14{,}968
\end{aligned}
$$

EXAMPLE 5 *(concluded)*

Since lower cost curves exist, each must be checked against the minimum cost generated by 70 cases at $18 each. In order to buy at $17 per case, at least 80 cases must be purchased. (Because the TC curve is rising, 80 cases will have the lowest TC for that curve's feasible region.) The total cost at 80 cases will be:

$$TC_{80} = (80/2)4 + (816/80)12 + 17(816) = \$14,154$$

To obtain a cost of $16 per case, at least 100 cases per order are required, and the total cost will be:

$$TC_{100} = (100/2)4 + (816/100)12 + 16(816) = \$13,354$$

Therefore, since 100 cases per order yields the lowest total cost, 100 cases is the overall optimal order quantity.

When carrying costs are expressed as a percentage of price, the procedure for determining the best purchase quantity is:

1. Beginning with the lowest price, compute the EOQs for each price range until a feasible EOQ is found (i.e., until an EOQ is found that falls in the quantity range for its price).
2. If the EOQ for the lowest price is feasible, it is the optimal order quantity. If the EOQ is not the lowest price range, compare the total cost at the price break for all *lower* prices with the total cost of the feasible EOQ. The quantity that yields the lowest total cost is the optimum.

EXAMPLE 6

Surge Electric uses 4,000 toggle switches a year. Switches are priced as follows: 1 to 499, 90 cents each; 500 to 999, 85 cents each; and 1,000 or more, 82 cents each. It costs approximately $18 to prepare an order and receive it, and carrying costs are 18 percent of purchase price per unit on an annual basis. Determine the optimal order quantity and the total annual cost.

Solution

See Figure 10–11.

EXAMPLE 6 *(continued)*

FIGURE 10–11

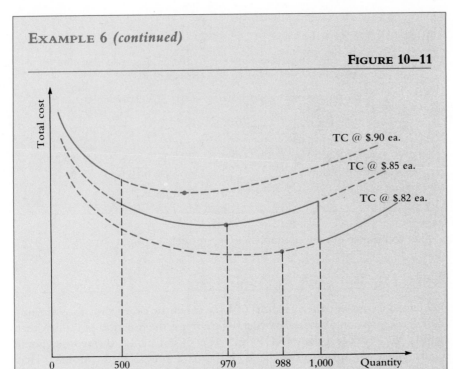

$$D = 4,000 \text{ switches per year}$$
$$S = \$18$$
$$H = 0.18P$$

Range	Unit price	H
1 to 499	\$0.90	0.18(0.90) = 0.1620
500 to 999	\$0.85	0.18(0.85) = 0.1530
1,000 or more	\$0.82	0.18(0.82) = 0.1476

a. Find the EOQ for each price, starting with the lowest price, until a feasible EOQ is located.

$$\text{EOQ}_{0.82} = \sqrt{\frac{2DS}{H}} = \sqrt{\frac{2(4,000)18}{0.1476}} = 988 \text{ switches}$$

Since 988 switches will cost \$0.85 each rather than \$0.82 each, 988 is not a feasible EOQ. Next, try \$0.85 per unit:

$$\text{EOQ}_{0.85} = \sqrt{\frac{2(4,000)18}{0.153}} = 970 \text{ switches}$$

This is feasible; 970 switches falls in the \$0.85 range of 500 to 999.

EXAMPLE 6 *(concluded)*

b. Compute TC for 970, and compare it to the total cost of the minimum quantity necessary to obtain a price of $0.82 per switch:

$$TC = \text{Carrying costs} + \text{Ordering costs} + \text{Purchasing costs}$$

$$= \left(\frac{Q}{2}\right)H + \left(\frac{D}{Q}\right)S + PD$$

$$TC_{970} = (970/2)(0.153) + (4,000/970)18 + 0.85(4,000) = \$3,548$$
$$TC_{1,000} = (1,000/2)(0.1476) + (4,000/1,000)18 + 0.82(4,000) = \$3,426$$

Thus, the minimum-cost order size is 1,000 switches.

This completes our discussion of EOQ models.

WHEN TO REORDER

EOQ models answer the question of how much to order, but they do not address the question of when to order. The latter is the function of models that identify the **reorder point (ROP)** in terms of a *quantity:* the reorder point occurs when the quantity on hand drops to a prespecified amount. That amount generally includes expected demand during lead time and perhaps an extra cushion of stock, which serves to reduce the probability of experiencing a stock-out during lead time.

There are four determinants of the reorder point quantity:

1. The rate of demand (usually based on a forecast).
2. The length of lead time.
3. The extent of demand and lead time variability.
4. The degree of stock-out risk acceptable to management.

We will consider reorder point models for these cases.

1. Constant demand rate, constant lead time.
2. Variable demand rate, constant lead time.
3. Constant demand rate, variable lead time.
4. Variable demand rate and variable lead time.

The following symbols are used in the various models:

Demand	*Lead time*
d = Constant demand rate	LT = Constant lead time
$\bar{d}$ = Average demand rate	$\overline{LT}$ = Average lead time
σ_d = Standard deviation of demand rate or forecast error	σ_{LT} = Standard deviation of lead time

The models generally assume that any variability in either demand rate or lead time can be adequately described by a normal distribution. However, this is not a strict requirement—the models provide approximate reorder points even in cases where actual distributions depart substantially from normal.

The discussion begins with the simplest case (demand and lead time both constant) and proceeds to models that can be used when either demand or lead time, or both, are variable.

Constant Demand Rate and Constant Lead Time

When both the demand (usage) rate and lead time are constant, there is no risk of a stock-out created by increased demand or lead times longer than expected. In such a case, the ROP is equal to the product of usage rate and lead time; no extra cushion of stock is needed.

EXAMPLE 7

Tingly takes Two-a-Day vitamins, which are delivered to his home by a routeman seven days after an order is called in. At what point should Tingly telephone his order in?

Solution

$$\text{Usage} = 2 \text{ vitamins per day}$$
$$\text{Lead time} = 7 \text{ days}$$
$$\text{ROP} = \text{Usage} \times \text{Lead time}$$
$$= 2 \text{ vitamins per day} \times 7 \text{ days} = 14 \text{ vitamins}$$

Thus, Tingly should reorder when 14 vitamin tablets are left.

Variable Demand Rates and/or Variable Lead Times

The concept of reorder points is easy to grasp when both demand rate and lead time are constant. In fact, this is the main reason for discussing that case, since under normal circumstances, one or the other of these, or both, exhibit some variability. In order to discuss these more realistic cases, two additional concepts must be introduced: *safety stock* and *service level*.

Safety Stock. When there are variations in either the demand rate or the lead time, the possibility of stock-outs must be dealt with. Unlike the case of constant demand and lead time, it is no longer known exactly how much stock will be needed to satisfy demand during lead time. Variations in the demand rate can result in a temporary surge in demand, which will drain inventory more quickly than expected, and variations in delivery times can lengthen the time a given supply must cover. In order to compensate for uncertainties in either demand rate or lead time, additional stock must be carried to reduce the risk of a stock-out during the lead time interval. This buffer, or **safety stock,** is stock that is held in excess of expected demand. In essence, it is a form of insurance.

Figure 10–12 illustrates how safety stock can reduce the risk of a stock-out during lead time (LT). Note that stock-out protection is needed only during lead time. If there is a sudden surge at any point during the cycle, this will trigger another order, and once that order is received, the danger of an imminent stock-out is negligible.

In general, when variations exist in either usage or lead time the ROP is:

$$\text{ROP} = \frac{\text{Expected demand}}{\text{during lead time}} + \text{Safety stock} \qquad (10\text{--}10)$$

EXAMPLE 8

Paul's Plant Place uses an average of 200 plastic bags per day, and lead time averages four days. Because both usage rate and lead times are variable, Paul carries a safety stock of 100 bags to lessen the chance of a stock-out. Determine the ROP.

Solution

$$\text{ROP} = \frac{\text{Expected demand}}{\text{during lead time}} + \text{Safety stock}$$
$$= 200 \text{ bags per day} \times 4 \text{ days} + 100 \text{ bags} = 900 \text{ bags}$$

Thus, Paul should reorder when existing stock equals 900 bags.[3]

Service Level. Because it costs money to hold safety stock, a manager must carefully weigh the cost of carrying safety stock against the reduction in stock-out risk it provides, since the service level increases as the risk of stock-out decreases. Order cycle **service level** can be defined as the probability that demand will not exceed supply during lead time (i.e., that the amount of stock on hand will be sufficient to meet demand). Hence, a service level of 95 percent implies a probability of 95 percent that demand will not exceed supply during lead time. An equivalent statement is that demand will be satisfied in 95 percent of such instances. It does *not* mean that 95 percent of demand will be

---

[3] This answer assumes that demand rates and lead times are independent. The same assumption underlies all of the ROP models described in this chapter.

FIGURE 10–12

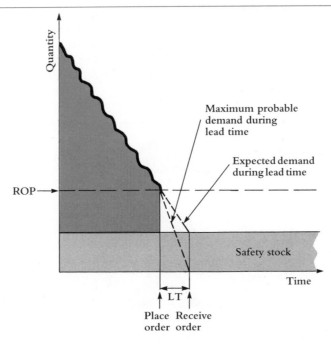

satisfied. The risk of a stock-out is the complement of service level; a customer service level of 95 percent implies a stock-out risk of 5 percent. In general,

$$\text{Service level} = 100 \text{ percent} - \text{Stock-out risk}$$

A bit later we will see how the order cycle service level relates to the *annual* service level.

The amount of safety stock that is appropriate for a given situation depends on the following factors:

1. The average demand rate and average lead time.
2. Demand and lead time variabilities.
3. The desired service level.

For a given order cycle service level, the greater the variability in either demand rate or lead time, the greater the amount of safety stock that will be needed to achieve that service level. Similarly, for a given amount of variation in demand rate or lead time, achieving an increase in the service level will require increasing the amount of safety stock. Selection of a service level may reflect stock-out costs (e.g., lost sales, customer dissatisfaction), or it might simply be a policy variable (e.g., the manager wants to achieve a specified service level for a certain item).

Variable Demand Rate, Constant Lead Time.   This model assumes that demand during lead time is composed of a series of *independent* daily demands that can be described by a normal distribution. In order to use the model, it is necessary to know the average daily demand rate and its standard deviation. That information is then used to determine the expected demand and standard deviation of demand for the lead time period.

FIGURE 10–13

Total demand during lead time is normally distributed with a mean equal to the sum of daily means and a variance equal to the sum of daily variances

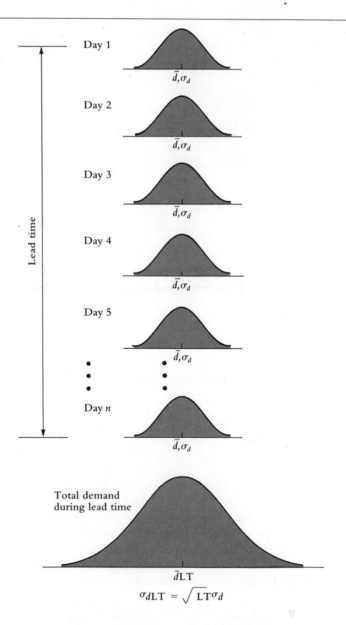

Figure 10–13 illustrates daily rates that are normally distributed. In effect, each day's demand is analogous to a random draw from a normal distribution, and we want to estimate demand for the entire lead time interval.

Expected demand is nothing more than the sum of average daily demands during lead time. Thus, if average daily demand is 7 units per day, and if lead time is 10 days, then expected total demand during lead time is 7 units per day times 10 days, or 70 units. This quantity will tend to be normally distributed and have a variance that is equal to the sum of the individual (daily) variances.[4] If the daily variance equals 4 (i.e., the daily standard deviation equals 2), the total variance for lead time is $4 \times 10 = 40$. Then the standard deviation of the total demand is the square root of 40, which is 6.32. (*Note:* This assumes that daily demands are independent.)

For variable demand with constant lead time, the reorder point is:

$$\text{ROP} = \begin{array}{c} \text{Expected demand} \\ \text{during lead time} \end{array} + \begin{array}{c} \text{Safety} \\ \text{stock} \end{array} \qquad (10–11)$$
$$= \bar{d}\text{LT} + z\sqrt{\text{LT}}\,(\sigma_d)$$

where

$$\bar{d} = \text{Average demand rate}$$
$$\text{LT} = \text{Lead time}$$
$$\sigma_d = \text{Standard deviation of demand rate}$$

Note that the standard deviation of lead time demand is $\sqrt{\text{LT}}\,(\sigma_d)$. The service level is equal to the probability that demand will not exceed the quantity on hand at the reorder point. For a normal distribution, this amounts to the area under the curve to the left of ROP, as shown in Figure 10–14.

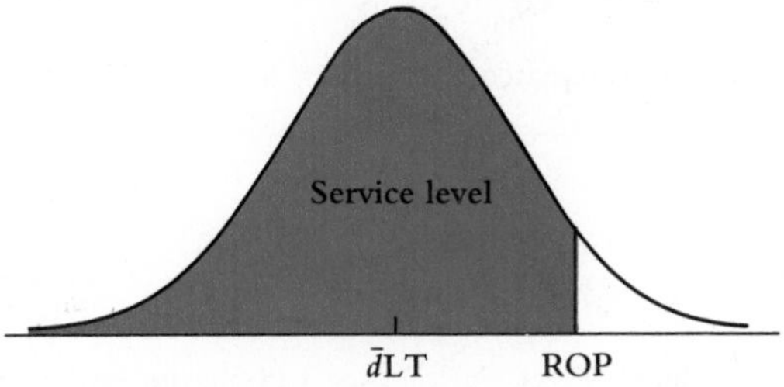

FIGURE 10–14

Service level is the probability that demand will not exceed the ROP amount

Service level

$\bar{d}\text{LT}$ ROP

---

[4] Variance = (Standard deviation)².

EXAMPLE 9

A pharmacy dispenses a generic drug at an average rate of 50 milligrams per day. An examination of pharmacy records suggests that daily demand is approximately normal and has a standard deviation of 5 milligrams per day. Lead time is four days, and the pharmacist wants a stock-out risk that does not exceed 1 percent.

1. Determine the ROP.
2. How much safety stock should be carried?
3. What service level would a reorder point of 215 mg provide?

Solution

$$\overline{d} = 50 \text{ mg per day}$$
$$\sigma_d = 5 \text{ mg per day}$$
$$\text{LT} = 4 \text{ days}$$

a. Service level = 100% − Risk = 99%; $z = 2.33$ (Appendix B, Table B)

$$\text{ROP} = \overline{d}\text{LT} + z\sqrt{\text{LT}}(\sigma_d)$$
$$= 50(4) + 2.33\sqrt{4}(5) = 223.3 \text{ mg}$$

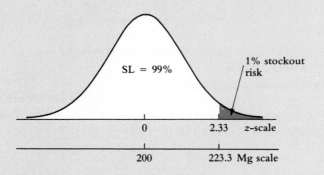

b. $\text{SS} = z\sqrt{\text{LT}}(\sigma_d) = 2.33\sqrt{4}(5) = 23.3 \text{ mg.}$

c. $z = \dfrac{\text{ROP} - \text{Expected demand}}{\sqrt{\text{LT}}(\sigma_d)} = \dfrac{215 - 200}{\sqrt{4}(5)} = 1.5$

This equates to a service level of .9332 (from Appendix B, Table B).

EXAMPLE 10

Jack's Pizza Parlor uses 1,000 large cans of tomatoes a month, at an average rate of 40 per day for each of the 25 days per month the parlor is open. Usage can be approximated by a normal distribution with a standard deviation of 3 cans per day. Lead time is constant at 4 days. Monthly carrying costs are $0.02 per can, and ordering costs are $2.

EXAMPLE 10 *(concluded)*

a. Determine the economic order quantity.

b. For a service level of 99 percent, how many cans of tomatoes should Jack have on hand when he reorders?

Solution

a. Ordinarily, demand and carrying costs will be in annual amounts. However, the fact that they are *both* expressed here in monthly amounts is acceptable and will not affect the answer if left in those units.

$D = 1,000$ cans per month $S = \$2$ $H = \$0.02$ per can per month

$$Q_0 = \sqrt{\frac{2DS}{H}} = \sqrt{\frac{2(1,000)2}{.02}} = 447 \text{ cans}$$

b. $\bar{d} = 40$ cans per day $\sigma_d = 3$ cans per day $LT = 4$ days

$$\text{ROP} = \bar{d}LT + z\sqrt{LT}\,(\sigma_d) = 40(4) + 2.33\sqrt{4}(3) = 174 \text{ cans}$$

Constant Demand Rate, Variable Lead Time. A variable lead time can assume any of a variety of patterns. For purposes of illustration, let's assume it can be described by a normal distribution. When lead time is normally distributed, the expected demand during lead time is normally distributed, but its variance does not encompass any summing of variances, as in the preceding model. The reason is that the actual lead time in any given cycle will be *one* number (e.g., two weeks) rather than a series of numbers (i.e., lead time demands).

FIGURE 10–15

With constant demand and normally distributed lead time, total usage during lead time will be normally distributed

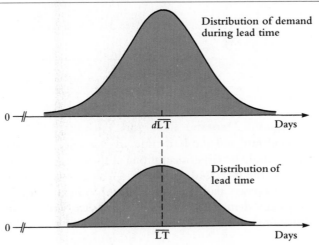

In this case, the expected demand during lead time is equal to $d\overline{\text{LT}}$, and the standard deviation of demand during lead time is equal to $d\sigma_{\text{LT}}$ (see Figure 10–15). The reorder point is:

$$\text{ROP} = d\overline{\text{LT}} + zd\sigma_{\text{LT}} \qquad (10\text{–}12)$$

where

$$d = \text{Constant demand rate}$$
$$\overline{\text{LT}} = \text{Average lead time}$$
$$\sigma_{\text{LT}} = \text{Standard deviation of lead time}$$

EXAMPLE 11

An automatic burner uses 2.1 gallons of oil per day. Lead time is normally distributed with a mean of six days and a standard deviation of two days. Determine the ROP to have a service level of 98 percent. How much of that quantity is safety stock?

Solution

$$d = 2.1 \text{ gallons per day} \qquad \overline{\text{LT}} = 6 \text{ days} \qquad \sigma_{\text{LT}} = 2 \text{ days}$$

$$\begin{aligned}
\text{ROP} &= d\overline{\text{LT}} + zd\sigma_{\text{LT}} \\
&= 2.1(6) + 2.055(2.1)2 \\
&= 12.6 + 8.63 = 21.23 \text{ gallons} \qquad \text{Safety stock} = 8.63 \text{ gallons}
\end{aligned}$$

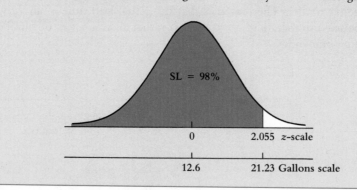

Variable Demand Rate and Variable Lead Time. When both the demand rate and the lead time are variable, it seems reasonable that safety stock should be larger than if one of these were constant, in order to compensate for the increased variability. In this case, expected demand during lead time is average daily demand multiplied by average lead time (in days).

If daily demand is normally distributed and if lead time is also normally distributed, then total demand during lead time will be normally distributed with a mean equal to $\overline{d}(\overline{LT})$. Its variance is actually the sum of the variances of demand and lead time, and the standard deviation is the square root of that sum:

$$\text{Standard deviation of total} \atop \text{demand during lead time} = \sqrt{\sigma_{\text{demand}}^2 + \sigma_{\text{lead time}}^2} \quad (10\text{--}13)$$

where

$$\sigma_{\text{demand}} = \sqrt{\overline{LT}}\ \sigma_d$$
$$\sigma_{\text{lead time}} = \overline{d}\sigma_{LT}$$

Hence,

$$\sigma_{dLT} = \sqrt{(\sqrt{\overline{LT}}\ \sigma_d)^2 + (\overline{d}\sigma_{LT})^2} = \sqrt{\overline{LT}\sigma_d^2 + \overline{d}^2\sigma_{LT}^2} \quad (10\text{--}14)$$
$$\text{ROP} = \overline{d}(\overline{LT}) + z\sqrt{\overline{LT}\sigma_d^2 + \overline{d}^2\sigma_{LT}^2} \quad (10\text{--}15)$$

(Note that every variable under the square root sign is squared except $\overline{LT}$.)

EXAMPLE 12

Consumption of Mug Beer at a local tavern is known to be normally distributed with a mean of 150 bottles per day and a standard deviation of 10 bottles per day. Delivery time is also normally distributed with a mean of six days and a standard deviation of one day. How many bottles of Mug should be on hand at reorder time in order to be 90 percent sure of not running out before the delivery arrives?

Solution

$$\overline{d} = 150 \text{ bottles per day} \qquad \overline{LT} = 6 \text{ days}$$
$$\sigma_d = 10 \text{ bottles per day} \qquad \sigma_{LT} = 1 \text{ day}$$
$$\text{ROP} = \overline{d}(\overline{LT}) + z\sqrt{\overline{LT}\sigma_d^2 + \overline{d}^2\sigma_{LT}^2}$$
$$= 150(6) + 1.28\sqrt{6(10)^2 + 150^2(1)^2}$$
$$= 900 \quad + 1.28\sqrt{23,100} = 1,095 \text{ bottles}$$

Shortages and Service Levels

The ROP computation does not reveal the expected *amount* of shortage for a given lead time service level. The expected number of units short can, however, be very useful to a manager, sometimes even more useful than the service level figure. This quantity can easily be determined from the same information that is used to compute the ROP, with one additional piece of information, which is contained in Table 10–3. Use of the table assumes that the distribution of lead time demand can be adequately represented by a normal distribu-

TABLE 10–3

Normal distribution service levels and unit normal loss function

z	Lead time service level	E(z)	z	Lead time service level	E(z)	z	Lead time service level	E(z)	z	Lead time service level	E(z)
−2.40	.0082	2.403	−0.80	.2119	0.920	0.80	.7881	0.120	2.40	.9918	0.003
−2.36	.0091	2.363	−0.76	.2236	0.889	0.84	.7995	0.112	2.44	.9927	0.002
−2.32	.0102	2.323	−0.72	.2358	0.858	0.88	.8106	0.104	2.48	.9934	0.002
−2.28	.0113	2.284	−0.68	.2483	0.828	0.92	.8212	0.097	2.52	.9941	0.002
−2.24	.0125	2.244	−0.64	.2611	0.798	0.96	.8315	0.089	2.56	.9948	0.002
−2.20	.0139	2.205	−0.60	.2743	0.769	1.00	.8413	0.083	2.60	.9953	0.001
−2.16	.0154	2.165	−0.56	.2877	0.740	1.04	.8508	0.077	2.64	.9959	0.001
−2.12	.0170	2.126	−0.52	.3015	0.712	1.08	.8599	0.071	2.68	.9963	0.001
−2.08	.0188	2.087	−0.48	.3156	0.684	1.12	.8686	0.066	2.72	.9967	0.001
−2.04	.0207	2.048	−0.44	.3300	0.657	1.16	.8770	0.061	2.76	.9971	0.001
−2.00	.0228	2.008	−0.40	.3446	0.630	1.20	.8849	0.056	2.80	.9974	0.0008
−1.96	.0250	1.969	−0.36	.3594	0.597	1.24	.8925	0.052	2.84	.9977	0.0007
−1.92	.0274	1.930	−0.32	.3745	0.576	1.28	.8997	0.048	2.88	.9980	0.0006
−1.88	.0301	1.892	−0.28	.3897	0.555	1.32	.9066	0.044	2.92	.9982	0.0005
−1.84	.0329	1.853	−0.24	.4052	0.530	1.36	.9131	0.040	2.96	.9985	0.0004
−1.80	.0359	1.814	−0.20	.4207	0.507	1.40	.9192	0.037	3.00	.9987	0.0004
−1.76	.0392	1.776	−0.16	.4364	0.484	1.44	.9251	0.034	3.04	.9988	0.0003
−1.72	.0427	1.737	−0.12	.4522	0.462	1.48	.9306	0.031	3.08	.9990	0.0003
−1.68	.0465	1.699	−0.08	.4681	0.440	1.52	.9357	0.028	3.12	.9991	0.0002
−1.64	.0505	1.661	−0.04	.4840	0.419	1.56	.9406	0.026	3.16	.9992	0.0002
−1.60	.0548	1.623	0.00	.5000	0.399	1.60	.9452	0.023	3.20	.9993	0.0002
−1.56	.0594	1.586	0.04	.5160	0.379	1.64	.9495	0.021	3.24	.9994	0.0001
−1.52	.0643	1.548	0.08	.5319	0.360	1.68	.9535	0.019	3.28	.9995	0.0001
−1.48	.0694	1.511	0.12	.5478	0.342	1.72	.9573	0.017	3.32	.9995	0.0001
−1.44	.0749	1.474	0.16	.5636	0.324	1.76	.9608	0.016	3.36	.9996	0.0001
−1.40	.0808	1.437	0.20	.5793	0.307	1.80	.9641	0.014	3.40	.9997	0.0001
−1.36	.0869	1.400	0.24	.5948	0.290	1.84	.9671	0.013			
−1.32	.0934	1.364	0.28	.6103	0.275	1.88	.9699	0.012			
−1.28	.1003	1.328	0.32	.6255	0.256	1.92	.9726	0.010			
−1.24	.1075	1.292	0.36	.6406	0.237	1.96	.9750	0.009			
−1.20	.1151	1.256	0.40	.6554	0.230	2.00	.9772	0.008			
−1.16	.1230	1.221	0.44	.6700	0.217	2.04	.9793	0.008			
−1.12	.1314	1.186	0.48	.6844	0.204	2.08	.9812	0.007			
−1.08	.1401	1.151	0.52	.6985	0.192	2.12	.9830	0.006			
−1.04	.1492	1.117	0.56	.7123	0.180	2.16	.9846	0.005			
−1.00	.1587	1.083	0.60	.7257	0.169	2.20	.9861	0.005			
−0.96	.1685	1.049	0.64	.7389	0.158	2.24	.9875	0.004			
−0.92	.1788	1.017	0.68	.7517	0.148	2.28	.9887	0.004			
−0.88	.1894	0.984	0.72	.7642	0.138	2.32	.9898	0.003			
−0.84	.2005	0.952	0.76	.7764	0.129	2.36	.9909	0.003			

tion. If it can, the expected number of units short in each order cycle is given by this formula:

$$E(n) \;=\; E(z)\sigma_{d\mathrm{LT}} \qquad\qquad (10\text{--}16)$$

where

$E(n)$ = Expected number of units short per order cycle
$E(z)$ = Standardized number of units short listed in Table 10–3
$\sigma_{d\mathrm{LT}}$ = Standard deviation of lead time demand

---

EXAMPLE 13

The standard deviation of lead time demand is known to be 16 units. Lead time demand is approximately normal.
a. For a lead time service level of 90 percent, determine the expected number of units short for any order cycle.
b. What lead time service level would an expected shortage of 2 units imply?

Solution

$$\sigma_{d\mathrm{LT}} = 16 \text{ units}$$

a. Lead time (cycle) service level = .90. From Table 10–3, $E(z) = 0.048$. Using Formula 10–16, $E(n) = 0.048(16 \text{ units}) = 0.768$ unit.
b. For the case where $E(n) = 2$, we must solve for $E(z)$ and then use Table 10–3 to determine the lead time service level that implies. Thus, $E(n) = E(z)\, \sigma_{d\mathrm{LT}}$, so $E(z) = E(n) \,/\, \sigma_{d\mathrm{LT}} = 2/16 = 0.125$. From Table 10–3, this implies a service level of approximately 78 percent (interpolating).

The expected number of units short is just that—an expected or *average* amount; the exact number of units short in any given cycle will be an amount close to that. Moreover, if discrete items are involved, the number of units short in any cycle must be an integer.

Having determined the expected number of units short for an order cycle, we can now determine the expected number of units short per year. It is simply the product of the expected number of units short per cycle and the number of cycles (orders) per year. Thus,

$$E(N) \;=\; E(n)\frac{D}{Q} \qquad\qquad (10\text{--}17)$$

where $E(N)$ = Expected number of units short per year.

EXAMPLE 14

Given the following information, determine the expected number of units short per year.

$$D = 1,000 \qquad Q = 250 \qquad E(n) = 2.5$$

Solution

Using the formula $E(N) = E(n)\dfrac{D}{Q}$

$$E(N) = 2.5 \left(\frac{1,000}{250}\right) = 10.0 \text{ units per year}$$

It is sometimes convenient to think of service level in annual terms. For instance, one definition of annual service level is the percentage of demand filled directly from inventory. Thus, if $D = 1,000$, and 990 units were filled directly from inventory (shortages totaling 10 units over the year were recorded), the annual service level would be $990/1,000 = 99$ percent. Annual service level is related to, but generally more than, lead time service level. The two service levels can be related using the following formula:

$$E(N) = (1 - SL_{annual})D \tag{10-18}$$

Using Formula 10–17 and 10–16, $E(N) = E(n)D/Q = E(z)\,\sigma_{dLT}D/Q$. Thus,

$$(1 - SL_{annual}) = \frac{E(z)\sigma_{dLT}}{Q} \tag{10-19}$$

EXAMPLE 15

Given a lead time service level of .90, $D = 1,000$, $Q = 250$, and $\sigma_{dLT} = 16$, determine the annual service level.

Solution

From Table 10–3, $E(z) = 0.048$ for a 90 percent lead time service level. Using Formula 10–19, we find:

$$(1 - SL_{annual}) = \frac{0.048(16)}{250}$$

$$= .003$$

Solving for the annual service level yields

$$SL_{annual} = 1 - .003 = .997$$

Note that in the preceding example, a lead time service level of 90 percent provided an annual service level of 99.7 percent. Naturally, different values of D, Q, and $\sigma_{d\text{LT}}$ will tend to produce different results for a cycle service level of 90 percent. Nonetheless, in general, the annual service level will be greater than the cycle service level. In addition, since the annual service level as we have defined it relates to the percentage of units short per year, it may make sense to base cycle service levels on a specified annual service level. This would mean setting the annual level, using Formula 10–19 to solve for $E(z)$, and then using that value to obtain the service level for the order cycles.

HOW MUCH TO ORDER: FIXED-ORDER-INTERVAL MODEL

When inventory replenishment is based on EOQ/ROP models, *fixed quantities* of items are ordered at varying time intervals. Just the opposite occurs under the **fixed-order-interval (FOI)** model: orders for *varying quantities* are placed at fixed time intervals (weekly, every 20 days, etc.).

There are a number of differences between these two approaches to reordering. For instance, both are sensitive to demand experience just prior to reordering, but in somewhat different ways. In the fixed-quantity model, a higher-than-normal demand causes a *shorter time* between orders, whereas in the fixed-interval model, the result would be a *larger order size*. Another difference is that the fixed-quantity model requires close monitoring of inventory levels in order to know *when* the amount on hand has reached the reorder point, and the fixed-interval model requires only a periodic review (i.e., physical inspection) of inventory levels just prior to placing an order to determine *how much* is needed.

Reasons for Using

Under certain conditions, the use of fixed order intervals is quite practical. In some cases, a supplier's policy might encourage orders at fixed intervals. Even if that is not the case, grouping orders for items from the same supplier can produce savings in shipping costs. Furthermore, some situations do not readily lend themselves to continuous monitoring of inventory levels. Many retail operations (e.g., drugstores, small grocery stores) fall into this category. The alternative for them is to use fixed order intervals, which require only periodic checks of inventory levels.

Determining the Amount to Order

If the demand rate and lead time are both constant, the fixed-interval model and the fixed-order-quantity model function identically. The differences in the two models become apparent only when examined under conditions of variability. As in the ROP model, there can be variations in demand only, in lead time only, or in both demand and lead time. However, for the sake of simplicity, and because it is perhaps the most frequently encountered situation, the discussion here will focus on only *variable demand and constant lead time.*

Figure 10–16 provides a comparison of the fixed-quantity and fixed-interval systems. Notice that in the fixed-quantity arrangement, and orders are triggered by a *quantity* (ROP), and in the fixed-interval arrangement, orders are triggered by a *time*. Because of this, the fixed-interval system must have stock-out protection for lead time plus the next order cycle, but the fixed-quantity system needs protection only during lead time since additional orders can be placed at any time and will be received shortly (lead time) thereafter. Consequently, there is a greater need for safety stock in the fixed-interval model than there is in the fixed-quantity model. Note, for example, the large dip into safety stock during the second order cycle with the fixed-interval model.

Order size in the fixed-interval model is determined by the following computation:

$$\begin{array}{ccccc} \text{Amount} \\ \text{to order} \end{array} = \begin{array}{c} \text{Expected demand} \\ \text{during protection} \\ \text{interval} \end{array} + \begin{array}{c} \text{Safety} \\ \text{stock} \end{array} - \begin{array}{c} \text{Amount on hand} \\ \text{at reorder time} \end{array}$$

$$= \quad \bar{d}(\text{OI} + \text{LT}) \quad + z\sigma_d\sqrt{\text{OI} + \text{LT}} - \qquad A$$

$$(10\text{–}20)$$

where

$$\text{OI} = \text{Order interval (length of time between orders)}$$
$$A = \text{Amount on hand at reorder time}$$

As in previous models, it is assumed that demand during the protection interval is normally distributed.

EXAMPLE 16

Given the following information, determine the amount to order.

$\bar{d}$ = 30 units per day	Desired service level = 99 percent
σ_d = 3 units per day	Amount on hand at reorder time = 71 units
LT = 2 days	OI = 7 days

Solution

$$z = 2.33 \text{ for 99 percent service level}$$

$$\begin{array}{c} \text{Amount} \\ \text{to order} \end{array} = \bar{d}(\text{OI} + \text{LT}) + z\sigma_d\sqrt{\text{OI} + \text{LT}} - A$$

$$= 30(7 + 2) + 2.33(3)\sqrt{7 + 2} - 71 = 220 \text{ units}$$

FIGURE 10—16

Comparison of fixed-quantity and fixed-interval ordering

A. Reordering fixed quantities

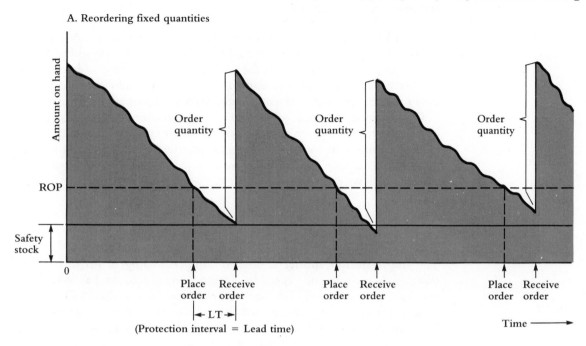

(Protection interval = Lead time)

B. Reordering at fixed intervals

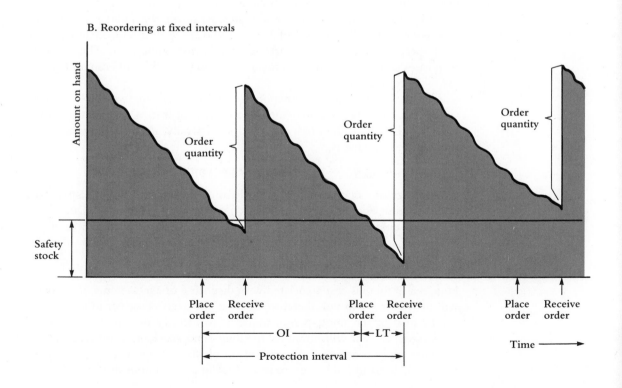

Benefits and Disadvantages

The fixed-interval system results in the tight control needed for A items in an A-B-C classification due to the periodic reviews it requires. In addition, when two or more items come from the same supplier, grouping orders can yield savings in ordering, packing, and shipping costs. Moreover, it may be the only practical approach if inventory withdrawals cannot be closely monitored.

On the negative side, the fixed-interval system necessitates a larger amount of safety stock for a given risk of stock-out due to the need to protect against shortages during an entire order interval plus lead time (instead of lead time only), and this increases the carrying cost. Also, there are the costs of the periodic reviews.

HOW MUCH TO ORDER: SINGLE-PERIOD MODEL

The **single-period model** is used to handle ordering of perishables (such things as fresh fruits and vegetables, seafood, and cut flowers) as well as items that have a limited useful life (such as newspapers and magazines.) What sets these items apart from those previously discussed is that unsold or unused items are not typically carried over from one period to the next, at least not without penalty. Day-old baked goods, for instance, are often sold at reduced prices, leftover seafood may be discarded, and out-of-date magazines may be offered to used book stores at bargain rates. At times, there may even be some cost associated with disposal of leftover goods. We can also include in the single-period category spare parts for specialized equipment. The *period* in such cases is the life of the equipment, assuming that the parts cannot be used for other equipment.

Analysis of single-period situations generally focuses on two costs: shortage and excess. Shortage cost may include a charge for loss of customer goodwill as well as the opportunity cost of lost sales. Generally, *shortage cost* is unrealized profit per unit. That is,

$$C_{\text{shortage}} = C_s = \text{Revenue per unit} - \text{Cost per unit}$$

If a shortage or stock-out relates to an item used in production or a spare part for a machine, then *shortage cost refers to the actual cost of lost production.*

Excess cost pertains to items left over at the end of the period. In effect, excess cost is the difference between purchase cost and salvage value. That is,

$$C_{\text{excess}} = C_e = \text{Original cost per unit} - \text{Salvage value per unit}$$

Note that if there is cost associated with disposing of excess items, the salvage will be negative and will therefore increase the excess cost per unit.

The goal of the single-period model is to identify the order quantity, or stocking level, that will minimize the long-run excess and shortage costs.

There are two general categories of problems that we will consider: those for which demand can be approximated using a continuous distribution (perhaps a theoretical one such as a uniform or normal distribution) and those for which demand can be approximated using a discrete distribution (say, historical frequencies or a theoretical distribution such as the Poisson). The kind of inventory in question can give an indication of which type of model might be appropriate. For example, demand for petroleum, liquids, and gases would tend to vary over some *continuous scale,* thus lending itself to description by a continuous distribution. Demand for houses, cars, and typewriters is expressed in terms of the *number of units* demanded and lends itself to description by a discrete distribution.

Continuous Stocking Levels

The concept of identifying an optimal stocking level is perhaps easiest to visualize when demand is *uniform.* Choosing the stocking level is similar to balancing a seesaw, but instead of having a person on each end of the seesaw, we have excess cost per unit (C_e) on one end of the distribution and shortage cost per unit (C_s) on the other. The optimal stocking level is analogous to the fulcrum of the seesaw; the stocking level equalizes the cost weights, as illustrated in Figure 10–17.

The *service level* is the *probability* that demand will not exceed the stocking level, and computation of the service level is the key to determining the optimal stocking level, S_o:

$$\text{Service level} = \frac{C_s}{C_s + C_e} \qquad (10\text{–}21)$$

where

$$C_s = \text{Shortage cost per unit}$$
$$C_e = \text{Excess cost per unit}$$

If actual demand exceeds S_o, there is a shortage; hence, C_s is on the right end of the distribution. Similarly, if demand is less than S_o, there is an excess, so C_e is on the left end of the distribution. When $C_e = C_s$, the optimal stocking level is halfway between the endpoints of the distribution. If one cost is greater than the other, S_o tends to be closer to the *larger* cost.

FIGURE 10–17

The optimal stocking level balances unit shortage and excess costs

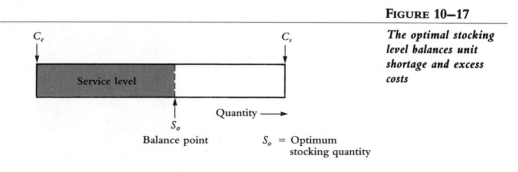

EXAMPLE 17

Sweet cider is delivered weekly to Pappy's Produce Stand. Demand varies uniformly between 300 liters per week and 500 liters per week. Pappy pays 20 cents per liter for the cider and charges 80 cents per liter for it. Unsold cider has no salvage value and cannot be carried over into the next week due to spoilage. Find the optimal stocking level and its stock-out risk for that quantity.

Solution

$$C_e = \text{Cost per unit} - \text{Salvage value per unit}$$
$$= \$0.20 \qquad - \$0$$
$$= \$0.20 \text{ per unit}$$

$$C_s = \text{Revenue per unit} - \text{Cost per unit}$$
$$= \$0.80 \qquad - \qquad \$0.20$$
$$= \$0.60 \text{ per unit}$$

$$SL = \frac{C_s}{C_s + C_e} = \frac{\$0.60}{\$0.60 + \$0.20} = .75$$

Thus, the optimal stocking level must satify demand 75 percent of the time. For the uniform distribution, this will be at a point equal to the minimum demand plus 75 percent of the difference between maximum and minimum demands:

$$S_o = 300 + 0.75(500 - 300) = 450 \text{ liters}$$

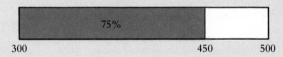

The stock-out risk is $1.00 - SL = 1.00 - 0.75 = 0.25$.

A similar approach applies if demand is normally distributed.

EXAMPLE 18

Pappy's Stand also sells a blend of cherry juice and apple cider. Demand for the blend is approximately normal with a mean of 200 liters per week and a standard deviation of 10 liters per week. $C_s = 60$ cents per liter, and $C_e = 20$ cents per liter. Find the optimal stocking level for the apple-cherry blend.

Solution

$$SL = \frac{C_s}{C_s + C_e} = \frac{\$0.60}{\$0.60 + \$0.20} = .75$$

EXAMPLE 18 *(concluded)*

This indicates that 75 percent of the area under the normal curve must be to the left of the stocking level. From Appendix B, Table B we see that a value of z between $+0.67$ and $+0.68$, say, $+0.675$, will satisfy this. Thus,

$$S_o = 200 \text{ liters} + 0.675(10 \text{ liters}) = 206.75 \text{ liters}$$

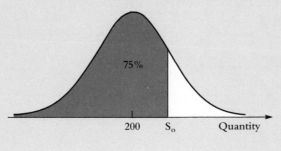

Discrete Stocking Levels

When stocking levels are discrete rather than continuous, the service level computed using the ratio $C_s/(C_s + C_e)$ usually does not coincide with a feasible stocking level (e.g., the optimal amount may be between, say, five and six units). The solution is to stock at the next highest level (e.g., six units). In other words, choose the stocking level so that the desired service level is equaled or *exceeded*. This concept is illustrated in Figure 10–18.

FIGURE 10–18

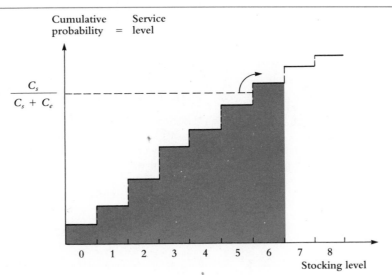

The service level achieved must equal or exceed the ratio

$$\frac{C_s}{C_s + C_e}$$

EXAMPLE 19

Historical records on the usage of spare parts for several large hydraulic presses are to be used as an estimate of usage for spares of a newly installed press. Stock-out costs involve downtime expenses and special ordering costs. These average $4,200 per unit short. Spares cost $800 each, and unused parts have zero salvage. Determine the optimal stocking level.

Numbers of spares used	Relative frequency	Cumulative frequency
0	.20	.20
1	.40	.60
2	.30	.90
3	.10	1.00
4 or more	.00	
	1.00	

Solution

$$C_s = \$4,200 \qquad C_e = \$800$$

$$\text{SL} = \frac{C_s}{C_e + C_s} = \frac{\$4,200}{\$800 + \$4,200} = .84$$

The cumulative frequency column indicates the percentage of time that demand did not exceed (was equal to or less than) some amount. For example, demand does not exceed one spare 60 percent of the time, or two spares 90 percent of the time. Thus, in order to achieve a service level of *at least* 84 percent, it is necessary to stock two spares (i.e., to go to the next highest stocking level).

EXAMPLE 20

Demand for long-stemmed red roses at a small flower shop can be approximated using a Poisson distribution that has a mean of four dozen per day. Profit on the roses is $3 per dozen. Leftover flowers are marked down and sold the next day at a loss of $2 per dozen. Assume that all marked-down flowers are sold. What is the optimal stocking level?

Solution

$$C_s = \$3 \qquad C_e = \$2 \qquad \text{SL} = \frac{C_s}{C_s + C_e} = \frac{\$3}{\$3 + \$2} = .60$$

EXAMPLE 20 *(concluded)*

Obtain the cumulative frequencies from the Poisson table (Table C in Appendix B) for a mean of 4.0:

Demand (dozen per day)	Cumulative frequency
0	.018
1	.092
2	.238
3	.434
4	.629
5	.785
⋮	⋮

Compare the service level to the cumulative frequencies. Stock four dozen in order to attain a service level that exceeds .60.

One final point about discrete stocking levels: If the computed service level is *exactly* equal to the cumulative probability associated with one of the stocking levels, there are two equivalent stocking levels in terms of minimizing long-run cost: the one with equal probability and the next higher one. For instance, in the preceding example, if the ratio had been equal to .629, we would be indifferent between stocking four dozen and stocking five dozen roses each day.

OPERATIONS STRATEGY

Inventories are a necessary part of doing business. However, they are best thought of as a necessary *evil*. One reason for this is that inventories tend to hide problems; they make it easier to "live with" problems rather than eliminate them. Another reason is that inventories are costly to maintain. Consequently, a wise operations strategy is to work toward reducing inventories. This can be accomplished by (1) reducing lot sizes and (2) reducing safety stocks.

Observers have noted that Japanese manufacturers seem to use smaller lot sizes than their Western counterparts. The reason for this is that the Japanese have adopted a slightly different perspective on inventory carrying costs. In addition to the usual components (storage, handling, obsolescence, etc.), they also recognize opportunity costs of disrupting work flow, the inability to place machines and workers closer together (which encourages cooperation, socialization, and communication), and hiding problems related to product quality and equipment breakdown. When these are factored in, carrying costs become higher—perhaps much higher—than before. The impact of an EOQ with revised (higher) holding costs is illustrated in Figure 10–19. Recall that carrying costs and ordering costs are equal at the EOQ. A higher carrying cost

FIGURE 10–19

Revised (increased) carrying costs result in a smaller EOQ

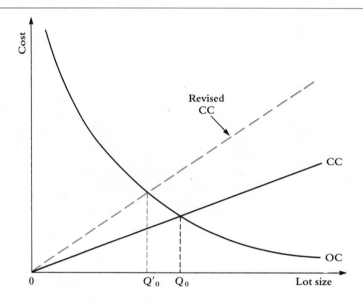

results in a steeper carrying-cost line, and the resulting intersection with the ordering-cost line occurs at a smaller quantity—hence a smaller EOQ.

Although it can be argued that these costs are not readily quantifiable, the point is that Western manufacturers should probably reassess holding costs under this new light and revise estimated holding costs upward.

FIGURE 10–20

Reductions in both ordering/setup cost and carrying cost result in much smaller lot sizes

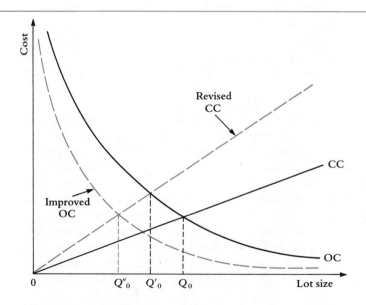

The second factor in the EOQ model that can contribute to smaller lot sizes is the setup or ordering processing cost. There are numerous examples of cases where these costs have been reduced through research efforts. Note, however, that whereas a reduction due to carrying costs stems from a reassessment of those costs, a reduction due to ordering or setup costs must come from actively pursuing improvement. Together, these cost reductions can lead to even smaller lot sizes, as illustrated in Figure 10–20.

Additional reductions in inventory can be achieved by reducing the amount of safety stock that is carried. Important factors in safety stock are lead time and lead time variability; reductions in these will result in lower safety stocks. Such reductions can often be realized by working with suppliers, by choosing suppliers that are located close to the buyer, and by shifting to smaller lot sizes. Note that if either lead time or lead time variability is zero, *no* safety stock will be needed!

In attempting to achieve the reductions discussed here, an A–B–C approach can be very beneficial. This means that all phases of operation should be examined, and those showing the greatest potential for improvement (i.e., "A items") should be attacked first. Early results will demonstrate the benefits of this strategy to both management and workers, making both parties more willing to lend their support to additional efforts.

Last, but certainly not least, it is important to make sure that inventory records be kept *accurate* and *up to date*. Estimates of holding costs, ordering costs, setup costs, and lead times should be reviewed periodically.

SUMMARY

Good inventory management is often the mark of a well-run organization. Inventory levels must be planned carefully in order to balance the cost of holding inventory and the cost of providing reasonable levels of customer service. Successful inventory management requires a system to keep track of inventory transactions, accurate information about demand and lead times, realistic estimates of certain inventory-related costs, and a priority system for classifying the items in inventory and allocating control efforts.

The models described in this chapter are relevant for instances where demand for inventory items is *independent*. Four classes of models are described: EOQ, ROP, fixed-interval, and single-period. The first three types are appropriate if unused items can be carried over into subsequent periods, and the single-period model is appropriate when items cannot be carried over. EOQ models address the question of *how much to order*. The ROP models address the question of *when to order* and are particularly helpful in dealing with situations that include variations in either demand rate or lead time. ROP models involve service level and safety stock considerations. When the time between orders is fixed, the FOI model is useful. The single-period model identifies a period stocking level that will balance the expected costs of shortage and excess resulting from variations in demand. The models presented in this chapter are summarized in Table 10–4.

TABLE 10–4

Summary of inventory formulas

Model	Formula	Symbols
1. Basic EOQ	$Q_0 = \sqrt{\dfrac{2DS}{H}}$ (10–2) $TC = \dfrac{Q}{2}H + \dfrac{D}{Q}S$ (10–1)	Q_0 = Economic order quantity D = Annual demand S = Order cost H = Annual carrying cost per unit
2. Economic run size	$Q_0 = \sqrt{\dfrac{2DS}{H}}\sqrt{\dfrac{p}{p-u}}$ (10–5) $I_{max} = \dfrac{Q_0}{p}(p - u)$ (10–6) $TC = \dfrac{I_{max}}{2}H + \dfrac{D}{Q}S$ (10–4)	Q_0 = Optimal run or order size p = Production or delivery rate u = Usage or demand rate I_{max} = Maximum inventory level
3. Reorder point under: a. Constant demand and lead time b. Variable demand rate c. Variable lead time d. Variable lead time and demand	$ROP = d(LT)$ $ROP = \bar{d}LT + z\sqrt{LT}\,(\sigma_d)$ (10–11) $ROP = \overline{dLT} + zd(\sigma_{LT})$ (10–12) $ROP = \overline{dLT} + z\sqrt{LT\sigma_d^2 + \bar{d}^2\sigma_{LT}^2}$ (10–15)	ROP = Quantity on hand at reorder point d = Demand rate LT = Lead time $\bar{d}$ = Average usage rate σ_d = Standard deviation of demand rate z = Standard normal deviation $\overline{LT}$ = Average lead time σ_{LT} = Standard deviation of lead time
4. ROP shortages a. Units short per cycle b. Units short per year c. Annual service level	$E(n) = E(z)\sigma_{dLT}$ (10–16) $E(N) = E(n)\dfrac{D}{Q}$ (10–17) $(1 - SL_{annual}) = \dfrac{E(z)\sigma_{dLT}}{Q}$ (10–19)	$E(n)$ = Expected number short per cycle $E(z)$ = Standardized number short σ_{dLT} = Standard deviation of lead time demand $E(N)$ = Expected number short per year SL_{annual} = Annual service level

TABLE 10–4

(concluded)

Model	Formula	Symbols
5. Fixed interval	$Q = \bar{d}(\text{OI} + \text{LT}) + z\sigma_d\sqrt{\text{OI} + \text{LT}} - A$	OI = Time between orders A = Amount on hand at order time
6. Single period	$SL = \dfrac{C_s}{C_s + C_e}$	C_s = Cost of shortage per unit C_e = Cost of excess per unit SL = Service level

KEY TERMS

A-B-C approach, 506
carrying cost, 504
continuous inventory system, 502
dependent demand, 499
economic order quantity
  (EOQ), 507
excess cost, 540
fixed-order-interval (FOI)
  model, 537
holding costs, 504
independent demand, 499

inventory, 498
ordering costs, 505
periodic system, 502
quantity discounts, 516
reorder point (ROP), 524
safety stock, 525
service level, 526
shortage costs, 505
single-period model, 540
two-bin system, 503
universal product code, 503

SOLVED PROBLEMS

1. *Basic EOQ.* A toy manufacturer uses approximately 32,000 silicon chips annually. The chips are used at a steady rate during the 240 days the plant operates. Annual holding cost is 60 cents per chip, and ordering cost is $24. Determine:
   a. The optimal order size.
   b. The number of workdays in an order cycle.

Solution

$$D = 32,000 \text{ chips per year}$$
$$S = \$24$$
$$H = \$.60 \text{ per unit per year}$$

a. $Q_0 = \sqrt{\dfrac{2DS}{H}} = \sqrt{\dfrac{2(32,000)\$24}{\$.60}} = 1,600 \text{ chips.}$

b. $\dfrac{Q_0}{D} = \dfrac{1,600 \text{ chips}}{32,000 \text{ chips/yr.}} = \dfrac{1}{20} \text{ year (i.e., 1/20} \times 240 \text{ days), or 12 days.}$

2.   *Noninstantaneous delivery.* The Dine Corporation is both a producer and a user of brass couplings. The firm operates 220 days a year and uses the couplings at a steady rate of 50 per day. Couplings can be produced at a rate of 200 per day. Annual storage costs are $1 per coupling, and machine setup costs are $35 per run.
   a.   Determine the economic run size.
   b.   Approximately how many runs per year will there be?
   c.   Compute the maximum inventory level.
   d.   Determine the length of the *pure consumption* portion of the cycle.

Solution

$$D = 50 \text{ units per day} \times 220 \text{ days per year} = 11,000 \text{ units per year}$$
$$S = \$35$$
$$H = \$1 \text{ per unit per year}$$
$$p = 200 \text{ units per day}$$
$$u = 50 \text{ units per day}$$

a. $Q_0 = \sqrt{\dfrac{2DS}{H}} \sqrt{\dfrac{p}{p-u}} = \sqrt{\dfrac{2(11,000)35}{1}} \sqrt{\dfrac{200}{200-50}} = 1,013 \text{ units.}$

b.   Number of runs per year: $D/Q_0 = 11,000/1,013 = 10.86$, or 11.

c. $I_{max} = \dfrac{Q_0}{p}(p-u) = \dfrac{1,013}{200}(200-50) = 759.3 \text{ or } 760 \text{ units.}$

d.   Length of cycle $= \dfrac{Q_0}{u} = \dfrac{1,013 \text{ units}}{50 \text{ units per day}} = 20.26 \text{ days}$

   Length of run $= \dfrac{Q_0}{p} = \dfrac{1,013 \text{ units}}{200 \text{ units per day}} = 5.065 \text{ days}$

   $\begin{array}{l}\text{Length of pure}\\ \text{consumption portion}\end{array} =$ Length of cycle $-$ Length of run

   $= 20.26 - 5.605 = 15.20 \text{ days.}$

3. *Quantity discounts.* A small manufacturing firm uses roughly 3,400 pounds of chemical dye a year. Currently the firm purchases 300 pounds per order and pays $3 per pound. The supplier has just announced that orders of 1,000 pounds or more will be filled at a price of $2 per pound. The manufacturing firm incurs a cost of $100 each time it submits an order and assigns an annual holding cost of 17 percent of the purchase price per pound.
   a. Determine the order size that will minimize the total cost.
   b. If the supplier offered the discount at 1,500 pounds instead of at 1,000 pounds, what order size would minimize total cost?

Solution

$$D = 3{,}400 \text{ pounds per year}$$
$$S = \$100$$
$$H = 0.17P$$

a. Compute the EOQ for $2 per pound:

$$Q_{\$2/pound} = \sqrt{\frac{2DS}{H}} = \sqrt{\frac{2(3{,}400)100}{0.17(2)}} = 1{,}414 \text{ pounds.}$$

Since this quantity is feasible at $2 per pound, it is the optimum.

b. When the discount is offered at 1,500 pounds, the EOQ for the $2/pound curve is no longer feasible. Consequently, it becomes necessary to compute the EOQ for $3 per pound and compare the total cost for that order size with the total cost using the price break quantity (i.e., 1,500).

$$Q_{\$3/pound} = \sqrt{\frac{2DS}{H}} = \sqrt{\frac{2(3{,}400)100}{0.17(3)}} = 1{,}155 \text{ pounds}$$

$$TC = \left(\frac{Q}{2}\right)H + \left(\frac{D}{Q}\right)S + PD$$

$$TC_{1,155} = \left(\frac{1{,}155}{2}\right)0.17(3) + \left(\frac{3{,}400}{1{,}155}\right)100 + 3(3{,}400)$$

$$= \$294.53 + \$294.37 + \$10{,}200 = \$10{,}789$$

$$TC_{1,500} = \left(\frac{1{,}500}{2}\right)0.17(2) + \left(\frac{3{,}400}{1{,}500}\right)100 + 2(3{,}400)$$

$$= \$255 + \$226.67 + \$6{,}800 = \$7{,}282$$

Hence, because it would result in a lower total cost, 1,500 is the optimal order size.

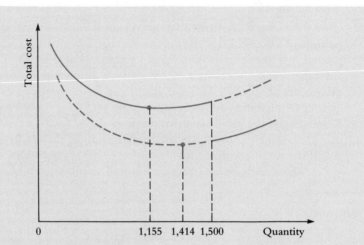

4. *ROP for variable demand and constant lead time.* The housekeeping department of a motel uses approximately 400 washcloths per day. The actual amount tends to vary with the number of customers who stay on any given night. Usage can be approximated by a normal distribution that has a mean of 400 and a standard deviation of 9 washcloths per day. A linen supply company delivers towels and washcloths with a lead time of three days. If the motel policy is to maintain a stock-out risk of 2 percent, what is the minimum number of washcloths that must be on hand at reorder time, and how much of that amount can be considered safety stock?

Solution

$\bar{d}$ = 400 washcloths per day   LT = 3 days
σ_d =   9 washcloths per day   Risk = 2%, so service level = 98%

From Appendix B, Table B, the z value that corresponds to an area under the normal curve to the left of z for 98 percent is about $+2.055$.

$$\text{ROP} = \bar{d}\text{LT} + z\sqrt{\text{LT}}\sigma_d = 400(3) + 2.055\sqrt{3}(9)$$
$$= 1,200 + 32.03, \text{ or approximately } 1,232$$

Safety stock is approximately 32 washcloths.

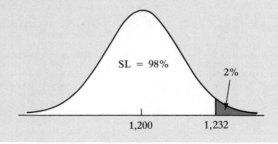

5. *ROP for constant demand and variable lead time.* The motel in the preceding example uses approximately 600 bars of soap each day, and this tends not to vary by more than a few bars either way. Lead time for soap delivery is normally distributed with a mean of six days and a standard deviation of two days. A service level of 90 percent is desired. Find the ROP.

Solution

$$d = 600 \text{ bars per day}$$
$$\underline{SL} = 90\%, \text{ so } z = +1.28 \text{ (from Appendix B, Table B)}$$
$$\overline{LT} = 6 \text{ days}$$
$$\sigma_{LT} = 2 \text{ days}$$
$$ROP = d\overline{LT} + zd(\sigma_{LT})$$
$$= 600(6) + 1.28(600)2$$
$$= 5{,}136 \text{ bars of soap}$$

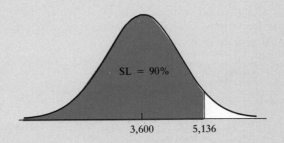

SL = 90%

3,600   5,136

6. *ROP for variable demand rate and variable lead time.* The motel replaces broken glasses at a rate of 25 per day. In the past, this quantity has tended to vary normally and have a standard deviation of 3 glasses per day. Glasses are ordered from a Cleveland supplier. Lead time is normally distributed with an average of 10 days and a standard deviation of 2 days. What ROP should be used to achieve a service level of 95 percent?

Solution

$$\bar{d} = 25 \text{ glasses per day} \qquad \overline{LT} = 10 \text{ days}$$
$$\sigma_d = 3 \text{ glasses per day} \qquad \sigma_{LT} = 2 \text{ days}$$
$$SL = 95\%, \text{ so } z = +1.65 \text{ (Appendix B, Table B)}$$
$$ROP = \bar{d}\overline{LT} + z\sqrt{\overline{LT}\sigma_d^2 + \bar{d}^2\sigma_{LT}^2}$$
$$= 25(10) + 1.65\sqrt{10(3)^2 + (25)^2(2)^2}$$
$$= 334 \text{ glasses}$$

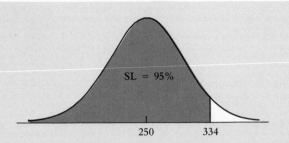

7. *Shortages and service levels.* The manager of a store that sells office supplies has decided to set an annual service level of 96 percent for a certain model of telephone answering equipment. The store sells approximately 300 of this model a year. Holding cost is $5 per unit annually, ordering cost is $25, and $\sigma_{dLT} = 7$.

  a. What average number of units short per year will be consistent with the specified annual service level?

  b. What average number of units short per cycle will provide the desired annual service level?

  c. What lead time service level is necessary for the 96 percent annual service level?

Solution

$SL_{annual} = 96\%$ $D = 300$ units $H = \$5$ $S = \$25$ $\sigma_{dLT} = 7$

a. $E(N) = (1 - SL_{annual})D = (1 - .96)(300) = 12$ units.

b. $E(N) = E(n)\dfrac{D}{Q}$. Solving for $E(n)$, we have

$$E(n) = E(N)/\left(\frac{D}{Q}\right) = 12/\left(\frac{300}{Q}\right)$$

$$Q = \sqrt{\frac{2DS}{H}} = \sqrt{\frac{2(300)(25)}{5}} = 54.77 \text{ (round to 55)}$$

Then $E(n) = 12/\left(\dfrac{300}{55}\right) = 2.2$.

c. In order to find the lead time service level, we need the value of $E(z)$. Since we know the value of $E(n)$ is 2.2 and that $E(n) = E(z)\sigma_{dLT}$, we have $2.2 = E(z)(7)$. Solving gives us $E(z) = 2.2/7 = 0.314$. Interpolating in Table 10–3 gives us the approximate lead time service level. Thus,

$$\frac{0.307 - 0.314}{0.307 - 0.324} = \frac{.5793 - x}{.5793 - .5636}$$

Solving, $x = .5728$.

[To interpolate, find the two values between which the computed number falls in the $E(z)$ column. Then find the difference between the computed value and one end of the range, and divide by the difference between the two ends of the range. Perform the corresponding calculation on the two service levels using x for the unknown value, and solve for x. Often, simply "eyeballing" the unknown value will suffice.]

8. *Fixed-order-interval model.* A lab orders a number of chemicals from the same supplier every 30 days. Lead time is 5 days. The assistant manager of the lab must determine how much of one of these chemicals to order. A check of stock revealed that eleven 25-ml jars are on hand. Daily usage of the chemical is approximately normal with a mean of 15.2 ml per day and a standard deviation of 1.6 ml per day. The desired service level for this chemical is 95 percent.

   a. How many bottles of the chemical should be ordered?

   b. What is the average amount of safety stock of the chemical?

Solution

$\bar{d}$ = 15.2 ml per day, OI = 30 days, SL = 95% requires z = 1.65
σ_d = 1.6 ml per day, LT = 5 days, A = 11 jars × 25 ml per jar
   = 275 ml

a.
$$\text{Amount to order} = \bar{d}(\text{OI} + \text{LT}) + z\sigma_d\sqrt{\text{OI} + \text{LT}} - A$$

$$= 15.2(30 + 5) + 1.65(1.6)\sqrt{30 + 5} - 275$$

$$= 272.62 \text{ ml}$$

Convert this to number of jars: $\dfrac{272.65 \text{ ml}}{25 \text{ ml per jar}} = 10.90$ or 11 jars.

b.
$$\text{Safety stock} = z\sigma_d\sqrt{\text{OI} + \text{LT}}$$

$$= 1.65(1.6)\sqrt{30 + 5} = 15.62 \text{ ml.}$$

9. *Single-period model.* A firm that installs cable TV systems has a certain piece of equipment that it carries two spare parts for. The parts cost $500 each and have no salvage value. Part failures can be modeled by a Poisson distribution with a mean of two failures during the useful life of the equipment. Holding and disposal costs are negligible. Estimate the apparent range of shortage cost.

Solution

C_s is unknown C_e = $500

Using the Poisson table (Appendix B, Table C) for a mean of 2, we obtain these values:

Number of failures	Cumulative probability
0	.135
1	.406
2	.677
3	.857
4	.947
5	.983
⋮	⋮

We know that for the optimal stocking level, the service level must usually be rounded up to a feasible stocking level. Hence, we know that the service level must have been between .406 and .677 in order to make two units the optimal level. By setting the service level equal first to .406 and then to .677, we can establish bounds on the possible range of shortage costs:

$$\frac{C_s}{C_s + \$500} = .406, \text{ so } C_s = .406(\$500 + C_s)$$

Solving, we find $C_s = \$341.75$. Similarly,

$$\frac{C_s}{C_s + \$500} = .677, \text{ so } C_s = .677(\$500 + C_s)$$

Solving, we find $C_s = \$1,047.99$. Hence, the apparent range of failure or shortage cost is $341.75 to $1,047.99.

DISCUSSION AND REVIEW QUESTIONS

1. What are the primary reasons for holding inventory?

2. What are the requirements for effective inventory management?

3. Briefly describe each of the costs associated with inventory.

4. Contrast independent and dependent demand with respect to inventories.

5. List the major assumptions of the EOQ model.

6. Why isn't price considered explicitly in the basic EOQ model? How is it sometimes indirectly included?

7. How would you respond to the criticism that EOQ models tend to provide misleading results because values of D, S, and H are, at best, educated guesses?

8. What are quantity discounts? What three costs enter into the order quantity decision when discounts are available?

9. What is safety stock, and why is it held?

10. Under what circumstances would the amount of safety stock held be:
   a. Large?
   b. Small?
   c. Zero?

11. What is the single-period model, and when is it appropriate?

12. What is meant by the term *service level?* Generally speaking, how is service level related to the amount of safety stock held?

13. Can the optimal stocking level in a single-period model ever be less than expected demand? Explain briefly.

14. Describe briefly the A–B–C approach to inventory control.

15. The purchasing agent for a company that assembles and sells air-conditioning equipment in a Latin American country has noted that the cost of compressors has increased significantly each time they have been reordered. The company uses an EOQ model to determine order size. What are the implications of this price escalation with respect to order size? What factors other than price must be taken into consideration?

16. Explain how a decrease in setup time can lead to a decrease in the average amount of inventory a firm holds, and why that would be beneficial.

PROBLEMS

1. A large bakery buys sugar in 100-pound bags. The bakery uses an average of 1,344 bags a year. Preparing an order and receiving a shipment of sugar involves a cost of $3 per order. Annual carrying costs are $14 per bag.
   a. Determine the economic order quantity.
   b. What is the average number of bags on hand?
   c. How many orders per year will there be?
   d. Compute the total cost of ordering and carrying sugar.

2. A gasoline pump is used to remove water from construction sites 300 days a year. The generator consumes 80 liters of fuel each day. Storage and handling costs are $4 per liter a year, and ordering and receiving the shipments of fuel involves a cost of $12 each.
   a. Find the optimal order size.
   b. Compute the annual ordering cost and the annual carrying cost.
   c. Are the annual ordering and carrying costs always equal at the EOQ?
   d. If storage and handling costs increase to $5 per liter per year, by how much will the total cost change?

3. Garden Variety Flower Shop uses 800 clay pots a month. The pots are purchased at $1 each. Annual carrying costs are estimated to be 15 percent of cost, and ordering costs are $30 per order.
   a. Determine the economic order quantity and the total annual carrying and ordering costs.
   b. The manager believes it is possible to substantially reduce ordering cost but feels that the benefit could not exceed $147 a year. Consequently, the manager is reluctant to expend the effort to do this. Is the manager correct concerning the potential savings? Explain.
   c. Suppose an analysis shows the actual carrying costs are roughly three times the current estimate. What impact would this have on the total annual carrying and ordering costs?

4. A produce distributor uses 800 packing crates a month, which it purchases at a cost of $10 each. The manager has assigned an annual carrying cost of 25 percent of the purchase price per crate. Ordering costs are $28. Currently the manager orders once a month. How much could the firm save annually in ordering and carrying costs by using the EOQ?

5. A chemical firm produces sodium bisulfate in 100-pound bags. Demand for this product is 20 tons per day. The capacity for producing the product is 50 tons per day. Setup costs $100, and storage and handling costs are $5 per ton a year. The firm operates 200 days a year.

   a. How many bags per run is optimal?
   b. What would the average inventory be for this lot size?
   c. Determine the approximate length of a production run, in days.
   d. About how many runs per year would there be?
   e. How much could the company save annually if the setup cost could be reduced to $25 per run?

6. A food processor uses approximately 27,000 glass jars a month for its fruit juice product. Because of storage limitations, a lot size of 4,000 jars has been used. A safety stock of 500 jars is kept to reduce the risk of running out of jars before a new shipment arrives. Monthly holding cost is 18 cents per jar, and reordering cost is $60 per order. The company operates an average of 20 days a month.

   a. What penalty is the company incurring by its present order size?
   b. The manager would prefer ordering 10 times each month but would have to justify any change in order size. One possibility is to simplify order processing to reduce the ordering cost. What ordering cost would enable the manager to justify ordering every other day?
   c. Suppose that after investigating ordering cost, the manager is able to reduce it to $50. How else could the manager justify using an order size that would be consistent with ordering every other day?

7. The Friendly Sausage Factory (FSF) can produce hot dogs at a rate of 5,000 per day.

FSF supplies hot dogs to local stores and restaurants at a steady rate of 250 per day. The cost to prepare the equipment for producing hot dogs is $22. Annual holding costs are 15 cents per hot dog. The factory operates 300 days a year. Find:

   a. The optimal run size.
   b. The number of runs per year.
   c. The length (in days) of a run.

8. A firm that trains crane operators guarantees its graduates an annual salary of at least $10,000, which it pays from the time of graduation until the student is employed. Demand for graduates is steady throughout the year and averages 100 per year. The cost per class for the firm is $4,100, regardless of class size.

   a. What is the optimal class size?
   b. How often should the course be offered?

9. A jewelry firm buys semiprecious stones that it uses in making bracelets and rings. The supplier quotes a price of $8 per stone for quantities of 600 stones or more, $9 per stone for orders of 400 to 599 stones, and $10 per stone for lesser quantities. The jewelry firm operates 200 days per year. Usage rate is 25 stones per day, and ordering costs are $48.

   a. If carrying costs are $1 per year for each stone, find the order quantity that will minimize total annual cost.
   b. If annual carrying costs are 17 percent of unit cost, what will the optimal order size be?
   c. If lead time is six working days, at what point should the company reorder?

10. A mail-order house buys gummed labels in boxes of 8,000. The firm uses 18,000 boxes a year. Carrying costs are 20 cents per box a year, and ordering costs are $32. The following price schedule applies. Determine:

   a. The optimal order quantity.
   b. The number of orders per year.

Number of boxes	Price per box
1,000 to 1,999	$1.25
2,000 to 4,999	1.20
5,000 to 9,999	1.18
10,000 or more	1.15

11. A charitable organization assembles and sells novelty items. Annual demand is 80,000 units, ordering and preparation costs run $60, and carrying costs are 30 percent of unit price per year. For quantities of 5,000 units or fewer, the cost is 12 cents per unit; for 5,001 to 9,800 units, the cost is 10 cents per unit; and for larger orders, the cost is 8 cents per unit. Find the optimal order size.

12. A manufacturer of baby strollers purchases the seat portion of the stroller from a supplier who lists these prices: less than 1,000 seats, $5 each; 1,000 to 3,999, $4.95 each; 4,000 to 5,999, $4.90 each; and 6,000 or more, $4.85 each. Ordering costs are $50, annual carrying costs are 20 percent of purchase cost, and annual usage is 4,900 seats. Determine an order quantity that will minimize total cost.

13. A newspaper publisher uses roughly 800 feet of baling wire each day to secure bundles of newspapers while they are being distributed to carriers. The paper is published Monday through Saturday. Ordering lead time is six workdays. What is the appropriate reorder point quantity, given that the company desires a service level of 95 percent, assuming that stock-out risk for various levels of safety stock are as follows: 1,500 feet, 0.10; 1,800 feet, 0.05; 2,100 feet, 0.02; and 2,400 feet, 0.01.

14. Demand for walnut fudge ice cream at the Sweet Cream Dairy can be approximated by a normal distribution with a mean of 21 gallons per week and a standard deviation of 3.5 gallons per week. The new manager desires a service level of 90 percent. Lead time is two days, and the dairy is open seven days a week. (*Hint:* Work in terms of weeks.)

    a. If an ROP model is used, what ROP would be consistent with the desired service level?

    b. If a fixed-interval model is used instead of an ROP model, what order size would be needed for the 90 percent service level with an order interval of 10 days and a supply of 2 gallons on hand at the order time?

15. A large accounting firm uses five 100-sheet boxes of letterhead stationery a week. Experience suggests that usage can be well approximated by a normal distribution with a mean of five boxes per week and a standard deviation of one-half box per week. Two weeks are required to fill an order for letterhead stationery. Ordering cost is $2, and annual holding cost is 20 cents per box.

    a. Determine the economic order quantity for minimizing ordering and carrying costs, assuming a 52-week year.

    b. If the firm reorders when the supply on hand is 12 boxes, compute the risk of a stock-out.

    c. If, instead of an ROP, a fixed interval of seven weeks is used for reordering, what risk of stock-out does the firm incur if it orders 36 boxes when the amount on hand is 12 boxes?

16. A large automotive repair shop uses an average of 40 repair kits per week. Usage can be described by a normal distribution that has a mean of 40 and a standard deviation of 6. Lead time for ordering the repair kits is also normal, with a mean of seven days and a standard deviation of one-half day. A stock-out risk of 1 percent is being used. The workweek is seven days.

    a. What ROP is appropriate?

    b. How much could safety stock be cut if average lead time could be reduced to one day? How much additional reduction would a risk of 5 percent yield?

c. What are some possible ways that lead time might be reduced?

17. The manager of a furniture manufacturing plant hopes to achieve a better allocation of inventory control efforts by adopting an A–B–C approach to inventory control. Given the monthly usages listed in the following table, classify the items in A, B, and C categories according to dollar usage.

Item	Usage	Unit cost
4021	50	$1,400
9402	300	12
4066	40	700
6500	150	20
9280	10	1,020
4050	80	140
6850	2,000	15
3010	400	20
4400	7,000	5

18. Ned's Natural Foods sells unshelled peanuts by the pound. Historically, Ned has observed that daily demand is normally distributed with a mean of 80 pounds and a standard deviation of 10 pounds. Lead time also appears normally distributed with a mean of eight days and a standard deviation of one day. What ROP would provide a 90 percent lead time service level? What is the expected number of units (pounds) short per cycle? (*Hint:* Use Formula 10–14 for σ_{dLT}.)

19. Regional Supermarket is open 360 days per year. Daily use of cash register tape averages 10 rolls. Usage appears normally distributed with a standard deviation of 2 rolls per day. Ordering tape involves a cost of $1, and carrying costs are 40 cents per roll a year. Lead time is three days.

a. What is the EOQ?

b. What ROP will provide a lead time service level of 96 percent?

c. What is the expected number of units short per cycle with 96 percent? Per year?

d. What is the annual service level?

20. An automatic machine produces rivets from bar stock at a rate of 1,200 per day, 250 days a year. The order size is 2,000 feet. Fifteen rivets can be cut from one foot of stock. Delivery lead time on stock is known to be normally distributed with a mean of nine days and a standard deviation of two days.

a. How much bar stock is used per day?

b. How much safety stock is needed for a stock-out risk of 3 percent for each order cycle? (Use $\sigma_{dLT} = d\sigma_{LT}$.)

c. What is the annual service level?

d. By how much could safety stock be reduced if average lead time could be reduced by five days and lead time variability could be cut in half?

21. A service station uses 1,200 cases of oil a year. Ordering cost is $40, and annual carrying cost is $3 per case. The station owner has specified an *annual* service level of 98 percent. What ROP is appropriate if lead time demand is normally distributed with a mean of 80 cases and a standard deviation of 4 cases? What is the lead time service level?

22. A drugstore uses fixed order cycles for many of the items it stocks. The manager likes a service level of .98. Determine the order size that will be consistent with this service level for these items for an order interval of 14 days and a lead time of 2 days:

Item	Average daily demand	Standard deviation	Quantity on hand
K033	60	5	420
K144	50	4	375
L700	8	2	160

23. Demand for jelly doughnuts on Saturday mornings at Don's Doughnut Shoppe is shown below. Determine the optimal number of doughnuts, in dozens, to stock if labor, materials, and overhead are estimated to be 80 cents per dozen, doughnuts are sold for $1.20 per dozen, and leftover

doughnuts at the end of each day are sold the next day for one-half off. What is the resulting service level?

Demand (dozens)	Relative frequency
19	.01
20	.05
21	.12
22	.18
23	.13
24	.14
25	.10
26	.11
27	.10
28	.04
29	.02

24. A public utility intends to buy a turbine as part of an expansion plan and must now decide on the number of square parts to order. One part, no. X135, can be purchased for $100 each. Carrying and disposal costs are estimated to be 145 percent of the purchase price over the life of the turbine. A stock-out would cost roughly $88,000 due to downtime, ordering, and "special purchase" factors. Historical records based on the performance of similar equipment operating under similar conditions suggests that demand for spares will tend to approximate a Poisson distribution with a mean of 3.2 parts for the useful life of the turbine. Find the optimal number of spares to order.

25. Skinner's Fish Market buys fresh Boston bluefish daily for $1.40 per pound and sells it for $1.90 per pound. At the end of each business day, any remaining bluefish is sold to a producer of cat food for 80 cents per pound. Daily demand can be approximated by a normal distribution with a mean of 80 pounds and a standard deviation of 10 pounds. Determine the optimal stocking level.

26. A small grocery store sells fresh produce, which it obtains from a local farmer. During the strawberry season, demand for

fresh strawberries can be reasonably approximated using a normal distribution with a mean of 40 quarts per day and a standard deviation of 6 quarts per day. Excess costs run 35 cents per quart. The grocer orders 49 quarts per day. What is the inplied cost of shortage per quart? Why might this be a reasonable figure?

27. Demand for devil's food whipped-cream layer cakes at a local pastry shop can be approximated using a Poisson distribution with a mean of six per day. The manager estimates it costs $3 to prepare each cake. Fresh cakes sell for $4, and day-old cakes sell for $3 each. What stocking level is appropriate if one half of the day-old cakes are sold and the rest thrown out?

28. Burger Prince buys top-grade ground beef for $1.00 per pound. A large sign over the entranceway guarantees that the meat is fresh daily. Any leftover meat is sold to the local high school cafeteria for 80 cents per pound. Four hamburgers can be prepared from each pound of meat. Burgers sell for 60 cents each. Labor, overhead, meat, buns, and condiments cost 50 cents per burger. Demand is normally distributed with a mean of 400 pounds per day and a standard deviation of 50 pounds per day. What daily order quantity is optimal? (*Hint:* Shortage cost must be in dollars per pound.)

29. Demand for rug cleaning machines at Clyde's U-Rent-It is shown below. Machines are rented by the day only. Profit on the rug cleaners is $10 per day. Clyde has four rug-cleaning machines.

Demand	Frequency
0	.30
1	.20
2	.20
3	.15
4	.10
5	.05
	1.00

a. Assuming that Clyde's stocking decison is optimal, what is the implied range of excess cost per machine?

b. Your answer from part *a* has been presented to Clyde, and he protests that the amount is *too low*. Would this suggest an increase or a decrease in the number of rug machines he stocks? Explain.

c. Suppose now that the $10 mentioned as profit is instead the excess cost per day for each machine and that the shortage cost is unknown. Based on the assumption that four machines is optimal, what is the implied range of shortage cost per machine?

30. Refer to Solved Problem 9. For what range of shortage cost would carrying no spare parts be the best strategy?

SELECTED BIBLIOGRAPHY

Buffa, Elwood, and James S. Dryer. *Essentials of Management Science/Operations Research*. New York: John Wiley & Sons, 1978.

Chase, Richard B., and Nicholas J. Aquilano. *Production and Operations Management*. 4th ed. Homewood, Ill.: Richard D. Irwin, 1985.

Fogarty, Donald W., and Thomas R. Hoffmann. *Production and Inventory Management*. Cincinnati, Ohio: South-Western Publishing Co., 1983.

Love, Stephen F. *Inventory Control*. New York: McGraw-Hill, 1979.

Peterson, R., and E. A. Silver. *Decision Systems for Inventory Management and Production Planning*. 2d ed. New York: John Wiley & Sons, 1984.

Tersine, Richard J. *Principles of Inventory and Materials Management*. 3d ed. New York: Elsevier North-Holland, 1987.

Vollman, Thomas E.; William L. Berry; and D. Clay Whybark. *Manufacturing Planning and Control Systems*. 2d ed. Homewood, Ill.: Richard D. Irwin, 1988.

CASE

THE DEWEY STAPLER COMPANY

From: Martin Crane, Sales Manager

To: Allen Grace, President

Dear Allen:

Well, it has been a very disappointing year. We've missed our quota by 10 or 15 percent in virtually every district and this is the year I had such high hopes for. When we decided to open up four branch warehouses rather than shipping from our central location only, I was convinced that this would give us better customer service. The last of the warehouses was opened up last May, just before our peak summer season, so perhaps some of the problem is just not having enough experience with branch warehouses. But I think it goes deeper than that.

Our warehouse people are authorized to keep a one-month supply of inventory on hand. While I know you feel strongly that the substantial increase in inventory we had during the year was due to the warehouse program, I can't see why it requires any more inventory to a keep a month's supply on hand in four branches and a main location than it did to keep a month's supply on hand back at the main location. A month's supply is a month's supply no matter how you look at it.

To my way of thinking, the real problem is customer service. Our salespeople are demoralized. They simply can't get the stock shipped out of the warehouses because the warehouses don't have it on hand. Forty percent of our customer orders, of course, are still being shipped out of the main location. Our warehouse people tell me that these customer orders get preference and their stock replenishment orders are pushed aside.

Allen, we've got to solve this problem. There's no sense in having a sales force if we can't have the stock to back them up. I propose the plant location be required to ship warehouse stocking orders just the same as they ship customer orders. They should treat the warehouses like a customer. In fact, the warehouses are their *biggest* customer and should be serviced accordingly. I propose also that the one-month inventory guideline be removed. Let the warehouse people stock whatever they think they need to support the salesforce. I would volunteer to have my district managers sit with the branch warehouse people to give them some idea of what they should really be ordering.

Allen, this branch warehouse program has been as big a disappointment to me as it has to you. I know you're concerned about the fact that inventories have been going up, but I frankly attribute that to poor management back at the plant. And, quite honestly, Allen, I don't think that people at the plant realize our problems out here in the field and are giving us the kind of support we need. Without it, we have no chance of making the sales quota. Instead of selling, I'm spending most of my time playing chaplain to a bunch of demoralized salespeople.

Sincerely,

Martin

From: Robert Ellers, Inventory Manager

To: Allen Grace, President

Dear Mr. Grace:

You asked me what my plans were to respond to Martin Crane's letter of January 5. I don't know where to start. This warehouse program has really torn us apart.

We thought that when branch warehouses were added, we would simply have to split some of the stock we had among the warehouses. Instead, we've had to build up the inventory very substantially. We don't get any plans from the warehouses at all. All we see is orders. We have no idea what their inventory position is when we get the orders and we only get them two to three weeks before we have to ship them. Then comes the moment of truth. We have a shortage on a particular item. Here's a customer order and also a warehouse stock replenishment order. Does the warehouse really need it? We know the customer does. In practice, I must admit we wind up waiting until the warehouse screams

although we know we may very well be hurting customer service at the branch warehouses.

Mr. Grace, I'm more worried about *this* year than I was about last. Some of the warehouses that had been on the air since year before last showed a disturbing tendency to keep their inventories low during the off-season so that they could boast about their inventory turnover. Then during the peak season, they expect me to turn the faucet on back at the plant. We don't have enough storage space at the plant to build up the inventory required during the off-season in order to keep people working at a steady rate. We need this inventory buildup in order to give good service during the peak season. I've been told repeatedly by plant management that we must keep people working at a steady rate.

All this squabbling about inventory levels prompts me to suggest an approach. We normally would manufacture in a lot size that would be equivalent to about a three-month's supply. When we do that, why don't I just ship a three-month's supply out to each branch warehouse, and then we won't have to bother worrying about them until the next lot is manufactured. Then they can't complain that they're not getting their fair share.

One of the disturbing elements that you may not have heard about is that Frank, our traffic manager, has now suggested that we ship to the West Coast warehouses by sea. This would mean going through the Panama Canal and would substantially increase our lead time and reduce our flexibility. He says, "Flexibility is like motherhood. I'm talking a $50,000 savings in transportation costs, and if you guys have to work a little harder to make that happen, so be it."

Mr. Grace, I really am almost at my wit's end. Perhaps one of the things we ought to consider would be a computer system for tying all of the warehouses together so we could cover a shortage at one warehouse by shipping from another warehouse. Last September, I checked on items that were out of stock in the Atlanta warehouse and I found that virtually everyone of them was in adequate supply throughout the system; i.e., we either had them

in Dallas, Los Angeles, Chicago, or back at the main plant. This type of computer system would be expensive, but perhaps this is the answer to our service problem.

Sincerely,

Robert Ellers

Question

The Dewey Stapler Company has some very serious problems. There are a number of misconceptions about inventory management in the company that need to be corrected. Take the position of a consultant being called in by Allen Grace, the president. You have enough information in these letters to give him some very helpful recommendations. Write a memo outlining your thoughts. Include a discussion of what will happen to service levels if total inventory investment remains constant.

Source: Reprinted by permission from Oliver W. Wright, *Production and Inventory Management in the Computer Age* (Boston: Cahners, 1974).

MATERIALS MANAGEMENT AND PURCHASING

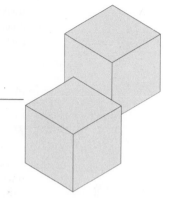

LEARNING OBJECTIVES

After completing this supplement, you should be able to:

1. Define *materials* and briefly describe the materials management function.
2. Describe how purchasing interfaces with other areas of the organization and with suppliers.
3. Outline the objectives of purchasing.
4. Describe the purchasing cycle, especially determination of price and sources of supply.
5. Discuss the issue of centralized purchasing versus decentralized purchasing.
6. Describe and discuss value analysis.
7. Discuss the importance of good vendor relations, and compare suppliers as partners versus suppliers as adversaries.
8. Discuss the logistics aspects of materials management.

SUPPLEMENT OUTLINE

Materials are physical items used during the production process. They include not only the parts and raw materials that become the finished goods, but also the physical items needed to support the production process, such as fuels, lubricants, tools, machinery, forms, and anything else that is purchased, moved, stored, or shipped. **Materials management** is concerned with purchasing, storage, and movement of materials during production and with distribution of finished goods. Figure 10S–1 provides an overview of the range of materials management.

The subject matter in this supplement is organized into two major topics: purchasing and logistics.

PURCHASING

Purchasing is responsible for obtaining material inputs for the operating system. This supplement describes the purchasing function as it operates in most organizations. It begins by discussing how purchasing interacts with other functional areas of the organization and with outside suppliers. Determination of sources of supply and price are examined along with the concept of value analysis.

Purchasing Interfaces

As a service function, purchasing has interfaces with a number of other functional areas, as well as with outside suppliers. Purchasing is the connecting link between the organization and its suppliers. In this capacity, it exchanges information with suppliers and functional areas. The interactions between purchasing and these other areas are briefly summarized in the following paragraphs.

Operating units constitute the main source of requests for purchased materials, and close cooperation between these units and the purchasing people is

FIGURE 10S–1

Overview of materials management

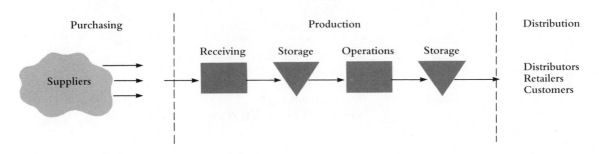

mandatory if quality, quantity, and delivery goals are to be met. Changes in specifications, cancellations, or changes in quantity or delivery times must be communicated immediately in order for purchasing to be effective.

The purchasing department may require the assistance of the *legal* department in contract negotiations as well as in drawing up bid specifications for nonroutine purchases. In addition, the legal department may be called on to help interpret legislation on pricing, product liability, and contracts with suppliers.

Accounting is responsible for handling payments to suppliers and must be notified promptly when goods are received in order to take advantage of possible discounts. In many firms, *data processing* is handled by the accounting department, which involves keeping inventory records, checking invoices, and monitoring vendor performance.

Design and *engineering* usually prepares material specifications, which must be communicated to purchasing. Because of its contacts with suppliers, purchasing is often in a position to pass information about new products and materials improvements on to design personnel. Also, design and purchasing people may work closely in determining if changes in specifications, design, or

FIGURE 10S–2

Purchasing interfaces with functional areas of the firm and with suppliers

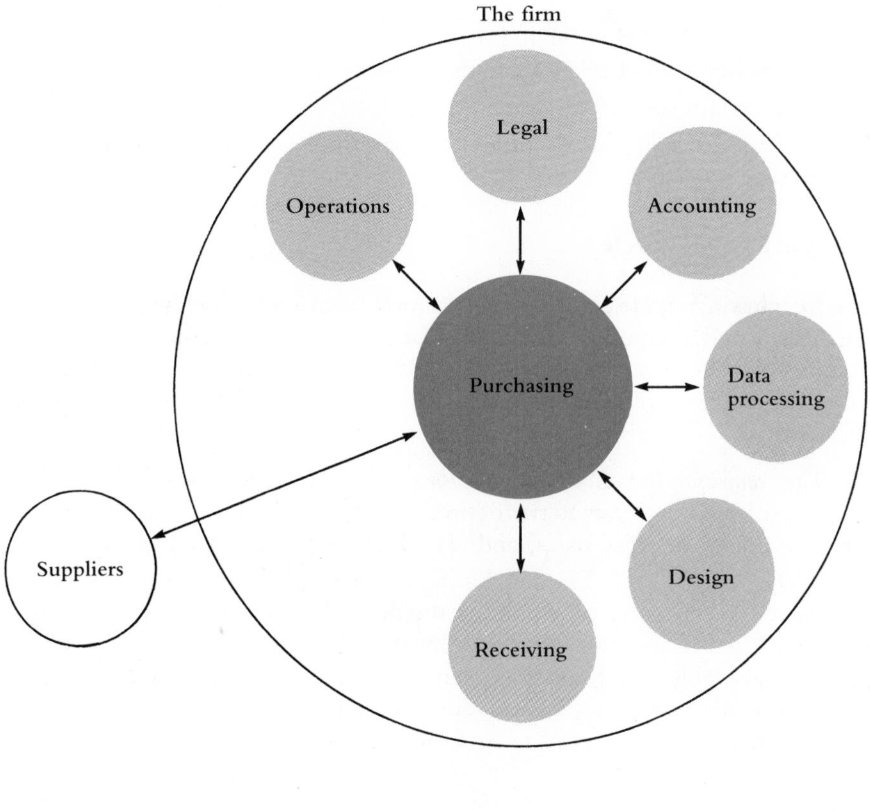

materials can reduce the cost of purchased items (see the following section on value analysis).

Receiving checks incoming shipments of purchased items to determine if quality, quantity, and timing objectives have been met and moves the goods to temporary storage. Purchasing must be notified when shipments are late; accounting must be notified when shipments are received so that payments can be made; and both purchasing and accounting must be apprised of current information on continuing vendor evaluation.

Suppliers or vendors work closely with purchasing to learn what materials will be purchased and what kinds of specifications will be required in terms of quality, quantity, and deliveries. Purchasing must rate vendors on cost, reliability, and so on (see the following section on vendor analysis). Good supplier relations can pay dividends on rush orders and changes, and vendors provide a good source of information on product and material improvements.

Figure 10S–2 summarizes the purchasing interfaces.

Purchasing Objectives

The basic objectives of purchasing can be summarized as follows:

1. To determine the quality and quantity needed and when an item is needed.
2. To obtain the best possible price.
3. To maintain good relations with suppliers.
4. To maintain sources of supply.
5. To be knowledgeable on prices, new products, and new services that become available.

The Purchasing Cycle

The **purchasing cycle** begins with a request from within the organization to purchase material, equipment, supplies, or other items from outside the organization, and the cycle ends when the purchasing department is notified that a shipment has been received in satisfactory condition. The main steps in the cycle are:

1. *The requisition is received by purchasing.* The requisition includes (*a*) a description of the item or material desired, (*b*) the quantity and quality necessary, (*c*) desired delivery dates, and (*d*) who is requesting the purchase.

2. *A supplier is selected.* The purchasing department must identify suppliers who have the capability of supplying the desired goods. If no suppliers are currently listed in the files, new ones must be sought. If one or more suppliers are available, vendor ratings may be referred to in choosing among vendors, or perhaps rating information can be relayed to the vendor with the thought of upgrading future performance.

3. *The order is placed with a vendor.* If the order involves a large expenditure, particularly for a one-time purchase, say, of equipment, vendors will usually be asked to bid on the job, and operating and design personnel may be asked to assist in negotiations with a vendor. Large-volume, continuous-usage items may be covered by blanket purchase orders, which often involve annual negotiation of prices with deliveries subject to request throughout the year. Moderate-volume items may also have blanket purchase orders, or they may be handled on an individual basis. Small purchases may be handled directly between the operating unit requesting the item and the supplier, although care must be taken so that some control is exercised over those purchases. Otherwise, they tend to get out of hand.

4. *Monitoring orders.* Routine follow-up on orders, particularly large orders or those with lengthy delivery schedules, allows the purchasing department to foresee delays and relay this information to the appropriate operating units. Likewise, changes in quantity and delivery needs of the operating units must be relayed to suppliers so that they can have time to adjust their plans.

5. *Receiving orders.* Incoming shipments from vendors must be checked for quality and quantity. Purchasing must be notified, as must accounting and the operating unit that requested the goods. If the goods are not received in satisfactory condition, they may have to be returned to the supplier for credit or replacement or subjected to detailed inspection. Again, purchasing, accounting, and the operating unit must be notified. In either case, vendor evaluation records must be updated.

Value Analysis

Value analysis involves an examination of the *function* of purchased parts and materials in an effort to reduce the cost and/or improve the performance of those items. Typical questions that would be asked as part of the analysis include: Could a cheaper part or material be used? Is the function necessary? Can the function of two or more parts or components be performed by a single part for a lower cost? Can a part be simplified? Could product specifications be relaxed, and would this result in a lower price? Could standard parts be substituted for nonstandard parts? Table 10S–1 provides a checklist of questions that can be used to guide a value analysis.

Naturally, such an investigation cannot be performed each time materials are ordered. However, value analysis should be conducted periodically on large dollar-volume items because of the potential savings.

Although purchasing does not ordinarily have the authority to implement changes on the basis of a value analysis, it can make suggestions to operating units, to designers, and to suppliers, which may lead to improved performance of purchased goods and/or reduce the cost of those goods. Purchasing people can offer a different perspective to the analysis, and purchasing people, because of their association with suppliers, possess information not known to others

TABLE 10S–1

Value analysis overview	1. Select an item that has a high annual dollar-volume. This can be a purchased part or material or a service.
	2. Identify the function of the item.
	3. Obtain answers to questions such as these:

       a. Is the item necessary; that is, does it add value, or can it be eliminated?

       b. Are there alternative sources for the item?

       c. Can it be provided internally?

       d. What are the advantages of the present arrangement?

       e. What are the disadvantages of the present arrangement?

       f. Could another part, material, or service be used instead?

       g. Can specifications be made less stringent to save cost or time?

       h. Can two or more items be combined?

       i. Can more (less) processing be done on the item to save on cost?

       j. Do suppliers/providers have suggestions for improvements?

       k. Do employees have suggestions for improvements?

       l. Can packaging be improved or made less costly?

4. Analyze the answers obtained plus answers to other questions that arise, and make recommendations.

---

within the organization. If a fair amount of technical knowledge is required to review a part or product, a team can be formed with representatives from design and/or operations to work with purchasing in conducting the analysis.

Make or Buy

There are times when an organization must consider whether to make or buy a certain item. There are a number of ways in which this issue can arise, such as in response to unreliable suppliers, idle capacity of an organization, the desire to achieve greater control over the production process, and increasing costs.

Generally, the factors that are taken into account in deciding whether to make or buy are the following:

1. Cost to make versus cost to buy, including startup costs.
2. Stability of demand and possible seasonality.
3. Quality available from suppliers compared to a firm's own quality capabilities.
4. The desire to maintain close control over operations.
5. Idle capacity available within the organization.
6. Lead times for making versus buying.
7. Who has patents, expertise, and so on, if these are factors.
8. Stability of technology; if a technology is changing, it may be better to use a supplier.
9. The degree to which the necessary operations are consistent with, or in conflict with, current operations.

Evaluating Sources of Supply (Vendor Analysis)

In many respects, choosing a vendor involves taking into account many of the same factors associated with making a major purchase (e.g., a car or a stereo system). A company considers price, quality, the supplier's reputation, past experience with the supplier, and service after the sale. The main difference is that a company, because of the quantities it orders and because of production requirements, often provides suppliers with detailed specifications of the materials or parts it wants instead of buying items off the shelf, although even large companies buy standard items that way.

The main factors firms look at when they select vendors are:

1. *Price.* This is the most obvious factor, along with any discounts offered, although it may not be the most important factor.

2. *Quality.* A company may be willing to spend more money to obtain desired-quality parts.

3. *Services.* Special services can sometimes be very important in choosing a supplier. Replacement of defective items, instruction in the use of equipment, repair of equipment, and similar services can be instrumental in selecting one supplier over another.

"The instructions are pasted on the back."

Reprinted from *The Wall Street Journal;* permission Cartoon Features Syndicate.

4. *Location.* Location of a supplier can have impact on shipping time, transportation costs, and response time for rush orders or emergency service. Local buying can create goodwill in the community by helping the local economy.

5. *Inventory policy of supplier.* If a supplier maintains an inventory policy of keeping spare parts on hand, this could be helpful in case of an emergency breakdown of equipment.

6. *Flexibility*. The willingness and ability of a supplier to respond to changes in demand, as well as a willingness to accept design changes, could be important considerations.

Determining Prices

There are essentially three ways that prices are determined: published price lists, competitive bidding, and negotiation.

In many instances, organizations buy products and services that have fixed or *predetermined prices*. This is generally the case for standard items that are bought infrequently and/or in small quantities.

For large orders of standard products and services, *competitive bidding* is often used. This involves sending requests for bids to potential suppliers, which ask vendors to quote a price for a specified quantity and quality of items or for a specified service to be performed. Government purchases of standard goods or services are usually made using competitive bidding.

Negotiated purchasing is used for special purchasing situations, such as cases where specifications are vague, when one or a few customized products or services are involved (e.g., space exploration), and when few potential sources exist. There are several myths concerning negotiated purchasing that should be recognized:

1. Negotiation is a win–lose confrontation.
2. The main goal is to obtain the lowest possible price.
3. Each negotiation is an isolated transaction.[1]

Realistically speaking, no one likes to be taken advantage of. Futhermore, contractors and suppliers need a reasonable profit to survive. Therefore, a take-it-or-leave-it approach or one that capitalizes extensively on the weaknesses of the other party will serve no useful purpose and may have detrimental effects that surface at a later time. The most reasonable approach is one of give and take, with each side giving and receiving some concessions.

Centralized versus Decentralized Purchasing

Centralized purchasing means that purchasing is handled by one special department. **Decentralized purchasing** means that individual departments or separate locations handle their own purchasing requirements.

Centralized purchasing may be able to obtain lower prices than decentralized units if the higher volume created by combining orders enables it to take advantage of quantity discounts offered on large orders; it may also be able to obtain better service and closer attention from suppliers. In addition,

---

[1] Richard J. Tersine, *Production/Operations Management: Concepts, Structure, and Analysis,* 2nd ed. (New York: Elsevier North-Holland Publishing, 1985), p. 598.

centralized purchasing often enables companies to assign certain categories of items to specialists, who tend to be more efficient because they are able to concentrate their efforts on relatively few items instead of spreading themselves across many items.

Decentralized purchasing has the advantage of being aware of differing "local" needs and being better able to respond to those needs. Decentralized purchasing usually can offer quicker response than centralized purchasing. In the case of widely scattered locations, decentralized purchasing may be able to save on transportation costs by buying locally, which has the added attraction of creating goodwill in the community.

Some organizations manage to take advantage of both centralization and decentralization by permitting individual units to handle certain items while centralizing purchases of other items. For example, small orders and rush orders may be handled locally, or by departments, and centralized purchases would be used for high-volume, high-value items for which discounts would be applicable or for which specialists could provide better service than local buyers or departments could.

Vendor Relations

American firms are becoming increasingly aware of the importance of building good relations with their vendors. In the past, too many firms regarded their vendors as adversaries and dealt with them on that basis. One lesson many have learned from the Japanese is that there can be numerous benefits from having good vendor relations. Among them are vendor flexibility in terms of accepting changes in delivery schedules, quality, and quantities. Moreover, vendors can often help in identifying problems and offer suggestions for solving them. Thus, simply choosing and switching vendors on the basis of price is a very shortsighted approach for handling an ongoing need.

Many Japanese firms rely on one or a few vendors to handle their needs. In contrast, many U.S. firms deal with numerous vendors. Perhaps they want to remain flexible, and possibly there are some advantages in playing one off against the others. However, it would appear that, in many instances, firms have too many vendors to deal with, although reducing that number to one or a few, as the Japanese have done, may be too extreme. A more realistic approach would be to move in the direction of a reduction in the number of vendors used.

Keeping good relations with suppliers is being increasingly recognized as an important factor in maintaining a competitive edge. Many companies are adopting a view of suppliers as partners rather than as adversaries. This viewpoint stresses a stable relationship with relatively few reliable suppliers who can provide high-quality supplies, maintain precise delivery schedules, and remain flexible relative to changes in productive specifications as well as delivery schedules. A comparison of these two contrasting views of suppliers is provided in Table 10S–2.

TABLE 10S–2

The supplier as partner versus adversary

Aspect	Partner	Adversary
Number of suppliers	One or a few	Many; play one off against the others
Length of relationship	Long-term	May be brief
Low price	Moderately important	Major consideration
Reliability	High	May not be high
Openness	High	Low
Quality	Insured at the source; vendor-certified	Buyer inspects; may be unreliable
Volume of business	High	May be low due to many suppliers
Location	Nearness may be stressed for short lead times and service	Widely dispersed
Flexibility	Relatively high	Relatively low

LOGISTICS

Logistics refers to the movement of materials within a production facility and to incoming and outgoing shipments of goods and materials.

Movement within a Facility

Figure 10S–3 provides an overview of the many instances that materials must be moved within a production facility, beginning with removing materials from incoming vehicles and placing them in a receiving area. There are numerous instances of materials movement:

1. From incoming vehicles to receiving.
2. From receiving to storage.
3. From storage to the point where they will be used (e.g., work center, office, maintenance).
4. From one work center to the next, or to temporary storage.
5. From the last operation to final storage.
6. From storage to packaging/shipping.
7. From shipping to outgoing vehicles.

Note that in some instances, the goods being moved are supplies; in other instances, the goods will be actual products or partially completed products; and in still other instances, the goods will be raw materials or purchased parts.

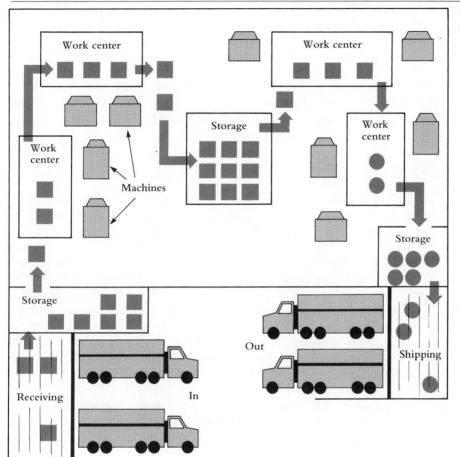

Overview of materials movement

Movement of materials must be coordinated so that they arrive at the appropriate destinations at appropriate times. Care must be taken so that items are not lost, stolen, or damaged during movement.

Incoming and Outgoing Shipments

Overseeing the shipment of incoming and outgoing goods comes under the heading of **traffic management.** This function handles schedules and decisions on shipping methods and times, taking into account costs of various alternatives, government regulations, the needs of the organization relative to quantities and timing, and such external factors as potential shipping delays or disruptions (e.g., highway construction, truckers' strikes).

Computer tracking of shipments often helps to maintain knowledge of the current status of shipments as well as provide other up-to-date information on costs and schedules.

Distribution

Distribution is the shipping of goods from the company through a distribution system to warehouses, retail customers, or final customers. Often, distribution is managed by the *marketing* function rather than the production function.

SUMMARY

Materials management is the management of materials over the entire range of the production process, beginning with purchasing and ending with distribution. It covers movement of materials within the organization as well as storage.

Purchasing is responsible for obtaining material inputs for the organization. This includes the actual purchasing of materials as well as vendor selection and conducting value analyses on purchased items. The basic design question in purchasing is whether to centralize or decentralize it. Centralization provides for closer control and may produce certain economies, whereas decentralized purchasing tends to produce quick response and may better serve local needs. Value analysis may be performed periodically to assure that purchased item cost–benefit is being optimized. Vendors are evaluated for cost, service after the sale, reliability, and quality.

Logistics involves movement of materials within the organization, incoming and outgoing shipments, and distribution.

KEY TERMS

centralized purchasing, 572
decentralized purchasing, 572
distribution, 576
logistics, 574
materials, 566

materials management, 566
purchasing cycle, 568
traffic management, 575
value analysis, 569
vendor analysis, 571

DISCUSSION AND REVIEW QUESTIONS

1. Briefly describe the materials management function.

2. Briefly describe how purchasing interacts with other functional areas of the firm such as accounting and design.

3. Describe value analysis. Why is purchasing a good location for this task?

4. Should the supplier with the highest quality–lowest price combination always be selected over others? Explain.

5. Discuss the issue of centralization versus decentralization as it applies to the purchasing function.

6. Discuss the determination of prices.

7. Discuss the importance of good vendor re-

lations. Compare the vendor-as-partner versus vendor-as-adversary viewpoints.

8. Describe the logistics aspects of materials management.

SELECTED BIBLIOGRAPHY

Ammer, Dean S. *Material Management and Purchasing*. Homewood, Ill.: Richard D. Irwin, 1980.

Hall, Robert. *Zero Inventories*. Homewood, Ill.: Dow Jones-Irwin, 1983.

Heinritz, Stuart F.; Paul V. Farrell; and Clifton Smith. *Purchasing: Principles and Applications*. Englewood Cliffs, N.J.: Prentice-Hall, 1986.

Kraljic, Peter. "Purchasing Must Become Supply Management." *Harvard Business Review*, September–October 1983, p. 109.

Leenders, M. R., et al. *Purchasing and Material Management*. 8th ed. Homewood, Ill.: Richard D. Irwin, 1985.

Riggs, James L. *Production Systems: Planning, Analysis and Control*. 3rd ed. Santa Barbara, Calif.: Wiley/Hamilton, 1981.

Tersine, Richard J. *Materials Management and Inventory Systems*. 3rd ed. New York: Elsevier North-Holland Publishing, 1987.

READING

SHAPING UP YOUR SUPPLIERS
Joel Dreyfuss

Small manufacturing companies are in crisis. Their main customers, the big boys of U.S. industry, have been humbled by global competition and are seeking their salvation in higher standards of quality and productivity. The big companies can't find redemption alone. So, like passionate converts, they are spreading the gospel of efficiency to their suppliers. Suddenly, small companies whose greatest concern was once to simply get the product out the door are under pressure to adopt the latest technologies, use quality control methods, *and* slash prices.

The suppliers often do not understand the new processes and management techniques their customers want them to embrace. Says L. Joseph Thomas, professor of manufacturing at Cornell's Johnson School of Management: "Small companies are less likely than large companies to have made improvements for productivity. They're concerned about

meeting the payroll and not about the longer term." Besides, if the suppliers do manage to come up to their customers' idea of quality, they expect to be paid more, not less. They're not the world's best experts in management.

Suppliers had better learn fast. Most large U.S. manufacturers are reducing their number of vendors in order to control quality. Says Charles E. Lucier, a Booz Allen & Hamilton vice president: "Most want two or three suppliers instead of ten or 12." They will give preference to those close to home. Russell W. Meyer, the chairman of Cessna Aircraft, the small-plane manufacturer headquartered in Wichita, says: "We spend a lot of time with subcontractors. It's a lot easier to work with someone in Wichita than with someone in Los Angeles."

To make the cut, suppliers will have to go through a rigorous survival drill. Buyers routinely send inspection teams to rate a small company's plants. They want to see Japanese-style just-in-time manufacturing and delivery techniques, statistical process controls that identify causes of defects, and the ability to handle data electronically.

Some small companies resist, either from ignorance or from fear. Says Joseph A. Bockerstette, a manufacturing specialist at consultant Coopers & Lybrand: "Many suppliers feel just-in-time is a way for FORTUNE 500 companies to dump on them." When a large company begins asking for three deliveries a day, a small supplier may end up stockpiling the goods the customer wants. Craig Skevington, president of Factory Automation & Computer Technologies, a consulting firm near Albany, New York, that specializes in manufacturing, says, "Just-in-time becomes just-in-case."

The stringent requirements could bring a wave of restructuring among little manufacturers as wrenching as the one the large companies went through. Because the small fry are great sources of innovation and new jobs, Skevington and others worry that a weakened small manufacturing sector could chill entrepreneurship and hurt the ability of the U.S. to generate new products.

Help is on the way. New organizations, sponsored by government and private companies, are coming to the rescue of manufacturing's embattled little guys. Among them:

■ The Cleveland Advanced Manufacturing Program, one of nine technology research centers financed by the state of Ohio's $250 million Thomas Edison Program, provides a free as-

sessment of a manufacturer's production line and recommends improvements.

■ In New York and Michigan, state-employed manufacturing experts roam industrial areas, offering small companies that can't afford consultants new ways to improve their manufacturing processes.

■ On Massachusett's Route 128, Coopers & Lybrand has started a manufacturing center to help local outfits solve their production-line problems.

■ In Cleveland, Troy, New York, and Columbia, South Carolina, regional manufacturing technology centers have sprung up. Funded through the National Institute of Standards and Technology (formerly the Bureau of Standards), they aim to transfer advanced manufacturing technology developed in government labs to smaller companies.

■ In Pennsylvania, government and corporations are raising $60 million for nine Industrial Resource Centers that help the state's small manufacturers by providing consultants on technology, management, and marketing.

■ In Wichita, the Center for Technology Application—financed by local companies, a regional economic development agency, and Wichita State University—offers training classes for computer machine tool operators, provides engineering advice, and promotes closer ties between large companies and small companies.

Source: Reprinted from Joel Dreyfuss, "Shaping Up Your Suppliers," *Fortune*, April 10, 1989, pp. 116–17. © 1989 The Time Inc. Magazine Company. All rights reserved.

11

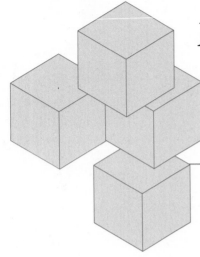

Material Requirements Planning

LEARNING OBJECTIVES

After completing this chapter, you should be able to:

1. Describe the conditions under which MRP is most appropriate.
2. Describe the inputs, outputs, and nature of MRP processing.
3. Constrast regenerative and net-change updating.
4. Explain how requirements in a master schedule are translated into material requirements for lower-level items.
5. Discuss possible uses of safety stock and safety time.
6. Explain how an MRP system is useful in capacity requirements planning.
7. Outline the potential benefits as well as some of the difficulties users have encountered with MRP.
8. Describe MRP II and how it relates to MRP.

Chapter Outline

Here are the views of managers in two companies that have tried material requirements planning (MRP):

"I don't know how we managed to get along without MRP for as long as we did. Our scheduling has gone from a state of turmoil to relative calm. We have achieved a substantial reduction in inventory size and cost, and yet our customer-service levels have actually improved quite a bit. We are more than satisfied with MRP; it allows us to *plan* instead of having to spend all of our time trying to *react* to one crisis after another. I would strongly recommend

that all manufacturing firms adopt MRP or some similar approach."

"We had heard so many good thing about MRP that we couldn't wait to get started, but so far, it seems like we've just been spinning our wheels. We're not even close to going online with it, and yet we've already exceeded our original time estimates and our costs are out of sight. Everyone is discouraged at this point, especially the brass. There is even some talk now of just scrapping the whole darn idea."

These two views reflect the range of reactions that typifies efforts of manufacturing firms to implement and use material requirements planning. This chapter examines the major issues of this current topic, including the need for this approach, the basic concepts of planning requirements, the benefits and limitations, and some of the reasons for the difficulties some firms have encountered in attempting to implement material requirements planning. It then goes on to describe MRP II. MRP II is an expanded approach to resource planning that incorporates MRP.

The preceding chapter focused on inventory management under conditions of *independent* demand. In this chapter, the focus is on managing inventories that have *dependent* or *derived* demand.

Dependent versus Independent Demand

As noted in the previous chapter, a major distinction in the way inventories are managed relates to the nature of demand for those items. When demand for items is *derived* from plans to make certain products, as it is in the case of raw materials, parts, and subassemblies used in producing a finished product, those items are said to have **dependent demand.** Hence, the parts and materials that go into the production of an automobile are examples of dependent demand since the total amount of parts and raw materials that will be needed during any time period is a function of the number of cars that will be produced. Conversely, demand for the finished cars is independent in the sense that a car is not a component of another item.

Independent demand is fairly stable, once allowances are made for seasonal variations, but dependent demand tends to be sporadic or "lumpy": large quantities are used at specific points in time with little or no usage at other times. Because of these tendencies, independent-demand items must be carried on a continual basis, but dependent-demand items need only to be stocked just prior to the time they will be needed in the production process. Moreover, the predictability of usage of dependent-demand items means that there is little or

FIGURE 11–1

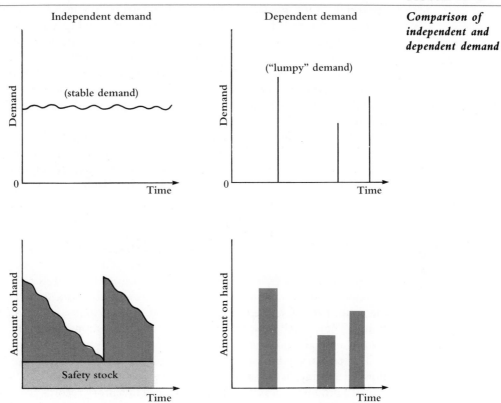

Comparison of independent and dependent demand

no need for safety stock. Figure 11–1 illustrates the contrasts in independent- and dependent-demand inventories.

AN OVERVIEW OF MRP

Material requirements planning (MRP) is a computer-based information system designed to handle ordering and scheduling of dependent-demand inventories (e.g., raw materials, component parts, and subassemblies). A production plan for a specified number of finished products is translated into requirements for component parts (raw materials, etc.) working backward, using lead time information to determine when and how much to order. Hence, requirements for end items generate requirements for lower-level components, which are broken down by planning periods (e.g., weeks) so that ordering, fabrication, and assembly can be scheduled for timely completion of end items while inventory levels are kept reasonably low.

Material requirements planning is as much a philosophy as it is a technique, and as much an approach to scheduling as it is to inventory control.

Historically, ordering and scheduling of assembled products suffered from two things. One was the enormous task of setting up schedules, keeping track of large numbers of parts and components, and coping with schedule and order changes. The other was that little effort was made to differentiate between independent demand and dependent demand; all too often, techniques that were designed for independent-demand items were being used to handle assembled items, which resulted in excessive inventories. Consequently, inventory planning and scheduling presented major problems for manufacturers.

In the last decade or so, manufacturers began to recognize the importance of the distinction between independent- and dependent-demand items and to approach these two categories of items in different ways. Much of the burden of record keeping and determining material requirements in many firms has now been transferred to computers, using techniques such as MRP. Much of the credit for publicizing MRP and educating potential users about MRP goes to Joseph Orlicky, author of the book *Material Requirements Planning* (New York: McGraw-Hill, 1975) and George Plossl, Oliver Wight, and the American Production and Inventory Control Society (APICS).

MRP begins with a schedule for finished goods that is converted into a schedule of requirements for the subassemblies, component parts, and raw materials that will be needed to produce the finished items in the specified time frame. Thus, MRP is designed to answer three questions: *what* is needed, *how much* is needed, and *when* is it needed.

The primary inputs of MRP are a bill of materials, which tells what a finished product is composed of; a master schedule, which tells how much finished product is desired and when; and an inventory records file, which tells how much inventory is on hand or on order.

This information is processed using various computer programs to determine the *net* requirements for each period of the planning horizon.

Outputs from the process include planned-order schedules, order releases, changes, performance-control reports, planning reports, and exception reports.

These topics are discussed in more detail in subsequent sections. An overview of an MRP system is provided in Figure 11–2.

MRP INPUTS

As illustrated in Figure 11–2, there are three major sources of information in an MRP system: a master schedule, a bill-of-materials file, and an inventory records file. Each of these inputs is described in this section, beginning with the master schedule.

The Master Schedule

The **master schedule** states which end items are to be produced, when these end items are needed, and what quantities are needed. Figure 11–3 illustrates a

FIGURE 11–2

Overview of MRP

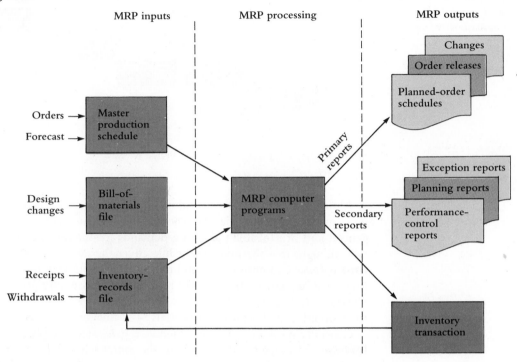

portion of a master schedule that shows planned output for end item X for the planning horizon. The schedule indicates that 100 units of X will be needed (e.g., for shipments to customers) at the *start* of week 4 and that another 150 units will be needed at the *start* of week 8.

The quantities in a master schedule can come from a number of different sources, including customer orders, forecasts, orders from warehouses to build up seasonal inventories, and external demand.

The master schedule separates the planning horizon into a series of time periods or time *buckets*. These are often in weeks. However, the time buckets need not be of equal length. In fact, the near-term portion of a master schedule may be in weeks, but later portions may be in months or quarters. Usually, plans for those more distant time periods are more tentative than near-term requirements.

FIGURE 11–3

A master schedule for end item X

	Week number							
Item: X	1	2	3	4	5	6	7	8
Quantity				100				150

FIGURE 11–4

The planning horizon must cover the cumulative lead time

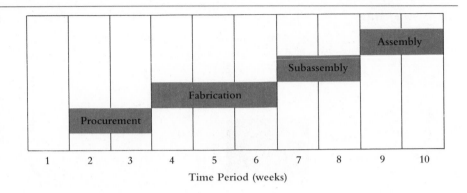

Although there is no set period of time that a master schedule must cover, most managers like to plan far enough into the future that they have some general idea of probable upcoming demands for the near future. It is important, though, that the master schedule cover the *stacked* or **cumulative lead time** necessary to produce the end items. This amounts to the sum of the lead times that sequential phases of the production or assembly process require, as illustrated in Figure 11–4, where a total of nine weeks of lead time is needed from ordering parts and raw materials until final assembly is completed.

Generally speaking, a master schedule is generated initially in terms of what is *needed* and not what is *possible,* so the initial schedule may or may not be feasible given the limits of the production system. Moreover, what appears on the surface to be a feasible master schedule may not be so when end items are translated into requirements for procurement, fabrication, and assembly. Unfortunately, the MRP system cannot distinguish between a feasible master schedule and a nonfeasible one. Consequently, it is often necessary to run a proposed master schedule through MRP processing in order to obtain a clearer picture of actual requirements, which can then be compared to available capacity. If it turns out that the current master schedule is not feasible, a decision may be made to increase capacity (e.g., through overtime or subcontracting) or to revise the master schedule. In the latter case, this may entail several revisions, each of which is run through the system until a feasible plan is obtained. At that point, the master schedule is *frozen,* at least for the near-term time periods, thus establishing a firm schedule from which to plan requirements.

The Bill-of-Materials File

A **bill of materials (BOM)** contains a listing of all of the assemblies, subassemblies, parts, and raw materials that are needed to produce one unit of a finished product. Thus, each finished product has its own bill of materials.

FIGURE 11–5

A product structure tree for end item X

Level

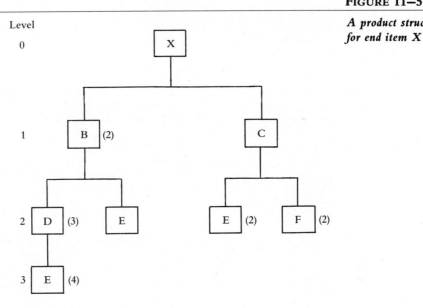

The listing in the bill-of-materials file is hierarchical; it shows the quantity of each item (in parentheses) needed to complete one unit of the following level of assembly. The nature of this aspect of a bill of materials is perhaps most readily grasped by considering a **product structure tree,** such as the one illustrated in Figure 11–5. We see that end item X is composed of two Bs and one C. Moreover, each B requires three Ds and one E, and each D requires four Es. Similarly, each C is made up of two Es and two Fs. These *requirements* are listed by *level,* beginning with level 0 for the end item, then level 1 for the next level, and so on. The items at each level are *components* of the next level up and are *parents* of their respective components. Note that the quantities of each item in the product structure tree refer only to the amounts needed to complete the assembly in the next level up.

A product structure tree is useful in illustrating how the bill of materials is used to determine the quantities of each of the ingredients (requirements) needed to obtain a desired number of end items.

EXAMPLE 1

Using the information presented in Figure 11–5, do the following:
a. Determine the quantities of B, C, D, E, and F needed to assemble one X.
b. Determine the quantities of these components that will be required to assemble 200 Xs.

EXAMPLE 1 *(concluded)*

Solution

a.

Component		Quantity
B . . . . 2 Bs per X		= 2
D . . . . 3 Ds per B × 2 Bs per X		= 6
E . . . . 4 Es per D × 3 Ds per B × 2 Bs per X		= 24
E . . . . 1 E per B × 2 Bs per X		= 2
C . . . . 1 C per X		= 1
E . . . . 2 Es per C × 1 C per X		= 2
F . . . . 2 Fs per C × 1 C per X		= 2

Note that E appears in three separate places; its total requirements can be determined by summing the separate amounts, which gives 28.

b.   In order to assemble 200 units of X, the quantities of each component must be multiplied by 200. Hence, there must be 200(2) = 400 Bs, 200(6) = 1,200 Ds, 200(28) = 5,600 Es, and so on.

When requirements are calculated in an MRP system, the computer, in effect, scans the product structure *level by level,* starting at the top. When a component (such as E in Figure 11–5) appears on more than one level, its total requirements cannot be determined until all levels have been scanned. From a

FIGURE 11–6

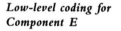

Low-level coding for Component E

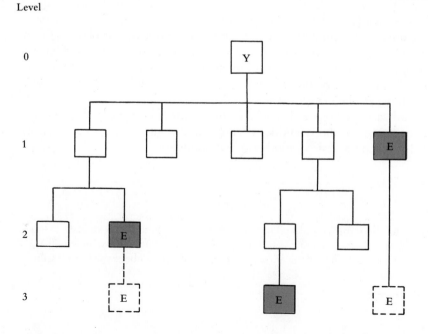

computational standpoint, this is somewhat inefficient. A simplification that is sometimes used to increase efficiency is **low-level coding,** which involves restructuring the BOM so that all occurrences of an item are made to coincide with the lowest level in which the item appears. Figure 11–6 illustrates how component E, which appears in three different levels of product Y, can be rearranged so that it appears at only one level.

Comment.   When the concept of low-level coding comes up, students are often puzzled by the following question: What happens if a component that appears at different levels is "buried" at an upper level and can't be lowered, as G seems to be in Figure 11–7? The answer, in terms of Figure 11–7, has two parts. One is that low-level coding is not limited to items at the end of "branches." The parent (G) and its components (and theirs, if necessary) can all be lowered, if need be, to achieve low-level coincidence. The other part of the answer lies in the fact that parent G should have the same components anywhere it appears in the product structure. In other words, the components H and I would always be required to assemble one G. If, for some reason, there is an exception to this, then one of the Gs should be given a different name; each name should carry a unique set of component requirements irrespective of where it appears in the product structure.

The Inventory Records File

The **inventory records file** is used to store information on the status of each item by time period. This includes gross requirements, scheduled receipts, and expected amount on hand. It also includes other details for each item, such as

FIGURE 11–7

One G seems to be buried, apparently preventing low-level coding

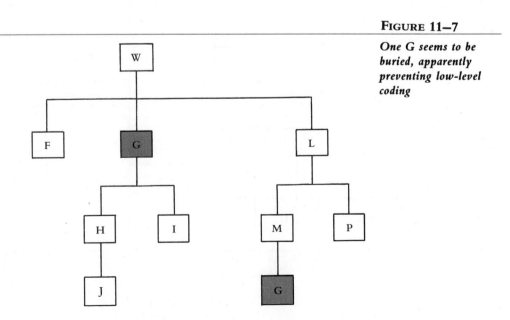

supplier, lead time, and lot size. In addition, changes due to stock receipts and withdrawals, canceled orders, and similar events are recorded in this file.

MRP PROCESSING

MRP processing involves taking the end-item requirements specified by the master schedule and "exploding" them into *time-phased* requirements for assemblies, parts, and raw materials using the bill of materials offset by lead times. The time-phasing of requirements can be readily seen in the assembly time chart in Figure 11–8. For example, raw materials D, F, and I must be ordered at the start of week 2, part C at the start of week 4, and part H at the start of week 5 in order to be available for delivery as planned.

The quantities that are generated by exploding the bill of materials are *gross requirements:* they do not take into account any inventory that is currently on hand or due to be received. The materials that must actually be acquired to meet the demand generated by the master schedule are the *net material requirements.*

FIGURE 11–8

Assembly time chart showing material order points needed to meet scheduled availability of the end item

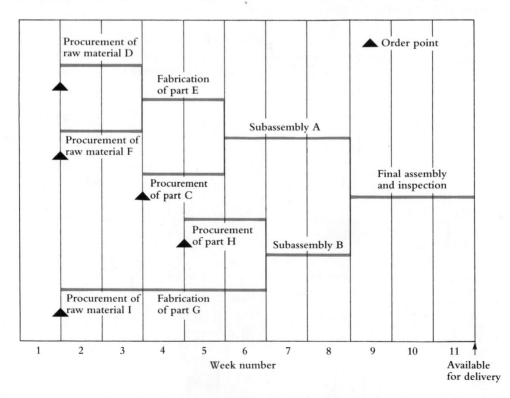

The determination of the net requirements *(netting)* is the core of MRP processing. It is accomplished by subtracting from gross requirements the sum of inventory on hand and any scheduled receipts and then adding in safety stock requirements, if applicable:

$$\begin{array}{c} \text{Net} \\ \text{requirements} \\ \text{in period } t \end{array} = \begin{array}{c} \text{Gross} \\ \text{requirements} \\ \text{in period } t \end{array} - \begin{array}{c} \text{Projected} \\ \text{inventory} \\ \text{in period } t \end{array} + \begin{array}{c} \text{Safety} \\ \text{stock} \end{array} \quad (11\text{--}1)$$

(For simplicity, safety stock is omitted from computations in examples and problems.) Net requirements are sometimes adjusted to include an allowance for waste, although, for simplicity, this is not included in examples or problems.

The timing and sizes of orders (i.e., materials ordered from suppliers or work started within the firm) are determined by *planned-order releases*. The timing of the receipts of these quantities is indicated by *planned-order receipts*. Depending on ordering policy, the planned-order releases may be multiples of a specified quantity (e.g., multiples of 50 units), or they may be equal to the quantity needed at that time. There are other possibilities, but these two seem to be the most widely used. The following example illustrates the difference between these two ordering policies as well as the general concepts of time-phasing material requirements in MRP. As you work through the example, you may find it useful to refer to the following list of terms.

Gross requirements: The total expected demand for an item or raw material during each time period. For end items, these quantities are shown in the master schedule; for components, these quantities equal the planned-order releases of their immediate "parents."

Scheduled receipts: Open orders scheduled to arrive from vendors or elsewhere in the pipeline.

Projected on hand: The expected amount of inventory that will be on hand at the *beginning* of each time period: Scheduled receipts + available from last period.

Net requirements: The actual amount needed in each time period.

Planned-order receipts: The quantity expected to be received by the *beginning* of the period in which it is shown. Under lot-for-lot ordering, this quantity will equal net requirements. Under lot-size ordering, this quantity may exceed net requirements. Any excess is added to available inventory in the *next* time period.

Planned-order-releases: Indicates a *planned* amount to order in each time period; equals planned-order receipts offset by lead time. This amount generates gross requirements at the next level in the assembly or production chain. When an order is executed, it is removed from the "planned-order receipts" and "planned-order release" rows and entered in the "scheduled receipts" row.

These quantities are used in a time-phased plan in this format:

Week number:	1	2	3	4	5	6	7	8
Item:								
Gross requirements								
Scheduled receipts								
Projected on hand								
Net requirements								
Planned-order receipts								
Planned-order releases								

EXAMPLE 2

A firm that produces wood shutters and bookcases has received two orders for shutters: one for 100 shutters and one for 150 shutters. The 100-unit order is due at the start of week 4 of the current schedule, and the 150-unit order is due for delivery at the start of week 8. Each shutter consists of four slatted wood sections and two frames. The wood sections are made by the firm, and fabrication takes one week. The frames are ordered, and lead time is two weeks. Assembly of the shutters requires one week. There is a scheduled receipt of 70 wood sections in (i.e., at the beginning of) week 1. Determine the size and timing of planned-order releases necessary to meet delivery requirements under each of these conditions:

1. Lot-for-lot ordering (i.e., order size equal to net requirements).
2. Lot-size ordering with a lot size of 320 units for frames and 70 units for wood sections.

Solution

a. Develop a master schedule:

Week number:	1	2	3	4	5	6	7	8
Quantity:				100				150

b. Develop a product structure tree:

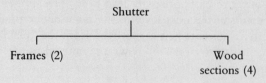

EXAMPLE 2 *(continued)*

c. Develop an assembly-time chart:

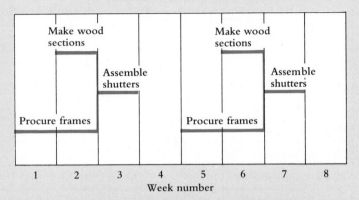

d. Using the master schedule, determine gross requirements for shutters. Next, compute net requirements. Assuming *lot-for-lot ordering,* determine planned-order receipt quantities and the planned-order release timing to satisfy the master schedule (see Figure 11–9).

Since the master schedule calls for 100 shutters to be ready for delivery at the start of the fourth week, and since no shutters are projected to be on hand at that time, the net requirements are also 100 shutters. Therefore, planned receipts for the fourth week equal 100 shutters. Since shutter assembly requires one week, this means a planned-order release at the start of the third week. Using the same logic, 150 shutters must be assembled during the seventh week in order to be available for delivery at the start of the eighth week.

The planned-order release of 100 shutters at the start of the third week means that 200 frames (gross requirements) must be available at that time. Since none are expected to be on hand, this generates net requirements of 200 frames and necessitates planned receipts of 200 frames by the start of the third week. With a two-week lead time, this means that 200 frames must be ordered at the start of the first week. Similarly, the planned-order release of 150 shutters at week 7 generates gross and net requirements of 300 frames for week 7 as well as planned receipts for that time. The two-week lead time means frames must be ordered at the start of week 5.

The planned-order release of 100 shutters at the start of the third week also generates gross requirements of 400 wood sections at that time. However, because 70 wood sections are expected to be on hand, net requirements are 400 − 70 = 330. This means a planned receipt of 330 by the start of the third week. Since fabrication time is one week, the fabrication must start (planned-order release) at the beginning of week 2.

Similarly, the planned-order release of 150 shutters at week 7 generates gross requirements of 600 wood sections at that point. Since no on-hand inventory of wood sections is projected, net requirements are also 600, and planned-order receipt is 600 units. Again, the one-week lead time means 600 sections are scheduled for fabrication at the start of the sixth week.

EXAMPLE 2 *(continued)*

FIGURE 11–9

MRP schedule with lot-for-lot ordering

Master schedule for shutters:

Week number	1	2	3	4	5	6	7	8
Quantity				100				150

Shutters:
LT = 1 week

	1	2	3	4	5	6	7	8
Gross requirements				100				150
Scheduled receipts								
Projected on hand								
Net requirements				100				150
Planned-order receipts				(100)				(150)
Planned-order releases			(100)				(150)	

times 2 (week 3) · times 2 (week 7)

Frames:
LT = 2 weeks

	1	2	3	4	5	6	7	8
Gross requirements			200				300	
Scheduled receipts								
Projected on hand								
Net requirements			200				300	
Planned-order receipts			(200)				(300)	
Planned-order releases	(200)				(300)			

times 4 · times 4

Wood sections:
LT = 1 week

	1	2	3	4	5	6	7	8
Gross requirements			400				600	
Scheduled receipts	70							
Projected on hand	70	70	70					
Net requirements			330				600	
Planned-order receipts			(330)				(600)	
Planned-order releases		(330)				(600)		

e. Under *lot-size ordering,* the only difference is the possibility that planned receipts will exceed net requirements; the excess is recorded as projected inventory in the following period. For example, in Figure 11–10, the order size for frames is 320 units. Net requirements for week 3 are 200; thus, there is an excess of 320 − 200 = 120 units, which become projected inventory in the next week. Similarly, net frame requirements of 180 units are 140 less

EXAMPLE 2 *(concluded)*

than the 320 order size; again, the excess becomes projected inventory in week 9. The same thing happens with wood sections: an excess of planned receipts in periods 3 and 7 is added to projected inventory in periods 4 and 8. Note that the order size must be in *multiples* of the lot size; for week 3 it is 5 times 70, and for week 7 its is 9 times 70.

FIGURE 11—10

MRP schedule with lot sizes for components

Master schedule for shutters:

Week number	1	2	3	4	5	6	7	8
Quantity				100				150

Shutters:
LT = 1 week
Lot size = None

	1	2	3	4	5	6	7	8
Gross requirements				100				150
Scheduled receipts								
Projected on hand								
Net requirements				100				150
Planned-order receipts				(100)				(150)
Planned-order releases			(100)				(150)	

times 2   times 2

Frames:
LT = 2 weeks
Lot size = 320

	1	2	3	4	5	6	7	8
Gross requirements			200				300	
Scheduled receipts								
Projected on hand				120	120	120	120	140
Net requirements			200				180	
Planned-order receipts			(320)				(320)	
Planned-order releases	(320)				(320)			

times 4   times 4

Wood sections:
LT = 1 week
Lot size = 70

	1	2	3	4	5	6	7	8
Gross requirements			400				600	
Scheduled receipts	70							
Projected on hand	70	70	70	20	20	20	20	50
Net requirements			330				580	
Planned-order receipts			(350)				(630)	
Planned-order releases		(350)				(630)		

Another perspective on the process of determining material requirements for subassembly components is given in Figure 11–11.

Example 2 is useful for describing some of the main features of MRP processing, but it understates the enormity of the task of keeping track of material requirements, especially in situations where the same subassemblies, parts, or raw materials are used in a number of different products. Differences in timing of demands and quantities needed, as well as revisions caused by late deliveries, high scrap rates, and canceled orders, all have an impact on processing.

FIGURE 11–11

Net requirements at each level determine gross requirements at the next

Master schedule for shutters

Week number	1	2	3	4	5	6	7	
Quantity								

Item: Shutters							
Gross requirements							
Scheduled receipts							
Projected on hand							
Net requirements							
Planned-order receipts							
Planned-order releases							

Item: Frames							
Gross requirements							
Scheduled receipts							
Projected on hand							
Net requirements							
Planned-order receipts							
Planned-order releases							

Item: Wood sections							
Gross requirements							
Scheduled receipts							
Projected on hand							
Net requirements							
Planned-order receipts							
Planned-order releases							

FIGURE 11–12

Bracket G is used in three different products

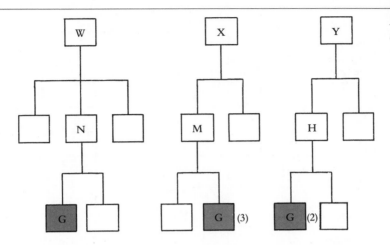

Consider, for example, bracket G, which is used for end items W, X, and Y, as shown by the product trees in Figure 11–12. For the sake of simplicity, assume that all lead times are one week. Suppose that the master schedule for these products is as shown in Figure 11–13. Note that these are the *gross requirements* for these end items; *net requirements* will be less by the amount of any on-hand inventories. The same holds true for net requirements for sub-assemblies N, M, and H. Each of these factors must be taken into account in calculating net material requirements for G. The gross requirements for G by parent might look something like the schedule shown in Figure 11–14, with the net requirements for G equal to the sum of these amounts minus any projected on-hand inventory of G, which is also shown in Figure 11–14. (*Note:* the on-hand quantities of the end items are not given, nor are those quantities given for parents N, M, and H. However, the point here is *not* the computations, but that gross requirements for bracket G are generated by the net requirements of all of its "parents." See the lower portion of Figure 11–14.)

The term **pegging** is used to denote working this process in reverse, that is, identifying the parent items that have generated a given set of material requirements for some item such as G. Although the process may appear simple

FIGURE 11–13

Master schedule for end items that use bracket G

				Week number			
End item	1	2	3	4	5	6	7
W			50		70		60
X			200			100	
Y		30			80	90	

FIGURE 11–14

Net Requirements for bracket G

Net requirements for G due to:	1	2	3	4	5	6	7
N	40		50		40		
M	120			240			
H				160	120		
Total	160		50	400	160		

	1	2	3	4	5	6	7
Gross requirements	160		50	400	160		
Projected on hand	200	40	40	0	0		
Net requirements			10	400	160		

Week number

enough given the product trees and schedules shown here, when this information is computerized, special efforts must be made so that requirements can be traced to specific parents.

The importance of the computer becomes quite evident when you stop to realize that a typical firm would have not one but many end items for which it needs to develop material requirements plans, each with its own set of components. Inventories on hand and on order, schedules, order releases, and so on must all be updated as changes and rescheduling occur. Without the aid of a computer, the task would be quite hopeless; with the aid of a computer, all of these things can be accomplished with a lot less difficulty.

Updating the System

There are two basic approaches to updating MRP records: *regenerative* and *net change*. A **regenerative system** is one that is updated periodically; a **net-change system** is one that is continuously updated.

A regenerative system is essentially a batch-type system that compiles all changes (e.g., new orders, receipts) that occur within the time interval (e.g., week) and periodically updates the system. Using that information, a revised production plan is developed (if needed), in the same way that the original plan was developed (i.e., exploding the bill of materials, level by level, etc.).

In a net-change system, the basic production plan is modified to reflect changes as they occur. Hence, if some purchased parts had to be returned to a vendor because they were defective, this information is entered into the system as soon as it becomes known. Only the *changes* would be exploded through the system, level by level; the basic plan would not be regenerated.

The regenerative system is best suited to systems that are fairly stable, whereas the net-change system is best suited to systems that have frequent changes. The obvious disadvantage of a regenerative system is the potential amount of lag between the time information becomes available and the time it can be incorporated into the material requirements plan. On the other hand, processing costs are typically less using regenerative systems, and there is the possibility that changes that occur in a given time period will end up canceling each other, thereby avoiding the need to modify the plan and then remodify it. The disadvantages of the net-change system relate to the computer processing costs involved in continuously updating the system and the fact that many small changes can keep the system in a constant state of flux. One way around this is to enter minor changes periodically, but enter major changes immediately. The primary advantage of the net-change system is that management can have up-to-date information for planning and control purposes.

MRP OUTPUTS

MRP systems have the ability to provide management with a fairly broad range of outputs. These are often classified as *primary reports,* which are the main reports, and *secondary reports,* which are optional outputs.

Primary reports concern production and inventory planning and control. These reports normally include the following:

1. A schedule of **planned orders,** which indicates the amount and timing of future orders.
2. **Order releases,** which authorize the execution of planned orders.
3. **Changes** to planned orders, which can include revisions of due dates or order quantities as well as cancellations of orders.

Secondary reports concern such things as performance control, planning, and exceptions:

1. **Performance-control reports** are used to evaluate system operation. They aid managers by measuring deviations from plans, including missed deliveries and stock-outs, and by providing information that can be used to assess cost performance.
2. **Planning reports** are useful in forecasting future inventory requirements. They include purchase commitments and other data that can be used to assess future material requirements.
3. **Exception reports** call attention to major discrepancies such as late and overdue orders, excessive scrap rates, reporting errors, and requirements for nonexistent parts.

The wide range of outputs generally permits users to adapt MRP to their particular needs.

OTHER CONSIDERATIONS

Aside from the main details of inputs, outputs, and processing, there are a number of other aspects of MRP that the manager must be knowledgeable about. These include the question of whether to hold safety stock, lot sizing choices, and the possible use of MRP for items that are not finished products.

Safety Stock

Theoretically, inventory systems with dependent demand should not require safety stock below the end-item level. In fact, this is one of the main advantages of an MRP approach. Supposedly, safety stock is not needed because usage quantities can be projected once the master schedule has been established. Practically speaking, however, there may be exceptions to this. For example, a bottleneck process or one with varying scrap rates can cause shortages in downstream operations. Furthermore, shortages can occur if orders are late or fabrication or assembly times are longer than expected. On the surface, these are the kinds of conditions that lend themselves to the use of safety stock to maintain smooth operations. However, the problem is somewhat complicated when dealing with multiechelon items (i.e., multiple-level items such as assembled products) by the fact that a shortage of *any* component will prevent manufacture of the final assembly. However, a major advantage of MRP would be lost by holding safety stock for all lower-level items.

   MRP systems deal with these problems in several ways. The first step is for a manager to identify those activities or operations that are subject to variability and then to determine the extent of that variability. When lead times are variable, the concept of safety *time* is often used instead of safety *stock*. This results in scheduling orders for arrival or completion sufficiently ahead of the time they are needed to eliminate or substantially reduce the chance of having to wait for those items. When quantities tend to vary, some safety stock may be called for. However, the manager must carefully weigh the need and cost of carrying the extra stock. Frequently, managers elect to carry safety stock for end items, because these are subject to random demand, and for selected lower-level operations when safety time is not feasible, say, because of capacity limitations.

Lot Sizing

An important issue in inventory management, whether for independent- or dependent-demand items, is choosing a lot size to order or for production. This is called **lot sizing.** For independent-demand items, economic order sizes and economic run sizes are widely used. However, for dependent-demand systems, there is a much wider variety of plans used for determining lot sizes, mainly because no one plan has a clear advantage over the others. Some of the most popular plans for lot sizing are described in this section.

FIGURE 11–15

Demand for part K

	\multicolumn{5}{c}{Period}
	1	2	3	4	5
Demand	70	50	1	80	4
Cumulative demand	70	120	121	201	205

For either independent- or dependent-demand systems, a primary goal of inventory management is to minimize the sum of ordering cost (or setup cost) and holding cost. It is often the case with independent demand that demand is uniformly distributed throughout the planning horizon (e.g., six months, year). Demand tends to be much more lumpy for dependent demand, and the planning horizon shorter (say, three months), so that economic lot sizes are usually much more difficult to identify. Consider the situation depicted in Figure 11–15. Period demands vary from 1 to 80 units, and no demand size repeats, at least over the horizon shown.

Economies can be realized by grouping order or run sizes. This would be the case if the additional cost incurred by holding the extra units until they were used led to a savings in setup or ordering cost. This determination can be very complex at times, for several reasons. One is that combining period demands into a single order, particularly for middle-level or end items, has a cascading effect down through the product tree. That is, in order to achieve this grouping, items at lower levels in the tree must also be grouped. Hence, their setup and holding costs must also be incorporated into the decision. Another reason is the uneven period demands and the relatively short planning horizon. These factors require a continual recalculation and updating of lot sizes. Not surprisingly, the methods used to handle the lot sizing question range from complex ones, which attempt to include all relevant costs, to very simple ones, which are easy to use and understand. And in certain cases, the simple models seem to approach cost minimization, although generalizations are difficult. Let's consider some of these models.

Lot-for-lot ordering is perhaps the simplest of all the approaches used. The order or run size for each period is set equal to demand for that period. This method was demonstrated in Example 2. Not only is the order size obvious, but it also virtually eliminates holding costs for parts carried over to other periods. Its two chief drawbacks are that it usually involves many different order sizes and so cannot take advantage of economies associated with a fixed order size (e.g., standard containers and other standardized procedures), and it involves a setup for each run. If setup costs can be significantly reduced, this approach may approximate a minimum-cost result.

Economic order quantity models (covered in Chapter 10) are sometimes used. They can lead to minimum costs if usage is fairly uniform. This is sometimes the case for lower-level items that are common to different parents and for raw materials. However, the more lumpy demand is, the less appropriate such an approach is. Since demand tends to be most lumpy at the end-item level, EOQ models tend to be less useful for end items than for items and materials at the lowest levels.

Fixed-period ordering provides coverage for some predetermined number of periods (e.g., two or three). In some instances, the span is simply arbitrary; in other cases, a review of historical demand patterns may lead to a more rational designation of a fixed period length. A simple rule would be: Order to cover a two-period interval. The rule can be modified when common sense suggests a better way. For example, take a look at the demands shown in Figure 11–15. Using a two-period rule, an order size of 120 units would cover the first two periods. The next two periods would be covered by an order size of 81 units. However, the demands in periods 3 and 5 are so small, it would make sense to combine them both with the 80 units and order 85 units.

The *part period* model represents another attempt to balance setup and holding costs. The term *part period* refers to holding a part or parts over a number of periods. For instance, if 10 parts were held for two periods, this would be $10 \times 2 = 20$ part periods. The economic part period (EPP) can be computed as the ratio of setup costs to the cost to hold a unit for one period. Thus, the formula for computing the EPP is:

$$EPP = \frac{\text{Setup cost}}{\text{Unit holding cost per period}} \qquad (11-2)$$

In order to determine an order size that is consistent with the EPP, various order sizes are examined for a planning horizon, and each one's number of part periods is determined. The one that comes closest to the EPP is selected as the best lot size. The order sizes that are examined are based on cumulative demand. The following example illustrates this approach.

EXAMPLE 3

Use the *part period* method to determine order sizes for this demand schedule:

	Period							
	1	*2*	*3*	*4*	*5*	*6*	*7*	*8*
Demand	60	40	20	2	30	—	70	50
Cumulative demand	60	100	120	122	152	152	222	272

Setup cost is $47 per run for this item, and unit holding cost is $.56 per period.

EXAMPLE 3 *(concluded)*

Solution

1. First compute the EPP: EPP = $47/$.56 = 83.93, which rounds to 84 part periods.
2. Next, try the cumulative lot sizes, beginning with 60, until the part periods approximate the EPP. Continue this process for the planning horizon. This leads to the following:

Period	Lot size	Extra inventory carried	× Periods carried	= Part periods	Cumulative part periods
1	60	0	0	0	0
	100	40	1	40	40
	120	20	2	40	80
	122	2	3	6	86*[closest to 84]
5	30	0	0	0	0
	100	70	2	140	140*[closest to 84]
8	50	0	0	0	0

The computations of part periods indicate that 122 units should be ordered to be available at period 1, and 100 units should be ordered to be available at period 5. The next lot will be ordered for period 8, but we do not have enough information now to determine its size.

   The lot sizes considered for period 1 correspond to cumulative demand. Once the best lot size has been identified, the cumulative demand is set equal to zero and then summed beginning for the next period. In this case, the lot size of 122 covers the first four periods, so cumulative demand is started next for period 5. That next lot size covers through period 7, and the count begins again at period 8.

   The process works quite well for the first lot size since the cumulative number of part periods is quite close to the EPP, but the effect of lumpy demand is very apparent for the second lot size of 100 (140 part periods is not very close to 84 part periods).

The *Wagner-Whitin algorithm* attempts to minimize the sum of ordering and carrying costs using dynamic programming to select the ordering strategy to cover net requirements in each period for the complete net-requirements schedule. The advantage of this approach is that the algorithm identifies a relatively few strategies, which it then compares, selecting the one that minimizes total costs. The disadvantage of the technique is that its complexity makes it highly unlikely that the average user will be able to understand it, which not only decreases the chance of having the technique selected for use in the first place, but also increases the risk of misusing it or misinterpreting the results.

   The choice of a lot sizing technique must take into account the nature of demand (degree of uniformity), the relative importance of carrying costs versus ordering costs, and any other considerations that affect ordering. It appears that no one technique is suited to all conditions.

Regardless of the lot sizing technique in use, there is always the possibility of adjustments in order sizes due to allowance for shrinkage or scrap, minimum and maximum order quantities established by management (e.g., do not order more than five months' supply), operating or shipping constraints (e.g., 200 pieces per run or 12 dozen per shipment) that require rounding of order sizes (usually up) to these amounts, and similar factors.

CAPACITY REQUIREMENTS PLANNING

One of the most important features of MRP is its ability to aid managers in capacity planning. As noted previously, a master schedule that appears feasible on the surface may turn out to be far from feasible in terms of resource requirements needed for fabrication and/or subassembly operations of lower-level items.

Capacity requirements planning is the process of determining short-range capacity requirements. The necessary inputs include planned-order releases for MRP, the current shop load, routing information, and job times. Outputs include load reports for each work center. When variances (underloads or overloads) are projected, remedies such as alternative routings, changing or eliminating lot sizing or safety stock requirements, and lot splitting may be considered. Moving production forward or backward can be very challenging due to precedence requirements as well as availabilities of components.

An overview of the capacity planning process is presented in Figure 11–16. The process begins with a proposed or tentative master schedule that must be tested for feasibility and possibly adjusted before it becomes permanent. The proposed schedule is processed using MRP to ascertain the material requirements that such a schedule would generate. These are then translated into resource (i.e., capacity) requirements, often in the form of a series of **load reports** for each department or work center that compare known and expected future capacity requirements with projected capacity availability. The nature of a load report is illustrated in Figure 11–17. It shows expected resource requirements (i.e., usage) for jobs currently being worked on, for planned orders, and for expected orders for the planning horizon. Given this sort of information, the manager can more easily determine whether there is sufficient capacity to satisfy these requirements. If there is enough capacity, the portion of the master schedule that generates these requirements can be frozen. In the load report illustrated in Figure 11–17, planned-order releases in the fourth time period will cause an overload. However, it appears possible to accommodate demand by slightly shifting some orders to adjacent periods. Similarly, an overload appears likely in period 11, but that too can be handled by shifting some jobs to adjacent time periods. In cases where capacity is insufficient, a manager may be able to increase capacity (by scheduling overtime, transferring personnel from other areas, or subcontracting some of the

FIGURE 11–16

Using MRP to assist in planning capacity requirements

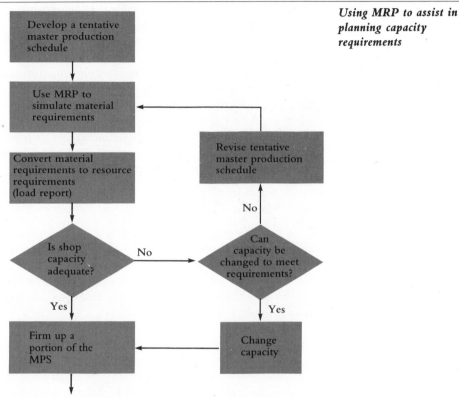

Source: Stephen Love, *Inventory Control* (New York: McGraw-Hill, 1979), p. 164. Reprinted by permission.

FIGURE 11–17

A hypothetical ídepartment load report

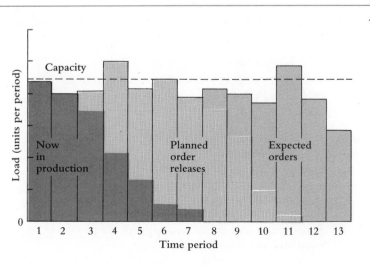

work) if this is possible and economical, or else revise the master schedule and repeat the process until an acceptable master schedule is obtained.

If the master schedule must be revised, this generally means that the manager must assign priorities to orders, since some orders will be finished later than originally planned.

An important aspect of capacity requirements planning is the conversion of quantity requirements into labor and machine requirements. This is accomplished by multiplying each period's quantity requirements by standard labor and/or machine requirements per unit. For instance, if 100 units of product A are scheduled in the fabrication department, and each unit has a labor standard time of 2 hours and a machine standard time of 1.5 hours, the 100 units of A convert into these capacity requirements:

$$\text{Labor} \quad 100 \text{ units} \times 2 \text{ hours/unit} = 200 \text{ labor hours}$$
$$\text{Machine} \quad 100 \text{ units} \times 1.5 \text{ hours/unit} = 150 \text{ machine hours}$$

These capacity requirements can then be compared to available department capacity to determine the extent to which capacity will be utilized by this product. For example, if the department has 200 labor hours and 200 machine hours available, labor utilization will be at 100% because all of the labor capacity will be required by this product. However, machine capacity will be underutilized:

$$\frac{\text{Required}}{\text{Available}} \times 100 = \frac{150 \text{ hours}}{200 \text{ hours}} \times 100 = 75\%.$$

Underutilization may mean that unused capacity can be used for other jobs; overutilization indicates that available capacity is insufficient to handle requirements. To compensate, production may have to be rescheduled, or overtime may be needed.

BENEFITS AND LIMITATIONS OF MRP

MRP offers a number of benefits of the typical manufacturing or assembly type of operation. These generally include:

1. Low levels of in-process inventories.
2. The ability to keep track of material requirements.
3. The ability to evaluate capacity requirements generated by a given master schedule.
4. A means of allocating production time.

The benefits of MRP depend in large measure on the use of a computer to maintain up-to-date information on material requirements.

In order to implement and operate an effective MRP system, it is necessary to have:

1. A computer and the necessary software programs to handle computations and maintain records.

2. Accurate and up-to-date:
   a. Master schedules.
   b. Bills of materials.
   c. Inventory records.
3. Integrity of file data.

Unfortunately, some of the firms that have attempted to install an MRP system have seriously underestimated the importance of these items. In many cases, bills of materials have been outdated because design changes were not incorporated into the records, leading to parts lists that did not correspond to what is actually required to assemble the finished product. In addition, it is not unusual for a firm to discover that the same part is being carried under different part numbers, making it difficult to develop meaningful records. Moreover, some firms have encountered resistance from foremen and others, often along the line of: "We've managed for 30 years without this stuff, so why bother with it now?"

Because of these obstacles, it can take a year or more to implement MRP, taking into account employee education, training, and *convincing,* and correction of record-keeping deficiencies.

On the whole, the introduction of MRP has led to major improvements in scheduling and inventory management. Nonetheless, it has not proved to be the cure-all that many hoped it would be. Consequently, manufacturers are beginning to take a much broader view of resource planning. One such approach is referred to as MRP II.

MRP II

In the early 1980s, materials requirements planning was expanded into a much broader approach for planning and scheduling the resources of manufacturing firms. This expanded approach has been dubbed MRP II, which refers to **manufacturing resources planning.** It has not replaced MRP, nor is it an improved version of MRP. Rather, it represents an effort to expand the scope of production resource planning and to involve other functional areas of the firm in the planning process. Marketing and finance are the two most notable areas that are impacted by—and have an impact on—the manufacturing plan.

In too many instances, production, marketing, and finance operate without complete knowledge or seeming regard for what the other areas of the firm are doing. Obviously, to be most effective, all areas of the firm need to focus on a common set of goals. A major purpose of MRP II is to integrate these primary functions as well as other functions such as personnel, engineering, and purchasing in the planning process.

Material requirements planning is at the heart of the process, which is illustrated in Figure 11–18. The process begins with an aggregation of demand from all sources (e.g., firm orders, forecasts, safety stock requirements). Production, marketing, and finance personnel work toward developing a master schedule. Although manufacturing people will have a major input in

FIGURE 11–18

An overview of MRP II

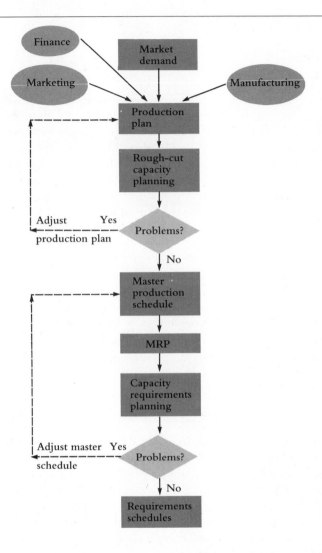

determining that schedule and a major responsibility for making it work, marketing and finance will also have important inputs and responsibilities. The rationale of having these functional areas work together is the increased likelihood of developing a plan that will work and one that everyone can live with. Moreover, because each of these functional areas has been involved in formulating the plan, they will have reasonably good knowledge of the plan and work toward achieving it.

In addition to the obvious manufacturing resources needed to support the plan, financing resources will be needed and must be planned for, both in amount and timing. Similarly, marketing resources will also be needed in varying degrees throughout the process. In order for the plan to work, it must be determined that all of these necessary resources will be available as needed. Often, an initial plan must be revised based on an assessment of the availability of various resources. Once these have been decided, the master schedule can be firmed up.

At this point, material requirements planning comes into play, generating material and schedule requirements. Then more detailed capacity requirements planning must be done to determine if these more specific capacity requirements can be met. Again, some adjustments in the master schedule may be required.

As the schedule unfolds and actual work begins, a variety of reports are generated that help managers to keep a pulse on how well actual experience complies with plans and to make any necessary adjustments to keep operations on track.

In effect, this is a continuing process, with the master schedule being updated and revised as necessary to achieve corporate goals. The business plan that governs the entire process also usually undergoes changes, although these tend to be less frequent than the changes made at lower levels (i.e., the master schedule).

Finally, it should be noted that most MRP II systems have the capability to do simulation. This enables managers to answer a variety of "what if" questions, thereby gaining a better appreciation of available options and their consequences.

Since MRP is at the heart of MRP II, the computer is an important tool in MRP II, one that is heavily relied on for information processing.

SUMMARY

Material requirements planning (MRP) is an information system used to handle ordering of dependent-demand items (i.e., components of assembled products). The planning process begins with customer orders, which are used along with any backorders to develop a master schedule that indicates the timing and quantity of finished items. The end items are exploded using the bill of materials, and material requirements plans are developed which show quantity and timing for ordering or producing components.

The main features of MRP are the time-phasing of requirements, the identification of components, and planned-order releases. In order to be successful, MRP requires a computer program and accurate master schedules, bills of materials, and inventory data. Firms that have not had reasonably accurate records or schedules have experienced major difficulties in trying to implement MRP.

MRP II is a second-generation approach to planning that incorporates MRP; it has a broader scope to manufacturing resource planning in that it links business planning, production planning, and the master schedule.

KEY TERMS

SOLVED PROBLEMS

1. The following product structure tree indicates the components needed to assemble one unit of product W. Redraw the tree so that it conforms to low-level coding, and determine the quantities of each component that will be needed to assemble 100 units of W.

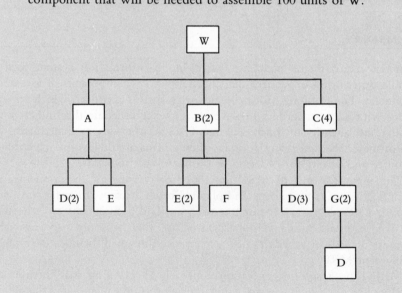

Solution

An easy way to compute and keep track of component requirements is to do it right on the tree, as illustrated below. Using low-level coding, it is then relatively simple to group like items in order to determine overall requirements.

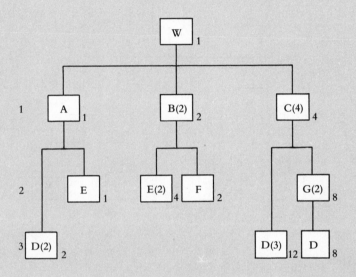

Summary:

Level	Item	(1 W) Quantity	(100 W) Quantity
0	W	1	100
1	A	1	100
	B	2	200
	C	4	400
2	E	5	500
	F	2	200
	G	8	800
3	D	22	2,200

2. The product structure tree for end item E is shown below. The manager wants to know the material requirements for ordered part R that will be needed to complete 120 units of E by the start of week

5. Lead times for items are: one week for level 0 items, one week for level 1 items, and two weeks for level 2 items. There is a scheduled receipt of 60 units of M at the *end* of week 1 and 100 units of R at the *beginning* of week 1. Lot-for-lot ordering is used.

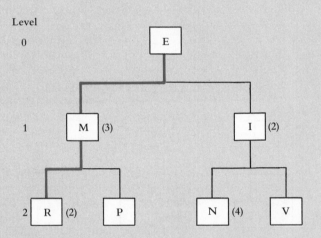

Solution

A *partial* assembly-time chart that includes R and leads to completion of E by the start of week 5 looks like this:

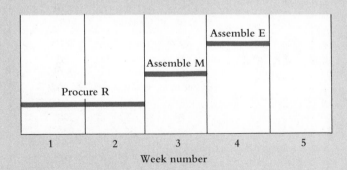

The master schedule for E and requirements plans for E, M, and R follow.

Master schedule for E

Week number:	1	2	3	4	5
Quantity					(120)

Item: E LT = 1 week					
Gross requirements					(120)
Scheduled receipts					
Projected on hand					0
Net requirements					120
Planned-order receipts					(120)
Planned-order releases				(120)	

Multiplied by 3
(see product tree)

Item: M LT = 1 week					
Gross requirements				(360)	
Scheduled receipts		60			
Projected on hand		60	60	60	
Net requirements				300	
Planned-order receipts				(300)	
Planned-order releases			(300)		

Multiplied by 2
(see product tree)

Item: R LT = 2 weeks					
Gross requirements			(600)		
Scheduled receipts	100				
Projected on hand	100	100	100		
Net requirements			500		
Planned-order receipts			(500)		
Planned-order releases	(500)				

The table entries are arrived at as follows:

Master schedule: 120 units of E to be available at the start of week 5.

Item E: Gross requirements equal quantity specified in master schedule. Since there is no on–hand inventory, net requirements also equal 120 units. Using lot-for-lot ordering, 120 units must be scheduled to be available at the start of week 5. Since there is a one-week lead time for assembly of Es, an order will need to be released (i.e., work started) at the beginning of week 4.

Item M: The *gross* requirements for M are three times E's *net* requirements since each E requires three Ms. These must be available at the start of week 4. The net requirements are 60 units less due to the 60 units expected to be on hand at that time. Hence, 300 additional units of M must be available at the start of week 4. With the one week lead time, there must be an order release at the start of week 3.

Item R: Since each M requires two units of R, 600 Rs will be needed to assemble 300 units of M. However, 100 units will be on hand, so only 500 need to be ordered. Since there is a lead time of two weeks, the 500 Rs must be ordered at the start of week 1.

3. *Capacity requirements planning.* Given the following production schedule in units and the production standards for labor and machine time for this product, determine the labor and machine capacity requirements for each week. Then compute the percent utilization of labor and machines in each week if labor capacity is 200 hours per week and machine capacity is 250 hours per week.

Production schedule:

Week	1	2	3	4
Quantity	200	300	100	150

Standard times:

Labor	.5 hours/unit
Machine	1.0 hours/unit

Solution

Convert the quantity requirements into labor and machine requirements by multiplying the quantity requirements by the respective standard times (i.e., multiply each quantity by .5 to obtain the labor hours and multiply each quantity by 1.0 to obtain the machine hours):

Week	1	2	3	4
Quantity	200	300	100	150
Labor hours	100	150	50	75
Machine hours	200	300	100	150

To compute utilization, divide the capacity requirements by the available capacity and multiply by 100. The results are:

Week	1	2	3	4
Labor	50%	75%	25%	37.5%
Machine	80%	120%	40%	60%

Note that machine capacity in week 2 is overutilized (i.e., capacity is insufficient) because the utilization exceeds 100 percent.

DISCUSSION AND REVIEW QUESTIONS

1. Contrast independent and dependent demand.
2. When is MRP appropriate?
3. Briefly define or explain each of these terms:
   a. Master schedule.
   b. Bill of materials.
   c. Inventory records file.
   d. Gross requirements.
   e. Net requirements.
   f. Time-phased plan.
   g. Low-level coding.
4. What is meant by the term *level-by-level processing?* Why does it require low-level coding?
5. What factors can create safety stock requirements in an MRP system?
6. What is meant by the term *safety time?*
7. Contrast *net-change* systems and *regenerative* systems for MRP.

8. Briefly discuss the requirements for effective MRP.
9. What are some of the main advantages and limitations of MRP?
10. How can the use of MRP contribute to productivity?
11. Briefly describe MRP II and indicate how it relates to MRP.
12. What is lot sizing, and why is it an issue with lumpy demand?
13. What is the goal of lot sizing? What are some of the methods used for lot sizing in MRP systems? At what level is an economic lot size usually most relevant? Why?
14. Contrast planned-order receipts and scheduled receipts.

PROBLEMS

1. Given the product structure tree at the top of the next page, do the following:
   a. Redraw the tree so that it conforms to low-level coding.
   b. Determine the quantities of each of the components that will be required to assemble 60 units of P.

Tree for Problem 1

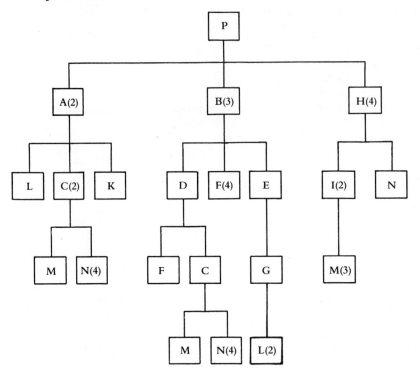

2. Given the following listing of parents and components, construct two product structure trees using low-level coding, and then determine what quantity of each item will be required to make 125 units of end item W and 50 units of end item Y.

W	Y
A(2)	A
B(4)	B(2)
C(4)	K(3)

A	A
D(2)	D(2)
E	E

B	B
F(2)	F(2)

D	D
F(4)	F(4)
E(2)	E(2)
G(4)	G(4)

C	K
H	L
G(2)	C(4)

C
H
G(2)

3. Determine material requirements plans for parts N and V and subassembly I as described in Solved Problem 2.

   a. Assume that there are currently 100 Ns on hand and scheduled receipts of 40 Is and 10 Vs at the beginning of week 3. No Es are on hand; 120 Es are needed at the start of week 5.

b. Assume on-hand and scheduled receipts as in part *a*. But now suppose that 100 Es are needed at the start of week 5 and 50 at the start of week 7. Also, use multiples of these order sizes: N, 800; V, 200. Use lot-for-lot ordering for I.

4. A firm that produces electric golf carts has just received an order for 200 carts, which are to be ready for delivery at the start of week 8. Information concerning the product structure, lead times, and quantities on hand is shown in the following table. Using this information, do each of the following:
   a. Construct a product tree.
   b. Construct an assembly time chart.
   c. Develop a material requirements plan that will provide 200 golf carts by week 8 assuming lot-for-lot ordering.

Parts list for electric golf cart	Lead time	Quantity on hand
Electric golf cart	1	0
Top	1	40
Base	1	20
Top		
Supports (4)	1	200
Cover	1	0
Base		
Motor	2	300
Body	3	50
Seats (2)	2	120
Body		
Frame	1	35
Controls	1	0
Wheel assemblies (4)	1	240

5. (Refer to the previous problem.) Assume there has been a change in the quantity and timing of orders for golf carts, which is apparently due to unusually mild weather.

The revised plan calls for 100 golf carts at the start of week 6, 100 at the start of week 8, and 100 at the start of week 9.
   a. Develop a master schedule for this revised plan.
   b. Determine the timing and quantities for orders for tops and bases.
   c. Assume now that due to equipment problems, capacity for assembling bases is 50 units per week. Revise your material plan for bases to reflect this, but still meet delivery dates.

6. Assume that you are the manager of Assembly, Inc. and that you have just received an order for 40 units of an industrial robot, which are to be delivered at the start of week 7 of your schedule. Using the following information, determine how many units of subassembly G should be ordered and the timing of those orders, given that subassembly G must be ordered in multiples of 80 units. Assume that there is no other use for the components of this particular robot.

Item	Lead time (weeks)	On hand	Components
Robot	2	10	B,G,C(3)
B	1	5	E,F
C	1	20	G(2),H
E	2	4	—
F	3	8	—
G	2	15	—
H	1	10	—

7. A manufacturing firm buys a certain part in varying quantities throughout the year. Ordering cost is $11 per order, and carrying cost is $.14 per piece per month. Given the following demand schedule for the part for the next eight months, what order sizes would be indicated using an economic part period approach, and when should each order be received? (See the next page.)

Period	Demand
1	—
2	80
3	10
4	30
5	—
6	30
7	—
8	30

8. A firm periodically produces a part that is a basic component of an assembled product it makes. Each time the part is run, a fixed cost of $125 is incurred. The cost to carry one unit for a week has been estimated to be $1.65. For the demand schedule shown, determine the quantity and timing of runs that would be consistent with an economic part-period approach. Assume a one-week lead time for each run.

Week	Demand
1	40
2	20
3	100
4	20
5	—
6	20
7	80

9. Assume that you are the manager of a shop that assembles power tools. An order has just been received for 50 chain saws, which are to be shipped at the start of week 8. Pertinent information on the saws is:

Item	LT (weeks)	On hand	Components
Saw	2	15	A(2),B(1),C(3)
A	1	10	E(3),D(1)
B	2	5	D(2),F(3)
C	2	30	E(2),D(2)
D	1	20	
E	1	10	
F	2	30	

Develop a product structure tree, an assembly time chart, and a master schedule. Also, develop the material requirements plan for component E.

10. End item P is composed of three subassemblies: K, L, and W. K is assembled using 3 Gs and 4 Hs; L is made of 2 Ms and 2 Ns; and W is made using 3 Zs. On-hand inventories are 20 Ls, 40 Gs, and 200 Zs. Scheduled receipts are 10 Ks at the start of week 3 and 30 Ks at the start of week 6.

One hundred Ps are to be shipped at the start of week 7. Lead times are two weeks for subassemblies and one week for components G, H, and M. Final assembly of P requires two weeks. Develop each of the following:
   a. A product structure tree.
   b. An assembly time chart.
   c. A master schedule for P.
   d. A material requirements plan for K, G, and H.

11. Product P is made of three subassemblies, A, B, and C: Two As, three Bs, and 4 Cs are needed for each P. Each A requires three Ms and four Ns; each B requires four Cs and five Ds. If twenty-five Ps are needed and there are 10 units of each subassembly and component part on hand currently, how many additional Cs will be needed?

12. The MRP Department has a problem. Their computer "died" just as it spit out the following information: Planned order release for item J27 = 640 units in week two. The firm has been able to reconstruct all the information they lost except the Master Schedule for end item 565. The firm is fortunate because J27 is used only in 565's. Given the following product structure tree and associated inventory status record information, determine what master schedule entry for 565 was exploded into the material requirements plan that killed the computer.

Part #	On hand	Lot size	Lead time
565	0	Lot-for-lot	1 week
X43	60	120	1 week
N78	0	Lot-for-lot	2 weeks
Y36	200	Lot-for-lot	1 week
J27	0	Lot-for-lot	2 weeks

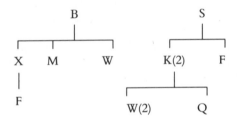

13. The Bloomington Bike Co. produces two models—the Basic and the Supra. Herb Hoosier, the owner, plans to assemble 15 Basics and 10 Supras each week during periods 4–8. Product structure trees for each bike are shown below.

B
X   M   W
F
K(2)   F
W(2)   Q

S

Develop the material requirements plan for component parts K and W over the next 8 weeks. Data on all lead times, current inventory, and ordering rules are given below.

Item	LT (weeks)	On hand	Lot-sizing rule
B	2	5	Lot-for-lot
S	2	2	Lot-for-lot
X	1	5	Q = 25
W	2	2	Multiples of 12
F	1	10	Q = 30
K	1	3	Lot-for-lot
Q	1	15	Q = 30

Scheduled receipts are as follows:

Period 1: 20 Bs; 18 Ws
Period 2: 20 Ss; 15 Fs

14. A company that manufactures paving material for driveways and parking lots projects the demand for its product for the next four weeks to be as follows:

Week	1	2	3	4
Material (tons)	40	80	60	70

The company's labor and machine standards and available capacities are:

	Labor	Machine
Production standard (hour/ton)	4	3
Weekly production capacity (hours)	300	200

a. Determine the capacity utilization for both labor and machine for each of the four weeks.

b. In which weeks do you foresee a problem? What options would you suggest to resolve these? What costs would be relevant in making a decision on choosing an option?

15. A company produces two very similar products that both go through a three-step sequence that involves fabrication, assembly, and packaging. Each step requires one day for a lot to be completely processed and moved to the next department. Processing requirements for the departments (hours per unit) are:

	Fabrication		Assembly		Packaging	
Product	Labor	Machine	Labor	Machine	Labor	Machine
A	2	1	1.5	1	1	.5
B	1	1	1	1	1.5	.5

Department capacities are all 700 hours of labor and 500 hours of machine time, except for Friday, when capacities are 200 hours for both labor and machine time. The production schedule for next week is:

Day	Mon	Tues	Wed	Thurs	Fri
A	200	400	100	300	100
B	300	200	200	200	200

a. Develop a production schedule for each department that shows the capacity re-

quirements for each product and the total load for each day. Ignore changeover time.

b. Evaluate the projected loading for the first three days of the week. Is the schedule feasible? What suggestions can you make in terms of balancing the load?

SELECTED BIBLIOGRAPHY

Blumberg, D. F. "Factors Affecting the Design of a Successful MRP System." *Production and Inventory Management* 21, no. 4 (4th quarter 1980), pp. 50–62.

Fox, Robert E. "OPT vs. MRP: Thoughtware versus Software." *Inventories & Production Magazine* 3, no. 6 (November–December 1983).

———. "MRP, Kanban, or OPT: What's Best?" *Inventories & Production Magazine* 2, no. 4 (July–August 1982).

LaForge, R. C. "MRP and the Part-Period Algorithm." *Journal of Purchasing Management,* Winter 1982, pp. 21–26.

Love, Stephen. *Inventory Control.* New York: McGraw-Hill, 1979.

Orlickly, Joseph. *Material Requirements Planning.* New York: McGraw-Hill, 1975.

Schulz, T. "MRP to BRP: The Journey of the 80's." *Production and Inventory Management Review and APICS News* 1 (October 1981), p. 29.

Theisen, E. C., Jr. "New Game in Town—The MRP Lot Size." *Production and Inventory Management,* 2nd quarter 1974, pp. 1–13.

Vollmann, Thomas E.; Berry, William L.; and Whybark, D. Clay. *Manufacturing, Planning and Control Systems.* 2nd ed. Homewood, Ill.: Richard D. Irwin, 1988.

Wight, Oliver W. *The Executive's Guide to Successful MRP II.* Williston Vt.: Oliver Wight Limited Publications, 1982.

12

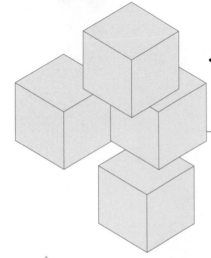

Just-in-Time Systems

LEARNING OBJECTIVES

After completing this chapter, you should be able to:

1. Explain what is meant by the term *just-in-time (JIT) production system.*
2. List each of the key elements of a JIT system and explain its importance.
3. List the benefits of JIT systems.
4. Outline the considerations important in converting a traditional mode of production to a JIT sytem.
5. List some of the obstacles that might be encountered in attempting to convert to a JIT system.

CHAPTER OUTLINE

Over the last decade, a new approach to repetitive manufacturing emerged that is now drawing considerable attention throughout the world. Called the **just-in-time (JIT)** approach, it emphasizes continual effort to remove waste and inefficiency from the production process through small lot sizes, high quality, and teamwork. In this chapter, the basic elements of this new and exciting approach are examined, along with its benefits and limitations and thoughts on implementing the approach in places that now use more traditional methods.

INTRODUCTION

The JIT approach was developed at the Toyota Motor Company of Japan by Mr. Taiichi Ohno (who eventually became vice president of manufacturing) and several of his colleagues. The development of JIT in Japan was probably due to the fact that Japan is a crowded country with few natural resources. Not surprisingly, the Japanese have become very sensitive to waste and inefficiency. They regard scrap and rework as waste, and they regard inventory as an evil because it takes up space and ties up resources.

The name *just-in-time* refers to a production system in which operations (processing, movement of materials and goods, etc.) occur just as they are needed or demanded. The result is very little inventory (i.e., an idle resource); production is very much a hand-to-mouth type of operation. The following article provides a glimpse of how such a system works.

THE NUTS AND BOLTS OF JAPAN'S FACTORIES

Urban C. Lehner

"If American automobile king Henry Ford I were alive today, I am positive he would have done what we did with our Toyota production system."
— Taiichi Ohno in his 1978 book
The Toyota Production System

TOYOTA CITY, Japan—Groping to explain "how Japan does it," experts have made much of the close ties between business and government and of the loyalty of Japan's highly skilled workers to their employers. They've noted the fierce competitiveness of Japanese companies in their home market, the nation's high savings rate, even the relative scarcity of lawyers.

Doubtless these are among the pieces needed to solve the puzzle. But some management consultants who've studied how Japan makes such high-quality, competitively priced products say there's another piece often overlooked. The Japanese, they say, have proved themselves increasingly adroit at organizing and running manufacturing operations. Japanese managers may lack the MBAs or the ability to plot big-picture business strategy of their American counterparts. But they know how to run factories.

"There's a growing acceptance that Japanese success is based at least in part on the development of manufacturing techniques that often tend to outrun our own," says management consultant Rex Reid, head of A T. Kearney's Toyota office.

One of the most interesting examples of Japanese production management skills is a concern quite familiar to Americans: Toyota Motor Co., the largest-selling foreign auto maker in the U.S.

Believe in Their System

Toyota officials resist claiming that their way of building autos is better than anyone else's. They're somewhat embarrassed by the exuberant projections of Henry Ford's behavior essayed by their former chief production executive, Taiichi Ohno, in his 1978 book. But Toyota men clearly remain believers in what Mr. Ohno called "the Toyota production system."

For a first-hand look at the system, take a walk through the Tsutsumi plant here in Toyota City, a town of 280,000 in central Japan that's the site of 8 of Toyota's 10 factories. Over here, Muneo Nakahara, 26 years old and an 8-year Toyota veteran, is doing his job. With the help of an overhead crain that Mr. Nakahara controls from a hand-held device, he hoists auto engines onto a conveyor belt that will take them to be matched up with auto bodies.

Mr. Nakahara is lifting the engines onto the conveyor from a small flat-bed truck that has brought them from the engine plant. Only two trucks carrying only 12 engines apiece park at Mr. Nakahara's post at any given time, so every few minutes an empty truck drives back to the engine plant and a new one takes its place.

That's the first feature of the Toyota system: no inventories. Toyota's factories keep on hand only that amount of parts needed for immediate production, from a few minutes' worth up to a few hours' worth, depending on the part. When fresh parts are needed—and only when they're needed—they're delivered from other Toyota plants or from outside suppliers directly to the production line.

Outsiders who've seen Toyota in action often call this the "kanban system," *kanban* being the Japanese word for the piece of paper enclosed in clear plastic that accompanies each bin of parts. (When a worker on the line begins drawing from a new bin, he re-

moves the kanban and routes it back to the supplier, for whom it serves as an order for a new bin of parts.) But Toyota officials say the pieces of paper are just tools. They call this inventory control aspect of their broader system the "just-in-time" system.

The same philosophy guides the meshing of operations within each plant. An assembly line that is building subcomponents makes just that number of subcomponents immediately needed at the next stage of production. When it's made enough, it's changed over to build some other kind of subcomponent for a while. Likewise, the final assembly line first builds one kind of car, then another, in small lots—only as much as called for in actual orders from Toyota's sales unit. Toyota engineers "average" and "level" production among the lines to coordinate output without building inventories. They compare auto assembly to rowing a boat: Everybody has to be pulling on the oars at the same rate.

"They concentrate very heavily on avoiding end-item and intermediate-item storage," says a Ford official in Detroit who's seen the system at work. "They throw out the whole concept of mass production."

The benefits are substantial. Toyota doesn't need space for inventory, people to handle and control inventory, or borrowed money to finance inventory. "It cuts costs in a lot of ways," says an official of Nissan Motor Co., Japan's second-largest automaker, which has adopted an inventory control system similar to its rival's in some plants.

Then there are the side benefits. Because Toyota is constantly changing over its machines to make new things, its workers have become fast at repair and changeover. In his book, Mr. Ohno cites a mold on a press that took two to three hours to change in the 1940s. Today "it takes only three minutes to change the mold," Mr. Ohno says.

Aside from its emphasis on holding down inventories, Toyota's system stresses quality controls. Throughout the Tsutsumi plant are boards with electric lights to indicate conditions on each assembly line. A red light means a line has been stopped because of a problem. Every worker has a button or cord with which he can stop the line, and he's told to use it whenever he thinks something's wrong with the operation of the line or when he spots defects in the product.

"We lose production temporarily this way," concedes Fujio Cho, manager of the production control department at Toyota's headquarters. "But in our experience stopping lines helps us detect problems early and avoid bad practices."

Another feature that becomes clear is the company's penchant for training workers to do more than one job. The man who runs one machine switches off every few moments to run another. The man who feeds rear windows to a robot also "tags" car shells with instructions telling workers farther down the line what to install in them. This versatility allows Toyota to realign its work force more efficiently when business is bad.

Indeed, "recession" thinking underlies a big part of Toyota's system. Much of the system originated in the late 1940s and early 1950s, when Toyota was producing exclusively for a domestic market that wasn't very strong. The company has been operating on the conventional assumption that it's most efficient to produce in large lots, "but that kind of thinking has pushed us close to bankruptcy, because the large lots we were producing couldn't be sold," says Mr. Cho. Toyota couldn't lay off workers—Japan's a "life-time" employment system—so Toyota executives hit upon the simple yet radical idea that still pervades its operations: Overproduction is waste.

Special Relationship

It is, of course, open to question whether Toyota's is the best way to make cars, and Toyota officials

themselves doubt whether other auto makers could adopt it readily. They note among other problems that it takes a special kind of relationship with suppliers to make the system work.

Fully 50 of Toyota's 250 suppliers are headquartered in Toyota City, and almost all have plants here. They have to be close to make all those deliveries every day. It still shocks Toyota officials to be told that American auto makers buy parts from suppliers all over the United States and even from suppliers in Europe and Japan. Toyota's most distant supplier is a five-hour drive away.

Then, too, suppliers must have close working relations with Toyota to adjust to Toyota's peculiar needs. It isn't surprising that many of Toyota's suppliers do all or most of their business with Toyota, and that Toyota owns large blocks of the stock of some of its most important suppliers. Many suppliers, even those Toyota doesn't own, have adopted Toyota's production system for their own operations. It improves coordination with Toyota and helps them avoid getting stuck with the inventory buildup that Toyota refuses to get stuck with.

The point isn't whether Toyota's system is best. The point is that it's very good and that Toyota is in many ways typical of Japanese manufacturers in its continual striving to improve production techniques. When experts talk about the competitiveness of Japanese products in international markets, that's something that shouldn't be forgotten.

This article provides a number of very important insights on the just-in-time approach to manufacturing, along with some reasons for the successes Japanese manufacturers have achieved. Let's take a close look at the important elements of the system.

KEY ELEMENTS OF JIT SYSTEMS

The essence of JIT production is a smooth flow of product through the system using minimal inventories. The key elements of JIT systems are:

1. A fixed, steady rate of production.
2. Low inventories.
3. Small lot sizes.
4. Quick, low-cost setups.
5. Layout.
6. Preventive maintenance and repair.
7. Multifunctional workers.
8. High quality levels.
9. A cooperative spirit.
10. Reliable vendors.
11. A *pull system* of moving goods.
12. Problem solving.
13. Continual improvement.

Let's examine each of these elements.

A Fixed, Steady Rate of Production

A JIT system of production requires a uniform flow of goods through the system to achieve a meshing of the different operations and the movement of goods and materials from the supplier to the final output. Every activity must be carefully coordinated because such systems have very little slack. Therefore, production schedules must be fixed over a time horizon (often a month) in order for production and purchasing schedules to be established. Once plans are set, they generally are not allowed to change. Obviously, there is great pressure to provide good forecasts and to develop realistic schedules because here, unlike more traditional manufacturing, there is not much inventory to help overcome disruptions in the system.

Low Inventories

People readily associate the term *just-in-time* with low inventories. And, in fact, one of the hallmarks of JIT systems is low inventories—of purchased parts and raw materials, work in process, and finished goods.

There are three important aspects of low inventories. Two reflect benefits of JIT systems, and one reflects a basic requirement of JIT systems. The obvious benefit of low inventories is the savings in space—warehouse space and space in work areas. Savings are also realized by not having to tie up money in idle inventory. The second benefit is more subtle but is a key aspect of the JIT philosophy. Inventories are buffers that tend to cover up problems that keep recurring and are never resolved, partly because they aren't obvious and partly because the presence of inventory makes them seem less serious. Thus, when a machine breaks down, it won't disrupt the system if there is a sufficient inventory of the machine's output to feed into the next workstation. Using inventory as the "solution" can lead to increasing amounts of inventory if breakdowns increase. A better solution would be to investigate the *causes* of machine breakdowns and focus on eliminating them. Similar problems with quality, unreliable vendors, and scheduling can also be "solved" by having ample inventories to fall back on. However, carrying all that extra inventory creates a tremendous burden in cost and space and allows problems to go unresolved.

The JIT approach is to pare down inventories gradually to uncover the problems. Once they are uncovered and solved, more inventory is removed, additional problems are found and solved, and so on. A useful analogy is a boat on a pond that has large, hidden rocks. The rocks represent problems that can hinder production (boat). The water in the pond that covers the rocks is the inventory in the system. As the water level is slowly lowered, the largest rocks are the first to appear (i.e., those problems are the first to be identified). At that point, efforts are undertaken to remove these rocks from the water (i.e., resolve these problems). Once that has been accomplished, additional water is removed from the pond, revealing the next layer of rocks, which are then worked on. As more and more of the rocks are removed, the need for water to cover them diminishes. Likewise, as more and more of the major production problems are solved, there is less and less need to rely on inventory. These concepts are illustrated in Figure 12–1.

The third important aspect of low inventories reflects a basic requirement of JIT systems—that to be able to operate with low inventories, the major problems must have already been resolved. Thus, low inventories are the result of a *process* of successful problem solving, one that has occurred over time. Furthermore, because it is unlikely that all problems will be found and resolved, it is necessary to have the capability to deal quickly with problems when they do occur. Hence, there is a continuing need to identify and solve problems in a short time span to prevent new problems from disrupting the smooth flow of work through the system.

FIGURE 12–1

Large rocks are hidden by a high water level (A). Once the rocks are removed, the water level (inventory) can be lowered (B).

A.

B.

Small Lot Sizes

JIT systems are characterized by small lot sizes, both in the production process and in deliveries from suppliers. These small lot sizes yield a number of benefits that enable JIT systems to operate effectively. One is that with small lots moving through the system, in-process inventory is considerably less than with large lots. This reduces carrying costs as well as space requirements. Another advantage of small lots is that there is less clutter in the workplace. A third advantage is that when problems with quality occur, inspection and rework costs are less because there are fewer items in a lot to inspect and rework.

Small lots also permit greater flexibility in scheduling. Repetitive systems typically produce a variety of products. In more traditional systems, this generally means long production runs of each product, one after the other. Although this spreads the setup cost for a run over many items, it also results in long cycles over the entire range of products. For instance, suppose a firm has three products, A, B, and C. In a traditional system, there would be a long run of product A (say, covering two or three days or more), then a long run of product B, and then a long run of product C before the sequence would repeat. In contrast, a JIT system, using small lots, would frequently shift from producing A to producing B and C. This gives JIT systems greater flexibility in scheduling, enabling them to respond more quickly to changing customer demands for output. In this way, JIT systems can produce just what is needed, when it is needed. The constrast between small and large lot sizes is illustrated in Figure 12–2.

It is worthwhile to note that in the JIT philosophy, the ideal lot size is one unit. Although that quantity may not always be a realistic goal because of practical considerations that require minimum lot sizes (e.g., machines that process multiple items simultaneously, heat-treating equipment that processs multiple items simultaneously, and machines with very high setup times), the goal is still to try to reduce the lot size as much as possible because small lot sizes have numerous benefits.

FIGURE 12–2

JIT versus large lot run sizes

JIT approach

AAA   BBBBBBB   CC   AAA   BBBBBBB   CC   AAA   BBBBBBB   CC   AAA   BBBBBBB   CC

Time →

Large-lot approach

AAAAAAAAAAAAAA   BBBBBBBBBBBBBBBBBBBBBBBBBBBBBBB   CCCCCCCCC   AAAAAAAAAAAA

Time →

Quick, Low-Cost Setups

Small lots and changing product mixes require frequent setups. Unless these are quick and relatively inexpensive, the time and cost to accomplish them would be prohibitive. Often, workers are trained to do their own setups. Moreover, programs to reduce setup time and cost are used to achieve the desired results; a deliberate effort is required, and workers are usually a valuable part of the process.

Setup tools and equipment, as well as setup procedures, must be simple and standardized. Multipurpose equipment or attachments can help to reduce setup time. For instance, a machine with multiple spindles that can easily be rotated into place for different job requirements can drastically reduce job changeover time. Moreover, *group technology* may be used to reduce setup cost and time by capitalizing on similarities in recurring operations. For instance, parts that are similar (in shape, materials, etc.) may require very similar setups. Processing them in sequence on the same equipment can reduce the need to completely change a setup; minor adjustment may be all that is necessary.

Layout

Traditional factories often use layouts based on processing requirements (i.e., work centers designed to handle a certain type of processing, such as drilling, cutting, or packaging). Consequently, in traditional manufacturing systems, a group of parts moved from one processing center to the next. Each move adds to the time in which parts are in the system, as lots wait to be moved, wait at the next center to be processed, and so on. This also adds to the amount of inventory in the system. In such systems, the time devoted to actually working on a part may constitute less than 5 percent of the time a part is in the system. For the remaining 95 percent of the time, no useful purpose is served by having the part in the system; no value is added. In a real sense, there is a considerable amount of waste and inefficiency.

JIT systems commonly use layouts based on product requirements. Equipment is arranged to handle streams of similar products with similar processing or assembly requirements. This avoids having to move large lots of parts around the work area; parts pass in small lots from one work center to the next with little or no waiting and with substantially less need for in-process inventory. Moreover, material handling costs are greatly reduced, as is the space needed to support a given level of output. Factories tend to be smaller and more efficient, and machines can be moved closer together, which has the further benefit of enhancing communication among workers.

Preventive Maintenance and Repair

Because JIT systems have very little in-process inventory, equipment breakdowns can be very disruptive. To minimize breakdowns, companies use **preventive maintenance** programs, which emphasize maintaining equipment in good operating condition and replacing parts that have a tendency to fail before they actually fail. Workers are often responsible for maintaining their own equipment.

Even with preventive maintenance, there will be occasional equipment failures. Consequently, it is necessary for companies to be prepared for this and to be able to quickly return equipment to working order. This may mean maintaining supplies of critical spare parts and making other provisions for emergency situations, such as maintaining a small force of repair people or training workers to do certain repairs themselves.

Note, too, that when breakdowns do occur, they are a further indication of a potential area for improvement. Thus, breakdowns become an opportunity to be exploited in a JIT system.

Multifunctional Workers

In traditional production systems, it is not unusual to find that a worker is trained for a relatively narrow set of tasks. For instance, some workers are trained to operate machinery, others to handle setups, and still others to perform maintenance and repair. JIT systems feature **multifunctional workers,** trained to handle all of those tasks. That does not mean that workers are trained as master mechanics; major repairs are usually handled by repair people. However, workers are expected to be able to handle adjustments and minor repairs as well as do their own setups. Remember, though, that under JIT systems, efforts are made to simplify setups, making it more appropriate to assign them to operators.

Workers in JIT systems are often trained to handle more than one production operation. That way, if a worker falls behind, others will be able to assist him or her in maintaining the schedule.

Workers are also responsible for checking the quality of their own work and monitoring the quality of work they receive as input to their stations. Workers are also expected to participate in problem solving. Note, however, that in spite of all this worker involvement, there is the expectation that workers will strictly adhere to schedules, and if a worker believes that he or she has discovered an improved way of doing a task, that idea is to be submitted to others and approved before it is implemented. Hence, workers are not permitted to alter established methods or routines on their own.

Flexible workers is a concept that has much to offer, but it is not without a downside. One negative aspect is the training cost and time that may be required to crosstrain highly skilled workers. Another is that workers may resist flexibility for reasons such as loss of job security and the burden involved in learning new skills. Older workers may be shunted off to early retirement rather than retrained because their benefit time would be much shorter than that of younger workers. Thus, it will be important for companies to carefully consider which jobs are best suited to multifunctional workers, and which are not. In all likelihood, the lowest skilled jobs will be the ones that will lead to the benefits of flexible workers.

High Quality Levels

JIT systems require high quality levels. The systems are geared to a smooth flow of work; the appearance of problems due to poor quality creates disruption in this flow. In fact, because small lot sizes and the absence of buffer stock result in low in-process inventories, if problems occur, production must cease until they have been resolved. Obviously, shutting down an entire process is costly and cuts into planned output levels, so it becomes imperative to avoid any shutdowns or to quickly resolve problems when they do appear.

JIT systems use a three-pronged approach to deal with quality. One prong is to design quality into the product and the production process. The fact that JIT systems produce standardized product leads to standardized job methods, workers who are very familiar with their jobs, and the use of standardized equipment, all of which contribute to high quality levels. Moreover, the cost of product design quality (i.e., building quality in at the *design* stage) can be spread over many units, yielding a low cost per unit.

A second prong of the approach is to insist that vendors provide high-quality materials and parts to minimize disruptions due to problems with incoming goods. Once a high degree of confidence in vendor quality has been achieved, the time and cost of inspecting incoming goods can be practically eliminated.

The third prong of the approach is to make workers responsible for producing goods of high quality. This requires providing adequate equipment and tools to do the work, providing proper training in work methods, providing training in measuring quality and detecting errors, supporting and encouraging worker efforts to improve quality, and enlisting workers in the problem solving effort when problems are found.

A Cooperative Spirit

JIT systems require a cooperative spirit among workers, management, and vendors. Unless that is present, it is doubtful that a truly effective JIT system can be achieved. The Japanese have been very successful in this regard, partly because in the Japanese culture, respect and cooperation are ingrained. In Western cultures, workers, managers, and vendors have historically been strongly at odds with each other. Consequently, a major consideration in operating under a JIT system is to achieve and maintain a spirit of mutual respect and cooperation. This requires an appreciation of the importance of cooperation and a tenacious effort to instill and maintain that spirit.

Reliable Vendors

Most JIT systems extend to vendors. Vendors are required to deliver high-quality parts and/or materials, in small lots, at fairly precise intervals.

Traditionally, buyers have assumed the role of monitoring the quality of purchased goods, inspecting shipments for quality and quantity, and returning poor-quality goods to the vendor for rework. Under JIT production, there is little slack, so poor-quality goods will cause a disruption in the smooth flow of work. Moreover, having to inspect incoming goods is viewed as inefficient because it does not add value to the product. For these reasons, the burden of ensuring quality is shifted to the vendor. Buyers work with vendors to help them achieve the desired quality levels and to impress upon them the importance of consistent, high-quality goods. The ultimate goal of the buyer is to be able to *certify* a vendor as a producer of high-quality goods. The implication of this certification is that a vendor can be relied on to deliver high-quality goods *without the need for buyer inspection.*

Suppliers must also be willing and able to ship in small lots on a regular basis. Ideally, suppliers themselves will be operating under JIT systems. Buyers can often help suppliers convert to JIT production based on their own experiences. In effect, the supplier becomes part of an extended JIT system that integrates the facilities of buyer and supplier. If a supplier is dedicated to only one or a few buyers, this will make integration easier. Practically speaking, a supplier is likely to have many different buyers, some using traditional systems and others using JIT. Consequently, compromises may have to be made by both buyers and vendors.

Such a spirit of cooperation between buyer and seller has not traditionally been present. In fact, traditionally, buyers and vendors have had a somewhat adversarial relationship. Buyers have generally regarded price as a major determinant in sourcing. Moreover, buyers have typically used *multiple-source* purchasing, which means having a list of potential vendors and buying from several to avoid getting locked into a sole source. In this way, buyers can play vendors off against each other to get better pricing arrangements or other concessions. The downside of this is that vendors cannot rely on a long-term relationship with a buyer; therefore, vendors have not felt loyalty to a particular buyer. Furthermore, vendors have often sought to protect themselves from losing a buyer by increasing the number of buyers they supply.

Under JIT purchasing, good vendor relationships are very important. Buyers take measures to reduce their lists of suppliers, concentrating on maintaining close working relationships with a few good ones. In addition, because of the need for frequent, small deliveries, many buyers attempt to find local vendors to shorten the lead time for deliveries as well as to reduce lead time variability. An added advantage of dealing with nearby vendors is quick response when problems do arise.

JIT purchasing is enhanced by *long-term* relationships between buyers and vendors. Vendors are more willing to commit resources to the job of shipping according to a buyer's JIT system given a long-term relationship. Moreover, price often becomes secondary to the other aspects of the relationship (e.g., consistent high quality; flexibility; frequent, small deliveries; and quick response to problems).

Push versus Pull

The terms *push* and *pull* are used to describe two different systems for moving work through a production process. In a **push system,** when work is finished at a workstation, the output is *pushed* to the next station; or, in the case of the final operation, it is pushed on to final inventory. Conversely, in a **pull system,** control of moving the work rests with the *following* operation; each workstation *pulls* the output from the preceding station as it is needed. Output of the final operation is pulled by customer demand or the master schedule. Thus, in a pull system, work is moved in response to demand from the next stage in the process, whereas in a push system, work is pushed on as it is completed, with no regard for whether the next station is ready for the work. Consequently, work may pile up at workstations that fall behind schedule, say, because of equipment failure or the detection of a problem with quality.

JIT systems use the pull approach to control the flow of work, with each workstation gearing its output to the demand presented by the next workstation. Traditional production systems use the push approach for moving work through the system. In JIT systems, there is communication backward through the system from station to station, so that work moves "just in time" for the next operation; the flow of work is thereby coordinated, and the accumulation of excessive inventories between operations is avoided. Of course, some inventory is usually present because operations are not instantaneous. That is, if a workstation waited until it received a request from the next workstation before *starting* its work, the next station would have to wait for the preceding station to perform its work. Therefore, by design, each workstation produces just enough output to meet the (anticipated) demand of the next station. This can be accomplished by having the following workstation communicate its need for input sufficiently ahead of time to allow the preceding station to do the work. Or there can be a small buffer of stock between stations; when the buffer decreases to a certain level, this signals the preceding station to produce enough output to replenish the buffer supply. The size of the buffer depends on the cycle time at the preceding work station: if the cycle time is short, little or no buffer will be needed; if the cycle time is long, a considerable amount of buffer will be needed. Note, however, that production occurs only in response to *usage* of the following station; work is *pulled* by the demand generated by the next operation.

An important feature of a pull system is that work flow is dictated by "next-step demand." There are a variety of ways in which such demand can be communicated, including a shout or a wave, but by far the most commonly used device is the **kanban** card. *Kanban* is a Japanese term that means *signal* or *visible record*. When a worker needs materials or work from the preceding station, he or she uses a kanban card to communicate this. In effect, the kanban card is the authorization to move or work on parts. In Kanban systems, no part or lot can be moved or worked on without one of these cards.

The system works in this way: A kanban card is affixed to each container. When a workstation needs to replenish its supply of parts, a worker goes to the area where these parts are stored and withdraws one container of parts. Each container holds a predetermined quantity. The worker removes the kanban card from the container and posts it in a designated spot where it will be clearly visible, and the worker then moves the lot to the workstation. The posted kanban is then picked up by a stock person who replenishes the stock with another container, and so on down the line. Demand for parts triggers a replenishment, and parts are supplied as usage dictates. Similar withdrawals and replenishments occur all the way up and down the line from finished goods inventory to vendors, all controlled by kanbans. In fact, if supervisors decide the system is too loose because inventories are building up, they may decide to withdraw some kanbans, thereby tightening the system. Conversely, if the system seems too tight, additional kanbans may be introduced to bring the system into balance.

It is apparent that the number of kanban cards in use is an important variable. The ideal number of kanban cards can be computed using this formula:

$$N = \frac{DT(1 + X)}{C}$$

where

N = Total number of containers
D = Planned usage rate of using work center
T = Average waiting time for replenishment of parts plus average production time for a container of parts
X = Policy variable set by management that reflects possible inefficiency in the system (the closer to 0, the more efficient the system)
C = Capacity of a standard container (should be no more than 10 percent of daily usage of the part)

Note that D and T must use the same time units (e.g., minutes, days).

EXAMPLE 1

Usage at a work center is 300 parts per day, and a standard container holds 25 parts. It takes an average of .12 day for a container to complete a circuit from the time a kanban card is received until the container is returned empty. Compute the number of kanban cards needed if $X = .20$.

EXAMPLE 1 *(concluded)*

Solution

$$N = ?$$
$$D = 300 \text{ parts per day}$$
$$T = .12 \text{ day}$$
$$C = 25 \text{ units}$$
$$X = .20$$

$$N = \frac{300(.12)(1 + .20)}{25} = 1.728 \text{ (round to two containers)}$$

Note that rounding down will cause the system to be tighter, and rounding up will cause it to be looser. Generally, rounding up is used.

Problem Solving

Problem solving is a cornerstone of any JIT system. Of interest are problems that interrupt, or have the potential to interrupt, the smooth flow of work through the system. When such problems surface, it becomes important to resolve them quickly. This may entail *temporarily* increasing inventory levels while the problem is investigated, but the intent of problem solving is to *eliminate* the problem, or at least greatly reduce the chances of it recurring.

Problems that occur during production must be dealt with quickly. Some companies use a light system to signal problems; in Japan, such a system is called **andon.** Each workstation is equipped with a set of three lights. A green light means no problems, an amber light means a worker is falling a little bit behind, and a red light indicates a serious problem. The point of the light system is to keep others in the system informed and to enable workers and supervisors to immediately see when and where problems are occurring.

Japanese companies have been very successful in forming teams composed of workers and managers that routinely work on problems. Moreover, workers are encouraged to report problems and potential problems to the teams. Teams may use **brainstorming** to generate possible solutions, where members meet and share thoughts and ideas on how problems might be resolved. The essence of these sessions is to encourage free thinking, so criticism is discouraged. Furthermore, a group may prefer to withhold analysis of ideas when they are presented in order to keep from stifling initiative or creating an atmosphere in which there is hesitancy in presenting potential solutions.

Groups may also use various statistical tools and quality control techniques (described in Chapter 16) such as sampling, control charts, and cause-and-effect diagrams.

It is important that management at all levels actively support and become involved in problem solving. This also requires a willingness to provide financial support and to recognize achievements. It is desirable to formulate goals with the help of workers, publicize the goals, and carefully document accomplishments. Goals give workers something tangible to strive for, and recognition can help maintain worker interest and morale.

Continual Improvement

The central theme of a true just-in-time approach is to work toward continual improvement of the system (i.e., reducing inventories, reducing setup cost and time, improving quality, increasing the output rate, and generally cutting waste and inefficiency). Toward that end, problem solving becomes a way of life—a "culture" that must be assimilated into the thinking of management and workers alike. It becomes a never-ending quest for improving operations as all members of the organization strive to improve the system.

JIT versus Traditional Manufacturing

The preceding pages have described JIT systems and compared them to traditional manufacturing systems. Table 12–1 provides a brief overview of those comparisons.

TABLE 12–1

Comparison of JIT and typical U.S. manufacturing philosophies

Factors	JIT	American philosophy
Inventory	A liability. Every effort must be expended to do away with it.	An asset. It protects against forecast errors, machine problems, late vendor deliveries. More inventory is "safer."
Lot size	Immediate needs only. A minimum replenishment quantity is desired for both manufactured and purchased parts.	Formulas. We're always revising the optimum lot size with some formula based on the trade-off between the cost of inventories and the cost of setup.
Setups	Make them insignificant. This requires either extremely rapid changeover to minimize the impact on production or the availability of extra machines already set up. Fast changeover makes small lot sizes practical and allows a wide variety of parts to be made frequently.	Low priority. Maximum output is the usual goal. Rarely does similar thought and effort go into achieving quick changeover.

TABLE 12–1 *(concluded)*

Comparison of JIT and typical U.S. manufacturing philosophies

Factors	JIT	American philosophy
Queues	Eliminate them. When problems occur, identify the causes and correct them. The correction process is aided when queues are small.	Necessary investment. Queues permit succeeding operations to continue in the event of a problem with the feeding operation. Also, by providing a selection of jobs, factory management has a greater opportunity to match varying operator skills and machine capabilities, combine setups, and, thus, contribute to the efficiency of the operation.
Vendors	Co-workers. They're part of the team. Multiple deliveries for all active items are expected daily. The vendor takes care of the needs of the customer, and the customer treats the vendor as an extension of the factory.	Adversaries. Multiple sources are the rule, and it's typical to play them off against each other.
Quality	Zero defects. If quality is not 100%, production is in jeopardy.	Tolerate some scrap. We usually track what the actual scrap has been and develop formulas for predicting it.
Equipment maintenance	Constant and effective. Machine breakdowns must be minimal.	As required. Not critical because we have queues available.
Lead times	Keep them short. This simplifies the job of marketing, purchasing, and manufacturing, as it reduces the need for expediting.	The longer the better. Most foremen and purchasing agents want more lead time, not less.
Workers	Management by consensus. Changes are not made until consensus is reached, whether or not a bit of arm twisting is involved. The vital ingredient of "ownership" is achieved.	Management by edict. New systems are installed in spite of the workers, not thanks to the workers. Then we concentrate on measurements to determine whether or not they're doing their jobs.

Source: Modern Materials Handling, Copyright 1982 in article by Walter E. Goddard, Oliver Wight Education Associates, by Cahners Publishing Company, Division of Reed Holdings, Inc.

MRP II VERSUS KANBAN[1]

Although the goals of MRP II and kanban are essentially the same (i.e., to improve customer service, reduce inventories, and increase productivity), their approaches are quite different. Neither MRP nor kanban is a stand-alone

---

[1] Based on an article by Walt Goddard, "Kanban versus MRP II—Which Is Best for You?" *Modern Materials Handling,* November 5, 1982.

system—each exists within a larger framework. MRP II is basically a computerized system; kanban is a manual system.

Kanban systems generally involve very small lot sizes, short lead times, and high-quality output, and they exemplify teamwork. Kanban is essentially a two-bin type of inventory; supplies are replenished semiautomatically when they reach a predetermined level. MRP II is more concerned with projecting requirements and with planning and leveling capacity via the computer.

A major benefit of the kanban system is its simplicity; a major benefit of MRP II is its ability to handle complex planning and scheduling quickly and efficiently. It also handles changes fairly easily. In addition, MRP II is capable of simulation (i.e., it enables management to answer "what if" questions) for capacity planning.

A comparison of how eight manufacturing functions are controlled by kanban and MRP II is presented in Table 12–2. Note that the two are the same in terms of employing a master schedule (products to be built) but differ in

TABLE 12–2

Comparison of kanban and MRP II

Functions	*Categories*	*Kanban system*	*MRP II*
Rates of output	Families of products	Leveling	Production plan
Products to be built	Finished goods for make-to-stock, customer orders for make-to-order	Master production schedule	Master production schedule
Materials required	Components—both manufactured and purchased	Kanban cards	Material requirements planning (MRP)
Capacity required	Output for key work centers and vendors	Visual	Capacity requirements planning (CRP)
Executing capacity plans	Producing enough output to satisfy plans	Visual	Input/output controls (I/O)
Executing material plans—manufactured items	Working on right priorities in factory	Kanban cards	Dispatching reports
Executing material plan—purchased items	Bringing in right items from vendors	Kanban cards and unofficial orders	Purchasing reports
Feedback information	What cannot be executed due to problems	Andon	Anticipated delay reports

Note: The same functions are performed by every manufacturing company; however, the tools used by kanban differ greatly from the MRP II tools. Under kanban, the tools are manual—kanban cards, andon lights, visual checks, and oral orders. Under MRP II, the most important tool is the computer.
Source: Reprinted from Walt Goddard, "Kanban versus MRP II—Which Is Best for You?" *Modern Materials Handling,* November 5, 1982.

terms of every other function. Note, too, that the kanban approach is considerably less formal than MRP II.

Another difficulty is that the philosophies that underlie JIT systems are quite different from the philosophies that manufacturers have traditionally held. Hence, a major effort to change will be required. That will not occur without the support of top management, and, even then, it will undoubtedly require much effort on all levels to overcome the ingrained resistance to such management changes. Chief among these management philosophies is that inventories of safety stocks should be maintained "just in case" something goes wrong. Realistically speaking, the focus has to shift from "who's to blame?" to "let's fix this so it won't happen again."

Whether manufacturers should adopt the kanban method is debatable. Some form of it may be useful, but kanban is merely an information system; by itself it offers little in terms of helping manufacturers become more competitive and/or productive. By the same token, MRP by itself will not achieve those results either. Instead, it is the overall approach to manufacturing that is crucial; it is the commitment and support of top management and the continuing efforts of all levels of management to find new ways to improve their manufacturing planning and control techniques, and then to adapt those techniques to fit their own particular set of circumstances, that will determine the degree of success. What can be said is that problems must be identified and eliminated in the manufacturing cycle and that improved methods of production planning and control are needed—improvements that will come about only through effort and determination.

BENEFITS OF JIT SYSTEMS

JIT systems have a number of important benefits that are attracting the attention of companies that produce using more traditional methods. The main benefits are:

1. Reduced levels of in-process inventories, purchased goods, and finished goods.
2. Reduced space requirements.
3. Increased product quality and reduced scrap and rework.
4. Reduced manufacturing lead times.
5. Greater flexibility in changing the production mix.
6. Smoother flow of production, with fewer disruptions caused by problems due to quality; shorter setup times; multiskilled workers who can help each other and substitute for others in case of absenteeism.
7. Increased productivity levels and utilization of equipment.
8. Worker participation in problem solving.
9. Pressure to build good relationships with vendors.
10. Reduction in the need for certain indirect labor, such as material handlers.

CONVERTING TO A JIT SYSTEM

The success of JIT systems in Japan has attracted keen interest among U.S. manufacturers. A number of well-known firms have converted a portion of their operations to JIT systems.

To increase the probability that conversion will be successful, companies should adopt a carefully planned approach that includes the following elements:

1. Make sure top management is committed to the conversion and that they know what will be required. Furthermore, make sure that management is willing to provide *visible* support. Make sure that management knows what it will cost and how long it will take to complete the conversion, and what results can be expected.

2. Study the operations carefully; decide which parts will need the most effort to convert.

3. Obtain the support and cooperation of workers. Prepare training programs that include sessions on setups, maintenance of equipment, cross-training for multiple tasks, cooperation, and problem solving. Make sure workers are fully informed on what JIT is and why it is desirable. Reassure workers that their jobs are secure.

4. Begin by trying to reduce setup times while maintaining the current system. Enlist the aid of workers in identifying and eliminating existing problems (bottlenecks, poor quality, etc.).

5. Gradually convert operations, beginning at the *end* of the process and working *backward*. At each stage, make sure the conversion has been relatively successful before moving on. Do not begin to reduce inventories until major problems have been resolved.

6. Convert suppliers to JIT as one of the last steps. Be prepared to work closely with them. Start by narrowing the list of vendors, identifying those who are willing to embrace the JIT philosophy. Give preference to vendors who have long-term track records as being reliable. Try to use vendors located nearby if quick response time is important. Establish long-term commitments with vendors. Insist on high standards of quality and adherence to strict delivery schedules.

7. Be prepared to encounter obstacles to conversion.

Obstacles to Conversion

There can be numerous obstacles to conversion. Among the most crucial are the following:

1. Management may not be totally committed or may be unwilling to devote the necessary resources to conversion. This is perhaps the most serious impediment; the conversion is likely to be doomed without it.

2. Workers and/or management may not display a cooperative spirit. The system is predicated on cooperation. Managers may resist because JIT shifts some of the responsibility from management to the workers and gives workers more control over the work. Workers themselves may resist because shared responsibility and cooperation is alien to them and because people generally resist change, preferring the known to the unknown.

3. Suppliers may resist, for several reasons:
   a. Buyers may not be willing to commit the resources necessary to help the supplier adapt to the JIT systems.
   b. They may be uneasy about long-term commitments to a buyer.
   c. Frequent, small deliveries may be difficult, especially if the supplier has other buyers that are not using JIT systems.
   d. The burden of quality control will shift to the supplier.
   e. Frequent engineering changes may have to be made as the result of continuing JIT improvements on the part of the buyer.

Converting to a JIT system can sometimes be a formidable undertaking, as illustrated by the following reading.

AUTO MAKERS HAVE TROUBLE WITH "KANBAN"

DETROIT—Sushi may be sweeping the West Coast, but here in Motor City the latest craze is *Kanban.*

Kanban is the word for Japanese auto manufacturers' precise methods of controlling inventories so that suppliers deliver needed parts to the assembly line "just in time." Holding inventories of engines, axles, and other parts to an absolute minimum saves Japanese auto makers hundreds of dollars per car in storage and carrying costs.

American car makers would dearly love such savings, but, like raw fish, Kanban may be difficult to swallow. As they get deeper into it, the domestic auto companies are finding that their system of manufacturing cars favors large stockpiles of parts. Changing that system is going to be a difficult and expensive process.

Over the long haul, altering the inventory system probably will be worth the effort. Robert Burrows, a specialist in inventory management at Booz, Allen & Hamilton, Inc., estimates that it costs General Motors well over $3 billion a year to carry its approximately $9 billion in worldwide inventories. The costs include storage, handling, staffing, freight charges, and losses due to obsolescence, defects, and tying up of inventory funds that otherwise could be earning a profitable return. GM, Mr. Burrows says, could cut those expenses by more than two thirds.

Some success

Progress comes easy at first. Anthony E. Ewert, director of materials management at GM's Buick Motor division, found he could reduce stocks of metal body stampings at Buick's Flint assembly plant merely by switching to truck delivery from rail delivery. Trucks now make three deliveries of stampings a day, usually keeping the plant's inventory under 700. For years, stampings had been delivered every two days on rail cars, and the plant's inventory often totaled more than 4,000.

Other auto makers have had some success, too. Ford Motor Co. says it has reduced its stock by $750 million in the past two years, slashing its carrying costs by more than $250 million. Chrysler claims a $200 million reduction in inventories in the past six months.

But as they solve the easy problems, auto executives in charge of installing the new system are encountering other obstacles, including the different geographic distribution of U.S. factories and widespread resistance to change within their companies.

In Japan, most suppliers are clustered around auto makers' assembly plants, making timely delivery cheaper and more reliable. U.S. assembly plants and suppliers are scattered around the country. Some parts take weeks to be shipped, which increases both the amount of inventory in transit and the supplies needed to guard against interrupted deliveries. A GM executive estimates that at any time more than half of the company's inventory is on trucks and trains.

Demand and supplies

Another difficulty for domestic auto makers has been to set accurate production forecasts. Faced with sputtering demand, the car companies have had trouble judging how many parts to order. "You need about 20 days of orders in hand to set a smooth schedule," says William J. Harahan, Ford's manager of manufacturing planning. "But lately we've been lucky to get 10 days."

The Japanese, on the other hand, have been able to run their plants at near full capacity, allowing them to schedule production weeks in advance and to send exact instructions to their suppliers. "They've got it down to where they can tell a vendor they want a certain number of parts delivered next week at a specified hour," says GM's Mr. Ewert. "We can't do that."

The Japanese system also is simpler to manage because the companies rely on fewer suppliers. Toyota Motor Co. has less than 250. By comparison GM has more than 3,500 suppliers just for its assembly operations, an amount it hopes to reduce.

Stocking for options

The drive to trim inventories at U.S. plants goes against long-standing practices. For years, marketing departments in auto companies have demanded numerous options and different trim packages so that customers can practically design their own cars. Manufacturing executives usually agreed to the idea of options because it didn't add much to the amount of labor that went into a car.

But the effect on inventories has been enormous. A buyer of one of Chrysler's Omni subcompacts can choose among several different chrome strips to go on the car doors. Because the strips require different mountings, the assembly plant has to stock several kinds of chrome strips as well as several kinds of doors.

Incentive systems in manufacturing also don't support inventory control. Robert Stone, a GM vice president, says a program to reduce stock at one plant ran into trouble because the production superintendent refused to turn off his equipment when the factory was building too many parts. The reason: His salary was based on the efficiency of his output.

Even the layout of their plants is an obstacle for U.S. auto makers. The Buick assembly plant in Flint, for example, was built in 1946 to accommodate mostly rail deliveries. Now that Mr. Ewert is trying to switch more deliveries to trucks, one of his biggest headaches is moving trucks in and out of the plant's small loading docks. If sales pick up, the loading docks could be swamped.

So far, most of the steps U.S. auto makers have taken involve their costliest parts: engines, transmissions, and axles. "That's the area to begin," says Buick's Mr. Ewert. "You can affect about 90 percent of the dollars you have tied up by tightening down on 10 percent of the parts."

GM claims success at some of its Midwestern assembly plants with a new procedure to control the supply of major components by ordering each morning only the parts needed that day. Previously, the parts were shipped based on a average daily requirement, which often varied significantly from the actual production.

Ford, however, recently had to abandon a similar system for shipping engines from a factory in Dearborn, Michigan, to a nearby assembly plant. A Ford official says sporadic production at the car plant was hurting the engine factory's ability to produce at a smooth, efficient rate.

Auto makers are confident that the new procedures will work better when car sales pick up. But they still see a long fight in the battle against inventories. "It took Toyota 10 years to implement their system," says Ford's Mr. Harahan. "We've really just begun."

Firms must decide whether a JIT approach will be advantageous. The next article makes some interesting points on this.

JIT HITS AMERICAN INDUSTRY— BUT NOT WITHOUT DRAWBACKS

JIT fever is catching. That is, nearly 65% of the buyers contacted by PURCHASING Magazine correspondents nationwide say their firms employ some facet of JIT or plan to do so in the near future. Compare that to a similar PURCHASING survey taken a year ago when 35% of respondents said their firms had a just-in-time system in place or were getting ready to implement one.

Why the jump in numbers? The reasons are as varied as the companies that employ JIT. Says William Cuilty, director of material at Rockwell Semiconductor Products Division, Newport Beach, Calif.: "The basic drive to implement JIT was the need to respond to our customers. We needed to react quickly to the different mix of our customers and JIT gives us the latitude to do that."

Schwinn Bicycle Co., Chicago, is working toward a customized JIT system because it means "better asset management for the company as a whole" and allows for "better control of the manufacturing process," says Steven Bina, manager of purchasing administration and domestic operations.

But "if you define JIT as 'arrive today—use tomorrow,' then it is not our goal," continues Bina. "If you mean timing deliveries more closely to the manufacturing process, then Schwinn is going in that direction—but it will take time to build a good system."

JIT American-style. Schwinn is not alone— American firms are indeed doing JIT their way. Robert D. Miller, corporate materials manager, FMC Corp., Chicago, best sums up the consensus: "Every one of our operations implements some aspect of JIT; few, if any, embrace all the philosophies. But we would like to make that happen. That's what we're working towards."

Says Bill Eisenman, operations director, NCR

Corp., Columbia S.C., "we use 'short cycle manufacturing' and JIT is part of this cycle." He estimates that about 10-million of 92-million parts delivered are on an "as needed" basis. "It [JIT] makes you eliminate waste and become more concerned with the quality of your pieces. It's different from the old days of matching inventory with product until it worked."

Quality and flexibility were cited by respondents as the big benefits. "You don't get encumbered with vast inventories—sins of the past—and it is easy to change to new products," says FMC's Miller. "It has made FMC more competitive in some markets . . . We don't view JIT as an inventory reduction tool here at FMC, but it happens. And the reduction in the overall cost of the product is also a major effect."

While there definitely appear to be advantages to JIT, buyers report that there are still some kinks that need to be worked out of the system. For example, Ford Motor Co.'s Dearborn, Mich., production parts facility ships auto bumpers to one of its assembly plants in Atlanta via an outside warehouse. Purchasing agent Bill Britts says this system was initiated to cut inventory costs and improve product quality. But, he says, there are problems. "The union here is on strike because that warehouse uses non-union labor. I'm standing here talking to you about the system while I can see picketers outside walking against it."

NCR's Eisenman says that a company must weigh freight costs when considering implementing JIT. "In the Southeast, you go great distances to get parts because few suppliers are located nearby. It's not like Japan where everybody's close by—most of our suppliers are on the West coast and in Florida and Texas."

He adds: "I don't want one screw to hold up a

$20,000 product, so I make sure I have those screws in my inventory." And John Heard, purchasing agent at Mead Corp. in Atlanta, concurs, "I don't want my employees out of work because I think there's a train sitting in the yard with materials and I find it's not there. I have to have back-up."

FMC's Miller believes that "the only potential drawback is in the implementation of JIT, not in JIT itself . . . It's hard to get everyone on board agreeing to its value. There are some champions but disagreement tends to fractionalize management. If you can get people with years of experience to buy into it, it won't be a negative situation. But if you can't accomplish that, there could be problems."

At McDonnell Douglas Corp.'s Aircraft division in St. Louis, John Calhoun, director of manufacturing engineering, takes that idea one step further: "Any decision must consider leadtimes, parts values, and capacity and a management team not willing to make a commitment to excellence will not witness anything from JIT."

It's not for everyone. Joe Tew, assistant director of materials, Lockheed-Georgia Co., Marietta, Ga., says he looked into the possibilities of using JIT, but dismissed the idea because it doesn't suit his company's situation. "For JIT you need a constantly moving assembly line. We move an entire airplane from station to station, and there are 20 stations in building a C-5A aircraft."

Buyers at Burgess-Norton Mfg. Co., a division of Amsted Industries (manufacturers and marketers of products for the construction and building markets, railroads, and general industry) in Chicago haven't jumped on the JIT bandwagon either. Reason: Burgess-Norton uses one raw material (steel) in uncommon grades and specialized diameters. Says PM George Lissy: "We have been contacted by service centers to talk about commonizing supplies and having the end user draw from that, but because our needs are so specialized no one will hold that type of inventory."

Source: *Purchasing,* September 11, 1986, p. 18. Reprinted by permission.

OPERATIONS STRATEGY

The JIT philosophy of production offers new perspectives on manufacturing that must be given serious consideration by managers in repetitive manufacturing who wish to be competitive.

Potential adopters should carefully study the requirements and benefits of JIT systems, as well as difficulties and strengths of their current systems, before making a decision on whether or not to convert to JIT. Careful estimates of time and cost to convert are essential, as is an assessment of how likely workers, managers, and suppliers are to cooperate in such an approach.

The decision to convert can be sequential, giving management an opportunity to gain firsthand experience with portions of JIT without committing themselves wholesale. For instance, improving vendor relations, reducing setup times, and improving quality are all worthwhile goals on their own. Similarly, efforts to reduce waste and inefficiency are also desirable goals. Moreover, a level production schedule is a necessary element of a JIT system, and achieving that will also be useful under a traditional system of operation.

The important thing is to not dismiss the concept of JIT production without giving it serious consideration, for it may turn out to be a formidable competitive advantage, either for one's own company or for one's competitors.

SUMMARY

Just-in-time (JIT) is a system of production used mainly in repetitive manufacturing, in which goods move through the system and tasks are completed just in time to maintain the schedule. Such systems require very little inventory because successive operations are closely coordinated.

JIT systems require that sources of potential disruption to the even flow of work be eliminated. High quality is stressed because problems with quality can disrupt the process. Quick, low-cost setups; special layouts; allowing work to be pulled through the system rather than pushed through; and a spirit of cooperation are all important features of JIT systems. So, too, are problem solving aimed at reducing disruptions and making the system more efficient, and an attitude of working toward continual improvement.

Key benefits of JIT systems are reduced inventory levels, high quality, flexibility, reduced lead times, increased productivity and equipment utilization, reduced amounts of scrap and rework, and reduced space requirements.

JIT differs in many ways from traditional systems used by many companies. The benefits of JIT systems have attracted the attention of U.S. manufacturers, causing them to consider converting their operations to JIT. In doing so, careful attention must be given to obtaining the support of top management, achieving a cooperative spirit throughout the organization, reducing setup times, and establishing good relationships with a small number of vendors.

KEY TERMS

andon, 636
brainstorming, 636
just-in-time (JIT), 624
kanban, 634

multifunctional workers, 631
preventive maintenance, 630
pull system, 634
push system, 634

SOLVED PROBLEM

Determine the number of containers that would be appropriate for a workstation that uses 100 parts per hour if the time for a container to complete a cycle (move, wait, empty, return, fill) is 90 minutes and a standard container holds 84 parts. An efficiency factor of 0.10 is currently in use.

Solution

$$N = ?$$
$$D = 100 \text{ parts per hour}$$

$$T = 90 \text{ minutes (1.5 hours)}$$
$$C = 84 \text{ parts}$$
$$X = 0.10$$

$$N = \frac{D(T)(1 + X)}{C} = \frac{100(1.5)(1 + .10)}{84} = 1.96 \text{ (round to 2) containers}$$

DISCUSSION AND REVIEW QUESTIONS

1. List the major elements of just-in-time systems, and briefly indicate how JIT systems differ from traditional production systems on each of those elements.

2. What are the main benefits of a JIT system?

3. Describe the philosophy that underlies JIT (i.e., what is JIT intended to accomplish?).

4. What are some of the main obstacles that must be overcome in attempting to convert from a traditional system to JIT?

5. Briefly discuss vendor relations in JIT systems in terms of the following issues:
   a. Why they are important.
   b. How they tend to differ from the more adversarial relations of the past.
   c. Possible reasons that vendors might be hestitant about JIT purchasing.

6. It has been said by some Japanese that Henry Ford's assembly line provided some of the rationale for JIT. What features of assembly lines are common to JIT systems?

7. Explain the kanban aspect of a JIT system.

8. Contrast push and pull methods of moving goods and materials through production systems.

9. What difficulties did U.S. automobile manufacturers encounter when they tried to use a kanban approach? Why did they have these difficulties?

10. Explain this statement: A key aspect of JIT systems is problem solving.

11. Explain this statement: Excessive inventories tend to inhibit system improvement.

12. Why are small lot sizes a goal of JIT systems?

PROBLEMS

1. A manager wants to determine the number of containers to use for a kanban system that will be installed next month. The process in question will have a usage rate of 80 pieces per hour. Because the process will be new, the manager has assigned an efficiency factor of .35. Containers each hold 45 pieces and take an average of 75 minutes to complete a cycle. How many containers should be used? Also, as the system improves, will more containers or fewer be required?

2. A JIT system uses kanban cards to authorize production and movement of materials. In one portion of the system, a work center uses an average of 100 pieces per hour while running. The manager has assigned an efficiency factor of .20 to the center. Standard containers are designed to hold six dozen parts each. The cycle time for parts containers is about 105 minutes. How many containers are needed?

3. A machine cell uses 200 pounds of a certain

material each day. Material is transported in vats that hold 120 pounds each. Cycle time for the vats is about two hours. The manager has assigned an efficiency factor of .08 to the cell. The plant operates on an eight-hour day. Determine the number of vats to use.

SELECTED BIBLIOGRAPHY

Alster, Norm. "What Flexible Workers Can Do." *Fortune* (February 13, 1989), pp. 62–66.

Burton, Terence T. "JIT/Repetitive Sourcing Strategies: 'Tying the Knot' with Your Suppliers." *Production and Inventory Management* (fourth quarter 1988), pp. 38–41.

Connell, Gale W. "Quality at the Source: The First Step in Just-in-Time Production," *Quality Progress* (November 1984), pp. 44–45.

Crosby, Leon B. "The Just-in-Time Manufacturing Process: Control of Quality and Quantity." *Production and Inventory Management* (fourth quarter 1984), pp. 21–33.

Goddard, Walter E. "Kanban versus MRP II— Which is Best for You?" *Modern Materials Handling* (November 5, 1982), pp. 40–48.

Hall, Robert W. *Attaining Manufacturing Excellence.* Homewood, Ill.: Richard D. Irwin, 1987.

Hannah, Kimball H. "Just-in-Time: Meeting the Competitive Challenge." *Production and Inventory Management* (third quarter, 1987), pp. 1–3.

Monden, Yasuhiro. "What Makes the Toyota Production System Really Tick?" *Industrial Engineering* 13, no. 1 (January 1981), pp. 38–46.

Nakane, J., and Robert W. Hall. "Management Specs for Stockless Production." *Harvard Business Review* (May–June 1983), pp. 84–91.

Schonberger, Richard J. *Japanese Manufacturing Techniques: Nine Hidden Lessons in Simplicity.* New York: Free Press, 1982.

————. *World Class Manufacturing.* New York: Free Press, 1986.

Stalk, George, Jr. "Time—The Next Source of Competitive Advantage." *Harvard Business Review* (July–August 1988), pp. 41–51.

Weiss, Andrew. "Simple Truths of Japanese Manufacturing." *Harvard Business Review* (July–August 1984), pp. 119–25.

13

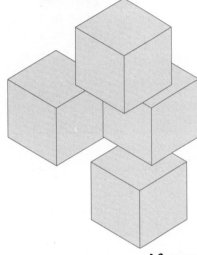

Scheduling

LEARNING OBJECTIVES

After completing this chapter, you should be able to:

1. Explain what scheduling involves and the importance of good scheduling.
2. Discuss scheduling needs in high-volume systems.
3. Discuss scheduling needs in job shops.
4. Use and interpret Gantt charts, and use the assignment method for loading.
5. Discuss and give examples of commonly used priority rules.
6. Describe some of the unique problems encountered in service systems, and describe some of the approaches used for scheduling service systems.

CHAPTER OUTLINE

Scheduling involves the *timing* of specific operations. It includes the use of equipment and facilities as well as human activities. Regardless of the nature of an organization's activities, scheduling is generally an important task. For example, manufacturers must schedule workers, purchases, production, and so on. Hospitals must schedule admissions, surgery, nursing staff, and support functions such as meal preparation and service, cleaning, building maintenance, grounds crews, office personnel, and security staff. Doctors, dentists, lawyers, hairdressers, and others must schedule appointments as well as other duties. Educational institutions must schedule classrooms, instructors, and students.

In the decision making hierarchy, scheduling decisions are the final step before actual output is achieved. The process essentially begins as capacity planning, when many decisions regarding facilities and equipment acquisition are made. These are often long-term decisions. In the aggregate-planning stage, decisions regarding the general use of facilities, personnel, and subcontracting are made. It still remains, however, to develop *specific* work assignments and other decisions related more precisely to the work itself. This sequence of planning is outlined in Figure 13–1. The transition from aggregate planning to scheduling can perhaps be clarified in terms of a master schedule, which was discussed in a previous chapter in the context of MRP. Note, however, that a master schedule is simply a mechanism for stating planned output, and that it serves a useful function that is not limited to MRP systems. Thus, both manufacturing and services generally rely on master schedules for planning purposes. In effect, the master schedule is a *disaggregation* of the aggregate plan; it converts those more general plans into specific plans for final output of goods or services. Recognize, though, that the master schedule does not complete the job of scheduling: the overall schedule must itself be translated into requirements for the individual goods and services that will be needed in the transformation process.

At each level in the process from capacity planning to scheduling, the constraints become narrower and more defined. In part, this is due to the lead

FIGURE 13–1

Overview of the capacity scheduling chain

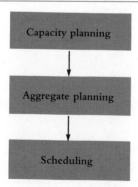

time needed to achieve changes. Consequently, scheduling decisions are usually made in a highly constrained environment.

Generally speaking, the objectives of scheduling are to achieve trade-offs among conflicting goals, which include efficient utilization of staff, equipment, and facilities, and minimization of customer waiting time, inventories, and process times.

Scheduling tasks are largely a function of the volume of system output. High-volume systems require approaches substantially different from those required by job shops, and project scheduling requires still different approaches. In this chapter, we will consider scheduling for high-volume systems, intermediate-volume systems, and low-volume (job-shop) scheduling. We will leave until the next chapter of the subject of project scheduling.

SCHEDULING IN HIGH-VOLUME SYSTEMS

Scheduling encompasses allocating workloads to specific work centers and determining the sequence in which operations are to be performed. High-volume systems are characterized by standardized equipment and activities that provide identical or highly similar operations on customers or products as they pass through the system. Consequently, the goal is to obtain a smooth rate of flow of goods or customers through the system in order to get a high utilization of labor and equipment. High-volume systems are often referred to as **flow systems.** Examples of high-volume products include autos, typewriters, radios and televisions, stereo equipment, toys, and appliances. In process industries, examples include petroleum refining, sugar refining, mining, waste treatment, and the manufacturing of fertilizers. Examples of services include cafeteria lines, news broadcasts, and mass inoculations. Because of the highly repetitive nature of these systems, many of the loading and sequencing decisions are determined during the design of the system. The use of highly specialized tools and equipment, the arrangement of equipment, the use of specialized material-handling equipment, and the division of labor are all designed to enhance the flow of work through the system, since all items follow virtually the same sequence of operations.

A major aspect in the design of flow systems is *line balancing,* which concerns allocating the required tasks to workstations so that they satisfy technical (sequencing) constraints and are balanced with respect to equal work times among stations. Highly balanced systems result in the maximum utilization of equipment and personnel as well as the highest possible rate of output. Line balancing is discussed in Chapter 7.

In setting up flow systems, designers must consider the potential discontent of workers related to the specialization of job tasks these systems entail: high work rates are often achieved by dividing the work into a series of relatively simple tasks that are assigned to different workers. The resulting jobs tend to be boring and monotonous and may give rise to fatigue, absenteeism, turnover, and other problems, all of which have a tendency to reduce productivity and disrupt the smooth flow of work through the system. These problems and potential solutions are elaborated on in Chapter 8, which deals with the design of work systems.

In spite of the built-in attributes of flow systems related to scheduling, there remain a number of problems with respect to scheduling. One stems from the fact that few flow systems are *completely* devoted to a single product or service. Most must handle a variety of sizes and models. Thus, an automobile manufacturer will assemble many different combinations of cars—two-door and four-door models, some with air conditioning and some not, some with deluxe trim and others with standard trim, some with tape decks, some with tinted glass, and so on. The same can be said for producers of appliances, electronic equipment, toys, and so on. Each change involves slightly different inputs that must be scheduled into the line, such as different parts and materials and different processing requirements. If the line is to operate smoothly, the flow of materials and the work must be coordinated. This amounts to scheduling the inputs, the processing, and the outputs, as well as scheduling purchases. In addition to achieving a smooth flow, it is important to avoid excessive buildups of inventories. Again, each variation in size or model will tend to have somewhat different inventory requirements, so that additional scheduling efforts will be needed.

Another source of scheduling requirements are disruptions to the system that generate less than the desired amount of output. These can be caused by equipment failures, material shortages, accidents, and absences. Practically speaking, it is usually not possible to increase the rate of output to compensate for these factors, mainly due to the fact that flow systems are designed to operate at a given rate. Instead, strategies involving subcontracting or overtime are often required, although subcontracting on short notice is not always feasible. Sometimes work that is partly completed can be made up off the line.

The reverse situation can also impose scheduling problems, although less severe. This happens when the desired amount of output is less than the usual rate. However, instead of slowing the rate of output, it is usually necessary to operate the system at the usual rate, but for fewer hours. For instance, a production line might operate for seven hours a day instead of eight for a while.

High-volume systems usually involve automated or specialized equipment for processing and handling. Moreover, they perform best when there is a high, uniform output. Consequently, the following factors often determine the success of such a system:

1. *Process and product design.* Here, cost and manufacturability are important, as is achieving a smooth flow through the system.
2. *Preventive maintenance.* Keeping equipment in good operating order can minimize breakdowns that would disrupt the flow of work.
3. *Rapid repair when breakdowns occur.* This can require specialists as well as stocks of critical spare parts.
4. *Optimal product mixes.* Techniques such as linear programming can be used to determine optimal blends of inputs to achieve desired outputs at

minimal costs. This is particularly true in the manufacture of fertilizers, animal feeds, and diet foods.

5. *Minimization of quality problems.* Quality problems can be extremely disruptive, requiring shutdowns while problems are resolved. Moreover, when output fails to meet quality standards, the labor, material, time, and other resources that went into it have been wasted, in addition to the loss of output.

6. *Reliability and timing of supplies.* Shortages of supplies is an obvious source of disruption and must be avoided. On the other hand, if the solution is to stockpile supplies, that can lead to high carrying costs. Shortening supply lead times, developing reliable supply schedules, and carefully projecting needs are all useful in this regard.

SCHEDULING IN INTERMEDIATE-VOLUME SYSTEMS

Intermediate-volume system outputs fall between the standardized type of output of the high-volume systems and the made-to-order output of job shops. Like the high-volume systems, intermediate-volume systems typically produce standard outputs. And if manufacturing is involved, the products may be made for stock rather than for special order. However, the volume of output in such cases is not large enough to justify devoting continual production. Instead, it is more economical to process these items *intermittently*. Thus, intermediate-volume work centers periodically shift from one job to another. In contrast to a job shop, though, the run sizes are relatively large. Examples of products made in these systems include canned foods, baked goods, paint, and cosmetics.

The two basic questions in these systems are what *run size* to use and in what *sequence* jobs should be processed.

In part, the question of run size can be answered using a model such as the economic run size model discussed in Chapter 10. The run size that would minimize setup and inventory costs is

$$Q_0 = \sqrt{\frac{2DS}{H}} \sqrt{\frac{p}{p - u}} \qquad (13\text{--}1)$$

This approach works well in the context of a single product but must be modified somewhat when multiple products are involved. One reason is that setup costs can be dependent on the order of processing: some products will have similar setups, so it can be less expensive to process them in sequence to take advantage of that. Another difficulty arises because usage is not always as smooth as assumed in this model. Consequently, some products will tend to be used up faster than expected and have to be replenished sooner. Also, because multiple products are to be processed, it is not always possible to schedule production to correspond with optimum run intervals.

Therefore, a second approach, called **runout time,** is often used. It may be used in conjunction with the economic run size model or without it. There are several variations of this model. The concept of this approach is expressed by the following version:

$$\text{Runout time} = \frac{\text{Current inventory}}{\text{Demand rate}} \qquad (13\text{--}2)$$

Runout time indicates how long it will be before a given item will incur a stockout. The runout time is computed for each product, and the products are ranked according to this measure. The lower the runout time, the more crucial it is to replenish the supply of an item. Here is an example of the calculations:

Product	Inventory (units)		Demand (units/week)		Runout time (weeks)
A	400	÷	100	=	4.0
B	120	÷	100	=	1.2
C	50	÷	20	=	2.5

Product A has a runout time of 4.0 weeks, product B has a runout time of 1.2 weeks, and product C has a runout time of 2.5 weeks. Consequently, the processing order would be B-C-A.

Modifications to the economic run size formula to allow for multiple products and dependent setups, and elaboration of the runout time approach are somewhat beyond the scope of this text. However, both topics are covered in more detail in the references found at the end of this chapter, if you are interested.

SCHEDULING IN LOW-VOLUME SYSTEMS

The characteristics of low-volume systems (job shops) are quite different from those of high- and intermediate-volume systems. Products are made to order, and orders usually differ considerably in terms of processing requirements, materials needed, processing time, and processing sequence and setups. Because of these circumstances, scheduling and controlling in job shops is usually fairly complex. This is compounded by the fact that it is impossible to establish firm schedules prior to receiving the actual job orders.

Job shop processing gives rise to two basic issues for schedulers: how to distribute the workload among work centers and what job processing sequence to use.

Loading

Loading refers to the assignment of jobs to processing (work) centers. In cases where a job can only be processed by a specific center, loading presents little difficulty. However, problems arise when two or more jobs are to be processed and there are a number of work centers capable of performing the required work. In such cases, the operations manager needs some way of assigning jobs to the centers.

In making assignments, managers often seek an arrangement that will either minimize processing and setup costs, minimize idle time among work centers, or minimize job completion time, depending on the situation.

A number of approaches are used for loading, ranging from pure intuition to linear programming. Two of these approaches are described in the following sections: the use of Gantt charts and the assignment method of linear programming.

Gantt charts are visual aids used for a variety of purposes related to loading and scheduling. They derive their name from Henry Gantt, who pioneered the use of charts for industrial scheduling in the early 1900s. Gantt charts can be used in a number of different ways, two of which are illustrated in Figure 13–2, which shows scheduling classrooms for a semester and scheduling hospital operating rooms for a day.

FIGURE 13–2

Examples of charts used for scheduling

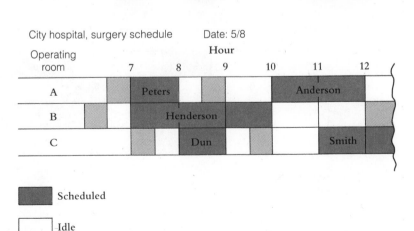

Classroom schedule: Fall — Friday

Room	8	9	10	11	12	1	2	3	4	5
A100	Stat 1	Econ 101	Econ 102	Fin 201	Mar 210	Acct 212			Mar 410	
A105	Stat 2	Math 2a	Math 2b			Acct 210	CCE – – – – – – –			
A110	Acct 340	Mgmt 250	Math 3		Mar 220					
A115	Mar 440		Mgmt 230			Fin 310	Acct 360			

City hospital, surgery schedule — Date: 5/8

Operating room	7	8	9	10	11	12
A		Peters			Anderson	
B		Henderson				
C		Dun			Smith	

■ Scheduled

□ Idle

▨ Cleaning and make ready

The purpose of Gantt charts is to organize and clarify the actual or intended use of resources in a *time framework*. In most cases, a time scale is represented horizontally, and resources to be scheduled are listed vertically. The use of the resources is reflected in the body of the chart.

Managers may use the charts for trial-and-error schedule development to get an idea of what different arrangements would involve. Thus, a tentative surgery schedule might reveal insufficient allowance for surgery that extends beyond its expected duration and can be revised accordingly. Use of the chart for classroom scheduling would help avoid assigning two different classes to the same room at the same time.

There are a number of different types of Gantt charts. Two of the most commonly used are the *load chart* and the *schedule chart*.

A **load chart** depicts the loading and idle times of a group of machines or a list of departments. A typical load chart is illustrated in Figure 13–3. This particular chart indicates that work center 3 is completely loaded for the entire week, center 4 will be available after noon on Tuesday, and the other two centers have idle time scattered throughout the week. This information can help a manager rework loading assignments to better utilize the centers. For instance, if all centers perform the same kind of work, the manager might want to free one center for a long job or for a rush order. It also shows when certain jobs are scheduled to start and finish and where idle time is expected.

A **schedule chart** is often used to monitor the progress of jobs. The vertical axis on this type of Gantt chart shows the orders or jobs in progress, and the horizontal axis shows time. The charts indicate which jobs are on schedule and which are behind or ahead.

A typical schedule chart is illustrated in Figure 13–4. It shows the current status of a landscaping job along with planned and actual starting and finishing times for the five stages of the job. We can see from the chart that approval was on schedule, as was ordering of trees and shrubs. The site preparation was a bit

FIGURE 13–3

A Gantt load chart

Work center	Mon.	Tues.	Wed.	Thurs.	Fri.
1	Job 3			Job 4	
2		Job 3	Job 7		⊠
3	Job 1	⊠		Job 6	Job 7
4	Job 10				

 Processing

⊠ Center not available (e.g., maintenance)

FIGURE 13–4

Progress chart for landscaping job

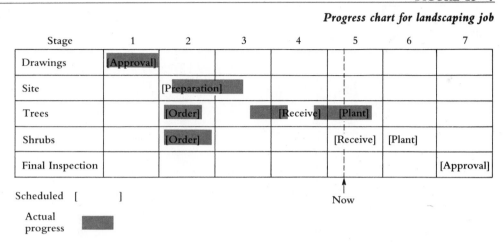

behind schedule. The trees were received earlier than expected, and planting is ahead of schedule. However, the shrubs have not yet been received. The chart indicates some slack between scheduled receipt of shrubs and shrub planting, so if the shrubs arrive by the end of the week, it appears the schedule can still be met.

In spite of the obvious benefits of these charts, they also possess certain limitations, the chief one being the need to repeatedly update the chart to keep it current. In addition, a chart does not directly reveal costs associated with alternative loadings. Finally, a job's processing time may vary depending on the work center involved: certain stations or work centers may be capable of processing some jobs faster than other stations. Again, that situation would increase the complexity of evaluating alternative schedules. Nonetheless, Gantt charts are the most widely used devices for scheduling.

The **assignment method** is a special-purpose linear programming model that is useful in situations that call for assigning tasks or other work requirements to resources. Typical examples include assigning jobs to machines or workers, territories to salespeople, and emergency calls to telephone repair crews. The idea is to obtain an optimum *matching* of tasks and resources. Commonly used criteria include costs, profits, efficiency, and performance.

A typical problem is illustrated in Table 13–1, where four jobs are to be assigned to four machines. The problem is arranged in a format that will facilitate evaluation of assignments. The numbers in the body of the table represent the value or cost associated with each job-machine combination. In this case, the numbers represent costs. Thus, it would cost $8 to do job 1 on machine A, $6 to do job 1 on machine B, and so on. If the problem involved minimizing the cost for job 1 alone, it is apparent that it would be assigned to

TABLE 13–1

A typical assignment problem

		Machine			
		A	**B**	**C**	**D**
Job	*1*	8	6	2	4
	2	6	7	11	10
	3	3	5	7	6
	4	5	10	12	9

machine C since that combination has the lowest cost. However, that assignment does not take into account the other jobs and their potential costs, which is important since the lowest-cost assignment for any one job may not be consistent with a minimum-cost assignment when all jobs are considered.

If there are to be *n* matches, there are *n!* different possibilities. In this case, there are 4! = 24 different matches. One approach would be to investigate each match and select the one with the lowest cost. However, even for a problem of this small size, considerable time and effort would be called for. Instead, a much simpler approach is to use the assignment method to identify the lowest-cost solution.

To be able to use the assignment method, a one-for-one matching is required. Each job, for example, must be assigned to only one machine. It is also assumed that every machine is capable of handling every job, and that the costs or values associated with each assignment combination are known and fixed (i.e., not subject to variation).

Once the relevant cost information has been acquired and arranged in tabular form, the basic procedure of the assignment method is:

1. Subtract the smallest number in each row from every number in the row. Enter the results in a new table.
2. Subtract the smallest number in each column of the new table from every number in the column. Enter the results in another table.
3. Test to see if an optimum assignment can be made. This is accomplished by determining the *minimum* number of lines that are needed to cover all zeros. If the number of lines equals the number of rows, an optimum assignment is possible. In that case, go to step 6. Otherwise go on to step 4. Note that "cover" means "cross out."
4. If the number of lines is less than the number of rows, modify the table in this way:
   a. Subtract the smallest uncovered number from every uncovered number in the table.

    b. Add the smallest uncovered number to the numbers at *intersections* of covering lines.

5. Repeat steps 3 and 4 until an optimal table is obtained.

6. Make the assignments. Begin with rows or columns with only one zero. Match items that have zeros, using only one match for each row and each column. Cross out both the row and the column after the match.

EXAMPLE 1

    Determine the optimum assignment of jobs to machines for the following data below (from Table 13–1).

		Machine				Row
		A	**B**	**C**	**D**	minimum
	1	8	6	2	4	2
	2	6	7	11	10	6
Job	*3*	3	5	7	6	3
	4	5	10	12	9	5

Solution

a. Subtract the smallest number in each row from every number in the row, and enter the results in a new table. The result of this *row reduction* is:

		Machine			
		A	**B**	**C**	**D**
	1	6	4	0	2
	2	0	1	5	4
Job	*3*	0	2	4	3
	4	0	5	7	4
Column minimum		0	1	0	2

b. Subtract the smallest number in each column from every number in the column, and enter the results in a new table. The result of this *column reduction* is:

EXAMPLE 1 *(continued)*

Machine

		A	B	C	D
	1	6	3	0	0
Job	2	0	0	5	2
	3	0	1	4	1
	4	0	4	7	2

c. Determine the minimum number of lines needed to cover (cross out) all zeros. (Try to cross out as many zeros as possible when drawing lines.)

Machine

		A	B	C	D
	1	6	3	0	0
	2	0	0	5	2
Job	3	0	1	4	1
	4	0	4	7	2

d. Since only three lines are needed to cover all zeros, this is not the optimum.
e. Subtract the smallest uncovered value (in this case, 1) from every uncovered number, and add it to numbers that are at the intersections of covering lines. The results are:

Machine

		A	B	C	D
	1	7	3	0	0
Job	2	1	0	5	2
	3	0	0	3	0
	4	0	3	6	1

f. Determine the minimum number of lines needed to cover all zeros (four). Since this equals the number of rows, the optimum assignment can be made.

EXAMPLE 1 *(concluded)*

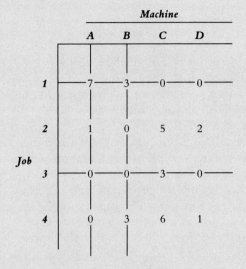

g. Make assignments: Start with rows and columns with only one zero. Match jobs with machines that have a zero cost:

	Machine			
Job	A	B	C	D
1	7	3	⬚0	0
2	1	⬚0	5	2
3	0	0	3	⬚0
4	⬚0	3	6	1

As you can see, the process is relatively simple compared to some of the other linear programming techniques. One extension of this technique that is worth knowing is the ability to prevent undesirable assignments. For example, union rules may prohibit one person's assignment to a particular job, or a manager might wish to avoid assigning an unpleasant job to the person who did it last. Whatever the reason, specific combinations can be avoided by assigning a relatively high cost to that combination. For instance, in the previous example, if combination 1–A is to be avoided, assigning a cost of $50 to that combination will achieve the desired effect because $50 is much greater than the other costs. In a situation involving profits instead of costs, the profits can be converted to *relative costs* by subtracting every number in the table from the largest number and then proceeding as in a minimization problem.

The simplicity of the assignment method belies its usefulness when the assumptions are met. Not only does it provide a rational method for making assignments, it guarantees an optimal solution, often without the use of a computer. In fact, computers are necessary only for fairly large problems.

Sequencing

Although loading decisions determine the machines or work centers that will be used to process specific jobs, they do not indicate the *order* in which the jobs waiting at a given work center are to be processed. **Sequencing** is concerned with determining job processing order.

If work centers are lightly loaded and if jobs all require the same amount of processing time, sequencing presents no particular difficulties. However, for heavily loaded work centers, especially in situations where relatively lengthy jobs are involved, processing order can be very important in terms of costs associated with jobs waiting for processing and in terms of idle time at the work centers. In this section, we will examine some of the ways in which jobs are sequenced.

Typically, a number of jobs will be waiting for processing. **Priority rules** are simple heuristics used to select the order in which the jobs will be processed. Some of the most common are listed in Table 13–2. The rules generally involve the assumption that job setup cost and time are *independent* of processing sequence. In using these rules, job processing times and due dates are important pieces of information. **Job time** usually includes setup and processing times. Jobs that require similar setups can lead to reduced setup times if the sequencing rule takes this into account (the rules described here do not). Due dates may be the result of delivery times promised to customers, MRP processing, or managerial decisions. They are subject to revision and must be kept current to give meaning to sequencing choices. Also, it should be noted that due dates associated with all rules except S/O and CR are for the operation about to be performed; due dates for S/O and CR are typically final due dates for orders rather than intermediate, departmental deadlines.

TABLE 13–2

Possible priority rules

FCFS (first come, first served): Jobs are processed in the order in which they arrive at a machine or work center.

SPT (shortest processing time): Jobs are processed according to processing time at a machine or work center, shortest job first.

DD (due date): Jobs are processed according to due date, earliest due date first.

CR (critical ratio): Jobs are processed according to smallest ratio of due date to processing time.

S/O (slack per operation): Jobs are processed according to average slack time (time until due date minus remaining time to process). Compute by dividing slack time by number of remaining operations, including the current one.

Rush: Emergency or preferred customers first.

The effectiveness of any given sequence is commonly judged in terms of one of three measures: average completion time, average job lateness, or average number of jobs at a work center. Two of these measures, average completion time and average number of jobs at a work center, are directly correlated. Hence, to use both for a given case would be redundant. In the examples and problems, both are employed simply for purposes of illustration.

Of these rules, Rush scheduling is quite simple and needs no explanation. The other rules are illustrated in the following two examples.

EXAMPLE 2

Processing times (including setup times) and due dates for six jobs waiting to be processed at a work center are given in the following table. Determine the sequence of processing according to each of these rules:

a. FCFS.
b. SPT.
c. DD.
d. CR.

Job	*Processing time (days)*	*Due date (days)*
A	2	7
B	8	16
C	4	4
D	10	17
E	5	15
F	12	18

Assume jobs arrived in the order shown.

Solution

a. The FCFS sequence is simply A–B–C–D–E–F. The measures of effectiveness are:

(1) *Average completion time:* 120/6 = 20 days.
(2) *Average job lateness:* 54/6 = 9 days.
(3) *Average number of jobs at the work center:* 120/41 = 2.93.

Job sequence	*(1) Processing time*	*(2) Flow time*	*(3) Due date*	*(2) − (3) Days late [0 if negative]*
A	2	2	7	0
B	8	10	16	0
C	4	14	4	10
D	10	24	17	7
E	5	29	15	14
F	12	41	18	23
	41	120		54

EXAMPLE 2 *(continued)*

The flow time column indicates *cumulative* processing time, so summing these times and dividing by the total number of jobs processed indicates the average time each job spends at the work center. Similarly, the average number of jobs at the center is found by summing the flow times and dividing by the total processing time.

b. Using the SPT rule, the job sequence is A-C-E-B-D-F (see the following table). The resulting values for the three measures of effectiveness are:

(1) *Average completion time:* 108/6 = 18 days.
(2) *Average job lateness:* 40/6 = 6.67 days.
(3) *Average number of jobs at the work center:* 108/41 = 2.63.

Sequence	(1) Processing time	(2) Flow time	(3) Due date	(2) − (3) Days late [0 if negative]
A	2	2	7	0
C	4	6	4	2
E	5	11	15	0
B	8	19	16	3
D	10	29	17	12
F	12	41	18	23
	41	108		40

c. Using earliest due date as the selection criterion, the job sequence is C-A-E-B-D-F. The measures of effectiveness are (see table):

(1) *Average completion time:* 110/6 = 18.33 days.
(2) *Average job lateness:* 38/6 = 6.33 days.
(3) *Average number of jobs at the work center:* 110/41 = 2.68.

Sequence	(1) Processing time	(2) Flow time	(3) Due date	(2) − (3) Days late [0 if negative]
C	4	4	4	0
A	2	6	7	0
E	5	11	15	0
B	8	19	16	3
D	10	29	17	12
F	12	41	18	23
	41	110		38

d. Using the critical ratio (due date ÷ processing time), the job sequence is C-F-D-B-E-A, and the resulting values for the three measures of effectiveness are:

(1) *Average completion time:* 160/6 = 26.67 days.
(2) *Average job lateness:* 85/6 = 14.17 days.
(3) *Average number of jobs at the work center:* 160/41 = 3.90.

EXAMPLE 2 *(concluded)*

Sequence	(1) Critical ratio	(2) Processing time	(3) Flow time	(4) Due date	(3) − (4) Days late
C	1.0	4	4	4	0
F	1.5	12	16	18	0
D	1.7	10	26	17	9
B	2.0	8	34	16	18
E	3.0	5	39	15	24
A	3.5	2	41	7	34
		41	160		85

The results of these four rules are summarized in Table 13–3.

TABLE 13–3

Comparison of the four rules

Rule	Average completion time (days)	Average lateness (days)	Average number of jobs at the work center
FCFS	20.00	9.00	2.93
SPT	18.00	6.67	2.63
DD	18.33	6.33	2.68
CR	26.67	14.17	3.90

In this example, the SPT rule was the best according to two of the measures of effectiveness and a little worse than the DD rule on average lateness. The CR rule was the worst in every case. For a different set of numbers, the DD rule (or perhaps another rule not mentioned here) might prove superior to SPT in terms of average job lateness or some other measure of effectiveness. However, SPT is always superior in terms of minimizing flow time and, hence, in terms of minimizing the average number of jobs at the work center and completion time. It is best for each shop or organization to consider carefully its own circumstances and the measures of effectiveness it feels are important in selecting a rule to use.

Generally speaking, the FCFS rule and the CR rule turn out to be the least effective of the rules.

The primary limitation of the FCFS rule is that long jobs will tend to delay other jobs. If a process consists of work on a number of machines, machine idle time for downstream workstations will be increased. However, for service systems in which customers are directly involved, the FCFS rule is by far the dominant priority rule, mainly because of the inherent "fairness" but also perhaps because of the inability to obtain realistic estimates of processing times for individual jobs. The FCFS rule also has the advantage of simplicity.

Because the SPT rule always results in the lowest average completion time, it can result in lower in-process inventories. And because it often provides the lowest average lateness, it can result in better customer service levels. Finally, since it always involves a lower average number of jobs at the work center, there tends to be less congestion in the work area. SPT also minimizes downstream idle time.

The major disadvantage of the SPT rule is that it tends to make long jobs wait, perhaps for rather long times (especially if new, shorter jobs are continually added to the system). Various modification may be used in an effort to avoid this (e.g., after waiting for a given time period, any remaining jobs are automatically moved to the head of the line). This is known as the *truncated SPT* rule.

The DD rule directly addresses due dates and usually minimizes lateness. Although it has intuitive appeal, its main limitation is that it does not take processing time into account. One possible consequence is that it can result in some jobs waiting a long time, which adds both to in-process inventories and to shop congestion.

The CR rule is easy to use and has intuitive appeal, but it often turns out to be the poorest in terms of average flow time and job lateness.

Let's take a look now at the S/O (slack per operation) rule.

EXAMPLE 3

Use the S/O rule to schedule the following jobs. Note that processing time includes the time remaining for the current and subsequent operations. In addition, we will need to know the number of operations remaining, including the current one.

Job	Remaining processing time	Due date	Remaining number of operations
A	4	14	3
B	16	32	6
C	8	8	5
D	20	34	2
E	10	30	4
F	18	30	2

Solution

Determine the difference between the due date and the processing time for each operation. Divide the amount by the number of remaining operations, and rank them from low to high. This yields the sequence of jobs:

EXAMPLE 3 *(concluded)*

Job	(1) Remaining processing time	(2) Due date	(3) (2) − (1) Slack	(4) Remaining number of operations	(5) (3) ÷ (4) Ratio	(6) Rank
A	4	14	10	3	3.33	3
B	16	32	16	6	2.67	2
C	8	8	0	5	0	1
D	20	34	14	2	7.00	6
E	10	30	20	4	5.00	4
F	18	30	12	2	6.00	5

The indicated sequences (see column 6) is: C–B–A–E–F–D.

Using the S/O rule, the designated job sequence may change after any given operation, so it is important to reevaluate the sequence after each operation. Note than any of the previously mentioned priority rules could be used on a station-by-station basis for this situation; the only difference is that the S/O approach incorporates downstream information in arriving at a job sequence.

In actuality, there are many priority rules available to sequence jobs, and some other rule might provide superior results for a given set of circumstances. The purpose of examining these few rules was to provide insight into the nature of sequencing rules.

In the following section, a special-purpose algorithm that can be used to sequence a set of jobs that must all be processed at the same two machines or work centers is described.

Sequencing Jobs through Two Work Centers

Johnson's rule is a technique that can be used to minimize the throughput (completion) time for a group of jobs that are to be processed on two machines or at two successive work centers.[1] It also minimizes the total idle time at the work centers. In order for the technique to be used, several conditions must be satisfied:

1. Job time (including setup and processing) must be known and constant for each job at each work center.
2. Job times must be independent of the job sequence.
3. All jobs must follow the same two-step work sequence.
4. Job priorities cannot be used.

---

[1] S. M. Johnson, "Optimal Two- and Three-Stage Production with Setup Times Included," *Naval Research Quarterly* 1 (March 1954), pp. 61–68.

Determination of the optimum sequence involves these steps:

1. List the jobs and their times at each work center.
2. Select the job with the shortest time. If the shortest time is at the first work center, schedule that job first; if the time is at the second work center, schedule the job last. Break ties arbitrarily.
3. Eliminate the job and its time from further consideration.
4. Repeat steps 2 and 3, working toward the center of the sequence, until all jobs have been scheduled.

Example 4

A group of six jobs are to be processed through a two–step operation. The first operation involves degreasing, and the second involves painting. Determine a sequence that will minimize the total completion time for this group of jobs. Processing times are as follows:

| | *Processing time (hours)* | |
Job	*Work center 1*	*Work center 2*
A	5	5
B	4	3
C	8	9
D	2	7
E	6	8
F	12	15

Solution

a. Select the job with the shortest processing time. It is job D, with a time of two hours.
b. Since the time is at the first center, schedule job D first. Eliminate job D from further consideration.
c. Job B has the next shortest time. Since it is at the second work center, schedule it last and eliminate job B from further consideration. We now have:

1st	2d	3d	4th	5th	6th
D					B

d. The remaining jobs and their times are:

Job	*1*	*2*
A	5	5
C	8	9
E	6	8
F	12	15

EXAMPLE 4 *(concluded)*

Note that there is a tie for the shortest remaining time: job A has the same time at each work center. It makes no difference, then, whether we place it toward the beginning or the end of the sequence. Suppose we place it toward the end arbitrarily. We now have:

1st	2d	3d	4th	5th	6th
D				A	B

e. The shortest remaining time is six hours for job E at work center 1. Thus, schedule that job toward the beginning of the sequence (after job D). Thus,

1st	2d	3d	4th	5th	6th
D	E			A	B

f. Job C has the shortest time of the remaining two jobs. Since it is for the first work center, it is placed third in the sequence. Finally, the remaining job (F) is assigned to the fourth position and the result is:

1st	2d	3d	4th	5th	6th
D	E	C	F	A	B

g. The easiest way to determine the throughput time and idle times at the work centers is to construct a chart:

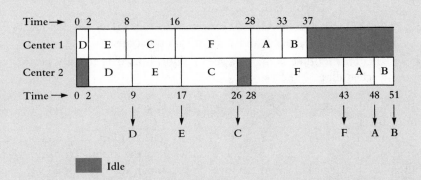

Idle

Thus, the group of jobs will take 51 hours to complete. The second work center will wait two hours for its first job and also wait two hours after finishing job C. Center 1 will be finished in 37 hours. Of course, idle periods at the beginning or end of the sequence could be used to do other jobs or for maintenance or setup/teardown activities.

When significant idle time at the second work center occurs, job splitting at the first center just prior to the occurrence of idle time may alleviate some of it and also shorten throughput time. In the preceding example, this was not a problem. The last solved problem at the end of this chapter illustrates the use of job splitting.

Optimized Production Technology

Optimized Production Technology (OPT) is a proprietary software package owned by Creative Output, Inc. of Milford, Connecticut. Information on the package is somewhat limited due to the proprietary nature of the technique. However, it is said to involve the use of mathematical programming, networking, and simulation.

A basic feature of OPT is the special attention it directs to bottleneck operations. The rationale of OPT is that bottleneck operations have an impact on an entire plant, and the best way to schedule a plant is to identify the bottleneck operations and try to optimize their use. The nonbottleneck operations are not critical and can therefore be treated differently. The OPT philosophy contends that the standard costs of bottleneck operations are understated because they don't take into account the fact that these operations constrain the entire system. Hence, OPT begins its scheduling procedure with the bottleneck operations and attempts to maximize their output. In essence, OPT is a finite loading procedure.

OPT consists of four basic modules:

1. *Buildnet.* This contains data on a plant's raw materials, purchased parts, products, work center capabilities, and customer orders.
2. *Serve.* This module identifies the bottleneck operations by running load profiles for each operation or work center.
3. *Split.* This module divides the system into two categories: critical operations (i.e., bottlenecks) and noncritical operations.
4. *Brain.* This module contains a set of algorithms that actually perform the scheduling.

OPT simulates different schedules and then selects a schedule based on the simulations.

There are two lot sizes in the OPT approach, a *process batch* and a *transfer batch*. The process batch is a lot size released to the shop. To optimize the output of bottlenecks, large batches (few setups) are run. However, since nonbottleneck operations have idle time, it does not make sense to attempt to maximize their output; there is nothing to gain by increasing idle time. Consequently, smaller lot sizes and more frequent setups can be used on such operations. The small batch sizes are the transfer lots. Hence, OPT deliberately schedules a variety of lot sizes, unlike more conventional approaches that use a single lot size throughout a shop for a job. You might think of this as lot splitting with multiple split sizes. An important feature of the software is selection of the appropriate lot size for each operation.

As you might expect, OPT directs its use of both safety stock and safety time to facilitate flow through bottleneck operations. By concentrating these resources, it seeks to gain the maximum benefit from them and generally minimize inventories otherwise devoted to this purpose.

Since OPT is still relatively new, widespread experience on its use is not yet available. Nonetheless, users have reported a number of benefits. One is that OPT appears to be quicker and less costly to implement than a system such as MRP. Like MRP, OPT requires extensive preliminary effort to obtain accurate, up-to-date information in data files on work standards, machine capabilities, product structures, and so on. OPT seems to require more detail than MRP, and many view the process of going through this effort as an important benefit because of the improved data base it produces.

SCHEDULING IN SERVICE SYSTEMS

Scheduling service systems presents certain problems not generally encountered in manufacturing systems. This is due primarily to (1) the inability to store or inventory services and (2) the random nature of customer requests for service. In some situations, the second difficulty can be moderated by using appointment or reservation systems, but the inability to store services in most cases is a fact of life that managers must contend with.

An important goal in service systems is to match the flow of customers and service capabilities. An ideal situation is one in which there is a smooth flow of customers through the system. This would occur if each new customer arrives at the precise instant that the preceding customer's service is completed, in a case such as a physician's office, or, in a case such as air travel, where the demand just equals the number of available seats. In each of these situations, customer waiting time would be minimized, and there would be full utilization of the service system staff and equipment. Unfortunately, because of the random nature of customer requests for service that generally prevails in service systems, it is nearly impossible to provide service capacity that will match demand. Moreover, if service times are subject to variability—say, because of differing processing requirements—the inefficiency of the system is compounded. The inefficiencies can be reduced if arrivals can be scheduled (e.g., appointments), as in the case of doctors and dentists. However, there are many situations in which appointments are not practical (supermarkets, gas stations, theaters, hospital emergency rooms, repair of equipment breakdowns). Chapter 15, on queuing analysis, focuses on those kinds of situations. There, the emphasis is on intermediate-term decisions related to service capacity. In this section, we will concern ourselves with short-term *scheduling,* in which much of the capacity of a system is essentially fixed, and the goal is to achieve a certain degree of customer service by efficient utilization of that capacity.

Appointment Systems

Appointment systems are intended to control the timing of customer arrivals in order to minimize customer waiting while achieving a high degree of capacity utilization. A doctor can use an appointment system to schedule office patients during the afternoon, leaving the mornings free for hospital duties. Similarly, an attorney can schedule clients around court appearances. Even with appointments, however, problems can still arise due to lack of punctuality on the part of patients or clients, no-shows, and the inability to completely control the length of contact time (e.g., a dentist might run into complications in filling a tooth and have to spend additional time with a patient, thus backing up later appointments). Some of this can be avoided—say, by trying to match the time reserved for a patient or client with the specific needs of that case rather than setting appointments at regular intervals. Even with the problems of late arrivals and no-shows, the appointment system is a tremendous improvement over allowing random arrivals.

Reservation Systems

Reservation systems are designed to enable service systems to formulate a fairly accurate estimate of the demand on the system for a given time period and to minimize customer disappointment generated by excessive waiting or inability to obtain service. Reservation systems are widely used by resorts, hotels and motels, and restaurants as well as in some modes of transportation (airlines, car rentals). In the case of restaurants, reservations enable management to spread out or group customers so that demand matches service capabilities. As with appointment systems, late arrivals and no-shows can disrupt the system. An approach to the no-show problem is illustrated in Chapter 6, using a decision matrix. The problem can also be viewed as a single-period inventory problem, as described in Chapter 10.

Scheduling Multiple Resources

In some situations, it is necessary to coordinate the use of more than one resource. For example, hospitals must schedule surgeons, operating rooms, operating room staffs, recovery room staffs, admissions, special equipment, nursing staffs, and so on. Similarly, educational institutions must schedule faculty, classrooms, audiovisual equipment, and students. As you might guess, the greater the number of resources that must be scheduled, the greater the complexity of the problem, and the less likely it becomes that an optimum schedule can be achieved. The problem is further complicated by the variable nature of such systems. For example, educational institutions frequently change their course offerings, student enrollments change, and students exhibit different course-selection patterns.

Some schools and hospitals are using computer programs to assist them in devising acceptable schedules, although many appear to be using intuitive approaches, with varying degrees of success.

Airlines are another example of service systems that require the scheduling of multiple resources. Flight crews, aircraft, baggage handling equipment, ticket counters, gate personnel, boarding ramps, and maintenance personnel all have to be coordinated. Furthermore, government regulations on the number of hours a pilot can spend flying place an additional restriction on the system. Another interesting variable is the fact that, unlike most systems, the flight crews and the equipment do not remain in one location. Moreover, the crew and the equipment are not usually scheduled as a single unit. Flight crews are often scheduled so that they return to their base city every two days or more often, and rest breaks must be considered. On the other hand, the aircraft may be in almost continuous use except for periodic maintenance and repairs. Consequently, flight crews commonly follow different trip patterns from that of the aircraft.

SUMMARY

Scheduling involves the timing and coordination of operations. Such activities are fundamental to virtually every organization. Scheduling problems differ according to whether a system is designed for high volume, intermediate volume, or as a job shop. Scheduling problems are particularly complex for job shops because of the variety of jobs these systems are required to process.

The two major problems in scheduling job shops are assigning jobs to machines or work centers and designating the sequence of job processing at a given machine or work center. Gantt load charts are frequently employed to help managers visualize workloads, and they are useful for describing and analyzing sequencing alternatives. In addition, both heuristic and optimizing methods are used to develop loading and sequencing plans. For the most part, the optimization techniques can be used only if certain assumptions can be made.

Customer requirements in service systems generally present very different circumstances from those encountered in manufacturing systems. Appointment and reservation systems can sometimes be used for scheduling purposes, although not all systems are amenable to this. When multiple resources are involved, the task of balancing the system can be fairly complex.

KEY TERMS

assignment method, 659
flow systems, 653
Gantt charts, 657
job time, 664
Johnson's rule, 669
load charts, 658
loading, 656

Optimized Production
  Technology, 672
priority rules, 664
runout time, 655
schedule chart, 658
sequencing, 664

SOLVED PROBLEMS

1. *The assignment method.* The following table contains information on the cost to run three jobs on four available machines. Determine an assignment plan that will minimize opportunity costs.

		\multicolumn{4}{c}{**Machine**}			
		A	**B**	**C**	**D**
Job	**1**	12	16	14	10
	2	9	8	13	7
	3	15	12	9	11

Solution

In order for us to be able to use the assignment method, the numbers of jobs and machines must be equal. To remedy this situation, add a *dummy* job with costs of 0, and then solve as usual:

		\multicolumn{4}{c}{**Machine**}			
		A	**B**	**C**	**D**
	1	12	16	14	10
Job	**2**	9	8	13	7
	3	15	12	9	11
(dummy)	**4**	0	0	0	0

a. Subtract the smallest number from each row. The results are:

		\multicolumn{4}{c}{**Machine**}			
		A	**B**	**C**	**D**
	1	2	6	4	0
Job	**2**	2	1	6	0
	3	6	3	0	2
	4	0	0	0	0

b. Subtract the smallest number in each column. (Because of the dummy zeros in each column, the resulting table will be unchanged.)

c. Determine the minimum number of lines needed to cover the zeros. One possible way is:

	Machine			
Job	A	B	C	D
1	2	6	4	0
2	2	1	6	0
3	6	3	0	2
4	0	0	0	0

d. Since the number of lines is less than the number of rows, modify the numbers.

(1) Subtract the smallest uncovered number (1) from each uncovered number.

(2) Add the smallest uncovered number to numbers at line intersections.

The result is:

	Machine			
Job	A	B	C	D
1	1	5	4	0
2	1	0	6	0
3	5	2	0	2
4	0	0	1	1

e. Test for optimality:

	Machine			
Job	A	B	C	D
1	1	5	4	0
2	1	0	6	0
3	5	2	0	2
4	0	0	1	1

Since the minimum number of lines equals the number of rows, an optimum assignment can be made.

f. Assign jobs to machines. Start with rows 1 and 3, since they each have one zero, and columns A and C, also with one zero each. The result is:

	Machine			
Job	A	B	C	D
1	1	5	4	[0]
2	1	[0]	6	0
3	5	3	[0]	2
4	[0]	0	1	1

g. Compute total costs, referring back to the original table:

$$
\begin{array}{ll}
\text{1-D} & \$10 \\
\text{2-B} & 8 \\
\text{3-C} & 9 \\
\text{4-A} & \underline{0} \\
& \$27
\end{array}
$$

h. The implication of assignment 4–A is that machine A will not be assigned one of these jobs. It may remain idle or be used for another job.

2. *Priority rules.* Job times (including processing and setup) are shown in the following table for five jobs waiting to be processed at a work center:

Job	Job time (days)	Due date (days)
a	12	15
b	6	24
c	14	20
d	3	8
e	7	6

Determine the processing sequence that would result from each of these priority rules:

a. FCFS.

b. SPT.

c. DD.

d. CR.

Solution

(Assume job times are independent of processing sequence.)

a. FCFS:

Job	Order
a	1
b	2
c	3
d	4
e	5

b. SPT:

Job	Job time	Order
a	12	4
b	6	2
c	14	5
d	3	1
e	7	3

c. DD:

Job	Due date	Order
a	15	3
b	24	5
c	20	4
d	8	2
e	6	1

d. CR:

Job	CR	Order
a	1.25	2
b	4.00	5
c	1.43	3
d	2.67	4
e	0.86	1

3. *S/O rule.* Using the following information, determine an order processing sequence using the S/O priority rule.

Order	Processing time remaining (days)	Due date (days)	Number of operations remaining
A	20	30	2
B	11	18	5
C	10	6	2
D	16	23	4

Solution

(Assume times are independent of processing sequence.)

Order	(1) Remaining processing time	(2) Due date	(3) (2) − (1) Slack	(4) Number of operations	(5) Ratio	(6) Rank (sequence)
A 20		30	10	2	5.00	4
B 11		18	7	5	1.40	2
C 10		6	−4	2	−2.00	1
D 16		23	7	4	1.75	3

(Note that one ratio is negative. When negatives occur, assign the *lowest* rank to the *most negative* number.)

4. *Sequencing jobs through two work centers.* Use Johnson's rule to obtain the optimum sequence for processing the jobs shown through work centers A and B.

Job	Job times (hours) Work center A	Work center B
a 2.50		4.20
b 3.80		1.50
c 2.20		3.00
d 5.80		4.00
e 4.50		2.00

Solution

a. Identify the smallest time: job b (1.50 hours at work center B). Since the time is for B, schedule this job last.

b. The next smallest time is for job e (2.00 hours at B). Schedule job e next to last.

c. Identify the smallest remaining job time: job c (2.20 hours at center A). Since the time is in the A column, schedule job c first. At this point, we have:

$$c, \underline{\hspace{1em}}, \underline{\hspace{1em}}, e, b$$

d. The smallest time for remaining jobs is 2.50 hours for job a at center A. Schedule this job after job c. The one remaining job (job d) fills the remaining slot. Thus, we have:

$$c\text{-}a\text{-}d\text{-}e\text{-}b$$

5. For the previous problem, determine what effect splitting jobs c, d, e, and b in work center A would have on the idle time of work center

B and on the throughput time. Assume that each job can be split into two equal parts.

Solution

We assume that the processing sequence remains unchanged and proceed on that basis. The solution from the previous problem is shown in the following chart. The next chart shows job processing at center B when splitting is used.

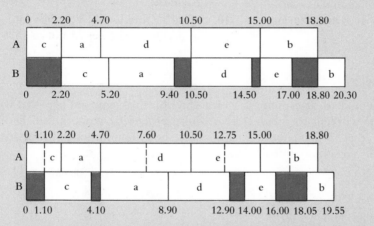

An inspection of these two figures reveals that throughput time has decreased from 20.30 hours to 19.55 hours. In addition, the original idle time was 5.6 hours, and after splitting certain jobs it was reduced to 4.85 hours. Hence, some improvement was achieved. Note, though, that for jobs toward the end of the sequence, processing times at B are generally less than at A. As a result, jobs such as e and b at B were scheduled so that they were *centered* around the finishing times of e and b, respectively, at A, in order to avoid having to break the jobs due to waiting for the remainder of the split job from A. Thus, the greatest advantage from job splitting generally comes from splitting earlier jobs when Johnson's rule is used for sequencing.

DISCUSSION AND REVIEW QUESTIONS

1. Why is scheduling fairly simple for continuous systems but fairly complex for job shops?

2. What are the main decision areas of job shop scheduling?

3. What are Gantt charts? How are they used in scheduling? What advantages and limitations are associated with Gantt charts?

4. What are the basic assumptions of the assignment method of linear programming?

5. Briefly describe each of these priority rules:
   a. FCFS.
   b. SPT.
   c. DD.
   d. S/O.
   e. Rush.
6. Why are priority rules needed?
7. What problems do service systems present for scheduling the use of resources that are not generally found in manufacturing systems?

8. Doctors' and dentists' offices frequently schedule patients at regularly spaced intervals. What problems can this create? Can you suggest an alternative approach that might reduce these problems? Under what circumstances would regularly spaced appointments constitute a reasonable approach to patient scheduling?
9. How are scheduling and productivity related?
10. What factors would you take into account in deciding whether or not to split a job?

PROBLEMS

1. Use the assignment method to determine the best way to assign workers to jobs, given the following cost information. Compute total cost for your assignment plan.

		Job		
		A	B	C
	1	5	8	6
Worker	2	6	7	9
	3	4	5	3

2. Rework the previous problem treating the numbers in the table as profits instead of costs. Compute the total profit.
3. Assign trucks to delivery routes so that total costs are minimized, given the cost data shown. What are total costs?

		Route				
		A	B	C	D	E
	1	4	5	9	8	7
	2	6	4	8	3	5
Truck	3	7	3	10	4	6
	4	5	2	5	5	8
	5	6	5	3	4	9

4. Develop an assignment plan that will minimize processing costs, given the information shown, and interpret your answer.

		Machine		
		A	B	C
	1	12	8	11
	2	13	10	8
Job	3	14	9	14
	4	10	7	12

5. Use the assignment method to obtain a plan that will minimize the processing costs in the following table under these conditions:
   a. The combination 2-D is undesirable.
   b. The combinations 1-A and 2-D are undesirable.

		Machine				
		A	B	C	D	E
	1	14	18	20	17	18
	2	14	15	19	16	17
Job	3	12	16	15	14	17
	4	11	13	14	12	14
	5	10	16	15	14	13

6. The following table contains information concerning four jobs that are awaiting processing at a work center.

Job	Job time (days)	Due date (days)
A	14	20
B	10	16
C	7	15
D	6	17

   a. Sequence the jobs using (1) FCFS, (2) SPT, (3) DD, and (4) CR. Assume the list is by order of arrival.
   b. For each of the methods in part a, determine (1) the average completion time, (2) the average lateness, and (3) the average number of jobs at the work center.
   c. Is one method superior to the others? Explain.

7. Using the information presented in the table shown, identify the processing sequence that would result using (1) FCFS, (2) SPT, (3) DD, and (4) CR. For each method, determine (1) average job completion time, (2) average job lateness, and (3) average number of jobs in the system.

Job	Operation time (hours)	Due date (hours)
a	7	4
b	4	10
c	2	12
d	11	20
e	8	15

8. The following table shows orders to be processed at a machine shop as of 8 A.M. Monday. The jobs have different operations they must go through. Processing times are in days. Jobs are listed in order of arrival.

   a. Determine the processing sequence at the first work center using each of these rules: (1) FCFS, (2) S/O.
   b. Compute the effectiveness of each rule using each of these measures: (1) average completion time, (2) average job lateness, and (3) average number of jobs at the work center.

Job	Processing time (days)	Due date (days)	Remaining number of operations
A	8	20	2
B	10	18	4
C	5	25	5
D	11	17	3
E	9	35	4

9. A wholesale grocery distribution center uses a two-step process to fill orders. Tomorrow's work will consist of filling the seven orders shown. Determine a job sequence that will minimize the time required to fill the orders.

	Time (hours)	
Order	Step 1	Step 2
A	1.20	1.40
B	0.90	1.30
C	2.00	0.80
D	1.70	1.50
E	1.60	1.80
F	2.20	1.75
G	1.30	1.40

10. The times required to complete each of eight jobs on two machines are shown in the table that follows. Each job must follow the same sequence, beginning with machine A and moving to machine B.
    a. Determine a sequence that will minimize throughput time.
    b. Construct a chart of the resulting sequence, and find B's idle time.

c. For the sequence determine in (a), how much could B's idle time be reduced by splitting the last two jobs in half?

Job	Time (hours)	
	Machine A	Machine B
a	16	5
b	3	13
c	9	6
d	8	7
e	2	14
f	12	4
g	18	14
h	20	11

11. Given the operation times provided:
    a. Develop a job sequence that minimizes idle time at the two work centers.
    b. Construct a chart of the activities at the two centers, and determine each one's idle time, assuming no other activities are involved.

	Job times (in minutes)					
	A	B	C	D	E	F
Center 1	20	16	43	60	35	42
Center 2	27	30	51	12	28	24

12. A shoe repair operation uses a two-step sequence that all jobs in a certain category follow. For the group of jobs listed,
    a. Find the sequence that will minimize total completion time.
    b. Determine the amount of idle time for workstation B.
    c. What jobs are candidates for splitting? Why? If they were split, how much of a reduction in idle time and throughput time would there be?

	Job times (in minutes)				
	a	b	c	d	e
Station A	27	18	70	26	15
Station B	45	33	30	24	10

13. A foreman has determined processing times at a work center for a set of jobs and now wants to sequence them. Given the information shown, do the following:
    a. Determine the processing sequence using (1) FCFS, (2) SPT, (3) DD, and (4) CR. For each sequence, compute the average job lateness, the average completion time, and the average number of jobs at the work center. The list is in FCFS order.
    b. Using the results of your calculations in part a, show that the average completion time and the average number of jobs measures are equivalent for all four sequencing rules.

Job	Job time (days)	Due date	Operations remaining
a	4.5	10	2
b	6.0	17	4
c	5.2	12	3
d	1.6	27	5
e	2.8	18	3
f	3.3	19	1

14. Given the information in the following table, determine the processing sequence that would result using the S/O rule.

Job	Remaining processing time (days)	Due date	Remaining number of operations
a	5	8	2
b	6	5	4
c	9	10	4
d	7	12	3
e	8	10	2

15. Use the runout method to designate the order in which the following jobs are to be processed and interpret your results.

Job	Inventory (pounds)	Demand (pounds per day)
A	450	40
B	210	20
C	180	30
D	760	80

16. A department has a mixing machine that has limited capacity. Five products are mixed using this machine. The manager uses a variation of the runout formula to determine runout times. It involves dividing the sum of production capacity and inventory by the demand rate. Interpret your results.

Given the following information, develop a processing order for the products listed using the runout time method.

Product	Production capacity (units)	Inventory (units)	Demand rate (units per week)
A	400	300	200
B	500	400	300
C	350	150	100
D	250	250	250
E	150	100	200

17. (Refer to the formula mentioned in the previous problem.) Given this information on production rates, inventory, and demand rates, determine processing order for the products listed using the runout method.

Product	Production rate (units/hour)	Inventory (units)	Demand rate (units/day)
A	40	200	70
B	50	150	80
C	30	100	80
D	20	100	90

Available production capacity is seven hours. Interpret your results.

18. Given this information on job times and due dates, determine the optimal processing sequence using (1) FCFS, (2) SPT, (3) DD, and (4) CR. For each method, find the average job completion time and the average job lateness.

Job	Job time (hours)	Due date (hours)
a	3.5	7
b	2.0	6
c	4.5	18
d	5.0	22
e	2.5	4
f	6.0	20

19. The Budd Gear Co. specializes in heat treating gears for many of the automobile companies. This morning at 8 A.M., when Budd's shop opened, there were five orders (listed in order of arrival) waiting to be processed.

Order	Order size (units)	Per unit time in heat treatment (minutes/unit)	Due date (min. from now)
A	16	4	160
B	6	12	200
C	10	3	180
D	8	10	190
E	4	1	220

a. If the Due Date rule is used, what sequence should be used?
b. What will be the average job lateness?
c. What will be the average number of jobs in the system?
d. Would the SPT rule produce better results in terms of lateness?

SELECTED BIBLIOGRAPHY

Baker, K. R. *Introduction to Sequencing and Scheduling.* New York: John Wiley, 1974.

Buffa, Elwood S., and Jeffery G. Miller. *Production-Inventory Systems: Planning and Control.* 3rd ed. Homewood, Ill.: Richard D. Irwin, 1979.

Chase, Richard, and Nicholas Aquilano. *Production and Operations Management.* 5th ed. Homewood, Ill.: Richard D. Irwin, 1989.

Fogarty, Donald W., and Thomas R. Hoffmann. *Production and Inventory Management.* Cincinnati, South-Western Publishing, 1983.

McClain, John O., and L. Joseph Thomas. *Opera-*

tions Management: Production of Goods and Services. 2nd ed. Englewood Cliffs, N.J.: Prentice-Hall, 1985.

Schonberger, Richard J. *Operations Management: Planning and Control of Operations and Operating Resources.* Plano, Tex.: Business Publications, 1981.

Tersine, Robert J. *Production/Operations Management: Concepts, Structure, and Analysis.* 2nd ed. New York: Elsevier-North Holland Publishing, 1985.

Vollmann, Thomas E.; William L. Berry; and D. Clay Whybark. 2nd ed. *Manufacturing Planning and Control Systems.* Homewood, Ill.: Richard D. Irwin, 1988.

MAINTENANCE

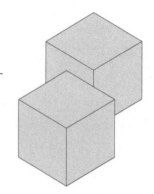

LEARNING OBJECTIVES

After completing this supplement, you should be able to:

1. Explain the importance of maintenance in production systems.
2. Describe the range of maintenance activities.
3. Discuss preventive maintenance and the key issues associated with it.
4. Discuss breakdown maintenance and the key issues associated with it.
5. State how the Pareto phenomenon pertains to maintenance decisions.

SUPPLEMENT OUTLINE

Maintaining the production capability of an organization is an important function in any production system. **Maintenance** encompasses all those activities that relate to keeping facilities and equipment in good working order, and making necessary repairs when breakdowns occur, so that the system can perform as intended.

Maintenance activities are often organized into two groups: (1) buildings and grounds and (2) equipment maintenance. Buildings and grounds people are responsible for the appearance and functioning of buildings, parking lots, lawns, fences, and the like. Equipment maintenance people are responsible for maintaining machinery and equipment in good working condition and making any necessary repairs.

INTRODUCTION

The goal of maintenance is to keep the production system in good working order at minimal cost. Decision makers have two basic options with respect to maintenance. One is to deal with breakdowns or other problems when they occur. This is referred to as **breakdown maintenance.** The other option is to reduce breakdowns though a program of lubrication, adjustment, cleaning, inspection, and replacement of worn parts. This is referred to as **preventive maintenance.**

Decision makers try to make a trade-off between these two basic options that will result in minimizing their combined cost. With no preventive maintenance, breakdown and repair costs would be tremendous. However, beyond a certain point, preventive maintenance activities are wasteful. For instance, if a person never had the oil changed in his or her car, never had it lubricated, and never had the brakes or tires inspected, simply having repairs done when absolutely necessary, preventive costs would be negligible, but repair costs could be quite high, considering the wide range of parts (engine, steering, transmission, tires, brakes, etc.) that could fail. In addition, property damage and injury costs may be incurred, plus there would be the uncertainty of when failure might occur (e.g., on the expressway during rush hour, or late at night). On the other hand, having the oil changed and the car lubricated every morning would obviously be excessive because automobiles are designed to perform for much longer periods without oil changes and lubrication. Hence, the best approach is to seek a balance between preventive maintenance and breakdown maintenance. The same concept applies to maintaining production systems: Strike a balance between prevention costs and breakdown costs. This concept is illustrated in Figure 13S–1.

The age and condition of facilities and equipment, the degree of technology involved, the type of production process, and similar factors enter into the decision of how much preventive maintenance is desirable. Thus, in the case of a new automobile, very little preventive maintenance may be needed since there is little risk of breakdowns. However, as the car ages and becomes worn through use, the desirability of preventive maintenance increases because the risk of breakdowns increases. Thus, when tires and brakes begin to show signs

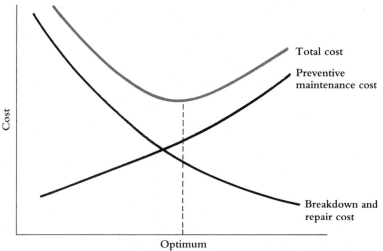

Total maintenance cost as a function of preventive maintenance effort

of wear, they should be replaced before they fail; dents and scratches should be periodically taken care of before they begin to rust; and the car should be lubricated and have its oil changed after exposure to high levels of dust and dirt. Also, inspection and replacement of critical parts that tend to fail suddenly should be performed before a road trip to avoid disruption of the trip and costly emergency repair bills.

PREVENTIVE MAINTENANCE

The goal of preventive maintenance (PM) is to reduce the incidence of breakdowns or failures in the plant or equipment to avoid the associated costs. Those costs can include loss of output; idle workers; schedule disruptions; injuries; damage to other equipment, products, or facilities; and repairs, which may involve maintaining inventories of spare parts, repair tools and equipment, and repair specialists.

Preventive maintenance is *periodic*. It can be scheduled according to the availability of maintenance personnel and to avoid interference with operating schedules. Preventive maintenance is generally scheduled using some combination of the following:

1. The result of planned inspections that reveal a need for maintenance.
2. According to calendar (passage of time).
3. After a predetermined number of operating hours.

Ideally, preventive maintenance will be performed just prior to a breakdown or failure because this will result in the longest possible use of facilities or equipment without a breakdown. **Predictive maintenance** is an attempt to determine when to perform preventive maintenance activities. It is based on historical records and analysis of technical data to predict when a piece of equipment or part is about to fail. The better predictions of failures are, the more effective preventive maintenance will be. A good preventive maintenance effort relies on complete records for each piece of equipment. Records must include such information as date of installation, operating hours, dates and types of maintenance, and dates and types of repairs.

In the broadest sense, preventive maintenance extends back to design and selection stage of equipment and facilities. Durability and ease of maintenance can have long-term implications for preventive maintenance programs. Training of employees in proper operating procedures and in how to keep equipment in good operating order (and providing the incentive to do so) are also important. More and more, organizations are transferring routine maintenance (cleaning, adjusting, inspecting) to the users of equipment, in an effort to give them a sense of responsibility and awareness of the equipment they use and to cut down on abuse and misuse of the equipment.

BREAKDOWN PROGRAMS

The risk of a breakdown can be greatly reduced by an effective preventive maintenance program. Nonetheless, occasional breakdowns may still occur. Consequently, even firms with good preventive practices have some need for breakdown programs. Of course, some organizations rely less on preventive maintenance than others, so they have an even greater need for effective ways of dealing with breakdowns.

Unlike preventive maintenance, breakdowns cannot be scheduled but must be dealt with on an irregular basis (i.e., as they occur). Among the major approaches used to deal with breakdowns are the following:

1. *Standby or backup equipment* that can be quickly pressed into service.
2. *Inventories of spare parts* that can be installed as needed, thereby avoiding lead times involved in ordering parts, and buffer inventories, so that other equipment will be less likely to be affected by short-term downtime of a particular piece of equipment.
3. *Operators* who are able to perform at least minor repairs on their equipment.
4. *Repair people* who are well trained and readily available to diagnose and correct problems with equipment.

The degree to which an organization pursues any or all of these approaches depends on how important a particular piece of equipment is to the overall production system. At one extreme is equipment that is the focal point of a system (e.g., printing presses for a newspaper; or vital operating parts of a car, such as brakes, steering, transmission, ignition, and engine). At the other extreme is equipment that is seldom used because it does not perform an important function in the system and equipment for which substitutes are readily available. Also included in this category is equipment that is less expensive to replace than to repair, for example, a simple calculator that sells for about $10 or a ball point pen. Similar examples exist in most business settings.

The implication is clear: Breakdown programs are most effective when they take into account the degree of importance a piece of equipment has in the production system and the ability of the system to do without it for a period of time. (Note that the Pareto phenomenon tends to exist in such situations: a relatively few pieces of equipment will be extremely important to the functioning of the systems, thereby justifying considerable effort and/or expense; some will require moderate effort or expense; and some will justify little effort or expense.)

SUMMARY

Maintaining the productive capability of an organization is an important function. Maintenance includes all of the activities related to keeping facilities and equipment in good operating order and to maintaining the appearance of buildings and grounds.

The goal of maintenance is to minimize the total cost of keeping the facilities and equipment in good working order. Maintenance decisions typically reflect a trade-off between preventive maintenance, which seeks to reduce the incidence of breakdowns and failures, and breakdown maintenance, which seeks to reduce the impact of breakdowns when they do occur.

KEY TERMS

breakdown maintenance, 688
maintenance, 688

predictive maintenance, 690
preventive maintenance, 688

DISCUSSION AND REVIEW QUESTIONS

1. What is the goal of a maintenance program?
2. List the costs generally associated with breakdown of equipment.
3. What are three different ways in which preventive maintenance is scheduled?
4. Explain the term *predictive maintenance* and the importance of good records.
5. List the major approaches organizations use to deal with breakdowns.

6. Explain how the Pareto phenomenon applies to:
   a. Preventive maintenance.
   b. Breakdown maintenance.
7. Discuss the key points of this supplement with respect to maintenance of an automobile.

SELECTED BIBLIOGRAPHY

Hall, Robert W. "Total Productive Maintenance—Essential to Maintain Progress." *Target* 3, no. 3 (Fall 1987), pp. 4–11.

Hora, Michael E. "The Unglamorous Game of Managing Maintenance." *Business Horizons* 30, no. 3 (May–June 1987), pp. 67–75.

Mann, Lawrence, Jr. *Maintenance Management*. Rev. ed. Lexington, Mass.: Lexington Books, 1983.

Nolden, Carol. "Predictive Maintenance: Route to Zero Unplanned Downtime." *Plant Engineering* 41, no. 4 (February 1987), pp. 38–43.

Wireman, Terry. *Preventive Maintenance*. Reston, Va.: Reston, 1984.

14

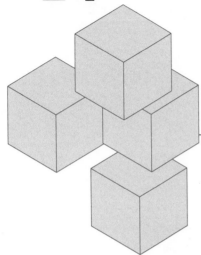

Project Management

LEARNING OBJECTIVES

After completing this chapter, you should be able to:

1. Give a general description of PERT/CPM techniques.
2. Construct simple network diagrams.
3. List the kinds of information that a PERT or CPM analysis can provide the manager.
4. Analyze networks with deterministic times.
5. Analyze networks with probabilistic times.
6. Describe activity "crashing" and solve simple problems.
7. Discuss the behavioral aspects of projects in terms of project personnel and the project manager.

Chapter Outline

Managers typically oversee a variety of operations. Some of these involve routine, repetitive activities, and others tend to vary with the task. Under the latter heading are **projects:** unique, one-time operations designed to accomplish a specific set of objectives in a limited time frame. Examples of projects include constructing a shopping complex, installing a new computer system, moving a firm to a new location, launching a space shuttle, and introducing a new product or service to the marketplace.

Most projects have certain elements in common. Often they involve considerable cost. They usually have a long time horizon, and they involve a large number of activities that must be carefully planned and coordinated in order for the project to be completed within time, cost, and performance guidelines. Goals must be established, and priorities must be set. Tasks must be identified, and time estimates must be made. Resource requirements must also be projected, and budgets must be prepared. Once underway, progress must be monitored to assure that project goals and objectives will be achieved.

The project approach enables an organization to focus attention and concentrate efforts on accomplishing a narrow set of objectives within a limited time and budget framework. This can produce significant benefits relative to other approaches that might be considered. Even so, projects present a manager with a host of problems that differ in many respects from those encountered with more routine types of activities. The problems of planning and coordinating project activities can be quite formidable for large projects, which typically have hundreds or even thousands of activities that must be carefully planned and monitored if a project is to proceed according to schedule and at a reasonable cost.

The chapter introduces the basic concept of project management. It begins with a brief discussion of some of the behavioral aspects of project management, along with some of the difficulties project managers are apt to encounter. The main portion of the chapter is devoted to a description of graphical and computational methods that are used for planning and scheduling projects.

BEHAVIORAL ASPECTS OF PROJECT MANAGEMENT

Project management differs from management of more traditional activities, mainly because of its limited time framework, which gives rise to a host of rather unique problems. This section considers more fully the nature of projects and their behavioral implications. Special attention is given to the role of the project manager.

The Nature of Projects

Projects go through a series of stages (i.e., a life cycle), which include project planning, execution of major activities, and project phaseout. During this life cycle, a variety of skill requirements are involved. An analogous set of circumstances exists in constructing a house. Initially a site must be found, and plans must be drawn up and approved by the owner and possibly a town building commission or other regulatory agency. Then a succession of personnel become involved, starting with those doing the site preparation, laying the foundation, erecting the frame, roofing, constructing exterior walls, wiring and plumbing, installing kitchen and bathroom fixtures and appliances, interior finishing work, and painting and carpeting work. Similar sequences are found on large construction projects, in R&D work, in the aerospace industry, and in virtually every other instance where projects are being used.

In effect, projects bring together personnel with diverse knowledge and skills, most of whom remain associated with the project for less than its full life. Some personnel go from project to project as their contributions become needed, and others are "on loan," either on a full-time or part-time basis, from their regular jobs. The latter is usually the case when a special project exists within the framework of a more traditional organization. Certain kinds of organizations tend to be involved with projects on a regular basis. Examples include consulting firms, architects, writers and publishers, and construction firms. In fact, it is not uncommon to have organizations or departments spending virtually all of their time involved with projects, with little or no "continuous" work.

Some organizations use a *matrix organization* that allows them to integrate the activities of a variety of specialists within a functional framework. For instance, they have certain people who prepare proposals, others who concentrate exclusively on engineering, others who devote their efforts to marketing, and so on.

The Project Manager

The central figure in the project is the project manager. He or she bears the ultimate responsibility for the success or failure of the project. The role of the project manager is one of an organizer—a person who is capable of working through others to accomplish the objectives of the project.

The job of project manager can be both difficult and rewarding. The manager must coordinate and motivate people who sometimes owe their allegiance to other managers in their functional areas. In addition, the people who work on a project frequently possess specialized knowledge and skills that the project manager does not have. Nevertheless, the manager is expected to guide and evaluate their efforts. Project managers must often function in an environment that is beset with uncertainties. Even so, budgets and time constraints are usually imposed, which can create additional pressures on project personnel. Finally, the project manager may not have the authority he or she needs to accomplish all of the objectives of the project. Instead, the manager must sometimes rely on persuasion and the cooperation of others to realize project goals.

The rewards of the job of project manager come from the benefits of being associated with a successful project as well as the personal satisfaction of seeing it through to its conclusion, the challenge of the job, and working with other people.

The Pros and Cons of Working on Projects

People are selected to work on special projects because the knowledge or abilities they possess are needed on them. In some instances, however, their supervisors may be reluctant to allow them to interrupt their regular jobs, even on a part-time basis, because it may require training a new person to do a job that will be temporary. Moreover, managers don't want to lose the output of good workers. The workers themselves are not always eager to participate in projects because it may mean working for two bosses, disruption of friendships and daily routines, and risking the possibility of being replaced on the current job. Furthermore, there may be fear of being associated with an unsuccessful project because of the adverse effect it might have on career advancement. In too many instances, when a project is phased out and the project team disbanded, team members tend to drift away from the organization for lack of a new project and the difficulty of returning to former jobs. This tendency is more pronounced after involvement with lengthy projects and is less likely to occur when a team member works on a part-time basis, although that approach has its own drawbacks in terms of divided loyalty and dual bosses.

In spite of the potential risks of being involved in a project, there are certain potential rewards that attract people to them. One is the dynamic environment that surrounds a project, often a marked contrast to the more staid environment in which some may feel trapped. Some individuals seem to thrive in more dynamic environments; they welcome the challenge of working under pressure and solving new problems. Then, too, projects may present opportunities to meet new people and to increase future job opportunities, especially if the project is at all successful. And being associated with a project can be a source of status among fellow workers. Finally, working on projects frequently inspires a team spirit, increasing morale and motivation to achieve successful completion of project goals.

PLANNING AND SCHEDULING WITH GANTT CHARTS

The Gantt chart is a popular tool for planning and scheduling *simple* projects. It enables a manager to initially schedule project activities and then to monitor progress over time by comparing planned progress to actual progress. A Gantt chart for a bank's plan to establish a new direct marketing department is illustrated in Figure 14–1. To prepare the chart, the vice president who was in charge of the project had to first identify the major activities that would be required. Next, time estimates for each activity were made, and the sequence of activities was determined. Once completed, the chart indicated which activities were to occur, their planned duration, and when they were to occur. Then, as the project progressed, the manager was able to see which activities were ahead of schedule and which activities were delaying the project. This enabled the manager to direct attention where it was needed most to speed up the project in order to finish on schedule.

FIGURE 14—1

Gantt chart for bank example

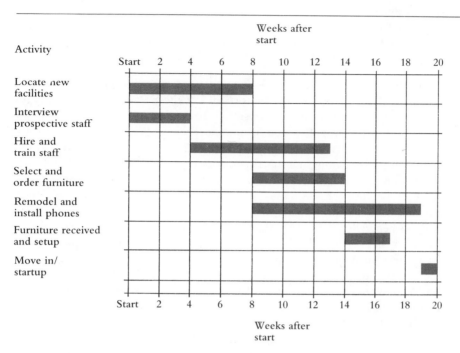

The obvious advantage of a Gantt chart is its simplicity, and this accounts for its popularity. However, Gantt charts fail to reveal certain relationships among activities that can be crucial to effective project management. For instance, if one of the early activities in a project suffers a delay, it would be important for the manager to be able to easily determine which later activities would have to be delayed because they could not start until that activity was completed. Conversely, some activities may safely be delayed without affecting the overall project schedule. Again, a Gantt chart does not directly reveal this. Consequently, Gantt charts are most useful for simple projects, say, where activities are simultaneous or where a string of sequential activities is involved. On more complex projects, Gantt charts can be useful for initial project planning, which then gives way to the use of *networks,* the subject of the following sections.

PERT AND CPM

PERT (program evaluation and review technique) and **CPM** (critical path method) are two of the most widely used techniques for planning and coordinating large-scale projects. By using PERT or CPM, managers are able to obtain:

1. A graphical display of project activities.
2. An estimate of how long the project will take.

3. An indication of which activities are the most critical to timely project completion.

4. An indication of how long any activity can be delayed without lengthening the project.

PERT and CPM were developed independently during the late 1950s. PERT evolved through the joint efforts of Lockheed Aircraft, the U.S. Navy Special Projects Office, and the consulting firm of Booz, Allen & Hamilton in an effort to speed up the Polaris missile project. At the time, there was considerable concern on the part of the U.S. government that the Soviet Union might be gaining nuclear superiority over the United States, and early completion of the project was given top priority by the Department of Defense. The project was a huge one, with over 3,000 contractors involved, and many thousands of activities. The use of PERT was quite successful: PERT is generally credited for shaving two years off the length of the project. Partly for that reason, PERT or some similar technique is now required on all large government projects.

CPM was developed by J. E. Kelly of the Remington Rand Corporation and M. R. Walker of Du Pont to plan and coordinate maintenance projects in chemical plants.

Although these two techniques were developed independently, they have a great deal in common. Moreover, many of the initial differences between the two techniques have disappeared as users borrowed certain features from one technique for use with the other. For example, PERT originally stressed probabilistic activity time estimates, because the environment in which it was developed was typified by high uncertainty. In contrast, the tasks for which CPM was developed were much less uncertain, so CPM originally made no provision for variable time estimates. At present, either technique can be used with deterministic or probabilistic times. Other initial differences concerned the mechanical aspects of developing project networks. However, from a conceptual standpoint, most of these differences were relatively minor. To avoid confusion, we will not delve into the differences here. For practical purposes, the two techniques are the same; the comments and procedures described will apply to CPM analysis as well as to PERT analysis of projects.

The Network Diagram

One of the main features of PERT and related techniques is their use of a *network* or **precedence diagram** to depict major project activities and their sequential relationships. Recall the bank example that used a Gantt chart (see Figure 14–1). A network diagram for that same problem is shown in Figure 14–2. The diagram is composed of a number of arrows and nodes. The arrows represent the project activities. Note how much clearer the sequential relationship of activities is with a network chart instead of a Gantt chart. For instance, it is apparent that ordering the furniture and remodeling both require that a location for the office has been identified. Likewise, interviewing must

FIGURE 14–2

*A simple project
network diagram*

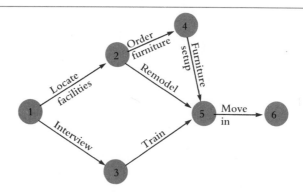

precede training. However, interviewing and training can take place independently of activities associated with locating a facility, remodeling, and so on. Hence, a network diagram is generally the preferred approach for visual portrayal of project activities.

You should know that there are two slightly different conventions for constructing these network diagrams. Under one convention, the *arrows* are used to designate activities; under the other convention, the *nodes* are used to designate activities. These conventions are referred to as **activity-on-arrow (A-O-A)** and **activity-on-node (A-O-N).** To avoid confusion, the discussion here will focus primarily on the activity-on-arrow convention. Then, later in the chapter, a comparison of the two conventions will be given. For now, we shall use the arrows for activities. **Activities** consume resources and/ or *time*. The nodes in the A-O-A approach represent the starting and finishing of activities, which are called **events.** Events are points in time. Unlike activities, they do not consume either resources or time.

Activities can be referred to in either of two ways. One is by their endpoints (e.g., activity 2–4) and the other is by a letter assigned to an arrow (e.g., activity c). Both methods are illustrated in this chapter.

The network diagram describes sequential relationships among major activities on a project. For instance, activity 2-4 cannot be started, according to the network, until activity 1-2 has been completed. A **path** is a sequence of activities that leads from the starting node to the finishing node. Thus, the sequence 1-2-4-5-6 is a path. There are two other paths in this network: 1-2-5-6 and 1-3-5-6. The length (of time) of any path can be determined by summing the expected times of the activities on that path. The path with the longest time is of particular interest because it governs project completion time. In other words, expected project duration equals the expected time of the longest path. Moreover, if there are any delays along the longest path, there will be corresponding delays in project completion time. Conversely, attempts to shorten project completion must focus on the longest sequence of activities. Because of its influence on project completion time, the longest path is the **critical path,** and its activities are referred to as **critical activities.**

Paths that are shorter than the critical path can experience some delays and still not affect the overall project completion time as long as the ultimate path time does not exceed the length of the critical path. The allowable slippage for any path is called the path *slack,* and it reflects the difference between the length of a given path and the length of the critical path. The critical path, then, has zero slack time.

Network Conventions

Developing and interpreting network diagrams requires some familiarity with networking conventions. Although there are many that could be mentioned, the discussion here will concentrate on some of the most basic, and most common, features of network diagrams. This will provide sufficient background for understanding the basic concepts associated with precedence diagrams and allow you to solve typical problems.

One of the main features of a precedence diagram is that it reveals which activities must be performed in *sequence* (i.e., there is a precedence requirement) and which can be performed independently of each other. For example, in the following diagram, activity a must be completed before activity b can begin, and activity b must be completed before activity c can begin.

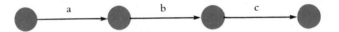

If the diagram had looked like this, both activity a and activity b would have to be completed before activity c could begin, but a and b could be performed at the same time; performance of a is independent of performance of b.

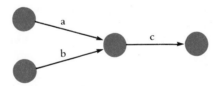

If activity a must precede b and c, the appropriate network would look like this:

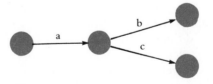

When multiple activities enter a node, this implies that all those activities must be completed before any activities that are to begin at that node can start. Hence, in this diagram, activities a and b must both be finished before either activity c or activity d can start.

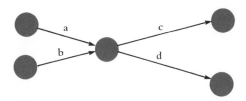

When two activities both have the same beginning and ending nodes, a *dummy* node and activity is used to preserve the separate identity of each activity. In the diagram below, activities a and b must be completed before activity c can be started.

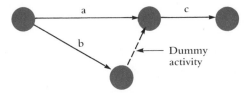

Separate identities are particularly important for computer analysis, because most computer programs identify activities by their endpoints; activities with the same endpoints could not be distinguished from each other, although they might have quite different expected times.

There are actually a number of different uses of dummy activities. Another common use is depicted below:

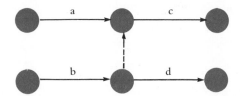

In this situation, activities a and b must both precede activity c. However, d's start is dependent only on completion of activity b, and *not* on activity a's completion.

The primary function of dummy activities is to clarify relationships. As far as time is concerned, a dummy activity has an activity time equal to zero.

For reference purposes, nodes are numbered typically from left to right:

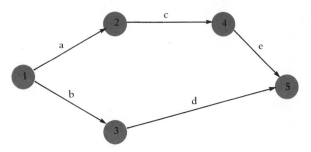

Starting and ending arrows are sometimes used during development of a network for increased clarity.

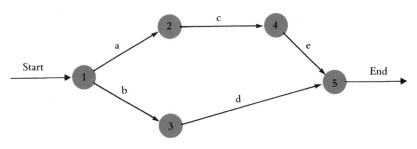

DETERMINISTIC TIME ESTIMATES

The main determinant of the way PERT and CPM networks are analyzed and interpreted is whether activity time estimates are *probabilistic* or *deterministic*. If time estimates can be made with a high degree of confidence that actual times will not differ significantly, we say the estimates are **deterministic.** On the other hand, if estimated times are subject to variation, we say the estimates are **probabilistic.** Probabilistic time estimates must include an indication of the extent of probable variation.

This section describes analysis of networks with deterministic time estimates. A later section deals with probabilistic times.

One of the best ways to gain an understanding of the nature of network analysis is to consider a simple example.

EXAMPLE 1

Given the information provided in the accompanying network diagram, determine each of the following:

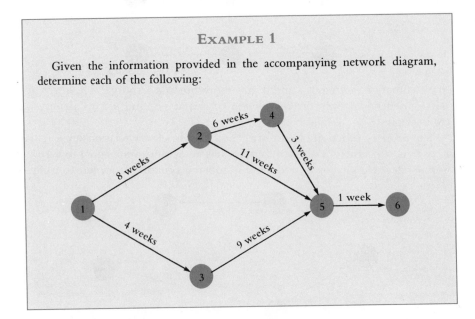

EXAMPLE 1 *(concluded)*

a. The length of each path.
b. The critical path.
c. The expected length of the project.
d. Amount of slack time for each path.

Solution

a. As shown in the following table, the path lengths are 18 weeks, 20 weeks, and 14 weeks.
b. The longest path (20 weeks) is 1-2-5-6, so it is the critical path.
c. The expected length of the project is equal to the length of the critical path (i.e., 20 weeks).
d. The slack for each path is found by subtracting its length from the length of the critical path, as shown in the last column of the table. (*Note:* It is sometimes desirable to know the slack time associated with activities. The next section describes a method for obtaining those slack times.)

Path	Lenth (weeks)	Slack
1-2-4-5-6	8 + 6 + 3 + 1 = 18	20 − 18 = 2
1-2-5-6	8 + 11 + 1 = 20*	20 − 20 = 0
1-3-5-6	4 + 9 + 1 = 14	20 − 14 = 6

* Critical path length.

A COMPUTING ALGORITHM

Many real-life project networks are much larger than the simple network illustrated in the preceding example; they often contain hundreds or even thousands of activities. Because the necessary computations can become exceedingly complex and time-consuming, large networks are generally analyzed by computer programs rather than manually. The intuitive approach just demonstrated does not lend itself to computerization because, in many instances, path sequences are not readily apparent. Instead, an algorithm is used to develop four pieces of information about the network activities:

ES, the earliest time activity can start, assuming all preceding activities start as early as possible.

EF, the earliest time the activity can finish.

LS, the latest time the activity can start and not delay the project.

LF, the latest time the activity can finish and not delay the project.

Once these values have been determined, they can be used to find:

1. Expected project duration.
2. Slack time.
3. Which activities are on the critical path.

The three examples that follow illustrate how these values are computed using the precedence diagram of Example 1, which is repeated here for convenient reference.

Computing ES and EF Times

Computation of earliest starting and finishing times is aided by two simple rules:

1. The earliest finish time for any activity is equal to its earliest start time plus its expected duration, t:

$$EF = ES + t \qquad (14\text{--}1)$$

2. For nodes with one entering arrow, ES for activities at such nodes is equal to EF of the entering arrow. For nodes with multiple entering arrows, ES for activities leaving such nodes equals the largest EF of the entering arrow.

EXAMPLE 2

Compute the earliest starting time and earliest finishing time for each activity in the diagram shown in Figure 14–3.

FIGURE 14–3

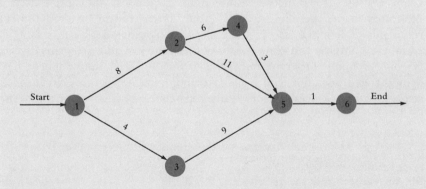

Solution

Assume an ES of 0 for activities without predecessors. Thus, activities 1-2 and 1-3, as initial activities, are assigned early starting times equal to zero. The earliest finishing times for these activities are:

EXAMPLE 2 *(concluded)*

$$EF_{1-2} = 0 + 8 = 8 \quad \text{and} \quad EF_{1-3} = 0 + 4 = 4$$

The EF of activity 1-2 becomes the ES for the two activities that follow it: 2-4 and 2-5. Likewise, the EF of activity 1-3 becomes the ES for activity 3-5. Thus:

$$ES_{2-4} = 8, \quad ES_{2-5} = 8, \quad \text{and} \quad ES_{3-5} = 4$$

The corresponding EF times for these activities are:

$$EF_{2-4} = 8 + 6 = 14$$
$$EF_{2-5} = 8 + 11 = 19$$
$$EF_{3-5} = 4 + 9 = 13$$

Activity 4-5 has an early starting time equal to EF_{2-4}, or 14, and an early finish time of $14 + 3 = 17$. Finally, activity 5-6, with three predecessors, has an early starting time equal to the *largest* EF of the three activities that precede it. Hence, it has an ES of 19. Its EF time is $19 + 1 = 20$.

These results are summarized in the following table.

Activity	Duration	ES	EF
1-2	8	0	8
1-3	4	0	4
2-4	6	8	14
2-5	11	8	19
3-5	9	4	13
4-5	3	14	17
5-6	1	19	20

Note that the latest EF is the project duration. Thus, the expected length of the project is 20 weeks.

Computing LS and LF Times

Computation of the latest starting and finishing times is aided by the use of two rules:

1. The latest starting time for each activity is equal to its latest finishing time minus its expected duration:

$$LS = LF - t \tag{14–2}$$

2. For nodes with one leaving arrow, LF for arrows entering that node equals the LS of the leaving arrow. For nodes with multiple leaving arrows: LF for arrows entering that node equals the smallest LS of leaving arrows.

Finding ES and EF times involves a "forward pass" through the network; finding LS and LF times involves a "backward pass" through the network. Hence, we must begin with the EF of the last activity and use that time as the LF for the last activity. Then we obtain the LS for the last activity by subtracting its expected duration from its LF.

EXAMPLE 3

Compute the latest finishing and starting times for each activity shown in Figure 14–3.

Solution

Set LF of the last activity equal to the EF of that activity. Thus,

$$LF_{5-6} = EF_{5-6} = 20 \text{ weeks}$$

Next, compute the latest starting time:

$$LS_{5-6} = LF_{5-6} - t$$
$$= 20 - 1 = 19$$

In order for activity 5-6 to start no later than week 19, all immediate predecessors must finish no later than that time. Thus,

$$LF_{4-5} = LF_{2-5} = LF_{3-5} = 19$$

The respective LS times for each activity are:

$$LS_{4-5} = 19 - 3 = 16$$
$$LS_{2-5} = 19 - 11 = 8$$
$$LS_{3-5} = 19 - 9 = 10$$

Similarly, $LF_{2-4} = LS_{4-5} = 16$, and $LS_{2-4} = 16 - 6 = 10$. Hence, there are two arrows leaving node 2: 2-4, with LS = 10, and 2-5, with LS = 8. The latest finish for activity 1-2 thus becomes 8, which is the smallest LS for a leaving arrow. The LF for 1-3 is equal to the LS for 3-5:

$$LF_{1-3} = LS_{3-5} = 10$$

The LS for activity 1-3 is:

$$LS_{1-3} = 10 - 4 = 6$$

The LS for activity 1-2 is:

$$LS_{1-2} = LF_{1-2} - t$$
$$= 8 - 8 = 0$$

The LS and LF computations are summarized in the following table.

Activity	Duration	LF	LS
5-6	1	20	19
4-5	3	19	16
2-5	11	19	8
3-5	9	19	10
2-4	6	16	10
1-2	8	8	0
1-3	4	10	6

Computing Slack Times

The slack time can be computed in either of two ways:

$$\text{Slack} = \text{LS} - \text{ES} \quad \text{or} \quad \text{LF} - \text{EF} \qquad (14\text{--}3)$$

EXAMPLE 4

Compute slack times for the precedence diagram of Figure 14–3.

Solution

We have the option of using either the starting times or the finishing times. Suppose we choose the starting times. Using ES times computed in Example 2 and LS times computed in Example 3, slack times are:

Activity	LS	ES	(LS − ES) Slack
1-2	0	0	0
1-3	6	0	6
2-4	10	8	2
2-5	8	8	0
3-5	10	4	6
4-5	16	14	2
5-6	19	19	0

The critical path using this computing algorithm is denoted by activities with zero slack time. Thus, the table in the preceding example indicates that activities 1-2, 2-5, and 5-6 are all critical activities, which agrees with the results of the intuitive approach demonstrated in Example 1.

Knowledge of slack times provides managers with greater detail for planning allocation of scarce resources and for directing control efforts toward those activities that might be most susceptible to delaying the project than the more simplistic intuitive approach does. In this regard, it is important to recognize that the activity slack times are based on the assumption that all of the activities on the same path will be started as early as possible and not exceed their expected times. Furthermore, if two activities are both on the same path (e.g., activities 2-4, and 4-5 in the preceding example) and have the same slack (e.g., two weeks), this will be the *total* slack *available to both*. In essence, the activities have *shared slack*. Hence, if the first activity uses all this slack, there will be zero slack for the other activity, and that much less slack for all following activities on that same path.

As noted above, this algorithm lends itself to computerization. A computer printout for this problem would appear something like the one shown in Table 14–1.

TABLE 14–1

Computer printout

ACTIVITY	TIME	STARTING SCHEDULE				SLACK
		EARLY		LATE		
		ES	EF	LS	LF	
1-2	8.00	0.00	8.00	0.00	8.00	0.00
1-3	4.00	0.00	4.00	6.00	10.00	6.00
2-4	6.00	8.00	14.00	10.00	16.00	2.00
2-5	11.00	8.00	19.00	8.00	19.00	0.00
3-5	9.00	4.00	13.00	10.00	19.00	6.00
4-5	3.00	14.00	17.00	16.00	19.00	2.00
5-6	1.00	19.00	20.00	19.00	20.00	0.00

THE CRITICAL PATH SEQUENCE IS:

SNODE	FNODE	TIME
1	2	8.00
2	5	11.00
5	6	1.00
		20.00

PROBABILISTIC TIME ESTIMATES

The preceding discussion assumed that activity times were known and not subject to variation. While that assumption is appropriate in some situations, there are many others where it is not. Consequently, those situations require a probabilistic approach.

The probabilistic approach involves *three* time estimates for each activity instead of one:

1. **Optimistic time:** The length of time required under optimum conditions. Represented by the letter *a*.

2. **Pessimistic time:** The amount of time that will be required under the worst conditions. Represented by the letter *b*.

3. **Most likely time:** The most probable amount of time that will be required. Represented by the letter *m*.

These time estimates should be made by managers or others with knowledge about the project.

The **beta distribution** is commonly used to describe the inherent variability in time estimates (see Figure 14–4.) Although there is no real theoretical justification for using the beta distribution, it has certain features that make it attractive in practice: The distribution can be symmetrical or skewed to either the right or the left according to the nature of a particular activity, the mean and variance of the distribution can be readily obtained from the three time estimates listed above, and the distribution is unimodal with a high concentration of probability surrounding the most likely time estimate.

FIGURE 14–4

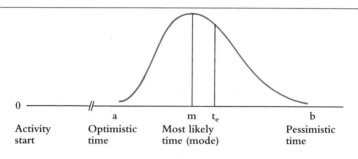

A beta distribution is used to describe probabilistic time estimates

Of special interest in network analysis are the average or expected time for each activity t_e, and the variance of each activity time, σ_i^2. The expected time is computed as a weighted average of the three time estimates.

$$t_e = \frac{a + 4m + b}{6} \qquad (14\text{–}4)$$

The standard deviation of each activity's time is estimated as one sixth of the difference between the pessimistic and optimistic time estimates. (Analogously, essentially all of the area under a normal distribution lies within three standard deviations of the mean, which is a range of six standard deviations.) The variance is found by squaring the standard deviation. Thus,

$$\sigma^2 = \left[\frac{(b - a)}{6}\right]^2 \qquad \text{or} \qquad \frac{(b - a)^2}{36} \qquad (14\text{–}5)$$

The size of the variance reflects the degree of uncertainty associated with an activity's time: the larger the variance, the greater the uncertainty. Hence, an activity with a variance of 16 would have more uncertainty as to its eventual duration than one with a variance of 6.

It is also desirable to compute the standard deviation of the expected time for *each path*. This can be accomplished by summing the variances of the activities on a path and then taking the square root of that number. That is,

$$\sigma_{\text{path}} = \sqrt{\Sigma(\text{variances of activities on path})} \qquad (14\text{–}6)$$

EXAMPLE 5

The network diagram for a project is shown in the accompanying figure, with three time estimates for each activity. Activity times are in months. Do the following:

a. Compute the expected time for each activity and the expected duration for each path.
b. Identify the critical path.
c. Compute the variance for each activity and the variance for each path.

EXAMPLE 5 *(concluded)*

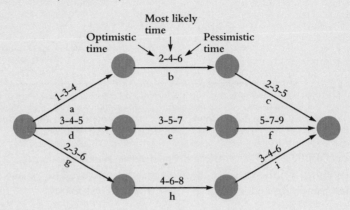

Solution

a.

		Times			$t_e = \dfrac{a + 4m + b}{6}$	Path
Path	Activity	a	m	b		total
a-b-c	a	1	3	4	2.83 ⎱	
	b	2	4	6	4.00 ⎰	10.00
	c	2	3	5	3.17 ⎰	
d-e-f	d	3	4	5	4.00 ⎱	
	e	3	5	7	5.00 ⎰	16.00
	f	5	7	9	7.00 ⎰	
g-h-i	g	2	3	6	3.33 ⎱	
	h	4	6	8	6.00 ⎰	13.50
	i	3	4	6	4.17 ⎰	

b. The path that has the longest expected duration is the critical path. Since path
d-e-f has the largest path total, it is the critical path.

c.

		Times			$\sigma^2_{act.} = \dfrac{(b - a)^2}{36}$	σ^2_{path}	σ_{path}
Path	Activity	a	m	b			
a-b-c	a	1	3	4	$(4 - 1)^2/36 = 9/36$ ⎱		
	b	2	4	6	$(6 - 2)^2/36 = 16/36$ ⎰	34/36 = 0.944	0.97
	c	2	3	5	$(5 - 2)^2/36 = 9/36$ ⎰		
d-e-f	d	3	4	5	$(5 - 3)^2/36 = 4/36$ ⎱		
	e	3	5	7	$(7 - 3)^2/36 = 16/36$ ⎰	36/36 = 1.00	1.00
	f	5	7	9	$(9 - 5)^2/36 = 16/36$ ⎰		
g-h-i	g	2	3	6	$(6 - 2)^2/36 = 16/36$ ⎱		
	h	4	6	8	$(8 - 4)^2/36 = 16/36$ ⎰	41/36 = 1.139	1.07
	i	3	4	6	$(6 - 3)^2/36 = 9/36$ ⎰		

Knowledge of the expected path times and their standard deviation enables a manager to compute probabilistic estimates of the project completion time, such as:

The probability that the project will be completed within 17 months of its start is about 84 percent.

The probability that the project will take longer than 18 months is approximately 2 percent.

Statements of this sort are based on the assumption that the duration time of a path is a random variable that is normally distributed around the expected path time. The rationale for a normal distribution is that we are summing activity times (random variables), and sums of random variables tend to be normally distributed when the number of items being summed is large. However, even when the number of items is relatively small, the normal distribution provides a reasonable approximation to the actual distribution.

The next example illustrates the use of a normal distribution to determine the probabilities for various completion times. Before we look at that example, it is important to make note of two points. One relates to **independence.** It is assumed that path duration times are independent of each other. In essence, this requires two things: Activity times are independent of each other, and each activity is only on one path. For activity times to be independent, the time for one must not be a function of another's time; if two activities were always early or late together, they would not be considered independent. The assumption of independent *paths* is usually considered to be met if only a *few* activities in a large project are on multiple paths. Even then, common sense should govern the decision of whether the independence assumption is justified.

A second important point is that a project is not completed until all of its activities have been completed, not just those on the critical path. It sometimes happens that another path requires more time than the critical path, in which case the project runs longer than expected. Hence, it can be risky to focus exclusively on the critical path. Instead, one must consider the possibility that at least one other path will delay timely project completion. This requires determining the probability that *all* paths will finish by a specified time. To do that, find the probability that each path will finish by the specified time, and multiply the resulting probabilities. Note that only paths with expected times that are relatively close to that of the critical path need to be considered, since it would be highly unlikely that a path with a much shorter expected time would exceed the critical path's time. A simple rule of thumb is to treat the probability of timely completion of a path as 100% if its expected time plus 2.5 of *its* standard deviations is less than the specified time. These concepts are illustrated in the following example.

EXAMPLE 6

Using the information from the preceding example, answer the following questions:

a. Can the paths be considered independent? Why?
b. Determine the probability that the project can be completed within 17 months of its start.
c. Determine the probability that the project will be completed within 15 months of its start.
d. What is the probability that the project will not be completed within 15 months of its start?

Solution

a. Yes, the paths can be considered independent since no activity is on more than one path and we have no information that would suggest that any activity times are interrelated.
b. To answer questions of this nature, we must take into account the degree to which the path distributions "overlap" the specified completion time. This concept is illustrated in the accompanying figure, which shows the three path distributions, each centered on that path's expected duration, and the specified completion time of 17 months.

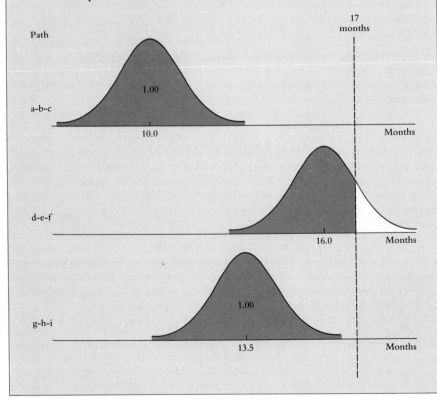

EXAMPLE 6 *(continued)*

The shaded portion of each distribution corresponds to the probability that the part will be completed within the specified time. Observe that paths a–b–c and g–h–i are well enough to the left of the specified time that it is highly likely that both will be finished by month 17 but that the critical path overlaps the specified completion time. Hence, we need consider only the distribution of path d–e–f in assessing the probability of completion by month 17. To do so, we must first compute the value of z using the relationship

$$z = \frac{\text{Specified time} - \text{Expected time}}{\text{Path standard deviation}} \qquad (14\text{--}7)$$

In this instance, we find

$$z = \frac{17 - 16}{1.00} = +1.00$$

Turning to Appendix B, Table B with $z = +1.00$, we see that the area under the curve to the left of z is .8413. Hence, the probability of the project finishing within 17 months of its start is 84.13 percent.

c. This question illustrates how to handle a problem in which more than one of the distributions overlap the specified time. Note in the accompanying figure

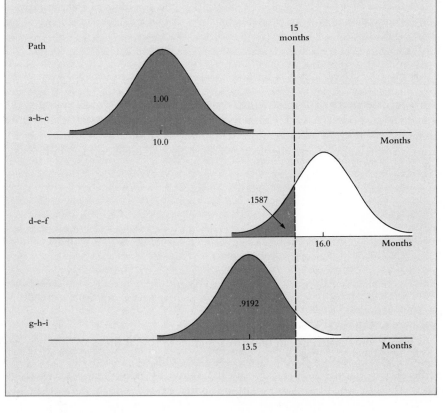

EXAMPLE 6 *(concluded)*

that paths d-e-f and g-h-i overlap month 15. This means that both paths have the potential for delaying the project beyond the 15 months.

Although the figure is useful in expressing the concept of overlapping paths, we need a more rigorous approach to determine which paths to consider and what each path's probability of completion is. This requires computing a value of z using Formula 14–7 for each path. Then, any path with a z of more than $+2.50$ is treated as having a completion probability of 100%; the others will be used to determine the *joint* probability of all finishing by the specified time. For this problem, with a specified time of 15 months, the z values are:

Path	$z = \dfrac{15 - \textit{Expected path duration}}{\textit{Path standard deviation}}$	*Probability of completion in 15 months*
a-b-c	$\dfrac{15 - 10.00}{0.97} = +5.15$	1.00
d-e-f	$\dfrac{15 - 16.00}{1.00} = -1.00$	.1587
g-h-i	$\dfrac{15 - 13.50}{1.07} = +1.40$	.9192

From Appendix B, Table B, the area to the *left* of $z = -1.00$ is .1587, and the area to the *left* of $z = +1.40$ is .9192. The joint probability of all finishing before month 15 is the product of their probabilities: $1.00(.1587)(.9192) = .1459$.

ACTIVITY-ON-NODE DIAGRAM

An alternate method for drawing network diagrams involves placing the activities on nodes (A-O-N) rather than on arrows. The result is a slightly different diagram. We can begin to get an appreciation for the differences by comparing the two approaches to a given problem. Consider this set of project activities:

Activity	*Precedes*
a	c
b	d,e
c	f
d	g
e	g
f	End
g	End

Figure 14–5 illustrates both types of networks.

One obvious difference in the two approaches is that there are more nodes in the A-O-N approach. Generally speaking, this will be the rule. A second difference is that the A-O-A network has a dummy arrow that is necessary to correctly show the precedence relationship that exists. A-O-N networks elim-

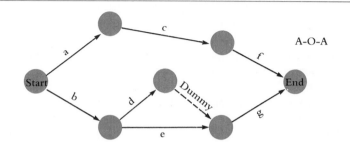

A-O-A

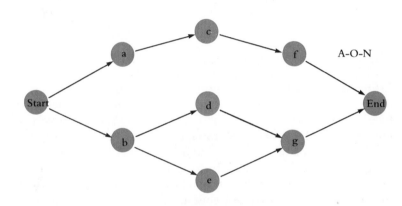

A-O-N

inate the need for dummy activities, which is an advantage of having activities on nodes.

In practice, both approaches are used. Most PERT/CPM computer programs can handle either convention, but some require one or the other. Often the choice of method depends more on personal preference or established procedures.

SIMULATION

The preceding section illustrated a method for computing the probability that a project would be completed in a specified length of time. That discussion assumed that the paths of the project were *independent;* that is, the same activities are not on more than one path. If an activity were on more than one path and it happened that the completion time for that activity far exceeded its expected time, all paths that included that activity would be affected, and, hence, their times would not be independent. In situations where activities are on multiple paths, one must consider if the preceding approach can be used. For instance, if only a few activities are on multiple paths, and particularly if the paths are *much* shorter than the critical path, that approach may still be reasonable. Moreover, for purposes of illustration, as in the text problems and examples, we treat the paths as being independent when, in fact, they may not be.

In practice, when *dependent* cases occur, an approach that is often used is *simulation*. It amounts to a form of repeated sampling wherein many passes are made through the PERT network. In each pass, a randomly selected value for each activity time is made based on the characteristics of the activity's probability distribution (e.g., its mean, standard deviation, and distribution type). After each pass, the expected project duration is determined by adding the times along each path and designating the time of the longest path as the project duration. After a large number of such passes (say, several hundred), there is enough information to prepare a frequency distribution of the project duration times. This distribution can be used to make a probabilistic assessment of the actual project duration, allowing for the fact that some activities are on more than one path. The last problem in the supplement to Chapter 15 illustrates this.

TIME-COST TRADE-OFFS: CRASHING

Estimates of activity times for projects usually are made for some given level of resources. In many situations, it is possible to reduce the length of a project by injecting additional resources. The impetus to shorten projects may reflect efforts to avoid late penalties, to take advantage of monetary incentives for timely completion of a project, or to free resources for use on other projects. In many cases, however, the desire to shorten the length of a project merely reflects an attempt to reduce the indirect costs associated with running the project, such as facilities and equipment costs, supervision, and labor and personnel costs. Managers often have certain options at their disposal that will allow them to shorten, or **crash,** certain activities. Among the most obvious options are the use of additional funds to support additional personnel or more efficient equipment and the relaxing of some work specifications. Hence, a project manager may be able to shorten a project, thereby realizing savings on indirect project costs, by increasing *direct* expenses to speed up the project. The goal in evaluating time-cost trade-offs is to identify a plan that will minimize the sum of the indirect and direct project costs.

In order to make a rational decision on which activities (if any) to crash, and on the extent of crashing desirable, a manager needs certain information:

1. Regular time and crash time estimates for each activity.
2. Regular cost and crash cost estimates for each activity.
3. A list of activities that are on the critical path.

Activities on the critical path are potential candidates for crashing, since shortening noncritical activities would not have an impact on total project duration. From an economic standpoint, activities should be crashed according to crashing costs: crash those with the lowest costs first. Moreover, crashing

FIGURE 14–6

Crashing activities*

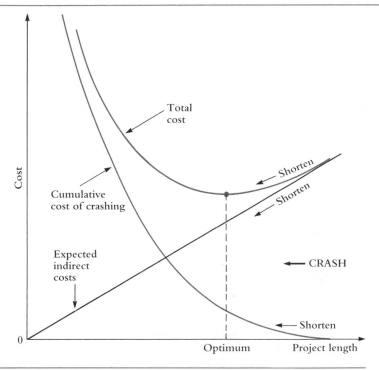

*Crashing activities reduces indirect project costs and increases direct costs; the optimum amount of crashing results in minimizing the sum of these two types of costs.

should continue as long as the cost to crash is less than the benefits received from crashing. These benefits might take the form of incentive payments for early project completion as part of a government contract, or they might reflect savings in the indirect project costs, or both. Figure 14–6 illustrates the basic relationships between indirect, direct, and total project costs due to crashing.

The general procedure for crashing is:

1. Obtain estimates of regular and crash times and costs for each activity.
2. Determine the lengths of all paths and path slack times.
3. Determine which activities are on the critical path.
4. Crash critical activities, in order of increasing costs, as long as crashing costs do not exceed benefits. (Note that two or more paths may become critical as the original critical path becomes shorter, so that subsequent improvements will require simultaneous shortening of two or more paths. In some cases, it will be most economical to shorten an activity that is on two [or more] of the critical paths. This is true whenever the crashing cost for a joint activity is less than the sum of crashing one activity on each separate path.)

EXAMPLE 7

Using the following information, develop an optimum time-cost solution. Assume that indirect project costs are $1,000 per day.

Activity	Normal time	Crash time	Cost per day to crash
a	6	6	—
b	10	8	$500
c	5	4	300
d	4	1	700
e	9	7	600
f	2	1	800

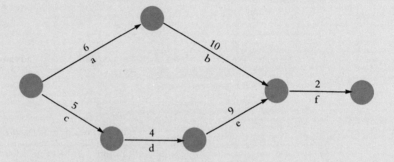

Solution

a. Determine which activities are on the critical path, its length, and the length of the other path:

Path	Length
a-b-f	18
c-d-e-f	20 (critical path)

b. Rank the critical path activities in order of lowest crashing cost, and determine the number of days each can be crashed.

Activity	Cost per day to crash	Available days
c	$300	1
e	600	2
d	700	3
f	800	1

c. Begin shortening the project, one day at a time, and check after each reduction to see which path is critical. (After a certain point, another path may equal the length of the shortened critical path.)
Thus:
(1) Shorten activity c one day at a cost of $300. The length of the critical path now becomes 19 days.

EXAMPLE 7 *(concluded)*

(2) Activity c cannot be shortened any more. Shorten activity e one day at a cost of $600. The length of path c-d-e-f now becomes 18 days, which is the same as the length of path a-b-f.

(3) Since the paths are now both critical, further improvements will necessitate shortening one activity on each.

The remaining points for crashing and their costs are:

Path	Activity	Crash cost (per day)
a-b-f	a	No reduction possible
	b	$500
	f	800
c-d-e-f	c	No further reduction possible
	d	$700
	e	600
	f	800

At first glance, it would seem that crashing f would not be advantageous, since it has the highest crashing cost. However, f is on both paths, so shortening f by one day would shorten *both* paths (and hence, the project) by one day for a cost of $800. The option of shortening the least expensive activity on each path would cost $500 for b and $600 for e, or $1,100. Thus, shorten f by one day. The project duration is now 17 days.

(4) At this point, no additional improvement is feasible. The cost to crash b is $500 and the cost to crash e is $600, for a total of $1,100, and that would exceed the project costs of $1,000 per day.

(5) The crashing sequence is summarized below:

Path	n = 0	1	2	3
		Length after crashing n days:		
a-b-f	18	18	18	17
c-d-e-f	20	19	18	17
Activity crashed		c	e	f
Cost		$300	$600	$800

ADVANTAGES AND LIMITATIONS OF PERT

PERT and similar project scheduling techniques can provide important services for the project manager. Among the most useful features are:

1. Use of these techniques forces the manager to organize and quantify available information and to recognize where additional information is needed.

2. The techniques provide a graphical display of the project and its major activities.

3. They identify (*a*) activities that should be closely watched because of the potential for delaying the project and (*b*) other activities that have slack time and so can be delayed without affecting project completion time. This raises the possibility of reallocating resources in order to shorten the project.

No analytical technique is without limitations. Among the more important limitations of PERT are the following:

1. In developing the project network, one or more important activities may be omitted.
2. Precedence relationships may not all be correct as shown.
3. Time estimates may include a fudge factor; managers feel uncomfortable about making time estimates because they appear to commit themselves to completion within a certain time period.
4. The use of a computer is essential for large projects.

SUMMARY

Projects are composed of a unique set of activities established to realize a given set of objectives in a limited time span. The nonroutine nature of project activities places a set of demands on the project manager, which are different in many respects than those required for the manager of more traditional operations activities, both in planning and coordinating the work in the human problems encountered.

PERT and CPM are two commonly used techniques for developing and monitoring projects. Although each technique was developed independently and for expressly different purposes, time and practice have erased most of the original differences, so that now little distinction can be made between the two. Either one provides the manager with a rational approach to project planning along with a graphical display of project activities. Both depict the sequential relationships that exist among activities and reveal to managers which activities must be completed on time in order to achieve timely project completion. Managers can use that information to direct their attention toward the most critical activities.

Two slightly different conventions can be used for constructing a network diagram. One designates the arrows as activities; the other designates the nodes as activities. To avoid confusion, this chapter emphasized only one approach, the activity-on-arrow model.

The task of developing and updating project networks quickly becomes complex for projects of even moderate size, so that the task is often handled through the use of computer programs, which involves the use of some computing algorithm.

A deterministic approach is used for determining project duration estimates when activity times can be fairly well established. However, when activity times are subject to some uncertainty, a probabilistic approach is more realistic, and estimates of the length of such projects should be couched in probabilistic terms.

In some instances, it may be possible to shorten the length of a project by shortening one or more of the project activities. Typically, such gains are achieved by the use of additional resources, although in some cases, it may be possible to transfer resources among project activities. Generally, projects are shortened to the point where the cost of additional reduction would exceed the benefit of additional reduction, or to the point where further improvements, although desirable, would be physically impossible.

KEY TERMS

SOLVED PROBLEMS

1. The following table contains information related to the major activities of a research project. Use the information to do the following:

   a. Draw a precedence diagram.

   b. Find the critical path.

   c. Determine the expected length of the project.

Activity		*Precedes*	*Expected time (days)*
a	. . . .	c,b	5
c	. . . .	d	8
d	. . . .	i	2
b	. . . .	i	7
e	. . . .	f	3
f	. . . .	j	6
i	. . . .	j	10
j	. . . .	End	8
g	. . . .	h	1
h	. . . .	k	2
k	. . . .	End	17

Solution

a. In constructing networks, these observations can be useful:
  (1) Activities with no predecessors are at the beginning (left side) of the network.
  (2) Activities with multiple predecessors are located at path intersections.

Start the network diagram by identifying and charting all activities with no predecessors:

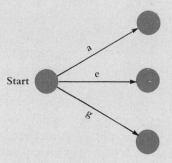

Next, complete the diagram in sections. Go down the activity list, in order when possible, to avoid overlooking any activities. The process is illustrated in the following diagram.

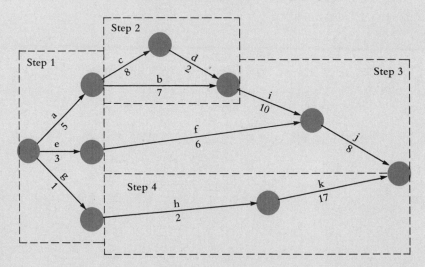

Here are some additional hints for constructing a precedence diagram:
  (1) Use pencil.
  (2) Start with a single node, and end with a single node.

(3)   Try to avoid having paths cross each other.
(4)   Number nodes from left to right.
(5)   Have activities going from left to right.
(6)   Use only one arrow between any pair of nodes.

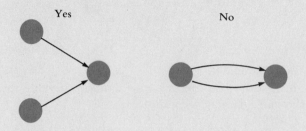

Yes   No

b. and *c.*

Path	Length (days)
a–c–d–i–j*	5 + 8 + 2 + 10 + 8 = 33†
a–b–i–j	5 + 7 + 10 + 8 = 30
e–f–j	3 + 6 + 8 = 17
g–h–k	1 + 2 + 17 = 20

*Critical path.
†Expected project duration.

2.   Using the computing algorithm, determine the slack times for the following diagram. Identify the activities that are on the critical path.

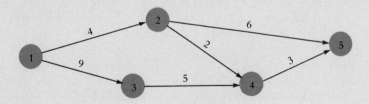

Solution

The task of determining ES, EF, LS, and LF times can be greatly simplified by setting up two brackets for each activity, as illustrated below:

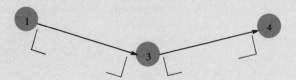

The bracket at the left end of each activity will eventually be filled in with the earliest and latest *starting* times, and the bracket at the right end of each activity will be filled in with the earliest and latest *finishing* times:

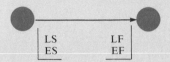

This is accomplished in a two-step process. First, the earliest starting times and earliest finishing times are determined, working from left to right, as shown in the following diagram.

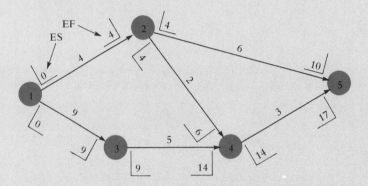

Thus, activity 1-2 can start at 0. With a time 4, it can finish at $0 + 4 = 4$. This establishes the earliest start for all activities that begin at node 2. Hence, 2-5 and 2-4 can start no earlier than 4. Activity 2-5 has an early finish of $4 + 6 = 10$, and activity 2-4 has an early finish of $4 + 2 = 6$. At this point, it is impossible to say what the earliest start is for 4-5: that will depend on which activity, 3-4 or 2-4, has the latest EF. Consequently, it is necessary to compute ES and EF along the lower path. Assuming an ES of 0 for 1-3, its EF will be 9, so 3-4 will have an ES of 9 and an EF of $9 + 5 = 14$.

Considering that the two activities entering node 4 have EF times of 6 and 14, the earliest that activity 4-5 can start is the *larger* of these, which is 14. Hence, activity 4-5 has an ES of 14 and an EF of $14 + 3 = 17$.

Now compare the EFs of the activities entering the final node. The largest of these, 17, is the expected project duration.

The LF and LS times for each activity can now be determined by working backward through the network (i.e., from right to left). The LF for the two activities entering node 5 is 17—the project duration. In other words, in order for the project to finish in 17 weeks, these last two activities must both finish by that time.

In the case of activity 4-5, the LS necessary for an LF of 17 is $17 - 3 = 14$. This means that both 2-4 and 3-4 must finish no later than 14. Hence, their LF times are 14. Activity 3 has an LS time of $14 - 5 = 9$, making the LF of activity 1-3 equal to 9, and its LS equal to $9 - 9 = 0$.

Activity 2-4, with an LF time of 14, has an LS time of $14 - 2 = 12$. Activity 2-5 has an LF of 17 and therefore an LS of $17 - 6 = 11$. Thus, the latest 2-5 can start is 11, and the latest 2-4 can start is 12 in order to finish by week 17. Since activity 1-2 precedes *both* of these activities, it can finish no later than the *smaller* of these, which is 11. Hence, 1-2 has an LF of 11 and an LS of $11 - 4 = 7$.

The ES, EF, LF, and LS times are shown on the following network.

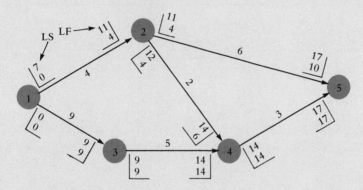

The slack time for any activity is the difference between *either* LF and EF *or* LS and ES. Thus,

Activity	LS	ES	Slack	or	LF	EF	Slack
1-2	7	0	7		11	4	7
2-5	11	4	7		17	10	7
2-4	12	4	8		14	6	8
1-3	0	0	0		9	9	0
3-4	9	9	0		14	14	0
4-5	14	14	0		17	17	0

The activities with zero slack times indicate the critical path. Thus, the critical path is 1-3-4-5.

When working problems of this nature, keep in mind the following:

a. For nodes with multiple entering activities, the ES time for leaving activities of that node is the *largest* EF of the entering activities.

b. For nodes with multiple leaving activities, the LF for an entering activity for that node is the *smallest* LS of the leaving activities.

3. Expected times and variances for the major activities of an R&D project are depicted in the following PERT chart. Determine the probability that project completion time will be:
   a. Less than 50 weeks.
   b. More than 50 weeks.

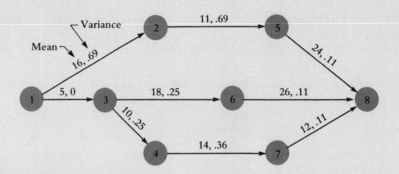

Solution

a. Compute the mean and standard deviation for each path:

Path	Expected time (weeks)	Standard deviation (weeks)
1-2-5-8 . . .	$16 + 11 + 24 = 51$	$\sqrt{.69 + .69 + .11} = 1.22$
1-3-6-8 . . .	$5 + 18 + 26 = 49$	$\sqrt{.00 + .25 + .11} = 0.60$
1-3-4-7-8 . .	$5 + 10 + 14 + 12 = 41$	$\sqrt{.00 + .25 + .36 + .11} = 0.85$

b. Compute the z score for each path for the length specified. For any path that has a score of more than $z = +2.50$, treat its probability of completion before the specified time as 1.00. Use

$$z = \frac{50 - t_{path}}{\sigma_{path}}$$

The probability that each path will be completed in 50 weeks or less is shown in the corresponding diagram. (Probabilities are from Appendix B, Table B.) The probability that the project will be completed in 50 weeks or less depends on all three paths being completed in that time. Because z for path 1-3-4-7-8 is greater than $+2.50$, it is treated as having a probability of completion in 50 weeks of 100 percent. It is less certain that the other two paths will be completed in that time. The probability that *both* will not exceed 50 is the *product* of their individual probabilities of completion. Thus, $.2061(.9525) = .1963$.

The probability that the project *will* exceed 50 weeks is the complement of this number, which is $1.000 - .1963 = .8037$.

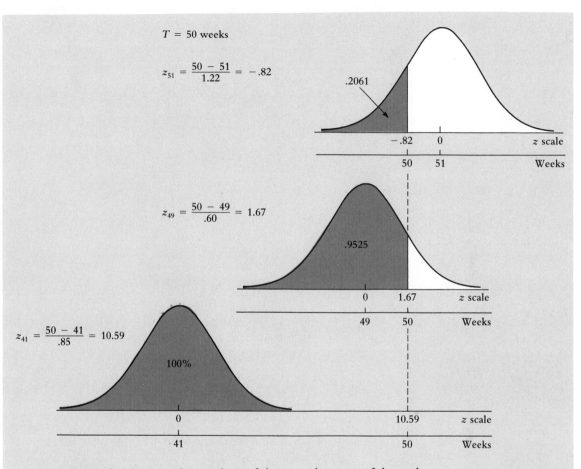

$T = 50$ weeks

$$z_{51} = \frac{50 - 51}{1.22} = -.82$$

.2061

$$z_{49} = \frac{50 - 49}{.60} = 1.67$$

.9525

$$z_{41} = \frac{50 - 41}{.85} = 10.59$$

100%

(Note that it is *not* the product of the complements of the path probabilities.)

4. Indirect costs for a project are $12,000 per week for as long as the project lasts. The project manager has supplied the cost and time information shown. Use the information to:

a. Determine an optimum crashing plan.

b. Graph the total costs for the plan.

Activity	Crashing potential (weeks)	Cost per week to crash
a 3		$11,000
b 3		3,000 first week, $4,000 others
c 2		6,000
d 1		1,000
e 3		6,000
f 1		2,000

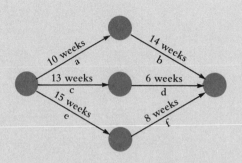

Solution

a. (1) Compute path lengths and identify the critical path:

Path	Duration (weeks)
a–b	24 (critical path)
c–d	19
e–f	23

(2) Rank critical activities according to crashing costs:

Activity	Cost per week to crash
b	$ 3,000
a	11,000

Activity b should be shortened one week since it has the lowest crashing cost. This would reduce indirect costs by $12,000 at a cost of $3,000, for a net savings of $9,000. At this point, paths a–b and e–f would both have a length of 23 weeks, so both would be critical.

(3) Rank activities by crashing costs on the two critical paths:

Path	Activity	Cost per week to crash
a–b	b	$ 4,000
	a	11,000
e–f	e	6,000
	f	2,000

Choose one activity on each path to crash: b on a–b and f on e–f, for a total cost of $4,000 + $2,000 = $6,000 and a net savings of $12,000 − $6,000 = $6,000.

(4) Check to see which path(s) might be critical: a–b and e–f would be 22 weeks in length, and c–d would still be 19 weeks.

(5) Rank activities on the critical paths:

Path	Activity	Cost per week to crash
a–b	b	$ 4,000
	a	11,000
e–f	e	6,000
	f	(no further crashing possible)

Crash b on path a–b and e on e–f for a cost of $4,000 + $6,000 = $10,000, for a net savings of $12,000 − $10,000 = $2,000.

(6) At this point, no further improvement is possible: paths a–b and e–f would be 21 weeks in length, and one activity from each path would have to be shortened. This would mean a at $11,000 and e at $6,000 for a total of $17,000, which would exceed the $12,000 potential savings in indirect costs.

b. The following table summarizes the results, showing the length of the project after crashing *n* weeks:

Path	n = 0	1	2	3
a–b	24	23	22	21
c–d	19	19	19	19
e–f	23	23	22	21
Activity crashed		b	b,f	b,e
Crashing costs ($000)		3	6	10

A summary of costs for the preceding schedule would look like this:

Project length	Cumulative weeks shortened	Cumulative crashing costs ($000)	Indirect costs ($000)	Total costs ($000)
24	0	0	24(12) = 288	288
23	1	3	23(12) = 276	279
22	2	3 + 6 = 9	22(12) = 264	273
21	3	9 + 10 = 19	21(12) = 252	271
20	4	19 + 17 = 36	20(12) = 240	276

The graph of total costs is as follows.

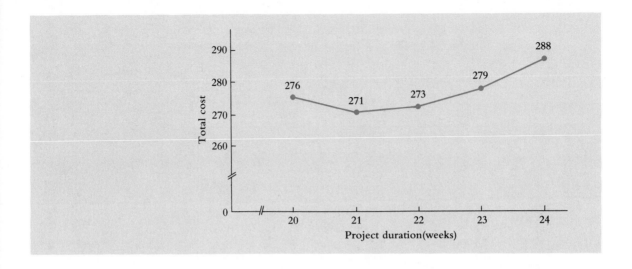

DISCUSSION AND REVIEW QUESTIONS

1. What are some of the basic differences between project planning and scheduling and production planning and scheduling?

2. "A probabilistic approach to estimating project duration is generally preferred." Comment.

3. Identify the term being described for each of the following:
   a. A sequence of activities in a project.
   b. The longest time sequence of activities in a project.
   c. Used when two activities have the same starting and finishing points.
   d. The difference in time length of any path and the critical path.
   e. Used to denote the beginning or end of an activity.
   f. The statistical distribution used to describe variability of an activity time.
   g. The statistical distribution used to describe project variability.
   h. Shortening an activity by allocating additional resources.

4. Explain the concept of shared slack.

5. Can you envision a situation in which resources might be *subtracted* from a project, in a kind of reverse time-cost trade-off? Explain briefly.

6. List the main advantages of PERT. List the main limitations.

7. What are dummy activities, and why are they used?

8. Why might a probabilistic estimate of a project's completion time based solely on the variance of the critical path be misleading? Under what circumstances would it be acceptable?

9. Define each of these terms, and indicate how each is determined.
   a. Optimistic time estimate.
   b. Most likely time estimate.
   c. Pessimistic time estimate.
   d. Expected activity time.
   e. Variance of an activity time.
   f. Standard deviation of a path's time.

10. Could PERT or CPM be used to schedule nonproject activities? Explain your reasoning briefly.

11. Why might a person wish to be associated with a critical path activity? What are some of the reasons one might have for not wanting such an association?

12. What are some of the potential benefits of working on a special project in one's firm? What are some of the risks?

13. What are some of the aspects of the pro-ject manager's job that make it more demanding than that of a manager working in a more traditional organizational framework?

14. What is the main benefit of a project organization over more traditional forms of operations management for project work?

PROBLEMS

1. For each of the following network diagrams, determine both the critical path and the expected project duration. The quantities on the arrows represent expected activity times.

a.

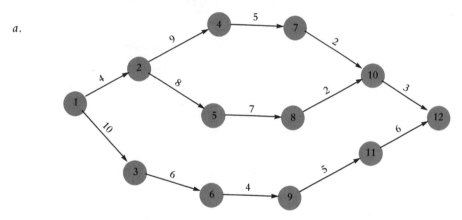

b.

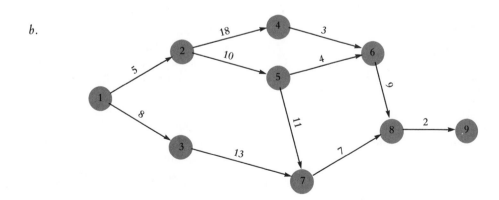

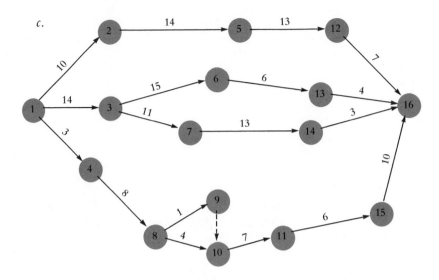

c.

2. Using the information provided in the accompanying table, do the following:
a. Construct a network diagram.
b. Determine which activities are on the critical path.
c. Compute the length of the critical path.

Activity	Estimated time (days)
1-2	5
2-3	6
2-4	4
3-6	9
6-7	2
4-5	4
4-7	18
5-7	10

3. The information shown pertains to a project that is about to commence. As the project manager, which activities would you be concerned with in terms of timely project completion? Explain.

Activity	Precedes	Estimated time (days)
a . . . . . b		15
b . . . . . c,d		12
c . . . . . e		6
d . . . . . End		5
e . . . . . End		3

Activity	Precedes	Estimated time (days)
f . . . . g,h		8
g . . . . i,j		8
h . . . . j		9
i . . . . End		7
j . . . . k		14
k . . . . End		6

4. Use the computational algorithm to determine the slack time for each activity in:
a. Problem 1a.
b. Problem 1b.
c. Explain shared slack time, referring to 1a or 1b.

5. For each of the problems listed, determine the following quantities for each activity: earliest start time, latest start time, earliest finish time, latest finish time, and slack. List the activities that are on the critical path, and determine the expected duration of the project.
a. Problem 2.
b. Problem 3.

6. Reconsider the network diagram of Problem 1a. Suppose that after 12 weeks, activities 1-2, 1-3 and 2-4 have been finished, 2-5 is 75 percent finished, and 3-6 is half finished. How many weeks after the original start time should the project be finished?

7. Three recent college graduates have formed a partnership and have opened an advertising firm. Their first project consists of activities listed in the following table.

a. Draw the precedence diagram.

b. What is the probability that the project can be completed in 24 days or less? In 21 days or less?

c. Suppose it is now the end of the seventh day and that activities a and b have been completed while d is 50 percent completed. Time estimates for the completion of d are 5, 6, and 7. Activities c and h are ready to begin. Determine the probability of finishing the project in 24 days and the probability of finishing in 21 days.

Activity	Pre-cedes	Time in days		
		Opti-mistic	Most likely	Pessi-mistic
a c		5	6	7
b ..... h		8	8	11
c ...... e		6	8	11
d ..... f		9	12	15
e ..... End		5	6	9
f ...... g		5	6	7
g ..... End		2	3	7
h i		4	4	5
i ..... End		5	7	8

8. The new director of special events at a large university has decided to completely revamp graduation ceremonies. Toward that end, a PERT chart of the major activities has been developed. The chart has five paths with expected completion times and variances as shown in the table. Graduation day is 17 weeks from now. Assuming the project begins now, what is the probability that the project will be completed before:

a. Graduation time?

b. The end of week 16?

c. The end of week 13?

Path	Expected duration (weeks)	Variance
A	10	1.21
B	8	2.00
C	12	1.00
D	15	2.89
E	14	1.44

9. The following precedence diagram reflects three time estimates for each activity. Determine:

a. The expected completion time for each path and its variance.

b. The probability that the project will require more than 49 weeks.

c. The probability that the project can be completed in 46 weeks or less.

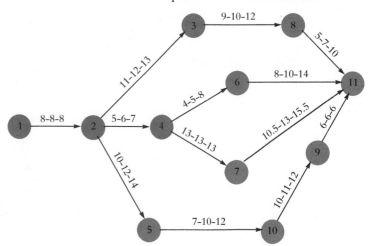

10. A project manager has compiled a list of major activities that will be required to install a computer information system in her firm. The list includes estimated completion times for activities and precedence relationships:

Acitivty	Precedes	Estimated times (weeks)
a	. . . . . d,f	2-4-6
d	. . . . . e	6-8-10
e	. . . . h	7-9-12
h	. . . . End	2-3-5
f	. . . . . g	3-4-8
g	. . . . End	5-7-9
b	 i	2-2-3
i	. . . . . . j	2-3-6
j	. . . . . k	3-4-5
k	. . . . End	4-5-8
c	. . . . . m	5-8-12
m	. . . . . n	1-1-1
n	. . . . o	6-7-11
o	. . . . End	8-9-13

If the project is finished within 27 weeks of its start, the project manager will receive a bonus of $1,000; and if the project is finished within 28 weeks of its start, the bonus will be $500. Find the probability of each bonus.

11. Construct an activity-on-node diagram for the set of activities listed in Problem 3.

12. Construct an activity-on-node diagram for the set of activities listed in Problem 2. To facilitate this, replace the activity designations (1-2, 2-3, etc.) with letters (a, b, c, etc.).

13. The project manager of a task force planning the construction of a domed stadium had hoped to be able to complete construction prior to the start of the next college football season. After reviewing construction time estimates, it now appears that a certain amount of crashing will be needed to insure that the project is completed before the season opener. Given the following time and cost estimates, determine a minimum-cost crashing schedule that will shave five weeks off the project length.

Activity	Precedes	Normal time (weeks)	Crashing costs First week	Crashing costs Second week
a	b	12	$15,000	$20,000
b	k	14	10,000	10,000
c	d,e,f	10	5,000	5,000
d	g	17	20,000	21,000
e	h	18	16,000	18,000
f	i	12	12,000	15,000
g	m	15	24,000	24,000
h	n,p	8	—	—
i	j	7	30,000	—
j	p	12	25,000	25,000
k	End	9	10,000	10,000
m . . .	End	3	—	—
n	End	11	40,000	—
p	End	8	20,000	20,000

14. A construction project has indirect costs totaling $40,000 per week. Major activities in the project and their expected times are shown in this precedence diagram:

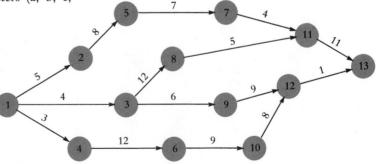

Crashing costs for each activity are:

Activity	Crashing costs ($000)		
	First week	Second week	Third week
1-2	$18	$22	$—
2-5	24	25	25
5-7	30	30	35
7-11	15	20	—
11-13	30	33	36
1-3	12	24	26
3-8	—	—	—
8-11	40	40	40
3-9	3	10	12
9-12	2	7	10
12-13	26	—	—
1-4	10	15	25
4-6	8	13	—
6-10	5	12	—
10-12	14	15	—

a. Determine the optimum time-cost crashing plan.
b. Plot the total-cost curve that describes the least expensive crashing schedule that will reduce the project length by six weeks.

15. Chuck's Custom Boats (CCB) builds luxury yachts to customer order. CCB has just landed a contract with a mysterious New York banker (Mr. T). Relevant data are shown below. The complication is that Mr. T wants delivery in 32 weeks or he will impose a penalty of $375 for each week his yacht is late.

Activity	Precedes	Normal time (weeks)	Crashing costs	
			1st week	2nd week
K	L,N	9	$410	$415
L	M	7	125	—
N	J	5	45	45
M	Q	4	300	350
J	Q	6	50	—
Q	P,Y	5	200	225
P	Z	8	—	—
Y	End	7	85	90
Z	End	6	90	—

Develop a crashing schedule.

SELECTED BIBLIOGRAPHY

Bierman, Harold, Jr.; Charles P. Bonini; and Warren H. Hausman. *Quantitative Analysis for Business Decisions.* 6th ed. Homewood, Ill.: Richard D. Irwin, 1981.

Buffa, Elwood, and James S. Dyer. *Essentials of Management Science/Operations Research.* New York: John Wiley & Sons, 1978

Burman, P. J. *Precedence Networks for Project Planning and Control.* New York: McGraw-Hill, 1972.

Hoare, H. R. *Project Management Using Networks.* New York: McGraw-Hill, 1973.

Kerzner, Harold. *Project Management for Executives.* New York: Van Nostrand Reinhold, 1984.

Levin, Richard I.; Charles A. Kirkpatrick; and David S. Rubin. *Quantitative Approaches to Management.* 5th ed. New York: McGraw-Hill, 1982.

Moder, J.; E. W. Davis; and C. Phillips. *Project Management with CPM and PERT.* New York: Van Nostrand Reinhold, 1983.

Reeser, Clayton. *Management: Functions and Modern Concepts.* Glenview, Ill.: Scott, Foresman, 1973.

Wiest, J. D., and F. K. Levy. *A Management Guide to PERT/CPM.* 2nd ed. Englewood Cliffs, N.J.: Prentice-Hall, 1977.

CASE

THE CASE OF THE MEXICAN CRAZY QUILT

"The mission of the project which you will head is to get our new Mexican subsidiary company ready for take-over by Mexican managers. My hope is that you will be able to do this in about two years," explained Robert Linderman, president of Linderman Industries, Inc., to Carl Conway, newly appointed project manager for "Operation Mexicano." Conway had been hired specifically for this assignment because of his experience in managing large defense projects in the aerospace industry.

"The first thing that I will have to do is put a project team together," said Conway. "I imagine that you have in mind my drawing people from the functional divisions."

"Yes, I have already sent memoranda to the division managers informing them that you will be asking for some of their key people to work under you for about two years," said Linderman. "In addition, I have advised them to be prepared to process work orders from Operation Mexicano with the personnel and equipment of their organizations. Later on in the project's life, you will begin to get Mexican personnel, both managers and technicians, into your organization. These people will have Mexican supervisors, but until the the mission is accomplished, they also will report to you. I will have to admit that you are going to have some complex authority relationships, especially as you personally will be responsible to the president of the subsidiary, Felix Delgado, as well as to me."

Conway began to make his plans for the project team. The plant building was available and empty in Mexico City, and it was important to get equipment purchased and installed as soon as possible. A plant layout would have to be prepared, but before that could be done there would have to be a manufacturing plan. Therefore, he needed to recruit an industrial engineer, a production planner, and an equipment buyer. They, in turn, would have to build their own staffs.

He made an appointment with Sam Sargis, corporate manager of industrial engineering. "I have had a preliminary talk with Bob Cates about his joining Operation Mexicano, and he is quite inter-

est," Carl said. "Will you release him to me?"

"Why, I'm grooming Cates to take over my job when I retire," replied Sargis. "He is my best man. Let me pick someone else for you, or better still, you just tell me what industrial engineering work you want done, and I will have it done for you."

"Sorry, I want Cates," said Carl firmly. "And besides, you are not due to retire for five years. This will be good experience for him."

For production planning, Carl had in mind Bert Mill, an older man with extensive experience in managing production operations, but Mill rejected his offer. "I talked it over with my wife," he said, "and we feel that at my age I shouldn't take a chance on not having a job to come back to when Operation Mexicano is finished."

Carl next talked to Emil Banowetz, who was assistant to Jim Burke, the vice president for manufacturing, and Banowetz decided that he would like to join the project team. However, Burke told Conway that if Banowetz were forcibly taken away from him, he would give Mr. Linderman his resignation, so Carl decided to back down. He finally accepted a man that Burke recommended.

Filling the equipment buyer's slot was easy. The director of procurement phoned Carl and said that a senior buyer, Humberto Guzman, had requested permission to ask for the assignment, and that he strongly recommended him. Guzman had been purchasing agent for a large mining company in Mexico for about 10 years.

Carl had about the same experiences in getting the people he wanted for the functions of engineering, quality control, cost, marketing, and advertising as he did for the first three positions; in other words, he won some confrontations with the division managers and lost some. For personnel, he got Dr. Juan Perez, who was slated to be personnel director of the subsidiary company, to affiliate temporarily with the project team.

The first brush that Project Mexicano had in getting a functional division to do work for it came when Carl's engineering man, Frank Fong, reported to him that the engineering vice president, who was formally Fong's boss, refused to authorize top priority to the changing of dimensions in the production drawings to the metric system. Carl had to take this issue to Linderman, who ruled in his favor. The defeated vice president, of course, did not take kindly to the decision.

The next incident revolved about Carl's desire to have a pilot run of products made with metric measurements for shipment to Mexico. The purpose was to test the market acceptance of the Linderman articles. Jim Burke stated flatly that there was no way that his production workers could be trained to work with metric drawings. Carl quickly saw that this was an issue that he was not going to win, so he had his buyer, Guzman, work with the newly appointed manufacturing manager for the subsidiary in getting a run of the products subcontracted in Mexico City.

Bob Cates made a special trip from Mexico City to present Carl with an interesting problem. The Mexican industrial engineer, whom Bob was supposed to be training, had his own ideas about plant layout. When they differed from Bob's, as they usually did, he would take his complaint directly to Felix Delgado, the president of the Mexican subsidiary. Because Delgado's competence was primarily in finance, he would not know how to decide the argument and would simply table it. Carl took examples of some of the disagreements to Bob's formal boss, Sam Sargis, who quite unexpectedly ruled against Bob's proposed methods. Carl saw that there was bad feeling by Sargis against Bob for leaving his department, which boded ill for Bob's return. To solve the immediate problem, however, Carl asked Dr. Perez to try to reconcile the situation in Mexico City.

Despite these problems, and many more of a similar nature, Project Mexicano was successful, and the transition to Mexican management was made in just a little over two years. By a curious twist, through Dr. Perez's intercession Felix Delgado became very impressed by Bob Cates and convinced him to accept the job of director of industrial engineering for the Mexican company. Humberto Guzman also stayed on to head the procurement operation.

Other members of the project team were not so fortunate. Linderman Industries was laying off personnel when the project ended in 1970, and only the project production man was able to get a job in the company at as high a level as the one he had when he joined the team. The cost expert elected to leave Linderman because he said the glamour of Project Mexicano had spoiled him for any routine job.

Carl Conway had a difficult decision of his own to make. Robert Linderman said that he was extremely pleased with his performance and that something good would open up in the company for him soon. In the meantime, there was a staff assignment available for him. Carl had seen enough project managers in the aerospace industry who had figuratively rotted on staff assignments when their projects were completed to be somewhat wary.

Questions

1. Was Linderman Industries' adoption of project organization an appropriate one for getting the Mexican subsidiary started?

2. In consideration of Robert Linderman's letting the division manager know that the project manager would be asking for some of their key people, why would Conway have any difficulty in getting the ones he wanted?

3. Would you expect that many people would turn a chance to join a project organization, as Bert Mill did?

4. Why would Conway take his problem with the engineering vice president to Linderman and have it resolved in his favor, yet back down in two disputes with the manufacturing vice president?

5. What could Linderman Industries have done to assure good jobs for the people coming off Project Mexicano, including Carl Conway, the project manager?

Source: *Management: The Key to Organizational Effectiveness,* rev. ed. by Clayton Reeser and Marvin Loper.
Copyright © 1978, Scott, Foresman and Company.
Reprinted by permission.

15

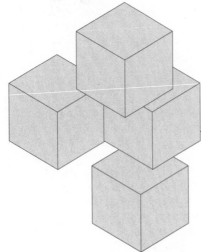

Waiting Lines

LEARNING OBJECTIVES

After completing this chapter, you should be able to:

1. Explain why waiting lines form in underloaded systems.
2. Identify the goal of queuing (waiting-line) analysis.
3. List the measures of system performance that are used in queuing.
4. Discuss the assumptions of the basic queuing models presented.
5. Solve typical problems.

Chapter Outline

WAITING—A NEW POPULAR PASTIME
MISS MANNERS

by Judith Martin

Many things in life are worth waiting for, but not all that long. Miss Manners would put a time limit on how long one should wait for salespeople to finish their conversations with each other before writing up one's order, or for a spouse who has departed with someone else to realize what a terrible mistake that was.

Nevertheless, waiting is now in a class with working as a popular pastime. A *waitologist* has estimated that the average adult spends one tenth of his or her waking moments waiting, at a minimum. There are waits for buses, banks, stores, theaters, gas stations, court cases, elevators, driver's licenses, and dentist appointments.

One could easily pass one's life enduring just such basic waits. But there are also intermediary waits, such as waiting for the rain to stop, and advanced waits, such as waiting for your ship to come in. Some of these go in fashions. There was a time when all of America was waiting to be discovered by a movie talent scout in a drug store, and now everyone is waiting for a television camera to come along and ask it to tell the world what it thinks.

It is the elementary, and comparatively short-term wait with which Miss Manners is concerned. If you want to hear about the others, you will just have to wait.

It is perfectly correct, although not many people realize it, to refuse to wait on the telephone. When Miss Manners is asked "Can you hold on for a minute?" she often replies, "No," and it is too bad that the person on the other end ties up his own line by putting her on hold anyway, because that person has not waited for Miss Manners' reply.

One should also refuse to wait for inefficient or indefinite service. A restaurant should be able to tell you how long the wait will be, and a service person should not keep you waiting except to attend a previous customer.

It is rude to refuse to wait by announcing that one's needs take precedence over those of other waiting people. Miss Manners can think of no circumstances in which a person transacting the ordinary business of life can plead with legitimacy that it is more outrageous to expect him to wait than to expect it of others. "Let me go through, please—I'm in labor," perhaps, but then what are you doing at the stockings sale, anyway?

The only polite way to wait, if one must do so, is to bring one's own portable work or amusement. An unoccupied person waiting in line is by definition a potential raving maniac. A nice Jane Austen novel ready-to-go has preserved even the naturally tranquil spirits of Miss Manners. Even using conversations as a means to pass the time is dangerous, in Miss Manners' opinion. Two people quietly discussing what a shame it is to have to wait are, by the same definition, a potential mob.

The preceding article pokes fun at one of life's realities: having to wait in line. No doubt those waiting in line would all agree that the solution to the problem is obvious: simply add more servers or else do something to speed up service. Although both ideas may be potential solutions, there are certain subtleties that must be dealt with. For one thing, most service systems have the capacity to process more customers over the long run than they are called on to process. Hence, the problem of waiting is a short-term phenomenon. The other side of the coin is that a certain times the system is empty, and *servers* are idle, waiting for customers. Thus, by increasing the service capacity, the server idle time would increase even more. Consequently, in designing service systems, the designer must weigh the cost of providing a given level of service capacity against the potential (implicit) cost of having customers wait for service.

The planning and analysis of service capacity frequently lends itself to **queuing theory,** which is a mathematical approach to the analysis of waiting lines. Such waiting lines are commonly found wherever customers arrive *randomly* for services. Some examples of waiting lines we encounter in our daily lives include the lines at supermarket checkouts, fast-food restaurants, airport ticket counters, theaters, post offices, and toll booths. In many business situations, the "customers" are not people but orders waiting to be filled, trucks waiting to be unloaded, jobs waiting to be processed, or equipment awaiting repairs. Still other examples include ships waiting to dock, planes waiting to land, hospital patients waiting for a nurse, and cars waiting at a stop sign.

The foundation of modern theory is based on studies made in the early part of this century by Danish telephone engineer A. K. Erlang involving automatic dialing equipment. Prior to World War II, there were very few attempts to apply queuing theory to business problems. However, since that time, queuing theory has been applied to a wide range of problems.

The mathematics of queuing can be quite complex, and for that reason, the emphasis here will not be on the mathematics but on the concepts that underlie the use of queuing in analyzing waiting line problems. We shall rely on the use of formulas and tables for analysis.

We shall begin our discussion of queuing with an examination of what is perhaps the most fundamental issue in waiting line theory: Why is there waiting?

WHY IS THERE WAITING?

Many people are surprised to learn that waiting lines tend to form *even though a system is basically underloaded.* For example, a fast-food restaurant may have the capacity to handle an average of 200 orders per hour and yet experience waiting lines even though the average number of orders is only 150 per hour. The key work here is *average.* In reality, customers arrive at random intervals rather than at evenly spaced intervals, and some orders take longer to fill than others. In other words, both arrivals and service times exhibit a high degree of variability. As a result of this variability, there are times when the system becomes temporarily overloaded, and that gives rise to waiting lines. By the same token, there are other times when the system is idle because there are no customers. Thus, although a system may be *underloaded* from a *macro* standpoint, because of variabilities in arrivals and service there will be times when the system is *overloaded* from a *micro* standpoint. It follows, then, that in systems where variability is minimal or nonexistent (say, because arrivals can be scheduled and service time is constant), waiting lines do not ordinarily form.

GOAL OF QUEUING ANALYSIS

The goal of queuing is essentially to minimize total costs. There are two basic categories of cost in a queuing situation: those associated with customers waiting for service and those associated with capacity. Capacity costs relate to maintaining the ability to provide service. Examples include the number of bays in a car wash, the number of checkouts in a supermarket, the number of repairmen to handle equipment breakdowns, and the number of lanes on a highway. Note that when a service facility is idle, there is a loss of capacity since it cannot be stored. The costs of customer waiting include the salaries paid to employees while they wait for service (mechanics waiting for tools, the drivers of trucks waiting to unload), the cost of the space for waiting (size of doctor's waiting room, length of driveway at a car wash, fuel consumed by planes waiting to land), and any loss of business due to customers refusing to wait and possibly going elsewhere in the future.

A practical difficulty that is frequently encountered is pinning down the cost of customer waiting time, especially since major portions of that cost are not a part of accounting data. One approach that is sometimes used is to treat waiting times or line lengths as a policy variable: a manager simply specifies an acceptable level of waiting and directs that capacity be established to achieve that level.

The goal of queuing analysis is to balance the cost of providing a level of service capacity with the cost of customers waiting for service. This concept is

FIGURE 15–1

The goal of queuing analysis is to minimize the sum of two costs: customer waiting costs and service capacity costs

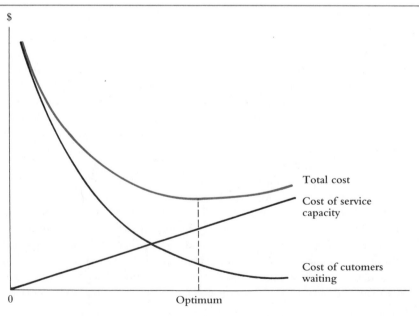

illustrated in Figure 15–1. Note that as capacity increases, its cost increases. For simplicity, the increase is shown as a linear relationship, although a step function is often more appropriate. However, use of a straight line does not significantly distort the picture. As capacity increases, the number of customers waiting, and the time they wait, tends to decrease, thereby decreasing waiting costs. As is the case with trade-off cost relationships, total costs can be represented as a U-shaped curve. The goal of analysis is to identify a level of service capacity that will minimize total cost. (Unlike the situation in the inventory EOQ model, the minimum point on the total cost curve is *not* usually where the two cost lines intersect.)

SYSTEM CHARACTERISTICS

There are numerous queuing models from which an analyst can choose. Naturally, much of the success of the analyst will depend on choosing an appropriate model. Model choice is dependent on the characteristics of the system under investigation. The main characteristics are:

1. The population source.
2. The number of servers (channels).
3. Arrival and service patterns.
4. The queue discipline (order of service).

Population Source

The approach used to analyze a queuing problem depends on whether or not there is a limit to the potential number of customers. There are two possibilities: *infinite-source* and *finite-source* populations. In an **infinite-source** situation, the potential number of customers greatly exceeds system capacity. Infinite-source situations exist whenever service is *unrestricted*. Typical examples include supermarkets, drugstores, banks, restaurants, theaters, amusement centers, and toll bridges. Theoretically, large numbers of customers from the "calling population" can request service at any time. When the potential number of customers is limited, a **finite-source** situations exists. Examples include a repairer responsible for a certain number of machines (the potential number of machines that might need repairs at any one time cannot exceed the number of machines assigned to the repairer). Similarly, an operator may be responsible for loading and unloading a bank of four machines, a nurse may be responsible for answering patient calls for a 10-bed ward, a secretary may be responsible for taking dictation from three executives, and a company shop may perform repairs as needed on the firm's 20 trucks.

Number of Servers (Channels)

The capacity of a queuing system is a function of the capacity of each server and the number of servers being used. The terms *server* and **channel** are

FIGURE 15–2

A single-channel queuing system

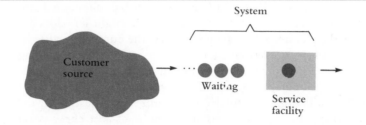

synonomous, and it is generally assumed that each channel can handle one customer at a time. Systems can be either *single-* or *multiple-channel*. (If a group of servers work together as a team, such as a surgical team, that is treated as a single-channel system.) Examples of single-channel systems are small grocery stores with one checkout counter, most theaters, single-bay car washes, and drive-in banks that have one teller. Figure 15–2 illustrates a single-channel

FIGURE 15–3

Four common variations of queuing systems

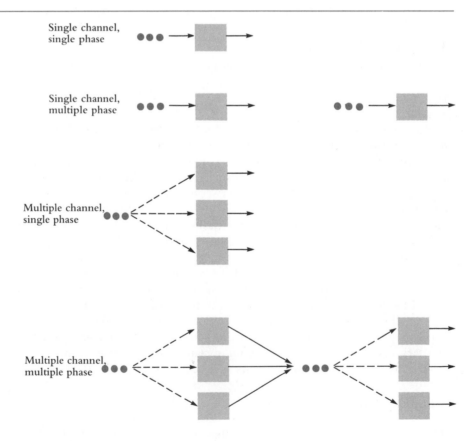

queuing system. Multiple-channel systems (those with more than one server) are commonly found in banks, at airline ticket counters, at auto service centers, and at gas stations.

A related distinction is the number of steps or *phases* in a queuing system. For example, at some college registrations, students go from desk to desk to have courses assigned and then move to final checkers and the bursar's table. Each location constitutes a separate phase where queues can (and usually do) form.

Figure 15–3 illustrates some of the most common queuing systems found in practice. Because it would not be possible to cover all of these cases in sufficient detail in the limited amount of space available here, our discussion will focus on *single-phase* systems.

Arrival and Service Patterns

Queues are a direct result of arrival and service variability. Waiting lines are created because random, highly variable arrival and service patterns produce systems that are temporarily overloaded. In many instances, the variabilities can be described by theoretical distributions. In fact, the most commonly used models assume that the customer arrival *rate* can be described by a Poisson distribution and that the service *time* can be described by a negative exponential distribution. These distributions are illustrated in Figure 15–4.

It is interesting to note that the Poisson and negative exponential distributions are alternate but equivalent ways of presenting the same basic information. If service time is exponential, then the service rate is Poisson. Similarly, if the customer arrival rate is Poisson, then the arrival time (i.e., the time between arrivals) is exponential. For instance, if a service facility can process 12 customers per hour (rate), average service time is five minutes. Similarly, if the arrival rate is 10 per hour, then the average time between arrivals is six minutes. Hence, the models described here generally require that arrival and service rates lend themselves to description using a Poisson distribution, or equivalently, that interarrival and service times lend themselves to description using a negative exponential distribution. In practice, it is necessary to verify that these assumptions are met. Sometimes this is done by collecting data and plotting them, although the preferred approach is to use a chi-square goodness-of-fit test for that purpose. A discussion of the chi-square test is beyond the scope of this text. However, most basic statistics textbooks cover the topic.

Research has shown that these assumptions are often appropriate for customer arrivals but less likely to be appropriate for service. In situations where the assumptions are not reasonably satisfied, the alternatives would be: (1) attempt to develop a more suitable model, (2) search for a better (and usually more complex) existing model, or (3) resort to computer simulation. Each of these alternatives requires more effort or cost than the ones presented here.

FIGURE 15–4

Poisson and negative exponential distributions

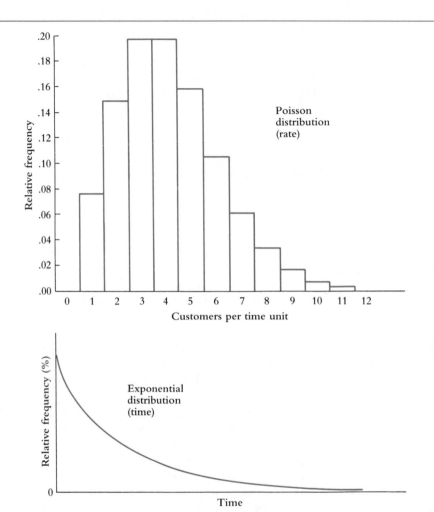

Queue Discipline

Queue discipline refers to the order in which customers are processed. All but one of the models described here assume that service is provided on a *first-come, first-served* basis. This is perhaps the most commonly encountered rule. We find first-come service at banks, stores, theaters, restaurants, four-way stop signs, registration lines, and so on. Examples of systems that do not serve on a first-come basis include hospital emergency rooms, rush orders in a factory, and computer processing of programs. In these and similar situations, customers do not all represent the same waiting costs; those with the highest costs (e.g., most seriously ill) are processed first, even though other customers arrived earlier.

MEASURES OF SYSTEM PERFORMANCE

The operations manager typically looks at five measures when evaluating existing or proposed service systems. Those measures are:

1. The average number of customers waiting, either in the line or in the system.
2. The average time customers wait, either in line or in the system.
3. System utilization, which refers to the percentage of capacity utilized.
4. The implied cost of a given level of capacity and its related waiting line.
5. The probability that an arrival will have to wait for service.

Of these measures, system utilization bears some elaboration. It reflects the extent to which the servers are busy rather than idle. On the surface, it might seem that the operations manager would want to seek 100 percent utilization. However, as illustrated in Figure 15–5, increases in system utilization are achieved at the expense of increases in both the length of the waiting line and the average waiting time. In fact, these values become exceedingly large as utilization approaches 100 percent. The implication is that under normal circumstances, 100 percent utilization is not a realistic goal. Instead, the operations manager should try to achieve a system that minimizes the sum of waiting costs and capacity costs.

QUEUING MODELS: INFINITE-SOURCE

There are many queuing models available for a manager or analyst to choose from. The discussion here will include four of the most basic and most widely used models. The purpose is to provide an exposure to a range of models

FIGURE 15–5

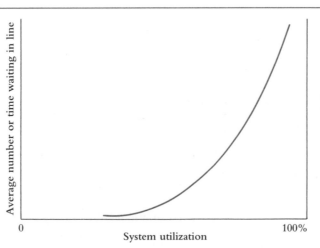

The average number waiting in line and the average time customers wait in line increase exponentially as the system utilization increases

rather than an extensive coverage of the field. The four models described here are listed below. All assume a Poisson arrival rate. Moreover, the models pertain to a system operating under *steady state* conditions; that is, they assume the average arrival and service rates are stable. The models are:

1. Single channel, exponential service time.
2. Single channel, constant service time.
3. Multiple channel, exponential service time.
4. Multiple priority service.

To facilitate your use of queuing models, Table 15–1 provides a list of the symbols used for the infinite-source models.

Basic Relationships

There are certain basic relationships that hold for all infinite-source models. Knowledge of these basic relationships can be very helpful in deriving desired performance measures, given a few key values. These basic relationships are:

1. The average number being served is the ratio of arrival rate to service rate:

$$r = \frac{\lambda}{\mu} \qquad (15\text{–}1)$$

   [*Note:* λ and μ must be in the same units (e.g., rate per hour, rate per minute)]

2. The average number in the system is the average number in line plus the average number being served:

$$L_s = L_q + r \qquad (15\text{–}2)$$

TABLE 15–1

Infinite-source symbols	Symbol	*Represents*
	λ	Customer arrival rate
	μ	Service rate
	L_q	The average number of customers waiting for service
	L_s	The average number of customers in the system (waiting or being served)
	ρ	The system utilization
	W_q	The average time customers wait in line
	W_s	The average time customers spend in the system (waiting in line and service time)
	$1/\mu$	Service time
	P_0	The probability of zero units in the system
	P_n	The probability of n units in the system
	M	The number of servers (channels)
	L_{max}	The maximum expected number waiting in line

3. The average time in line is the average number in line divided by the arrival rate:

$$W_q = \frac{L_q}{\lambda} \qquad (15–3)$$

4. The average time in the system is the sum of the time in line plus service time:

$$W_s = W_q + \frac{1}{\mu} \qquad (15–4)$$

5. System utilization is the ratio of arrival rate to service capacity:

$$\rho = \frac{\lambda}{M\mu} \qquad (15–5)$$

All infinite-source models require that system utilization be less than 1.0; the models apply only to underloaded systems.

The average number waiting in line, L_q, is a key value because it is a determinant of some of the other measures of system performance, such as the average number in the system, the average time in line, and the average time in the system. Hence, L_q will usually be one of the first values to be determined in problem solving.

EXAMPLE 1

Customers arrive at a bakery at an average rate of 18 per hour on weekday mornings. The arrival distribution can be described by a Poisson distribution with a mean of 18. Each clerk can serve a customer in an average of four minutes; this time can be described by an exponential distribution with a mean of 4.0 minutes.

a. What are the arrival and service *rates?*
b. Compute the average number of customers being served at any time.
c. Suppose it has been determined that the average number of customers waiting in line is 3.6. Compute the average number of customers in the system (i.e., waiting in line or being served), the average time customers wait in line, and the average time in the system.
d. Determine the system utilization for $M = 2$, 3, and 4 servers.

Solution

a. The arrival rate is given in the problem: $\lambda = 18$ customers per hour. The service time can be changed to a comparable *hourly* rate by first restating the time in hours and then taking its reciprocal. Thus, (4 minutes per customer)/(60 minutes per hour) $= 1/15 = 1/\mu$. Its reciprocal is $\mu = 15$ customers per hour.

EXAMPLE 1 *(concluded)*

b. $r = \dfrac{\lambda}{\mu} = \dfrac{18}{15} = 1.2$ customers.

c.   Given: $L_q = 3.6$ customers.

   $L_s = L_q + r = 3.6 + 1.2 = 4.8$ customers

   $W_q = \dfrac{L_q}{\lambda} = \dfrac{3.6}{18} = 0.20$ hours per customer, or 0.20 hours
   $\times$ 60 minutes/hour = 12 minutes

   $W_s = $ Waiting in line plus service

   $= W_q + \dfrac{1}{\mu} = 0.20 + \dfrac{1}{15} = 0.267$ hours, or approximately 16 minutes

d.   System utilization is $\rho = \dfrac{\lambda}{M\mu}$

   For $M = 2$, $\rho = \dfrac{18}{2(15)} = .60$

   For $M = 3$, $\rho = \dfrac{18}{3(15)} = .40$

   For $M = 4$, $\rho = \dfrac{18}{4(15)} = .30$

Hence, as the system capacity as measured by $M\mu$ increases, the system utilization for a given arrival rate decreases.

Model 1: Single Channel, Exponential Service Time

The simplest model involves a system that has one server (or a single crew). The queue discipline is first-come, first-served, and it is assumed that the customer arrival rate can be approximated by a Poisson distribution and service time by a negative exponential distribution. There is no limit on length of queue.

TABLE 15–2

Formulas for basic single-server model

Performance measure	Equation	
Average number in line	$L_q = \dfrac{\lambda^2}{\mu(\mu - \lambda)}$	(15–6)
Probability of zero units in the system	$P_0 = 1 - \left(\dfrac{\lambda}{\mu}\right)$	(15–7)
Probability of n units in the system	$P_n = P_0 \left(\dfrac{\lambda}{\mu}\right)^n$	(15–8)

Table 15–2 lists the formulas for the single-channel model, which should be used in conjunction with formulas 15–1 through 15–5.

EXAMPLE 2

An airline is planning to open a satellite ticket desk in a new shopping plaza, staffed by one ticket agent. It is estimated that requests for tickets and information will average 15 per hour, and requests will have a Poisson distribution. Service time is assumed to be exponentially distributed. Previous experience with similar satellite operations suggests that mean service time should average about three minutes per request. Determine each of the following.

a.   System utilization.
b.   Percent of time the server (agent) will be idle.
c.   The expected number of customers waiting to be served.
d.   The average time customers will spend in the system.
e.   The probability of zero customers in the system and the probability of four customers in the system.

Solution

$$\lambda = 15 \text{ per hour}$$

$$\mu = \frac{1}{\text{Service time}} = \frac{1 \text{ customer}}{3 \text{ minutes}} \times 60 \text{ minutes per hour}$$

$$= 20 \text{ customers per hour}$$

a. $\rho = \dfrac{\lambda}{M\mu} = \dfrac{15}{1(20)} = .75$

b.   Percentage idle time $= 1 - \rho = 1 - .75 = .25$, or 25%

c. $L_q = \dfrac{\lambda^2}{\mu(\mu - \lambda)} = \dfrac{15^2}{20(20 - 15)} = 2.25$ customers

d. $W_s = \dfrac{L_q}{\lambda} + \dfrac{1}{\mu} = \dfrac{2.25}{15} + \dfrac{1}{20} = 0.20$ hours, or 12 minutes

e. $P_0 = 1 - \dfrac{\lambda}{\mu} = 1 - \dfrac{15}{20} = .25; \quad P_4 = P_0 \left(\dfrac{\lambda}{\mu}\right)^4 = .25 \left(\dfrac{15}{20}\right)^4 = .079$

Model 2: Single Channel, Constant Service Time

As noted previously, waiting lines are a consequence of random, highly variable arrival and service rates. If the variability of either or both can be reduced or eliminated, waiting lines can be shortened noticeably. A case in point is a system with constant service time. The effect of a constant service time is to cut in half both the average number of customers waiting in line and the average time customers spend waiting in line. Similar improvements can be realized by smoothing arrival times (e.g., by use of appointments). In effect, the formulas 15–1 through 15–6 can be used for problems with constant service time as long as the computed value of L_q is divided by 2.

EXAMPLE 3

Wanda's Car Wash & Dry is an automatic, five-minute operation with a single bay. On a typical Saturday morning, cars arrive at a mean rate of eight per hour, with arrivals tending to follow a Poisson distribution. Find:

a. The average number of cars in line.
b. The average time cars spend in line and service.

Solution

$$\lambda = 8 \text{ cars per hour}$$
$$\mu = 1 \text{ per 5 minutes, or 12 per hour}$$

a. $\quad L_q = \dfrac{\lambda^2}{2\mu(\mu - \lambda)} = \dfrac{8^2}{2(12)(12 - 8)} = 0.667 \text{ cars}$

b. $\quad W_s = \dfrac{L_q}{\lambda} + \dfrac{1}{\mu} = \dfrac{0.667}{8} + \dfrac{1}{12} = 0.167 \text{ hours, or 10 minutes}$

Model 3: Multiple Channel

A multiple-channel system exists whenever there are two or more servers working *independently* to provide service to customer arrivals. Use of the model involves the following assumptions:

1. A Poisson arrival rate and exponential service time.
2. Servers all work at the same average rate.
3. Customers form a single waiting line (in order to maintain first-come, first-served processing).

Formulas for the multiple-channel model are listed in Table 15–3.

Obviously, the multiple-channel formulas are more complex than the single-channel formulas, especially the formulas for L_q and P_0. However, these formulas are shown primarily for completeness; actual determination of their values can be made using Table 15–4, which gives values of L_q and P_0 for selected values of λ/μ and M.

To use Table 15–4, compute the value of λ/μ and round according to the number of decimal places given for that ratio in the table. Then simply read the value of L_q and P_0 for the appropriate number of channels, M. For instance, if $\lambda/\mu = 0.50$ and $M = 2$, the table provides a value of 0.033 for L_q and a value of .600 for P_0. These values can then be used to compute other measures of

TABLE 15-3

Performance measure	Equation		Multiple-channel queuing formulas
Average number in line	$$L_q = \frac{\lambda\mu\left(\dfrac{\lambda}{\mu}\right)^M}{(M-1)!(M\mu-\lambda)^2}P_0$$	(15–9)	
Probability of zero units in the system	$$P_0 = \left[\sum_{n=0}^{M-1}\frac{\left(\dfrac{\lambda}{\mu}\right)^n}{n!} + \frac{\left(\dfrac{\lambda}{\mu}\right)^M}{M!\left(1-\dfrac{\lambda}{M\mu}\right)}\right]^{-1}$$	(15–10)	
Average waiting time for an arrival not immediately served	$$W_a = \frac{1}{M\mu-\lambda}$$	(15–11)	
Probability that an arrival will have to wait for service	$$P_w = \left(\frac{\lambda}{\mu}\right)^M\frac{P_0}{M!\left(1-\dfrac{\lambda}{M\mu}\right)}$$	(15–12)	

system performance. Note that the formulas in Table 15–3 and the values in Table 15–4 yield *average* amounts (i.e., expected values). Note also that Table 15–4 can also be used for single-channel problems (i.e., $M = 1$).

TABLE 15-4

Inifinite-source values for L_q and P_0 given λ/μ and M

λ/μ	M	L_q	P_0	λ/μ	M	L_q	P_0	λ/μ	M	L_q	P_0
0.15	1	0.026	.850	0.65	1	1.207	.350	1.0	2	0.333	.333
	2	0.001	.860		2	0.077	.509		3	0.045	.364
0.20	1	0.050	.800		3	0.008	.521		4	0.007	.367
	2	0.002	.818	0.70	1	1.633	.300	1.1	2	0.477	.290
0.25	1	0.083	.750		2	0.098	.481		3	0.066	.327
	2	0.004	.778		3	0.011	.495		4	0.011	.367
0.30	1	0.129	.700	0.75	1	2.250	.250	1.2	2	0.675	.250
	2	0.007	.739		2	0.123	.455		3	0.094	.294
0.35	1	0.188	.650		3	0.015	.471		4	0.016	.300
	2	0.011	.702	0.80	1	3.200	.200		5	0.003	.301
0.40	1	0.267	.600		2	0.152	.429	1.3	2	0.951	.212
	2	0.017	.667		3	0.019	.447		3	0.130	.264
0.45	1	0.368	.550	0.85	1	4.817	.150		4	0.023	.271
	2	0.024	.633		2	0.187	.404		5	0.004	.272
	3	0.002	.637		3	0.024	.425	1.4	2	1.345	.176
0.50	1	0.500	.500		4	0.003	.427		3	0.177	.236
	2	0.033	.600	0.90	1	8.100	.100		4	0.032	.245
	3	0.003	.606		2	0.229	.379		5	0.006	.246
0.55	1	0.672	.450		3	0.030	.403	1.5	2	1.929	.143
	2	0.045	.569		4	0.004	.406		3	0.237	.211
	3	0.004	.576	0.95	1	18.050	.050		4	0.045	.221
0.60	1	0.900	.400		2	0.277	.356		5	0.009	.223
	2	0.059	.538		3	0.037	.383	1.6	2	2.844	.111
	3	0.006	.548		4	0.005	.386		3	0.313	.187

TABLE 15—4

(continued)

λ/μ	M	L_q	P_0	λ/μ	M	L_q	P_0	λ/μ	M	L_q	P_0
	4	0.060	.199		7	0.018	.061	3.9	4	36.859	.002
	5	0.012	.201	2.9	3	27.193	.008		5	1.830	.015
1.7	2	4.426	.081		4	1.234	.044		6	0.485	.019
	3	0.409	.166		5	0.293	.052		7	0.153	.020
	4	0.080	.180		6	0.081	.054		8	0.050	.020
	5	0.017	.182		7	0.023	.055		9	0.016	.020
1.8	2	7.674	.053	3.0	4	1.528	.038	4.0	5	2.216	.013
	3	0.532	.146		5	0.354	.047		6	0.570	.017
	4	0.105	.162		6	0.099	.049		7	0.180	.018
	5	0.023	.165		7	0.028	.050		8	0.059	.018
1.9	2	17.587	.026		8	0.008	.050		9	0.019	.018
	3	0.688	.128	3.1	4	1.902	.032	4.1	5	2.703	.011
	4	0.136	.145		5	0.427	.042		6	0.668	.015
	5	0.030	.149		6	0.120	.044		7	0.212	.016
	6	0.007	.149		7	0.035	.045		8	0.070	.016
2.0	3	0.889	.111		8	0.010	.045		9	0.023	.017
	4	0.174	.130	3.2	4	2.386	.027	4.2	5	3.327	.009
	5	0.040	.134		5	0.513	.037		6	0.784	.013
	6	0.009	.135		6	0.145	.040		7	0.248	.014
2.1	3	1.149	.096		7	0.043	.040		8	0.083	.015
	4	0.220	.117		8	0.012	.041		9	0.027	.015
	5	0.052	.121	3.3	4	3.027	.023		10	0.009	.015
	6	0.012	.122		5	0.615	.033	4.3	5	4.149	.008
2.2	3	1.491	.081		6	0.174	.036		6	0.919	.012
	4	0.277	.105		7	0.052	.037		7	0.289	.130
	5	0.066	.109		8	0.015	.037		8	0.097	.013
	6	0.016	.111	3.4	4	3.906	.019		9	0.033	.014
2.3	3	1.951	.068		5	0.737	.029		10	0.011	.014
	4	0.346	.093		6	0.209	.032	4.4	5	5.268	.006
	5	0.084	.099		7	0.063	.033		6	1.078	.010
	6	0.021	.100		8	0.019	.033		7	0.337	.012
2.4	3	2.589	.056	3.5	4	5.165	.015		8	0.114	.012
	4	0.431	.083		5	0.882	.026		9	0.039	.012
	5	0.105	.089		6	0.248	.029		10	0.013	.012
	6	0.027	.090		7	0.076	.030	4.5	5	6.862	.005
	7	0.007	.091		8	0.023	.030		6	1.265	.009
2.5	3	3.511	.045		9	0.007	.030		7	0.391	.010
	4	0.533	.074	3.6	4	7.090	.011		8	0.133	.011
	5	0.130	.080		5	1.055	.023		9	0.046	.011
	6	0.034	.082		6	0.295	.026		10	0.015	.011
	7	0.009	.082		7	0.091	.027	4.6	5	9.289	.004
2.6	3	4.933	.035		8	0.028	.027		6	1.487	.008
	4	0.658	.065		9	0.008	.027		7	0.453	.009
	5	0.161	.072	3.7	4	10.347	.008		8	0.156	.010
	6	0.043	.074		5	1.265	.020		9	0.054	.010
	7	0.011	.074		6	0.349	.023		10	0.018	.010
2.7	3	7.354	.025		7	0.109	.024	4.7	5	13.382	.003
	4	0.811	.057		8	0.034	.025		6	1.752	.007
	5	0.198	.065		9	0.010	.025		7	0.525	.008
	6	0.053	.067	3.8	4	16.937	.005		8	0.181	.008
	7	0.014	.067		5	1.519	.017		9	0.064	.009
2.8	3	12.273	.016		6	0.412	.021		10	0.022	.009
	4	1.000	.050		7	0.129	.022	4.8	5	21.641	.002
	5	0.241	.058		8	0.041	.022		6	2.071	.006
	6	0.066	.060		9	0.013	.022		7	0.607	.008

TABLE 15—4

(continued)

λ/μ	M	L_q	P_0	λ/μ	M	L_q	P_0	λ/μ	M	L_q	P_0
	8	0.209	.008		12	0.012	.004		10	0.285	.001
	9	0.074	.008	5.7	6	16.446	.001		11	0.115	.001
	10	0.026	.008		7	2.264	.002		12	0.046	.001
4.9	5	46.566	.001		8	0.721	.003	6.6	7	13.770	.000
	6	2.459	.005		9	0.266	.003		8	2.420	.001
	7	0.702	.007		10	0.102	.003		9	0.825	.001
	8	0.242	.007		11	0.038	.003		10	0.285	.001
	9	0.087	.007		12	0.014	.003		11	0.130	.001
	10	0.031	.007	5.8	6	26.373	.001		12	0.052	.001
	11	0.011	.077		7	2.648	.002	6.7	7	19.532	.000
5.0	6	2.938	.005		8	0.823	.003		8	2.796	.001
	7	0.810	.006		9	0.303	.003		9	0.932	.001
	8	0.279	.006		10	0.116	.003		10	0.363	.001
	9	0.101	.007		11	0.044	.003		11	0.147	.001
	10	0.036	.007		12	0.017	.003		12	0.060	.001
	11	0.013	.007	5.9	6	56.300	.000	6.8	7	31.127	.000
5.1	6	3.536	.004		7	3.113	.002		8	3.245	.001
	7	0.936	.005		8	0.939	.002		9	1.054	.001
	8	0.321	.006		9	0.345	.003		10	0.409	.001
	9	0.117	.006		10	0.133	.003		11	0.167	.001
	10	0.042	.006		11	0.051	.003		12	0.068	.001
	11	0.015	.006		12	0.019	.003	6.9	7	66.055	.000
5.2	6	4.301	.003	6.0	7	3.683	.001		8	3.786	.001
	7	1.081	.005		8	1.071	.002		9	1.191	.001
	8	0.368	.005		9	0.392	.002		10	0.460	.001
	9	0.135	.005		10	0.152	.002		11	0.188	.001
	10	0.049	.005		11	0.059	.002		12	0.077	.001
	11	0.017	.006		12	0.022	.002	7.0	8	4.447	.001
5.3	6	5.303	.003	6.1	7	4.394	.001		9	1.347	.001
	7	1.249	.004		8	1.222	.002		10	0.517	.001
	8	0.422	.005		9	0.445	.002		11	0.212	.001
	9	0.155	.005		10	0.173	.002		12	0.088	.001
	10	0.057	.005		11	0.068	.002	7.1	8	5.270	.000
	11	0.021	.005		12	0.026	.002		9	1.525	.001
	12	0.007	.005	6.2	7	5.298	.001		10	0.581	.001
5.4	6	6.661	.002		8	1.397	.002		11	0.238	.001
	7	1.444	.004		9	0.504	.002		12	0.099	.001
	8	0.483	.004		10	0.197	.002	7.2	8	6.314	.000
	9	0.178	.004		11	0.078	.002		9	1.729	.001
	10	0.066	.004		12	0.030	.002		10	0.652	.001
	11	0.024	.005	6.3	7	6.480	.001		11	0.268	.001
	12	0.009	.005		8	1.598	.001		12	0.112	.001
5.5	6	8.590	.002		9	0.571	.002	7.3	8	7.675	.0003
	7	1.674	.003		10	0.223	.002		9	1.963	.0005
	8	0.553	.004		11	0.089	.002		10	0.732	.0006
	9	0.204	.004		12	0.035	.002		11	0.300	.0007
	10	0.077	.004	6.4	7	8.077	.001		12	0.126	.0007
	11	0.028	.004		8	1.831	.001	7.4	8	9.511	.0003
	12	0.010	.004		9	0.645	.002		9	2.233	.0005
5.6	6	11.519	.001		10	0.253	.002		10	0.820	.0006
	7	1.944	.003		11	0.101	.002		11	0.337	.0006
	8	0.631	.003		12	0.040	.002		12	0.142	.0006
	9	0.233	.004	6.5	7	10.341	.001	7.5	8	12.109	.0002
	10	0.088	.004		8	2.102	.001		9	2.546	.0004
	11	0.033	.004		9	0.730	.001		10	0.920	.0005

TABLE 15—4

(concluded)

λ/μ	M	L_q	P_0	λ/μ	M	L_q	P_0	λ/μ	M	L_q	P_0
	11	0.377	.0005		12	0.224	.0004		11	0.811	.00025
	12	0.160	.0005	7.9	8	75.827	.00003		12	0.347	.00026
7.6	8	16.039	.0002		9	4.474	.00023	8.3	9	8.884	.00011
	9	2.912	.0004		10	1.457	.00031		10	2.341	.00019
	10	1.031	.0004		11	0.586	.00035		11	0.903	.00022
	11	0.421	.0005		12	0.251	.00036		12	0.386	.00024
	12	0.179	.0005	8.0	9	5.227	.00020	8.4	9	10.960	.00009
7.7	8	22.636	.0001		10	1.637	.00028		10	2.647	.00017
	9	3.343	.0003		11	0.653	.00031		11	1.006	.00020
	10	1.157	.0004		12	0.280	.00033		12	0.429	.00021
	11	0.471	.0004	8.1	9	6.161	.00017	8.5	9	13.891	.00007
	12	0.201	.0004		10	1.841	.00025		10	3.003	.00015
7.8	8	35.898	.0001		11	0.728	.00028		11	1.121	.00018
	9	3.856	.0002		12	0.312	.00029		12	0.476	.00019
	10	1.298	.0004	8.2	9	7.344	.00014				
	11	0.525	.0004		10	2.074	.00022				

EXAMPLE 4

Alpha Taxi and Hauling Company has 10 cabs stationed at the airport. It has been determined that during the late-evening hours on weeknights, customers request cabs at a rate that follows the Poisson distribution with a mean of 9.6 per hour. Service time is exponential with a mean of 50 minutes per customer. Assume that there is one customer per cab. Find each of the performance measures listed in Table 15–3 and the system utilization.

Solution

$$\lambda = 9.6 \text{ per hour} \qquad M = 10 \text{ cabs (servers)}$$

$$\mu = \frac{1 \text{ customer per trip}}{50 \text{ minutes per trip} \div 60 \text{ minutes per hour}}$$
$$= 1.2 \text{ customers per hour per cab}$$

$\lambda/\mu = 8.0$. From Table 15–4, with $M = 10$; $L_q = 1.637$ and $P_0 = .00028$

a. $L_q = 1.637$ customers

b. $L_s = L_q + \dfrac{\lambda}{\mu} = 1.637 + 8.0 = 9.637$ customers

c. $W_q = \dfrac{L_q}{\lambda} = \dfrac{1.637}{9.6} = 0.17$ hours

d. $W_s = W_q + \dfrac{1}{\mu} = 0.17 + 0.833 = 1.0033$ hours

e. $P_0 = .00028$ (from Table 15–4)

EXAMPLE 4 *(concluded)*

f. $W_a = \dfrac{1}{M\mu - \lambda} = \dfrac{1}{10(1.2) - 9.6} = 0.4167$ hours

g. $P_w = \left(\dfrac{\lambda}{\mu}\right)^M \dfrac{P_0}{M!\left(1 - \dfrac{\lambda}{M\mu}\right)} = (8)^{10}\dfrac{.00028}{10!\left(1 - \dfrac{9.6}{10(1.2)}\right)} = .414$

The process can also be worked in reverse. That is, an analyst can determine the capacity needed to achieve specified levels of various performance measures. This approach is illustrated in the following example.

EXAMPLE 5

Alpha Taxi and Hauling also plans to have cabs at a new rail station. The expected arrival rate is 4.8 customers per hour, and the service rate (including return time to the rail station) is expected to be 1.5 per hour. How many cabs will be needed to achieve an average time in line of 20 minutes or less?

Solution

$$\lambda = 4.8 \text{ customers per hour}$$
$$\mu = 1.5 \text{ customers per hour}$$
$$M = ?$$

$$r = \frac{\lambda}{\mu} = \frac{4.8}{1.5} = 3.2$$

$$W_q \text{ (desired)} = 20 \text{ minutes, or } 0.333 \text{ hour.}$$

Using $L_q = \lambda W_q$, we can solve for L_q: 4.8/hour(0.333 hour) = 1.6 units. Thus, the average number waiting should not exceed 1.6 customers. Referring to Table 15–4, with $r = 3.2$, we find $L_q = 2.386$ for $M = 4$ and 0.513 for $M = 5$. Hence, five cabs will be needed.

Another question that often comes up in capacity planning is the amount of space to allocate for waiting lines. Theoretically, with an infinite population source, the waiting line can become infinitely long. This implies that no matter how much space is allocated for a waiting line, one can never be completely sure that the space requirements won't exceed that amount. Nonetheless, as a practical matter, one can determine a line that will not be exceeded a specified proportion of the time. For instance, an analyst may wish to know the length of line that will probably not be exceeded 98 percent of the time, or perhaps 99 percent of the time, and use that number as a planning value.

The approximate line length that will satisfy a specified percentage can be determined by solving the following equation for *n:*

$$n = \frac{\log K}{\log \rho} \quad \text{or} \quad \frac{\ln K}{\ln \rho} \qquad \text{where } K = \frac{1 - \begin{array}{c} \text{Specified} \\ \text{percentage} \end{array}}{L_q(1 - \rho)} \qquad (15\text{–}13)$$

The resulting value of n will not usually be an integer. Generally, round *up* to the next integer and treat that value as n. However, as a practical matter, if the computed value of n is less than 0.10 above the next lower integer, round down. Thus, 15.2 would be rounded to 16, but 15.06 would be rounded to 15.

EXAMPLE 6

Determine the maximum length of a waiting line for specified probabilities of 95 percent and 98 percent for a system in which $M = 2$, $\lambda = 8$ per hour, and $\mu = 5$ per hour.

Solution

$$r = \frac{8}{5} = 1.6 \quad \text{and} \quad \rho = \frac{8}{2(5)} = .80$$

From Table 15–4, $L_q = 2.844$ customers. For 95 percent, using Formula 15–13,

$$K = \frac{1 - .95}{2.844(1 - .80)} = .088$$

$$n = \frac{\ln .088}{\ln .80} = \frac{-2.4304}{-.2231} = 10.89, \text{ which rounds to 11.}$$

For 98 percent

$$K = \frac{1 - .98}{2.844(1 - .80)} = .035$$

$$n = \frac{\ln .035}{\ln .80} = \frac{-3.352}{-.2231} = 15.03, \text{ which rounds to 15.}$$

Model 4: Multiple Priorities

In many queuing systems, processing occurs on a first-come, first-served basis. However, there are situations in which that rule is not appropriate. The reason is that the cost or penalty incurred is not the same for all customers. For example, in a hospital emergency waiting room, there can be a wide variety of injuries and illnesses that need treatment. Some may be minor (sliver in finger), and others may be much serious, even life-threatening. It would seem reasonable to treat the most serious cases first, letting the nonserious cases wait until all serious cases have been treated. Similarly, computer processing of jobs often follows rules other than first-come, first-served (e.g., shortest job first). In such cases, a **multiple-priority model** is useful for describing system behavior.

In these systems, arriving customers are assigned to one of several *priority classes,* or categories, according to a predetermined assignment method (e.g., heart attacks, serious injuries, and unconscious persons are assigned to the highest priority class; sprains, minor cuts, bruises, rashes, etc. are assigned to the lowest class; and other problems are assigned to one or more intermediate classes). Customers are then processed by class, highest class first. Within each class, processing is first-come, first-served. Thus, all customers in the highest class would be processed before those in the next lower class, then processing would move to that class, and then to the next lower class. Exceptions would occur only if a higher priority customer arrived; that customer would be processed *after* the customer currently being processed (i.e., service would not be *preemptive*).

This model incorporates all of the assumptions of the basic multiple-server model except that priority serving is used rather than first-come, first-served. Arrivals to the system are assigned a priority as they arrive (e.g., highest priority = 1, next priority class = 2, next priority class = 3, and so on). An existing queue might look something like this:

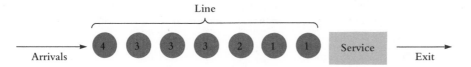

Within each class, waiting units are processed in the order they arrived (i.e., first-come, first-served). Thus, in this sequence, the first #1 would be processed as soon as a server was available. The second #1 would be processed

Performance Measure	Formula	Formula Number	
			TABLE 15–5
System utilization	$\rho = \dfrac{\lambda}{M\mu}$	(15–14)	*Multiple-server priority service model*
Intermediate values (L_q from Table 15–4)	$A = \dfrac{\lambda}{(1 - \rho)L_q}$	(15–15)	
	$B_k = 1 - \displaystyle\sum_{c=1}^{k}\dfrac{\lambda_c}{M\mu}$	(15–16)	
	$(B_0 = 1)$		
Average waiting time in line for units in kth priority class	$W_k = \dfrac{1}{A \cdot B_{k-1} \cdot B_k}$	(15–17)	
Average time in the system for units in the kth priority class	$W = W_k + \dfrac{1}{\mu}$	(15–18)	
Average number waiting in line for units in the kth priority class	$L_k = \lambda_k \cdot W_k$	(15–19)	

when that server, or another one, became available. If, in the interim, another #1 arrived, it would be next in line *ahead of the first #2*. If there were no new arrivals, the only #2 would be processed by the next available server. At that point, if a new #1 arrived, it would be processed ahead of the #3s and the #4. Similarly, a new #2 would be processed ahead of the #3s and the #4. Conversely, if a new #4 arrived, it would take its place at the end of the line.

Obviously, a unit with a low priority could conceivably wait a rather long time for processing. In some cases, units that have waited more than some specified time are reassigned a higher priority.

The appropriate formulas for this multiple-channel priority service model are given in Table 15–5.

EXAMPLE 7

A machine shop handles tool repairs in a large company. As each job arrives in the shop, it is assigned a priority that is based on the urgency for that tool. Requests for repair can be described by a Poisson distribution. Arrival rates are: $\lambda_1 = 2$ per hour, $\lambda_2 = 2$ per hour, and $\lambda_3 = 1$ per hour. The service rate is one tool per hour for each server, and there are six servers in the shop. Determine the following information.

a.   The system utilization.
b.   The average time a tool in each of the priority classes will wait for service.
c.   The average time a tool spends in the system for each priority class.
d.   The average number of tools waiting for repair in each class.

Solution

$$\lambda = \Sigma\lambda_k = 2 + 2 + 1 = 5 \text{ per hour}$$
$$M = 6 \text{ servers}$$
$$\mu = 1 \text{ customer per hour}$$

a. $\rho = \dfrac{\lambda}{M\mu} = \dfrac{5}{6(1)} = .833$

b.   Intermediate values ($\lambda/\mu = 5/1 = 5$; from Table 15–4, $L_q = 2.938$)

$$A = \frac{5}{(1 - .833)2.938} = 10.19$$
$$B_0 = 1$$
$$B_1 = 1 - \frac{2}{6(1)} = \frac{2}{3} = .667$$
$$B_2 = 1 - \frac{2 + 2}{6(1)} = \frac{1}{3} = .333$$
$$B_3 = 1 - \frac{}{6(1)} = \frac{}{6} = .167$$
$$W_1 = \frac{1}{A \cdot B_0 \cdot B_1} = \frac{1}{10.19(1)(.667)} = 0.147 \text{ hours}$$

EXAMPLE 7 *(concluded)*

$$W_2 = \frac{1}{A \cdot B_1 \cdot B_2} = \frac{1}{10.19(.667)(.333)} = 0.442 \text{ hours}$$

$$W_3 = \frac{1}{A \cdot B_2 \cdot B_3} = \frac{1}{10.19(.333)(.167)} = 1.765 \text{ hours}$$

c. Average time in system $= W_k + 1/\mu$. In this case, $1/\mu = 1/1 = 1$. Thus, we have:

Class	$W_k + 1 = W$ *(hours)*
1	$0.147 + 1 = 1.147$
2	$0.442 + 1 = 1.442$
3	$1.765 + 1 = 2.765$

d. The average number of units waiting in each class is $L_k = \lambda_k \cdot W_k$. Thus, we have:

Class	$\lambda_k \cdot W_k = L_k$ *(units)*
1	$2(0.147) = 0.294$
2	$2(0.442) = 0.884$
3	$1(1.765) = 1.765$

Revising Priorities.   If any of the waiting times computed in the preceding example are deemed too long by management (e.g., a waiting time of 0.147 hours for tools in the first class might be too long), there are several options. One is to increase the number of servers. Another is to attempt to increase the service rate, say, by introducing new methods. If such options are not feasible, another approach would be to reexamine the membership of each of the priority classifications. The reason for this is that if some repair requests, say, in the first priority class can be reassigned to the second priority class, this will tend to decrease the average waiting times for repair jobs that retain the highest priority classification simply because the arrival rate of those items will be lower.

EXAMPLE 8

Suppose the manager of the repair shop, after consulting with the managers of the departments that use the shop's services, has been able to revise the list of tools that are given the highest priorities. This would be reflected by revised arrival rates. Suppose that the revised rates are: $\lambda_1 = 1.5$, $\lambda_2 = 2.5$, and λ_3 remains unchanged at 1.0. Determine the following information:

a. The system utilization.
b. The average waiting time for units in each priority class.

EXAMPLE 8 *(concluded)*

Solution

$$\lambda = \Sigma\lambda_k = 1.5 + 2.5 + 1.0 = 5.0$$
$$M = 6$$
$$\mu = 1$$

(Note that these values are the same as in the previous example.)

a. $\rho = 5.0/6(1) = .833$, which is the same as in the previous example.

b. The value of A, since it is a function of M, μ, and λ, is the same as in the preceding example because these values are the same. Therefore, $A = 10.19$ and:

$$B_0 = 1 \text{ (always)}$$
$$B_1 = 1 - \frac{1.5}{6(1)} = .75$$
$$B_2 = 1 - \frac{1.5 + 2.5}{6(1)} = .333$$
$$B_3 = 1 - \frac{1.5 + 2.5 + 1.0}{6(1)} = .167$$

Then:

$$W_1 = \frac{1}{10.19(1)(.75)} = 0.131 \text{ hours}$$
$$W_2 = \frac{1}{10.19(.75)(.333)} = 0.393 \text{ hours}$$
$$W_3 = \frac{1}{10.19(.333)(.167)} = 1.765 \text{ hours}$$

In the preceding example, we find several interesting results. One is that through reduction of the arrival rate of the highest priority class, the average waiting time for units in that priority class has decreased. Hence, removing some members of the highest class and placing them into the next lower priority class reduced the average waiting time for units that remained in the highest class. Note, though, that the average waiting time for the second priority class also was reduced, even though units were added to that class. Although this may appear counterintuitive, it is necessary to recognize that the *total* waiting time (when all arrivals are taken into account) will remain unchanged. We can see this by noticing that the average *number* waiting (see Example 7, part *d*) is .294 + .884 + 1.765 = 2.943. In Example 8, using the average waiting times just computed, the average number waiting in all three classes is

$$\sum_{k=1}^{3} \lambda_k W_k = 1.5(.131) + 2.5(.393) + 1.0(1.765) = 2.944$$

Aside from a slight difference due to rounding, the totals are the same.

Another interesting observation is that the average waiting time for customers in the third priority class did not change from the preceding example. The reason for this is that the *total* arrival rate for the two higher-priority classes did not change, and the average arrival rate for this class did not change. Hence, units assigned to the lowest class must still contend with a combined arrival rate of 4 for the two higher-priority classes.

QUEUING MODEL: FINITE-SOURCE

The finite-source model is appropriate for cases in which the calling population is limited to a relatively small number of potential calls. For instance, one person may be responsible for handling breakdowns on 15 machines. Hence, the size of the calling population is 15. There may be more than one server or channel, though. For instance, due to a backlog of machines awaiting repairs, the manager might authorize an additional person to work on repairs.

As in the infinite-source models, arrival rates are required to be Poisson and service times exponential. A major difference between the finite- and infinite-source models is that the arrival rate of customers in a finite situation is *dependent* on the length of the waiting line: the arrival rate decreases as the length of the line increases simply because there is a decreasing proportion of the population left to generate calls for service. The limit occurs when *all* of the population are waiting in line; at that point the arrival rate is zero since no additional units can arrive.

Because the mathematics of the finite-source model can be quite complex, finite-queuing tables are often used in conjunction with simple formulas to analyze these systems. Table 15–6 contains a list of the key formulas and definitions. You will find it helpful to study the diagram of a cycle that is presented in the table.

Table 15–7 is an abbreviated finite-queuing table that is used to obtain values of D and F. (Most of the formulas require a value of F.) In order to use the finite-queuing table, follow this procedure:

1. List the values for:
   a. N, population size.
   b. M, number of servers/channels.
   c. T, service time.
   d. U, time between calls for service, per customer.
2. Compute the service factor, $X = T/(T + U)$.
3. Locate the section of the finite-queuing tables for N.
4. Using the value of X as the point of entry, find the values of D and F that correspond to M.
5. Use the values of N, M, X, D, and F as needed to compute the desired measures of system performance.

TABLE 15–6

Finite-source queuing formulas and notation

Formulas		Notation†
Service factor	$X = \dfrac{T}{T + U}$ (15–20)	D = Probability that a customer will have to wait in line
Average number waiting	$L = N(1 - F)$ (15–21)	F = Efficiency factor: $1 -$ percentage waiting in line
Average waiting time	$W = \dfrac{L(T + U)}{N - L} = \dfrac{T(1 - F)}{XF}$ (15–22)	H = Average number of customers being served
Average number running	$J = NF(1 - X)$ (15–23)	J = Average number of customers not in line or in service
Average number being serviced	$H = FNX$ (15–24)	L = Average number of customers waiting for service
Number in population	$N = J + L + H$ (15–25)	M = Number of service channels
		N = Number of potential customers
		T = Average service time
		U = Average time between customer service requirements per customer
		W = Average time customers wait in line
		X = Service factor

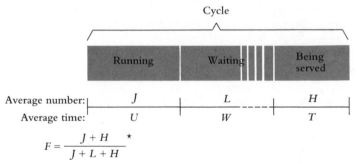

$$F = \frac{J + H}{J + L + H} \quad \star$$

⋆ The purpose of this formula is to provide an understanding of F. Because the value of F is needed to compute J, L, and H, the formula cannot be used to actually compute F. The finite queuing tables must be used for that purpose.

---

† Adapted from L. G. Peck and R. N. Hazelwood, *Finite Queuing Tables* (New York: John Wiley & Sons, 1958). Reprinted by permission.

TABLE 15—7

Finite-queuing tables

X	M	D	F	X	M	D	F	X	M	D	F	X	M	D	F
POPULATION 5				.135	1	.505	.907	.290	3	.079	.992	.520	4	.073	.991
.012	1	.048	.999	.140	2	.102	.992		2	.362	.932		3	.359	.927
.019	1	.076	.998		1	.521	.900		1	.856	.644		2	.779	.728
.025	1	.100	.997	.145	3	.011	.999	.300	4	.008	.999		1	.988	.384
.030	1	.120	.996		2	.109	.991		3	.086	.990	.540	4	.085	.989
.034	1	.135	.995		1	.537	.892		2	.382	.926		3	.392	.917
.036	1	.143	.994	.150	3	.012	.999		1	.869	.628		2	.806	.708
.040	1	.159	.993		2	.115	.990	.310	4	.009	.999		1	.991	.370
.042	1	.167	.992		1	.553	.885		3	.094	.989	.560	4	.098	.986
.044	1	.175	.991	.155	3	.013	.999		2	.402	.919		3	.426	.906
.046	1	.183	.990		2	.123	.989		1	.881	.613		2	.831	.689
.050	1	.198	.989		1	.568	.877	.320	4	.010	.999		1	.993	.357
.052	1	.206	.988	.160	3	.015	.999		3	.103	.988	.580	4	.113	.984
.054	1	.214	.987		2	.130	.988		2	.422	.912		3	.461	.895
.056	2	.018	.999		1	.582	.869		1	.892	.597		2	.854	.670
	1	.222	.985	.165	3	.016	.999	.330	4	.012	.999		1	.994	.345
.058	2	.019	.999		2	.137	.987		3	.112	.986	.600	4	.130	.981
	1	.229	.984		1	.597	.861		2	.442	.904		3	.497	.883
.060	2	.020	.999	.170	3	.017	.999		1	.902	.583		2	.875	.652
	1	.237	.983		2	.145	.985	.340	4	.013	.999		1	.996	.333
.062	2	.022	.999		1	.611	.853		3	.121	.985	.650	4	.179	.972
	1	.245	.982	.180	3	.021	.999		2	.462	.896		3	.588	.850
.064	2	.023	.999		2	.161	.983		1	.911	.569		2	.918	.608
	1	.253	.981		1	.683	.836	.360	4	.017	.998		1	.998	.308
.066	2	.024	.999	.190	3	.024	.998		3	.141	.981	.700	4	.240	.960
	1	.260	.979		2	.117	.980		2	.501	.880		3	.678	.815
.068	2	.026	.999		1	.665	.819		1	.927	.542		2	.950	.568
	1	.268	.978	.200	3	.028	.998	.380	4	.021	.998		1	.999	.286
.070	2	.027	.999		2	.194	.976		3	.163	.976	.750	4	.316	.944
	1	.275	.977		1	.689	.801		2	.540	.863		3	.763	.777
.075	2	.031	.999	.210	3	.032	.998		1	.941	.516		2	.972	.532
	1	.294	.973		2	.211	.973	.400	4	.026	.997	.800	4	.410	.924
.080	2	.035	.998		1	.713	.783		3	.186	.972		3	.841	.739
	1	.313	.969	.220	3	.036	.997		2	.579	.845		2	.987	.500
.085	2	.040	.998		2	.229	.969		1	.952	.493	.850	4	.522	.900
	1	.332	.965		1	.735	.765	.420	4	.031	.997		3	.907	.702
.090	2	.044	.998	.230	3	.041	.997		3	.211	.966		2	.995	.470
	1	.350	.960		2	.247	.965		2	.616	.826	.900	4	.656	.871
.095	2	.049	.997		1	.756	.747		1	.961	.471		3	.957	.666
	1	.368	.955	.240	3	.046	.996	.440	4	.037	.996		2	.998	.444
.100	2	.054	.997		2	.265	.960		3	.238	.960	.950	4	.815	.838
	1	.386	.950		1	.775	.730		2	.652	.807		3	.989	.631
.105	2	.059	.997	.250	3	.052	.995		1	.969	.451	POPULATION 10			
	1	.404	.945		2	.284	.955	.460	4	.045	.995	.016	1	.144	.997
.110	2	.065	.996		1	.794	.712		3	.266	.953	.019	1	.170	.996
	1	.421	.939	.260	3	.058	.994		2	.686	.787	.021	1	.188	.995
.115	2	.071	.995		2	.303	.950		1	.975	.432	.023	1	.206	.994
	1	.439	.933		1	.811	.695	.480	4	.053	.994	.025	1	.224	.993
.120	2	.076	.995	.270	3	.064	.994		3	.296	.945	.026	1	.232	.992
	1	.456	.927		2	.323	.944		2	.719	.767	.028	1	.250	.991
.125	2	.082	.994		1	.827	.677		1	.980	.415	.030	1	.268	.990
	1	.473	.920	.280	3	.071	.993	.500	4	.063	.992	.032	2	.033	.999
.130	2	.089	.933		2	.342	.938		3	.327	.936		1	.285	.988
	1	.489	.914		1	.842	.661		2	.750	.748	.034	2	.037	.999
.135	2	.095	.993	.290	4	.007	.999		1	.985	.399		1	.302	.986

TABLE 15—7

(continued)

X	M	D	F	X	M	D	F	X	M	D	F
.036	2	.041	.999	.100	1	.776	.832	.180	4	.066	.996
	1	.320	.984	.105	3	.064	.997		3	.238	.978
.038	2	.046	.999		2	.279	.978		2	.614	.890
	1	.337	.982		1	.800	.814		1	.975	.890
.040	2	.050	.999	.110	3	.072	.997	.190	5	.016	.999
	1	.354	.980		2	.301	.974		4	.078	.995
.042	2	.055	.999		1	.822	.795		3	.269	.973
	1	.371	.978	.115	3	.081	.996		2	.654	.873
.044	2	.060	.998		2	.324	.971		1	.982	.522
	1	.388	.975		1	.843	.776	.200	5	.020	.999
.046	2	.065	.998	.120	4	.016	.999		4	.092	.994
	1	.404	.973		3	.090	.995		3	.300	.968
.048	2	.071	.998		2	.346	.967		2	.692	.854
	1	.421	.970		1	.861	.756		1	.987	.497
.050	2	.076	.998	.125	4	.019	.999	.210	5	.025	.999
	1	.437	.967		3	.100	.994		4	.108	.992
.052	2	.082	.997		2	.369	.962		3	.333	.961
	1	.454	.963		1	.878	.737		2	.728	.835
.054	2	.088	.997	.130	4	.022	.999		1	.990	.474
	1	.470	.960		3	.110	.994	.220	5	.030	.998
.056	2	.094	.997		2	.392	.958		4	.124	.990
	1	.486	.956		1	.893	.718		3	.366	.954
.058	2	.100	.996	.135	4	.025	.999		2	.761	.815
	1	.501	.953		3	.121	.993		1	.993	.453
.060	2	.106	.996		2	.415	.952	.230	5	.037	.998
	1	.517	.949		1	.907	.699		4	.142	.988
.062	2	.113	.996	.140	4	.028	.999		3	.400	.947
	1	.532	.945		3	.132	.991		2	.791	.794
.064	2	.119	.995		2	.437	.947		1	.995	.434
	1	.547	.940		1	.919	.680	.240	5	.044	.997
.066	2	.126	.995	.145	4	.032	.999		4	.162	.986
	1	.562	.936		3	.144	.990		3	.434	.938
.068	3	.020	.999		2	.460	.941		2	.819	.774
	2	.133	.994		1	.929	.662		1	.996	.416
	1	.577	.931	.150	4	.036	.998	.250	6	.010	.999
.070	3	.022	.999		3	.156	.989		5	.052	.997
	2	.140	.994		2	.483	.935		4	.183	.983
	1	.591	.926		1	.939	.644		3	.469	.929
.075	3	.026	.999	.155	4	.040	.998		2	.844	.753
	2	.158	.992		3	.169	.987		1	.997	.400
	1	.627	.913		2	.505	.928	.260	6	.013	.999
.080	3	.031	.999		1	.947	.627		5	.060	.996
	2	.177	.990	.160	4	.044	.998		4	.205	.980
	1	.660	.899		3	.182	.986		3	.503	.919
.085	3	.037	.999		2	.528	.921		2	.866	.732
	2	.196	.988		1	.954	.610		1	.998	.384
	1	.692	.883	.165	4	.049	.997	.270	6	.015	.999
.090	3	.043	.998		3	.195	.984		5	.070	.995
	2	.216	.986		2	.550	.914		4	.228	.976
	1	.722	.867		1	.961	.594		3	.537	.908
.095	3	.049	.998	.170	4	.054	.997		2	.886	.712
	2	.237	.984		3	.209	.982		1	.999	.370
	1	.750	.850		2	.571	.906	.280	6	.018	.999
.100	3	.056	.998		1	.966	.579		5	.081	.994
	2	.258	.981	.180	5	.013	.999		4	.252	.972

TABLE 15–7

(concluded)

X	M	D	F	X	M	D	F	X	M	D	F
.280	3	.571	.896	.420	6	.130	.987	.580	4	.937	.684
	2	.903	.692		5	.341	.954		3	.994	.517
	1	.999	.357		4	.646	.866	.600	9	.010	.999
.290	6	.022	.999		3	.905	.700		8	.072	.994
	5	.093	.993		2	.994	.476		7	.242	.972
	4	.278	.968	.440	7	.045	.997		6	.518	.915
	3	.603	.884		6	.160	.984		5	.795	.809
	2	.918	.672		5	.392	.943		4	.953	.663
	1	.999	.345		4	.698	.845		3	.996	.500
.300	6	.026	.998		3	.928	.672	.650	9	.021	.999
	5	.106	.991		2	.996	.454		8	.123	.988
	4	.304	.963	.460	8	.011	.999		7	.353	.954
	3	.635	.872		7	.058	.995		6	.651	.878
	2	.932	.653		6	.193	.979		5	.882	.759
	1	.999	.333		5	.445	.930		4	.980	.614
.310	6	.031	.998		4	.747	.822		3	.999	.461
	5	.120	.990		3	.947	.646	.700	9	.040	.997
	4	.331	.957		2	.998	.435		8	.200	.979
	3	.666	.858	.480	8	.015	.999		7	.484	.929
	2	.943	.635		7	.074	.994		6	.772	.836
.320	6	.036	.998		6	.230	.973		5	.940	.711
	5	.135	.988		5	.499	.916		4	.992	.571
	4	.359	.952		4	.791	.799	.750	9	.075	.994
	3	.695	.845		3	.961	.621		8	.307	.965
	2	.952	.617		2	.998	.417		7	.626	.897
.330	6	.042	.997	.500	8	.020	.999		6	.870	.792
	5	.151	.986		7	.093	.992		5	.975	.666
	4	.387	.945		6	.271	.966		4	.998	.533
	3	.723	.831		5	.553	.901	.800	9	.134	.988
	2	.961	.600		4	.830	.775		8	.446	.944
.340	7	.010	.999		3	.972	.598		7	.763	.859
	6	.049	.997		2	.999	.400		6	.939	.747
	5	.168	.983	.520	8	.026	.998		5	.991	.625
	4	.416	.938		7	.115	.989		4	.999	.500
	3	.750	.816		6	.316	.958	.850	9	.232	.979
	2	.968	.584		5	.606	.884		8	.611	.916
.360	7	.014	.999		4	.864	.752		7	.879	.818
	6	.064	.995		3	.980	.575		6	.978	.705
	5	.205	.978		2	.999	.385		5	.998	.588
	4	.474	.923	.540	8	.034	.997	.900	9	.387	.963
	3	.798	.787		7	.141	.986		8	.785	.881
	2	.978	.553		6	.363	.949		7	.957	.777
.380	7	.019	.999		5	.658	.867		6	.995	.667
	6	.083	.993		4	.893	.729	.950	9	.630	.938
	5	.247	.971		3	.986	.555		8	.934	.841
	4	.533	.906	.560	8	.044	.996		7	.994	.737
	3	.840	.758		7	.171	.982				
	2	.986	.525		6	.413	.939				
.400	7	.026	.998		5	.707	.848				
	6	.105	.991		4	.917	.706				
	5	.292	.963		3	.991	.535				
	4	.591	.887	.580	8	.057	.995				
	3	.875	.728		7	.204	.977				
	2	.991	.499		6	.465	.927				
.420	7	.034	.993		5	.753	.829				

Source: L. G. Peck and R. N. Hazelwood, *Finite Queuing Tables* (New York: John Wiley & Sons, 1958). Reprinted by permission.

EXAMPLE 9

One operator loads and unloads a bank of five machines. Service time is exponentially distributed with a mean of 10 minutes per cycle. Machines run for an average of 70 minutes between loading and unloading, and this time is also exponential. Find:

a. The average number of machines waiting for the operator.
b. The expected number of machines running.
c. Average downtime.
d. The probability that a machine will not have to wait for service.

Solution

$$N = 5 \qquad\qquad M = 1$$
$$T = 10 \text{ minutes}$$
$$U = 70 \text{ minutes}$$

$$X = \frac{T}{T + U} = \frac{10}{10 + 70} = .125$$

From Table 15–7, with $N = 5$, $M = 1$, and $X = .125$, $D = .473$ and $F = .920$.

a. Average number waiting, $L = N(1 - F) = 5(1 - .92) = 0.40$ machines.
b. Expected number of running, $J = NF(1 - X) = 5(.92)(1 - .125) = 4.025$ machines.
c. Downtime = Waiting time + Service time:

$$\text{Waiting time, } W = \frac{L(T + U)}{N - L} = \frac{.40(10 + 70)}{5 - .40} = 6.957 \text{ minutes}$$

Downtime = 6.957 minutes + 10 minutes = 16.957 minutes.
d. Probability of not waiting = 1 − Probability of waiting
$$= 1 - D$$
$$= 1 - .473 = .527$$

EXAMPLE 10

Suppose that in the previous example, operators are paid $10 per hour, and machine downtime costs $16 per hour. Should the department add another operator if the goal is cost minimization?

Solution

Compare the total cost of the present system with the expected total cost of the proposed system:

EXAMPLE 10 *(concluded)*

M	Average number down, N − J	Average down cost (per hour), (N − J)$16	Operator cost (per hour)	Total cost (per hour)
1	.975	$15.60	$10	$25.60
2	.651	10.42	20	30.42

Hence, the present system is superior because its total cost is less than the expected total cost using two operators.

OTHER APPROACHES

The discussion in this chapter has focused on designing service systems that achieve a balance between service capacity and customer waiting time. The implication is that an appropriate level of service capacity can be determined. In certain instances, such an approach may not be practical, for a variety of reasons. One is that the system may be currently in operation and indicated design changes may be too costly, or there may be space restrictions such that changes cannot reasonably be made. One alternative that is particularly suited for queuing systems in which the customers are people rather than inanimate objects is to provide some form of diversion so that the waiting time becomes more tolerable. For example, magazines and newspapers can be placed in waiting rooms, as is usually the case in doctors' and dentists' offices. Auto repair shops sometimes use radio or television, and airlines may provide in-flight movies to help occupy the time. Airlines also serve meals and snacks, which helps to make the time spent waiting more pleasant. Some less obvious measures include placing mirrors where people wait for elevators and asking people to fill out forms, which makes waiting somewhat constructive.

Carrying this concept one step further, it is sometimes possible to derive some benefit from customer waiting. For instance, supermarkets position impulse items near checkout counters and gain additional sales, banks advertise current rates and place brochures describing bank services within easy reach of waiting customers, and restaurants have bars where customers can relax and spend money while waiting for their tables.

The implication in these approaches is that imagination and creativity can often play an important role in system design and that mathematical approaches are not the only ones worth considering.

SUMMARY

Analysis of waiting lines can be an important aspect of the design of service systems. Waiting lines have a tendency to form in such systems even though, in a macro sense, the system is underloaded. The arrival of customers at random times and variability of service times combine to create temporary overloads. When this happens, waiting lines appear. By the same token, at various times, the servers will be idle.

A major consideration in the analysis of queuing systems relates to whether the number of potential customers is limited (finite-source) or whether entry to the system is unrestricted (infinite-source). Five basic queuing models are described in the chapter, four dealing with infinite-source populations and one dealing with finite-source populations. In general, the models assume that customer arrival rates can be described by a Poisson distribution and that service time can be described by a negative exponential distribution.

KEY TERMS

channel, 745
finite source, 745
infinite source, 745

multiple-priority model, 760
queue discipline, 748
queuing theory, 743

SOLVED PROBLEMS

1. *Infinite source.* One of the features of a new machine shop will be a well-stocked tool crib. The manager of the shop must decide on the number of attendants needed to staff the crib. Attendants will receive $9 per hour in salary and fringe benefits. Mechanics' time will be worth $30 per hour, which includes salary and fringe benefits plus lost work time caused by waiting for parts. Based on previous experience, the manager estimates requests for parts will average 18 per hour with a service capacity of 20 requests per hour per attendant. How many attendants should be on duty if the manager is willing to assume that arrival and service rates will be Poisson-distributed? (Assume the number of mechanics is very large, so an infinite-source model is appropriate.)

Solution

$$\lambda = 18 \text{ per hour}$$
$$\mu = 20 \text{ per hour}$$

The solution requires a trial-and-error approach that reveals the total cost of feasible alternatives (i.e., a utilization less than 100 percent) and selection of the lowest-cost alternative. Note that the total-cost curve will always be U-shaped; increase the number of servers until the total cost shows an increase over the previous value. The optimum will be the number of servers that produced the previous total cost value. Thus,

Number of servers, M	L_q*	$L_q + \dfrac{\lambda}{\mu} = L_s$	M($9): Server cost (per hour)	L_s($30): Mechanic cost (per hour)	Total cost (per hour)
1	8.1	8.1 + 0.9 = 9.0	$ 9	$270	$279
2	0.299	0.299 + 0.9 = 1.129	$18	$ 33.87	$ 52†
3	0.03	0.03 + 0.9 = 0.93	$27	$ 27.9	$ 55†

* L_q: from Table 15–4, with $r = \lambda/\mu = 18/20 = 0.9$.
† Rounded.

Hence, two servers will produce the lowest total cost.

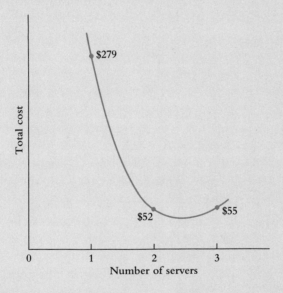

2. *Infinite source.* The following is a list of service times for three different operations:

Operation	Service time
A	8 minutes
B	1.2 hours
C	2 days

    a. Determine the service rate for each operation.
    b. Would the calculated rates be different if these were interarrival times rather than service times?

Solution

a.   The service rate is the reciprocal of service time. Thus, the rates
are:
A: 1/8 per minute = .125 per minute, or .125/min. × 60 min./
hr. = 7.5 per hour
B:/1/1.2 per hour = .833 per hour
C: 1/2 per day = .50 per day

b.   No. In either case, the rate is simply the reciprocal of the time.

3.   *Finite source.* A group of 10 machines is loaded and unloaded by one
of three servers. The machines run for an average of six minutes per
cycle, and average time to unload and reload is nine minutes. Each
time can be described by an exponential distribution. While running,
the machines produce at a rate that would yield 16 units per hour if
they did not have to pause to wait for a server and be loaded and
unloaded. What is the average hourly output of each machine when
waiting and serving are taken into account?

Solution

$$T = 9 \text{ minutes}$$

$$U = 6 \text{ minutes}; \quad X = \frac{T}{T + U} = \frac{9}{9 + 6} = .60$$

$$M = 3 \text{ servers; from Table 15–7, } F = .500$$
$$N = 10 \text{ machines}$$

a.   Compute the average number of machines running:

$$J = NF(1 - X) = 10(.500)(.40) = 2$$

b.   Determine the percentage of machines running, and multiply by
output while running:

$$\frac{J}{N} \times (16 \text{ per hour}) = \frac{2}{10} \times (16 \text{ per hour}) = 3.2 \text{ per hour}$$

DISCUSSION AND REVIEW QUESTIONS

1.   In what kinds of situations is queuing analysis most appropriate?

2.   Why do waiting lines form even though a service system is underloaded?

3.   What are the most common measures of system performance in a queuing analysis?

4.   What effect would decreasing arrival and service variability have on the effective capacity of a system?

5.   What approaches do supermarkets use to offset variations in customer traffic intensity?

6. Contrast *finite* and *infinite* population sources.
7. Will doubling the service rate of a single-channel system reduce the average waiting time in line by a factor of one half? Explain briefly.
8. In a multiple-channel system, what is the rationale for having customers wait in a single line, as is now being done in many banks and post offices, rather than multiple lines? (*Hint:* The average waiting time is unaffected.)
9. What happens to the length of a waiting line in a highly variable (queuing) setting if a manager attempts to achieve a high percentage of capacity utilization?

PROBLEMS

1. Repair calls are handled by one repairman at a photocopy shop. Repair time, including travel time, is exponentially distributed with a mean of two hours per call. Requests for copier repairs come in at a mean rate of three per eight-hour day (assume Poisson). Determine the following:
   a. The average number of customers awaiting repairs.
   b. System utilization.
   c. The amount of time during an eight-hour day that the repairman is not out on a call.
   d. The probability of two or more customers in the system.

2. A vending machine dispenses hot chocolate or coffee. Service time is 30 seconds per cup and is constant. Customers arrive at a mean rate of 80 per hour, and this rate is Poisson-distributed. Determine:
   a. The average number of customers waiting in line.
   b. The average time customers spend in the system.
   c. The average number in the system.

3. A small town with one hospital is supplied ambulance service via the hospital's two ambulances. Requests for ambulances during nonholiday weekends average 0.8 per hour and tend to be Poisson-distributed. Travel and assistance time averages one hour per call and follows an exponential distribution. Find:

   a. System utilization.
   b. The average number of customers waiting.
   c. Average customer waiting time.
   d. The probability that *both* ambulances will be busy when a call comes in.

4. The following information pertains to telephone calls to a motel switchboard on a typical Tuesday. Determine the average time callers wait to have their calls connected for each period and the probability that a caller will have to wait for each period.

Period	Incoming rate (calls per minute)	Service rate (calls per minute per operator)	Number of operators
Morning	1.8	1.5	2
Afternoon	2.2	1.0	3
Evening	1.4	0.7	3

5. For each case in the previous problem, determine the maximum line length for a probability of 96 percent.

6. Trucks arrive at the loading dock of a wholesale grocer at the rate of 1.2 per hour. A single crew consisting of two men can load a truck in about 30 minutes. Crew members receive $10 per hour in wages and fringe benefits, and trucks and drivers reflect an hourly cost of $60. The manager is thinking of adding another member to the crew. The service rate would then be 2.4

trucks per hour. Assume rates are Poisson. Would the third crew member be economical? Would a fourth member be justifiable if the resulting service capacity were 2.6 trucks per hour?

7. A branch location of a large savings bank is open on Saturdays from 10 A.M. until 2 P.M. During that time, four tellers are on duty. Tellers can handle customer deposits and withdrawals at the rate of 28 customers per hour each. Customers arrive to do their banking at the rate of 84 per hour during this period. Determine each of the following, assuming arrival and service rates are Poisson:

   a. The average number of customers waiting in line for a teller.
   b. The expected length of time customers wait in the system.
   c. The average waiting time for customers who are not served immediately.
   d. The maximum number waiting, for a confidence (probability) of 97 percent.

8. During slow hours, a certain post office branch uses three clerks, each of whom can process customers at a rate of 1.26 per minute (Poisson). The average time between customer arrivals is 25 seconds (exponential). Determine each of the following:

   a. System utilization.
   b. The percentage of time clerks are idle.
   c. The average number of customers in line and the average waiting time for those who must wait.
   d. The maximum number waiting, for a probability of 98 percent.
   e. The manager is contemplating using only two clerks. What impact would this have on the average number waiting in line, the average waiting time, and the maximum number waiting (98 percent probability)?

9. One field representative services five customers for a computer manufacturer. Customers request assistance at an average (Poisson-distributed) rate of once every

four working days. The field representative can handle an average (Poisson-distributed) of one call per day. Determine:

   a. The expected number of customers waiting.
   b. How long customers must wait, on the average, from the time a request for service is made until the service has been completed?
   c. The percentage of time the service rep will be idle.
   d. By how much would your answer to part a be reduced if a second field rep were added?

10. Two operators handle adjustments for a group of 10 machines. Adjustment time is exponentially distributed and has a mean of 14 minutes per machine. The machines operate for an average of 86 minutes between adjustments. While running, each machine can turn out 50 pieces per hour. Find:

   a. The probability that a machine will have to wait for an adjustment.
   b. The average number of machines waiting for adjustment.
   c. The average number of machines being serviced.
   d. The expected hourly output of each machine, taking adjustments into account.
   e. Machine downtime represents a cost of $70 per hour; operator cost (including salary and fringe benefits) is $15 per hour. What is the optimum number of operators?

11. One operator services a bank of five machines. Machine running time and service time are both exponential. Machines run for an average of 90 minutes between service requirements, and service time averages 35 minutes. The operator receives $10 per hour in salary and fringe benefits, and machine downtime costs $35 per hour per machine.

   a. If each machine produces 60 pieces per hour while running, find the average hourly output of each machine, when waiting and service times are taken into account.

b. Determine the optimum number of operators.

12. The manager of a regional warehouse must decide on the number of loading docks to request for a new facility in order to minimize the sum of dock costs and driver-truck costs. The manager has learned that each driver-truck combination represents a cost of $300 per day and that each dock plus loading crew represents a cost of $1,100 per day. How many docks should be requested if trucks arrive at the rate of four per day, each dock can handle five trucks per day, and both rates are Poisson?

13. For the preceding problem, if the cost for waiting space is $100 per day, how many docks would be optimum if a probability of .95 is used for the maximum line length?

14. Customers arriving at a service center are assigned to one of three categories (1, 2, or 3, with category 1 given the highest priority) for servicing. Records indicate that an average of nine customers arrive per hour and that one third are assigned to each category. There are two servers, and each can process customers at the rate of five per hour. Arrival and service rates can be described by Poisson distributions.

a. What is the utilization rate for this system?

b. Determine the average waiting time for units in each class.

c. Find the average number of customers in each class that are waiting for service.

15. A manager must determine requirements for waiting space for customers. A priority system is used to process customers, who are assigned to one of two classes when they enter the processing center. The highest-priority class has an arrival rate of four per hour; the other class has an arrival rate of two per hour. Both can be described as Poisson-distributed. There are two servers, and each can process customers in an average of six minutes.

a. What is the system utilization?

b. Determine the number of customers of each class that are waiting for service.

c. Determine the average waiting time for each class.

d. If the manager could alter the assignment rules so that arival rates of the two classes were equal, what would be the revised average waiting time for each priority class?

16. A priority waiting system assigns arriving customers to one of four classes. Arrival rate (Poisson) of the classes are shown in the following table:

Class	Arrivals per Hour
1	2
2	4
3	3
4	2

Five servers process the customers, and each can handle three customers per hour.

a. What is the system utilization?

b. On the average, how long do customers in the various classes wait for service? How many are waiting in each class, on the average?

c. If the arrival rate of the second priority class could be reduced to three units per hour by shifting some arrivals into the third priority class, how would your answers to part b change?

d. What observations can you make based on your answers to part c?

17. Referring to the preceding problem, suppose that each server could handle four customers per hour. Answer the questions posed in the preceding problem. Explain why the impact of reassigning customers is much less than in the preceding problem.

Selected Bibliography

Buffa, Elwood. *Operations Management*. 3rd ed. New York: John Wiley & Sons, 1972.

Chase, Richard, and Nicholas Aquilano. *Production and Operations Management*. 5th ed. Homewood, Ill.: Richard D. Irwin, 1989.

Griffin, W. *Queuing: Basic Theory and Applications*. Columbus, Ohio: Grid Publishing, 1978.

Hillier, Frederick S., and Gerald J. Lieberman. *Introduction to Operations Research,* 3rd ed. San Francisco: Holden–Day, 1980.

Peck, L. G., and R. N. Hazelwood. *Finite Queuing Tables*. New York: John Wiley & Sons, 1958.

Stevenson, William J. *Introduction to Management Science*. Homewood, Ill.: Richard D. Irwin, 1989.

SIMULATION

LEARNING OBJECTIVES

After completing this supplement, you should be able to:

1. Explain what is meant by the term *simulation*.
2. List some of the reasons for simulation's popularity.
3. Explain how and why random numbers are used in simulation.
4. Outline the advantages and limitations of simulation as a tool for decision making.
5. Describe the alternatives that a manager would reject before choosing simulation as a decision-making tool.
6. Solve typical problems that require the use of simulation.

SUPPLEMENT OUTLINE

Simulation is a descriptive technique that involves developing a model of a process and then conducting experiments on the model to evaluate its behavior under certain conditions. Unlike many of the other models that have been described in this text, simulation is not an optimizing technique. In fact, simulation does not produce a solution per se. Instead, it enables decision makers to test *their* solutions on a model that reasonably duplicates a real process; simulation models enable decision makers to experiment with decision alternatives using a *what if* approach.

The use of simulation as a decision-making tool is fairly widespread, and you are undoubtedly familiar with some of the ways it is used. For instance, space engineers simulate space flight in laboratories to permit future astronauts to become accustomed to working in a weightless environment. Similarly, airline pilots often undergo extensive training with simulated landings and takeoffs before being allowed to try the real thing. Many universities use management games as a means of simulating business environments. Tire designers evaluate alternative tread designs using machines that simulate conditions that produce tire wear and handling problems. There are many other examples of applications of simulation techniques; these few are mentioned to illustrate the nature and diversity of their use.

There are a number of reasons for the popularity of simulation. Among the most important ones are:

1. Many situations are too complex to permit development of a mathematical solution. The degree of simplification needed would seriously affect the results. However, simulation models are often able to capture the richness of a situation without sacrificing simplicity, thereby enhancing the decision process.
2. Simulation models are fairly simple to use and to understand.
3. Simulation enables the decision maker to conduct experiments that will help in understanding the model's behavior while avoiding the risks inherent in conducting tests on the model's real-life counterpart.
4. Extensive computer software packages are available, making it easy to use fairly sophisticated models.
5. Simulation can be used for a wide range of situations.
6. There have been numerous successful applications of these techniques.

STEPS IN THE SIMULATION PROCESS

Regardless of the type of simulation involved, there are certain basic steps used for all simulation models:

1. Identify the problem and set objectives.
2. Develop the simulation model.
3. Test the model to be sure that it reflects the system being studied.

4. Develop one or more experiments (conditions under which the model's behavior will be examined).
5. Run the simulation and evaluate the results.
6. Repeat steps 4 and 5 until you are satisfied with the results.

The first step in problem solving of any sort is to clearly *define the problem and set objectives* that the solution is intended to achieve; simulation is no exception. A clear statement of the objectives can provide not only guidance of model development but also the basis for evaluation of the success or failure of a simulation. In general, the goal of a simulation study is to determine how a system will behave under certain conditions. The more specific a manager is about what he or she is looking for, the better the chances that the simulation model will be designed to accomplish that. Toward that end, the *scope* and *level of detail* of the simulation must be decided on. This will provide an indication of the required degree of complexity of the model as well as the information requirements of the study.

The next step in simulation is *model development*. Typically this involves making decisions on the structure of the model and then writing a computer program to carry out the simulations. (Note that for instructional purposes, the examples and problems in this chapter are primarily *manual,* but in most real-life applications, computers are used to conduct the simulations. This stems from the need for large numbers of runs, the complexity of simulations, and the need for record keeping of results.) Data gathering is an important aspect of model development. The amount and type of data needed are a direct function of the scope and level of detail of the simulation. The data are needed for both model development and evaluation. Naturally, the model must be designed to enable evaluation of key decision alternatives.

The *validation* phase is closely related to model development. Its main purpose is to determine if the model adequately depicts real system performance. This is usually accomplished by comparing the results of simulation runs with known performance of the system under the same circumstances. If such a comparison cannot be made, say, because real-life data are difficult or impossible to obtain, an alternative is to employ a test of reasonableness, in which the judgments and opinions of individuals familiar with the system or similar systems are relied on for confirmation that the results are plausible and acceptable. Still another aspect of validation is careful consideration of the assumptions of the model and the values of parameters used in testing the model. Again, the judgments and opinions of those familiar with the real-life system and those who must use the results are essential. Finally, note that model development and model validation go hand in hand: model deficiencies uncovered during validation prompt model revisions, which lead to the need for futher validation efforts and perhaps further revisions.

The fourth step in simulation is *designing experiments*. Experiments are the essence of a simulation. They help answer the *what if* questions posed in simulation studies. By going through the process, the manager or analyst is able to learn about system behavior.

The fifth step in simulation is to *run the simulation model*. If a simulation model is deterministic, and all parameters are known and constant, only a single run will be needed for each *what if* question. If the simulation is probabilistic, with parameters subject to random variability, multiple runs will be needed to obtain a clear picture of the results. In this text, probabilistic simulations are the focal point of the discussion, and we shall limit comments to that sort of simulation. Probabilistic simulation is essentially a form of random sampling, with each run representing one observation. Consequently, statistical theory can be used to determine appropriate sample sizes. In effect, the larger the degree of variability inherent in simulation results, the greater the number of simulation runs needed to achieve a reasonable level of confidence that the results are truly indicative of model behavior.

The last step in the simulation process is to *analyze and interpret the results*. Interpretation of the results depends to a large extent on the degreee to which the simulation model approximates reality; the closer the approximation, the less need there is to "adjust" the results. Moreover, the closer the approximation of the model to reality, the less the risk inherent in applying the results.

MONTE CARLO SIMULATION

There are many different kinds of simulation techniques. Our discussion will focus on probabilistic simulation using the **Monte Carlo method.** The technique gets its name from the famous Mediterranean resort often associated with games of chance. In fact, the chance element is an important aspect of Monte Carlo simulation; this approach can be used only when a process has a **random,** or chance, component.

In the Monte Carlo method, a probability distribution is developed that reflects the random component of the system under study. Random samples taken from this probability distribution are analogous to observations made on the system itself. As the number of observations increases, the results of the simulation will more closely approximate the random behavior of the real system, provided an appropriate model has been developed. Sampling is accomplished by the use of random numbers.

The basic steps in the process are as follows:

1. Identify a probability distribution for each random component of the system.
2. Work out an assignment so that intervals of random numbers will correspond to the probability distribution.
3. Obtain the random numbers needed for the study.
4. Interpret the results.

The random numbers used in Monte Carlo simulation can come from any source that exhibits the necessary randomness. Typically, they come from one of two sources: large studies depend on computer-generated random numbers,

	1	2	3	4	5	6	7	8	9	10	11	12
1	18	20	84	29	91	73	64	33	15	67	54	07
2	25	19	05	64	26	41	20	09	88	40	73	34
3	73	57	80	35	04	52	81	48	57	61	29	35
4	12	48	37	09	17	63	94	08	28	78	51	23
5	54	92	27	61	58	39	25	16	10	46	87	17
6	96	40	65	75	16	49	03	82	38	33	51	20
7	23	55	93	83	02	19	67	89	80	44	99	72
8	31	96	81	65	60	93	75	64	26	90	18	59
9	45	49	70	10	13	79	32	17	98	63	30	05
10	01	78	32	17	24	54	52	44	28	50	27	68
11	41	62	57	31	90	18	24	15	43	85	31	97
12	22	07	38	72	69	66	14	85	36	71	41	58

and small studies commonly make use of numbers from a table of random digits like the one shown in Table 15S–1. The digits are listed in pairs for convenience, but they can be used singly, in pairs, or in whatever grouping is called for in a given problem.

There are two important features of sets of random numbers that are essential to simulation. One is that the numbers are uniformly distributed. This means that for any size grouping of digits (e.g., two–digit numbers), every possible outcome (e.g., 34, 89, 00) has the same probability of appearing. The second feature of these sets is that there are no discernible patterns in sequences of numbers to enable one to predict numbers further in the sequence (hence the name *random* digits). This feature holds for any sequence of numbers; the numbers can be read across rows as well as up or down columns.

An important point in using the table is to avoid always starting in the same spot; that would result in the same sequence of numbers each time. Various methods exist for choosing a random starting point. One involves using the serial number of a dollar bill to select the row, column, and direction of number selection. Another approach is to use rolls of a die to choose the starting point. For our purposes, the starting point will be specified in each example or problem so that we may all obtain the same results.

The process of simulation will become clearer as we work through some simple problems.

EXAMPLE S–1

The manager of a machine shop is concerned about machine breakdowns. A decision has been made to simulate breakdowns for a 10-day period. Historical data on breakdowns over the last 100 days are given in the following table:

EXAMPLE S–1 *(continued)*

Number of breakdowns	Frequency
0	10
1	30
2	25
3	20
4	10
5	5
	100

Simulate breakdowns for a 10-day period. Read two-digit random numbers from Table 15S–1, starting at the top of column 1 and reading down.

Solution

a. Develop a cumulative probability distribution for breakdowns:

(1) Convert frequencies into probabilities by dividing each frequency by the sum of the frequencies. Thus, 10 becomes 10/100 = .10, 30 becomes 30/100 = .30, and so on.

(2) Develop cumulative probabilities by successive summing. The results are shown in the following table:

Number of breakdowns	Frequency	Probability	Cumulative probability
0	10	.10	.10
1	30	.30	.40
2	25	.25	.65
3	20	.20	.85
4	10	.10	.95
5	5	.05	1.00
	100	1.00	

b. Assign random-number intervals so that they correspond to the cumulative probabilities for breakdowns. (*Note:* Two-digit numbers are used because the probabilities are given to two decimal places.) We want there to be a 10 percent probability of obtaining the event "0 breakdowns" in our simulation. Therefore, we must designate 10 percent of the possible random numbers as corresponding to that event. Since the numbers are evenly distributed between 00 and 99 (i.e., there are 100 two-digit numbers), we assign the 10 numbers 00 to 09 to that event.

Similarly, we assign the numbers 10 to 39 to "one breakdown," 40 to 64 to "two breakdowns," 65 to 84 to "three breakdowns," 85 to 94 to "4 breakdowns" and 95 to 99 to five breakdowns." (Note that the ending digit of each random-number interval is 1 less than the cumulative probability, and the interval begins at the cumulative probability for the last event, except for the first one, which begins at 00.) The results are as follows:

EXAMPLE S–1 *(concluded)*

Number of breakdowns	Frequency	Probability	Cumulative probability	Corresponding random numbers
0	10	.10	.10	00 to 09
1	30	.30	.40	10 to 39
2	25	.25	.65	40 to 64
3	20	.20	.85	65 to 84
4	10	.10	.95	85 to 94
5	5	.05	1.00	95 to 99
	100	1.00		

c. Obtain the random numbers from Table 15S–1, column 1, as specified in the problem:

18   25   73   12   54   96   23   31   45   01

d. Convert the random numbers into numbers of breakdowns:

18 falls in the interval 10 to 39 and corresponds, therefore, to one breakdown on day 1.

25 falls in the interval 10 to 39, which corresponds to one breakdown on day 2.

73 corresponds to three breakdowns on day 3.

12 corresponds to one breakdown on day 4.

54 corresponds to two breakdowns on day 5.

96 corresponds to five breakdowns on day 6.

23 corresponds to one breakdown on day 7.

31 corresponds to one breakdown on day 8.

45 corresponds to two breakdowns on day 9.

01 corresponds to no breakdowns on day 10.

These results are summarized in the following table:

Day	Random number	Simulated number of breakdowns
1	18	1
2	25	1
3	73	3
4	12	1
5	54	2
6	96	5
7	23	1
8	31	1
9	45	2
10	01	0
		17

The mean number of breakdowns for this 10-period simulation is 17/10 = 1.7 breakdowns per day. Compare this to the *expected* number of breakdowns based on the historical data:

$$0(.10) + 1(.30) + 2(.25) + 3(.20) + 4(.10) + 5(.05) = 2.05 \text{ per day}$$

Several points are worth noting:

1. This simple example is intended to illustrate the basic concept of Monte Carlo simulation. If our only goal were to estimate the average number of breakdowns, we would not have to simulate; we could base the estimate on the historical data alone.

2. The simulation should be viewed as a *sample;* it is quite likely that additional runs of 10 numbers would produce different means.

3. Because of the variability inherent in the results of small samples, it would be unwise to attempt to draw any firm conclusions from them; in an actual study, much larger sample sizes would be used.

In some cases, it can be helpful to construct a flowchart that describes a simulation. This is especially true if the simulation will involve periodic updating of system values (e.g., amount of inventory on hand), as illustrated in the following example.

EXAMPLE S–2

The manager of a small truck dealership wants to acquire some insight into how a proposed policy for reordering trucks might affect order frequency. Under the new policy, two trucks are to be ordered whenever the number of trucks on hand is five or fewer. Due to the nearness of the dealer to the home office, orders can be filled overnight. According to the dealer's records, the probability distribution for daily demand is:

Demand, x	P(x)
0	.50
1	.40
2	.10

a. Construct a flowchart that describes a 10-day simulation.
b. Use two-digit random numbers from Table 15S–1, column 11, reading down. Assume a beginning inventory of seven trucks.

EXAMPLE S–2 *(continued)*

Solution

a.

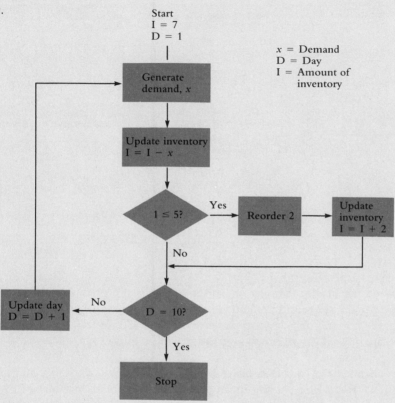

b. (1) Assign digits to probabilities:

x	P(x)	Cumulative P(x)	Digits
0	.50	.50	00–49
1	.40	.90	50–89
2	.10	1.00	90–99

(2) Obtain random numbers, convert to demand, update inventory accordingly, and reorder when necessary:

EXAMPLE S–2 *(concluded)*

Day	Random number	Demand, x	Beginning inventory	Ending inventory
1 54		1	7	6
2 73		1	6	5 (reorder 2; new beginning inventory = 5 + 2)
3 29		0	7	7
4 51		1	7	6
5 87		1	6	5 (reorder 2; new beginning inventory = 5 + 2)
6 51		1	7	6
7 99		2	6	4 (reorder 2; new beginning inventory = 4 + 2)
8 18		0	6	6
9 30		0	6	6
10 27		0	6	6

Simulating Theoretical Distributions

In many instances, a simulation will involve the use of theoretical distributions. Among the most frequently encountered theoretical distributions are the Poisson, normal, and exponential distributions. Consequently, an ability to simulate these distributions will greatly enhance knowledge and appreciation of simulation.

For simulation of a Poisson distribution, the mean of the distribution is required. Knowledge of the mean enables one to obtain cumulative probabilities for the distribution from Appendix B, Table C, which provide the basis for random-number assignments. Table 15S–1 can be used to obtain random numbers, three-digit random numbers must be read from Table 15S–1 to achieve correspondence. The following example illustrates these concepts.

EXAMPLE S–3

The number of lost-time accidents at a large plant has been determined from historical records to be two per day. Moreover, it has been determined that this accident rate can be well approximated by a Poisson distribution that has a mean of 2.0. Simulate five days of accident experience for the plant. Read random numbers from columns 1 and 2 of Table 15S–1.

EXAMPLE S–3 *(concluded)*

Solution

First obtain the cumulative distribution from Appendix B, Table C for a mean of 2.0, and make the range assignments:

x	Cumulative probability	Random number ranges
0	.135	000 to 134
1	.406	135 to 405
2	.677	406 to 676
3	.857	677 to 856
4	.947	857 to 946
5	.983	947 to 982
6	.995	983 to 994
7	.999	995 to 998
8	1.000	999

Next obtain three-digit numbers from Table 15S–1. Reading from columns 1 and 2 as instructed, we find 182, 251, 735, 124, and 549.

Finally, convert the random numbers into number of lost-time accidents using the established set of ranges. Hence, since 182 falls in the second range, it corresponds to one accident on day 1. The second random number, 251, falls in the same range, indicating one accident on day 2. The number 735 falls between 677 and 856, which corresponds to three accidents on day 3; 124 corresponds to 0 accidents on day 4; and 549 corresponds to two accidents on day 5.

The normal distribution can be important in many problems. There are a number of ways to simulate a normal distribution, but perhaps the simplest is to use a table of normally distributed random numbers, such as Table 15S–2.

TABLE 15S–2

Normally distributed random numbers

	1	2	3	4	5	6	7	8	9	10
1	1.46	0.09	−0.59	0.19	−0.52	−1.82	0.53	−1.12	1.36	−0.44
2	−1.05	0.56	−0.67	−0.16	1.39	−1.21	0.45	−0.62	−0.95	0.27
3	0.15	−0.02	0.41	−0.09	−0.61	−0.18	−0.63	−1.20	0.27	−0.50
4	0.81	1.87	0.51	0.33	−0.32	1.19	2.18	−2.17	1.10	0.70
5	0.74	−0.44	1.53	−1.76	0.01	0.47	0.07	0.22	−0.59	−1.03
6	−0.39	0.35	−0.37	−0.52	−1.14	0.27	−1.78	0.43	1.15	−0.31
7	0.45	0.23	0.26	−0.31	−0.19	−0.03	−0.92	0.38	−0.04	0.16
8	2.40	0.38	−0.15	−1.04	−0.76	1.12	−0.37	−0.71	−1.11	0.25
9	0.59	−0.70	−0.04	0.12	1.60	0.34	−0.05	−0.26	0.41	0.80
10	−0.06	0.83	−1.60	−0.28	0.28	−0.15	0.73	−0.13	−0.75	−1.49

The basis of the table is a normal distribution with a mean of 0 and a standard deviation of 1.00. Like all such tables, the numbers are arranged randomly, so that when they are read in any sequence they duplicate "randomness." In order to use the table, we must have the parameters of a normal distribution (i.e., its mean and standard deviation) in mind. Numbers obtained from the random number table can then be converted to "actual" values by multiplying the standard deviation by the random number and adding this amount to the mean. That is:

$$(15S\text{--}1)$$

Simulated value = Mean + Random number × Standard deviation

In effect, the random number equates to a normal z value, which indicates how far a particular value is above or below the distribution mean.

EXAMPLE S–4

It has been determined that the time required to perform a certain task can be described by a normal distribution that has a mean of 30 minutes and a standard deviation of 4 minutes. Simulate times for three jobs using the first three values in column 1 of Table 15S–2.

Solution

The first three values are: 1.46, −1.05, and 0.15. The simulated values are:

For 1.46, 30 + 1.46(4) = 35.84 minutes.
For −1.05, 30 − 1.05(4) = 25.80 minutes.
For 0.15, 30 + 0.15(4) = 30.60 minutes.

It is important to recognize that the last example involves a continuous variable, whereas the previous examples have involved discrete variables. (Remember that discrete variables typically take on only integer values, whereas continuous variables can take on integer and noninteger values.) Whenever possible, a model of a continuous variable should be able to simulate noninteger values as well as integer values.

FIGURE 15S–1

A uniform distribution

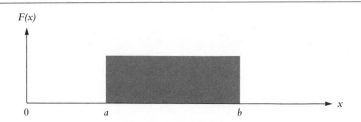

Another continuous type of distribution we can consider is the uniform distribution, in which values may occur anywhere over a continuous range between two extremes, *a* and *b,* as illustrated in Figure 15S–1.

Simulated values for a uniform distribution are determined in this way:

$$(15S–2)$$

Simulated value $= a + (b - a)$(Random number as a percentage)

Converting the random number to a percentage simply involves placing a decimal point to the left of the number. For example, 77 becomes .77.

EXAMPLE S–5

Job times vary uniformly between 10 and 15 minutes. Use Table 15S–1 to simulate job times for four jobs. Read numbers from column 9, going down.

Solution

$a = 10$ minutes, $b = 15$ minutes, $a - b = 5$ minutes

a. Obtain the random numbers: 15, 88, 57, and 28.
b. Convert to simulated values:

Random number	Computation	Simulated value (minutes)
15	$10 + 5(.15) =$	10.75
88	$10 + 5(.88) =$	14.40
57	$10 + 5(.57) =$	12.85
28	$10 + 5(.28) =$	11.40

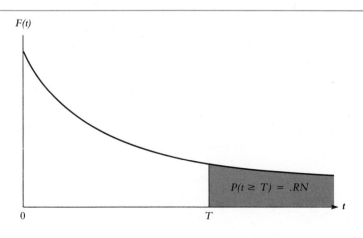

A negative exponential distribution

A third continuous distribution is the exponential distribution. We will concern ourselves with simulating values of negative exponential distributions, as portrayed in Figure 15S–2.

With a negative exponential distribution, the probability is fairly high that the random variable will assume a value close to zero. Moreover, the probability decreases as the specified value of the random variable increases. The probability that a random variable will take on a value greater than some specified value T, given that the variable can be described by an exponential distribution with a mean equal to $1/\lambda$, is given by the equation.

$$P(t \geq T) = e^{-\lambda t} \qquad (15S-3)$$

To simulate exponential values, we select a random number, place a decimal point to the left of it, set this equal to the probability $P(T)$, and solve Formula 15S–3 for t. The result is a simulated value from an exponential distribution with a mean of λ.

We can obtain an expression for t by taking the natural logarithm of both sides of the equation. Thus, with $P(T) = .RN$ (for *random number*), we have

$$\ln(.RN) = \ln(e^{-\lambda t})$$

The natural logarithm of a power of e is equal to the power itself, so

$$\ln(.RN) = \ln(e^{-\lambda t}) = -\lambda t$$

Then

$$t = -\frac{1}{\lambda} \ln(.RN) \qquad (15S-4)$$

This concept is illustrated in Figure 15S–2.

Values of random numbers can be obtained using Table 15S–1, as demonstrated in the following example.

EXAMPLE S–6

Times between breakdowns of a certain type of equipment can be described by an exponential distribution with a mean of five hours. Simulate the time between two breakdowns. Read two-digit random numbers from column 3 of Table 15S–1.

Solution

The mean, $1/\lambda$, is 5 hours. The random numbers are 84 and 05. Using Formula 15S–4, the simulated times are:

For 84, $t = -5[\ln(.84)] = -5[-0.1744] = 0.872$ hours.
For 05, $t = -5[\ln(.05)] = -5[-2.9957] = 14.979$ hours.

Note that the smaller the value of the random number, the larger the simulated value of t.

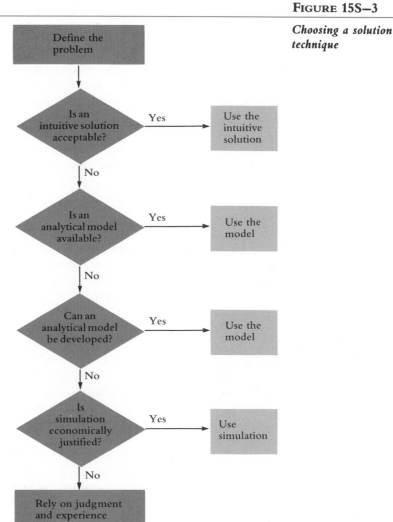

SIMULATION APPLICATIONS

Simulation has applications across a broad spectrum of operations management problems. In some instances, the simulations are quite modest, and in others, they are rather involved. Their usefulness, however, depends on the degree to which decision makers are able to answer their *what if* questions.

Generally speaking, the simulation approach is used either because optimization techniques are unavailable or because the assumptions required by an optimizing technique are not reasonably satisfied in a given situation. Queuing problems are a good example of the latter reason. Although waiting-line problems are pervasive, the rather restrictive assumptions of arrival and service distributions in many cases are simply not met. Very often, analysts will then turn to simulation as a reasonable alternative for obtaining descriptive information about the system in question.

If you were to go down the list of operations management topics, you would find that most have simulation applications. For instance, simulation is often helpful in product design and testing, facilities layout, line balancing, job design, aggregate planning, testing alternative inventory policies, scheduling, and project management. Actually, the list is quite long. The books and articles noted in the bibliography of this chapter give an indication of the richness and breadth of those applications and offer the interested reader an opportunity to explore this fascinating and useful subject in more detail.

COMPUTER SIMULATION

Although the emphasis in this supplement has been on manual simulation, in order to convey the main concepts, most real-life simulations involve the use of a computer. Computers offer relatively quick and easy means of obtaining results. Many real-life applications involve fairly complex simulation models that have substantial record-keeping requirements, and computers offer a practical solution.

Over the years, a number of simulation languages have been developed that make the task of writing simulation programs much simpler compared to the use of such standard programming languages as FORTRAN and BASIC. Some of the more widely used specialty languages are SIMSCRIPT, GPSS, GASP, and DYNAMO. In addition, there are a number of other simulation packages, some of which have very narrow focuses that relate to queuing or network problems. Most of the simulation packages have certain features in common. For example, they generally provide for random number generation from a variety of statistical distributions, as well as collection and tabulation of simulation results and time keeping.

It should be noted that some managers prefer to write their own simulations, or have a member of their staff do so, using a standard programming language rather than a simulation language. In cases where simulation is used infrequently, it can be more practical to use that approach rather than go through the time and effort required to use a specialty language. For simple problems, the slight inefficiency related to the use of a standard language is not usually an important consideration.

ADVANTAGES AND LIMITATIONS OF USING SIMULATION

Among the main advantages of simulation are the following:

1. It lends itself to problems that are difficult or impossible to solve mathematically.
2. It permits an analyst to experiment with system behavior while avoiding possible risks inherent in experimenting with the actual system.

3. It compresses time so that managers can quickly discern long-term effects.

4. It can serve as a valuable tool for training decision makers by building up their experience and understanding of system behavior under a wide range of conditions.

There are also certain limitations associated with simulation. Some of the chief limitations are:

1. Simulation does not produce an optimum solution; it merely indicates an *approximate* behavior for a given set of inputs.

2. For large-scale simulation, it can require considerable effort to develop a suitable model as well as considerable computer time to obtain simulations.

3. Monte Carlo simulation is applicable only in situations that have elements that can be described by random variables.

Because simulation produces an approximate answer rather than an exact solution, and because of the cost of running a simulation study, simulation is not generally the first choice of a decision maker. Instead, depending on the complexity of the situation, intuitive or analytical methods should first be investigated. Very often in simple cases, an intuitive solution will be acceptable. In more complex cases, an analytical solution would be preferable, assuming an appropriate technique is available. If not, it may be feasible to attempt to develop an analytical model that could be used to generate a solution. If these measures are rejected, simulation becomes the next logical possibility. However, its use may not be economically justifiable, in which case the decision maker will have to resort to the use of judgment and experience. In effect, after reevaluating all the alternatives, the decision maker must revert to an intuitive solution, even though initially that approach did not appear acceptable. This process is outlined in Figure 15S–3.

KEY TERMS

Monte Carlo method, 782   simulation, 780
random, 782

SOLVED PROBLEMS

1. The number of customers who arrive at a transmission repair shop can be described by a Poisson distribution that has a mean of three per hour. Assuming the distribution holds for an entire eight-hour day, simulate customer arrivals for the first four hours of a day. Read random numbers from Table 15S–1, columns 4 and 5, going down.

Solution

a. Obtain cumulative probabilities of the Poisson distribution from Appendix B, Table C for the mean specified. (Those values are given below for convenience.) Determine the random number ranges.

x	Cumulative probability
0	.050
1	.199
2	.423
3	.647
4	.815
5	.916
6	.966
7	.988
8	.996
9	.999
10	1.000

b. Obtain the random numbers: 299, 642, 350, and 091. (*Note:* Three-digit numbers are needed because the probabilities are given to three decimal places.)

c. Convert the random numbers to numbers of arrivals. Note where each number falls in the random number range list. For instance, 299 falls between 199 and 423. Interpret this to mean two customers arrive in the first hour. Similarly, 642 is interpreted to mean three customers arrive in the second hour, 350 implies two customers in the third hour, and 091 implies one customer in the fourth hour.

In sum, the number of customers per hour for the four-hour simulation is:

Hour	Number of arrivals
1	2
2	3
3	2
4	1

2. Jobs arrive at a workstation at fixed intervals of one hour. Processing time is approximately normal and has a mean of 56 minutes per job and a

standard deviation of 4 minutes per job. Using the fifth row of the table of normallly distributed random numbers (Table 15S–2), simulate the processing times for four jobs, and determine the amount of operator idle time and job waiting time. Assume the first job arrives at time $= 0$.

Solution

a. Obtain the random numbers from the table: 0.74, -0.44, 1.53, and -1.76.

b. Convert the random numbers to simulated processing times:

Random number	Computation	Simulated time
0.74	56 + 4(0.74) =	58.96
−0.44	56 + 4(−0.44) =	54.24
1.53	56 + 4(1.53) =	62.12
−1.76	56 + 4(−1.76) =	48.96

Note that three of the times are less than the interarrival times for the jobs, meaning the operator may be idle after those three jobs. One time exceeds the one-hour interval, so the next job must wait, and possibly the job following it if the waiting plus processing time exceeds 60 minutes.

c. Compute waiting and idle times:

Job number	Arrives at	Processing time, t (minutes)	60 − t Operator idle (minutes)	t − 60 Next job waits (minutes)
1	0	58.96	1.04	—
2	60	54.24	5.76	—
3	120	62.12	—	2.12
4	180	48.96	8.92*	—
			15.72	2.12

*60 − 2.12 − 48.96 = 8.92

3. The time between mechanics' requests for tools in a large plant is normally distributed with a mean of 10 minutes and a standard deviation of 1 minute. The time to fill requests is also normal with a mean of 9 minutes per request and a standard deviation of 1 minute. Mechanics' waiting time represents a cost of $2 per minute, and servers represent a cost of $1 per minute. Simulate arrivals for the first nine mechanic requests and their

service times, and determine the mechanics' waiting time, assuming one server. Would it be economical to add another server? Explain. Use Table 15S–2, column 8 for requests and column 9 for service.

Solution

a. Obtain random numbers and convert to times [see columns (a) and (b) in the following table for requests and columns (f) and (g) for service].

	Customer arrivals				Service		
(a)	(b)	(c)	(d)	(e)	(f)	(g)	(h)
			(e − c)				(e + g)
Random → number	Time between arrivals	Cumulative arrival time	Customer waiting time	Service begins	Random → number	Service time	Service ends
−1.12	8.88	8.88	0.00	8.88	1.36	10.36	19.24
−0.62	9.38	18.26	0.98	19.24	−0.95	9.05	28.29
−1.20	8.80	27.06	1.23	28.29	0.27	9.27	37.56
−2.17	7.83	34.89	2.67	37.56	1.10	10.10	47.66
0.22	10.22	45.11	2.55	47.66	−0.59	8.41	56.07
0.43	10.43	55.54	0.53	56.07	1.15	10.15	66.22
0.38	10.38	65.92	0.30	66.22	−0.04	8.96	75.18
−0.71	9.39	75.31	0.00	75.31	−1.11	7.89	83.20
−0.26	9.74	85.05	0.00	85.05	0.41	8.59	93.64
			8.62				

b. Determine arrival times [column (c)] by successive adding to times between arrivals in column (b).

c. Use arrival times for service start *unless service is still in progress on a previous request.* In that case, determine how long the arrival must wait (e − c). Column (e) values are the sum of starting time and service time [column (g)], which is the time service ends [column (h)]. Thus, service on each new request begins [column (e)] at the same time that service on the previous request ends [column (h)].

d. The simulation and resulting waiting times for the first nine arrivals are shown in the table. Total waiting time is 8.26 minutes.

e. The total cost for the 93.64 minutes (end of service on the ninth request) of the simulation is:

Waiting cost . . . . . . 8.26 minutes at $2 per minute = $ 16.52
Server cost   . . . . . . 93.64 minutes at $1 per minute =   93.64
$110.16

f. Usually, a second simulation with two servers would be needed (but with the same arrival times so that the results would be comparable). However, in this case it is apparent that a second server would increase server cost by about $93 but could not eliminate more than $16.52 of waiting cost. Hence, the second server would not be justified.

DISCUSSION AND REVIEW QUESTIONS

1. What is a simulation?
2. What are some of the primary reasons for the widespread use of simulation techniques in practice?
3. What are some of the ways simulation can be used?
4. What role do random numbers play in Monte Carlo simulations?
5. How would you respond to the following comment?

"I ran the simulation several times, and each run gave me a different result. Therefore, the technique does not seem to be useful. I need answers!"

6. Briefly discuss the main advantage of simulation.
7. What are some of the limitations of simulation as a tool for decision making?

PROBLEMS

1. The number of jobs received by a small shop is to be simulated for an eight-day period. The shop manager has collected the following data:

Number of jobs	Frequency
2 or less	0
3	10
4	50
5	80
6	40
7	16
8	4
9 or more	0
	200

Use the third column of Table 15S–1 and read two-digit numbers, going down. Determine the average number of jobs per day for the eight-day simulation period.

2. Jack M. sells insurance on a part-time basis. His records on the number of policies sold per week over a 50-week period are:

Number sold	Frequency
0	8
1	15
2	17
3	7
4	3
	50

Simulate three five-day periods. Use Table 15S–1, column 6 for the first simulation, column 7 for the second, and column 8 for the third. In each case, read two-digit numbers, beginning at the *bottom* of the column and going *up*. For each simulation, determine the percentage of days on which two or more policies are sold.

3. After a careful study of requests for a special tool at a large tool crib, an analyst has concluded that demand for the tool can be adequately described by a Poisson distribution with a mean of two requests per day. Simulate demand for a 12-working-day period for this tool using Table 15S–1. Read three-digit numbers from columns 5 and 6 combined, starting at the *top* and reading *down* (e.g., 917, 264, 045).

4. The number of lost-time accidents at a logging firm can be described using a Poisson distribution that has a mean of four accidents per month. Using the last two columns of Table 15S–1 (e.g., 540, 733, 293), simulate accidents for a 12-month period.

5. The time a physician spends with patients can be modeled using a normal distribution that has a mean of 20 minutes and a standard deviation of 2 minutes. Using the table of normally distributed random numbers (Table 15S–2), simulate the times the doctor might spend with the next seven patients. Use column 4 of the table; start at the bottom of the column and read up.

6. Jobs are delivered to a workstation at random intervals. The time between job arrivals tends to be normally distributed with a mean of 15 minutes and a standard deviation of 1 minute. Job processing time is also normally distributed with a mean of 14 minutes per job and a standard deviation of 2 minutes.

   a. Using Table 15S–2, simulate the arrival and processing of five jobs. Use column 4 of the table for job arrival times and column 3 for processing times. *Start each column at row 4.* Find the total times jobs wait for processing.

   b. The company is considering the use of new equipment that would result in processing time that is normal with a mean of 13 minutes and a standard deviation of 1 minute. Job waiting repre-

sents a cost of $3 per minute, and the new equipment would represent an additional cost of $.50 per minute. Would the equipment be cost justified? (*Note:* Use the same arrival times and the same random numbers for processing times.)

7. Daily usage of sugar in a small bakery can be described by a uniform distribution with endpoints of 30 pounds and 50 pounds. Assuming usage is independent of the day of the week, simulate daily usage for a 10-day period. Read four-digit numbers from Table 15S–1, columns 5 and 6, going up from the bottom.

8. Weekly usage of spare parts for a specialized machine can be described by a Poisson distribution with a mean of 2.8 parts per week. Lead time to replenish the supply of spare parts is two weeks (constant). Simulate the total usage of parts during lead time 10 times, and then determine the frequency of lead time demands (i.e., what percentage of times was the demand equal to 2, 3, 4, etc.?). Read four-digit numbers from Table 15S–1, columns 8 and 9, going down.

9. (Computer exercise.) Repeat the previous problem for 100 lead time periods.

10. A repair shop breaks an average of 0.6 tools per day. The average number of days required to obtain replacements is six. (Parts are delivered by mail once each day.) Both breakages and delivery times can be described by Poisson distributions. Tools are reordered whenever three or more must be replaced.

   a. Draw a flowchart to describe this process.

   b. Simulate breakage, ordering, and receipt for a 12-day period. Read three-digit numbers from Table 15S–1, columns 5 and 6, going down (e.g., 917, 264), for tool breakage, and columns 7 and 8, going down (e.g., 643, 200), for delivery time. Assume zero tools in inventory to start.

11. (Computer exercise.) Repeat the previous problem for 150 days.

12. Customers arrive randomly at a catalog department of a large store. The time between arrivals varies uniformly between 10 and 20 minutes. Service time is normal with a mean of 15 minutes and a standard deviation of 2 minutes.

    a. Simulate processing and waiting times for nine customers. Read three-digit numbers going down columns 9 and 10 of Table 15S–1 for arrivals (e.g., 156, 884, 576). Use column 8, Table 15S–2, for processing time.

    b. If management can reduce the range of arrival times to between 13 and 17 minutes, what would the impact be on customer waiting times? (Use the same service times and the same random numbers for arrival times from part *a*.) Round arrival times to two decimal places.

13. Probabilities have been determined for the movements of the ball in a pinball game. These are shown in the accompanying table, along with the points awarded if the ball strikes a given position. Simulate the paths of three balls, and compute the number of points awarded for each ball. Use column 1 of Table 15S–1 for the first ball, column 2 for the second ball, and column 3 for the third ball, reading down the columns.

Path	Probability	Path	Probability
S to A	.30	C to A	.10
B	.30	B	.15
C	.25	C	.20
D	.10	D	.15
E	.04	E	.25
F	.01	F	.15
A to A	.25	D to A	.10
B	.25	B	.05
C	.25	C	.25
D	.10	D	.20
E	.10	E	.25
F	.05	F	.15
B to A	.30	E to A	.05
B	.20	B	.10
C	.20	C	.15
D	.15	D	.15
E	.10	E	.20
F	.05	F	.35

(*Hint:* Construct a cumulative probability distribution for each of the six cases. Each new random number indicates the next position to move on. Each ball must start at S.)

14. Repeat the previous problem using columns 1, 2, and 3 for the next three balls, reading *up* from the bottom.

15. An anaylst found that the length of telephone conversations in an office could be described by an exponential distribution with a mean of four minutes. Reading two-digit random numbers from Table 15S–1, column 6, simulate the length of five calls and compute the simulated average time. Why is the simulated average different from the mean of four minutes?

16. The length of time between calls for service of a certain piece of equipment can be described by an exponential distribution with a mean of 40 minutes. Service time can be described by a normal distribution with a mean of 8 minutes and a standard deviation of 2 minutes. Simulate the time until the first breakdown and the times between four

Position	Points
A	400
B	300
C	200
D	100
E	50
F	20

breakdowns, as well as the four service times. For breakdowns, read two-digit numbers from Table 15S–1, row 7; for service times, read numbers from Table 15S–2, row 8.

17. The number of jobs per day that a repair shop gets can be described by a Poisson distribution with a mean of 3.0. Repair time per job can be described by an exponential distribution with a mean of six hours. Simulate the number of jobs received for a four-day period and the repair time for each job. What is the simulated total repair time per day? For number of jobs received, read two-digit numbers from Table 15S–1, row 1; for repair times, read two-digit numbers from row 2 of the same table.

18. A service operation consists of three steps. The first step can be described by a uniform distribution that ranges between five and nine minutes. The second step can be described by a normal distribution with a mean of seven minutes and a standard deviation of one minute, and the third step can be described by an exponential distribution with a mean of five minutes. Simulate three cycles using two-digit numbers from Table 15S–1, row 4 for step 1; Table 15S–2, row 6 for step 2; and two-digit numbers from column 4 of Table 15S–1 for step 3. Determine the simulated time for each of the three cycles.

19. A project consists of eight major activities, as illustrated in the accompanying diagram. Activity times are normally distributed with means and standard deviations as

shown in the following table. Note that there are two paths through the project: 1-2-3-5 and 1-2-4-5. Project duration is defined as the largest sum of times along a path. Simulate 12 times for each activity. Use columns 1 and 2 of Table 15S–2 for activity 1-2, columns 3 and 4 for activity 2-3, columns 5 and 6 for activity 2-4, columns 7 and 8 for activity 3-5, and columns 9 and 10 for activity 4-5. Determine the project duration for each of the 12 sets, and then prepare a frequency distribution of project duration. Use categories of 25 to less than 30, 30 to less than 35, 35 to less than 40, 40 to less than 45, and 45 or more. Determine the proportion of time that a simulated duration of less than 40 days occurred. How might this information be used?

Activity	Mean (days)	Standard deviation (days)
1-2	10	2
2-3	12	2
2-4	15	3
3-5	14	2
4-5	8	1

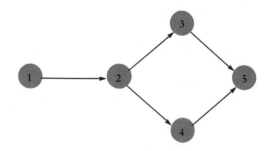

SELECTED BIBLIOGRAPHY

Barton, R. *A Primer on Simulation and Gaming.* Englewood Cliffs, N.J.: Prentice-Hall, 1970.

Buffa, Elwood. *Operations Management.* 3rd ed. New York: John Wiley & Sons, 1972.

Chase, Richard, and Nicholas Aquilano. *Production and Operations Management.* 5th ed. Homewood, Ill.: Richard D. Irwin, 1989.

Graybeal, W., and U. Pooch. *Simulation: Principles and Methods.* Cambridge: Winthrop Publishers, 1980.

Law, A. M., and W. D. Kelton. *Simulation Modeling and Analysis*. New York: McGraw-Hill, 1982.

Meier, R. C.; W. T. Newell; and H. L. Pazer. *Simulation in Business and Economics*. Englewood Cliffs, N.J.: Prentice-Hall, 1969.

Schmidt, J. W., and R. E. Taylor. *Simulation and Analysis of Industrial Systems*. Homewood, Ill.: Richard D. Irwin, 1970.

Shannon, Robert E. *Systems Simulation: The Art and Science*. Englewood Cliffs, N.J.: Prentice-Hall, 1975.

Smith, David E. *Quantitative Business Analysis*. New York: John Wiley & Sons, 1977.

Watson, Hugh J. *Computer Simulation in Business*. New York: John Wiley & Sons, 1981.

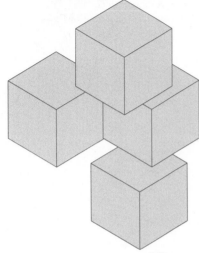

Quality Assurance

After completing this chapter, you should be able to:

1. Define the term *quality* and tell why quality is important for the organization.
2. Discuss the determinants of quality and some of the avenues available for improving quality.
3. Describe quality circles and their potential benefits.
4. Discuss the major inspection decisions managers must make.
5. Contrast *variables* and *attributes* inspection.
6. Describe the major features of acceptance sampling.
7. Differentiate acceptance sampling and process control.
8. List and briefly explain the elements of the control process.
9. Explain how control charts are used to monitor a process and the concepts that underlie the use of control charts.
10. Use and interpret control charts.
11. Use run tests to check for nonrandomness in process output.

Chapter Outline

Establishing quality levels for goods or services and assuring that those levels are achieved are vital tasks for virtually every type of business organization and government agency. Quality—or lack of quality—can have far-reaching consequences. In profit-oriented firms, quality can have a strong impact on differentiation among competitors and, ultimately, on the profits and losses firms experience. This is true whether the firm is engaged in manufacturing, banking, transportation, tourism, health care, or repair work. By the same token, quality is important in nonprofit organizations such as schools, state and local governments, and federal agencies, where political, economic, and social pressures have an impact. Moreover, social services, including public safety, postal services, waste removal and disposal, highway planning and construction, and fire protection are coming under increasing scrutiny, in terms of both cost and quality. In addition, legal and professional standards may fix minimum acceptable quality levels.

Quality assurance is concerned with the entire range of production, beginning with product or service design, continuing through the transformation process, and extending to service after delivery. The current view of quality assurance is that in order for it to be successful, it must be all-inclusive.

The chapter begins with a definition of quality, a list of reasons for the importance of quality, a discussion of the major determinants of quality, and an outline of some ways of improving quality. Since measurement is a key factor in control, the subject of inspection is discussed with emphasis on the major managerial decisions that must be made. The remainder of the chapter is divided into two parts. The first of these is acceptance sampling, which relates to inspection of lots or batches of previously produced goods or services. The second part concerns process control, which involves monitoring an ongoing process for the purpose of deciding when corrective action is necessary so that future output will be acceptable.

INTRODUCTION

Decisions on quality are among the most important ones that managers are called on to make. In this section, we examine how quality is defined and why decisions on quality are so important.

Defining Quality

The term *quality* is used in a variety of ways. Sometimes it refers to the *grade* of a product, as in "USDA Prime" and "grade A" eggs. At other times, it refers to materials, workmanship, or special features, as in "fine leather," "expertly handcrafted," or "waterproof." As a practical matter, we can define two major categories of quality: *quality of design* and quality of *conformance*.

Quality of design refers to the intention of the designer to include or exclude certain features in a good or service. For instance, the general purpose of an automobile is to provide transportation. However, models and manufacturers differ in terms of size, comfort, fuel economy, appearance, roominess, road handling ability, and performance. These are the result of deliberate choices made by designers that affect the quality of design.

Quality of conformance refers to the degree to which goods and services conform to (i.e., achieve) the intent of design. This is affected by such factors as the capability of equipment used to produce the good or service, the training and skills of workers, the extent to which design lends itself to production, the degree of monitoring of output to assess conformance, and the motivation of workers.

Both aspects of quality are important; the best design in the world cannot overcome poor workmanship, nor can workmanship, however good, overcome a poor design. Since the remainder of the chapter concentrates on achieving quality of conformance, it will be helpful to at least mention some of the salient aspects of quality of design.

Design choices are usually the result of marketing input (what do consumers want?) and operations (what can we produce or provide?). Naturally, a firm has to consider if it can produce at a cost that will enable it to make a reasonable profit. Maximizing profit generally does not mean achieving the highest design quality that is technically feasible. Consumers would not generally appreciate that level of quality, nor would they be willing to pay the price. Thus, it may be technically feasible to produce a stick of bubble gum that would retain its flavor forever, but at $300 a piece, not many people would stand in line to buy it. Hence, the goal of selecting the design quality is to maximize the *difference* between the cost to provide quality and the value (price) to the consumer. This is illustrated in Figure 16–1.

FIGURE 16–1

The optimum design quality

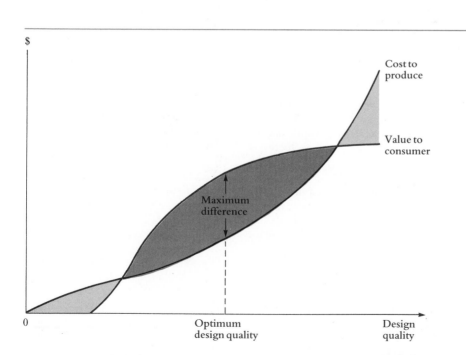

From the consumers' perspective, what is desired is a reasonable quality level and a reasonable price. Generally speaking, consumers are interested in one or more of the following, depending on the item in question: how it looks, how well it works, and how long it will last. In other words, the quality of a good or service is often perceived by the consumer in terms of:

1. Appearance.
2. Operation.
3. Reliability.

These are viewed by consumers as determinants of "fitness for use." Table 16–1 illustrates how these three dimensions of quality might apply to a color TV, clothing, and a restaurant meal.

In some cases, one or two of these dimensions might be considerably more important than the other two or one. For example, a painting would be judged primarily on appearance, attic insulation on how well it insulates (operation), and a truck tire on how long it lasts; the other dimensions tend to be secondary in such cases. On the other hand, there are many examples of products or services in which all three dimensions are important, including automobiles, kitchen appliances, house paint, and dental care.

In essence, **quality** can be defined in terms of how well a product or service serves its intended function.

TABLE 16–1

Examples of dimensions of quality	*Product/service*	*Appearance*	*Operation*	*Reliability*
	Color TV	Cabinetry, position of controls, exterior workmanship	Clarity, sound, ease of adjustment, reception, realistic colors	Frequency of repair
	Clothing	Seams matched, no loose threads or missing buttons, pattern matched, fit, style	Warm/cool, resistance to wrinkles, color-fastness	Durability
	Restaurant meal	Color, arrangement, atmosphere, cleanliness, friendliness of servers	Taste and consistency of food	Indigestion?

THE IMPORTANCE OF QUALITY

As a rule, consumers are influenced by three major factors when making buying decisions: price, availability, and quality. Hence, to compete effectively in the marketplace, businesses must pay careful attention to these factors; the decisions and trade-offs managers make will be a major determinant of demand for a firm's goods and services.

It is important for management to recognize the different ways in which the quality of a firm's products or services can affect the organization and to take this into account in developing and maintaining a quality assurance program. Some of the major ways that quality affects an organization are:

1. Reputation and image.
2. Liability.
3. Productivity.
4. Costs.

An organization's *reputation and image* are generally associated with the cost and quality of the goods or services it provides. Failure to devote adequate attention to quality can damage the organization's image and perhaps lead to a decreased share of the market, in the case of a profit-oriented firm, or increased criticism and/or controls, in the case of a government agency or other non-profit organization. In many instances, consumers are unable to assess product quality directly. Instead, they tend to rely on price, brand name, and a company's reputation when making choices.

Organizations must pay special attention to their potential *liability* due to damages or injuries resulting from either faulty design or poor workmanship. This applies to both products and services. Thus, a poorly designed steering arm on a car might cause the driver to lose control of the car, but so could improper assembly of the steering arm. However, the net result is the same. Similarly, a tree surgeon may be called to cable a tree limb. If the limb later falls and causes damage to a neighbor's car, the accident might be traced to a poorly designed procedure for cabling or to improper workmanship. Liability for poor quality has been well established in the courts. The organization's liability costs can often be substantial, especially if large numbers of items are involved, as is the case in the automobile industry, or if potentially widespread injury or damage (e.g., an accident at a nuclear power plant) is involved. Negligence is often a key issue, although "foreseeable" use or misuse can also be an important issue. Express written warranties as well as implied warranties generally guarantee the product as safe when used as intended. The courts have tended to extend this to uses that are *foreseeable*, even if the product has been used incorrectly or misused. In the health care field, medical malpractice claims and insurance costs are having an impact on skyrocketing costs and have drawn the attention of both doctors and legislators.

Productivity and quality are often closely related. Poor quality can adversely affect productivity during the manufacturing process if parts are defective and have to be reworked or if an assembler has to try a number of parts before finding one that fits properly. Similarly, poor quality in tools and equipment can lead to injuries and defective output, which must be reworked or scrapped, thereby reducing the amount of usable output for a given amount of input. Conversely, improving and maintaining good quality can have a positive effect on productivity.

Poor quality increases certain *costs* incurred by the organization. These include scrap and rework costs, warranty costs, replacement and repair costs after purchase, and any other costs expended in transportation, inspection in the field, and payments to customers or discounts used to offset the inferior quality. In some instances, the costs can be substantial. Liability claims and legal expenses are perhaps obvious. However, other costs can also be substantial, even if those two items are not factors. For instance, rework costs involve the salaries of workers and the additional resources needed to perform the rework (e.g., equipment, energy, raw materials). Beyond those costs are such items as inspection of reworked parts, disruption of schedules, the added costs of parts and materials in inventory waiting for reworked parts, and the paperwork needed to keep track of the items until they can be reintegrated into the process. Aside from these out-of-pocket costs are opportunity costs related to lost sales due to dissatisfied customers who switch their business to competitors.

Quality also has international implications. If a company is to compete effectively in the world marketplace, its products must compare favorably with its competitors' products in terms of price, quality, and availability. If the products of a country's major industries are consistently inferior to those of other industrial nations, that country can lose out at home and abroad. The result will be a drain of capital needed for construction of facilities and to provide employment opportunities for its people. This points up the need for government and industries to recognize the importance of the quality issue and to work together to improve the quality of products and services. Favorable tax status and support of research are two possible avenues. Another is encouragement and support of exchange programs that enable manufacturers to acquire firsthand information on techniques used in other countries.

DETERMINANTS OF QUALITY

A few pages back it was noted that the ultimate definition of quality is consumer perception of how well a product or service does—or will—perform its intended function and that performance often manifests itself in terms of such dimensions as appearance, operation, and reliability.

Any realistic effort to achieve specific quality goals or to improve quality must be predicated on the factors that determine quality. The degree to which a product or service successfully satisfies its intended purpose has four primary determinants. They are:

1. Design.
2. Conformance to design.
3. Consumer education.
4. Service after delivery.

These four determinants essentially define the scope of quality assurance.

The design phase is the starting point for the level of quality that is eventually achieved. Design involves decisions regarding specific characteristics of a product or service (size, shape, location, and so on), as well as methods, materials, processes, and equipment that will be employed. Design decisions must take into account the wants and needs of the consumer (perhaps determined by market research), production and service capabilities, safety and liability both during production and after delivery, and projected costs, profits, or other relevant considerations.

Poor design can result in difficulties in production or service. For example, materials might be difficult to obtain, specifications might be difficult to meet, or procedures difficult to follow. Moreover, if a design is inadequate or inappropriate for the circumstances, the best workmanship in the world may not be enough to achieve the desired quality. Thus, we cannot expect a surgeon to achieve good results if the given tools or procedures are inadequate. Likewise, it is wrong to criticize a social service agency for failure to achieve specified results if funding is inadequate. This can occur if local funding does not enable the agency to meet state-mandated guidelines.

Once the desired quality level has been specified, the responsibility for quality becomes one of conformance, which involves ensuring that operations follow through as intended. This involves workmanship, inspection, and corrective action when necessary.

As noted, the importance of workmanship is equivalent to the importance of design—the best design in the world can be easily negated by inferior workmanship. Furthermore, it matters not to the consumer whether poor quality is due to design or workmanship; the end result is the same. Good workmanship is the product of selection and training of employees, supervision of work, and development and maintenance of favorable attitudes toward quality standards.

Inspection and control are vital links in quality assurance. The objective of inspection is to provide an indication to management when output does not conform to expectations. Even with good design and workmanship, problems can still occur that will lead to poor quality. For example, equipment can malfunction, materials received from suppliers can be inferior or incorrect, materials can deteriorate after being received, tools can wear out more quickly than expected, and human beings can make mistakes. Consequently, it is necessary to inspect at least a portion of the output at various stages of completion—partly to correct defects that have already occurred, but primarily to know when corrective action is needed to avoid future deficiencies.

Whenever problems are discovered, it becomes necessary to undertake appropriate corrective action. This typically involves an investigation into the causes, selection of an action that can be expected to rectify the situation, implementation of the corrective action, and following up to insure that the desired changes have been realized.

The determination of quality does not stop once the product or service has been sold or delivered. Customer education is necessary to increase the chances (but not guarantee) that a product will be used for its intended purposes and used in such a way that it will continue to function properly and safely. (Companies involved in liability litigation often argue that injuries and damages occurred because the user misused the product.) Much the same reasoning can be applied to services. If customers, patients, clients, or other users are not clearly informed on what they should or should not do, there is the danger that they will take some action that will adversely affect quality. Typical examples include the doctor who fails to specify that a medication should be taken *before* meals and *not* with orange juice, the TV installer who doesn't take enough time to show the owner how to properly adjust the color, and the attorney who neglects to inform a client of a deadline for filing a claim.

Much consumer education takes the form of printed instructions and labeling. Thus, it is important for manufacturers to ensure that directions for unpacking, assembling, using, maintaining, and adjusting the product—and what to do if something goes wrong (e.g., flush eyes with water, call a physician, induce vomiting, do not induce vomiting, nontoxic, disconnect set immediately, no consumer-serviceable parts)—are *clearly visible* and *easily understood*.

Products do not always perform as expected, and services do not always yield the desired results, for a variety of reasons. Whatever the reason, it is important from a quality standpoint to remedy the situation—either through recall and repair of the product, adjustment, replacement or buyback, or reevaluation of a service—and then do whatever is necessary to bring the product or service up to standard.

While each of these factors is an important determinant of quality, it is important to recognize that *management* has the ultimate responsibility for quality; it is management that initially establishes the desired level of quality being sought, and it is management that provides the necessary funding for selection and training of workers, for inspection and control, and for follow-up after delivery to correct problems. Furthermore, management is responsible for creating a supportive environment, for conveying to employees the importance of quality, and for seeing that employees reflect this in their work.

THE EVOLUTION OF QUALITY CONTROL

Prior to the Industrial Revolution, production was carried out by skilled craftsmen. Pride of workmanship and reputation often provided the necessary motivation to see that a job was done right. Lengthy apprenticeships required by guilds caused this attitude to carry over to new workers. Moreover, one person or a small group of people were responsible for an entire product.

The Industrial Revolution was accompanied by a division of labor; each worker was responsible for only a small portion of each product. Price of workmanship became less meaningful since workers could not readily identify with the final product. The responsibility for quality control shifted to the foremen. Inspection was either nonexistent or haphazard, although in some instances 100 percent inspection was used.

In 1924, W. Shewhart of Bell Telephone Laboratories introduced statistical control charts that could be used to monitor production. Then, around 1930, H. F. Dodge and H. G. Romig, also of Bell Labs, introduced tables for acceptance sampling. However, statistical quality control procedures were not widely used until World War II, when the U.S. government began to require vendors to use them.

Just after the war, the American Society for Quality Control was founded. Throughout the years, the society has promoted quality control with its publications, conferences, and training programs.

Armand Feigenbaum's book *Total Quality Control* was published in 1961. Up to that time, quality efforts were directed toward correction. Feigenbaum's book expanded the concept of quality control to encompass the entire range of production, from design to sale, and to include *prevention* as well as corrective action.

During the 1950s and 1960s, W. Edwards Deming is credited with introducing statistical quality control methods to Japanese manufacturers. Prior to that time, much of the output by the Japanese was of inferior quality. However, by the late 1970s, the Japanese began to acquire a reputation of high quality in automobiles, appliances, steel, and electronics, some of which can be attributed to quality control efforts. Now, Japanese manufacturers are formidable competitors in the world marketplace. One consequence is that manufacturers in other industrialized countries have intensified their efforts to improve the quality of their products.

During the 1960s and 1970s, quality assurance methods spread to service organizations, such as banks, government agencies, health care, and hotels.

The current thinking on achieving consistently high levels of quality in both goods and services stresses a *total* approach to quality, from the design, procurement, production, and delivery stages to service after the sale, as well as consumer education. More and more, firms that once overlooked the importance of quality are recognizing its importance and attempting to achieve higher quality levels.

IMPROVING QUALITY

For many reasons, most organizations are constantly striving to improve the quality of their products or services. Competitive pressures, complaints from clients or customers, professionalism, and the desire to increase sales and/or market share all have a potential for instigating quality improvements. Some of the major sources of improvements are research and development, competitors, customers, and employees.

Research and development involves exploring new or different designs for products or services or new or different equipment, materials, processes, methods, or packaging that have the potential for yielding quality improvements. Organizations are sometimes reluctant to commit large sums of money to these efforts because of the high risks of failure (i.e., not obtaining the desired results), because the funds are needed elsewhere, or because stockholders often prefer the more tangible returns afforded by higher dividends. During the 1970s, the amount of funding large corporations allocated to R&D decreased steadily. However, more and more companies are beginning to recognize the merits of research and development and are committing the necessary funds.

Competitors are often sources for quality improvements, although at first glance, it may seem unethical to adopt another firm's ideas. To be sure, patent and copyright laws are designed to provide protection from the wholesale absorption of another's technology or techniques. However, there is nothing inherently wrong with noting how a competitor is able to achieve higher reliability, that the competitor uses special packaging to reduce damage during shipment, or that the competitor uses newer and more efficient methods or offers free in-home repair service. In other words, it is often possible to accomplish the same results without violating another's rights. Other examples of this include observing that a competitor offers more convenient sizes, expends more effort to educate customers in the use of the product, or uses better materials or ingredients.

Customers or consumers can often be a valuable source of ideas for quality improvement, either via suggestions they offer or via complaints received. Through careful analysis, perhaps using follow-up surveys, much can be learned about how users perceive quality and what changes they would be receptive to. Professional societies use customer or patient complaints to identify potential sources of poor quality and usually attempt to institute corrective measures.

Employees can often provide suggestions for improvements both in the design of a product or service and in the way the product or service is processed. One obvious advantage that workers possess is that they are intimately familiar with the process and the product or service, which can give them valuable insight that other sources may lack. Some organizations have made use of employee suggestions all along, while many others have more or less tended to ignore this input. Fortunately, more and more organizations are beginning to recognize the potential of employee suggestions. One of the ways companies are tapping this potential is with the use of **quality circles,** which are voluntary groups of employees who get together periodically to discuss ways of improving both the quality of their product and ways of improving working conditions. This can also yield indirect benefits by improving worker attitudes about quality. Japan is noted for its use of quality circles, and some American firms are patterning their quality circles along the same lines as the Japanese. One possible benefit of management's support and encouragement of these groups is that it communicates to employees the importance of quality in the eyes of management, and this can motivate them in their own work as well as motivate them to search for ways of improving quality. Another possible benefit often noted is the potential for making the worker feel like an important part of the system, one whose opinion and counsel are sought on something that is important to the organization. However, quality circles are neither a panacea nor a "quick fix," as the following reprint explains.

QUALITY CONTROL CIRCLES: THEY WORK AND DON'T WORK

Kenichi Ohmae

Quality control circles, so spectacularly successful in Japan in recent years, hold little promise of short-term gains. They take generations to bear fruit and cannot be expected to succeed if they are ordered by edict. Moreover, the scope of their achievement, though impressive over time, is limited.

A QC circle is a group of about 10 relatively autonomous workers from the same division of a company who volunteer to meet for an hour or so once or twice a month. After work (usually they are paid overtime), they discuss ways to improve the quality of their products, the production process in their part of the plant, and the working environment. Their long-term objective is to build a sense of responsibility for improving quality, but the immediate goal is to exchange ideas in a place uninhibited by barriers of age, sex, or company rank.

Japan's experience has revealed several preconditions for the success of QC circles. Some may be indigenous.

First, the work force must be intelligent and reasonably well educated. Members of the circles must be able to use statistical and industrial engineering analysis. They must know what it takes to make things work on a nuts and bolts level, and they must be able to brainstorm together. It is no coincidence that the Japanese companies that have been most successful with these circles and other participatory methods for improving productivity (Hitachi, Teijin, Asahi Glass, and Nippon Kokan) are also well known for their fine recruiting and internal training programs.

Second, management must be willing to trust workers with cost data and important information, and to give them the authority to implement their ideas. At Japanese companies with successful QC programs, managers have tended to work their way up through the ranks: They really believe in their work force. It is no surprise to them that groups of workers, if given information and authority to experiment by trial and error, will be able to reduce downtime, waste, or reworking—the sorts of questions that the circles are most effective in addressing.

Third, workers must be willing and eager to cooperate with each other. Unlike the suggestion box and other worker incentive programs that reward individuals, QC programs reward groups. A genuine "team spirit" is therefore necessary: Workers must be willing to express themselves and find fulfillment by reaching agreement.

Moreover, if authority in production decisions is to be decentralized down to the level of these circles, then the circles have to be able to cooperate with each other lest they work at cross purposes. Unless there is a spirit of cooperation within the work force, an attitude that talking a problem through with peers is more rewarding than taking it up to management, a company is better off using individual carrots instead of the circles. Otherwise, it may find night shifts undoing the improvements of day shifts.

One of the most important features of QC circles in Japan is that they did not originate with senior management. They spring rather from a voluntary, grass-roots movement of workers and middle managers from across the nation.

The spearhead has been the Union of Japanese Scientists and Engineers, or Nikka-Giren. In 1962 it began publishing a magazine, later named FQC, that called for quality control circles among factory workers and foremen and helped precipitate a change from the Western concept of quality control as the prerogative of technical experts. The magazine circulated widely among industrial workers, who bought it themselves (it cost them about the same as a pack of cigarettes) rather than receiving it through their employers, and read it together—in a circle. The magazine, together with a generation of supervisors familiar with QC concepts from the 1950s, helped initiate massive training of nonsupervisors.

The Nikka-Giren Union continues to have great influence. It publishes case histories of successful QC circles and sponsors regional and national conferences, where circle participants from different companies share their experiences.

Since most Japanese companies are very secretive with each other, this openness seems a paradox. But the movement was initially popular in the steel and ship-building industries, where there was a tradition of letting other companies freely inspect production methods and facilities. Had the movement started in the Japanese camera or auto industry, it is doubtful whether the current openness and cross-fertilization would have developed. Today, cross-fertilization is one of the keys to the success of the circles in Japan— the exchanges not only encourage but also keep workers interested in the process.

Quality control circles don't run themselves. They must be revitalized. Most important is the specific set of goals they are given and a strong manager who coordinates QCC changes with corporate objectives. In companies that use both the suggestion box and quality control circle, management can gather directly from workers ideas that may require significant capital expenditures and at the same time use suggestion box successes to encourage QCC efforts.

Management spends more time today on sustaining existing circles than starting new ones, understanding that their effects are incremental and cumulative. In 1951 Toyota received 700 proposals from its new worker participation program. Today it gets 500,000 per year, which saves a reported $230 million.

But there are limits to what the circles can do. The abrupt quantum leaps in cost reduction that the Japanese have achieved in industries as diverse as steel and consumer electronics do not result from QC circles. Instead they come from major strategic decisions about new technologies and plants and entirely new ways of producing and delivering a product.

At Ricoh, for example, it wasn't a circle that figured out how to redesign the business system by changing the technology, manufacturing, and marketing to completely change the game in plain paper copiers. Nor was it the circles that led to the elimination of inventory ("Kanban" system) at Toyota. QC circles, composed of workers from a single division, can't come up with these bold strokes.

A Single-Minded Focus

Nor can they replace strategy. Indeed, in many industries a single-minded focus on productivity improvements and concomitant quality control activities may be less important for success than focused R&D and targeted marketing.

Quality control circles work best when they are part of what the Japanese call total quality control, which embraces concerns about the entire spectrum of a business. And they are one of a number of productivity improvement techniques that work best when put together. As the Japanese would say, it's like collecting dust to make a mountain. But somebody has to envision the mountain, and know which way the wind is blowing.

Source: *The Wall Street Journal*, March 29, 1982. Reprinted by permission of *The Wall Street Journal*, © Dow Jones & Company, Inc. 1982. All rights reserved.

Management is the key factor in quality improvements. It is management that decides if quality improvements are needed, which sources will be used, and how much emphasis will be placed on achieving them. Hence, if quality circles are formed but management pays only lip service to them while ignoring their advice, that approach is doomed to failure. Although it might seem irrational for management to ignore employee input, some managers are fearful of permitting employees to have a say in how things are done because they feel they will lose control of the situation or be criticized for not recognizing the potential improvements themselves. Also, some managers prefer to retain all initiative for changes and improvements rather than share it with others.

Similarly, a doctor may receive complaints from patients or staff but choose to ignore them or attempt to rationalize his or her behavior instead of making an effort to improve the situation. The same can be said for teachers, lawyers, dentists, and other professionals.

When consumers encounter substandard quality in either goods or services, there is a tendency to blame workers' attitudes. However, workers generally reflect the attitudes of their managers and/or lack training, which is also the responsibility of management. Hence, management is the key factor in improving and maintaining quality output.

Dr. W. Edwards Deming suggests a number of actions that management can take to improve quality.[1] Among them are:

1. Adopt a long-term perspective.
2. Don't go along with the philosophy of an "irreducible percentage of defectives."
3. Demand quality from vendors.
4. Use statistical methods to identify sources of poor quality and then take corrective action. Train employees to use statistical techniques.
5. Improve supervision.
6. Don't emphasize output at the expense of good quality.
7. Make sure that employees have the proper training to do their jobs.

Other points can be added to the list. An important one is for top management to visibly support quality efforts. Philip Crosby offers some additional suggestions.[2] Among them are:

1. Top management must demonstrate its commitment to quality and its willingness to give support to achieve good quality.
2. Management must be persistent in efforts to achieve good quality.
3. Management must spell out very clearly what it wants in the way of quality and what workers must do to achieve that.
4. Make it (or do it) right the first time.

Marketing is another key factor in quality improvements. Marketing is responsible for determining consumers' wants and needs and for communicating this

---

[1] W. Edwards Deming, "Dr. Deming's Cure for U.S. Management," *WARD'S Auto World,* November 1981, p. 16.

[2] Philip Crosby, *Quality without Tears: The Art of Hassle-Free Management* (New York: McGraw-Hill, 1984).

to operations. Moreover, it is important for marketing people to understand the capabilities as well as the limitations of operations. Thus, it is necessary for these two areas to work together.

CAUSE OF QUALITY-CONTROL PROBLEMS MIGHT BE MANAGERS—NOT WORKERS

Ed Bean

A company's widgets continue to roll off the assembly line with loose screws and flaky paint. Who is at fault?

The stubborn union? The slipshod school system? Careless suppliers?

Blame the chairman and the chief executive officer, suggest quality experts.

Too many companies, consultants say, still equate quality control with having more inspectors at the end of the assembly line. Or with plastering factory walls with posters that exhort employees to take pride in their work.

Those old notions of quality control came under scrutiny as the Japanese carved out even bigger niches in the U.S. markets. Following the doctrines of such consultants as W. Edwards Deming, the 84-year-old crusader for quality and productivity and the man who often gets credit for much of Japan's success with quality control, more U.S. companies are now controlling quality through prevention.

That means better training for workers. It may mean re-engineering the product and redesigning the workplace. Above all, it means reshaping attitudes, from board room to loading dock, so that quality becomes more important than getting the product out the door. On all these fronts, consultants say, management has to take the initiative.

Outside Help

Tennant Co., a Minneapolis manufacturer of maintenance equipment for industrial floors, was one of the earliest U.S. companies to adopt such tactics. Too many of its machines were rolling off the assembly line with defects, says John Davis, Ten-

nant manager for quality. In 1979 the company sought outside help.

Tennant became the first client of Philip Crosby, a management consultant in Winter Park, Florida. Since 1979, Mr. Crosby has advised more than 350 companies on quality control. His theory: A company gets what it asks for. If management decides it can live with a 10 percent defect rate, management will get a 10 percent defect rate.

Mr. Crosby advised Tennant to start its quality program by assigning a dollar value to the additional production time and service visits caused by defects. Study groups by workers and managers then identified specific problems.

Leaking joints in hydraulic lines were a consistent headache. A study group found that management hadn't adequately trained assembly workers how to install the joints. Further study showed that Tennant engineers hadn't kept up with the latest technology in hydraulics circuits. Relations with suppliers of the joints were simplified when the number of suppliers was reduced to 2 from 16. The company also reduced the variety of joints it used.

Mr. Davis warns that self-examination can be painful. Suppliers were often blamed for the poor quality of some parts. But when Tennant discussed its problems with suppliers, the company found that it often hadn't given accurate specifications. In some cases, Tennant was using parts that unnecessarily exceeded specifications.

By the end of 1984, manufacturing defects had decreased 52 percent. The cost of correcting error (the company calls it the "cost of quality") was cut to 8.9 percent of sales at the end of 1984, down from 17 percent in 1980. The company's goal: Reduce that to 2.5 percent by 1988. But such progress hasn't come easily. "We grossly underestimated the time required to implement this," Mr. Davis says.

All of the company's 1,200 employees received at least 40 hours of classroom training in the first year, and much more time was devoted to studying business and production processes. The big change, though, was reshaping attitudes so that employees realized management was giving quality more than lip service. "People had a lot of questions," says Mr. Davis. "Are you going to provide us with the tools we need? How will it impact my performance review? Is this a one-shot deal?"

Carolina Freight Corp., a Cherryville, N.C., trucking company, also had problems convincing employees that its new push for quality wasn't just a fad. Middle and lower-level managers, such as dock supervisors, were the most skeptical, says Doug Wiles, Carolina's director of quality. To prove its commitment, the company spent about $250,000 on its program in the first year.

The company, which started thinking about quality in late 1983, sought help from Leadership Education & Development Services Inc., management consultants in Orlando, Fla.

The biggest concern at Carolina and most other trucking companies was claims for damages and shortages. Although a forklift driver or dock worker often seemed to be the culprit, the company eventually recognized that the workers had received little training in the art of loading a trailer.

Many problems were embarrassingly simple: Someone didn't pay attention. The company found that late deliveries usually were caused by someone failing to read the paperwork that listed when a shipment was promised. Drivers ran out of fuel because broken fuel gauges were never repaired. The latter was a $25,000-a-year inconvenience that disappeared.

Other problems required more sophisticated approaches. Haphazard routing that often left trucks half empty was corrected with computer scheduling.

Like Tennant, Carolina is finding that quality programs only work if everyone from the chief executive to the hourly employee is involved. "We used to think mistakes were just a part of doing business," Mr. Wiles says.

The chief executive's response to such a challenge may determine how a company regards quality, says David Garvin, a Harvard University associate professor who has studied quality in the United States and Japan. "He may make speeches about quality and say he's interested, but I look at how he spends his time. If he meets with the quality people once every six months, he's not serious. If he sits down with them once a week for three hours, that's a good indicator."

Traditional Views

Even with a strong commitment, a company shouldn't expect to see big improvements for several years, Mr. Garvin says. U.S. managers have traditionally viewed quality control as a defensive strategy to control costs, he says. Now, he says, management must learn that quality is becoming a competitive strategy that will separate the winners from the losers.

Tennant Co. had so many outside executives ask about its quality program that it organized a conference several years ago where companies could share information. Last year the two-day meeting attracted 170 executives. This fall Tennant is expecting 600.

Mr. Garvin thinks U.S. industry is making great strides, particularly auto and electronics companies. But he cautions that they're shooting at a moving target. The Japanese are also getting better.

Mr. Crosby, the consultant, estimates that the U.S. auto industry is about 60 percent of the way in its bid to catch the Japanese. But too much of the improvement has come with better inspection, rather than prevention, he laments. "It's been plain old hard work, like dragging a sled behind you with no wheels."

When Detroit does achieve parity with its foreign competition, consumers will forgive and forget, Mr. Crosby says. "It's like Scrooge," he says. "As soon as he changed, everyone accepted him and forgot he had been rotten for 20 years."

Tools for Improvement

Organizations can approach quality problems in a variety of ways. Some have found quality circles to be useful, others use more specialized groups, and still others try to involve everyone in the organization. Regardless of the particular approach that is used, there are certain tools that can be very helpful in solving problems. Among the most useful are brainstorming, check sheets, Pareto analysis, and cause-and-effect diagrams.

Brainstorming is a technique in which a group of people share thoughts and ideas on problems in a way that encourages unrestrained collective thinking. The idea is to achieve a relaxed atmosphere that will generate a free flow of ideas on identifying problems and finding causes, solutions, and ways to implement solutions. In successful brainstorming, criticism is forbidden, one or a few members are not allowed to dominate sessions, and all ideas are welcomed.

Check sheets provide a format that enables users to record and organize data in a way that facilitates collection and analysis. Check sheets are designed on the basis of what the users are attempting to learn by collecting data. They facilitate data collection by providing a format in which data can be recorded by means of checkmarks or other simple symbols.

There are many different formats that can be used for a check sheet and many different types of sheets. One frequently used form of check sheet deals with type of defect, another with location of defects. Both are illustrated in Figure 16–2.

The first check sheet shows tallies that denote the type of defect and the time of day each occurred. It appears that problems with missing labels tend to occur early in the day and that smeared print tends to occur late in the day, whereas off-center labels are found throughout the day. Identifying types of defects and when they occur can help in pinpointing causes of the defects.

The second check sheet makes it very easy to see where on the product defects are occurring. In this case, defects seem to be occurring on the tips of the thumb and first finger, in the finger valleys (especially between the thumb and first finger), and in the center of the gloves. Again, this may help determine why the defects occur and help correct the problems.

Pareto analysis is a technique for focusing attention on the most important problem areas. The Pareto concept, named after the 19th-century Italian economist Vilfredo Pareto, is that a relatively few factors generally account for a large percentage of the total cases (e.g., complaints, defects, problems). The implication is to classify the cases according to degree of importance and then focus efforts on resolving those that are most important, leaving the less important ("trivial many"). Often referred to as the 80–20 rule, it states that approximately 80 percent of the problems (or value, cost, etc.) come from 20 percent of the items (or other factors). For instance, 80 percent of machine breakdowns come from 20 percent of the machines, and 80 percent of the product defects come from 20 percent of the causes of defects.

FIGURE 16–2

Two examples of check sheets

A. Label defects on packages

Type of Defect

Day	Time	Missing label	Off center	Smeared print	Loose or folded	Other	Total
M	8–9	////	//				6
	9–10		///				3
	10–11	/	///	/			5
	11–12		/		/	/ (TORN)	3
	1–2		/				1
	2–3		//	///	/		6
	3–4		//	++++ /			8
Total		5	14	10	2	1	32

B. Defect location on work gloves
(results of tests performed on 1,000 gloves.)

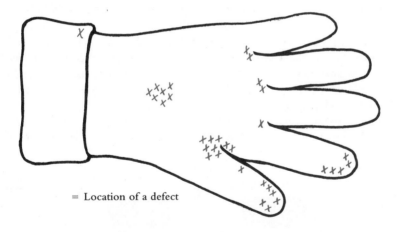

X = Location of a defect

Often, it is useful to prepare a chart that shows the number of occurrences by category, arranged in order of frequency. Figure 16–3 illustrates such a chart corresponding to the first check sheet shown in Figure 16–2. The dominance of the problem with off-center labels becomes apparent. Presumably, efforts would be focused on trying to resolve this problem. Once that is accomplished, the remaining defects would be addressed in similar fashion; "smeared print" would be the next major category to be resolved, and so on. Additional check sheets would be used to collect data to verify that the defects in these categories have been eliminated or greatly reduced. Hence, in later Pareto diagrams, categories such as "off center" may still appear but would be much less prominent.

FIGURE 16–3

A Pareto diagram based on data in Figure 16–2.

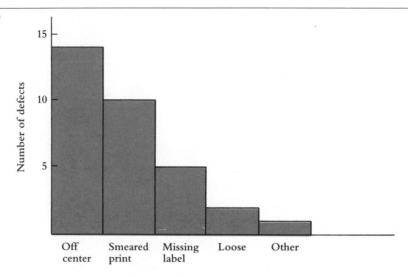

Cause-and-effect diagrams offer a structured approach to problem solving. They are also referred to as **fishbone diagrams,** because of their shape, or *Ishikawa diagrams,* after Japanese Professor Kaoru Ishikawa, who developed the approach to help workers who were overwhelmed in problem solving by the number of factors that needed to be examined. The diagrams help organize problem-solving efforts by providing several layers of *categories* that may be factors in causing problems.

Often, cause-and-effect diagrams are used after brainstorming sessions to organize the ideas generated. They may also be used in conjunction with

FIGURE 16–4

One format of a cause-and-effect diagram

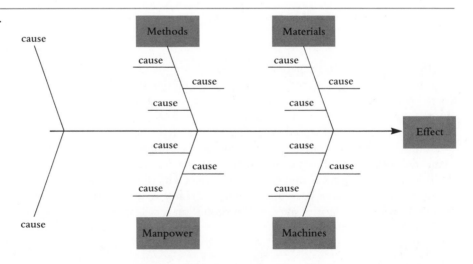

brainstorming, with quality circles, or by individuals to help organize their thinking. One form of a cause-and-effect diagram is illustrated in Figure 16–4.

An example of an application of such a cause-and-effect diagram is shown in Figure 16–5. Each of the factors listed in the diagram is a potential source of ticket errors. Some are more likely causes than others, depending on the nature of the errors. If the cause is still not obvious at this point, additional investigation into the *root cause* may be necessary, involving a more in–depth analysis. Often, more detailed information can be obtained by asking *who, what, where, when, why,* and *how* questions about factors that appear to be the most likely sources of problems.

Fail-safe methods can improve both design quality and quality during production. Fail-safe methods are like a combination lock, which will not open unless the correct sequence of numbers is used, or like the warning light for a seatbelt. Fail-safe methods provide additional warnings or guidance that increase the probability that output will possess intended quality levels. They can also be applied to automatic inspection during production: all items are inspected, and defective work or items are caught before additional work is performed.

Simple fail-safe methods can have a major impact on reduction of human error in work and on reduction of costs. However, many operations probably do not need fail-safe methods. Those that do are ones that have high costs associated with failure.

FIGURE 16–5

Cause-and-effect diagram for airline ticket errors

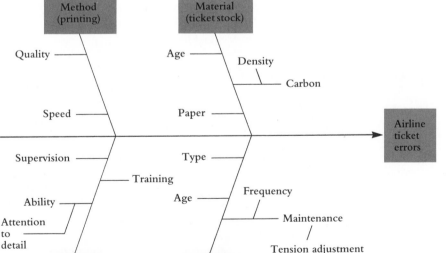

Reprinted from Howard Gitlow, Shelly Gitlow, Alan Oppenheim, and Rosa Oppenheim, *Tools and Methods for the Improvement of Quality* (Homewood, Ill.: Richard D. Irwin, 1989), p. 384, by permission.

Taguchi Methods

Traditionally, quality control efforts have focused on process control and the use of control charts. More recently, quality efforts have been extended to include improvement in both product and process design. Japanese statistician Genichi Taguchi has proposed a system of steps, known as **Taguchi Methods,** to (1) develop product specifications, (2) incorporate the specifications into a process and/or a product, and (3) obtain output that actually surpasses those specifications.

Under the Taguchi approach, quality costs are measured relative to *society* (i.e., customers, producer, and the community) rather than to just the producer. Taguchi defines quality in terms of the *loss* imparted to society by a product. This loss is made up of two parts: the cost of producing a product with given parameters and the cost to both the customer and the community of inferior quality. Hence, quality improvement is desirable as long as its cost is less than the savings to society (which is greater than the savings to the firm alone).

According to Taguchi, there are unwelcome costs associated with *any* deviation from a nominal or target value (e.g., width equal to 3 inches), even though the deviation may be within tolerances. In fact, the cost of a deviation is thought to be proportional to the *square* of the deviation, implying that large deviations are much more serious than small deviations. The necessary attitude, then, is one of continually working to reduce *any* deviation from a target value.

Taguchi advocates experimental design as a way of determining the optimal product or process. However, due to the number of interacting variables, that can require testing of a substantial number of combinations. Hence, anything that can reduce the number of variables (such as customer suggestions, quality circles, and copying competitors) is valuable.

QUALITY OF CONFORMANCE

The remainder of this chapter deals with quality of conformance, which refers to making sure that goods and services exhibit "fitness for use" (i.e., conform to the intent of design).

There are three points in the production process where monitoring takes place: before production, during production, and after production. The logic of checking conformance before production is to make sure that inputs are acceptable. The logic of checking conformance during production is to make sure that the conversion of inputs into outputs is proceeding in an acceptable manner. The logic of checking conformance of output is to make a final verification of conformance before passing goods on to customers.

Monitoring before and after production involves *acceptance sampling* procedures; monitoring during the production process is referred to as *process control*. These procedures are explained in detail in the following pages. Figure

FIGURE 16—6

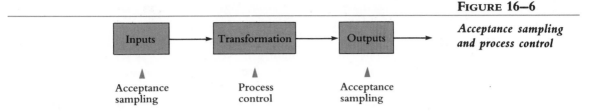

16—6 gives an overview of where these two procedures are applied in the production process.

For both acceptance sampling and process control, inspection provides key data for decision making.

INSPECTION

To determine if a process is functioning as intended, or to verify that a shipment of raw materials or final products does not contain more than a specified percentage of defectives, it is necessary to physically examine at least some of the items in question. The purpose of inspection is to provide information concerning the degree to which items conform to a standard. The basic issues in inspection are:

1. How much to inspect and how often.
2. At what points in the process inspection should occur.
3. Whether to inspect in a centralized location or on site.
4. Whether to inspect attributes or variables.

Consider, for example, inspection at an intermediate step in the manufacture of electric typewriters. Because inspection costs are often significant, the question naturally arises of whether it is necessary to inspect every typewriter, or whether a small sample of typewriters will suffice. Moreover, although there are numerous points in the production process where inspections could be made, it is not generally cost-effective to inspect at every point. Hence, the question comes up of which points to inspect at. Once these have been identified, a decision must be made on whether to remove the typewriters from the line and take them to a lab, where specialized equipment might be available to run certain tests, or whether to test them where they are being made. These points are expanded on in the following sections.

How Much to Inspect and How Often

The amount of inspection can range from no inspection whatsoever to inspecting each item numerous times. Low-cost, high-volume items such as paper clips, roofing nails, and wooden pencils often require little inspection because (1) the cost associated with passing defectives is quite low and (2) the processes that produce these items are usually highly reliable, so that defectives are rare. Conversely, high-cost, low-volume items that have large costs associated with passing defectives often require more intensive inspections. Thus, critical components of a manned-flight space vehicle are closely scrutinized because of the risk to human safety and the high cost of mission failure. One option that may be employed in high-volume systems is *automated* inspection.

The majority of quality control applications lies somewhere between these two extremes. Most require some inspection, but it is neither possible nor economically feasible to critically examine every part or activity for control purposes. The cost of inspection, resulting interruptions of a process or delays caused by inspection, and the manner of testing typically outweigh the benefits of 100 percent inspection. However, the cost of letting undetected defectives slip through is high enough that inspection cannot be completely ignored. The amount of inspection needed is governed by the costs of inspection and the expected costs of passing defective items. As illustrated in Figure 16–7, if inspection activities increase, inspection costs increase, but the costs of un-detected defectives decrease. The goal, of course, is to minimize the sum of these two costs. In other words, it may not pay to attempt to catch every defective, particularly if the cost of inspection exceeds the penalties associated with letting some defectives get through.

As a rule, operations that have a high proportion of human involvement necessitate more inspection effort than mechanical operations because the latter tend to be more reliable.

The frequency of inspection depends largely on the rate at which a process may go out of control or the number of lots being inspected. A stable process will necessitate only infrequent checks, whereas an unstable one, or one that has recently given trouble, will require more frequent checks. Likewise, many

FIGURE 16–7

The amount of inspection is optimal when the sum of the costs of inspection and of passing defectives is minimized

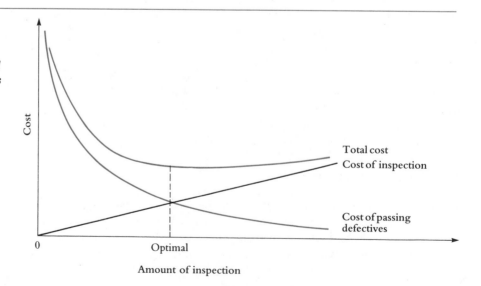

small lots will require more samples than a few large lots because it is important to obtain sample data from each lot.

Where in the Process to Inspect

In many operations, there are many possible inspection points. Because each inspection adds to the cost of the product or service, it is important to restrict inspection efforts to the points where they can do the most good. In manufacturing, some of the typical inspection points are:

1. *Raw materials and purchased parts.* There is little sense in paying for goods that do not meet quality standards and little sense in expending time and effort on material that is bad to begin with.
2. *Finished products.* Customer satisfaction and the firm's image are at stake here, and repairing or replacing products in the field is usually a good deal more costly than when it is done at the factory. Likewise, the seller is usually responsible for shipping costs on returns, and payments may be held up pending delivery of satisfactory goods.
3. *Before a costly operation.* The point is to not waste costly labor or machine time on items that are already defective.
4. *Before an irreversible process.* In many cases, items can be reworked up to a certain point, but beyond that point they cannot. For example, pottery can be reworked prior to firing. After that, defectives must be discarded or sold as seconds at a lower price.
5. *Before a covering process.* Painting, plating, and assemblies often hide defects.

In the service area, inspection points are incoming purchased materials and supplies, personnel, service interfaces (e.g., service counter), and outgoing completed work (e.g., repaired appliances, automobiles). Table 16–2 illustrates a number of examples.

Each situation is different. The operations manager must weigh the costs and benefits of inspections at each potential point in a process when deciding to assign inspections.

Centralized versus On-Site Inspection

Some situations require that inspections be done *on site*. For example, inspecting the hull of a ship for cracks requires inspectors to visit the ship. At other times, specialized tests can best be performed in a lab. This is the case, for example, with many medical tests, and it also applies to various tests in business and industry (analyzing food samples, testing metals for hardness, running viscosity tests on lubricants, and so on).

The central issue in the decision of whether to inspect on site is whether the advantages of specialized lab tests are worth the time and interruption needed to obtain the results. Arguments favoring on-site inspection are quicker deci-

TABLE 16–2

Examples of inspection points in service organizations

Type of business	Inspection points	Characteristics
Fast food	Cashier	Accuracy
	Counter area	Appearance, productivity
	Eating area	Cleanliness, no loitering
	Building and grounds	Appearance, safety hazards
	Kitchen	Cleanliness, purity of food, food storage, health regulations
	Parking lot	Safe, well-lighted
Hotel/motel	Accounting/billing	Accuracy, timeliness
	Building and grounds	Appearance and safety
	Main desk	Appearance, waiting times, accuracy of bills
	Maid service	Completeness, productivity
	Personnel	Appearance, manners, productivity
	Reservations/occupancy	Over/underbooking, percent occupancy
	Restaurants	Kitchen, menus, meals, bills
	Room service	Waiting time, quality of food
	Supplies	Ordering, receiving, inventories
Supermarket	Cashiers	Accuracy, courtesy, productivity
	Deliveries	Quality, quantity
	Produce	Freshness, well-stocked
	Aisles and stockrooms	Uncluttered
	Inventory control	Stock-outs
	Shelf stock	Ample supply, rotation of perishables
	Shelf displays	Appearance
	Checkouts	Waiting time
	Shopping carts	Good working condition, ample supply, theft/vandalism
	Parking lot	Safe, well-lighted
	Personnel	Appearance

sions and avoidance of introduction of extraneous factors (e.g., damage or other alteration of samples during transportation to the lab). On the other hand, specialized equipment and a more favorable testing environment (less noise and confusion, lack of vibrations, absence of dust, and workers "helping" with inspections) offer strong arguments for using a lab.

In unit (one-by-one) production, some companies rely on self-inspection by operators if errors can be traced back to specific operators. This places responsibility for errors at their source.

Attributes versus Variables Inspection

Quality characteristics are the focal point of inspection. They can be classified as either *attributes* or *variables*. **Attributes** yield pass/fail data, such as defective/nondefective and acceptable/not acceptable. Thus, attribute data are *count* data. For attribute data, a discrete distribution such as the binomial or Poisson serves as the basis for statistical inference. **Variables** can be present in varying degrees (e.g., length, height, thickness, tensile strength). As such, they must be *measured* rather than counted. Often, a normal distribution serves as the basis for statistical inference.

Inspection and control procedures differ somewhat, depending on whether the quality characteristic of interest is an attribute or a variable.

ACCEPTANCE SAMPLING

Acceptance sampling is a form of inspection that is applied to lots or batches of items either before or after a process instead of during the process. In the majority of cases, the lots represent incoming purchased items or final products awaiting shipment to warehouses or customers. The purpose of acceptance sampling is to decide if a lot satisfies predetermined standards. Lots that are judged to satisfy standards are passed or *accepted;* those that do not are *rejected.* Rejected lots may be subjected to 100 percent inspection, or they may be returned to the supplier for credit or replacement (especially if destructive testing is involved).

Acceptance sampling procedures are most useful when one or more of the following conditions exist:

1. A large number of items must be processed in a short time.
2. The cost consequences of passing defectives are low.
3. Destructive testing is required.
4. Fatigue or boredom caused by inspecting large numbers of items leads to inspection errors.

Acceptance sampling procedures can be applied to both attribute and variable inspection. However, inspection of attributes is perhaps more widely used, so for purposes of illustration, the discussion here will focus exclusively on attribute sampling plans.

Sampling Plans

Sampling plans specify the lot size, N, the sample size, n, the number of samples to be taken, and the acceptance/rejection criteria. There are a variety of sampling plans in use. Some plans call for selection of a single sample, and others call for two or more samples, depending on the nature of the plan. Some different kinds of plans are briefly described in the following paragraphs.

Single-Sampling Plans.   In a single-sampling plan, one random sample is drawn from each lot, and every item in the sample is examined and classified as either "good" or "defective." If any sample contains more than a specified number of defectives, c, that lot is rejected.

Double-Sampling Plans.   A double-sampling plan allows for the opportunity to take a second sample if the results of the initial sample are inconclusive. For example, if the quality of the initial sample is high, the lot can be accepted without need for a second sample. If the quality in the initial sample is poor, sampling can also be terminated and the lot rejected. For results between those two cases, a second sample must be taken and the items inspected, after which the lot is either accepted or rejected on the basis of the evidence obtained from both samples. A double-sampling plan specifies the lot size, the size of the initial sample, accept/reject criteria for the initial sample (e.g., $c_1 = 2$, $c_2 = 5$: if two or fewer defectives are found, accept the lot; if more than five defectives are found, reject the lot; and if three, four, or five defectives are found, take a second sample), the size of the second sample, and a single acceptance number (e.g., $c_3 = 6$: accept the lot if the total number of defectives found in both samples is six or fewer; otherwise, reject the lot).

Multiple-Sampling Plans.   Multiple-sampling plans are very similar to double-sampling plans, except that more than two samples may be required. A sampling plan will specify each sample size and two limits for each sample. The values increase with the number of samples. If, for any sample, the cumulative number of defectives found (i.e., those in the present sample plus those found in all previous samples) exceeds the upper limit specified for that sample, sampling is terminated and the lot is rejected. If the cumulative number of defectives is less than or equal to the lower limit, sampling is terminated and the lot is passed. If the number is between the two limits, another sample is taken. The process continues until the lot is either accepted or rejected.

Choosing a Plan.   The cost and time required for inspection often dictate the kind of sampling plan used. The two primary considerations are the number of samples needed and the total number of observations required. Single-sampling plans involve only a single sample, but the sample size is large relative to the total number of observations taken under double- or multiple-sampling plans. In a situation where the cost to obtain a sample is relatively high compared to the cost of analyzing the observations, a single-sampling plan would be more desirable. For instance, if a sample of moon soil is needed, clearly the cost of returning for a second or third sample would far outweigh the cost of analyzing a single large sample. Conversely, in situations where item inspection costs are relatively high, such as destructive testing, it may be better to use double or multiple sampling, because the average number of items inspected per lot will be lower. This stems from the fact that if the lot quality is either very good or very poor, this will often show up initially, and sampling can be terminated.

Operating Characteristic Curve

An important feature of a sampling plan is how well it discriminates between lots of high quality and lots of low quality. The ability of a sampling plan to discriminate is described by its **operating characteristic (OC) curve.** A typical curve for a single-sampling plan is shown in Figure 16–8. The curve shows the probability that use of the sampling plan will result in lots with various *fractions defective* being accepted. For example, we can see from the graph that a lot with 3 percent of defectives (i.e., a fraction defective of .03) would have a probability of about .90 of being accepted (and, hence, a probability of $1.00 - .90 = .10$ of being rejected). Note that there is a downward relationship: as lot quality decreases, the probability of acceptance decreases, although the relationship is not linear. For instance, if a lot contains 20 percent defectives, the probability of acceptance drops to about .04.

It is interesting to note that even lots containing more than 20 percent defectives still have some probability of being accepted, whereas lots with as

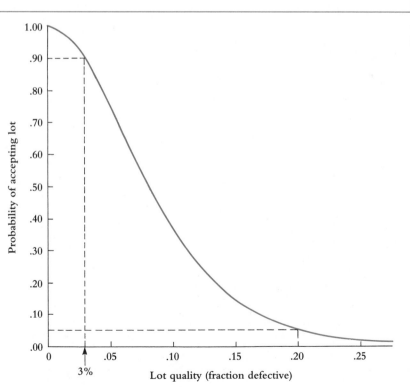

FIGURE 16–8

A typical OC curve for proportions

Probability of accepting lot

Lot quality (fraction defective)

3%

few as 3 percent defectives stand some chance of being rejected. In other words, a sampling plan does not provide prefect discrimination between good and bad lots; some low-quality lots will invariably be accepted, and some lots with very good quality will invariably be rejected.

The degree to which a sampling plan discriminates between good and bad lots is a function of the steepness of the graph's OC curve: the steeper the curve, the more discriminating the sampling plan. This is illustrated in Figure 16–9. Note the curve for an ideal plan (i.e., one that can discriminate perfectly between good and bad lots). In order achieve that, it would be necessary to inspect 100 percent of each lot. Obviously, if you are going to do that, theoretically *all* of the defectives can be eliminated (errors and boredom might result in a few defectives remaining). However, the point is that 100 percent inspection provides a perspective from which to view the OC curves of other sampling plans.

It should be noted that the cost and the time that would be needed to conduct 100 percent inspection often rule out 100 percent inspection, as does destructive testing, leaving acceptance sampling as the only viable alternative.

For these reasons, consumers are generally willing to accept lots that contain small percentages of defective items as "good," especially if the cost related to a few defectives is low. Often this percentage is in the neighborhood of 2 percent to 4 percent defective. This figure is known as the **acceptable quality level (AQL).** Because of the inability of random sampling to clearly

---

FIGURE 16–9

The steeper the OC curve, the more discriminating the sampling plan

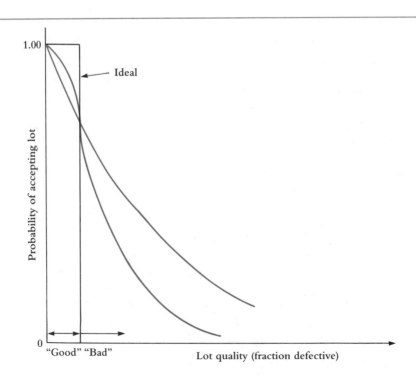

identify lots that contain more than this specified percentage of defectives, consumers recognize that some lots that actually contain more will be accepted. However, there is usually an upper limit on the percentage of defectives that a consumer is willing to tolerate in accepted lots. This is known as the **lot tolerance percent defective (LTPD).** Thus, the consumer would like quality equal to or better than the AQL, and is willing to live with some lots with quality as poor as the LTPD, but would prefer not to accept any lots that have a defective percentage that exceeds the LTPD. The probability that a lot containing defectives exceeding the LTPD will be accepted is known as the **consumer's risk,** or beta (β), or the probability of making a **Type II error;** the probability that a lot containing the acceptable quality level will be rejected is known as the **producer's risk,** alpha (α), or the probability of making a **Type I error.** Many sampling plans are designed so that they have a producer's risk of 5 percent and a consumer's risk of 10 percent; although other combinations are also used. It is possible to use trial and error to design a plan that will provide selected values for alpha and beta given the AQL and the LTPD. However, standard references such as the government MIL-STD tables are widely used to obtain sample sizes and acceptance criteria for sampling plans. Figure 16–10 illustrates an OC curve with the AQL, LTPD, producer's risk, and consumer's risk.

FIGURE 16–10

The AQL indicates "good" lots, and the LTPD indicates "bad" lots

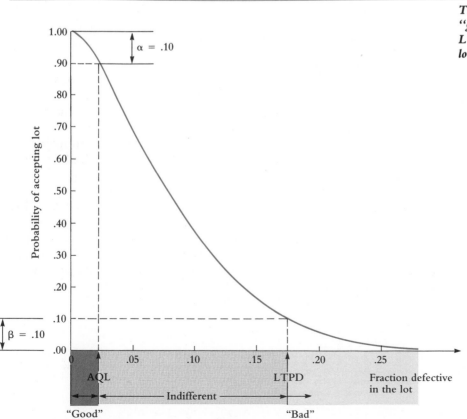

A certain amount of insight can be gained by actually constructing an OC curve. Suppose we want the curve for a situation in which a sample of $n = 10$ items is drawn from lots containing $N = 2,000$ items, and a lot is accepted if no more than $c = 1$ defective is found. Because the sample size is small relative to the lot size, it is reasonable to use the binomial distribution to obtain the probabilities that a lot will be accepted for various lot qualities.[3] A portion of the cumulative binomial table found in Appendix B, Table D is reproduced below to facilitate the discussion.

						Fraction defective, p						
n	x	.05	.10	.15	.20	.25	.30	.35	.40	.45	.50	.55	.60
10 ... 0	.5987	.3487	.1969	.1074	.0563	.0282	.0135	.0060	.0025	.0010	.0003	.0001
1	.9139	.7361	.5443	.3758	.2440	.1493	.0860	.0464	.0233	.0107	.0045	.0017
2	.9885	.9298	.8202	.6778	.5256	.3828	.2616	.1673	.0996	.0547	.0274	.0123
3	.9990	.9872	.9500	.8791	.7759	.6496	.5138	.3823	.2660	.1719	.1020	.0548

$c = 1 \rightarrow$ (row for x = 1)

To use the table, select various lot qualities (values of p listed across the top of the table), beginning with .05, and find the probability that a lot with that percentage of defectives would be accepted (i.e., the probability of finding zero or one defective in this case). Hence, for $p = .05$, the probability of one or no defectives is .9139. For a lot with 10 percent defectives (i.e., a fraction defective of .10), the probability of one or fewer defectives drops to .7361, and for 15 percent defectives, the probability of acceptance is .5443. In effect, we simply read the probabilities across the row for $c = 1$. By plotting these points (e.g., .05 and .9139, .10 and .7361) on a graph and connecting them, we obtain the OC curve illustrated in Figure 16–11.

When $n > 20$ and $p < .05$, the Poisson distribution is useful in constructing operating characteristic curves for proportions. In effect, the Poisson distribution is used to approximate the binomial distribution. The Poisson approximation involves treating the mean of the binomial distribution (i.e., np) as the mean of the Poisson (i.e., μ):

$$\mu = np \tag{16–1}$$

As with the binomial distribution, various values of lot quality, p, are selected, and the probability of accepting a lot (i.e., finding two or fewer defectives) is determined by referring to the cumulative Poisson table. Values of p in increments of .01 are often used in this regard. The following example illustrates this use of the Poisson table.

---

[3] Since sampling is generally done "without replacement," if the ratio n/N is 5 percent or more, the hypergeometric distribution would be more appropriate since the probability of finding a defective would vary from observation to observation. We shall only consider the more general case of the binomial distribution (i.e., for $n/N < 5$ percent).

FIGURE 16–11

OC curve for n = 10, c = 1

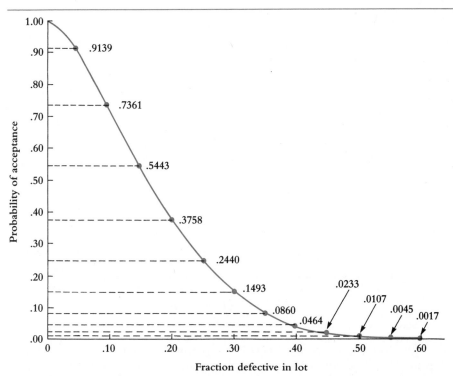

Fraction defective in lot

EXAMPLE 1

Use the cumulative Poisson table to construct an OC curve for this sampling plan:

$$N = 5{,}000$$
$$n = 80$$
$$c = 2$$

Solution

Selected values of p	$\mu = np$	P_{ac} [P(x ≤ 2) from Appendix B, Table C]
.01	80(.01) = 0.8	.953
.02	80(.02) = 1.6	.783
.03	80(.03) = 2.4	.570
.04	80(.04) = 3.2	.380
.05	80(.05) = 4.0	.238
.06	80(.06) = 4.8	.143
.07	80(.07) = 5.6	.082
.08	80(.08) = 6.4	.046

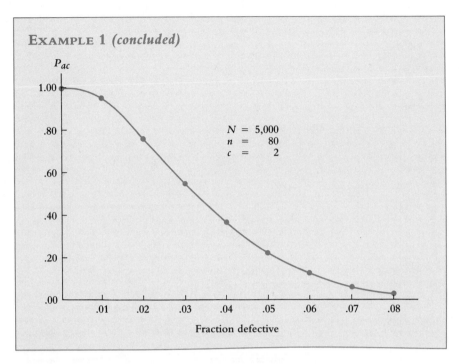

EXAMPLE 1 *(concluded)*

$N = 5{,}000$
$n = 80$
$c = 2$

Operating characteristic curves can be constructed for variables sampling plans as well as for attributes sampling plans. It is beyond the scope of this presentation to go into detail on this. The purpose here is merely to illustrate the concept of an OC curve and to show how its construction is based on an underlying *sampling distribution*.

Average Quality of Inspected Lots

An interesting feature of acceptance sampling is that the level of inspection automatically adjusts to the quality of lots being inspected, assuming rejected lots are subjected to 100 percent inspection. The OC curve reveals that the greater the percentage of defectives in a lot, the less likely the lot is to be accepted. Generally speaking, good lots have a high probability of being accepted, and bad lots have a low probability of being accepted. If the lots being inspected are mostly good, few will end up going through 100 percent inspection. But the poorer the quality of the lots, the greater the number of lots that will come under closer scrutiny. This tends to improve overall quality of lots by weeding out defectives. In this way, the level of inspection is affected by lot quality.

If all lots have some given percentage of defectives, p, the *average outgoing quality* (AOQ) of the lots can be computed using the following formula, assuming defectives are replaced with good items.

$$AOQ = P_{ac} \times p \left(\frac{N - n}{N} \right) \qquad (16\text{--}2)$$

where

P_{ac} = Probability of accepting the lot
p = Fraction defective
N = Lot size
n = Sample size

In practice, the last term is often omitted since it is usually close to 1.0 and therefore has little effect on the resulting values. The formula becomes:

$$AOQ = P_{ac} \times p \qquad (16\text{--}3)$$

Use this formula instead of the preceding one for computing AOQ values.

By allowing the percentage, p, to vary, a curve such as the one in the following example can be constructed in the same way that an OC curve is constructed. The curve illustrates the point that if lots are very good or very bad, the average outgoing quality will be high. The maximum point on the curve becomes apparent in the process of calculating values for the curve.

EXAMPLE 2

Construct the AOQ curve for this situation:

$$N = 500, \qquad n = 10, \qquad c = 1$$

Solution

Let values of p vary from .05 to .50 in steps of .05. The probabilities of acceptance, P_{ac}, can be read from Appendix B, Table D.

$$AOQ = P_{ac} \times p$$

p	P_{ac}	AOQ
.05	.9139	.046
.10	.7361	.074
.15	.5443	.082
.20	.3758	.075
.25	.2440	.061
.30	.1493	.045
.35	.0860	.030
.40	.0464	.019

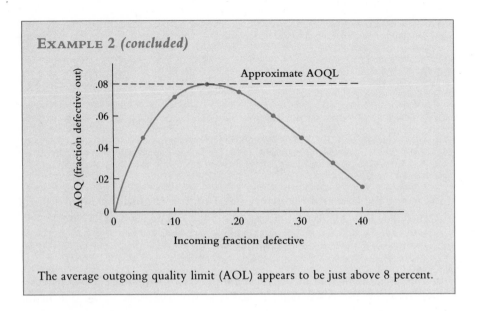

EXAMPLE 2 *(concluded)*

The average outgoing quality limit (AOL) appears to be just above 8 percent.

PROCESS CONTROL

Process control is concerned with assuring that *future* output is acceptable. Toward that end, periodic samples of process output are taken and evaluated. If the output is acceptable, the process is allowed to continue; if the output is not acceptable, the process is stopped, and corrective action is instituted. The primary tool of evaluation is the control chart.

The Control Process

The basic elements of control are the same whether the intent is to control quality, costs, personnel, accidents, or anything else. In each case, effective control requires these steps:

1. Define.
2. Measure.
3. Compare to a standard.
4. Evaluate.
5. Take corrective action if necessary.
6. Evaluate corrective action.

Define in as much detail as possible what it is that is to be controlled. It is not sufficient, for example, to simply refer to a painted surface. The paint can have a number of characteristics that might be of interest, such as its thickness, resistance to fading or chipping, and hardness. Different characteristics may require different approaches for control purposes.

Only those characteristics that can be counted or measured are candidates for control. Thus, it is important to consider how measurement will be accomplished.

There must be a standard of comparison that can be used to evaluate the measurements. This will relate to the level of quality being sought.

A definition of *out of control* must be established. Even a process that is functioning as it should will not yield output that conforms exactly to a standard, simply because of the natural (i.e., random) variations that are inherent in all processes, whether they are manual or mechanical. In other words, a certain amount of variation is inevitable. The main task of quality assurance is to distinguish random from nonrandom variability, because nonrandom variability means that a process is out of control.

In the event that a process is judged to be out of control, corrective action must be taken. This involves uncovering the cause of nonrandom variability (worn equipment, incorrect methods being used, failure to follow specified procedures, and so on).

To ensure that corrective action is effective, it is necessary to closely monitor the output of a process for a sufficient period of time to verify that the problem has been eliminated.

In a nutshell, control is achieved by inspecting a portion of the goods or services, comparing the results to a predetermined standard, evaluating departures from the standard, taking corrective action when necessary, and following up to insure that problems have been corrected.

Variations and Control

All processes that provide a good or a service exhibit a certain amount of variation that is inherent or "natural" in their output. The variations are created by the combined influences of countless minor factors, each one so unimportant that even if it could be identified and eliminated, the decrease in process variability would be negligible. In effect, this natural or inherent variability cannot be reduced—the operations manager must learn to live with it. It is often referred to as *random* or **chance variability.** The amount of inherent variability differs from process to process. For instance, older machines generally exhibit a higher degree of natural variability than newer machines, partly because of worn parts and partly because newer machines may incorporate design improvements, which lessen variability.

A second kind of variability is called **assignable variation.** Unlike natural variation, the main sources of assignable variation can usually be identified (assigned to a specific cause) and eliminated. Such factors as tool wear, equipment that needs adjustment, defective materials, and human factors (carelessness, fatigue, failure to follow correct procedures, and so on) are commonly encountered sources of assignable variation.

In terms of quality control, a process that exhibits only random variability is said to be statistically *in control,* and one that exhibits nonrandom (i.e., assignable) variations is said to be *out of control*. The objective of quality control is to distinguish the two kinds of variations so that appropriate corrective action can be taken when necessary to insure desirable future output. Thus, if a process exhibits nonrandom variations, that is an indication of a probable need for corrective action.

Control Charts

Control charts are graphical tools used to differentiate random and nonrandom process output. There are different kinds of control charts (e.g., for means, for ranges) for different kinds of situations. Each kind of chart is constructed in a slightly different way. However, on the surface they are quite similar. Each chart has a center line, which represents the process average, and upper and lower lines, called **control limits,** which define the range of random output. Use of the charts involves taking periodic samples, computing the appropriate sample statistic (e.g., sample mean for a mean chart, sample range for a range chart), and plotting that value on the chart. Values that fall within the control limits suggest (but do not prove) that the process is in control (i.e., process variations are random), whereas one or more values on or outside of the control limits suggests the process is out of control (i.e., process variations are nonrandom). For example, consider the control chart for means illustrated in Figure 16–12. Because all of the sample means fall within the control limits, it appears the process is statistically stable, or "in control." A second means chart is illustrated in Figure 16–13. Unlike the previous one, this chart has a sample mean that is beyond the upper control limit, which suggests that the process is not "in control."

Underlying every control chart is a related sampling distribution (based on sample size and type of data—e.g., means) that indicates the extent to which sample statistics such as the mean or range will tend to vary from the process average solely as a result of chance. In effect, the sampling distribution provides a *standard of comparison* against which sample statistics can be judged: those that fall within the bounds (control limits) of the sampling distribution

FIGURE 16–12

Since all of the sample means are within the control limits, it appears that the process is performing properly

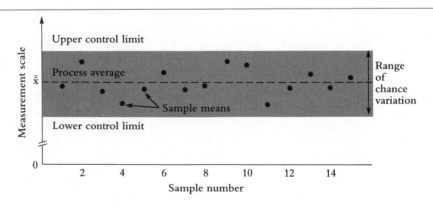

FIGURE 16–13

The process is out of control

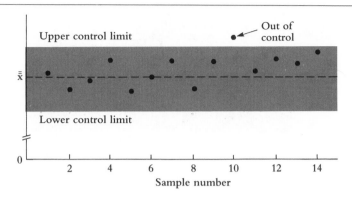

suggest randomness, and those beyond the bounds suggest nonrandom output.

We shall consider four commonly used control charts: mean, range, percent defective, and number of defects. The first two pertain to variables, and the last two pertain to attribute or count data. Recall that variables generate continuous data (e.g., thickness, length, weight) and that use of attribute data involves counting the number of occurrences in a sample (e.g., five defectives in a sample of 200).

Control Charts for Variables

Mean and range charts are used to monitor variables. Control charts for means reflect the *central tendency* of a process, and control charts for the range reflect process dispersion.

Mean Charts.   **Mean control charts,** or $\overline{x}$ (*x*-bar) charts, are based on a normal distribution. The theoretical foundation for this is the **central limit theorem,** which states roughly that the distribution of sample means taken from a process will be normal if the process distribution is normal, and it will be approximately normal even if the process is nonnormal, if the sample size is large enough. In most cases, a sample size of 30 is large enough, and often sample sizes in the range of 10 to 20 observations will suffice. Not only is the sampling distribution of the means normal, but its variability is also less than the variability of the process being sampled. These concepts are illustrated in Figure 16–14.

Control limits are based on the sampling distribution, and in effect, each sample mean plotted on a control chart represents a test of whether the process mean has shifted (see Figure 16–15).

In selecting control limits, it is important to recognize that just because all observations are within the limits, this does not guarantee that assignable variations are not present, and that just because an observation appears outside one of the control limits, this does not guarantee that assignable variations are

FIGURE 16–14

The sampling distribution of means is normal, and it has less variability than the process

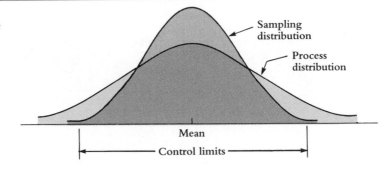

present. For example, if two-sigma limits are used, 95.5 percent of the sample means should be within the limits and 4.5 percent should be outside of the limits, when *only* random variations are present. Using wider limits (e.g., three-sigma limits) will reduce the risk of concluding that the process is out of control when in fact only random variations account for points outside the control limits. However, wider limits make it more difficult to detect nonrandom variations when they occur. Thus, the process average might shift (assignable cause of variation) enough to be readily apparent at the two-sigma level but not at the three-sigma level. Hence, the risk with wide limits is that assignable variations may go unnoticed. Concluding a process is out of control when it really isn't is called a *Type I error,* and concluding it is in control when it isn't is called a *Type II error.* In theory, the costs of these two kinds of error should be balanced in the selection of control limits. However, in practice either two- or three-sigma limits are commonly used, mainly because of the difficulties associated with determining what probability of a Type II error is appropriate.

If the process mean and standard deviation are known (there may be considerable historical data on which to base these values), control limits can

FIGURE 16–15

Each observation on a control chart tests whether the process average has changed

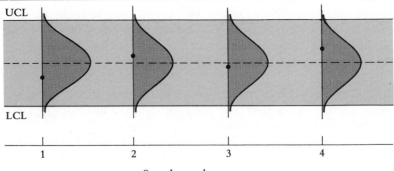

be computed using these formulas:

$$\text{Upper control limit (UCL): } = \mu + z\sigma_{\bar{x}}$$
$$\text{Lower control limit (LCL): } = \mu - z\sigma_{\bar{x}}$$ (16—4)

where $\sigma_{\bar{x}} = \sigma/\sqrt{n}$

and

$\sigma_{\bar{x}}$ = Standard deviation of distribution of sample means
σ = Process standard deviation
n = Sample size
z = Standard normal deviate
μ = Process mean

The following example illustrates the use of these formulas.

EXAMPLE 3

A process for making aluminum rods has a mean of 2 centimeters. The process variability is approximately normal and has a standard deviation of 0.1 centimeter. Determine control limits that will include 99.74 percent of sample means if the process is generating random output for:

1. $n = 16$.
2. $n = 25$.

Solution

$\mu = 2$ cm, $\quad \sigma = 0.1$ cm, $\quad z = 3$ (from Appendix B, Table A)
$\text{UCL} = \mu + z(\sigma/\sqrt{n})$
$\text{LCL} = \mu - z(\sigma/\sqrt{n})$

1. $n = 16$: UCL $= 2 + 3(0.1/\sqrt{16}) = 2 + 0.075 = 2.075$
   LCL $= 2 - 3(0.1/\sqrt{16}) = 2 - 0.075 = 1.925$
2. $n = 25$: UCL $= 2 + 3(0.1/\sqrt{25}) = 2 + 0.06 = 2.06$
   LCL $= 2 - 3(0.1/\sqrt{25}) = 2 - 0.06 = 1.94$

Note that increasing the sample size results in control limits that are closer to the process mean.

If the process mean and/or process standard deviation are unknown, two alternative approaches are available. One is to substitute *sample estimates* of the unknown parameters in Formula 16—4. For instance, if the mean of the process is unknown, the average of the sample means, $\bar{\bar{x}}$, can be used in its place. Similarly, if the process standard deviation is unknown, the sample standard deviation can be used in its place.

TABLE 16—3

Factors for three-sigma control limits for $\bar{x}$ and R charts

Number of observations in subgroup, *n*	Factor for $\bar{x}$ chart, A_2	Factors for R chart	
		Lower control limit, D_3	Upper control limit, D_4
2	1.88	0	3.27
3	1.02	0	2.57
4	0.73	0	2.28
5	0.58	0	2.11
6	0.48	0	2.00
7	0.42	0.08	1.92
8	0.37	0.14	1.86
9	0.34	0.18	1.82
10	0.31	0.22	1.78
11	0.29	0.26	1.74
12	0.27	0.28	1.72
13	0.25	0.31	1.69
14	0.24	0.33	1.67
15	0.22	0.35	1.65
16	0.21	0.36	1.64
17	0.20	0.38	1.62
18	0.19	0.39	1.61
19	0.19	0.40	1.60
20	0.18	0.41	1.59

Source: Adapted from Eugene Grant and Richard Leavenworth, *Statistical Quality Control,* 5th ed. (New York: McGraw-Hill, 1980).

A second approach is to use the sample *range* as a measure of process variability. The appropriate formulas for control limits are:

$$\text{UCL} = \bar{\bar{x}} + A_2 \bar{R}$$
$$\text{LCL} = \bar{\bar{x}} - A_2 \bar{R} \qquad (16\text{--}5)$$

Values of A_2 can be obtained from Table 16–3.

EXAMPLE 4

Twenty samples of $n = 8$ have been taken from a milling process. The average sample range for the 20 samples was 0.016 centimeters, and the average mean was 3 centimeters. Determine three-sigma control limits for this process.

EXAMPLE 4 *(concluded)*

Solution

$\overline{\overline{x}} = 3$ cm, $\overline{R} = 0.016$, $A_2 = 0.37$ for $n = 8$ (from Table 16–3)

$$\text{UCL} = \overline{\overline{x}} + A_2\overline{R} = 3 + 0.37(0.016) = 3.006 \text{ cm}$$
$$\text{LCL} = \overline{\overline{x}} - A_2\overline{R} = 3 - 0.37(0.016) = 2.994 \text{ cm}$$

Note that this approach assumes that the range is in control.

Range Charts.   **Range control charts** are used to monitor process variability; they are sensitive to changes in process dispersion. Although the underlying sampling distribution is not normal, the concepts for use of range charts are much the same as those for use of means charts. Control limits for range charts are found using the average sample range in conjunction with the formulas:

$$\text{UCL}_R = D_4\overline{R}$$
$$\text{LCL}_R = D_3\overline{R} \qquad (16\text{–}6)$$

where values of D_3 and D_4 are obtained from Table 16–3.

EXAMPLE 5

Twenty-five samples of $n = 10$ observations have been taken from a milling process. The average sample range was 0.01 centimeter. Determine upper and lower control limits for sample ranges.

Solution

$$\overline{R} = 0.01 \text{ cm}, \qquad n = 10$$

From Table 16–3, for $n = 10$, $D_4 = 1.78$ and $D_3 = 0.22$.

$$\text{UCL}_R = 1.78(0.01) = 0.0178 \text{ or } 0.018$$
$$\text{LCL}_R = 0.22(0.01) = 0.0022 \text{ or } 0.002$$

In the preceding example, a sample range of 0.018 centimeters or more would suggest that the process variability had increased. A sample range of 0.002 or less would imply that the process variability had decreased. In the former case, this would mean that the process was producing too much variation and we would want to investigate this in order to remove the cause of variation. In the latter instance, even though decreased variability is desirable, we would want to determine what was causing it. Perhaps an improved method has been used, in which case we would want to identify it. Possibly the improved quality has come at the expense of productivity, which would not generally be desirable. Or this may only be a random occurrence; we would expect these about 1 percent of the time. Hence, it can be beneficial to investigate points beyond the lower limit as well as the upper limit in a range chart.

Using Mean and Range Charts.   Mean control charts and range control charts provide different perspectives on a process. Mean charts are sensitive to shifts in the process mean, whereas range charts are sensitive to changes in

FIGURE 16–16

Mean and range charts used together complement each other

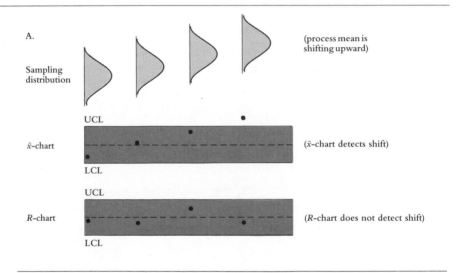

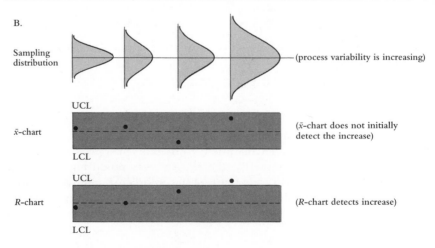

process dispersion. Because of the difference in perspective, both types of charts might be used to monitor the same process. The logic of using both is readily apparent in Figure 16–16. In diagram A, the mean chart picks up the shift in the process mean, but because the dispersion is not changing, the range chart fails to indicate a problem. Conversely, in diagram B, a change in process dispersion is less apt to be detected by the mean chart than by the range chart. Hence, use of both charts provides more complete information than either chart alone. Even so, in some cases, a single chart may suffice. For example, a process may be more susceptible to changes in the process mean than it is to changes in dispersion, so it might not be necessary to monitor dispersion. Because of the time and cost involved in constructing control charts, gathering the necessary data, and evaluating the results, only those aspects of a process that have a tendency to cause problems should be monitored.

Once control charts have been set up, they can serve as a basis for deciding when to interrupt a process and search for assignable causes of variation. To determine initial control limits, the following procedure can be used:

1. Obtain 20 to 25 samples. Compute the appropriate sample statistic(s) for each sample (e.g., mean).
2. Establish preliminary control limits using the formulas and graph them.
3. Plot the sample statistics on the control chart(s), and note if any points fall outside of the control limits.
4. If all points are within limits, assume that the process is in control. If not, investigate and correct assignable causes of variation. Then discard those points for which assignable causes have been found and recompute the control limits, or resume the process and collect another set of observations upon which control limits can be based.

Control Charts for Attributes

Control charts for attributes are used when the process characteristic is *counted* rather than measured. For example, the number of defective items in a sample would be counted, whereas the length of each item would be measured. There are two types of attribute control charts, one for the percentage of defective items in a sample (a *p*-chart) and one for the number of defects (called a *c*-chart). A *p*-chart is appropriate when both the defectives and nondefectives can be counted. For instance, if glass bottles are inspected for chipping and cracking, both the good bottles and the defective ones can be counted. However, one can count the number of accidents that occur during a given period of time but *not* the number of accidents that did not occur. Similarly, one can count the number of scratches on a polished surface, the number of bacteria present in a water sample, and the number of crimes committed during the month of August, but one cannot count the number of nonoccurences. In such cases, a *c*-chart is appropriate.

p-**Chart.** A *p*-**chart** is used to monitor the proportion of defectives generated by a process. The theoretical basis for a *p*-chart is the binomial distribution, although for large sample sizes, the normal distribution provides a good approximation to it. Conceptually, a *p*-chart is constructed and used in much the same way as a mean chart.

The center line on a *p*-chart is the average fraction defective in the population, *p*. The standard deviation of the sampling distribution when *p* is known is:

$$\sigma_p = \sqrt{\frac{p\,(1 - p)}{n}}$$

Control limits are computed using the formulas:

$$UCL_p = p + z\sigma_p$$
$$LCL_p = p - z\sigma_p$$

(16–7)

If *p* is unknown, it can be estimated from samples. That estimate, $\bar{p}$, replaces *p* in the preceding formulas, as illustrated in the following example.

EXAMPLE 6

Using the following information, construct a control chart that will describe 95.5 percent of the chance variation in the process when the process is in control. Each sample contains 100 items.

Sample	Number of defectives	Sample	Number of defectives
1	14	11	8
2	10	12	12
3	12	13	9
4	13	14	10
5	9	15	11
6	11	16	10
7	10	17	8
8	12	18	12
9	13	19	10
10	10	20	16
			220

Solution

z for 95.5% is 2.00 (from Appendix B, Table A).

$$\bar{p} = \frac{\text{Total number of defectives}}{\text{Total number of observations}} = \frac{220}{20(100)} = .11$$

EXAMPLE 6 *(concluded)*

$$\hat{\sigma}_p = \sqrt{\frac{\bar{p}(1 - \bar{p})}{n}} = \sqrt{\frac{.11(1 - .11)}{100}} = .03$$

Control limits are:

$$UCL_p = \bar{p} + z\,(\hat{\sigma}_p) = .11 + 2.00(.03) = .17$$
$$LCL_p = \bar{p} - z\,(\hat{\sigma}_p) = .11 - 2.00(.03) = .05$$

Plotting the control limits and the sample percentages, we can see that the process is initially in control, although the last point is close to the upper limit.

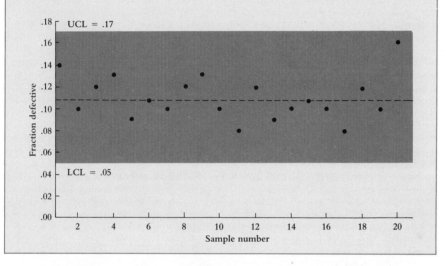

If the computed LCL is negative, use zero as the lower limit.

c-Chart.   When the goal is to control the number of defects per unit, a *c-chart* is used. Units might be automobiles, hotel rooms, typed pages, or rolls of carpet. The underlying sampling distribution is the Poisson distribution. Use of the Poisson distribution assumes that defects occur over some *continuous* region and that the probability of more than one defect at any particular spot is negligible. The mean number of defects per unit is *c,* and the standard deviation is $\sqrt{c}$. For practical reasons, the normal approximation to the Poisson is used. The control limits are:

$$UCL_c = c + z\sqrt{c}$$
$$LCL_c = c - z\sqrt{c} \tag{16-8}$$

If the process average is unknown, it can be estimated from sample data, using $\bar{c}$ = Number of defects/Number of samples.

EXAMPLE 7

Rolls of coiled wire are monitored using a *c*-chart. Eighteen rolls have been examined, and the number of defects per roll has been recorded in the following table. Is the process in control? Plot the values on a control chart that uses $z = 2$.

Sample	Number of defects	Sample	Number of defects
1	3	10	1
2	2	11	3
3	4	12	4
4	5	13	2
5	1	14	4
6	2	15	2
7	4	16	1
8	1	17	3
9	2	18	1
			45

Solution

$$\bar{c} = 45/18 = 2.5$$
$$\text{UCL}_c = \bar{c} + 2\sqrt{\bar{c}} = 2.5 + 2\sqrt{2.5} = 5.66$$
$$\text{LCL}_c = \bar{c} - 2\sqrt{\bar{c}} = 2.5 - 2\sqrt{2.5} = -0.66 \rightarrow 0$$

When the computed lower control limit is negative, the effective lower limit is zero, since negative observations cannot occur. (The reason the calculation sometimes produces a negative lower limit is due to the use of the normal distribution to approximate the Poisson distribution: the normal is symmetrical whereas the Poisson is not symmetrical when $\bar{c}$ is close to zero.)

Tolerances, Control Limits, and Process Variability

There are three commonly used terms that refer to the variability of process output. Each term relates to a slightly different aspect of that variability, so it is important to differentiate these terms.

Tolerances are specifications established by engineering design or customer requirements. They indicate a range of values in which individual units of output must fall in order to be acceptable.

Control limits are statistical limits that reflect the extent to which *sample statistics* such as means and ranges can vary due to randomness alone.

Process variability reflects the natural or inherent variability in a process. It is also referred to as **process capability.**

Control limits and process variability are directly related: control limits are based on sampling variability, and sampling variability is a function of process variability. This relationship can be seen in the way control limits are calculated. For example, control limits for an $\bar{x}$-chart are computed using the formula:

$$\text{Control limits} = \frac{\text{Process}}{\text{mean}} \pm z \frac{\text{Process variability}}{\sqrt{n}}$$

On the other hand, there is no direct link between tolerances and either control limits or process variability. Tolerances are specified in terms of a product or service, not in terms of the *process* by which the product of service is generated. Hence, in a given instance, the output of a process may or may not conform to specifications, even though the process may be statistically "in control." For example, consider the three cases illustrated in Figure 16–17. In the first case, process capability and output specifications are well matched, so that nearly all of the process output can be expected to meet the specifications. In the second case, the process variability is much less than what is called for, so that virtually 100 percent of the output should be within tolerance. However, in the third case, the specifications are tighter than what the process is capable of, so that even when the process is functioning as it should, a sizable percentage of the output will fail to meet the specifications. In other words, in the third case, the process could be "in control" and still be generating unacceptable output. Thus, we cannot automatically assume that a stable process will provide desired output. Instead, we must specifically check to see if a process is *capable* of meeting specifications, and not simply set up a control chart to monitor it. A process should be in control and within specifications

FIGURE 16–17

Process capability and specifications may or may not match

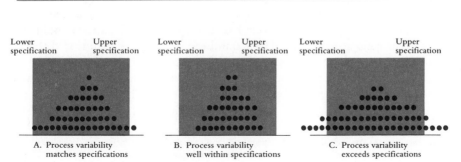

A. Process variability matches specifications

B. Process variability well within specifications

C. Process variability exceeds specifications

before production begins. In essence, "Set the toaster right at the start. Don't burn the toast and then scrape it!"

Run Tests

When a process is stable, or in statistical control, the output it generates will exhibit natural variability over a period of time. The presence of patterns, such as trends, cycles, or bias in the output, indicates that assignable, or nonrandom, causes of variation exist. Hence, a process that produces output with such patterns is not in a state of statistical control. This is true even though all of the points on a control chart may be within the control limits. For this reason, it is usually prudent to subject control chart data to run tests to determine if patterns can be detected.

A **run** is defined as a sequence of observations with a certain characteristic, followed by one or more observations with a different characteristic. The characteristic can be anything that is observable. For example, in the series A A A B, there are two runs: a run of three As followed by a run of one B. Underlining each run helps in counting them. In the series A̲ A̲ B̲ B̲ B̲ A̲, there are three runs, as indicated by the underlining.

Two useful run tests involve examination of the number of runs *up and down* and the number of runs with respect to the *median*.[4] In order to count these runs, first transform the data into a series of Us and Ds (for "up" and "down") and into a series of As and Bs (for "above" and "below" the median). Consider the following sequence, which has a median of 36.5. With respect to the median, the first two values are below it, the second two are above it, the second to last is below, and the last is above. Thus, there are four runs:

$$\begin{array}{cccccc} 25 & 29 & 42 & 40 & 35 & 38 \\ \underline{B} & \underline{B} & \underline{A} & \underline{A} & \underline{B} & \underline{A} \end{array}$$

In terms of up and down, there are three runs in the same data. The second value is up from the first value, the third is up from the second, the fourth value is down from the third, and so on.

$$\begin{array}{cccccc} 25 & 29 & 42 & 40 & 35 & 38 \\ - & \underline{U} & \underline{U} & \underline{D} & \underline{D} & \underline{U} \end{array}$$

(The first value does not receive either a U or a D, since nothing precedes it.)

To determine if any patterns are present in control chart data, one must transform the data into both As and Bs and Us and Ds and then count the number of runs in each case. These numbers must then be compared to the number of runs that would be expected in a completely random series. For both the median and the up/down run tests, the expected number of runs is a function of the number of observations in the series. The formulas are:

---

[4] The median and mean are approximately equal for control charts. The use of the median depends on its ease of determination; use the mean instead of the median if it is given.

$$E(r)_{med} = \frac{N}{2} + 1 \qquad\qquad (16\text{--}9a)$$

$$E(r)_{u/d} = \frac{2N - 1}{3} \qquad\qquad (16\text{--}10a)$$

where N is the number of observations.

The actual number of runs in any given set of observations will vary from the expected number, due to chance and to any patterns that might be present. Chance variability is measured by the standard deviation of runs. The formulas are:

$$\sigma_{med} = \sqrt{\frac{N - 1}{4}} \qquad\qquad (16\text{--}9b)$$

$$\sigma_{u/d} = \sqrt{\frac{16N - 29}{90}} \qquad\qquad (16\text{--}10b)$$

Distinguishing chance variability from patterns requires use of the sampling distributions for median runs and for up/down runs. Both distributions are approximately normal. Consequently, we know, for instance, that 95.5 percent of the time a process that is random will produce an observed number of runs that is within two standard deviations of the expected number. If the observed number of runs falls in that range, we can conclude that there are probably no nonrandom patterns; for observed numbers of runs beyond such limits, we begin to suspect that patterns are present. Hence, either too few or too many runs can be an indication of nonrandomness.

In practice, it is often easiest to compute the number of standard deviations, z, by which an observed number of runs differs from the expected number. This z value would then be compared to the value ± 2 (z for 95.5 percent) or some other desired value (e.g., ± 1.96 for 95 percent, ± 2.33 for 98 percent). A test z that exceeds these limits indicates patterns are present. (See Figure 16–18.) The computation of z takes the form:

$$z_{test} = \frac{\text{Observed number of runs} - \text{Expected number of runs}}{\text{Standard deviation of number of runs}}$$

FIGURE 16–18

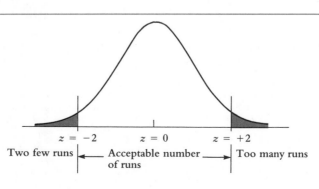

z = −2   z = 0   z = +2

Two few runs |← Acceptable number →| Too many runs
of runs

A sampling distribution for runs is used to distinguish chance variation from patterns

For the median and up/down tests, z is found using the formulas:

Median:
$$z = \frac{r - [(N/2) + 1]}{\sqrt{(N - 1)/4}}$$
(16–11)

Up and down:
$$z = \frac{r - [(2N - 1)/3]}{\sqrt{(16N - 29)/90}}$$
(16–12)

where

N = Total number of observations

r = Observed number of runs of either As and Bs or Us and Ds, depending on which test is involved.

It is desirable to apply both run tests to any given set of observations because each test is different in terms of the types of patterns it can detect. Sometimes both will pick up a certain pattern, but sometimes only one will detect nonrandomness. If either does, the implication is that some sort of nonrandomness is present in the data.

EXAMPLE 8

Twenty sample means have been taken from a process. The means are shown in the following table. Use median and up/down run tests with $z = 2$ to determine if assignable causes of variation are present. Assume the median is 11.0.

Solution

The means are marked according to above/below median and up/down. The solid lines represent the runs.

Sample	A/B	Mean	U/D	Sample	A/B	Mean	U/D
1	B	10.0	—	11	B	10.7	D
2	B	10.4	U	12	A	11.3	U
3	B	10.2	D	13	B	10.8	D
4	A	11.5	U	14	A	11.8	U
5	B	10.8	D	15	A	11.2	D
6	A	11.6	U	16	A	11.6	U
7	A	11.1	D	17	A	11.2	D
8	A	11.2	U	18	B	10.6	D
9	B	10.6	D	19	B	10.7	U
10	B	10.9	U	20	A	11.9	U

A/B: 10 runs   U/D: 17 runs

The expected number of runs for each test is:

$$E(r)_{med} = \frac{N}{2} + 1 = \frac{20}{2} + 1 = 11$$

EXAMPLE 8 *(concluded)*

$$E(r)_{u/d} = \frac{2N - 1}{3} = \frac{2(20) - 1}{3} = 13$$

The standard deviations are:

$$\sigma_{med} = \sqrt{\frac{N - 1}{4}} = \sqrt{\frac{20 - 1}{4}} = 2.18$$

$$\sigma_{u/d} = \sqrt{\frac{16N - 29}{90}} = \sqrt{\frac{16(20) - 29}{90}} = 1.80$$

The z_{test} values are:

$$z_{med} = \frac{10 - 11}{2.18} = -0.46$$

$$z_{u/d} = \frac{17 - 13}{1.80} = +2.22$$

Although the median test does not reveal any pattern, since its z_{test} value is less than ± 2, the up/down test does; its value exceeds $+2$. Consequently, we conclude that nonrandom variations are present in the data and, hence, that the process is not in control.

If ties occur in either test (e.g., a value equals the median, or two values in a row are the same), assign A/B or U/D in such a manner that z_{test} is as large as possible. If z_{test} still does not exceed ± 2 (± 1.96, etc.) then you can be reasonably confident that a conclusion of randomness is justified.

OPERATIONS STRATEGY

Emphasis on the quality of goods and services is increasingly becoming a part of business strategy. Over the years, quality efforts have evolved from focusing mainly on inspection, to quality control, and now to product and process design. Whereas initial efforts were aimed at *finding* poor quality, and then at *correcting* problems, much current effort is aimed at *preventing* problems. This shift in emphasis reflects the growing attitude that prevention is better than correction, and that the best approach is "right from the start."

Quality problems are not only costly to correct, they are disruptive to production. In just-in-time systems, such disruptions can easily negate the benefits of the system, which is why that approach places heavy emphasis on achieving high levels of product quality.

Quality has become a major element of competition, and consumers are becoming more quality conscious in making buying decisions.

It is perhaps obvious that businesses should formulate a strategy for quality and that all phases of the business should support that strategy. Moreover, if the strategy is to be successful, it must also have the complete and continuing support of top management. Beyond that, workers and managers should understand the importance of quality, they should be trained in the methods and concepts of quality assurance, they should be encouraged to offer suggestions for improvement of quality, and they should be instilled with the idea that quality is everyone's job. The challenge for operations management is to develop a strategy that achieves these goals. Part of this must be to identify and resolve problems as quickly as possible so that the damage caused by the problems is minimal.

SUMMARY

Quality assurance is a comprehensive approach to quality that begins with product or service design, continues through the transformation process, and extends to service after delivery.

Among other things, successful quality assurance depends on clear definition of what constitutes desired quality. This chapter discussed the definition of quality, the determinants of quality, problem solving, and potential sources of ideas for improving quality. The remainder of the chapter covered quality of conformance.

TABLE 16–4

Summary of quality assurance formulas

Acceptance sampling	$AOQ = P_{ac} \times p$

Control charts

Mean	Symbol	Control limits	
Mean	$\bar{x}$	$\mu \pm z\dfrac{\sigma}{\sqrt{n}}$	or $\quad \bar{\bar{x}} \pm A_2\bar{R}$
Range	R	$UCL = D_4\bar{R}, \qquad LCL = D_3\bar{R}$	
Percent defective	p	$p \pm z\sqrt{\dfrac{p(1-p)}{n}}$	
Number of defects	c	$c \pm z\sqrt{c}$	

Run tests

Name	Number of runs		Standard deviation	z
	Observed	Expected		
Median	r	$\dfrac{N}{2}+1$	$\sqrt{\dfrac{N-1}{4}}$	$\dfrac{r-[(N/2)+1]}{\sqrt{(N-1)/4}}$
Up/down	r	$\dfrac{2N-1}{3}$	$\sqrt{\dfrac{16N-29}{90}}$	$\dfrac{r-[2N-1)/3]}{\sqrt{(16N-29)/90}}$

The primary concern of quality control is the assurance that goods and services conform to standards. Quality control efforts are directed toward detecting departures from standards and instituting corrective or remedial action whenever it becomes necessary. Since it is not usually feasible to examine every single item, the task of identifying departures from standards relies on inspection of sampled items.

Quality control is largely based on statistical procedures. There are two main areas of quality control: acceptance sampling and process control. Acceptance sampling involves sampling previously produced output with the goal of deciding whether to pass or reject an entire lot. Operating characteristic curves can be used to describe the ability of a given sampling plan to discriminate between good and bad lots. Sampling plans exist for both variables and attributes. This chapter focused on single-sampling plans for percent defectives since they are widely used and easily understood.

Process control involves the monitoring of an ongoing process, partly to check on current quality, but primarily to determine if future output is likely to be acceptable. The main tool is the control chart, which is a statistical aid for distinguishing between random variations in output and those which can be traced to specific causes and eliminated. Four different control charts were described: means, ranges, fraction defectives, and number of defects. Control charts are based on sampling distributions that indicate the extent of chance or random variation. Run tests are sometimes used in conjunction with control charts to check for patterns in sample data that would suggest nonrandomness.

The formulas used in this chapter are summarized in Table 16–4.

KEY TERMS

acceptable quality level (AQL), 832
acceptance sampling, 829
assignable variation, 839
attributes, 829
brainstorming, 820
c-chart, 849
cause-and-effect diagram, 822
central limit theorem, 841
chance variability, 839
check sheet, 820
consumer's risk, 833
control charts, 840
control limits, 840, 851
fail-safe methods, 823
fishbone diagram, 822
lot tolerance percent defective
   (LTPD), 833
mean control chart, 841
operating characteristic (OC)
   curve, 831

Pareto analysis, 820
p-chart, 848
process capability, 851
process control, 838
process variability, 851
producer's risk, 833
quality, 808
quality assurance, 806
quality circles, 814
quality of conformance, 807
quality of design, 806
range control charts, 845
run, 852
sampling plans, 829
Taguchi methods, 824
tolerances, 851
Type I error, 833
Type II error, 833
variables, 829

SOLVED PROBLEMS

1. *Inspection.* A process for manufacturing shock absorbers for light trucks produces 5 percent defectives. Inspection cost per shock is $0.40, and 100 percent inspection generally catches all defectives, due to the nature of the inspection and the small volume produced. Any defectives installed on trucks must eventually be replaced at a cost of $12 per shock. Is 100 percent inspection justified?

Solution

Five percent of the output is defective. The expected cost per shock for replacement is thus 0.05($12) = 60 cents. Since this is greater than the inspection cost per shock of 40 cents, 100 percent inspection is justified.

2. *Acceptance sampling.* Shipments of 300 boxes of glassware are received at a warehouse of a large department store. Random samples of five boxes are checked, and the lot is rejected if more than one box reveals breakage. Construct the OC curve for this plan.

Solution

When the sample size is less than five percent of the lot size, the binomial distribution can be used to obtain P_{ac} for various lot percentages defective. Here, $n/N = 5/300 = .017$, so the binomial can be used. A portion of the cumulative binomial table is shown on this page and the next. Note that $c = 1$.

Cumulative binomial probabilities

	n	x	.05	.10	.15	.20	.25	.30
					p = *Fraction defective*			
	5 ...	0	.7738	.5905	.4437	.3277	.2373	.1681
$c = 1$ →		1	.9974	.9185	.8352	.7373	.6328	.5282
		2	.9988	.9914	.9734	.9421	.8965	.8369
		3	1.0000	.9995	.9978	.9933	.9844	.9692
		4	1.0000	1.0000	.9999	.9997	.9990	.9976
		5	1.0000	1.0000	1.0000	1.0000	1.0000	1.0000

The table indicates that $P_{ac} = .9974$ when lot quality is 5 percent defective, .9185 for 10 percent defective, .8352 for 15 percent, and so on. The resulting curve is:

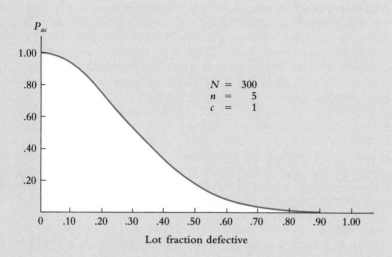

$$N = 300$$
$$n = 5$$
$$c = 1$$

3. Develop the AOQ curve for the previous problem.

.35	.40	.45	.50	.55	.60	.65	.70	.75	.80
.1160	.0778	.0503	.0313	.0185	.0102	.0053	.0024	.0010	.0003
.4284	.3370	.2562	.1875	.1312	.0870	.0540	.0308	.0156	.0067
.7648	.6826	.5931	.5000	.4069	.3174	.2352	.1631	.1035	.0579
.9460	.9130	.8688	.8125	.7438	.6630	.5716	.4718	.3672	.2627
.9947	.9898	.9815	.9688	.9497	.9222	.8840	.8319	.7627	.6723
1.0000	1.0000	1.0000	1.0000	1.0000	1.0000	1.0000	1.0000	1.0000	1.0000

Solution

$$AOQ = P_{ac} \times p$$

(Values of lot quality, p, are taken from the portion of the binomial table shown.)

p	P_{ac}	AOQ
.05	. . .9974	.050
.10	. . .9185	.092
.15	. . .8352	.125
.20	. . .7373	.147
.25	. . .6328	.158
.30	. . .5258	.158
.35	. . .4284	.150
.40	. . .3370	.135
.45	. . .2562	.115
.50	. . .1875	.094
.55	. . .1312	.072
.60	. . .0870	.052
.65	. . .0540	.035
.70	. . .0380	.027
.75	. . .0156	.012
.80	. . .0067	.005

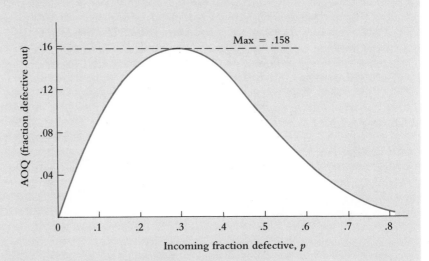

4. *Control chart for means when μ and σ are known.* An industrial process that makes 3-foot sections of plastic pipe produces pipe with an average inside diameter of 1 inch and a standard deviation of 0.05 inches.
   a. If one piece of pipe is randomly selected, what is the probability that its inside diameter will exceed 1.02 inches (assuming the population is normal).
   b. If a random sample of 25 pieces of pipe is selected, what is the probability that the sample *mean* will exceed 1.02 inches?

Solution

$$\mu = 1.00, \qquad \sigma = 0.05$$

$$a. \quad z = \frac{x - \mu}{\sigma} = \frac{1.02 - 1.00}{0.05} = 0.4$$

Using Appendix B, Table B, $P(x > z) = 1.0000 - .6554 = .3446$.

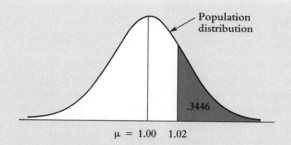

b. $z = \dfrac{\overline{x} - \mu}{\sigma/\sqrt{n}} = \dfrac{1.02 - 1.00}{0.05/\sqrt{25}} = 2.00$

Using Appendix B, Table B,

$$P(\overline{x} > z) = 1.0000 - .9772 = .0228$$

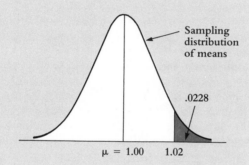

5. *Control charts for means and ranges when* μ *and* σ *are unknown.* Drop-forged steel handles have a designed weight of 10 ounces. Five samples of four observations each have been taken. Use the sample data in conjunction with Table 16–3 to construct upper and lower control limits for both a mean chart and a range chart. Is the process in control?

	Sample 1	Sample 2	Sample 3	Sample 4	Sample 5
	10.2	10.3	9.7	9.9	9.8
	9.9	9.8	9.9	10.3	10.2
	9.8	9.9	9.9	10.1	10.3
	10.1	10.4	10.1	10.5	9.7
Totals	40.0	40.4	39.6	40.8	40.0

Solution

a. Determine the mean and range of each sample.

$$\bar{x} = \frac{\Sigma x}{n}, \qquad \text{Range} = \text{Largest} - \text{Smallest}$$

Sample	Mean	Range
1	$40.0/4 = 10.0$	$10.2 - 9.8 = 0.4$
2	$40.4/4 = 10.1$	$10.4 - 9.8 = 0.6$
3	$39.6/4 = 9.9$	$10.1 - 9.7 = 0.4$
4	$40.8/4 = 10.2$	$10.5 - 9.9 = 0.6$
5	$40.0/4 = 10.0$	$10.3 - 9.7 = 0.6$

b. Compute the average mean and average range:

$$\bar{\bar{x}} = \frac{10.0 + 10.1 + 9.9 + 10.2 + 10.0}{5} = \frac{50.2}{5} = 10.04$$

$$\bar{R} = \frac{0.4 + 0.6 + 0.4 + 0.6 + 0.6}{5} = \frac{2.6}{5} = 0.52$$

c. Obtain factors A_2, D_4, and D_3 from Table 16–3 for $n = 4$:

$$A_2 = 0.73, \; D_4 = 2.28, \; D_3 = 0$$

d. Compute upper and lower limits:

$$\text{UCL}_{\bar{x}} = \bar{\bar{x}} + A_2\bar{R} = 10.04 + 0.73(0.52) = 10.42$$
$$\text{LCL}_{\bar{x}} = \bar{\bar{x}} - A_2\bar{R} = 10.04 - 0.73(0.52) = 9.66$$
$$\text{UCL}_R = D_4\bar{R} = 2.28(0.52) = 1.19$$
$$\text{LCL}_R = D_3\bar{R} = 0(0.52) = 0$$

e. Plot sample means and ranges on their respective control charts, or otherwise verify that points are within limits.

The smallest sample mean is 9.9, and the largest is 10.2. Both are well within the control limits. Similarly, the largest sample range is 0.6, which is also within the control limits. Hence, we conclude the process is in control. Note, however, that for illustrative purposes, the number of samples was deliberately small; 20 or more samples would give a clearer indication of control limits and whether the process was in control.

6. *Type I error (alpha risk).* After several investigations of points outside control limits revealed nothing, a manager began to wonder about the probability of a Type I error for the control limits being used ($z = 1.90$).

a. Determine the alpha risk for this value of z.

b. What z would provide an alpha risk of about 2 percent?

Solution

a. Using Appendix B, Table A, we find that the area under the curve between $z = 0$ and $z = +1.90$ is .4713. Therefore, the area (probability) of values *within* -1.90 to $+1.90$ is $2(.4713) = .9426$, and the area *beyond* these values is $1 - .9426 = .0574$.

b. The alpha risk (Type I error probability) is always specified as an *area* in the tail(s) of a distribution. With control charts, we are involved with two-sided control limits. Consequently, half of the risk lies in each tail. Hence, the area in the right tail is 1 percent, or .0100. This means that .4900 should be the area under the curve between $z = 0$ and the value of z we are looking for. The closest value is .4901 for $z = +2.33$. Thus, control limits based on $z = \pm 2.33$ would provide an alpha risk of about 2 percent.

7. p-*chart and* c-*chart*. Using the appropriate control chart, determine two-sigma control limits for each case:

a. An inspector found an average of 3.9 scratches in the exterior paint of each of the automobiles being prepared for shipment to dealers.

b. Before shipping lawnmowers to dealers, an inspector attempts to start each mower and notes any that do not start on the first try. The lot size is 100 mowers; and an average of 4 did not start (4 percent).

Solution

The choice between these two types of control chart relates to whether *two* types of results can be counted (*p*-chart) or whether *only occurrences* can be counted (*c*-chart).

a. The inspector can only count the scratches that occurred, not the ones that did not occur. Consequently, a *c*-chart is appropriate. Because the process average is unknown, the sample average of 3.9 scratches per car must be used. Two-sigma control limits are found using the formula:

$$\text{UCL} = \bar{c} + z\sqrt{\bar{c}}$$
$$\text{LCL} = \bar{c} - z\sqrt{\bar{c}}$$

where

$$\bar{c} = 3.9$$
$$z = 2$$

Thus,

$$UCL = 3.9 + 2\sqrt{3.9} = 7.85 \text{ scratches}$$
$$LCL = 3.9 - 2\sqrt{3.9} = -0.05 \text{ (0 scratches)}$$

(Note: Only round to zero if the lower limit is *negative*.)

b. The inspector can count both the lawnmowers that started and those that did not start. Consequently, a *p*-chart is appropriate. Because the process average is unknown, the sample average must be used. Two-sigma control limits can be computed using the following:

$$UCL = \bar{p} + z\sqrt{\frac{\bar{p}(1 - \bar{p})}{n}}$$

$$LCL = \bar{p} - z\sqrt{\frac{\bar{p}(1 - \bar{p})}{n}}$$

where

$$\bar{p} = .04$$
$$n = 100$$
$$z = 2$$

Thus,

$$UCL = .04 + 2\sqrt{\frac{0.04(.96)}{100}} = 0.079$$

$$LCL = .04 - 2\sqrt{\frac{.04(.96)}{100}} = 0.001$$

8. *Run tests.* The number of defectives per sample for 11 samples is shown below. Determine if nonrandom patterns are present in the sequence.

		Sample										
		1	*2*	*3*	*4*	*5*	*6*	*7*	*8*	*9*	*10*	*11*
Number of defectives		22	17	19	25	18	20	21	17	23	23	24

Solution

Since the median isn't given, it must be estimated from the sample data. To do this, array the data from low to high; the median is the middle value. (In this case, there are an odd number of values. For an even number of values, average the middle two to obtain the median.) Thus,

17 17 18 19 20 21 22 23 23 24 25
(5 below)   ↑   (5 above)
median

The median is 21.

Next, code the observations using A/B and U/D:

Sample	A/B	Number of defectives	U/D
1	|A	22	—
2	|B	17	|D
3	|B	19	|U
4	|A	25	|U
5	|B	18	|D
6	|B	20	|U
7	—	21	|U
8	|B	17	|D
9	|A	23	|U
10	|A	23	—
11	|A	24	|U

Note that with each test there are tied values. How these are resolved can affect the number of observed runs. Suppose we adhere to this rule: Assign a letter (A or B, U or D) in such a way that the resulting difference between the observed and expected number of runs is as large as possible. To accomplish this, it will be necessary to initially ignore ties and count the runs to see whether there are too many or too few. Then return to the ties and make the assignments. The rationale for this rule is that it is a conservative method for retaining data; if we can conclude the data are random using this approach, we can be reasonably confident that the data are random and that our method has not "created" randomness. With this in mind, assign a B to sample 7 since the expected number of runs is:

$$E(r)_{med} = N/2 + 1 = 11/2 + 1 = 6.5$$

and the difference between the resulting number of runs, 5, and 6.5 is greater than 6.5 and 7 (which occurs if A is used instead of B). Similarly, in the up/down test, a U for sample 10 produces 6 runs, whereas a D produces 8 runs. Since the expected number of runs is:

$$E(r)_{u/d} = (2N - 1)/3 = (22 - 1)/3 = 7$$

it makes no difference which one we use: they both yield a difference of 1. For the sake of illustration, suppose we assign a D.

The computations for the two tests are summarized below. Since neither test reveals nonrandomness, we conclude the data are random.

	Runs observed	$E(r)$	σ_r	z	Conclude
Median	5	6.5	1.58	-0.95	Random
Up/down	8	7.0	1.28	0.78	Random

DISCUSSION AND REVIEW QUESTIONS

1. Define the term *quality*, and explain why quality is important to most organizations.
2. What are the primary determinants of quality?
3. What are some sources of ideas for improving quality?
4. Explain the term *quality circle*, and list some of the potential benefits of quality circles.
5. For each item listed below, indicate how you would define quality.
   a. Family car.
   b. Lawn care.
   c. Tree.
   d. Answering service.
6. Inspection is an integral part of quality control.
   a. What level of inspection is optimal?
   b. What factors often guide the decision of how much to inspect?
   c. What are the main considerations in choosing between centralized on on-site inspection?
   d. What points are potential candidates for inspection?
7. What is meant by the term *fitness for use?*
8. How are quality and productivity related?
9. Compare and contrast design quality and quality of conformance.
10. What is the objective of acceptance sampling?
11. What is an operating characteristic curve?
12. What general factors govern the choice of single- versus multiple-sampling plans?
13. Briefly explain each of these terms:
    a. AOQ.
    b. AOQL.
    c. LTPD.
    d. Alpha risk.
    e. Beta risk.
14. How does process control differ from lot control?
15. List the elements in the control process.
16. Quality control is an example of management by exception. Explain.
17. What are the concepts that underlie the construction and use of control charts?
18. What is the purpose of control charts?
19. Why is order of observation important in process control?
20. What is a run? How are run tests useful in process control?
21. Why is it usually desirable to use both an up/down run test and a median run test on the same data?
22. If neither the up/down nor the median test indicates nonrandomness, does that guarantee that the process is random? If

one or both tests indicate nonrandom variations in the data, does that prove that the process is not in control? Explain.

23. Contrast tolerances, control limits, and process variability.

24. Explain this statement: "A process may be out of control even though all observations are well within the control limits."

25. A customer has recently modified specifications on a part your company supplies. The specs are now much narrower than the machine generally used for the job is capable of. Briefly discuss the alternatives the operations manager might consider to resolve this problem. (See Figure 16–17C.)

26. A new order has just come into the department. The capability of the machine used for this type of work is such that virtually all of the output can be expected to be well within specs. (See Figure 16–17B.)
    a. What benefits might be derived by analyzing this situation?
    b. What alternatives should be considered in this sort of situation?

PROBLEMS

1. An assembly operation for trigger mechanisms of a semiautomatic spray gun produces a small percentage of defective mechanisms. Management must decide whether to continue the current practice of 100 percent inspection or whether to replace defective mechanisms after final assembly, when all guns are inspected. Replacement at final assembly costs $30 each; inspection during trigger assembly costs $12 per hour for labor and overhead. The inspection rate is one trigger per minute.
   a. Would 100 percent inspection during trigger assembly be justified if there are (1) 4 percent defective? (2) 1 percent defective?
   b. At what point would management be indifferent between 100 percent inspection of triggers and only final inspection?

2. Random samples of $n = 20$ circuit breakers are tested for damage caused by shipment in each lot of 4,000 received. Lots with more than one defective are pulled and subjected to 100 percent inspection.
   a. Construct the OC curve for this sampling plan.

   b. Construct the AOQ curve for this plan, assuming defectives found during 100 percent inspection are replaced with good parts. What is the approximate AOQL?

3. Auditors use a technique called *discovery sampling* in which a random sample of items is inspected, and if any defectives are found, the entire lot of items being sampled is subjected to 100 percent inspection.
   a. Draw an OC curve for the case where a sample of 15 credit accounts will be inspected out of a total of 8,000 accounts.
   b. Draw an OC curve for the case where 150 accounts out of 8,000 accounts will be examined. (*Hint:* Use $p = .001$, .002, .003, ...)
   c. Draw the AOQ curve for the preceding case, and estimate the AOQL.

4. Random samples of lots of textbooks are inspected for defectives just prior to shipment to the warehouse. Each lot contains 3,000 books.
   a. On a single sheet of graph paper, construct OC curves for $n = 100$ and (1) $c = 0$, (2) $c = 1$, and (3) $c = 2$. (*Hint:* Use $p = .001, .002, .003, ...$)

b. On a single sheet of graph paper, construct OC curves for $c = 2$ and (1) $n = 5$, (2) $n = 20$, and (3)$n = 120$.

c. Construct AOQ curves for the first two cases in part b.

5. Manufacturing specifications call for motor housings that weigh between 24 and 25 pounds. The housings are cast using a process that produces castings that have a mean of 24.5 pounds and a standard deviation of 0.2 pounds. The distribution of output is normal.

a. What percentage of housings will not meet the weight specs?

b. Determine three-sigma control limits for this process if $n = 16$.

6. An automatic filling machine is used to fill 1-liter bottles of cola. The machine's output is approximately normal with a mean of 1.0 liters and a standard deviation of 0.01 liters. Output is monitored using means of samples of 25 observations.

a. Determine upper and lower control limits that will include roughly 95.5 percent of the sample means when the process is in control.

b. Graph the control chart and plot these sample means: 1.005, 1.001, 0.998, 1.002, 0.995, and 0.999. Is the process in control?

7. A grinding and deburring operation is monitored using a mean and a range chart. Six samples of $n = 20$ observations have been obtained and the sample means and ranges computed:

Sample	Mean	Range
1	3.06	0.42
2	3.15	0.50
3	3.11	0.41
4	3.13	0.46
5	3.06	0.46
6	3.09	0.45

a. Using the factors in Table 16–3, determine upper and lower limits for mean and range charts.

b. Is the process in control?

8. Using samples of 200 observations each, a quality inspector found the following:

Sample	1	2	3	4
Number of defectives	4	2	5	9

a. Determine the fraction defective in each sample.

b. If the true fraction defective for this process is unknown, what is your estimate of it?

c. What is your estimate of the mean and standard deviation of the sampling distribution of fractions defective for samples of this size?

d. What control limits would give an alpha risk of .03 for this process?

e. What alpha risk would control limits of 0.047 and 0.003 provide?

f. Using control limits of 0.047 and 0.003, are any of the sample fractions defective beyond the control limits? If so, which one(s)?

g. Suppose now that the long-term fraction defective of the process is known to be 2 percent. What are the values of the mean and standard deviation of the sampling distribution?

h. Construct a control chart for the process, assuming a fraction defective of 2 percent, using two–sigma control limits. Are any of the samples beyond the control limits? If so, which one(s)?

9. A continuous process cuts plastic tubing into nominal lengths of 80 centimeters. Samples of five observations each have been taken, and the results are as listed. Using factors from Table 16–3, determine upper and lower control limits for mean

and range charts, and decide if the process is in control.

			Sample		
1	*2*	*3*	*4*	*5*	*6*
79.2	80.5	79.6	78.9	80.5	79.7
78.8	78.7	79.6	79.4	79.6	80.6
80.0	81.0	80.4	79.7	80.4	80.5
78.4	80.4	80.3	79.4	80.8	80.0
81.0	80.1	80.8	80.6	78.8	81.1

10. An automatic screw machine produces 2-inch hex nuts. Using the following sample data and $n = 200$, construct a control chart for the fraction defective using two-sigma limits. Is the process in control? If not, eliminate any values that are outside of the limits, and compute revised limits.

				Sample								
1	*2*	*3*	*4*	*5*	*6*	*7*	*8*	*9*	*10*	*11*	*12*	*13*

Number of
defectives . . . 1 2 2 0 2 1 2 0 2 7 3 2 1

11. The postmaster of a small western city receives a certain number of complaints about mail delivery each day. Assume that the distribution of daily complaints is Poisson. Construct a control chart with three-sigma limits using the following data. Is the process in control?

						Day							
1	*2*	*3*	*4*	*5*	*6*	*7*	*8*	*9*	*10*	*11*	*12*	*13*	*14*

Number of
complaints . . . 4 10 14 8 9 6 5 12 13 7 6 4 2 10

12. Construct a control chart with three-sigma limits for the number of defects per spool of cable, given the following data. Is the process in control?

Observation	Number of defects
1	2
2	3
3	1
4	0
5	1
6	3
7	2
8	0
9	2
10	1
11	3
12	1
13	2
14	0

13. During long runs of canned vegetables through a labeling machine, a few labels invariably fail to adhere properly and eventually fall off. Using the following sample data, which are based on samples of 100 observations each, construct a control chart for the fraction defective using 95 percent control limits, and determine if the process is in control.

Sample	Number of defectives
1	5
2	3
3	6
4	7
5	4
6	6
7	8
8	4
9	5
10	8
11	3
12	4
13	5
14	6
15	6
16	7

14. Tolerances for a metal shaft are much wider than the process used to machine the shafts is capable of. Consequently, the decision has been made to allow the cutting tool to wear a certain amount before replacement. The tool wears at the rate of 0.004 centimeters per piece. The process has a natural variation, σ, of 0.01 centimeters and is normally distributed. Tolerances are 15 to 17 centimeters, and $n = 1$. For two–sigma limits, how many shafts can the process turn out before tool replacement becomes necessary? (See diagram.)

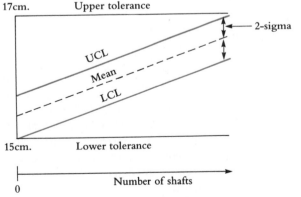

15. Tolerances for the plastic tubing mentioned in Problem 9 are 78 centimeters and 81 centimeters. Based on the data given in the problem, are the tolerances being met? Estimate the percentage of process output that can be expected to fall within the tolerances.

16. A process that produces bars of soap is to be investigated. Historically, the process has had a standard deviation equal to 0.146. The means of 39 samples of $n = 14$ are:

Sample	Mean	Sample	Mean
1	3.86	21	3.84
2	3.90	22	3.82
3	3.83	23	3.89
4	3.81	24	3.86
5	3.84	25	3.88
6	3.83	26	3.90
7	3.87	27	3.81
8	3.88	28	3.86
9	3.84	29	3.98
10	3.80	30	3.96
11	3.88	31	3.88
12	3.86	32	3.76
13	3.88	33	3.83
14	3.81	34	3.77
15	3.83	35	3.86
16	3.86	36	3.80
17	3.82	37	3.84
18	3.86	38	3.79
19	3.84	39	3.85
20	3.87		

a. Construct an $\bar{x}$-chart for this process with three-sigma limits. Is the process in control?

b. Analyze the data using a median run test and an up/down run test. What can you conclude?

17. For each of the accompanying control charts, analyze the data using both median and up/down run tests with $z = \pm 1.96$ limits. Are nonrandom variations present? Assume the center line is the long-term median.

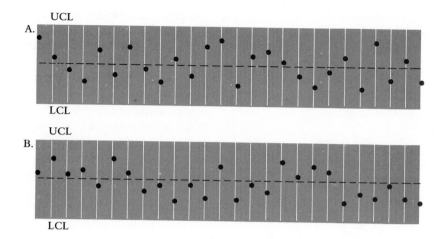

18. Analyze the data in the problems listed below using median and up/down run tests with $z = \pm 2$.
    a. Problem 13.
    b. Problem 11.

19. Use both types of run test to analyze the daily expense voucher listed. Assume a median of $31.

Day	Amount	Day	Amount
1	$27.69	21	28.60
2	28.13	22	20.02
3	33.02	23	26.67
4	30.31	24	36.40
5	31.59	25	32.07
6	33.64	26	44.10
7	34.73	27	41.44
8	35.09	28	29.62
9	33.39	29	30.12
10	32.51	30	26.39
11	27.98	31	40.54
12	31.25	32	36.31
13	33.98	33	27.14
14	25.56	34	30.38
15	24.46	35	31.96
16	29.65	36	32.03
17	31.08	37	34.40
18	33.03	38	25.67
19	29.10	39	35.80
20	25.19	40	32.23

Day	Amount	Day	Amount
41	26.76	51	37.78
42	30.51	52	34.16
43	29.35	53	38.28
44	24.09	54	29.49
45	22.45	55	30.81
46	25.16	56	30.60
47	26.11	57	34.46
48	29.84	58	35.10
49	31.75	59	31.76
50	29.14	60	34.90

20. A company has just negotiated a contract to produce a part for another firm. In the process of manufacturing the part, as the cutting tool wears, the inside diameter of successive parts becomes smaller and smaller. However, the specs are so wide relative to machine capabilities that it is possible to initially set the diameter at a large value and let the process run for a while before replacing the cutting tool. (This situation is somewhat similar to the one described in Problem 14.)

The inside diameter decreases at an average rate of 0.001 cm per part, and the process has a standard deviation of 0.01 cm. The variability is approximately normal. Assuming three-sigma control limits, how frequently must the tool be replaced if the process specs are 3 cm and 3.5 cm and the initial setting is the upper spec? Use $n = 1$.

21. (Refer to Solved Problem 5.) Suppose the process specs are 9.65 and 10.35. Based on the data given, does it appear that the specs are being met? If not, what should one look for?

22. A production process consists of a three-step operation. The scrap rate of the first step is 10 percent, and the rate is 6 percent for the other two steps.
   a. If the desired daily output is 450 units, how many units must be started to allow for loss due to scrap?
   b. If the scrap rate for each step could be cut in half, how many units would this save in terms of the scrap allowance?
   c. If the scrap represents a cost of $10 per unit, how much is it costing the company per day for the original scrap rate?

23. (Refer to the data in Example 7.) Two additional observations have been taken. The first resulted in three defects, and the second had four defects. Using the set of 20 observations, perform run tests on the data. What can you conclude about the data?

24. A manufacturer receives shipments of several thousand parts from a supplier every week. The manufacturer has the option of conducting a 100 percent inspection before accepting the parts or not. The decision is based on a random sample of 15 parts. If parts are not inspected, defectives become apparent during a later assembly operation, at which time replacement cost is $6.25 per unit. Inspection cost for 100 percent inspection is $1 per unit.
   a. At what fraction defective would the manufacturer be indifferent between 100 percent inspection and leaving discovery of defectives until the later assembly operation?
   b. For the sample size being used, what is the maximum number of sample defectives that would cause the lot to be

passed without 100 percent inspection (based on your answer to part a)?
   c. If the shipment actually contains 5 percent defectives:
      (1) What is the probability that it would be accepted without 100 percent inspection?
      (2) What is the probability it would be rejected in favor of 100 percent inspection?
      (3) What would the correct decision be?
      (4) What is the probability of a Type I error? Type II error?
   d. Answer the questions in part c for a shipment that contains 20 percent defectives.

25. (Refer to the preceding problem, part c). Suppose there are two defectives in the sample.
   a. If the acceptance number is $c = 1$, what decision should be made? What type of error is possible?
   b. If the acceptance number is $c = 3$, what decision should be made? What type of error is possible?
   c. Determine the average outgoing quality for each of these percent defectives if $c = 1$.
      (1) 5 percent.
      (2) 10 percent.
      (3) 15 percent.
      (4) 20 percent.

26. A machine operator has obtained the following measurements:

Sample			
1	2	3	4
4.5	4.6	4.5	4.7
4.2	4.5	4.6	4.6
4.2	4.4	4.4	4.8
4.3	4.7	4.4	4.5
4.3	4.3	4.6	4.9

   a. Determine the mean of each sample.
   b. If the process parameters are unknown,

estimate its mean and standard deviation.

c. Estimate the mean and standard deviation of the sampling distribution.

d. What would three-sigma control limits for the process be? What alpha risk would they provide?

e. What alpha risk would control limits of 4.14 and 4.86 provide?

f. Using limits of 4.14 and 4.86, are any sample means beyond the control limits? If so, which one(s)?

g. Construct control charts for means and ranges using Table 16–3. Are any samples beyond the control limits? If so, which one(s)?

h. Explain why the control limits are different for means in parts d and g.

i. If the process had a known mean of 4.4 and a known standard deviation of 0.18, what would three-sigma control limits be for a mean chart? Are any sample means beyond the control limits? If so, which one(s)?

SELECTED BIBLIOGRAPHY

Baker, Thomas R. "Quality Engineering by Design." *Quality Progress,* December 1986, pp. 32–42.

Duncan, A. J. *Quality Control and Industrial Statistics.* 4th ed. Homewood, Ill.: Richard D. Irwin, 1974.

Enrick, Norbert L. *Quality, Reliability, and Process Improvement.* 8th ed. New York: Industrial Press, 1985.

Garvin, David A. "Quality on the Line." *Harvard Business Review,* September–October 1983, p. 64.

Gitlow, Howard S.; Shelly Gitlow; Alan Oppenheim; and Rosa Oppenheim. *Tools and Methods for the Improvement of Quality.* Homewood, Ill.: Richard D. Irwin, 1989.

Gitlow, Howard S., and Paul T. Hertz. "Product Defects and Productivity." *Harvard Business Review,* September–October 1983, p. 131.

Grant, Eugene L., and Richard S. Leavenworth. *Statistical Quality Control.* 5th ed. New York: McGraw-Hill, 1980.

Hall, Robert W. *Attaining Manufacturing Excellence.* Homewood, Ill.: Dow Jones-Irwin, 1987.

Juran, J. M. "The Quality Trilogy." *Quality Progress* 19, no. 8 (August 1986), pp. 19–24.

Juran, J. M., and F. M. Gryma, Jr. *Quality Planning and Analysis.* 2nd ed. New York: McGraw-Hill, 1980.

Kackar, Raghu N. "Taguchi's Quality Philosophy: Analysis and Commentary." *Quality Progress,* December 1986, pp. 21–29.

Kume, Hitoshi. *Statistical Methods for Quality Improvement.* Tokyo: AOTS Chosakai, 1985.

Leonard, Frank S., and Earl Sasser. "The Incline of Quality." *Harvard Business Review,* September–October 1982, pp. 163–71.

Reddy, Jack, and Abe Berger. "Three Essentials of Product Quality." *Harvard Business Review,* July–August 1983, pp. 153–59.

Schein, Lawrence, and Melissa A. Berman, eds. *Total Quality Performance.* Research Report No. 909. New York Conference Board, 1988.

Reading

Transformation of Western Style of Management

W. Edwards Deming

The decline of Western industry can only be halted by transformation of the Western style of management by following the 14 points of management.

The Crisis of Western Industry

The decline of Western industry, which began in 1968 and 1969, a victim of competition, has reached little by little a stage that can only be characterized as a crisis. The decline is caused by Western style of management, and it will continue until the cause is corrected. In fact, the decline may be ready for a nose dive. Some companies will die a natural death, victims of Charles Darwin's inexorable law of survival of the fittest. In others, there will be awakening and conversion of management.

What happened? American industry knew nothing but expansion from 1950 till around 1968. American goods had the market. Then, one by one, many American companies awakened to the reality of competition from Japan.

Little by little, one by one, the manufacture of parts and materials moves out of the Western world into Japan, Korea, Taiwan, and now Brazil, for reasons of quality and price. More business is carried on now between the U.S. and the Pacific Basin than across the Atlantic Ocean.

A sudden crisis like Pearl Harbor brings everybody out in full force, ready for action, even if they have no idea what to do. But a crisis that creeps in catches its victims asleep. Some awaken in a drowse; some awaken to action; others will go on sleeping.

A Declining Market Exposes Weaknesses

Management in an expanding market is fairly easy. It is difficult to lose when business simply drops into the basket. But when competition presses into the market, knowledge and skill are required for survival. Excuses ran out. By 1969, the comptroller and the legal department began to take charge for survival, fighting a defensive war, backs to the wall. The comptroller does his best, using only visible figures, trying to hold the company in the black, unaware of the importance for management of figures that are unknown and unknowable. The legal department fights off creditors and predators that are on the lookout for an attractive takeover. Unfortunately, management by the comptroller and the legal department only brings further decline.

Forces that Feed the Decline

The decline is accelerated by the aim of management to boost the quarterly dividend, and to maximize the price of the company's stock. Quick returns, whether by acquisition, or by divestiture, or by paper profits or by creative accounting, are self-defeating. The effect in the long run erodes investment and ends up as just the opposite to what is intended.

A far better plan is to protect investment by plans and methods that will improve product and service, accepting the inevitable decrease in costs that accompany improvement of quality and service, thus reversing the decline, capturing the market with better quality and lower price. As a result, the company stays in business and provides jobs and more jobs.

For years, price tags and not total cost of use governed the purchase of materials and equipment. Work standards, quotas, exhortations, numerical goals devoid of methods to achieve them, failure to invest in knowledge, failures of training and supervision, have added their contribution to the decline.

Other forces are still more effective.

1. Lack of constancy of purpose to plan product and service that will have a market and keep the company in business, and provide jobs.

2. Emphasis on short-term profits: short-term thinking (just the opposite from constancy of purpose to stay in business), fed by fear of unfriendly takeover and by push from bankers and owners for dividends.

3. Personal review system, or evaluation of performance, merit rating, annual review, or annual

appraisal, by whatever name, for people in management, the effects of which are devastating.

4. Mobility of management; job hopping from one company to another.

5. Use of visible figures only for management, with little or no consideration of figures that are unknown or unknowable.

Peculiar to industry in the United States.

6. Excessive medical costs.

7. Excessive costs of warranty, fueled by lawyers that work on contingency fee [Grant 1984].

Anyone could add more inhibitors. One, for example, is the choking of business by laws and regulations, the effect of which is too often to nullify the work of standardizing committees of industry, government, and consumers.

Still another force is the system of detailed budgets which leave a division manager no leeway. In contrast, the manager in Japan is not bothered by detail. He has complete freedom except for one item; he cannot transfer to other uses his budget for education and training.

Remarks on Evaluation of Performance of the So-Called Merit Rating

Many companies in America have systems by which everyone in management or in research receives from his superiors a rating every year. Some government agencies have a similar system. Management by objective, on a go no-go basis, is another name for the same evil. Management by fear would be a better name, as someone in Germany suggested. The effect is devastating.

- It nourishes short-term performance, annihilates long-term planning, builds fear, demolishes teamwork; nourishes rivalry and politics.

- It leaves people bitter, others despondent and dejected, some even depressed, unfit for work for weeks after receipt of rating, unable to comprehend why they are inferior. It is unfair, as it ascribes to the people in a group differences that may be caused totally by the system that they work in.

The idea of a merit rating is alluring. The sound of the words captivates the imagination: pay for what you get; get what you pay for; motivate people to do their best, for their own good.

The effect of the merit rating is exactly the opposite of what the words promise. Everyone propels himself forward, or tries to, for his own good, on his own life preserver. The organization is the loser.

Moreover, a merit rating is meaningless as a predictor of performance, except for someone that falls outside the limits of differences attributable to the system that the people work in.

Other Obstacles

1. Hope for quick results (instant pudding).

2. The excuse that "our problems are different."

3. Inept teaching in schools of business.

4. Failure of schools of engineering to teach statistical theory.

5. Statistical teaching centers fail to prepare students for the needs of industry. Students learn statistical theory for enumerative studies, then see them applied in class and in textbooks to analytic problems. They learn to calculate estimates of standard errors of the result of an experiment and in other analytic problems where there is no such thing as a standard error. They learn tests of hypothesis, null hypothesis, and probability levels of significance. Such calculations and the underlying theory are excellent mathematical exercises, but they provide no basis for action, no basis for evaluation of the risk of prediction of the results of the next experiment, nor of tomorrow's product, which is the only question of interest in a study aimed at improvement of performance of a process or of a product.

   Meanwhile, people with master's degrees in statistical theory accept jobs in industry and government to work with computers. It is a vicious cycle. Statisticians that do not know what statistical work is are satisfied to work with computers. Management likewise has no knowledge about statistical work in industry, and somehow supposes that computers are the answer. Statisticians and management thus misguide each other and keep the vicious cycle rolling.

Statisticians and other technical people can reach maximal usefulness in industry, including service industries, only by adopting as their main purpose help to management, to make the changes that are necessary for survival.

6. The supposition by management that the work force could turn out quality if they would only apply full force their skill and effort. The fact is that nearly everyone in Western industry, management and work force, is impeded by barriers to pride of workmanship.

7. Reliance on QC-Circles, employee involvement, employee participation groups, quality of work life, anything to get rid of the problems of people. These shams, without management's participation, deteriorate and break up after a few months. The big task ahead is to get the management involved in management for quality and productivity. The work force has always been involved. There will then be quality of work life, pride of workmanship, and quality.

Remarks on Use of Visible Figures

The comptroller runs the company on visible figures. This is a sure road to decline. Why? Because the most important figures for management are not visible: they are unknown and unknowable. Do courses in finance teach students the importance of the unknown and unknowable loss

- from a dissatisfied customer?
- from a dissatisfied employee, one that, because of correctible faults of the system, cannot take pride in his work?
- from the annual rating on performance, the so-called merit rating?
- loss from absenteeism (purely a function of supervision)?

Do courses in finance teach their students about the increase in productivity that comes from people that can take pride in their work? Do they teach students about the multiplying effect of a happy customer?

Condensation of the 14 Points for Management

There is now a theory of management. No one can say now that there is nothing about management to teach. If experience by itself would teach management how to improve, then why are we in this predicament? Everyone doing his best is not the answer that will halt the decline. It is necessary that everyone know what to do; then for everyone to do his best.

The 14 Points apply anywhere, to small organizations as well as to large ones, to the service industry as well as to manufacturing.

1. Create constancy of purpose toward improvement of product and service, with the aim to stay in business, and to provide jobs.

2. Adopt the new philosophy. We are in a new economic age, created by Japan. Transformation of Western style of management is necessary to halt the continued decline of industry.

3. Cease dependence on inspection to achieve quality. Eliminate the need for inspection on a mass basis by building quality into the product in the first place.

4. End the practice of awarding business on the basis of price tag. Purchasing must be combined with design of product, manufacturing, and sales, to work with the chosen supplier, with the aim to minimize total cost, not merely initial cost.

5. Improve constantly and forever every activity in the company, to improve quality and productivity, and thus constantly decrease costs.

6. Institute training and education on the job, including management.

7. Institute supervision. The aim of supervision should be to help people and machines and gadgets to do a better job.

8. Drive out fear, so that everyone may work effectively for the company.

9. Break down barriers between departments. People in research, design, sales, and production must work as a team, to foresee problems of production and in use that may be encountered with the product or service.

10. Eliminate slogans, exhortations, and targets for the work force asking for zero defects and new levels of productivity. Such exhortations only create adversarial relationships, as the bulk of the causes of low quality and low productivity belong to the system and thus lie beyond the power of the work force.

11. Eliminate work standards that prescribe numerical quotas for the day. Substitute aids and helpful supervision.

12. **a.** Remove the barriers that rob the hourly worker of his right to pride of workmanship. The responsibility of supervisors must be changed from sheer numbers to quality.

    b. Remove the barriers that rob people in management and in engineering of their right to pride of workmanship. This means, *inter alia,* abolishment of the annual or merit rating of management by objective, and management by the numbers.

13. Institute a vigorous program of education and retraining. New skills are required for changes in techniques, materials, and service.

14. Put everybody in the company to work in teams to accomplish the transformation.

What Is Required for Change?

The first step is for Western management to awaken to the need for change. Change may not be easy for everybody.

Top management will agree to carry out the new philosophy. They will explain by seminars and other means to a critical mass of people in the company why change is necessary, and that the change will involve everybody. Everyone must understand the 14 points, the deadly diseases, and the obstacles. Top management and everyone else must feel pain and dissatisfaction with past performance, and must have the courage to change. Top management must break out of line, even to the point of exile amongst their peers.

What about Great Accomplishments within the Existing System?

As everyone knows, applications of techniques within the system as it exists often accomplish spectacular results, great improvements in quality and productivity, and reduction of waste. Anyone that attends a meeting of the American Society for Quality Control may well come away convinced that the great problems of the country are already solved. It is easy to be fooled. An example (not mine) is a simple change in the tracker for the seat of an automobile with eventual reduction of failures from 42 percent to 2 percent. Another simple example saved a company $186,000 per day, calculations for which were accomplished in less than half an hour. The fact is that the management of the company must somehow save 30 times this amount to become competitive.

The sad fact is that in spite of the accomplishments posted, however spectacular they be, they are insignificant in comparison with the losses caused by Western style of management. What these colossal accomplishments do is to prolong by a few months the life of the patient, whose demise in one form or another is assured by Western style of management.

References

Deming, W. Edwards 1985, *Out of the Crisis,* Center for Advanced Engineering Study, Massachusetts Institute of Technology, Cambridge, Massachusetts.

Grant, Eugene L. 1984, Interview, *Quality* (March).

Source: *Interfaces* 15, no. 3 (May–June 1985), pp. 6–11. Copyright © 1985, The Institute of Management Sciences

CASE

MARION CAMP MEMORIAL HOSPITAL

The Marion Camp Memorial Hospital provides convalescent care for patients with long-term illnesses as well as for patients who require extended periods of physical therapy. The average length of stay at the hospital is four months. The hospital is supported through a combination of state and federal funding, medicare payments, and private donations. Less than 10 percent of the hospital's revenue is derived from patients.

The hospital director, H. John ("Big Jack") Pace, has become increasingly concerned with the number of complaints the hospital is receiving on various aspects of its health care, and he recently made this the main topic at the monthly staff meeting. In attendance at the meeting were Alan Carter, chief physician; Nancy Ames, supervisor of nursing; Phil Rogers, manager of support services; and Charlotte James, assistant director.

Mr. Pace began the meeting with a brief statement outlining some of the many complaints he'd received, which ranged from cold meals to beds not being changed often enough. Some of the complaints were from hospital employees themselves. Mr. Pace indicated that he hoped that this wasn't the start of a decline in the quality of health care. However, his main concern was an upcoming inspection for reaccreditation by the state. In his words, "You know how they can pick up on something like this and blow it all out of proportion."

Charlotte James, who has been investigating the problem, reported that she was having difficulties because "doctors, nurses, dietitians, and support people all have different definitions of quality." She also noted that most of the complaints seemed to relate to support services rather than medical care, and Phil Rogers tended to agree with her, but he indicated that he had not been able to "turn things around." He pointed out that support people (nurses' aids, kitchen workers, janitors, painters, etc.) were unskilled or semiskilled personnel who generally received the minimum wage. He noted that turnover was high, morale was low, there were no professional standards, and few workers viewed themselves as a part of the "health care team." According to Phil, "Most of my people are bored with their jobs, and they lack any positive attitude toward quality. In fact, I'm not even sure they know what quality means!"

At this point, Nancy Ames mentioned that her husband was involved in quality control for a local candy manufacturer, and she wondered if perhaps some of those techniques might be useful. Although she was not completely familiar with those techniques, she promised to ask her husband to drop by to discuss the problems.

Mr. Pace closed the meeting, tabling the discussion until they could meet with Mr. Ames.

The meeting with Mr. Ames took place late the following week. At the meeting, Mr. Ames stressed the importance of defining quality, illustrated the use of control charts, and wondered if some of the increase in complaints could be attributed to seasonal factors. He also suggested that the hospital develop a short questionnaire for patients and staff, which might enable them to, in his words, "get a better handle on the problems before wasting any time trying to solve them."

Question

Assume that you have been called in as a consultant on this case. Your job is to identify the main problem and to make recommendations for solving it.

CASE

ANYONE FOR SUSHI?

The operations manager of a firm that produces frozen dinners had received numerous complaints about the firm's Chick-n-Gravy dinners from supermarkets that sell this item. The manager then asked Ann to investigate the matter and to report her recommendations.

Ann's first task was to sift through the list of complaints to determine what problems were gener-

ating the complaints. The majority of complaints centered on five defects: underfilled packages, a missing item, spills/mixed items, unacceptable taste, and packages improperly sealed.

Next, she took samples of dinners from the production line and examined each sample, making note of any defects that she found. A summary of those results is shown in the accompanying table.

				Defect Observed			
Date	Time	Line	Underfilled	Missing item	Spill/ mixed	Unacceptable taste	Improperly sealed
5/12	0900	1		√√	√	√√√	
5/12	1330	2			√√		√√
5/13	1000	2				√	√√√
5/13	1345	1	√√		√√		
5/13	1530	2		√√	√√√		√
5/14	0830	1		√√√		√√√	
5/14	1100	2	√		√	√√	
5/14	1400	1			√		√
5/15	1030	1		√√√		√√√√√	
5/15	1145	2			√	√√	
5/15	1500	1	√		√		
5/16	0845	2				√√	√√
5/16	1030	1		√√√	√	√√√	
5/16	1400	1					
5/16	1545	2	√	√√√√√	√	√	√√

The data resulted from inspecting approximately 800 frozen dinners. What should Ann recommend to the manager?

Case 1: Elysian Cycles

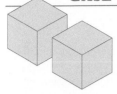

Elysian Cycles (EC), located in a major southwestern city, is a wholesale distributor of bicycles and bicycle parts. Its primary retail outlets are located in eight cities within a 400-mile radius of the distribution center. These retail outlets generally depend on receiving orders for additional stock within two days after notifying the distribution center (if the stock is available). The company's management feels this is a valuable marketing tool that aids survival in a highly competitive industry.

EC distributes a wide variety of finished bicycles, but these are all based on five different frame designs. Table 1 gives a breakdown of the product options available to the retail outlets.

EC receives these different styles from a single manufacturer overseas, and shipments may take as long as four weeks from the time an order is made by telephone or telex. With the cost of communication, paperwork, and customs clearance included, EC estimates that each time an order is placed it incurs a cost of $65. The cost per bicycle is roughly 60 percent of the suggested list price for any of the styles available.

Demand for the bicycles is somewhat seasonal in nature, heavier in the spring and early summer and tapering off through the fall and winter seasons (except for a heavy surge in the six weeks prior to Christmas). A breakdown of the previous year's business with the retail outlets usually forms the basis for EC's yearly operations plan. A growth factor (either positive or negative) is used to refine further the demand estimate by reflecting the upcoming yearly market for bicycle sales. By developing a yearly plan and updating it when appropriate, EC can establish some reasonable basis for obtaining any necessary financing from the bank. Last year's monthly demand for the different bicycle styles EC distributes is shown in Table 2.

Owing to the increasing popularity of bicycles for recreational purposes and for supplanting some automobile usage, EC believes that its market may grow

Table 1

Bicycles stocked

Frame style	Suggested list price (complete bicycle)
A	$ 99.95
B	124.95
C	169.95
D	219.95
E	349.95

Source: Adapted from James A. Fitzsimmons and Robert S. Sullivan, *Service Operations Management* (New York: McGraw-Hill, 1982), pp. 419–21. Reprinted by permission.

TABLE 2

Monthly demand

Month	Frame style					
	A	*B*	*C*	*D*	*E*	*Total*
January	0	3	5	2	0	10
February	2	8	10	3	1	24
March	4	15	21	12	2	54
April	4	35	40	21	3	103
May	3	43	65	37	3	151
June	3	27	41	18	2	91
July	2	13	26	11	1	53
August	1	10	16	9	1	37
September	1	9	11	7	1	29
October	1	8	10	7	2	28
November	2	15	19	12	3	51
December	3	30	33	19	4	89
Total	26	216	297	158	23	720

by as much as 25 percent in the upcoming year. However, because there have been years when the full amount of expected growth did not materialize, EC has decided to base its plan on a more conservative 15 percent growth factor to allow for variations in consumer buying habits and to ensure that it is not excessively overstocked if the full market does not occur. Holding costs associated with inventory of any bicycle style is estimated to be about 0.75 percent of the unit cost of a bicycle per month.

Questions

Develop an inventory control plan for Elysian Cycles to use as the basis for its upcoming yearly plan. Be sure to justify your reasons for choosing a particular type (or combination of types) of inventory system(s). On the basis of your particular plan, specify the safety stock requirements if EC institutes a policy of maintaining a 95 percent service level.

CASE 2:   COQUILLE REFINERY CORPORATION

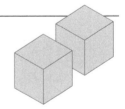

The Coquille Refinery Corporation is contemplating building a crude-oil storage and docking facility on the southern coast of France. They plan to import crude oil by ship from the Middle East and distribute this crude oil by pipeline to refineries in the area.

Source: James A. Fitzsimmons and Robert S. Sullivan, *Service Operations Management* (New York: McGraw-Hill, 1982), pp. 78–80. Reprinted by permission.

The construction of this facility represents a substantial capital investment. Furthermore, the cost of such a facility is principally determined by its crude-oil storage capacity. You have been asked to study the problem and recommend an appropriate storage capacity; bear in mind that too large a capacity represents an unnecessary expense, but too small a capacity will result in costly later additions to the facility.

A long-term contract has been made with the Middle East supplier to furnish an average daily supply of 300,000 barrels of crude oil. Because its fleet of ships consist of 200,000-barrel tankers, the supplier expects that the arrival of its tankers will follow the distribution below:

Tanker arrivals per day	Probability
0	0.1
1	0.5
2	0.2
3	0.2

A review of past production records of refineries in the area suggests the following distribution of crude-oil demand per day:

Barrels per day	Probability
100,000	0.1
200,000	0.2
300,000	0.3
400,000	0.4

Questions

1. Consider the following issues before you simulate:
   a. What is the expected daily demand for crude oil? Why must this be so?
   b. What assumptions concerning the timing of crude-oil receipts and deliveries would require the greatest oil storage capacity?
   c. What assumption concerning receipts and deliveries would require the least oil storage capacity?
   d. Give a reason based on systems-analysis considerations why back orders should be filled from the next day's receipts rather than considered as lost sales.

2. Develop a Monte Carlo simulation model for Coquille that will generate information useful for resolving the storage capacity problem and simulate 10 days of capacity.

3. Assume a computer program was written to simulate 10,000 days of activity under the assumptions listed in question 1b. From the results of

such a simulation the following distribution of oil in storage, after a day's receipts, is determined. (Note: Negative figures represent back orders.)

Oil in storage, in thousands	Probability
−300	0.01
−200	0.04
−100	0.06
0	0.07
⋮	⋮
1000	0.09
1100	0.08
1200	0.07
1300	0.05
1400	0.03
1500	0.02
	1.00

a. What level of crude-oil safety stock should be carried to ensure 95 percent protection against stock-outs (1 stock-out in 20 days)?

b. If Coquille decides to use the above safety stock, what should be the oil storage capacity to ensure 90 percent protection against overruns (i.e., sufficient capacity to accommodate completely receipts 9 days out of 10)?

4. Note two ways one might determine if the simulation run length of 10,000 days is adequate.

5. Make a list of cost factors that would influence the final selection of oil storage capacity.

CASE 3: CLEARMOUNT SOUTHERN INCORPORATED

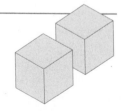

A forecast of expected business volume and prices for the coming fall season, and a review of production standards, had produced the information in Table 1 for the production of fabric.

The profits are based on expected costs and prices. More specifically they represent so-called operating profit, also known as *variable margin, contribution to profit and overhead,* and *gross profit* and were determined from the difference between expected selling price and expected variable costs.

In order to effectively direct sales efforts, keeping in mind the expected profits per yard, the anticipated sales volume on certain styles for which

Source: Professor Norbert L. Enrick, Ph.D., Administrative Sciences, Kent State University, Ohio. Reprinted by permission.

TABLE 1

Marketable fabric styles, demand limits on sales, productive requirement, and productive capacity

Market-able styles	Sales limit 1,000s of yards per week	Profit[a] per 100,000 yards (in dollars)	Production time needed per 100,000 yards of fabric per production process in 100's of delivery hours[b]						
			Cards	Drawing	Roving	Spinning	Loom 40″	Loom 40″	Loom 60″
A	3.0	9020	3.3	2.0	35.2	1348	28.4		
B	6.0	6420	3.7	2.2	34.5	794	22.6		
C	10.0	5480	3.5	2.1	37.7	1128	31.0		
D		4790	4.4	2.7	47.8	1162	33.4		
E		2690	3.1	1.8	34.3	1050		28.4	
F		5620	3.8	2.3	41.4	1228		28.7	
G	10.0	5130	4.5	2.7	42.3	1071		23.7	
H	30.0	6890	5.1	3.1	55.6	1354		34.7	
I	7.5	9080	3.9	2.4	42.9	1468			34.1
J	5.0	7290	2.9	1.7	31.2	1064			25.6
K	4.0	10530	3.6	2.1	38.9	1334			30.8
L	3.0	12040	3.8	2.3	41.8	1436			30.8
M		6900	3.3	2.0	30.9	794			20.5
Normal capacity per 120-hour week in 1,000s of delivery hours			27.0	14.4	257	7204	155	21.7	16.3

[a] Estimated from expected selling price less expected variable costs.
[b] Successive processing through carding, drawing, roving, spinning and the loom group shown (40-inch, 46-inch or 60-inch). Fabric styles cannot be switched from wider to narrower looms or vice versa. A "delivery" is an output position. For example, a roving frame has some 100 spindles or "deliveries."

demand was considered limited, as well as productive requirements and capacity, it was desired to ascertain:

1. Optimal yardage to be sold (as a goal or target) for each style.
2. Resultant profit, per style and overall.
3. Resultant utilization of productive facilities, cards through looms.

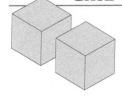

CASE 4:   WHITE SNOW GREETING CARD COMPANY

In 1960, after moving to Denver, Ted Barber founded White Snow Greeting Card, Incorporated. Ted had graduated from college three years earlier with a degree in commercial art and was interested in starting his own business. He obtained a loan from a local bank, leased an old plant in the industrial section

Source: Vincent A. Mabert and Michael J. Showalter, *Cases in Operations Management* (Plano, TX.: Business Publications, 1984), pp. 71–74.

of Denver, and purchased a used press from a bankrupt printing shop. Two months after the company moved into the plant, the first cards were being shipped to customers.

In the years that followed, the business expanded rapidly through internal growth and acquisitions. The current year's forecast of more than 200 million cards was the best in the company's history. White Snow distributes and sells cards nationally, with all printing, packaging, and shipping being done at the Denver plant. The plant has been expanded over the years and is currently in need of another addition.

Operations

Like most companies in this industry, White Snow manufactures a full line of greeting cards, i.e., Christmas, Valentines, birthday, get well, etc. By 1989 the product line included more than 1,500 designs.

The greeting card business is very seasonal, with the bulk of sales occurring during the Christmas holiday period. The sales of the recently completed year are shown in Exhibit 1, along with forecasts for the next two years.

The manufacturing and shipping of all cards is done by 186 employees at the Denver plant. The plant is fully integrated, meaning that all activities are carried out at White Snow, from the design of a 5-by-7 inch card right down to the packaging of 2,500 cards in a box measuring 30 inches by 15 inches by 10 inches for shipment. The plant operates at full capacity most of the time. Occasionally, subcontracting to outside printers is necessary to relieve temporary backlog conditions.

Envelope Machine Acquisition

At an executive committee meeting on January 5, Ted Barber raised the question of whether White Snow should purchase an envelope machine from the Gray Tool Company. Up to this point, White Snow has always purchased its entire supply of envelopes. Gray is offering to sell them a machine that has an expected life of about 10 years. The price tag on the machine is $900,000. Ted estimates that the machine running at full capacity could make enough envelopes to cover next year's expected card sales.

Ted's assistant, Tom Marshall, has already collected some information on

EXHIBIT 1

Actual and forecasted sales (millions of cards)

| | Quarter | | | | |
Year	1st	2nd	3rd	4th	Total
Current	47.5	19	28.5	95	190 mil (actual)
1	50	20	39	100	200 mil (forecasted)
2	55	22	33	110	220 mil (forecasted)

EXHIBIT 2

Interdepartmental communication

TO: Ted Barber, President   FROM: Tom Marshall
                                          Administrative Assistant
                                          to the President

DEPT: DEPT:

SUBJECT: New Envelope Machine   DATE: January 10

    During our January 5 meeting you directed me to gather more detailed information on the proposed envelope machine now under consideration. This memo summarizes my investigations. Most of the information was gathered from John Deutsch, Plant Manager; Jill Thomas, Personnel Director; and Phil McKenzie, Materials Manager.

    I spent two hours with John the other day and discussed the issue of the new machine. He thought our initial estimates of staffing requirements were correct. He wondered if it is all right to run the machine on overtime. He knows there is a 50 percent premium for Saturday and 100 percent premium for Sunday overtime, but feels he might have to use it when production falls behind. He mentioned that breakdowns and the two-week August vacation shutdown always cause problems in meeting shipping schedules. He hopes the financial budget will allow him some flexibility.

    John also reviewed the records of the current machines in the plant. He estimates that power and maintenance costs would be about 65 cents/thousand envelopes run. However, that figure could be expected to increase as the machine gets older.

    Later that day I met with Jill Thomas. We discussed the current wage structure in our plant. She mentioned that our workers currently average about $4.50 per hour in wages and there is a 25 percent fringe benefit package also in force under the current union contract. However, they expect a 5 to 10 percent wage increase when the new contract talks occur next year. Jill also mentioned that we pay shift differentials. Employees on the evening shift get an added 10 percent, while night workers receive 15 percent extra per hour shift differential.

    The final item of interest came from Phil McKenzie. Our current envelope vendor has just provided us with a new price list on orders. They must have heard we plan to make our own envelopes. Listed below is the new price schedule for a placed order, which may have different color and size specifications.

Price	Order size	
$4.50/thousand	Less than 20 million	
$4.30/thousand	20–40 million	
$4.10/thousand	Above 40 million	QQT

the proposed acquisition and operating requirements. Mr. Marshall figures that seven men would be required to run the machine. A two-man crew would be needed to operate the machine on each of three daily shifts five days per week. Each worker would earn $4.50 per hour. One supervisor, earning $7 per hour, would be required to coordinate and schedule the three shifts. Mr. Marshall estimated that paper and glue would run $2.42 per 1,000 envelopes.

The question of available space was also raised at the executive meeting. There is just enough room at the plant for the new machine. However, space for seasonal envelope inventory is limited. They could possibly rent space at the public warehouse down the street at $2 per square foot per year, but would be required to rent in minimum space lots of 1,000 square feet.

At the close of the meeting Ted Barber directed Tom Marshall to gather more information on this important proposal within the next two weeks. A few days later, Marshall sent Ted Barber an update memo (Exhibit 2).

Questions

1. Evaluate the envelope machine's capacity to meet White Snow's greeting card business. Is it sufficient?

2. What are your recommendations to Mr. Barber? Should White Snow purchase the new machine?

CASE 5: MONOLITH PRODUCTIONS

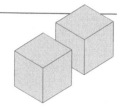

The traffic flowing into downtown Burbank on Monday, August 20, was even worse than usual. The summit meeting at Monolith Productions started promptly at 10:45 A.M. The president of the company, Hugo Monolith III, called the meeting of his vice presidents to order.

"Ladies and gentlemen, thank you for meeting here on such short notice. A most important contract has been won by our company. As you may know, George Walters, our vice president of project development, has been negotiating with the Broadcasting Association of America (BAA). The fruit of that work has been the signing of Monolith to produce a new made-for-TV version of Charles Dickens's *A Christmas Carol*. The movie will be broadcast during prime time on the nationwide BAA Network.

Monolith's announcement was met by enthusiastic applause. He then continued.

"Details of the agreement are not of immediate importance. Suffice it to say that BAA has agreed to *pay* us $1.25 million for the completed 90-minute movie. The first installment of $250,000 will be received when the project starts. An additional $350,000 will be received on November 1, and the balance will be received the day the film is to air.

Source: Vincent A. Mabert and Michael J. Showalter, *Cases in Operations Management* (Plano, TX.: Business Publications, 1984), pp. 257–62. Reprinted by permission.

"We are in complete control of the project. We will write a screenplay version of the story (with the BAA having final approval), produce the film, and support BAA's promotion of the film. We also have the rights to release a picture book based upon the film.

"We are here today to begin development of the project's production budget. The project will be coordinated by John Quinn. I've asked John to give a brief presentation summarizing the project. John?"

"Thank you, Mr. Monolith," stated Mr. Quinn. "I would like to give everyone an overview of our 'Christmas Carol.' The production of the film will be the responsibility of the director. We have been fortunate enough to recruit Steven Playhill for that task. Steven will present his ideas later. I will pesonally handle the promotion, and I will follow Steven's discussion. We will then hear from Madeline Crawford, who will be in charge of production and release of the picture book. Please feel free to ask questions at any time during the presentation. It is now my privilege to introduce one of the most popular film directors of our time, Steven Playhill. Steven?"

The introduction of Playhill brought further applause. It was acknowledged by a slight, bearded man in rumpled casual clothing who walked to the front of the conference room and started to speak.

"Thank you. As Mr. Monolith said, we are here today to develop a budget for this made-for-TV film. I would like to detail the production process which must be accomplished. We are targeting the completion of the film for December 17. The film is to be shown on the evening of December 24, but BAA wants one week in case last-minute rescheduling during Christmas week is necessary. At this time we are at the very beginning of the project; we have yet to start anything."

"Well, we have Mr. Dickens's original book," chuckled Mr. Monolith. "I signed a $25,000 check just this morning for the rights. The check went to the Dickens Foundation, 221C Baker Street, London."

"Yes, but you can't have the people stand and read the book verbatim over the air," Playhill replied. "The first task is to have a screenplay written. I have chosen a couple of writers who worked on my last feature film, 'Paws.' The screenplay, with revisions, should take three weeks to complete."

"Excuse me," interrupted Felix Birschfeld, vice president of accounting, "but how much will these undoubtedly fine writers cost us?"

"The writing team usually receives $20,000 for a feature-length screenplay. This is a little more than the going rate, but the quality of their work allows me to forego an additional week of review and rewrite."

"And what is that going rate?" asked Felix.

"About $10,000. Are there additional questions about the screenplay? Very well. The next step is to cast the leading roles according to the screenplay. Casting for this project will proceed in two stages because filming will take place in two stages. Interior scenes requiring only the primary characters can be shot at a studio using soundstages. Exterior shots, depicting the streets of 19th century London, will be filmed on location."

"Wait a minute," said Charles Hume, vice president of data processing. "Aren't there outdoor soundstages available for the exterior work? Location shooting in London sounds quite expensive."

"Actually, shooting the exterior scenes at a studio would be more expensive. A London set is not available at any studio, so we'd have to build one. Construction would be more expensive than location work because a bank loan from Burbank National Bank at 15 percent would be required to finance it. Also, what would we do with the set after shooting? None of the studios may want to buy it."

"But, to fly everyone to London . . ."

"Unnecessary. There are areas in Boston that can be used for the filming. The architecture in the Beacon Hill and Cambridge areas is well suiited for this film. The traveling expenses would be lower . . ."

"Speaking of expenses . . ."

"Yes, Mr. Birschfeld. Soundstage rentals average about $30,000 per week. I expect we can comfortably complete the interior scenes in about four weeks."

"Thirty thousand dollars! Steven, how long would it take to complete the interiors, say, working longer days, or on weekends?" Birschfeld asked.

"Well, the four weeks is a very rough estimate. After reading the story over, I can see us using six interior scenes."

Playhill went to the blackboard and drew the following table:

Scene	Days needed	Characters
Cratchet Home 1	2–3	Whole Cratchet Family
Scrooge Office 1	2–3	Scrooge, Bob Cratchet
Cratchet Home 2	2–3	Mrs. Cratchet, Children
Scrooge Office 2	2–3	Scrooge
Scrooge Bedroom 1	4–5	Scrooge, Ghosts
Cratchet Home 3	6–8	Cratchet Family, Scrooge

"As you can see, this schedule can take anywhere from four to five weeks," Playhill continued. Union rules say any work on Saturday or Sunday means a 50 percent bonus for all off-stage labor involved. So, if we shoot one Saturday, everybody gets 150 pecent of their daily pay for that Saturday.

"The shooting in Boston will probably take about three weeks. However, we want good amounts of fog and some snow available, so we cannot begin Boston shooting before November. Rental of the locations, including traffic and crowd control, is about $45,000 per week. We cannot shorten the time the location shooting will require."

Talk of expenses had subdued the audience's enthusiasm. Mr. Monolith cleared his throat and asked, "Are there any other nonpersonnel expenses which are needed for shooting?"

"Let's see . . . well, some props would have to be constructed. I'd say that should take a week but could be done prior to renting shooting sites. The cost would be about $10,000. Costume rental and fitting will cost about $20,000. Lighting, filming, and sound equipment can be rented for about $7,000 per week for soundstage and $10,000 per week for location work."

Jill Habaersham, vice president of marketing, made a comment. "Steve, you mentioned that casting would be handled around the shooting schedule."

"Yes, thank you for reminding me. Casting of the primary roles, such as Scrooge, will be for both the interior and exterior shooting. The payroll for Scrooge and the Cratchet Family should run about $15,000 per week. Secondary roles and extras are another matter. The interior scenes will require minimal use of extras. In Boston many local people should be hired as extras to provide background crowds. Most of these people could probably be paid a total of from $2,000 to $3,000 per week. They can be hired just for the Boston work, so auditions can be held anytime before that. However, the casting director should probably do this work immediately prior to the Boston shooting. This would insure that the extras will be available and ready when shooting begins. Casting should take about one week at each stage.[1]

"The other people are the technical, backstage staff. We formed a company of the people who normally work in my crew. They know my directing style and we've worked well together in the past. The fee is $300,000, including my $60,000, for the film."

"Are there any other processes during this project which will require time to complete the film?"

"Yes, Mr. Hume. After each stage of filming is completed we will need at least one week to edit the film which was shot. We'll need an additional week at each stage for shooting any retakes. Has anyone requested a preview?"

Mr. Monolith spoke up. "BAA always requires their films to be previewed. Why?"

"Because we should allow another week for staging the preview here in Burbank and processing any re-edits they request. That should produce us a made-for-TV film. Any questions? Thank you."

Playhill took his seat and Quinn began to discuss the promotion of the film.

"BAA has requested two forms of promotion. They would like us to produce a 60-second and a 30-second commercial including actual film footage. The 60-second spot must include scenes from both interior and location shooting. The 30-second spot should contain only close-ups of the primary characters. They want to run these commercials from December 3 through December 24. The cost of the commercials will be around $20,000, and I have set aside a week to complete this task. The commercials could be completed in as little as three days. But the production staff size would have to expand, probably increasing the commercial cost to around $37,000."

"John, does that mean the film must be completed by December 3?"

"No, it means we'll take some action shots during the editing stage, produce copies, and expect those shots to appear in the film," Quinn replied.

---

[1] Casting of the primary roles could be cut to four days rather than making an extensive search. Big name talent could be signed, but payroll costs would probably double.

"The second phase of promotion also kicks off on December 3, BAA airs several talk shows, including Donny Parson and David Postman. They would like two or three of the stars of the movie to make the rounds of these shows after shooting is completed. They will appear, discuss the film, and introduce a film clip. The film clip accompanying a star has to spotlight that star. Because filming of such shows is done two weeks in advance, all these spots must be completed by December 10.

"That does it for the promotion. Now Madeline Crawford from our Phantom Books Publishing wing will discuss the picture book."

"Thank you, John. Ladies and gentlemen, this portion of the project is not exactly a 'picture book.' What we plan to do is develop a novella from the film screenplay. Basically, we're editing Dickens into an action novel. Then we will combine this prose with color photos taken from the film. Similar products have been quite successful. Since we have total control over this part of the project, we are its sole benefactor and collect all revenues. We anticipate sales of about 150,000 to 250,000 copies priced at $1.80 per copy. The book should be finished and shipped to outlets by the beginning of the last week of November to reap maximum sales. A delay of one week would cost us about 100,000 copies."

"Madeline, are you saying now that the film has to be done by the third week of November?"

"No, all that must be completed is the filming. Like the commercials, we can then take stills from the footage. Once we have the photos, it will take one week to put the photos in the book and print copies."

"Excuse me, but about the cost of printing . . ."

"Yes, Mr. Birschfeld. Printing a book like this requires an initial outlay of $100,000 for the first 10,000 copies. Then, every 100,000 copies printed costs an additional $80,000."

"What about the prose portion of the book, Madeline?"

"The book has to be written from the original screenplay. Although some changes may occur during shooting, such changes should not affect the book significantly. The 'prose-ifying' of the screenplay should take about two weeks. We need another three weeks to choose an appropriate layout and composition for the book. Then it's all done except photos and printing. Are there any questions?"

Mr. Monolith rose to wrap up the meeting. "Ladies and gentlemen, we have one week to schedule and budget this project. We plan to let the people who made presentations here begin their work one week from today.

"We will meet again Thursday. Between now and Thursday, my assistant, Jennifer Wilson, will put together a preliminary plan. The report will include a schedule, budget, and cash flow. We will discuss, revise if necessary, and approve a plan. And now, it's almost noon, so let's adjourn to the executive dining room for luncheon and informal discussions."

The vice presidents and other executives filed out of the room, leaving a rather nervous Jennifer Wilson bending a paper clip and wondering what to do next. Jennifer had recently graduated from college and wanted to do well on her first job at Monolith Productions. She knew that working with the executive group of the firm was a tremendous opportunity to learn the industry and demonstrate her capabilities.

Questions

1. What analytical tools can Jennifer Wilson use to schedule the project? Is any tool more advantageous than others?
2. Are there ways of shortening the time it will take to complete the project? Is it more profitable to shorten the project time?
3. Can the project support its own weekly cash needs?

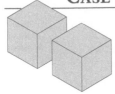

CASE 6:   ONTARIO PACKAGING

"It looks to me that we are agreed. The process investment proposals before us are sound in principle providing we can increase throughput from present levels by some 40 percent, as indicated in the supporting details. I know this is no easy task, but all market segments are getting more difficult and, if we are to survive and maintain current performance levels, then this type of challenge will be illustrative of many future corporate decisions. From these initial discussions it appears that the extra volume is available, even though it places a great emphasis on price. The new process will help, in part, to reduce costs, but higher volumes are essential if we are to maintain the group's payback requirements, and protect the above-average return on investment performance we have achieved in the past." Norm Phillips, chief executive officer of Ontario Packaging, was summing up a meeting on manufacturing investment proposals, which was intended to be the initial phase of a modernization program within the company.

Background

Ontario Packaging is part of Texet Industries, a large group of companies with diverse interests in food, cosmetics, engineering, and toys, besides a growing stake in retail holdings and other nonmanufacturing businesses. Taken over in 1984, Ontario Packaging is now one of several packaging companies within the Group, but the first within the Province.

Having given the company time to settle down within the new corporate structure and allowed Norm Phillips to gain an understanding of the business

Source: Terry Hill, *Manufacturing Strategy* (Homewood, Ill.: Richard D. Irwin, 1989), pp. 427–31. Reprinted by permission.

since his transfer from within the Group, some 12 months before, the Executive Group of Texet had recently asked the company to review its position. The review was to include an assessment of its current markets and to include any future process investment proposals it thought to be necesssary with an indication of why they should take place, the anticipated impact on the business as a whole, and on the various return on investment measures used within the Group, in particular.

Manufacturing

Ontario Packaging produces a fairly wide range of cartons and other forms of packaging. Its manufacturing capability comprises various forms of printing, laminating, cutting, creasing, glueing, and other auxiliary processes, together with a whole range of in-house support functions.

The investment proposals under review concern replacing current laminating equipment with an up-to-date process which would provide the same capability (see Exhibit 1). The cartons which use this process account for some 30 percent of total production volumes (standard machine hours). At a cost of $2.5 million, the investment would give labor, material, and other savings to provide a payback of 6.5 years on current volumes. However, in order to meet the Texet investment payback norm of four years it would necessitate increasing current sales revenue for these cartons by some 40 percent. It is this higher level of volumes on which the investment proposals have been based.

Besides the basic gains accruing from increased throughput speed (a principal source of savings) and reduced material wastage, the new process would offer few additional technical advantages (setup times were marginally faster), other than those associated with the reduced performance on existing processes resulting from wear and tear with age.

While the utilization of the current process was less than 60 percent, the target set in the proposal for the new investment was 80–85 percent, based on higher volumes.

Marketing

"Ontario Packaging has, over the years, increasingly positioned itself in the higher quality end of all its markets,"explained Rod Shaw, the marketing director, who has been with the company for over 15 years. "The cartons under review are no exception. While the technical features of the final carton are slightly less demanding than many of the rest of the product range, there is the same demand for high, reliable quality. While the manufacturing process currently used is able to consistently provide the quality requirements of our products, no doubt the new process will enable us to achieve these more easily.

"A recent marketing survey on the relative importance of different purchasing criteria to carton users revealed that in the segment to which this invest-

EXHIBIT 1

_Details of the invest-
ment proposal under
review_

As part of a strategy to upgrade its processes (as well as increase its process capability where appropriate) Ontario Packaging was proposing to invest in a state-of-the-art laminating process, which would replace the existing process capacity. Currently, some 30 percent of the total production volumes (standard machine hours) were laminated.

The new laminator would offer significant savings in direct labor (through reduced staffing), lower material costs within the laminating process, and a reduced maintenance bill (with, however, a corresponding increase in depreciation costs).

However, in order to achieve the group payback norm of four years, the company would need to increase its sales of laminated products by about 40 percent on current levels.

While setup (or make-ready) times for the new process were similar to the existing equipment, throughput speeds were more than twice as fast. The order quantities currently processed averaged about seven hours and ranged from 2.0 to 60.0 hours.

Current sales were split roughly half and half between those which were not price-sensitive and those where price was an order-winning criterion at some level. However, the latter orders varied in their degree of price sensitivity, with two thirds of this segment where price was given a weighting of 20 points or less.

It was recognized that the proposed increase in sales of laminated products of about 40 percent of current levels would be achieved in segments where price would increasingly be the important order winner. The company, although recognizing that this would require significant sales effort, has identified the segments and customers that are available and consider the achievement of these higher volumes to be a realistic target within the required timescales.

Notes:
1. Laminations consist of sheets of material (varying with individual specifications) that are glued together.
2. Due to space restrictions and to maintain the current, sensible flow of materials through the manufacturing process, the proposed new process will be installed where the existing equipment is positioned.
3. The current equipment comprises two machines and is run on a two-shift basis. It is also proposed to run the single replacement process on a two-shift basis.

---

ment proposal relates, providing prompt quotations and samples, together with high delivery reliability and a willingness to meet schedule changes, are critical features and ones which our company has proved to be better at providing than our competitors." This represents the view our customers expressed in the survey.

"While price is not an important factor in winning current orders for these products, it would increasingly be so for the new orders we would need to secure to achieve the additional volume called for by the output levels under-pinning the process investment proposals being considered. However, to compensate we would be moving into higher volume orders, which would reinforce the gains inherent in the new process in terms of the cost savings available, while obviously providing the overall volume levels associated with the whole proposal. I know we can get these additional orders, providing the price is right and we maintain all the other features of the product and necessary levels of customer service. It's a tall order, so to speak, but I know we can do it."

Answers to Selected Problems

Chapter 2: Decision Making

1. *a.* Expand (80).
  b. Do nothing (50).
  c. Indifferent between do nothing and subcontract (55).
  d. Subcontract (10).

2. *a.* Expand (62).
  b. $9.

3. Do nothing: $P(high) < .50$.
  Subcontract: $.50 < P(high) < .67$.
  Expand: $P(high) > .67$.

4. *a.*

5. Large for $\dot{P}(low) < .55$.
  Small for $P(low) > .55$.

6. *a.* Relocate.
  b. Renew.
  c. Relocate.

7. *a.* Renew.
  c. Yes.

9. *a.* Build large.
  b. Build small.
  c. $12.4.
  d. Build small for $P(high) < .721$.
  Build large for $P(high) > .721$.

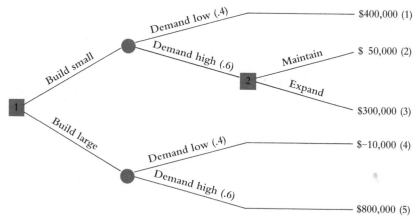

b. $164,000.

10. Buy two ($113.5).

11. Expand ($1.57).

12. $4.

13. *a.* New staff.
    b. Redesign.
    c. New staff.
    d. New staff or redesign.

16. *b.* Alternative *c*.
    c. $P(2) > .625$.
    d. $P(1) < .375$.

Chapter 2 Supplement: Linear Programming

1. *a.* $x = 0$, $y = 12$, Profit = $240.
    b. $A = 25.45$, $B = 18.18$, $Z = \$207.25$.

2. *a.* $T = 20$, $S = 8$, $Z = \$58.40$.
    b. $C = 4.6$, $D = 14.4$, $Z = \$24.18$.

3. $H = 132$ units, $W = 36$ units, Profit = $6,360.

4. Deluxe = 90 bags, Standard = 60 bags, Profit = $243.

5. $x = 327.27$, $y = 163.64$, $Z = \$1,636.36$.

6. 500 apple, 200 grape, Revenue = $990. Fifty cups of sugar will be unused.

7. Final tableau:

C		10	20	0	0	
	Variables in solution	x_1	x_2	s_1	s_2	Solution quantity
0	s_1	3.0	0.0	1.0	−0.5	16.0
20	x_2	1.0	1.0	0.0	0.3	12.0
	Z	20.0	20.0	0.0	5.0	240.0
	C − Z	−10.0	0.0	0.0	−5.0	

8. *a.* (1) 485.72 to 800.
       (2) 750 to 1,080.
       (3) 145.45 to infinity.
    b. (optimality).
       C_A: $3.75 to $12.
       C_B: $1.50 to $4.80.

9. Final tableau:

C		40	30	0	0	
	Variables in solution	H	W	s_1	s_2	Solution quantity
40	H	1.0	0.0	0.3	−0.1	132
30	W	0.0	1.0	−0.1	0.2	36
	Z	40.0	30.0	9.0	2.0	6,360
	C − Z	0.0	0.0	−9.0	−2.0	

    a. Fabrication 160 to 960.
       Assembly: 300 to 1,800.
    b. (optimality).
       H: $10 to $60.
       W: $20 to $120.

10. Final tableau:

C		4	2	0	0	0	
	Variables in solution	x	y	s_1	s_2	s_3	Solution quantity
2	y	0.0	1.0	0.0	0.0	−0.4	163.64
0	s_2	0.0	0.0	−0.1	1.0	1.0	695.46
4	x	1.0	0.0	−0.0	0.0	0.3	327.27
	Z	4.0	2.0	0.0	0.0	0.4	1,636.36
	C − Z	0.0	0.0	−0.0	0.0	−0.4	

a. Casting: 32,000 to 41,016.
   Grinding: 1,555 to infinity.
   Drilling: 2,871 to 4,050.
b. (optimality).
   C_x: $2.67 to $4.50.
   C_y: $1.78 to $3.00.

11. a. Final tableau:

C		10.5	11.75	10.8	0	0	0	
	Variables in solution	x	y	z	s_1	s_2	s_3	Solution quantity
0.00	s_1	0.0	5.6	1.6	1.0	−0.7	0.0	507.14
10.50	x	1.0	1.3	1.3	0.0	0.1	0.0	178.57
0.00	s_3	0.0	−2.1	0.9	0.0	−0.6	1.0	5.71
	Z	10.5	13.5	13.5	0.0	1.5	0.0	1875.00
	C − Z	0.0	−1.8	−2.7	0.0	−1.5	0.0	

b. Stapling, since the optimum solution exhausts that resource.

12. Final tableau:

C		2.40	2.50	3.00	0	0	0	
	Variables in solution	a	b	c	s_1	s_2	s_3	Solution quantity
2.50	b	1.2	1.0	0.0	0.2	0.0	−0.1	80
0.00	s_2	0.2	0.0	0.0	−0.3	1.0	−0.1	380
3.00	c	0.0	0.0	1.0	−0.1	0.0	0.1	50
	Z	3.0	2.5	3.0	0.2	0.0	0.1	350
	C − Z	−0.6	0.0	0.0	−0.2	0.0	−0.1	

C_a (insignificance): $0 to $3.00.
C_b (optimality): $2.00 to $3.50.
C_c (optimality): $2.00 to $5.00.

13. *a.* Final tableau:

C		21	18	999	0.0	999	0.0	
Variables in solution		x_1	x_2	a_1	s_1	a_2	s_2	Solution quantity
18	x_2	0.0	1.0	0.1	−0.1	−0.3	0.3	6.7
21	x_1	1.0	0.0	−0.1	0.1	0.7	−0.7	6.7
	Z	21.0	18.0	1.0	−1.0	8.0	−8.0	260.0
	C − Z	0.0	0.0	998.0	1.0	991.0	8.0	

b. Final tableau:

C		5	2	3	999	0	999	0	999	0	
Variables in solution		x	y	z	a_1	s_1	a_2	s_2	a_3	s_3	Solution quantity
3	z	1.0	0.0	1.0	0.1	−0.1	−0.1	0.1	0.0	0.0	12.56
0	s_3	2.1	0.0	0.0	−0.2	0.2	0.7	−0.7	−1.0	1.0	11.16
2	x	−0.1	1.0	0.0	−0.2	0.2	0.2	−0.2	0.0	0.0	11.40
	Z	2.6	2.0	3.0	0.1	−0.1	0.1	−0.1	0.0	0.0	60.47
	C − Z	2.4	0.0	0.0	999	0.1	999	0.1	999	0.0	

16. *a.* board = 0, holder = 50.
 b. Cutting = 16 minutes, gluing = 0 minutes, finishing = 210 minutes.

17. *a.* A = .7143, B = 7.7143, Cost = $.91.
 b. Carbohydrates by 20 grams.

19. Radio = 24, TV = 12, Newspaper = 8.

20. Bookcases = 31.11, food carts = 3.33, z = $1413.

21. z = $433.

22. *a.* $.12; 1,000 pounds to 2,000 pounds.
 b. $.48.
 c. No.
 d. Optimal quantities would not change; z would increase by $40.

23. *a.* $1.50; range is 450 to 750.
 b. $1.50/pound.
 c. $0; range 375 to infinity.
 d. None.
 e. 150 pounds of pine bark.
 f. Optimal quantities would not change; z would increase by $75.

Chapter 3: Forecasting

2. *b.* (1) 20.86, (2) 19, (3) 19.26, (4) 20.
 d. Demand did not exceed supply.

4. *a.* 88.16 percent.
 b. 88.54 percent.

5. *a.* Starting forecast is (800 + 810 + 808 + 812)/4 = 807.5; F_9 = 809.68 cases.
 b. 804 cases.

7. *a.* 700,000 sq. ft.   *b.* 760,000 sq. ft.

8. *a.* Increasing by 15,000 bottles per year.
 b. 275 (i.e., 275,000 bottles).

9. *b.* 1,320 trees.

10. 500 − 18.18t.

11. *a.* Y_t = 204.09 + 19.76t.   *c.* 500.49.

12. Q_1: 158; Q_2: 175; Q_3: 126; Q_4: 325.

13. Y_{11}: 267.63; Y_{12}: 274.13; Y_{13}: 280.63; Y_{14}: 287.13

14. Use periods 1 through 4 for model development.
TAF = 224
T = 8

Period	Forecast
5	223.62
6	234.79
7	233.25
8	247.32
9	251.04
10	259.72
11	272.58

17. Fri. = 0.79, Sat. = 1.34, Sun. = 0.87.

22.

Day	Relative
1	.902
2	.836
3	.919
4	1.034
5	1.416
6	1.487
7	.427

24.

Jan.	800
Feb.	810
Mar.	750
Apr.	810
May	826
Jun.	850
Jul.	850
Aug.	855
Sep.	865
Oct.	900
Nov.	806
Dec.	900

27. *b.* $29,000.

28. *b.* $17.90.

29. *a.* $Y = 12.35 + .543x$. *b.* $r = .539$.
c. Yes.

30. *a.* $Y = 334.57 - 22.286x$. *c.* $r = -.974$.

31. *b.* $Y = 66.33 + .584x$. *c.* Yes.
d. 90.27. *e.* 90.27 ± 10.04.

32. *a.* $r = +.94$. *b.* $Y = .955 + 5.276x$.
c. 11.51 mowers.

34. *a.* $MAD_5 = 5$ *b.* $TS_5 = 1.40$
$MAD_6 = 5.9$ $TS_6 = -0.17$
$MAD_7 = 4.73$ $TS_7 = -0.63$
$MAD_8 = 3.911$ $TS_8 = -0.26$
$MAD_9 = 4.238$ $TS_9 = -1.42$
etc.   etc.

35. *a.*

	MSE	MAD
Forecast 1	10.44	2.8
Forecast 2	42.44	3.6
Naive	156	10.7

36. *a.* Initial MAD = 4.727. The tracking signal for month 15 is 4.087, so at that point, the forecast would be suspect.
b. Σ errors = -1, Σ errors^2 = 345. Control limits: 0 ± 12.38 (in control). Plot reveals cycles in errors.

Chapter 4: Product and Service Design

1. *a.* .81.   *b.* .9801.   *c.* .9783.

2. .9033.

3. .9726.

4. .93.

5. *a.* .9315.   *b.* .9953.   *c.* .994.

6. *a.* .7876.

7. *a.* Plan 2 (.9934).

8. .996.

9. .995.

10. .006.

11. *a.* (1) .2725.   *b.* (1) .6671.
(2) .2019.   (2) .3935.
(3) .1353.   (3) .1813.
c. (1) 21 months.   (3) 90 months.
(2) 57 months.   (4) 138 months.

12. *a.* .6321.   *b.* Three months or 90 days.

13. *a.* .3012.   *b.* .1813.   *c.* .5175.

14. *a.* .2231.   *b.* .8647.
c. .0878.   *d.* .0302.

15. *a.* .2266.   *b.* .4400.   *c.* .3830.

16. *a.* (1) .9772. *b.* Approximately zero.
(2) .5000.
(3) .0013.

Chapter 5: Location Planning

1. Kansas City: $256,000.
2. *a.* A: 16,854; B: 17,416; C: 17,753.
   b. C: $14,670.
3. *a.* 120 units. *b.* A: 0 to 119; B: 121+.
4. *a.* B: 0 to 33; C: 34 to 400; A: 400+.
5. C($270,000).
6. Biloxi ($160,000).
7. *a.* (1) outside; (2) city. *b.* 230 cars.
9. A.
10. *a.* B = C > A.
   b. B > C > A.

Chapter 5 Supplement: The Transportation Model

1.

	A	B	C
1	15		25
2	15	45	
3			50

2.

	A	B	C
1			40
2		25	35
3	30	20	

3.

	A	B	C	D
1	10	30		
2	80			
3		50	30	50

4.

	A	B	C	D	Dummy
1	13		35		
2	28	2		20	6
3		32			

5.

	A	B	C	D
1		40		
2	80	10		
3		30	30	50
Dummy	10			

6.

	A	B	C	D	Dummy
1	41		7		
2			56		
3		32			
Balt.		2	28	4	16

	A	B	C	D	Dummy
1	41		7		
2		2	54		
3		32			
Ph.		28	6		16

8.

	A	B	C	Dummy
1		500		
2	400			
N1		100	350	50

	A	B	C	Dummy
1		500		
2	400			
N2		100	350	50

9.

	A	B	C
1			210
2	140		
3	80	60	10
Tol.		160	

	A	B	C
1			210
2	60	80	
3		140	10
Cin.	160		

Chapter 6: Process Selection and Capacity Planning

1. *a.* 46,000 units. *b.* (1) $3,000,
   (2) $8,200.
   c. 126,000 units. *d.* 25,556 units.
2. *a.* A: 8,000 units. *b.* 10,000 units.
   B: 7,500 units.
   c. A: $20,000.
   B: $18,000.
3. *a.* 39,683 units. *b.* $1.71 (rounded up).
4. *a.* A: $82.
   B: $92.
   C: $100.
   c. A: 0 to less than 178.
   B: Never.
   C: 178+.

5. ⅓ day, ⅔ evening.
6. *a.* Additional plant. *b.* Do nothing.
   c. Do nothing.
   d. Do nothing.
7. *a.* Buy 200. *b.* Do nothing.
   c. Buy 80.
   d. (1) Buy 80.
   (2) Buy 80.
8. *b.* Overbook 1 for maximin; indifferent for maximax.
   c. Overbook 1 ($19.2).

Chapter 6 Supplement: Financial Analysis

1. *a.* 11%. *b.* 12%.
2. *a.* Seven years.
   b. $PV_a = \$181,800$, $PV_b = \$241,550$.
3. PV_{buy}: $7,112; PB_A: $6,914; PV_B: $6,748.40.
4. *a.* PV_A: $4,250, PV_B: $7,164.
   b. PV_A: $5,538, PV_B: $7,935.
5. A: 4.8 years; B: 5 years.
6. A: 20%; B: 18%; C: 22%.
7. PV_A: $1,910; PV_B: $-\$13,300$; PV_C: $-\$3,800$.
8. *a.* (1) $217,800.
   (2) $-\$1,346,400$.
   b. Approximately 12%.
   c. Eight years.
9. Remodel ($58,168).

Chapter 7: Facilities Layout

1. *a.* Minimum is 2.4 minutes, maximum is 18 minutes.
   b. 25 units to 187.5 units. *c.* Eight.
   d. 3.6 minutes. *e.* (1) 50 units.
   (2) 30 units.
2. *c.* 11.54%. *d.* 323 units per day.
3. *a.* 2.3 minutes. *c.* 182.6 units per day.
   d. 91.3 units per day.

4. *b.* 1 minute. *c.* Three stations.
5. *c.* (1) 11.1%. (2) 11.1%. (3) 33.33%.
7.

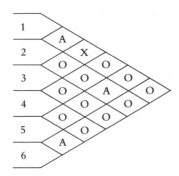

8.

3	5	4
1	8	7
6	2	

10.

3	1	8
9	7	4
5	2	6

11.

6	2	5
3	1	4

TC = $52,080.

13. A: 3; B: 5; C: 1; D: 4; E: 6; F; 2.
14. A: 1; B: 2; C: 5; D: 4; E: 9; F: 8; G: 6;
H: 10; I: 7; J: 3.

Chapter 8: Design of Work Systems

1. 15.08 minutes.
2. *a.* 1.2 minutes.
   b. 1.14 minutes.
   c. 1.27 minutes.

3.

Element	OT	NT	ST
1	0.46	0.414	0.476
2	1.505	1.280	1.472
3	0.83	0.913	1.050
4	1.16	1.160	1.334

4. 5.85 minutes.
5. 7.125 minutes.
7. 57 observations.
8. 14 cycles.
9. *a.* 12%. *b.* 163 observations.
10. 377 observations.
11.

Hour	Minute
1	0
1	47
1	56
3	38
4	24
4	27
6	26
7	15

Chapter 8 Supplement: Learning Curves

1. *a.* 178.8 hours.
   b. 1,121.4 hours.
   c. 2,914.8 hours.
2. *a.* 41.47 hours.
   b. 60.55 hours.
   c. 72.20 hours.
3. *a.* 56.928 days.
   b. 42.288 days.
   c. 37.512 days.
4. *a.* P = 85 percent.
   b. 23.5 minutes.
5. 87.9 minutes.
6. 201.26 minutes.
7. *a.* 10.57 hours.
   b. 13.05 hours.
   c. 12.29 hours.

8. *a.* $80.31.
   b. 10 units.
9. 31.63 days.
10. B and C.

Chapter 9: Aggregate Planning

3. B: $18,870.
   C: $18,860.
4. $18,525.
5. $18,530.50.
6. $18,190.
7. *b.* $6,350.
8. *a.* $4,670.
   b. $4,800.
9. $4,680.
10. $4,970.
12. $124,960.
13. $123,830.
14. $124,060.

Chapter 10: Inventory Management

1. *a.* 24 bags.
   b. 12 bags.
   c. 56.
   d. $336.
2. *a.* 379.47 liters.
   d. Increase by $179.
3. *a.* 1,960 pots.
4. $176.
5. *a.* 10,328 bags.
   b. 3,098 bags.
   c. 10.33 days.
   d. 7.75.
7. *a.* 4,812.
   b. 15.6.
   c. 0.96 days.
8. *a.* 9.
   b. 11 times per year.

9. *a.* 693 stones.
   b. 600 stones.
10. *a.* 10,000 boxes.
   b. 1.8 orders.
11. 20,000 units.
12. 1,000 seats.
13. 6,600 feet.
14. *a.* 8.39 gallons.
   b. 40 gallons.
15. *a.* 72 boxes.
   b. .0023.
   c. .0228.
16. 56 kits.
18. 749 pounds; 4.078 pounds.
19. *a.* 134 rolls.
   b. 36 rolls.
   c. .055 per cycle $[\sigma_{dLT} = \sqrt{LT}\sigma_d]$.
   d. .9996.
20. *a.* 80 feet per day.
   b. 301 feet.
   c. .999.
21. ROP = 77 cases.
22. KO33: 581.
   K144: 458.
   L700: 0.
23. 25 dozen.
24. Nine spares.
25. 78.9 pounds.
26. $4.89 per quart.
27. Five cakes.
28. 421.5 pounds.
29. *a.* $0.53 to $1.76.
   c. $56.67 to $190.00.
30. $0 to $78.03.

Chapter 11: Material Requirements Planning

1. *b.*

Level	Item	Quantity
0	P	60
1	A	120
	B	180
	H	240
2	K	120
	D	180
	E	180
	I	480
3	C	420
	F	900
	G	180
4	L	480
	M	1,860
	N	1,920

2.

Level	Item	Quantity
0	W	125
	Y	50
1	A	300
	B	600
	K	150
2	D	600
	C	1,100
	L	150
3	F	3,600
	E	1,500
	G	4,600
	H	1,100

3. *a.*

Master Schedule for E

Week number	1	2	3	4	5	6	7	8
Quantity					120			

Item: E LT = 1 week

Gross requirements					120			
Scheduled receipts								
Available								
Net requirements					120			
Planned order receipt					120			
Planned order release				120				

Item: I(2) LT = 1 week

Gross requirements				240				
Scheduled receipts			40					
Available			40	40				
Net requirements				200				
Planned order receipt				200				
Planned order release			200					

Item: N(4) LT = 2 weeks

Gross requirements			800					
Scheduled receipts								
Available	100	100	100	100				
Net requirements			700					
Planned order receipt			700					
Planned order release	700							

Item: V LT = 2 weeks

Gross requirements			200					
Scheduled receipts			10					
Available			0					
Net requirements			190					
Planned order receipt			190					
Planned order release	190							

5. *c.*

Master schedule for golf carts

Week number	1	2	3	4	5	6	7	8	9
Quantity						100		100	100

Item: Golf cart LT = 1 week	1	2	3	4	5	6	7	8	9
Gross requirements						100		100	100
Scheduled receipts									
Available									
Net requirements						100		100	100
Planned order receipt						100		100	100
Planned order release					100		100	100	

Item: Bases LT = 1 week		1	2	3	4	5	6	7	8	9
Gross requirements							100		100	100
Scheduled receipts										
Available	20	20	20	20	20	50	100	50	100	50
Net requirements							0		0	50
Planned order receipt				30	50	50	50	50	50	
Planned order release			30	50	50	50	50	50		

6. Order 160 units in week 2.

7. Order 120 units in period 2 and 60 units in period 6.

8. EPP = 75.76. Produce 60 units in week 0; 140 in 2; 80 in 3

Chapter 12: Just-in-Time Systems
Chapter 12: Just-in-Time Systems

1. 3.

2. 3.

Chapter 13: Scheduling

1. 1-A, 2-B, 3-C.

2. 1-B, 2-C, 3-A.

3. 1-A, 2-E, 3-D, 4-B, 5-C; or 1-A, 2-D, 3-E, 4-B, 5-C.

4. 1-B, 2-C, 3-D, 4-A.

5. *a.* 1-A, 2-B, 3-C, 4-D, 5-E.
   b. 1-E, 2-B, 3-C, 4-D, 5-A.

6. *b.*

	FCFS	SPT	DD	CR
Av. compl. time	26.5	19.75	21	26.50
Av. job lateness	11	6	6	7.33
Av. no. of jobs	2.86	2.14	2.27	2.86

7. FCFS: a–b–c–d–e.
SPT: c–b–a–e–d.
DD: a–b–c–e–d.
CR: a–d–e–b–c.

	FCFS	SPT	DD	CR
Av. compl. time	17.40	14.80	16.80	22.60
Av. job lateness	5.20	5.40	4.60	9.00
Av. no. of jobs	2.72	2.31	2.63	3.53

9. B–A–G–E–F–D–C.

10. *a.* e–b–g–h–d–c–a–f.
c. Two hours.

11. *a.* B–A–C–E–F–D.

12. *a.* b–a–c–d–e.
b. 37 minutes.
c. 15 minutes.

13. *a.*

	FCFS	SPT	DD	CR
Av. compl. time	15.25	11.12	15.60	15.68
Av. job lateness	1.7	2.33	0.55	0.30
Av. no. of jobs	3.91	2.85	4.00	4.02

14. b–c–e–a–d.

Chapter 14: Project Management

1. *a.* 1–3–6–9–11–12: 31.
b. 1–2–4–6–8–9: 37.
c. 1–2–5–12–16: 44.

2. *b.* 1–2–4–7.
c. 27.

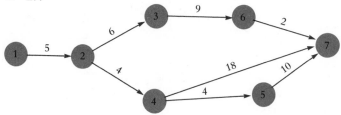

4. *a.* Summary:

Activity	ES	EF	LF	LS	Slack
1- 2	0	4	11	7	7
2- 4	4	13	21	12	8
4- 7	13	18	26	21	8
7-10	18	20	28	26	8
10-12	21	24	31	28	7
2- 5	4	12	19	11	7
5- 8	12	19	26	19	7
8-10	19	21	28	26	7
1- 3	0	10	10	0	0
3- 6	10	16	16	10	0
6- 9	16	20	20	16	0
9-11	20	25	25	20	0
11-12	25	31	31	25	0

b. Summary:

Activity	ES	EF	LF	LS	Slack
1-2	0	5	5	0	0
2-4	5	23	23	5	0
4-6	23	26	26	23	0
6-8	26	35	35	26	0
8-9	35	37	37	35	0
2-5	5	15	17	7	2
5-6	15	19	26	22	7
5-7	15	26	28	17	2
7-8	26	33	35	28	2
1-3	0	8	15	7	7
3-7	8	21	28	15	7

7. *b.*   24 days: .9686; 21 days: .2350.

8. *a.*   .8755.
   b.   .6881.
   c.   .0204.

9. *b.*   .0262.
   c.   .2296.

10.

Path	Mean	Standard deviation
a-d-e-h	24.34	1.354
a-f-g	15.50	1.258
b-i-j-k	14.83	1.014
c-m-n-o	26.17	1.658

27 weeks: .6742; 28 weeks: .8698.

13. Crash schedule (1 week each): c, c, f, f, e, p.

14. *a.*   Crash four weeks:
   (1) 7-11, (2) 1-2, (3) 7-11 and 6-10, (4) 11-13 and 4-6.

Chapter 15: Waiting Lines

1. *a.*   2.25 customers.
   b.   75 percent.
   c.   Two hours.
   d.   .5625.

2. *a.*   0.67 customers.
   b.   One minute.
   c.   1.33 customers.

3. *a.*   40 percent.   *d.*   .2288.
   b.   0.1523.
   c.   0.19 hour.

4. Morning: 0.3749 minutes; .450.
   Afternoon: 0.6776 minutes; .539.
   Evening: 0.6349 minutes; .444.

5. M: 4; A: 8; E: 5.

6. Three optimum.

7. *a.*   1.5282 customers.
   b.   0.054 hour.
   c.   0.0357 hour.

8. *a.*   63.5 percent.
   b.   36.5 percent.
   c.   0.688 customers; 0.725 minutes.
   d.   Six customers.
   e.   17.587 customers, 7.32 minutes, 76 customers.

9. *a.*   0.995 customers.
   b.   2.24 days.
   c.   31.1 percent.
   d.   0.875 customers.

10. *a.*   .437.
   b.   0.53 machines.
   c.   1.33 machines.
   d.   40.72 pieces.
   e.   Three.

11. *a.*   28.56 pieces.
   b.   Two.

12. One dock.
13. Two docks.
14. *a.* .90.
    b. W_1 = .12 hour.
       W_2 = .3045 hour.
       W_3 = 2.13 hours.
    c. L_1 = .36.
       L_2 = .91.
       L_3 = 6.39.
15. *a.* 30.
    b. L_1 = .034.
       L_2 = .025.

Chapter 15 Supplement: Simulation

1. 5.375 jobs.
2. 1: 80 percent, 2: 40 percent, 3: 40 percent.
5.

Patient	Time
1.	19.44
2.	20.24
3.	17.92
4.	19.38
5.	18.96
6.	16.48
7.	20.66

7.

Day	Usage
1.	43.932
2.	48.036
3.	34.908
4.	32.758
5.	42.186
6.	30.438
7.	33.298
8.	41.678
9.	33.526
10.	30.904

8.

Period	Usage
1	2
2	1
3	3
4	1
5	1
6	4
7	5
8	3
9	1
10	2

10. *b.*

Day	Order size
1	—
2	—
3	—
4	—
5	3
6	—
7	—
8	1
9	—
10	—
11	3
12	—

13. Ball 1: 1,320 points; ball 2: 1,120 points; ball 3: 1,170 points.
14. Ball 1: 3,320 points; ball 2: 720 points; ball 3: 970 points.

Chapter 16: Quality Assurance

1. *a.* (1) Yes. (2) Yes. *b.* .0067.
2. *b.* .0390.
3. *c.* .0024.
5. *a.* .0124. *b.* 24.35 pounds and 24.65 pounds.
6. *a.* LCL: 0.996 liters. *b.* Not in UCL: 1.004 liters. control.
7. *a.* Mean: LCL is 3.019, UCL is 3.181. Range: LCL is 0.1845, UCL is 0.7155.
   b. Yes.

9. Mean: LCL is 78.88 cm.
   UCL is 81.04 cm.
 Range: LCL is 0 cm.
    UCL is 3.946 cm.
 Process is in control.

10. LCL: 0
 UCL: .0234
 Revised limits based on 12 samples:
 LCL: 0
 UCL: .0197

11. Yes, UCL = 16.266, LCL = 0.

12. Yes, UCL = 5.17, LCL = 0.

13. Yes, UCL = .098, LCL = .010.

14. 490 pieces.

15. One in 30 is "out." Tolerances seem to be met. Approximately 97% will be acceptable.

16. a. LCL: 3.73
   UCL: 3.97
   Out of control.
 b. Random variations.

17.

	Test	Number of runs Observed	Expected	Standard deviation	z	Conclude
a.	Med 18		14	2.50	1.6	Okay
	U/D 17		17	2.07	0	Okay
b.	Med 8		14	2.50	−2.40	Nonrandom
	U/D 22		17	2.07	2.41	Nonrandom

18. a. Med: $z = -0.52$
   U/D: $z = -1.47$
 b. Med: $z = -1.11$
   U/D: $z = -1.36$

19. Med: $z = -2.34$
 U/D: $z = -1.45$

20. 440 pieces.

22. a. 566 units.
 b. 62 units.
 c. $1,160.

23. Med: $z = +0.917$
 U/D: $z = +0.556$

24. a. 0.16.
 b. 2.
 c. (1) .9638.
   (2) .0362.
   (3) Ac.
   (4) Both are zero.

26. b. 4.5, .192.
 c. 4.5, .086.
 d. 4.242 to 4.758.
 f. None.

APPENDIX

B

Tables

Table A

Areas under the normal curve, 0 to z

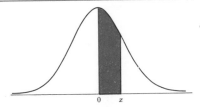

z	.00	.01	.02	.03	.04	.05	.06	.07	.08	.09
0.0	.0000	.0040	.0080	.0120	.0160	.0199	.0239	.0279	.0319	.0359
0.1	.0398	.0438	.0478	.0517	.0557	.0596	.0636	.0675	.0714	.0753
0.2	.0793	.0832	.0871	.0910	.0948	.0987	.1026	.1064	.1103	.1141
0.3	.1179	.1217	.1255	.1293	.1331	.1368	.1406	.1443	.1480	.1517
0.4	.1554	.1591	.1628	.1664	.1700	.1736	.1772	.1808	.1844	.1879
0.5	.1915	.1950	.1985	.2019	.2054	.2088	.2123	.2157	.2190	.2224
0.6	.2257	.2291	.2324	.2357	.2389	.2422	.2454	.2486	.2517	.2549
0.7	.2580	.2611	.2642	.2673	.2703	.2734	.2764	.2794	.2823	.2852
0.8	.2881	.2910	.2939	.2967	.2995	.3023	.3051	.3078	.3106	.3133
0.9	.3159	.3186	.3212	.3238	.3264	.3289	.3315	.3340	.3365	.3389
1.0	.3413	.3438	.3461	.3485	.3508	.3531	.3554	.3577	.3599	.3621
1.1	.3643	.3665	.3686	.3708	.3729	.3749	.3770	.3790	.3810	.3830
1.2	.3849	.3869	.3888	.3907	.3925	.3944	.3962	.3980	.3997	.4015
1.3	.4032	.4049	.4066	.4082	.4099	.4115	.4131	.4147	.4162	.4177
1.4	.4192	.4207	.4222	.4236	.4251	.4265	.4279	.4292	.4306	.4319
1.5	.4332	.4345	.4357	.4370	.4382	.4394	.4406	.4418	.4429	.4441
1.6	.4452	.4463	.4474	.4484	.4495	.4505	.4515	.4525	.4535	.4545
1.7	.4554	.4564	.4573	.4582	.4591	.4599	.4608	.4616	.4625	.4633
1.8	.4641	.4649	.4656	.4664	.4671	.4678	.4686	.4693	.4699	.4706
1.9	.4713	.4719	.4726	.4732	.4738	.4744	.4750	.4756	.4761	.4767
2.0	.4772	.4778	.4783	.4788	.4793	.4798	.4803	.4808	.4812	.4817
2.1	.4821	.4826	.4830	.4834	.4838	.4842	.4846	.4850	.4854	.4857
2.2	.4861	.4864	.4868	.4871	.4875	.4878	.4881	.4884	.4887	.4890
2.3	.4893	.4896	.4898	.4901	.4904	.4906	.4909	.4911	.4913	.4916
2.4	.4918	.4920	.4922	.4925	.4927	.4929	.4931	.4932	.4934	.4936
2.5	.4938	.4940	.4941	.4943	.4945	.4946	.4948	.4949	.4951	.4952
2.6	.4953	.4955	.4956	.4957	.4959	.4960	.4961	.4962	.4963	.4964
2.7	.4965	.4966	.4967	.4968	.4969	.4970	.4971	.4972	.4973	.4974
2.8	.4974	.4975	.4976	.4977	.4977	.4978	.4979	.4979	.4980	.4981
2.9	.4981	.4982	.4982	.4983	.4984	.4984	.4985	.4985	.4986	.4986
3.0	.4987	.4987	.4987	.4988	.4988	.4989	.4989	.4989	.4990	.4990

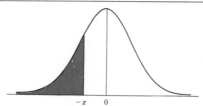

.09	.08	.07	.06	.05	.04	.03	.02	.01	.00	z
.0002	.0003	.0003	.0003	.0003	.0003	.0003	.0003	.0003	.0003	−3.4
.0003	.0004	.0004	.0004	.0004	.0004	.0004	.0005	.0005	.0005	−3.3
.0005	.0005	.0005	.0006	.0006	.0006	.0006	.0006	.0007	.0007	−3.2
.0007	.0007	.0008	.0008	.0008	.0008	.0009	.0009	.0009	.0010	−3.1
.0010	.0010	.0011	.0011	.0011	.0012	.0012	.0013	.0013	.0013	−3.0
.0014	.0014	.0015	.0015	.0016	.0016	.0017	.0018	.0018	.0019	−2.9
.0019	.0020	.0021	.0021	.0022	.0023	.0023	.0024	.0025	.0026	−2.8
.0026	.0027	.0028	.0029	.0030	.0031	.0032	.0033	.0034	.0035	−2.7
.0036	.0037	.0038	.0039	.0040	.0041	.0043	.0044	.0045	.0047	−2.6
.0048	.0049	.0051	.0052	.0054	.0055	.0057	.0059	.0060	.0062	−2.5
.0064	.0066	.0068	.0069	.0071	.0073	.0075	.0078	.0080	.0082	−2.4
.0084	.0087	.0089	.0091	.0094	.0096	.0099	.0102	.0104	.0107	−2.3
.0110	.0113	.0116	.0119	.0122	.0125	.0129	.0132	.0136	.0139	−2.2
.0143	.0146	.0150	.0154	.0158	.0162	.0166	.0170	.0174	.0179	−2.1
.0183	.0188	.0192	.0197	.0202	.0207	.0212	.0217	.0222	.0228	−2.0
.0233	.0239	.0244	.0250	.0256	.0262	.0268	.0274	.0281	.0287	−1.9
.0294	.0301	.0307	.0314	.0322	.0329	.0336	.0344	.0351	.0359	−1.8
.0367	.0375	.0384	.0392	.0401	.0409	.0418	.0427	.0436	.0446	−1.7
.0455	.0465	.0475	.0485	.0495	.0505	.0516	.0526	.0537	.0548	−1.6
.0559	.0571	.0582	.0594	.0606	.0618	.0630	.0643	.0655	.0668	−1.5
.0681	.0694	.0708	.0721	.0735	.0749	.0764	.0778	.0793	.0808	−1.4
.0823	.0838	.0853	.0869	.0885	.0901	.0918	.0934	.0951	.0968	−1.3
.0985	.1003	.1020	.1038	.1056	.1075	.1093	.1112	.1131	.1151	−1.2
.1170	.1190	.1210	.1230	.1251	.1271	.1292	.1314	.1335	.1357	−1.1
.1379	.1401	.1423	.1446	.1469	.1492	.1515	.1539	.1562	.1587	−1.0
.1611	.1635	.1660	.1685	.1711	.1736	.1762	.1788	.1814	.1841	−0.9
.1867	.1894	.1922	.1949	.1977	.2005	.2033	.2061	.2090	.2119	−0.8
.2148	.2177	.2206	.2236	.2266	.2296	.2327	.2358	.2389	.2420	−0.7
.2451	.2483	.2514	.2546	.2578	.2611	.2643	.2676	.2709	.2743	−0.6
.2776	.2810	.2843	.2877	.2912	.2946	.2981	.3015	.3050	.3085	−0.5
.3121	.3156	.3192	.3228	.3264	.3300	.3336	.3372	.3409	.3446	−0.4
.3483	.3520	.3557	.3594	.3632	.3669	.3707	.3745	.3783	.3821	−0.3
.3859	.3897	.3936	.3974	.4013	.4052	.4090	.4129	.4168	.4207	−0.2
.4247	.4286	.4325	.4364	.4404	.4443	.4483	.4522	.4562	.4602	−0.1
.4641	.4681	.4721	.4761	.4801	.4840	.4880	.4920	.4960	.5000	−0.0

TABLE B *(concluded)*

2. *Areas under the standardized normal curve from* $-\infty$ *to* $+z$

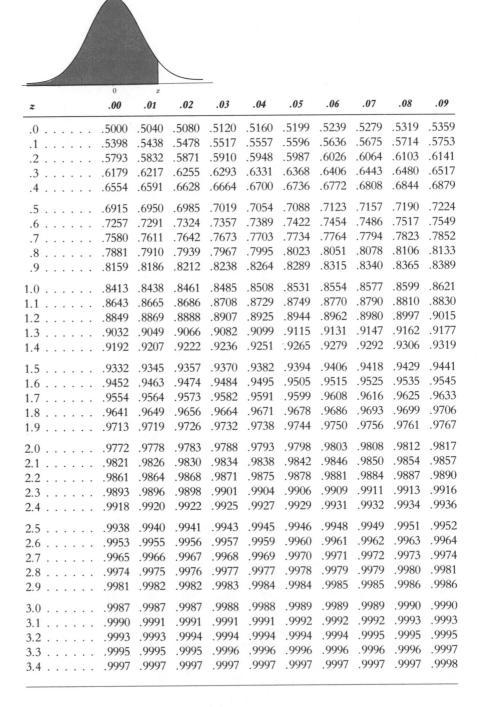

z	.00	.01	.02	.03	.04	.05	.06	.07	.08	.09
.0	.5000	.5040	.5080	.5120	.5160	.5199	.5239	.5279	.5319	.5359
.1	.5398	.5438	.5478	.5517	.5557	.5596	.5636	.5675	.5714	.5753
.2	.5793	.5832	.5871	.5910	.5948	.5987	.6026	.6064	.6103	.6141
.3	.6179	.6217	.6255	.6293	.6331	.6368	.6406	.6443	.6480	.6517
.4	.6554	.6591	.6628	.6664	.6700	.6736	.6772	.6808	.6844	.6879
.5	.6915	.6950	.6985	.7019	.7054	.7088	.7123	.7157	.7190	.7224
.6	.7257	.7291	.7324	.7357	.7389	.7422	.7454	.7486	.7517	.7549
.7	.7580	.7611	.7642	.7673	.7703	.7734	.7764	.7794	.7823	.7852
.8	.7881	.7910	.7939	.7967	.7995	.8023	.8051	.8078	.8106	.8133
.9	.8159	.8186	.8212	.8238	.8264	.8289	.8315	.8340	.8365	.8389
1.0	.8413	.8438	.8461	.8485	.8508	.8531	.8554	.8577	.8599	.8621
1.1	.8643	.8665	.8686	.8708	.8729	.8749	.8770	.8790	.8810	.8830
1.2	.8849	.8869	.8888	.8907	.8925	.8944	.8962	.8980	.8997	.9015
1.3	.9032	.9049	.9066	.9082	.9099	.9115	.9131	.9147	.9162	.9177
1.4	.9192	.9207	.9222	.9236	.9251	.9265	.9279	.9292	.9306	.9319
1.5	.9332	.9345	.9357	.9370	.9382	.9394	.9406	.9418	.9429	.9441
1.6	.9452	.9463	.9474	.9484	.9495	.9505	.9515	.9525	.9535	.9545
1.7	.9554	.9564	.9573	.9582	.9591	.9599	.9608	.9616	.9625	.9633
1.8	.9641	.9649	.9656	.9664	.9671	.9678	.9686	.9693	.9699	.9706
1.9	.9713	.9719	.9726	.9732	.9738	.9744	.9750	.9756	.9761	.9767
2.0	.9772	.9778	.9783	.9788	.9793	.9798	.9803	.9808	.9812	.9817
2.1	.9821	.9826	.9830	.9834	.9838	.9842	.9846	.9850	.9854	.9857
2.2	.9861	.9864	.9868	.9871	.9875	.9878	.9881	.9884	.9887	.9890
2.3	.9893	.9896	.9898	.9901	.9904	.9906	.9909	.9911	.9913	.9916
2.4	.9918	.9920	.9922	.9925	.9927	.9929	.9931	.9932	.9934	.9936
2.5	.9938	.9940	.9941	.9943	.9945	.9946	.9948	.9949	.9951	.9952
2.6	.9953	.9955	.9956	.9957	.9959	.9960	.9961	.9962	.9963	.9964
2.7	.9965	.9966	.9967	.9968	.9969	.9970	.9971	.9972	.9973	.9974
2.8	.9974	.9975	.9976	.9977	.9977	.9978	.9979	.9979	.9980	.9981
2.9	.9981	.9982	.9982	.9983	.9984	.9984	.9985	.9985	.9986	.9986
3.0	.9987	.9987	.9987	.9988	.9988	.9989	.9989	.9989	.9990	.9990
3.1	.9990	.9991	.9991	.9991	.9991	.9992	.9992	.9992	.9993	.9993
3.2	.9993	.9993	.9994	.9994	.9994	.9994	.9994	.9995	.9995	.9995
3.3	.9995	.9995	.9995	.9996	.9996	.9996	.9996	.9996	.9996	.9997
3.4	.9997	.9997	.9997	.9997	.9997	.9997	.9997	.9997	.9997	.9998

TABLE C

Cumulative Poisson probabilities

$$P(x \le c) = \sum_{x = 0}^{x = c} \frac{\mu^x e^{-\mu}}{x!}$$

μ \ x	0	1	2	3	4	5	6	7	8	9
0.05	.951	.999	1.000							
0.10	.905	.995	1.000							
0.15	.861	.990	.999	1.000						
0.20	.819	.982	.999	1.000						
0.25	.779	.974	.998	1.000						
0.30	.741	.963	.996	1.000						
0.35	.705	.951	.994	1.000						
0.40	.670	.938	.992	.999	1.000					
0.45	.638	.925	.989	.999	1.000					
0.50	.607	.910	.986	.998	1.000					
0.55	.577	.894	.982	.998	1.000					
0.60	.549	.878	.977	.997	1.000					
0.65	.522	.861	.972	.996	.999	1.000				
0.70	.497	.844	.966	.994	.999	1.000				
0.75	.472	.827	.960	.993	.999	1.000				
0.80	.449	.809	.953	.991	.999	1.000				
0.85	.427	.791	.945	.989	.998	1.000				
0.90	.407	.772	.937	.987	.998	1.000				
0.95	.387	.754	.929	.984	.997	1.000				
1.0	.368	.736	.920	.981	.996	.999	1.000			
1.1	.333	.699	.900	.974	.995	.999	1.000			
1.2	.301	.663	.880	.966	.992	.998	1.000			
1.3	.273	.627	.857	.957	.989	.998	1.000			
1.4	.247	.592	.833	.946	.986	.997	.999	1.000		
1.5	.223	.558	.809	.934	.981	.996	.999	1.000		
1.6	.202	.525	.783	.921	.976	.994	.999	1.000		
1.7	.183	.493	.757	.907	.970	.992	.998	1.000		
1.8	.165	.463	.731	.891	.964	.990	.997	.999	1.000	
1.9	.150	.434	.704	.875	.956	.987	.997	.999	1.000	
2.0	.135	.406	.677	.857	.947	.983	.995	.999	1.000	
2.2	.111	.355	.623	.819	.928	.975	.993	.998	1.000	
2.4	.091	.308	.570	.779	.904	.964	.988	.997	.999	1.000
2.6	.074	.267	.518	.736	.877	.951	.983	.995	.999	1.000
2.8	.061	.231	.470	.692	.848	.935	.976	.992	.998	.999

TABLE C (concluded)

μ\x	0	1	2	3	4	5	6	7	8	9	10	11	12	13	14	15	16	17	18	19	20
3.0	.050	.199	.423	.647	.815	.916	.966	.988	.996	.999	1.000										
3.2	.041	.171	.380	.603	.781	.895	.955	.983	.994	.998	1.000										
3.4	.033	.147	.340	.558	.744	.871	.942	.977	.992	.997	.999	1.000									
3.6	.027	.126	.303	.515	.706	.844	.927	.969	.988	.996	.999	1.000									
3.8	.022	.107	.269	.474	.668	.816	.909	.960	.984	.994	.998	.999	1.000								
4.0	.018	.092	.238	.433	.629	.785	.889	.949	.979	.992	.997	.999	1.000								
4.2	.015	.078	.210	.395	.590	.753	.868	.936	.972	.989	.996	.999	1.000								
4.4	.012	.066	.185	.359	.551	.720	.844	.921	.964	.985	.994	.998	.999	1.000							
4.6	.010	.056	.163	.326	.513	.686	.818	.905	.955	.980	.992	.997	.999	1.000							
4.8	.008	.048	.143	.294	.476	.651	.791	.887	.944	.975	.990	.996	.999	1.000							
5.0	.007	.040	.125	.265	.441	.616	.762	.867	.932	.968	.986	.995	.998	.999	1.000						
5.2	.006	.034	.109	.238	.406	.581	.732	.845	.918	.960	.982	.993	.997	.999	1.000						
5.4	.005	.029	.095	.213	.373	.546	.702	.822	.903	.951	.978	.990	.996	.999	1.000						
5.6	.004	.024	.082	.191	.342	.512	.670	.797	.886	.941	.972	.988	.995	.998	.999	1.000					
5.8	.003	.021	.072	.170	.313	.478	.638	.771	.867	.929	.965	.984	.993	.997	.999	1.000					
6.0	.003	.017	.062	.151	.285	.446	.606	.744	.847	.916	.957	.980	.991	.996	.999	.999	1.000				
6.2	.002	.015	.054	.134	.259	.414	.574	.716	.826	.902	.949	.975	.989	.995	.998	.999	1.000				
6.4	.002	.012	.046	.119	.235	.384	.542	.687	.803	.886	.939	.969	.986	.994	.997	.999	1.000				
6.6	.001	.010	.040	.105	.213	.355	.511	.658	.780	.869	.927	.963	.982	.992	.997	.999	.999	1.000			
6.8	.001	.007	.030	.082	.173	.301	.450	.599	.729	.830	.915	.955	.978	.990	.996	.998	.999	1.000			
7.0	.001	.007	.030	.082	.173	.301	.450	.599	.729	.830	.901	.947	.973	.987	.994	.998	.999	1.000			
7.2	.001	.006	.025	.072	.156	.276	.420	.569	.703	.810	.887	.937	.967	.984	.993	.997	.999	.999	1.000		
7.4	.001	.005	.022	.063	.140	.253	.392	.539	.676	.788	.871	.926	.961	.980	.991	.996	.998	.999	1.000		
7.6	.001	.004	.019	.055	.125	.231	.365	.510	.648	.765	.854	.915	.954	.976	.989	.995	.998	.999	1.000		
7.8	.000	.004	.016	.048	.112	.210	.338	.481	.620	.741	.835	.902	.945	.971	.986	.993	.997	.999	1.000		
8.0	.000	.003	.014	.042	.100	.191	.313	.453	.593	.717	.816	.888	.936	.966	.983	.992	.996	.998	.999	1.000	
8.2	.000	.003	.012	.037	.089	.174	.290	.425	.566	.692	.796	.873	.926	.960	.979	.990	.995	.998	.999	1.000	
8.4	.000	.002	.010	.032	.079	.157	.267	.400	.537	.666	.774	.857	.915	.952	.975	.987	.994	.997	.999	1.000	
8.6	.000	.002	.009	.030	.074	.150	.256	.386	.523	.653	.763	.849	.909	.949	.973	.986	.993	.997	.999	1.000	
8.8	.000	.002	.007	.024	.062	.128	.226	.348	.482	.614	.729	.822	.889	.935	.964	.981	.990	.995	.998	.999	1.000
9.0	.000	.001	.006	.021	.055	.116	.207	.324	.456	.587	.706	.803	.876	.926	.959	.978	.989	.995	.998	.999	1.000
9.5	.000	.001	.004	.015	.040	.089	.165	.269	.392	.522	.645	.752	.836	.898	.940	.967	.982	.991	.996	.998	.999

TABLE D

Cumulative binomial probabilities

$$P(x \le c) = \sum_{x=0}^{c} \binom{n}{x} p^x (1-p)^{n-x}$$

n	x	.05	.10	.15	.20	.25	.30	.35	.40	.45	.50	.55	.60	.65	.70	.75	.80	.85	.90
1	0	.9500	.9000	.8500	.8000	.7500	.7000	.6500	.6000	.5500	.5000	.4500	.4000	.3500	.3000	.2500	.2000	.1500	.1000
	1	1.0000	1.0000	1.0000	1.0000	1.0000	1.0000	1.0000	1.0000	1.0000	1.0000	1.0000	1.0000	1.0000	1.0000	1.0000	1.0000	1.0000	1.0000
2	0	.9025	.8100	.7225	.6400	.5625	.4900	.4225	.3600	.3025	.2500	.2025	.1600	.1225	.0900	.0625	.0400	.0225	.0100
	1	.9975	.9900	.9775	.9600	.9375	.9100	.8775	.8400	.6975	.7500	.6975	.6400	.5775	.5100	.4375	.3600	.2775	.1900
	2	1.0000	1.0000	1.0000	1.0000	1.0000	1.0000	1.0000	1.0000	1.0000	1.0000	1.0000	1.0000	1.0000	1.0000	1.0000	1.0000	1.0000	1.0000
3	0	.8574	.7290	.6141	.5120	.4219	.3430	.2746	.2160	.1664	.1250	.0911	.0640	.0429	.0270	.0156	.0080	.0034	.0010
	1	.9928	.9720	.9393	.8960	.8438	.7840	.7183	.6480	.5748	.5000	.4253	.3520	.2818	.2160	.1563	.1040	.0608	.0280
	2	.9999	.9990	.9966	.9920	.9844	.9730	.9571	.9360	.9089	.8750	.8336	.7840	.7254	.6570	.5781	.4880	.3859	.2710
	3	1.0000	1.0000	1.0000	1.0000	1.0000	1.0000	1.0000	1.0000	1.0000	1.0000	1.0000	1.0000	1.0000	1.0000	1.0000	1.0000	1.0000	1.0000
4	0	.8145	.6561	.5220	.4096	.3164	.2401	.1785	.1296	.0915	.0625	.0410	.0256	.0150	.0081	.0039	.0016	.0005	.0001
	1	.9860	.9477	.8905	.8192	.7383	.6517	.5630	.4752	.3910	.3125	.2415	.1792	.1265	.0837	.0508	.0272	.0120	.0037
	2	.9995	.9963	.9880	.9728	.9492	.9163	.8735	.8208	.7585	.6875	.6090	.5248	.4370	.3483	.2617	.1808	.1095	.0523
	3	1.0000	.9999	.9995	.9984	.9961	.9919	.9850	.9744	.9590	.9375	.9085	.8704	.8215	.7599	.6836	.5904	.4780	.3439
	4	1.0000	1.0000	1.0000	1.0000	1.0000	1.0000	1.0000	1.0000	1.0000	1.0000	1.0000	1.0000	1.0000	1.0000	1.0000	1.0000	1.0000	1.0000
5	0	.7738	.5905	.4437	.3277	.2373	.1681	.1160	.0778	.0503	.0313	.0185	.0102	.0053	.0024	.0010	.0003	.0001	.0000
	1	.9974	.9185	.8352	.7373	.6328	.5282	.4284	.3370	.2562	.1875	.1312	.0870	.0540	.0308	.0156	.0067	.0022	.0005
	2	.9988	.9914	.9734	.9421	.8965	.8369	.7648	.6826	.5931	.5000	.4069	.3174	.2352	.1631	.1035	.0579	.0266	.0086
	3	1.0000	.9995	.9978	.9933	.9844	.9692	.9460	.9130	.8688	.8125	.7438	.6630	.5716	.4718	.3672	.2627	.1648	.0815
	4	1.0000	1.0000	.9999	.9997	.9990	.9976	.9947	.9898	.9815	.9688	.9497	.9222	.8840	.8319	.7627	.6723	.5563	.4095
	5	1.0000	1.0000	1.0000	1.0000	1.0000	1.0000	1.0000	1.0000	1.0000	1.0000	1.0000	1.0000	1.0000	1.0000	1.0000	1.0000	1.0000	1.0000
6	0	.7351	.5314	.3771	.2621	.1780	.1176	.0754	.0467	.0277	.0156	.0083	.0041	.0018	.0007	.0002	.0001	.0000	.0000
	1	.9672	.8857	.7765	.6554	.5339	.4202	.3191	.2333	.1636	.1094	.0692	.0410	.0223	.0109	.0046	.0016	.0004	.0001
	2	.9978	.9842	.9527	.9011	.8306	.7443	.6471	.5443	.4415	.3438	.2553	.1792	.1174	.0705	.0376	.0170	.0059	.0013
	3	.9999	.9987	.9941	.9830	.9624	.9295	.8826	.8208	.7447	.6563	.5585	.4557	.3529	.2557	.1694	.0989	.0473	.0159
	4	1.0000	.9999	.9996	.9984	.9954	.9891	.9777	.9590	.9308	.8906	.8364	.7667	.6809	.5798	.4661	.3446	.2235	.1143
	5	1.0000	1.0000	1.0000	.9999	.9998	.9993	.9982	.9959	.9917	.9844	.9723	.9533	.9246	.8824	.8220	.7379	.6229	.4686
	6	1.0000	1.0000	1.0000	1.0000	1.0000	1.0000	1.0000	1.0000	1.0000	1.0000	1.0000	1.0000	1.0000	1.0000	1.0000	1.0000	1.0000	1.0000
7	0	.6983	.4783	.3206	.2097	.1335	.0824	.0490	.0280	.0152	.0078	.0037	.0016	.0006	.0002	.0001	.0000	.0000	.0000
	1	.9556	.8503	.7166	.5767	.4449	.3294	.2338	.1586	.1024	.0625	.0357	.0188	.0090	.0038	.0013	.0004	.0001	.0000
	2	.9962	.9743	.9262	.8520	.7564	.6471	.5323	.4199	.3164	.2266	.1529	.0963	.0556	.0288	.0129	.0047	.0012	.0002
	3	.9998	.9973	.9879	.9667	.9294	.8740	.8002	.7102	.6083	.5000	.3917	.2898	.1998	.1260	.0706	.0333	.0121	.0027
	4	1.0000	.9998	.9988	.9953	.9871	.9712	.9444	.9037	.8471	.7734	.6836	.5801	.4677	.3529	.2436	.1480	.0738	.0257
	5	1.0000	1.0000	.9999	.9996	.9987	.9962	.9910	.9812	.9643	.9375	.8976	.8414	.7662	.6706	.5551	.4233	.2834	.1497
	6	1.0000	1.0000	1.0000	1.0000	.9999	.9998	.9994	.9984	.9963	.9922	.9848	.9720	.9510	.9176	.8665	.7903	.6794	.5217
	7	1.0000	1.0000	1.0000	1.0000	1.0000	1.0000	1.0000	1.0000	1.0000	1.0000	1.0000	1.0000	1.0000	1.0000	1.0000	1.0000	1.0000	1.0000

TABLE D (continued)

Cumulative binomial probabilities

n	x	.05	.10	.15	.20	.25	.30	.35	.40	.45	.50	.55	.60	.65	.70	.75	.80	.85	.90
8	0	.6634	.4305	.2725	.1678	.1001	.0576	.0319	.0168	.0084	.0039	.0017	.0007	.0002	.0001	.0000	.0000	.0000	.0000
	1	.9428	.8131	.6572	.5033	.3671	.2553	.1691	.1064	.0632	.0352	.0181	.0085	.0036	.0013	.0004	.0001	.0000	.0000
	2	.9942	.9619	.8948	.7969	.6785	.5518	.4278	.3154	.2201	.1445	.0885	.0498	.0253	.0113	.0042	.0012	.0002	.0000
	3	.9996	.9950	.9786	.9437	.8862	.8059	.7064	.5941	.4470	.3633	.2604	.1737	.1061	.0580	.0273	.0104	.0029	.0004
	4	1.0000	.9996	.9971	.9896	.9727	.9420	.8939	.8263	.7396	.6367	.5230	.4059	.2936	.1941	.1138	.0563	.0214	.0050
	5	1.0000	1.0000	.9998	.9988	.9958	.9887	.9747	.9502	.9115	.8555	.7799	.6848	.5722	.4482	.3215	.2031	.1052	.0381
	6	1.0000	1.0000	1.0000	.9999	.9996	.9987	.9964	.9915	.9819	.9648	.9368	.8936	.8309	.7447	.6329	.4967	.3428	.1869
	7	1.0000	1.0000	1.0000	1.0000	1.0000	.9999	.9998	.9993	.9983	.9961	.9916	.9832	.9681	.9424	.8999	.8322	.7275	.5695
	8	1.0000	1.0000	1.0000	1.0000	1.0000	1.0000	1.0000	1.0000	1.0000	1.0000	1.0000	1.0000	1.0000	1.0000	1.0000	1.0000	1.0000	1.0000
9	0	.6302	.3874	.2316	.1342	.0751	.0404	.0207	.0101	.0046	.0020	.0008	.0003	.0001	.0000	.0000	.0000	.0000	.0000
	1	.9288	.7748	.5995	.4362	.3003	.1960	.1211	.0705	.0385	.0195	.0091	.0038	.0014	.0004	.0001	.0000	.0000	.0000
	2	.9916	.9470	.8591	.7382	.6007	.4628	.3373	.2318	.1495	.0898	.0498	.0250	.0112	.0043	.0013	.0003	.0000	.0000
	3	.9994	.9917	.9661	.9144	.8343	.7297	.6089	.4826	.3614	.2539	.1658	.0994	.0536	.0253	.0100	.0031	.0006	.0001
	4	1.0000	.9991	.9944	.9804	.9511	.9012	.8283	.7334	.6214	.5000	.3786	.2666	.1717	.0988	.0489	.0196	.0056	.0009
	5	1.0000	.9999	.9994	.9969	.9900	.9747	.9496	.9006	.8342	.7461	.6386	.5174	.3911	.2703	.1657	.0856	.0339	.0083
	6	1.0000	1.0000	1.0000	.9997	.9987	.9957	.9888	.9750	.9502	.9102	.8505	.7682	.6627	.5372	.3993	.2618	.1409	.0530
	7	1.0000	1.0000	1.0000	1.0000	.9999	.9996	.9986	.9962	.9909	.9805	.9615	.9295	.8789	.8040	.6997	.5638	.4005	.2252
	8	1.0000	1.0000	1.0000	1.0000	1.0000	1.0000	.9999	.9997	.9992	.9980	.9954	.9899	.9793	.9596	.9249	.8658	.7684	.6126
	9	1.0000	1.0000	1.0000	1.0000	1.0000	1.0000	1.0000	1.0000	1.0000	1.0000	1.0000	1.0000	1.0000	1.0000	1.0000	1.0000	1.0000	1.0000
10	0	.5987	.3487	.1969	.1074	.0563	.0282	.0135	.0060	.0025	.0010	.0003	.0001	.0000	.0000	.0000	.0000	.0000	.0000
	1	.9139	.7361	.5443	.3758	.2440	.1493	.0860	.0464	.0233	.0107	.0045	.0017	.0005	.0001	.0000	.0000	.0000	.0000
	2	.9885	.9298	.8202	.6778	.5256	.3828	.2616	.1673	.0996	.0547	.0274	.0123	.0048	.0016	.0004	.0001	.0000	.0000
	3	.9990	.9872	.9500	.8791	.7759	.6496	.5138	.3823	.2660	.1719	.1020	.0548	.0260	.0106	.0035	.0009	.0001	.0000
	4	.9999	.9984	.9901	.9672	.9219	.8497	.7515	.6331	.5044	.3770	.2616	.1662	.0949	.0473	.0197	.0064	.0014	.0001
	5	1.0000	.9999	.9986	.9936	.9803	.9527	.9051	.8338	.7384	.6230	.4956	.3669	.2485	.1503	.0781	.0328	.0099	.0016
	6	1.0000	1.0000	.9999	.9991	.9965	.9894	.9740	.9452	.8980	.8281	.7340	.6177	.4862	.3504	.2241	.1209	.0500	.0128
	7	1.0000	1.0000	1.0000	.9999	.9996	.9984	.9952	.9877	.9726	.9453	.9004	.8327	.7384	.6172	.4744	.3222	.1798	.0702
	8	1.0000	1.0000	1.0000	1.0000	1.0000	.9999	.9995	.9983	.9955	.9893	.9767	.9536	.9140	.8507	.7560	.6242	.4557	.2639
	9	1.0000	1.0000	1.0000	1.0000	1.0000	1.0000	1.0000	.9999	.9997	.9990	.9975	.9940	.9865	.9718	.9437	.8926	.8031	.6513
	10	1.0000	1.0000	1.0000	1.0000	1.0000	1.0000	1.0000	1.0000	1.0000	1.0000	1.0000	1.0000	1.0000	1.0000	1.0000	1.0000	1.0000	1.0000

Table D (concluded)

Cumulative binomial probabilities

n	x	.05	.10	.15	.20	.25	.30	.35	.40	.45	.50	.55	.60	.65	.70	.75	.80	.85	.90
15	0	.4633	.2059	.0874	.0352	.0134	.0047	.0016	.0005	.0001	.0000	.0000	.0000	.0000	.0000	.0000	.0000	.0000	.0000
	1	.8290	.5490	.3186	.1671	.0802	.0353	.0142	.0052	.0017	.0005	.0001	.0000	.0000	.0000	.0000	.0000	.0000	.0000
	2	.9638	.8159	.6042	.3980	.2361	.1268	.0617	.0271	.0107	.0037	.0011	.0003	.0001	.0000	.0000	.0000	.0000	.0000
	3	.9945	.9444	.8227	.6482	.4613	.2969	.1727	.0905	.0424	.0176	.0063	.0019	.0005	.0001	.0000	.0000	.0000	.0000
	4	.9994	.9873	.9383	.8358	.6865	.5155	.3519	.2173	.1204	.0592	.0255	.0093	.0028	.0007	.0001	.0000	.0000	.0000
	5	.9999	.9978	.9832	.9389	.8516	.7216	.5643	.4032	.2608	.1509	.0769	.0338	.0124	.0037	.0008	.0001	.0000	.0000
	6	1.0000	.9997	.9964	.9819	.9434	.8689	.7548	.6098	.4522	.3036	.1818	.0950	.0422	.0152	.0042	.0008	.0001	.0000
	7	1.0000	1.0000	.9994	.9958	.9827	.9500	.8868	.7869	.6535	.5000	.3465	.2131	.1132	.0500	.0173	.0042	.0006	.0000
	8	1.0000	1.0000	.9999	.9992	.9958	.9848	.9578	.9050	.8182	.6964	.5478	.3902	.2452	.1311	.0566	.0181	.0036	.0003
	9	1.0000	1.0000	1.0000	.9999	.9992	.9963	.9876	.9662	.9231	.8491	.7392	.5968	.4357	.2784	.1484	.0611	.0168	.0022
	10	1.0000	1.0000	1.0000	1.0000	.9999	.9993	.9972	.9907	.9745	.9408	.8796	.7827	.6481	.4845	.3135	.1642	.0617	.0127
	11	1.0000	1.0000	1.0000	1.0000	1.0000	.9999	.9995	.9981	.9937	.9824	.9576	.9095	.8273	.7031	.5387	.3518	.1773	.0556
	12	1.0000	1.0000	1.0000	1.0000	1.0000	1.0000	.9999	.9997	.9989	.9963	.9893	.9729	.9383	.8732	.7639	.6020	.3958	.1841
	13	1.0000	1.0000	1.0000	1.0000	1.0000	1.0000	1.0000	1.0000	.9999	.9995	.9983	.9948	.9858	.9647	.9198	.8329	.6814	.4510
	14	1.0000	1.0000	1.0000	1.0000	1.0000	1.0000	1.0000	1.0000	1.0000	1.0000	.9999	.9995	.9984	.9953	.9866	.9648	.9126	.7941
	15	1.0000	1.0000	1.0000	1.0000	1.0000	1.0000	1.0000	1.0000	1.0000	1.0000	1.0000	1.0000	1.0000	1.0000	1.0000	1.0000	1.0000	1.0000
20	0	.3585	.1216	.0388	.0115	.0032	.0008	.0002	.0000	.0000	.0000	.0000	.0000	.0000	.0000	.0000	.0000	.0000	.0000
	1	.7358	.3917	.1756	.0692	.0243	.0076	.0021	.0005	.0001	.0000	.0000	.0000	.0000	.0000	.0000	.0000	.0000	.0000
	2	.9245	.6769	.4049	.2061	.0913	.0355	.0121	.0036	.0009	.0002	.0000	.0000	.0000	.0000	.0000	.0000	.0000	.0000
	3	.9841	.8670	.6477	.4114	.2252	.1071	.0444	.0160	.0049	.0013	.0003	.0000	.0000	.0000	.0000	.0000	.0000	.0000
	4	.9974	.9568	.8298	.6296	.4148	.2375	.1182	.0510	.0189	.0059	.0015	.0003	.0000	.0000	.0000	.0000	.0000	.0000
	5	.9997	.9887	.9327	.8042	.6172	.4164	.2454	.1256	.0553	.0207	.0064	.0016	.0003	.0000	.0000	.0000	.0000	.0000
	6	1.0000	.9976	.9781	.9133	.7858	.6080	.4166	.2500	.1299	.0577	.0214	.0065	.0015	.0003	.0000	.0000	.0000	.0000
	7	1.0000	.9996	.9941	.9679	.8982	.7723	.6010	.4159	.2520	.1316	.0580	.0210	.0060	.0013	.0002	.0000	.0000	.0000
	8	1.0000	.9999	.9987	.9900	.9591	.8867	.7624	.5956	.4143	.2517	.1308	.0565	.0196	.0051	.0009	.0001	.0000	.0000
	9	1.0000	1.0000	.9998	.9974	.9861	.9520	.8782	.7553	.5914	.4119	.2493	.1275	.0532	.0171	.0039	.0006	.0000	.0000
	10	1.0000	1.0000	1.0000	.9994	.9961	.9829	.9468	.8725	.7507	.5881	.4086	.2447	.1218	.0480	.0139	.0026	.0002	.0000
	11	1.0000	1.0000	1.0000	.9999	.9991	.9949	.9804	.9435	.8692	.7483	.5857	.4044	.2376	.1133	.0409	.0100	.0013	.0001
	12	1.0000	1.0000	1.0000	1.0000	.9998	.9987	.9940	.9790	.9420	.8684	.7480	.5841	.3990	.2277	.1018	.0321	.0059	.0004
	13	1.0000	1.0000	1.0000	1.0000	1.0000	.9997	.9985	.9935	.9786	.9423	.8701	.7500	.5834	.3920	.2142	.0867	.0219	.0024
	14	1.0000	1.0000	1.0000	1.0000	1.0000	1.0000	.9997	.9984	.9936	.9793	.9447	.8744	.7546	.5836	.3828	.1958	.0673	.0113
	15	1.0000	1.0000	1.0000	1.0000	1.0000	1.0000	1.0000	.9997	.9985	.9941	.9811	.9490	.8818	.7625	.5852	.3704	.1702	.0432
	16	1.0000	1.0000	1.0000	1.0000	1.0000	1.0000	1.0000	1.0000	.9997	.9987	.9951	.9840	.9556	.8929	.7748	.5886	.3523	.1330
	17	1.0000	1.0000	1.0000	1.0000	1.0000	1.0000	1.0000	1.0000	1.0000	.9998	.9991	.9964	.9879	.9645	.9087	.7939	.5951	.3231
	18	1.0000	1.0000	1.0000	1.0000	1.0000	1.0000	1.0000	1.0000	1.0000	1.0000	.9999	.9995	.9979	.9924	.9757	.9308	.8244	.6083
	19	1.0000	1.0000	1.0000	1.0000	1.0000	1.0000	1.0000	1.0000	1.0000	1.0000	1.0000	1.0000	.9998	.9992	.9968	.9885	.9612	.8784
	20	1.0000	1.0000	1.0000	1.0000	1.0000	1.0000	1.0000	1.0000	1.0000	1.0000	1.0000	1.0000	1.0000	1.0000	1.0000	1.0000	1.0000	1.0000

INDEX

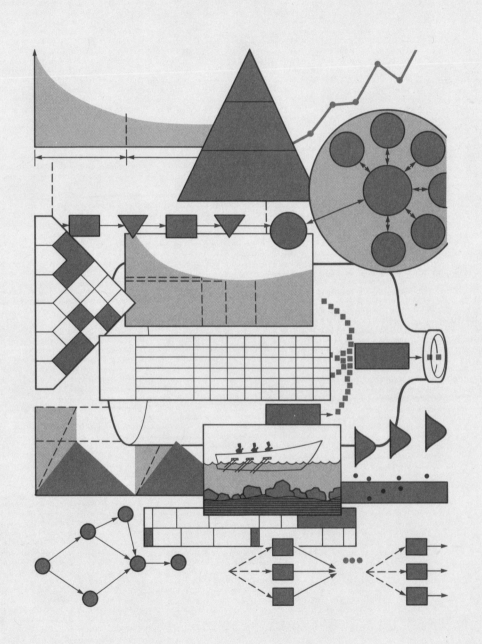